W9-AXW-497

Understanding Sociology

Understanding Sociology

Craig Calhoun
University of North Carolina at Chapel Hill

Donald Light
University of Medicine and Dentistry of New Jersey
Rutgers University

Suzanne Keller
Princeton University

Douglas Harper
University of South Florida
Visual Sociology Consultant

GLENCOE

McGraw-Hill

New York, New York   Columbus, Ohio   Woodland Hills, California   Peoria, Illinois

UNDERSTANDING SOCIOLOGY

Imprint 1998

Send all inquiries to:
Glencoe/McGraw-Hill
936 Eastwind Drive
Westerville, Ohio 43081

Printed in the United States of America

This book is printed on acid-free paper.
Text and photo credits appear on pages 619–623, and on this page by reference.

6 7 8 9 10 11 12   071   02 01 00 99 98

ISBN 0-07-011225-8

ABOUT THE AUTHORS

Craig Calhoun is Professor of Sociology and History at the University of North Carolina, Chapel Hill. He is also Chair of the Curriculum in International Studies and Director of the Program in Social Theory and Cross-Cultural Studies. A preacher's son, Professor Calhoun grew up in several communities in Kentucky, Illinois, and Indiana; learning about each new home was his first training in sociology. After studying at the University of Southern California and Columbia University, he won a scholarship to England and received his doctorate from Oxford University. He has taught in Chapel Hill since 1977.

Professor Calhoun is the author of *The Question of Class Struggle: The Social Foundations of Popular Radicalism in the Industrial Revolution* (Chicago, 1982) and *Beijing Spring: Students and the Struggle for Democracy in China* (California, forthcoming). He is also the editor of such books as *Structures of Power and Constraint* (with W. R. Scott and M. W. Meyer, Cambridge, 1990), *Habermas and the Public Sphere* (M.I.T. Press, 1992), *Bourdieu: Critical Perspectives* (with M. Postone and L. LiPuma, Chicago, 1993), and *Social Theory and the Politics of Identity* (Blackwells, 1993). Professor Calhoun is currently engaged in comparative historical research on nationalism and movements for democracy.

Teaching is a central part of Professor Calhoun's work. In addition to teaching a range of sociology classes, he was the founding professor in UNITAS, an experiment in multicultural living and learning at UNC. In 1988, UNC undergraduates elected him to their honor society, the Order of the Golden Fleece.

Donald Light is Professor of Sociology at Rutgers University and Professor of Social and Behavioral Medicine in the Department of Psychiatry at the University of Medicine and Dentistry of New Jersey. Born and raised in Massachusetts, Professor Light went to college at Stanford and completed his graduate work in sociology at the University of Chicago and Brandeis University. Along the way, he helped to implement President Kennedy's Equal Employment Opportunity Program for minority workers and became increasingly interested in the field of education and health. He is now conducting research on the sociological changes taking place in the American health-care system.

Professor Light's first appointment was to the faculty of Princeton University, where he taught the introductory course in sociology as well as courses in education, deviance, and professions. It was there he met and became friends with Suzanne Keller and subsequently developed the first edition of this text. He has published a well-known study of medical training entitled *Becoming Psychiatrists: The Professional Transformation of Self* (Norton, 1980). His latest book, *Political Values and Health Care*, is published by M.I.T. Press. He is the author of numerous articles, which have appeared in *The American Journal of Sociology*, *The Journal of Health and Social Behavior*, *The Administrative Science Quarterly*, *Daedalus*, and *The New England Journal of Medicine*.

Suzanne Keller is Professor of Sociology at Princeton University, where she has served as Chairperson of the Department of Sociology. She was born in Vienna, came to the United States as a child, but has spent a good part of her professional life in Europe. She received a Ph.D. in sociology from Columbia University in 1953. In 1957, she became an Assistant Professor at Brandeis University, where she taught courses in social theory, stratification, and the sociology of religion. A Fulbright Lectureship in 1963 at the Doxiadis Center of Ekistics in Athens marked the beginning of her interest in architecture and community planning. At the completion of her Fulbright in 1965, Professor Keller joined the Center, where she remained until 1967. That year she came to Princeton University as a Visiting Professor, and in 1968 she was the first woman to be appointed to a tenured Professorship there. She has held several elective offices in the American Sociological Association, including that of Vice-President, and most recently as President of the Eastern Sociological Society.

At Princeton, Suzanne Keller teaches courses on contemporary elites, comparative family systems, theories of gender, and social psychiatry. The author of numerous articles and several books, Professor Keller helped launch the program in Women's Studies at Princeton. She is currently completing a book on the creation of community and embarking on a study of contemporary elites. A consultant to many universities, corporations, and government agencies, both here and abroad, Professor Keller has received a number of fellowships and honors, including a Guggenheim Award. She currently chairs the board of the DBH Foundation, for the advancement of humane and safe living environments.

CONTENTS IN BRIEF

CONTENTS

BOXES

Making Choices

Global Issues/Local Consequences

Key Concepts in Action

General

PREFACE

The writing of *Understanding Sociology* has returned us to the joys of our first encounters with sociology. What attracted us then were the possibilities for understanding the connections between huge global issues and the problems we saw face to face. We were impressed by the fact that sociologists didn't limit themselves to one dimension of human existence, such as economics or psychology, but rather compared a wide range of societies, institutions, groups, organizations, and patterns of interaction in order to understand social life in its fullness. In sociological theory we found concepts that helped us make sense of a host of issues, from the antiwar movement of the 1960s to the problems of developing societies.

In preparing this book, our main task has been to make sociology as intellectually exciting and engaging for students in the mid-1990s as it has always been for us. We have been helped in this task by the fact that in the 1990s sociology itself has entered a new phase of intellectual excitement and engagement with practical issues. Sociology generates more enthusiasm in schools now than at any time since the 1960s—partly because of the centrality of such current sociological issues as cultural diversity, gender relations, violent crime, white-collar unemployment, and the resurgence of nationalism in the wake of communism's collapse. We have worked hard in this book to show how sociology helps people understand all these matters and more besides.

Moreover, we have tried to present sociological thinking in its full richness and diversity, while also revealing the power of the intellectual orientation that unites the field. We have tried to make sure that the book really speaks to the student concerns and intellectual agendas of the 1990s. We have also worked hard to make sure that the text's definitions are clear and precise, its examples interesting and pointed, its explanations easy to follow. We have tried, in other words, to make this a book students will want to read as well as a book from which they will learn about the best of contemporary and classical sociology.

NEW THEORETICAL FRAMEWORK: FIVE KEY CONCEPTS

This effort has meant a careful appraisal of how best to present the key concepts of sociology. As a result, we have chosen to analyze modern sociological theories and principles on the basis of five key concepts.

The traditional notion of three major schools of thought—functionalism, conflict theory, and symbolic interactionism—just doesn't do justice to current work in sociology. For one thing, it gives students the impression that sociology is divided into three incompatible camps, whereas of course practicing sociologists draw insights from all theoretical and analytic traditions. For another, that old way of presenting theoretical approaches leaves out some of the most active, exciting, and cental parts of sociology. Where does social structure fit in, for example, or culture? Last but not least, the concentration on those old categories made theoretical debates seem completely separate from empirical research, rather than showing how theoretical concepts are aspects of empirical understanding.

Accordingly, throughout the book, the concepts of ***functional integration***, ***power***, ***social action***, ***social structure***, and ***culture*** are presented as major tools of sociological work. These key concepts appear in ***bold italic*** type the first time they are used in any substantive discussion. Examples show how the key concepts are used in building theory, conducting empirical research, and formulating practical solutions to social problems. A series of boxes headed "Key Concepts in Action" shows how sociological thinking illuminates major public issues and research topics. At the end of each chapter, a brief review headed "Thinking Back on the Key Concepts" helps students relate the specific topics they study to these broad themes of sociological understanding.

The introduction of the key-concepts framework is evolutionary, not revolutionary. ***Functional integration***, ***power***, and ***social action*** are adaptations of the familiar terms *functionalism*, *conflict theory*, and *symbolic interaction*;

however, as the new usage indicates, these are not just competing theories or "isms," but tools that all sociologists can use. ***Power*** replaces the closely related term *conflict* because the former denotes more clearly the underlying issue. And ***social structure*** and ***culture*** bring into focus major aspects of sociological analysis that were obscured by the old three-perspective model. When this scheme was tried out in the classroom, we were amazed at how much clearer students find it, and how much quicker they make it a part of their own "sociological imaginations."

FOCUS ON VISUAL SOCIOLOGY

In cultivating students' sociological imaginations, words are certainly not our only tools. We also urge our students to look at the world around them through new eyes. This book helps in that process by presenting graphic images as a basic part of its sociology, not as mere decorations.

Douglas Harper of the University of South Florida is largely responsible for this new approach to visual sociology. A widely published and award-winning photographer as well as a distinguished sociologist, Doug took some of the photographs reprinted in this edition and selected the others in order to ensure that the visual images were used to their full potential. His captions make the images a fully realized part of the introduction to sociology offered by the book.

The graphs and other line drawings have been designed to make quantitative data easy to absorb and understand. In presenting quantitative data, we try to help students develop the skills they need in order to make sense of the tables, charts, figures, and statistics they will encounter on the job, in newspapers and magazines, and on television.

EMPHASIS ON CROSS-CULTURAL UNDERSTANDING AND SOCIAL CHOICES

Some of the other innovations in *Understanding Sociology* reflect the directions taken in the 1990s by social change and sociology alike. The book is internationally oriented, for example, with a chapter on the Third World and global inequality, a series of high-interest special features headed "Global Issues/Local Consequences," and cross-cultural examples in every chapter. The collapse of Soviet and Eastern European communism and the problems that have ensued get systematic attention. Our treatment of race and ethnic relations develops a broad picture of a multicultural United States.

The text is written to show how sociological research and analysis inform the choices that people face both in everyday life and in public policy. This emphasis is reflected in a series of boxes headed "Making Choices" and is also brought out in Chapter 19, which integrates population and environment, and in a variety of other places.

ACKNOWLEDGMENTS

A number of people have helped in the effort to ensure that the book is both readable and informative. Perhaps the most important are the three people who at different stages worked with us to make the writing come alive without sacrificing clarity: Cecilia Gardner, Ann Levine, and Mary Marshall.

Thomas Gieryn played a major role in this edition, as in previous ones. A gifted teacher of introductory sociology, he tested various ideas in the classroom. He also wrote out for use in this book some of the illustrations, explanations, and examples that he has developed in his teaching.

James Crawford, Cindy Hahamovitch, Tim Henderson, and Steve Pfaff were tireless and resourceful research assistants. Leah Florence provided wide-ranging and very helpful editorial assistance throughout the project. Phil Butcher was (and is) a devoted sponsoring editor at McGraw-Hill. Sylvia Shepard and Melissa Mashburn offered very useful advice in planning the revision as well as critiquing the first drafts. Speaking of critics, none were more valuable than the academic reviewers who are listed on page xxvii. They were advocates not only for clarity but also for good sociology, urging us—to cite one crucial example—not to be bashful about highlighting the key concepts within the text or about reviewing the key-concept coverage at the end of every chapter.

Craig Calhoun
Donald Light
Suzanne Keller

ACADEMIC REVIEWERS

Donald J. Adamchak
Kansas State University

Nicky Ali
Purdue University–Calumet

Ernest K. Alix
Southern Illinois University at Carbondale

David V. Baker
Riverside Community College

Richard P. Barasch
Rancho Santiago College

Gerry R. Cox
Fort Hays State University

Joseph R. DeMartini
Washington State University

David L. Ellison
Rensselaer Polytechnic Institute

William Feigelman
Nassau County Community College

William Finlay
University of Georgia

Mark Gottdiener
CUNY–Hunter College

Sharon E. Hogan
Longview Community College

M. Drew Hurley
Santa Fe Community College

Lawrence H. Joyce
State University of New York–College of Agriculture and Technology at Cobleskill

Irwin Kantor
Middlesex County College

Hugh F. Lena
Providence College

Patrick McNamara
University of New Mexico

David R. Maines
Wayne State University

Robert E. Meyer
Arkansas State University

Fred Pampel
University of Colorado–Boulder

Travis Patton
University of Nebraska at Omaha

Novella Perrin
Central Missouri State University

Jeffrey P. Rosenfeld
Nassau County Community College

Robert L. Seufert
Miami University

Brad Simcock
Miami University

Regina Spires-Robin
New York City Technical College

Stephan Spitzer
University of Minnesota

Larry Stern
Collin County Community College

John Stirton
San Joaquin Delta Community College

Robert Turley
San Bernardino Valley College

Theodore C. Wagenaar
Miami University

Mark Wehrle
Central Missouri State University

William M. Wentworth
Clemson University

S. Mont Whitson
Morehead State University

Stuart A. Wright
Lamar University

Surendar Yadava
University of Northern Iowa

Glyn Young
East Carolina University

Joan Cook Zimmern
College of Saint Mary

Understanding Sociology

PART 1

The Study of Sociology

CHAPTER 1

The Sociological Perspective

On August 2, 1990, shortly after midnight, 100,000 Iraqi troops crossed the border into the neighboring kingdom of Kuwait. Rolling down a six-lane highway toward the capital city virtually unopposed, Iraqi tanks quickly surrounded the main government buildings. In less than 6 hours Iraq had control of Kuwait.

Leaders from around the world were quick to condemn Iraq's action. The United Nations Security Council voted first to impose a strict economic embargo on Iraq, and later to authorize the use of force if Iraq did not withdraw from Kuwait by January 15, 1991. Combined American, Arab, and European troops assembled across the border in Saudi Arabia. When negotiation and intimidation failed, the allies began bombing Baghdad on January 16.

From the beginning of the Persian Gulf crisis, attention and blame focused on one man, Iraq's President Saddam Hussein. U.S. President George Bush said that half a century ago, "our nation and the world paid dearly for appeasing an aggressor [Adolf Hitler] who should, and could, have been stopped. We are not going to make the same mistake again" (quoted in Miller and Mylroie, 1990, p. xii). Secretary of State James Baker echoed this view: The crisis in the gulf was "about a dictator who, acting alone and unchallenged, could strangle the global economic order" (quoted in Miller and Mylroie, 1990, p. xiii). The media, too, focused on the individual. "What kind of man would cold-bloodedly gobble up a neighboring country?" asked *Time* magazine (August 13, 1990, p. 23). "Saddam is a tyrant and a bully," declared *Newsweek* (August 13, 1990, p. 17). To many Americans, Saddam Hussein became the personification of evil, and the war in the Persian Gulf was "Saddam's war."

There is little doubt that Saddam Hussein ordered the invasion of Kuwait and bears personal responsibility for the bloodshed and destruction that followed. But can one man single-handedly create an international crisis and alter the course of history? Sociologists think not. They argue that to understand events like the invasion of Kuwait we need to look beyond individuals to the social forces that shape human behavior. Even when certain people play critical roles in history, we need to understand the social factors that enable them to do so. Thus, the crisis in the gulf was not caused by a single villain acting alone, but was the result of preexisting tensions, cultural misunderstandings, political miscalculations, and a struggle for power in a region of strategic and economic importance. If Saddam Hussein were to disappear tomorrow, the problems in the Middle East would not suddenly disappear with him.

We begin this chapter with an overview of sociology. What does the sociological perspective add to our understanding of world events and our own lives? This section introduces five key sociological concepts that you will encounter throughout this book: social structure, social action, functional integration, power, and culture. Next we show these key concepts and the sociological imagination at work, analyzing the crisis in the Persian Gulf. In the third section we trace these concepts back to their roots in the writings of the founders of sociology. In the last section we discuss the role sociology plays in contemporary public life.

SOCIOLOGICAL IMAGINATION

Sociology is the study of human society, including both social action and social organization. Sociologists use scientific research methods and theories, and study social life in a wide variety of settings. Sociology offers us not only information, but a distinctive way of looking at the world and our place in it. Whereas most people try to explain events by analyzing the motives of those involved, sociologists encourage us to look beyond individual psychology to the many recurring patterns in people's attitudes and actions, and how these patterns vary across time, cultures, and social groups. Sociologists do not ask simply, "What kind of person is Saddam Hussein?" Instead they ask, "What social conditions enabled Saddam to rise to power?" "Why did the Iraqi people answer his call to arms?" "What caused other participants in the gulf crisis to respond as they did?" Sociologists do not ignore individuals. They show that to understand the actions of individuals—and our own experiences—we have to understand the social context in which they take place.

Take the experiences of American soldiers who served in the Persian Gulf. They were very different from the experiences of soldiers who served in Vietnam. Was this just because the wars were experienced by different people with different personalities? No. The different experiences arose from different social circumstances. These included different methods of recruitment (an all-volunteer army versus the draft), different ways of deploying troops (assignment for the duration of the conflict versus a limited tour of duty), different characteristics of enemy combatants (traditional soldiers versus a local population, including women and children), and different levels of support back home (very high versus very low). All these social circumstances, beyond each individual's control, were critical in shaping American soldiers' experiences.

Understanding this point is a basic illustration of what the great American sociologist C. Wright Mills called **sociological imagination**. Sociological imagination is a way on the Persian Gulf crisis—a matter of social relationships, social positions, and population distribution.

A map of the region shows it neatly divided into independent countries with clear-cut boundaries (see Figure 1.1), but this "map structure" is only one aspect of the real social structure and was largely imposed from outside. From A.D. 1500 to 1900, most Arabs were ruled by the Turkish Ottoman Empire. When Europeans defeated the Turks in World War I, the Middle East was "awarded" to the British and French under the auspices of the League of Nations. The borders of the countries we know as Iraq, Jordan, Syria, Kuwait, and Saudi Arabia were drawn by European officials to serve their own interests, often with little regard for the histories and sentiments of local peoples. There has never been an accepted border between Oman or Yemen and Saudi Arabia. Under Ottoman rule southern Iraq and Kuwait were part of a single administrative district called Basra. The decision to separate Kuwait from Iraq was made in 1919 by an agent of the British colonial government of India who wanted to use Baghdad as a base and a Bedouin chief who sought British protection.

This separation of Kuwait and Iraq on maps does not correspond to structures of social relations. Bedouin tribespeople have moved across what are now considered borders for centuries. Kinship bonds join cousins who officially reside on opposite sides of the borders. Much of the land in question is desert and very sparsely settled. To the inhabitants of these territories, many of whom were nomads, the borders were little more than "lines in the sand" that might blow away with the next wind. The 1990–1991 conflict was only the most recent in a long series of clashes that arose partly from social-structural instabilities. In particular, the structure of formal positions (the borders of countries, their political systems, citizenship) did not correspond closely to the structure of social relations (such as kinship and employment) or the distribution of population.

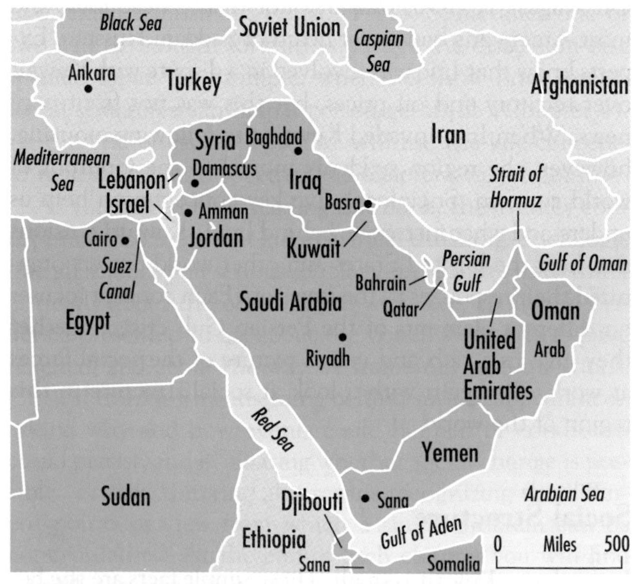

FIGURE 1.1 / Countries of the Middle East

Since oil was discovered in Kuwait, the situation had grown even more extreme. Most of the people living in Kuwait were not its citizens, but rather temporary workers brought in to serve the small ruling elite of official Kuwaitis. At the time of Iraq's invasion, the population of Kuwait included large numbers of Egyptians, Palestinians, Indians, Pakistanis, and Filipinos. The government of Kuwait did not recognize any of these people as having the rights of citizens, even if their families had lived in Kuwait for a hundred years. Many of these people actually welcomed the arrival of the Iraqis.

Other social-structural factors also impose divisions on the Middle East. One factor is differences in the political systems. Kuwait (along with Saudi Arabia, Jordan, and the sheikdoms of the Arabian peninsula) is a *monarchy*, in which the right to rule is based on inheritance. Most important political positions are awarded to members of the royal families, and they and their relatives maintain controlling interests in major industries (especially oil). By contrast, Iraq (along with Egypt, Syria, and Sudan) is a *republic*, in which the opportunity to rule is theoretically open to any citizen (as in the United States). Iraq is not a democracy (though Egypt is). But who becomes president (or dictator) is not determined by membership in a royal family. Ironically, Saddam Hussein lived out the "American dream" of a poor boy from a small, rural town who grew up to be president. At the time of the invasion, most Arabs knew that Saddam was a ruthless dictator. But the fact that he was a self-made leader, as opposed to an oil-rich, ultra-privileged sheik, appealed to many Arabs. Social-structural differences thus helped to explain not only why Iraq and Kuwait were in conflict but also why many Arabs were more sympathetic to Iraq.

Finally, of all the countries in the region, only Iraq, Egypt, and Syria have enough water and arable land to support large populations. Although not as rich as Saudi Arabia or even tiny Kuwait, these three countries can field large armies. At the time of the invasion there were more soldiers in Iraq's army than there were native civilians—men, women, and children—in Kuwait, a social-structural fact that made Kuwait very vulnerable to attack. Although heavily armed, neither Kuwait nor Saudi Arabia had the potential troop strength to oppose Iraq and so had to call in foreign troops.

Social action emerges in new situations and often brings people together who otherwise have little in common. The social actions of American supporters of the Persian Gulf war had a profound impact on the U.S. government's ability to wage the war; but they were also fleeting and did not lead to lasting social arrangements. If the war had gone differently—if, for example, the invasion had led to a lengthy ground war with heavy casualties on both sides—the nature of such social action would undoubtedly have been different.

Social Action

Although social structure set the stage for ***social action*** in the Persian Gulf, the war still depended on the intentions, decisions, and understandings of a wide range of social actors from ordinary Iraqi citizens to the U.S. and other governments.

Saddam Hussein did not invade Kuwait by himself. He needed the cooperation of millions of Iraqis. War is a socially organized action involving coordination among many different people (also called a *collective action*, see Chapter 21). To understand why it occurred in the Persian Gulf, we must ask why hundreds of thousands of Iraqi men, some of them only teenagers, answered Saddam's call to arms, and why the Iraqi population was willing to fight another war so soon after its war with Iran. The answers involve the way that people interpreted their situations, and the decisions they made in response to those understandings.

One important aspect of how Iraqis interpreted their situations was their perception that they were surrounded by enemies. To the east lay Iran. After a bloody eight-year war (1980–1988), with a million or more casualties, Iran and Iraq had reached a cease-fire, but not true peace. To the west, just beyond a thin strip of Jordan, lay Israel. Iraq and Israel had existed in a state of undeclared war for decades. Also to the west lay Syria, the only Arab state that had sided with Iran against Iraq. To the north was Turkey, a member of NATO that was seeking admission to the European Economic Community. Iraq depended on pipelines through Turkey to export much of its oil, but could not count on Turkey remaining loyal to its Arab neighbors.

Countries that see themselves surrounded by enemies often gravitate toward strong leaders. They are also more likely to tolerate censorship, restrictions on civil liberties, and police action. Insiders described Iraq under Saddam's rule as a "republic of fear," in which torture, public hangings, assassinations, and mass killings had become common (al-Khalil, 1990). The state-controlled media promoted a siege mentality. It broadcast that the United States was plotting against Iraq and that attack by Israel was imminent.

Social action against Kuwait was also made more likely because of the ways that Iraqis perceived and interpreted the actions of the Kuwaiti people. Wealthy beyond the imagination of the average Arab, the Kuwaitis flaunted their riches where others could see and resent them. Given their country's desert climate (often 115°F in the summer), Kuwaitis loved to travel—to the French Riviera, the Swiss Alps, and London. Their jet-set lifestyle abroad seemed in flagrant violation of Islamic laws (such as the prohibition against alcohol). The Kuwait government did give financial aid to other Arab nations and causes, but it also made huge investments abroad. Many Arabs felt that its economic policies were geared more toward protecting those investments than toward supporting the Arab world.

Saddam also believed that the United States would not intervene militarily. During the Iraq–Iran war that preceded the Persian Gulf war, the United States had remained officially neutral but leaned toward Iraq, restoring full diplomatic relations, extending $300 million annually in credits for the purchase of grain, and quietly providing Iraq with secret information on Iranian troop positions. The United States had condemned Saddam for violations of human rights within Iraq. But the United States also continued to give some forms of support almost up to the moment of the invasion. The primary concern of the U.S. government was stability in the region. Aware that U.S. support for Israel angered many Arabs, Saddam reasoned that the United States would tread softly. If the United States did threaten or use force, he thought, other Arabs would side with Iraq.

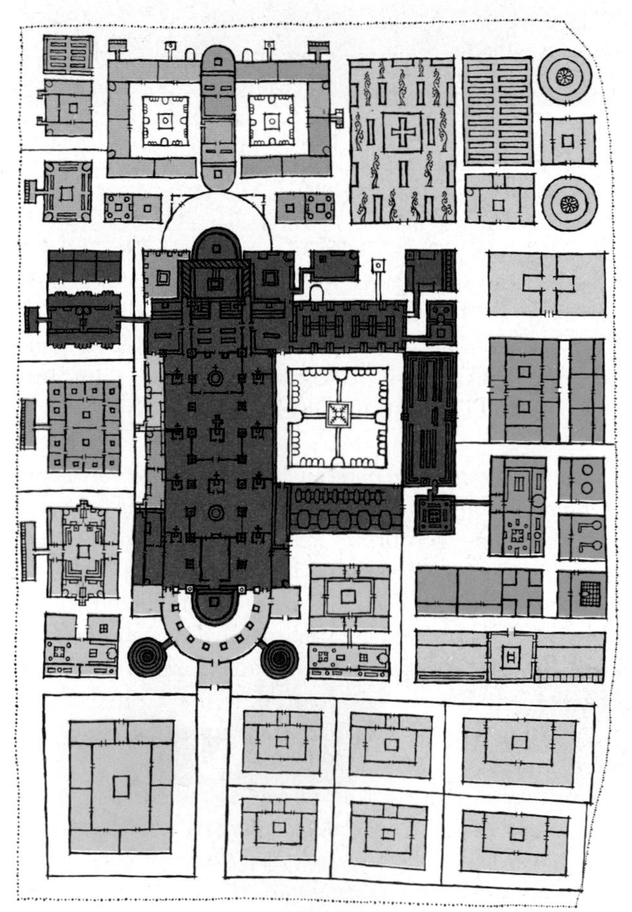

This architectural plan shows how the ninth-century Benedictine monastery of St. Gall in Switzerland is functionally integrated: it represents a built environment in which subsistence and socialization needs are carefully organized to make the community self-sufficient and self-perpetuating. The red areas represent the church and its outbuildings; yellow, livestock barns and gardens; dark green, crafts, milling, and baking; lavender, health and medicine; blue, education; and light green, reception and visitors' quarters.

In the spring of 1990 Iraqi leaders began blaming Kuwait for standing in the way of its economic recovery after the war with Iran. With some justification, Saddam charged that Kuwait was producing more than its allotted quota of oil and thus lowering the price of oil on the world market. On the grounds that Iraqis had "shed blood" to protect their Arab brothers from their ancient Persian enemy and to halt the spread of militant Islamic fundamentalism, Saddam demanded that Kuwait forgive Iraq's $15 billion war debt. He also reopened an old territorial dispute, claiming a historical right to two uninhabited islands blocking Iraq's access to the Persian Gulf. Unmoved, Kuwaiti officials rejected both Saddam's appeals and his threats.

One might speculate about what would have happened if Kuwait had agreed to some of Iraq's demands, if Arab leaders had put more collective pressure on either country, or if the United States had stated directly, publicly, and repeatedly that it would defend Kuwait. Apparently, none saw the situation exactly as the Iraqis did or anticipated what the Iraqis would do. Far from being only an individual's decision or an irrational act, the invasion of Kuwait took place within a web of conflicting expectations and interpretations, moves and countermoves.

Functional Integration

We explained earlier that ***functional integration*** is the mutual interdependence of the different parts of a social system. Most social systems exist in a state of *dynamic equilibrium*, in which each part is constantly adjusting to the others, keeping its functions integrated with those of the other parts so that the system continues to operate. When this delicate balance is upset, it can send shock waves through the whole system. This is what happened as a result of the gulf crisis. It upset the social equilibrium not only in the Middle East, but in other parts of the world too because of the strategic positions Kuwait and Iraq hold in the global economic order. The structure of the modern, industrialized world means that countries depend on oil for survival, and huge oil deposits lie in Kuwait and Iraq. This is why Iraq's invasion of Kuwait had such significance. If the Central American nation of Guatemala had invaded its neighbor Belize to gain access to the Atlantic Ocean (something it has frequently threatened to do), the whole world—or much of it—would not have taken up arms. Belize's main export is sugar, not oil.

Actions can also be planned to disrupt functional integration, that is, to deliberately create dysfunctions or disintegration in a social system. This was an important part of the U.S. strategy against Iraq. When the deadline for withdrawal from Kuwait passed, the United States and its allies did not attack the Iraqi troops in Kuwait directly (as Iraq apparently expected). Rather, they launched an air assault designed to destroy Iraq's command centers, radar installations, power plants, telephone exchanges, broadcast antennas, roads, and bridges—in short, to destroy the functional integration of its military machine. As a result, communications between Iraqi commanders and their field units were cut off, as was the flow of supplies to Kuwait. Broken into isolated segments, the Iraqi army was unable to function. When allied ground troops moved into Kuwait, they found Iraqi soldiers half-starved, disorganized, and thoroughly demoralized.

In January, when the war began, the Iraqi leaders did not anticipate such devastation. In fact, they still hoped that their invasion of Kuwait would help to mend a major economic dysfunction that had arisen as a result of the previous war with Iran. In that war, Iraq had acquired military might but had also accumulated a huge foreign debt, estimated at $88 billion (Marr, 1991). By annexing Kuwait, Iraq would have gained additional oil fields, a port on the Persian Gulf, and more control over the price of oil on the world market. In addition, invading Kuwait was a way of warding off a major social-economic dysfunction that would result if the Iraqi army had to be dismantled. Iraq had mobilized a vast army (almost 5 percent of its total population) to fight Iran. For eight years, nearly a million Iraqi men had been fed, clothed, housed, and paid by the government. Iraq could not demobilize these soldiers without creating mass unemployment and the likelihood of civil unrest (Marr, 1991). One solution to these problems was to invade Kuwait.

The U.S. reaction to the invasion can also be looked at in terms of the disintegration it helped to prevent. The United States depends on oil, about half of which is imported. The possibility that one government would control the vast reserves of both Iraq and Kuwait (and maybe those of Saudi Arabia, too, if Saddam were not opposed) threatened the American economic system. Furthermore, the U.S. economy was sliding into a recession. The federal budget deficit, the savings-and-loan crisis, the increasing numbers of homeless people, and even the growing market for drugs were symptoms of underlying economic problems the nation had not begun to address. Operation Desert Storm may not have resolved the budget deficit (and, indeed, probably increased it), but it certainly functioned as a diversion. Once the fighting began, Americans were glued to their TV sets, waiting for the latest news. The recession was still there, of course, but for a time Americans had more important things on their minds. On another level, the war allowed the country to demonstrate that, even with its economic problems, it was still a

This photograph shows daily life in a monastery that has been in continual existence in Holland since 1134. The functional integration of the monastery results from its ability to organize multiple roles for its members, such as providing and preparing food and maintaining the physical environment.

superpower. It also helped to restore the confidence and pride that Americans had lost during the war in Vietnam. The gulf war was partly a defense of the functional integration of the U.S. and world economies.

Power

Power relations were clearly basic to the conflict in the Persian Gulf. They can be analyzed on several levels. Within Iraq, Saddam Hussein exercised a near monopoly of power (Marr, 1991; Peretz, 1990). When he became president in 1979, one of his first acts was to execute twenty-two former officials for alleged treason. By 1990, Saddam had eliminated virtually all sources of dissent inside Iraq. Criticism of the president was punishable by imprisonment or worse. Some groups resented Saddam's rule, but they had little power to resist.

Saddam had helped to make Iraq one of the most powerful countries in the Middle East; only Iran was a real competitor for regional leadership. The two countries' brutal war during the 1980s had ended in a draw.

Iraq's power derived from its oil wealth, its large population, its army (at the time, the fourth largest in the world), and the impressive arsenal of weapons it had amassed, some of which it produced itself. The creation of this Iraqi "military-industrial complex" helped ensure that a balance of power could not be established in the Middle East. Iraq had simply grown too strong.

Contributing to America's power to act in the region was the decline of the Soviet Union as a world power. During the cold war, the United States and the USSR had acted as countervailing powers in the Middle East. Each had "client" states, which it armed but usually held in check to avoid confrontation with each other. Middle Eastern states often obtained arms or aid by playing the superpowers against each other. But by 1990 the USSR was no longer in a position to dictate policy or intervene militarily. Had the UN Security Council voted to take economic and then military action against Iraq in 1980, it is likely that the Soviet Union would have exercised its veto power. In 1990, it did not.

In terms of military technology, President Bush's power base was far stronger than Saddam's. But in terms of internal control, it was in some ways more limited. Unlike the Iraqi leader, Bush had to convince the American public and Congress that war was right and necessary before a shot was fired. In choosing military strategies, he had to consider how many casualties the American public would accept and how long it would support a war far from home. Moreover, to maintain credibility and avoid the appearance of being an international bully, both at home and abroad, Bush had to maintain a fragile ad hoc coalition among Arab and European allies, including such former enemies of the United States as Iran and Syria. The UN deadline for Iraq's withdrawal from Kuwait was set for January 15 in part because this date fell between Christmas and the Islamic holy month of Ramadan, which began on March 17. Thus, President Bush had the power to wage war, but his ability to exercise this power was limited by law, by political considerations, and by culture.

While social power is often measured by concrete, observable factors such as available firepower, sociologists recognize that social power may also emerge from intangible forces such as commitment and collective action. Between 1975 and 1979, the Sandinista revolutionary party fought a guerilla campaign, using handguns and homemade grenades, against the well-equipped army of the Nicaraguan government. Despite their lack of modern equipment, the Sandinistas were militarily successful.

Culture

Shared ***culture*** links together people in many different Middle Eastern countries. As we have mentioned, the people there have not always thought of themselves as "Iraqis," "Kuwaitis," or "Saudis"; nor is this the only way they think of themselves today. For many Middle Easterners, their cultural identity as "Arab" is more important than citizenship in any state. Although spread across many countries, Arabs share a common language, history, worldview, religion, values, and way of life: in short, a common culture. In addition to Arab culture, the Islamic religion is shared by most Arabs and many others in the Middle

East. Iranians, for example, are not Arabs but they are Muslims (followers of Islam, the religion of the prophet Mohammed).

When Europe was still in the Dark Ages, Arabs possessed a rich literary and philosophical tradition (Pfaff, 1991). It was Arabs who preserved Greek philosophy and introduced Aristotle and Plato to medieval Europe. They developed advanced theoretical science, preparing the groundwork for modern physics and astronomy; they invented the zero, multiplication, division, and the square root, laying the foundation for modern mathematics. (We still use Arabic numerals today.) Before his death in A.D. 632, the prophet Mohammed had unified most of the Arabian peninsula. After his death, Arabs swept northward into Gibraltar and Spain and eastward through Turkey, Afghanistan, and central Asia, almost to China. They repelled waves of European Crusaders to the Holy Land. Thus, only a thousand years ago, the Mediterranean world—north and south—was largely Arab and Muslim.

Today this glorious past lives on in Arab cultural memory, but so does awareness that the recent history of the Arab world has been one of humiliation and defeat—by the Ottoman Turks, by the European colonial powers, and in recent decades by the state of Israel (backed by the United States). The combination of earlier glory and more recent humiliation helps to promote the shared cultural ideals of pan-Arab and pan-Islamic brotherhood and unity. Many Arab nationalists believe that Arabs are one people and should have a single Arab state or a pan-Arab federation. This was one of the declarations made by Saddam Hussein. Also helping to bind Arabs together is a common resentment of foreign, "imperialist" intervention in Middle Eastern affairs, of Western technological superiority, and of Western cultural exports. All these are shared elements of a pan-Arab culture.

This poster, entitled "Flag of the Nation," is for a 1929 Soviet film called World Sensation, *about the struggle of American industrial workers against capitalism. We seldom think of our own culture as the subject of criticism and comment by other countries, and our own cultural bias limits our understanding of the visual metaphors employed in the poster. Why is the figure holding a joker with a dollar sign? Is he a capitalist or a worker? How are we to interpret his expression?*

The gulf war brought these elements of culture into clear view. To Westerners, Iraq's invasion of Kuwait was a blatant violation of national integrity—equivalent to Germany invading Belgium. For many Arabs, however, cultural beliefs and values caused them to see national borders as no more significant than state lines within the United States. They perceived the invasion of Kuwait as an internal matter, which should be settled among Arabs, and the invitation of foreign troops to fight on Arab soil as a far greater crime. Even before the war began, Muslim clerics preached against the presence of foreign troops as an invasion of "atheists" and "infidels," descendants of the Crusaders and defenders of Israel.

Also an outgrowth of Arab-Islamic culture was the perception that the Kuwaitis and neighboring Saudis had sold out to the West. Their lavish spending on opulent Western imports and their secularized royal families offended traditional Muslim values. In the words of one Jordanian official: "We resent the fact that they buy everything—technology, protection, ideas, people, respectability. Most Arabs now say that Saudi Arabia has disappeared and America alone is running things in the Gulf. . . . Have the Saudis no shame?" (Viorst, 1991, p. 46). The same words could have been spoken about Kuwaitis.

Finally, the image of Saddam standing up to world powers appealed to a deep cultural tradition of personal honor among Arabs. In Arab culture insults cannot be ignored, which is why Arabs seem (to Westerners) so obsessively polite in public. According to an old Arab saying, "Never spit on a man's moustache unless it is on fire" (Newhouse, 1991). In a sense, Saddam filled a cultural vacuum. Since the death of Egyptian President Gamal Abdel Nasser in 1970, the Arab world had lacked a strong leader who was willing and able to stand up to Israel and the West, a leader who would not be "spat upon." Nasser's successor, Anwar el-Sadat, was seen as a hero in the West for going to Jerusalem and signing a peace agreement with Israel in 1977. But although Sadat regained the Sinai Desert for Egypt, he surrendered his honor in the eyes of many Arabs. Saddam Hussein, in contrast, refused to back down. He lived up to his first name, which means "one who confronts," and, despite his losses, is remembered as a hero in parts of the Arab world. The reason, again, has to do with Arab cultural values.

The Western nations allied against Iraq were operating according to a different set of cultural values and guidelines. The United States was founded on the principle of separation of church and state, religion and politics. "Holy wars" are something from the distant past (as in the Crusades). Americans understand only two reasons to fight: to defend honorable principles, such as freedom and democracy, and to rebuff dishonorable greed, such as desire for national territory. Even though Americans have fought wars for national territory as the nation expanded across the North American continent, they now condemn those who invade other countries' territory. They consider a war just insofar as the aims are clear and the violence is in proportion to the reasons for fighting (Dowd, 1991). The idea of a holy war, in which there are no limits to slaughter or sacrifice because it is God's will to vanquish the infidel, seems foreign to Americans. Furthermore, American culture endorses pragmatism over personal honor—that is, when the odds are against the nation, it is willing to compromise and try to make the best deal possible, rather than fight for a "lost cause."

Negotiations to avert war in the Persian Gulf failed in part because of cultural stereotypes, misunderstandings, and miscalculations—on both sides. Apparently, Iraqi leaders misunderstood the role of public debate in a democracy and underestimated President Bush's ability to rally public opinion. Apparently, Bush misunderstood the importance of honor in Arab culture. By refusing to negotiate with Saddam directly (and thus grant him public recognition as an important head of state), by sending more than half a million troops to Saudi Arabia, and by using such colloquial expressions as "kick ass," the Bush administration was delivering an insult that Saddam could only interpret as a challenge he could not ignore. In his interview with U.S. Ambassador April Glaspie days before the invasion, Saddam declared, "[W]hen we feel that you want to injure our pride and take away the Iraqis' chance of a high standard of living, then we will cease to care, and death will be the choice for us. Then we would not care if you fired 100 missiles for every missile we fired. Because without pride life would have no value" (in Oberdorfer, 1991, p. 39). U.S. officials heard Saddam's words but, because of their own cultural understandings, did not take what he said seriously.

Summing Up the Sociological Perspective on the Persian Gulf War

In summary, the sociological perspective shows that the crisis in the Persian Gulf was largely produced by a collision of social forces over which no individual or nation had complete control. To be sure, Saddam Hussein played a central role in this historic drama. But to focus solely on Saddam's personal responsibility for all that happened is shortsighted. Saddam could not have become president-for-life of Iraq or mobilized a million-man army if many segments of the Iraqi population had not agreed with his aims. He would not have been cheered in the streets of Amman, Cairo, Tunis, Damascus, and Rabat if large numbers of Arabs had not felt disenchanted with their leaders and disinherited from their rightful place in history and current events. And Saddam's troops would not have ravaged Kuwait to the extent they did if they had not believed that their neighbors were their enemies.

The five key concepts around which we organized this extended example—social structure, social action, functional integration, power, and culture—are part of the very foundation of sociology. As you will see again in the chapters that follow, these concepts help sociologists to look beyond individual personalities and events and analyze the social dimension of both history and biography.

THE ORIGINS OF SOCIOLOGY

Sociology was born in the late eighteenth and early nineteenth centuries, a period of sweeping social change in Western societies. The world that Europeans had known for centuries was disappearing, and the "modern era" had begun.

Until the eighteenth century, most Europeans lived in small, semiautonomous, agricultural villages. These villages were part of larger countries whose rulers—generally kings—had begun to build empires and to promote international trade. But affairs of state and imported goods had little impact on the average man and woman. Most people lived their entire lives in the village where their parents, grandparents, and more distant ancestors had been born.

Every villager knew every other villager (and minded everyone else's business). Nearly everybody attended the same church. Travel was rare: There were no railroads or even stage coaches, and highway robbery was a real danger. Gossip was local: There were no newspapers or regular postal deliveries, much less radios or telephones.

The family was the heart of village life, providing and caring for its own (Laslett, 1973). Home served as a combination storehouse, workshop, school, hospital, and old-age home. Nearly all families were farmers, though most did not own the land they worked. Rather, they rented from a landlord (often a member of the aristocracy) under agreements dating back centuries. This social order was thought to be ordained by God and was seldom questioned. A few people were born to rule, while the great majority were born to toil. Fathers had authority over their families, landlords over their tenants, and monarchs over all their subjects. People knew their duty and their place. Little changed from one generation to the next.

Life in these preindustrial villages was far from idyllic. Landlords exploited their tenants, often taxing them to the brink of starvation. Neighbors argued with neighbors, and family feuds sometimes spanned generations. Sanitation was poor, medical care primitive, and early death common.

But however hard life was, the boundaries and contours were known. Though some long-term changes were always taking place, they were generally slow and not very visible to ordinary people. In a few places, the sixteenth and seventeenth centuries brought the seeds of modern life. The Protestant Reformation encouraged new ideas, and agricultural improvements brought a higher standard of living. But for most everyday purposes, people could still predict the future from the past.

The Revolutionary Context of Sociology

Change gathered speed in early modern Europe. Scientific thinking and research, new inventions, the growth of cities, and the conquest of colonies were all important. But it took two dramatic political events in the late eighteenth century to really shock people into realizing how the traditional social order had been challenged.

The American and French revolutions showed that old notions of duty, tradition, and submission to authority were being replaced with new ideas of individual rights, equality, and freedom, threatening monarchs everywhere. At the same time, a new class of capitalist entrepreneurs was gaining wealth and power, pushing aside the old landed aristocracy. The political term *revolution* was soon applied to these rapid social and economic changes.

The Industrial Revolution altered both the physical and the social landscape. In the nineteenth century, factories were built, coal mines opened, and railroads and telegraph lines laid, destroying the isolation that had sheltered traditional agricultural communities. Pushed by inventions that reduced the need for farm labor, and pulled by the lure of wages, people left their ancestral villages in ever-increasing numbers. Factory towns appeared almost overnight, and urban populations mushroomed. By 1850, more people in Great Britain lived in towns and cities than in the countryside. (The United States did not become predominantly urban until the twentieth century.)

Traditional social relationships were torn apart in the process. Social interaction in factory towns was far more impersonal than in small rural villages. Often people did not know many of their neighbors and co-workers, much less have face-to-face dealings with their employers. Machine production put many people out of work. Urban riots and squalor created an unsettling image of mass poverty and the threat of crime or rebellion within European societies.

In addition to sweeping changes at home, the growth of colonial empires and international trade brought Europeans into contact with peoples whose customs and values were quite different from their own. Most Europeans believed that their own culture was clearly superior. They believed that they were rational creatures while others were slaves to superstition or to primitive, animal passions. But scholars were perplexed by cultural diversity. Where had European civilization come from, and where was it headed?

It was from this social and intellectual turmoil that sociology was born. Common-sense explanations of the world, based on past experience, no longer applied. Social philosophy, which dealt with what society *should* be like, could not explain what was currently happening in the real world. What governments, businesses, and ordinary citizens needed was a *science* of society—a large body of factual information put into perspective by systematically tested theories—that would help them understand and adapt to the modern era (Nisbet and Perrin, 1977). And so a new discipline—which the pioneering French thinker Auguste Comte (1798–1857) called sociology—came into being.

The rise of scientific thinking was itself one of the major social changes in Europe. The early sociologists were both part of the scientific tide that was sweeping Europe and observers of it. Adapting ideas and methods from the physical sciences, they gathered empirical data and constructed theories that are still influential today. They developed the key concepts of social structure, social action, functional integration, power, and culture. In the following section we will examine the ideas of those who have had—and continue to have—the greatest influence on sociology's development.

Rational-Choice Theory and Social Action

One of sociology's ancestors, Adam Smith (1723–1790), also helped to create modern economics. His concern, and that of many other thinkers of the era, was how individual decisions—social action—could add up to the beneficial organization of a whole society. Smith (1776/1976) believed that people make choices (what to buy, what to manufacture, what career to enter) on the basis of very rational cost/benefit calculations. In doing so, they consider mainly the consequences to themselves, not how their actions will affect others. Yet in a free-market system, Smith maintained, economic choices motivated purely by self-interest ultimately lead to the efficient production of the goods consumers want and a corresponding rise in society's wealth. This occurs because competition works like an "invisible hand" to streamline production, maximize profits, and guide labor and investment into areas where demand is greatest. Smith's version of rational-choice theory uses the key concept of functional integration. Smith saw society as a self-regulating system in which many different parts, all acting in their own interest, are meshed together through market forces to form an integrated whole that functions for the common good.

Smith's work helped to found rational-choice theory because his method of analysis was not just to study the actual choices people made, but to construct models of what a *rational* actor would do, given certain interests, abilities, and conditions. Actual behavior could then be compared with these models. Cultural patterns could be evaluated to see whether they led people astray by obscuring their true interests or were in accord with what unbiased rational actors would choose. Smith argued, for example, that the feelings that bind us to other members of our culture sometimes lead us away from rational decisions, as when we impose taxes that raise the prices of goods imported from foreign countries.

The British philosopher Jeremy Bentham (1748–1832) expanded and systematized Smith's analysis of rational decision making. Bentham (1789/1970) stressed that humans everywhere are motivated to obtain pleasure and avoid pain. He argued that people try to evaluate their different experiences so as to act in ways that maximize pleasure over pain. Bentham disagreed with Smith's view that individual decisions, made on the basis of self-interest, automatically add up to the greatest good for society as a whole. To Bentham, the public good (defined as the greatest benefit at the lowest cost for the greatest number of people) could best be achieved by scientifically planned government action—what he called a "visible hand." Cooperation among social actors does not automatically occur, he claimed, even when it would produce greater benefit for more people. If a government with the power to demand cooperation does not intervene, conflict among actors is likely to break out, with each trying to gain at the expense of the others. This view made Bentham an early thinker about the key sociological concept of power.

The rational-choice theory that Smith and Bentham pioneered is still influential in sociology. Rational-choice theory holds that, in making decisions, people weigh the gains to be made from a particular action against the costs incurred. Only when they perceive the gains as outweighing the costs do they adopt the behavior. Rational-choice theory stresses the role of individual decisions in shaping social facts (J. S. Coleman, 1990b). As you will see in later chapters, this approach has been applied to how businesses make market decisions, how people decide to invest in more education, and even how young people choose whom to date and marry (J. S. Coleman, 1992). Rational-choice theory is particularly important in public-policy analysis, where it helps to identify who will gain or lose from any new public program.

In many ways, however, rational-choice theory was part of the established view against which other sociological theories developed. Challenging the idea that social patterns can be explained as the sum of individual actions, other sociological thinkers stressed the role of groups, large-scale social structure culture, and historical change in creating the conditions for social action.

Marx on Class Conflict and the Social Structure of Capitalism

An economic historian, social theorist, and revolutionary, Karl Marx (1818–1883) is best known as the father of modern communism. In addition, Marx made enormous contributions to the fields of sociology and economics.

Marx (1867/1976) believed that the most significant social fact about the industrial societies of his time was their capitalist social structure. The means of production were privately owned and used to produce profits. These societies were divided into two opposing classes: the **capitalists** or **bourgeoisie**, who owned the land, factories, and machines, and the **proletariat** or workers, who actually produced economic goods through their labor.

This structural division of society into opposing classes had strong implications for power relations, as Marx was quick to point out. To Marx the interests of the capitalists and the proletariat were inherently contradictory. Capitalists were driven to maximize profits by exploiting workers and holding their wages at the lowest possible levels. Workers suffered, and therefore were driven to overthrow the capitalist system, seize the means of production, and establish a classless society in which wealth would be distributed evenly. Of course, the capitalists and the governments they supported would use all the power they could muster to stop workers from changing the social order. Workers, accordingly, would need the power that came from their numbers in order to resist, and they would probably have to engage in prolonged conflict with their oppressors in order to overthrow them. Thus, revolution might or might not occur, but friction and struggle over social values and goals were inevitable. According to Marx, class conflict is built into a capitalist system.

Marx argued that social structure, rooted in economic production and class relations, always shaped social action and even culture. Thus, the agricultural, peasant economies of the Middle Ages gave rise to strong communities and religious faith, while the industrial, capitalist economies of the modern era bred individualism and a more scientific outlook. Marx further held that class conflict is "the engine of history," the primary source of social change. There is room for social action in his view, but it is never free from the influence of previous actions and above all social structure. "Men make their own history," Marx wrote, "but they do not make it under circumstances chosen by themselves, rather under circumstances directly encountered, given, and transmitted from the past" (Marx, 1852/1979, p. 103).

One of Marx's central contributions to sociology was his emphasis on collective struggle as a kind of social action. Because a small elite controls most of the wealth in society, most individuals have relatively little power by themselves. But workers would gain the power to change this social structure if they joined together in unions and political parties. This called not just for action, but for a change in culture. Workers had to break free of capitalism's idea that everyone should be considered only as an individual; they had to develop **class consciousness**, a sense of their shared interests and problems. Until then,

Residents of an English children's home in the 1870s. These boys were vagrants, crippled by industrial accidents and homeless because their families had fallen apart. They became wards of a charitable organization, which could address only a small portion of the immense social problems caused by industrial capitalism.

In Karl Marx's view, capitalist society is dominated by those who control the means of production and reap profits from the labor of others. The deep division between social classes leads to struggles over social power and eventually to revolution.

the capitalists would use their power to shape the workers' religious beliefs, leisure activities, and consumer preferences. This would foster a "false consciousness" among the proletariat, a misleading cultural orientation that would prevent them from realizing that they were being exploited. Culture thus reinforced the power of elites in capitalism's class-divided social structure. Unless workers could change that structure, Marx argued, they could not gain power. This is why he advocated revolution—to seize government and use its power to change social structure.

Many contemporary sociologists are influenced by Marx. Few are Marxists in the sense of accepting his entire doctrine and its politics, especially in view of the recent collapse of communism in Eastern Europe. But many follow Marx in focusing on the importance of capitalism as a social structure yielding unequal economic power. Many also agree with his emphasis on how people who are weak as individuals gain in power when they are socially organized.

Durkheim on Functional Integration and Culture

Another early sociologist with enormous influence was the Frenchman Émile Durkheim (1858–1917). While Durkheim did not agree with Marx's strong emphasis on the economy as the basis of social structure, or on the inevitability of class divisions, he did share Marx's concern for the forces that bind people together, or what he called **social solidarity** (Durkheim, 1893/1985). For Durkheim the key to social solidarity was functional integration. In Durkheim's view, there were two basic forms of social solidarity. **Mechanical solidarity** is based on strongly shared beliefs, values, and customs. This is what holds together small, simple, tribal societies and traditional agricultural villages, where everyone views the world in much the same way and engages in the same activities. Large, complex, modern societies, in contrast, are knit together by what Durkheim called **organic solidarity**, an interdependence that is based on a complex division of labor. In a modern society each person earns money from a specialized occupation and then uses that money to buy goods and services that thousands of others have specialized roles in producing. The social bonds this system creates are extremely strong. People are interconnected because differences in their skills and roles make them need each other to survive. Functional integration is greatest in modern societies that are based on organic solidarity.

Durkheim (1895/1982) argued that society forms a whole that is greater than the sum of its parts, and the study of society is at a different level from the study of individuals. To clarify these points, he used the analogy of a living organism (hence the term *organic* solidarity). A whole person is more than the sum of the cells and organs that make up the body; there are characteristics of the interconnected living system that transcend its collection of parts. And so it is with societies. Yet we can profitably study the parts and how each is important to the functioning of the whole system. Along with the British sociologist Herbert Spencer, Durkheim pioneered sociology's use of the key concept of functional integration. He emphasized the ways in which different social activities and institutions (like families, schools, and courts) fit together and support one another—even when no one plans the whole. The whole, in Durkheim's functionalist view, is held together through the interrelated workings of its parts.

Using the same functionalist reasoning, Durkheim argued that shared values and practices derived from culture also play a role in knitting society together (Durkheim, 1912/1965; Alexander, 1988). For example, religious services are occasions not only for worshiping God but also for affirming social bonds among members of the congregation and between the congregation and society as a whole. Religion and other elements of culture also function to provide people with a sense of rules and limits, with ideas about what they can reasonably expect. In times of rapid

Émile Durkheim believed that shared social bonds hold modern society together. Mutual trust and interdependency create a "collective conscience," or sense of belonging, and help to make society as a whole greater than, and distinct from, the sum of its individual members.

social change—such as the Industrial Revolution—these ideas are challenged. When expectations deviate too far from realities, society suffers from **anomie**—a state in which breakdowns of social norms or rules make it difficult for people to maintain a clear sense of who they are, where their lives will take them, and what it all means. According to Durkheim, even our most private feelings are shaped by society. The key concepts that Durkheim emphasized were the ones that pertain to the broadly shared features of social life—culture, social structure, and especially functional integration. His approach tells us relatively little about power.

Weber on Social Action and Power

Max Weber (1864–1920) was one of the most important German intellectuals of his day. Like the other early sociologists, Weber (1904/1958) believed that social facts must be analyzed using scientific methods. In contrast to Durkheim, he maintained that social facts are nothing more (or less) than the cumulative result of the social actions of individuals. Sociological explanations, he argued, must derive from an understanding of why individual people choose the actions they do. Where rational-choice theory stressed analysis of actors' "objective" interests, however, Weber stressed their subjective understanding and motivation. Sociologists must try to see actions from the point of view of the actor, looking beyond objective behavior to the subjective thoughts and feelings that shape particular actions. They must interpret, not just observe. Weber called this approach ***verstehen***, a German word that means empathetic understanding.

Like Marx and Durkheim, Weber wanted to understand the rapid social changes occurring in his time. He believed that the most significant trend in the modern era was an increasing *rationalization* of social action and social institutions. More specifically, Weber (1922/1978) saw the history of Western society in terms of a shift from traditional orientations (in which people accept the wisdom of the past as a guide to the future and strive to follow the ways of their ancestors) to more rational orientations (in which people make a logical assessment of the consequences of an act in deciding how to behave) (Brubaker, 1984; Roth and Schluchter, 1979). The rise of science as the principal means of acquiring knowledge, the emergence of governments based on the rule of law, and the development of capitalism were all signs of this trend. For example, capitalism requires people to analyze markets, maximize the efficiency of production, calculate returns on investment, and create financial institutions to support economic expansion, all of which demand a logical, reasoned approach to the world. This rationalization is basic, Weber said, to a dramatic increase in the power of formal organizations from governments to giant corporations.

Max Weber focused on the interplay of economic, political, and cultural factors in producing the distinctive social organization of the modern West. He stressed that for this type of organization, individuals had to adopt a more rational and less traditional orientation to social action.

Weber is often said to be engaged in an argument with the ghost of Marx. He tried to show that Marx put too much emphasis on economic structure. While Weber shared an interest in social structure, he tried to supplement it with a stress on culture to help understand capitalism. More specifically, he saw capitalism as produced by cultural changes, particularly changes in religious beliefs and values. He maintained that the Protestant Reformation, which held individuals responsible for their own salvation and promoted the work ethic, laid the groundwork for capitalism (see Chapter 16). In Weber's view, people's cultural ideas play independent and important roles in shaping their actions, and thus determining the structure of society, including the economic system. Thus, economic changes sometimes *follow* cultural changes, not the other way around as Marx claimed.

Weber disagreed with Marx in other ways as well. Although like Marx he believed that power and conflict are fundamental elements of social life, he argued that people's economic identities are not always important in determining how the lines of the power struggle will be drawn. Often, he said, we care more about other social factors—such as race, religion, and personal tastes—in defining where people fit in the social hierarchy. These other social factors are the basis of **status groups**. Weber thought that status groups were at least as important as economic class when it came to political activity. In the United States, for instance, working-class whites might try to maintain their superior status over working-class blacks even at the expense of the economic interests they share. Such racial status distinctions hinder the two groups' ability to join together politically to improve their economic lot. In contrast, stressing status-group differences works in favor of elites. When a person must go to the right schools, speak with the right accent, and have the right manners in order to be included at the top, many newly wealthy people will be barred from elite status, and elite groups will remain small and privileged.

Mead and Symbolic Interactionism: Culture and Social Action

Other twentieth-century sociologists have shared with Weber a stress on the importance of both social action and culture. But whereas Weber was concerned mainly with large-scale organization patterns in his analyses of action and culture, these other sociologists have focused particularly on the ways that people construct face-to-face interactions. This focus is called **interactionism**.

One root of interactionism is a school of philosophy called **phenomenology**, which developed in Europe at the turn of the century. Phenomenological sociologists wanted to get away from a one-sided focus on large-scale generalizations about social behavior, such as those made by Marx and Durkheim. Instead, they concentrated on how people construct their own social realities, subjectively experiencing and understanding their social worlds (Schutz and Luckmann, 1973). These sociologists also wanted to know how different people come to share a common definition of reality. This encouraged many to study language, the major means by which humans communicate their thoughts and feelings to each other.

An American school of sociology called **symbolic interactionism** developed a similar approach, incorporating much of phenomenology and also an American philosophy called *pragmatism* that emphasized how we learn from practical action. Two founders of this school were George Herbert Mead (1863–1931) and W. I. Thomas (1863–1947), both of the University of Chicago. They began with the idea that much of human behavior is determined not only by the objective facts of a situation but also by how people define that situation—that is, by the meanings they attribute to it. The most famous statement of this position comes from Thomas: "If men define situations as real, then they are real in their consequences" (Thomas and Thomas, 1928, p. 572). Suppose, for example, that you define American city streets as too dangerous to walk on at night. As a result, you never venture out after dark. In this case, an objective fact (the actual crime rate) is not determining your behavior as much as your understanding of what the crime rate is. That understanding is real for you because it keeps you home. Interestingly, our definitions of situations can sometimes become self-fulfilling prophecies (Merton, 1968a). If most people think it's too dangerous to go out after dark and so stay indoors, the lack of people on the streets can actually make the streets more dangerous because there are fewer people to observe or deter crimes.

Everyday human interactions were of major interest to George Herbert Mead. He viewed words, gestures, and expressions as symbols of what we think and feel; these symbols constitute the very foundations of social life.

Elaborating on the importance of our understandings of social situations, Mead reasoned that we learn what behavior and events mean through *interaction* with others. Through such interaction we come to learn our "places" in the social world and the roles we are expected to play in different situations. Even our sense of identity or self is shaped through social interaction, Mead (1934) asserted. By this he meant that we come to know ourselves largely by seeing how others react to us. But a person's thoughts and feelings are not directly accessible to others. Rather, we communicate by way of *symbols*—words, gestures, facial expressions, and other sounds and actions that have common, widely understood interpretations. Thus, much human behavior is shaped by *symbolic interaction.*

Symbolic interactionists focus on everyday behavior, such as what happens when you approach your instructor after class with a question. You first assess what the instructor is doing in order to determine how best to make your approach. If the instructor is talking to another student, you probably interpret this to mean that she is busy, and you remain silent, waiting for a more appropriate time. When you do speak, you monitor your words and actions and your instructor's responses to them. If the instructor smiles and leans slightly toward you, you probably assume she is being encouraging, so you continue confidently. If, however, she frequently glances out the window or at her watch as you speak, you probably read her actions as signs of impatience and may cut short what you have to say. In this way you exchange tentative cues and feedback as you fashion your social behavior. The result is the emergence of a shared understanding of what the situation means. Such shared understandings are essential to social life and of primary concern to interactionists (Blumer, 1969/1986). They may also be an important condition of the rational give-and-take between individuals emphasized by rational-choice theory (Coleman, 1990b; Cook, 1990). We will examine this approach in greater depth in Chapter 4.

Founding Theories and Contemporary Sociology

The work of these early thinkers—Marx, Weber, Durkheim, and Mead and other interactionists, the rational-choice theorists—helped to lay a foundation for modern sociology. Along with many nineteenth- and early twentieth-century thinkers, they created sociology as a scientific discipline. Each cast light on important aspects of social life. Each helped to develop the key concepts of sociology, as well as other, less central concepts. Each also offered an integrated perspective on the nature of modern society and its problems. Sociologists continue to read their works both for numerous specific insights and for the general wisdom that comes from seeing how their overall perspectives worked. Though subject to modification, their analytic frameworks retain a great deal of validity today.

For a long time after sociology's founders made their contributions, three major perspectives dominated the field. One emphasized functional integration and social structure, and was called **structural-functionalism**. The great American theorists Talcott Parsons (1951, 1960) and Robert K. Merton (1968a, 1982) were its two most important developers. They drew especially on Durkheim and Weber. Another perspective, which came to be labeled **conflict theory**, criticized structural-functionalism's limitations. It argued that structural-functionalism ignored the importance of power and conflict and also underestimated the problems brought about by economic and social inequalities. This approach was shaped especially by Marx and Weber. Finally, in American sociology especially, there have long been followers of Mead and *symbolic interactionism* (Blumer, 1969/1986). In Europe, the influence of phenomenology was stronger, but the impact was similar in creating a perspective that stressed the interpretation of culture and social action and that often used face-to-face observation as a major method of studying social life.

Sociologists, however, have never divided neatly into these three schools of thought. There were always those who crossed the boundaries or who didn't fit into any group. In addition, sociologists have always shared a great deal despite their different orientations. As sociology has grown larger and more international, there is even less adherence to the idea of three main perspectives.

Every sociologist must develop his or her own perspective on social life. That perspective need not be written out as a formal theory, but it must orient the sociologist's observations, shape the questions he or she asks, and guide his or her attempts to answer those questions systematically. The work of the founding sociologists—and of all the other sociologists who have written since—is available for inspiration and as a source of concepts to build on, analytic tools, and unresolved questions to answer. Developing one's own sociological perspective involves the type of imagination we discussed at the beginning of this chapter. A sociological perspective cannot simply be a set of rules to follow, like a recipe in a cookbook. It must be a way of looking at the world that helps one make sense of one's own problems, the ethical and moral challenges of life, and the overall workings of society. The sociological imagination is involved whenever a sociologist thinks about the relationship of social structure to social action, the relationship of culture to power and conflict, or the possibilities and failures of functional integration.

One thing you will see as you read this book is that the theoretical perspective a sociologist develops greatly influences the kind of research questions he or she asks. Choosing what questions to ask about social life is like choosing where to point a camera and whether to use a wide-angle or a telephoto lens. It all depends on what you want to highlight in the scene you see. By focusing on certain questions, you may ignore others that might also be valid. Reconsidering the founding theories again and again is one way in which contemporary sociologists keep renewing their own perspectives and reminding themselves of the need to ask different questions. At the same time, their new empirical knowledge and the new problems they study keep sociological theory moving forward.

SOCIOLOGY AND PUBLIC LIFE

Sociologists are both students of society and members of the societies they study. As such, they have a professional as well as a personal responsibility to take part in public life.

Sociologists as Researchers, Policy Analysts, and Interpreters

Sociologists contribute to public debate and public policy by performing three main roles: those of researchers, policy analysts, and interpreters (Marris, 1990).

As researchers, sociologists provide scientific evidence on social conditions. They attempt to give precise, accurate, comprehensive observations of social phenomena, refuting false stereotypes and assumptions. In some cases sociologists serve as expert witnesses in courtrooms and on committees appointed by the president or Congress to report on social issues. More generally, sociologists publish the results of their research in both technical articles and books written for other scientists, and in more popular works written for the general public. They conduct the U.S. census, which is the primary data base about the U.S. population. Such decisions as how many seats in the House of Representatives will be allocated to a given geographic area and where federal funds will be spent are based on census data. Public opinion polls conducted by sociologists inform political decision makers about where the public stands on issues from war to welfare. They have also become an integral (and controversial) part of local, state, and federal election campaigns. When the media want information on such issues as crime, divorce, health care, and housing and the homeless, they regularly turn to sociologists for data on the dimensions of the problem, its social causes, and possible solutions.

As policy analysts, sociologists play a direct role in designing, implementing, and evaluating solutions to problems. They may develop antipoverty programs for state or local governments, act as negotiators and arbitrators between unions and management, conduct marketing surveys for advertising agencies, and much more. For example, sociologists served on a team of researchers that advised the U.S. Navy on the physical design and social organization of battleships and aircraft carriers. These huge naval vessels are like small cities, with 5,000 or more people living and working in a confined space that has no exits. Often they are at sea for months at a time, with little to do beyond maintenance chores (from swabbing the decks and peeling potatoes to keeping computers, radar equipment, and weapons operational). The Navy had to grapple with the problems of providing for the sailors' social and physical needs, preventing or minimizing interpersonal conflict in crowded quarters, and keeping the sailors alert and ready for action through long stretches of inactivity and boredom. Sociologists helped to provide solutions.

As interpreters, sociologists interpret what is going on in social life and help us make sense of the facts learned by scientific research and observed in daily interaction. Sociological interpretations integrate "knowledge of what happened with understanding of why it happened and a sense of what it means to us" (Marris, 1990, p. 81). They use a careful, systematic collection of information to make sure the pictures they draw are accurate, and they use theory to show how specific facts and observations fit into the larger picture. Sociologists offer us interpretative frameworks that we can use in our own efforts to make sense of social life.

Sociologists contribute to public debate by challenging popular assumptions, questioning government decisions and policies, and offering diverse perspectives on social issues. For example, a leading public issue for contemporary America is: Why do a disproportionate number of African-Americans remain poor thirty years after most forms of overt discrimination were outlawed by the Civil Rights Act? Why are a quarter of black Americans trapped in persistent poverty, even while another third have risen into the middle class? U.S. Senator Daniel Patrick Moynihan (1986), who is also a sociologist, blames the breakdown of the black family. He points to the fact that a majority of black children today are born to single mothers, and to the decline of once-strong cultural traditions of mutual support in black families. Other sociologists, like Charles V. Willie (1983), trace the problem to "institutionalized racism." According to this view, racial inequality is the built-in, unintended consequence of doing business as usual—for example, the widespread custom of hiring people through an "old-boy network"—without any plan or wish to discriminate. William Julius Wilson (1987) argues that poor blacks are the victims of the deindustrialization of the U.S. economy. Stranded in dying cities, and poorly educated and thus unable to earn a living wage in an increasingly sophisticated job market, members of the so-called underclass are especially vulnerable to crime, drugs, and other social problems. Charles Murray (1984) blames government welfare programs for promoting the idea that it is all right to live on handouts, thus undermining the work ethic.

Each of these sociologists has not simply asserted his personal view of the problem, but has conducted research and brought to light objective information about poverty among black Americans. No matter what your opinion on this issue, the chances are that your views have been shaped by their writings and public comments. They clarify which arguments and items of evidence support the various interpretations of the issue.

Global Issues, Local Consequences

One of the important lessons of contemporary sociology is that global issues have local consequences. The Persian Gulf crisis made this abundantly clear. As a result of the U.S. military response to Iraq's invasion of Kuwait, everyday life was totally disrupted in towns like Hinesville, Georgia, near Fort Stewart. Sales in local stores plummeted. Wives and mothers (and some husbands and fathers) became single parents, and grandparents, aunts, and uncles stepped in as surrogate parents. Teachers found that children of service personnel could not concentrate on their schoolwork. Even children whose parents were not sent overseas worried about war, death, and abandonment. Special counseling services were set up to help parents and other caregivers deal with their children's—and their own—fears.

To clarify the relationship between global issues and local consequences, several chapters in this book contain boxes exploring a particular issue. In Chapter 5, for example, we look at the way in which workers' expectations have changed when Japanese car companies have set up factories in America. Because American workers and Japanese managers have been socialized in different cultures, each group has had to learn a great deal about the other's culture in order to get along. Because of the increasing internationalization of the economy, this sort of interaction is becoming more common. In Chapter 7, we discuss how the international drug trade produces local consequences both in American communities where drug use and associated crime are serious problems and in Third World communities where growing and processing drugs offer a rare chance to make money, but at high social and political cost.

Making Choices

Social facts and social forces also influence personal choices. During the gulf crisis, the rate of enlistment in the U.S. military rose dramatically. Apparently, the highly favorable coverage of the war in the mass media helped to wipe out the negative image of military service left over from the war in Vietnam. At the same time, however, small but persistent groups protested the war and called for a peaceful solution. Many people said that they opposed the war because the burden was not shared equally. A disproportionate number of soldiers came from poor, minority, and working-class backgrounds, as in the Vietnam war (a statistic revealed through sociological research). At the same time, research showed that whites were more active in the antiwar protests than were blacks.

In a series of boxes entitled Making Choices, we will show how sociological imagination can inform personal choices. In Chapter 4, for example, we will look at the sociological aspects of choosing an occupation.

In short, sociology is both an academic discipline, dedicated to producing new scientific knowledge, and a practical one, committed to teaching students and the public at large how to put sociological knowledge to use in public and private life. Because sociology deals with the most basic features of human social life, the sociological perspective is crucial for an understanding of the world. But because that social world is constantly changing and subject to many interpretations, sociological knowledge is never fixed. Rather, it is subject to continual updating, revision, and dispute. In the chapters that follow we offer the most up-to-date information on American society in its global context. Even more important, we offer the key concepts or intellectual tools that will enable you to apply sociological imagination to the public and private issues you will face in the years to come.

SUMMARY

1. Sociology is the study of human society and behavior in social settings. C. Wright Mills coined the term *sociological imagination* to describe the ability of people to view their personal experiences in the context of what is happening in the world around them.

2. Social facts are enduring properties of social life that shape or constrain the actions individuals can take. Social facts don't arise from individuals in isolation, but result from the interactions of individuals and groups.

3. Five key concepts have proved extremely useful in helping sociologists to understand our complex, ever-changing social world. These concepts are ***social structure*** (relatively stable, enduring patterns of social relationships, of social positions, and of numbers of people); ***social action*** (conscious behavior that is in response to, coordinated with, or oriented toward the actions of others); ***functional integration*** (the ways in which the different parts of a social system are often so closely interrelated that what happens in one affects the others, and is influenced by them in turn); ***power*** (the ability of a social actor to control the actions of others, either directly or indirectly); and ***culture*** (the shared norms, values, beliefs, knowledge, and symbols that make possible meaningful understanding of one's own actions and those of others).

4. In contrast to common-sense explanations of people and events, sociology is grounded in the scientific method—that is, in the systematic collection of data and the construction of theories, which seek to explain relationships among different phenomena and to identify cause and effect.

5. The five key concepts can be used to analyze the war in the Persian Gulf. They show that that conflict was the result of a collision of social forces over which no one person had complete control.

6. Sociology emerged during the eighteenth and nineteenth centuries, a period of rapid social change that raised urgent questions about the workings of society. The views of the sociological thinkers of this period remain influential today.

7. Adam Smith was a founder of rational-choice theory, which holds that in making decisions people choose the course of action that is most advantageous to them. Jeremy Bentham expanded this concept. He maintained that government intervention is needed to help society function smoothly and to allow as many people as possible to benefit from society's resources.

8. Karl Marx believed that the economic system of a society shapes all other aspects of social life and breeds persistent social conflict. According to Marx, power in a capitalist system is in the hands of the capitalists, who dominate the workers. The only way for workers to overcome their oppression is through planned social action and revolution.

9. Émile Durkheim focused on the social forces that bind a society together, a phenomenon he called social solidarity. Mechanical solidarity is based on a strong sharing of values, customs, and beliefs. Organic solidarity is interdependence that is based on a complex division of labor. Durkheim emphasized the functional relationships among different parts of society and warned of the dangers of anomie.

10. Max Weber is important for introducing into sociology an awareness of the subjective nature of social life, for balancing Marx's emphasis on economic forces with an equal stress on culture, and for balancing Durkheim's emphasis on functional integration with attention to power. To Weber, the most fundamental trend in the modern era is an increasing rationalization of social action and social institutions.

11. George Herbert Mead and the interactionists, who focused on language and symbolic communication, maintained that people address and respond to others depending on how they interpret the social situation.

12. Every sociologist must develop his or her own perspective on social life. The work of the founding sociologists—and of all the other sociologists who have written since—is available for inspiration and as a source of concepts to build on, analytical tools, and unresolved questions to answer.

13. Sociologists play an active role in public life, as researchers (providing informed testimony on social conditions), policy analysts (designing and evaluating social programs), and interpreters (explaining and interpreting social phenomena).

REVIEW QUESTIONS

1. Define the five key concepts in sociology, and give an example of each.

2. How does sociology differ from common sense?

3. Outline the origins of sociology by comparing and contrasting rational-choice theory, Marx's perspective, Durkheim's perspective, Weber's perspective, and Mead's perspective.

4. Briefly compare the structural-functionalist, conflict, and symbolic-interactionist perspectives.

5. Give examples of how sociologists are involved in public life.

CRITICAL THINKING QUESTIONS

1. How would the sociological imagination apply to some experience that you have had? Use at least one social fact in your response. Show how the sociological approach goes beyond common sense in accounting for your experience.

2. Which two of the five key concepts do you think are the most important, and why?

3. Select a major current event and apply the five key concepts to it, similar to the chapter's analysis of the Persian Gulf crisis.

4. Find a newspaper story about some social issue. How might common sense and sociology explain the issue?

5. How would each of the early perspectives in sociology—rational-choice theory, Marx's perspective, Durkheim's perspective, Weber's perspective, and Mead's perspective—help explain some contemporary social issue, such as unemployment, poverty, alienation, or responses to the AIDS epidemic?

6. How would the five key concepts each help explain some issue on your campus, such as sexual harassment, crime, increasing tuition rates, or academic dishonesty?

7. Do you think sociologists should be more involved in public decisions about social life? Why or why not?

GLOSSARY

Anomie Disruption in the rules and understandings that guide and integrate social life and give individuals a sense of their place in it.

Bourgeoisie The social class in a capitalist industrialized society that owns and controls the means of production (the land, factories, machinery, and so forth).

Capitalists Members of the bourgeoisie.

Class consciousness A sense of shared interests and problems among members of a social class.

Conflict Altercations that occur when the exercise of power meets resistance.

Conflict theory A general perspective in sociology that stresses the importance of power and conflict in social relationships, as well as the problems brought about by social and economic inequalities.

Critical thinking The attempt to develop an understanding that goes behind surface appearances to ask why and how events happen or conditions persist, whether social conditions could be changed, and in which different ways a given problem can be conceptualized.

Culture The learned norms, customs, values, knowledge, artifacts, language, and symbols that are constantly communicated among people who share a common way of life.

Functional integration The ways in which the different parts of a social system are often so closely interrelated that what happens in one affects the others, and is influenced by them in turn.

Interactionism The branch of sociology emphasizing the analysis of concrete interpersonal encounters and the use of this analysis to explain broader social patterns. See Symbolic interactionism.

Mechanical solidarity Solidarity that is based on common beliefs, values, and customs.

Organic solidarity Interdependence among a group of people that is based on an intricate division of labor.

Phenomenology A philosophy that holds that people construct their own social reality in accordance with the ways they experience and understand their social world.

Power The ability of a social actor to control the actions of others, either directly or indirectly.

Proletariat The members of a capitalist industrialized society who have no control over the means of production—primarily the workers.

Scientific method The rules, principles, and methods of science that are used for the systematic pursuit of knowledge.

Social action Behavior which is shaped by a person's understandings, interpretations, and intentions and which is in response to, coordinated with, or oriented toward the actions of others.

Social facts Enduring properties of social life that shape or constrain the actions individuals can take.

Social solidarity The condition that results when underlying social forces bind people together.

Social structure Relatively stable, enduring patterns of social relationships, or social positions, and of numbers of people; patterns over which individuals have little control.

Sociological imagination A way of looking at our personal experiences in the context of what is going on in the world around us.

Sociology The study of human society, including both social action and social organization.

Status groups Groups based on race, religion, personal tastes, and other noneconomic factors, which help establish a social hierarchy.

Structural-functionalism A general perspective in sociology that places its main emphasis on functional integration and social structure.

Symbolic interactionism An approach to human behavior as constructed in interaction and interpreted through culture, stressing the collective attribution of meaning to social life. The most widespread theoretical orientation within interactionism.

Theory A systematic attempt to explain how two or more phenomena are related.

Verstehen Weber's term for an empathetic understanding of what people are thinking and feeling.

CHAPTER 2

Methods of Sociological Research

Research in sociology begins whenever someone tries to be systematic in observing social life. Sociological researchers are always trying to produce highly accurate descriptions of the social world, descriptions that are less random and limited in scope than casual observations allow. Distinguishing different aspects of social life is a first step in this effort—for example, by using the five key concepts of social structure, social action, functional integration, power, and culture that we discussed in Chapter 1. Frequently, too, researchers are trying to understand the *why* of social life. Why are groups, institutions, and society structured in the ways they are? How do cultural differences or patterns of relationships with other people help to explain why humans act as they do? Answers to the question "why" usually involve causal explanations.

The French sociologist Émile Durkheim had both accurate description and causal explanation in mind when he set out to study suicide nearly a century ago. He wanted to explore systematically the social patterns related to suicide, to find out when and where suicide is most common and what social characteristics suicide victims tend to share. By collecting this information he hoped to gain insights into why people kill themselves. In Durkheim's day, as in our own, suicide was usually explained in individual terms: The victims were assumed to be depressed, mentally ill, or stricken with some unbearable loss. But Durkheim knew that suicide was more common among some groups than others, and he suspected that social factors were causing these patterns. Systematic collection of data would help him test this suspicion. So he gathered information about the rates of suicide in different countries, in different seasons, and among people who belonged to different social categories and groups. He used government records that listed numbers of suicides and gave statistics about the victims: their age, sex, marital status, nationality, religion, and so forth.

Upon analyzing this information, Durkheim found that the usual explanations for suicide were inadequate. Suicide rates varied between countries, between times of year, and between groups. If suicide were caused merely by personal problems, why was there so much variation in its rates? It could not simply be that some groups had higher rates of mental illness, for mental illness rates and suicide rates did not always vary in consistent ways. Some groups shared high rates of mental illness but little suicide; other groups shared high rates of both. Durkheim also noticed that women were more likely than men to be diagnosed as mentally ill but less likely to commit suicide. Other contradictory information surfaced: Durkheim discovered that most people committed suicide during warmer, sunnier times of the year, not, as might be expected, during the cold, gloomy days of winter.

The facts and statistics that he collected led Durkheim to conclude that suicide, at least in part, depended on social circumstances. As he wrote in his classic study, *Suicide* (1897/1951, p. 145), suicide is based on "social causes and is itself a collective phenomenon." Characteristics of the *social group* in which people find themselves make suicide more or less likely; self-destruction is not simply a private act.

In analyzing his information, Durkheim looked for the social conditions under which suicide occurred. People with few ties to a community were likely to commit what Durkheim called **egoistic suicide**, or suicide related to social isolation and individualism. In contrast, there were some people whose ties to their group were so strong that they died as heroes for it, in effect committing suicide for the good of the group, called **altruistic suicide**. There were also those who lived in stressful and disrupted times that resulted in a state of anomie (see Chapter 1) and encouraged **anomic suicide**. Finally, some people committed **fatalistic suicide** to end what seemed an inevitably bleak and depressing fate (such as life imprisonment or an incurable illness). Durkheim's analysis of these different types of suicide marked the beginning of a revolution in our thinking about social life.

THE RESEARCH PROCESS

In pursuing his study of suicide, Durkheim shaped sociology as an *empirical* science: a discipline with the capacity to analyze data objectively. Durkheim established signposts for a clear **methodology** (the procedures that guide research) and a clearly sociological way of knowing things. His research followed seven "model" steps: defining the problem, reviewing the literature, forming a hypothesis, choosing a research design, collecting data, analyzing the data, and drawing conclusions (see Figure 2.1). Each of these steps is crucial, but they do not always occur in precisely the model order.

Defining the Problem

The first step, defining the problem in a precise way, can be harder than you might think. For example, Durkheim had to define what counted as an act of suicide. He concluded that *suicide* referred to "all cases of death resulting directly or indirectly from a positive or negative act of the victim himself, which he knows will produce this result"

Durkheim classified suicide into four types according to the motivation for self-destruction. The death of Marilyn Monroe, which captured media attention around the world, is an example of egoistic suicide. The Japanese kamikaze pilots of World War II, some of whom are shown posing before their fatal mission, gave their lives in altruistic suicide. The panic of crowds on Wall Street during the 1929 stock market crash preceded widespread despair that led to cases of anomic suicide. Killing oneself in a seemingly hopeless situation, such as in prison, is an act of fatalistic suicide.

(Durkheim 1897/1951, p. 44). By "positive act," Durkheim meant such things as jumping off a bridge or shooting oneself. By "negative act," he meant such things as not taking necessary medicine or not getting out of the way of a moving vehicle. With this definition, a soldier's sacrifice of his own life to save his comrades counted as a case of (altruistic) suicide, even though many people might not have thought of it as suicide at all.

Many of the things scientists study can be classified as **variables**—that is, as factors capable of change. In sociology, a variable is any aspect of social life that can fluctuate over time, or appear in different amounts or frequencies. The suicide rate is a variable because it fluctuates from one period to another, as well as across different groups. Durkheim assumed that the suicide rate *depended* on other variables, which he was trying to identify. Thus, in Durkheim's study, the suicide rate was the **dependent variable**, and the other factors that influence it were the **independent variables** (those that fluctuate for other reasons—i.e., independently of changes in the rate of suicide). It is

FIGURE 2.1 / Steps in the "Model" Research Process

1. Defining the Problem
Selecting a topic for research and defining key concepts

2. Reviewing the Literature
Familiarizing oneself with the existing theory and research on a topic

3. Forming a Hypothesis
Defining the relationship between measurable variables so that they can be measured and the hypothesis tested

4. Choosing a Research Design
Selecting a method for study: experiment, survey, field observation, or a historical approach

5. Collecting the Data
Collecting the information that will test the hypothesis

6. Analyzing the Data
Working with and examining the data to shed light on the hypothesis

7. Drawing Conclusions
Summarizing the outcome of the study, indicating its significance, relating the findings to existing theory and research, and identifying problems for future research

useful to think in terms of variables when defining a research problem, because variables can be easily compared with one another and used to help explain observed differences in other variables.

It is important that researchers know whether their own definition of a variable matches the definition of other researchers studying the same topic. The fact that two researchers use different definitions of a variable can help explain important differences in their findings. For instance, a researcher who excludes "negative acts" of self-destruction from her definition of suicide might find that the suicide rate is relatively low among people with terminal illnesses. But if failure to take prescribed medications is very common in this population, then another researcher, who uses Durkheim's definition, will find that suicide is actually frequent among the terminally ill.

Not only must researchers define the variables that they want to study; they must also specify what they want to understand about those variables. In other words, they must state their research *problem*. Durkheim's problem—the focus of his attention—was not the question of what suicide meant to those who killed themselves, nor how it made their families feel. His problem was explaining the variation in suicide rates. Why do certain times, certain places, and certain social groups have higher or lower suicide rates than others?

Reviewing the Literature

Sociologists decide what research questions to ask largely on the basis of a review of the literature concerning the topic of interest to them. Good researchers look to see what is already known about a subject. Durkheim, for instance, looked to see what was known about suicide. He found few existing studies regarding the causes of group differences in suicide rates. This told him that his proposed research was not an unnecessary duplication of effort. It would fill an important gap. His review of the literature also enabled Durkheim to design his research so that it tested a number of existing theories. For instance, some people had claimed that because suicide was a product of depression, it probably occurred most often in the bleak, cold months of winter. Durkheim tested this idea and it turned out *not* to be true. Durkheim also tested the theory that suicide is encouraged largely by the power of suggestion; that people decide to kill themselves because others put the idea of suicide into their heads. Durkheim's findings provided evidence that although suggestion may play a part, it probably is not a major cause of suicide. Thus, Durkheim's research both evaluated some old theories of suicide and explored the value of new ones. In this way, he helped advance scientific knowledge on the subject.

Forming a Hypothesis

As you learned in Chapter 1, Durkheim's view of social life centered on the concept of functional integration. He believed that some of the most important influences on people stemmed from how well integrated their social groups were—that is, on the degree of close interconnection among the group members. Well-integrated groups, Durkheim argued, were able to provide their members with effective social supports, a clear set of values, and a strong sense of self-identity. These ideas enabled Durkheim to form a hypothesis about suicide. A **hypothesis** is a tentative statement about how two or more variables affect, or are related to, each other. Durkheim's main hypothesis was that the more integrated people are into social groups, the less apt they are to commit suicide. The two variables involved in this hypothesis are (1) the degree of integration in a social group and (2) the rate of suicide. Durkheim proposed that the first of these variables is inversely related to the other: that is, the *lower* the level of social integration, the *higher* the rate of suicide.

Choosing a Research Design and Collecting Data

To test their hypotheses, researchers need facts, statistics, study results, and other pertinent information. The first step in gathering these **data** is to figure out how to observe (and if possible measure) the different variables to be studied. How would you observe and measure social integration, for instance? Because this concept is so abstract, it is not easy to say. When researchers study such abstract concepts, they need to identify some concrete indicators of them. An **indicator** is something that can be measured empirically in order to get information about a more abstract variable that is related to the indicator but is difficult to measure directly. To measure social integration, Durkheim chose as indicators such things as marital status and church membership. He reasoned that people who are married and active members of a church are more integrated into society than those who are single and have no church ties. Thus, Durkheim essentially defined social integration in terms of the indicators of it he selected. This is called developing an **operational definition**.

The next step in gathering data is to choose a research design—that is, an actual plan for collecting the information that is needed. Some researchers conduct surveys and ask questions of many different people. Some choose participant observation; the investigators live and work among the people being studied to learn firsthand how they think and behave. Some researchers conduct experiments; that is, they create an artificial situation in which they can observe how people respond to different stimuli. Still other researchers use historical records to gather data. For many problems, the best approach involves a combination of several research strategies: surveys plus observation plus document searches. Researchers can also draw on the results of previous research to supplement the new data that they collect. We discuss all these specific data-gathering methods in the concluding section of this chapter.

Whatever research design is used, the researchers' crucial task is to gather enough information on which to base a sound understanding of the problem and to test their hypothesis. Although this may sound simple and straightforward, it can often be very difficult. Not only can a researcher encounter problems in collecting data, but a given set of data can often be interpreted in several different ways. Durkheim, for example, chose to rely on official government records that listed causes of death. But this meant that he had to accept the interpretations that government officials, physicians, and family members gave of why a person died. Because people generally base their observations about society on their interpretations of what others do, a researcher must take care to evaluate "the facts" with as much objectivity as possible.

Analyzing the Data and Drawing Conclusions

Once sociologists have collected their data, the next step is to analyze this information, which is often in the form of *statistics* or data expressed in numbers. Analysis is the process of looking to see which parts go together to form a pattern or whole, and how these pieces are related. To analyze statistics, sociologists use a number of measures (see the box "Basic Statistical Concepts"). However, analysis begins well before data are gathered. In a sense, it begins with defining the research problem, for there the sociologist decides just what factors to study and how to measure them.

In analyzing his data Durkheim looked for the social conditions under which suicide occurred more often and those under which it occurred less often. He found that Protestants committed suicide three times more often than Catholics, and Catholics more often than Jews. Single people committed suicide more often than married people, and married people with children least often of all. Durkheim reasoned that suicide rates are higher when people feel few or weak ties to a social group or community. The Jewish community was more tightly knit than the Catholic, the Catholic more tightly knit than the Protestant. Married people, especially those with children, had stronger social attachments than single people. Durkheim also saw that suicides increased when there were sharp economic reversals or upturns, and decreased when there was stability. He reasoned that any change that causes people stress—whether economic boom or bust—makes suicides more likely. When times are stable, people feel better integrated into the social fabric and more committed to social norms.

The final step in the research process is to draw conclusions based on the results of analysis. Depending on what patterns have emerged, and how these patterns are interpreted, the hypothesis may be confirmed, rejected, or left unsettled. Durkheim's analysis confirmed his hypothesis that suicide rates rise when people's attachments to sig-

Basic Statistical Concepts

To analyze statistics derived from research projects and experiments, sociologists use a number of measures. The most basic of these measures are averages and correlations.

Averages

Researchers distinguish three kinds of central tendencies, or averages, in the data that they collect.

The **mode** is the figure that occurs most often in a set of data. For example, a researcher studies seven families and finds their yearly incomes are:

$6,000
$6,000
$15,000
$18,000
$22,000
$30,000
$180,000

In this group, the modal income is $6,000 a year. The mode provides no information about the range of the data but is useful for discerning which statistic appears most frequently.

The **mean**, commonly referred to as the "average," is found by adding all the figures in a set of data and then dividing the sum by the number of items. The mean income of the seven families is $39,571 ($277,000/7). The mean is useful because it reflects all the available data, but it can be misleading: The $180,000 income of one of the families obscures the fact that the other six families all have incomes of $30,000 a year or less. The mean is most helpful when the range of data does not include extremes.

The **median** is the number that falls in the middle of a sequence of data. For the seven families here, the median income is $18,000. Unlike the mean, this measure does not allow extremes to mask the central tendency. Researchers often calculate both the mean and the median to present an accurate impression of their findings.

Sociologists may also want to find out to what extent a statistic varies from the mean (or another central point). Variation from the mean is measured by units of **standard deviation**. When taking this measurement, investigators calculate how far other recorded instances fall from the mean and then express whether each instance falls into the group closest to the mean, second closest to the mean, and so forth. The findings might be expressed as something like, "Most of the families in the study are within one standard deviation of the mean."

Correlations

A correlation, as discussed in the text, refers to a regular relationship between two variables. The strength of a correlation is usually expressed as a **correlation coefficient**, a decimal number between zero and one. When there is no correlation between variables (that is, the two have no relationship to each other), the correlation coefficient is zero. When two variables are found together all the time, there is a perfect positive correlation, expressed as +1.0. When two variables are inversely related (that is, the presence of one is always associated with the absence of the other), there is a perfect negative correlation. This is expressed as −1.0. Usually, in the real world, researchers do not find perfect correlations. They usually find less extreme examples of association between variables.

The most common questions in analysis concern whether two variables that are correlated have any *causal* connection to one another. It is always possible that a correlation is coincidental or the result of some third variable that is influencing the other two. Correlations therefore have to be checked for a possible independent cause. This is one way of checking validity (sometimes called *statistical independence*).

nificant groups are weakened and fall when they are strengthened. The stronger the ties people have to social groups, the more they depend on these groups and the more likely they are to take other people into account when making decisions. People who have few ties to their community are more likely to take their own lives than people who are deeply involved with their community.

The research process allows sociologists to evaluate one another's conclusions independently. Thus conclusions are not regarded as final, but are always open to question and reinvestigation. When research makes a significant contribution to sociological knowledge, it is usually published and made available for use by other sociologists.

Subsequent Research

No one research project ever exhausts an important topic. There is always room for work by subsequent researchers. These researchers may look at the subject from a different theoretical perspective. They may use better measures or different indicators of important variables. They may ask additional questions and gather additional data. Sociological knowledge grows through this process of continuing research in which many different investigators study closely related problems. Thus, Durkheim did not provide the last word on suicide. In fact, a contemporary American sociologist, David Phillips, has discovered that one of the theories of suicide Durkheim found in his review of the literature seems to have more merit than Durkheim thought. This theory holds that suicide is encouraged by the power of suggestion—that people sometimes decide to commit suicide when they hear about others who have done so.

To test this theory, Phillips (1974) selected a number of famous suicide cases, like that of Marilyn Monroe. He measured the amount of front-page press coverage that each of these suicides received. Then he compared the number of expected suicides during the following month with the actual number of suicides. He found a direct corelation between a highly publicized suicide and an increase in the suicide rate. But he was not finished yet. He had to test alternative hypotheses.

Perhaps all the publicity merely prompted people who were already set upon suicide to take their own lives right away. Perhaps people who were already so bereaved or depressed as to be virtually certain to kill themselves responded to the publicity by going ahead with the act (Phillips and Carstensen, 1986). If so, Phillips expected to find first a peak in suicides after the publicity and then an abnormal drop. But he found no such drop. Another hypothesis was that perhaps coroners became suggestible after so much publicity about suicide and classified more deaths as suicides and fewer as homicides or accidents. If so, Phillips expected to find a proportionate decrease in the rates of other causes of death. He didn't find that either. Maybe, then, the increase in suicides had to do with other conditions. If so, the suicides should not peak just after a front-page story, and the amount of publicity should not correlate with the increase in suicides. But the suicides did peak, and the variables did correlate. Finally, perhaps the increase was caused not by imitation but by grief. Phillips selected a sample of widely admired people whose suicides should have generated an unusual amount of grief, but he found that the suicide rate was no more affected by the stories of these deaths than it was affected by the suicides of less well-known people. (The box "How to Read a Table" includes two tables from Phillips's research.)

How to Read a Table

Social scientists frequently choose to depict their research findings in tables. These tables, which often appear in journal articles, textbooks, newspapers, and magazines, provide an overview of information and express relationships between variables. As popular as tables are, however, they raise a number of questions: How valid is the information in tables? Can tables be used to draw conclusions? What should one look for when interpreting a table? The following steps for interpreting Table 2.1 are general guides that can be applied to any table or chart.

1. *Read the table title to find out what data are in the table and how this information is presented.* In Table 2.1, the data are presented as numbers, but in other tables the data may appear as percentages or as some other measurement.

2. *To assess the quality of the data, look for headnotes and footnotes that may explain how the data were collected, why certain variables were studied, and whether data were collected differently for certain variables.* The source of the data, usually given at the bottom of a table or chart, is another potential measure of quality. The sources for Table 2.1 are (1) sociologist David Phillips's published article, "The Influence of Suggestion on Suicide," and (2) suicide statistics published by the federal government. If the source had been a group with a vested interest in the subject, such as a suicide prevention agency, you might suspect bias.

3. *Read the labels for each column (i.e., up and down) and row (i.e., across) to learn exactly what data appear in the table.* Table 2.1, which depicts the rise in suicides after stories of suicides appeared in the *New York Times*, lists the names of well-known people who committed suicide, the date on which the story appeared in the newspaper, the numbers of actual suicides and expected suicides in the month following a publicized suicide, and whether the suicide rate was higher or lower than expected.

4. *Look at the patterns in the data.* Note that some publicized suicides were followed by rises in the overall suicide rate, while some were not. The suicide of the film star Marilyn Monroe, for example, led to almost 200 more suicides than expected the following month.

5. *Draw conclusions about the information in the table, and consider what other questions the data raise.* Do suicides in fact increase after highly publicized stories of suicides? Is there some imitative effect, contrary to what Durkheim concluded? If so, does the *amount* of publicity have further influence? In other words, if a suicide is publicized on the front page for more than one day, is there a correspondingly greater increase in imitative suicides? David Phillips checked this question, and the data he found appear in Table 2.2.

TABLE 2.1

Rise in the Number of Suicides after Stories on the Front Page of the New York Times

Name of Publicized Suicide	Date of Suicide Story	Observed No. of Suicides in Month after Suicide Story	Expected No. of Suicides in Month after Suicide Story	Rise in Suicides after Suicide Story (Observed Minus Expected No. of Suicides)
Lockridge, author	March 8, 1948	1510	1521.5	−11.5
Landis, film star	July 6, 1948	1482	1457.5	24.5
Brooks, financier	August 28, 1948	1250	1350.0	−100.0
Holt, betrayed husband	March 10, 1948	1583	1521.5	61.5
Forrestal, ex-Secretary of Defense	May 22, 1949	1549	1493.5	55.5
Baker, professor	April 26, 1950	1600	1493.5	106.5
Lang, police witness	April 20, 1951	1423	1519.5	−96.5
Monroe, film star	August 6, 1962	1838	1640.5	197.5
Graham, publisher, and Ward, implicated in Profumo affair	August 4, 1963	1801	1640.5	160.5
Burros, Ku Klux Klan leader Morrison, war critic	November 1, 1965 November 3, 1965	1710	1652.0	58.0

Source: From Phillips (1974, p. 344). Original source of suicide statistics: U.S. Department of Health, Education, and Welfare, Public Health Service (yearly volumes, 1947–1968).

TABLE 2.2

Rise in the Number of Suicides after Stories on the Front Page of the New York Daily News

	NUMBER OF DAYS ON PAGE 1 OF THE NEWS[a]				
	0	1	2	3	4
Average rise in United States suicides after each suicide story[b]	25.26	28.54	35.25	82.63	197.5

Source: From Phillips (1974, p. 345) with permission. Original source of suicide statistics: U.S. Department of Health, Education, and Welfare, Public Health Service (yearly volumes, 1947–1968).

[a]The suicide stories carried in the New York Times and listed in Table 2.1 fall into the following categories: 0 days—Lockridge, Baker, Lang, Graham, Morrison; 1 day—Landis, Brooks, Forrestal, Burros; 2 days—Holt; 3 days—Ward; 4 days—Monroe.
[b]Ward and Graham died on the same day, August 4, 1963. Half the rise in suicides in August 1963 has been credited to Ward and half to Graham. A similar procedure has been followed for Burros and Morrison, who died on November 1 and November 3, 1965.

Phillips kept up his systematic investigation of patterns of imitation. He found that the rates of fatal motor-vehicle accidents also rise after publicized suicides (Phillips, 1986). He found imitation after widely publicized stories of robberies and assaults. Even heavyweight championship boxing matches are followed by a rise in murders, with victims looking more like the loser of the prizefight than one would statistically expect. Phillips has discovered that teenagers are especially vulnerable to this social imitation. In the week following substantial TV coverage of a celebrity suicide, the suicide rate among teenagers leapt by over 22 percent on average (Phillips and Carstensen, 1988).

Of course, Phillips's findings about imitative suicide don't invalidate Durkheim's conclusion that suicide rates are related to degree of social integration. They simply show that Durkheim's theory isn't the whole story. Neither is imitation. Combining the influence of both social integration *and* imitation enables us to explain more of the variance in suicide rates than considering just one of these factors alone. Sociologists hope that by combining the impacts of a relatively small number of independent variables they can explain much of the variance in their dependent variables. Only very rarely can they explain *all* the variance, however. Influences on human behavior are so numerous and complex that some things are inevitably overlooked. There may also be inaccuracies in data that distort assessments, and distortions due to chance may enter in as well. This is why there is always room for more research, more efforts to refine our knowledge of the social world.

Frequently, the work of one researcher raises questions that others find intriguing and want to try to answer. Phillips's work, for example, suggests several new questions for future research: What other types of behavior does publicity trigger? Does it encourage prosocial as well as antisocial actions? Should the government regulate the publicity given to violence, or the way it is reported, to minimize imitation? When other researchers try to answer such questions they build on Phillips's findings, and so sociological knowledge grows.

The tragedy of teenage suicide is often believed to be imitative. That is, the actions of significant others, or even the widely publicized suicides of famous people, may lead to increases in suicide rates.

CHALLENGES IN DOING SOCIOLOGICAL RESEARCH

The study of suicide highlights some of the challenges that researchers face when studying social behavior. Like all other scientific studies, those of suicide must be assessed in terms of their validity and reliability. **Validity** is the degree to which a study measures what it is attempting to measure—for example, the degree to which Durkheim actually measured social integration by using indicators like marriage rates. **Reliability** is the degree to which a study yields the same results when repeated by the original researcher or by other scientists.

Subsequent studies of suicide rates have shown Durkheim's results to be reliable, but critics have questioned whether Durkheim's data were valid (Pescosolido and Mendelsohn, 1986). Might the data have been distorted? Perhaps Catholics appear to have fewer suicides than Protestants because they disguise and cover up their suicides better. A good case could be made for the hypothesis that the better integrated a person is within society, the less likely it is that his or her death will be *classified* as a suicide. For example, officials in a close-knit community might respect a family's wish to avoid embarrassment and record the suicide as a death resulting from natural causes. Or the officials might not suspect suicide because the person was deemed a leading citizen of the community (Douglas,

1967). Such concerns undermine Durkheim's argument.

Another challenge that researchers confront is specifying the relationship between variables. Ideally, sociologists are most interested in specifying cause-and-effect relationships, or relationships in which a change in one variable is caused by a change in another.

In many cases, however, sociologists may not be able to determine a causal relationship between variables. They may only be able to show that two variables change together—are *correlated*—in some measurable way. A **correlation** refers to a regular relationship between two variables. For example, if a high value of one variable (say, the divorce rate) is found together with a high value of another variable (say, the suicide rate), the two are said to be positively correlated.

The discovery of a correlation between variables, however, does not prove that they have a cause-and-effect relationship. Two variables may be correlated but have no causal link to one another. This is known as a **spurious correlation**, and it is a source of error in research. A crucial part of sociological analysis is distinguishing meaningful from spurious correlations. For example, someone might ask whether the relationship that Durkheim found between suicide rates and religious affiliation had a causal basis or if the connection was a spurious one. Perhaps both variables are the result of some third factor, such as differences in wealth or geographic region. Durkheim was aware that some third variable might explain his findings, and he tried to establish that this was not the case.

Related to the difficulties of determining causal relationships is the fact that people, unlike many objects of study in the natural sciences, are not reducible to simple cause-and-effect equations. Because people engage in ***social action***, and because their action is shaped by different ***cultures***, social variables may not remain constant over time or from place to place. The law of gravity and the composition of water are the same everywhere, the same today as they were yesterday. But no two families, for example, are exactly alike, and ideas about what the family should be vary enormously from one culture to another.

Finally, sociologists face the challenge of creatively combining social theory and social research. Research and theory are inseparable in sociology. Theories are especially crucial in defining problems to be studied, formulating hypotheses, analyzing data, and drawing conclusions about them. Theories help to synthesize and bring order to research findings. At the same time, they are constantly revised in response to the knowledge that research provides. Without data derived from research, theories are simply unproven speculations and not part of science. Research can test propositions contained in a theory, and it can bring to light new empirical data that call for new or modified theories. In this way social theories are updated and refined.

Different theoretical perspectives can lead to research projects that complement each other by shedding light on different aspects of a problem. Thus, Durkheim's study of suicide (guided by an emphasis on functional integration)

In 1978, Jim Jones, the leader of the People's Temple, and about 900 of his followers—believing that their movement was about to be destroyed by hostile reports from visiting U.S. government officials and journalists—killed themselves by drinking poison at their compound in Guyana. To understand such a peculiar and tragic event, a sociologist needs to learn how the event was defined by the people involved. This can be done by examining any messages left by the participants and by studying similar occurrences.

and Phillips's study of it (guided by a focus on the role of imitation in social action) each help us to understand variation in suicide rates. The most extensive possible knowledge about an aspect of social life often requires the use of several research methods and several theoretical approaches. For example, a sociologist with the key concepts of culture and social action in mind might notice that Durkheim's research on suicide neglected questions about the meaning of suicide both to those who commit it and to the members of groups to which the victims belonged. Such a sociologist—perhaps a follower of George Herbert Mead and symbolic interactionism—could design a study to look closely at how each of a number of suicides occurred and what it meant to those involved. This would not replace Durkheim's approach, of course, for it would not tell us anything about suicide *rates*. But it could give us insights into how suicide is related to social integration, and so complement Durkheim's work.

RESEARCH METHODS

Sociological research can be divided into two basic types: quantitative and qualitative. In **quantitative research,** sociologists count the instances of some social phenomenon and try to relate them to other social factors in statistical terms. Quantitative researchers employ a variety of statistical techniques to establish relationships between variables and to test for causal connections. (The box "Basic Statistical Concepts" discusses some simple but important statistical measures.) David Phillips's work on the statistical relationship between highly publicized celebrity suicides and a rise in the general suicide rate is an example of quantitative research. So is Durkheim's work on suicide. Durkheim would have found computers and the many sophisticated statistical procedures available today of enormous help in analyzing his data.

Of course, not all social phenomena can be counted or measured in quantitative ways. (You can quantitatively measure the rate of suicide, for instance, but not the meanings that the act of suicide has for those who commit it.) As a result, **qualitative research** is also important in sociology. In qualitative research, sociologists examine instances of some social phenomenon in detail, or try to interpret general patterns of social life in nonstatistical ways. A researcher who observes work groups to determine how leadership roles emerge, or who interviews young children to discover the meaning they attach to their parents' divorce, is doing qualitative research.

For both quantitative and qualitative research, there are many different methods of gathering data—from conducting surveys to making firsthand observations; from drawing on historical records to carrying out experiments. In the following sections we will examine the most important of these data-gathering methods and show how each is particularly well suited to answering certain kinds of questions.

Surveys

Sociologists use surveys to measure public opinion, to test assumptions about behavior, and to predict how people will act. **Surveys** are the systematic gathering of anwers to standardized questions from a designated sample of respondents. Respondents may be asked to answer questionnaires by mail, over the phone, or in face-to-face interviews. Surveys are especially useful when sociologists want information about events that they cannot measure directly. For example, sociologists may want to know how many people in the United States believe that elective abortion should be illegal. Most people will never be in a position to act on such a belief—that is, to vote on whether or not abortion should be outlawed. But public opinion often influences the decisions of policymakers.

Surveys are common in the United States; their results turn up often on the nightly news and in popular magazines. (An interesting survey from *Business Week* magazine is presented in Chapter 13.) Sociological surveys, however, involve much more than simply asking people a few questions. If the results are to be reliable and valid, sociologists have to be systematic in choosing *whom* to question and *how* to ask the questions.

Choosing a Survey Sample

Most surveys are designed to collect information from a small number of people that can be used to make generalizations about the attitudes, behavior, or other characteristics of a much larger population. The **population** of any survey is simply the total number of people who share a characteristic that the sociologist is interested in studying. Say that a team of sociologists is interested in comparing attitudes toward abortion between younger (defined as aged twenty to thirty) and older (defined as aged fifty to sixty) American women. The survey population in this case would be all the women living in the United States between the ages of twenty and thirty and between the ages of fifty and sixty.

Because it is usually too costly and time-consuming to interview everyone in a population, sociologists canvass a

The increasing power of personal computers and the availability of quantitative data, whether the results of questionnaire research or a census, make analysis of sociological questions ever more practical, even to those who work in isolated settings.

sample—a limited subset of the population being studied. The sociologists studying abortion, for example, might choose a sample of American women from the two age groups. Usually a sample is designed to be as representative as possible. This means that relevant social characteristics—age, race, social class, and so forth—appear in the same proportions in the sample as they do in the larger population. When a sample is representative, the responses of people in it give a good idea of the distribution of attitudes among the population as a whole.

Many people think that a large sample is more representative than a smaller one, but this is not always so. Perhaps the most famous counterexample was an attempt to predict the outcome of the 1936 presidential election. A popular magazine, *Literary Digest*, sent postcard ballots to 10 million people whose names were collected from telephone directories and car registrations. From the 2 million postcards returned, the magazine predicted that Alfred Landon would beat Franklin D. Roosevelt by a landslide. Meanwhile, a young man named George Gallup sampled a mere 50,000 people and correctly predicted that Roosevelt would win. In this case, the smaller sample was more representative of the population at large. For one thing, in 1936, deep in the Great Depression, many voters did *not* own cars or telephones. These people—most of whom voted for Roosevelt—were excluded from the *Literary Digest* sample. Gallup used a **random sample**, in which everyone within the population had an equal chance of being selected.

Designing a representative sample is a real challenge. If you wanted to survey the students at your school to find out their career plans (or their views on suicide or abortion or presidential candidates), you would be making a mistake if you arbitrarily polled the first 100 students to walk out of a campus building. What about the possibly large number of students who never use that building? You would have a more genuinely representative sample if you randomly chose 100 names from the complete roster of students at your school.

Constructing and Asking Survey Questions

The very wording and sequence of the questions that sociologists ask in interviews or on questionnaires affect the validity and reliability of the data that they get (Schuman and Presser, 1981).

WORDING The choice of words in survey questions can and does affect the results of the research. At first glance, for instance, it would seem that questions with the words "forbid speeches" and "allow speeches" would be logical opposites. But apparently the connotations of the words are different. In 1976, some respondents were asked, "Do you think the United States should forbid public speeches against democracy?" Others were asked, "Do you think the United States should allow public speeches against democracy?" The responses did not dovetail: only 21.4 percent said that they would "forbid" the speeches, but 47.8 percent said that they would not "allow" the speeches (Schuman and Presser, 1981).

SEQUENCE The order in which sociologists ask questions can affect the pattern of responses. Issues raised in earlier questions can affect how respondents think about later questions. Sometimes sociologists get different results just by reversing the order of two questions. For example, people were asked the following two questions: (a) "Do you think the United States should let newspaper reporters from communist countries come here and send back to their papers the news as they see it?" and (b) "Do you think a communist country like Russia should let American newspaper reporters come there and send back to America the news as they see it?" When people were asked question *a* first, 54.7 percent said yes to it. But when people were asked question *b* first, 74.6 percent said yes to question *a* (Schuman and Presser, 1981).

FORM OF RESPONSE On surveys people can answer questions in one of two forms. In a *closed response* question, respondents must choose from the set of answers provided by the researchers. In an *open response* question, respondents answer in their own words. For example, sociologists might want to know what people most prefer in a job.

They can ask this in a closed form: "Would you please look at this card and tell me which thing on this list you would most prefer in a job?" The card then lists five choices: high income, no danger of being fired, short working hours, chances for advancement, and satisfying work that gives a feeling of accomplishment. The question can also be asked in an open form: "People look for different things in a job. What would you most prefer in a job?" When people were actually asked these questions, the answers differed with the form of presentation. For example, 17.2 percent of the respondents chose "chances for advancement" when they saw it among the responses. But only 1.8 percent volunteered this answer when they were asked the question in an open form. Sociologists have to be aware that the wording, sequence, and form of survey questions affect research results.

Interviewing

When survey researchers need more information than a short questionnaire allows, they may interview people by phone or in person. An **interview** is a conversation in which a researcher asks a series of questions or discusses a topic with another person. If they use open response questions, interviewers can tell when to probe for more information and when to move to the next question. Good interviewers also know that the validity and reliability of interviews depend on the interaction between interviewer and respondent. They learn to tailor the tone or the pace of an interview to different kinds of respondents.

The sociologist Harriet Zuckerman was interested in investigating the careers of scientists who had won a Nobel Prize. She wanted to interview members of this ultra-elite group about their family histories, education, relationships with other scientists, organizational affiliations, and the changes in their lives since winning the Nobel Prize (Zuckerman, 1972). Zuckerman managed to interview forty-four of the fifty-five Nobel laureates living in the United States in 1963. She prepared thoroughly for each interview, not only constructing in advance the set of questions that she would ask but also researching the background of each scientist. She made sure to establish rapport during the interview—avoiding sensitive topics, using scientific language, and framing questions to establish continuity within the interview ("You said earlier that. . .").

These talks with Nobel laureates were *semistructured interviews*—that is, the general and specific issues to be covered were worked out in advance but the subjects were free to talk about each topic in the terms most meaningful to them. In contrast, *structured interviews* are ones in which the wording and sequence of questions are carefully planned in advance. In an *unstructured interview*, the questions and precise topics are not predetermined, and the interviewer and the subject engage in free-flowing conversation.

Experiments

The **experiment** offers scientists the most effective technique for establishing a cause-and-effect relationship. In experiments, social scientists can test a hypothesis—that one variable (*X*) causally influences another variable (*Y*)—by exposing subjects to a specially designed situation that allows the researchers to control the factors that may affect the variables. For instance, sociologists may wish to test the hypothesis that people who undergo a severe initiation to gain admission to a group (variable *X*) develop a strong attachment to the group (variable *Y*) (Aronson and Carlsmith, 1968; Aronson and Mills, 1959). In choosing to perform an experiment to test their hypothesis, the sociologists are thinking about the problem in these terms: If you change one variable (*X*) and another variable (*Y*) also changes and if all the other factors have been held constant (controlled), the change in *Y* must have been caused by the change in *X*.

Thus, in order to test a hypothesis, researchers (1) systematically manipulate one variable (*X*) and (2) observe the effect of the manipulation on the other variable (*Y*). The factor that is systematically varied is the independent variable; it is assumed to be the causal factor in the relationship being studied. The factor being studied is the dependent variable; it is the factor that is affected by the manipulation of the independent variable. In our illustration, the initiation condition would be the independent variable and the intensity of the subjects' attachment to the group would be the dependent variable.

Sociologists rely on two kinds of experiments—laboratory and field.

Laboratory Experiments

In laboratory experiments, sociologists bring subjects into artificial conditions that can be regulated carefully by the investigator. That is, the person doing the research can control for the effects of some factors while isolating the factor or factors that are of experimental importance. For example, social psychologist Bibb Latané and his associates (1979) studied the behavior called *social loafing* under laboratory conditions. Social loafing is the tendency for peo-

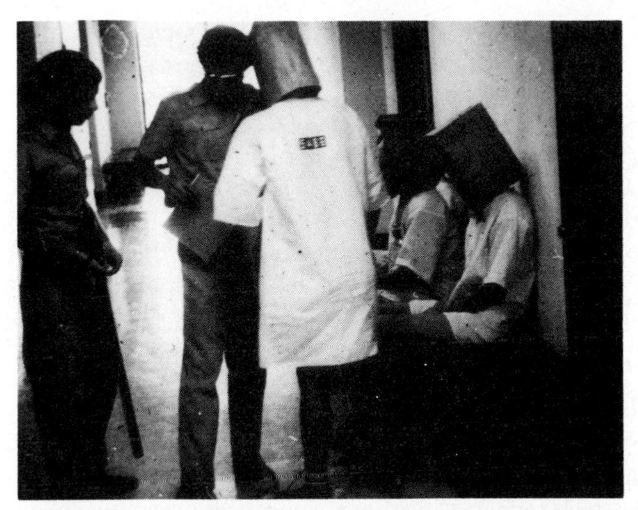

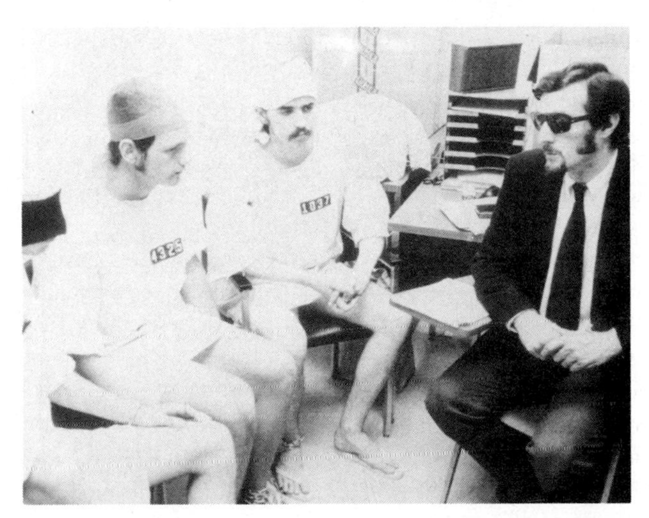

In the early 1970s Philip Zimbardo, a social psychologist, set up a mock prison in which student volunteers were assigned the roles of either prisoners or guards. The "guards" took their assigned roles very seriously, behaving aggressively and abusively toward the "prisoners," most of whom became passive and depressed. The methodology of Zimbardo's experiment revealed much about conformity to social roles, but it also raised ethical issues about the treatment of human subjects. Stricter rules are now in place to guide researchers in designing their experiments.

ple to work less hard when they are in a group than when they are not. It is a concept with social significance; for instance, the researchers wondered whether it might be related to the relatively low productivity of American factory workers.

First, Latané and his associates brought volunteers into the laboratory, where they were asked to cheer and clap (the task) alone and in groups of two, four, and six people. When the researchers measured the sound of the cheering and clapping, they found that the amount of sound from each person diminished as the size of the group increased. The experiment showed that an increase in group size (the independent variable) *caused* people to participate less in the task (the dependent variable). In other words, the larger the group, the more the social loafing. This was true even when the researchers tried to control for any annoyance the noise may have caused the participants. Since the researchers studied only Americans, however, they did not control for the effects of cultural differences. (Individualistic Americans might behave differently from more group-oriented Japanese, for example.)

To get the data about social loafing, the researchers had to deceive the volunteers. The researchers said that the purpose of the experiment was to see how well people in crowds could judge sound levels. Had the volunteers been told that this was a study of social loafing, they might have acted in ways that would have invalidated the results of the experiment.

This kind of "deceptive methodology" has been common in laboratory social experiments. But in the last few decades the issue of protecting people from harm in research has raised new and sometimes disturbing questions. Do researchers have the right to deceive people or cause them anxiety or humiliation in the name of scientific inquiry? In response to these concerns, the federal government has tightened regulations on human research, and universities have set up review boards to approve experiments involving people. Current guidelines for this type of research are clear: Explain the experiment or procedure to the subject; do not lie; warn the subject about any hazards; describe how the data are to be used; ensure the subject's confidentiality; make certain that, before a subject gives consent, he or she is fully informed about the experiment.

Field Experiments

Is it possible to do social experiments in real-world ("field") settings? Without the controlled conditions of a laboratory, where sociologists can measure precisely the effects and changes in independent variables, it is harder, but not impossible, to establish a cause-and-effect relationship.

The most famous field experiment of all time illustrates the difficulty. In the 1930s, researchers set out to study whether factors like better lighting would increase the productivity of work groups at Western Electric's Hawthorne plant in Illinois (Roethlisberger and Dickson, 1939/1961). Mysteriously, every work group studied became more productive, no matter what aspect of the work environment was changed. Eventually, the researchers realized that the workers were simply responding to the attention they were receiving: Being studied by social scientists made them feel important and valued. This "Hawthorne effect" revealed the need for researchers to control for the effects of their own presence. The main way to do this is to compare two groups that are treated exactly the same in all respects except for the factor being studied. Thus, the *experimental group* might get brighter lighting while the *control group* did not, but both would get the same amount of extra attention.

In the largest sociological field experiment ever undertaken, researchers used these improved methods to test whether the amount of government money poor people received or the way they received it made more of a difference in their efforts to find better-paying jobs (in Hunt, 1985). The experimental group (those who actually underwent the experimental conditions) got a guaranteed annual income. The control group got traditional welfare benefits. Interviews and monthly reports of income and expenses provided the researchers with information about, first, whether a guaranteed income was a more efficient way to distribute money than a traditional welfare system and, second, whether a guaranteed income would discourage people from finding better-paying jobs. The experiment yielded some unexpected results.

People who were given a higher guaranteed annual income earned less on their own than those who received a lower guaranteed income, but the evidence did not suggest that guaranteed incomes discouraged people from trying to find better-paying jobs. Surprisingly, more marital breakups occurred among the families receiving guaranteed incomes than among welfare recipients. Although income maintenance may have increased family stability among some of the participants in the study, it may also have made the poorest of the nonworking women less dependent on their partners and thus more likely to seek a divorce or separation.

These findings raise a number of ethical questions. When the experiment began, the researchers could not predict its outcome. Some of the study's effects, such as increased marital instability, might be seen as harmful. Is it fair to ask people to participate in research when they may be hurt by it? Other ethical questions focus on the issue of privacy. The researchers asked the subjects highly personal questions, such as: Have you ever committed a crime? Had an abortion? Although the sociologists were concerned with gathering as much relevant data as possible, did certain questions nonetheless constitute an invasion of privacy? Finally, some subjects in the experimental group got more financial rewards than others. Is it right for some people to have to make do with less money because they have been placed in the control group? Undoubtedly, experiments in the real world as well as in the laboratory raise serious questions about research ethics. However, they do offer new knowledge.

Ethnographies

In experiments, sociologists attempt to influence or change people's behavior. In ethnographies, this is not usually the case. **Ethnographies** are studies in which researchers observe people in everyday settings, usually over a considerable period of time. The researchers' goal is to provide detailed descriptions and interpretations of social life as it happens—among, for example, children on playgrounds, homosexual men in bathhouses, or street gangs in urban neighborhoods. Ethnographic studies provide the kind of eyewitness accounts of social life that are not possible in experimental designs.

Overt Participant Observation

In **overt participant observation**, the investigator participates in the social life of his or her subjects and the investigator's role is made known to the people under study. The sociologist William Corsaro (1985) acted as an overt participant observer of children's play. For several months, he watched and recorded how nursery school children played together. He did not try to hide his purpose. The children thought of him as a "big person" who acted more like them than other adults, and this perception gave him access to the children's culture.

In conducting the participant observation, Corsaro had to solve some problems of method. How could he enter the children's world without upsetting or changing it? He had to remain unobtrusive, but not so distant as to lose sight of how the children themselves understood their social world. Before he could even enter the playground, Corsaro had to negotiate with the "gatekeepers"—the school director, secretary, teachers, and parents. Once on the playground, Corsaro played with the children but did not affect the nature or the flow of their play episodes. (He considered play episodes the central unit of behavior in his study.) He never tried to start an activity or to substantially

The man on the left is a rail tramp looking for work as a cowboy. The one on the right is a sociologist studying the culture of the tramp. Both have ridden freight trains illegally the night before to a "jungle"—a gathering place for tramps. In order to understand the point of view of the subject, it is often necessary for sociologists to place themselves in the same setting and to experience the same reality as the subject.

redirect one. He never settled children's conflicts.

Like other ethnographers, Corsaro had a dual purpose: to understand the subjective meaning of events to his subjects and to remain analytical, systematic, and *sociological* in his investigation.

Covert Participant Observation

Sociologists sometimes do not tell their subjects that they are being observed for an ethnography. In **covert participant observation,** sociologists enter social worlds without identifying themselves as researchers and try to pass as bona fide members of the groups they are studying. The research subjects usually do not learn the sociologist's true identity or purpose. Sociologists have posed as members of cults prophesying the end of the world, as practitioners of "open marriages" who exchange sex with other married couples, and in a variety of other roles. Covert participation solves the problem of intrusion (that the sociologist's presence might alter the group's behavior) and allows sociologists to observe groups that are usually closed to outsiders. But this research method, in turn, raises serious ethical questions. Is it ethical to deceive people deliberately by pretending to belong to their group when, in fact, the real intent is to study them? Is a covert operation by definition an invasion of privacy?

Nonparticipant Observation

A variation on covert participant observation is **nonparticipant observation,** in which sociologists do not join in the activities of the group under study. They simply observe the group in its everyday settings as its members go about their daily business. When nonparticipant observers are successful, the group does not notice that it is being studied. However, observing behavior from a distance may make it difficult to perceive all the nuances involved.

Content Analysis

Sociologists often employ **content analysis** to uncover relevant information in historical and contemporary materials. Content analysis may be applied to almost any type of recorded communication—letters, diaries, autobiographies, memoirs, laws, novels, song lyrics, constitutions, newspapers, even paintings, all of which can reveal much about people's behavior. This research method is especially useful in historical studies, because it provides a way to systematically organize and summarize both the manifest and latent content of communication. The computer, which allows researchers to analyze content from many perspectives, has proved a powerful research tool.

As an example of how content analysis works, suppose that a group of researchers has decided to study the images of men and women in rock music videos. Because they cannot study every music video ever made, the investigators begin by collecting a representative sample of rock videos. Next, they list all the possible categories of content, such as song lyrics, clothing styles, gestures, and so forth. They then examine the sample videos, noting as many specific items of content as possible. So far, the researchers have relied heavily on qualitative research—research that depends on interpretations. Once sufficient data have been collected, the researchers can move to statistically based—or quantitative—research methods; for example, they can count the frequency with which women appear in subordinate roles to men, and they can check to see whether these instances correlate with other variables. Researchers have actually carried out this particular content analysis and have found that music videos often portray women in subordinate roles, as sexual objects, or as targets of violence (Brown and Campbell, 1986; Sherman and Dominick, 1986).

You can—and should—conduct informal content analyses of the photographs in this book, which have been chosen for their sociological interest. The accompanying box explains how you can "read" a photograph for its sociological significance.

Comparative Methods and Cross-Cultural Studies

Some sociological studies make comparisons between different societies, social groups, or social categories of people. Such studies may involve any of the other research methods we have discussed. They may be qualitative or quantitative. They may use data gathered from surveys, experiments (though very seldom), participant observation, historical approaches, or content analysis. What is crucial is the element of comparison (Ragin, 1987). Durkheim used comparative methods when he contrasted the suicide rates of Protestants, Catholics, Jews, and others, searching for social characteristics that could affect the propensity toward suicide. Other sociologists compare men and women to see if there are differences in their education levels; blacks, whites, and Hispanics to examine their voting preferences; and different age groups to see how their income levels vary. Comparison is implicit whenever researchers study a society or social group other than their own. An American studying Brazil will necessarily clarify some of the differences between the two societies, as well as the similarities. This is an example of international or **cross-cultural research**. Even studies done of one's own society or group can later be used for comparative analyses by other researchers.

One of the goals of comparative studies is to avoid overgeneralizing from the characteristics of one society or social group. For example, researchers comparing university students in America, Europe, and Japan are implicitly assuming that the characteristics of one group are not necessarily shared by the others. Comparative researchers also seek to assess the effects of variables they might not be able to assess if they focused on only one group or society. Why, for instance, do many employees in Japan seem to be more loyal to their companies and more diligent workers than American employees? One possibility is that Japanese culture instills these work habits, whereas American culture does not. Another is that the ways in which Japanese firms are organized tend to encourage high productivity and commitment among workers. Which of these explanations is more valid makes a great deal of difference. If national culture is the main explanation, there is little that Americans can do to increase loyalty and commitment among workers. This is because making cultural changes would be a slow, unpredictable process. If, however, the cause lies more in business organization, then American managers could introduce changes that would help to boost both loyalty and worker output. A comparative study of Japanese and American workers in several companies has helped provide the answer (Lincoln and Kalleberg, 1990). It has found that many approaches to business organization have effects on worker loyalty and output that are independent of national culture. This finding was made possible only by doing comparative research.

Some comparative research projects are mainly statistical comparisons of large numbers of countries. For example, sociologists interested in slowing world population

How to "Read" a Photograph Sociologically

Photographs in books and magazines are fun to look at, but they can also be valuable sources of information and insight. The photographs in this book have been chosen to illuminate the sociological concepts discussed in each chapter. Take a minute or two to "read" each photograph, rather than just glancing at it, and use the caption as a guide; you will soon find yourself discovering the sociological significance of the image shown in the photograph.

For practice, look at the two photographs shown below and ask yourself the following questions:

1. *Who is shown in the picture?* Photo A shows Chinese student protesters; photo B shows the changing of the guard at Buckingham Palace in London. This much is obvious—but look closer. In photo A, for instance, notice that most of the demonstrators are young males—a sociologically significant fact.
2. *What is happening?* Are the subjects of the photo part of an event, and if so, what kind of activity is it? Both of our sample photos involve public performances; the subjects have not been surprised in private. However, in photo A the performance is spontaneous and somewhat chaotic, while the action in photo B is organized and ceremonial. Clues such as the way people are dressed can help you figure out what is going on.
3. *Where was the picture taken?* "China" and "England" are the obvious answers, but a more specific awareness of the setting can help you interpret the photographs. The protesters in photo A are marching down a street—in fact, one of the main streets of Beijing, China's capital. In photo B, the changing of the guard is taking place in front of a palace.
4. *When was the picture taken?* Often the caption must provide the factual information you need here. Photo A was taken in mid-May of 1989, just a couple of weeks before China's elderly communist leadership brutally crushed the pro-democracy movement. Photo B was taken in 1993, while the British royal family's marital problems were making headlines.
5. *Why did this event happen, and why was it significant?* Often the photograph provides clues about why the subjects are doing what they're doing and why the photographer thought the action was noteworthy. In photo A, for example, one marcher is wearing a headband that evokes Patrick Henry's famous words, "Give me liberty or give me death!" Members of China's pro-democracy movement made such English-language signs precisely to attract the attention of Western photojournalists.

Every photograph—like a painting or a poem—means different things to different people. Nevertheless, careful analysis, using these questions, will bring out the sociological content of any photograph.

A

B

growth have tried to find the factors that best explain reductions in the number of children per mother in some countries. Careful statistical comparisons are used to see which independent variables have the greatest effect on the dependent variable of fertility (a statistically standardized measure of birth rates for women of childbearing age). Their studies show that the most important independent variables include educational and employment opportunities for women, quality of health care, the overall economic level of the country, and the availability of contraceptives.

Other comparative research focuses on a smaller number of cases in order to develop more detailed pictures of each case. This is particularly important where statistics are unreliable (as is true for much of the nonindustrialized world) or not strictly comparable (as when different governments use different definitions to collect data on their countries), or where so many factors are involved that it is hard to control them all statistically. As we will see with historical methods, focused case studies are also valuable when there are only a few cases of an important phenomenon, like revolutions. A good example is the recent transformation in some communist societies. The sociologists Victor Nee and David Stark (1989) wanted to compare the ways in which previously communist societies began to introduce freer markets and other reforms. They looked in detail at China and Hungary and somewhat more generally at several other Eastern European societies. They found some crucial similarities, such as cycles of reform (in both China and Eastern Europe a wave of reform in the 1950s anticipated that of the 1980s). They also found differences, such as China's greater success in introducing market reforms for some goods even though it remained a poorer and more restrictive country.

Comparative international or cross-cultural research is growing rapidly in contemporary sociology. The first reason is that there is a great diversity of human cultures and forms of social organization. To use findings from just one limits the range of variation being studied. This could lead to spurious generalizations. If you only looked at Americans, for example, you might think that shaking hands is the natural form of human greeting. But in fact there are many other forms of greeting around the world: bowing (as in Japan), kissing (as in some social groups in Europe), even thumping one another on the chest (as among the Yanomamö of Brazil). Similarly, if we took the American kinship or religious or educational or political systems to be "natural" and failed to compare them with others in the world, we would have a very limited view of the range of human social organization.

The second reason for using international or cross-cultural comparison is that the people of the world are coming into closer relationship with one another. The economies of all countries are being drawn increasingly into a single global system. The media are becoming increasingly international, as Americans watch shows from Britain, Egyptians watch *Dallas*, and Michael Jackson is revered as a star in Japan. Most important, people are tied together by the reality that armed conflict taking place in one part of the world can threaten to spread around it. Comparative research enables sociologists to study these processes of **globalization**. Throughout this book, we will report on research that broadens our perspective by examining globalization or by describing social patterns in other societies.

Historical Studies

Sociologists can only observe in the here and now. But understanding the past is often extremely useful for understanding the present, as Durkheim demonstrated when he used historical records of deaths in his study of suicide. Because sociologists are also concerned with the changes that take place in institutions, groups, and societies, they turn to historical materials—data about actions, structures, ideas, and events that have shaped human behavior in the past. By understanding historical settings, sociologists seek to avoid faulty generalizations when comparing and contrasting phenomena in different societies and at different times in one or more societies.

Sociologists are more likely to choose a historical approach when studying sociological phenomena that do not occur frequently. In such instances, sufficient statistical data might not be available, and interviews and surveys may be impossible to conduct. To observe the effects of a rare event, a sociologist might have to wait decades for a chance to gather fresh information. For example, it makes little sense for sociologists to postpone their research on revolutions until one occurs. And in the event of an actual revolution, the conditions surrounding it might make sociological research dangerous or impractical.

Sociologists also conduct historical studies to analyze events that unfold over extended periods of time. Most sociological research focuses on fairly brief events, like marriage and divorce, adolescence, or the creation of new businesses. Other phenomena of great importance, however, happen over longer time frames. Industrialization, immigration to the United States, the creation of the modern form of the family, and the spread of popular democracy are a few examples of developments that took many centuries to unfold. If sociologists looked only at present-day cases, they not only would be led to faulty generalizations but would miss the larger historical pattern of the events.

A major source of data for sociologists doing historical and other research is documents created for other purposes. Like historians, sociologists study business records, old newspapers, diaries, church records on births and deaths, and data and statistics collected by government agencies. (For example, Durkheim and others investigating suicide have used coroners' reports.) Sociologists may also draw on the published works of historians, especially when an investigation covers a long period of time or several different countries are being compared. This method, called **secondary analysis**, includes the analysis of data that were originally collected for another reason. In some cases, a sociologist might reinterpret data collected by another sociologist with different research objectives.

Combining Historical and Comparative Methods

Theda Skocpol's *States and Social Revolutions* (1979) is among the most admired and consequential books written in sociology during the last twenty years or so. It is an excellent model for illustrating how sociologists actually use historical and comparative methodologies in their research; combining methodological strategies in this way is a common and successful approach.

Skocpol began as any sociologist must: by defining the phenomenon to be studied—in this case, "social revolutions." She defined social revolutions as "the rapid, basic transformation of a society's state and class structure accompanied and in part carried through by class-based revolts from below" (Skocpol, 1979, p. 33). Without going too far into the details, this definition is a demanding one in that many social processes often called "revolutions" would not qualify under Skocpol's meaning. A social revolution requires fundamental transformation of *political* institutions (the state structure) and of *economic* institutions (the class structure, that is, the distribution of wealth or property). Political violence, *coups d'état*, and violent strikes would not necessarily be considered social revolutions unless they changed both the state structure and class structure in basic ways.

One methodological consequence of this demanding or restrictive definition of social revolution is the actual instances of the phenomenon to be studied are few and far between. Social revolutions are rare events, and to come up even with three cases for analysis, Skocpol needed to take a long historical view. That is, Skocpol's methodological decision to adopt a *historical* research design was necessitated by the fact that she could find a sufficient number of bona fide examples of social revolutions only by looking through history over a considerable period. The three cases she chose are France between 1787 and the early 1800s, Russia between 1917 and the 1930s, and China between 1911 and the 1960s.

Importantly, Skocpol did not want to abandon the pursuit of a generalizable, causal theory of social revolution. It might have been tempting—with only three cases at hand—to do what historians have typically done: tell the "story" of what happened and when in France, Russia, and China during their revolutionary years. Skocpol was not satisfied to write historical narrative, a kind of blow-by-blow account of events. Instead, she sought a theoretical understanding of social revolutions that would identify the common causes to be found in each of her three cases. This theoretical goal led Skocpol to the other half of her research methodology: A *comparative* analysis of France, Russia, and China would be needed.

In developing her analysis, Skocpol relied on many specific, detailed studies by historians who took the considerable time it takes to go through the many pamphlets, broadsides, edicts, and newspaper stories from long ago. Skocpol was able to draw on these narrower studies as she developed her broader analysis of the three social revolutions. This strategy—known as secondary analysis and defined earlier in this chapter—is a familiar one in comparative-historical studies.

However, Skocpol knew that this secondary analysis could be accomplished only with a prior commitment to theoretical assumptions that would allow her to separate important from trivial details as she read through the historians' work. Once again (saving the details for our consideration of revolution to Chapter 17), Skocpol's theory set down three stipulations.

- First, an adequate theory of social revolution must treat states (that is, the machinery of national governments, which are the institutions of central power) as autonomous social units, independent to some degree from class structures in the societies they govern. So Skocpol considered how state regimes try to survive and do their best to manage society even when their success runs counter to the interests of the nation's elite, powerful social classes. In other words, she looked at the balance of power between different elite groups, not just between elites and ordinary people or between the bourgeoisie and the proletariat (as Marx had suggested).

■ Second, Skocpol insisted that an adequate theory of social revolution must anchor these state structures in the *international* political and economic world order. The strength or weakness of a state depends on the international context—on the presence of war, debts, allies, and the like.

■ Third, Skocpol believed that an adequate theory of social revolution must emphasize ***social-structural*** causes. That is, the sources of revolution are to be found in the patterned relations among social groups and classes and in the institutionalized machinery of state agencies. This last stipulation implies that the causes of revolution are not likely to be found in the realm of ***culture***—say, in the changing beliefs, attitudes, satisfactions, and interpretations of people who lived through the French, Russian, and Chinese revolutions (although Skocpol does see culture as important in shaping the aftermath of revolutions). It also means that Skocpol did not place much stress on the revolutionary actions of individuals, although she agreed that such actions were necessary. She argued, for example, that Lenin did not make the Russian Revolution by himself, any more than Saddam Hussein (as we saw in Chapter 1) made the 1991 Persian Gulf war by himself.

With these three theoretical stipulations clearly announced, Skocpol compared the three revolutions, looking for elements they had in common and elements unique to one or another example. In addition, as kind of check on her developing causal model, Skocpol compared these three successful social revolutions with other historical situations where not-quite-revolutions failed to fundamentally alter both the political and economic structures in a society. Ideally, in this comparative method, Skocpol would hope to find certain elements found in each of the three successful cases—France, Russia, and China—but absent from cases where the revolutions failed. She found three such causes of social revolutions: (1) the collapse of an autocratic (or dictatorial) monarchy resulting from the inability of the state's machinery to deal with international pressures and crises; (2) mass uprisings of peasants as an immediate or precipitating factor; (3) conflicts among elites to establish a new state structure on the ashes of the fallen ancien regime (inevitably becoming as centralized as what preceded it).

What Skocpol's research methods enabled her to do was to go beyond telling the story of any one revolution. Her book is an account of causal factors that are important in all social revolutions. Other sociologists have stressed additional causal factors, including ideology and population (see Chapter 21), but they continue to use the method of combining comparative and historical research.

SUMMARY

1. In his study on suicide, Émile Durkheim set an important precedent for examining a problem from a sociological point of view.

2. The first step in the research process is to define the problem. Defining a concept in measurable terms produces an operational definition.

3. Sociologists formulate questions to ask in their studies on the basis of a review of the literature in the field—a survey of the findings of other researchers who have studied a particular subject.

4. After a review of the literature, a researcher forms a hypothesis, a statement that predicts how two or more variables affect, or are related to, one another.

5. The first step in gathering data, or information, is to choose a research design. It can employ either a quantitative or a qualitative approach, or a combination of both. The design, in turn, depends on the questions one is asking. Among research designs are survey, participant observation, and experiment.

6. A study is valid when it measures what it is attempting to measure. A study is reliable when repeated research produces the same findings.

7. Sociological knowledge develops as research generates additional theories and more research. One example of continuing research is David Phillips's studies of imitation as a factor in suicide. His findings add to the knowledge that Durkheim provided.

8. Sociologists face a number of challenges in doing research. They must make sure that their studies are both reliable and valid. They must accurately specify the relationships between variables. They must deal with a topic of study—human social life—that does not remain constant over time or from place to place. And finally, they must cope with the challenge of creatively combining social theory and social research.

9. A survey is a systematic gathering of answers to standardized questions from a designated sample of respondents. A sample is a representative subset of the population being studied. In a random sample, everyone within a population has an equal chance of being selected. Survey responses can be affected by the wording of questions, the sequence in which they are asked, and the form of response that is permitted.

10. The sociological interview may be structured (with the questions elaborated in advance), semistructured, or unstructured. Interviewing is a technique that depends to some extent on the skill of the interviewer.

11. In an experiment, one or more independent variables are manipulated so the researcher can examine the effect on a dependent variable. In laboratory experiments, sociologists carefully manipulate people under artificial conditions. In field experiments, real-world conditions are manipulated. Instances of deceptive methodology have led to stricter federal and university guidelines for research.

12. Ethnographies are studies in which researchers observe groups in their everyday settings, usually for long periods of time. Overt participant observers study others' behavior openly; covert participant observers do so without revealing themselves as sociologists. In nonparticipant observation, investigators simply note the behavior of others without participating in their activities.

13. In historical studies, sociologists use data about actions, structures, ideas, and events that have shaped human behavior in the past. Historical studies are valuable for analyzing rare events and events that unfold over a long period of time.

14. Content analysis provides a way to systematically organize and summarize both the manifest and latent content of communication. It is an example of research that combines qualitative and quantitative approaches.

15. Some sociological research makes comparisons between different societies, social groups, or categories of people. Research that compares different countries or other types of societies, each with a distinctive culture, is called cross-cultural research. Such research is increasingly important because peoples of the world are being drawn into closer relationship with one another.

REVIEW QUESTIONS

1. Outline the steps in the research process.

2. Explain why it is important to clearly distinguish independent from dependent variables and why these variables must be clearly indicated in a hypothesis.

3. Define validity and reliability.

4. Compare random with nonrandom samples and explain why random samples are preferable.

5. Provide some advice for effective survey questions.

6. Suggest topics that would be best studied by each of the basic methods: survey, experiment, ethnography, historical study, content analysis, and comparative methods and cross-cultural studies.

CRITICAL THINKING QUESTIONS

1. Select a topic of interest. Briefly outline how you would complete the study, following the steps of the research process. Explain why you made the choices you made.

2. Present a case for either reliability or validity being more important.

3. Explain why some people feel that establishing causality in the social sciences is more difficult than in the other sciences.

4. Find a study in the newspaper or one of the newsweeklies. Describe the sampling method used and discuss its strength and weaknesses.

5. Some people argue that we should not "experiment" on people. Present your feelings about using the experimental method to do research.

GLOSSARY

Altruistic suicide Durkheim's term for suicide that results from extreme commitment to a group or community.

Anomic suicide Durkheim's term for suicide that results from a condition of social normlessness known as anomie.

Content analysis A research method that provides a way to systematically organize and summarize both the manifest and latent content of communication.

Correlation A regularly occurring relationship between two variables.

Correlation coefficient A decimal number between zero and one that is used to indicate the strength of a correlation.

Covert participant observation A research technique in which people's activities are observed without their knowledge and the investigators never identify themselves as sociologists.

Cross-cultural research Studies that describe social patterns in societies other than the researchers' own.

Data Facts, statistics, study results, and other pieces of observable information that are collected and used to construct theories.

Dependent variable In an experiment, the quality or factor that is affected by one or more independent variables.

Egoistic suicide Durkheim's term for suicide that results from social isolation and individualism.

Ethnographies Studies in which researchers observe people in their everyday settings, usually over an extended period of time.

Experiment A research method in which subjects are exposed to a specially designed situation that allows the researchers to control the factors that may affect the hypothetical cause-and-effect relationship among the variables they are studying. Experiments may be done in laboratories or field settings.

Fatalistic suicide The taking of one's own life to avoid what seems to be an inevitably bleak future if one goes on living.

Globalization The process by which the peoples of the world are being drawn into closer relationship with one another.

Hypothesis A tentative statement that predicts how two or more variables affect, or are related to, one another.

Independent variable In an experiment, the quality or factor that affects one or more dependent variables.

Indicator Something that can be clearly measured as an approximation of some other, more complex variable.

Interview A conversation through which an investigator seeks information from a research subject. An interview may be structured, semistructured, or unstructured.

Mean The average; obtained by adding all figures in a series of data and dividing the sum by the number of items.

Median The number that falls in the middle of a sequence of figures.

Methodology The procedures that guide research.

Mode The figure that occurs most often in a series of data.

Nonparticipant observation A research technique in which the investigators observe behavior closely but do not actually participate in the activities of the group under study.

Operational definition A measurable indicator for one of the variables in a hypothesis.

Overt participant observation A research technique in which the investigator participates in the activities of those being observed and the investigator's role is made known.

Population In a survey, the total number of people who share a characteristic that is being studied.

Qualitative research Research that depends primarily on subjective interpretations by the investigator of the material or event.

Quantitative research Research that relies on statistical analyses of data.

Random sample In a survey, a method used to draw a sample in such a way that every member of the population being studied has an equal chance of being selected.

Reliability The degree to which a study yields the same results when repeated by the original or other researchers.

Sample A limited number of people selected from the population being studied who are representative of that population.

Secondary analysis Research that reanalyzes data drawn from previous research projects.

Spurious correlation A correlation between two variables that has no meaningful causal basis.

Standard deviation A statistical measurement of how far other recorded instances fall from the mean or another central point.

Survey A research method using questionnaires or interviews, or both, to learn how people think, feel, or act. Good surveys use random samples and pretested questions to ensure high reliability and validity.

Validity The degree to which a scientific study measures what it attempts to measure.

Variable Any factor that is capable of change.

CHAPTER PROJECTS

1. **Individual Project** Choose a topic that you would like to research. Study the steps in the research process as outlined on page 31 and tell how you would explore your topic and what you would do to complete each of the seven steps in the process.

2. **Cooperative Learning Project** Work in teams of four to design a survey analyzing television viewing patterns and preferences among the students in your school. Be certain to follow the guidelines given in this chapter for constructing and asking survey questions. Conduct the surveys and present your findings to the class. Did all the teams draw the same conclusions from their survey results?

CHAPTER 3

Culture

In a recent television advertisement, a sleek new car surges over the crest of a hill and along an open road. A lone male driver skillfully maneuvers around a smooth bend, as wide rays of sunlight fall onto the auto, giving it a spiritual aura. A rapidly changing montage of driving scenes follows. The car rolls effortlessly past the neon lights of a city street at night; we see it easing to a graceful stop before an elegant restaurant; we glimpse it as it crosses a magnificent bridge with a powerful river below. In the end the lone driver, now in the foothills of a mountain range, steps from the car and gazes out across an expansive plain. The song that accompanies these pictures tells the viewer that the American road "belongs to Buick."

The agency that created this TV advertisement demonstrated a keen appreciation of American culture. The ad reflects not only what it means to own a Buick, but what it means to be an American. Americans own more cars than any other people in the world. We celebrate our cars in movies (*Corvette Summer*, *Cadillac Man*, *The Love Bug*), songs ("Little Deuce Coupe," "Maybelline," "Fast Car"), and sporting contests (from the Indianapolis 500 to stock-car racing). Chrysler Corporation chairman Lee Iaccoca became a national hero through his appearances in car commercials and his best-selling autobiography. Many of us still agree with GM president Charles Wilson's 1953 statement, "What's good for the country is good for General Motors, and vice versa."

As we saw in Chapter 1, **culture** is defined broadly as the learned norms, values, knowledge, artifacts, language, and symbols that are constantly communicated among people who share a common way of life. The TV ad for Buick is a part of American culture because it embodies a whole array of symbols, the meaning of which Americans share. The moving car, the open road, the lone driver, the unpopulated landscape all symbolize to us a sense of freedom and independence that we as Americans revere. At the same time, this material object, a luxury car, is imbued with cultural messages about gender, status, privilege, affluence, and social class. The man who drives it is considered a cut above the rest. One reason advertising is so prominent in our culture is that it is so successful in communicating these kinds of messages (Schudson, 1984). It is a primary means by which information about the social meaning of material objects gets distributed throughout our population. As such, "advertising is not just a business expenditure undertaken in the hope of moving some merchandise off the store shelves, but is rather an integral part of modern culture" (Leiss, Kline, and Shelly, 1986).

Culture includes our beliefs about what is important in life, and it shapes our interpretations of what events mean. We praise democracy, worship one God, and value competition in part because our culture teaches us to do so. Falling in love is another cultural phenomenon, in that how we act when we are in love is something we learn from our culture—its books, magazines, movies, television shows, song lyrics, and so forth. In some parts of the world the rather flighty and obsessive behavior that we call "falling in love" is virtually unknown. Selecting a wife or husband is considered a much more practical matter. Like other beliefs, attitudes, and behavior that people in a society share, romantic love is a product of culture (Brain, 1976; Luhmann, 1986).

Culture also encompasses common, trivial, everyday habits that we so take for granted we hardly notice them. For instance, Americans commonly answer the telephone by saying "Hello"; the British, in contrast, typically answer by stating their telephone number or their name. We expect people in certain jobs (for example, flight attendants) to smile constantly and people in other occupations (lawyers and surgeons) to act serious, regardless of their true feelings (Hochschild, 1983). Each must control his or her emotions in accord with cultural expectations. We would be shocked if a lawyer in a murder trial smiled and seemed to enjoy himself—even if the trial was truly exciting and a big step up in his career.

Sociologists study the entire range of culture, both "high" or elite culture and popular culture. They may look at cultural objects and activities (such as books, paintings, museums, and concerts) that are related to cultural values, beliefs, symbols, and knowledge, or they may explore the cultural dimensions of other social phenomena (such as elections, schools, or jobs).

The sociology of culture shows that our hopes and fears, our likes and dislikes, our beliefs and habits, are very much social creations, strongly influenced by the time and place in which we live. This is not to say that culture *dictates* thoughts and behavior. It leaves room for action. Culture is something people *develop* and *use*. The sociologist Howard Becker (1986) captures this idea in describing culture as "shared understandings that people use to coordinate their activities." By creating and expressing the elements of our culture, by living them day to day, we are constantly communicating to each other an understanding of our social world. In the process, there is also room for reshaping culture, for adapting it to meet new demands and situations. As a result, culture is never static. It is constantly changing.

In this chapter, then, we focus on ***culture***, both as one of sociology's key concepts and also as a specific field of sociological research. It is important to keep in mind that culture is always related to the rest of social life and therefore to the other key concepts. We will see, for example, how some groups exercise ***power*** by controlling the definitions of what counts as elite culture and how the power of certain influentially placed people (agents, producers, gallery owners) helps determine what movies get made, what songs become popular, and what paintings sell for thousands of dollars. We will see how various cultural values—achievement, individualism, community—are ***functionally integrated*** into American society and how the existence of different cultural groups creates the challenge of achieving cultural integration while respecting diversity. We will see how language helps to make ***social action*** possible and how new aspects of culture are produced through social action. We will see how culture is shaped by ***social structure***; for example, American culture is currently being shaped by the presence of large numbers of immigrants in our society and by the aging of the baby-boom generation. At the same time, we will note how culture affects social structure by influencing which group boundaries are maintained—for example, by shaping the rates at which members of different ethnic groups intermarry.

THE ELEMENTS OF CULTURE

The particular content of culture varies from place to place, but all human cultures have the same basic elements. These include knowledge, language, symbols of all kinds, values, norms, and artifacts (the physical objects that people make). People use this cultural "tool kit" (Swidler, 1986) both to maintain and to change their way of life.

Material and Nonmaterial Culture

Sociologists commonly distinguish between two aspects of culture, the material and the nonmaterial. **Material culture** consists of all the physical objects, or artifacts, that people make and attach meaning to—books, clothing, schools, churches, and guided missiles, to name just a few. Natural objects are not part of material culture, but how people see and use them are shaped by culture. For example, to pioneers of European descent, the prairies of the American West were part of nature—a great, untouched wilderness. To the Native Americans (or Indians) who lived there, however, the hills and mountains, trees and wildlife, were rich with meaning. When Spanish and Anglo homesteaders carved the plains into ranches and farms, the land took on new meaning for them. What Native Americans had seen (and still see) as a communal homeland, settlers saw as "private property"—a distinctly European cultural concept.

Nonmaterial culture consists of human creations that are not embodied in physical objects—values, norms, knowledge, systems of government, the languages we speak, and so on. The value that Americans place on in-

This decorative ax is used in ceremonies of the Kwakiutl people of the Pacific Northwest. Non-Native Americans take such objects out of their cultural context and place them in museums and galleries, where they are seen as beautiful objects rather than as meaningful, vital elements of another culture.

dividualism, for instance, is not embodied in any one tangible thing. Rather, it is an abstract idea that guides our thoughts and actions. But the line between material and nonmaterial culture is never sharp. Thus, the value we place on individualism helps to explain our infatuation with cars. With a car, we can pick up and go any time we like (as opposed to depending on public transportation). Moreover, people express their individual tastes in the kinds of cars they buy. In the sections that follow we look more closely at nonmaterial elements of culture, beginning with values.

Values

The Tangu of New Guinea play a game called *taketak*. The equipment consists of two groups of coconut stakes that look like bowling pins and a toplike object made from a dried fruit. The players divide into two teams, and the members of the first team take turns throwing the top at their group of stakes. Every stake they hit is removed. Then the members of the second team toss the top at their stakes. Surprisingly (to us), the object of the game is not to knock over as many stakes as possible. Rather, the game continues until both teams have removed the same number of stakes. To Americans, who value competition so highly, such a game seems senseless. But to the Tangu, this game makes perfect sense. The Tangu value equivalence, not competition (Burridge, 1957). They are bothered by the idea of one group winning and another losing, for they believe this situation causes ill will. When Europeans brought soccer to New Guinea, the Tangu changed the rules so that the object was for the two teams to score the same number of goals. Sometimes their soccer games went on for days! American games, in contrast, are highly competitive; there are always winners and losers.

A **value** is a general idea that people share about what is good or bad, desirable or undesirable. The values people hold tend to color their overall way of life; they transcend any one particular situation. Thus, Americans tend to be competitive not only in sports but also in politics, in business, in the classroom, and in their social lives. For example, if there is no clear winner in a political election, a runoff is held. Similarly, U.S. electoral procedures do not permit the formation of a coalition government (say, with a Republican president and Democratic vice president).

Competition is one of the basic or core American values

Courtesy Standard Brands, Inc.

This advertisement, which appeared in newspapers and on billboards in the 1930s, is an example of both material and nonmaterial culture. It is also an attempt by the advertiser to sway public opinion. Rather than relying on facts about tea, it shows a romanticized image. It is designed to instill in readers the opinion that drinking this tea will somehow make their lives more exciting. Do you think modern ads attempt to sway public opinion?

identified some years ago by the sociologist Robin M. Williams, Jr. (1970). Others he noted include achievement and success, activity and work, humanitarianism, efficiency and practicality, progress, material comfort, equality, freedom, conformity, science and rationality, nationalism and patriotism, democracy, individuality, and racial and ethnic group superiority. Williams's list of values is not necessarily shared by all Americans, nor does it exhaust all the possibilities. In addition, because values change over time, some on Williams's list may be declining. Nonetheless, his compilation is still regarded as a distinctively American set of core values.

Sometimes values reinforce one another. For example, Americans value material comfort, so it makes sense that they would also value the success that can buy that comfort, as well as the hard work needed to achieve success. Other American values, however, are not so compatible (see the Making Choices box). In seeming contradiction, we value both conformity and individuality, both racial harmony and racial separation. How do people manage to live with these contradictions? Often by applying different values in different situations. For example, most Americans today accept and approve of racial equality in the workplace. Yet relatively few extend the value of racial equality to their family lives; they would not approve of a member of their own family marrying a person of another race or adopting a child of another race.

When values are repeatedly in sharp conflict, and reconciliation is difficult, pressure for social change may build. The civil rights movement of the 1950s and 1960s focused national attention on the conflict between the values of "freedom and justice for all" and racial segregation. Protesters awakened the nation's conscience by repeatedly confronting white segregationists, who often responded violently to peaceful protests, in full view of the media. As a result, the "separate but equal" doctrine was overturned by the U.S. Supreme Court and new laws were passed banning discrimination in schools, public accommodations, employment, and housing (see Chapter 21). These laws prompted new behaviors that, in turn, helped to shift values. Values also change as social events and circumstances change. For example, in 1989 nearly 80 percent of college freshmen said that being very well off financially was very important to them, whereas in 1970 only about 50 percent voiced this opinion (Astin, Korn, and Berz, 1989). Perhaps a change in economic conditions (greater competition in the job market, for instance) has prompted students to place more value on achievement and material success. Whatever the reason, these figures show that values are not static. Like all aspects of culture, values undergo change.

Norms

Values provide the framework within which people in a society develop norms of behavior. A **norm** is a specific guideline for action; it is a rule that says how people should behave in particular situations. Sometimes norms are made explicit, as in written laws or biblical commandments. But more often, norms are unspoken customs that people implicitly know and follow. For example, when someone you don't particularly like and find physically unattractive asks you out on a date, you don't say, "I think you're dumb and ugly and never want to go out with you." Rather, you make an excuse such as "I'm busy that night" or "I'm seeing someone else." Only if that person ignores your polite refusals and continues pestering you do you say directly, "I don't want to go out with you." No one has ever explicitly told you about this social convention. It is a norm that you implicitly grasped in the process of learning your culture.

Like values, norms can vary greatly from society to society. Polite and appropriate behavior in one society may be disgraceful in another. For example:

> Among the Ila-speaking peoples of central Africa, girls are given houses of their own at harvest time where they may play at being wife with boys of their choice. It is said that among these people virginity does not exist beyond the age of ten. [In contrast] among the Tepoztlan Indians of Mexico, a girl's life becomes "crabbed, cribbed, confined" from the time of her first menstruation. A girl is not to speak to or encourage boys in the least way. To do so would be to court disgrace, to show oneself to be crazy. (Ember and Ember, 1988, p. 306)

Norms also vary from group to group within a single society. Just think of the difference in dating norms between American teenagers and American adults. Norms, like values, vary over time as well; they seldom remain the same indefinitely. A good example is how much American norms regarding smoking have changed in the last few decades. In the 1950s, it would not have occurred to smokers in a restaurant to sit away from nonsmokers. The custom of segregating smokers from nonsmokers was simply not a norm. Today, of course, all this has changed with the increased awareness of the hazards of inhaling secondhand smoke.

Most norms are situational; that is, they apply to specific circumstances and settings. For instance, we employ the norm of shaking hands upon meeting or leaving someone, not midway through a conversation (unless perhaps we are cementing an agreement). Similarly, the norm of quietly raising a hand and waiting to be called upon to speak is

MAKING CHOICES

Why Get Involved?

The tension between the values of individualism (or "taking care of number one") and community (or getting involved) has always been a part of American culture. The individual's right to "life, liberty, and the pursuit of happiness" is enshrined in our Constitution. We hold sacred the right to think for ourselves, judge for ourselves, make our own decisions, and live our lives as we see fit. We believe that individuals should be free from arbitrary authority (whether by government, employers, or family), free from having other people's values, ideas, or tastes forced upon them, free from unwanted entanglements and obligations—in short, free to "do their own thing."

At the same time, however, we are nostalgic for the small towns of the past—for harmonious communities in which families put down roots and stayed for generations. People in these communities knew their minister, schoolteachers, grocer, pharmacist, and mail carrier personally; neighbors helped one another without being asked; and it was safe to walk the streets at night. Sunday church services, town meetings, and holidays like the fourth of July brought people together to reaffirm communal values. Public life and private life were intertwined.

A number of contemporary sociologists have argued that our highly individualistic culture neglects basic human needs for community and connection (e.g., Riesman, 1951; Slater, 1976). When Robert Bellah and his colleagues interviewed more than 200 white, mostly upper-middle-class Americans, they found that individualism remains a dominant feature of our culture (Bellah et al., 1985). In their popular and highly acclaimed book *Habits of the Heart*, they argued that although individualists are often thoughtful, admirable people, they also tend to be lonely and isolated. One of the strong individualists among their subjects was Margaret Oldham. A psychotherapist with an impressive academic and professional record, Oldham has struggled to overcome a rigid, moralistic upbringing. She places a high value on autonomy, and sees self-knowledge as a guiding principle, in both her work and her personal life. She believes that to become your own person you must separate yourself from values imposed both by your past and by your present social milieu. And she believes that, like herself, other people should be free to have their own standards and live their lives however they choose. As a therapist, she is not in the business of changing people, but rather of helping them to better understand themselves. But Oldham's ethic of tolerance has a darker underside. "I do think it's important for you to take responsibility for yourself," she says. "I mean people do take care of each other, people help each other, you know, when somebody's sick, and that's wonderful. But in the end you're really alone. . ." (p. 15). The cost of Oldham's individualism, according to Bellah, is loss of community.

By "community" Bellah means more than a neighborhood. A community depends, first, on shared memories of how the community came into being, of men and women who embodied its virtues, and what its hopes and fears are. Second, a community depends on "practices of commitment"—on rituals, moral codes, and aesthetic tastes that define people's loyalties and obligations. For example, Angelo Donatello was raised in a traditional Italian family in East Boston. Like many children of immigrants, Angelo wanted first and foremost to be an "American." After finishing school he moved out of the old neighborhood, married a woman of Irish descent, and started a business of his own, taking the individualistic route. He thought he had left his past behind. When some old friends began talking about forming a chapter of the Sons of Italy, he attended

appropriate in a classroom but not in a group of friends. Part of the process of acquiring a culture is learning exactly when each of the norms that are part of that culture is expected of us.

Much of the time, people follow norms more or less automatically. Alternatives never occur to them. This is particularly true of unspoken norms that seem self-evident, such as answering a person who addresses you. People conform because it seems right, because to violate the norm would damage their self-image or hurt their conscience, and because they want approval and fear ridicule, ostracism, and punishment. Of course, people don't always automatically follow a norm. It depends on the particular norm and the particular person. For example, there are many Americans who don't wear seatbelts in automobiles even though wearing seatbelts has become a norm in our society. Similarly, many Christians don't follow the norm of attending church each Sunday even though they believe they *should*. Here the desire to follow the norm competes with other motivations, such as a desire to sleep late or go fishing on Sunday mornings.

It is important to understand the difference between norms and values. Consider a man at a baseball game when the national anthem is sung. He stops talking with his friends, removes his hat, and stands quietly facing the flag. He is following the norms that prescribe how one should meetings reluctantly. The turning point for Angelo came when the group attempted to buy land for a hall and was refused, on the grounds that Italians are drunken and rowdy. This unexpected experience of ethnic prejudice led Angelo to believe there was more to life than becoming successful on his own. He began fighting for the Italian-American community he had tried to forget, became involved in local politics, and today serves as a town selectman. Grounded in community, Angelo Donatello thinks in terms of long-term commitments and a collective vision of the good life. His life has purpose and direction; in contrast, Margaret Oldham seems isolated and adrift.

Sociologist Herbert Gans (1988) has studied the tension between individualism and community among white working- and lower-middle-class people who make up the bulk of our population. Middle Americans, Gans found, value privacy. They want to be free to choose whether or not to be neighborly; to join or not join a church, union, or other organizations; and "to reject unwelcome advice or demands for behavior change from the spouse, employer, or anyone else" (p. 3). The great Middle American dream is to own a house of one's own. Although they are focused on their own lives, Gans holds, Middle Americans are neither selfish, narcissistic, nor materialistic. Nor are they lonely. Most are deeply committed to their immediate family and involved in a variety of social networks and informal groups. But they distrust big government, big business, and formal organizations in general. They are not joiners or activists. Aside from voting (which they may or may not do), few play an active role in the political life of their community or the nation as a whole. The reason, according to Gans, is not so much that they do not care about such social problems as crime, drugs, and poverty. Rather, they feel powerless to do anything about the big issues, and so dismiss collective or even individual action on the grounds that "you can't beat the system." Gans points out that disengagement from public affairs can become a self-fulfilling prophecy. People do not participate in collective action because they do not believe that one individual can make a difference; but because they do not participate, collective action fails, and this failure confirms their original (but untested) belief that collective action is futile. (Bellah's Angelo Donatello is an exception to this rule.)

Over the course of a lifetime, each of us faces numerous choices between individualism and community. As a student, do you participate in school activities and speak out on school issues, or do you put all your time and energy into earning top grades? As a consumer, do you shop for products that are environmentally safe or buy whatever is most convenient and attractive? As a neighborhood resident, do you help organize or participate in a neighborhood crime patrol or invest in an expensive security system for yourself? As a worker, do you protest unsafe conditions and discrimination on the job or keep quiet and collect your paycheck?

These aren't always easy choices to make (you might get fired for speaking up). But neither are they always either/or decisions. For example, you may believe that a strong public education system is vital to a healthy, productive society. As a student, however, you want the best possible education and may decide to attend a private school. But you can still pay attention to school issues in your community, vote for school board members you think will do a good job, or volunteer to tutor children who cannot afford private school. Individualism and community, in short, need not be incompatible values.

act in this particular situation. If asked why he does these things, he will probably tell you it is "right" to show respect for the nation; to do otherwise would be unpatriotic. Here the man is assessing his behavior according to a broad, abstract value: patriotism. Norms, then, are the rules that govern behavior in particular contexts, while values are the broad, internalized standards against which we evaluate behavior.

Norms vary in the importance that people assign to them and in the way they react to violations. **Folkways** are norms that are simply everyday habits and convention. People obey them without giving much thought to the matter. For example, we cover our mouths when we yawn, shake hands when introduced, and eat dessert at the end rather than the beginning of a meal because these are American folkways. People who violate folkways may be labeled eccentrics or slobs, but as a rule they are tolerated. In contrast, violations of mores provoke intense reactions. **Mores** are the norms people consider vital to their well-being and to their most cherished values. Examples are the prohibitions against incest, cannibalism, and sexual abuse of children. People who violate mores are considered unfit for society and may be ostracized, beaten, locked up in a prison or a mental hospital, exiled, or even executed.

Some norms are formalized into **laws**, which are rules enacted by a political body and enforced by the power of

We tend to see our own small interactions, such as greeting rituals, as "normal," but when we are in a different cultural setting we soon realize that a norm we have accepted as natural is just one of an infinite number of possibilities. In Japan, for example, people traditionally greet one another by bowing, where we would shake hands. Think about how such minor actions contribute to a culture's typical "personality."

the state. Whereas folkways and mores are typically enforced by the collective and spontaneous actions of the members of the community, laws are enforced by the police, the military, or some other specialized organization. Laws may formalize folkways (as some traffic regulations do) or back up mores (as laws against murder and treason do). Political authorities may also attempt to introduce new norms by enacting laws such as those governing the disposal of toxic wastes or the extension of civil rights to various minorities. In general, the laws that are most difficult to enforce are those that are not grounded in folkways or mores—for example, laws against gambling or drinking before age twenty-one.

Symbols

In addition to giving us guidelines for behavior and ideas about what is "good" and "right," culture also gives us notions about what things in our world mean. These meanings may involve **symbols**—objects, gestures, sounds, or images that represent something other than themselves. Geometrically, for example, a cross is merely two intersecting lines, but for Christians a cross symbolizes sacrifice, pain and suffering, faith, and the hope of salvation. Similarly, an American flag is nothing more than a rectangle of tricolored fabric, but for people around the world it symbolizes a powerful nation and that nation's entire way of life. Words, too, are symbols with meanings that people share. The word *green*, for instance, is just a string of sounds with no inherent meaning, but for speakers of English these sounds symbolize a certain family of colors.

As the examples we have given illustrate, symbols do not necessarily look like, sound like, or otherwise resemble what they stand for. Granted, symbols may sometimes derive their meaning partly from their inherent qualities (a lion symbolizing a powerful empire, for instance). But the meaning given to symbols is frequently quite arbitrary, simply a matter of tradition and consensus. That is why, in different cultures, different symbols are often used to represent the same concept. In some societies, for instance, black is the color of mourning, while in others white or red suggests grief. There is nothing about these colors that dictates their meaning. The meaning is arbitrarily assigned.

When meanings are arbitrarily assigned to symbols, those meanings can more easily be changed. For example, in England the index and middle fingers held in a V with the palm facing inward is considered a rude insult. During World War II, Churchill turned this symbol around (palm facing outward) and made it stand for victory. Two decades later, students protesting the Vietnam war made this same gesture a symbol for peace. In 1989, the "V" or peace sign was adopted by prodemocracy protesters in China and Eastern Europe.

Even when people think they assign the same meaning to a symbol, their meanings may in fact be somewhat dif-

To Americans, the Stars and Stripes symbolizes their nation's values, ideals, and place in the world. The flags of other countries, of course, serve the same purpose for their citizens.

ferent. For instance, in the United States a gold band worn on the third finger of someone's left hand symbolizes that he or she is married. To some, this suggests that the person had made an exclusive, lifelong commitment. To others it means a commitment to stay together only as long as the relationship "works." Thus, each of us brings our own interpretations to the cultural meaning of symbols.

But the act of personally interpreting symbols should not be taken to mean that each of us defines them idiosyncratically. If people are to align their actions with one another, they must have reasonably similar understandings of the world. That is why the collective creation and use of symbols is the very heart of social life. As Clifford Geertz has written:

> Undirected by . . . organized systems of significant symbols . . . man's behavior would be virtually ungovernable, a mere chaos of pointless acts and exploding emotions, his experience virtually shapeless. Culture, the accumulated totality of such [symbols], is not just an ornament of human existence but . . . an essential condition for it. (Geertz, 1973, p. 46)

Language

A **language** is a system of verbal and, in many cases, written symbols with rules about how those symbols can be strung together to convey more complex meanings. It is impossible to overstate the importance of language in the development, elaboration, and transmission of culture (see Figure 3.1). Language enables people to store meanings and experiences and to pass this heritage on to new generations. Through language, we are able to learn about and from the experiences of others. In addition, language enables us to transcend the here and now, preserving the past and imagining the future. It also makes possible the formulation of complex plans and ideas. People could reason only on the most primitive level if they did not possess language. These capacities that language enables are augmented by the use of writing.

Some sociologists focus on the structure of language. These researchers analyze how language is put together—how it is built up from smaller speech sounds into words, and from words into meaningful phrases and sentences. Such analysis shows that the structure of language is an essential factor in conveying meaning. We cannot arbitrarily rearrange the sounds in a word or the words in a sentence and create a statement that another person is likely to comprehend. Languages have rules of grammar and syntax that must be followed if we want to be understood. Moreover, words often take their meaning from a structure of opposites: We understand white partly through contrast to black, male to female, tall to short, and so on. But words simply name things; to communicate we must

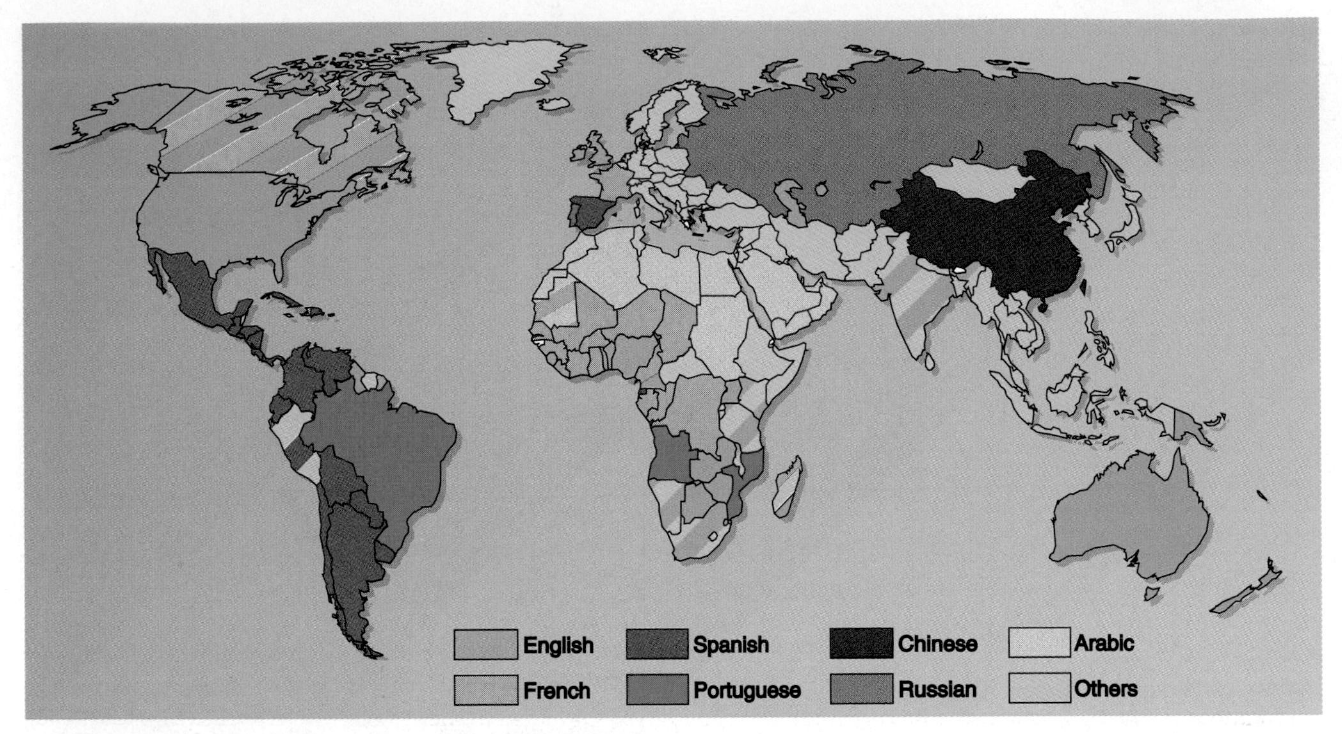

FIGURE 3.1 / A Comparative Look at Languages

The world's people speak thousands of different languages, though many have died out. A few have become especially widespread as a result of trade, conquest, and colonialism. This map shows regions in which several of the world's major languages are widely spoken. Of course, not everybody in each region speaks the dominant language, and for some it may be only a second language. Russian is spoken throughout the former Soviet Union, for example, because the old government demanded that it be taught in schools. But in the different republics that have succeeded the Soviet Union a number of different languages are the primary bases for communication.

Sources: *The Europa Year Book*, 1980; *Guinness Book of Answers*, 1985.

master the structure of language, which allows us to communicate in meaningful ways.

Other sociologists look at the role of language in ***social action***, focusing on how people use language to coordinate their activities and to create and confirm social understandings (Bourdieu, in press; Levinson, 1983). One discovery is that people seem to change their patterns of speech as social contexts change. For instance, a woman asking her son to mow the lawn might give a direct order ("Get that lawn mowed!") but use indirect phrasing when addressing her husband ("Isn't it your turn to mow the lawn?"). Such indirect phrasing is considered more polite and therefore more appropriate between adults of equal status. A frequent mistake that people make in learning to speak a new language is to overlook cultural conventions about how that language should be used in different social contexts. Thus, Germans sometimes sound domineering when they speak English because their native language encourages more direct phrasing of requests and complaints than English does (House and Kasper, 1981).

When people use aspects of language to interpret a situation, they are employing language as a kind of social marker (Scherer and Giles, 1979). A **social marker** is any pattern of behavior that provides indications about who people are, what groups they belong to, and what their understanding of a situation is. In other words, it identifies where a person or group fits into a ***social structure***. Imagine, for instance, that after a week in a new job you are asked to attend a staff meeting. Having no idea what a staff meeting entails, you approach it in a cautious, exploratory manner, searching for clues about how you should act. Among these would be linguistic clues. Do the participants at the meeting use formal language? Do they follow a fairly rigid format of who speaks when and for how long, or are their interactions more loosely structured, as in casual conversations? Such clues would give you a good idea of what kind of meeting this is.

Pronunciation, word choice, tone of voice, and grammar would alert you to the status of the people at the meeting. A person in authority usually conveys dominance by phrasing things in an assertive manner ("Get that information by tomorrow"). A subordinate is likely to adopt a

The public tends to think of the homeless as living in a cultural vacuum. This tramp, however, lives in a complex cultural world, whose meaning he interprets through cultural knowledge and a specialized and extensive vocabulary.

more tentative style of speaking, liberally sprinkled with linguistic "hedges" ("It seems to me. . . ," "Maybe. . . ," "You know. . .") and rising intonations at the end of declarative statements (as in answering "Thursday?" to a question about when a report will be ready). Often without realizing it, we categorize people on the basis of these speech patterns (Andrews, 1984). Thus, to a large extent a person's social identity is established and maintained through the patterns of language that he or she uses (Gumperz, 1982).

Knowledge

Knowledge is the body of facts, beliefs, and practical skills that people accumulate over time. It consists partly of procedural information, such as how to drive a car or operate a computer. It also consists of information about places, people, and events (Where is the Rose Bowl? Who was our first president? What happens when milk is poured on Rice Krispies?). Often we have knowledge about things that we cannot verify for ourselves but that we accept as "truths." In our society, this includes knowledge that atomic energy can be harnessed and that germs cause disease. However, one person's "true" knowledge may be another person's "mere" belief. Witness the debates over the biblical story of creation and evolutionary theories of human origin. All these kinds of knowledge are part of our culture, our shared heritage.

Modern society is accumulating knowledge at a fantastically rapid pace. This is partly due to the contributions of the various branches of science, the fundamental goal of which is to provide new knowledge. The amount of knowledge that science could generate would be greatly limited, however, if it were not for modern methods of storing data. Modern books, microfilm, magnetic tapes, computer disks, and so forth, can store vast quantities of information for long periods of time. People in widely separated locations can then have easy access to these data. Some sociologists think that control over all this accumulated knowledge is central to a modern "information society" such as ours (Bell, 1980; Giddens, 1990).

Not all knowledge takes the form of information that can be explained in words or formulas or that can be written down and stored. Much *practical knowledge* is largely nonverbal. Knowing how to swim and how to shoot a hook shot in basketball are examples. A person does not need to know the physics and muscles involved in these activities. Even the best swimmers and basketball players have difficulty explaining to others how they perform so well; they just do it. Practical knowledge is important in many areas of social life, from making judgments of taste, to making business deals, to making love (Bourdieu, 1990b).

CULTURAL INTEGRATION AND DIVERSITY

> On a leafy side street in the Los Angeles suburb of Glendale, parents and children are playing out the American ritual of going back to school. About 30 [youngsters] file into John Robertson's fifth-grade classroom, where the walls are decorated with Presidential portraits, diagrams of the 50 states, and Navajo sand drawings. From all appearances a traditional setting. But appearances are deceiving.

> That becomes evident when Robertson addresses his charges, with names like Aram, Razmik, Sarkis, Su Chin, Pierre, and Angela. The classroom, a typical one in the new California, is filled with immigrant children from Soviet Armenia, Mexico, El Salvador, Korea, and Hong Kong, plus a few Americans. At the rear, a Filipino-American teacher's aide, Nanette Morales, prepares to help Armenian and Korean children learn English. (Reinhold, 1991)

Part of the task Robertson has been given is to help bring these mostly foreign-born children into the American cultural fold, while teaching them awareness and respect for our cultural diversity. This job was mandated by the California Board of Education when it adopted a new framework for teaching history and social studies. That framework requires public school teachers to "accurately portray the cultural and racial diversity of our society," while stressing the "centrality of Western civilizations as the source of American political institutions, laws, and ideology" (Reinhold, 1991).

This teaching goal in California, and elsewhere in the United States, highlights a tension that has long existed in American society. On the one hand, there are social forces that encourage **assimilation**, the process by which newcomers to America, as well as other "outsiders," give up their culturally distinct beliefs, values, and customs and take on those of the dominant culture. On the other hand, there is a tendency to preserve cultural diversity, to keep one's own personal heritage alive and to respect the right of others to do so. This tension between assimilation and diversity exists not just for those who must make individual choices about who they are and how they will act. It also exists for the larger society when it makes decisions about how much cultural diversity is "good" for the social order, how much can be accepted without it starting to weaken the fabric of society. California's decision to teach diversity while stressing the centrality of Western values is one example of how this tension is constantly being resolved. (See further discussion of American cultural diversity in Chapter 10.)

Cultural Integration

One result of cultural assimilation is **cultural integration**. This term refers to the degree to which a culture is a ***functionally integrated*** system, so that all the parts fit together well. On another level, the elements of culture are functionally integrated with *other* facets of society, such as social structure and power relations. When people have a well-integrated culture, there are few contradictions in the ways they think and act. Their religious, economic, and family lives are all of one piece. Simply by following established traditions, they can carry out the business of living with minimal inner conflict. Yet, as the anthropologist Ralph Linton (1947) has stressed, a highly integrated culture is extremely vulnerable. The customs, beliefs, values, and technology are interdependent. Changes in one area invariably affect other areas, sometimes throwing the entire system out of balance.

For example, when European missionaries succeeded in converting large numbers of natives of Madagascar to Christianity, theft became commonplace and people no longer diligently cared for their homes and villages. The reason? Traditional sanctions against theft, littering, and shabbiness lost their power in light of the newly adopted European beliefs and practices: "The fear of hell and the police are a poor substitute," Linton explained, "for the fear of ancestral ghosts who know everything and who punish an evil doer with sickness on earth and exclusion from the ancestral village in the hereafter" (Linton, 1947, p. 357).

Similarly, the introduction of steel virtually destroyed the highly integrated Stone Age culture of the Australian aborigines. To the Europeans who introduced them, steel axes were simply tools that were technically superior to stone implements. But to the aborigines the ax was more than a tool: Relations between families and tribes were based on the ceremonial exchange of cherished stonework (Arensberg and Niehoff, 1964). These patterns of exchange were undermined when the aborigines abandoned their stone implements for those made of steel.

Most cultures are more loosely integrated than those of the traditional Madagascans or the Australian aborigines. This is especially true in large, diverse societies like our own that include people from many different racial and ethnic backgrounds. American culture is more loosely integrated than that of Japan, which for generations has been a very closed society that discourages immigration and preserves traditions despite its many economic ties with the rest of the world. Intermediate in cultural integration is a society like England. England has experienced immigration from various parts of the Commonwealth, so it has more cultural diversity than Japan does. But immigration to England has been on a small scale compared with immigration to the United States, so England is less culturally diverse than America is. Of course, immigration is not the only source of diversity; people of similar ethnic backgrounds may choose different lifestyles. And some common values and beliefs can integrate people despite diversity on other dimensions. Cultural integration, then, is always a matter of degree. To some extent, it depends on how diverse or homogeneous a society has been throughout its history.

Cultures that are very heterogeneous and loosely integrated involve a certain amount of internal contradiction. "Cultures," Linton (1947, p. 358) wrote, "like personalities, are perfectly capable of including conflicting elements and logical inconsistencies." We saw examples of such inconsistencies within American culture in our earlier discussion of values. Many other large, heterogeneous societies live with similarly contradictory elements of culture. Diversity may reduce cultural integration, but it can also be a source of creativity and freedom of choice.

Cultural Diversity and Subcultures

There are two main reasons that some societies remain culturally diverse over long periods of time (Marger, 1991). One is that cultural minorities do not *want* to assimilate into the **dominant culture**, or the set of values, norms, traditions, and outlooks that are treated as normal for the society as a whole. They value their separate beliefs, customs, and cultural identities. These minorities want to retain their group boundaries, while enjoying free and equal participation in politics and the economy. This goal is aided by legislation that protects minorities from discrimination. In other cases, however, cultural diversity endures because the dominant groups in society seek to maintain their ***power*** and privilege by keeping certain minority groups separate and unequal (see Chapter 10). Sometimes this is done by limiting contact between majority and minority, as the South African government tried to do for many years with its policy of apartheid. The result is a society with enclaves of cultural minorities that are denied equal access to economic and political life. Very often, of course, both these reasons for enduring cultural diversity coexist: Members of the dominant culture limit chances for assimilation, but at the same time members of cultural minorities don't wish to lose their distinctive identities by assimilating completely.

The distinctive norms, values, knowledge, language, and symbols that members of a cultural minority share, and that they use to distinguish themselves from the dominant culture, constitute a **subculture** (Fine, 1987; Fine and Kleinman, 1979). For a subculture to exist, people must identify with the subcultural group (though they may have other identifications too). They must also have opportunities for communicating with one another, both directly (in face-to-face contact) and indirectly (through the mass media). This makes subcultures the products of symbolic interaction (see Chapters 1 and 4).

In the process of interacting with one another, members of subcultures not only identify with their own groups; they also *de*identify with the dominant culture (the culture whose members wield power and influence, not necessarily the numerical majority). For instance, from the point of view of homosexuals, the dominant culture in America (and the one they feel like outsiders to) is a heterosexual culture. Similarly, from the point of view of atheists, the dominant culture is religious; from the point of view of African-Americans, the dominant culture is that of white people of Western European heritage; from the point of view of someone homeless and unemployed, the dominant culture is middle class and financially well off. The dominant American culture, then, is a mix of various elements. Many Americans share in it in some ways, but not in others.

Ethnic Subcultures: The Case of Hispanics

Ethnicity is a major source of subcultural identification in the United States. Jews, African-Americans, Chinese-Americans, Hispanic-Americans, and many other ethnic groups think of themselves as having customs, language, beliefs, and values distinctive in many ways from those of the dominant culture. Take Hispanic-Americans, for example, who in 1990 made up nearly 9 percent of the U.S. population. The term *Hispanic* refers not to a single people, but to various groups who came to this country at different times in its history from different Spanish-speaking parts of the Western Hemisphere. Some are descendants of Spaniards who settled in the Southwest in the 1500s, long before the United States annexed that territory in the Mexican-American War (1848). Others are part of a steady stream of migration of Mexican farm workers, which continues today. Some are political refugees. Still others are not fleeing political persecution or poverty, but simply seeking a better life for themselves and their children. Their cultural roots lie in Mexico, Cuba, Puerto Rico, and Central and South America. (See Figure 3.2.) Nevertheless, these varied cultures have common threads that distinguish Hispanics from the Anglo-American mainstream.

Hispanic culture emphasizes obligation, loyalty, and respect toward the family above all else, even political ambition and career. By "family," Hispanics mean the extended family that includes not just parents and children but also grandparents, aunts, uncles, and cousins by blood or by marriage. Hispanics also place a high value on the dignity and worth of the individual. They tend to believe that a high degree of respect is owed to oneself and others, and they react strongly to personal insults or scorn. Spiritual values often take precedence over materialistic ones. Hispanics tend "to think in terms of transcendent qualities, such as justice, loyalty, or love, rather than in terms of practical arrangements which spell out justice or loyalty in the concrete" (Fitzpatrick, 1971, pp. 91–92). Hispanic culture also emphasizes highly personal, one-to-one relationships more than the Anglo culture does.

Compared with other groups of immigrants to the United States, Hispanics have been among the least inclined to become assimilated into the dominant culture (*Oxford Analytica*, 1986). Hispanics who were born in this country and speak English in school and at work tend to speak Spanish at home. Said a Mexican-American librarian who is teaching her young son Spanish as well as English, "It is a sign of respect to my parents that we carried our culture from our parents to our children" (in Mydans, 1991). Those who can afford to live almost anywhere often choose to remain in Hispanic neighborhoods and communities, where they can shop at Hispanic stores, join Hispanic clubs, and in other ways maintain a network of personal relationships with other Hispanics. Many regularly travel back and forth to their homelands, maintaining ties with relatives who have not emigrated. In part because of geographical closeness, in part because of modern transportation and communications, and in part because of commitment, Hispanics have been able to maintain their traditional culture to a greater degree than most other immigrant groups (Mydans, 1991).

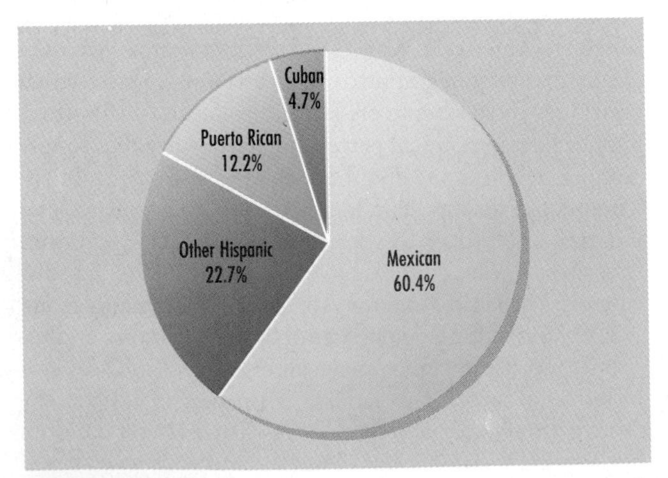

FIGURE 3.2 / People of Hispanic Origin in the United States

Source: U.S. Department of Commerce, Bureau of the Census, Release CB91-216 (June 12, 1991).

Other Subcultures

Ethnic and religious groups are not the only source of subcultures. Subcultures also form out of occupational groups, socioeconomic groups, age groups, and so on. Adolescents, for example, are active creators of subcultures revolving around music, dating, and the shared experience of being not quite adults and yet no longer children. Similarly, medical students share common experiences, goals, and problems and hence a common viewpoint. Subcultures typically arise when people in similar circumstances find themselves isolated from the mainstream world. They may be isolated physically (such as inmates in prison, soldiers on a military base, poor people in a ghetto) or isolated by what they do and think, that is, by their shared worlds of meanings.

Tensions often develop between members of the dominant culture and one or more subcultures, especially subcultures that directly oppose dominant norms and values. Members of the dominant group usually call these subcultures *deviant*. Examples are a drug subculture, a homosexual subculture, or an inner-city gang subculture. Of course, from the point of view of those who participate in these subcultures, they are not "deviant" in the sense of being morally bad or wrong. They are simply outside the mainstream of American life.

Sometimes subcultures develop that are not just distinct from the dominant culture, but that are oriented toward challenging that culture or deliberately trying to change it. These are called **countercultures**. A good example is the student counterculture of the 1960s. Its members actively rejected the hard work–success ethic, the materialistic focus, the deferred gratification, and the sexually restrictive morality of the "establishment." Religious groups like Hare Krishna likewise have many countercultural overtones. So do American Nazi groups.

Of course, countercultures are not the only kinds of subcultures that can bring about change in the dominant culture. Tacos and pizza have found their way from ethnic minority subcultures to become widely accepted elements of mainstream American culture. And this is just one small example of how subcultures can quietly change the face of a dominant culture. Much depends on how open members of the dominant culture are to new customs and ideas. One of the important features of American culture has long been its tolerance—even sometimes its celebration—of subcultural diversity. Members of the dominant culture have not always used their power in the service of intolerance and repression.

Cultural change is everywhere, even in a counterculture. "Hard-core" music evolved from punk, which in turn was a response to the artificiality and commercialism of disco. The norms of a hard-core concert differ from those for other forms of rock music. For example, dancing consists mainly of jumping up and down, which anyone can do. Members of the audience may join the band on the stage and then leap off, trusting that they will be caught by other fans.

Ethnocentrism and Cultural Relativism

When members of a dominant culture become suspicious of subcultures and seek to isolate or assimilate them, it is often because the members of the dominant culture are making value judgments about the beliefs and practices of the subordinate groups. Most Anglo-Americans, for instance, see the extensive family obligations of Hispanics as a burdensome arrangement that inhibits individual freedom. Hispanics, in contrast, view the isolated nuclear family of Anglo-Americans as a lonely institution that cuts people off from the love and assistance of their kin. This tendency to view one's own cultural patterns as good and right and those of others as strange or even immoral is called **ethnocentrism**.

Accounts of the first European contacts with black Africa are a study in ethnocentrism. The letters and journals of fifteenth- and sixteenth-century explorers, merchants, and missionaries overflowed with lurid descriptions of cannibalism, incest, and "unbridled lust." Since the Africans did not practice Christianity, they were labeled "heathens"; since their laws were not of a European style, they were said to be "lawless"; and since their marriage and family practices differed from those prevalent in Europe, they were judged to be "savages" and "barbarians." The Europeans viewed the Africans as objects of loathing. Ethnocentrism led them to overlook the accomplishments of great African kingdoms, such as the Sonniki dynasty in Ghana, which was founded in the second century A.D. Not untypical was the following account by a European:

> The majority of them . . . are entirely savage and display the nature of the wild beast . . . and are as far removed as possible from human kindness to one another, and speaking as they do with a shrill voice and cultivating none of the practices of civilized life as these are found among the rest of mankind, they present a striking contrast when considered in light of our own customs. (quoted in George, 1968, p. 25)

Ironically, such accounts tell us more about the biases of the Europeans than about the behavior of the Africans.

For most people, culture operates outside awareness. Their own customs, beliefs, and values are so deeply ingrained that they consider these learned elements of culture part of "human nature." Such ethnocentric attitudes promote group solidarity and loyalty, improve morale, encourage conformity, and foster nationalism and patriotism. At the same time, however, ethnocentric sentiments increase hostility toward outsiders, foster conflict among groups, engender racism, and intensify resistance to change. In sum, although ethnocentrism is a source of unity and stability within groups, it is a source of misunderstanding and friction between groups.

Social scientists contend that in order to understand a culture fully, we must do more than just try to suspend our ethnocentrism. We must also strive to consider the elements of that culture on their own terms, in their own setting, and in light of the social forces that impinge on the people who have created and who use those cultural traditions. This perspective is called **cultural relativism**. Cultural relativism stresses that any element of culture is meaningful in relation to a particular time, place, and set of circumstances. If we try to analyze that element outside the cultural context in which it evolved, we will probably distort its meaning. For example, to Westerners the Hindu ban on slaughtering cattle and eating meat may seem absurd, particularly in India where so many people go hungry. This view ignores not only the religious meaning of cattle to Hindus but also the functional integration of this reverence for cattle with other aspects of Indian life and with certain material benefits. In fact, live cattle do more to support life than they would if sliced into steaks. Cattle consume food that is inedible for humans. Oxen pull plows; cows give milk; and cattle dung provides both fertilizer and fuel. In context, the "sacred cow" makes sense (M. Harris, 1975). Social scientists adopt cultural relativism when studying the customs of people in societies different from their own. But this is a matter of understanding and not necessarily of approval. To some extent, we can separate our attempt to understand another culture from our evaluation of it (Taylor, 1992).

The tension between cultural relativism on the one hand and ethnocentrism on the other is closely tied to the tension between assimilation and cultural diversity. Cultural relativism encourages tolerance for the beliefs and customs of different subcultures (thereby allowing diversity), whereas ethnocentrism encourages dominant groups to impose their norms and values on others (thereby fostering assimilation). Of course, ethnocentrism can lead toward separation rather than assimilation, if groups are able to minimize their contact. As with resolving the tension between assimilation and diversity, resolving the tension between cultural relativism and ethnocentrism is a matter of finding a workable middle ground. Few culturally heterogeneous societies can afford to be totally ethnocentric or totally tolerant toward *all* subcultural differences. Tolerance of differences must coexist with some shared elements of culture, which give rise to a reasonable amount of cultural integration.

THE PRODUCTION OF CULTURE

Sociologists do not view culture as spontaneous or "given," but as the product of ***social action***. Herbert Blumer had an opportunity to study the women's fashion industry. He was impressed by the fact that fashion trends are not created on the drawing boards of famous fashion designers. Instead, these trends are the end result of a complex social process by which a large number of potential new "looks" are screened and selected. As Blumer described one of the later stages in that process:

> At a seasonal opening of a major Parisian fashion house there may be presented a hundred or more designs of women's evening wear before an audience of from one to two hundred buyers [representatives of retail stores that sell women's clothing]. The managerial staff of the fashion house is able to indicate a group of about thirty designs of the entire lot, inside of which will fall the small number, usually about six to eight dresses, that are chosen by the buyers. But the managerial staff is typically unable to predict this small number on which the choices converge. Now, these choices are made by the buyers—a highly competitive and secretive lot—independently of each other and without knowledge of each other's selections. Why should their choices converge on a few designs as they do? When the buyers were asked why they chose one dress in preference to another—between which my inexperienced eye could see no appreciable difference—the typical, honest, yet largely uninformative answer was that the chosen dress was "stunning." (Blumer, 1969/1986, pp. 278–279)

Blumer's study focuses on the fascinating topic of how new items get introduced into an existing culture—that is, on how cultural innovations are produced. An important finding is that new elements of culture don't get added in a freewheeling, "anything goes" manner. Fashion house managers could consistently predict the dresses in a show on which the buyers' attention would focus. The buyers, in turn, although never conferring, would invariably agree on which of those were "stunning." Somehow the decisions of designers and buyers are channeled and constrained; they are not solely the product of independent choices and tastes. These constraints are imposed by a complex set of social forces, especially previously existing elements of culture.

As we've already mentioned, the fate of a cultural innovation is determined partly by the degree to which it conforms to shared ideas and expectations that are part of existing culture (Griswold, 1989). Fashion designers, for instance, could conceivably design clothing that bears no resemblance at all to what we are accustomed to wearing. But no designers who are successful depart from the norm in such a radical way. Instead, most create styles that are reasonably in line with the fashion industry's (and the public's) expectations. To do otherwise would usually mean dooming one's cultural innovations to obscurity. Thus, the basic Chanel jacket has remained essentially unchanged for decades, and Ralph Lauren produces variations on "American country" themes season after season.

The women's fashion industry is just one example of how new facets of culture are produced. Richard Peterson (1979) argues that in advanced industrialized societies like our own, new elements of culture are often deliberately created and disseminated by people who specialize in this task. The fashion designer is one such specialist. Others are artists, scientists, and members of the legal profession, all of whom are in the business of adding new ideas to culture. Peterson and others seek to analyze how these people introduce, market, and distribute new cultural elements from the time these elements are first conceived to the time that others use them.

The success of a cultural innovation is also affected by the ***social structure*** and especially ***power*** relationships in society. Of special importance are those who have a hand in disseminating new ideas. Such people are called **cultural gatekeepers** because they have the power to regulate the flow of new elements of culture into society. Gatekeepers decide which of a huge number of proposed cultural innovations will end up getting widespread exposure through traditional distribution channels. The retail buyers of new clothing designs that Herbert Blumer wrote about are gatekeepers of the fashion world. Their decisions determine which of hundreds of fashion designs actually get displayed on retail store racks.

When sociologist Paul Hirsch (1971) studied the creation of new products in three entertainment industries (book publishing, popular records, and movies), he likewise found that gatekeepers play an important role. Because producers in these industries are uncertain about what the ingredients of a "blockbuster" are, they hedge their bets by issuing many more new releases than consumers would ever want. They certainly cannot afford to give each one of these new products a large advertising budget. So they depend on independent gatekeepers (book reviewers, disc jockeys, film critics, talk-show hosts) to bring the products to public attention. The fate of any given product is decided at this strategic checkpoint. In the world of fashion, buyers for stores and fashion magazine editors perform this function. They are the ones who decide which new styles will be displayed to the public and therefore have a chance of being accepted into the mainstream culture. In the world of art, gallery owners and museum administrators are the gatekeepers (Becker, 1984).

What role do public tastes play in the acceptance of new elements of culture? Public tastes are just as important as the exposure given to particular innovations by cultural gatekeepers. Because of public tastes, *Star Wars* played in more movie theaters than any European "art" film released in the same year. Because of public tastes, Madonna gets more radio and TV airtime than the very best singers of medieval madrigals. But note that people's cultural preferences are partly a result of what they are repeatedly exposed to. When cultural gatekeepers barrage us with certain kinds of products, we are apt to decide that these are in fact the products we like best. Often, then, our role as "consumers" of culture is simply to decide among the relatively small number of new cultural items that gatekeepers choose for our consideration (Hirsch, 1971). Moreover, personal tastes are influenced by such social factors as time, place, and social class. The Key Concepts in Action box applies the five key sociological concepts to the social factors that influence tastes in art.

CULTURE AND THE MEDIA

Studies of the production of culture remind us that culture is never a static, "finished" product. Instead, it undergoes constant change as a result of decisions made by many different people who are both creators and consumers of culture. Among the most important agents of cultural change in today's world are the mass media, especially television. Television and other electronic media are the latest step in a long line of innovations aimed at helping people communicate.

Language was the first distinctly human medium of communication. When people developed language, they set their lives on a different course from that followed by their nonspeaking relatives (the forebears of today's apes). Language dramatically changed the nature of society. It enabled people to create complex cultures, to share a variety of beliefs, values, knowledge, and symbols, and to pass those cultural elements on to future generations. None of these changes came about overnight; they occurred gradually. But in the end, the essence of human life had been

KEY CONCEPTS IN ACTION

Culture, Tastes, and Social Class

"If I'd seen this pile of bricks on the side of the road I'd never have thought it was art."

"But now that you've seen it in an art gallery, do you think it's art?"

"Well, I suppose it must be if they think so. Somebody must think so or else they wouldn't have paid so much money for it."

"Well, it may be art to them, but it isn't to me. It's still just a pile of bricks. Why do they put this rubbish on show instead of some real art?" (adapted from R. Williams, 1982, pp. 131–132)

Tastes—we all have them. You prefer certain styles of art, certain kinds of food and clothing, certain types of music, certain ways of decorating your room. The list could go on and on. *De gustibus non est disputandum,* the old saying goes—there is no accounting for taste. Tastes just seem to spring from somewhere inside us, rather mysteriously. We can't really say why we prefer rock to Mozart, burgers to paté, jeans to neatly pressed slacks. These tastes are simply part of us, our individual selves. But tastes are also part of ***culture***, which is a broader social phenomenon.

Consider tastes in art. The very notion of "art"—the idea that art objects should be consecrated, placed in museums and galleries, and treated with reverence—does not exist in most cultures. People everywhere try to make objects beautiful. But the African masks and Indian gourds we place in museums were designs to be used in rituals and everyday activities, not to be admired from afar.

What we consider art depends in part on the context. For instance, the fact that the conversation above occurs in an art gallery makes an enormous difference to what the people present say and think. Had they seen the same pile of bricks at a construction site, no one would have given it a second glance, much less talked about it as art. But because the pile of bricks *is* being exhibited as art, the observers feel obligated to debate its artistic merits. It is important, too, that more than one person is viewing the brick sculpture. When in the company of others we are much more concerned about voicing the "right" opinions. Thus, the person who hesitantly expresses the view that this must be art might be doing so simply to keep others from thinking that he or she lacks sophistication.

Our attitudes toward art also reflect ***social structure***—specifically, our own position in our society's class hierarchy. For example, people from upper social classes or with a higher level of education are more likely to appreciate abstract art, or at least make an effort to understand it. Because their education often includes some introduction to art, they may find it easier to grasp the "point" of a work that looks like nothing more than an interesting arrangement of shapes and colors. People with less formal education or from lower-class backgrounds are less likely to appreciate abstract art. In fact, they may consider lack of clarity, or the failure of a painting or sculpture to tell a recognizable story, a sign of bad art. The last speaker in the art-gallery conversation above expresses this point of view. This person's dislike for the brick sculpture is not just a personal preference: It is very much the product of a certain social background. Because social background so strongly influences people's tastes in art, sociologists can predict with a fair degree of accuracy the social characteristics of those who will like or dislike a given work of art.

Why do upper-class, better-educated people prefer art that has less appeal to lower-class people? According to Pierre Bourdieu (1984; Bourdieu and Darbel, 1990), a leading sociologist of culture, it is not simply a matter of exposure to and knowledge about art. It also has to do with ***power***, ***social action***, and efforts on the part of social elites to distinguish themselves from people of lower social status. To members of the elite, the ability to appreciate abstract art is considered an indication of their higher education and breeding. So they cultivate a taste for art that appeals more to the intellect than it does to the emotions and the senses. The same preference can be seen in elites' taste in furniture. Whereas working-class people tend to prefer furniture that is comfortable (a large-cushioned velour sofa, for instance), elites tend to prefer pieces that have beauty of form but may be much less pleasing to the body (such as a finely carved but straight-backed antique chair). Elites use their knowledge and appreciation of abstract art, antiques, rare wines, and the like, not only to reaffirm their own claims to upper-class status but also to deny that status to others. Thus a *nouveau riche* millionaire, who lacks the "cultural capital" to match his or her economic capital, will be treated with disdain.

The producers and consumers of art are part of a ***functionally integrated*** system that is organized so that each person's actions, even though self-interested, tend to reproduce the whole system. If an artist tries something new, many people help to determine whether it will catch on: gallery owners, critics, museum curators, art magazine editors, and others. All these people occupy statuses in the art world that make them dependent on one another as well as on people who buy paintings or go to museums.

Finally, tastes in art are the product of a particular time and place. What is proclaimed an excellent drawing in one culture may be considered primitive doodling in another; what is dismissed as a pile of bricks in one era may be tomorrow's masterpiece sculpture. For example, many of the novels that are considered classics today (such as Henry Fielding's *Tom Jones* and Emily Brontë's *Wuthering Heights*) were considered trashy at the time they were published (see Figure 3.3). Social factors shape not just what specific works we consider to be "good" art, but what kinds of work we consider to be art at all. Thus, when photography was first invented, it was seen as a way to produce copies of reality, not as art. By the early twentieth century, however, some photographers were coming to be considered important artists. Today, a distinction is made between "art" photographers and "news," "portrait," and other professional photographers. Even within the ranks of those who aim to produce art, there are distinctions. At the top are the relatively small number of photographers whose work is considered serious art, in part because of the level of technical difficulty it entails. Then there are the countless amateur photographers, whose work may occasionally win prizes or be exhibited in local galleries, but connoisseurs consider only "middle-brow art" (Bourdieu, 1990a). In these ways a new art form, and a new means of social distinction, has been added to our culture.

Work	Review
HAMLET WILLIAM SHAKESPEARE 1601	It is a vulgar and barbarous drama, which would not be tolerated by the vilest populace of France, or Italy . . . one would imagine this piece to be the work of a drunken savage. Voltaire (1768), in *The Works of M. de Voltaire* 1901
TOM JONES HENRY FIELDING 1749	A book seemingly intended to sap the foundation of that morality which it is the duty of parents and all public instructors to inculcate in the minds of young people. Sir John Hawkins, *Life of Samuel Johnson* 1787
WUTHERING HEIGHTS EMILY BRONTË 1847	. . . wild, confused, disjointed and improbable . . . the people who make up the drama, which is tragic enough in its consequences, are savages ruder than those who lived before the days of Homer. *The Examiner*
ON **EDGAR ALLAN POE**	After reading some of Poe's stories one feels a kind of shock to one's modesty. We require some kind of spiritual ablution to cleanse our minds of his disgusting images. Leslie Stephen, *Hours in a Library* 1874
ON **WALT WHITMAN**	He is morally insane, and incapable of distinguishing between good and evil, virtue and crime. Max Nordau, *Degeneration* 1895
LADY CHATTERLEY'S LOVER D. H. LAWRENCE 1928	D. H. Lawrence has a diseased mind. He is obsessed by sex . . . we have no doubt that he will be ostracized by all except the most degenerate coteries in the literary world. John Bull
THE CATCHER IN THE RYE J. D. SALINGER 1951	Recent war novels have accustomed us all to ugly words and images, but from the mouths of the very young and protected they sound peculiarly offensive . . . the ear refuses to believe. *New York Herald Tribune Book Review*

FIGURE 3.3 / *Excerpts from Literary Reviews Written by Contemporary Critics*

Source: Bill Henderson (ed.), *Rotten Reviews: A Literary Comparison* (Penguin, New York, 1987).

The student pro-democracy demonstration in Beijing's Tiananmen Square in 1989 was an extraordinary example of both the internationalization of student culture and the impact of worldwide mass media on the production of culture. This photograph of a student demonstrator facing down Chinese Army tanks became world-famous overnight.

transformed because of the creation of a medium of communication.

Compared with spoken language, subsequent developments in communications media seem pale. Nevertheless, these innovations, in their turn, have had a marked effect on how people live. The invention of writing made possible the long-term storage of information. No longer did people have to hold in their heads all the knowledge of their culture. They could turn to written records for information, and they could study and analyze ideas at their leisure. Then came the printing press, an invention usually attributed to Johannes Gutenberg, a fifteenth-century German goldsmith. The printed word enormously increased the distribution of books. A skilled copyist, working by hand, required six months to produce a book, whereas a printer, working on a Gutenberg press, could turn out dozens or even hundreds of copies in the same time (Eisenstein, 1979). With books available to a wider audience, new ideas spread rapidly. It is no wonder that Francis Bacon, the English philosopher and statesman, said that printing (along with the compass and gunpowder) "changed the appearance and state of the whole world."

In this century, the new electronic media of communication have again transformed culture. TV is only one of the electronic inventions that enable people to collect, process, and exchange information with one another (Rogers, 1986). Others include the radio, the telephone, the tape recorder, the motion picture, the computer, the VCR, and the camcorder. The electronic media have greatly extended the speed and distance over which people can "talk" to one another, as well as the size of the audiences involved in communications. At the same time, the electronic media have dramatically altered how we think about the world and how we relate to other people.

Consider, for example, TV news. Compared with print, television is an image-oriented medium; it is produced largely to be *seen*. As a result, decisions about what will appear on the evening news, and how it will be framed, are based in part on what visual impact it will make. If a news story has no exciting visual content to speak of, visual content will be created with graphics or "stock footage." This dramatic, action-packed format makes TV messages much more fragmented and disconnected than messages in print. The goal is to keep the material constantly moving, filled with exciting glimpses into different events. The average length of a "sound bite," the portion of a statement by a politician or other public figure selected for broadcast, dropped from 43 seconds in 1968 to 8.9 seconds in 1988 (Hallin, in Rosen, 1991; Postman, 1986). The entire transcript of a nightly news broadcast contains only as much text as one and a half columns on the front page of *The New York Times* (Meyrowitz, 1985). The result is a rapidly changing kaleidoscope of images. Nothing is dwelled on long enough to become boring. But at the same time, nothing is given enough attention to be analyzed in any depth. Television, in contrast to the written word, is a medium of communication best suited for drama, not analysis (Eisslin, 1982).

J. Meyrowitz (1985) holds that TV is also undermining our sense of distance from what it shows us. Dan Rather is not actually in our living rooms every evening telling us the news of the day, but television makes us feel as if he were. We hear his words, we see his face, we watch his expressions and experience his style in much the same way that we would if he were sitting right on the living-room sofa. As a result, Meyrowitz argues, people come to feel that they "know" those they meet on television in the same way they know their friends. Similarly, live TV coverage can make us feel as if we are there. The night the air war in the Persian Gulf began, for example, millions of Americans watched the Cable News Network (CNN) staff in Baghdad peer cautiously out the window and, now and then, dive for the floor. The fact that cameras, cables, and other equipment were in full view made the broadcast seem even more immediate. Thus, we have the illusion of knowing firsthand what we only glimpse thirdhand.

Some observers are concerned that these characteristics of television are shaping the way that Americans view other aspects of the world. Critic Neil Postman (1986) believes that ours is becoming an entertainment culture, in which people believe that law enforcement, politics, education, and so forth, should be diverting and amusing, just as we expect of TV. As a result, we may so blur the distinction between reality and entertainment that we fail to take important public matters seriously enough. Postman (1986, pp. 93–97) gives numerous examples of this trend: a Catholic priest and radio personality who mixes religious teachings with rock and roll on the grounds that "you don't have to be boring to be holy"; a broadcast of triple-bypass surgery, complete with a play-by-play and "color" man to keep viewers informed about what was happening (as on sports broadcasts); an actual rape trial aired during the hours viewers normally watch soap operas, which the trial closely resembled; and debates between presidential candidates, in which the winner and loser are decided more for reasons of style ("how they looked, fixed their gaze, smiled, delivered one-liners") than of content. Postman believes that the line between show business and serious public affairs is becoming increasingly fuzzy. "Our priests and presidents," he writes, "our surgeons and lawyers, our educators and newscasters need worry less about satisfying the demands of their discipline than the demands of good showmanship" (p. 98). He thinks that this pervasive show-business outlook arises in large part from our constant exposure to television.

THE INTERNATIONALIZATION OF CULTURE

One of the most significant consequences of the growth of the mass media has been the *internationalization* of culture. That is, distinctive local cultures are being replaced by a single global culture in which everyone participates. People watch Donald Duck cartoons in Indonesia, read French newspapers in Africa, dance to Michael Jackson records in Brazil, eat egg rolls, tacos, and couscous in Paris and New York, and listen to the British Broadcasting Corporation news on radios all over the world. This process of cultural diffusion is a two-way street: New tastes and styles flow both from developed to less developed countries (primarily through TV and other mass media) and vice versa (primarily through migration and tourism). (See Chapter 22.) Today few places on earth are immune to outside cultural influences.

The internationalization of culture is not entirely new. The great empires of the past and the spread of world religions introduced people of widely different cultures to common sets of laws, customs, beliefs, and symbols. But in the twentieth century the process of internationalization has become much more rapid. Thanks to the electronic media, new cultural items can circle the globe in a matter of days, even hours. Large-scale immigration is another social force contributing to the internationalization of culture in recent times. Thousands of Indians and Pakistanis have moved to Britain, West Africans to France, and Mexicans to the United States. Immigration not only creates subcultures (as we saw in the case of Hispanic-Americans); it also fosters the development of a new international culture.

A convergence of tastes (such as the worldwide demand for jeans, Coca-Cola, and rock music) is only part of the story. The international culture has played a critical role in important world events. The prodemocracy movement that erupted in China in 1989 is an example. After the death of Mao Zedong in 1976, the new leaders of China had opened its doors. For the first time in decades foreign tourists, businesspeople, and scholars were invited into China; Chinese officials and students were encouraged to travel abroad; and foreign goods, from translations of the works of Jefferson and Freud to Sony Walkman cassette players and polo shirts with designer logos, were offered for sale in Chinese markets. By the mid-1980s, many young, urban Chinese had bought the entire Western package, "from discos to democracy" (Schell, 1989, p. 73).

In the spring of 1989 students occupied Beijing's huge Tiananmen Square and organized massive demonstrations and hunger strikes. Inspired by Western cultural notions of democracy, freedom of speech, and human rights, they called on the government to listen to their point of view. The students drew on symbols from the international culture (such as the "V" peace sign and the thirty-foot "Goddess of Democracy," fashioned after the Statue of Liberty) and carried signs in French ("Vive la liberté"), English ("Give me liberty or give me death"), and other languages. This was particularly surprising in China, a society in which hierarchy and order are highly valued and young people are expected to respect and defer to their elders, not demand to be heard. In 1989 Chinese students saw themselves (in part) as participating in an international youth movement as well as in an international movement for democracy.

Equally significant, the rest of the world was watching on live TV broadcasts. No other internal uprising in a Third World country, before or since, has commanded as much attention from the international media. This media coverage mobilized overseas Chinese, who were able to circumvent censorship within China by faxing news reports back to the students. It rallied international support for the movement (and perhaps nostalgia for the student movements of the 1960s in the United States and Europe). And it preserved on videotape a chapter of history for future scholars and political activists.

The prodemocracy movement in China ended abruptly on the night of June 3, when government troops surrounded Tiananmen Square and thousands of students were killed as they tried to flee. Student leaders were arrested, and old restrictions on freedom of speech and assembly were reinstated. But the image of unarmed students and civilians standing up to the soldiers and tanks of an authoritarian government helped to inspire the successful protest movements against communist regimes in Eastern Europe, which began that fall. Thus, the student protesters in China were both products of and contributors to international culture (Calhoun, 1989).

In a very different way, the internationalization of culture contributed to the furor over Salman Rushdie's 1989 novel, *The Satanic Verses* (Kramer, 1991). Born in Bombay, India, to Muslim parents, Rushdie was educated at Cambridge University and has spent most of his adult life in Britain. His early novels were translated into many languages and earned international acclaim (including a prize in Iran). *The Satanic Verses* is a novel about Indian emigrants, especially film stars and writers who, like Rushdie himself, participate in international culture. One section describes a dream in which the prophet Mohammed may have been tempted by the devil (a possibility Islamic scholars have debated for centuries).

The novel was published on September 26; on October 5 it was banned in India, where the government feared it would spark riots between Hindus and Muslims. (Pakistan and some twenty other nations followed suit for similar reasons.) The idea to protest the book's publication apparently originated in India but spread quickly by phone and fax to Britain. In December, Muslims in the Yorkshire cities of Bradford and Bolton staged book burnings and succeeded in attracting the spotlight of the world press. When this was brought to the attention of the aging Ayatollah Khomeini in Iran, he issued a *fatwa* (or death sentence) on Rushdie, later backed by a $5 million bounty for any Muslim who executed the sentence. In fear for his life, Rushdie went into hiding, where, except for a few guarded public appearances, he remains today. Saudi Arabian leaders denounced the *fatwa* but financed demonstrations protesting the book. In May, 50,000 British Muslims marched on Parliament, demanding that the book be banned. Soon afterward, Muslim clerics and leaders began calling for a separate system of Islamic law, within the British system, for that country's million or more Muslim immigrants.

In the furor Rushdie's novel caused, as well as its contents, we can see the effects of the internationalization of culture: the spread of news (through informal networks as well as mass media), the "immigrant problem" (including the gap between assimilated immigrants and traditional subcultures), the clash of beliefs, and a struggle for cultural dominance as some attempted to defend their ideal of freedom of the press and others their religious beliefs (see Chapter 14). What is clear is that all cultural products—from a social movement like that in China to a novel—are now potentially part of an international process of communication and reception, consumption and critique.

Thinking Back on the Key Concepts

In this chapter we focused on ***culture***, one of the key concepts in sociology as well as a specific field of sociological research. However, it is important to keep in mind that culture is interwoven with other aspects of social life and thus with the other key concepts. Cultural values such as achievement, individualism, and community are ***functionally integrated*** into American society. Our values exert a powerful impact on the way we act and think, the relationships we form, and the goals we pursue. The existence of many different cultural groups in the United States poses a special challenge, as we seek to balance the twin goals of achieving cultural integration and respecting cultural diversity.

New cultural items and trends do not simply happen; they are created through ***social action***, or people influencing and being influenced by one another. We found that certain people (agents, producers, gallery owners, and other cultural gatekeepers) have the ***power*** to determine which fashions people wear, which movies are made, what songs become popular, and which paintings sell for thousands of dollars. We also saw how social elites use their power to control what counts as fine art or gourmet cooking and thus affirm their own high social status while excluding others.

Culture is also influenced by ***social structure***. Our own culture is being shaped by the influx of new immigrants and by the aging of the baby-boom generation. Both of these trends are changing the markets for various cultural products and thus are causing shifts in cultural values. For example, when the large baby-boom cohort was in its infancy, child-rearing books such as those by Dr. Spock topped the best-seller lists; today, as this generation moves into middle age, books on money management and staying fit are the best-sellers.

Finally, the diffusion of cultural ideals has stimulated people to challenge the existing **social structure**, not only in China and other nations from the old communist bloc but also in democratic countries such as Great Britain.

SUMMARY

1. The term *culture* refers to a people's entire learned way of life, including the physical objects they make (material culture) and their values, norms, symbols, language, and knowledge (nonmaterial culture).

2. Values are general ideas that people share about what is good or bad. Americans typically share a number of values, among them achievement and success, practicality, progress, material comfort, democracy, and individuality. When values are in conflict, people tend to apply them selectively.

3. Norms are specific guidelines for action that say how people should behave in particular situations. Norms are often unspoken customs that people implicitly know and follow. Norms vary from society to society and also from group to group within a single society.

4. Symbols are objects, gestures, sounds, or images that represent something other than themselves. The meaning given symbols is often arbitrary, and particular symbols may have slightly different meanings for different people.

5. A language is a system of verbal (and, in many cases, written) symbols with rules about how those symbols can be strung together to convey more complex meanings. Language is extremely important in the development, elaboration, and transmission of culture. Language often offers many clues to the meaning of social interactions.

6. Knowledge is our stored body of facts, beliefs, and practical skills. Modern society is generating and storing knowledge at a very rapid rate. In addition to that which can be expressed in language, numbers, or other explicit symbols, much knowledge is maintained only in the form of practical abilities.

7. The degree to which the parts of a culture form a consistent and interrelated whole is termed *cultural integration*. In a highly integrated culture, customs, beliefs, values, and technology are interdependent. In large, diverse societies such as the United States, culture is very loosely integrated.

8. In large, heterogeneous societies there is also usually a tension between assimilation (the process by which newcomers and other "outsiders" give up their distinctive elements of culture and take on those of the dominant culture) and a desire to preserve cultural diversity. In a society as culturally diverse as the United States, there are a great many subcultures, each with its own distinctive values, norms, knowledge, language, and symbols.

9. Ethnocentrism is the tendency to see one's own cultural patterns as the good and right ones and the standard by which to judge others. Ethnocentric attitudes promote group solidarity and loyalty, but increase hostility toward outsiders and foster conflict among groups.

10. Cultural relativism stresses that any element of culture is relative to a particular time, place, and set of circumstances. Cultural relativism fosters understanding of other groups and tolerance of their practices.

11. Cultural innovations are shaped by a variety of decisions about what is desirable and good. The production of culture is always a social process: Cultural innovators always act within a social context. Cultural gatekeepers are people who decide which of a number of proposed cultural innovations will be accepted.

12. The electronic media have had a great impact on Western culture, dramatically increasing the speed and range of communication. Some have argued that television, with its orientation to images rather than rational discussion, is changing how people view the world.

13. The mass media have also contributed to the internationalization of culture. As a result, tastes may become standardized, political events in distant places are "brought home" via TV, and cultural dissent is exported via immigrant networks.

REVIEW QUESTIONS

1. Show how values and norms are closely linked. Use examples in your answer.
2. Distinguish among folkways, mores, and laws. Give examples of each.
3. List some forces that promote cultural integration and some forces that promote cultural diversity.
4. Explain why someone might be ethnocentric or a cultural relativist.
5. Show how the media both reflect and affect culture.

CRITICAL THINKING QUESTIONS

1. Describe how the values and norms of your dominant culture or subculture differ from one other culture or subculture.
2. Describe the symbols that are special to you and explain why they are special.
3. Present an argument that there is greater cultural integration or greater cultural diversity in the United States than there is in most other countries.
4. Develop the essential ingredients of a program to reduce ethnocentrism on your campus.
5. Present a case pro or con that the media accurately reflect our culture.
6. Indicate general ways in which the internationalization of culture can benefit people and other ways in which it can hurt people. What distinguishes the situations producing good and bad effects?

GLOSSARY

Assimilation The process by which newcomers or members of a subculture give up their distinctive cultural patterns and take on those of the dominant culture of the society in which they live.

Counterculture A group whose norms, attitudes, values, and lifestyle directly challenge or seek to change those of the dominant or mainstream culture.

Cultural gatekeepers People who regulate the flow of new elements of culture into society.

Cultural integration The degree to which the parts of a culture form a consistent and interrelated whole.

Cultural relativism The idea that any element of culture is understandable only in relation to the rest of its cultural context and to a particular time, place, and set of circumstances.

Culture The learned norms, values, knowledge, artifacts, language, and symbols that are constantly communicated among people who share a common way of life.

Dominant culture The group whose values, norms, traditions, and outlooks are imposed on the society as a whole.

Ethnocentrism The tendency to view one's own cultural patterns as good and right and to judge other cultural patterns by those standards.

Folkways Norms that are everyday habits and conventions.

Knowledge The body of facts and beliefs people accumulate over time.

Language A system of verbal (and usually also written) symbols with rules about how those symbols can be strung together to convey more complex meanings.

Laws Norms that are enacted as formal rules by a political body and enforced by the power of the state.

Material culture All the physical objects, or artifacts, that people make and attach meaning to.

Mores Norms that people consider vital to their well-being and to their most cherished values.

Nonmaterial culture Human creations, such as values, norms, knowledge, systems of government, language, and so on, that are not embodied in physical objects.

Norms Specific guidelines for action that say how people should behave in particular situations.

Social marker Any pattern of behavior that provides indications about who people are, what groups they belong to, and what their understanding of a situation is.

Subculture A set of distinctive norms, values, knowledge, artifacts, language, and symbols that a particular group in society uses to distinguish itself from the dominant culture.

Symbol An object, gesture, sound, image, or design that represents something other than itself.

Values General ideas that people share about what is good or bad, desirable or undesirable.

CHAPTER 4

Interaction and Social Structure

John Anderson, a college senior, is on his way to his first job interview. The RAM Computer Corporation is looking for sales trainees. John believes the future belongs to computers and is eager for the job. Flushed from running, slightly damp with perspiration, he arrives 15 minutes late for his appointment. Even before he thinks to shake hands with the interviewer, he starts to apologize. The interviewer responds with an impassive face and gestures John toward a chair. John sits down, still talking rapidly about traffic jams and parking problems. Abruptly, the interviewer asks to see his résumé. John fumbles through his pockets and then realizes that he left his freshly typed résumé in the car. He has only a rough draft with him in his coat pocket. Again he apologizes profusely. Squirming in his seat, John fiddles with the cord of the phone on the interviewer's desk while she skims over the piece of paper. The interviewer stares at the twisted phone cord and then glances briefly at her watch.

"Thank you, Mr. Anderson." She pushes her chair back from her desk and stands. John jumps to his feet.

"I've had a lot of experience with computers . . . ," John stammers.

"Yes, I see. Thank you. Good day."

John backs to the door and hurries out.

You certainly know that this interview got off to a bad start, from which it never recovered. But how did you come to this conclusion? What makes you sure that John will not be offered the job? The answer lies in your implicit understanding of social interactions. The interviewer's unenthusiastic greeting conveyed clear annoyance with John's lateness, which we assume she interpreted as a sign of disorganization, undependability, or lack of interest in the job. John tried to change her opinion by explaining why he was late, but the interviewer's cool response indicated that she considered his excuses lame. The crumpled résumé merely confirmed her first impression. John, in turn, signaled his lack of confidence by squirming and fidgeting with the phone cord. The interviewer's glance at her watch told him that he had no chance of salvaging the situation. Even though very few words were spoken, meanings were understood and communicated.

What intrigues sociologists who take an interactionist perspective is how, in the course of their daily lives, people shape and give meaning to their social encounters by their interrelated actions (Taylor and Sniezek, 1984). These actions are always ordered; they do not occur at random. The interview itself is an example of ***social action***, in which the job applicant and employer jointly seek to realize their individual goals. But their action is shaped by a number of social forces that transcend the intentions and desires of two individuals.

First, all interactions are ordered by socially defined expectations about how people should act in a given situation. During the job interview, for instance, the interviewer was very businesslike. She judged John briskly in terms of his qualifications (including traits like punctuality) and did not waste valuable time when she found him unsuitable. In our ***culture*** such an efficient approach is expected in a job interview. We believe that a job seeker should be judged on his or her work qualifications. In other cultures, however, people consider it normal and appropriate to select workers on the basis of their age, gender, or family connections.

Second, social behavior is ordered by the characteristics that people bring to an interaction; these characteristics are partly the result of particular positions they occupy in the ***social structure***. These positions, called *social statuses*, are the places where individuals "fit" within a group, organization, or society. Each social status is accompanied by a set of behaviors, attitudes, obligations, and privileges known as a *role*. Statuses and roles transcend any particular set of people or episodes of interaction; in a sense, they exist outside the people who occupy and play them. Because she is in the position of job provider and John is in the position of job seeker, the interviewer takes charge from the beginning. If they were playing different roles—say, if he were a swimming instructor and she were one of his pupils—their interaction would be altogether different.

Third, interpersonal connections, or *networks*, also shape social behavior. For example, if John had been recommended for the job by his father, who just happened to be one of the company's best customers, the interviewer might have been inclined to overlook his tardiness and general state of disarray. Exploiting networks of influential family members and friends is one way applicants can increase their ***power*** during a job interview. While the interviewer retains the formal power to hire or not hire, that decision could be shaped by a network of powerful people who pressure or even force the company to give the job to a less-than-suitable applicant.

Finally, interactions take place within a much broader social structural context, which also shapes their direction and outcome. The computer firm that employs the interviewer is part of an economy in which thousands of companies compete for both consumer dollars and talented employees. Likewise, John is one of thousands of men and women who each year leave high schools and colleges in search of jobs. The markets for computers and for workers nicely illustrate the key concept of ***functional integra-***

tion—how different parts of society are interrelated, such that changes in one part are likely to bring about changes in other parts. If the economy is booming and the number of well-educated job seekers is relatively small, corporations may be so desperate for workers that they would even hire a person who seems disorganized and ill-prepared. However, if the economy is in a slump or the number of new college graduates soars, a sizable number will not get jobs, even if they are well-qualified, arrive on time, and create a good first impression.

Thus, our job interview is hardly a unique and random event. It is very orderly and predictable because of the many social forces influencing the people involved in it. Sociologists are interested in all the different levels at which social forces operate. In general, they distinguish between two basic levels: the micro level and the macro level. **Microsociology** focuses mainly on small-scale, everyday patterns of behavior and face-to-face interactions. **Macrosociology** looks at large-scale social arrangements, examining how they are structured and what long-term effects they have. In between are a number of levels of investigation, including the study of the webs of relationships called *networks*. We will consider these three levels in this chapter, starting with the micro, then moving to the level of social networks, and ending with a macro perspective.

However, the fact that we are primarily considering one level at a time does not mean that these different levels of study are unrelated. Social life takes place on *all* levels simultaneously, and what occurs at one level inevitably affects (and in turn is affected by) what occurs at other levels. Thus, what happens in face-to-face interactions during job interviews is inseparable from the market structure of job seekers and available positions in the economy. Similarly, the way in which students and instructors interact in a college classroom is intimately tied to the overall organization of education in our society. In the end, distinctions among various levels of sociological analysis are simply devices to help achieve greater clarity of thinking. With this in mind, let us continue our look at the micro level of social interaction.

SOCIAL INTERACTION

We all engage in countless behaviors during our daily lives. We cough, laugh, scratch our heads, grimace when we struggle to carry a heavy package, to name just a few routine behaviors. Other people sometimes see our behaviors and alter their own accordingly. In response to our cough, they turn away to avoid catching our cold; in response to our laugh, they smile; in response to our grimace, they offer help. Aware of the responses we have triggered in others, we, in turn, may adjust our behavior. We cover our mouth and explain that our cough is just a tickle in the throat, thank the person who offers to help, and so on. **Social interaction** is this process of people orienting themselves to others and acting in response to what others say and do. The word *social* implies that more than one person is involved, while *interaction* means that all parties are mutually influencing one another. Physical proximity is not necessary for social interaction to occur. People interact when they communicate via letter, phone, or fax. Moreover, just being near others does not always mean that social interaction will take place. You could be hurrying through a crowded train station, surrounded by hundreds of people, and never even make eye contact with a single one.

Social interaction is purposive: People act and react to each other in their pursuit of goals. In some interactions, the participants have different goals. In our opening example, the interviewer may have a dozen job candidates to evaluate that day and may want to do the job as quickly and efficiently as possible, whereas the candidate wants to capture her interest and extend the interview so that he can impress her with his many qualifications. Different goals, of course, do not always lead to conflict. Sometimes different goals are complementary. For instance, if John had made a good impression, the interview might have ended happily with her offering him a job and his accepting. In still other situations, participants in social interaction intentionally work together with a common aim. Two college roommates, for example, may share information on which job recruiters are coming to campus that week and what qualifications each is looking for. But that interaction might shift from cooperative to competitive if the roommates keep information to themselves because they fear the other might get the job they want. In still another kind of social interaction, the goals of one party are imposed or forced on others who would rather not pursue them—as when a supervisor tells employees they must work until 6 p.m., rather than 5 o'clock, or they will be fired. As this example makes clear, ***power*** differences are another element of social interaction.

Whether social interaction is complementary or cooperative, competitive or coercive, it is always ordered by patterns of ***social structure*** and ***culture***. When people get together, they generally fall into routinized schemes of expected behavior. Thus, even if you have never gone on a job interview, you know a good deal about how to prepare for one and what to expect. Chances are, very little that

Social interaction involves "reading" other people's facial expressions and responding appropriately. Our behavior is shaped in part by our expectations about, and the cues we take, from another person's smiles and frowns. Here, different types of smiles, as studied by Paul Ekman, convey different sorts of messages. How would you respond to the genuine smile at left and to the false smiles above?

happens on your first job interview will come as a complete surprise. Similarly, even at a party, there is order and predictability to interaction; it is never completely free form. The party-goer who sits on a couch reading, or keeps asking everyone to quiet down and get serious, will be thought distinctly odd. At parties you are expected to be sociable and to have fun.

Most of us take these routines of everyday behavior for granted. Sociologists do not. How do people know how to act the first time they meet a person or encounter a new situation? Why is social interaction so orderly and predictable, at least most of the time? Sociologists have developed five different micro-level perspectives on the sources of order in social interaction.

Defining the Situation

One approach to studying social interaction is to look at how people *define* the situation. In our opening example, for instance, both people had important guidelines concerning appropriate behavior. Just knowing that the situation was a job interview told them that the interviewer was in charge, that she was expected to ask most of the questions and decide when the meeting was over. It also told them that certain topics had to be covered (the candidate's background, skills, and experience, and—if the interview had gone better—a description of the job and mention of the starting salary), whereas other topics were taboo (one doesn't discuss the details of one's sex life in a job interview). Apparently, there is a good deal of agreement concerning whether other topics of conversation are appropriate or not. In one study of campus recruitment interviews, the candidates were often asked about their extracurricular activities, but rarely about their family background, which was probably assumed to be too "private" to discuss (Taylor and Sniezek, 1984).

How does a simple definition of a situation allow people to know so much about what is expected of them? The answer lies in the large stock of cultural knowledge about social life that we acquire through socialization (the subject of Chapter 5). This knowledge is shared—we *all* have internalized it—and we can draw on it at any time. That isn't to say that we explicitly define a new situation in an overt way. John certainly didn't say to the interviewer:

"This is a job interview, you know, which means that you're in charge and I should be deferential." We do, however, *implicitly* keep such cultural knowledge in mind and let it help guide our actions.

The definition of a situation, however, isn't always obvious. If a classmate asks you to go with him or her to the library, is this a date or just an effort to get your help with an assignment? It is sometimes hard to say. In some cases, both parties are unclear about what is going on; in other cases, people have definite but *different* definitions of the situation. When different definitions exist, the participants can be thought of as inhabiting different social realities (Schutz and Luckmann, 1973). Suppose you are a personnel representative for a corporation. Shortly before noon a man dressed in a black leather jacket and carrying a white paper bag enters your office. You assume he is delivering your lunch from the deli and ask him, "How much will that be?" The man looks puzzled, puts down the bag, and takes a résumé from his pocket. Apparently, he is here to inquire about job possibilities (this is *his* social reality). You apologize for your mistake, interview him briefly, but do not offer him a job. In initially defining the man as a delivery person, you created a social reality of your own that made him seem inappropriate for the kind of job openings you had.

This example illustrates an important sociological point: In the words of the sociologist W. I. Thomas, if people "define situations as real, they are real in their consequences" (Thomas and Thomas, 1928, p. 572). The Thomas theorem, as this point is called, says that once we define a situation, that definition determines not only some of our actions but also some of the consequences of what we do. It doesn't matter that you were wrong in defining the job applicant as a delivery person. He won't get the job because your error created a social reality biased against him.

Most of the situations we encounter are ambiguous to some extent. As a result, we must constantly "test out" actions and modify them based on feedback as we strive toward a more precise, collective definition of what is going on. Thus, definitions of a situation are best seen as a form of **negotiated order**. Shared expectations impose limits (or social structure) on interactions, but these limits are not engraved in stone. There is always room for improvisation and negotiation (social action). Negotiations, however, tend to create new rules that impose constraints on future interactions (and thus establish more social structure).

Donald Roy (1960) discovered the full power of negotiated order when he became a participant observer among a small group of factory machine operatives. Roy's job was to operate a punch machine. This meant:

> standing all day in one spot beside three old codgers [George, Ike, and Sammy] in a dingy room looking out through barred windows at the bare walls of a brick warehouse, leg movements largely restricted to the shifting of body weight from one foot to the other, hand and arm movements confined, for the most part, to a simple repetitive sequence of place the die, —punch the clicker, —place the die, —punch the clicker, and intellectual activity reduced to computing the hours to quitting time. (Roy, 1960, p. 160)

The job was so unremittingly dull that Roy considered quitting before the first day was over. Then he discovered how his co-workers made a game of work. The company imposed certain restraints on employees (they had to be on time, meet production quotas, and so on). But within this formal structure, they had room to improvise. Every day Sammy would announce "peach time," produce two peaches from his lunch box, and divide them among the four workers, who invariably would complain about their poor quality. About an hour later Ike would sneak behind Sammy's machine, extract a banana from Sammy's lunch box, shout "banana time!" and gulp the whole thing himself, over Sammy's loud protests. Like a cuckoo clock with a series of varied movements, these interruptions came at regular, hourly intervals. At first Roy found this horseplay childish and silly, but gradually he began to understand its function. The men had developed a set of informal interactions to break up the long day's grind.

What Roy did not realize (at first) was that these games had rules. The negotiated order contained elements of both free choice and creativity, constraint and regulation. When the rules were broken, the relationships among these machine operators proved to be fragile. This was revealed on "Black Friday," when an innocent bit of needling went overboard and destroyed (for a time) the convivial relations among the workers. George's daughter had recently married a college professor, and he was full of pride. George often told stories about their lavish wedding and about his long Sunday afternoon walks with his son-in-law. For George, a blue-collar worker, his daughter's marriage to a college professor was obviously a matter of considerable prestige on the shop floor. On the day that came to be known as Black Friday, Roy and Ike decided to tease George about his relationship with the professor. Ike announced that he had seen George's son-in-law teaching at a school for *barbers*! Insulted, George stopped speaking to Ike and began complaining of Sammy's sloppy work; Ike stopped singing and joking; peach and banana time disappeared; lunch passed in stony silence. Too late, Roy realized that the friendly banter in the clicker room was governed by unspoken rules the men had negotiated over years of working together, rules as strict in their own way as the company's regulations. Unknowingly, Roy had crossed the line from humor to insult. The informal, often unspoken definition of a situation, arrived at through repeated social interaction, can become as rigid and unyielding as a formal set of rules and regulations; today's negotiations can become tomorrow's social structure.

Symbolic Interaction

A different interpretation of the sources of order in everyday social life is found in symbolic interactionism, the theoretical perspective pioneered by George Herbert Mead (1934) (see Chapter 1). Mead's approach to social interaction rested on three basic premises (Blumer, 1969/1986). The first is that people act toward the things they encounter on the basis of what those things mean to them. (*Things*, in this context, refers not just to objects, but also to people, activities, and situations.) Second, we learn what things mean by observing how other people respond to them—that is, through social interaction. Third, as a result of ongoing interaction, the sounds (or words), gestures, facial expressions, and body postures we use in our dealings with others acquire symbolic meanings that are shared by people who belong to the same culture. The meaning of a **symbolic gesture** extends beyond the act itself. A handshake, for instance, is a symbolic gesture of greeting in Western societies. As such, it conveys more than just a mutual grasping of fingers and palms. It expresses both parties' shared understanding that a social interaction is beginning. (In other cultures, such as Japan, willingness to interact is expressed or symbolized in a bow.) *Not* accepting a handshake, on the other hand, expresses unwillingness to interact and a desire to maintain social distance in our culture. Mead believed that it is such shared symbolic meanings that give order and predictability to everyday social interaction.

A single social action can have vastly different meanings, depending on the context. Dunking a member of the community in a body of water can signify a victory celebration after a boat race; a test for witchcraft (floating proves witchcraft; drowning proves innocence); or the religious sacrament of baptism. In these public actions, each individual, like an actor, plays a given role—and plays it to an audience consisting of all the other people involved.

Acquiring our many shared symbolic meanings is not easy, because the same symbol can have different meanings, depending on the context. When you stare at someone who pushes in front of you as you wait to get on a bus, your look will probably be interpreted as a sign of anger. But when you stare at a member of the opposite sex across a barroom floor, your look is likely to be read as a sign of romantic interest. Contemporary followers of Mead have investigated the form and functions of such symbolic gestures in the laboratory. For instance, researchers who study eye contact in face-to-face interaction report a common pattern: When partners have unequal amounts of power and prestige, the one who first breaks initial eye contact is sending a symbolic message of deference or submission to the other (Ridgeway, Berger, and Smith, 1985). The lower-status person is also more likely to maintain eye contact when listening to the partner, but to look down or away when speaking. As a general rule, in man–woman interaction, the woman is most likely to signal deference by breaking eye contact. But when the woman is in a position of superior power (as in the job-interview example that opened this chapter), the reverse is true. We easily make such adjustments in our everyday interactions depending upon the particular situation and the people involved in them.

Mead held that interpreting symbolic messages depends on our ability to take the role of the other person. **Role-taking** involves imagining ourselves in the other person's place, judging how that person is thinking and feeling, and anticipating what further actions he or she might take. Role-taking is an important part of fully understanding the meanings that others intend to convey. Consider Donald Roy's mistake, described above. When he proposed the joke about the professor, he did not stop to look at the situation through George's eyes. In talking about the professor, George was not only basking in his son-in-law's reflected glory but also describing the kind of person he himself would like to have been. To understand what the professor meant to George, Roy would have had to put himself in George's position.

Role-taking also helps us to tailor our words and actions to those of other people. In our opening example, John fully realized that the interviewer was forming a negative impression of him, but did not take that extra step of looking at the situation from her perspective. If he had thought about a time when he had a busy schedule and someone had kept him waiting, it might have occurred to him to ask whether it would be more convenient to reschedule the interview. This gesture of consideration, in turn, might have modified the interviewer's first impression of John. In most social interactions, we rapidly rehearse several responses to what other people say and do and then pick the response that is likely to "go over" best or bring us closer to our goals.

The Dramaturgical Approach

Mead stressed our ability to role-play in our minds. Other sociologists have also used the role-playing concept, but with a different slant. They emphasize not how people mentally analyze their own and others' behaviors but rather how all of us are performers, much like actors on a stage. This view of social interaction is called the **dramaturgical approach**.

Writing about his experiences as a dishwasher in a Paris restaurant, the author George Orwell described how a maitre d' is transformed as he leaves the noisy confusion of the kitchen, where his job is to keep things running smoothly, and enters the elegant dining room, where his job is to "serve" the diners:

> As he passes the door a sudden change comes over him. The set of his shoulders alters; all the dirt and hurry and irritation have dropped off in an instant. He glides over the carpet, with a solemn priest-like air. I remember our assistant maitre d'hotel, a fiery Italian, pausing at the dining-room door to address an apprentice who had broken a bottle of wine. Shaking his fist above his head he yelled (luckily the door was more or less soundproof):
>
> "Tu me fais! Do you call yourself a waiter, you young bastard? You a waiter! You're not fit to scrub floors in the brothel your mother came from, Marquereau!"
>
> Then he entered the dining-room and sailed across it dish in hand, graceful as a swan. Ten seconds later he was bowing reverently to a customer. And you could not help thinking, as you saw him bow and smile, with that benign smile of the trained waiter, that the customer was put to shame by having such an aristocrat to serve him. (Orwell, 1933/1972, pp. 68–69)

The maitre d' is playing two different roles. In his position as supervisor of the restaurant staff, he rants and raves, struts and fumes, portraying intense anger. Then he steps through the door to the dining room and his whole demeanor changes. He is like a performer who assumes a new character as he steps through the curtain onto the stage. Now he becomes the elegant, smiling maitre d' who treats his customers with refinement and elaborate courtesy.

Like Orwell, a number of sociologists think it is useful to look at social interaction as a kind of theatrical performance. One of the leaders of this dramaturgical ap-

We usually think of a drama as entertainment, or perhaps as a commentary on life. Erving Goffman developed the insight that social life itself resembles the performances of a play. We assemble a role to make our way through a series of "acts" which constitute daily life. For many of these acts, we know our role well and the play goes as planned. For many other acts, our roles are more ambiguous and the play goes less smoothly.

proach was the American sociologist Erving Goffman (1959, 1974). Goffman saw social life as a series of improvisational plays or skits. Every social situation has a script, which outlines in general terms what is supposed to happen and what roles need to be played. But in contrast to real theater, there is no director. So the actors (the participants in social interaction) have to negotiate among themselves who will play which role. They also must interpret and play their roles in ways that will elicit the desired responses from others, so that the play (the interaction) will have a "happy ending."

In an actual theater, actors strive to convince the audience that they are the characters they are playing. In much the same way, participants in social interaction work to convince the audience (other participants) that the roles they are trying to play are genuine. Goffman coined the term **impression management** to describe people's efforts to control what others think about them. In the search for a job, for example, impression management begins even before an interview, with the résumé. As a popular how-to-get-a-job manual suggests, "Telling the facts about yourself is never enough. You have to market yourself as a product" (Petras and Petras, 1989, p. 31). (See Figure 4.1.) You also have to "dress for success"—in most cases, in a suit, not a leather jacket.

Goffman's important insight is that impression management is not confined to such formal situations as a job interview, but goes on all the time. Someone who goes around in tattered jeans and the same old sweatshirt is trying to create an impression ("I'm too busy to worry about fashion" or "I'm a rebel!") every bit as much as the person whose expensive-looking outfits are always carefully coordinated, and who never wears the same thing two days in a row. Decisions about where we live, what kind of car we buy, even whether we eat hamburgers or pasta, are all aspects of impression management, "props" that support the identity we want to project.

One of the puzzles of social interaction is why others usually go along with a person's "act," even when they realize it is contrived. Goffman believed the answer is that each person's success at impression management depends on other people playing complementary roles. You cannot present yourself successfully as a maitre d', for example, if waiters and customers ignore you. Nor can you successfully be a restaurant diner if the maitre d' refuses to seat you and the waiter never takes your order. In an effort to maintain each other's performances, people try hard to "buy" what the other participants are doing. If someone makes an inadvertent mistake, others try to gloss it over. For instance, if the maitre d' in an elegant restaurant accidentally burps as he greets some customers, they pretend not to notice (what Goffman called "studied nonobservance"). If a waiter spills salad in a diner's lap, the maitre d' quickly steps in to remove the evidence of a bungled performance.

FIGURE 4.1 / Writing a Résumé That Sells

Source: Adapted from Kathryn Petras and Ross Petras, *The Only Job Hunting Guide You'll Ever Need* (Poseidon Press, New York, 1989), chap. 2.

Think of your resume as a marketing tool to sell yourself as a product
Your goal is to sell your way into an interview, or to sell yourself to an interviewer. Continually ask yourself what qualities the employer is looking for, and present your own background and experience to suit. Remember to **be selective**. Do not clutter up your résumé with unimportant facts.

More specifically, you should include:

1. Personal data: Give name, address, and phone number only; anything else is a waste of space. **Tip:** Print personal data in the upper right-hand corner, not the middle of the page, so that when someone flips through a stack of résumés your name is immediately noticeable.

2. Career objectives: A brief, clear statement of your immediate goals. If you are not sure about your goals, skip this section.

3. Work experience: List past jobs and accomplishments presented so as to show that you have the qualities a prospective employer wants. If you have a steady record of employment and advancement, choose a chronological format, putting your current job first. If your employment record is spotty, or you do not have much work experience, consider a functional format, with headings that indicate areas of expertise. **Example:** A recent college graduate applying for a position as a management trainee used his accomplishments as a part-time salesperson in a gourmet food shop to illustrate his management skills (trained new personnel; supervised other part-time workers; managed the shop on weekends; devised a new inventory system).

4. Education: List school, degree(s), year graduated, major, and any awards or honors received. If you are a student or recent graduate, put this section before work experience and expand with such information as college activities and courses related to the position you want. **Example:** A young woman applying for an executive trainee position in a department store listed computer courses she had taken because she knew buyers at the company had to use computers. **Tip:** If you worked during your college years, include the percentage of your college expenses you earned yourself; this shows prospective employers your maturity, independence, and initiative.

5. Activities: List outside activities, memberships in organizations, volunteer work, and the like. Do not write this category off as fluff; activities make you stand out as an individual. Focus on things that relate to the job you are seeking or illustrate general qualities that employers like to see. Be sure to include examples of productivity (or profit-mindedness), patterns of accomplishment and upward movement, examples that show you are a team player, and evidence of stability and direction. **Tip:** Avoid mentioning groups that are overtly political or controversial.

6. Presentation and style: Stick with a clear, readable typeface, white or off-white bond paper, and black print. A résumé should be at least one page long. If you do not have much information, use spacing and wide margins to fill the page. If you have a lot of information, do not crowd the page; leave space between sections and paragraphs within sections. A résumé should demonstrate your ability to communicate by presenting information clearly and concisely. Use short words, sentence fragments, and active verbs, and omit the personal pronoun (salesperson rather than I was a salesperson); everyone knows the résumé is about you.

Diners do not stare at people eating at other tables or eavesdrop on their conversations, but act as if they were the only diners in the room (a pattern Goffman called "civil inattention"). In these and countless other ways, parties to the interaction keep their roles and the elegance of the situation intact. In Goffman's words:

> Much of the activity during an encounter can be understood as an effort on everyone's part to get through the occasion and all the unanticipated and unintentional events that can cast participants in an undesirable light, without disrupting the relationships of participants. (Goffman, 1967, p. 41)

But it is hard to be on stage every minute. This is why social life has both "frontstage" and "backstage" regions. In a frontstage region, people are required to play their roles with all the skill they can muster. The dining room is frontstage for waiters. No matter how harried, annoyed, or exhausted they feel, waiters are expected to remain polite and helpful toward their customers. Once in the kitchen, however, waiters are backstage. Here they can joke about returning some dropped food to a plate. The kitchen is where waiters relax and prepare themselves for their next performance. Virtually every role has a backstage to which a person can retreat. The doctors' lounge is backstage to physicians at a hospital, as is the teachers' room to teachers at a school. Backstage in their dorms students laugh about their professors, while backstage in their offices professors joke about their students.

Does this mean that most frontstage behavior is phony and insincere, that the face people present to the world is merely a mask? Not necessarily. Goffman argued that all people must project some image, even if it is the image of someone who is unconcerned about images. Moreover, the more we play a role, the more genuine it feels, until eventually we are as convinced as our audience that we are the person we portray. As sociologist Peter Berger has explained it:

> One feels more ardent by kissing, more humble by kneeling and more angry by shaking one's fist. That is, the kiss not only expresses ardor but manufactures it. Roles carry with them both certain actions and emotions and attitudes that belong to these actions. The professor putting on an act that pretends to wisdom comes to feel wise. The preacher finds himself believing what he preaches. The soldier discovers martial stirrings in his breast as he puts on his uniform. In each case, while the emotion or attitude may have been present before the role was taken on, the latter inevitably strengthens what was there before. (Berger, 1963, p. 96)

In short, Goffman held that implicit "scripts," based on past experience and shared understandings, are what give order and predictability to social interactions. Scripts, in other words, provide social structure. But the outcome of social interaction depends on people interpreting one another's behavior correctly and supporting one another's performances (social action). Indeed, Goffman believed that people have to "work at" interaction, particularly in unfamiliar social situations where they must negotiate the identities and roles they will play.

Ethnomethodology

Like Goffman, sociologist Harold Garfinkel (1967) focused on the routines of everyday social life. But where Goffman observed social interaction from a distance, somewhat like a critic watching a play, Garfinkel attempted to analyze it from the inside, as if he were a novice actor stepping onstage for the first time. This is not an easy perspective to take, for none of us is truly a novice at social interaction; we have all been interacting with others since the day we were born. As a result, we have grown so accustomed to our culture's scripts that we aren't even aware they exist. For example, without thinking about it, most Americans walking on a busy sidewalk keep to the right (just as they do in their cars) to avoid colliding with others. This shared understanding is just one of the millions of tacit, taken-for-granted bits of knowledge that provide order and structure to our social interactions.

To reveal the unconscious understandings that structure social life, Garfinkel and his students deliberately violated social expectations and then observed the consequences. Garfinkel called this approach **ethnomethodology**. (*Ethnos* is a Greek word meaning "people" or "culture.") So the word "ethnomethodology" refers to the methods or ways in which people make sense out of everyday interactions. These methods are also known as "practical reasoning."

In one experiment, Garfinkel asked some of his students to act as if they were guests when they visited their families. For fifteen minutes to an hour, the students maintained a polite distance—talking about general topics, rather than personal ones; asking permission to use the bathroom or to get a glass of water; expressing gratitude to

Harold Garfinkel introduced the study of "practical reasoning," which came to be known as ethnomethodology. Studies like his help us realize the enormous number of small behaviors that constitute the unrecognized practical reasoning of daily life. They help us become more sensitive to such ideas as how difficult it would be to suddenly live as a member of the other gender—as did the well-known travel writer Jan Morris, who had lived until well into adulthood as James Morris before surgically changing her sexual identity.

the "host" and "hostess" for their kind hospitality. Two of the forty-nine families thought the students were joking; one ignored the behavior; the remainder were upset and annoyed. "Family members demanded explanations: What's the matter? What's gotten into you? Did you get fired? Are you sick? What are you being superior about? Why are you mad? Are you out of your mind or just being stupid?" (Garfinkel, 1967, pp. 47–48). In one way or another, the students' families tried to restore "normal" relations and in doing so they revealed some of their unstated assumptions about family interaction.

In other experiments, Garfinkel's students "made trouble" by attempting to bargain for items in a store (something Americans generally do not do); by breaking the rules in a game of tic-tac-toe (erasing the opponent's first move); and by closing in during a conversation so that they were nose to nose with the unsuspecting subject. Each of these violations of the rules of interaction produced confusion and often anxiety (in the students as well as in the "victim") and frequently culminated in an angry rebuke. These intense reactions confirmed for Garfinkel the degree to which people depend on tacit, often unconscious, rules of interaction to structure their social encounters.

A newer line of ethnomethodology shifts attention from the content to the *mechanics* of social interaction (Atkinson, 1988). Instead of investigating what social actors think or mean, or what they unconsciously assume, researchers analyze what social actors do, in minute detail. Some have observed the flow of traffic on a sidewalk, or the way people form a line to wait for a movie (Livingston, 1987).

Perhaps the most interesting work in this vein has focused on conversations. How, ethnomethodologists ask, do people manage the rather complicated business of holding a conversation, avoiding gaps and silences on the one hand and "collisions" (both talking at once) on the other? Sociologists have discovered regular, clear patterns of conversation in classrooms (McHoul, 1978; Mehan, 1979), courtrooms (Atkinson and Drew, 1979), and clinics (West, 1984). In all these settings, those who enjoy superior power and authority (the teacher, the judge, the physician) claim the right not only to speak first (and last) but also to direct the conversation and silence interruptions. Conversations between the sexes also tend to be asymmetrical (Fishman, 1978; West and Zimmerman, 1977). In general, men hold the floor, and women often seek permission before they interrupt or change the subject. In certain situations, however—for example, when the female is the boss and the male her assistant or secretary—this pattern is reversed.

Social Exchange

Both Goffman and Garfinkel studied the taken-for-granted and invisible underpinnings of human social interaction. They tried to pull back the veil from social life and lay bare its otherwise hidden rules and mechanisms. We gain a quite different view of what makes interaction orderly from theorists such as Peter M. Blau (1964) and George C. Homans (1974). These sociologists analyzed a wide range of social behaviors as processes of exchange. Although exchange can take many forms, it is usually guided by the norm (or rule) of reciprocity (Gouldner, 1973). When someone does us a favor or gives us something of worth, reciprocity requires that we repay the kindness, balancing the social ledger. The original giver then has an obligation to reciprocate in response to us, to keep the relationship going. Whatever form the reciprocation takes, however, it strengthens a social bond and keeps the interaction alive by creating new social obligations.

Social-exchange theorists see mutual reciprocation as the most basic form of human interaction. It can be observed everywhere, Peter Blau argues:

> not only in market relations but also in friendship and even in love . . . as well as in many social relations between these extremes of intimacy. Neighbors exchange favors; children, toys; colleagues, assistance; acquaintances, courtesies; politicians, concessions; discussants, ideas; housewives, recipes. (Blau, 1964, p. 88)

To Blau and other social-exchange theorists, reciprocity is part of what gives social life its order and predictability.

The social-exchange perspective on interaction is partly rooted in rational-choice theory, introduced in Chapter 1. According to the rational-choice model, people weigh the anticipated gains from their actions against the possible costs before deciding how to act. From this perspective, social action is "premeditated." Although we do not keep an actual ledger for each of our relationships, we do keep track of social "credits" and "debits" and have a good sense of who "owes" whom.

But the rational-choice model does not easily explain such apparently irrational behavior as love, which often entails self-denial in pursuit of someone else's welfare (Emerson, 1976). Why do close friendships and marriages endure over long periods when one or the other partner is unable or unwilling to reciprocate? To explain the emotional and habitual aspects of social interaction, Homans and others turn to the school of psychology known as *behaviorism*. According to the psychological principle of operant conditioning, people tend to repeat behavior for

Exchange theorists focus on how social interaction is guided by a norm of reciprocity, which means that two or more parties each get the equivalent of whatever they give. The Kwakiutl Indians of the Pacific Northwest are socially integrated through ceremonies called potlatches, in which guests receive gifts (which over the years have varied widely in lavishness) from their hosts. What seems on the surface to be one-sided giving should really be understood as an exchange: The host is paying his guests for the service of witnessing his high social status, and the guests, by accepting the gifts, validate that status.

which they have been rewarded in the past and to avoid behavior for which they have been punished. From this perspective, the persistence of a relationship that is unreciprocated is not dependent upon the rational calculation of anticipated gains. Rather, it is shaped by past patterns of reinforcement. For example, if a husband and wife had a whirlwind courtship and the "honeymoon" continued through the early years of their marriage, they are likely to stay together during periods when one of them doesn't have much time or energy to devote to the other. Old friendships can endure separations, lapses in "good manners," and even occasional quarrels. Past rewards keep these relationships going.

The combination of rational choice and operant conditioning helps to shape many patterns of social interaction. Suppose you were offered two jobs as a reporter: one for a famous big-city newspaper and one for the local paper in your rural hometown. Your decision would be based in part on rational calculation: Which job pays more? Could you live as well in the city as you could in the country on the salaries offered? And which job is most likely to lead to a promotion in the near future? Past experience and conditioning would also enter into your decision. Have you found moving and making new friends easy or difficult in the past? Have you learned to work best in a highly competitive situation (the city paper) or a more relaxed, cooperative one (your hometown paper)? Thus, what interactions we choose to enter into and what relationships we seek to maintain depend on both rational calculation and psychological conditioning.

NETWORKS: WEBS OF SOCIAL RELATIONSHIPS

The processes of social interaction just described are the bases for creating **social relationships**—relatively enduring patterns of interaction between two or more people. Most people have many social relationships, from casual acquaintances to intimate friendships and close family bonds. These acquaintances, friends, and relatives, in turn, interact with others, and so establish more or less enduring sets of cross-cutting ties, which link together large numbers of people. A web of relationships among a set of people who are linked together, directly and indirectly, through their various communications and dealings is called a **network**.

The study of networks moves us away from micro-level analysis of human interaction toward a more macro-level look at social structure. Networks are actually a middle ground between social interaction and larger-scale structural aspects of society. Networks arise from regularized, repeated interactions, but like elements of structure they form a context that constrains and shapes how people act toward others.

Studying Network Patterns

Networks have been described as the basic social context—the interpersonal environment—in which people live (Marsden, 1987). Network data have been used to investigate such diverse topics as occupational achievement (Lin, Ensel, and Vaughn, 1981), psychological mood and well-being (Fischer, 1982; Kadushin, 1983), willingness to contribute to causes (Oliver, 1984), and the spread of innovations (Rogers, 1979). How do sociologists collect and analyze data on networks?

Identifying Networks

A sociologist knocks on your door and asks if you would be willing to answer a few questions about your friends and acquaintances. You agree and invite her to come in and sit down. She begins:

> From time to time, most people discuss important matters with other people. Looking back over the last six months, who are the people with whom you discussed matters important to you? Just tell me their first names or initials. (Marsden, 1987)

Go ahead and make a list of names. Next, write down the answers to the following questions about the first person on your list.

How close are you to this person?

How often do you see one another?

How long have you known each other?

What is the nature of your relationship (relative, co-worker, neighbor, member of the same organization, "just friend," etc.)?

What is this person's age, sex, race/ethnicity, level of education, and religious preference?

Now answer the same questions for the second, third, fourth, and fifth people on your list (stopping at five). Fi-

Like other social ties, attraction and love, say social exchange theorists, are governed by reciprocity. Like does tend to attract like: Partners do tend to pair off according to perceived similarities in attractiveness. But regardless of the basis on which these bonds are formed, they are sure to be part of a broad network of relationships in each partner's life.

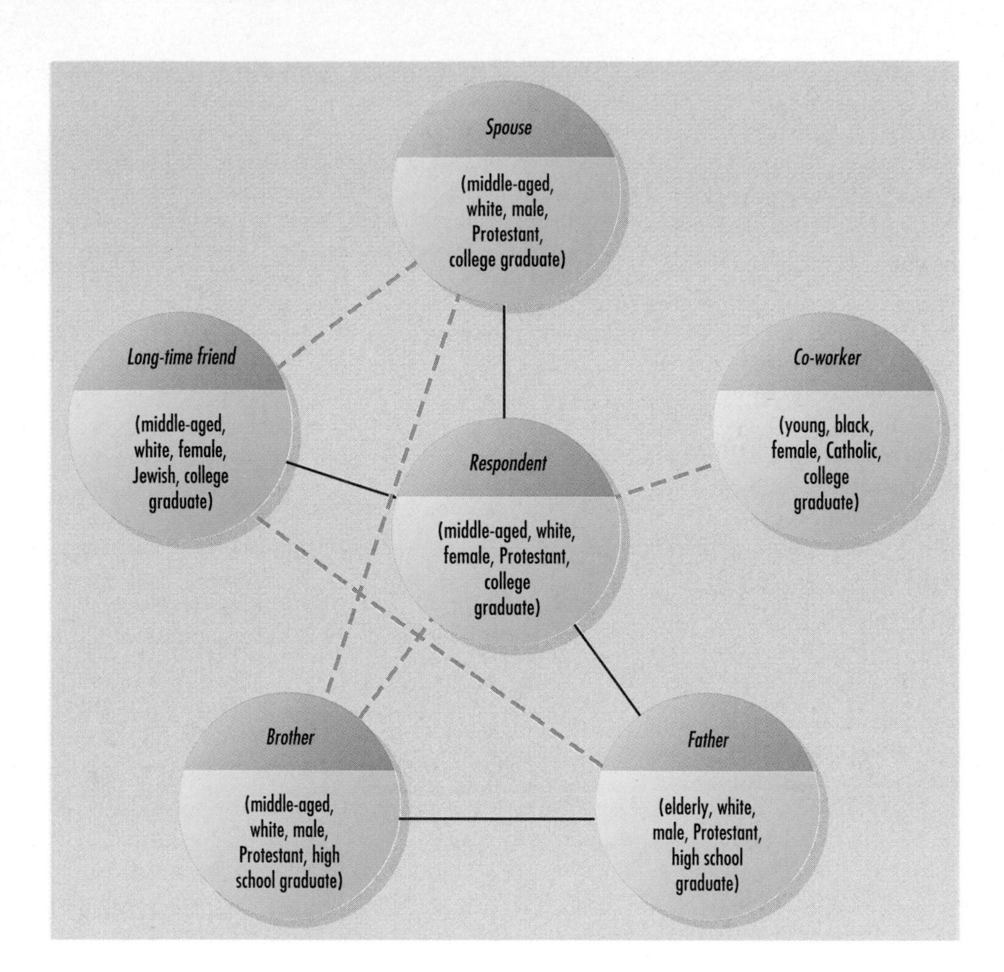

FIGURE 4.2 / Sample Interpersonal Discussion Network

nally, answer the following questions about relationships among the various people to whom you talk, considering them one at a time in relation to each of the others:

Does this person know the other people on your list?

Are they extremely close, moderately close, or total strangers?

When you have answered these questions, the network interview is complete.

This exercise was not just made up for this textbook. These questions, almost exactly as worded here, were asked of a random sample of 1,534 American adults as part of the 1985 General Social Survey, or GSS (Burt, 1990; Marsden, 1987, 1990a). The responses—yours as well as theirs—describe an "interpersonal discussion network." To see what your network looks like, take out a piece of paper. Put yourself, as respondent, in the center. In a circle around you, put the people to whom you talk about important matters. Draw a solid line connecting you to those people with whom you have especially close relationships, and a dotted line to indicate a more distant relationship. Now do the same to indicate the strength of ties between the five other people in your network; no line means two people do not know each other. If you wish, fill in data on each person and the nature of your relationships with him or her. You have created a network sociogram. (To help you complete the exercise, a sample sociogram is shown in Figure 4.2.)

How close is your interpersonal discussion network to those collected in the General Social Survey? We will discuss the results of this survey shortly. But first we must introduce some of the concepts sociologists use in analyzing network data.

Analyzing Networks: Basic Concepts

In order to compare social networks, sociologists have developed several useful conceptual tools (Marsden, 1990b). These concepts allow us to distinguish between (a) the different types of units that make up a network, (b) the different kinds of ties linking these units, and (c) the different kinds of overall network patterns. Let's look at each of these in turn.

In the discussion network you just constructed, the units involved are individual people. Sociologists call these units in a network **nodes**, to distinguish them from the ties (the links or associations) that connect nodes. In many network studies, nodes are individuals, but nodes can also be collective actors like groups, organizations, or even nation-states. For example, a sociologist interested in studying changes in the American economy might construct networks of the fifty largest corporations during each of several historical periods, linking together those corporations that do a certain minimum volume of business with each other. Comparisons of these networks over time might show changes in the nodes (which corporations make the top fifty list) as well as in the connections between them. This, in turn, might suggest new insights into changes in the American economy. The idea that network analysis can explore linkages among corporations (or labor unions, political parties, voluntary associations, what have you) greatly expands the usefulness of this sociological tool.

Just as nodes can vary in what they represent (individuals or collective actors), so the ties connecting nodes can also vary from network to network.

- One way in which they can vary is in terms of *content*. Studies have looked at networks of people linked by friendship, frequency of interaction, conversations at work, proximity of residence, and many other factors. In some cases, several different kinds of ties exist between the same two people. Your best friend might also be a member of your volleyball team and a member of your church (what sociologists call "multiplex" ties).

- Network ties can vary in *strength* as well. Stronger ties generally entail more frequent contact, involve more emotional intensity or intimacy, and make greater demands on both parties (for example, time demands). But weaker ties, of the "friend-of-a-friend" sort, can be important too, as we will show when we describe using networks to find a job.

- Ties also vary in terms of *reciprocity*. Suppose your sociology professor collected and compared all the networks from your class. If the person you listed first as someone with whom you discuss important issues also listed you first, then the tie is reciprocal. But that person may not have listed you at all, making the tie nonreciprocal. Reciprocity (or the lack of reciprocity) is particularly important for understanding friendship networks. In general, the more often someone is mentioned in other people's networks, the more popular and visible he or she is; the more nonreciprocal ties a person has, the more peripheral or marginal that individual is.

- Finally, ties can vary in their degree of *symmetry*. Symmetrical ties link nodes that are equivalent in such characteristics as age, level of education, sex, and income, while asymmetrical ties link nodes that differ in these or other socially significant ways.

So far we have discussed different types of nodes and ties in networks. But how do networks as a whole vary one from another? One way is in terms of *size*. Size is usually measured by the number of nodes in a network (or in some cases, the number of ties). Thus, in an interpersonal discussion network some people might list only one or even no confidants, suggesting that they are socially isolated, whereas others might list ten or more confidants, indicating that they are highly integrated into their family, workplace, neighborhood, and/or other social settings.

Other differences in networks are illustrated in Figure 4.3. The *density* of a network is measured by the ratio of actual ties to all possible ties, or whether all possible linkages are "filled." If all the people you listed in your interpersonal discussion network know one another (as might be the case if you listed all family members, for example), the density would be 100 percent (as in Figure 4.3a). High density indicates that a network is tightly linked. *Reachability* is closely related to density. For any node, reachability is the number of direct ties a person must pass through to reach any other node in the network. In Figure 4.3a the reachability of person E to person A is 1, whereas in Figure 4.3c it is 4, indicating greater social distance. Finally, *range* and *centrality* refer to the relative position of different nodes in a network. For any given node, range refers to the absolute number of ties that person has with others in the network, while centrality refers to the proportion of all possible links the person actually has made. Both measures are useful for distinguishing people who are always in the center of the action (high range and centrality, as for person C in Figure 4.3b) from those who are more peripheral (low range and centrality, as for person A in both Figures 4.3b and 4.3c).

With all these variations in mind, let's go back to the General Social Survey.

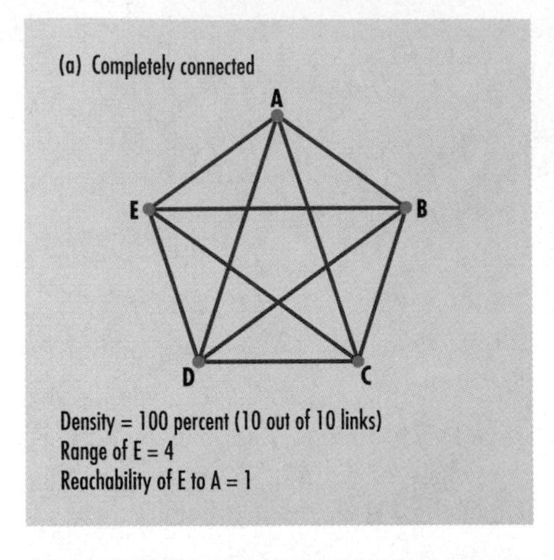

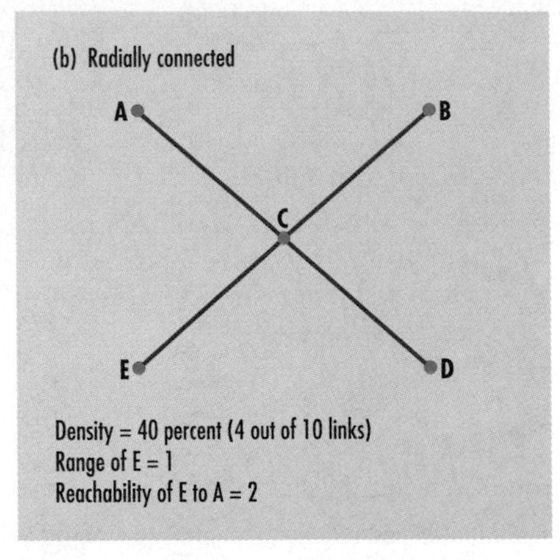

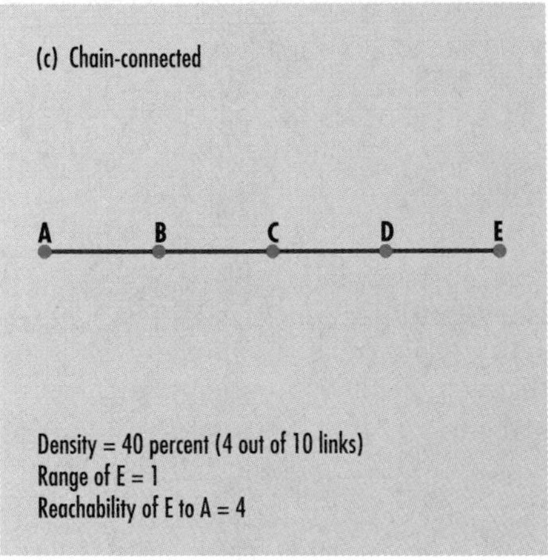

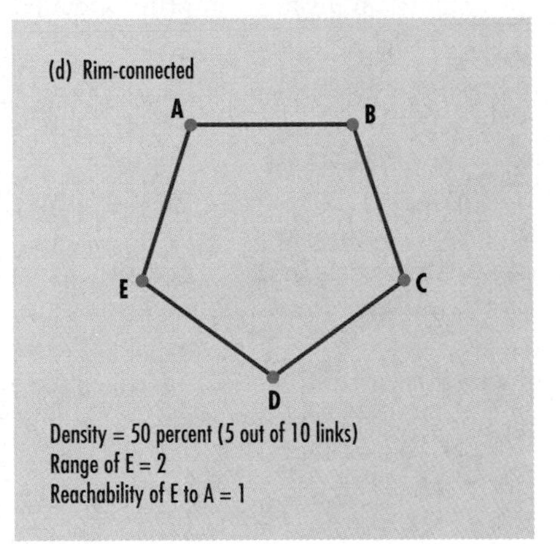

FIGURE 4.3 / Four Types of Networks

Who Talks to Whom: Results of the General Social Survey

How does your interpersonal network compare with those generated by the General Social Survey? Is the network of people with whom you discuss important matters typical or unusual?

According to the GSS, the typical American discussion network is small (containing an average of only three people), kin-centered (about half of the confidants in the average network were relatives, and nearly a third of all respondents mentioned only kin), relatively dense (most respondents said that two out of three of their confidants knew each other, and about half saw their confidants daily), and homogeneous (Burt, 1990; Marsden, 1987, 1990a). The racial and ethnic homogeneity of networks was particularly striking. Only ninety-six out of the 1,534 respondents said that they had talked about important matters with someone from a different racial or ethnic group, usually at work. The same pattern applied whether the person was white, black, Hispanic, or Asian. In terms of who talks to whom, American society may be more racially polarized than other measures have indicated. To some degree young, urban college graduates departed from the typical GSS patterns. Their discussion networks were generally larger and more diverse, but less dense: They were more likely to include people they saw infrequently and people who did not know one another.

How do network patterns affect people's opportunities and the actions they engage in? How do they influence the functioning of society as a whole? In the section that follows, we will focus on one social activity that often critically involves networks: getting a job.

Using Networks to Search for a Job

Karl E. is an engineer just out of college. His father, also an engineer, heard from a colleague that there was a job

> opening in a nearby company. The colleague had heard about this opening from a salesman who had visited the company and heard of it from a secretary. The secretary had heard from her boss. Karl applied and was later accepted for the job. (Granovetter, 1974, p. 57)

Social networks helped Karl E. to find his first job out of college. The process began with one relationship in Karl's own personal network, that with his father. Through this tie he was in turn linked to overlapping networks of friends and acquaintances—his father's colleague, a salesman the colleague knew, a secretary with whom the salesman was acquainted, and the secretary's boss. All these people played a role in Karl's successful job search. This example suggests that getting a job is as much a matter of *who* you know (the network of personal contacts you maintain) as of *what* you know. But is Karl E.'s case typical? Do most people get jobs through networks of personal contacts?

Mark Granovetter (1974) studied professional, technical, and managerial workers who had changed jobs within the preceding five years. He found that, like Karl E., 56 percent of the men he studied had found their present job through personal networks. Only about 19 percent had used formal, impersonal channels, such as responding to an advertisement or using an employment agency. Another 19 percent had applied directly to the employer, without having seen an ad or heard about a specific job. (The remaining 6 percent used other approaches.) The only thing unusual in Karl E.'s (fictionalized) experience was the number of people involved—that is, the length of the chain of contacts—five, counting Karl's father. Usually, the number of connections is relatively small—nearly always fewer than three.

Why did so many of the job seekers Granovetter studied choose the network route? They claimed that they got more accurate information from personal contacts than they would have through ads or agencies or through inquiries made to a company directly. Friends told them whether co-workers at the firm were congenial, whether the boss was neurotic, whether the company was moving forward, and the like. Most also said that their contact had "put in a good word" for them, as well as telling them about the job.

Granovetter's research pointed to a second important finding, this one regarding the *nature* of the ties between job seekers and their contacts. Common sense suggests that a network of strong ties would give the most assistance. People you are close to, after all, are strongly motivated to give your needs high priority. But Granovetter found just the opposite. Generally speaking, the people who are most useful in providing us with job leads are not those with whom we are the closest, but rather those linked to us by weak ties (Granovetter, 1974, 1984). Of those respondents who had found jobs through networks, only about 17 percent reported that they saw their contact often (a strong tie), while 83 percent reported that they saw their contact occasionally or rarely (weak ties). Indeed, in many cases, the contact was on the outer margins of the person's current network—say, an old college friend or a former employer seen only sporadically over the years. Typically, a mutual friend or chance encounter renewed the contact and gave rise to the job lead.

Why are weak ties so important to a job search? The answer lies in the benefit of broadening one's sources of information. The closest ties in your social network tend to be connected to many of the same people you are connected to. Consequently, if *they* know about a job opening, the chances are *you* do too. In contrast, your weak ties have links to many people whom you do not know. As a result, they can offer a greater range of information than your close friends and family can.

Are networks important to the search for a job in other countries and cultures? Often they are, but different kinds of networks may be involved. For instance, in Japan the nodes of many job-seeking networks are high schools and corporations, not individuals as in the United States (Rosenbaum and Kariya, 1989; Rosenbaum, Kariya, Settersten, and Maier, 1991). Put another way, the Japanese often rely on *institutional* networks, whereas Americans use *interpersonal* ones. Many Japanese firms have long-term arrangements with certain high schools. Each year they distribute job offers to these schools, offering the most and the best jobs to the schools they rank highest (based on the job performance of past graduates). Teachers nominate students for these jobs, matching the individual student's skills to the particular job openings, and ranking them in order of whom they consider best qualified. Employers then interview the school's nominees and, in eight out of ten cases, select one for the job. This system has advantages for both the schools and the employers. The schools know that as long as they continue to nominate only qualified graduates for jobs, they will continue to be able to place their students. Even during slow periods, when they do not need new workers, employers hire some graduates, just to keep the relationships going with the "client" schools. Employers, in turn, are virtually guaranteed a steady flow of new employees in the years ahead. Students, of course, have little say in this process. Still, if their grades are good, students are virtually guaranteed employment, which is strong motivation to work hard in school.

On the surface, the Japanese hiring system seems entirely different from our own. But in both countries information about potential jobs flows through networks. In the

Japanese institutional networks, as in the American interpersonal ones, the system works because of both communication and trust. Whether Americans would be willing to switch to the Japanese system is questionable, however. Although we do appreciate security in finding a job, our culture values freedom of choice even more highly.

Position and Power in Networks

Where does social ***power*** come from? Why are some people able to tell others what to do or what to think—and get away with it? One answer looks at the attributes of powerful people: Perhaps it is because they are bigger or smarter, more skillful or wealthier, that they have power to control others. Another answer traces power back to the authority that goes with an office in a formal organization or bureaucracy: Presidents, chief executive officers, and chairmen (and women) of the board have power to tell other members of their organizations what to do. A third, quite different, explanation of the roots of power focuses on the individual's position in a social network.

To say "X has power" has no meaning unless we specify power over whom. Thus, power is not an attribute of an individual, but a property of a social relationship (Emerson, 1962). Most social relationships in a network entail the exchange of valued items—whether tangible things like money, goods, and jobs, or intangible things like love, friendship, approval, and information (Cook, Emerson, Gillmore, and Yamagishi, 1983). Differences in power among people in a network depend on the degree to which some of those people control these valued resources. And control of valued resources depends in large part on where a person is located in the network. In many networks, the more centrally located someone is, the more power he or she typically has over those at the periphery or margins. Look again at network b in Figure 4.3. Which person in this network has the most power? Obviously C. Because of C's central location, all exchanges—whether of love, information, money, or goods—must go through this person. Suppose, for example, that A and B are manufacturers of compact disks, and D and E are consumers. C is the classic "middleman." All the other people in this network are dependent on C to provide what they need (a market or source for compact disks). Put another way, then, power is the result of (other people's) dependency.

Sociologists have explored power–dependence relationships in social networks (Markovsky, Willer, and Patton, 1988; Marsden, 1983; Yamagishi, Gillmore, and Cook, 1988). In exchange networks, power–dependence relationships can be positive or negative (facilitating or hindering exchange). Imagine a three-person network, A-B-C, in which A and C have direct ties to B but not to each other. Suppose, further, that A manufactures compact disks, B is a retailer who sells compact disks, and C is a consumer who wants to buy one. In this case, B is a positive link, facilitating exchange. But in other cases, the same three-person network can result in very different power relations. Suppose now that this is a classic love triangle, where both A and C are in love with B. This gives B the power to choose between A and C. If B decides to marry A (and we assume marital fidelity), then further amorous exchanges with C are cut off. Or B may string both along—the familiar case of a person in the middle of a network "playing off" the others against each other. Here B is a negative link, limiting exchange.

In all these cases, the power of B comes from his or her position in the network. Simply being in the middle makes others dependent on you and generally gives you power over them. But even though position in a network gives a person *potential* power over others, it does not determine whether or how that power will be used. The actual use of power is shaped by many factors other than position in a network, such as variations in interactive skills (being a smooth talker), information processing (recognizing one's power potential), and willingness to take risks (Molm, 1990).

SOCIAL STRUCTURE

So far, we have examined social interaction and shown how, in some cases, interaction becomes the basis for relatively long-lasting arrangements known as social relationships and networks. These relatively stable and enduring social arrangements, which constrain individual choices, can be thought of as a transition between social interaction and social structure. In this section, we focus on ***social structure***—its various elements and the effects it has on people's actions.

Statuses and Roles

A **social status**, as we have said, is a position in the social structure—any position that determines where a person "fits" into the organized whole of a group, organization, or society. In everyday conversation, we often use the word *status* to mean "prestige." The job of surgeon is said to be of "higher status" than the job of hospital orderly. In sociology, however, status refers to *any* position in the social structure, however it might be ranked. A job seeker, a waiter, a student, a mother, a child, and a friend are all social statuses. Of course, attached to most social statuses is a certain degree of power (high in the case of U.S. president, for example, low in the case of convicted felon), as well as a certain set of rights, responsibilities, and interests.

Every person occupies a number of different statuses at any given time. You are not just a student but also (perhaps) a male, a son, a fiancé, a Protestant, a Caucasian, and so on. Taken together, the full range of positions occupied by any single person at a given time is called a **status set**. Although each of us has statuses that are similar to those of others, every person's status set is uniquely his or her own. Status sets thus serve to differentiate among people.

Sociologists are particularly interested in how people "move into" social statuses. Some statuses are assigned to people without effort on their part; these are called **ascribed statuses**. Being male or female, a Mexican-American, a Rockefeller, and a senior citizen are examples of ascribed statuses. You have almost no control over whether or not you occupy these kinds of social positions. You are born a Rockefeller (or adopted into that family), just as you are born white or black, male or female, beautiful or plain. The meanings attached to ascribed statuses do change, however. For example, the cultural significance of being an American female has changed greatly in recent years, as more opportunities have become available to women (see Chapter 11).

In contrast to an ascribed status, an **achieved status** is a position a person attains largely through personal effort. Physician, politician, artist, teacher, town drunk, or Boston strangler—each of these is an achieved status. Ascribed and achieved statuses are not completely separate, however. What people achieve is partly shaped by their ascribed characteristics (and the meanings assigned to these statuses), as well as the opportunities available to them. For example, only 20 percent of the physicians in the United States are female, but 95 percent of the nurses are (U.S. Department of Labor, 1988). Why? How does "being female" (an ascribed status) affect a young woman's chances of becoming either a doctor or a nurse (achieved statuses)? A full answer must consider ***social action*** as well as social structure. Women make occupational choices (social action) that depend in part on their understandings of the chances for success in particular fields. Their opportunities, in turn, may be limited by patterns of discrimination (elements of social structure) (S. Cole, 1986).

Sometimes a particular status (either ascribed or achieved) determines many of a person's other statuses. This kind of status, called a **master status**, shapes a person's identity throughout life. (See the Making Choices box.) Being the Prince of Wales, for instance, is a master status because it determines so many other social positions for the person who occupies it (ceremonial leader, military officer, even husband and father since a future king must have heirs). In recent years, being diagnosed as having acquired immunodeficiency syndrome (AIDS) has become a master status for those suffering from this disease. AIDS victims may, for example, be denied jobs, housing, and even friendship.

Sociologists distinguish between master status and **salient status**—a social position that dominates in a particular social context. For instance, when you step into a college classroom, your status of student comes to the fore and is the major influence on your attitudes, behavior, and interactions. It is not particularly important that you are also a friend, a son or daughter, a part-time employee, and so forth. In the classroom context, your student status is salient. In contrast, when you visit your parents, your student status recedes to the background and your position in the family takes the foreground (is salient).

Every status carries with it a socially prescribed **role**—that is, a set of expected behaviors and attitudes, obligations and privileges. For instance, we expect friends to be helpful, sharing, loyal, and concerned about our problems, because that is the role that we associate with the status of friend. The difference between a status and a role is that we *occupy* a status but *play* a role (Linton, 1947). A status is a position; a role is how we think and act in that position.

People learn how to play their roles by observing and interacting with others more experienced than themselves. This process, discussed in Chapter 5, is known as *socialization*. Socialization into the role of student is one familiar example. From the age of five, American children are taught to raise their hands in order to speak in a classroom, to do their homework, to study for tests, and to avoid cheating—all part of the role of student.

No role is cast in stone, however. Within certain limits, individuals are free to interpret the roles they play, giving them their own personal styles. You can see this in the way that different classmates play the role of student. Some study constantly, and others study only when they must; some initiate class discussions, and others wait to be called upon. But despite such variations, most students conform to the basic expectations for the student role. (Those who do not do so are likely to find themselves expelled from the student status.) In addition, roles change over time. College students were once expected to stand when their professor entered the lecture hall; that is not appropriate role behavior today.

MAKING CHOICES

Choosing an Occupational Status

Among the most consequential of all the social statuses you will ever acquire is your occupational status—the job at which you work. In our society, a person's job is often his or her master status, at least during the middle adult years. Acquiring an occupational status is not just a matter of getting the necessary training and making the right "connections." No matter how prepared you may be, no matter how many people you know, you cannot move into a particular occupation unless there is a vacancy in that line of work. This constraint that the "job market" imposes on career choices is an excellent illustration of how ***social structure*** limits and shapes ***social actions***.

Take, for instance, the job market for broadcast journalists, who work in radio and television. People who are trained to work as broadcast journalists constitute the supply of workers available in this field, while the number of vacant positions for broadcast journalists constitutes the demand for them. When the supply exceeds the demand, some people trained in broadcast journalism might end up driving taxis. On the other hand, when the demand exceeds the supply, qualified people can pick and choose among opportunities, and probably earn a higher-than-average income as well.

How can people accurately estimate future job opportunities for each of the various occupations they might be interested in? Fortunately, sociologists and economists have made the task relatively easy.

The U.S. Department of Labor's Bureau of Labor Statistics (BLS) regularly forecasts future job opportunities in all fields of employment. This information is contained in various publications available at many college libraries. For instance, the *Occupational Outlook Handbook* provides detailed discussions of hundreds of jobs: the kinds of work they entail, the skills and training they require, the personalities best suited to them, and the demand for them—whether it is rising or falling.

It is quite a complicated task to make this kind of job forecast. The BLS begins by estimating what the labor force will be like in the years ahead—its overall size and a breakdown of workers by age, sex, race, years of education, types of degrees obtained, and so forth. It then projects the future performance of the economy: What will the gross national product be in *x* number of years, and how will it be affected by patterns of consumption, business investment, foreign trade, and government spending? Next the BLS tries to anticipate factors that will specifically affect the demand for workers in each of the 226 "producing sectors" it has identified (factors like an important technological innovation). All this information, taken together, gives a good idea of supply and demand in different kinds of occupations.

Some of the best opportunities today are in fields that didn't even exist just a few years ago. A good example is desktop publishing. In the mid-1980s most Americans had never heard of desktop publishing, but today it is one of the fastest-growing career areas in the field of computers. The person employed in desktop publishing uses a personal computer, plus sophisticated text and graphics software, to design and lay out professional-looking documents that can then be printed or reproduced in volume. Desktop publishers produce books, magazines, newspapers, advertisements, brochures and fliers, instruction manuals, reports, and more. In the process, they save companies millions of dollars in conventional typesetting and page layout costs.

The emergence of a new career often means that some old careers will be forced into decline. According to the BLS, there will be little or no growth in the years ahead in occupations such as typesetter, compositor, and pasteup artists due to the continuing development and use of desktop publishing technology. Thus, social-structural elements help determine how many people will get the job that they want, and how many others will be forced to take whatever job is offered.

Another important fact about roles is that they exist in relation to each other. The role of daughter cannot be understood apart from the role of parent, the role of lawyer apart from the role of client, the role of professor apart from the role of student, the role of police officer apart from the role of lawbreaker. In effect, the statuses of two people are linked together via role relationships—patterned behaviors and attitudes expected of each participant. Furthermore, a single status may involve several roles, called a **role set**, depending upon the other people with whom the person in that status is interacting. A personnel manager, for instance, plays one role in relation to the company president, another in relation to a department manager, a third in relation to a sales representative, a fourth in relation to a new employee, a fifth in relation to an administrative assistant, and a sixth in relation to a product manager. (See Figure 4.4 for an illustration of this role set.) Similarly, the status of college student simultaneously involves role relationships with roommates, classmates, professors, administrative officials, and dining hall workers.

Sometimes a person has trouble meeting the obligations of a role or role set. **Role strain** occurs when the obligations of a role associated with *a single* status are too demanding for the resources that a person has (Goode, 1960). Elliot Liebow found cases of role strain when he studied a group of black men who hung out on a Washington, D.C., street corner, many of whom were unemployed or worked only sporadically. Whereas most of the men had married at a young age with high hopes of being good husbands and fathers, most had failed at these roles—at first financially, then emotionally. "Where the father lives with his own children, his occasional touch or other tender gesture is dwarfed by his unmet obligations. No matter how much he does, it is not enough" (Liebow, 1967, p. 87). Apparently, their inability to play the role of "good provider" caused so much stress in these men's lives that they failed at their nurturant, loving role as well.

In this one moment, England's Prince Andrew (at left, with the rose in his teeth) is simultaneously playing the roles of son (to Queen Elizabeth and Prince Philip), Duke of York, officer in the Royal Navy—and ham. In years to come, he would take on the additional roles of husband, father, and divorce.

Sociologists distinguish between role strain and role conflict. **Role conflict** is defined as competing or incompatible demands in roles stemming from *two different* social statuses. A classic example occurs in the world of business when a manager hires a close friend. The demands of the role attached to the status of manager (giving employees directives, criticizing their work when needed, not showing favoritism) can conflict with the demands of being a good friend. Another example of role conflict occurs when the demands of a high-powered career (total dedication, long hours at the office) clash with the demands of being a good spouse and parent. In such situations, people often try to insulate one set of role expectations from the other—"leaving the job at the office," for example. Role conflict may also be lessened somewhat by "prioritizing"—

FIGURE 4.4 / A Simplified Role Set of a Manager

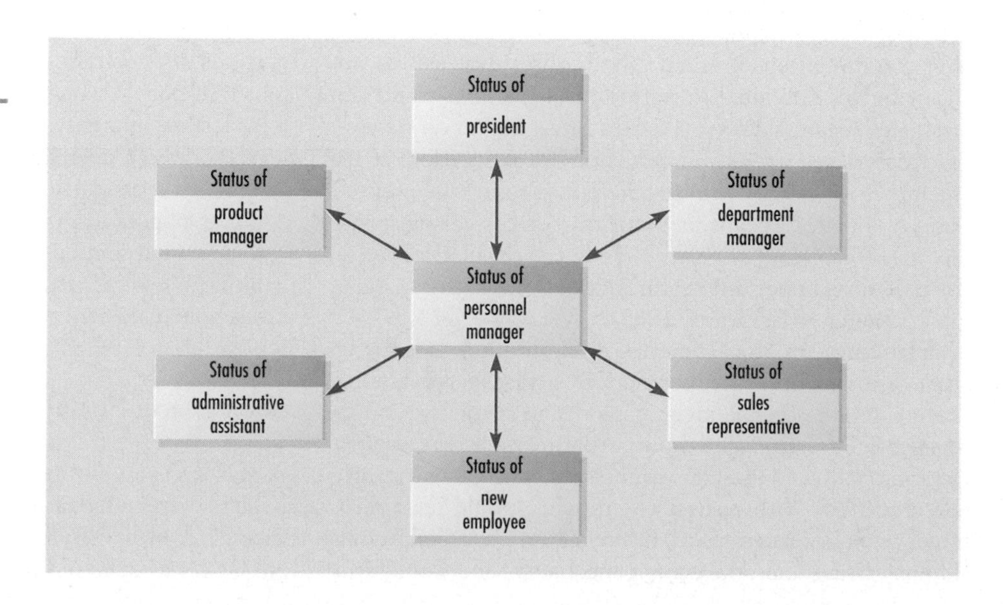

such as deciding that job requirements must temporarily take precedence over family obligations. Neither insulation nor prioritization is completely effective in eliminating role conflict, however, as many overwhelmed working parents can attest.

Sometimes role strain or role conflict becomes so great that people choose (or are forced) to leave one or more of their social statuses. In her book *Becoming an Ex,* Helen Fuchs Ebaugh (1987) defines **role exit** as the process of disengaging from a role that was central to one's identity, redefining relationships with former role-set partners, ceasing to think of oneself in the former role, and reestablishing an identity in a new role. Retirees, alumni, and widows go through this process, as do divorced partners, ex-convicts, ex-nuns, ex-doctors, ex-alcoholics, and transsexuals. In studying a variety of "exes," Ebaugh found that the ease or difficulty of role exit depended on numerous factors, including whether the change was voluntary, how central the former role was to the person's identity, whether the change was reversible, how much time the person had to prepare for the change, and whether other people were going through the same transition. Role exit is more common today than in the past, when people tended to stay in one marriage, one occupation, one religion, and one geographic locale for life, regardless of how satisfied they were with these statuses.

Population and Social Structure

Still another element of ***social structure*** derives from the numbers of people occupying different statuses in a population. Peter M. Blau holds that the overall composition of a population creates opportunities for, and places limits on, the formation of social relationships. Just as we can describe an individual in terms of that person's status set (female, Asian, lawyer, aged thirty-five, and so on), so we can describe a society in terms of the proportion of its members who occupy these different statuses (the proportion of females, Asians, lawyers, thirty-five-year-olds, and so on). For Blau, this distribution of the population is one of the most important features of social structure (Blau, 1977; Blau and Schwartz, 1983).

Blau suggests that societies differ in their degree of *heterogeneity* (how the population is distributed among such categories as sex, race, religion, and ethnicity) and in their degree of *inequality* (how people are ranked by wealth, income, or power). For example, a society with high heterogeneity with respect to ethnicity would have relatively equal proportions of individuals from several ethnic groups. In a society with high inequality, one would find many people living in poverty and a few enjoying extraordinary wealth.

Blau argues that a high degree of heterogeneity promotes intergroup relations, such as intermarriages. With the population spread out evenly among a variety of ethnic, racial, and religious categories, there are simply more opportunities for contact with people from different categories, contact that may develop into social relationships. Suppose, for example, that a woman lives in a society such as Japan, which has very little racial heterogeneity. Her chances of meeting a potential husband from a different race than her own are obviously slim. But suppose this Japanese woman moves to San Francisco. That city's racial heterogeneity makes it more likely that she will meet and date men of other races. Thus, racial heterogeneity greatly increases the chances of an interracial marriage, regardless of cultural norms about proper marriage partners.

The degree of inequality in a population also affects social relations among people of different social classes. Suppose, for example, that a young woman attends a private high school where all the students come from middle-income families. In this setting, her chances of dating young men from other economic classes are virtually nil. But suppose that afterward she goes to a state college where there are students from all social classes. Now the chances of her meeting and dating men from different economic backgrounds have risen from almost zero to a significant percentage. Structural inequality has become an influential force in the kinds of relationships she forms.

The major point in Blau's analysis is his emphasis on how large-scale social-structural patterns affect people's interactions and social relationships. He is not concerned with the psychological motivations that draw people together or push them apart. Rather, he focuses on the proportions of people in different social statuses. To the extent that people who come into contact with each other are socially different (say, of different races and income levels), intergroup relationships are promoted. Blau believes such cross-cutting relationships help to bind a large complex population (such as our own) into a more integrated and harmonious whole. In the following section we will take a look at other sociological perspectives on what holds human societies together.

Society and Social Institutions

A **society** is an autonomous grouping of people who inhabit a common territory, have a common culture (a shared set of beliefs, values, customs, and so forth), and are linked to one another through routinized social inter-

Large-scale social-structural patterns profoundly affect people's interactions and social relationships. For example, the Netherlands has achieved an unusually high level of racial and ethnic integration as people from its former colonies have settled in Amsterdam and other Dutch cities. Note that most of the people shown here attending a concert in Amsterdam appear to have come from Turkey, northern Africa, or southeast Asia. Yet they have gathered in a nonthreatening environment to enjoy the same music.

actions and interdependent statuses and roles. Americans form a society, as do the people of Japan or Egypt. In the modern world, the borders of nation-states usually define the boundaries of societies. This is not necessarily the case, however. Human societies existed for thousands of years before modern nation-states were created; some separate societies still exist *within* the boundaries of states, and some extend *across* national borders.

The question of what integrates a society—what binds it together as a whole—is a fundamental one in sociology. In Blau's view, cross-cutting relationships between different groups are important in tying together a society's various parts; these relationships serve to link dissimilar elements into an integrated whole. But many sociologists believe that cross-cutting relationships, by themselves, aren't enough to hold a society together. They argue that ***functional integration*** among social institutions is critical.

A **social institution** consists of patterned behaviors and status/role relationships that fulfill certain basic societal needs. Institutions respond to the fundamental requirements of all human societies by organizing behavior and relationships in a way that satisfies those requirements. Tasks essential for the survival of the society as a whole are "assigned" to people who occupy designated statuses in the social structure and play the accompanying social roles. (See Figure 4.5.)

What functions do social institutions serve? One is a need to reproduce new members and to teach them the customs, beliefs, and values shared by those who live in their world. This task falls mainly upon the institution of the family. The traditional American family consists of parents and children. The parents' role is to produce the children, to nurture and provide for them until they reach adulthood, and to teach them "right from wrong." The children's role is essentially that of learner, a kind of trainee for the society's next generation. In other societies, the parents' roles are more likely to extend beyond the nuclear family, being performed also by other kin (grandparents, aunts, and uncles), and even close friends and neighbors.

Another basic need in all societies is to mobilize scarce resources in order to produce and distribute the goods and

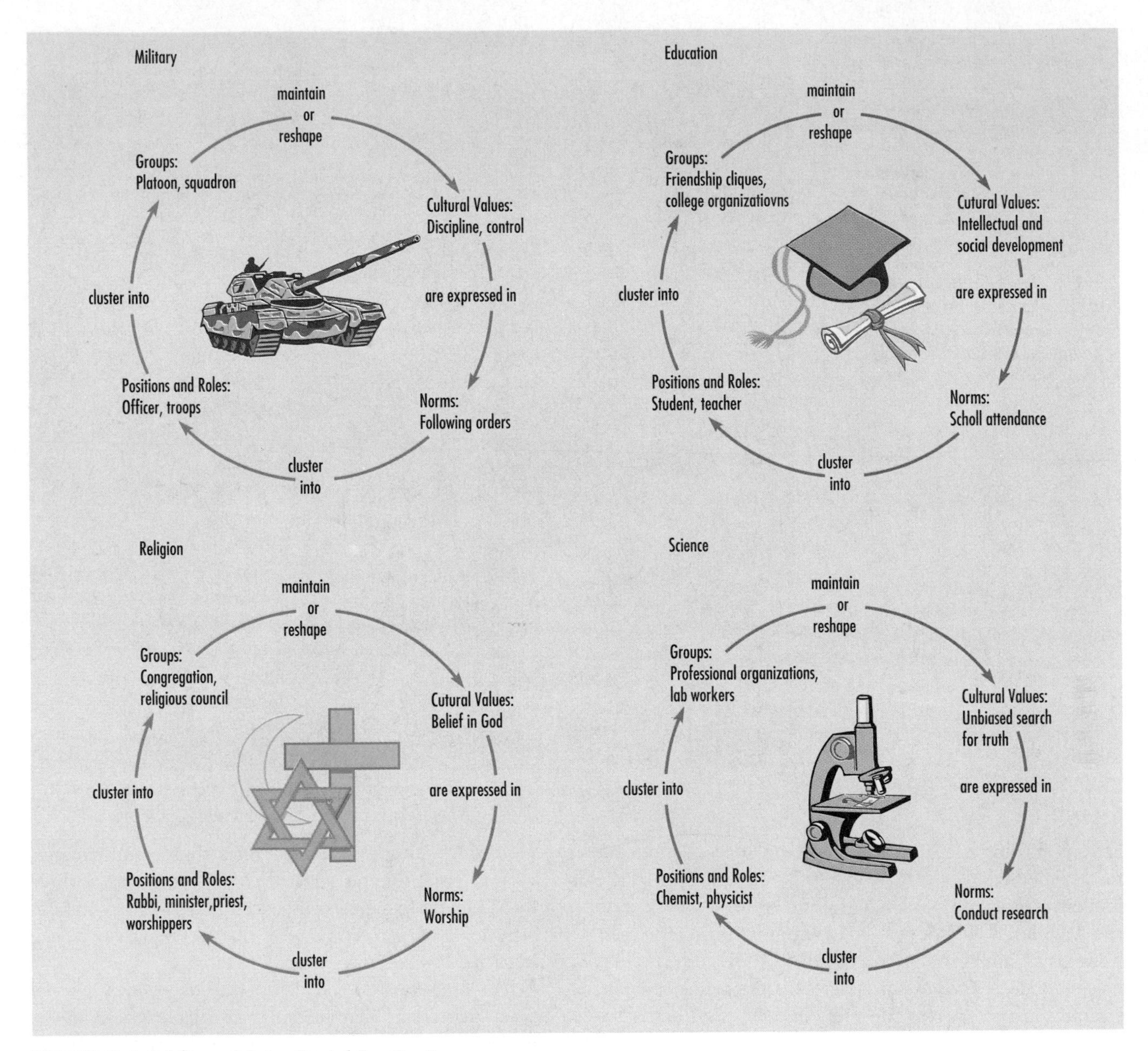

FIGURE 4.5 / Some Major Social Institutions

services that people want. This need is largely met by our economic institutions. A third societal need involves protecting people from external threats, such as military invasions, and from internal threats, such as crime. In our society this need is the province of our political institutions. Societies also need to teach people about certain statuses and roles, especially those that have to do with being a citizen and a worker. This is a primary function of our educational institutions. Equally important, societies need to motivate people to perform their social roles by giving life meaning and purpose. Religious institutions are deeply involved in fulfilling this requirement. Finally, all societies need to be able to acquire and communicate new knowledge, as well as to be able to apply some of that knowledge to obtaining raw materials and transforming them into usable goods. In modern societies, these last two functions are filled by the institutions of science and technology.

Following Durkheim's functional view, some sociologists maintain that societal integration is a matter of all these various institutions successfully filling the basic needs that they evolved to serve. When institutions are meeting these important requirements, when people adequately perform their role expectations, society is a smoothly running, well-put-together whole. But other sociologists, working from a Marxist perspective, see society through different eyes. They believe that societies are never smoothly functioning and well-put-together because conflict is an inherent feature of them. The social order that exists, these sociologists contend, results from the imposition of ***power*** by some people over others. In their view, groups that control scarce resources manipulate social institutions to further their own interests.

Although sociologists don't agree on the extent to which social institutions help to tie a society together into a smoothly functioning whole, there is widespread agreement that institutions do serve as important locuses of change within societies. For example, in many preindustrial societies, the creation and development of new knowledge falls within the institutional domain of religion. "Witch doctors," seers, shamans, and prophets are looked to as the major sources of information about the nature of the world and the people who inhabit it. In modern industrial societies, in contrast, this function is typically assigned to the institution of science, although religion persists as a source of ultimate values that provide meaning and purpose to life. Thus, over the course of social evolution, this important change in institutional functions has taken place.

The shape of social institutions may change. In the 1950s a majority of American households were composed of "Ozzie and Harriet" families—a working husband, stay-at-home wife, and two children. Today such families are in the minority, and alternative arrangements—such as cohabiting couples, single parents, and blended families created through remarriage—have become more common. Thus families have changed, but the *institution* of the family lives on, continuing to perform the same functions of regulating sexual behavior, rearing children, and preparing the next generation for their adult lives.

Relationships between institutions have changed as well. For example, the "distance" between family and economic institutions has widened as human societies have moved from agricultural to industrial economies. The traditional farm household was both the center of economic production and the center for child-rearing and socialization. Today, the roles associated with family and economic institutions are kept apart. Most people "produce" at their workplace and rear their children at home.

But despite these kinds of historical and evolutionary changes, social institutions are also a major source of continuity and stability in societies. The essential needs of human societies have remained the same for thousands of years: to produce the basic necessities of life, to socialize new generations, to allocate scarce resources, and to make decisions about the future. The relatively stable set of statuses and roles and of values and norms that are embodied in social institutions make certain that these essential tasks get done. The people who occupy these statuses, play these roles, and adhere to these norms and values come and go, but in each new generation the same work gets accomplished, the same societal needs get filled.

Thinking Back on the Key Concepts

In this chapter we have covered a remarkable amount of ground. We began by considering patterns in the interaction between two people involved in a face-to-face conversation. We ended by considering social institutions so enduring and so "big" that they have been essential parts of social structure since human societies began. The task of sociologists is to understand *all of this*, from the most microscopic social interactions to the macroscopic elements of social structure. In this respect, sociologists are not very different from physicists. Some physicists study patterns of motion and change in the largest entities of the universe (planets, solar systems, galaxies), while others study the smallest entities (subatomic particles like quarks and leptons). Physicists believe that all these entities are ultimately governed by the same mechanisms, but the search for a single unifying theory has so far frustrated even the greatest minds. Sociologists, too, have not been able to find a single unifying theory, one that can explain both face-to-face interaction and institutional change. Instead, many different concepts and theoretical orientations explain bits and pieces of human social life. Still, most sociologists agree that what goes on in social interactions cannot be completely understood without taking into account social structure, just as an understanding of social structure requires an investigation of social interaction.

This chapter's exploration of interaction and social structure raised two fundamental questions. First, how are the actions and choices of individuals shaped, limited, or enabled by wider forces in the society at large? Second, what holds society together? Answers to these questions bring us back to the key concepts introduced in Chapter 1.

We began the chapter with a classic example of social interaction: the job interview. Both applicant and employer were engaged in ***social action***. To achieve their individual goals (find a job, hire a worker), the participants had to orient their behavior toward each other, communicate their intentions, and attempt to manage the situation. ***Culture*** makes social action possible by enabling people to communicate meaningfully and achieve common understanding of what is going on. These elements of culture are not made from scratch each time two people try to get something done; rather, culture (for example, the English language) has an existence of its own, independent of episodes of interaction. Social action is also shaped by ***social structure***. The outcome of an interaction such as the job interview depends on the four main elements of social structure discussed in this chapter: networks (Does the applicant have "connections"?), statuses and roles (How well does the applicant play the role of prospective worker?), population characteristics (How many qualified graduates are seeking jobs?), and social institutions (How many jobs are available in the economy?).

The key concepts also make it possible to answer the second question, What holds society together? Some sociologists argue that social order depends on the ***functional integration*** of social institutions. Social institutions—the economy, education, the family, the government—are designed to fulfill certain essential needs in an interdependent way. By assigning institutional tasks to individuals who occupy social statuses—manager, teacher, parent, president—societies make certain that the whole survives. Other sociologists suggest that whatever order exists in society is the result of the exercise of ***power***. Some groups and individuals have the means to organize society in a way that serves their own interests. Still other sociologists maintain that what holds society together is ***culture***. A certain measure of social order is achieved if people speak the same language, draw on a common stock of knowledge, and share the same beliefs and values. Finally, Peter Blau offers a ***social-structural*** explanation of social order. Relationships among people in very different social statuses—blacks interacting with whites, young people with old—knit societies together in a way that prevents endless conflict and chaos. The likelihood of these cross-cutting ties, in his view, depends not just on cultural beliefs and values but also on the composition of the population.

SUMMARY

1. We engage constantly in social interaction—orienting ourselves to other people and acting in response to them. Social interaction occurs for the purpose of accomplishing some aim and is always directed toward specific other people. Whether complementary or cooperative, competitive or coercive, it is always ordered. Sociologists have developed five different perspectives on the sources of order in social interaction.

2. One approach focuses on how people arrive at a definition of the situation. In some cases, the meaning of an interaction is clear, but often it is ambiguous. Through frequent interaction, participants may arrive at a negotiated order.

3. Symbolic interaction, a sociological approach founded by George Herbert Mead, focuses on the symbolic aspects of social interaction. Only through symbolic gestures and role-taking are people able to coordinate their behavior.

4. The dramaturgical approach sees social interaction as a kind of theatrical performance, with a frontstage and backstage area and numerous props. To some degree, we all engage in impression management.

5. Ethnomethodology looks at social interaction from the inside, focusing on the ways that people make sense out of everyday interactions by applying shared, often unconscious, rules to different situations.

6. Social exchange theory views reciprocity as the most basic form of human interaction. It is rooted in rational-choice theory, which holds that people weigh the gains their actions bring against the costs they incur, and behaviorism, which holds that anticipated gains may be the result of prior conditioning.

7. The web of social relationships among a set of people who are linked together, directly and indirectly, through their various communications and dealings is called a network. In analyzing networks, sociologists look at the nodes, ties or links, and overall patterns. Networks differ from one another in size, density, reachability, and range and centrality. Research on networks has found that even weak links can be important (for example, in finding a job), and that social power depends in part on location within a network.

8. Social structure consists of the stable and enduring features of social organization over which individuals have little control and which shape or constrain their behavior. In addition to networks, elements of social structure discussed in this chapter are statuses and roles, the distribution of people among social statuses, and social institutions.

9. Every person occupies a number of different statuses at any given time. Some statuses are ascribed (assigned to people without effort on their part) and others are achieved (attained largely by personal effort). Every status carries with it a socially prescribed role—a set of expected behaviors, attitudes, obligations, and privileges. Within limits, people are free to interpret the roles they play, giving them their own personal styles.

10. The distribution of people among social statuses in a society as a whole affects patterns of social relationships. In particular, Peter Blau argues that a society's degree of inequality and heterogeneity affects how (and whether) intergroup relationships are promoted. Such cross-cutting relationships help to bind a large, complex society together.

11. A society is an autonomous grouping of people who live in a common territory, share a common culture, and are linked to one another through routinized social interactions and interdependent statuses and roles.

12. Some sociologists believe that societies are held together by specialized subsystems called institutions: the family, the government, religion, and so on. Institutions are a set of patterned behaviors and status/role relationships that fulfill basic societal needs. They are a source of both stability and change in human societies.

REVIEW QUESTIONS

1. Describe what sociologists mean by definition of the situation.

2. Distinguish these perspectives on social interaction: symbolic interaction, the dramaturgical approach, ethnomethodology, and social exchange.

3. Explain why networks constitute the basic social context of people's lives.

4. Show how your own network ties might vary by content, strength, reciprocity, and symmetry.

5. Indicate how social networks as a whole vary one from another.

6. Distinguish status from role by definition and example.

CRITICAL THINKING QUESTIONS

1. You have been asked to prepare a report for Congress on possible solutions to poverty. Explain why you would take either the microsociological or the macrosociological approach in your report.

2. Do you believe that some animals have social interaction as described in the chapter? Explain why or why not.

3. Select a role or experience that is particularly meaningful for you, such as being a partner, going to a party, being a student, or meeting someone new. Explain how you have defined that particular situation so that it made sense to you and so that you could respond to the demands of that particular role or social experience.

4. Select an experience you remember well from high school, such as a flunking grade, a particular date, or an argument with a teacher. Take each of the following perspectives to interpret your experience: symbolic interaction, the dramaturgical approach, ethnomethodology, and social exchange.

5. Assess your hometown in terms of heterogeneity and inequality and their effects on you.

GLOSSARY

Achieved status A status a person attains largely through personal effort.

Ascribed status A status assigned to people without effort on their part.

Dramaturgical approach A sociological perspective in which social interaction is viewed as resembling a theatrical performance in which people "stage" their behavior in such a way as to elicit the responses they desire from others.

Ethnomethodology A viewpoint on social interaction developed by Harold Garfinkel that focuses on the ways people make sense out of everyday interactions.

Impression management Erving Goffman's term for the efforts people make to control how others see and respond to them.

Macrosociology The large-scale analysis of sociological data derived from studies of the structure and effects of overall social arrangements.

Master status One status that largely determines a person's social identity.

Microsociology The small-scale analysis of data derived from studies of everyday behavior and face-to-face social interaction.

Negotiated order A shared definition of a situation arrived at by "testing out" actions and modifying them based on feedback from others.

Network The web of relationships among a set of people who are linked together, directly or indirectly, through their various communications and dealings.

Nodes The connected units within a social network.

Role A set of behaviors, attitudes, obligations, and privileges expected of anyone who occupies a particular status.

Role conflict Competing or incompatible role demands stemming from two different social statuses.

Role exit The process of disengaging from a role that was central to a person's identity.

Role set The cluster of different roles associated with a particular status.

Role strain Difficulty in meeting the obligations of a role associated with a single social status.

Role-taking Imagining oneself in the role of another and thereby helping to understand the meanings that the other intends to convey.

Salient status A status that dominates in a certain social context.

Social institutions Patterned behaviors and status/role relationships that fulfill certain basic societal needs.

Social interaction The process of people orienting themselves to others and acting in response to each other's behavior.

Social relationships Relatively enduring patterns of interaction between two or more people.

Social status A position in a social structure that determines where a person fits within the social order.

Society An autonomous grouping of people who share a common territory and participate in a common culture, and who are linked to one another through routinized social interactions and interdependent statuses and roles.

Status set The full range of social positions occupied by any one person at a given time.

Symbolic gesture A gesture that has acquired symbolic meaning shared by people who belong to the same culture.

CHAPTER PROJECTS

1. Individual Project One of the most important ways in which potential employers judge applicants is by reading their résumés. Study the chart on page 83. Then write your own résumé. Share your résumé with the class.

2. Cooperative Learning Project Working in groups of four, choose a country in Asia or Africa. Research the meanings of symbolic gestures in that society and contrast those symbolic gestures with those prevalent in American society. Share your findings with the class.

PART 2

The Individual and Society

CHAPTER 5

Socialization

In a primary school in China third-graders are busily employed in their school workshop. The workshop is associated with a nearby factory that makes, among other things, wooden pieces for the game of Chinese chess. Squads of youngsters work diligently on a series of consecutive tasks: shaping the edges of the pieces, stamping characters on them, painting them, and finally packing them into boxes. Older children in the school spend more time in the workshop; younger children less. But they are all proud to be contributing "productive labor" to the state. They tell a team of American social scientists who have come to observe education in China that their efforts are "serving the people" (Kessen, 1975).

In a Japanese nursery school, the scene is also very different from what we usually find in the United States. The teacher asks the children to paint a series of pictures that work together to tell a story. After the children decide what story they want to tell, the teacher reminds them that they must make different pictures that fit together; they are not all to make their own separate pictures, as American nursery schoolers typically do. The teacher places paints in the center of the table, where they might be spilled if there are scuffles, and deliberately provides fewer brushes than there are children. As the children work, they confer with one another about what part of the story they will paint next and eagerly await their turn at the paints and brushes (Lewis, 1989).

Every society shapes its children in the image of its own culture. In ancient Sparta, young boys were taught discipline, obedience, physical prowess, and self-denial through harsh treatment and deprivation. In nearby Athens, parents raised their sons to be artistically sensitive and broadly educated as well as athletic. These practices produced quite different individuals as well as different societies (Berger and Berger, 1979). In modern times, middle- and upper-class Americans encourage children to cultivate their individual abilities and compete with their peers for success. The Chinese foster group loyalty and a willingness to endure self-sacrifice for the good of society. The Japanese instill the value of cooperation in managing problems and working together to complete projects and attain goals. The process of instilling such fundamental elements of culture in a society's members is called **socialization**.

Through socialization, people develop distinctive orientations to ***social action***. These include the broad styles characteristic of their ***culture***, as we have just seen in comparing Japan, China, and the United States. Socialization also shapes the distinctive characteristics of individuals, because socialization is a process not only of learning but also of developing an identity. As people grow up, they may even influence their own future socialization—for example, by seeking out opportunities such as going to college. Socialization processes help maintain a society's ***functional integration*** by ensuring that individual members have the necessary skills, education, and motivation to participate effectively in the society's economy and other institutions. The ***social structure*** influences socialization both by determining what kinds of skills or motivations are needed by the society (whether it be a large and complex industrial society or a small farming community) and by determining who gets access to what sorts of socialization. It is no accident, in other words, that within a society there are differences in the socialization of rich and poor or men and women. These differences reflect both the divisions characteristic of the social structure and the influence of ***power***. For example, when the American South was a slave society, teaching slave children to read or write was forbidden. The place allocated to most African-Americans in the social structure—as slaves—did not allow for socialization into such skills as reading and writing or into the many social roles that depended on those skills. When we see the effects of power and social structure, we realize that although socialization is somewhat different in the experience of each person, and is affected by our choices, it is not something we can freely choose; rather, it is a process in which we are shaped both by our society as a whole and by our particular place within it.

This chapter explores the process of socialization. In the first section we place socialization in a broader context by considering how it interacts with genetic potential to help make us who we are. In the second section we look at different theories of how socialization works and what it accomplishes. Next, we examine how American socialization differs by social class, and we ask if these differences help perpetuate class status across generations. The fourth section explores the major agents of childhood socialization, the groups and organizations that teach young people the elements of their culture. The last section deals with socialization in adulthood, especially the process by which the norms and values of adults are aligned with those of the organizations they join.

SOCIALIZATION: NATURE AND NURTURE

Is a person's behavior determined largely by biological makeup ("nature") or by the environment in which he or she lives ("nurture")? For many years scientists have debated this question. On one side are those who hold that the human infant is largely a blank slate, waiting to be written on. According to them, the kind of person a baby becomes is determined almost entirely by environment. The most famous statement of this position came from the American psychologist John B. Watson (1878–1958). "Give me a dozen healthy infants," Watson wrote, ". . . and my own specific world to bring them up in and I'll guarantee to take any one at random and train him to become any type of specialist I might select—a doctor, lawyer, artist, merchant, chief, yes even a beggarman and thief, regardless of his talents, penchants, tendencies, abilities, vocations, and the race of his ancestors" (Watson, 1925/1970, p. 104).

On the opposite side of this issue are those who argue that many human behaviors have strong biological roots. According to this view, experience can modify these behaviors somewhat, but it seldom can change them completely. The most recent version of this perspective comes from a group of scientists known as **sociobiologists**. Sociobiologists hold that just as humans have evolved certain physical characteristics that give them a survival advantage (such as a large brain and very deft fingers), so have they also evolved certain behavioral traits that help them survive and flourish. One example sociobiologists cite is the avoidance of incest, which is prohibited in virtually every human society (E. O. Wilson, 1978). Sociobiologists reason that because inbreeding tends to produce inferior offspring, natural selection has favored people who avoid sexual relations with close kin. The transmission of this avoidance behavior through thousands of generations has resulted in making the incest taboo a cultural universal. This universally shared element of culture, sociobiologists claim, is an instinct based on genes (the unit of heredity).

But most sociologists reject the more extreme claims of sociobiologists. Many point to the fact that the boundaries of incest taboos vary widely among societies. First cousins can legally marry in some societies but not in others. Another objection is the rapid way in which social behavior can change, sometimes transforming itself completely from one generation to the next. For example, under the influence of Christian missionaries, some Polynesian peoples gave up their uninhibited sexual ways and took up premarital chastity. How could this happen if sexual mores were largely genetically based? It is more reasonable to assume that such social behaviors are *created* by people and passed on in their culture because they help them adapt to environmental situations and to human biology. Environmental pressures, in short, tend to encourage different forms of human social action.

Does this mean that genes play no role whatsoever in the development of our social behavior? No, of course not. It simply means that genes never completely dictate how humans act toward one another. Rather, genes enable a range of *possible* responses on which the environment works to help determine which of many potential behaviors will ultimately be adopted. In the following section we take a closer look at this critical interaction of genes and environment.

The Interaction of Heredity and Environment

The best examples of how genetic potential interacts with environment to give rise to human social behavior can be seen in the development not of *shared* behavior patterns but rather of the *distinctive* styles of social interaction that each of us possesses, our so-called personalities. People come into the world with behavioral predispositions—known as **temperaments**—which many researchers think are largely genetic in origin (Smolak, 1986). From the first days of life, babies differ in their activity levels, "soothability," "talkativeness," attention spans, fearfulness in new situations, and frequencies of positive and negative emotions (Bates, 1987; Rothbart, 1986).

These behavioral predispositions do not dictate what a child becomes. In fact, as a general rule, these patterns of infant temperament do not remain stable as a baby grows older, suggesting that many environmental influences subsequently act upon them (Belsky, Fish, and Isabella, 1991). Some of these environmental influences stem from the traits of the adults who care for a child. For instance, confident, easygoing parents will help to make a fussy baby calmer by being patient and soothing in their caregiving style. In contrast, parents who are anxious and under a great deal of stress will probably do just the opposite. At the same time, an infant's own behavior influences the behavior of adults. The "talkative," cheerful infant, for example, tends to elicit positive attention from others, whereas the cranky, easily distracted baby may not. The result is a complex interplay of genes and environment that gives rise to a child's characteristic ways of responding. Figure 5.1 gives another good example of how environment interacts with inherited potential to give rise to a person's level of intelligence, as measured by IQ tests.

A similar interaction of genes and environment occurs in the development of *shared* patterns of social behavior—that is, in the development of culture. For example, humans have a biological potential for developing a complex spoken system of communication (we have the vocal ap-

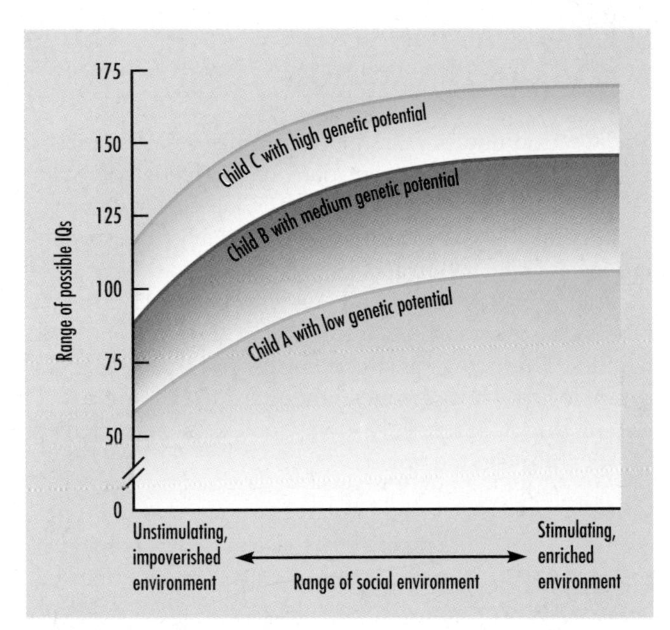

FIGURE 5.1 / *The Interaction of Inherited Potential and Social Environment*

Although inherited potential establishes the range of socialization, social environment greatly affects the extent to which inherited potential can be realized. This is particularly true for child "C," who has the greatest potential range of the three children in the figure above. With an impoverished environment, a child "C" might develop less than a child "A" who has an advantageous environment.

paratus to produce a wide variety of speech sounds and the large, highly developed brains required to create a language's vocabulary and syntax). However, the particular language that a people develop is by no means innate. It depends on various aspects of the world in which they live. (For instance, Americans wouldn't have coined such words as *transistor* and *tomography* if our society had not developed into a very technologically advanced one.)

Similarly, humans seem endowed with a biological tendency to form "pecking orders" of some kind, but the particular hierarchy of positions they establish is largely shaped by their social structure, power relations, and culture. For instance, the legacy of slavery left the United States with a racist culture that included a rigid division between dominant whites and subordinate blacks in the late nineteenth century. Those in power encouraged even the lowest-status whites to think they were better than blacks. But there was also a hierarchy among whites. As the most recent immigrants at that time, the Irish generally found themselves at the bottom of the white group.

Another example of the heredity–environment connection can be seen in marriage customs. Humans seem to have a biological inclination to form mating pairs of some kind. However, the specific norms that surround these unions depend on social forces. (The practice of polyandry, for instance, in which one woman is simultaneously married to two or more men, tends to occur in societies where, for one reason or another, men significantly outnumber women.)

Genes, then, never rigidly determine how people behave. Instead, what we inherit at birth is a set of developmental *possibilities*, all of which are then shaped by the world in which we live. Human patterns of social behavior are not inborn and fixed. They are constantly open to change through environmental influences. It is these environmental influences on behavior that sociologists study and that are central to the process of socialization.

Socialization through the Life Course

Socialization is particularly important during childhood. Without it at this early stage of life, we would not become social beings. No social scientists would raise an infant without socialization—that is, in total isolation from other people—just to find out what kind of person that child would become. Some people, however, suffer extreme neglect, spending their early years almost completely alone. These people provide dramatic natural evidence about the importance of childhood socialization (Curtiss, 1977).

One such person was Anna, the illegitimate and unwanted child of a farmer's daughter (K. Davis, 1949). After trying unsuccessfully to place her in a foster home or an institution, Anna's mother confined her to a windowless room in the attic. She fed the child enough milk to keep her alive, but rarely talked to her and never cuddled or played with her. This appalling neglect continued for five years. When social workers discovered Anna, she was so apathetic they thought she was deaf, mentally retarded, or both. She did not walk or talk. She didn't know how to dress or feed herself, or even how to chew. She never laughed or cried. Observers felt that there was something inhuman about her. And there was. Anna's socialization did not begin until the age of six, when she was placed in a foster home. With care and attention, she slowly began to talk, walk, run, and play with other children. She also began learning how to take care of herself. In other words, she began to develop human interests and abilities.

However, she had not completely overcome her early years of neglect before she died of jaundice at the age of eleven.

Other evidence for the importance of childhood socialization comes from less extreme cases of neglect. For instance, René Spitz (1951) conducted a classic study of infants in orphanages. The babies got adequate physical care—good food, regular baths and diaper changes, clean sheets, bright and airy nurseries—but they had little meaningful interaction with adults. When tested at age one, most were mentally retarded. They hardly ever smiled or cried and made no effort to speak. Other similar studies report the same results (Bowlby, 1973). Physical care is not enough for children to develop normally. They need socialization as much as they need food if they are to develop into full-fledged human beings.

While socialization is most visibly an issue for children and adolescents, it is an ongoing process that continues throughout life. Sometimes adult socialization involves fairly modest changes in roles, as when a person who has been working as a cashier in a supermarket takes a new job behind the counter of a dry cleaner's. Under some circumstances, however, adult socialization is intense. For instance, when recent college graduates start their first jobs, there are a great many totally new norms of behavior to master. We will say more about this major life-course transition later in this chapter.

Another intense form of adult socialization occurs when people immigrate to other countries. Learning a new language, acquiring new customs and values, and often experiencing barriers to economic success are major challenges that can be very stressful. Some immigrants liken the experience to a "second childhood" (Portes and Rumbaut, 1990). The Hmong refugees who came to the United States in the late 1970s are an example of an immigrant group that had trouble becoming socialized to a new way of life. In Laos they had a traditional, homogeneous, nonliterate, agrarian peasant society. Suddenly they had to adapt to a literate, highly technological, urban, and heterogeneous one. As one Hmong immigrant explained: "I feel like a thing which they say drops in the fire but won't burn and drops in the river but won't flow" (Portes and Rumbaut, 1990, p. 143).

Adding to the challenge is the fact that Hmong children were attending American schools and carrying new patterns of behavior back to their families. Often they pressured their parents to "Americanize" faster—demonstrating that, while parents play a major role in their children's socialization, the process is a two-way street. Few parents (even nonimmigrant ones) emerge from the experience of raising children without some *re*socialization, or changes in their own attitudes and behaviors (see Chapter 6).

SOCIALIZATION AND SOCIAL INTERACTION

Socialization always takes place in social relationships—relationships in which even young children are active participants. We develop our most basic ideas of who we are as individuals—our identities—and our most basic orientations to social action and ways of relating to other people through participating in and trying to understand important social relationships, starting with those in our birth families. This point was stressed by each of the three social psychologists who were most important in shaping socialization theory: Charles Horton Cooley, George Herbert Mead, and Sigmund Freud.

Cooley: The Looking-Glass Self

Each of us possesses a sense of **self**—that is, a sense of having a distinct identity, of being set apart from other things and people. Like other aspects of social life, this sense of self is not inborn. Instead, we actively construct it from our interactions with others.

Charles Horton Cooley (1864–1929) was one of the first theorists to consider the social origins of the self. Observing his own children, Cooley developed the idea of the **looking-glass self**. We acquire our sense of self, he said, by seeing ourself reflected in other people's attitudes and behaviors toward us and by imagining what they think of us.

According to Cooley (1956, 1964), the looking-glass self has three parts: what we think others see in us; how we imagine they judge what they see; and how we feel about those judgments. For instance, a fourteen-year-old boy may think his classmates see him as a "brain" and imagine that they judge braininess as "weird." This reflected image may make him feel bad about himself and wish he were more athletic, or it may make him feel pleased that he is different from the pack. Note that the looking-glass self is not a *direct* reflection of what other people see in us. It is a mixture of social actions—observation, imagination, and subjective interpretation. It is also a social construction, involving our class, or position in the social structure, and the values we have learned from the culture.

Cooley distinguished primary relationships (family, close friends) from secondary relationships (casual acquaintances). He also emphasized that we are concerned about how we appear to others all the time—in relation to strangers on the street as well as in relation to people we really care about. This is because we are interested in

Since the 1920s sociologists have proposed explanations of how individual identity emerges from social action. Charles Cooley suggested that we see ourselves reflected in the actions people direct toward us. George Herbert Mead also stressed how we take the role of "the other" when we interact, but added that this role taking is often strongly associated with significant others. To reflect on these theories, try to put yourself behind the eyes of both the grandmother and the child as they perform their carefully coordinated dance.

how we appear to ourselves, and we see ourselves by imagining what others—family, friends, and total strangers—think of us.

Mead: Role-Taking

Building on Cooley's analysis, George Herbert Mead (1863–1931) traced the development of self-awareness to early social interaction (Mead, 1934). (We discussed Mead in Chapter 1 as the founder of symbolic interactionism.) Mead argued that almost from the beginning, infants realize that they are dependent on others to satisfy their needs, and that their own actions influence how others behave toward them. They learn, for example, that crying brings food and smiles bring cuddling. Over time, they learn more ways of eliciting desired behavior from others, ways that involve first gestures (looking, reaching, pointing) and later words. Mead called these words and gestures **significant symbols**. He believed that human social interaction cannot exist without symbols, and that symbols gain significance only in social interaction. Through symbolic interaction, children learn to anticipate what other people expect, and to evaluate and adjust their own behavior accordingly.

Out of early social interaction a sense of self emerges, which is composed of two parts, according to Mead. He called these parts the "I" and the "me." The "I" is the self as subject, or initiator of thoughts and actions. The "me" is the self as object, the part that the I and others observe, respond to, and assess. When people say hello to you, they are talking to your "me," but your "I" is the one that evaluates the tone of the "me's" reply. Social interaction depends on this kind of self-monitoring. Without it we would lack the feedback needed to tune our social actions to other people's.

Children have developed the concept of "me" when they are able to understand themselves as the object of others' attention ("Mommy and Daddy are smiling at *me*"). But at this early stage they are not yet able to take the role of another person and look at themselves. That is to say, they do not yet have a sense of "I." Gradually, however, they begin to distinguish between such notions as "*I* am hungry" and "Mommy feeds *me*." The play of early childhood helps to sharpen the "I/me" distinction. Young children spend much of their time role playing. They make-believe that they are doctors, police officers, fire fighters, and fantasy characters like Cinderella or Ninja Turtles. Often they take the roles of people important in their lives, what sociologists call **significant others** (H. S. Sullivan, 1953). Young children are especially fond of playing mothers fussing over babies, fathers lecturing children on their behavior, and teachers presenting a lesson to the class. This play allows them to see themselves from another person's perspective (as son or daughter from a parent's perspective, as student from a teacher's point of view). In doing so, their sense of "I" matures.

From taking the role of specific others, children eventually advance to taking what Mead called the role of the **generalized other**. Now they begin to think about what people *in general* will think about a certain action. They learn, for example, to cover their mouths when coughing because people in general think it is a good idea. Soon they are able to reflect on themselves in light of cultural norms and values and to monitor their behavior in accordance with general social expectations. This is the ultimate goal of childhood socialization.

Freud: The Internal Dynamics of Socialization

No theory of socialization has had a greater impact on Western thought than that of Sigmund Freud (1856–1939), a giant of twentieth-century psychology. Freud (1920/1953, 1923/1947) saw socialization as a lifelong struggle within a person's mind. This struggle, in his view, involved three forces: the **id**, a reservoir of innate biological drives aimed at obtaining physical pleasure; the **ego**, the rational part of the self, which mediates between the id and reality; and the **superego**, essentially a person's conscience, which embodies the moral standards of society. The ego's job, as Freud saw it, was to find safe ways to satisfy the id without causing guilt or remorse to the superego.

In Freud's view, people are not born with an ego or a superego. These parts of the psyche develop through social action, particularly the child's interaction with parents. Freud believed that at birth humans are irrational, amoral creatures, with nothing more to guide them than their pleasure-seeking impulses. But it isn't long before a baby begins to learn that biological drives cannot always be gratified immediately—food is not available on demand, for example. It is through such discoveries that the ego begins to develop. The ego's role is to channel id impulses toward outlets that are realistic and safe. Freud argued that through this basic ego function the mind develops and refines all its higher intellectual capabilities: perceiving,

In Freud's view, toilet training is important in shaping our individual and cultural personalities because it is the imposition of the society, here in the form of a mother, onto the individual. To become a mature individual is to resolve the conflict between the id's drive for pleasure and the ego's acceptance of the need for self-control.

learning, remembering, problem solving, decision making, and planning.

The third aspect of the psyche in Freudian theory, the superego, develops through a child's encounters with the demands of the larger culture as conveyed by parents and other adults. Freud focused on societal demands that curb the child's natural drive to obtain sensual pleasure. One such demand is toilet training, which occurs in the late toddler period. Freud argued that how conflicts between id drives and parental demands are resolved is what shapes a child's personality. According to Freud, a final coalescing of the superego occurs around the fifth year, when the child finally accepts the enormous power of parents. To avoid constantly being embroiled in conflicts over demands that the parents impose, the child seeks vicarious power by adopting the parents' moral attitudes and values.

While Cooley and Mead saw socialization as a gradual, complementary merger of individual and society, Freud saw it as a perennial battle between society and a person's biological inclinations. All three, however, recognized the individual's active role in the socialization process. We become social beings, members of a group, by actively thinking about and interpreting ourselves in relation to others. Although Freud believed that much of this process occurs on an unconscious level, he still saw it as central to becoming a fully socialized adult. All three also recognized that the influence of society was not the same for everyone, but rather varied among different families, cultural groups, and classes.

SOCIAL CLASS AND THE TRANSMISSION OF VALUES

> I used to dream about how I'd grow up and get married and live in one of those big, beautiful houses like they show in the magazines—you know, magazines like *House Beautiful*. God, all the hours I spent looking at those magazines, and dreaming about how I would live in one of those houses with all that beautiful furniture, and everything just right. . . . Life turns out a lot different in the end, doesn't it? (Thirty-six-year-old cannery worker, mother of three, married twenty years, quoted in L. B. Rubin, 1976, p. 43)

Although in every generation there is some movement up and down the social ladder, leaps from "rags to riches" are extremely rare. Most adults end up in the same social class into which they were born. Why does this happen? Why aren't dreams and hard work enough to win most working-class people the life to which they aspire? Aspects of social structure, like access to education or opportunities in the job market, play a big role. At the same time, sociologists have asked, does socialization reinforce social-class differences generation after generation?

In the last twenty years, sociologists concerned with the impact of social class on socialization have attempted to answer this question. Comparing lower-, middle-, and upper-class families, researchers have found that there are indeed differences in how children are socialized. Some of these differences have to do with the values parents instill. Differences among social classes in the transmission of values may help to channel children into the same kinds of occupations their parents hold.

That social-class positions are partly perpetuated by the values parents teach is suggested by the work of sociologist Melvin Kohn, who has extensively studied this subject over a period of many years. He and his co-workers have found very consistent differences in the values people hold for themselves and their children depending upon their social class (Kohn, 1959; Kohn and Schooler, 1983). Figure 5.2 presents some of the different values that working-

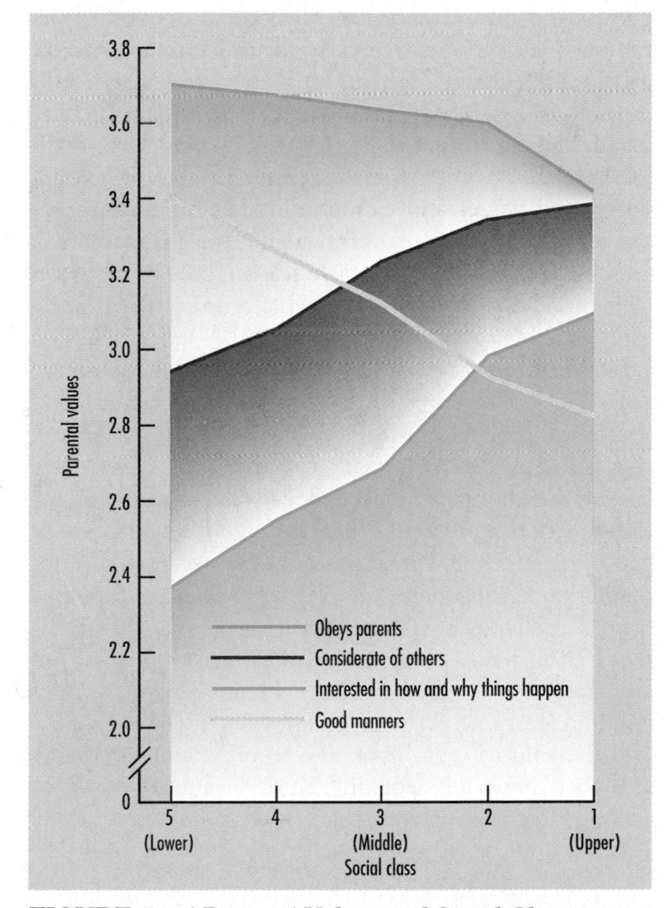

FIGURE 5.2 / Parents' Values and Social Class

Source: Melvin L. Kohn and Carmi Schooler, *Work and Personality: An Inquiry into the Impact of Social Stratification* (Ablex, Norwood, N.J., 1983).

class and middle-class parents stress. Working-class parents place more value on manners, neatness, good behavior in school, honesty, and obedience. Middle-class parents, in contrast, place more value on consideration, interest in how and why things happen, responsibility, and self-control.

Comparing the items on these lists suggests a basic difference between the two value systems. People in higher social classes are more likely to value traits that involve self-direction, while people in lower social classes are more likely to value traits that involve conformity to external authority. Valuing manners, for example, involves caring about whether a child follows the rules of etiquette that society sets for people, whereas valuing consideration involves caring about whether a child feels empathy for others. The first value stresses conformity to an *external* authority; the second value stresses the development of one's own *internal* standards.

Where do these different sets of values come from? Why do working-class parents want their children to follow established conventions and obey with no questions asked, while middle-class parents are more concerned with instilling self-direction and internalized standards? Kohn's research has shown that these class-based differences are directly related to the parents' experiences at work (Kohn, 1976, 1981; Kohn and Schooler, 1978). Work that provides opportunities for independent thought, initiative, and judgment—occupational self-direction—tends to foster middle-class values. Work that restricts these opportunities tends to encourage working-class values. Certain aspects of work are especially important in this regard (see Figure 5.3). When a person is not closely supervised, deals with data or people instead of with things, and has work that is complex enough to allow various approaches, he or she has the job-related independence conducive to valuing self-direction. Apparently, this same chain of influences operates in other countries besides the United States. Kohn found that in Japan, for example, a non-Western capitalist state, as well as in socialist Poland, people in more advantaged social classes placed more value on flexibility and occupational self-direction both for themselves and for their children (Kohn et al., 1990; Kohn et al., 1986).

If the value of self-direction is so important to holding a higher-status job, couldn't this value be stressed in schools? In this way, working-class children might have a better chance of acquiring the personal outlook needed to climb the occupational ladder. Such a program is certainly possible. The question is how much society wants to broaden the opportunities for working-class children. We will return to this question in Chapter 13, which explores education.

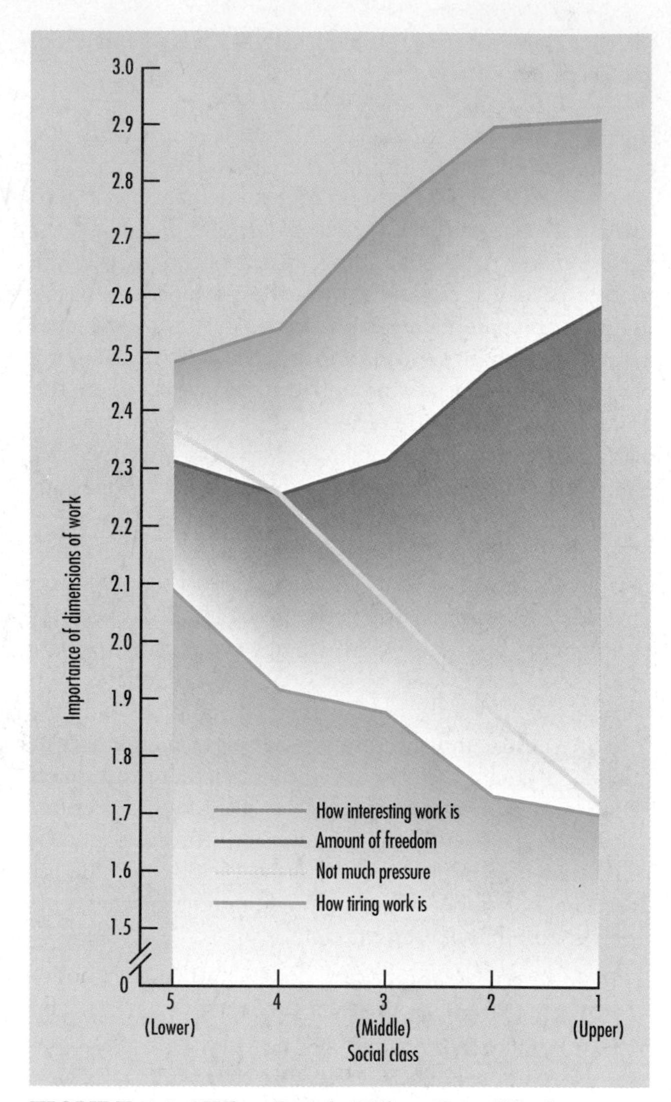

FIGURE 5.3 / What People Value about Work

Source: Melvin L. Kohn and Carmi Schooler, *Work and Personality: An Inquiry into the Impact of Social Stratification* (Ablex, Norwood, N.J., 1983).

AGENTS OF CHILDHOOD SOCIALIZATION

Childhood socialization occurs in many different settings, through interactions with many different people, groups, and organizations (Elkin and Handel, 1984). Agents of childhood socialization—those who do the socializing—play different roles, have different aims, and have different

We tend to think of social class as a reality largely created in adult worlds. As sociologists, we need to understand how social class is recreated in the worlds of children as they learn the nuances of behavior that are the day-to-day realities of social life. Notice, in these photographs, differences in setting, in posture, and in the reactions of the children to the camera and photographer. Even very young children have already learned to inhabit certain kinds of environments in which they have vastly different responsibilities, pressures, and expectations.

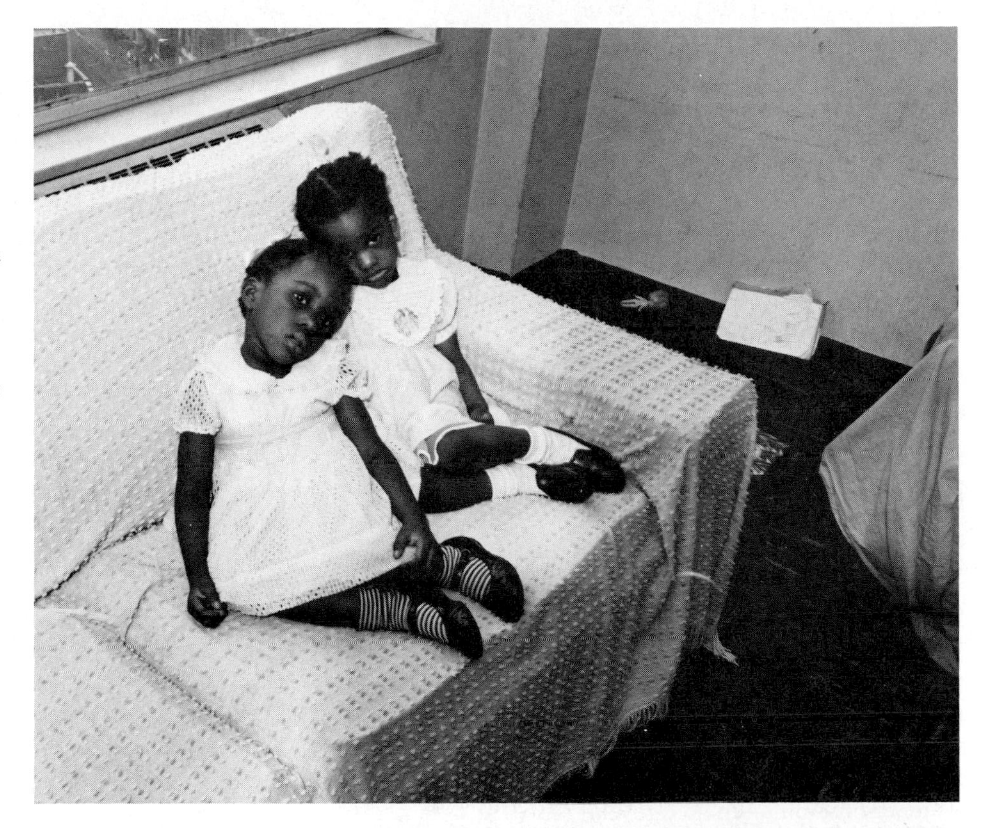

impacts on development. They may reinforce one another on some issues and contradict one another on others. For example, parents may want their children to see males and females as equals, and teachers may support this aim. But situation comedies, advertisements, and rock videos on television glamorize and "humorize" the differences between the sexes, and peer groups often demand sex-stereotyped behavior (girls who play with guns are ignored, while boys who play with dolls are ridiculed).

The influences that different agents of socialization have can be intentional or unintentional. A mother who insists that her preschool boy return a toy to its owner may be concerned about teaching him to get along with peers, but unwittingly she is also teaching him to respect "private ownership." Certainly she does not intend a lesson on the principles of capitalism, but that is a latent function of her actions. Similarly, parents may intend to teach a child that a person's race or religion doesn't matter, but their actions (the friends they have, the groups they join, the neighborhood they live in, and their comments on other people's lifestyles) may convey a different message. Thus, socialization seldom follows a clear-cut path to a preselected goal (Wrong, 1961). However, the various agents of socialization do need to be somewhat congruent (if not identical) in their teaching and to supply certain basic needs (such as motivating people to work), or there will be problems for the overall ***functional integration*** of a society.

There are many overlapping and unrecognized influences on a child's social development, and many possible outcomes. With this in mind, let's turn to four major agents of childhood socialization: the family, peers, the mass media, and schools. The relative importance of these four agents differs depending on ***social structure***. In most societies, the family is the all-important agent of socialization; but in modern Western societies like our own, the media and schools are also very influential.

The Family

The family is the first social world a child encounters, and family members are the mirror in which children begin to see themselves. To be sure, the family doesn't play the all-encompassing role in socialization that it once did. Schools and various other social agencies have taken over many of its functions. Children used to start school at age six; now most go to kindergarten or nursery school at age four or five, and many attend day-care centers as infants and toddlers. Television, a widely used baby-sitter in American society, has also encroached on the family's role in socialization. Still, the family remains the primary agent of childhood socialization—for important reasons (Elkin and Handel, 1984).

The family introduces children to intimate, personal relationships and gives them their first experience of being treated as distinct individuals. The family is children's first reference group, the first group whose norms and values they adopt as their own and refer to in evaluating behavior. The family also introduces children to group life. Living together in a family means learning to share family resources, including space, objects, and parental time and attention.

Fathers and mothers tend to have different ways of relating to children and so provide different socialization experiences (Easterbrooks and Goldberg, 1984). For instance, with infants and toddlers, fathers tend toward physical play and inventing new games, while mothers tend toward verbal interaction and familiar games like peek-a-boo. Patterns of socialization in the home also reflect the parents' relationship with one another and the general family environment. Whether "interaction in the family is characteristically relaxed and good-humored or tense and guarded, whether it emphasizes or minimizes the distance between parents and children or between males and females, whether it is typically cooperative or competitive," all affect the socialization that children experience at home (Elkin and Handel, 1984, p. 132).

The birth of siblings adds new complexities to family life. Through interaction with siblings, children gain experience in cooperation and conflict, negotiation and bargaining, inequalities based on size and experience, and the limits of other people's tolerance. In addition, how parents respond to a child depends not only on that child's disposition but also on the youngster's birth-order position. In one study, mothers were found to spend twice as much time with first-born children as with later-born ones, a pattern that surely must have some effect on each sibling's socialization experiences (White, Kaban, and Attanucci, 1979). There are other ways that birth order affects socialization. The arrival of a sibling arouses competitive feelings in first-borns, which can cause them "to be more conscientious, achieve higher scholastically, and go to school longer than later-borns" (Forer, 1976, p. 11; see also Blake, 1986). In contrast, second-borns must learn to work their way around an older, stronger sibling, so they often become adept at diplomacy and negotiation (Jiao, Ji, and Jing, 1986). Parents, moreover, usually discipline a second-born less strictly, which can encourage the child to have relaxed relationships with people (Snow, Jacklin, and Maccoby, 1981).

Of course, family influences on children are not static. Families, like individuals, go through transitions. The birth or adoption of a child (or the departure of one from the family home), the entry of an elderly grandparent into the home, or the death of a family member changes family structure in important ways, which in turn fosters new socialization experiences. Divorce, single parenthood, remarriage, and "blended" families also have marked impacts on socialization within the family. In fact, children today are often socialized not just by one family, but by a series of different families as the lives of their parents change (Kalmuss and Seltzer, 1989).

It is important, too, to get a broader perspective on the family as a socializing agent. The family introduces children into society, locating them on the social map. To be born into a particular family is to acquire a social status. Whether a child's parents are wealthy or on welfare strongly affects how people view that child. Moreover, a family's values, attitudes, and lifestyles reflect the social class, religion, ethnic group, and region of the country of which it is a part. This means that children acquire selected versions of their society's culture depending on the background and experiences of their particular family.

Studies of birth order show that parents give their children different levels and degrees of attention, depending on their order of birth. These differing patterns of attention and involvement show up in the children's general patterns of success or failure as adults. Much speculation has surrounded the impact of birth order on the Kennedy brothers.

Peers

Three fourth-graders, Bonnie, Norman, and Craig, are trying to decide how to divide up some candy bars that they have received as a reward for making three bracelets apiece. Their division of the candy must also include a younger child, Dennis, who made only one bracelet. Dennis is not present for the deliberations:

> *Bonnie:* We should get a bigger reward because we made more. . . .
> *Norman:* He [Dennis] is little. . . . Besides, we're not thinking about him. *You're* not thinking about him. You're leaving him out and just thinking about us three. Just because he's not here doesn't mean you shouldn't think about him.
> *Craig:* I didn't say that.
> *Norman:* I know. But you didn't say anything. We're the ones bickering and arguing about it and you're sitting there not saying a single word.
> *Bonnie:* Craig, what do you want to do? One for Dennis and three for the rest of us?
> *Craig:* I want to give Dennis the same as us.
> *Bonnie:* It's the only fair way—I think we should. (Damon, 1977)

Peer groups provide children with their first experience of equal-status relationships. Because adults are older, stronger, "wealthier" (they control such resources as the refrigerator and the television dial), and presumably wiser than children, adult–child relationships are always asymmetrical. At home and in school, children are always subordinate to adults. In contrast, they are—by definition—the social equals of their peers. This equal status makes peer groups ideal settings for learning norms of sharing and reciprocity. The three children above are clearly socializing each other regarding the norms of distributive justice as they apply to particular situations. If an adult had been involved, he or she would probably just have *required* the children to split the candy four ways. But this might have kept them from accepting the "rightness" of the decision as readily as they did when they made the choice themselves.

By school age, children have developed and internalized a wide range of beliefs, norms, and values, including a concept of friendship and the behaviors that friendship entails. They use these ideas both as a guide for their own behavior and as a standard against which to assess the behavior of peers. This leads to more sharply defined role expectations. Children now feel they know what can be expected from friends and how they themselves should act in a friendship. Of course, children's concepts of "good" and "right" behavior do not always match those of adults. Children sometimes develop their own distinctive norms and values, their own peer outlooks on things. As a result, they are sometimes challenged to decide which norms or values to follow in which situations. This is a crucial skill for adulthood (Corsaro and Eder, 1990).

The experience of childhood is primarily one of subordination to adults. When children form relationships with people their own age, they create a world that is, for the first time, largely of their own making. Thus peer groups have a vast and significant impact on how children view the world and behave in it. Institutions such as sports are the basis of many peer groups, both those which are directed by adults and those which emerge on their own.

The study of norms and values in Little League baseball reveals some of the distinctive aspects of children's culture (Fine, 1987). For example, Little Leaguers have their own ideas about appropriate emotions, which they expect one another to follow. A boy who cries after a game because he performed poorly, even though his team won, is labeled "strange." Similarly, one who smiles nervously after striking out is called "crazy." In general, Little Leaguers expect one another to control negative feelings. They should try not to show anger, frustration, disappointment, or even pain when they get hurt. Someone who excessively displays these emotions is told to "shape up." Yet a competitive desire to win is obligatory among Little Leaguers. Boys who fail to hustle and to get involved in the game are scorned. "Ratting" or "tattling" on a teammate to an adult is also against the rules. So is acting superior to your teammates. A boy who brags about his ability is cut down to size with sarcastic remarks. In these and other ways elementary school children create their own special peer culture to which they become socialized.

The elementary school years are the time when peer socialization tends to occur in groups exclusively of one sex or the other. Boys tend to form larger peer groups and engage in more aggressive and competitive play, usually organized around sports. Girls generally form smaller, more intimate peer groups. At this stage, children are constructing a social structure; cultivating, testing, and maintaining friendships; and developing social identity through interaction with their peers.

By early adolescence, being with friends has taken on major importance, and the issues of acceptance, popularity, and group solidarity are paramount. Adolescent boys tend to spend time with a group of male friends, while adolescent girls often gravitate to a single "best" girlfriend, to whom they disclose their problems, concerns, and fears. For both sexes, friends tend to be chosen from those of the same age, social class, race, and ethnic group (Dornbusch, 1989). In peer groups, adolescents develop a set of symbols—language, music, haircuts, clothing styles, and so forth—to express the self. They use these collective symbolic actions to make sense of confusion, to form judgments and ways of thinking, and to guide their behavior (Willis, 1990).

In seeking to define themselves, adolescents often come into conflict with the power and expectations of their parents and other adults. Even when they do not join movements of active resistance (as in the youth culture of the 1960s), they tend to test the boundaries of what will be tolerated—by experimenting with alcohol or illegal drugs, for example. Adolescents are also likely to resist parental power in matters of taste, like fashion and musical preferences. And there are often conflicts over whether parents will grant responsibilities, such as using the car and engaging in sexual relationships, that adolescents believe they are ready to handle.

Nonetheless, adolescents often remain responsive to the preferences of their parents concerning future life goals and core values (Davies and Kandel, 1981; Krosnick and Judd, 1982). In fact, more often than not, peer values reinforce parental values, rather than oppose them. In later adolescence, as peer–adult conflict begins to wane, adolescents generally choose a peer group that reflects values with which they feel comfortable, values that are often very similar to the ones they grew up with in the family. At this point, peer and family socialization may begin to parallel each other.

There are numerous cross-cultural differences in peer-group socialization. Several researchers compared adolescent groups in the United States and the Soviet Union (before its breakup). In one study, students were asked if they would go along with their friends in hypothetical bad conduct, such as lying or cheating. They were told that their answers would be shown only to peers involved in the study, not to adults. American students tended to go along with the misconduct, but Soviet students did not (Grusec and Lytton, 1988). Apparently, in America, it was more important not to be a tattletale than to correct improper behavior. The values of the adolescent peer group were at variance with the official standards of adult society. In the Soviet Union, in contrast, young people were willing to correct undesirable behavior in their classmates—that is, the peer group would act to reinforce the society's publicly stated values. The end of the Soviet Union has brought changes to schools. Many place a new stress on freedom and individuality; it will be interesting to see if future studies continue to find this pattern.

The Mass Media

Children are exposed to a variety of mass media, the forms of communication that reach large numbers of people: television, radio, movies, videos, records, tapes, books, magazines, and newspapers. While all the mass media are important agents of socialization, the most influential is probably television. Overall, children in the United States (and other Western nations) spend more time watching television than they spend in school, or, very likely, in direct communication with their parents (Winn, 1985).

Parents and others are concerned about how television is socializing children. They are unhappy with the content of many shows, especially the amount of violence they contain and their persistent portrayal of gender and other stereotypes. On television, women tend to be portrayed as submissive and domesticated; men are shown as knowledgeable and independent; elders are presented as lacking common sense. Thus, major network programming often provides an impoverished version of American culture, with implicit and detrimental messages about race, marriage, divorce, and the family.

Television is not alone in encouraging stereotypes. In one study, for instance, researchers analyzed how the two sexes were presented in prize-winning books for preschoolers. They studied books published between 1980 and 1985 and then compared their analysis with a similar one conducted for books published between 1967 and 1979 (Williams, Vernon, Williams, and Malecha, 1987). They found that while the number of female characters had begun to equal the number of male ones, *central* male characters still outnumbered central female characters two to one. Moreover, males were still portrayed as independent, creative, and active, while females, typically, were still portrayed as just the opposite (dependent, submissive, passive). Outdated ideas about men's and women's work also prevailed in these children's stories. Only one woman in all the books studied had a job outside the home, and she was a waitress.

Although stereotypes in the mass media are upsetting to many parents, an even greater concern is their excessive depiction of violence. This concern focuses especially on television. Numerous studies suggest that watching television violence encourages aggression in children. One long-term study of teenagers found that a preference for violence on television was a more accurate predictor of aggressive behavior than socioeconomic background, family relationships, IQ, or any other single factor (Cater and Strickland, 1975). It is difficult to say which comes first, the aggressive behavior or the preference for violent shows, but a link between the two does exist.

Many social scientists are especially concerned with the effects that TV violence may be having on very young children. Some have found that heavy television viewing in the preschool years puts a child at risk for problem be-

resocialization. Typically resocialization is preceded by **desocialization**, the process whereby people are stripped of the values and self-conceptions acquired in the past.

The Case of College Athletes

The transition of college athletic recruits to their new role as campus "jocks" is a good example of desocialization and resocialization at work. Peter Adler and Patricia Adler (1985) have extensively studied this transition. Peter Adler spent four years as a participant observer at a Midwestern university with a "big-time" basketball team. As the team sociologist, he gained the confidence of players and coaches and was able to track not only the athletes' careers but also their attitudes toward college and themselves.

The Adlers found that, contrary to popular belief, most athletes enter college with high educational ideals and a strong desire to graduate. Recruiters tell them that their athletic skills are their ticket to academic and occupational success, and parents and society reinforce this expectation. In the words of one freshman: "If I can use my basketball ability to open up the door to get an education, hopefully I can use my degree to open up the door to get a good job. . . . " (Adler and Adler, 1985, p. 243). The first few semesters in college suggest that this isn't just an empty dream. During the freshman year, coaches protect athletes from academic problems by arranging special programs for them, making sure they get "sympathetic" instructors, providing them with tutors when needed, and otherwise buffering them from academic demands.

The dream *is* commonly an illusion, however, and this becomes painfully apparent in the athletes' sophomore year. Now, as academic demands increase, the coach can no longer shelter "his" athletes from regular academic standards. The sophomore year is best described as a period of desocialization, in which the athletes are stripped of their former expectations, ideals, and beliefs. They come to realize that they will not automatically graduate from college, that their high school backgrounds may not have prepared them for doing college work. They also realize that they are not going to be as popular on campus as they thought they would be (based on their high school experiences). Because of their height, and their racial and socioeconomic status, other students see them as "different." The majority of students at the university that the Adlers studied were white, suburban, and middle class. In contrast, most of the athletes were working class or lower-middle class, and 70 percent were black. Adding to this sense of being different, of not "fitting in," is the fact that college athletes are often physically isolated as well. At some schools, they must live in a special dormitory located on a remote part of campus. Long hours of practice, frequent trips away from school, and other athletic functions cut them off from college social life.

With all these social forces working on them, it is not surprising that college athletes in their sophomore year feel disillusioned, alienated, and adrift. They are no longer sure of who they are and where they are going. They feel distanced from the role of student and the norms and values of student life. Most of those who chose business, engineering, or other professional majors switch to easier courses. Others simply quit studying and dream of being drafted by a professional team (a remote possibility even for college stars). The desocialization of the athletes is now complete.

The stage is set for resocialization to a new set of values and beliefs, as well as a new self-image. This resocialization comes largely from the subculture of the athletes' dorm.

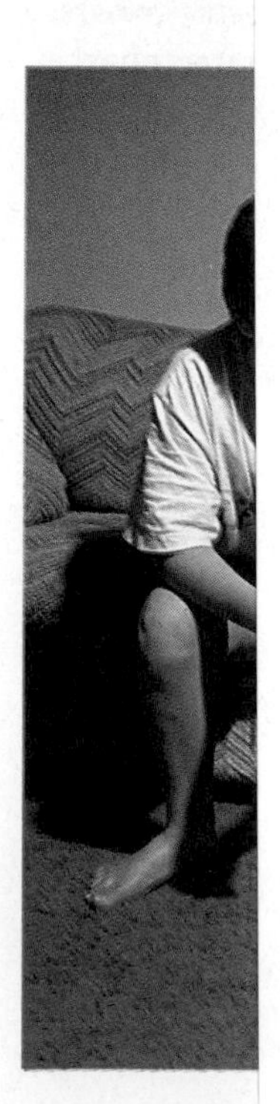

When people enter total institutions such as convents they must be resocialized—literally recreated as social beings. When such resocialization is voluntary, we are likely to assume that it presents no problems. However, learning to operate within a whole new set of social expectations pushes an individual's definitions of self to an extreme.

High-steel workers must learn from their workmates how to overcome fear. Sociologists have studied this work culture to learn about how norms emerge in an intimate group that is held together by the need for cooperation in an extremely dangerous and difficult situation.

Here the outlook is anti-intellectual and anti-academic. Dorm members scorn the importance of grades, provide excuses and justifications for academic failure, and mock those who keep on trying. In the end, the athlete embraces the stereotyped role of "dumb jock" who eats, sleeps, and breathes sports.

The Adlers' study clearly shows that processes of socialization do not necessarily benefit individuals or society. They can even have very negative effects, such as convincing young people they cannot succeed outside the world of sports. According to the Adlers, all college athletes are subjected to this negative resocialization, regardless of their academic potential. They believe that the system is not unchangeable, however. The cycle of disillusionment and detachment could be broken if athletes were integrated into regular dorms, given academic role models and advisers (not athletic personnel masquerading as advisers), and protected from media attention which tends to glorify the "jock" role.

Total Institutions

Even more extreme cases of desocialization and resocialization occur in organizations that deliberately close themselves off from the outside world and lead a highly insular life that is formally organized and tightly controlled. Such organizations are often called **total institutions** because they so totally dominate the thoughts and actions of their members. Examples are prisons, mental hospitals, and military boot camps. In all such settings, people are segregated as completely as possible—emotionally, mentally, and physically—from other environments. Often the total institution becomes the *only* reality for its members.

Newcomers to a total institution undergo a process of desocialization that sociologist Erving Goffman (1961) has called **mortification**. The newcomers are methodically stripped of clothes, adornments, and personal possessions that help express their former identities. In exchange, they receive standard, nondescript, and often ill-fitting attire—a uniform or hospital gown and robe. Their hair may be shaved to further erase any vestiges of their former selves. The spirit of new members is also obliterated. The institution compels them to perform meaningless tasks, to submit to arbitrary and unreasonable commands, and to endure personal abuse (verbal or physical). At the same time, newcomers are deprived of the sense of privacy that normally helps to set them apart as individuals. They must undergo a debasing physical exam when admitted, after which they eat, sleep, and shower with the group. They are under constant supervision and surveillance. Every moment of every day is planned by others.

These procedures destroy people's feelings of self-worth and train them for deference to their superiors. In this way, total institutions foster psychological regression: They promote childlike feelings of helplessness and dependence to facilitate the institution's control over members' lives. At this point, members are ready to be resocialized to a new role, one that the total institution has designed.

Why do total institutions carry out such extreme and rigid desocialization? Goffman suggests several reasons. First, the members of a total institution have low social status. Convicted criminals, the mentally ill, and even "raw" recruits for the army are seldom among those to whom society gives great deference. As a result, those who operate a total institution feel they can take many liberties in running these people's lives. Second, the relatively small staff of a total institution must control a large number of people. This control is easier when extreme desocialization and resocialization take place. Third, means tend to become ends, almost without intention. Procedures that started as ways of facilitating control gradually get carried out largely for their own sake. When this happens, the measures used to desocialize new members have become more important than meeting the institution's original goals.

Occupational Socialization

Schools give children only a very general preparation for their future careers. When children become adults and enter the world of work, they always receive some "on-the-job" training—if not formal classes, then at least an informal initiation into what is expected of them. Socialization to a job, called **occupational socialization**, imparts not only specific job-related skills but also a set of values and ethics that applies to a person's work, the unofficial rules of the workplace that the person is entering, and knowledge of the ways that people in the organization are expected to relate to one another depending on their statuses and roles.

Whether a person is socialized to a job individually or in a group makes a significant difference. In an army boot camp or a large sales training program, people go through the experience with others. Here peer relations and informal group norms become very important and sometimes encourage resistance to the organization's goals. In contrast, when people are socialized individually rather than in groups, they are more dependent on the superiors who are doing the "breaking in" (Mortimer and Simmons, 1978; Van Maanen, 1976; Wheeler, 1966).

Often people try to prepare themselves for socialization to a new work role. For example, new college graduates about to embark on their first "real" jobs in large corporations mentally rehearse what the new experience might be like. If possible, they talk to other employees at the particular firms to get a feel for what working there involves. In subtle ways they may start to adopt new, more conservative values and behaviors in anticipation of those they believe their companies will expect of them. All these changes are collectively called **anticipatory socialization**. Essentially, the graduates are starting to "recast" themselves in anticipation of the socialization they are about to undergo.

We now understand that socialization is not confined to childhood but continues through our lives, centered in institutions such as our jobs. Interest in occupational socialization has increased as sociologists and others attempt to understand why the work forces of most industrialized nations outperform that of the United States.

GLOBAL ISSUES/LOCAL CONSEQUENCES

East Meets West in Mazda's Detroit Plant

In recent decades the world has entered a new economic era. Worldwide trade has existed for hundreds of years, but today it has taken on a whole new structure. Large, modern corporations no longer feel that they "belong" to the country where their headquarters are. They do not view themselves as American, Japanese, or West German. Instead, they see themselves as *multinational* organizations, with the entire world as their economic base. This means that the modern corporation not only buys and sells goods abroad but also manufactures its products wherever in the world it makes economic sense to do so.

The recent opening of Japan's Mazda car plant in Detroit is just one example of this new global economic order. Mazda executives believe that producing cars in the United States is an efficient way of helping supply the American portion of their market. This global economic decision was made purely on the basis of costs and profits. It was not specifically intended to change the lives of American workers. Yet as a by-product, it is having precisely this result. The fact that the top executives of Mazda are all Japanese is affecting how Americans hired to work for Mazda are being socialized. The Japanese style of occupational socialization is not the same as that of Americans. Consequently, Americans who find jobs at the new Mazda plant must adapt to a set of norms and values in many ways foreign to them.

For instance, the Japanese system of production is organized into work teams, consisting of from six to ten people each. The members of a team are jointly responsible for getting their assigned tasks done. Each member is expected to show dedication and commitment to the job that exceeds what is expected in the American system. Japanese managers expect people to continue working even when slightly ill, and they expect them to willingly take on extra work when a member of their team is absent. Absent workers must be genuinely ill, as verified by a doctor. At the Detroit plant, as in Mazda plants around the world, there is no provision for a standard number of "sick days" off that workers may take at their own discretion.

American workers at Mazda are being socialized to other new norms and values too. One is a different style of corporate decision making. The Japanese strive for consensus in decision making; they don't favor decisions that are simply imposed from above. Consequently, all Mazda employees are expected to participate in decision-making meetings where both workers and managers collectively come to agreements about ways to improve production. Socialization into the Mazda plant also involves a new way of looking at the employee's relationship to the firm. Employees are expected to merge their own individual interests with those of the larger group (as they would in a family), and they are expected to make personal sacrifices for the good of the company. In keeping with this approach, wages at the new Mazda plant were set at 15 percent below those of the "Big Three" American carmakers. Some American workers have trouble with this different way of thinking. Most have long considered large corporations impersonal bureaucracies (the very opposite of a family), where workers are sometimes adversaries of the firm.

Of course, the cultural adjustments occurring at Mazda's new American plant are not just in one direction. Japanese executives must also come to terms with differences between American and Japanese employees that are very difficult to erase. For instance, Japanese workers make little distinction between "should" and "must," between what would be appropriate to do if they wished to and what they are required to do. American workers, in contrast, want this distinction to be clear. As a result, they will not automatically clean up their work stations after their shift is done, nor will they voluntarily use their "break time" to attend a problem-solving session. Japanese managers must adapt to this and other aspects of American culture if the new Detroit operation is to run smoothly.

The designers of Mazda's new plant hope to create a "third culture," one that combines various elements of Japanese and American cultures. While it is too early to tell if their efforts have succeeded, it is clear that members of each society are being socialized to the norms and values of the other.

Source: Joseph J. Fucini and Suzy Fucini, *Working for the Japanese. Inside Mazda's American Auto Plant* (The Free Press, New York, 1990).

But anticipatory socialization is seldom enough when a life transition is major. In the case of adapting to a first corporate job, people almost never fully anticipate what they will encounter. Edgar Schein (1978) has found that this transition entails four very difficult tasks. The first is coming to terms with the reality of a bureaucratic organization. New employees soon discover that others in the organization are often a roadblock to what they want to get done. Co-workers do not seem as bright, competent, or productive as they should be. Too often they appear to be illogical, irrational, and unmotivated. The new employee must learn to accept the human organization with all its weaknesses. "Selling," "compromising," and "politicking" become essential skills.

The second task is learning to cope with resistance to change within the organization. New employees complain that their good ideas are undermined, sidetracked, and sabotaged, or simply ignored. They discover that their recommendations, which seem so technically sound, are not implemented for one reason or another. The degree to which new employees learn to cope with resistance to change has important consequences for their future career paths.

The third task for new employees is resolving ambiguity related to their work. They find that some aspects of their jobs are poorly defined. They also have trouble getting the feedback needed to judge their own performance. Carving out a niche in the organization is a critical part of adapting to it.

Finally, new employees must learn how to get ahead in their organizations. They must discover how to relate to their bosses, establishing a balance between overdependence and rebellion. At the same time, they must figure out the reward system: They must discover what is really expected of them, what is really rewarded in their organizations, and how much they can trust what official statements tell them.

Once people are over the initial hurdle of indoctrination into a new job, they begin to internalize the values and folkways of their organizations. (See the Global Issues/Local Consequences box.) The degree to which this internalization occurs depends on people's involvement in their work. Involvement in work, in turn, is encouraged by a number of factors, one of which is degree of autonomy on the job. The more autonomous people are (the more they can set their own goals and make their own choices), the more likely they are to feel committed to their work. Job involvement also tends to be related to newness at an occupation. In general, involvement is intense in the early years of a career and then stabilizes.

Thinking Back on the Key Concepts

The year is 1973; the place China. A 12-year-old boy named Tan Xanli is in the fifth grade. For some time he has been pestering his parents for a new bookcase because his old one is falling apart. Then, through his school, he has a chance to talk with members of the People's Liberation Army (PLA). They praise self-sacrifice, productive labor, and people who are more than just consumers. Tan Xanli is deeply impressed by this experience. He applies the words of the PLA members to his own life and decides that he should repair his old bookcase rather than get a new one. His classmates learn of his decision and commend it over the school public-address system. As a result of this incident Tan Xanli becomes a somewhat different person. (Based on Kessen, 1975)

This anecdote is clearly an instance of socialization, but how should sociologists analyze it? The five key concepts introduced in Chapter 1 suggest several possibilities.

First, Tan Xanli is being taught two important values: the value of self-sacrifice and the value of productive labor. Both are elements of his ***culture***. Such transmission of values and other elements of culture is one of the most important functions of the socialization process. We saw this also in the way in which different socialization patterns of working-class and middle-class children reflect different class cultures. Families, peers, schools, and the mass media all transmit culture as they socialize young people. And in adult life, people are resocialized as they learn how to fit into new occupations and the specific cultures of different companies and workplaces. Sometimes, as in the case of Japanese companies operating in the United States, this can involve socialization into aspects of a very different national culture as well as a different occupational culture.

Second, Tan Xanli's socialization is contributing to ***functional integration***. It is producing the kind of person suited to the Chinese society of twenty years ago. The roles of self-sacrificing citizen and productive worker fit the social order and help to functionally integrate it. Similarly, in American culture, families, schools, and peers teach more individualistic values that are suited to survival in a competitive society.

Third, a struggle for ***power*** has determined which values are being taught. In the China of Tan Xanli's youth, the People's Liberation Army was widely present in schools and villages as part of a campaign to change people's values. This was the result of a power struggle in the Communist party called the Great Proletarian Cultural Revolution. Under the guidance of Chairman Mao Zedong, an older Chinese emphasis on books and scholarship was replaced with a stress on practical skills related to work and economic production. Thus, Tan Xanli is being taught the values of those who have the upper hand in an ideological battle to influence people's thinking. Wielders of power in capitalist society also influence what children are taught, most obviously by emphasizing the importance of work and the necessity of being economically self-supporting.

Fourth, the ***social structure*** of China is determining the agents that leaders like Chairman Mao can use to impart new values to the population. China of the late 1960s and early 1970s had a People's Liberation Army that infiltrated other social organizations and was ever-ready to socialize citizens. American social structure influences socialization by providing different kinds of schooling for rich, poor, and middle-class students, and by providing distinctly different social environments for children on the basis of social class.

Finally, Tan Xanli is not just the passive recipient of other people's values. He thinks about and interprets the ideas he hears, and he plays an active role in his own socialization. His ***social action*** of repairing the bookcase is a response to his talk with the PLA members and may even have an influence on the actions of other students, for stories like his were widely used to reinforce the teachings of the Cultural Revolution. An American youth, in contrast, might get a job to earn money to buy a new bookcase—a social action that will lead to further socialization experiences in a competitive capitalist society.

SUMMARY

1. Socialization is the process of instilling fundamental elements of culture in a society's members. It is one of the basic forces that shape human social behavior. Another is a person's inherited biological potential. This potential establishes a range of behavioral possibilities on which environmental influences then work.

2. Socialization is particularly important during early childhood. Without it in the first few years of life, people would not become social beings. But socialization is certainly not confined to childhood. It continues throughout life and is especially important during major life transitions, such as starting a new job or getting divorced.

3. Sociologist Charles Horton Cooley analyzed socialization using the concept of a looking-glass self. He argued that we acquire our sense of self by seeing ourselves reflected in other people's behaviors toward us and by imagining what they think we are like. Sociologist George Herbert Mead built on this perspective when he stressed that, through symbolic interaction with others, children learn both to anticipate what other people expect and to evaluate and adjust their own behavior accordingly. Another influential theory of socialization is that of Sigmund Freud. He saw socialization as a struggle between biologically based drives for pleasure and the rules of acceptable conduct society imposes on us.

4. Socialization tends to reinforce social-class differences generation after generation, so that children tend to be channeled into the same kinds of occupations as their parents hold. One factor underlying this process may be that children of different social classes are instilled with different values. Because lower-class children are taught to value obedience and conformity more than middle-class children are, they may be socialized more for lower-status jobs that offer few opportunities for independent thought. Lower social status may also be perpetuated across generations because working-class parents do not assist their children much in the critical socialization process that occurs in schools.

5. The family is a primary agent of socialization. It introduces children to intimate relationships and group living, and it gives them a status in society. Cultural norms and values are also strongly instilled by children's peer groups. Norms and values related to fairness, sharing, and reciprocity are particularly suited to being learned in the egalitarian relationships that exist among peers. Although children's peer groups often develop their own norms and values, on important issues the norms and values of parents and children usually coincide. The mass media are also important agents of childhood socialization, as are schools. The official function of schools is to teach children "academics," but the classroom conveys a great many values as well.

6. When adults must internalize new norms and values very different from their old ones, the process is called resocialization. Often, *re*socialization is preceded by *de*socialization, the process whereby people are stripped of the values and self-conceptions held in the past in preparation for replacing these with new values and self-images. Extreme cases of desocialization occur in total institutions, organizations that deliberately close themselves off from the outside world and lead a highly insular life that is formally organized and tightly controlled. Examples are prisons, mental hospitals, and military boot camps. An important aspect of socialization in adulthood is teaching people the norms and values they need in their particular jobs. This is called occupational socialization.

REVIEW QUESTIONS

1. Summarize the nature–nurture argument.

2. Compare Cooley's looking-glass self-concept, Mead's ideas on role-taking, and Freud's analysis of the internal dynamics of socialization.

3. Show how social class affects socialization.

4. Briefly describe the role of each of the following in the socialization process: the family, peers, the mass media, and schools.

5. Differentiate desocialization from resocialization by definition and example.

CRITICAL THINKING QUESTIONS

1. Describe the relative importance of nature and nurture in your own socialization. Provide specific examples.

2. Give examples of socialization that you have experienced since beginning college.

3. Differentiate the role of the following in your own socialization: your family, your peers, the mass media, and the schools you have attended. Identify the most important one and give reasons for your choice.

4. Present an argument pro or con regarding this issue: Schools should become more like total institutions so that they can more effectively educate children. Evaluate your argument. Which parts of it are facts? Which are opinions?

5. Some have argued that we should more extensively regulate the socialization of young children, perhaps by having mandatory parenting classes or having children start preschool at a very early age. Present your ideas on this proposition, using some of the concepts from the chapter.

6. Which future occasion for resocialization seems likely to affect you most deeply: entering your career, getting married, or entering a retirement community? Why?

GLOSSARY

Anticipatory socialization The process of starting to adjust one's belief, norms, and values in anticipation of new socialization one is about to undergo.

Desocialization The process of shedding one's self-image and values, usually followed by resocialization to a different set of values and view of the self.

Ego Sigmund Freud's term for the practical, reality-oriented part of the human psyche, which finds socially acceptable ways of satisfying biologically based pleasure-seeking drives.

Generalized other An internalized general impression of what society as a whole expects of us.

Id Sigmund Freud's term for the reservoir of innate biological drives aimed at obtaining physical pleasure.

Looking-glass self Charles Horton Cooley's term to explain how others influence the way we see ourselves. We gain an image of ourselves by imagining what other people think about us.

Mortification Erving Goffman's term for the process of desocialization that occurs in total institutions.

Occupational socialization The process of aligning the norms, values, and beliefs of a new worker with those of the organization or occupation in which he or she is employed.

Resocialization The internalization of a new set of norms and values that are very different from those held in the past.

Self The sense of having a distinct identity that sets us apart from other people and objects.

Significant others People who are emotionally important in someone's life.

Significant symbols George Herbert Mead's term for gestures and words acquired in early childhood that elicit desired responses from others and make social interaction possible.

Socialization The process by which new members of a society are instilled with the fundamental elements of their culture.

Sociobiologists Scientists who hold that humans have certain genetically evolved behavioral traits that provide a survival advantage and so have tended to endure.

Superego Sigmund Freud's term for conscience, the part of the human psyche that internalizes society's views of right and wrong.

Temperament The behavioral predisposition with which a child is born.

Total institutions Organizations that deliberately close themselves off from the outside world and lead a highly insular life that is formally organized and tightly controlled. Examples are prisons, mental hospitals, and army boot camps.

CHAPTER 6

The Life Course: From Childhood to Old Age

Remember the cartoon version of a python that swallows a pig? The snake's jaws open wide, then they snap shut, and the mouth bulges out. Slowly the bulge moves through the python's body, from head to middle to tail. This image of the pig-in-the-python is useful for understanding the generation known as "baby boomers" (L. Y. Jones, 1980).

GENERATIONS AND THE LIFE COURSE

The Baby Boomers

From colonial times until now, the birth rate in the United States has steadily declined. On average, people have had fewer children. There was one huge exception to this trend. Starting in 1946, just nine months or so after the end of World War II, couples started having babies in unprecedented numbers. At first, sociologists thought that couples were simply "making up for lost time" and having babies they could not have during the war. But the birth explosion continued for another two decades, and by 1964 (when the birth rate once again began to drop steadily), 76 million babies had been added to the American population.

People born between 1946 and 1964 are the baby boomers. Generations born before and after them are smaller in number. Because of this, baby boomers make a bulge in the American population structure (look ahead to Figure 6.1). As they age, they are like that pig passing through the python. The bulge slowly moves along from infancy, through childhood and adolescence, through the various stages of adulthood, and finally to retirement and old age. This slowly moving bulge has so far covered four decades of tumultuous times in American society. Many baby boomers were children during the Eisenhower years, the launching of the first spacecraft (*Sputnik*), and the cold war. For many, adolescence roughly began with John F. Kennedy's assassination and ended with the Vietnam war and Woodstock. Then came young adulthood during Nixon's Watergate era, and for many a comfortable status as young, urban professionals ("Yuppies"). Today, however, the "young" is starting to fade from the "Yup," a process that began in 1991 when the first of the baby boomers turned forty-five (Shapiro, 1991).

The experience of the baby boomers gets at the heart of sociological perspectives on the human life course. By **life course,** sociologists mean the sequence of stages in a life, from birth to death (Elder, 1987; O'Rand and Krecker, 1990). Just as the year is divided into seasons, so a human life can be divided into stages: infancy, childhood; adolescence; early, middle, and later adulthood; and old age. Sociologists see a close interdependence between a person's experiences during the life course and historical changes in society (M. W. Riley, 1987). What happens to someone depends in part on *when* that person was born—that is, on the historical events that are going on as the person reaches life's major milestones. (What happens to someone also depends on whether that person is male or female, rich or poor, American or Chinese, and so forth, but we will address these issues later.) Baby boomers, in short, are the product of a *particular* time and place. Indeed, to talk about *the* baby boomers is an overgeneralization, for the oldest boomers are in many ways different from the youngest ones because they were at different ages when different important events occurred. The oldest boomers, for instance, were twenty-two when Martin Luther King, Jr., was assassinated in 1968, while the youngest ones were only four.

Consider just a few examples of the unique experiences that baby boomers have had so far in their lives. One is the introduction of television during their childhood. The boomers were children when television first became widely available. In contrast, most of those born before 1946 first experienced "the tube" as adults, while those born after 1964 grew up with television as a well-established modern institution. Being the *first* generation to pass through childhood with TV gave baby boomers a unique experience, which in turn gave rise to patterns of behavior, attitudes, and values distinctively their own. Baby boomers were also the first generation of children to grow up mainly in suburbs, a fact perhaps related to our present mania for shopping malls and drive-through services. Just as male baby boomers were reaching the age when they were eligible to be drafted into the army, the highly controversial Vietnam war arose. Not surprisingly, the baby-boom generation took the lead in antiwar protests. Thus, a whole series of historical events—the advent of television, the growth of suburbs, the waging of a very unpopular war, to name just a few—occurred at specific points in the lives of baby boomers so as to make them in many ways different from any other generation.

But the baby-boom generation is not just a passive product of the times it has lived through. It has also helped to shape those times, sometimes quite dramatically. Because baby boomers outnumber the generations that preceded and followed them, they have caused social change at each stage of their development. In the late 1940s and early 1950s baby boomers crowded maternity wards and nursery schools, making Dr. Spock and Dr. Seuss household names. Later in the 1950s and into the 1960s, they over-

The collective experience of "baby boomers," born between 1946 and 1964, has largely defined modern American society. The election of Bill Clinton as president in 1992 formally shifted power to the generation that first grew up with television, went to college during the countercultural years of the 1960s, and, as adults, have formed the extremes of materialistic yuppies and "New Age" spiritual awareness groupies.

loaded elementary schools. Then gradually, in the 1970s, elementary schools in the United States started emptying out, as the bulge of baby boomers left childhood behind. The baby-boom generation has had an enormous impact on the marketplace as well. During the baby boomers' adolescence, for example, sales of acne medication and rock music skyrocketed. American tastes and values have also been affected by the baby boomers. Compared with older generations, baby boomers are more likely to go to movies, believe in the paranormal (such as unidentified flying objects and psychic phenomena), go to parties, and listen to records; but they are *less* likely to do volunteer work, to read, or to garden and do other tasks around the yard (Gerber et al., 1989; P. Light, 1988; D. Q. Mills, 1987; J. Schwartz, 1991; L. Wilson, 1988). Boomers delayed having children of their own, but enough of them have started families to create an "echo" of their own baby boom—another, much smaller, bulge of Americans that began to come on board in the late 1980s (Koretz, 1989).

What other social changes might we expect as the baby-boom generation moves into later adulthood and approaches old age (Russell, 1987)? Inevitably, when the boomers begin to reach their sixties (not long after the start of the next century), the number of retired people will soon exceed the number still working. Perhaps there will be labor shortages in the year 2015. Perhaps society will not be able to produce enough goods and services to support an increasingly dependent elderly population. The possibility exists that government programs designed to assist the elderly (like Medicare and Social Security) will not have enough money to survive. The housing market might respond to the baby-boom bulge by building huge retirement communities, new nursing homes, and more convalescent centers.

By Contrast: Growing Up in the Great Depression

The baby-boom generation is not unique in the way it has been shaped by its particular historical context, and in turn has influenced the social world of which it is a part. These important processes occur for each generation, regardless of how relatively small or large it is. Another excellent example can be seen in Glen Elder's study *Children of the Great Depression* (Elder, 1974; also Elder, 1978, 1987). Elder did not study an entire generation, which usually spans about twenty years, but rather a sample of Americans born during a two-year period, 1920 to 1921. People born in the same year, or in a small number of consecutive years, are called a **birth cohort.** The birth cohort on which Elder focused experienced the depths of the Great Depression of the 1930s as young adolescents. This historical accident affected their attitudes and behaviors, not only immediately, but in their future lives as well. Cohort membership, after all, doesn't just influence people as children. "It affects them at every age, through the groups to which they belong, the others with whom they interact, and the social and cultural conditions to which they are exposed" (M. W. Riley, 1987).

In the Great Depression, families suffered a great deal from economic deprivation; but many people who grew up during the 1930s remember their families drawing together in meaningful and pleasurable ways.

As teenagers during the Great Depression, most of Elder's subjects experienced "hard times" in their families. Many of their parents had spells of unemployment and accompanying losses of income. But it may have been the perceived loss of prestige that hurt these families most, a subjective feeling of "coming down in the world" that could not be measured in dollars alone. Many families tried to hide the hardships they were suffering from the outside world. One of Elder's subjects recalled that his parents spent a considerable amount of money on new paint for the house, but were very tight when it came to buying food. Why? Because everyone in the neighborhood could see the house's condition, but they couldn't see the food that went on the table.

As for the young adolescents on whom Elder focused, about 40 percent remembered being expected to make significant contributions to family income through part-time jobs. As a result, many of them became acutely aware early in life of the cost of basic necessities like food, clothes, and housing. These early work experiences apparently instilled strong values of financial responsibility and conservativeness. Ideas like "money doesn't come easily" and "don't spend beyond your means" are, in general, heartily endorsed by people who experienced the Great Depression as working teenagers. Significantly, at the time of the Depression, these adolescents didn't usually respond with despair and resignation to the hardships they were suffering. Instead, they tended to react with positive responses, such as working harder.

In later years, the experiences of the Depression continued to affect Elder's subjects. Among men, Elder found a pattern of "vocational crystallization," in which they decided on a line of work early in life and then stuck with it. Especially for those men who came from very deprived family backgrounds, there was an early narrowing of interests, vision, and desires, a zeroing in on *some* stable occupation. This may have been a reaction to the severe poverty they had experienced as adolescents. Most of

Elder's male subjects, even those who had not experienced abject poverty, were very work-centered in their adult lives. They put a greater value on work achievements and success than on family, leisure, or community service. Among the women Elder studied, there was a strong preference for pursuing traditional female roles, generally centered on family and household responsibilities. Especially for those from very deprived family backgrounds, there was a tendency to marry at an early age and to give up employment outside the home, at least when the first child was born. Perhaps, for these women, a focus on the family was an attempt to undo the "psychic disruptions" to their childhood families during the Depression.

Interestingly, Elder found that people who experienced the Great Depression as teenagers were affected by it in dramatically different ways than those who experienced it as young children. When compared with those born between 1928 and 1929 (who were very young during the Depression), those born between 1920 and 1921 (who were teenagers at the time) were more helpful, self-directed, and confident about their futures. Generally, they also achieved more in their adult lives than those who were born eight or nine years later. It appears that the Depression had more negative life consequences for those who went through it as very young children than for those who went through it as adolescents. Why do you think this was so?

THE LIFE COURSE IN SOCIOLOGICAL PERSPECTIVE

Our discussions of the baby-boom generation and of children of the Great Depression illustrate two important features of sociological perspectives on the life course. First, as sociologists trace the experiences of people as they move from birth to death, they recognize that these experiences take place in distinctive historical, institutional, and cultural contexts. This means that the experiences vary depending on a person's generation, race and ethnic background, nationality, social class, gender, and so on. A black girl born tomorrow to impoverished parents living in Harlem will not have the same experiences at each stage of the life course as will a son born to Jewish parents who have recently immigrated to Israel from the Soviet Union to start new lives as shopkeepers in Tel Aviv.

Second, sociologists are interested in the social changes brought about as successive generations of people (born at different historical times) pass through life's stages. How did children of the Great Depression, as adults in the 1950s, affect the postwar recovery of our national economy? How did *their* children, some of the baby-boom generation, leave their mark on the Vietnam era and beyond? And how will children of the baby boomers, many born in the 1990s, change the social world? Perhaps, as adults, they will rebel against the norms and values of conventional society, much as their parents did during the late 1960s. Perhaps, as young adults, they will embrace the materialism and individualism that appealed to their parents in the 1980s (Seligman, 1988). Only time will tell.

In studying the life course, sociologists distinguish among age, aging, and age structure. To sociologists, **age** is not just the number of years since a person was born; it also involves a set of social definitions regarding what is required of and appropriate for people of different ages. These definitions differ from society to society, and they can change significantly with the passage of time. Aging, too, has a sociological meaning different from the everyday one. In everyday speech aging usually refers to the process of growing older in the later stages of life. But sociologists use the term more broadly. To them, **aging** is the process of growing older that begins on the day we are born. It is the process of moving through the entire life course, starting with birth, through infancy, childhood, and adolescence, and onward through the various stages of adulthood to death. Finally, **age structure** is the number of people in a society at each stage of the life course. Put another way, it is the distribution of a population by age: the number of people who are one year old, two years old, three years old, and so forth. The relative proportion of children to elderly adults—high in youthful societies, low in ones where older people predominate—significantly shapes all aspects of social life, from employment opportunities to leisure-time pursuits.

The five key sociological concepts will be helpful as we explore further the ideas of age, aging, and age structure. Age structure is a specific element of the ***social structure*** of all human societies. As we shall see, changes in the number of people at each age level have profound implications for how a society chooses to allocate its resources, how individuals make personal and private choices, and how people define the "proper" behavior for various ages. Historical or cultural differences in age structure create different contexts for ***social action*** by individuals and groups. The enormous size of the baby-boom generation created a situation in which age-specific protests against the Vietnam war attracted many young adults in the late 1960s (although other baby boomers chose to enter the armed forces and fight in Southeast Asia). Changes in age structure also bring about problems of ***functional integration***. Various social institutions, such as education or the economy, must adjust to increases in the proportion of older people and decreases in the proportion of children in the population. Differences in ***power*** come into play, too. Many observers wonder whether increases in the proportion of Americans over age sixty-five are creating a new and powerful voting bloc that prefers governmental programs designed to help their age group (for example, health care) over programs benefiting other age groups (such as schools or child care). The next section begins with a discussion of how the meanings of age—what is expected or allowed from children, teenagers, and adults—vary from one ***culture*** to another.

Social Definitions of Age

What does it mean when someone tells you to "act your age"? That frequently heard admonition suggests that there are behaviors and attitudes expected of people at different ages. Behavior appropriate for a two-year-old (like thumb sucking) can only be done as a joke by an ordinary forty-two-year-old. All cultures include sets of norms that define expected and appropriate behavior for people at each stage of life (Keith, 1990). As aspects of ***culture***, these norms vary from one society to another. They are not simply mandated by the biological characteristics associated with a particular stage (Clausen, 1986). For example, our society generally frowns on pregnancy in a twelve-year-old, but in some preindustrial societies (where life expectancy is often shorter) the same biological age might be defined as ideal for having a baby.

Age shapes the flow of people into and out of social roles and statuses (and the rights and responsibilities that go with them). In American society, you cannot drive a car until age sixteen, vote until age eighteen, drink alcohol until age twenty-one (in most places), or qualify for Social Security retirement benefits until age sixty-five. Every human society establishes timetables that define "normal" age ranges for major life events such as completing your education, leaving the home of your parents, getting your first full-time job, marrying, and retiring from the work force. Age also organizes the distribution of valued resources in a society—money, power, and prestige (O'Rand and Krecker, 1990). In many preindustrial societies, advanced age confers great prestige: The wisdom of the few remaining elders is considered very useful and is highly valued. By contrast, in modern societies such as our own, the wisdom of the more plentiful elders is often considered obsolete, and advanced age is no guarantee of high prestige.

The process of classifying people into social categories according to their age is known as **age grading**. Although age grading is widespread in our society, it has not always been so. The considerable importance we now attach to age and age differences first emerged in the late nineteenth century and took firm hold only in the early decades of this century (Chudacoff, 1989). Before 1850, age grading was simply not as significant as it is today in regulating and organizing people's behavior and society's institutions.

Take education. Schools were not age-graded until the 1870s. Before that time, it was not uncommon to find teenagers in the same classes with very young children. Students then did not enter and leave school at the precise ages that have, in the century and a half since, become routine: kindergarten at five, middle school at eleven or twelve, high school graduation at eighteen. Even colleges and universities were populated by a wider array of ages than is the typical pattern now. Boys of fourteen and men of twenty-five were not unusual at Harvard or Yale, and in 1804 the new president of the University of North Carolina at Chapel Hill was only twenty-four years old—younger than many of his students! Before the Civil War, then, someone's age was an unreliable predictor of that person's progress and placement in the educational system. These days, in contrast, most students march through school in lockstep with those the same age. (We say *most* students, because there are signs that this strict age grading is gradually starting to change in colleges and universities, a trend we'll discuss later in this chapter.)

A general trend toward increased age grading can be seen in other spheres of social life as well. For instance, most Americans today choose to marry someone about their own age, but this hasn't always been so. In Providence, Rhode Island, in 1864, almost half (47.1 percent) of the newly married couples were separated in age by six or more years; but that percentage had dropped to less than a quarter (23.1 percent) by 1921. Similarly, in Omaha, Nebraska, between 1875 and 1877, 46.0 percent of newly married couples were separated by six or more years, but that percentage was down to 26.5 percent by 1925 (Chudacoff, 1989).

What explains this changing pattern? The institutionalization of age-graded education meant that young people literally grew up with their age peers. They passed the same milestones of life together and shared common experiences. When it came time to marry, newlyweds-to-be chose from the pool of people they knew best: those of the same age. Also, between the 1860s and the 1920s, revolutions in communications and mass media (more widely available newspapers, magazines, and books) spread the words of educators, scientists, physicians, social reformers, and other advice-givers about the "healthy" or "proper" or "modern" choice of a husband or wife. People evidently listened when they were told that "robbing the cradle" to obtain a spouse ran counter to new social norms and values.

Norms regarding "appropriate" ages for major life events are also subject to change. For example, in a survey conducted in the late 1950s, 80 percent of the males and 90 percent of the females felt that the best ages for a man to marry were between twenty and twenty-five. By the late 1970s, however, only 42 percent of men and women agreed with that earlier consensus. Similarly, in the late 1950s, the overwhelming majority of people believed that nineteen to twenty-four were the best ages for a woman to marry. Two decades later, this view had fallen out of favor, especially among American women, only 36 percent of whom now agreed that nineteen to twenty-four were the ideal ages of marriage for a woman (Rosenfeld and Stark, 1987). Such changing norms often make it harder for people to decide whether or not their own lives are "on schedule" (Neugarten and Neugarten, 1987).

Of course, the scheduling of major life events varies not only over time but also between societies. Growing up Masai is not at all like growing up American. The Masai are a pastoral society in East Africa. Their traditional age-grading system is based on principles completely different from our own. The Masai recognize four age grades for males—boy, warrior, junior elder, and senior elder—and each grade is assigned specific rights and responsibilities. The boys, who are still under the authority of their parents, are responsible for herding their family's livestock. Warriors (called *morani*) range in age from fifteen to thirty, and live as bachelors in separate villages under the supervision of a committee of elders. Junior elders (about thirty to forty-five years old) are permitted to marry, own cattle, and establish their own homesteads. Senior elders (above forty-five) are responsible for the public affairs of the society. For males in Masai society, the allocation of roles—along with associated rights and responsibilities—is almost completely determined by age (Bernardi, 1955; Ole Saitoti and Beckwith, 1980; Spencer, 1988).

In most modern societies, by contrast, age is simply one characteristic among many used to allocate statuses and roles, rights and obligations. In fact, American society has instituted laws that limit the extent to which age can be a determining factor in the distribution of rights and opportunities. It is illegal, in many contexts, to deny employment or housing to someone simply because that person is too old or too young. Still, negative stereotyping based on age, called **ageism**, persists (Butler, 1989). Older people are the usual victims of ageism in American society,

Societies formally and informally separate their members into groups defined by their ages. The norms that define the interaction between age groups do evolve, but they seldom change radically. The film Harold and Maude *depicts a love affair between a man in his late teens and a woman in her sixties. The controversy that this movie provoked in the early 1970s derived from the fact that it mocked the age-graded (and gender-biased) patterns of social life that are taken for granted as foundations of the social order.*

where younger is defined as better and people invest fortunes in medical fountains of youth (face-lifts and cell therapies, for example). When a television newscaster is fired because of her wrinkles and gray hairs, ageism has led to outright **age discrimination**: the denial of rights, opportunities, and services to someone exclusively because of that person's age (Levin and Levin, 1980).

Aging: Transitions in the Life Course

In one important respect, age is fundamentally different from other ascribed statuses, such as race and gender. Being black or white, male or female, is a lifelong status, except in rare cases. Age, in contrast, is a **transitional status** because people periodically move from one age category to another. This process of a person moving through the life course, from birth to death, is called **aging**.

As people age, they face different sets of expectations and responsibilities, enjoy different rights and opportunities, and possess different amounts of power and control. Consequently, transitions from one age status to another are societally important. They are often marked by **rites of passage**, public ceremonies—full of ritual symbolism—that record the transition being made (van Gennep, 1908/

Rites of transition are often thought of as events in traditional societies, but American institutions also have rites of passage. Institutions that seek personal loyalty, such as sororities, have elaborate rituals intended to integrate members emotionally and psychologically into the group.

1961). Religious confirmations, graduation ceremonies, debutante balls and other coming-out parties, weddings, retirement dinners, and funerals are all examples of rites of passage in American society.

Rites of passage are important both for the individual who moves to a new age status and for the society in which he or she lives. The ceremonies typically use stories and symbols to explain the meaning of the change in age. In the process, both the individual and the society are reminded of the rights and responsibilities that go along with the new status. The importance of rites of passage can be seen in their persistence, even despite social changes that might tend to make them obsolete. For example, few people today would consider a thirteen-year-old mature enough to assume the many rights and responsibilities of adulthood. And yet among Jews, a boy still symbolically becomes a man at age thirteen through the bar mitzvah ceremony. The persistence of this ritual through centuries of Jewish life is an indication of the significance all cultures attach to their rites of passage.

Interestingly, although age grading has generally increased in our society, and people are more conscious of being "on time" for major life transitions (experiencing them when others their age do), in recent years there has been more variability in the ages at which people *actually* undergo certain rites of passage. For example, although our culture may still define twenty-one or twenty-two as the appropriate age to graduate from college, certain social changes—increasing divorce rates, increasing rates of female participation in the labor force, big swings in unemployment rates—are bringing older adults back to colleges and universities at nontraditional ages. If this trend continues, the American college graduation rite of passage will no longer be as age-graded as it has been in the recent past.

In societies like that of the Masai, where age grading more thoroughly determines appropriate behavior and opportunities, the timing of rites of passage is much more rigid than it is in America. In his classic 1908 analysis, French anthropologist Arnold van Gennep graphically described the initiation ceremonies in which Masai boys and girls became adults. Traditionally, the ceremony for boys took place every four or five years and involved young adolescents between the ages of twelve and sixteen:

> The candidates . . . smear themselves with white clay and wander from kraal to kraal [living areas] for two or three months. Their heads are shaved, and an ox or sheep is killed. The morning after the slaughter each candidate cuts down a tree which the girls plant in front of his hut. The following morning the boys go out into the cold air and wash with cold water. [Circumcision is then performed, using primitive tools.] The operator cuts the foreskin; an ox hide containing the blood which has been shed is placed on each boy's bed. The boys remain shut up for four days. Then they come out and tease the girls and often dress as women. . . . They adorn their heads with small birds and ostrich feathers. When they are healed, their

> heads are shaved; when their hair grows back sufficiently to be combed, they are called morani, or warriors. (van Gennep, 1908/1961, pp. 85–86)

The ceremony for girls involved excision of the clitoris, and, upon healing, the woman was "married off."

Do the initiation ceremonies of the Masai strike you as bizarre, ridiculously elaborate, even gruesome? If so, it is largely a matter of your cultural perspective, for some "coming of age" ceremonies in our own society have the same complexity and strangeness. Consider the debutante ball, Texas-style, with $20,000 gowns, as described by Molly Ivins (only somewhat tongue-in-cheek):

> Instead of a simple curtsy, Texas debs sink slowly to the floor (this requires really good quadriceps) and touch their foreheads to the floor in front of their "dukes." They then look up at the "duke" (you don't want to dwell too much on the symbolism of this posture), and with his permission they slowly rise from the floor (which takes *great* quadriceps). (Ivins, 1990)

Thus, elaborate rites of passage occur in every society, for everywhere people want to celebrate and reaffirm the importance of certain life-course transitions.

Age Structure: The Graying of America

Age structure refers to the distribution of a population by age—that is, the number of people at each age level. As we have noted, it is an important aspect of ***social structure***. In order to describe the age structure of a society, sociologists first count the people born in each year (who constitute a birth cohort) and then keep track of how many of them survive each subsequent year. Much can be learned about the life course of people and about historical changes in a society by comparing successive birth cohorts.

For example, people in different birth cohorts can have different life experiences simply because their cohorts vary in size. Many of those born in relatively small cohorts find that they are extended certain opportunities at an earlier age—promotions, important offices—than those born in larger cohorts. Those born in larger cohorts, generally speaking, face stiffer competition from age peers for desired positions or activities, and many must wait until a later age in order to enjoy them.

The size of birth cohorts also affects the ***functional integration*** of society—that is, the broad patterns of social organization. The age structure of our entire society is changing precisely because of size differences in birth cohorts during this century (see Figure 6.1). This change—

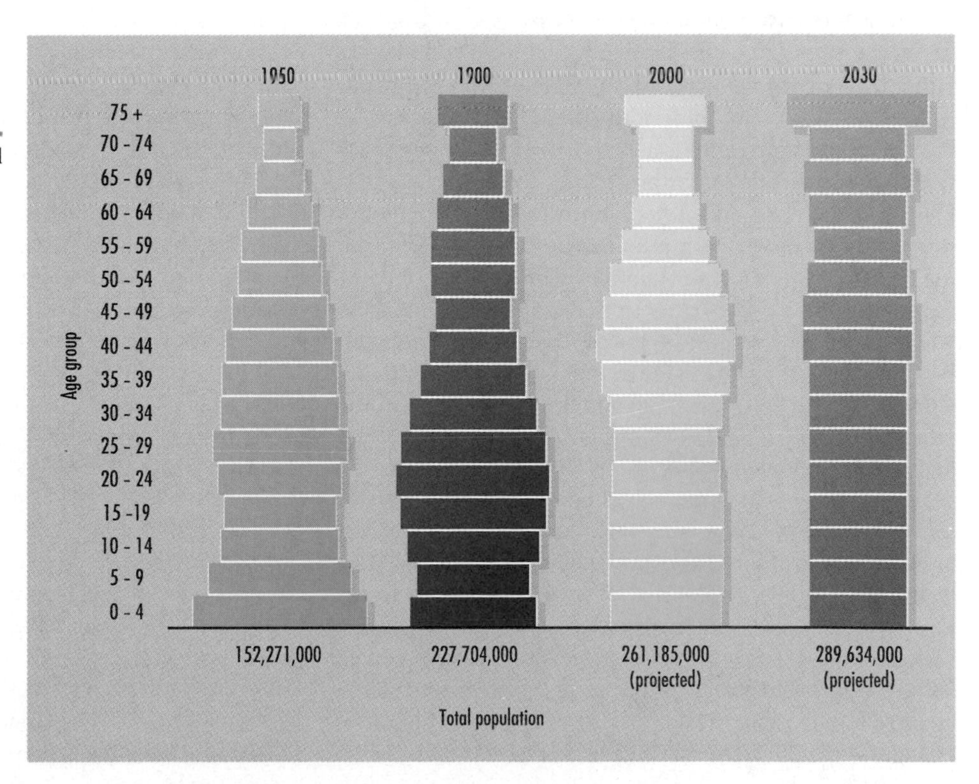

FIGURE 6.1 / The U.S. Population Pyramid Is Becoming a Rectangle

Source: U.S. Bureau of the Census and the World Bank.

which is causing a "graying" of American society (Myers, 1990)—can be seen in two simple statistics. One is the *median age* of the population, the age that divides the population in half, so that 50 percent are older than the median and 50 percent younger. The median age of Americans has increased throughout this century and promises to go even higher in the decades ahead. In 1900, the median age was 22.9 years; by 1950, it had risen to 30.2 years; and by 1990, it was 33.0 years. By the year 2020, the median age will be 40.2 years, and by 2050, it will be about 46.0 years! The same story is told if we look at the *proportion of Americans aged sixty-five or older*. That proportion has increased during this century, and will continue to go up as Americans move into the next one. In 1900, a mere 4.1 percent of the population was aged sixty-five or older; by 1950, the percentage had risen to 8.1 percent; and by 1990, it was 12.7 percent. Looking ahead, in the year 2020, 18.2 percent of the population will be sixty-five or older, and in 2050 that will rise to 24.9 percent. Children, adolescents, and even young adults will, as America moves into the next century, become an ever-diminishing proportion of the American population.

There are two fundamental causes of this graying of the American population. First, average life expectancy has increased through this century. A white male born in 1900 could, on average, expect to live forty-seven years, and a white female could expect to live forty-nine years. Today, men can expect to live to about seventy-two and women to almost eighty. Increasing life expectancy is due to improvements in the general standard of living (better nutrition and sanitation) and especially in medical care.

A second cause of the graying of the population is the baby-boom generation. Although the median age in the United States has increased from 1900 to the present, there was one exception to the trend. In the decades during and just after the baby boom, the median age actually declined, from 30.2 years in 1950, to 29.4 years in 1960, to 27.9 years in 1970 (after which it began to move consistently upward again). Interestingly, this short-term decline in the median age of the population occurred at the same time that the proportion of Americans aged sixty-five and older continued to increase! Such a pattern was possible because the large baby-boom generation statistically overwhelmed the relatively smaller birth cohorts moving through their sixties and seventies. Now the baby-boom bulge is moving toward its own "gray" years, however. The first baby boomers will reach age sixty-five in the year 2011. Because birth cohorts of younger people have been consistently smaller than those of the baby-boom years, an increasingly rapid graying of the American population is inevitable during the next half century.

What differences in social life can Americans expect from a graying age structure? One is a sharp decline in the demand for primary and secondary school teachers. The demand for college-level teachers, however, may not drop as much due to the increasing numbers of college students of nontraditional ages. By 1996, almost 60 percent of those enrolled in higher education will be twenty-two years or older, compared with only 38 percent in 1970 (U.S. Department of Education, 1990). Colleges and universities may well develop more "continuing education" programs for older students in order to keep their enrollments up. The graying of the population will also affect the practice of medicine. More physicians will become specialists in health problems and diseases that affect the elderly, for that is where the greatest demand will be. Other industries targeted to the senior market will also flourish—everything from retirement communities to convalescent aids.

But the graying of the American population may also precipitate economic crises in the years ahead. As the baby boomers grow old, government programs that provide benefits for the elderly will take an ever-increasing chunk of the federal budget. At the same time, the ratio of employed to unemployed people will continue declining, which means that fewer working Americans will be available to pay for senior citizen benefits out of their income tax dollars (Habib, 1990). A growing imbalance between workers and nonworkers is already visible. In 1945, each person receiving Social Security was supported by thirty-five workers, whereas, in 1985, each Social Security recipient was supported by *three* workers. This shift has caused many observers to wonder whether the system will be able to sustain itself by the middle of the twenty-first century. Adding to the economic crisis may be the spiraling costs of health care. If future increases in life expectancy are achieved by huge investments in high-tech medical treatments, there may be both a greatly expanded elderly population and a society in which a large proportion of its resources goes toward keeping elderly people alive (Callahan, 1987).

The Stages of Life: Erikson's Theory

We are now ready to look more closely at four major stages in the human life course: childhood, adolescence, adulthood, and old age. This particular way of dividing up the life course is characteristic of modern Western cultures such as our own. Some preindustrial cultures don't recognize a distinct stage of adolescence, and others don't make a sharp distinction between middle adulthood and old age. But since these four stages are the way our culture generally thinks about the life course, we will use them to organize our discussion in the remainder of this chapter.

A number of theorists have used these four major stages as a starting point for developing ideas about the social experiences people undergo during the course of their lives. One of these theorists is Erik Erikson. In his pathbreaking work *Childhood and Society* (1950), Erikson proposed eight challenges that people face as they pass through the life course (see Figure 6.2). Each challenge must be dealt with in some way, either positively or negatively, and how a person deals with a current challenge affects how well that person will cope with subsequent challenges.

With its roots in the psychoanalysis of Sigmund Freud, Erikson's theory of the life course is undeniably psychological. However, his theory can be extended in a sociological direction by asking: How do the hypothesized challenges at each stage of the life course differ for people who live in different historical or cultural contexts, or who differ in terms of race, gender, or social class? Thus, Erikson's theory will give us a framework for looking more deeply at the variations in people's experiences at each stage of human life. We'll begin our discussion of each stage with a brief review of Erikson's theory, highlighting the challenges he described as crucial. Then we'll consider sociological research on the actual life experiences of people—from our own society today, from the past, and from other cultures.

Stages	Developmental Tasks	Basic Strengths	Basic Antipathies
Infancy	Basic Trust vs. Basic Mistrust	Hope	Withdrawal
Early Childhood	Autonomy vs. Shame, Doubt	Will	Compulsion
Play Age	Initiative vs. Guilt	Purpose	Inhibition
School Age	Industry vs. Inferiority	Competence	Inertia
Adolescence	Identity vs. Identity Confusion	Fidelity	Repudiation
Young Adulthood	Intimacy vs. Isolation	Love	Exclusivity
Adulthood	Generativity vs. Stagnation	Care	Rejectivity
Old Age	Integrity vs. Despair	Wisdom	Disdain

FIGURE 6.2 / Erikson's Stages of Life and Developmental Issues

Source: Reproduced from *The Life Cycle Completed: A Review,* by Erik H. Erikson, by permission of W. W. Norton & Company, Inc. Copyright © 1982 by Rikan Enterprises, Ltd.

CHILDHOOD

In Erikson's theory, infants face the challenge of being totally dependent on others to provide for their basic needs. This sets the stage for the development of *basic trust versus mistrust.* Babies who receive care that is loving and reliable learn to trust other people and to see the world as essentially a safe and secure place. In contrast, those whose care is erratic come to view the world as unpredictable and harsh and acquire a basic mistrust of others. The second childhood challenge in Erikson's theory occurs during toddlerhood, when the child begins to strive for some independence from adults. The issue now is developing *autonomy versus shame and doubt.* Those who are encouraged to be independent learn to master simple tasks and develop a healthy sense of self-sufficiency. Those whose autonomy is thwarted may come to doubt their abilities and feel shame about the self.

Around the age of four or five another challenge begins, which leads to *initiative versus guilt.* At this stage, children increasingly initiate interactions with peers and try to take on more responsibilities, such as helping with household chores. If parents and others are supportive of these initiatives, children develop feelings of self-worth. But if their initiatives meet with rejection or ridicule, they punish themselves for their failures and feel guilt. Finally, when they reach school age, children struggle to acquire skills and information and to relate to a larger social circle. This challenge ends in the development of *industry versus inferiority.* Depending on their experiences, children may develop pride in their abilities and accomplishments and learn to pursue activity joyfully for its own sake; or they may begin to feel increasingly inferior and fear that if required to perform, they will inevitably fail.

Historical Perspectives on Childhood

The idea of childhood as a distinct stage in the life course is a fairly recent cultural invention. Childhood as we know

The idea of childhood is an invention of the European Renaissance. A picture of a peasant child would portray none of the special privileges and protections that these children of England's King Charles I and Queen Henrietta Maria were among the first to enjoy.

it simply did not exist in Europe in the Middle Ages. The privileged treatment of children as something more than miniature adults didn't begin until the Renaissance for upper social classes, and much later for other segments of society (Ariès, 1962). During the Middle Ages, parents rarely spent much time with their children. In wealthier medieval families, infants were sent out to live with wet nurses (where their odds of survival were often slim), and if they survived infancy and returned to the family as children, they were put under the care of servants until they were old enough to begin apprenticeships—usually by age seven. Children of peasants typically started working in the fields by the age of five. In effect, they moved quickly into their adult roles (Shorter, 1975). Very few of the special activities that we now take for granted as part of a happy childhood—songs, games, stories, abundant leisure—were available to children in this era.

The idea that children should be cherished, nurtured, protected, and distanced from the sometimes harsh realities of adult life took hold in upper-class families by the eighteenth century. For those lucky children, childhood was defined a time to learn, explore, and play. But these luxuries were denied to children of the middle and working classes for another century or more. Even at the turn of the twentieth century in the United States, 18.2 percent of all children aged ten to fifteen were employed in the work force, two-thirds of them in nonagricultural jobs (Fyfe, 1989). Industrialization created a huge demand for children to work in the new factories, and the American labor force gained over a million children between 1870 and 1900.

Early industrialization brought an exploitation of child labor every bit as brutal as the farm work that medieval peasant children did. George Washington wrote in his diary about a duck-cloth factory in Boston where "each spinner has a small girl to turn the wheel and where the whipping of these factory children was commonplace" (in Fyfe, 1989, p. 57). The additional income earned by children was vital for the well-being of many families. In the Philadelphia of 1880, for example, Irish children contributed between 38 and 46 percent of total family income. Laws prohibiting child labor and requiring compulsory primary education were not routinely enforced until the 1930s.

Between the 1870s (when children working in sweatshops was socially acceptable) and the 1930s (when such child labor had become immoral and illegal), the cultural meaning of childhood underwent a massive redefinition. Sociologist Viviana Zelizer (1985) has described this as a shift from the useful child to the useless—but priceless!—child. That is, in the 1870s, children were often valued for their wages and their economic contributions to the family. By the 1930s, children had become emotional and sentimental assets, removed from the spheres of economic life and wage earning.

What caused this shift in the definition of childhood?

To some extent it was a matter of economic forces and technological change. Between 1870 and 1930, new technologies eliminated many jobs once filled by children, in part, by increasing the skill level required of people working in factories. Also, especially during the prosperous 1920s, parents were often earning enough money that they could afford to let their children stay in school. Still, the stiff enforcement of child labor laws in the 1930s reflected a change in *attitudes and values*, not just a change in *economics*. Zelizer suggests that there was a "moral redefinition" of childhood, a kind of "sacralization" in which children were invested with sentimental and even religious value. Changing norms increasingly defined the working child as a victim of unloving parents and greedy industrialists. Certainly from the 1930s until today, middle-class children do work. But it is work for a weekly allowance rather than a wage, newspaper routes and baby-sitting rather than assembly-line jobs, and work intended to teach discipline and the value of money rather than to increase family income.

Industrialization led to brutal exploitation of children, which lasted for several generations in Europe and the United States. Not until the early twentieth century was child labor first regulated and then eliminated. This exploitation was not considered shameful because children were expected to contribute financially to their families.

Has Childhood Disappeared Again?

These days, we see childhood as a carefully bounded and separated period of learning and growth. Children are thought to have their own needs and their own sphere of activities. Parents invest huge amounts of time and money to guarantee a protected and stimulating environment for their children. Could Teenage Mutant Ninja Turtles and Barbie dolls be so phenomenally successful if ours were not a child-centered society?

Despite our ideals, it may be just a myth that American children today live in their own protected world. Consider the titles of several recent books: *The Disappearance of Childhood* (Postman, 1982), *The Erosion of Childhood* (Suransky, 1982), and *Children Without Childhood* (Winn, 1984). Is modern society in fact re-creating its distant cultural past, when childhood was not a cleanly separated stage in the life course, when children didn't enjoy special privileges and weren't spared the challenges and troubles of adulthood? Some observers think so. As evidence, they point to the initiation of many children into behaviors that carry with them "adult" responsibilities and complexitiesmsex, drugs, alcohol, even regular employment outside the home. This trend may herald a return to the view of children as miniature adults, a redefinition of childhood as no longer a period of protection, but a period of preparation for adult roles (Winn, 1984).

Several causes of the disappearance of childhood have been identified. One is a decline in parental authority (Winn, 1984). Parents increasingly doubt their ability to control their children's behavior, to prevent early experimentation with adult activities and lifestyles. Second, television is broadcasting information that was once the exclusive domain of adults (Postman, 1982). Postman calls TV an "open admission technology," which means that any viewer of any age can watch whatever is shown—sex, violence, drug use, and other aspects of adult life. Third, television, films, and contemporary literature (for example, the juvenile novels of Judy Blume) are increasingly portraying children as confronting adult themes and situations (Postman, 1982). Finally, the modern child-care industry may be in part responsible for children growing up without childhood. According to Suransky, "the business of child-care negates the being of the child, who emerges as the voiceless and helpless victim of a growing industry which is manipulating the child as a profit integer. . . . The child becomes objectified because it is not the human development of the child that is fostered, but rather, how many children can be contained within the structure for the greatest amount of money and smallest number of staff" (Suransky, 1982, p. 187).

Some observers are horrified at this erosion of childhood. They fear that when children are rushed into adulthood, they not only miss out on the simple pleasures of childhood, but are also prepared poorly for later years. Others disagree, however. Some believe that it is a mistake to shield children from the complexities of adulthood or to sugar-coat the tensions and challenges of modern life. They applaud portrayals in films, TV, and literature of children confronting difficult challenges, for they feel this helps to prepare young people for the important life decisions they must inevitably face. Also, some believe that complete economic dependence lessens the development of self-worth, competence, and autonomy during childhood. Finally, some argue that the "protected childhood" of maximum leisure and limited responsibilities simply does not fit well with other realities of modern family life. Increases in divorce and in households where both parents work may well require that children mature more quickly than was common, say, during the 1950s era of "Ozzie and Harriet" and "Leave It to Beaver."

No doubt this debate over the possible disappearance of childhood will continue unresolved for some time to come, partly because childhood experiences in the United States are so varied that it is difficult to generalize about them. It may be impossible to prescribe one best method for raising children in light of the differences in cultural beliefs, economic circumstances, and family structure that make American society heterogeneous. Recent sociological studies of childhood, however, may shape the future direction of this debate. In his studies of friendship networks among preschoolers in the United States and Italy, William Corsaro has found a distinctive "peer culture" that results from children's creative and selective borrowing of information from the adult world (Corsaro, 1985; Corsaro and Eder, 1990). Preschoolers don't simply imitate adults. Rather, they reshape adult ideas to meet the problems they face in dealing with their peers. Corsaro has suggested that childhood should not be seen as a period of apprenticeship that prepares a child for competent adulthood. Instead, childhood is a time when groups of children collectively build their own meaningful worlds, worlds in which they attempt to gain control of their lives, share that control with friends, and challenge adult authority.

ADOLESCENCE

For Erik Erikson, adolescents face the challenge of *identity versus role confusion*. **Identity** is an understanding of who one is and where one is going. As such, it is built on a sense of continuity about one's past, present, and future. To develop an identity is to coordinate one's view of the self with perceptions of the views of others. Adolescents who are unable to develop an identity experience role confusion.

The Invention of Adolescence

Adolescence is an even more recent cultural invention than childhood (Kett, 1977). Toward the end of the nineteenth century, social commentators began to describe the period between childhood and adulthood as a particularly dangerous and vulnerable stage in development. In one of his most detailed and important works, *Adolescence: Its Psychology and Its Relations to Physiology, Anthropology, Sociology, Sex, Crime, Religion, and Education* (1905/1981), the psychologist G. Stanley Hall described adolescence as a period of storm and stress, but also of possibility and promise. He argued that teenagers should be given a chance to experiment with and explore various roles available to them before being pushed into the adult world.

Hall's ideas were partly a product of changing social conditions. As twentieth-century America became increasingly urban and industrialized, and positions for unskilled laborers became scarce, education was no longer a luxury; it was a necessity. So instead of being rushed into adulthood, young people were urged to finish high school or even college. Later, during the Great Depression of the 1930s, staying in school was encouraged for another reason: It kept young people from crowding the shrinking job market. Thus, between 1900 and 1956, the proportion of Americans graduating from high school rose from 6.3 to 62.5 percent.

Adolescence as we know it today took shape in the 1940s and 1950s, when the segregation of young people in schools fostered the development of an "adolescent society," a teenage subculture with its own tastes and standards (Coleman, 1961). That subculture was in many ways the product of post–World War II affluence, which set the stage for a dizzying series of social changes and role redefinitions. For example, many teenagers now had access to cars, which meant that dating was no longer under the watchful eyes of adults. This change may in part account for the increase in teenage sexual activity.

Because an adolescent subculture has its own norms and values, the teenage years are a time when parents and children are more likely to bicker about what the children want to do. Despite these disagreements, teenagers still report that they feel close to and identify with their parents. Only about 10 percent experience deteriorating family relationships (Dornbusch, 1990; Gecas and Seff, 1990).

Contemporary American Adolescents

There are signs that the age at which children become adolescents is slowly creeping downward. The "bobby-

During the 1950s, the teen culture hit its stride and many of the age-graded social institutions that we now take for granted came into being.

soxers" who swooned over Frank Sinatra in the 1940s were fifteen to eighteen years old; the "teeny-boppers" who mobbed the Beatles in the 1960s were twelve to fourteen. The age at which teenagers begin dating and using cosmetics—and drugs—has dropped from fifteen or sixteen to only eleven or twelve (Neugarten and Neugarten, 1987).

The average age of first sexual experience is also moving downward, as young people leave childhood behind them earlier than in the past (Gelman, 1990; Zeman, 1990). In 1988, 80 percent of adolescent girls and 86 percent of adolescent boys had experienced sex by age nineteen, and sizable proportions had been sexually initiated much earlier than that (25 percent of the girls and 33 percent of the boys by age fifteen). Still, there is a substantial amount of variability in the age at which particular teenagers begin having sex. What explains these differences?

Sociologists have learned a great deal about the circumstances that lead a teenager to begin sexual activity earlier rather than later. First, some teenagers physically mature earlier than others do, and early puberty may be associated with a younger age of sexual initiation, especially for boys (Miller and Moore, 1990; Udry and Billy, 1987). Second, parents' sexual and marriage patterns affect the sexual behavior of their children. One study found that the younger a woman had been when she had her first sexual experience, the younger her daughter would be at *her* first sexual activity (Newcomer and Udry, 1984). Also, adolescent girls from one-parent families are likely to begin sexual activity sooner than girls from two-parent homes (Miller and Bingham, 1989). Third, various sociocultural factors influence a person's age of first sexual experience. For example, girls who are religiously devout and attend church regularly tend to report postponing sexual activity; girls who grow up in poverty tend to begin having sex early (Forste and Heaton, 1988; Hogan and Kitagawa, 1985). Fourth, the age at which teenagers begin having sex is affected by their friends. For example, white teenage girls who have not yet had sex are more likely to start if their girlfriends are already sexually active (Billy and Udry, 1985). Even enrolling in a school where sexual activity is common can prompt young people to decide to have sex themselves (Moffat, 1989).

Adolescents today are beset by violence in the schools, drugs and alcohol, sexual pressures, unstable families, and uncertainty in their futures. Yet in many ways these cultural traumas of the modern teen resemble those that American teens have always confronted.

The Transition to Adulthood

Beginning in the 1960s, as the first baby boomers reached college age, a growing proportion of college students were remaining financially dependent on their parents into their early twenties. Today, an increasing number of college graduates are returning home for a time to live with their parents. Among men and women eighteen to twenty-four years old, 68.3 percent live with parents or other relatives. About 40 percent in that age group have returned to their parents' home after leaving the nest (Riche, 1990). At the same time, the proportion of young middle-class people who "delay" (according to traditional life-course timetables) commitments to work and family has remained high.

Thus, adolescents today are facing contradictory messages: Many cultural signals tell them to grow up faster, but the lack of opportunities (the right job or mate, affordable housing) makes it difficult to assume complete adult independence as they move into their twenties. As a result, the adolescent years are being stretched out at both ends (Ianni, 1989). Children are being pushed into adolescence earlier and left there longer.

The length of the delay in taking on adult commitments varies from one individual to the next. In fact, there seems to be an increasing diversity in how and when adolescents make the transition to adulthood. In one study, Buchmann (1989) used three events to measure the achievement of adult status: completing one's education, getting married, and having a child. She compared those who graduated from high school in 1960 with those who graduated in 1980. Of the 1960 cohort, 23.4 percent had completed all three status changes within four years after high school graduation, but of the 1980 cohort only 11.0 percent had done so. Indeed, over a third of the more recent cohort had not yet experienced any of the three changes even by the end of the 1980s. Thus, there seems to be increasing variation in the timing and sequencing of events involved in becoming an adult. Buchmann describes this trend as a "partial destandardization" of the transition to adulthood (p. 83).

ADULTHOOD

Once considered a period of relative stability, adulthood is now recognized as a time of continuous challenge and change. Marriage, parenthood, family, and work mean different things to today's adults than they did to their parents and grandparents. And no wonder. As the twenty-first century approaches, Americans are increasingly unlikely to keep the same spouse, job, or home throughout their adult lives.

Erikson (1950, 1982) wrote that the challenge for young adults (ages twenty to forty) is *intimacy versus isolation*. Young adults must partially fuse their own identities with those of other people, forming deep friendships, falling in love and marrying, producing and raising children. The danger is that they will fail to commit themselves to others because they fear a loss of self, and thus they will feel isolated and lonely. In middle adulthood (ages forty to sixty) the challenge is *generativity versus stagnation*. Mature adults either feel that they are making a contribution to the world by being productive in their work and guiding younger generations or feel bored, self-centered, and stagnant. Although Erikson believed that these challenges arose for both men and women, the passage through adulthood is sufficiently different for the two sexes that we will look at them separately here.

Men Grow Up

Daniel Levinson (1978) was a pioneer in the systematic investigation of the adult life cycle, especially the shift from young or early adulthood to middle age. His major study, done in the late 1960s and early 1970s, has been both praised and criticized. He studied only men, aged thirty-five to forty-five, and though he chose his forty subjects from various backgrounds and walks of life (ten business executives, ten hourly wage workers, ten novelists, and ten university biologists), his sample cannot be considered representative of the male population as a whole. Levinson's work, however, was instrumental in turning attention to the life course in adulthood and in altering our conception of this time of life.

Like Erikson, Levinson saw two distinct stages within adulthood: early adulthood and middle age. Each has both stable (or structure-building) periods, in which a man reviews and evaluates his past choices and considers the future, and transition periods, in which he feels suspended between past and future and struggles to bridge the gap. Levinson argued that although the biological age at which men

Many American men are rejecting stereotyped masculine roles and are trying to discover their true maleness by participating in the men's movement.

enter a particular period may vary somewhat, most pass through the same stages in the same order (see Figure 6.3).

In the young man's transition into early adulthood (roughly speaking, during his twenties), he becomes a novice adult with a home base of his own. He begins to make choices about marriage, occupation, residence, and lifestyle that will define his place in the adult world. Around age thirty, these decisions take on a new seriousness. They can no longer be thought of as experimentation; now they are "for real." The late thirties are a time of settling down and settling in—establishing a niche in society, anchoring life more firmly, and advancing in a chosen occupation.

The midlife transition, according to Levinson, usually occurs between ages forty and forty-five. In early adulthood, men are at their physical and mental peak. Now they must face the signs and limitations of advancing age. For 70 to 80 percent of the men Levinson studied, the midlife transition—popularly called the "midlife crisis"—was psychologically wrenching. Suddenly they began to question their marriages, families, and careers. "What have I done with my life? What do I really get from and give to my wife, children, friends, work, community—and self? What is it I truly want for myself and others?" (p. 60). For some, the realization that their youthful dreams might never be realized was particularly agonizing.

Men who negotiated this transition well found middle adulthood the most creative time of their lives. They became more attached to others and more secure in themselves. Echoing Erikson, Levinson believed that the most successful middle-aged men develop generativity. They use their authority creatively and accept paternal responsibility for younger generations.

Other research confirms some of Levinson's findings but qualifies certain aspects of them. For instance, the Grant Study of Adult Development followed 270 Harvard freshmen into adulthood. George Vaillant (1977) interviewed ninety-four of these men at their twenty-fifth college reunion, when they were in their mid-forties, and again in their mid-fifties. (This study is subject to the same criticism as Levinson's is: It focused only on one age cohort of men.) Like Levinson, Vaillant found early adulthood to be a period of launching and consolidating families and careers, and midlife a period of inner turmoil. Indeed, he described midlife as a second adolescence, when "men leave the compulsive unreflective busywork of their occupational apprenticeships, and once more explore the world within"

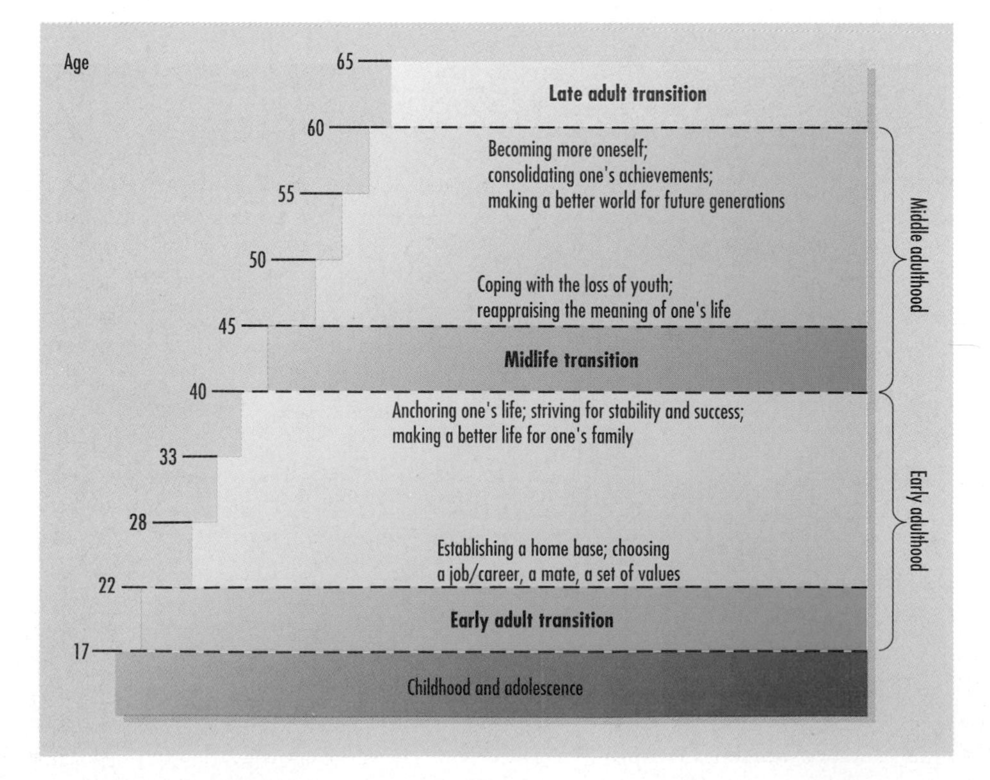

FIGURE 6.3 / Levinson's Adulthood Transition Chart

Source: Adapted from Daniel J. Levinson et al., *The Seasons of a Man's Life* (Knopf, New York, 1978), p. 57.

The "stages" of a woman's life are less clear-cut and more complicated by marriage and parenthood than are those of a man's life. Today's woman is more likely than her Victorian predecessor to be confronted with the decisions involved in juggling the roles of mother, career woman, and homemaker.

(p. 220). Unlike Levinson, however, Vaillant found that the age at which men began questioning their life choices varied by as much as a decade. Some became introspective at thirty; others, at age forty-five, were still struggling with unresolved issues of identity and intimacy (conflicts that Erikson associated with adolescence and early adulthood, not middle age). Vaillant argued that such self-questioning can occur at any point in the life course, and depends more on specific events in a person's life (such as divorce or failure to get a promotion) than on a person's age.

Women Grow Up

Available evidence suggests that the "ages-and-stages" approach may not apply as well to women as it does to men (Rosenfeld and Stark, 1987). This is primarily because the timing of childbearing can vary so much among women, which in turn affects decisions about work and career. A woman who has children in her twenties may not enter the work force until her late thirties, and so she reaches the stage of career consolidation in her middle to late forties, which is ten to fifteen years behind men. Another woman may concentrate on her career in her twenties and postpone motherhood until her thirties. In American society today, knowing a woman's age alone tells you very little about her marital, parental, or occupational status. However, if you also know when she had children and how many she had, this is a very good predictor of her participation in the work force and her occupational advancement (Hanson, 1983).

On the whole, it is not yet clear how the recent influx of women into the labor force and the trend for younger women to combine job and family roles will alter the female life course in adulthood—besides increasing its diversity. At this point, women still tend to be more identified with family life, and more centrally defined by family commitments and priorities, than men are. This is true at all stages of the life course and is not affected by involvement in careers (Lowenthal, Thurnher, and Chiriboga, 1975). The difference, however, is more noticeable at some stages than others. For instance, it tends to be most pronounced in adolescents and middle-aged people and least pronounced in newlyweds and those approaching retirement (Lowenthal et al., 1975). All in all, though, family roles tend to be more central for a woman than they are for a man.

But even if women don't go through specific stages in as predictable a way as men do, they seem to go through similar types of changes in adulthood. According to a longitudinal study of 132 graduates of Mills College, a women's college in California (Helson and Moore, 1987), women became more committed to duties and more self-disciplined in their twenties; more confident, assertive, and achievement-oriented in their thirties; and more generative and involved in affairs outside the family in their forties. This study also found that those women who were not committed either to family or to career changed less over their adult years than did women who were committed to these roles.

OLD AGE

The Abkhasians, a people living in the Caucasus Mountains in the former Soviet republic of Georgia, are famous for their longevity. Many maintain fully active and healthy lives well into their eighties and nineties, and an unusually large number of both men and women live to be over one hundred (Benet, 1976; Garb, 1984). Why?

Biological factors are partly responsible. The Abkhasian genetic makeup programs them for "late-blooming" at each stage of the life course; because of their genes they physically age more slowly and gradually than people elsewhere do. Diet may also make a contribution. Abkhasians eat large quantities of fresh fruits and vegetables, cornmeal and other grains, cottage cheese, and yogurt, while eating little saturated fat or refined sugar. Food is eaten in small quantities throughout the day, and obesity is regarded as an illness. The pace and pressures of life in the modern industrialized world are largely absent in this peasant society of simple farmers, where social change comes slowly. This undoubtedly reduces the Abkhasians' incidence of stress-related illness. Finally, the Abkhasians have no need for exercise gyms or jogging paths. The physical demands of farming and herding help keep them fit to a ripe old age.

The Abkhasians probably also stay active into old age because their ***culture*** *expects* them to do so. There is nothing negative about growing older in this society. The Abkhasians look forward to old age, and most continue to be interested in the world long after the age when most Americans have lost that enthusiasm. This is partly because the elderly are rarely detached from the ongoing life of the community; they remain integrated through networks of friends and kin. Old people are needed and valued among the Abkhasians. Older Abkhasians rarely complain about their physical ailments (according to one of their proverbs, "The ill-tempered don't live long"), nor do they rely on sophisticated health-care facilities to keep them alive. Instead, the everyday care and love from family and friends keep them in good health.

Now compare the life of an Abkhasian elder with this portrait of an elderly person in the United States.

> An older person thinks and moves slowly. He does not think as he used to or as creatively. He is bound to himself and to his past and can no longer change or grow. He can learn neither well nor swiftly and, even if he could, he would not wish to. . . . He dislikes innovations and is not disposed to new ideas. Not only can he not move forward, he often moves backward. He enters a second childhood, caught up in increasing egocentricity and demanding more from his environment than he is willing to give to it. . . . He becomes irritable and cantankerous, yet shallow and enfeebled. He lives in his past; he is behind the times. He is aimless and wandering of mind, reminiscing and garrulous. . . . He is often stricken by disease. . . . He has lost his desire and capacity for sex. His body shrinks, and so too does the flow of blood to his brain. . . . Feeble, uninteresting, he awaits his death, a burden to society, to his family and to himself. (Butler, 1975, p. 7)

Is this your image of life after sixty-five? For many younger Americans it is. As a culture, we idealize and glorify youth, fear and deny the inevitability of aging, and reject the aged. In Erik Erikson's model, the last stage of life—for those over sixty—is marked by the challenge of *integrity versus despair.* One can either work toward accepting oneself and one's past, and integrating the lived life into a coherent whole, or one can regret the past, feel helpless about the future, and fear death to the point of despair. Which culture seems to provide a better context for dealing with this last of Erikson's stages, Abkhasian or American?

Myths and Realities about the Elderly

Happily, the above portrait of old age in the United States seems to bear little resemblance to the actual experiences of later life for most Americans. If old age were as bad as all that, it would be difficult to explain pubic opinion polls which consistently find that people over sixty-five are extraordinarily satisfied with their *present lives* (C. H. Russell, 1989). According to one recent study, people who are sixty-five or older have "significantly higher levels of life satisfaction" when compared with younger people, even when differences in income, education, race, and sex are taken into account (Gove, Ortega, and Style, 1989).

Maybe the image of old people as senile, unproductive, lonely, dependent, inflexible, miserable, and sexless is just that—an image, or myth invented by a culture that defines the twenties or thirties as the prime of life. With this in mind, let us examine in more detail some of the realities of life among the elderly.

The elderly face loneliness and medical infirmity, yet they are also vital creators of new social worlds. The mall walkers shown warming up here have all lost their mates and have moved to a new part of the country, but they have established a new social group that provides them with meaningful social relations and, at the same time, helps them keep fit.

Lifestyles and Personal Relationships

At age ninety-six, Ethel Nixon is always on the go. She lives in a retirement village in California, but still does her own shopping and cleaning, and regularly drives to visit her two sons, five grandchildren, and six great-grandchildren. When Mrs. Nixon appeared on Johnny Carson's "Tonight Show," she became an overnight celebrity. Why? Because she defies the stereotype that people her age are confined to nursing homes, dependent on their middle-aged children, or neglected, abandoned, and alone.

Mrs. Nixon may be unusual in the vigor she shows at nearly one hundred years old, but her self-reliance is far from unique. A majority of the 2.5 million Americans aged eighty-five and older still maintain independent households, even though many are poor and most have no income other than Social Security. Only about 11 percent of those over eighty-five live with their children. Like so many other myths about the aged, the belief that they are a drain on their children's time and finances is generally false. A 1987 poll by Louis Harris & Associates found that older Americans are four times more likely to give financial aid to their children than to receive such aid themselves. Moreover, less than 1 percent of older people say that they would want to live with their children (Horn and Meer, 1987). Apparently, the shift to an "empty nest" is associated with significant improvements in marital happiness for parents (White and Edwards, 1990).

This self-reliance does not mean that the elderly necessarily feel cut off from their children. Many stay in close contact with their children, and both sides may derive satisfaction from the relationship. Friends, too, continue to be important sources of satisfaction and social support for older Americans. In one study, half the older subjects said that they had between eleven and forty friends on whom they could call for assistance in their daily lives (Quadagno, 1986). These relationships were reciprocal: Someone who had a car would drive friends to church or to the shopping mall; another would make a larger cake or pot of soup than she needed and share the surplus with her neighbors; still another would regularly read to a friend who had trouble with her eyes. The elderly do not see themselves as lonely, although many younger people assume they are. In one study, 88 percent of those over sixty-five did not think loneliness was a problem for them (C. H. Russell, 1989).

A small minority of the elderly ensure that they have an adequate social circle by living in retirement communities. This choice of lifestyle seems to have some benefits. Most studies show that people in retirement communities

CHAPTER 7

Deviance and Crime

Ivan Boesky was a classic example of the great American success story. The son of a Russian immigrant, he struggled to earn a degree from the Detroit School of Law. After serving unhappy stints as a law clerk and an accountant, he landed a job on Wall Street at the age of twenty-nine (G. Russell, 1986b). His wealthy father-in-law, who was then paying Boesky's rent, nicknamed him "Ivan the Bum." By age forty-nine, however, Boesky had amassed a personal fortune estimated at $200 million. On Wall Street he became known as "Ivan the Terrible."

Boesky rode to fortune on the wave of a new business phenomenon—the corporate takeover—that changed the very nature of American business. Rather than dealing directly with the officers of a company they sought to acquire, corporate "raiders" would purchase the target company's stock on the open market, often buying a controlling share before anyone realized what was happening. When news of a potential takeover became public, the price of stock would jump as the raiders and the company's management vied for control.

A superstar of takeover finance, Boesky had an uncanny ability to anticipate takeovers before they happened. For example, between May 22 and May 29, 1985, Boesky bought 377,000 shares of Nabisco Corporation. On May 30, Nabisco and R. J. Reynolds announced a merger, and Boesky sold his Nabisco shares for a profit of $4 million (G. Russell, 1986a). Boesky attributed his success at predicting takeovers to a combination of instinct and information. In fact, as was later revealed, his success was the result of fraud.

One of the rules of the investment business, enforced by the Securities and Exchange Commission (SEC), is that "insiders" are not allowed to profit from information that is unavailable to the general public. Boesky violated this rule on a grand scale. He agreed to pay investment banker David Levine huge sums for advance notice of takeover bids. When Levine was charged with insider trading in August 1986, he named Boesky as an accomplice. Over the next several months, with Boesky's cooperation, investigations revealed a web of insider trading—complete with Caribbean bank accounts, midnight raids on investment bankers' desk drawers, secret passwords, and briefcases loaded with cash (Sterngold, 1987). By spring, all of Wall Street was reacting to the discovery of deviance within its ranks.

Deviance is any action that is perceived as violating some widely shared norm of a society's or group's culture. As such, deviance is not just a matter of what is atypical or uncommon. (Sky diving, for instance, is uncommon, but it is not deviant.) For a behavior to be considered deviant, it must be seen as violating some socially defined standard. Since some standards are codified into law while others are not, deviance includes both criminal behavior (like Boesky's) and behavior that, although not illegal, is widely viewed as unethical, immoral, peculiar, unrespectable, or "sick."

Acts of deviance vary in how serious they are believed to be. Some generate strong public disapproval, while others are shrugged off. People who commit acts of deviance looked upon as very serious are often negatively labeled as "nuts," "sluts," "crooks," or "perverts." Those whose deviant behaviors are considered minor are viewed as "normal" people who occasionally lapse. So-called minor acts of deviance are very common. How many people do you know who never failed to return a library book or stole pens and paper from the office where they work? How many people do you know who never ran a red light, told a lie, or cheated on their income taxes? Clearly, when we include such minor violations of norms, as well as major ones, deviance is extremely widespread.

Acts of deviance can be analyzed in terms of our five key concepts. A deviant behavior is usually a ***social action*** in that it is oriented toward or coordinated with the actions of other people. Ivan Boesky's insider trading, for example, was both coordinated with the behavior of his accomplice David Levine and committed in response to the financial dealings of corporate managers and investors.

An act of deviance is, by definition, a violation of a norm of one's ***culture***. Boesky violated the norm that securities brokers are not allowed to use inside information to reap personal profits. This norm fosters another element of American culture: an attitude of trust in the financial system, a belief that this system is run with integrity and adherence to ethical standards. The discovery of insider trading involving Boesky and others shook the foundations of this cultural trust.

Deviance almost always involves ***power*** relations. The illegal use of inside information increases the power of dishonest brokers on Wall Street. In a modern economy such as that of the United States, both information and money are sources of power that can be turned to deviant uses. We will discuss the link between deviance and power more fully a little later in this chapter.

Deviant behavior takes place within the context of a ***social structure***—that is, within patterns of social relationships and social positions. Wall Street has a social structure that makes insider trading possible. A small number of investment brokers buy and sell billions of dollars'

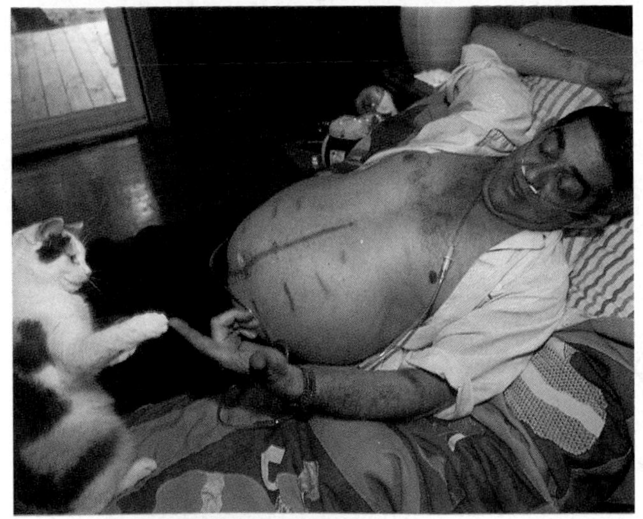

We typically think of deviance as relatively clear-cut instances of "right" or "wrong" behavior by individuals. Sociologists, however, suggest that deviance is much more complex and is always socially constructed. Thus, we can interpret these three photographs as examples of the unfortunate consequences of capitalism, or we can see them as depictions of the irresponsible use of natural resources (American corporations spend a tiny percentage of what other industrial countries spend to reclaim strip-mined land), the exploitation of wage labor (the back-breaking labor of workers creates huge profits for the coal industry), and the injury of workers (black lung disease is common among coal miners).

worth of securities. The elite members of this group all know one another, eat lunch at the same restaurants, and socialize at the same private clubs. They also have access to inside information about the corporate world by virtue of their social and family ties to the men who sit on corporate boards of directors. In this kind of tightly knit social structure, opportunities for insider trading abound.

The social structure in which deviance takes place often forms a ***functionally integrated*** system. The trading of stocks and bonds, for instance, is an integral part of the financial system on which American capitalism is based. Without an open market for the buying and selling of securities, large corporations couldn't raise the money they need to operate and expand. Acts of deviance within this system, like Boesky's insider trading, are a source of dysfunction that can upset the system's balance. But deviance, somewhat surprisingly, can also serve positive functions, a fact that we will explain in a later section.

In the rest of this chapter we look at deviance from a sociological perspective, often drawing on one or more of these key concepts to help us analyze and understand this complex phenomenon. In the first section we delve more deeply into the nature of deviance. We see how deviance is relative to different times, groups, and situations, how it involves power relations, serves important social functions, and entails a process of labeling the deviant. In the second section we consider different explanations of why some people behave deviantly more than others do. In the last section, we focus on crime, criminal justice, and the use of imprisonment to punish those who break the law.

THE NATURE OF DEVIANCE

Deviance Is a Matter of Social Definition

Deviance exists only in relation to the social norms that prevail in a particular place, time, group, and situation. Deviance, in other words, is in the eye of the beholder; it is a matter of *social definition.* As such, no behavior is inherently deviant. Deviance is a property that people confer on some forms of behavior because of the norms they have established and consider "good" and "right."

Variations in the Social Definition of Deviance

That deviance is a matter of social definition is revealed by the many variations in what is considered deviant (see Table 7.1). In the United States, for instance, what is considered deviant varies between different ethnic groups (to many Asians and Hispanics, for instance, failure to care at home for an elderly parent is considered the worst kind of deviance, but it is more accepted among whites); between different social classes (in urban ghettoes a young girl who gets pregnant is not likely to be considered deviant, but in middle-class settings she is); between different occupational groups (dating a patient is considered deviant for a psychoanalyst, but not for a dentist); between different geographic regions (in New York City it is deviant to greet strangers on the street, but in a small town in Georgia it is not); and between the two sexes (girls who regularly get into fistfights are considered much more deviant than boys who do the same). Thus, whether a particular act is considered deviant or not depends upon the socially defined norms of the group in which it occurs.

Deviance, moreover, varies not just from group to group but also from situation to situation even within the same group. For instance, in our society (and most others) killing is an act of deviance, *except* in self-defense or when the victim is a wartime enemy (Ben-Yehuda, 1985). Similarly, because the norms of societies and groups change over time, so do their definitions of deviance. For example, not too long ago in the United States living together with-

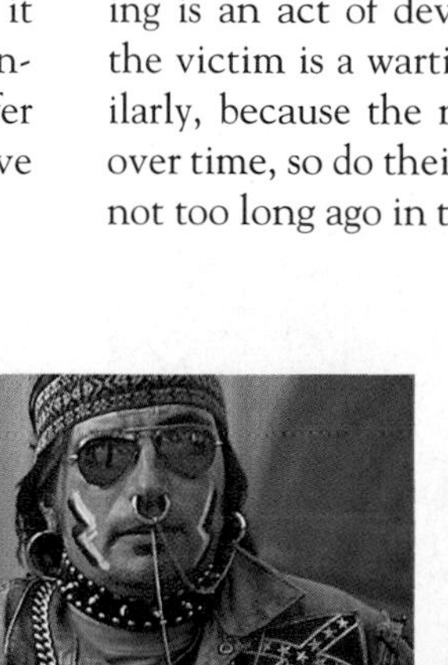

Behavior considered deviant in one culture may be considered normal in another. While the ornaments worn by these two people are strikingly similar, the person on the left is considered deviant by a large percentage of people in American society, while the ornamentation on the person on the right marks his normality in his social group.

out being married was widely considered deviant—even grounds for expulsion from college. Today, in contrast, many people find cohabitation socially acceptable, especially if the couple is young, childless, and heterosexual.

Changes in definitions of deviance are an important part of social change. Some occur when social norms gradually shift in response to changing conditions. The expansion of civil rights, for instance, has helped to ease strict norms against interracial dating. Other changes in definitions of deviance are more a matter of struggle, such as the struggle of gay men and lesbians to end condemnation of their sexual preferences and lifestyles. Much is at stake in struggles like these, for behavior defined as deviant is generally punished. Sometimes it is punished by making it a crime and using the government's law enforcement power to restrain it. Other times punishment is informal, as when people who object to interracial dating stare disapprovingly at interracial couples or make derogatory comments within their hearing. When definitions of deviance change so that previously impermissible behavior is more acceptable, people who engage in that behavior are less often targets of punishment.

Social Definitions of Deviance: The Case of Inner-City Gangs

That deviance is a matter of social definition—that it exists in the eye of the beholder and is not absolute—is clearly illustrated in the case of inner-city gangs. The term *inner-city gang* strikes fear in the minds of most middle-class Americans. Gangs to them are by definition lawless and deviant, perpetrators of often brutal acts of violence against rival gangs and others who are targets of their hate. There are parts of virtually every major city in the United States where middle-class citizens dare not walk for fear of being attacked by gangs. And yet, on the basis of a ten-year study of gangs in New York, Boston, and Los Angeles, Martin Sánchez Jankowski (1991) argues that gangs are *not* always considered deviant in their own social worlds. In the poor, minority neighborhoods in which gangs exist, residents often view gangs as normal aspects of everyday life.

Young men in these communities join gangs because to do so makes sense to them. They see it as a rational way of getting a larger share of the things they want in an environment of chronic scarcity and deprivation. Young men in inner cities want many of the same things that other Americans do: money, respect, and a sense of security. But their social situation makes these resources hard to obtain. American society has created ghettoes for members of ethnic minorities, and ghettoes offer few legitimate ways to fulfill ordinary wants. Gangs try to circumvent this problem. They attempt to create an effective social organization to deal with the pressures and challenges of living in some of the most difficult circumstances in American society. From this viewpoint, gang membership is not a sign of social disorganization, an absence of values, or a psychological defect. It is instead an effort to achieve widely desired goals.

TABLE 7.1

The Cultural Relativity of Deviance

Type of Act	PERCENTAGE WHO THINK ACT SHOULD BE PROHIBITED BY LAW[a]				
	India	Iran	Italy (Sardinia)	U.S.	Yugoslavia
Public, nonviolent political protest	33	77	35	6	46
Failure to help another person in danger	45	56	80	28	77
Air pollution caused by a factory	99	98	96	96	92

[a]*Percentages have been rounded off.*

Source: Adapted from Graeme Newman, Comparative Deviance: Perception and Law in Six Cultures *(Elsevier, New York, 1976), p. 116, table 4.*

For instance, membership in a gang increases a young man's chances of getting money on a regular basis from "business deals" in the community (usually illegal activities). At the same time, a gang gives its members anonymity in dealing with police. They are no longer separate individuals pulling off a deal; they are submerged in the protective cover of the group. Gangs also provide members and their families with aid in times of economic hardship. Street Dog, a fifteen-year-old gang member, explained this benefit to Jankowski:

> Hey, the club [gang] has been there when I needed help. There were times when there just wasn't enough food for me to get filled up with. My family was hard up and they just couldn't manage all of their bills and such, so there was some lean meals! Well I just needed some money to help for awhile. . . . They [the gang] was there to help. (Jankowski, 1991, p. 42)

In addition, there is the physical protection that gangs provide their members. When a young man is in a gang, others are less likely to threaten or harass him:

> Man, I joined the Fultons because there are a lot of people out there who are trying to get you and if you don't got protection you in trouble sometimes. My homeboys [fellow gang members] gave me protection, so hey, they were the thing to do. . . . Now that I got some business things going I can concentrate on them and not worry so much. I don't always have to look over my shoulder. (Jankowski, 1991, p. 45)

Finally, there is the social life that urban gangs offer. A gang has a clubhouse with a bar and a gameroom (pool tables, pinball machines, video games) and a place to hold parties. To Fox, a twenty-three-year-old who had been a member of the Bats for seven years, this social life, and the esteem that it afforded, was an important reason for joining:

> [A]ll the foxy ladies were going to [the Bats'] parties and hanging with them. Plus the parties were great. . . . Man, it was a great source of dope and women. Hell, they were the kings of the community so I wanted to get in on some of the action. (Jankowski, 1991, p. 43)

Jankowski stresses that those who join gangs are not marginal members of their communities and not rebels who reject the norms and values that exist there. In fact, they are *more* likely than those who don't join gangs to possess character traits admired in inner-city ghettoes. These traits include strong competitiveness, mistrust and wariness of others, self-reliance in getting what one wants, a tendency to maintain social distance and to fight for survival, and a defiant air when dealing with those who impose obstacles. Notice that these traits aren't opposite to those admired in mainstream American culture. The American ideal has always included the "rugged individualist"—tough, self-reliant, self-confident, ready to defy any challenge. These are the very traits that we find in gang members, just exaggerated by the experience of growing up in a world in which people must fight for everything they get.

The exaggerated toughness and self-reliance admired in the urban ghetto go hand in hand with acceptance of certain behaviors often considered deviant in other parts of American society. Take violence and aggression, for instance. In poor inner-city neighborhoods, where people must struggle for survival, showing that you are tough and ready to defend your rights is considered a key to avoiding being preyed upon by others. In the words of Jinx, a sixteen-year-old New York gang member:

> Take BiBi there. That man is got a reputation for being one tough dude. Nobody messes with him because the word's out that he's too much. You see he hardly ever gets into fights anywhere because of his rep. In fact, I ain't seen him ever fight. A lot of members don't get into fights 'cause they got reps, so that's what we all trying to do. You see, if you got yourself a rep, you don't have to worry as much as if you don't. (Jankowski, 1991, p. 143)

Of course, to get a reputation you must at some point earn it by showing your capacity for violence. As a result, a high level of violence is more common in the inner city than in the typical middle-class American community. This high level of violence is one of the greatest threats to young African-American and Hispanic men and the neighborhoods in which they live. Thus, a response that makes sense for the individual is not necessarily good for the group as a whole.

Just as violence and aggression are more accepted in the urban ghetto than elsewhere in American society, so too are theft and other illegal means of "getting ahead." In a world in which there are few opportunities to "make it" through legal means, capitalizing on illegal opportunities is regarded as a perfectly normal thing to do. Most gang members, in fact, see themselves as entrepreneurs, not much different from those who "hustle" in the corporate world. As Arrow, an eighteen-year-old gang member, explained when asked about ethics in his business dealings:

> Hey, man, what do you mean by ethics? Ethics don't pay bills, money pays bills, and I'm hustling to get money. There ain't nobody interested in ethics, morality, and all that shit—the bottom line is, did you make money or not? . . . Hey, it's dog eat dog, and if you ain't up to it, you get eaten, simple as that! And look at the corporate businesses, they ain't moral or ethical, they never have been and they ain't about to be either, 'cause they only know that they want money. Since nobody complains about them, nobody should complain about us. (Jankowski, 1991, p. 103)

People do complain, though, including people in the gang's own neighborhood. Church and community development groups argue that gangs stand in the way of community progress, not only because they increase levels of violence but also because the money they take often comes from the community and goes for the gangs' private purposes. These criticisms of gangs are sometimes greater in African-American communities, where gangs are somewhat likelier to be separate from other community organizations and to engage in high levels of violence, such as drive-by shootings. In Hispanic communities, in contrast, gangs have been more closely integrated into other social institutions, and their violence, therefore, has been somewhat more restrained.

Despite complaints about gangs, many inner-city residents still understand why young people join them. Orlando, a thirty-three-year old father of five employed as an apartment-house doorman, explained his view of gangs this way:

> Those who are in gangs do a lot of things that [outsiders] think is terrible, but I'm not against them because I know how they feel. You see they are just not going to sit around and accept what society says is your place. They going to resist that stuff all the time. . . . So I don't get down on them because I know how frustrating it can be to think that all you going to have in life is poverty. (Jankowski, 1991, p. 182)

Sometimes, gangs are actively accepted and appreciated by community members for the protection they provide, especially from drug addicts, loan sharks, unethical landlords or store owners, and other outsiders who try to rip off community residents. Wilma, a forty-eight-year-old resident of a poor neighborhood, is typical in her positive feelings:

> Well, the gangs have protected me and my family a couple of times when we were getting attacked by some dope addicts. They just came over and boy did they beat those guys. They beat them with clubs and chains and they didn't show any mercy. . . . You know that isn't nice, but it works and works better than the police, because with the police, they have to be concerned with the criminal's rights and all that. And even if they do catch them, nothing ever happens to them because the courts let them back on the street to do it all over again. But the gangs don't have to worry about rights and that stuff and they let criminals know that if they come back they can expect exactly the same or worse. . . . People can think what they want, but this has worked here. (Jankowski, 1991, p. 185)

Thus, in order to understand inner-city gangs, we need to realize that in a sense they are social organizations trying to cope with the fear, deprivation, and frustration of poverty-stricken neighborhoods. Gangs are functionally integrated into their social settings, and they are unlikely to disappear as long as those settings continue to be excluded from most of the benefits of American society. This view of gangs stresses that they are not simply groups of people who think and behave deviantly. Whether or not a gang's actions are considered deviant is a matter of social perspective. In inner-city ghettoes, gangs are considered more acceptable than they are in middle- and upper-class American communities. This is because inner-city residents are immersed in the world in which gangs exist and so are more likely to accept the norms by which gangs operate. Gangs, in other words, are not *always* looked upon as deviant. Definitions of deviance are relative to the particular time, place, and situation.

Deviance Can Serve Social Functions

The key concept of ***functional integration***, as we said before, can help us to analyze and understand deviance. Not only does deviance sometimes disrupt well-integrated social systems, but it can also, in the process, serve some positive social functions. Émile Durkheim (1895/1982), one of sociology's founders, was the first to discuss this seeming paradox. Durkheim argued that deviance is a natural part of social life, indeed "an integral part of all healthy societies" (1895/1982, p. 67). What did he mean by this? How can deviance be healthy for societies?

Durkheim's answer has two parts. First, in defining certain kinds of behavior as deviant, a group or community also defines what behavior is acceptable. The boundaries between acceptable and unacceptable are rarely hard and fast. Societies typically have a "permissive zone of variation" (in Durkheim's words) surrounding even strongly supported and quite specific norms. Most norms, however, are not expressed in highly specific ways. Rather, they are defined informally in the course of people's day-to-day activities. By testing the boundaries of permissiveness, deviants force other members of society to think about what they believe is normal and right.

Deviance can also serve a positive function by uniting a society's members in opposition to the deviant, thus reaffirming their social solidarity. When people in the Old West formed a posse, when parents unite to fight a pornography shop in their town, when citizens vote for a new, more honest politician, they are united by a sense of shared courage against a deviant—the outlaw who stole their horses, the merchant who opened the pornography store, the unethical politician who accepted bribes. Public opposition to and punishment of deviants not only reaffirm norms that were threatened but also allow members of a community to pour their collective energy into shoring up the social order.

Like the outlaw, the crooked politician, and the pornography merchant, the men arrested for insider trading on Wall Street performed positive functions for society through their acts of deviance. In the 1980s, the financial community underwent rapid and profound change. A revolution in personal computers and telecommunications allowed brokers to engage in new activities for which few rules had been written. The scandal involving Boesky and others provided an opportunity to stop and consider the boundaries of acceptable trading in stocks and bonds, and to reaffirm the ethical framework in which the financial community operates. In 1988, President Ronald Reagan signed into law the Insider Trading and Securities Fraud Enforcement Act. It was designed to ensure fuller disclosures on the part of brokers and investment advisers and to strengthen enforcement of prohibitions against insider trading. The search for unethical "insider" dealings has since been extended to other areas of public concern, such as savings and loan associations.

Just as deviance may help people reaffirm norms that are threatened, it may also serve as a catalyst for social change. This was true of acts in defiance of racial segregation during the 1950s. Earlier social changes encouraged such defiance. Throughout the first half of the twentieth century, African-Americans became increasingly integrated into the American economy. World War II saw many black Americans fighting alongside whites. Both economic and military integration made social segregation in schools, housing, transportation, and public facilities harder to accept. Some African-Americans responded by simply refusing to comply. Thus in 1955, when Rosa Parks of Montgomery, Alabama, refused to move to the back of a bus where blacks were required to sit, she engaged in an individual act of defiance and deviance. But this time, white attempts to punish the deviant and force her compliance did not have the usual effect of reaffirming traditional norms. Instead, Mrs. Parks's action became part of a wider movement to bring the social position of African-Americans into line with other aspects of social change. (We discuss the black civil rights movement in more detail in Chapter 21.)

Whether deviance leads to reaffirmation of existing norms or serves as a catalyst for new ones depends in part on the type of society in which that deviance occurs (Ben-Yehuda, 1985). The structure of simple, traditional societies tends to produce a high degree of consensus regarding acceptable behavior. In such societies, the punishment of deviance usually leads to increased commitment to the status quo. Complex, modern societies, in contrast, tend to be heterogeneous—that is, there are many competing lifestyles and moral points of view. "In such societies, values, norms, and moral boundaries are not given; they are negotiated" (Ben-Yehuda, 1985, p. 15). As a result, deviance can often lead to a renegotiation of norms and promote social change.

Definitions of Deviance Reflect Power Relations

If deviance is relative to the norms that exist in a particular time, place, and situation, an important question is, *Whose* norms prevail in society as a whole? That is, which particular people in a society have the ***power*** to define what the mainstream norms will be, and what behaviors deviate from them?

In American society, both wealth and race help determine who holds the power to influence definitions of deviance. For example, the activities of inner-city gangs are widely defined as deviant because middle- and upper-class whites have the power to label them such. Typically, the label of deviant is applied to those with relatively little power. Even when the powerful do significant damage to individuals and society, people are slow to label them deviant. For instance, although wealthy savings and loan executives defrauded Americans of over $200 million in the 1980s, deviant labels were not quickly or widely applied to them.

The relatively powerless who are more likely to be labeled deviant are not necessarily poor and nonwhite. For centuries men have had the power to label as deviants women who try to redefine the socially imposed boundaries of female behavior. Even women who are victims of rape, abuse by their husbands, or sexual harassment at work, and who dare to protest too loudly, have been labeled deviant.

Women now have more power than they did to contest these traditional male definitions, but the problem persists because men continue to hold most of the positions of greatest social power in American society. Thus, when Vice President Dan Quayle criticized the television show "Murphy Brown" because the central character became a single mother, he was attempting to use the power of his office to promote the norm that only married women should bear children and to define unmarried motherhood as deviant.

Karl Marx believed that a small ruling class of economic elites determines moral norms (and thus definitions of deviance) because moral norms can be used to support the existing economic order. According to Marx, the severity of society's response to the violation of its norms depends on how much the violation threatens established power relations. For example, drug addiction was widely tolerated by American elites as long as it affected mainly the poor and ethnic minorities. However, once drug use and drug-related problems increased among middle-class whites, social action against drugs intensified (Ben-Yehuda, 1990). Part of what happened was that the drug trade had become so large and profitable that those involved in it began to undermine the control of traditional power bases. The result was an effort on the part of elites to stop this encroachment.

Thus, viewed from the Marxist and other sociological perspectives that focus on power, law is a reflection first and foremost of the interests of the governing class (Chambliss and Seidman, 1972). The criminal justice system, according to this view, reflects the values and interests of those who have the power to control the legislatures, police, and courts. This perspective contrasts sharply with the ideal of justice as blind to differences in social power. How accurate an image of American society does this perspective paint? Does the American justice system often give special treatment to the powerful, sometimes to the point of ignoring the general good of the people?

Sociologist Amitai Etzioni estimates that two-thirds of America's 500 largest corporations break the law, in varying degrees, during any ten-year period (in Gellerman, 1986). In one case that has taken decades to resolve, investigators described the crimes of the Manville Corporation as a kind of murder. Manville was one of the oldest and largest manufacturers of asbestos in America. Evidence that exposure to asbestos dust causes debilitating, often fatal, lung disease began appearing in medical journals in the late 1920s. Executives at Manville knew about this information, but did nothing to warn or protect workers. To the contrary, they suppressed research on the dangers of working with asbestos, instructed company physicians not to tell workers when their chest x-rays showed symptoms of asbestosis, and quietly settled workers' claims out of court. This cover-up continued for forty years and resulted in numerous deaths (Calhoun and Hiller, 1988). And yet, during all that time, no legal force was brought to bear on Manville to change its policy toward asbestos. Apparently, the company's size and power influenced how it was treated under the law. Often, then, the degree to which a given act is viewed as deviant is a factor not of the amount of harm it causes, but of the power of those who have stepped across the line.

Of course, the power of elites is never complete. Especially in a democratic society that tends to be pluralistic, there are usually opportunities for groups outside the governing class to exert some influence on what is considered deviant. Beginning in the 1960s, for example, consumer protection groups (such as Ralph Nader's Center for Science in the Public Interest) began effectively to lobby the federal government to protect consumers against dangerous products, like asbestos and cancer-causing food additives. A current example is public pressure leading to stronger rules against cigarette smoking, despite objections by the corporations that profit from the sale of cigarettes. Thus, it is possible for the public, with enough collective effort, to define even the actions of powerful elites as deviant.

Deviance Is a Matter of Labeling

According to a sociological perspective called **labeling theory**, being labeled deviant has long-term consequences for a person's social identity (Lemert, 1951). It is central to turning **primary deviance** (an initial violation of a social norm, about which no inferences are made regarding a person's character) into **secondary deviance** (violations of norms that have become part of a person's lifestyle because that person thinks of the self as deviant due to other people's opinions). Primary deviance occurs all the time. Nearly everyone breaks the law occasionally or acts a little "odd" at times, but most people do not think of themselves as deviant. However, a small number of primary deviants are singled out and labeled as "criminal," "mentally ill," "homosexual," and so forth. Typically, people who have been given such labels are then excluded from the mainstream of life. The man who has been labeled a criminal cannot get an honest job; the woman who has been labeled a lesbian loses custody of her young children; and so on. This social rejection helps encourage the labeled people to define themselves as deviant and adopt a deviant lifestyle. In doing so, they are embracing the role that other people expect of them (Goffman, 1963). The labeling theory of deviance is an outgrowth of the social-interactionist perspective, which holds that people's self-concepts are largely the product of how they think *others* perceive them. In terms of the key concepts, a deviant label is a function of ***culture***; labeling is a ***social action*** that involves the exercise of ***power***.

Sociologist William Chambliss (1973) found the labeling process at work in the Missouri high school where he spent two years as an observer. Chambliss identified two cliques of boys at the school, which he nicknamed the Saints and the Roughnecks. The eight members of the Saints came from upper-middle-class families, were good students, and were active in school affairs. On weekends and on days when they cut classes, the Saints amused themselves with various forms of delinquency: heavy drinking, reckless driving, petty theft, vandalism, and games of "chicken." The people of the town considered them good boys who were sowing a few wild oats. The police didn't arrest one Saint in the two years Chambliss observed them. The six Roughnecks, in contrast, came from lower-class families and were not particularly good students. Most weekends they could be found hanging around the local drugstore, drinking alcohol from concealed bottles. About once a month they got into a fight (usually among themselves), they engaged in petty theft, and thus were constantly in trouble with the police. The townspeople considered them good-for-nothings.

Why did the townspeople excuse the Saints but condemn the Roughnecks? The Saints dressed well, drove expensive cars, and spoke politely to teachers, police, and other authority figures. Anyone could see that they were "good boys," tomorrow's leaders. The Roughnecks were different: "Everybody agreed that the not-so-well-dressed, not-so-well-mannered, not-so-rich boys were heading for trouble" (Chambliss, 1973, p. 27). In addition, the police knew that the Saints' parents would cause trouble if their sons were arrested, whereas the Roughnecks' parents lacked the power and influence to fight back. In short, the community's ***social structure*** (its social-class system) and its distribution of ***power*** protected the Saints but not the Roughnecks. Through selective perception and labeling, the poor, defiant "tough kids" were identified as "delinquents," whereas the equally delinquent upper-middle-class youth with socially influential parents were not.

With few exceptions, the members of both the Saints and the Roughnecks responded to the differential labeling by meeting the community's expectations. Several members of the Roughnecks were arrested repeatedly, not only as teenagers but also as young adults. In contrast, the Saints left adolescence behind them, moved along upper-middle-class pathways, and remembered their teenage delinquency fondly as a youthful fling.

These workers are moving toxic waste to a safe location. The corporate crime of dumping dangerous chemicals is widespread in the United States. The cost of the cleanup, paid for out of the Superfund, is ultimately borne by consumers—an example of how the costs of doing business in the United States are socialized while the profits remain private.

As this example suggests, deviant labels tend to become self-fulfilling prophecies (Merton, 1968a). This may happen even to children stigmatized by the labels their parents are given (Hagan and Palloni, 1990). The labeling process pushes people toward a deviant career, the adoption of a deviant lifestyle, and identity within a deviant subculture. Being cut off socially plays a key role in this outcome. Shunned by the mainstream, the addict begins to associate almost exclusively with other addicts, the prostitute with other prostitutes, the delinquent with other delinquents. Gradually they learn from more experienced offenders the various techniques for deviating. Equally important, they learn rationalizations for deviant behavior. Prostitutes, for example, grow to regard their work as a social service and consider those who condemn sex for money as hypocrites. Thus, by labeling certain people deviant and shutting them out of conventional life, society virtually ensures the behavior that it is trying to prevent.

Although labeling theory sheds some valuable light on how people drift into deviant careers, critics charge that it overstates some of the facts. Consider the mentally ill, for example. Labeling theory by itself would imply that the people who fill the wards of mental hospitals are there because someone decided, more or less arbitrarily, to label them sick. This image of rather arbitrary labeling overlooks the fact that most of the people in mental hospitals were unable to cope with their daily lives. Thus, they may have been labeled sick by others, which helped to seal their fate, but that label was not necessarily unwarranted. Sociological studies show that both families and authorities usually consider commitment to a mental hospital a last resort (Gove, 1975, 1979). Labeling theory thus needs to be supplemented with other explanations of deviance.

EXPLAINING WHO BECOMES DEVIANT

It is clear that the social definition of what is deviant varies with time, place, and situation. And labeling theory helps to explain why similar behaviors—like teenage drinking—are overlooked for the members of some groups but made the basis of a deviant label and possible deviant career for others. In some cases, however, there is widespread agreement that a certain behavior—from embezzling money to committing incest or murder—is deviant. Why do some people engage in such deviant acts, while others do not? Can we predict with reasonable accuracy who will behave deviantly and who won't? In answering these questions, we will look at four factors: a person's *nature* (his or her inherent traits), the *socialization* that he or she has experienced, aspects of *social structure* that cause strain on certain individuals, and *insufficient social control* that selectively affects particular people.

Looking at Nature

Over the years, many attempts have been made to explain who behaves deviantly in terms of people's inherent natures. In the nineteenth century, for example, Cesare Lombroso, an Italian criminologist, looked at the shape of criminals' skulls for evidence that they shared inherited deviant tendencies. His investigation suggested that many criminals had high cheekbones, large jaws, and prominent brow ridges, similar to the facial characteristics of apes. To Lombroso, this confirmed that criminals were throwbacks to an earlier stage of evolution, "savages" among civilized people. Lombroso made one fatal error, however. He examined only the skulls of criminals, not a representative sample of the entire population. Some years later, when the British physician Charles Goring compared the skulls of criminals with those of ordinary citizens, he found no difference between the two (Goring, 1913). Other evidence also supports the idea that criminals are generally "made," not born. For instance, Australia began as a British penal colony, and many present-day Australians are descended from this largely criminal population; yet modern Australians don't have a particularly high crime rate—so they don't seem to have inherited criminal tendencies (R. Hughes, 1987).

It would be a mistake, however, to conclude that biology plays no role in deviance. Recent advances in genetics, biochemistry, and neuropsychology have led to renewed scientific interest in biological explanations of deviance. Evidence is mounting that certain forms of deviance, especially mental disorders, are at least partly biological in origin (Moffitt, 1987; Moffitt and Mednick, 1988; Wender and Klein, 1981). For instance, people who suffer from schizophrenia inherit a neurological vulnerability to the disorder. When under stress, the nervous systems of these individuals overreact, creating chemical imbalances that lead to disordered thinking, hallucinations, and other symptoms. A similar pattern has been found in people with bipolar disorder (formerly called "manic depression"), who experience extreme mood swings. If genetic and biochemical abnormalities explain these deviations from normal behavior, it is reasonable to suspect that biology may play a role in certain other forms of deviance as well (Kamin, 1986; J. Q. Wilson, 1983).

Looking at Socialization

The way people are socialized—what they are taught about the norms and values of their culture—helps to determine who behaves deviantly. For instance, Sigmund Freud, the founder of psychoanalysis, argued that most people learn in the process of growing up how to inhibit or productively channel their innate drives toward pleasure and aggression. Some children, however, lack an appropriate adult with whom to identify, an adult whose moral norms and values they can adopt as their own. Such children, according to Freud's theory, fail to develop a strong superego, the part of the psyche that serves as a conscience in guiding behavior. These are the people who Freud believed are especially prone to deviance.

Social-learning theorists have studied how people learn deviant behaviors by observing and imitating others who behave deviantly, especially those they admire and respect. In one classic study, Albert Bandura and Richard Walters (1959) compared groups of delinquent and nondelinquent boys from financially stable homes. They found that the most aggressive boys typically came from families in which the parents encouraged or condoned aggression, sometimes unwittingly. Often the parents' own behavior, such as the use of physical punishment, served as an aggressive model that the children could copy when frustrated or angry. Bandura (1977, 1986) contends that repeated exposure to models of aggressive behavior helps explain why some people commit violent acts of deviance.

A more social-structural addition to learning theory is contained in the theory of **differential association**. This theory holds that people who behave deviantly tend to form social bonds with other deviants, from whom they learn deviant norms and values. According to this perspective, deviant behavior is produced by the same processes of socialization as conforming behavior is (Gaylord and Galliher, 1988; Sutherland, 1949). Every social group transmits its own cultural norms and values to new members through family influences and peer pressure. The new members adopt these norms and values as their own because they are immersed in them through close association with the group. Of course, when the norms of their own group contradict those of the larger society, especially regarding important moral issues, the new members are being socialized into a deviant subculture. Thus, through differential association with deviants, people can be socialized to a drug subculture, a delinquent gang subculture, an insider-trading subculture on Wall Street, or any number of other deviant lifestyles.

In his classic study of marijuana users, Howard Becker (1963) explored the role of differential association in acquiring a deviant habit. (Becker was writing at a time when marijuana was widely considered as dangerous as heroin and when use of the drug had not yet spread to the middle class.) He found that whether or not someone became a marijuana user depended on how much that person participated in the marijuana subculture. The more participation, the closer the social ties, the more likely that deviant drug use would develop. What did initiates to the marijuana subculture learn from those already in it? For one thing, they learned the norms of drug-using behavior. For instance, the first time people smoked marijuana, most

A pickup basketball game is harmless fun but, ironically, this kind of peer association creates loyalty and commitment that can easily be distorted if the group evolves into an adolescent gang. The positive feeling of belonging may become the basis for violent behavior if the gang feels that its turf or its members are threatened.

had either no reaction or an unpleasant one (spatial disorientation, sound distortion, extreme thirst, and so forth). Experienced users had to teach initiates how to smoke a joint, cultivate its effects, and learn to enjoy them. In addition, initiates to the marijuana subculture learned from experienced users the "right" attitudes to adopt. These included the belief that people who condemn marijuana are inappropriate role models (they are "squares" or "straights") and the belief that marijuana use is really all right because of the pleasure it brings. Thus, close association with experienced users was essential in order for this deviant behavior to be instilled.

Adolescents are particularly open to learning the norms, attitudes, and values of any subculture to which they are exposed—including one involved in deviance. As Akers (1985, p. 148) puts it, "The single best predictor of adolescent behavior, conforming or deviant, is the behavior of close friends." Both teenage drug use and teenage delinquency are primarily group behaviors. Thus, when an adolescent's friends take cocaine or vandalize for fun, it is more likely that that adolescent will engage in these behaviors too. Of course, it is not just that peers strongly influence a teenager's behavior. It is also that a teenager tends to choose as friends others who accept, even condone, what he or she already does. This pattern continues into adulthood. For instance, a gay man who "comes out" in a small town in Kansas may move to San Francisco to be with others who share his lifestyle. The homosexuality that was considered deviant in Kansas is less likely to be labeled deviant in San Francisco. Seeking out others who are supportive of one's lifestyle is not limited to those who are labeled deviant by the larger culture or some groups within it, but it is especially important to them. The result is that, through differential association, the attitudes and norms of the deviant subculture become even more deeply entrenched.

Just as differential association can help explain why certain individuals become prone to deviance, it can also help explain why entire groups of people sometimes do so. In other words, it can explain why the *rate* of deviance (how many deviant acts per unit of population) varies from group to group, neighborhood to neighborhood, or community to community. In one early study, for example, sociologists set out to understand why a high crime rate persisted in the same Chicago neighborhood for over twenty years as different ethnic groups came and went (Shaw, 1930). Obviously, ethnic cultural traditions could not explain the persistently high rate of crime. In a later study, Shaw and McKay (1969) discovered that new arrivals to the neighborhood were constantly learning deviant norms of behavior from those who already lived there, especially in children's play groups and teenage gangs. Then, once the newcomers had adopted the deviant norms, they passed them on to the next wave of immigrants, and so a deviant culture was sustained and transmitted.

Looking at Structural Strain

Another perspective on why certain people or groups are more prone to deviance than others is Robert Merton's theory of structural strain (Merton, 1968a). Merton based his theory on Durkheim's concept of anomie, a loss of faith in social norms and institutions. In his view, high rates of deviance are the result of a discrepancy between societal expectations and opportunities, between cultural goals and the means available for achieving them. Merton reasoned that to some degree all people internalize the goals that are considered worth striving for in their culture. Everyone also internalizes the norms that govern proper and legitimate ways of working toward those goals. But when legitimate opportunities for achieving culturally defined goals are limited or nonexistent, people may seek alternative ways to achieve those goals, or they may abandon the goals altogether. Merton's main point is that strains in the ***social structure*** invite deviance. "Some social structures," he wrote, "exert a definite pressure upon certain persons in the society to engage in nonconforming rather than conforming behavior" (Merton, 1968a, p. 132).

Merton's prime example was American society, which places tremendous emphasis on financial success. Children are taught that they can become well-to-do if they work hard enough. At the same time, however, legitimate opportunities to become wealthy are limited in American society. What do people do when confronted with this gap between cultural goals and legitimate means of achieving them? Merton identified five possibilities (see Figure 7.1):

1. Conformity: Continuing to seek culturally approved goals by culturally approved means, despite the discrepancy between expectations and opportunities. Bankers and brokers who adhered strictly to the rules against insider trading, even though they suspected that many of their most successful colleagues were bending the rules, are an example.

2. Innovation: Pursuing culturally approved goals by culturally disapproved means (including illegal activities). Boesky and the others who engaged in insider trading fall into this category. Jankowski's study shows how young people in inner-city neighborhoods join gangs as a means to achieve these goals. They all make money (a culturally approved goal) any way they can.

3. Ritualism: Conforming so strictly to socially prescribed means of achieving goals that the larger goals are forgotten. The deviance lies in conforming to such a degree that the negative consequences of doing so are ignored. The classic example of ritualism is the bureaucrat who rigidly adheres to rules and regulations even when they lead to inefficiency and stifle creativity.

4. Retreatism: Abandoning both the goals and the means of achieving them that one's culture prescribes. Retreatists are dropouts in the eyes of society—the people who give up looking for work and become skid-row bums, chronic drug addicts, and drifters.

5. Rebellion: Rejecting the approved goals and means of achieving them and embracing new, socially disapproved ones instead. An example are financial rebels on Wall Street who fashioned the new goal of restructuring American business and then invented a new means of achieving that end: the hostile corporate takeover. Yesterday's rebels, however, may become tomorrow's conformists. Virtually all Wall Street firms now have divisions that handle corporate mergers and acquisitions.

Modes of Adapting	Accepts Culturally Approved Goals	Accepts Culturally Approved Means
Conformist	Yes	Yes
Innovator	Yes	No
Ritualist	No	Yes
Retreatist	No	No
Rebel	No (creates new goals)	No (creates new means)

FIGURE 7.1 / Merton's Five Modes of Social Adaptation

Source: Adapted from Robert K. Merton, *Social Theory and Social Structure* (Free Press, New York, 1968), p. 194.

Merton's theory is partly a rational-choice model of why some people behave deviantly. Deviance, he claimed, is a rational option when a certain social-structural condition exists—namely, lack of legitimate channels to achieve culturally desirable goals. As long as this condition prevails and the costs of acting deviantly aren't too high (the risk of getting caught and punished is relatively low, or the negative evaluation of others doesn't matter very much), it makes sense for some people to try deviant ways of getting the same things that most other people want. In addition to this rational-choice component, Merton's theory has a social-psychological one. The absence of legitimate means to achieve culturally desirable goals produces frustration, Merton argued. This frustration, in turn, helps to fuel deviance because acting deviantly is a way for certain people to get back at the society that limits their opportunities. How much truth is there to this social-psychological motive for deviance, especially for criminal activity? Studies have found that although frustration encourages crime in some cases, it is not a major explanation of it (G. Walters, 1992, p. 223).

Critics have charged that Merton's theory has other shortcomings, too (see Johnson and Turner, 1984). For one thing, it can't explain some types of deviance (such as alcoholism or mental disorders). For another, it doesn't really explain why people who are thwarted in their efforts to succeed respond with deviant behavior sometimes, but not always. If structural-strain theory can't predict when deviant reactions will occur, it is less useful than some of its proponents would like it to be. Newer versions of strain theory try to get around this problem. Some suggest that the daily irritations and frustrations of life can help to predict when people who are predisposed to deviance will actually commit deviant acts (Agnew, 1990). Others add that a predisposition to deviance depends in part on the groups to which people belong and the pressures for or against deviance that exist in these groups (A. K. Cohen, 1965, 1966). Thus, both differential association and social stresses and strains probably play a role in encouraging people to engage in deviant behaviors.

One of the most important implications of structural-strain theory is that deviance cannot be explained by looking only at deviants. It is necessary to look at the overall ***social structure*** to see what pressures and incentives for deviance it provides. It is also necessary to look at the ***culture*** to see what goals and values it sets for people and which means to achieve them it defines as acceptable. And it is necessary to look at the ***functional integration*** of different parts of society to see where strains are likely to emerge, for example, strain is likely to emerge when schools teach people goals and expectations that the economy does not give them opportunities to fulfill legally.

Looking at Inadequate Social Control

Social control refers to the efforts of a group or society to regulate the behavior of its members in conformity with

The illegality of buying and selling certain drugs has fostered a complex social structure and an international underground that often appears to be beyond social control.

established norms. Although it is hoped that people will conform on their own because they've *internalized* the norms (absorbed them deeply into their way of thinking), such automatic compliance doesn't always occur. As a result, there must also be **sanctions**, or externally imposed constraints. Some of these are **informal sanctions**: unofficial pressures to conform. Positive informal sanctions involve rewards for conformity, such as a smile, a kiss, or a word of approval. Negative informal sanctions involve informal penalties for *not* conforming, such as ridicule or ostracism. When informal sanctions aren't enough, **formal sanctions** come into play. These are officially imposed pressures to conform, such as fines or imprisonment. Formal sanctions are especially needed in large, complex societies such as our own, where there tend to be competing ideas about appropriate behavior, and where most people do not live in small, closely knit communities that often secure near-universal conformity just through informal pressures.

Sociologist Travis Hirschi (1969) has made a major contribution by focusing on inadequate social control as a determinant of who commits crime and deviance. For example, very little crime is committed by young children because they are constantly under adult supervision (Gottfredson and Hirschi, 1990). It is not until adolescence that children are free enough from adult control to engage in criminal activity. Similarly, drug addicts tend to live in urban neighborhoods characterized by poverty, high crime rates, and large minority populations not simply because drug use leads to crime or because minorities are more likely to engage in both. A crucial factor is that in these neighborhoods social control is reduced: There is less police presence and more of a distance from the disapproving eye of "straight" society (Hirschi and Gottfredson, 1988). Here there is also a relatively high incidence of weak family structures (broken homes, negligent parents), which tend *not* to exert the controls against crime and drug use that strong family structures do.

Although Hirschi and his colleagues focus on an absence of external constraints against deviance, they also look at social control that comes from within a person. Through socialization and the internalization of cultural norms and values, most people learn to pursue socially accepted goals through socially accepted means, even without external sanctions. For some people, however, this social learning is faulty or incomplete, so deviance is more likely for them. People who engage in criminal behavior or become addicted to drugs are typically those who exhibit "an underlying tendency to pursue short-term, immediate pleasure" regardless of the fact that their aims and methods may be widely disapproved of (Hirschi and Gottfredson, 1988, p. 21).

CRIME AND CRIMINAL JUSTICE

Despite an elaborate and costly criminal justice system to maintain social control, crime is still a fact of life in American society, as Figure 7.2 shows. A **crime** is a violation of a norm that has been entered into law and is backed by the power and authority of the state to impose formal sanctions (fines, arrest, imprisonment). Norms that get entered into criminal statutes are those that are seen as protecting people from significant harm and those whose supporters have enough social ***power*** to get the state to enforce prohibitions against violating the norms in question.

Although not all deviant acts are crimes, willfully committing crimes is usually considered deviant. The exceptions are mainly cases in which the laws that are violated are widely considered illegitimate. For example, when civil rights protesters of the 1950s and 1960s violated segregation laws, Americans who agreed with the protesters' cause did not consider them deviants, even though their actions were officially crimes.

As the example of civil rights protesters suggests, crime is a socially defined concept that can change over time. Some crimes that were once considered serious, such as smoking marijuana, are no longer the focus of much concern. Other illegal activities that used to be largely overlooked, such as dumping industrial wastes in unauthorized areas, are now receiving much more public attention. Entirely new crimes can also spring up as society changes. For example, illegal dumping of toxic wastes and illegal insider trading on Wall Street are both products of important changes that have occurred in American society.

The overall trend in the United States has been toward more rather than fewer legal restrictions. States have passed more than 500,000 new criminal laws in this century (Callahan, 1979). This raises the question of whether the United States is becoming "overcriminalized" in its attempt to extend formal social control to more kinds of human behavior.

Types of Crime

The Federal Bureau of Investigation issues annual reports about two major categories of crime. The first (Type I)

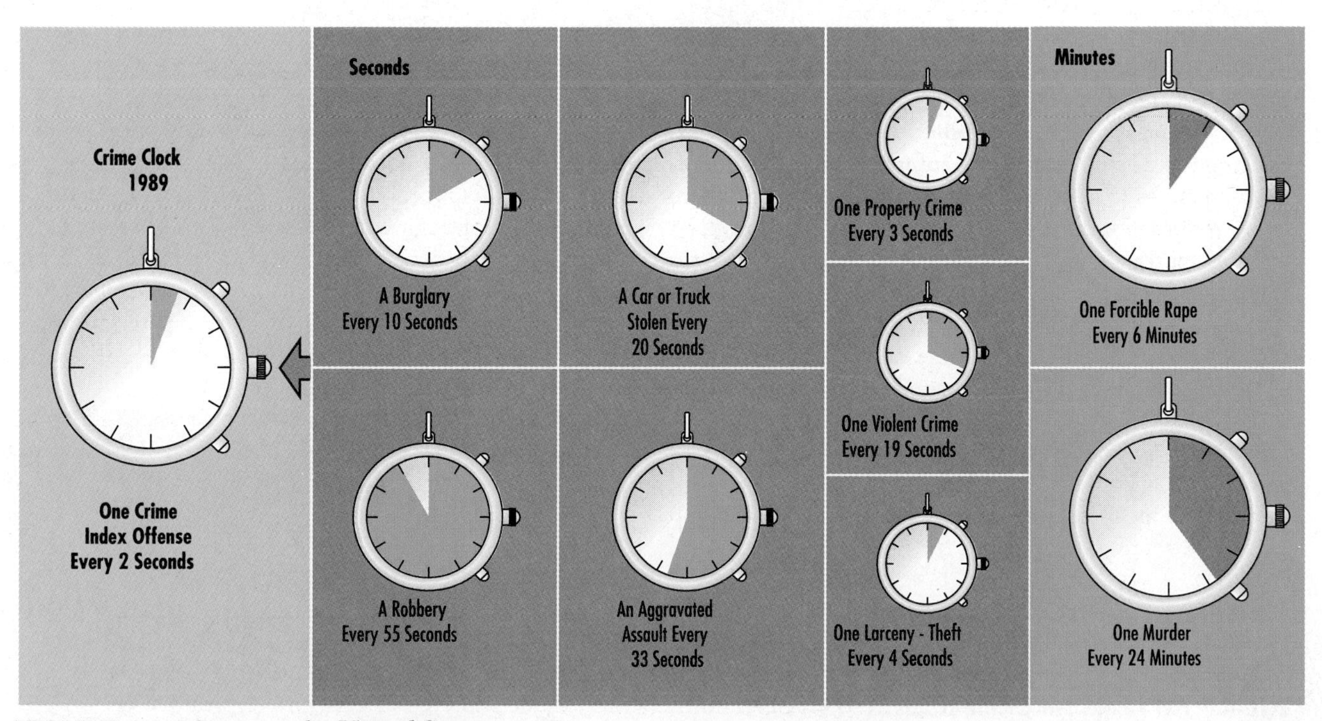

FIGURE 7.2 / Crime in the United States

Source: Federal Bureau of Investigation, *Uniform Crime Reports for the United States, 1991*, p. 4.

consists of crimes with criminal intent. These include both crimes against people—such as murder, rape, and assault—and crimes against property—such as burglary, theft, and arson (see Figure 7.3). Type II crimes do not usually involve criminal intent in the same way Type I crimes do. They include white-collar crime, prostitution, drug abuse, illegal weapons possession, sex offenses, gambling, vandalism, and receiving stolen property. In the United States, nearly all kinds of crime have been on the rise in recent years and are more common here than in other countries.

Violent Crimes

Most public attention focuses on **violent crimes**, such as murder, assault, and rape, even though violent crimes constitute only a little over 10 percent of all Type I offenses. The reason for this public concern is the fear that violent crime arouses. From an international perspective, American society *is* quite violent. The number of murders committed in Manhattan alone each year is equal to that committed in all of England and Wales. Between 1969 and 1991 in the United States the rates of several violent crimes increased substantially: murder and manslaughter by 36 percent, rape by 133 percent, and aggravated assault by 185 percent (*Uniform Crime Reports for the United States, 1991*).

The most likely victims of violent crime are black males of lower socioeconomic status (Adler, Mueller, and Laufer, 1991). Overall, African-Americans are 70 percent more likely than whites to be victims of violent crimes. In 1988, among each 100,000 Americans, fifty-eight black males and thirteen black females were murdered, compared with eight white males and three white females (*Uniform Crime Reports for the United States, 1991*). The murder rate for black teenagers is particularly alarming. In 1988, one in every 1,000 black male youths died in a homicide, more than five times the rate for young white males.

The widespread availability of firearms has been cited as one of the causes of these dramatic figures (*New York*

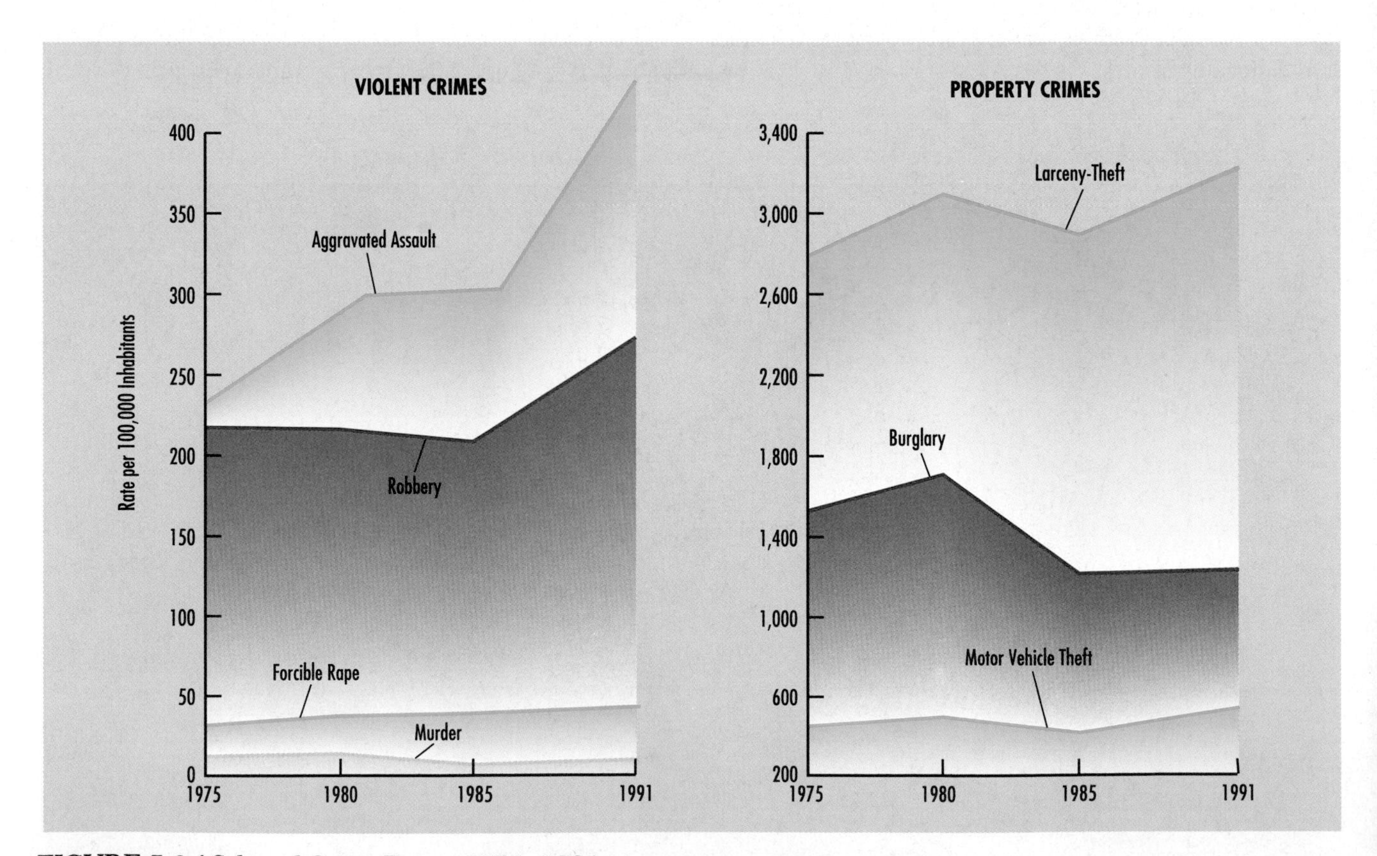

FIGURE 7.3 / Selected Crime Rates, 1975–1991

Source: *Statistical Abstract of the United States, 1992*, U.S. Department of Commerce, Bureau of the Census, Washington, D.C., p. 170.

Times, December 7, 1990). Half of all households in the United States have at least one weapon. But widespread ownership of guns doesn't necessarily lead to criminal violence. In countries such as Switzerland and Israel, where private ownership of handguns is also widespread, there are relatively low rates of violence with firearms.

Violent crimes are not the only source of public concern. Indeed, people are much more likely to be victims of property crimes like burglary and theft (see Figure 7.3). Every time a home is broken into or a car stolen, the public's sense of vulnerability increased. Such robberies are also costly. But even more costly are the large-scale thefts, embezzlements, and other kinds of white-collar crimes (which we will examine below).

Crime is not spread evenly among the American people. It affects the poor more than the rich. Crime rates are much higher in America's large cities than in the country as a whole (compare Table 7.2 with Figure 7.3). And in those large cities, African-Americans and members of other racial minorities are disproportionately likely to be the victims of crime.

Crimes without Victims

We think of crime as having an identifiable victim who suffers at the hands of another person. Some crimes, however, don't seem to have victims. These **victimless crimes** include prostitution, illegal acts among consenting adults, illicit drug use, and gambling (see Table 7.3). In this type of crime, there is usually no complainant—no one who feels he or she has been harmed. These acts are designated as criminal because the community as a whole, or powerful groups within it, regard them as morally repugnant. Those who hold different views of morality think that at least some of these behaviors should not be considered criminal.

Still others argue that victimless crimes really do have victims. Compulsive gamblers rob their families of needed income; prostitutes spread AIDS and other sexually transmitted diseases; drug users may resort to other crimes to support their habit. According to this view, society should control these kinds of behaviors because they *do* have harmful effects.

Crime rates are higher in large cities than in small towns. Size is not the only factor, however, as the range of variation in urban crime rates shows.

TABLE 7.2

Crime Rates of Large Cities in the United States, 1991 (per 100,000 Population)

Cities Ranked by Population Size	Crime Index Total	Violent Crime	Property Crime
New York	8,484	2,044	6,440
Los Angeles	7,622	1,795	5,826
Detroit	7,056	1,001	6,055
Dallas	10,039	1,333	8,705
Honolulu	5,958	240	5,718
Washington, D.C.	5,898	785	5,113
Boston	5,475	832	4,642
Columbus, Ohio	6,984	720	6,263
Denver	6,620	730	5,890
Seattle	7,153	596	6,557
Fort Worth	10,143	992	9,151
Kansas City	7,478	1,175	6,303
Atlanta	8,317	987	7,329
Portland, Oregon	6,778	798	5,980
Tucson	8,364	688	7,675
Oakland	7,458	1,037	6,421
Minneapolis	5,572	470	5,102
Charlotte	8,035	1,159	6,876
Sacramento	7,210	794	6,415
Newark, N.J.	6,623	1,028	5,594

Source: Uniform Crime Reports for the United States, 1991, *Federal Bureau of Investigation*, Washington, D.C.

TABLE 7.3

Arrests for Crimes without Victims, 1991

Prostitution and commercialized vice	76,974
Drug abuse violations (all)	706,097
Illegal gambling	11,626
Drunkenness	582,036
Curfew, loitering (juvenile)	68,080
Runaways (juvenile)	125,495

Source: Uniform Crime Reports for the United States, 1991, p. 217, *Federal Bureau of Investigation*, Washington, D.C.

Opponents answer that the government shouldn't try to legislate morality. Why should someone have the right to tell consenting adults what they can and can't do if they are not hurting or bothering anyone else? From a more pragmatic standpoint, what is gained by denying large segments of the population goods and services they want? Such laws are not only difficult to enforce; they also create black markets and opportunities for organized crime.

Organized Crime

Organized crime is a self-perpetuating conspiracy that operates for profit or power and that seeks to obtain immunity from the law through fear and corruption (Abadinsky, 1981). Organized crime differs from other businesses in its heavy involvement in illegal activities and its almost routine use of bribery and violence. It specializes in providing illegal goods and services—selling illegal drugs, fencing stolen or illegal items (such as illegal handguns and stolen credit cards), and loan sharking (lending money at interest rates above the legal limit). Organized crime also provides legal goods and services by illegal means. In many cities, for instance, crime syndicates monopolize garbage collection, vending machines, and taxi and limousine services. They achieved these monopolies by bribing public officials and threatening violence against potential competitors. In addition, legitimate companies are used to "launder" money earned through organized crime's illegal activities.

Crime syndicates often develop among immigrants who aren't familiar enough with the mainstream culture to participate in its economy and who are suspicious of the police and other authorities who don't speak their language. As a result, organized crime has followed the pattern of "ethnic succession." The Irish crime syndicates in nineteenth-century America were followed by those of European Jews, and then, in the 1920s, by Italian crime families that gained power during Prohibition. When alcohol was legalized again in the 1930s, the Italian syndicates had the capital, the experience, the personnel, and the overseas contacts to move into the heroin trade.

Italians remain prominent in American organized crime, but the ethnic picture has become more complex. One factor is the source of drugs, like heroin. In the 1960s, most heroin was made from opium grown in Turkey, processed in Marseilles, France, or Corsica, and then sold in the United States. In the 1970s, groups with contacts in other opium-producing countries—Mexico, Colombia, Pakistan, Iran, and countries of Southeast Asia—began to move in. Today's crime syndicates have been described as "a United Nations of drug smugglers, including Chinese,

The financial rewards of organized crime's illegal activities are so great that gang rivalries frequently turn violent. John Gotti (center), reportedly the head of organized crime in New York City, is serving a life sentence for the murder of a rival gangster.

GLOBAL ISSUES/LOCAL CONSEQUENCES

The International Drug Trade

A young black man in Washington, D.C., works at a trade in which his chances of being killed are a hundred times greater than in other occupations. One of the reasons for his choice is that the income from this work, about $24,000 a year, is several times more than he could otherwise earn (*The Economist*, July 14, 1990). In the mountains of Thailand, a Hmong woman tends a field of poppies that will bear crops for ten or twelve years, instead of only two or three years as does rice. Selling the harvest means additional income for her family. In Medellín, Colombia, a man who has become a billionaire from the profits of his business has diversified his investments to include vast real estate holdings and cattle ranches (Lee, 1989).

These three people, from very different cultural backgrounds, are all inextricably tied to one of the most dramatic social problems in the world today: drug trafficking. The drug trade, in turn, is linked to other serious social problems that run the gamut from an increase in the number of homeless, to babies who are born addicted to cocaine, to connections between government officials and organized crime, both in the United States and abroad. The drug trade also contributes to the perpetuation of gangs which use armed violence to achieve their aims. In addition, drug trafficking lures otherwise "respectable" middle- and upper-middle-class professionals into criminal activities that offer huge payoffs. Bankers may get involved in money-laundering schemes, and judges may accept bribes to throw out cases or impose lenient sentences. Police corruption is also encouraged by the drug trade, involving anyone from the cop on the beat up to station chiefs and even commissioners.

These local consequences are the result of a *global* industry that flourishes despite the fact that it has been illegal worldwide for more than thirty years. That industry is fueled by a constant and growing demand for drugs in the wealthy industrialized countries. People there are willing to pay high prices for illegal drugs, and so they make drug trafficking a big business. Americans are major contributors to this process. Not only are an estimated 6 million Americans regular drug users (*The Economist*, July 21, 1990); Americans also pay the most money for them and earn the greatest profits. Coca leaves (from which cocaine is made) cost $2.10 per kilogram at their source in the highlands of the Andes; at street level in the United States the price per kilo is $90,000. Most of that money stays in the hands of Americans.

Just as there is a constant and growing demand for drugs, there is also a ready supply. In the less developed countries of the world, where most people have few economic opportunities, drug production makes economic sense. For instance, in Peru, the money earned by poor peasants from the growth and sale of coca leaves can mean the difference between a near-starvation level of subsistence and a decent standard of living. Yet of the roughly $2 billion a year that returns to the cocaine-producing countries in Latin America, very little finds its way to the poor. It flows mainly to the druglords, who have amassed huge fortunes. These men often block economic programs that would give peasants a chance to earn money outside the drug trade. In this way, they ensure a continued supply of cheap agricultural labor.

The global drug industry also flourishes because it manipulates the press, the police, and the courts through bribes and terrorism. Latin American cocaine producers, for instance, have extensive ties to political power structures, and drug money often funds political campaigns, many times for the traffickers themselves. Most important, the druglords are often allied with right-wing military groups, which are eager to maintain the existing social order against left-wing guerrillas who seek to change it.

It is at this point that the U.S. government is often drawn into the picture. In its fight against communism in the Western Hemisphere, the United States has given military and financial support to "anticommunist" right-wing military groups, even though these groups often get money from the sale of drugs as well. The anticommunist "Contra" rebels in Nicaragua and former dictator Manuel Noriega in Panama were both long supported by the United States, despite their known drug connections. Thus, America's international policies have effectively thwarted American efforts to combat drugs at home. Military aid to nondemocratic Third World countries only encourages political corruption, protects foreign druglords, and helps ensure a continuing supply of illegal drugs. It also uses foreign aid that would be better spent on economic development programs to create *legal* jobs for the poor in Third World countries.

Some observers think the American government's efforts to reduce the drug trade should focus on the home front, not abroad (Scott and Marshall, 1991). But simply cracking down on dealers is not enough. There are always others willing to take their places. Long-term solutions probably lie in drug-treatment programs, drug education programs, and assistance to disadvantaged communities, so that a poor teenager in the South Bronx will not see a chance to make more money selling drugs than in other lines of work. In short, Americans need to attack the root causes of the drug trade at home and address the social and psychological issues that surround it. At the same time, developing countries need American help to provide people with non-drug-related opportunities for economic advancement. Although this is a global problem, we feel its consequences in our everyday lives, and therein may lie some of the answers to it.

Thais, Pakistanis, Indians, Iranians, Afghans, Nigerians, and Israelis" (P. Kerr, 1987, p. 1), as well as the Japanese Yakuza and black groups like el Rukns and the Jamaican "posses." The Global Issues/Local Consequences box describes the international drug trade in more detail.

White-Collar and Corporate Crimes

One man robs a gas station of $250 and is sent to prison for six months; another makes $2.5 million through illegal stock trading and is required only to return the money (plus "interest" in the form of fines). Terrorists who plant a bomb in a diplomat's car are charged with conspiracy and criminal homicide. Ford Motor Company sells millions of Pintos with rear-mounted gas tanks that the company knows may explode if the car is hit from behind. For the 500 people who are burned to death in accidents involving Pintos, Ford must pay millions in damages, but it is found innocent of criminal charges. Clearly, our society's responses to white-collar and corporate crime are quite different from its treatment of "common criminals."

The term **white-collar crime** was first used by the sociologist Edwin Sutherland to refer to "a crime committed by a person of respectability and high status in the course of his occupation" (Sutherland, 1949, p. 9). Embezzling, padding expense accounts, stealing from an employer, and evading personal income taxes all fall into this category. So does the misuse of public funds by government officials (accepting bribes, padding payrolls, and the like). One difference between white-collar and "common" crime is that white-collar crime seldom involves force or violence. White-collar crime, however, is more costly in dollars and cents. For example, bank embezzlers steal an average of $23,000 each, whereas bank robbers steal only about $3,000 or less (Clinard and Yeager, 1980). And yet only 3 percent of bank embezzlers go to prison, compared with 90 percent of those who rob banks (*Sourcebook of Criminal Justice Statistics*, 1989). When politicians talk about the need for more law and order, they usually mean more money for police to fight street crimes, not for federal investigators to fight white-collar crimes.

In contrast to white-collar crimes, which are committed by people for their own personal gain, **corporate crimes** are committed on behalf of a formal organization. Their primary goal is to boost company profits (or avoid losses). Unlike other criminals, corporations are not persons and cannot be jailed. Indeed, corporate crimes are often handled outside the court system by government regulatory agencies (the SEC, the Federal Trade Commission, the Environmental Protection Agency, and so forth). In most cases, sanctions take the form of fines that are small in relation to earnings. A standard $50,000 fine for price fixing doesn't mean much to a corporation that has revenues in excess of $1 billion a year (Ermann and Lundman, 1982).

The most obvious explanation of corporate crime is profit (Ermann and Lundman, 1982). For example, in 1972 it would have cost Johns-Manville $12 million to install the legally required equipment that would protect its workers from asbestos dust, and another $5 million annually to maintain that equipment. In contrast, paying workers' compensation cost the company only $1 million a year. Protecting workers was not "cost-effective" for Johns-Manville. The complex structure of corporations may also encourage corporate crimes by shielding those involved in them. Usually, no one person in a large corporation has authority over a particular action; responsibility, in other words, tends to be diffuse. This allows managers to go along with policies they might not otherwise approve of. At the same time, managers can establish norms and sanctions that make it hard for employees at lower levels to report corporate crime. The result is that corporate crime is quite widespread.

Controlling Crime

In a major study of crime, Charles Silberman found evidence to support Robert Merton's belief that people resort to deviant means when desirable goals are out of reach. Silberman puts it this way: "In the United States, the premium placed on winning—on success—encourages people to violate rules that get in the way, and to feel justified in doing so" (Silberman, 1980, p. 50). Those who are poor and discriminated against may be especially likely to respond in this way, for they have good reason to believe that they will never achieve "success" except through unlawful means. As criminal activities become an established part of the social environment in poor neighborhoods, children are socialized into a criminally deviant lifestyle, and crime gets culturally transmitted from one generation to the next.

Elliott Currie (1985) holds that conventional techniques for controlling crime, such as putting more police on the beat and sending more criminals to prison for longer sentences, will not be very successful. In his view, the only way to significantly reduce crime is to attack its root causes: unemployment, social and economic inequality, lack of community bonds, and family breakdown. Currie maintains that the government can bring about major and positive changes in social structure. Attractive jobs can be made more available to young people (especially minority youths), community life can be supported, and families can be helped to cope. Although such far-reaching changes require a major social commitment, a sizable number of people may be ready to make that commitment, because our police, courts, and prisons don't seem able to do the job alone. In the following sections we'll take a look at some of the major problems that exist in our current system of crime control and consider how that system can be made more effective in a comprehensive fight against crime.

Police as Agents of Control

Numerous studies have shown that increasing the number of police on duty, conducting random patrols, and instituting other conventional measures to combat crime have not had the desired results in most cases (Skolnick and Bayley, 1986). But this does not mean that the police cannot have *any* impact on crime. Today, some police departments are trying new approaches, with much more positive results. These approaches involve working with the community to improve conditions that tend to disrupt social, commercial, and political life. The strategy is now "problem-oriented" policing (trying to eliminate some of the causes of crime), in addition to the traditional "incident-oriented" policing (responding to incidents of crime as they occur and apprehending the lawbreaker) (Siegel, 1990).

In *The New Blue Line* (1986), Jerome Skolnick and David Bayley discuss the police force in Santa Ana, California, which began a series of reforms in the early 1970s to bring community and police together. These reforms included *civilianization* (using civilians from the community to help file reports); *community mobilization* (appointing block captains to serve as liaisons between the police and the community); and *substations* (combination police station/social service centers where residents can get information on how to handle personal and community problems). While the crime rate in Santa Ana did not fall dramatically (in part because more residents were willing to report crimes), neither did it rise as fast as in other cities.

But some police departments have not worked as hard on community relations and police behavior, and there are rising concerns over police brutality. In March 1991, an amateur photographer filmed Los Angeles patrol officers brutally beating a man, Rodney King, who suffered brain damage, internal bleeding, missing teeth, and a broken ankle. The videotape was shown repeatedly on network newscasts. Los Angeles Police Chief Daryl Gates steadfastly held that the incident was "an aberration," and his response angered many people. Gates had a long record of refusal to recognize police brutality and poor relations with the African-American community. He was eventually forced to resign and was replaced by Los Angeles's first black police chief. Four officers were tried for beating King, not in multiethnic Los Angeles, but in a nearly all-white

The use of force, even when it is sanctioned by a police uniform, is not always accepted by society.

suburb where they were found innocent. The verdict sparked riots and demonstrations in Los Angeles and around the country. The King affair brought renewed attention to the question of police violence. It also focused on the question of racism among police, for tapes of police radio calls during the King incident revealed racist jokes. Many minority groups feel that they cannot get justice in cases of police brutality. At the same time, many minority residents of South Central Los Angeles pointed out that during the riots the police did little to protect their community, a neglect that they say is typical.

Defenders of police often answer that drug-related crime has increased dramatically in the inner cities, and the criminals are often better armed than the police. Police work may now have become so dangerous that officers are beginning to snap under the pressure. In response, some police departments are providing violence-reduction courses in their training programs, and many are trying to screen out recruits who are psychologically unsuited to the job. Civilian complaint review boards that help identify problem officers have also been set up in many cities, and they provide another safeguard against police abuses. In addition, some police themselves are challenging the "blue code" against informing on each other in misconduct cases. Thus, both the police and the public are becoming increasingly aware that the problem of police abusing their power can be solved only by both sides working together.

The Criminal Justice Funnel

In 1989, just over half the cases of aggravated assault and rape in the United States led to arrests, as did fewer than a third of all the robbery cases and crimes against property (see Figure 7.4). Of those arrested, only a small percentage were ultimately imprisoned. For example, in one sample of seven states, only 40 percent of all persons arrested were eventually sentenced to and served terms in jail or prison (U.S. Department of Justice, 1989). In effect, the criminal justice system is a funnel, with a great many crimes reported at one end, a relatively large number of arrests in the middle, and few convictions and still fewer imprisonments at the other end. Why?

One study found that many felons are never prosecuted or convicted because their victims refuse to testify against them (Vera Institute of Justice, 1977). When people call the police, they often do so to frighten the offender and show their anger. Later, when it comes time to give testimony that may send the person to prison, either they have cooled off or they fear revenge. Many felons also never go to prison because their crimes are reduced to misdemeanors (less serious offenses) through **plea bargaining.** Plea bargaining is the process in which the district attorney offers to reduce charges if the suspect will plead guilty and relinquish the right to a trial. Plea bargaining saves the state time, expense, and trouble, but it puts some serious offenders back on the streets quickly and may also pressure some innocent people to plead guilty.

Poor nonwhites are disproportionately likely to get funneled through the criminal justice system. About a quarter of all African-American males between the ages of twenty and twenty-nine are in jail, on parole, or on probation (*Newsweek*, May 18, 1992, p. 37). Because subjective decisions are made throughout the criminal justice process, discrimination occurs, intentional or not. First, the police

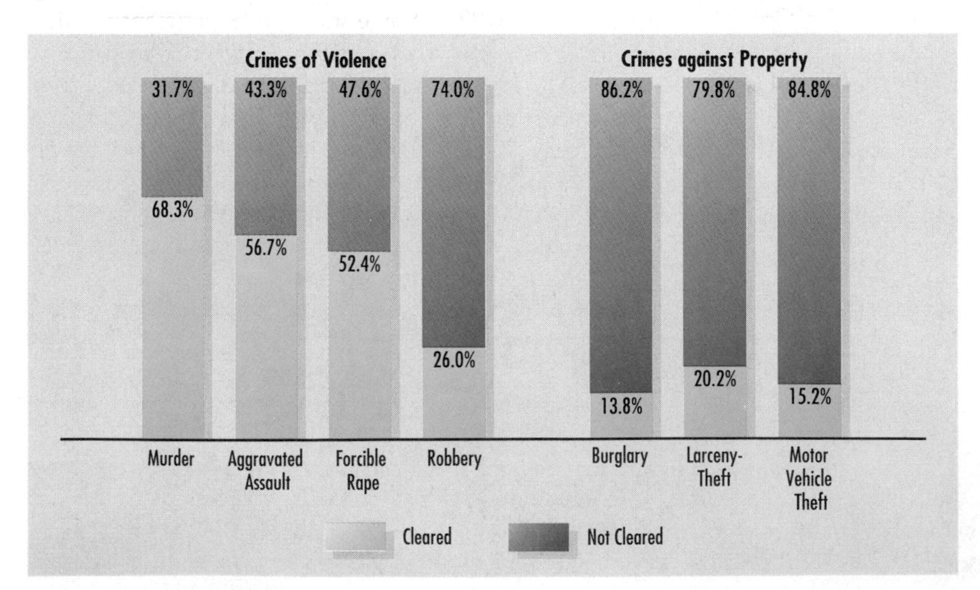

FIGURE 7.4 / Crimes Resolved by Arrest, 1991

Source: Federal Bureau of Investigation, *Uniform Crime Reports for the United States, 1991*, p. 204, Table 25.

The Swedish caption to this photograph reads: "This is a family visitation room in a Swedish prison in an experimental program for narcotics offenders. Some would argue that allowing prisoners to have private family time while incarcerated is too lenient; others point out that building prisons so that prisoners can maintain meaningful social contacts helps them reintegrate into society when their terms are up." Our own society tends to agree with the first argument: American prisons stress punishment rather than rehabilitation. Which approach do you think is more effective?

use their judgment in making arrests. Then public prosecutors use their judgment in offering plea bargains. Finally, judges decide which people are a danger to the community and so should be denied bail and sent to prison if convicted. This last stage in the process—sending offenders to prison—is the subject we take up in the final section of this chapter.

The Imprisoning Society

Public support for imprisonment is increasing. A recent Gallup Poll showed that more than 80 percent of Americans favored making it harder for those convicted of violent crimes to be paroled, and more than 65 percent believed that those accused of such crimes shouldn't be released on bail while awaiting trial (*Sourcebook of Criminal Justice Statistics*, 1989). In the 1980s, despite the fact that certain crime rates began to level off and even fall, rates of imprisonment still climbed steadily. Between 1980 and 1987, the number of inmates in U.S. prisons and jails more than doubled, reaching 712,563 in 1989. In that year, 2.2 percent of the total U.S. population was either in jail or on parole or probation (U.S. Department of Justice, *Correctional Population in the United States*, 1989). Prison systems have not been able to keep pace with the flood of inmates. Cells that were built to house one inmate now hold two or three, with the overflow being bedded in gyms, recreation rooms, corridors, basements, and tents. To ensure security, San Quentin, which was designed to hold 2,700 prisoners, confines its 3,900 inmates to their cells except for meals and showers (Logan, 1985).

Many of the problems surrounding the prison system stem from a confusion of purposes. Are prison sentences designed to deter people from committing crimes? To rehabilitate criminals and return them to society as reformed citizens? To punish offenders? To protect the public? In recent years, the pendulum has swung from a societal emphasis on rehabilitation to public demands for longer imprisonments, presumably to punish, deter, and protect.

Although there is little agreement on the goal of imprisonment, there is widespread agreement that the prison system is inadequate on many counts. For one thing, the harsh conditions tend to breed an excessive toughness, "the ability either to victimize others or to withstand victimization" (Silberman, 1980, p. 523). This kind of prison culture may actually socialize people into criminal deviance.

Alternatives to prison sentences are currently being tried (Lacayo, 1987). Some states are experimenting with giving certain criminals a choice between a prison sentence and a combination of fines and public service. Other states are putting some criminals under house arrest in which they are allowed to live in their own homes and go to work, but must obey strict curfews and meet frequently with corrections officers. Still other states are trying work-release centers, which require criminals to live in prison-like dormitories but also permit them to hold jobs.

Only a few alternatives to imprisonment have gotten beyond the idea stage, however. Judges seem reluctant to take chances. What if a person under house arrest commits another crime? As things stand now, social attitudes are not inclined toward leniency for criminals. Thus, imprisonment remains the most likely fate for those convicted of serious offenses (Applebombe, 1987). But neither crime in general nor serious offenses seem destined to vanish from America's main public concerns in the near future.

CHAPTER 8

Groups and Organizations

ociah
mal sanctions.
socially defined, which n
re must be people with the po
norm violations constitute deviance. In the United

SUMMARY

1. Deviance is behavior that members of a group or society see as violating their norms. Since norms are a matter of social definition, deviance is as well. Whether a particular act is considered deviant or not depends on the time, place, and social circumstances in which it occurs. Urban gangs, for instance, are considered deviant by the middle and upper classes, but not by many of the people who live in poor, inner-city neighborhoods.

2. The concept of functional integration also helps us to understand the nature of deviance. Émile Durkheim is among those who have argued that deviance serves some necessary social functions. For one thing, it tests the boundaries of permissiveness in a society, forcing people to think about what they believe is normal and right. In addition, acts of deviance unite communities in opposition to the deviant and so reaffirm people's sense of social solidarity. Deviant behavior can also serve as a catalyst for social change.

3. Determining whose definition of deviance prevails in a society involves power relations. By offering rewards and imposing penalties, some people and groups have the power to make their standards of right and wrong prevail even when others disagree with them. Karl Marx was particularly influential in developing this power perspective on deviance.

4. Not everyone who violates norms of acceptable behavior is singled out and labeled deviant by others. Those who are singled out tend to become excluded from the social mainstream and so begin to think of themselves as deviant and to adopt a deviant lifestyle. The idea that deviance is partly a product of labeling by others is an outgrowth of the social-interactionist perspective.

5. Some explanations of deviance focus on individuals' inherent traits: Certain genetic and biochemical abnormalities are associated with some forms of deviance. Differential association theory attributes deviance to socialization, holding that people are socialized into deviance when they associate mainly with th who act deviantly and adopt their norms and values. Structura strain theory holds that deviance arises when conformity to widely accepted norms of behavior fails to satisfy people's legitimate, culturally approved desires. Another theory maintains that inadequate social control fosters deviance, both externally (when the family or society fails to apply formal and informal sanctions as pressures on an individual to conform with established norms) and internally (when the individual has not been adequately socialized and has not fully internalized the culture's norms and values).

6. Crimes are acts that have been formally defined as illegal and are subject to formal sanctions by the state. Violent crimes receive widespread public attention because of the fear they arouse. America's rate of violent crime is relatively high compared with those of many other modern industrialized countries. Organized crime involves self-sustaining underground organizations that provide illegal goods and services and/or use violence and bribery to overcome their competition. White-collar and corporate crimes are illegal acts committed by employees of legitimate companies, either for their own personal gain or for the perceived good of their firms. Victimless crimes are those—like prostitution—that do not necessarily injure anyone but offend a community's moral standards.

7. Widespread dissatisfaction exists with our current system of crime control, causing people to look for ways to make the fight against crime more effective. Studies suggest that crime rates can be cut when police collaborate with the community in an effort to eliminate some of the causes of crime. Another approach to cutting the crime rate is to see that more offenders are convicted and imprisoned, rather than plea bargaining their way to reduced sentences. But some sociologists believe that alternatives to traditional prisons may be more effective in rehabilitating criminals and seeing that they repay their debts to society.

Come to the Tupperware party! Your neighbor down the street has invited you to one to be held at her house next Tuesday morning. Many of your friends from the neighborhood will be there, along with others you know from church. Bring the kids: Your "hostess" has hired a baby-sitter so that her guests with young children can relax. The party, she says, is just a friendly get-together over coffee and pastry, with absolutely no obligation to buy. She has made a "date" with a "distributor" from the Tupperware sales family (another woman who lives across town) who will be showing the latest in plastic food-storage products, along with old Tupperware favorites and the line of TupperToys. The guests will play games (an auction with play money), and one lucky person will receive a surprise gift (Hanson, 1987).

On one level, this Tupperware party is purely a social occasion—an informal gathering of friends and neighbors to talk and have fun. On another level, however, it is also big business. Tupperware—along with Mary Kay Cosmetics, Amway, Shaklee, Discovery Toys, and others—is a direct-sales organization, in which a salesperson (or "distributor") sells products or services in face-to-face interaction with consumers, typically in private homes. In one recent year, direct-sales organizations took in $8.36 billion in revenue and had 5.12 million distributors working for them.

Part of the reason for this stunning success may be that direct-sales organizations blur the usual separation between the personal world of family, friends, and feelings and the economic world of markets, products, and profits (Biggart, 1989). When you buy from Tupperware, or other organizations like it, you do not have the sense that you are buying from a large *formal organization*, such as Exxon or General Motors. Instead, you see yourself as part of a small social group of friends and neighbors.

The distinction between a group and a formal organization (or bureaucracy) is an important one in sociology. A **social group** is a set of people who identify with one another and interact in informally structured ways based on shared values, norms, and goals. The Tupperware party illustrates some of the characteristics of a group. The friends and neighbors who attend are linked by common values and practices (they might go to the same church, for example), share a common identity (as wives and mothers living in a certain neighborhood), and interact regularly in an informal way. Many of these same characteristics extend to Tupperware distributors as well. Distributors are organized into familylike groups in which friendly cooperation is valued more than competition, but great respect is also given to independent entrepreneurship. New distributors are recruited through networks of family and friends, with little formal evaluation of their potential performance. All distributors come together for rallies and an annual Jubilee, where prizes are given to top sellers and planning is done in a festive, informal atmosphere.

These social arrangements contrast sharply with those that exist in a typical, bureaucratically organized formal organization. A **formal organization** is a set of people whose activities are precisely and intentionally designed for the rational achievement of explicitly stated goals. Some features of direct-sales organizations make them resemble formal organizations more closely than social groups. For example, the games played at Tupperware parties are not just for fun. They are carefully designed to stimulate sales. Another set of rules governs the awarding of Tupperware prizes. For instance, a hostess who persuades friends to hold their own Tupperware parties wins Tupperware products herself. Tupperware distributors are also organized hierarchically for better control, direction, and motivation. Distributors at the top earn a percentage from each sale made by distributors "down the line" (whom the "higher-ups" have generally recruited into the organization). In addition, hundreds of people are involved in making Tupperware products in factories where workers are paid hourly wages for performing explicitly defined, closely supervised jobs. Finally, Tupperware as a corporation must conform to federal laws that govern business practices and that don't apply to informal groups (B. Brown, 1989).

In this chapter we take a detailed look at social groups and formal organizations. We begin with a section on the nature of groups—their defining characteristics, their dynamic processes, and their various types as identified by sociologists. Next we consider how people become committed to groups, sometimes to the point of giving up their individual identities. In the process, we explore commitment in the Amish community, a social group with an extremely high degree of loyalty. Then we shift our attention to formal organizations, discussing how bureaucracies emerge as ways of solving problems in the collective pursuit of goals. We explore the major features of bureaucracies and how they operate in the real world, as well as some of their failures. As the example of Tupperware suggests, some formal organizations flourish when they depart from the bureaucratic mold.

You will note that most of these topics link up to our five key sociological concepts. Both groups and organizations have their own patterns of ***social structure***, such as their size, distribution of power and authority, rules, and division of labor. These social-structural elements are never set in stone: Organizational innovations by individuals or by bureaucracies illustrate the concept of ***social action***. Such innovations are often brought about by changes in the external environment, as a group or organization becomes more (or less) ***functionally integrated*** with their wider society. The structure and processes of groups and organizations are also much affected by ***cultural*** factors, such as beliefs and values within the group or beliefs and values of the society within which an organization is established. Finally, there are similarities in how individuals acquire and retain ***power*** in social groups and in formal organizations.

THE NATURE OF SOCIAL GROUPS

William Golding's novel *Lord of the Flies* (1954) opens on an uninhabited tropical island after a plane carrying thirty English schoolboys, ranging in age from six to twelve, makes a crash landing. All the adults are killed, and the boys are left alone to organize themselves and try to be rescued. But things don't work out as the boys originally hope. A rational, democratic group organized by Ralph is overcome by an irrational and violent one led by Jack. The boys become consumed by groundless fears, intense competition and hatred, and the drive to experience immediate pleasures and express primitive aggressions.

Throughout the story, Golding shows how group experiences influence us to a remarkable degree. Social groups link our private lives to the larger society. They provide us with security and support; they shape our values, attitudes, and behavior; they organize us to accomplish tasks, make decisions, and control deviance. How we act within a group is seldom how we would act if we were entirely alone.

Group Characteristics

After the boys in *Lord of the Flies* crash-land on the tropical island, the first to emerge from the jungle is a fat, overprotected, intellectual boy nicknamed Piggy and a blond, athletic twelve-year-old named Ralph. At Piggy's suggestion, Ralph summons the other survivors by blowing into a large conch shell. Small boys, wearing tattered school uniforms, make their way out of the jungle and onto the beach. These boys do not yet constitute a social group. They are simply an **aggregate** of individuals who happen to be in the same place at the same time, much like pedestrians in a shopping mall or passengers on the same bus. However, the boys soon become a group by repeatedly interacting with one another, by developing an informal social structure, by agreeing on norms to guide their behavior, and by establishing a feeling of unity and belonging.

A social group has four characteristics. First, there is *regular interaction* among members. People who do not communicate with one another, and who barely acknowledge each other's existence, constitute a social aggregate, not a social group. In *Lord of the Flies*, the ragged collection of survivors starts to become a group only with the blowing of the conch and the calling of the first "assembly." After that, the boys routinely get together as a group, to discuss their situation and make decisions regarding their future.

A second characteristic of a social group is the *structured interactions* among members. People in a group don't deal with one another in a haphazard way. Each person typically assumes a certain status and adopts a certain role. These statuses and roles are not officially established, as they are in formal organizations. They tend to evolve informally and are open to renegotiation as people rethink their understandings of situations and engage in social interactions. Nevertheless, relationships in a group are structured in some way, as can be seen in *Lord of the Flies*. For instance, at the first assembly the oldest boys quickly take control; they become the group leaders. The youngest boys are deferential and obedient; they see themselves as followers, not leaders.

A third characteristic of a social group is *agreement on norms, goals, and values*. A collection of people who are at cross-purposes is unlikely to form a group. When Golding's young survivors initially agree on the need for orderly procedures and on the importance of being rescued, they are more of a group than when this consensus later begins to dissolve. A group's norms, goals, and values need not be explicitly stated; often they are implicit or taken for granted. But even implicit, shared understandings can strongly bind a group together.

Finally, the members of a social group feel a *sense of shared identity*. They think of themselves as united and interdependent, somewhat apart from other people. This sense of collective belonging quickly emerges on Golding's island, where the boys—separated from all other people—soon begin to see themselves as Robinson Crusoes sharing an adventure. "This is our island," proclaims Ralph to the others at their second assembly. "It's a good island. Until the grownups come to fetch us we'll have fun." The boys in Golding's novel thus form a set of individuals who identify with one another and who interact in informally structured ways based on norms, goals, and values they implicitly share—in short, they form a social group.

This fraternity at the University of Illinois reflects all the characteristics of a group: regular interaction among members; structured interactions, with informally assigned statuses and roles; agreement on norms, goals, and values; and a feeling of shared identity.

Group Dynamics

Although the boys in *Lord of the Flies* imagine a fun-filled adventure, their reality turns out differently. From the beginning, there is a struggle for control between the fair-haired, attractive Ralph, who represents civilized, rational, rule-governed society, and the tall, thin, ugly Jack, who represents the primitive, spontaneous instincts of violence and excitement. At first Ralph prevails; the boys are orderly and adopt a set of rules to help with their rescue. But gradually Jack gains the upper hand. In the end, most of the boys are persuaded to join Jack's "tribe," which then turns on the remaining "outsiders" and systematically enslaves or destroys them. Eventually, Ralph is the only voice of reason and civilization left on the island, and the others hunt him down like an animal. There appears to be no hope for Ralph until a naval cruiser happens by the island and the adult world intervenes.

Lord of the Flies provides some excellent examples of group dynamics at work. **Group dynamics** are the recurrent patterns of social interaction among the members of a group. These patterns are influenced by several factors, one of the most important of which is group size.

The Impact of Group Size

When Ralph and Piggy find each other, they think at first that they are the only two survivors of the crash. At that time, they form a **dyad**, or two-person group. Then Ralph blows into the conch shell, and six-year-old Johnny comes out of the brush. The dyad had now become a **triad**, or three-person group. This seemingly simple addition of one person (a change in group structure) significantly affects interactions within a group (see Table 8.1). For example, in a dyad both members must participate or the group ceases to exist, whereas in a triad one person may leave but the group lives on. This puts pressure on the members of a dyad to keep the interaction going if they want the group to survive. Golding shows this in *Lord of the Flies* when Piggy and Ralph first meet. Ralph is not very interested in Piggy's overtures of friendship. He does not view this fat, nearsighted, asthmatic child as a desirable companion. So Piggy is forced to follow doggedly as Ralph heads for the beach, coaxing Ralph into interaction. Since Ralph can end the relationship at any time simply by ignoring Piggy, Piggy must proceed carefully lest Ralph reject him completely. This threat of withdrawal by one member makes dyads more prone to tension than triads are.

TABLE 8.1

As Group Size Increases Arithmetically, the Number of Relationships Increases Geometrically

Size of Group	Number of Relationships
2	1
3	6
4	25
5	90
6	301
7	966

Source: A. Paul Hare, *Handbook of Small Group Research* (Free Press, Glencoe, Ill., 1976), p. 218.

Another difference between dyads and triads is that participants in a dyad cannot hide their responsibility for events that occur within the group. If one of two roommates eats the last candy bar that was stashed away, both know with certainty who did it. When three or more roommates live together, only the person who ate the candy bar can be sure wh
or more, one member can also re en
other members, whereas in a dyad der to
act as a mediator. However, a dyad d to deal
with the problem of intruders or spectato ıer of the
pair needs to perform for the benefit o party; nor
does either have to worry about giving a arty "equal
time." Finally, the possibilities of buildi alitions and
creating majorities distinguish dyads from ads. If Ralph
and Jack had been the only survivors in d *of the Flies*,
a division into two hostile camps could ver have occurred. But as soon as other boys come ou of the jungle, competition between leaders for the boys' yalty and support can begin.

As group size increases beyond three, so does the potential for a specialized division of labor. Early in Golding's novel, when all the boys are united into one large group, they successfully assign tasks to different people. Some boys are given the role of hunters; others are asked to be water carriers; still others are given the job of keeping a smoke signal going in case a ship sails near the island. But near the end of the book, when Jack has lured most of the boys into his breakaway tribe, Ralph is left with only a few followers. The elaborate division of labor breaks down. Ralph's now-tiny group cannot even keep the signal fire burning. The relatively complicated structure that was possible when the group was large is no longer feasible in a very small band.

Group dynamics change in other ways as the number of members increases. For instance, in large groups, there is a limit on the amount and quality of communication that can occur among all the members. At the first large assembly in *Lord of the Flies*, a handful of boys dominate the proceedings, and many have no chance to speak at all. In general, rank-and-file members are more inhibited—participating in fewer discussions—as a group's size increases. Problem solving also changes with group size. A large group has a greater variety of skills and resources for solving problems, but the average contribution of each member tends to be less than it would be in a small group. Because of diverse opinions, moreover, it is often difficult for members of a large group to reach consensus on a solution. Such differences in group dynamics, which occur entirely because of size, have an enormous impact on people's experiences in groups with different numbers of members.

Conformity and Control

The boys in *Lord of the Flies* at first form a harmonious social group that adopts the familiar norms of school and the adult world. At an early assembly Ralph points out:

> ". . . We can't have everybody talking at once. We'll have to have 'Hands up' like at school. . . . Then I'll give him the conch."
>
> "Conch?"
>
> "That's what this shell's called. I'll give the conch to the next person to speak. He can hold it when he's speaking." . . .
>
> Jack was on his feet.
>
> "We'll have rules!" he cried excitedly. "Lots of rules!" (Golding, 1954, p. 31)

The boys agree on rules concerning where the signal fire should be built, who will keep it burning, how food and water will be gathered, and so forth. Acceptance of such shared norms helps to bind a group together. The norms tell members how they should act and how group goals should be accomplished. With norms in place, it is possible for the group to exert pressure for conformity.

However, conformity to norms is rarely permanent. In *Lord of the Flies*, consensus and conformity begin to break down very quickly. Jack, who was put in charge of keeping the fire going, lures the fire tenders away from their task so that they can help him hunt wild pigs. The boys also become lackadaisical in their efforts to build sleeping shel-

Dyad members enjoy direct communication and immediate responsibility for each other. Triad members are able to form (or avoid) coalitions, share or avoid responsibility, and mediate disputes. In one context or another, each of us has experienced these basic units of social interaction.

ters and collect drinking water. Soon their orderly way of life becomes aimless and haphazard. Jack, with his aggressive, bullying ways, increasingly asserts himself. Conformity based on rules and consensus gives way to control by force (Goode, 1972). In a scene that marks this transition, Jack challenges the group's norm that only the person holding the conch can speak:

> Piggy had settled himself in a place between two rocks, and sat with the conch on his knees. . . .
>
> "I got the conch," said Piggy indignantly. "You let me speak!"
>
> "The conch doesn't count on top of the mountain," said Jack, "so you shut up."
>
> "I got the conch—"
>
> Jack turned fiercely.
>
> "You shut up!"

This threat of force works because of Jack's superior physical strength. Later on, Jack solidifies his control by destroying the conch and with it whatever meager authority Ralph still holds. Without the conch as a symbol of group consensus and shared rules, spears and stones become the instruments of control.

Leadership

Just as conformity and control change during the life of a group, so leadership patterns, or ***power*** relations, change as the group faces new situations. In *Lord of the Flies*, Ralph is first chosen as the leader. Not only is Ralph one of the oldest and biggest boys, he is also physically attractive and shows initiative in calling the survivors together. His easy self-assurance earns him respect. The other boys applaud when they elect him chief, and they look to him to call meetings, establish rules, and assign tasks. But as the story unfolds, it becomes increasingly clear that the leadership role is largely forced on Ralph by circumstances (his accidentally finding the conch, for example). Far from being a natural leader, Ralph is uncomfortable with the attention and responsibility that leadership brings. Often he is at a loss for what to do next. Jack soon emerges as a rival leader who appeals to the boys' needs for adventure and emotional release.

After careful observation of groups in the process of forming, Harvard sociologist Robert Bales and his students have concluded that groups need leaders for two reasons: to direct tasks and to maintain good spirits and relations among members (Secord and Backman, 1974). The first is known as **instrumental leadership**; the second as **expressive leadership**. In most groups, one person starts out by performing both roles, as Ralph does early in Golding's novel. Later, these roles get divided between two people. The expressive leader is usually a well-liked person. Ralph has the qualities of a good expressive leader. He values harmonious and democratic social relations; he protects Piggy and other underdogs; and he listens to everyone's ideas and needs. But he is less successful at directing important group tasks. In fact, Ralph has such a difficult time with the task of keeping the smoke signal going that he begins to neglect the expressive needs of the group. He is then vulnerable to Jack's seizure of power.

> "Look at us. How many are we? And yet we can't keep a fire going to make smoke. Don't you understand? Can't you see we ought to—ought to die before we let the fire go out?"
>
> There was a self-conscious giggling among the hunters. Ralph turned on them passionately. . . .
>
> "And another thing."
>
> Someone called out.
>
> "Too many things." . . .
>
> There was a row immediately. Boys stood up and shouted and Ralph shouted back. (Golding, 1954, p. 73)

Jack, greedy for power, senses the unmet needs of the group and moves into the leadership gap that Ralph has created by making a single, very tedious task assume overriding importance. While Ralph concentrates on keeping the fire going, Jack offers fun and adventure to those who will leave Ralph:

> "Bollocks to the rules! We're strong—we hunt! If there's a beast, we'll hunt it down! We'll close in and beat and beat and beat—!"
>
> He [Jack] gave a wild whoop and leapt down to the pale sand. At once the platform was full of noise and excitement, scramblings, screams and laughter. (Golding, 1954, p. 83)

Thus, leadership roles may change hands over time, but group members' instrumental and expressive needs still must be met.

Group Decision Making

The boys on Golding's island have no idea why events take the course they do. Things just happen; decisions get made. Sociologists who study group dynamics are more insightful. They have found that, whatever a group's composition or whatever task it must perform, the group typically goes through four stages in making choices (Bales and Strodtbeck, 1951).

The first stage involves orientation. Members analyze the task before them, exchange information, and suggest solutions. The second stage is evaluating the possibilities, and the third stage is eliminating the less desirable options and selecting the one that seems best. The fourth stage is restoring equilibrium—that is, normalizing group relationships after the tension of making a decision. When the boys in *Lord of the Flies* make the decision to remain on the island and await rescue, a period of joking and informal banter restores equilibrium, drawing into the fold even those who disagree with this choice.

The boys' decision to stay on the island is the best one under the circumstances. If they had fashioned a makeshift boat and ventured out on the ocean, they would have courted disaster. Not all decisions are this sound, however. Even when a group of highly intelligent adults analyzes reliable data, serious errors in judgment can occur. When are groups most prone to poor decision making? Social scientist Irving L. Janis (1982, 1989) believes that small, highly cohesive groups with forceful and respected leaders are prone to produce seriously flawed decisions. Such groups, according to Janis, can fall victim to **groupthink**—the tendency for members to be so intent on maintaining group unanimity that they overlook or dismiss as unimportant the flaws in their decisions. Victims of groupthink collectively rationalize their decisions and suppress their doubts. They insulate themselves from the opinions of knowledgeable outsiders, while negatively stereotyping views that are at odds with their own. As a result, they convince themselves that their decisions are sound and that their actions will inevitably bring success. Needless to say, they are often unpleasantly surprised.

A classic example of a groupthink-induced fiasco is the Bay of Pigs invasion carried out by President John F. Kennedy and his advisers in 1961. Fifteen hundred CIA-trained exiles were to land in Cuba and overthrow Fidel Castro's communist regime. The invasion, however, was a complete failure. It embarrassed the United States and solidified Cuba's alliance with the Soviet Union. In making its decision, the group considered only two plans. It failed to reconsider the second plan when the flaws of the first became apparent; it didn't consult with a wide range of experts on Cuba; it ignored contradictory information brought to its attention; and it failed to provide adequate contingency plans. Janis (1972) argues that the major reason for this debacle was a strong compulsion in the small, closely knit circle of Kennedy advisers to maintain unity

The term "groupthink" suggests how group members, when isolated from their social or moral environment, make decisions that appear from the inside to make perfect sense but are, in fact, fundamentally flawed. President Richard Nixon insulated himself with a small group of close advisers, who misread the American public's response to the series of government scandals collectively known as Watergate. Their groupthink ultimately led to the collapse of Nixon's presidency.

and agreement at all costs—in short, not to rock the boat. Another example of groupthink in American government is the Watergate scandal, which involved an attempt by President Richard Nixon's reelection advisers to cover up a politically motivated break-in at the Washington, D.C., offices of the Democratic National Committee. The poor decision making eventually led to Nixon's resignation in 1974.

The same pattern can be seen in *Lord of the Flies* when the boys persistently ridicule and suppress any views that contradict majority opinion. For instance, in one scene a perceptive boy named Simon tries to warn the others that the "beast" they are dismissing as nonexistent may actually lie within themselves (it is a mental creation that reflects the boys' own destructive potential). The other boys immediately scoff at Simon's warning and force him to drop the subject. Simon never publicly expresses his view again. Given such strong group pressures toward conformity, it is not surprising that the boys fail to confront the problem of the "beast" until they are overwhelmed by violent impulses. By then it is too late.

Types of Groups

Although similar patterns of interaction exist in many different groups, all groups are not the same. Sociologists have developed several ways of classifying groups. One involves the distinction between in-groups and out-groups.

In-Groups and Out-Groups

An **in-group** is one with which a person identifies and in which he or she feels at home. An **out-group** is one with which a person does not identify and toward which he or she feels like an outsider. In other words, we think of an in-group as "we" and an out-group as "they."

We are all constantly positioning ourselves in terms of in-groups and out-groups. How we do so can have profound effects on attitudes and public policies. An example is the current debate over health insurance in the United States (discussed in detail in Chapter 15). People who can afford private insurance or whose employers provide them with insurance coverage tend to form an in-group that has little sympathy for the millions of Americans in the out-group of the uninsured. The in-group's resistance to reform—and to the tax increases it would entail—is changing, however, as health-care costs spiral upward and the gaps in insurance coverage become more apparent.

The distinction between in-groups and out-groups draws attention to group *boundaries*, the implicitly understood lines separating those who are in from those who are out. Without boundaries, there would be no way of setting groups off from one another and distinguishing members from nonmembers. Boundaries serve two functions. They keep outsiders out (preventing them from interacting in certain ways with insiders), and they keep insiders in (inhibiting them from moving beyond the confines of the group and encouraging conformity to group norms for fear of possible expulsion).

Members work to maintain group boundaries and to make them clear to others. One way to do this is through the use of visible symbols. For instance, a fraternity T-shirt or a college decal placed on a car window announces one's insider status, symbolically telling the world that one "belongs." The slang and specialized vocabularies used within a group serve much the same purpose. Another very effective way to create and maintain group boundaries is through conflict with outsiders, as we saw in our example of Iraq in Chapter 1. A common enemy helps draw people together and encourages a sense of "we-ness." Even a sports rival can produce this effect.

In the concluding chapters of *Lord of the Flies*, Jack forms a tight in-group from which Ralph, Piggy, and a few other boys are excluded. The members identify themselves by dressing and acting like "savages" (wearing war paint, tying their long hair back from their foreheads, and dancing and chanting together). They also build a fortress to keep out "outsiders."

> "Tomorrow," went on the chief [Jack], "we shall hunt again."
>
> He pointed at this savage and that with his spear.
>
> "Some of you will stay here to improve the cave and defend the gate. I shall take a few hunters with me and bring back meat. The defenders of the gate will see that the others don't sneak in."
>
> A savage raised his hand and the chief turned a bleak, painted face toward him.
>
> "Why should they try to sneak in, Chief?"
>
> The chief was vague but earnest. "They will. They'll try to spoil things we do. So the watchers of the gate must be careful." (Golding, 1954, pp. 145–146)

In this episode, Jack actively exploits Ralph's and Piggy's enemy status (depicting them as a threatening out-group) to unify his band (the in-group).

Primary and Secondary Groups

Although we all identify with a number of different in-groups, we do not necessarily interact with all the members of these groups or even know them all intimately (see Figure 8.1). When a group has an especially close-knit nature, it is called a **primary group**. This term was introduced by Charles Horton Cooley (1909/1929), who described a primary group as having five features:

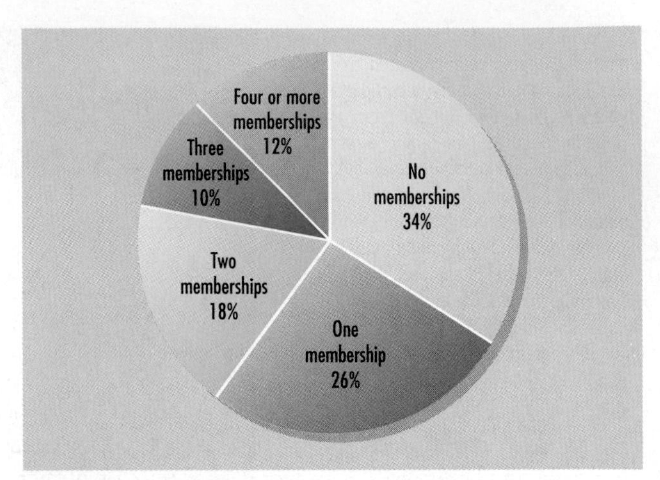

FIGURE 8.1 / Percentages of Americans Who Belong to Various Numbers of Voluntary Associations (Political, Professional and Occupational, Mutual Aid, Religious, and Charitable Groups)

Source: National Opinion Research Center, *General Social Surveys 1972–1990: Cumulative Guidebook* (National Opinion Research Center, Chicago, 1990), p. 369.

1. Continuous face-to-face interaction
2. Strong personal identity with the group
3. Strong ties of affection among group members
4. Multifaceted relationships
5. A tendency for the group to be very enduring

The nuclear family—wife, husband, and their children—is the ideal primary group. Members of a nuclear family engage in frequent face-to-face interaction. For them, the family is an important source of identity and purpose. Love and affection bind the family members together, and they have multifaceted relationships with one another (ranging from exchange of services—"You set the table; I'll wash the dishes"—to emotional support and physical protection). Finally, the family is enduring. Even when members move away from each other, they still consider themselves part of the unit.

Cooley chose the term *primary* to describe this kind of group because these groups are the primary, or "first," agents of socialization. They are the principal means by which people acquire their social selves. Cooley called primary groups "the nurseries of human nature." The values and norms people learn in their primary groups tend to remain with them for life. Golding illustrates this fact in a scene in which Roger and Maurice, two of the older boys, kick over sand castles that some little boys are making. In the process Maurice accidentally kicks sand in a little boy's eyes. The child whimpers, and Maurice feels guilt even though there is no adult around to reprimand him. Maurice had once been reprimanded by his parents for doing this very thing, which is why he feels guilty about doing it again. The socialization that occurred in that faraway primary group still affects the way he thinks and feels.

This example illustrates a second reason that groups such as the family are aptly called primary: It is in such groups that social norms are very often enforced. In their frequent and intimate interactions, members of primary groups have countless opportunities to scrutinize one another's behavior and to bring back into line those who deviate from the norms. They might do this with a look of displeasure, a word of rebuke, or a temporary withdrawal of affection. Maurice's parents did one or more of these things when they saw him kicking sand in another child's face. In such ways, primary groups serve as "frontline" agents of social control.

Primary groups are primary in a third sense as well: Relationships within them meet people's most basic emotional and psychological needs. Members of primary groups give one another a sense of love and security, a sense of recognition, companionship, and well-being. Such groups are our principal anchors in society. Without them, we would feel alone and vulnerable.

Secondary groups have the opposite characteristics of primary groups:

1. Limited face-to-face interaction
2. Modest or weak personal identity with the group
3. Weak ties of affection among group members
4. Limited, shallow relationships
5. A tendency not to be very enduring

An example of a secondary group is a student committee organized to choose movies for an upcoming campus film festival. Members of the committee meet infrequently, for only a few hours at a time, and for an explicit purpose; their interactions are not an end in themselves. In fact, the members will probably view digressions from their stated task with a good deal of impatience. Although members may hold similar attitudes and values, their basic ties are task-oriented, not emotional ones. Sometimes secondary groups become rather informal, and the members get to know one another fairly well. Even so, their friendships exist in a limited context; they are not intimately bound together by relationships on many levels.

Like many other distinctions in sociology, the distinction between primary and secondary groups is not hard and fast. The two types of groups often overlap in real life. Thus, although relations among these marketing specialists are limited to the workplace, their teamwork may contain the primary-group traits of intimacy, affection, and loyalty.

Like other distinctions in sociology, the one between primary and secondary groups is useful because it highlights social dimensions that we might not otherwise see. The distinction is not absolute, however. Often it is more accurate to view primariness and secondariness as matters of degree. For example, many work groups in businesses, although task-oriented, provide their members with close and warm relationships. In these groups, we see some primary-group traits within a basic secondary-group context. Such blending of features does not invalidate the distinction between primary groups and secondary groups. It just means that in real life group characteristics can be quite complex.

Reference Groups

People don't always *belong* to the groups with which they identify. **Reference groups** are those groups to which people refer when they evaluate their own behavior, even though they may not necessarily belong to them.

Reference groups serve two functions. One is to provide standards for evaluating ourselves and our life situations. This can be seen in *Lord of the Flies* when Piggy, Ralph, and Simon compare themselves and their own bungled efforts to the competent world of adults:

> "Grownups know things," said Piggy. . . . "They'd meet and have tea and discuss. Then things 'ud be all right—"

> "They wouldn't set fire to the island. Or lose—"
> "They'd build a ship—"
> The three boys stood in the darkness, striving unsuccessfully to convey the majesty of adult life.
> "They wouldn't quarrel—"
> "Or break my specs—"
> "Or talk about a beast—"

In comparison to this older, more mature reference group, the boys judge their own behavior to be pathetically inept.

Reference groups also serve a normative function—that is, they provide guidelines regarding appropriate thought and behavior. Because people hope to be identified with their reference groups (especially if they aren't members of them), they try to act like those they think typify these groups. If your reference group is the jocks on campus, you will dress, speak, and act quite differently than if your reference group consists of intellectuals. A reference group, in other words, helps to shape a person's outlook, appearance, and style.

Group Survival as a Matter of Commitment and Structure

Have you ever belonged to a group that just fell apart and ceased to exist altogether? What happened to it? Sociologists want to know why some groups last for years, even centuries, while others disappear almost as soon as they are formed. One critical factor is the level of commitment that a group inspires. Groups that last are good at getting members to contribute their time, energy, money, and other resources to the group. In groups that fail, members lose interest and refuse to provide the time and resources needed to keep the group alive.

The Old-Order Amish offer an excellent example of a group that inspires high levels of commitment (Hostetler, 1980). The Amish are simultaneously a social group, a church, a community, and a spiritual union. Their way of life has survived for nearly 300 years, with almost no changes in the customs, beliefs, and values established by their founder, Jacob Amman. The Amish believe it is necessary to separate themselves from the larger world, with its vices and temptations, in order to live the truly righteous life that is needed for eternal salvation. To the Amish, this means they must distance themselves from the values, beliefs, and material possessions of the larger society. Accordingly, they shun many "worldly" things, from modern styles of clothing, to personal adornments (jewelry, watches, makeup, haircutting or hair curling for women), to modern conveniences most of us take for granted (cars, electricity, running water, central heating, telephones). The Amish manage to maintain their traditional way of life despite the fact that modernity is all around them. In eastern Pennsylvania, for example, the exurbs of Philadelphia have encroached upon Amish farms, bringing with them all the temptations of late twentieth-century American culture. Still, only 6 percent of Amish young people choose to leave the fold. Much of the reason so few defect is that the Amish community demands total commitment from its members. It is what sociologist Lewis Coser (1974) calls a **greedy group**, one that makes all-encompassing claims on the hearts, minds, and loyalty of its members. Whereas most social groups claim only a small part of each member's life, groups like the Amish want the "whole" person.

How do the Amish and other groups like them manage to inspire this kind of commitment? To answer this question, Rosabeth Moss Kanter (1972) conducted a study of nineteenth-century utopian communities, some of which were similar to the Amish. She found that communities that lasted for a long time had created certain social arrangements that fostered commitment. In other words, commitment was encouraged through the ***social structure*** of the group. In Kanter's model, six important processes were woven into the social structure of enduring groups: sacrifice, investment, renunciation, communion, mortification, and transcendence. We will explore these processes in depth, illustrating each with examples from the Old-Order Amish.

Sacrifice means that group members are expected to give up something of value in order to join the group. The greater that sacrifice, Kanter argues, the stronger the members' devotion to the group, for people need to justify giving up so much. Sacrifice also builds commitment by weeding out potential members who are not prepared to devote themselves totally to the group. This leaves only those who are ready to commit themselves entirely. There are hundreds of examples of sacrifice among the Amish. For example, the Amish aren't allowed to own cars, radios, television sets, telephones, stereos, musical instruments, electric refrigerators, washing machines, and other household appliances. (They choose not to hook up with the electric power network because the Bible instructs them not to "yoke" themselves with nonbelievers.) The Amish are also forbidden to own "luxury" furnishings such as carpets, curtains, and wallpaper and to buy or make fashionable clothing or personal adornments of any kind. Members must sacrifice the chance of going to college (most Amish don't go to school beyond the eighth grade) and the chance of finding satisfying work in a field that involves "outsiders."

Sacrifice, investment, renunciation, communion, mortification, and transcendence—how many of these commitment-building processes identified by Kanter are at work in the Amish custom of a barn raising?

Investment means that members must contribute their resources to the group—either tangible resources such as property and money or intangible ones such as time and effort. The more people are required to invest in a group, the greater the stake they have in the group's survival. Investment also builds commitment by reminding people that the needs of the group take priority over selfish desires. Investment in Amish communities takes the form of contributions of time and labor. For instance, when fire destroys an Amish barn or house, all the Amish men in the area gather to rebuild what was lost. Similarly, when a death occurs in an Amish family, members of the community help out by doing the bereaved family's chores. Amish men are also called upon to serve as ministers of the church. The job does not pay a salary, but it is considered an honor. By investing their efforts in the community, the Amish heighten their sense of group commitment.

Renunciation means that members of a group are required to renounce (give up) relationships that interfere with obligations to the group or that cause them to question group beliefs and values. At its most extreme, renunciation leaves members only one another to interact with, thus strengthening group ties. To bring about renunciation, the Amish erect many symbolic boundaries between insiders and outsiders. One such boundary is a strict dress code. Amish men with their black suits, collarless shirts, and wide-brimmed hats and Amish women with their long dresses, black stockings, and traditional aprons and caps set themselves off from other twentieth-century Americans. This distinctive dress helps to foster a strong sense of "we-ness" and contributes to group commitment.

Communion involves the coming together of the group for joint activities, often in symbolic rituals that celebrate the power of the group over the individual. Like renunciation, communion builds commitment by enhancing a sense of "we," a view of the self as intermingled with others who are part of the group. But whereas renunciation requires that people give up relationships with outsiders, communion strengthens the bonds that remain among insiders. The Amish calendar is filled with communal occasions. Religious services for every adult and child in the district are held every other Sunday in Amish homes. Community sings are communal events that occur on a regular basis and help to build a sense of fellowship. Occurring less often, but extremely important for strengthening group commitment, is the baptism ritual. Upon being baptized into the Amish church, young adults make a solemn promise to uphold the rules of the Amish community and to strive to lead a virtuous life. For all those who attend this service, devotion to the group is renewed. Other Amish community rituals that enhance group commitment include weddings and funerals (often attended by everyone in the district) and the celebration of Christian communion, which for the Amish involves the ritual washing of one another's feet (just as Jesus washed the feet of his disciples at the Last Supper).

The root word of *mortification* is *mort*, or death. Kanter uses the term to mean "death of the private self." Some groups—especially greedy ones—demand that members let their private, autonomous selves perish and replace them with a self that is complete only as part of the group. Mortification builds group commitment because it makes members need the group in order to feel whole. The Amish encourage mortification through their practice of condemning self-pride. Neither women nor men are allowed to show pride in their physical appearance. (Even owning a mirror or having one's picture taken is strictly forbidden.) At school, Amish children are not to show pride in their academic achievements. To actively compete with other students and boast about good grades is considered the worst kind of self-aggrandizement. The Amish demand intense humility from one another. Calling special attention to the self is looked upon as vain and disgraceful.

Transcendence means that people feel a special power or virtue as a result of being part of the group. They have a sense that group membership allows them to transcend (rise above) the ordinary, giving their lives a higher meaning than is available to other people. Commitment is strengthened through transcendence, for members believe that they enjoy a "special" life that comes only through their bond with the group. Transcendence is built into the Amish way of life. The Amish consider their community the true Christian church, distinguished from the "fallen" church, which has become corrupt and displeasing to God. As members of the true church, the Amish strive to be a "peculiar" people, peculiar in the sense of being different from the rest of the world. Their distinctive life of righteous humility is the only route to eternal life in heaven, according to the Amish view.

The degree to which these six processes (sacrifice, investment, renunciation, communion, mortification, and transcendence) are present in a social group largely determines the level of commitment which that group enjoys. At least some commitment-building processes must exist in a social group, because otherwise groups tend to dissolve very quickly. When all six of these processes are woven into a group's social structure, commitment to that group tends to be strong and the group is likely to endure.

THE RISE OF FORMAL ORGANIZATIONS: BUREAUCRATIC INNOVATIONS

Ask most people what the word *bureaucracy* brings to mind and you won't get very favorable answers. They might tell you about waiting in a line for two hours, only to be told that they should have been waiting in the line across the hall. Or they might complain about being treated like a nine-digit number instead of a unique individual. In spite of these frustrating, dehumanizing features, bureaucracy is very common in modern social life. We literally spend our lives in formal organizations, moving from one bureaucracy to another. We are born in large hospitals, taught in formal educational complexes, employed by multinational corporations, governed by state and federal agencies, and even buried by large mortuary firms. Indeed, most of the crucial decisions affecting our lives—especially those having to do with economic matters and issues of war and peace—are made by large organizations. Surely there must be more to bureaucracy than incompetence and red tape.

In spite of their flaws and limitations, bureaucratically structured formal organizations enable people to work together to accomplish tasks that they couldn't accomplish in an informal, loosely structured group (see Figure 8.2). As the number of people involved gets larger, and as tasks become more diverse and complex, bureaucratic organization becomes the most efficient vehicle for ***social action***. Thus, bureaucratically structured formal organizations pervade modern society because certain aspects of them have been successful. They have given people a competitive advantage over others who are not bureaucratically organized. In this section, we consider several bureaucratic innovations that have proved to be extremely successful in helping people achieve their collective goals. These bureaucratic innovations solved three important problems: how to organize a large number of people in the pursuit of a goal, how to accomplish several diverse tasks simultaneously, and how to reduce opposition to an organization's aims.

Organizing Large Numbers of People: The Military

Napoleon I was among the greatest military leaders of all time. He oversaw every detail of a battle, often sleeping only a few hours each night. When awake, he was in constant motion: traveling from one strategic position to another, inspecting his troops, conferring with his subordinates, gathering information from civilians and prisoners of war, even doing his own reconnaissance, which sometimes brought him within firing distance of the enemy lines. At night he would pull together all the available data, formulate his plans, and compose his highly detailed orders. Sometimes he would dictate orders to four separate secretaries on four separate topics at once (Van Creveld, 1985). But even Napoleon's impressive powers of control began to break down as his army got bigger. At the battle of Austerlitz in 1805, Napoleon brilliantly controlled an army of 85,000 men, whereas at Jena a year later he lost control of a third to a half of his 150,000 troops (Van Creveld, 1985). The grand army that Napoleon assembled

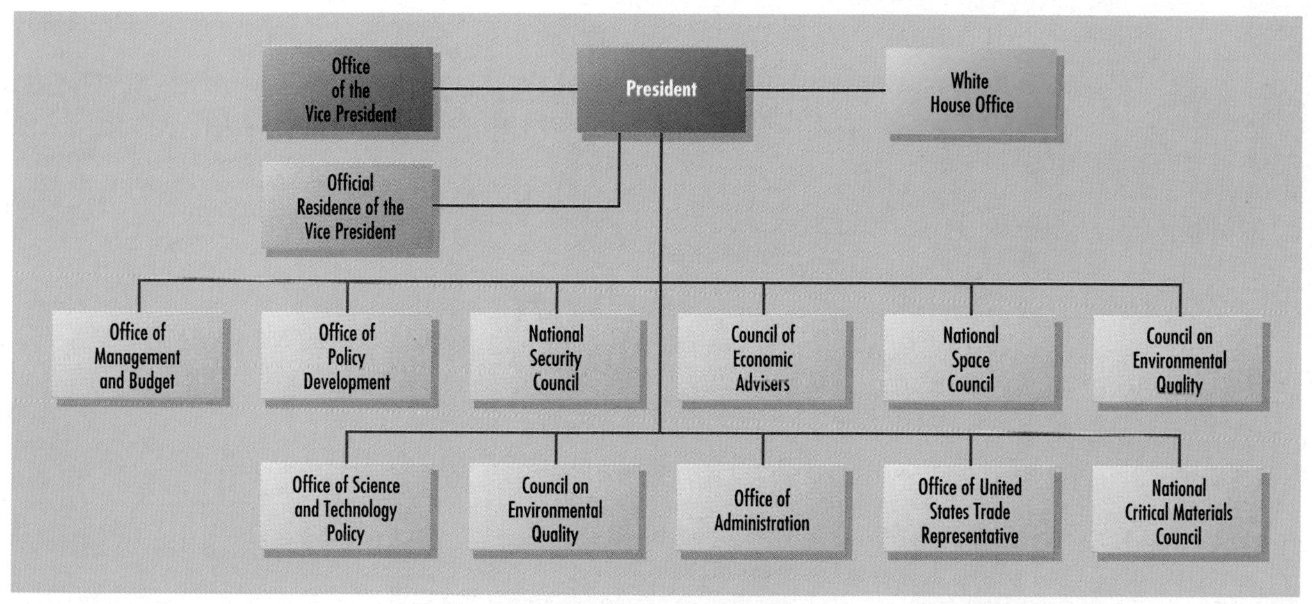

FIGURE 8.2 / The Bureaucratic Structure of a Formal Organization: The Organization Chart of the Executive Office of the President of the United States

Source: *Federal Register*, 1989, p. 86.

for his invasion of Russia had over 500,000 men. Not even Napoleon, with his computerlike mind, could keep track of such a huge fighting force; the invasion failed.

After Napoleon's defeat, Helmut von Moltke, chief of the Prussian general staff, tried to figure out a better way to exercise command over a large army. One of his innovations was uniform, specialized training for staff officers. No longer were young men given staff positions simply because they came from military families. Instead, potential staff officers were carefully selected from each year's graduates of the prestigious Kriegsakademie (War College). Moreover, even when appointed to the general staff, an officer spent several years on probation, during which time he was given further training in military strategy and execution. Only when von Moltke was fully satisfied with the man's performance was the young officer made a permanent member of the staff. In this way, von Moltke thoroughly trained his officers to think and respond as he would, much as a large corporation such as IBM trains its junior executives to think and act in "the IBM way." This unanimity of thought and action among staff members helped ensure their finely tuned coordination during warfare (Ropp, 1959). It also ensured that no one was indispensable, since all were highly trained and similarly skilled. Each of his officers was capable of doing whatever von Moltke ordered. Thus, the solitary, heroic general like Napoleon was replaced by a staff of "managers."

A second organizational innovation used by von Moltke was the standardization of the Prussian army's divisions. The divisional system was introduced during the Seven Years' War (1756–1763) by the French general Duke Victor de Broglie. De Broglie combined infantry brigades and artillery brigades, which had formerly been independent, into the same unit, which he called a division. These divisions allowed much better coordination among the various kinds of troops. In 1794, the French minister of war created divisions that included three types of troops: infantry, artillery, and cavalry. Within a few years this system was adopted throughout the French army, and not long thereafter the British and the Prussians also switched to a divisional system (Dupuy and Dupuy, 1986). Von Moltke carried the divisional idea to its ultimate by making divisions very similar to one another in size, composition, and structure (each division was even issued the same number of knives, forks, and spoons). Divisions in the Prussian army, in a sense, became interchangeable parts in a well-designed military machine.

The greater efficiency of von Moltke's system largely explains Prussia's rapid victory over France in the Franco-Prussian War (1870–1871). The two sides were relatively equal in armaments and manpower, but von Moltke's organizational innovations gave the Prussians a decisive edge. Von Moltke's innovations were soon copied throughout the West. Today all armies exploit von

The military was one of the origins of the modern bureaucracy. The military stresses roles rather than individuals, strict discipline, action without emotion, and standard "presentations of self," as these midshipmen are learning at the U.S. Naval Academy.

Moltke's basic bureaucratic system. They train their officers in a common set of tactics and procedures, and they standardize the makeup and structure of their military units. These organizational techniques are essential if modern armies are to fight efficiently.

Integrating Diverse Tasks: Swift and Company

The nineteenth century saw the birth not just of huge armies but also of huge industrial corporations. These companies were enormous in terms of their volume of output as well as the diversity of their operations. How were business executives to manage a sprawling enterprise that supplied its own raw materials, manufactured a large line of products, and marketed those products in diverse locations? The answers, again, came through new techniques of formal organization.

Swift and Company is a good example of how organizational techniques made it possible to integrate diverse operations (Chandler, 1962). Gustavus Swift was a butcher from Massachusetts who moved to Chicago in the mid-1870s. He knew that the demand for fresh meat in Eastern cities such as Boston, Philadelphia, and New York was greater than East Coast suppliers could satisfy. Swift hit upon the idea of using refrigerated railway cars to transport large quantities of Western-raised beef to the Eastern Seaboard. Selling this beef in the East was at first not an easy matter. People were wary of eating meat that had been so long in transport; they had to be convinced that refrigeration would keep the meat fresh. Because local meat shops weren't certain they should sell meat their customers didn't trust, Swift set up his own marketing operation in each of the major Eastern cities. Each city had a refrigerated warehouse for temporary storage of the arriving shipments, as well as a network of wholesalers and retail outlets to get the meat to consumers. Such a large and complicated system might have been hard to coordinate had it not been for another bureaucratic innovation: a vertical chain of command connecting the branch manager in each metropolitan area to the home office in Chicago. This **vertical integration** allowed information (about inventory, for example) to travel up from local warehouses to corporate managers at the highest levels. At the same time, it allowed important strategic decisions (say, to increase bacon production) to move from the top decision makers down to the various branches.

These two bureaucratic techniques—a diversity of operations conducted by a single firm and a vertical chain of command to integrate the entire system—seem commonplace to us today, but in Swift's time they were innovations. Other companies in the meat business had to copy Swift's organization in order to compete with him. Soon the industry was dominated by a few huge, well-organized firms, each of which integrated a variety of operations through vertical chains of command.

Reducing Opposition: A Government Agency

A persistent problem that formal organizations face is opposition to their programs and policies. Since their inception, formal organizations have had to find ways to reduce such opposition. One technique they have used is **cooptation**, the process of defusing potential opponents by bringing them into one's own organizational structure.

An excellent example of co-optation is the case of the Tennessee Valley Authority (TVA), a U.S. government-owned corporation established under the New Deal in 1933 to integrate the development of the Tennessee River basin (Selznick, 1949). The TVA was empowered to build dams to control flooding, to deepen river channels and make them more navigable, to produce and distribute inexpensive electricity and operate some fertilizer plants, and to plan for the proper use and conservation of the region's natural resources. Many people who lived in the region opposed the grand plans of the TVA. In an effort to overcome the resistance of area residents, representatives of powerful local groups and organizations were given positions on TVA decision-making boards. Many of these board members were initially opposed to the TVA, but by co-opting them into the organization, the TVA essentially eliminated their opposition and was able to survive in a very conservative region of the country (Blau and Meyer, 1987).

Co-optation, however, is a two-way street (Hall, 1982). Although an organization can defuse its opposition by giving potential critics a voice in its operation, this process increases the chances that the views of co-opted parties will find their way into the organization's policies. This is what happened with the TVA, which often favored the private interests of its directors over the public interests it had been created to support. For example, land with improved soil that bordered TVA reservoirs was allowed to be privately purchased, and reforested land that was meant to be left as undisturbed watershed area was allowed to be exploited by powerful lumber companies (Scott, 1981). Thus, co-optation may be a successful technique for helping an organization survive, but it can also change that organization's goals and policies.

THE NATURE OF BUREAUCRACY

These three examples—von Moltke's army, Swift and Company, and the TVA—show how certain bureaucratic innovations provided a competitive advantage. When the Prussian army standardized the training of its officers and the structure of its divisions, it was better able to control large numbers of people. When Swift and Company established hierarchies of personnel, it was better able to integrate diverse operations. And when the TVA co-opted its local opposition, it was better able to survive in a conservative part of the country. Thus, techniques of formal organization enabled those who used them to achieve important goals and to defeat rivals and opponents. As a result, these techniques were widely imitated and formal organization spread, so that today it exists throughout modern societies.

Weber's Ideal Type

It was left for Max Weber—the German sociologist writing in the early decades of this century—to synthesize these (and other) innovations into a definition of **bureaucracy**. To do so, Weber constructed an "ideal type," a model to highlight bureaucracy's major features. Weber's ideal type doesn't describe *all* bureaucracies as they actually function. As you'll see shortly, real-world bureaucracies are much too varied to fit into a single mold. Instead, Weber's ideal type is an analytical tool that calls attention to general features commonly found in bureaucracies. There are five such features:

1. *Specialization*

In bureaucracies, the work to be accomplished is broken down into a clear-cut division of labor, and people are trained to specialize in performing each task. It is assumed that such specialization is the most efficient way to get the job done. Gustavus Swift used specialization in his meat-marketing operation. Some employees specialized in purchasing cattle at the stockyards; others in butchering the beef; others in loading the meat onto train cars; others in running the warehouses in the East; and still others in selling the Swift and Company products to wholesale dealers and retail outlets. This system was far more efficient than having a team of workers follow each beef shipment from the Western prairies to grocery store counters in New York.

2. *Hierarchy of Offices*

Once an organization's operation is divided into smaller, more manageable tasks, the various activities must be coordinated—the gears of the machine must mesh. If they do not, people in one department might design a bolt an eighth of an inch larger than the nut designed in another department (Blau and Meyer, 1987). The solution is to organize workers into a hierarchy, with each person being

CHAPTER 9

Class and Stratification

Starting in the 1980s, the sidewalks of American cities became home to an increasing number of people. Shabbily dressed, sometimes smelly, they often carried all their worldly possessions around in plastic bags. Middle-class Americans sometimes offered them pocket change and sometimes were offended or frightened when homeless people begged too aggressively. Lawmakers announced programs to deal with "the homeless." Churches set up shelters. News programs discussed the causes of homelessness. Yet the homeless people did not vanish. The sociologist James Wright (1989) estimates that a million and a half people spend at least part of the year without a fixed address.

Now, in small towns as well as big cities, middle-class Americans have become accustomed to the presence of homeless people. Confronted with a homeless person on the way to lunch or shopping, most Americans stare straight ahead and keep walking. We may feel pity, fear, or disgust, or we may simply wish the homeless would go away. But when we stop to think about it, we are also puzzled: The homeless are a "visible mystery" (Schruger, 1990). It is hard to believe that such misery can exist in the richest nation on earth. Who are these people, and why are they living on the street?

Joseph Fisher is a frail, undernourished black man who looks considerably older than his thirty-three years. In his teens Mr. Fisher dropped out of high school to enlist in the Navy. After his discharge, he lived with his mother and younger sister and worked at a factory for a short time. But that was nearly ten years ago, and he has not been employed steadily since. Eventually, his mother asked him to move out. When interviewed, Mr. Fisher was sleeping at a mission shelter most nights and hawking newspapers to drivers stopped at downtown traffic lights, for which he earns between $10 and $15 a week. An alcoholic, Mr. Fisher spends most of what he earns on cheap wine, which he sometimes shares with other homeless men. When he is out of money, they share with him. Mr. Fisher sees no hope of a better future, often has no appetite, and frequently thinks about suicide.

Henry Kublik is a fifty-five-year-old white man. After graduating from high school, Mr. Kublik went to work in a steel mill, married, and fathered three children. Then, at age forty-four, he suffered a heart attack. Unable to return to the mill, he drifted from one sales job to another. His earnings dropped, his savings evaporated, and his marriage broke up. Since he lost his family, Mr. Kublik has worked at a series of low-paying, low-skill jobs, and moved back and forth between rooms in run-down hotels and beds in homeless shelters, depending on his income. He has not been in contact with his children for years. Mr. Kublik worries about his health. He believes he would not survive a second heart attack because, with no health insurance, he would not get proper care.

Frowzy and unkempt, thirty-five-year-old Ida Madigan looks more like fifty-five. When interviewed at a shelter on a hot day in July, she clutched a ragged wool coat over a wrinkled rayon dress. After graduating from high school, Ms. Madigan held a number of clerical jobs, the last for four years as a department store billing clerk. She lost that job when she began to suffer severe depressive episodes and could not get to work. Ms. Madigan checked herself into a psychiatric hospital out of fear that she would commit suicide. Discharged after six months, she received disability payments from Social Security at first, but these were abruptly terminated. Both of her parents are dead, and the sister with whom she lived before she was hospitalized has married and moved away. Ms. Madigan has been homeless for several years.

These portraits, drawn from the sociologist Peter Rossi's book *Down and Out in America* (1989, pp. 1–8), help us to see the personal tragedy of homelessness. Every homeless person has an individual story that describes the events that led to his or her predicament. But there is also a more sociological story. Homelessness is not just a tragedy for some individuals; it is a reflection of the sharp inequality that divides the experiences of different groups of Americans. Just as Americans are members of different races, genders, or religions, they are also members of different *social classes*—groupings based on their unequal places in the economic hierarchy. Some Americans have inherited vast wealth and spend much of their time on the golf course; others have worked hard to go to medical school and now enjoy high incomes as doctors; others are modestly paid schoolteachers, struggling small-business owners, blue-collar workers on assembly lines, or welfare recipients in inner cities. And some are chronically homeless because they can't afford housing even when they work.

We call the United States the land of equal opportunity, but in fact our chances in life are based largely on the class into which we are born. Our actions (and those of our parents and others) can move us from one class to another, but class is one of the most basic and enduring features of ***social structure***. In order to understand homelessness, or poverty in general, or the pressures on the middle class today, or our chances of becoming rich, we need to understand the structures of social inequality that have become part of the ongoing, institutionalized character of American society.

The contrast between extreme poverty and enormous prosperity has grown sharper in recent years (Rossi, 1989).

This photograph was taken by Nicole Mitchell, an eleven-year-old girl living in a shelter in Washington, D.C., as part of a project in which homeless children chronicled their social existence. The picture reminds us that many homeless people are children and most of them belong to minority groups.

More people became millionaires in the 1980s than in any previous decade. Yet in front of the glittering office towers built by the banks that manage the millionaires' money, homeless people rummage through garbage, sleep on ventilation grates, and beg from passersby. Millionaires, bankers, and beggars all have their place in the American system of social stratification.

WEALTH, POWER, AND PRESTIGE: THE DIMENSIONS OF STRATIFICATION

The study of social stratification is the attempt to explain institutionalized patterns of social inequality. As the sociologist Gerhard Lenski (1966) puts it, we want to know *who gets what, and why*. Part of the answer has to do with individual differences. In every society, individuals differ in their wisdom, skills, strength, beauty, and ambition. These qualities may affect their standard of living, the respect they enjoy from others, and the influence they wield. A system of social stratification, however, is based on more than differences among individuals.

Stratification refers to the division of a society into layers (or strata) of people who have unequal amounts of scarce but desirable resources, unequal life chances, and unequal social influence (Beteille, 1985). On each level, people occupy social statuses that give them access to different amounts of the three main dimensions of stratification: wealth (including income), power, and prestige. The status of banker is high on all three of these dimensions; that of homeless person is low on all three. Other statuses enjoy high scores on one dimension and low scores on the others. Most ministers in local churches, for example, have substantial prestige, or social esteem, in their communities, but their status generally does not bring them a great deal of power or wealth.

When we say that social stratification is institutionalized, we refer to the fact that inequalities are built into the social structure and may persist from generation to generation. A stratification system is considered **closed** to the extent that it is difficult or impossible to move up the social hierarchy. Under apartheid, the South African stratification system was largely closed for blacks. By contrast, the American system is relatively **open**; no positions are officially denied people because of their birth or other inherited characteristics (except that an immigrant cannot become president). American ideology says that class positions are mostly **achieved statuses** (see Chapter 4)—that is, they are the results of individual effort and accomplishment; but this is not really true. While individual achievements do matter, the class position of a person's parents remains the best predictor of the class position that person will occupy.

Social stratification does not occur by chance or just as a result of individual differences in ability; it is a systematic arrangement that serves the interests of some people above the interests of others. No human society has ever been found in which members are perfectly equal in their wealth, power, and prestige, though the degree of inequality varies enormously from society to society (Lenski, Lenski, and Nolan, 1991; Sahlins, 1958). Among the Bushmen of Africa's Kalahari desert, for example, there are few inequalities beyond age, family position, and gender (E. M. Thomas, 1959). Elders make most collective decisions, parents exercise authority over their children, and men enjoy power and privileges denied to women. In larger societies, with more accumulated wealth, whole groups are stratified into a stable hierarchy, and positions in this hierarchy are passed on from generation to generation by inheritance. The basis of such hierarchies varies widely (Smith, 1974, 1991). For example, material possessions are not always prized above spiritual status and other sources of cultural prestige. In India the prestige and power of Mahatma Gandhi were much greater than those of many wealthy businesspeople, even though he had few possessions, wore only a simple loincloth, and spent much of his life fasting. Indeed, the fact that he *chose* poverty contributed to his prestige and power. The caste system of traditional India also involved a basic emphasis on spiritual status rather than material wealth. In other settings, sacrifices like Gandhi's may not be equally valued, and power may instead be based on physical strength, wealth, educational credentials, or democratic elections.

In modern industrial societies like the United States, wealth and income play an especially strong role in stratification. This emphasis on economic differences is reflected in the term **social class**. A social class, as we saw above, is a group of people who occupy similar positions in the system of stratification because they occupy similar positions in the economy. Thus, when Americans speak of "the middle class," they mean people who are neither extremely rich nor extremely poor. Class position influences virtually every aspect of our lives, from the kind of food we eat to the quality of our housing, from our education, occupation, and income to our choice of marriage partners, our tastes in art, and even the number of years we live. We will examine the American class structure in more detail later in this chapter, and ask what chances Americans have to change their class position.

No system of social stratification, even those in which economic class is most influential, is ever so simple that each layer fits neatly and completely over the one beneath it in terms of wealth and income, power, and prestige. For example, a drug dealer may be rich, but we are reluctant to consider him or her upper class. Most of us consider the Reverend Billy Graham part of the elite even though he is not extremely wealthy. We recognize that power can come from control over a bureaucracy and not just from wealth. And we recognize that cultural factors such as racism may limit people's prestige and power independently of their wealth.

KEY CONCEPTS IN STRATIFICATION ANALYSIS

Social stratification has been a central concern of nearly all major sociological theorists because, as we noted earlier, it is one of the most basic dimensions of ***social structure***. Karl Marx pioneered modern studies of class and stratification by showing that even where the "free-enterprise system" gave individuals opportunities that earlier economies had not, people's life chances were still largely determined by their class position. In this section we begin by introducing Marx's theory. In addition to calling attention to the centrality of class structure, however, Marx argued that stratification was rooted overwhelmingly in capitalist economic production and that unequal class power would always lead to struggle and conflict between classes. While most other sociologists join Marx in emphasizing social structure, many have challenged his focus on economic classes and his prediction of inevitable class conflict. As we will see, these other theorists placed greater emphasis on the key concepts of ***functional integration, power***, and ***culture***. Finally in this section, we will look briefly at the different ways in which sociologists see the potential for stratification to be changed by ***social action***.

Class Structure

When modern stratification analysis started in the mid-nineteenth century, the biggest issue was the way in which early capitalism was producing a new division between rich and poor. Marx (1867/1976) argued that this division was new in two senses. First, capitalism produced new sources of wealth, including large-scale trade and, especially, industrial production. Merchants and factory owners grew spectacularly rich, seemingly overnight. Their wealth helped them gradually to replace the aristocrats of the old feudal era as the most influential class in society. Second, capitalism divided the rich from the poor in new ways. The old multilevel hierarchy (peasant, squire, knight, lord, king) based equally on religious, political, and economic dimensions was replaced by a two-level class structure based on private ownership of property. Capitalism divided society into owners of the means of production (capitalists) and people who could live only by selling their labor (workers). Many craft workers and small farmers who had been reasonably well-off and independent lost their traditional livelihoods and became landless laborers.

Most famously, as we saw in Chapter 1 (and will explore further in Chapter 16), Marx argued that capitalists had to exploit workers in order to survive and make profits. The two groups' interests were thus fundamentally opposed, a situation that could only lead to economic crises and class conflict. Marx acknowledged that capitalist industry produced vast new wealth and created more opportunities for people to escape from poverty than previous economic systems had. But Marx argued that instead of allowing this new wealth to be distributed to benefit all members of a society, capitalism required that it be accumulated as capital investments that benefited the owners of the means of production at the expense of the workers. Small-business owners might get their start by exceptionally hard work or bright ideas, but in the long run—as, for example, when the great-grandchildren of entrepreneurs have inherited their businesses—it is ownership of the means of production, rather than talent, hard work, or any other form of individual merit, that explains wealth.

Marx's theory is the foundation of modern stratification analysis, especially class analysis. He did more than any other thinker to show that structural inequality is central to social organization, and especially to capitalism. A number of modern researchers follow his emphases on the economic foundations of class structure and the conflict and problems produced by this inequality. But other sociologists have challenged Marx on each of these points, emphasizing the importance of other key concepts besides social structure.

Functional Integration

One of the best known of these challenges is the contention that inequality can actually contribute to the ***functional integration*** of society. This argument was advanced by the early functionalist sociologists Herbert Spencer (1974) and Émile Durkheim (1893/1985) and was developed by the American sociologists Kingsley Davis and Wilbert Moore (1945). Like Marx, Davis and Moore focused on the economic structure of society. But instead of emphasizing the formation of classes or the accumulation of inherited wealth, they stressed how opportunities to earn different levels of income would motivate people. This argument applied mainly to inequalities of income, not to inherited wealth, and so did not constitute a theory of the stratification system as a whole, with its institutionalized, structural hierarchy of classes. Thus it supplemented Marx's theory rather than completely refuting it. But it also challenged Marx's idea that the inequality of capitalism could be replaced by a completely egalitarian, nonhierarchical form of social organization.

Davis and Moore argued that some jobs are more important than others to the functional integration of complex societies. Since only a limited number of people have the talents, or are willing to invest in the education, needed to perform those jobs, it is necessary to pay them more than the average wages (or give them other extra rewards such as prestige, power, or pleasant working conditions) in order to motivate them. Therefore social inequality is functionally necessary. A society that failed to motivate people to perform these important jobs would collapse.

There is little doubt that people can be motivated to choose certain jobs by pay or other rewards; when computer scientists were in short suppply in the 1980s, their pay and working conditions improved dramatically as companies competed to attract them. Critics have called other aspects of the Davis and Moore theory into question, however (see Kerbo, 1991, pp. 129–134). For example, is it clear that the best-paid jobs in American society are really those that are functionally most important or those that require the most investment in education and training? We might agree that doctors are very important, need special talents, and must invest in a great deal of training, and perhaps that shoe shiners are not very important, do not need special talents, and are easy to train. So doctors get paid more than shoe shiners. But once we leave these extremes, it is much less clear whether the theory holds. It takes more education and arguably more talent to be a schoolteacher than a bank manager, but teachers are paid much less than bankers. Are truck drivers really more important than nurses, or are they paid more because most of them are men? Do lawyers get higher incomes than garbage collectors because they are functionally more important? In short, it is very difficult to assess functional importance objectively. At best, what Davis and Moore call functional importance is simply a reflection of what is valued in the labor market.

There is an even more basic objection, however. Davis and Moore completely ignore the effects of power, influence, and inheritance on the labor market (Collins, 1975). The children of doctors (and of other middle- and upper-class people) have a better chance of becoming doctors than do equally talented poor children who work equally hard at school. Some parents can buy their children expensive private educations that give them connections to other elite children (whether or not they offer better learning). Parents' income also affects their ability to pay for college and graduate school for their children. Individuals' chances in the labor market are further influenced by their race or ethnicity and gender.

Still another problem with theories emphasizing functional integration was suggested by Thorstein Veblen (1899). Veblen argued that the highest pay ought to go to people who do the most unpleasant work, the work no one else wants to do. On this basis, garbage collectors and ditch diggers would be highly paid; pay would be less for jobs that offered more interesting work, better working conditions, and higher prestige. In fact, of course, exactly the opposite happens. The jobs that have the highest prestige and intrinsic interest are usually the ones that also pay very well.

The Davis and Moore theory clearly is not an adequate substitute for Marx's theory. Indeed, it is not completely contradictory to Marx's. A Marxist could agree that inequality served as a motivator *within* capitalism even though it would eventually become so extreme that capitalism would suffer crises or revolutions. And those who emphasize functional integration could agree that the class system is dysfunctional to the extent that it makes inheritance of wealth or power interfere with motivating individuals to do the work society needs (Tumin, 1953). The difference in emphasis between the two theories is basic, however. Davis and Moore disregarded the question that Marx saw as central: Who owns the means of production (wealth)? In looking at how motivation could be functional for a society as a whole, they didn't pose the question of who benefited most from any particular structure of inequality. Had they done so, they might have been led to look at the role of power in shaping and maintaining systems of stratification.

Power

Another founder of sociology, Max Weber, argued that Marx had looked at ***power*** as only one of the ways in which economic stratification was maintained. In the long run, Marx thought, ownership of the means of production was the one crucial source of power. Weber contended, however, that there were other sources of power in modern societies and that power should be seen as a dimension of stratification in itself, not merely as a support for economic stratification.

Above all, Weber pointed to the power of those who are able to run the bureaucracies that have become ever more influential in modern societies (see Chapter 4). This is especially important to the analysis of communist societies. Although Marx had thought of communism as the building of a classless society (see Chapter 16), in reality the power of the government bureaucracy became the basis for a new form of inequality under communism. In the Soviet Union, China, and other communist countries, senior bureaucrats gained access to more and better food and other goods through special shops. They had privileges denied ordinary citizens, from travel opportunities to summer houses and chauffeur-driven cars. Those who controlled essential resources (such as access to good jobs or scarce apartments) were able to demand bribes and favors from people who needed their help. The bureaucrats were even able to get special educational and job opportunities for their children and thus turn their individual good fortunes into inherited class privileges (Lenski, Lenski, and Nolan, 1991).

Even in capitalist societies like the United States, bureaucratic power can be an important basis for stratification. There are many examples of corruption, of course, like state highway commissioners who take kickbacks from construction companies. But even without corruption, high public or bureaucratic office can be a source of wealth. Members of Congress and state legislatures not only establish their own salaries but often receive free trips to exotic resorts and other favors from lobbying groups. Retired admirals and generals often become rich as consultants to corporations that seek their influence in selling products to the military.

Weber's point, however, was not just that bureaucratic power can be converted into economic income or wealth. Rather, he wanted to emphasize that power is an independent dimension of social stratification, not only a reflection of ownership of the means of production. In modern capitalist societies, most big businesses are run not by their owners, but by professional managers (see Chapter 16). Millions of individuals, pension funds, and other corporations own stock in IBM, for example, but the company is a bureaucracy run by its chairman, president, and other top officials. These executives have connections to those in other corporations and to top government bureaucrats. By sharing their influence through such connections, they achieve a kind of class power (Domhoff, 1993).

As another example, consider elections. Each American citizen has the same power: one vote. This is democracy. But when it comes to money for advertising, capacity to influence what is reported in newspapers or on TV, or resources to run a campaign, all Americans are not equal. This is the stratification of power. It is based not only on wealth but also on control of bureaucracies and other organizations (see Chapter 17 on the role of wealth and power in politics).

Culture

Weber did not think that even wealth and power together could fully explain systems of stratification in modern societies. Factors involving ***culture*** must also be taken into consideration, both as a source of stratification and as a dimension of inequality in themselves. For example, the lower value that many cultures place on "women's work" results in lower pay for certain occupations—like nursing—regardless of ownership of the means of production (see also Chapter 11). Race and ethnicity are other cultural identities that can influence the workings of stratification systems. Weber used the term *status group* to describe such groups of people whose prestige derives from cultural rather than economic or political factors.

Prestige is the social esteem, respect, or approval that is awarded to people because they possess attributes that their society considers admirable (Goode, 1978). Different societies attach prestige to different attributes. In traditional Indian society, as we indicated earlier, spiritual qualities are given special prestige. But spiritual qualities are not all understood as individual accomplishments; for example, in India's traditional **caste system**, one's spiritual status and position in the social hierarchy were determined at birth (Gould, 1971); everyone was a member of a caste, generally obligated to marry a member of the same caste and to observe strict rituals according to caste rank. High-caste Indians, especially Hindus, were charged with keeping a certain formal distance from members of lower-caste groups. A member of the highest caste, a Brahman, would feel defiled, "impure," or dirtied by physical contact with a Harijan, or "untouchable" (the lowest group, composed of street sweepers, scavengers, and swineherds). The prestige attached to caste and purity operated separately from, and overrode, wealth and power. Despite government attempts to abolish the caste system and end discrimination against lower-caste Indians, cultural position still affects how people are treated. Low-caste Hindus who achieve great economic or political success are still shunned by members of higher castes, while a poor but high-caste Brahman is still regarded by many as pure and holy.

In the United States, spiritual purity is much less likely to confer prestige. Instead, Americans emphasize other cultural and social factors, such as how people earn their money (their occupation), how they spend it (their mode of consumption), who they are (their ancestry), whom they know, and how successful or well-known they are. Being a neurosurgeon, earning several hundred thousand dollars a year, owning a large home, having an Anglo-Saxon surname, belonging to the "right" clubs, and having friends in positions of power are all sources of prestige in American society. For most Americans, occupation is the main determinant of prestige. Americans value certain occupations for the honor they feel those occupations bring, not just for power or wealth.

Sociologists measure the prestige of occupations by asking representative samples of the population to rate the social standing of various jobs (for example, on a scale from excellent through average to poor). Researchers then translate these rankings into prestige tallies ranging from zero (lowest) to 100 (highest). The results of such occupational surveys tend to remain fairly stable over time. As Table 9.1 shows, Americans rate most highly those jobs that confer power on an individual, require professional skills, and provide high income. Doctors, professors, lawyers, and architects are among the top occupations; garbage collectors, janitors, and shoe shiners are at the bottom; carpenters, farmers, and sales managers are between the top and bottom groups.

In large corporations, there are many clues to employees' ranks in the prestige hierarchy. A corner office on a high floor, for example, is one sign of success. BankAmerica employees know that they have made it when they are given stationery with the bank's logo printed in gold rather than black ink. The Ford Motor Company has a particularly elaborate system of status classification. Employees are classified into grades from 1 (clerks and secretaries) to 27 (chairman of the board). Grade 9, the lowest executive level, confers the right to an outdoor parking space; grade 13 brings a larger office with windows, plants, an intercom system, and a secretary. Those who reach grade 16 receive an office with a private lavatory, a signed Christmas card from the chairman, an indoor parking space, and a company car.

Prestige is a widespread and important part of modern statification systems (Bourdieu, 1984). Doctors, lawyers, and college professors consider their highly educated professions especially prestigious, and many would be disappointed if their children took jobs in business, even if that meant earning as much or more money. Within such a profession, individuals may be motivated more by the

TABLE 9.1

Prestige Ranking of Occupations in the United States

Highest-Ranking Occupations	Score	Lowest-Ranking Occupations	Score
Physician	82	Auctioneer	32
College/university professor	78	Bus driver	32
Lawyer	76	Truck driver	32
Dentist	74	Cashier	31
Physicist/astronomer	74	File clerk	30
Bank officer	72	Upholsterer	30
Architect	71	Drill-press operator	29
Aeronautical/astronautical engineer	71	Furniture finisher	29
Psychologist	71	Retail salesperson	29
Airplane pilot	70	Midwife	23
Clergy	69	Gas station attendant	22
Chemist	69	Security guard	22
Electrical engineer	69	Taxi driver	22
Geologist	67	Elevator operator	21
Sociologist	66	Bartender	20
Secondary school teacher	63	Waiter/waitress	20
Mechanical engineer	62	Clothing presser	18
Registered nurse	62	Farm laborer	18
Dental hygienist	61	Household servant	18
Pharmacist	61	Car washer	17
Radiologic technician	61	Freight handler	17
Chiropractor	60	Garbage collector	17
Elementary school teacher	60	Janitor	16
Veterinarian	60	Bellhop	14
Postmaster	58	Shoe shiner	09

Source: Adapted from General Social Surveys, 1972-1983. Cumulative Codebook *(National Opinion Research Center, Chicago, 1983), pp. 338-349.*

pursuit of prestige among their colleagues than by the pursuit of wealth. This is, indeed, one of the basic differences between professions and fields like business. Running a record store is not any more or less prestigious than running a clothing store, nor is managing a steel mill more or less prestigious than managing an automobile factory. We judge these businesses and those who run them mainly by the money they make. But we do not expect doctors to judge one another mainly by the money they make. For example, if you ask someone who the best pediatrician in town is, you want that person to tell you which one takes the best care of children, not which one makes the most money. And doctors judge one another by the extent to which they keep informed about new techniques, follow accepted practices conscientiously, and put their patients' welfare above "merely financial" concerns. We think someone is a bad doctor if he or she refuses to treat someone in need, but we do not think a person is a bad grocer if that individual refuses to give vegetables to people with no money. The French sociologist Pierre Bourdieu (1984) has shown that while such considerations of prestige are strongest among professionals, they apply at all levels of the occupational hierarchy.

Indeed, Bourdieu has suggested that people accumulate not just wealth or power, but also what he calls "cultural capital"—resources that benefit an individual because of the prestige they confer. A college degree, for example, is not in itself a means of production or an instrument of power. Under some circumstances, however, it can be converted into wealth or power, as when it is used to get a good job or impress someone (Bourdieu, 1987). Sometimes cultural capital is effective where money isn't. A Harvard graduate, for example, might be able to join certain elite clubs that would be closed to people without college educations, even if they were millionaires. At these clubs, he or she can meet with other members of the elite in business, law, or government.

Cultural capital is as unequally distributed as wealth or power. Most Americans do not have college degrees. Still fewer have degrees from Harvard or other Ivy League colleges. And some elite college graduates can claim additional cultural distinctions—a year of study abroad, membership in the Phi Beta Kappa honorary society, or mastery of a foreign language.

Social Action

The example of cultural capital shows that class positions are shaped by ***social action***. Choosing to study abroad, working hard enough to get into Phi Beta Kappa, and spending the time to learn a foreign language are all actions. The chances to participate in those actions are influenced by class background, but they are also matters of individual choice. Such individual choices have a small impact on the class structure as a whole, but they can have great importance for the individuals who make them. Thus, dropping out of college can end your hopes of being middle class, but it would take hundreds of thousands of decisions to drop out to affect the class structure by lowering society's overall education level.

In different ways, Marx, Davis and Moore (and other functionalists), and Weber all considered the relationship of social stratification to social action. Marx made two main points. First, he showed that class inequality is not mainly a result of individual action. Some new entrepreneurs may become business leaders and other business owners may go bankrupt, but this does not change the system. Moreover, capitalists do not exploit workers because they are bad people, Marx said, but because that is the only way they can make a profit and survive in a capitalist system. Their actions—like trying to keep wages as low as possible—are determined by their position in the class structure. In the same way, workers could not all hope to become capitalists—or even middle class—simply by working hard and saving money. According to Marx, the capitalist system requires that there be a large number of workers and only a small number of capitalists. So while a few workers might succeed in rising from rags to riches, not enough of them could become rich by their individual actions (or luck) to bring an end to poverty or inequality. This fact brought up Marx's second point about the relationship of social action to stratification. The only way for workers to have a good chance to change their situation, Marx thought, was for them to stop competing with one another and join together to overturn the capitalist system. Marx thought that the inequality brought about by capitalism would be so extreme that workers would be led to choose revolution as a means of ending their exploitation (Marx and Engels, 1848/1967). This is what he meant by "class struggle." Instead of individual struggle to get ahead *within* capitalism, Marx called for struggle by the whole working class to replace the capitalist system with socialism. While individual action didn't matter much in his theory, this collective action did.

Looking at the problem of functional integration, Davis and Moore placed a heavier stress on individual action. As they saw it, motivating a society's members to work was too important to be left to chance or individual whim. There had to be a socially organized way to make sure people got the necessary education and did the necessary work, and the structure of inequality filled the bill. According to this theory, the class structure guided individuals to act in ways that contributed to the overall functional integration of society. Although Davis and Moore recognized that the class structure was slow to change, they pointed out that it did respond to new technology and other pressures. The development of the modern automobile and highway system lowered the prestige of railroad engineers and conductors, for example; when computers became crucial to economic and social organization, then computer programmers became high-status professionals.

Weber and other theorists who emphasized power and culture also stressed social action (as we saw in Chapter 1). While Marx was concerned with collective action to change the overall class structure, Weber was more concerned with individuals' efforts to change their own position, or that of their social group, within the class structure. These efforts inevitably involved competition with other individuals and groups—and therefore were a matter of the different amounts of power they had as well as the different strategies guiding their action. Weber discussed, for example, the ways in which some minority groups—especially religious minorities and groups of immigrants—form tight-knit communities and support one another's efforts to advance economically. Because they do not have much power as individuals, such groups need the strength that comes from coordinated social action (Parkin, 1976). Following Weber's lead, sociologists study the actions of subcultural groups like recent Asian immigrants to the United States. They point out that though these groups value the free enterprise system, they do not approach it in a completely individualistic way; their action is socially organized and oriented toward family and community. Members of such groups lend one another money to set up small businesses, hire family members as employees, save large percentages of their income, and make sacrifices to send children to college (D. Light, 1986). Through all

The business executive might argue that he achieved his high level of success through years of hard work and self-sacrifice—but will the same degree of struggle and self-sacrifice produce the same results for these migrant farm workers?

these actions they improve the class position of their families and their ethnic communities.

To sum up, modern sociologists generally follow Marx in emphasizing economic structure as the single most important factor in stratification. But they also follow Weber in seeing that stratification is not based only on wealth. Stratification of power and of cultural values such as prestige are also important and cannot be completely reduced to economic sources. While Marx stressed the ways in which structures of inequality produce conflict, sociologists also note that the same inequalities can be sources of motivation and at least some versions of functional integration. We address the most important forms of power stratification in Chapter 17 (on politics). Chapter 18 (on the Third World) reminds us that much of the most basic inequality in the world is found not within the United States and other rich countries, but between the rich and poor countries of the world—a matter of economics, power, and culture. Chapters 10 (on race and ethnicity), 11 (on gender), and 13 (on education) address various cultural dimensions of social stratification. In the discussion of the American class system that follows, we will not neglect culture, but we will place our major stress on economic aspects of stratification—that is, the structures of wealth and power. And we will consider the extent to which the actions of individuals and groups result in social mobility, or movement up and down the class hierarchy.

INEQUALITY AND SOCIAL MOBILITY

When Great Britain colonized the United States in the seventeenth and eighteenth centuries, it still gave special privileges to aristocrats and denied ordinary people the right to vote. From the time of the Revolution, Americans resisted such formal distinctions among citizens. In 1776, the founders of the United States declared that "All men are created equal," and a generation later the great French social theorist Alexis de Tocqueville traveled around America and declared that the United States was a model for the organization of a more equal, democratic society and thus a model for Europe's future. Of course, from the beginning there were exceptions. The phrase read "all *men* are created equal"; women were denied the vote and many economic privileges in American society until the twentieth century. Even more glaringly, the founders of the United States decided not to try to undo the system of slavery that denied not only citizenship but freedom to most African-Americans. Only after the Civil War nearly destroyed the country in 1861–1865 was slavery abolished and formal equality granted to African-Americans. Since then, generations of struggle have been required to break down the barriers to full equality—unfair voter registration tests, job discrimination, segregated schools. Today African-Americans—and other American minority groups—still suffer discrimination and a lower standard of living than the white majority.

American culture values equality, but also accepts a very unequal class structure as legitimate. Tension between the ideal and the reality is inevitable. Thus, Americans don't like rich people who think they are better than other people, but they do think it is all right for the grandchildren of wealthy entrepreneurs to inherit fortunes that mean the grandchildren will never have to work. Although most Americans believe in equality of opportunity, many resent government programs designed to increase the level of actual equality in American society.

The American Class Structure

Most Americans think of themselves as middle class, whether they are shop clerks or plumbers or engineers or doctors. They think of themselves as middle class so long as they work for a living and don't depend on either welfare or inherited millions. This distinction among work, wealth, and welfare is catchy, but it obscures important differences. Are a corporation chairman who makes more than $1 million a year and a housekeeper who makes $12,000 really in the same class just because both work full-time for their living?

As this question indicates, there is no one perfect way to decide how many classes there are in American society. The number of classes depends on our definitions and how precise we want to be. Sociologists commonly define classes by looking at people's wealth, income, and occupational characteristics.

Wealth refers to people's valuable property, to what they own. Wealth represents "stored-up purchasing power" that can be drawn upon in times of need and passed from one generation to the next (Oliver and Shapiro, 1990). **Income** refers to how much people *get* (rather than what they already have): It is the amount of money that flows into a household (regardless of how much flows out). If, for example, you own a house, that is wealth; if you rent that house to someone, the money you are paid is income. If you have a job, your salary or wages are income; but any shares of stock you may own are wealth. There are thus two main sorts of income: Wages and salaries are returns on labor; interest, dividends, and rent are returns on property or capital.

Wealth is most important in distinguishing the very top members of the American class structure. These are people who inherit much of what they own. Their income comes mainly from investments, not from work. This is what sets them apart from middle- and working-class Americans. The differences between middle- and working-class Americans have mainly to do with occupational characteristics—the kinds of jobs they hold, how much education their jobs require, how much the jobs pay, how prestigious they are, and how much authority (that is, power) an individual has at work.

The sociologist Harold Kerbo (1991, pp. 13–14) summarizes the American class structure this way:

- The **upper class** consists of families that own a great deal of property, with high authority flowing from such ownership. These are the old, established families with significant ownership of major corporations and real estate, such as the Rockefellers, the Du Ponts, the Mellons, and the Fords.

- The **corporate class** is made up of people who have great bureaucratic authority in major corporations (and often government), usually not based on ownership of these corporations. These people include top corporate executives and corporate board members. There is some evidence that the upper class is shrinking in importance while the corporate class is growing in importance.

- The **middle class** is composed of people who own relatively little property, but whose occupations give them high-to-middle income, prestige, and authority. The middle class is subdivided into the upper middle class (lesser corporate managers, doctors, lawyers) and lower middle class (office workers and salespeople).

- The **working class** consists of people who own little or no property and whose occupations give them middle-to-low income and prestige and little or no authority. The working class is largely composed of manual workers (subdivided into skilled and unskilled) and low-end clerical workers.

- The **lower class** includes those individuals with no property, who are often unemployed and have no authority and usually no prestige—that is, the poor.

The art of a society often reflects either the existing social arrangements or those which reformers or revolutionaries would like to achieve. The image on the left shows the social stratification of the medieval world, with the Duke of Berry presiding over his estate. The painting on the right, a twentieth-century mural, celebrates the possibility of a classless society organized around and sustained by workers.

These conceptual categories are useful to keep in mind as we look at official government figures on the distribution of wealth and income in the United States today. Bear in mind that the federal government does not collect data on classes as such (by the above or any other definition). Rather, its data refer to the income and wealth of fixed percentages of the population—like the richest (or poorest) 1 percent, 5 percent, or 20 percent. These correspond only approximately to the class definitions, above. Keep in mind also that some differences of wealth and income are not due to class position so much as stage of life: People in their twenties typically have steady incomes but little accumulated wealth. Conversely, retired people generally have accumulated assets (a home, car, and other property) but relatively small incomes. But the difference between the wealth of a working teacher or plumber (who is still paying the mortgage on her house) and that of a retired one (who owns the house outright) is tiny by comparison to the difference between teachers and plumbers on the one hand and very rich people like the Rockefellers and Du Ponts on the other.

The Distribution of Wealth and Income

The distribution of wealth in the United States is extremely lopsided (though not so unequal as in some Third World countries; see Chapter 18). Most Americans have very little wealth. To be sure, nearly two-thirds own their own home (though most owe a large part of its value to the bank that holds the mortgage). However, only a little over 20 percent of Americans own stocks or bonds, and just 10.5 percent own any real estate besides their homes. Most households have savings, checking, or retirement accounts, but the median value of these deposits is only about $3,500 (U.S. Bureau of the Census, 1991). Many have limited or no health insurance (a problem discussed in detail in Chapter 15). What all this means is that most Americans live very close to the edge of financial ruin. In an emergency like long-term unemployment or serious illness, they would have very little to fall back on.

The upper class does not have such worries. When Melvin Oliver and Thomas Shapiro (1990) analyzed the distribution of wealth in the United States, they looked at both net worth (all assets minus all debts) and net capital or productive financial assets (assets that could be used to generate income and wealth, excluding vehicles and homes). They found that the median net worth of the wealthiest 1 percent of the population is twenty-two times the median for the remaining 99 percent of the population. The disparity is even greater when we look at financial assets; the richest 1 percent of Americans have 237 times more productive wealth per person than do the other 99 percent. The wealthiest 0.05 percent of Americans (roughly 430,000 households) own 40 percent of all corporate stocks. By contrast, one-third of American households have zero or negative assets (that is, more debts than assets). Households with children, especially those headed by single or divorced women, are the least likely to have stocks, savings, or real estate.

Like the distribution of wealth, the distribution of income in the United States is very uneven. As shown in Figure 9.1, the bottom one-fifth of American families received 3.9 percent of the nation's total income in 1991, while the top one-fifth received 46.6 percent. The top 5 percent of households (including much of the corporate class) received 17.4 percent of all income—more than three times the share they would receive if income were distributed equally.

The gap between rich and poor widened significantly during the 1980s (Greenstein and Barancik, 1990; K. Phillips, 1991). The average income of the wealthiest one-fifth of Americans increased by 30 percent and that of the wealthiest 1 percent by 75 percent (an increase of $236,000 per person before taxes). Most American millionaires are members of the corporate class. *Business Week* magazine (April 26, 1993) surveyed the country's top corporate CEOs (chief executive officers) in 1993 and found that their average salary exceeds $1 million. When combined with bonuses and profits on stock options, the average CEO takes home $3.8 million a year. This is 158 times the average factory worker's income ($24,411), 112 times what the average teacher earns ($34,098), 66 times the average engineer's income ($58,240), and 19 times what the president of the United States is paid ($200,000). The richest 1 percent of Americans today receive almost as much income as the bottom 40 percent. That is, the 2.5 million wealthy Americans at the top end of the upper and corporate classes receive as much income as the more than 100 million members of the working and lower classes.

The incomes of the middle class, by contrast, increased only slightly in the 1980s—an average increase of 3 percent for the middle fifth of the population, or $900 a year before taxes. In most cases, however, middle-income families had to work more hours or send more household members into the work force to sustain their 1980 standard of living (Mishel and Simon, 1988). In effect, they had to run harder to stay in place. The situation was even worse

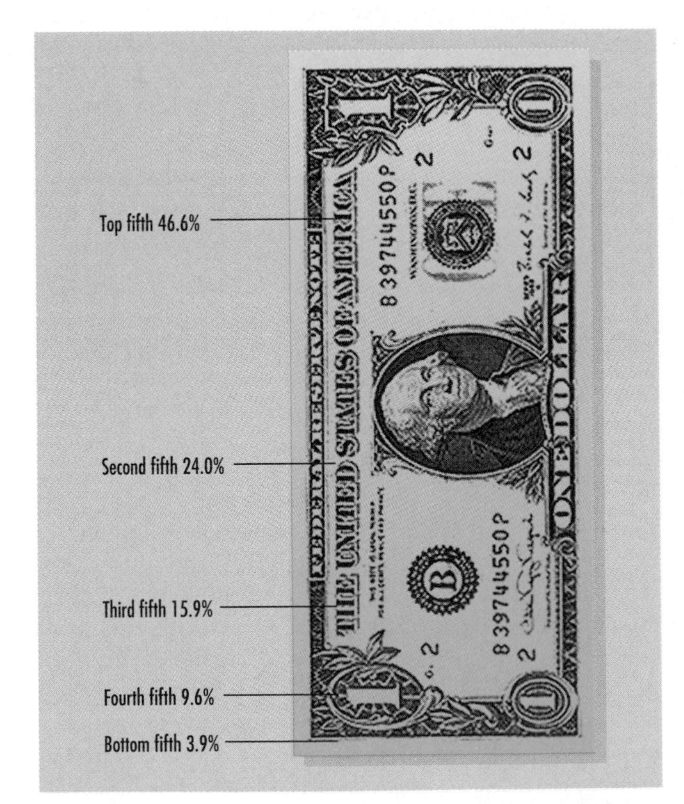

FIGURE 9.1 / Percentage of American Income Held by Population Fifths

Source: *Statistical Abstract of the United States, 1991*, Bureau of the Census, Washington, D.C., and *Current Population Reports*, Series P-60, no. 174 (November 1991).

for the working class; even with a dramatic increase in the number of two-income families, there was on average no increase in their income. The lower class actually lost ground in the 1980s: The average income for the bottom fifth of Americans dropped almost 4 percent, to $7,725, and that for the bottom tenth fell 9 percent, to $4,700 (Greenstein and Barancik, 1990).

To complete the damage, the proportion of income that poor households paid in taxes increased while it decreased for the upper and corporate classes. As shown in Figure 9.2, which is based on *after*-tax incomes, the 1980s clearly was a decade in which the rich got richer and the poor got poorer. One of the main reasons for this widening gap was that a greater share of Americans' national income came from property-based income or capital gains rather than wages. In other words, the return on investments increased while the return on labor wages paid to workers decreased (Mishel and Simon, 1988). We will take a closer look at the poverty that exists in the midst of our society's wealth later in this chapter.

First, we need to ask what is happening to working- and middle-class Americans, the people on whom our social and political systems most depend. The short answer, as we just saw, is that they are working harder without earning more. In addition, during the recession of the early 1990s, the middle class was hit harder by unemployment than at any other time since the Great Depression of the 1930s. Far more members of the working class have also experienced unemployment, which for many seems to be permanent as they face the effects of automation, the relocation of American manufacturing facilities overseas, and international competition. (We discuss these issues further in Chapter 16.)

Americans have always had the idea that they ought to be able to improve their situations—or at least their children's chances—by hard work and frugality. This is the American dream, but it is under challenge. In the prosperous years after World War II, members of the American working class—especially those who belonged to labor unions—won wage levels close to those of the lower middle class and obtained new educational opportunities for their children. The number of Americans in the middle class increased dramatically during the 1950s and 1960s. Now, however, working-class incomes are falling, and fewer children of the working class can move up into the middle class. Children born into middle-class families have to struggle to avoid dropping into the working class or even the lower class. Moving up cannot be taken for granted.

Social Mobility

Leonard Stern's father came to this country from Germany several decades ago. When his textile business got into trouble, the elder Stern and a friend decided to import canaries. They were moderately successful, but then their canary business also fell into debt. Meanwhile, Leonard had gone to college and acquired an M.B.A. in record time. He took over the business in 1959. The younger

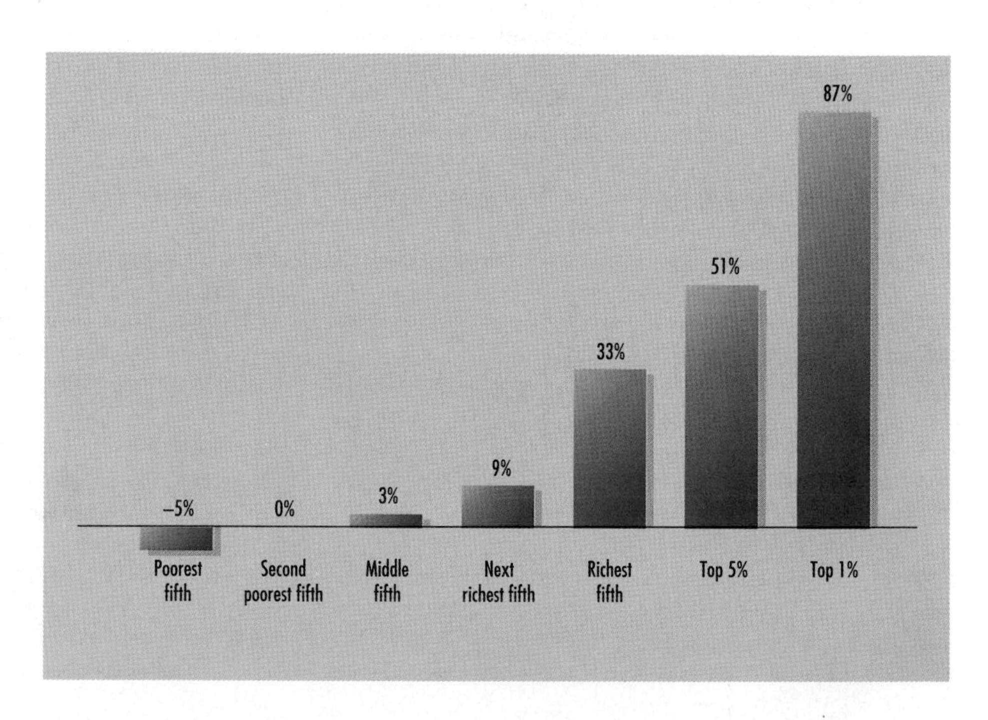

FIGURE 9.2 / Average After-Tax Income Gains and Losses between 1980 and 1990, by Household Income Groups

Source: *Congressional Budget Office*, in Melvin L. Oliver and Thomas M. Shapiro, "Wealth of a Nation: A Reassessment of Asset Inequality in America . . . ," *American Journal of Economics and Sociology* 49, no. 2 (1990): 129–151.

Stern built the family's Hartz Mountain Corporation into a $150-million-a-year pet-supplies business; by the time he was thirty-five he had amassed over half a billion dollars and was mingling with the elite of the business, social, and art worlds (Louis, 1973). Stern's story is a dramatic expression of the American dream of social mobility.

Social mobility refers to movement from one social position or level to another. It may take the form of a step up the social ladder, a climb to the top (as in Leonard Stern's case), or a step down. The nineteenth-century novelist Horatio Alger and other writers have popularized the American dream with stories of those rare people who went from rags to riches. Sociologists place a greater emphasis on *mobility rates*, general patterns of movement up or down the social scale. Their research shows that most upward mobility takes the form of small steps up the occupational or economic ladder, not leaps from the bottom to the top. The child of a factory worker becomes a factory supervisor; the child of a teacher becomes a college professor. Because of the relative openness of the American stratification system, movement both up and down the social hierarchy is common (Blau and Duncan, 1967; Featherman and Hauser, 1978). When the economy as a whole was growing, as it was during the 1960s, there was an abundance of opportunities; from the 1940s through the 1970s, most Americans' experience of poverty and downward mobility took the form of temporary setbacks (Duncan, 1984). Since then, downward mobility has been more permanent.

Sociologists also point out that social mobility in the United States often results from structural change, not individual success (Levy, 1987). **Structural mobility** refers to changes in the number and kinds of occupations available in a society, relative to the number of workers available to fill them. Structural mobility occurs as a result not of individual decisions to change jobs or lifestyles but of external changes in opportunities for stability or mobility. In some cases these changes may be cyclical, as when a periodic recession or depression causes large numbers of people to be temporarily unemployed or underemployed. In other cases, change is permanent and widespread, as when a new technology creates some new jobs but eliminates many others, or when an increase in international competition reduces sales of all kinds of domestic products.

Patterns of Social Mobility

Historically, the United States has been an upwardly mobile society. The labor market has grown dramatically, absorbing immigrants and creating opportunities for creativity and hard work to be rewarded with advancement. Since the turn of the century, the total number of jobs has more than doubled and the number of white-collar jobs has skyrocketed (Levy, 1987). Technology has opened whole new fields, expanding career opportunities for technicians, managers, and professionals.

Large-scale immigration stimulated occupational advancement in this expanding economy. Contrary to popular belief, immigrants do not always take jobs away from natives, but may help to create more and better jobs. For much of America's history, economic expansion has meant a relative shortage of labor—a problem that immigrants helped to solve. Many immigrants also became farmers, adding to America's agricultural wealth and to the market for the industrial goods produced in the cities. Finally, an influx of unskilled and semiskilled laborers, such as occurred in this country during the late nineteenth and early twentieth centuries, can enable experienced workers to move up the occupational ladder (see the Global Issues/Local Consequences box). For example, an artisan who once did all the work in the shop can hire assistants, expand operations, and become a manager.

The fact that white-collar workers tend to have fewer children than workers in other categories further stimulates upward mobility. Quite simply, white-collar workers have historically not produced enough children to replace themselves, let alone fill an expanding demand for white-collar and professional workers. This shortfall has given individuals from lower occupational groups a chance to move up.

Today, however, America's long-standing pattern of upward mobility is breaking up. The auto and steel industries—once the backbone of the U.S. economy—are in decline. Other industries, such as clothing manufacture, have moved most of their production facilities overseas. In addition, automation and the other technological advances that have contributed to the economy's growth are now eliminating more jobs than they are creating. These changes have put the previously stable or expanding working and middle classes under new pressure. In the 1980s and 1990s, both groups have begun to experience more permanent downward mobility, not just temporary setbacks (Newman, 1988).

Consider autoworkers. During the 1950s and 1960s, thousands of people moved to Detroit and other northern Midwest cities from the hills of Kentucky or dirt farms farther south. They sought escape from depressed home regions and a better life for themselves and their children. For a while the pilgrimage north was a success. These new workers readily found jobs in a growing and powerful industry, and enjoyed the benefits of membership in one of the best and strongest unions in the country. They put

GLOBAL ISSUES/LOCAL CONSEQUENCES

Immigration, Race, and Social Mobility

European immigrants who settled in the industrial cities of the northern United States after 1880 fared better, as a group, than did blacks who came to those same cities from the South. Traditionally, race has been considered the main reason for this difference. The European immigrants, despite differences in language, religion, and culture, "were after all *white* and a generation or two later it was possible for the descendants to shed as many of these markers as necessary" (Lieberson, 1980, p. xi). Blacks, by contrast, were permanently marked as different by their racial characteristics, which made them vulnerable to discrimination long after the European immigrants had blended in with the general population. An alternative explanation has maintained that the Europeans brought with them more cohesive family structures, a different work ethic, greater intelligence, and a more positive view of education as a means to advance in society.

In his book *A Piece of the Pie* (1980), Stanley Lieberson rejects both of these explanations. He cites data that suggest, for example, that blacks were at least as eager for education as European immigrants, and there was nothing inherent in their family structures that held them back. Nevertheless, blacks did suffer greater discrimination than European immigrants. Employers and labor unions generally preferred whites, despite linguistic and cultural differences. The question therefore becomes: To what extent does racial discrimination alone explain the differences between African-American migrants and European immigrants to the North?

Lieberson argues that race was not the determining factor in the failure of blacks to advance as swiftly as Europeans. Asian immigrants, he notes, were also distinguished by racial features and were victims of prejudice, and yet they have seen notable success. Lieberson's explanation involves two central ideas. First, the kind of work immigrants did was largely determined by the opportunities available in the place they came from. Those who left a desperately poor homeland were willing to accept work that was unacceptable to those who had had better work at home. Using mortality data—perhaps the only data available to measure quality of life—Lieberson suggests that conditions in the U.S. South (especially for black people) were worse than those in Southern, Central, and Eastern Europe. Thus, black immigrants to Northern cities were willing to settle for less. This would have put them at a disadvantage in earnings and mobility. It would also have earned them the hostility of white workers, who would have viewed them as competitors who could be exploited by employers to depress wages or break strikes.

Black migrants to the North thus started out in a disadvantaged position. To explain why they stayed behind over time, Lieberson offers his second central idea, the concept of *mobility niches*. He notes that different groups tended to concentrate in certain occupations: Italians became barbers; Irish became policemen and firemen; Swedes worked as carpenters; Greeks opened restaurants; Russians traded in furs; and so on. Such occupations gave those groups a base from which to advance. But "niches" could absorb only small percentages of immigrant groups. Although restrictions in immigration drastically curtailed the flow of immigrants from Europe and Asia during the 1920s and 1930s, black migration from the South continued unabated. Newcomers who found themselves excluded from mobility niches worked to undercut earlier and more successful immigrants, at the same time reinforcing negative stereotypes in the minds of the dominant class. Also, the attitudes of whites changed as the demographic balance changed; that is, continuing black migration helped reduce the negative attitudes of whites toward other whites. In Lieberson's words, "The presence of blacks made it harder to discriminate against the new Europeans because the alternative was viewed even less favorably."

Thus, in Lieberson's analysis, race was not the most important factor in explaining the greater social mobility of European immigrants. Economic conflict was more important, and race was resorted to simply because it was the most obvious feature available to justify discrimination. In short, "differences between blacks and whites—real ones, imaginary ones, and those that are the product of earlier race relations—enter into the rhetoric of race and ethnic relations, but they are ultimately secondary to the conflict for society's goodies" (p. 382).

down roots, buying houses and working to improve the local schools. Blacks and other minority-group members benefited from the fact that the auto industry was freer from discrimination than many others.

In the 1990s, American car manufacturers are in trouble, suffering from their inability to compete effectively with the Japanese and Europeans. In addition, automation in the auto industry is eliminating jobs. As a result, General Motors announced in December 1991 that it would close twenty-one plants nationwide and lay off 74,000 workers over the next three years. What will happen to those workers? Hardly any will get other jobs in the auto industry because Ford and Chrysler have been laying off workers themselves. The layoffs cut into what autoworkers

Modern capitalism is characterized by cycles in which periods of nearly full employment are followed by recessionary periods in which millions of workers lose their jobs. Here, hundreds of unemployed steel workers in a Pennsylvania mill town line up to apply for fifteen jobs.

can spend, so local businesses also suffer, closing or laying off workers. Some workers will look for better opportunities in other cities, but in the recession of the early 1990s, jobs are scarce everywhere, even in the once-booming Sunbelt cities—Phoenix, Atlanta, and Los Angeles. Laid-off workers also usually lack the skills for the best new jobs (Kasarda and Appold, 1990). Others will try to tough it out on unemployment pay and then maybe welfare, in the forlorn hope that someday they will be called back. Eventually many of these autoworkers—men and women who had worked hard every day for years—will realize that they are never going to have good jobs again. While they once earned $12, $15, or $20 an hour making cars, they will consider themselves lucky to get jobs making hamburgers at $4.50 an hour or cleaning offices at $6 an hour. This is the experience of downward mobility.

Downward mobility has affected the middle class, too (Newman, 1988, 1991). It has hit the families of airline pilots laid off when Pan Am went bankrupt—men who made $75,000 a year and will now lose seniority and be lucky to make $45,000 if they can land jobs with other airlines. It has affected the children of doctors who find the competition for medical school admissions tougher than when their parents got in, and the costs of opening a private practice much higher even if they do become doctors. It has hit graduate students from middle-class families who finish years of study for Ph.D.s only to find that colleges aren't hiring because of budget constraints.

Downward mobility has always existed, but before the 1980s it didn't attract much attention. It seemed the exception to the rule of upward mobility. People still assumed that they could live out the American dream. In fact, high rates of upward mobility were one reason American workers never developed much of the radical, socialist opposition to capitalism that Karl Marx expected. Even when they were getting a raw deal, workers could always expect that things would eventually get better, for their children if not for themselves.

Who Gets Ahead?

Sociologists are interested not only in what proportion of the total population experiences upward or downward mobility but also in the factors that determine which sorts of people are most likely to experience such changes. In a classic study, Peter M. Blau and Otis Dudley Duncan (1967) addressed the question of how social origin affects a person's ultimate status and whether factors other than social origin are involved. The researchers developed a measure known as the *socioeconomic index* that allowed them to compare fathers' educational and occupational attainments with those of their sons. Blau and Duncan concluded that social origin affects ultimate social status primarily by influencing the level of education a person attains. Educational achievement, they believed, was the mechanism by which status is passed from one generation to another.

The Blau and Duncan model of status attainment was amplified by William H. Sewell and his colleagues at the University of Wisconsin (Hauser et al., 1982, 1983; Sewell and Hauser, 1976). They followed, at periodic intervals, some 10,000 people who graduated from Wisconsin high schools in 1957. The researchers sought to determine how a person's social background influences his or her later career and what other mechanisms may intervene. They concluded that educational and occupational attainment are the outcome of two related processes: those that shape a person's status aspirations and those that convert the aspirations into a new status ranking. A family's class affects a child's later attainments through the personal influences that family members bring to bear on the child's status aspirations during adolescence. Parents' and teachers' encouragement to attend college and the college plans of the adolescent's best friend also influence an adolescent's status aspirations.

Once an individual has finished school, the impact of parents' social background becomes inconsequential. The level of the person's schooling then becomes the principal influence. Viewed in this fashion, occupational attainment is shaped by many links in a chain extending from birth across the life span: Parental status colors the adolescent's aspirations; aspirations contribute to the individual's educational attainment; educational attainment influences the person's first occupational placement; and the person's first job affects his or her later occupational opportunities.

The idea that status attainment is based on educational achievement rests on certain assumptions about society—most significantly, that *individual* qualifications are more important than the general labor market. The Blau and Duncan model suggests that a person who gets a good education will automatically get a good job with good pay. Research indicates that this is more commonly true for white men than for minorities and women, who generally receive a smaller return on their educational investment. Moreover, men and women, and blacks and whites, compete to some extent in different labor markets (see Chapter 16). For example, white male blue-collar workers are more often employed in high-paying unionized industries that produce "important" products, such as automobiles; white female blue-collar workers more often work in nonunion plants that produce less valuable items, such as clothing and toys. Regional differences in available opportunities may also affect status attainment. An understanding of status attainment must take into account the *structures* of opportunity within which individual social action, in the form of occupational achievement, can occur. Whereas the opportunity structure of the 1950s and 1960s made it seem relatively straightforward to translate aspirations into education and education into jobs, the economic changes of the 1980s and 1990s have made such action more difficult. Upward mobility can become common again only if the United States can regain a high growth rate that generates enough good jobs in an era when high-technology automation is common.

If rising from rags to riches is the American dream, falling into poverty is the American nightmare. Many Americans see poverty as a remote possibility, as a problem confined to a deviant minority, as something that happens only to "them" and never to "us" (Bane and Ellwood, 1989). This is not necessarily so, as the following section will explain.

POVERTY IN THE UNITED STATES

Poverty is relative. Compared to people starving in Somalia, even many poor Americans are well off. However, a corporate executive who is laid off may feel poor if he cannot afford to send his children to college. An unemployed worker may feel that getting just a minimum-wage job would help her to escape from poverty. In order to develop a more systematic picture of poverty in the United States, the government since the 1960s has calculated an official *poverty line* based on the minimum amount of money that families of different sizes and compositions need to purchase a nutritionally adequate diet, assuming that they spend one-third of their income for food (see Table 9.2). This measure is adjusted each year for inflation. In 1990, the poverty line for a family of four was $13,359 per year, or a little over $1,100 a month.

The use of the poverty line is controversial (Bane and Ellwood, 1989). Some critics argue that the poverty line is too high because it does not take into account such noncash or in-kind benefits as food stamps and school lunches, housing subsidies, and Medicaid. Other critics point out that the poverty line does not reflect regional differences in the cost of living: Presumably it costs more

TABLE 9.2

Adjusted Poverty Threshold, by Family Size, 1990

Number of Family Members	Poverty Line
1 person	$6,652
2 persons	8,509
3 persons	10,419
4 persons	13,359
5 persons	15,792
6 persons	17,839
7 persons	20,241

Source: U.S. Bureau of the Census, Current Population Reports, *Series P-60, no. 175 (1991).*

to live in New York City than in rural Mississippi. Nor does the poverty line consider changing patterns of family expenses, such as the rising cost of housing or the cost of child care in the increasing number of families with working mothers (Ruggles, 1990). Moreover, the poverty line lumps together families and individuals who are chronically poor with those who have suffered a temporary setback and combines families and individuals who have almost nothing with those who are struggling but managing to get by. In spite of these limitations, the official poverty line is still the best and most widely used index.

In 1960, when John F. Kennedy was elected president, 39.5 million Americans—more than 20 percent of the country's population—were living in poverty. The social scientist and activist Michael Harrington had just shocked both the government and the country with his account of this endemic poverty in *The Other America* (1959/1963). Harrington's book spurred the young and optimistic Kennedy administration into action; after Kennedy's death, Lyndon Johnson greatly expanded Kennedy's effort into the War on Poverty. The number of poor Americans fell throughout the 1960s, hitting a low of 24.1 million (9.5 percent) in 1969. Although the absolute numbers increased somewhat in the 1970s, the proportion stayed below 10 percent until 1980. During the Reagan and Bush presidencies in the 1980s, these improvements began to be eroded. In 1991, more than 36 million Americans—14.2 percent of the population—lived in poverty (see Figure 9.3). Many live far below the poverty line. A recent study showed that the average poor family fell almost $4,400 short of what the government believed it needed in a year for adequate nutrition (Littman, 1989).

To get a better idea of poverty in contemporary America, we will look at some general statistics about the poor. Then we will focus on three groups: the working poor, the ghetto poor, and the homeless. We will close the chapter with a look at the impact of poverty.

Who Are the Poor?

It is difficult to generalize about America's poor. Certainly the poor include unwed teenage mothers in inner-city ghettoes, but they are not the majority of poor people. Neither are the homeless. An accurate portrait of Americans living in poverty would include many farmers (60 percent of the poor live outside cities), many recently unemployed people with long histories of steady work, and many people who have suffered crises like divorce or death in the family. African-Americans and Hispanic-Americans are much more likely than whites to be poor, although the majority of poor Americans are white (*Statistical Abstract*, 1990, p. 458). About half are either children under sixteen or people over sixty-five. One of the biggest changes in America's poor population is the rapid increase in the number of poor children, and the almost simultaneous reduction in poverty among the elderly, for whom Social Security and private pensions have worked

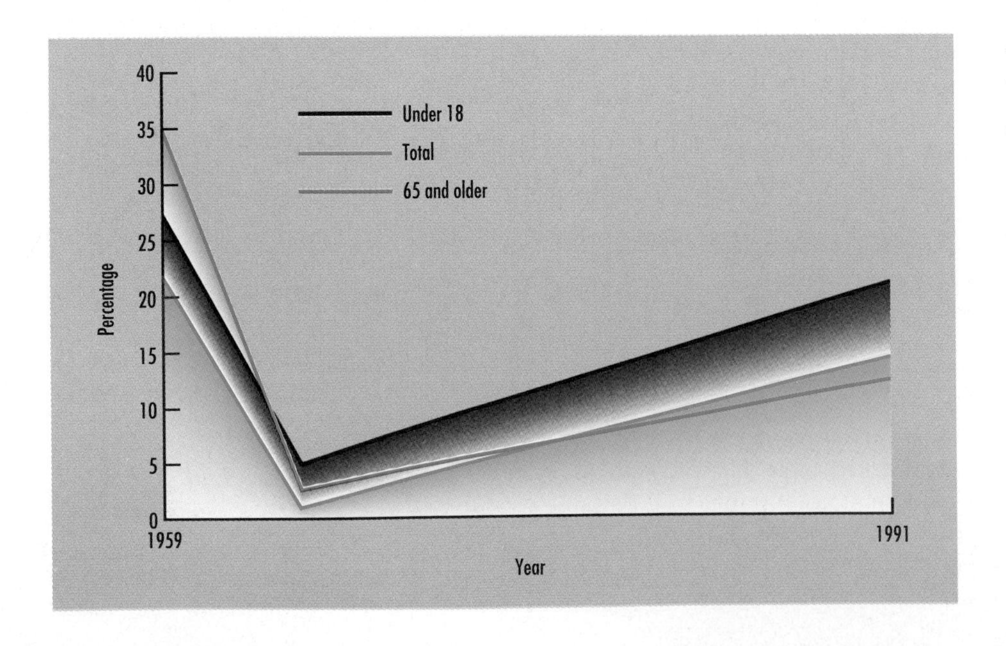

FIGURE 9.3 / *Percentage of Americans Living below the Poverty Line, 1959–1991*

Source: *Statistical Abstract of the United States, 1991*, U.S. Bureau of the Census, Washington, D.C.

wonders (Preston, 1984).

Nearly half the people who live below the poverty line are employed; 4 million of these "working poor" have full-time jobs (*Los Angeles Times*, July 15, 1990). Contrary to stereotypes, only just over a third of poor people receive welfare payments (not counting aid to the elderly and veterans; Harrington, 1988; *U.S. News & World Report*, October 15, 1990). In fact, no matter how poor they are, able-bodied men cannot receive any form of government welfare assistance other than food stamps. After children and their mothers, disabled people are the next largest group receiving government aid. Despite a rise in the number of children born to unwed mothers, there has not been a rise in the proportion of welfare recipients who are children in single-parent families (Bane and Elwood, 1989).

While it is a myth that the welfare rolls are dominated by single women having babies just to get more money, changes in family structure have increased the rate of welfare dependency. The sociologists David Eggebeen and Daniel Lichter (1991) examined the records of poor children from 1960 to 1988. They found that changing family structure—particularly the increase in female-headed households—accounted for nearly 50 percent of the rise in child poverty rates since 1980. Black children suffered three times as much as whites from this trend. The biggest factor enabling single-parent families to escape poverty is the combined availability of child care and employment opportunities for women.

The Working Poor

Middle-class Americans are divided on the reasons for poverty (Zinn and Eitzen, 1989). Some believe that most poor people are poor because they lack motivation and ambition or because they do not have the values and skills necessary to hold a job. Others believe that trying to hold the individual responsible amounts to "blaming the victim" for a situation over which individuals actually have little control (Ryan, 1976). The real culprits, they suggest, are plant closings and relocations, changing technologies, and discrimination. The one point on which most would agree is that people would not be poor if they held jobs. This may have been true in the past, but a job no longer guarantees that a worker and his or her family will not be poor (Bane and Ellwood, 1989). The number of Americans who worked full-time, year-round, but remained mired in poverty increased by 37 percent in the 1980s making this the fastest-growing group among the poor (Mishel and Simon, 1988).

Although there is no simple explanation for the growing number of working poor, two factors stand out. The first is the change in the occupational structure of the economy that we referred to in our discussion of downward mobility. In the 1970s and 1980s, the American economy's shift from manufacturing to services brought about numerous plant closings; new technologies reduced the need for manual labor; budget deficits forced all levels of government (a major employer) to cut their payrolls; and the labor market became polarized into low- and high-wage sectors. Job growth was mostly at the low-wage end, in service industries like retail trade, restaurants, health care, cleaning, and repair shops, which tended to pay near-minimum-wage salaries, offered few benefits (such as health insurance and pension plans), and provided little job security (see Figure 9.4). New jobs at the high end (in computers and engineering, for example) required skills that the millions of Americans who had lost their jobs in well-paid, unionized industries didn't have. Displaced workers frequently experienced long periods of unemployment and ended up in jobs that paid significantly less than the ones they had lost; new workers were unable to find the kinds of jobs that had been available a generation earlier (Klein and Rones, 1989). In 1989, the average wage for U.S. workers hit a new low of $4.80 per hour, down from a high of $5.38 in 1974 (in constant 1977 dollars). In 1989 dollars, working forty hours a week, fifty-two weeks a year at this wage would earn a person $14,539.20—below the poverty line for a family of five (*Statistical Abstract*, 1991, p. 418).

Second, the value of the minimum wage set by the government declined steadily in the 1980s (see Figure 9.5). Contrary to popular stereotypes, the majority of minimum-wage workers are not teenagers but adults, many of whom support dependents, and many of whom are among the working poor. As recently as 1979, the minimum wage was worth about half the average wage in purchasing power and was sufficient to keep a family of three above the poverty level. By 1987, the minimum wage was worth only a third of the average wage and did not pay enough to keep a family of two, much less three, above the poverty level. A family of four with one full-time and one part-time minimum-wage worker would end up almost $2,000 below the poverty line (Mishel and Simon, 1988). Returning the minimum wage to about half the average wage was an important part of President Clinton's 1993 economic plan (not yet enacted at the time this book went to press).

The working poor are especially common in rural America. The decline of the farm economy and the increasing dominance of large corporate farms have not only left small farmers hurting but have cut into income possibili-

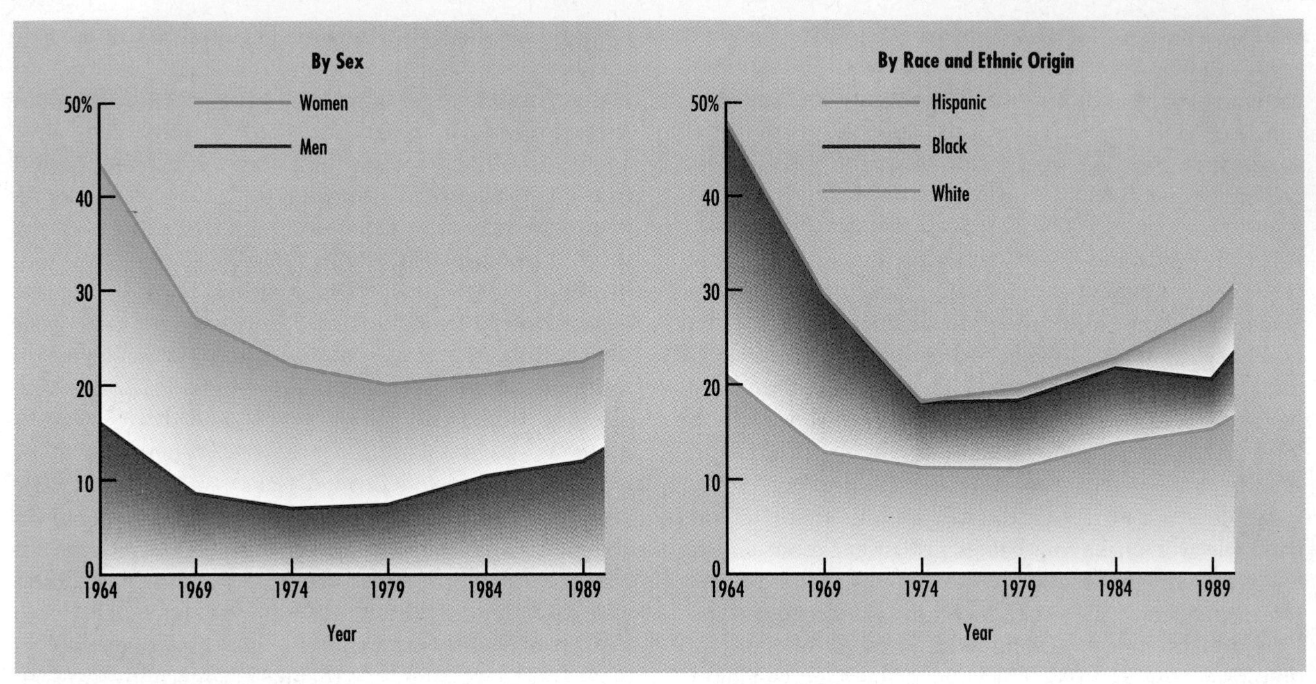

FIGURE 9.4 / Percentage of Low-Wage ($12,195 per Year or Less) Workers, by Sex and Race, 1964–1990

Source: U.S. Bureau of the Census, in *New York Times*, July 26, 1992.

ties for whole communities that once depended on farmers. Many jobs, like harvesting, are seasonal rather than year-round. Rural people often take work into their homes, addressing envelopes, embroidering jogging suits, or assembling stuffed toys to make enough money to get by. As Osha Gray Davidson writes, "Industrial homework is becoming to today's rural ghettos what sweatshops were to the immigrant tenements in the first half of this century: vehicles for the exploitation of a mostly female work force, characterized by low wages, unsafe working conditions, child labor, and little or no government regulation" (1990, p. 142). Such work enables people to stay on their farms, but seldom to escape poverty.

We have noted that, historically, a slide into poverty has been the result of a temporary crisis for many Americans (Duncan, 1984). Today, this slide more often appears

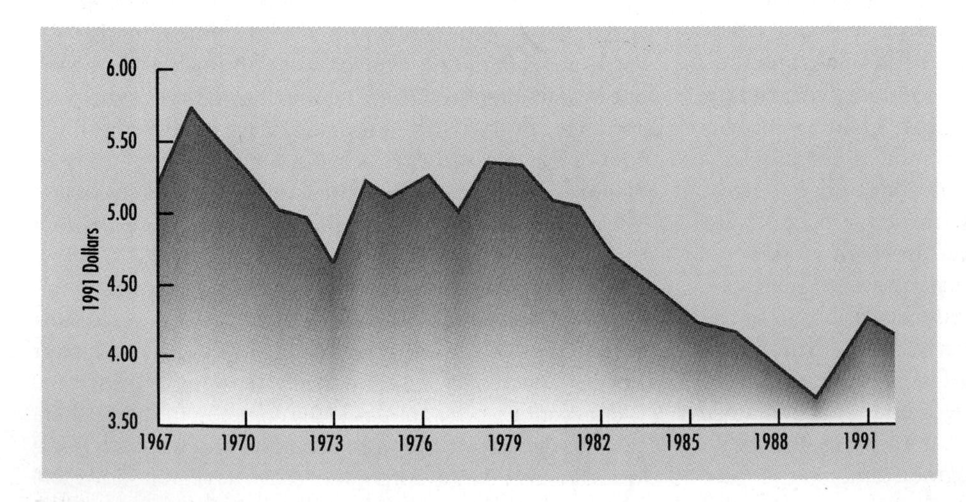

FIGURE 9.5 / Value of the Minimum Wage in 1991 Dollars, 1967–1992

Source: Economic Policy Institute, Washington, D.C., April 1993.

to be permanent. Structural changes in the economy and thus in the employment-opportunity structure combine with a lower minimum wage to make it harder for poor people to pull themselves and their families out of poverty even when they work full-time (Keyfitz, 1991). This problem is particularly acute for African-Americans, many of whom face the additional problems of life in inner-city ghettoes, where jobs are especially hard to come by.

The Ghetto Poor

On Chicago's predominantly black South Side, two out of three adults are unemployed; half have not completed high school; and six in ten are on welfare (A. Duncan, 1987; Wacquant, 1989). Median income is one-third the city average, and half of South Side households subsist on annual incomes of $7,500 or less. Stable families are also rare (Wacquant and Wilson, 1989; W. J. Wilson, 1987). Almost half of South Side adults are without a steady partner; six in ten babies are born out of wedlock; and two out of three households are headed by women. Rates of teenage pregnancy, violent and property crime, and drug abuse are higher than for any other section of the city.

Chicago's South Side is not unique. In most major American cities, both the number of ghetto poor and the severity of ghetto poverty increased during the 1970s and the 1980s, and social conditions deteriorated (Wilson, 1991). Why is extreme poverty concentrated in inner-city, predominantly black neighborhoods? Why, more than a quarter of a century after the passage of antidiscrimination legislation, are 2.5 million African-Americans still trapped in poverty? These issues spurred national concern about the "underclass"—the people at the very bottom of the class structure. As the sociologists William Julius Wilson (1991) and Herbert Gans (1990) have observed, however, the word *underclass* became misleading when some journalists used it to describe poor people whom they thought didn't deserve any better because they refused to work or do anything else to better themselves.

Wilson (1980, 1987, 1991), the leading authority on the subject, takes issue with the popular idea that the rise of ghetto poverty reflects the development of a "welfare mentality" or a "culture of poverty" among urban black people, or that African-Americans simply do not value education, work, and family as much as other Americans do. Emphasizing social structure rather than culture or voluntary action, he argues that nonconforming and deviant behavior among the ghetto poor is the result, not the cause, of their living conditions and of the restricted opportunities available to them.

In the past, manual labor, factory work, and government jobs provided a route out of poverty for African-Americans who had migrated to the city from the rural South and for those with a high school education or less. With the changes in the economy that we described above, these jobs became harder to find. Cities were particularly hard-hit because many of the surviving companies, along with retail stores and warehouses, moved out. Most inner-city African-Americans can't afford the cost of moving or commuting to the suburbs, where most entry-level blue-collar, clerical, and sales jobs are now located. Whereas the most common first job for their fathers a generation ago had been factory assembler or machine operator, the most common jobs reported by today's black male youths are janitor and waiter—if they work at all (Testa and Krogh, 1989). Nearly half of inner-city black youth aged sixteen to nineteen are out of school and unemployed.

A second factor in the rise of ghetto poverty, according to Wilson, was the migration of higher-income African-Americans out of the inner cities. As a result of legislation banning discrimination in housing, professional, middle-class, and working-class blacks were able to move to better neighborhoods within the city or to the suburbs. In the past, the presence of higher-income families in the ghettoes had provided a social buffer for poor families. In times of rising unemployment for low-income workers, better-off ghetto residents maintained such basic institutions as churches, schools, stores, banks, and recreational facilities. They also provided role models of stable, successful working families for children whose own families were worse off. Their departure led to greater social isolation of the most disadvantaged segments of the African-American community. Local institutions cut back services or closed their doors. Contact with people of different class and racial backgrounds became increasingly rare. Access to quality education and to job networks (the most common route to employment, as described in Chapter 4) was cut off. Because of unemployment, high mortality rates, and high rates of imprisonment, there is a shortage of marriageable men capable of supporting a family. These structural changes have led to unconventional family forms and welfare dependency.

Although he emphasizes structural factors, Wilson does not dismiss the impact of culture and socialization processes on ghetto poverty. The combination of social isolation and joblessness deprives young people of exposure to adults from whom they can learn the disciplined habits associated with steady work. Wilson draws on Pierre Bourdieu's earlier research (1965) to show how a job

This photograph, taken by Chris Heflin, a nine-year-old, homeless child living in a shelter in Virginia, is another from the project in which homeless children were taught photography so that they could record and reflect on their world. The photograph is sociologically meaningful because it shows how poor people accomplish routines such as play and because it reflects the point of view of the subjects.

provides a worker not only with an income but also with a framework for organizing daily life; conversely, unemployment or irregular employment makes rational daily planning more difficult. Moreover, when individuals are surrounded by others who are chronically unemployed, they may begin to doubt their own ability to accomplish conventional goals or to doubt that society will provide opportunities to exercise those skills.

Wilson does not deny that racial discrimination played a role in the rise of ghetto poverty. There is evidence that employers tend to perceive inner-city black males, especially, as uneducated, unstable, uncooperative, and dishonest, even when the employers do not express overtly racist attitudes (Neckerman and Kirschenman, 1990). However, Wilson points out that African-Americans with higher education have made significant progress in recent decades, a fact that tends to rule out discrimination as the sole or main factor in the rise of ghetto poverty. For example, in New York City between 1970 and 1985, 84,000 blacks lost jobs in manufacturing (which require low levels of education), but 104,000 gained jobs in public administration and professional services (which require higher education) (Bailey, 1989).

Although racism is real, it has been around too long to fully explain the recent worsening of the situation of the black ghetto poor. Before Wilson's research, the most common explanation started with the social disorganization of the ghetto. What Wilson did was to show that this disorganization was not simply a result of African-American culture or the idiosyncratic actions of individuals but rather of structural changes in urban economies. So long as the mismatch continues between the jobs available in cities and the skills of young ghetto residents, especially males, chronic ghetto poverty is likely to persist.

The Homeless

Homelessness is not a new phenomenon. During the Industrial Revolution in England, thousands of homeless people wandered from door to door, begging, and slept under bridges and in fields. Every American city has long had its skid row, and in times of economic hardship—such as the Great Depression—jobless people have lived on the streets and in public parks. As we saw earlier in this chapter, personal tragedies figure in the stories of many of today's homeless people. But changes in the ***social structure*** in four areas—employment opportunities, housing, welfare benefits, and mental health programs—are more important factors behind the numbers of today's homeless population.

The first and most basic cause of increased homelessness was a set of economic changes that increased the number of poor people. Poverty is the root cause of homelessness;

people who can afford housing seldom sleep on the sidewalks. Indeed, as we saw above, the number of poor Americans increased substantially during the 1980s, the same decade that saw the rapid increase in homelessness. In addition to a recession, structural changes in the American economy were at work (see Chapter 16). New technology and drives for industrial efficiency meant that fewer workers were needed. As factory workers and others were laid off, they took less skilled or demanding jobs that might previously have gone to more marginal workers. This trend forced more people into the ranks of the destitute.

A second crucial reason for the rapid increase in homelessness was a sharp reduction in the availability of low-cost housing (Kozol, 1988). In a study of twelve major U.S. cities, James D. Wright (1989) found that the number of low-income housing units dropped by about 30 percent during the late 1970s and early 1980s. Nationwide, as many as 1 million beds in inexpensive residential hotels were lost (Kasinitz, 1986; Lang, 1989; Levitas, 1990). Some were torn down to make room for urban renewal and gentrification (see Chapter 10); others were simply abandoned. At the same time, the Reagan administration cut government spending for low-income housing by 75 percent (Lang, 1989; National Housing Task Force, 1988).

Third, just as poverty was increasing, government assistance for poor people was being cut back. In the twelve largest U.S. cities, the number of poor people increased by 36 percent (more than 1 million persons) between 1979 and 1984 (Wright, 1989). At the same time, the real value of welfare benefits declined by nearly a third (Levitas, 1990). In addition, welfare reforms reduced the number of people eligible for benefits by half a million or more. This increased the demand for the cheapest housing, and those who couldn't get it were pushed out onto the streets.

Fourth, thousands of mentally ill people became homeless when they were released from hospitals without adequate community facilities to help them (Isaac and Armat, 1990; Johnson, 1990). Under a 1963 federal law, old state mental hospitals, where patients often were confined for life in deplorable conditions, were to be replaced by smaller, more humane community mental health centers that would provide both residential care and outpatient clinics. The idea was that community care, in combination with new antipsychotic drugs, would allow the mentally ill to lead more normal lives. The problem was that only half the program was implemented: All but the most severely ill patients were "deinstitutionalized," but because of budget cuts, most of the community centers were never established. Many former patients had nowhere to go, stopped taking medication, and ended up wandering the streets. Another law prohibiting involuntary commitment of nonviolent individuals exacerbated the problem by eliminating one way of getting care for people who couldn't function on their own. Although most homeless people do not suffer from severe, chronic mental illness, current estimates suggest that a quarter to a third do have serious, recurring problems (Kalifon, 1989). Moreover, a survey by researchers from Johns Hopkins University found that more than 70 percent of single homeless men and 95 percent of homeless women suffer from minor psychological disorders (Jacoby, 1991).

The homeless population exploded in the 1980s, in sum, because the poverty rate went up at the same time that three needed social supports were cut back: housing, welfare benefits, and mental health care. These are all structural factors. They do not explain the personal tragedies that shape the individual stories of homeless men, women, and children (as we saw at the beginning of the chapter). They do explain why tragedies struck more frequently and why many of the victims had nowhere to turn and became homeless when those tragedies struck. In this difficult time, the people who wound up homeless were those among the extremely poor who suffered what the sociologist Peter Rossi (1989) has called an "accumulation of troubles": chronic unemployment, mental illness, poor physical health, alcoholism, drug problems, criminal records. Two-thirds of the homeless people Rossi studied in Chicago had experienced three or more of these problems. Such difficulties not only make it harder for them to find work and get back on their feet; they make it less likely that relatives and friends will be able to provide them with shelter and support.

Poverty and Life Chances

Not all poor people are homeless, but homelessness is a condition that all poor people have to fear. Living close to the margin of survival, they could at any point find themselves without the means to keep a roof over their heads. This is just one of the many hazards to which poor people are more exposed than the rest of Americans.

The term **life chances** refers to the distribution within a social system of opportunities that affect people's health, survival, and happiness. Most Americans have access to such essentials as food and shelter, but those in the bottom strata have the worst life chances. Poverty affects not only how a person lives, but whether a person lives at all.

One of the most telling poverty statistics is the infant mortality rate (the number of babies per 1,000 live births who die before their first birthdays). Although the United States spends considerably more on health care than any other country, its infant mortality rate is the highest of all the developed nations (Hale, 1990). Infant mortality is not distributed evenly in American society. Nonwhite babies are twice as likely as white babies to die in infancy; they are also twice as likely to be born to poor mothers. Infant mortality rates are also higher in inner cities and rural counties, where poverty is concentrated. A black baby born in Boston's inner city has less chance of surviving his or her first year than a child born in Third World countries like Panama, North Korea, or Uruguay (K. Phillips, 1991).

Poor, minority children are more likely than other American children to die in infancy because they are more likely to be born to a mother who is teenaged, in poor physical health, malnourished, and dependent on drugs or alcohol, all of which place the baby at risk. Standard prenatal care could prevent many infant deaths. In virtually every other developed nation, the government guarantees health care to all pregnant women and their babies. At present, the U.S. government requires only that states make Medicaid health care available to single mothers with incomes below the poverty line (Hale, 1990). The quality of care offered is uneven; complex eligibility requirements vary from state to state and restrict access to free health care. Nationwide, the proportion of the poor covered by Medicaid dropped from about 65 percent in 1976 to 38 percent in 1986 (Harrington, 1988).

The health costs of poverty continue through childhood and adulthood into old age. Poor children typically receive less adequate nutrition, have fewer medical checkups, miss more days of school because of illness, have a higher rate of accidents (in part because they live in unsafe environments), and are more likely to suffer from impaired vision, impaired hearing, and iron and vitamin deficiencies than are other children (Baumeister, 1987; Coll, 1990). Poor adults often suffer from untreated acute or chronic health problems, miss days of work because of illness, and describe their health as only fair or poor.

The poor spend a much greater proportion of their incomes on food than other Americans do: on average, 40 percent for families earning less than $5,000 per year, compared with 13 percent for families with incomes of $30,000 or more (*Statistical Abstract*, 1990). Often the poor pay more for less: prices are higher and quality lower in inner-city grocery stores—partly because merchants face higher risks and insurance costs. Tight food budgets usually mean unhealthy diets, high in cheap, fatty meats and starches, low in fruits and vegetables.

The poor also pay proportionately more for housing. On average, families earning less than $5,000 pay 45 percent of their income for housing, compared with 10 percent for families with incomes of $30,000 or more (*Statistical Abstract*, 1990). After paying their rent, four-person poor families typically have only $230 a month left for everything else—food, clothing, transportation—for everyone in the household. According to the Physicians' Task Force on Hunger, in 1985 about 20 million Americans (including 12 million children) went hungry at some point each month (Harrington, 1988).

Thinking Back on the Key Concepts

We have seen in this chapter that social stratification is first and foremost a matter of ***social structure***. Despite 200 years of increasing national wealth, millions of Americans are still living in poverty. This is part of an unequal distribution of wealth that is basic to the American social structure. In 1990, there were about 950,000 millionaires in the United States; their combined wealth ran to more than $2,000 billion (*Fortune*, September 10, 1990). In that same year, 35.3 million Americans were living below the poverty line (*Statistical Abstract*, 1990, p. 458). If the millionaires had agreed to redistribute just the *interest* on their wealth, sacrificing none of their capital, every poor person in the country would have received $3,500—enough to lift most of them out of poverty (*Statistical Abstract*, 1990, pp. 458, 464).

The inequalities of wealth in American society also reflect other social factors. They reflect the fact that the ***functional integration*** of American society is organized through a capitalist, free-enterprise system that depends on unequal rewards to motivate people to invest for the future and to work hard. Greatly reducing poverty would depend on basic changes in the social system. Some changes have been made, such as the establishment of antipoverty programs in the 1960s. Such changes are often resisted, however, partly because they conflict with some models of how a capitalist economy will work most effi-

100
MEN
US (+)
COMMUNITY
CLUBS
TO 79th ST
WESTERN AVE
PLUS
ALL
ONE
COLOR
STOP THE KILLING

Seniors at the University of North Carolina (UNC) have a long-standing tradition of giving the university a class gift as they graduate. The class of 1987 decided to fill a space in front of the university's new library and commissioned a well-known sculptor to create a group of statues depicting student life.

In the fall of 1990, the statues were set in place. The outcry was immediate. The group of seven figures included two apparently African-American students—one balancing a book on her head and the other twirling a basketball on his fingertip. The single Asian-American student was primly dressed and carried a violin. Many students felt the statues reinforced racial and ethnic stereotypes. While African-American students were portrayed as athletes (and thus less serious than other students) with roots in a "primitive" culture (the black woman carrying a load on her head), Asian-Americans were portrayed as eggheads and nerds who spend their time practicing (the violin) and studying. The sculptor's attempt to capture the racial and ethnic diversity of today's university had backfired.

Tempers flared when someone knocked over one of the African-American statues and stole the basketball. The vandals were never caught. To this day no one knows whether they were racist whites who resented the inclusion of African-Americans in the group or African-American students protesting the stereotype of the black athlete. The chorus of complaints eventually led the chancellor to order the statues moved to a less visible spot on campus.

Sociology's five key concepts help to make sense of this dispute—and similar racial misunderstandings. The incident at the University of North Carolina showed how ***social action*** can take the form of a chain reaction: the decision of the graduating class motivating the sculptor, the sculptor unwittingly provoking the dispute, the vandals seizing the opportunity to protest, and the chancellor responding to the vandals. These social actions were, in turn, shaped by ***culture***: The fact that the figures reflected cultural stereotypes set off the dispute in the first place. The incident at UNC also reflected ***social structure***. Black students are underrepresented at the university compared with their numbers in the population of the state. A main reason is ***power***—specifically the power of the white elite, which refused to admit any black students to the university for over 150 years.

Functional integration also played a part in this social drama. The university needs money to operate. Alumni, legislators, and others tend to give more to a school when its teams are winning. So the administration encourages coaches to seek out star basketball players (many black) and perhaps make exceptions to usual academic standards for athletes. Sports scholarships enable poor minority students to attend college who otherwise might not be able to do so. This is a major reason why the percentage of African-Americans is higher on the basketball team than in the student body as a whole. And this overrepresentation in sports reinforces the racial stereotype of the black basketball player, setting off controversies like the one described here.

UNC was not alone. The statue incident was just one in a wave of racial and ethnic clashes that hit American colleges and universities in the late 1980s and early 1990s. Such episodes reflect the fact that America, ethnically diverse from its origin, has become a more multicultural society than ever, with members of numerous minorities struggling to have their special needs and abilities recognized. As we will see in this chapter, inequalities of race and ethnicity have been among our country's most difficult and enduring problems. They are the internal, domestic equivalents of the global cultural divisions that have produced many nationalist movements and both civil and international wars. We will also see, however, that cultural differences are among our country's greatest strengths and sources of creativity.

We will begin by looking at the sources of cultural diversity, emphasizing the role of immigration in the American experience. Then we will explore the different kinds of relations that exist between culturally different groups in a society, focusing on relations between dominant and minority groups. Finally, we will profile four of the most prominent minority groups in this country: African-Americans, Hispanic-Americans, Native Americans, and Asian-Americans.

CULTURAL DIVERSITY

The Pledge of Allegiance asserts that the United States is "one nation, indivisible." But our country is also culturally diverse. People who call themselves "American" have cultural roots in all other countries on earth and, in varying degrees, still identify with their ancestral heritage. As the incident at UNC illustrated so vividly, the ideal of cultural unity often clashes with the reality of cultural diversity. So it is in most modern nations.

The notion that all members of a society should share a common culture is a relatively recent one. Consider France, a nation many people view as highly unified and steeped in shared tradition. In reality, however, most people in France did not speak French until the 1850s (Weber,

American immigrants have often become important entrepreneurs, starting small businesses that serve the needs of their own communities (such as stores which sell foods from home cultures) as well as adding diversity to American communities.

1976). For centuries Burgundy, Britanny, Languedoc, and Provence each had its own provincial ruler, local traditions, and language or dialect. Even now clashes in values often erupt between, say, the Béarnaise in the hills of southwestern France and Parisians. But however much French people may differ from one another, they are certain that being French is quite different from being German.

The ideal of cultural unity often promotes *ethnocentrism*, the belief that one's own culture is superior to all others (see Chapter 3). In Europe ethnocentrism reached a dramatic and terrible peak in the Holocaust, the attempt by Nazi Germany to exterminate the Jews and Gypsies of Germany and Central Europe. Millions perished in Nazi death camps. But the Holocaust was not a unique or isolated event in Western history. The colonial period was also one of violent ethnocentrism. France, Britain, and other European powers sought not only to conquer the world politically but also to convert the world culturally. When local or "native" populations did not cooperate, they were displaced (in North America), subdued by force (in India and Africa), or slaughtered (in Latin America).

The current picture in Europe is mixed. On the one hand, the European Community agreements are uniting French, English, German, and other cultures in increasingly close economic, political, and cultural collaboration. All Europeans may eventually have one passport, one currency, perhaps even one official language. On the other hand, large numbers of migrants from former colonies are seeking to make Europe their home. Indians, Pakistanis, and Jamaicans move to Britain; Algerians and West Africans to France; Indonesians to the Netherlands. Germany is home to Poles, Spaniards, Turks, and many from Europe's poorer nations. Not all of today's migrants are poor: a growing number are highly trained, well-paid professionals who work in international relations or for global corporations. In any case, the new arrivals are not always welcome. In Germany, gangs have attacked immigrant housing complexes, in what some see as a revival of Nazism. Moreover, the breakdown of communist rule in Eastern Europe and the former Soviet Union has allowed old ethnic antagonisms to surface. In what used to be Yugoslavia, Serbian Christians have launched a program of "ethnic cleansing" to expel Bosnian Muslims from their homeland by whatever means necessary, including murder and rape.

The tension between the ideals of cultural unity and tolerance and the realities of cultural diversity and ethnocentrism is among the leading issues of our times. Four basic factors have contributed to this tension:

1. Most modern states have joined together populations that once considered themselves separate and distinct (as in France and the former Yugoslavia).

2. Although colonialism brought Europeans into contact with other cultures and Europeans learned much from the peoples they conquered, this period tended to reinforce ethnocentrism.

3. Modern states have attracted large numbers of immigrants, both from former colonies and from other, usually poorer, countries.

4. International relations and international business keep goods, ideas, and people flowing across national borders and cultural boundaries.

The United States is like European nations in some of these respects, but unique in others.

Immigration to the United States

The United States is one of the most culturally diverse nations in the world. Most Americans are descended from immigrants. (Indeed, so are Native Americans, or Indians, whose ancestors migrated from Asia across the Bering Strait to North America some 25,000 years ago.) Before the United States became an independent nation, French and Dutch as well as British settlers had founded colonies here. In addition to African slaves, waves of European, Latin American, and Asian immigrants have poured into the United States.

Since 1882, when Congress enacted the Chinese Exclusion Act, the United States has attempted to control both the number and the type of immigrants admitted to this country. For many years we had a quota system based on country of origin. Simply put, white Western Europeans were nearly always welcome, and nonwhite, non-Europeans (with a few exceptions) were not. Quotas were an attempt to maintain American cultural unity by admitting mostly people whom white Americans of European descent perceived to be like themselves—people who would readily be absorbed into mainstream American culture.

The 1965 Immigration Act abolished the national-origins quota system, but immigration regulations are still highly selective. Cultural and racial biases are maintained in several ways. First, although the United States no longer discriminates against people from specific nations, a system of regional quotas is still in effect. It is designed to admit roughly equal numbers of Europeans, Asians, Africans, and South Americans. On the surface, this policy seems even-handed, but in fact it is skewed. We admit as many immigrants from tiny Europe, with its relatively small population, as we do from heavily populated Asia.

Second, people who have close relatives in the United States are given preference over those who do not. Reuniting families is certainly a worthy goal, but it has the effect of favoring groups who are already here, most of which are European. However, some racial and ethnic minorities (such as Indians and Pakistanis) have also benefited.

Third, the American government uses immigration as a tool in foreign policy. Refugees—individuals who are fleeing political persecution in their homelands—are given special treatment. Individuals fleeing economic deprivation, even famine and starvation, are not considered refugees under U.S. regulations. Even decisions about who qualifies as a political refugee are selective. These decisions depend on which regimes the United States considers hostile or friendly. For example, in the 1980s the United States admitted most Nicaraguans who claimed to be fleeing persecution at the hands of the communist Sandinista government (which since then has been overthrown). But the U.S. government was far less willing to grant refugee status to people from the neighboring country of El Salvador, whose right-wing government was as repressive as the Nicaraguan government. The people from these two countries seeking asylum in the United States were alike in most ways (culturally, racially, socioeconomically). The crucial difference was that the government of El Salvador was an ally and the Nicaraguan government was an enemy.

The United States has been largely populated by immigrant groups, but the reception of immigrants has varied according to the employment situations and racial attitudes of the society at a given time. Currently, controversy over U.S. immigration policy centers on Haitians who flee their troubled homeland in crowded, rickety boats.

Other decisions about who counts as a refugee also reflect racial and cultural bias. Before the communist governments of Eastern Europe and the USSR collapsed, would-be immigrants from those countries were automatically considered refugees. The U.S. government did not grant the same privilege to people fleeing the Marxist regime in Ethiopia, even though they were far more likely to be imprisoned, tortured, or killed by their government than were Eastern Europeans. U.S. government officials acknowledged that America did not have the same strategic interest in northeast Africa that it had in Eastern Europe; but another, unstated reason was that Ethiopians are black. Even now the United States limits the number of refugees from the entire continent of Africa to 2,000 a year, regardless of famine, civil war, and other catastrophes.

Despite these attempts at control, immigration to the United States has climbed in recent decades—from 3 million in the 1960s, to 4.5 million in the 1970s, to almost 6 million in the 1980s (*Statistical Abstract*, 1991, p. 9). One reason is that immigration laws have been relaxed somewhat. Even with the restrictions noted above, the United States admits more Africans, Asians, and Latin Americans today than it did twenty-five years ago. Another reason is that the international situation has changed (Zolberg, 1991). First, the lives of millions of people around the world have been disrupted by political crises and transformations, civil wars, and natural catastrophes like famines and droughts. Second, the gap between the rich and poor countries of the world has widened (see Chapter 18), increasing the attractiveness of wealthy countries like the United States. This accounts for the steady flow of Mexican and Central American immigrants into the United States. Third, the increasing interconnections of the global economy and global culture are drawing people from different countries into closer relationships with one another. Some migrants, for example, work in highly internationalized fields of cultural production such as the film industry and journalism.

Immigration changes the ***social structure*** of a population. Just as the arrival of Irish and Italian immigrants brought diversity to late-nineteenth-century America, so the arrival of Latin American, Asian, and African immigrants provides diversity today. It may also promote economic dynamism. Studies show that immigrants are particularly likely to start small businesses, such as specialty stores catering to other immigrants and ethnic restaurants that all Americans enjoy. Immigration patterns clearly reflect ***social actions***, ranging from governmental decisions about foreign policy that affect immigration laws to individual decisions to leave one's homeland. Migration flows are also shaped by balances and imbalances in ***functional integration***: People leave places where overpopulation and economic underdevelopment limit their opportunities and go to places that have shortages of low-wage laborers and economic niches to be filled.

Minority Groups

One effect of successive waves of immigration to the United States has been the creation of a number of minority groups. A **minority group** is a category of people who, because of their physical appearance or cultural characteristics, are singled out from others in their society, held in low esteem, and subject to unequal treatment.

Many new immigrants were discriminated against in their early years in America. Gradually, most blended into the population at large, ceased to be objects of discrimination, and maintained their ethnic identity only loosely, as a matter of choice. Americans of German descent, for example, may take pride in their heritage, but most of them no longer speak German, live in primarily German-American communities, or suffer discrimination. Some groups, especially those who arrived more recently and encountered substantial hostility, have maintained stronger identities. Irish-Americans, though they have moved far from the definition of a minority group, are still concentrated in certain northeastern cities; in Boston, for example, they are a powerful influence on local politics. The same is true of the Poles in Chicago. The experience of the Holocaust and continued discrimination have contributed to the minority status of American Jews. A few groups, however, have been so discriminated against that they remain strongly identified with one another, in their own and society's eyes, even though they have deep roots in America. This is most obviously true of African-Americans; it is also true of Hispanic-Americans and Asian-Americans.

The concept of "minority group" does not refer to numerical size. Rather, it "refers to the degree of social power. Numerical majorities can be social minorities" (Wallerstein, 1991, p. 83). In South Africa, for example, blacks make up 80 percent of the population, but socially speaking they are a disadvantaged, overpowered minority group. Conversely, a small group may be able to establish its values, culture, and interests as dominant in a country. Thus white Anglo-Saxon men are a numerical minority in the United States, but they are not a minority group in the sociological sense because they are not singled out for discrimination. (Indeed, in federal and state legislatures and corporate boardrooms they often are a numerical majority.) By the same token, for certain purposes it makes sense to think of women as a minority group. Even though women outnumber men by 52 to 48 percent in America, they often are treated as a minority. Women's values and demands are regarded as "special interests," while those of white men are regarded as "the public interest" (see Chapter 11).

The distinction between a numerical and a social minority is an important one. In everyday usage we use the term *minority* loosely. But to say "South Africa has a minority government" (government by the few) does not mean the same thing as "Women are a minority group" (lower in status than men). The most common criteria for singling out a category of people for minority-group status are cultural differences, or *ethnicity*, and biological differences in appearance, or *race*.

Racial and Ethnic Groups

The definition of *race* seems obvious: a biological category made up of people who exhibit distinctive, hereditary characteristics, which are transmitted genetically. On closer examination, however, the limitations of this definition become clear. Obviously, people do differ physically, but these differences do not neatly and automatically divide them into racial groups. Why should skin color be more important as a basis for racial classification than hair or eye color, or why should facial features be more meaningful than height or build? Consider "black" Africans. The genetic and physical diversity within this category is enormous. Africa is home to some of the world's tallest people (the Tutsi) and some of the world's shortest (Pygmies). Africans themselves distinguish among a variety of skin colors, from purplish black to coffee brown. Some "black" Africans have the facial features that Americans consider typically "negroid," but others do not. Only the white Europeans who invaded Africa or raided it for slaves saw all Africans as belonging to a single race.

Thus, **race** denotes a category of people who perceive themselves and are perceived by others as distinctive on the basis of certain biologically inherited traits. Race is a social and cultural category, not simply a biological one. A race exists primarily in the perceptions and beliefs of its beholders.

Whereas race is based on the perception of *physical* differences, ethnicity is based on the perception of *cultural* differences. An **ethnic group** consists of people who perceive themselves and are perceived by others as sharing distinctive cultural traits such as language, religion, family customs, and food preferences. The term *ethnic group* is usually used to describe subgroups within a country. Polish-Americans, Navahos, French Canadians, and Ethiopian Jews are examples. The extent to which ethnic group members actually share unique cultural traits is less important than the fact that they and others believe they are "different." Ethnicity, like race, is a social label. There is a process of choice in claiming one's own identity, and a process of "ascription" or assignment in which others decide which identity they regard as appropriate. Both of these processes may outweigh seemingly objective factors, as sociologist Mary Waters found when studying Americans' "ethnic options" (see the Making Choices box).

The distinction between racial and ethnic groups is not always clear-cut. Are Hispanics, for example, a race or an ethnic group? What about Jews? The current debate over the terms *black American* and *African-American* illustrates this point. *Black* (or the earlier term *Negro*, which means "black" in Spanish) focuses on a physical attribute, while *African-American* emphasizes ancestry and cultural heritage. In addition, usages and identifications change. White Americans used to apply the term *colored* to people of African ancestry; today many blacks, or African-Americans, use the phrase *people of color* to emphasize their identification with all non-white, non-European peoples who have been colonized or enslaved.

PATTERNS OF INTERGROUP RELATIONS

Throughout history, contact between different societies and cultures has taken a variety of forms—from conflict and domination to acceptance and integration, and everything in between. Whether relations are friendly and cooperative or are hostile and exploitative is largely a matter of social ***power***.

Patterns of Conflict and Domination

When ethnocentrism combines with competition for territory and scarce resources, the results often are explosive. Ethnocentrism can fuel and "justify" competition; and competition can in turn heat up ethnocentrism, fanning the fires of racist ideologies and policies.

Colonialism

The takeover of a territory or population by a foreign government or nation, and the subsequent political and social domination of the native population, is called **colonialism**. European colonialism, which began in the fifteenth century, is history's prime example. At one time Europeans ruled most of the Southern Hemisphere and perhaps half the world's population. Under colonialism, the foreign elite pursued lives of leisure while local people were forced to labor in fields and mines or as servants. Traditional political systems, patterns of land use, production methods, and other elements of local culture were exploited or banned to suit European goals. Small numbers of natives might be hired as soldiers or given enough European education to serve as clerks, but no more.

Most European colonies won their independence in the decades following World War II. (We will discuss the aftermath of colonialism in Chapter 18.) But in a few "settler societies"—notably the United States, Australia, New Zealand, and South Africa—colonials seized control from the mother country and declared a new nation.

Displacement of Native Populations

In some cases the invading group does not stop at domination of the native population; it seeks to displace them. Displacement is most likely to occur in areas that are rich in natural resources and that possess a geography and climate similar to those of the homeland of the invading group (S. Lieberson, 1961; Van den Berghe, 1978). Displacement may take the form of attrition (the native group gradually moves on or dies out), forced population transfers, or genocide (deliberate extermination). All three played a role in the displacement of Native Americans.

Native Americans did not think of land as a commodity to be bought and sold. Consequently, they did not realize that white occupation of a piece of land meant a monopoly on its use. By the time this became clear, their very survival was threatened. They began to resist but were no match for the endless flood of white settlers with their vastly superior weapons (Spicer, 1980).

At first the whites attempted to resolve the conflict by moving the Native Americans west of the Mississippi. Later, on the Great Plains, they wiped out the buffalo, destroying the Native Americans' principal means of survival. Ultimately, a program of mass extermination reduced the Native American population by about two-thirds (D. Brown, 1971/1984).

Similar patterns have been repeated many times, in many places, and under a variety of circumstances. During World War II, the Soviet Union acquired territory and resources by expelling "disloyal nationalities" from their homelands. The Nazi slaughter of 6 million Jews was the culmination of hundreds of years of pogroms—organized massacres of Jews—across Eastern Europe. As the Nazi ex-

MAKING CHOICES

Ethnic Options: Selecting Identities in America

Every American has roots in at least one other culture (including Native Americans, who belong to many different nations or tribes). How do Americans decide their ethnic identity? If a woman has one German and one Italian parent, which ethnicity does she claim? What makes a man describe himself as Hispanic rather than specifically Mexican-American, Guatemalan, or Puerto Rican?

Mary Waters (1990) studied American ethnicity from the sociological perspective. She found that among later-generation Americans of European background, ethnic identities are in a state of flux. Intermarriage rates are high, and many people's ethnic identities are ambiguous. Parents may assign a different ethnic identity to their children than their children claim themselves; brothers and sisters may identify with different sides of the family; and individuals may claim different ethnicities in different situations (describing themselves as 100 percent American in relation to the Persian Gulf war, drawing on a father's Irish identity to fit in at work, and choosing to attend a Polish Catholic church because their mother strongly influenced their religious upbringing). People also claim different ethnic identities at different points in their lives, or they may pass themselves off as having a different ancestry of their own choosing. Ethnic flexibility is not confined to Americans of mixed ancestry. People whose ancestors all came from Ireland may see themselves as Irish to the core, or they may consider this background inconsequential and describe themselves simply as "American."

How do people choose? Parents may emphasize ethnicity ("We do this because we're Italian"), perhaps contrasting one side of the child's ancestry to the other ("That's your Irish temper," says an Italian mother when her half-Irish son misbehaves). A majority of adults claim the ethnic identity that matches their surname (which usually comes from the father's side of the family), but this is not always the case. Some ethnic identities are more popular among Americans than others. In the 1980s the favorite was Italian, followed by English, Irish, German, and Scottish. But ethnic identities tend to go in and out of vogue: For example, many more people claimed Native American ancestry on the census in 1990 than in 1980, an increase that neither birth nor immigration rates would explain.

In childhood and adolescence, young people usually mention all the ancestries they know in their background. In young adulthood, while they are getting married, starting a family, and raising children, increasing numbers settle on a single identity. Multiple identities tend to reemerge in middle age and then decline in old age.

One surprise is how few people describe themselves as simply "American," regardless of how long their families have lived here. The census form offers a choice of writing in a specific identity or checking "American" or "Don't Know"; in 1990 only 6 percent checked "American."

For Americans of European descent, ethnic identity is flexible, voluntary, and largely symbolic. This is not equally true for others. For African-Americans, Hispanic-Americans, Native Americans, and Asian-Americans, ethnic identity is not just a matter of personal choice. Ethnic labels are imposed by others, often on the basis of whether physical appearance deviates from white standards. This is one reason that nearly all children of mixed black and white marriages are considered black (Jencks, 1992).

Ethnicity, then, is largely a cost-free option for European-Americans and a more problematic issue for others. Yet all Americans tend to emphasize their ethnic identities even when not pressed to do so. Waters suggests that they do so because ethnicity helps to solve a basic contradiction in American culture, between individualism and community (see Chapter 3). An ethnic identity makes us feel special.

> *We are all aware that our ties with the European past grow increasingly feeble. Yet we feel uneasy before the prospect of becoming* just American [*emphasis added*]. *We feel uneasy before the prospect of becoming as undistinguishable from one another as our motel rooms are, or as flavorless and mass produced as the bread many of us eat. (L. Howe, 1977, p. 18)*

As individualists, we want to go our own way and do our own thing. Yet we long for community and need to feel that we come "from somewhere." Ethnic identities allow us to feel part of a community, but without enduring the constraints and demands of actual communities. In other words, they let us have it both ways. One of the women Waters interviewed expressed this quite clearly when asked to choose her ideal ethnic identity. (She was Scotch-Irish, which she described as "wishy-washy.")

> *"I would like to be a member of a group that is living a culture, like on an American Indian reservation, or a gypsy encampment . . . or an Italian neighborhood. Where there is meat to the culture. . . . [Laughs.] But flexible too, open to new ideas." (Waters, 1990, p. 152)*

Many Americans would like to have an ethnic community to which they could return when they felt lonely but which they could leave when they felt adventurous, without paying a price for entry or departure.

ample suggests, genocide and mass expulsions are not limited to territorial expansion. They also may occur within a country when the dominant group perceives a minority as threatening, when assimilation of the minority into the dominant group is viewed as impossible or undesirable, or when minority-group members are not considered essential (Dowty, 1987).

Slavery and Segregation

Displacing minority groups is not always in the best interests of the elites; often minority labor is essential to the economy. This was the case in the United States both during the slavery era and after its abolition. More than 10 million Africans were brought by force to America, where they were viewed as property and bought, sold, used, and abused at the will of the white majority. Slavery was rationalized on the grounds that Africans were a "backward," even "childlike," people, incapable of exercising the rights guaranteed to white men under the Constitution. At slavery's root, however, lay the economic interests of those who benefited from the cheap labor of slaves.

Slavery has long existed in human societies. The word, in fact, originates from "Slav," referring to eastern Europeans and Russians whom the Vikings captured and forced into bondage in the ninth and tenth centuries. But Africans have probably suffered more from slavery than any single group in human history, partly because African slavery became part of the colonization of both North and South America.

After the Civil War, the official freedom that had been granted to African-Americans did not reconcile white elites to the loss of cheap slave labor, or poorer whites to competition from free blacks. To defend their dominant status, whites instituted new boundaries and restrictions. They used legal mechanisms, like Jim Crow laws, which made it difficult for blacks to vote and barred them from public facilities. They used social pressure to reward black leaders who called on others to cooperate and to stop white liberals from encouraging blacks to demand more freedom and opportunity. When these efforts failed, they resorted to violence (cross burnings, evictions, lynchings). A central part of this strategy of domination was the effort to keep blacks from mixing with whites.

Segregation is the term for such enforced separation of racial or ethnic groups. It is a form of institutionalized discrimination, woven into the ***social structure***. In a segregated society, only certain types of contact between the dominant group and the minority group are allowed. Typically, members of the subordinate group are not allowed to live in the same neighborhoods as those in the dominant group, attend the same schools, work in the same occupations, join the same clubs, or use the same public facilities (hotels, restaurants, washrooms, even water fountains). Segregationists particularly fear intermarriage. Segregation is largely a strategy for maintaining the "purity" of elites (Tischler and Berry, 1978).

In the United States, segregation was rationalized on the grounds of "separate but equal" opportunities, as outlined by the Supreme Court in *Plessy* v. *Ferguson* (1896). Blacks had the same right to public education as whites, for example, but this did not mean blacks and whites had to attend the same schools. In practice, however, separate did not mean equal.

Prejudice and Discrimination

Prejudice is a rigid positive or negative opinion about a category of people, such as a racial or ethnic group, based on its members' real or imagined characteristics. Prejudice is rigid in the sense that it is independent of factual confirmation—it is literally a *pre*judgment. People are prejudiced when they are convinced that all members of a certain group have the same qualities, such as being immoral, violent, and backward; when they cannot see members of

These photographs graphically and metaphorically capture the social pain caused by efforts to integrate the United States. Top: *Jeering local whites pour sugar, ketchup, and mustard over the heads of nonviolent demonstrators at a segregated lunch counter in Jackson, Mississippi, in 1963.* Bottom: *In Boston in the 1970s court-ordered busing moved children to schools across neighborhood lines that were ethnically as well as racially distinct. Some Italian-Americans from Boston's South End and Irish-Americans from Charlestown mounted protests, often violent, against school integration.*

the group as individuals; and when they ignore evidence that would disprove their beliefs. Prejudice has a powerful effect on people's actions because it shapes their emotional responses as well as their thoughts.

Prejudices are not just individual attitudes; they are ***cultural*** norms. Racial prejudices, for example, are learned by American children from books, their parents' conversation and behavior, television, and other cultural sources, not merely their own observations. Often prejudices are maintained because people seldom come in contact with members of the scorned minority, except in unequal relationships (such as master and servant). When they do meet, people tend to perceive members of a devalued group in terms of their stereotypes (Lieberson, 1982).

Indeed, as the sociologist Robert K. Merton has observed, our prejudices can lead us to make very different evaluations of the same behavior, depending on whether it is seen in members of our own group (in-group) or another against which we are prejudiced (out-group):

> Did Lincoln work far into the night? This testifies that he was industrious, resolute, perseverant, and eager to realize his capacities to the full. Do the out-group Jews or Japanese keep these same hours? This only bears witness to their sweatshop mentality, their ruthless undercutting of American standards, their unfair competitive practices. Is the in-group hero frugal, thrifty, and sparing? Then the out-group villain is stingy, miserly, and penny-pinching. All honor is due to the in-group Abe for his having been smart, shrewd, and intelligent and, by the same token, all contempt is owing to the out-group Abes for their being sharp, cunning, crafty, and too clever by far. (Merton, 1957, p. 428)

One of the most common forms of prejudice is **racism**; the view that certain physical attributes are related to inferiority or superiority in moral, intellectual, and other nonphysical attributes (Van den Berghe, 1978). Racists often justify social avoidance and domination by claiming that relevant traits are biologically inherited and thus unalterable. They say, for example, that all black people are lazy, implying that laziness is somehow automatically associated with dark skin. Racist ideology also prescribes norms for the treatment of members of the allegedly inferior group. Thus, whites who agreed that blacks were lazy held the related notion that it was reasonable to beat blacks to make them work for the benefit of whites. Finally, racist ideology promotes belief in sharp divisions and boundaries. One is either white or black. If you are not one of "us," then you are one of "them."

One of the main results of prejudice against a racial or ethnic group is discrimination. **Discrimination** refers to significant social decisions about, and actions toward, people that are based on their presumed racial or ethnic identities. Thus, prejudice is a set of culturally based opinions; discrimination is a series of social actions based on those opinions.

Prejudice and discrimination can lead to a circular form of reasoning in which causes and effects become confused (Myrdal, 1944). People frequently use the *consequences* of prejudice and discrimination to prove that their negative evaluation was right. For example, African-Americans—on average—*do* live in poorer houses than whites, they *do* hold lower-paying jobs, and they *do* score lower on academic achievement tests. But rather than being any justification for prejudice and discrimination, these conditions are the *result* of prejudice and discrimination. Yet racist whites turn such facts around and use them as evidence that blacks are inferior to whites (see Figure 10.1).

As such reasoning suggests, overcoming prejudice and eliminating discrimination is extremely complicated. Policies and programs for creating equal opportunity—especially, affirmative action—have proved highly controversial (see the Key Concepts in Action box).

Resistance to Domination

Victims of prejudice and discrimination rarely accept abuse with complete passivity. In 1992, for example, when white policemen who had beaten a black motorist were acquitted of charges of brutality, a major riot broke out in Los Angeles, setting off protests and violence in other cities as well. Riots do not solve the minority's problems, but may call attention to their plight (see Chapter 21). In most cases, however, ***power*** relations prevent members of minorities from protesting or fighting back openly. They can only employ what James Scott (1985, 1987) has called "weapons of the weak."

One strategy is to avoid confrontation and unpleasant interaction by "self-segregation." Even where laws do not force them to stay separate, members of the minority group may choose mainly to stick together. Self-segregation has the advantage of strengthening support networks and reinforcing ethnic pride. These advantages are a major reason many of the best African-American students choose to attend primarily black colleges, and why black students at predominantly white schools often develop special institutions, such as fraternities, an African-American cultural center, or a black student movement.

Another strategy is covert resistance. For example, the minority may refuse to work harder than the dominant group forces them to—one source of the common myth

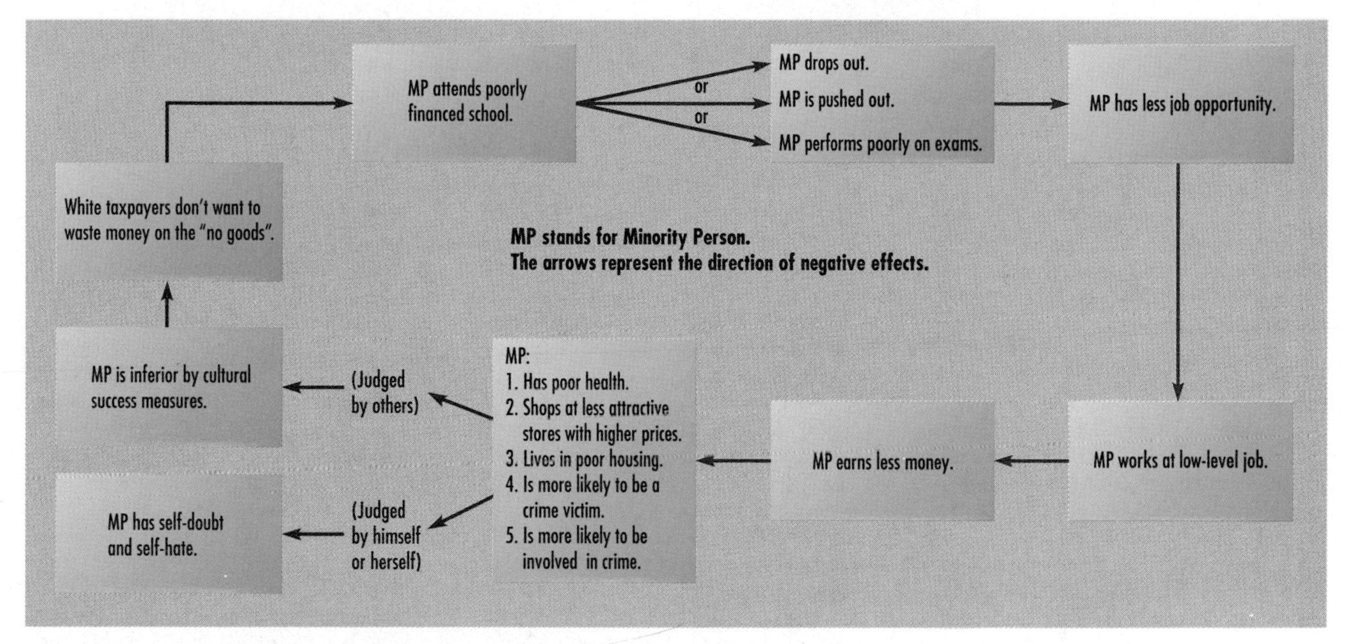

FIGURE 10.1 / The Vicious Cycle of Prejudice and Discrimination

Source: From Richard T. Schaefer, *Racial and Ethnic Groups*, 4th ed. Copyright © 1989 by Richard T. Schaefer. Reprinted by permission of Little, Brown and Company.

that members of minority groups are lazy. They may feign illness to avoid work and spread gossip about the dominant group. Still without risking open rebellion, they may sabotage equipment in factories, pass secrets to enemies of the dominant group, or steal from elites.

Minorities are not always so weak that they must limit themselves to indirect, more or less secret actions (Scott, 1987). In India, for example, Mahatma Gandhi developed the idea of nonviolent resistance as a form of protest against British colonial rule. Following the example of Jesus (whom Gandhi admired) as well as models from Indian culture, Gandhi and his followers would simply remain passive—go limp—when attacked by police. The basic goals of nonviolent resistance are, first, to disrupt existing patterns of social interaction and, second, to demoralize the police and make them look vicious in the eyes of the general public. These strategies are most often used when a group lacks the resources to win a pitched battle. Thousands of Indian demonstrators were jailed, injured, and even killed, but India eventually won independence through nonviolent revolution. Martin Luther King, Jr., urged similar tactics on the American civil rights movement of the 1950s and 1960s.

Nonviolent protest is still basically a weapon of the weak. It relies on the willingness of some members of dominant groups to recognize the suffering of the minority group and to acknowledge the justice of their cause. Thus, sit-ins in the American South not only raised black consciousness but also led many whites to withdraw support from racist, segregationist businesses and politicians. Divisions within the dominant population often are crucial to the success of nonviolent protest.

Sometimes members of a minority group are strong enough to attempt a full-fledged revolt. This is most likely when the social minority group is actually a numerical majority of the population. In Kenya and Rhodesia (now Zimbabwe), where black Africans greatly outnumbered British colonists, armed rebellion played a central role in the struggle for independence. The British had superior armies and weapons and fought the rebels, but eventually grew weary of the killing, the cost, and the absence of any prospect for peace on their terms. Most former colonies in Africa won independence through armed rebellion.

Acceptance and Integration

Although conflict between racial and ethnic groups is common, intergroup relations can also be characterized by tolerance and respect. When different groups join together in a common, socially interconnected population, the re-

KEY CONCEPTS IN ACTION

Prejudice, Discrimination, and Affirmative Action

African-Americans have protested discrimination for generations. But the decisive battle against segregation began in the South in the 1950s with the civil rights movement (see Chapter 21). After years of struggle, the laws that supported racial segregation were struck down by the Supreme Court, and new legislation outlawing discrimination was passed by Congress. Although legal enforcement of segregation (or **de jure segregation**) was ended, racial inequality and separation **(de facto segregation)** were not. Ironically, the former slave states of the South are now less segregated in many respects than the Northern states, where people of color live almost exclusively in central-city areas with very few white people (Massey and Denton, 1987). Why should this be? What can be done?

Sociology's five key concepts help to explain the current dilemma. To begin with, racial inequality is built into our country's ***social structure***. As a result of hundreds of years of discrimination, African-Americans do not occupy an equal position to that of white Americans. In general, they have less property, less education, and fewer ties to elite networks, so they start on a lower rung of society's ladder.

Some whites still use their ***power*** to prevent blacks from gaining equality. They may be prejudiced themselves or simply looking out for their own interests. Whatever the reason, they have the clout to influence decisions about hiring and promotion in business, admission to universities, chances to join private clubs where elite networks are forged, opportunities to live in good neighborhoods, and so on.

Old ***cultural*** prejudices do not disappear overnight simply because the laws have changed. Some white Americans still think that black people are lazy, ignorant, immoral, and otherwise unworthy of respect. Even if these bigots do not have much power, they can influence decisions by boycotting businesses and other establishments that practice equal opportunity. White people who do not have much power often feel most threatened by new opportunities for blacks. They, not the rich and powerful, are most likely to be hurt by competition from blacks for jobs. If blacks moving into a neighborhood drive housing values down (because prejudiced whites no longer want to buy there), these less powerful whites will suffer the most.

Patterns of discrimination are ***functionally integrated*** into the fabric of American life and would persist even if prejudice and discrimination could be eliminated tomorrow. This unintentional inequality is often called **institutional discrimination**. For example, many universities have long discriminated *in favor of* alumni's children. This policy of giving preference in admissions to the children of earlier graduates is functionally knit together with efforts to make those alumni feel loyal to the school and give money, and with the operation of networks based on old school ties. But the seemingly colorblind practice of favoring alumni's children in fact discriminates against blacks, whose parents did not have the opportunity to attend once-segregated schools.

Similarly, many companies base pay raises on seniority and, in hard times, follow a "last hired, first fired" policy, laying off workers with the least seniority. These seemingly impartial practices discriminate against African-Americans who have not been able to build seniority because they were not offered jobs in the past.

Affirmative-action programs were initiated in 1965 in the belief that African-Americans had endured prejudice and discrimination for so long that strong ***social action*** was needed to achieve racial equality. Simply ending de jure segregation was not enough. **Affirmative action** calls on employers and educational institutions to go beyond eliminating formal discrimination against blacks and other minorities and create positive programs for increasing minority representation.

Almost from the beginning, affirmative action has provoked intense public debate, pitting conservatives (both black and white) against liberals (both

sult is integration (the opposite of segregation). **Integration** exists to the extent that interaction between different racial and ethnic groups is frequent and social relationships are open and common (Blau and Schwartz, 1983). Such peaceful coexistence can take several forms. To some degree each form exists in the United States.

The Melting Pot?

In some societies members of different ethnic and racial groups mix freely, allow their various customs and values to blend, and intermarry, thus creating a totally new culture. This is what the playwright Israel Zangwill had in mind when he described the United States at the turn of the century as a *melting pot*: "There she lies, the great melting pot—listen! Can't you hear the roaring and bubbling? Ah, what a stirring and seething—Celt and Latin, Slav and Teuton, Greek and Syrian, Black and Yellow—Jew and Gentile" (1909, pp. 198–199). In Zangwill's romantic play, a poor Jewish immigrant man marries a beautiful Christian woman, all animosities between their families disappear, and the couple lives happily ever after.

black and white). In general, Americans believe that people should not be discriminated against because of race, ethnicity, religion, and the like. Instead, everyone should have an equal opportunity to succeed, and people should be evaluated on the basis of their individual merits. This is the crux of the debate. Most Americans agree that blacks were discriminated against in the past. But many see affirmative action as a form of "reverse discrimination"—that is, it mandates the selection of qualified blacks or other minorities (including women) over equally or more qualified white males. The sociologist Christopher Jencks (1992) has tried to sort out some of the evidence and arguments on sociological rather than ideological grounds.

Affirmative action may subtly reinforce racial stereotypes. For example, selective colleges want more African-American students and so may relax academic standards somewhat for black applicants compared with white applicants. Students usually enroll in the most selective college that accepts them, so blacks may end up at the bottom of their freshman class. A few overcome the odds, but many more earn lower grades than their white classmates and shy away from such difficult majors as chemistry and engineering. Conspicuous racial differences in performance not only reinforce stereotypes among whites, but may lower self-esteem among black students, contributing to their high dropout rates.

The same thing happens to athletes. In high school, there is almost no correlation between grades and athletic ability. "Jocks" do as well in class as everybody else. But because colleges discriminate in favor of athletes, they often end up in schools where they are outclassed academically. Since they have heavy practice schedules, it is difficult for athletes to keep up with their course work simply by studying more. Their relatively poor classroom performance is the result of the biased admissions policy, not of any negative relationship between intelligence and athletic ability. Nevertheless, jokes about slow-witted jocks become a staple of undergraduate humor.

In the heat of the debate over affirmative action, positive effects may be overlooked. Universities, for example, want students from many backgrounds because such diversity is educationally valuable for whites as well as minorities. And they want the faculty to reflect this diversity— not only so that minority students have role models and mentors but also so that members of the majority have experience with highly trained minority teachers. But black college teachers are in short supply, partly because of past discrimination and partly because fewer blacks attend college and graduate school. Should universities compete for black faculty, perhaps by offering them higher salaries? Should they lower their standards for hiring? In either case they would be accused of reverse discrimination.

Consider a police department in a city that is half black. "No sensible police chief wants to deploy an overwhelmingly white force in overwhelmingly black neighborhoods. . . . Most police chiefs believe that a racially mixed force is less likely to start riots and better able to keep order than an overwhelmingly white force" (Jencks, 1992, p. 60). The police department seems justified in hiring some blacks whose test scores are lower than those of some white applicants, because the black applicants' race is directly related to their ability to do their jobs. But this policy will antagonize whites, who will see themselves as victims of reverse discrimination, and thus it will increase racial tensions. How would the community react if the police chief of a white suburb favored white applicants on the same grounds?

There are no easy answers to these puzzles. Affirmative action was intended as a temporary measure that would quickly put blacks on an equal footing with whites. But racial inequality is so deeply entrenched in our culture and social structure that this ideal has not yet been realized. There is little doubt that affirmative-action programs can breed resentment. Yet Jencks's analysis (1992) suggests that without such programs, discrimination against blacks would increase again.

To what degree does the image of the melting pot apply to the United States? Certainly, a new and distinctively American culture has been created out of the many influences that different groups of migrants have brought to the country. It is also true, however, that America remains diverse: Racial, ethnic, and cultural differences have not simply melted away. Differences "melted" most among those people who (1) migrated earliest, (2) occupied more or less equal positions in the power structure, (3) had the most similar cultures to begin with, and (4) were most alike in physical traits labeled as racial (such as skin color). Thus, the differences between English, French, Irish, German, and Scandinavian ancestry do not figure prominently in American society today.

African-Americans are the most dramatic example of a group that has *not* blended in. European-Americans actively worked to limit black Americans' access to the dominant culture (first by not allowing slaves to learn how to read; later by denying blacks equal access to education). At the same time they prevented slaves from maintaining their traditional cultures in this country and treated all African cultures as essentially alike and equally "heathen."

Ironically, one of the best examples of a melting pot in the United States is the merging of different influences into a new and distinctive African-American culture. Blacks combined African rhythms and harmonies with adaptations of Christian hymns and folk music to create a uniquely American musical tradition—stretching from gospel, blues, and jazz to rock and roll and rap music. African-Americans have also made original contributions to technology, literature, and other arts.

Assimilation

Not all Americans have shared the melting-pot ideal. From the earliest days of this country, the Anglo-Saxon elite expected newcomers to adopt their customs and values. John Quincy Adams expressed the sentiment in the early nineteenth century:

> To one thing they [immigrants to the United States] must make up their minds, or they will be disappointed in every expectation of happiness as Americans. They must cast off the European skin, never to resume it. They must look forward to their posterity rather than backward to their ancestors; they must be sure that whatever their own feelings may be, those of their children will cling to the prejudices of this country. (Quoted in Gordon, 1978, p. 187)

Thus, immigrants have been expected not only to embrace the dominant culture but also to surrender their cultural heritage.

The adoption of prevailing norms and values is part of the process of **assimilation**—the incorporation of a minority group into the culture and social life of the dominant group so that the minority eventually disappears as a separate, identifiable unit. Assimilation is asymmetrical. Whereas advocates of the melting pot hold that all groups will be equally changed into something new, proponents of assimilation hold that minorities must conform to the existing majority culture.

The sociologist Robert E. Park (1925) described assimilation as a series of stages through which each new immigrant group was likely to pass. In the first stage newcomers, who are not familiar with the dominant culture, struggle for a foothold. They can only manage to secure what others do not want—the poorest land, the worst housing, the most menial jobs. Scorned and ridiculed by those who are better established, most immigrants gravitate to separate ethnic enclaves (often city slums) where they can feel safe and comfortable. In the second stage they, or more likely their children and grandchildren, begin to acquire the culture of the dominant group. The struggle for survival is converted to a struggle for respectability, better living conditions, and higher-paying, more prestigious jobs. This is an uphill battle, but gradually more

Many once-homogeneous European countries, such as Switzerland and the Netherlands (Holland), have become multicultural and succeeded in integrating vastly different ethnic groups into well-functioning societies. Switzerland's ethnic groups have long histories of migration and settlement, but the migration to the Netherlands, largely from former colonies, has been more recent. The new members of Dutch society have contributed new traditions, such as open-air markets and native foods.

members of the ethnic group achieve upward mobility, remnants of their traditional culture fade, and intergroup marriages occur. Assimilation is complete.

Not all groups have been "invited" to assimilate, as we saw in the case of African-Americans. And not all groups have wanted to assimilate. Hispanic-, Asian-, and Native Americans, in particular, have actively worked to keep their cultural traditions alive. In recent years more Americans have begun to see cultural differences as a source of strength, to be preserved rather than melted down or absorbed.

Pluralism and Multiculturalism

Another pattern of intergroup relations is **pluralism**; in which different racial and ethnic groups within a society maintain their own cultural identities and social networks, yet participate in shared political and economic systems (Kuper and Smith, 1969). In plural societies, each group has its own language, religion, cuisine, and so on, and members interact socially (date, marry, form close friendships) primarily among themselves. Yet all are part of a ***functionally integrated*** society.

In thinking about plural societies, it is important to distinguish between *functional* integration and *social* integration. Groups in a plural society are functionally integrated in the sense that they depend on one another. But this does not mean that all are equal or that they treat one another with respect. (That is, they are not necessarily socially integrated.) In the era of apartheid, South Africa was a plural society in that its economy depended on contributions from blacks, whites, Asians, and Coloureds, even though these groups were strictly segregated and wealth and power were distributed very unequally.

In Switzerland, by contrast, people of German, French, Italian, and Romansch heritage preserve their distinct cultural ways and separate communities, yet coexist peacefully and equally. Switzerland is an example of **multiculturalism**, in which different racial and ethnic groups within a society maintain their distinctive cultures, yet live together in mutual harmony, tolerance, and respect.

Advocates of multiculturalism see cultural diversity as good and desirable, as a source of strength. They call for new patterns of understanding and interaction that depend not on sameness but rather on respect for differences. For example, they advocate educational reforms that would encourage members of each ethnic group to learn more about the others, and full acknowledgment of the contributions of Africans, Hispanics, Asians, and Native Americans to American history and society. In a multicultural society, they maintain, members of each group must acknowledge the legitimacy and value of the others, not simply refrain from violence against them (Taylor, 1992). They believe people should be free to make choices about cultural identities rather than being forced into them by labels applied by others (Aronowitz, 1992; Warner, 1992).

Multiculturalism is more than a prescription for better intergroup relations in the United States. It is also a recognition of the increasingly multicultural nature of social relations in a more international, globally integrated world (Lee, 1991). Migration between countries is a basic fact of life in today's world; we all watch films and television programs from around the world; and the ease of travel and communication brings us into frequent contact with people of different cultures. Not least of all, the global marketplace requires American business executives to be prepared to deal with customers, colleagues, and competitors from Russia, Germany, Japan, and Saudi Arabia.

MINORITY GROUPS IN THE UNITED STATES

The racial and ethnic composition of the United States changed more in the 1980s than at any other time in the twentieth century (see Figure 10.2). Minority populations increased twice as fast as in the preceding decade. Immigration was one major reason; the other was higher-than-average birth rates among minorities. Whites of European background are still the largest group in the country (about 76 percent of the population; see Figure 10.3). But almost one in four Americans today is of African, Asian, Hispanic, or Native American ancestry. Hispanics may soon be a numerical majority in the states of New Mexico and California. By the year 2000, one-third of all school-age children will be members of non-European ethnic groups; they will grow up to become a large proportion of the twenty-first-century work force (*Report on Minorities in Higher Education*, 1988). Peaceful relations among racial and ethnic groups will be crucial for American social life and prosperity.

Unfortunately, intergroup hostility seems to be increasing instead. Behind these tensions are the facts that different ethnic groups have had very different experiences in the United States, have very different living conditions, and often feel themselves to be in competition with one another. This section will profile four major minority groups, focusing on their social history in the United States and current position in the American social structure.

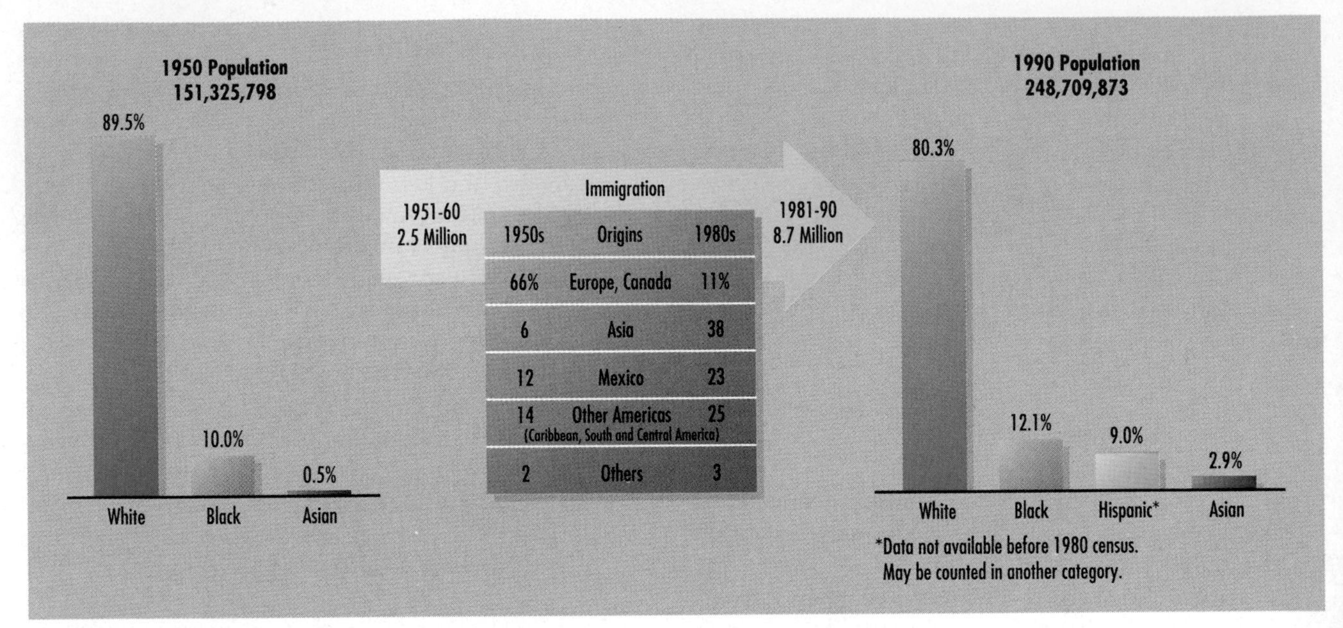

FIGURE 10.2 / The Increasing Diversity of the U.S. Population, as Fueled by Immigration, 1950–1990

Source: U.S. Bureau of the Census, U.S. Immigration and Naturalization Service, and the Urban Institute, in "Reinventing America," *Business Week* Special Issue, 1992.

African-Americans

Numbering 30 million, African-Americans are this country's largest racial minority. Their experience in America has been one of exploitation, poverty, and violence on the one hand and distinctive accomplishments, cultural innovations, and upward mobility on the other. African-Americans have been in this country since the 1600s and have participated in every major event in American history. Black Americans have been soldiers in America's major wars, pioneers in the westward migration, and part of the great trek from farms to cities and factories.

A Brief Social History

The contemporary situation of African-Americans is shaped by this history. Brought to this country against their will, they have endured the brutalities of slavery. Plucked from many different cultures by slave traders, Africans were thrown together indiscriminately in this country and forbidden to carry their native traditions forward. Thus, unlike recent Hispanic and Asian immigrants, they were deprived of two vital resources: their culture (at least in part) and preexisting social networks.

Nevertheless, African-Americans developed a unique subculture, which provided a framework for struggle. Ever since they were granted full citizenship and legal rights at the end of the Civil War, African-Americans have worked to make white Americans recognize those rights. The struggle was grounded in black churches and communities. At the same time, black individuals and families strove to get ahead, often moving from the rural South to the urban North to do so.

The struggle gathered focus and momentum with the civil rights movement, which began in the South in the 1950s (see Chapter 21). The movement achieved great legal victories—most notably, federal legislation in 1964 and 1965 that put an end to most forms of racial discrimination. But African-Americans soon discovered that the new laws were not enough. Whites did not give up their privileges willingly, and programs like affirmative action sometimes backfired.

Current Socioeconomic Status

In 1989 the National Academy of Sciences commissioned a major study of progress toward racial equality, under the leadership of the sociologist Robin Williams. The report,

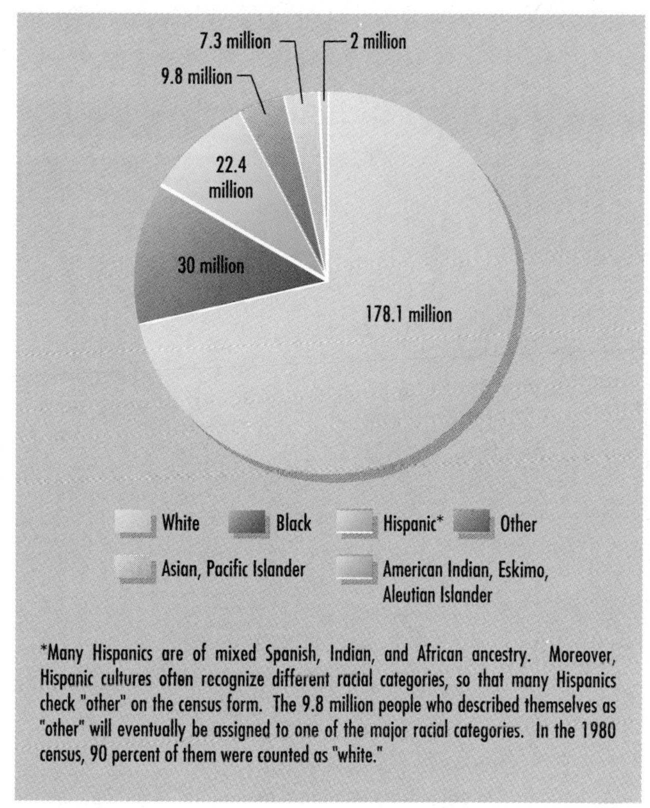

FIGURE 10.3 / American Ethnic Groups

Source: U.S. Bureau of the Census, 1991. Preliminary release of 1990 census data.

entitled *A Common Destiny*, concluded that the status of black Americans today could be described as a glass that is either half full (if compared with their situation before the civil rights movement) or half empty (if measured in terms of continuing inequalities between white and black Americans). Many African-Americans today are better educated, are better off financially, and have better job prospects than did their parents, or even their older brothers and sisters (W. R. Allen and Farley, 1986; R. Farley, 1984; O'Hare, Pollard, Mann, and Kent, 1991). But African-Americans as a group have not achieved full equality, and some are losing ground. Consider education, income, employment, political participation, and housing.

EDUCATION In some ways, the education gap between blacks and whites has narrowed. High school graduation rates for black and white youth today are almost equal (83 and 86 percent, respectively) (O'Hare et al., 1991). This does not mean, however, that they receive equal educations. On average, black students earn lower grades and score below the national average on standardized achievement tests. The primary reasons for unequal performance seem to be that low-income black children are educationally disadvantaged even before they enter kindergarten, attend schools that do little to encourage them to improve, and have little reason to believe that education will pay off for them (National Research Council, 1989).

Another education-related problem is that a high school diploma is worth less on the job market today than it used to be, and the percentage of African-Americans (especially males) who go on to college—and graduate—has been slipping (O'Hare et al., 1991). This means that a large proportion of African-American high school graduates may be confined to the low-wage service sector of the economy in the future. Even among men with five years of college or more, African-Americans are more likely to be unemployed and to work fewer hours than whites (R. Farley and Allen, 1987).

INCOME AND EMPLOYMENT In terms of income, an increasing number of African-Americans have made it into the middle class. The median income of younger black couples (family head aged twenty-five to forty-four) with college degrees is $54,000, not far behind the $58,800 median for similar white couples. In 1989 nearly one in seven African-American families had incomes of $50,000 or more, four times the number in 1967. Like affluent whites, prosperous blacks tend to be well-educated, married, two-career suburban homeowners (O'Hare et al., 1991).

Despite these gains, median income for all blacks is $18,676, only 60 percent of the $31,231 median income of whites (U.S. Bureau of the Census, 1990). The poverty rate among blacks has remained about three times that of whites for more than two decades. The experience of poverty is also likely to be different for African-Americans. They tend to be poorer than poor whites, to remain in poverty for longer, and to live in high-poverty, high-crime neighborhoods (O'Hare et al., 1991). (See the discussion of ghetto poverty in Chapter 9.)

The number of blacks without steady work, as well as the number who have dropped out of the labor force completely, has risen dramatically. Between 1963–1965 and 1985–1987 the proportion of blacks between ages twenty-five and fifty-four who did no paid work for an entire calendar year rose from 5 to 14 percent (Jencks, 1992, p. 35). In early 1992, the national unemployment rate stood at 7.7 percent but was 14.6 percent for African-Americans (U.S. Department of Labor, 1992). White males were twice as likely as black males to be managers; about one-third of employed black males hold menial, semiskilled jobs (see Figure 10.4).

Perhaps the area of employment that has come closest to black–white equality is the U.S. military, especially the

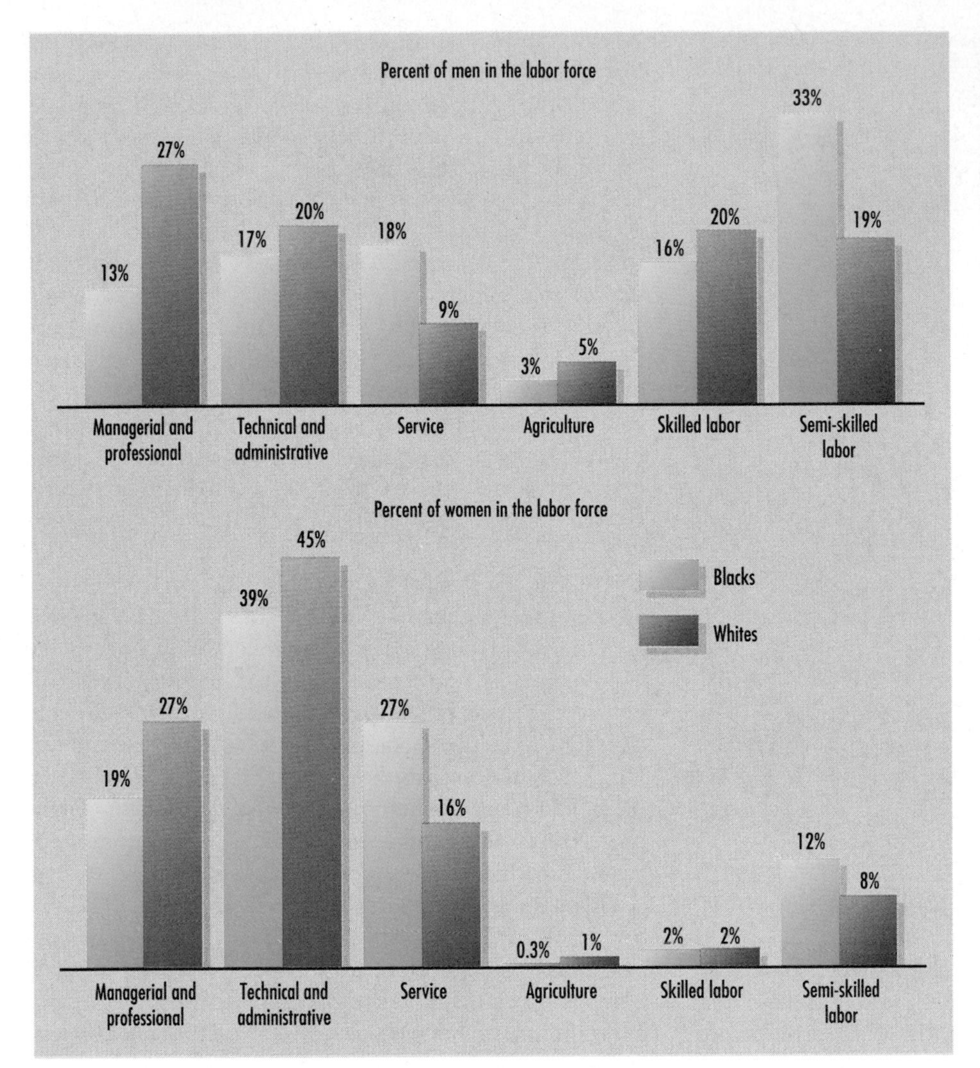

FIGURE 10.4 / The Occupations of Blacks and Whites, Men and Women, 1990

Source: U.S. Bureau of Labor Statistics, *Employment and Earnings* 38, no. 1 (1991), table 22.

army (see Table 10.1). Military recruitment, training, and advancement programs are color-blind, and blacks and whites work together on sometimes dangerous missions (such as the Persian Gulf war) that demand cooperation and mutual trust. The army is one of the few places where blacks often are in positions of authority over whites. Although the proportion of African-American officers is not equal to their proportion in either the population or the military, it has grown steadily.

POLITICAL PARTICIPATION Some hopeful signs are also visible in politics. The number of black elected officials has climbed from a few hundred in the 1960s to more than 7,000 in the 1990s. African-Americans have been elected to every office in the country except president and vice president and have won important elections in which the majority of voters were white (such as governor of Virginia and mayor of New York City). Black voting rates are as high as or higher than rates for whites of similar socioeconomic standing, and black–white coalitions have become an important part of the political scene (National Research Council, 1989).

HOUSING Housing is the area in which there has been the *least* progress toward integration. There has been virtually no change in the degree of residential segregation of African-Americans since 1970 (Massey and Denton, 1987; National Research Council, 1989; O'Hare et al., 1991). Nearly 30 percent—or 9 million blacks—live in almost complete racial isolation, primarily in inner cities. Studies comparing minority groups find that African-Americans are almost twice as segregated, or residentially

TABLE 10.1

Black Participation in the U.S. Army (as Percentage of Officers and Enlisted Personnel), 1962–1986

Rank	1962	1972	1980	1986
Officers				
General	—	0.7	5.4	7.0
Colonel	0.1	1.6	4.5	5.0
Lt. Colonel	0.9	5.1	4.9	4.4
Major	2.5	5.1	4.4	6.8
Captain	5.2	3.7	7.5	12.7
1st Lieutenant	4.3	2.9	10.2	14.4
2nd Lieutenant	2.3	2.5	10.4	11.4
Total	3.2	3.9	7.2	10.4
Enlisted				
Sergeant Major	2.9	7.0	20.5	30.9
Master Sergeant	5.5	14.0	25.3	24.4
Sergeant 1st Class	7.8	19.6	24.7	25.5
Staff Sergeant	12.7	23.9	23.9	35.7
Sergeant	15.7	16.6	31.2	36.0
Specialist 4	13.0	13.5	37.2	29.9
Private 1st Class	10.8	15.9	39.0	23.6
Private	13.3	17.9	37.0	22.2
Recruit	11.4	18.3	22.0	22.8
Total	12.3	17.0	32.5	29.6

Source: Charles C. Moskos and John S. Butler, "Blacks in the Military since World War II," paper prepared for the Committee on the Status of Black Americans, National Research Council, Washington, D.C., 1987, p. 27.

isolated, as Hispanic- or Asian-Americans (Massey and Denton, 1987).

Racial segregation in housing is not confined to cities, but follows blacks to the suburbs (Massey and Eggers, 1990.) For Hispanics and Asians, residential segregation declines as families move from immigrant to native status and from low to high socioeconomic levels. For African-Americans, segregation persists regardless of the length of time families live in urban society and regardless of their income and education (Denton and Massey, 1988). According to Donald Massey's and Nancy Denton's studies (1992), a black person who makes more than $50,000 a year will be virtually as segregated as a black person who makes only $2,500 a year.

Residential segregation has far-reaching consequences: It affects the schools children attend, the friends they and their parents make, the job networks to which they have access, the health-care and other services available in an emergency, and even the quality of the food and merchandise available for them to buy.

Racial Attitudes

Most polls show that white attitudes toward African-Americans have changed dramatically over the decades (National Research Council, 1989). The great majority of whites support equal opportunity for blacks, at least in principle. But they are less likely to support the *practice* of equality, particularly if it involves frequent, prolonged, or close social contact with significant numbers of blacks. Moreover, white support for programs and policies to implement equal opportunity is waning. Racial equality seemed like a good idea in the late 1960s, when the nation appeared prosperous enough to close the black–white economic gap at no cost to whites. But in the economically uncertain times since then, formerly "liberal" whites have been prone to argue that blacks have come far enough or that if they lag behind economically they have only themselves to blame (Landry, 1991).

In addition, many people of various political persuasions are troubled by the thought of relying for extended periods on programs like affirmative action. Indeed, a number of black conservatives, such as Stanford economist Thomas Sowell and Supreme Court Justice Clarence Thomas, now argue that government programs are not the best way to help blacks and that the source of black people's problems lies primarily in a breakdown of family values and other aspects of African-American culture.

Hispanic-Americans

Hispanics, or Spanish-speaking Americans, are the second-largest minority in the United States. At least 22.4 million Hispanics are legal residents of the United States; many more have immigrated without full legal documentation (U.S. Bureau of the Census, March 1990). Because immigration rates are high and because Hispanics now in this country tend to be young and to have more than the average number of children, the Hispanic population is growing rapidly. If current growth rates continue, by the turn of the century Hispanics will pass African-Americans as the largest minority in the United States (*Current Population Reports*, 1986).

The Diversity of Hispanic-Americans

Hispanic-Americans come from diverse backgrounds, as we noted in Chapter 3. Spanish settlers arrived on this continent before the British. Christopher Columbus was sent by the king and queen of Spain, and he was followed

A system based on exclusion of racial groups from the social order leads to structural strain that can produce riots and civil disorder. This photograph captures the terror and destruction of police repression of crowds in South Africa. The United States, too, has seen many race riots and much police violence.

by thousands of Spanish explorers, priests, and *conquistadors*. The Spanish established colonial outposts throughout the part of Mexico that is now the American Southwest. The United States acquired this territory by force in 1848, after the Mexican–American War. Likewise, the Philippines, a former Spanish colony, was acquired by military conquest in 1899, and Puerto Rico in 1898. In effect, both became U.S. colonies, though Puerto Rico became a commonwealth in 1952. (The Philippines gained independence in 1946.)

In the twentieth century, the United States has added Hispanic citizens mainly by immigration, not conquest, often as a result of political upheavals or economic hardship.

MEXICAN-AMERICANS Although some descendants of the original Spanish settlers remained in the Southwest, many others are more recent immigrants. Early in this century, Mexicans began entering the United States as seasonal workers to harvest cotton in Texas. Some came here legally under periodic agreements with the Mexican government; others illegally, by swimming or wading the Rio Grande. Over the years agricultural interests in the Southwest became increasingly dependent on these migratory workers, and the smuggling of illegal workers became highly organized and professional (Rumbaut, 1991).

Driven by population growth, high unemployment, and severe poverty in Mexico, and drawn by family connections and economic opportunity, the flow of legal and illegal immigrants continues. Increasingly, immigrants are bypassing the farms and ranches of the Southwest for urban jobs in the construction, light manufacturing, and service industries. Here, as on farms, Mexican nationals are particularly susceptible to exploitation and abuse because they fear being returned to Mexico or fired.

PUERTO RICANS The migration of Puerto Ricans to the U.S. mainland is relatively recent. All Puerto Ricans were declared American citizens in 1917. But only after World War II, when the airlines introduced lower fares, did increasing numbers of Puerto Ricans leave their island to seek their fortunes, especially in New York City. What makes the Puerto Rican situation unique is that immigration runs two ways: The island is part of the United States, so that entry and exit visas are not required, and it is also close enough for immigrants to return home, temporarily or permanently, as most do.

CUBAN-AMERICANS Cuban-Americans arrived in this country in three main waves: in the early 1960s, after Fidel Castro seized control of the Cuban government and declared the nation communist; in the late 1960s and early 1970s, when Castro permitted two "freedom flights" per day; and in 1980, as part of the "Mariel boatlift," a temporary opening of Cuba's ports that was apparently designed to relieve housing and job shortages within Cuba.

The Cuban-American population is concentrated in southern Florida and New York City. Cubans are the largest ethnic minority in Miami and have become a major force in that city's business and politics. Cubans have proved to be one of the most politically organized of Hispanic-American groups, focusing their efforts on persuading the U.S. government to keep the pressure on Castro's regime. Cubans are also among the most economically successful group of Hispanics, primarily because those who migrated (especially in the first two waves) were largely business and professional people, and many were able to bring substantial amounts of money and property with them.

Young Chicano men, particularly in the American Southwest, have developed a counterculture based largely on restoring and modifying American automobiles of the 1960s and 1970s. The "lowriders," as pictured here, are unremarkable sedans with stock engines and transmissions, but the young men modify them to develop individual statements along a consistent cultural theme. The lowrider phenomenon is considered to be a rejection of the American fascination with speed and power, and with standardization and efficiency. Yet it also symbolizes the partial assimilation of Mexican-Americans into mainstream American life.

Issues of Identity

By and large, different groups of Hispanic-Americans have remained distinct from one another as well as from the rest of the population. Immigrants from Central and South America are likely to retain a stronger sense of themselves as Indians than do Mexicans; neither Cubans nor Puerto Ricans have any significant Indian heritage. Despite their diversity, Hispanics share many cultural features, especially language, religion (Roman Catholicism), and commitment to family (as described in Chapter 3). Hispanics are less likely to get involved in civic affairs than are most other groups of Americans, and have relied less on public services. Instead they depend on the family for social activities and social support.

This attitude is beginning to change as Hispanics realize that in order to pursue their collective interests—and to preserve their cultural values—they need to become more active in American politics. One important issue for many Hispanic-Americans is the status of the Spanish language. Hispanics tend to resist pressure to assimilate to American society by speaking English. Many immigrants never learn English, and while their children usually do, they tend to speak Spanish as well. Many educators have argued that Hispanic schoolchildren are placed at a disadvantage when they are forced to attempt to master English in the early grades. They have called for multilingual schools, where Hispanic children could study academic subjects in Spanish while learning English. Some English speakers respond that their own ancestors had to "sink or swim" when it came to learning English, and that Hispanics and other immigrants should be expected to do the same. These critics argue that national unity requires a common language.

Current Socioeconomic Status

In general, Hispanics made modest social and economic gains in the 1980s, but few achieved equality with Anglo-Americans (Bureau of the Census, March 1990). In 1990, about 51 percent of Hispanics had completed high school (up from 46 percent in 1983, but still much lower than the proportions of black or white non-Hispanics), and approximately 9 percent had completed four or more years of college (compared with 21 percent of non-Hispanics).

Although the proportion of Hispanics in managerial, professional, and other white-collar occupations grew in the 1980s, Hispanics still tend to be employed in low-level occupations (see Table 10.2). The median household income for Hispanics in 1991 was $22,330 (compared with

TABLE 10.2

Occupational Employment by Hispanic Origin and Sex, Annual Averages, 1983–87

Occupation	HISPANIC Percent Distribution, 1987	HISPANIC Percent Change, 1983–87	NON-HISPANIC Percent Distribution, 1987	NON-HISPANIC Percent Change, 1983–87
Men, 18 years and older	100.0	25.0	100.0	8.3
Managerial and professional specialty	12.0	30.0	25.9	10.3
Technical, sales, and administrative support	15.7	37.5	20.3	10.4
Service occupations	13.9	17.0	9.2	5.9
Precision production, craft, and repair	20.5	21.0	19.9	8.7
Operators, fabricators, and laborers	29.1	21.1	20.2	8.7
Farming, forestry, and fishing	8.9	33.2	4.4	−9.2
Women, 18 years and older	100.0	33.7	100.0	13.2
Managerial and professional specialty	14.7	61.2	25.0	28.2
Technical, sales, and administrative support	39.9	27.4	45.5	11.7
Service occupations	23.3	40.1	17.8	7.7
Precision production, craft, and repair	3.7	22.3	2.2	14.6
Operators, fabricators, and laborers	16.9	27.5	8.4	2.9
Farming, forestry, and fishing	1.5	2.3	1.1	−7.1

Source: Peter Cattan, "The Growing Presence of Hispanics in the U.S. Work Force," Monthly Labor Review *(August 1988), p. 13, table 4.*

$36,920 for whites; U.S. Bureau of the Census, 1991). On average, Hispanics earned 67 cents for every dollar that non-Hispanics earned. Income was not distributed evenly among Hispanic subgroups, however; it varied from $16,200 for Puerto Ricans, to $22,439 for Mexican-Americans, to $25,900 for Cuban-Americans (see also Figure 10.5). Although the unemployment rate for Hispanics has declined (from a high of 16.5 percent during the 1983 recession to 8.2 percent in 1990), it is still higher than that for non-Hispanics (5.3 percent in 1990). Likewise, although the poverty rate for Hispanics is lower than in the early 1980s, 25 percent of Hispanics (compared with 9.5 percent of non-Hispanics) live below the poverty line.

The main reasons usually given for high rates of poverty among Hispanics are low levels of educational attainment, recent entry into the labor force, lack of English skills, and concentration in occupations that are vulnerable to recessions (Cattan, 1988). However, a recent study (Telles and Murguia, 1990) suggests that racist attitudes also play a part. Hispanics vary in appearance, from light to dark-skinned, and from Anglo to Indian or Native American in facial features. The researchers found that the darkest and most Indian-looking Mexican-Americans earned significantly less than those who might "pass" as Anglos, regardless of education, occupation, and other variables.

Native Americans

The first Americans were mistakenly called "Indians" by Christopher Columbus and other explorers who were seeking an ocean route to India. Even when Europeans realized that the land they reached was not India, but was a continent previously unknown to Westerners, the mistaken name persisted. So did the idea that Columbus "discovered" America and that the land was virtually empty before European colonization. In fact, America had been settled 20,000 to 40,000 years ago by migrants from Asia, the ancestors of the people whom we today call "Native Americans."

The migrants who first settled North America apparently came in a series of relatively small and distinct groups that gradually spread through North, Central, and South America. These Indian groups were and are diverse, ranging from the warlike Plains Indians to the fishermen of the Pacific Northwest, the trappers of the Northeast and Great Lakes regions, and the sendentary farmers in what are now the Carolinas, and from the great Inca Empire of Peru to the small tribes of hunter-gatherers in the Amazon.

The two greatest Native American empires, the Inca of Peru and the Aztec of Mexico and Guatemala, were among the most advanced civilizations of their day. They devel-

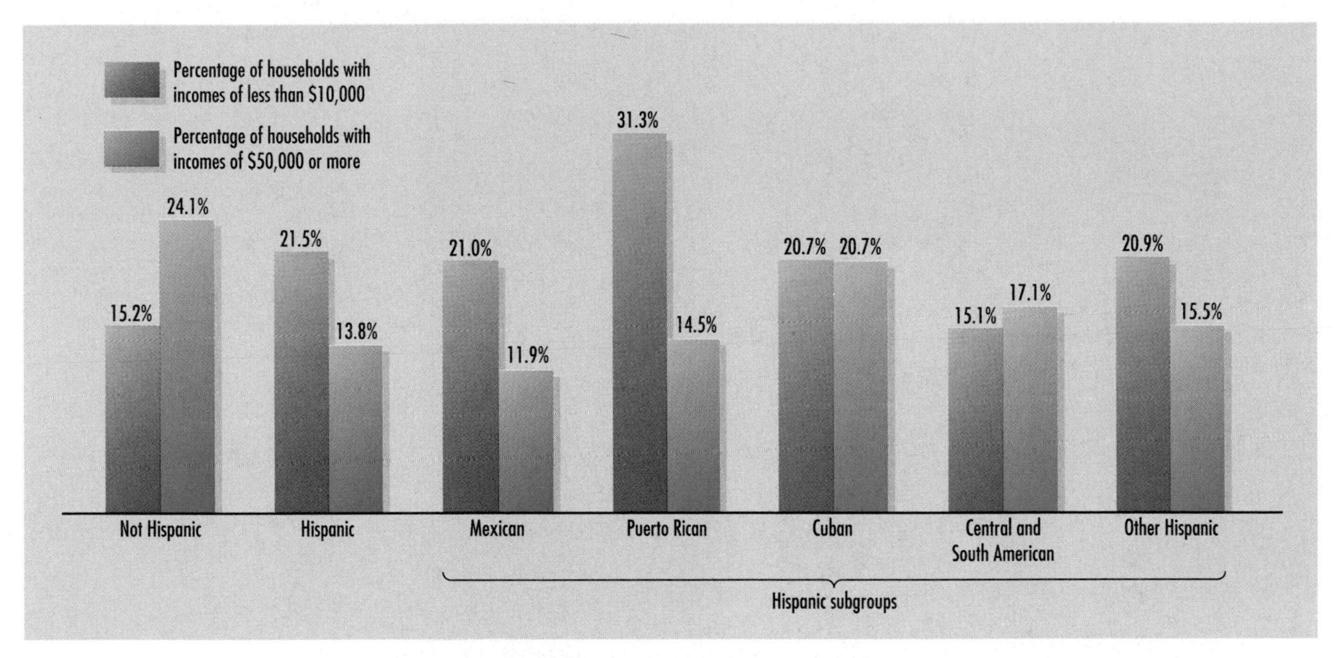

FIGURE 10.5 / Income Distribution for Hispanic Subgroups, 1989

Source: U.S. Bureau of the Census, *Current Population Reports.* Population Characteristics, Series P-20, no. 449 (1989), p. 5.

oped accurate calendars and time reckoning long before Europeans did. They built vast cities, advanced irrigation systems for agriculture, and far-reaching communication networks.

While the Inca and Aztec were like Europeans in their efforts to dominate nature, many North American Indians were highly sensitive to the environment. Their religions stressed respect for nature, and their social practices were geared toward preserving the environment. For example, they did not attempt to accumulate wealth beyond what they needed for subsistence. Only recently have their cultures and accomplishments been recognized by the descendants of European invaders.

A Brief Social History

Before Europeans came to America, Native American tribes shared more than 2 billion acres of land; by 1871 their territory had dwindled to 150 million acres and by 1980 to 90 million (Dorris, 1981). Native Americans were pushed from their traditional lands onto reservations—and when whites realized that those reservations contained valuable resources, some tribes were forced to move again. Typically the land they were left was considered worthless. (Some later proved to have value, however; the Navaho and Hopi reservations in the desert Southwest, for example, contain huge oil deposits.)

Persecution of Native Americans reached a peak toward the middle of the nineteenth century when the eastern United States was becoming crowded and the transcontinental railroad made travel westward easier. Gold was discovered in the Black Hills of South Dakota in 1874, and white settlers were demanding more lands for farms and ranches. The Plains Indians fought back harder than their eastern counterparts had done but they were outnumbered and outgunned by the U.S. Army. Disease and hunger multiplied the death toll. More than 500,000 Indians died before the century was over. The 300,000 who survived were forced onto inhospitable reservations administered by the white-run and corrupt Bureau of Indian Affairs (BIA).

About half of today's Native Americans live on reservations, where they have attempted to preserve their traditional way of life and such social structures as tribal councils and gatherings of elders. These Indians have a unique status in the United States. Rather than being considered simply as individual citizens or private organizations, they are considered members of tribes that relate to the U.S. government as sovereign nations. The government, however, has a long record of refusing to honor its

White Mountain Apaches in White River, Arizona, take sweatbaths in a plastic-covered sweathouse. Sweatbaths, which are part of nearly all Native American cultures, are taken not only for pleasure but also as part of complex medicinal procedures. For decades native people in America were discouraged from, even punished for, trying to preserve their cultural practices and beliefs. This process of cultural genocide has declined as native people have begun to assert their rights to their cultural practices and beliefs.

treaties with various Indian nations.

In return for yielding some of their sovereignty (for example, the right to an independent foreign policy), Indian tribes receive schools, health care, and other services from the BIA, funded by the federal government. But quality generally has been poor and budgets low. The BIA has also controlled much of what Indians were allowed to do with their land and other resources, usually in ways that benefited outsiders more than the tribes themselves (Yetman, 1992).

During the early 1970s, as militancy among African-Americans grew, Native Americans became more insistent in their demands that past wrongs be redressed. The American Indian Movement (AIM) used public protests and demonstrations to call attention to Native American claims. These radical tactics alienated more moderate tribe members and were forcibly repressed by the U.S. government. A more effective tactic has been to file lawsuits demanding either enforcement of long-standing treaties or compensation. For example, eight tribes of the Sioux nation were recently awarded $122.5 million in compensation for the illegal seizure of the Black Hills long ago. Such suits mark progress in the official acknowledgment of the injustices that Native Americans have suffered (Cornell, 1984).

As Indian tribes acquire new resources and legal clout, many have begun to take social policy into their own hands, suing the government for the right to manage their own lands and the services provided by the BIA. Many tribes are launching economic development programs based on the agricultural, water, timber, fishing, and energy resources formerly controlled by others. These new social actions require complex decisions. The tribes must decide, for example, whether to manage their resources as a trust on behalf of the entire tribe or as a corporation in which all tribe members own shares as individuals. For most Native Americans, however, the rewards of these efforts lie in the future.

Current Socioeconomic Status

The 1.74 million Native Americans today are among the poorest minority groups in the country (*Statistical Abstract*, 1991, p. 17). In many ways, those who live on reservations (about half) are worse off than those who don't. For example, among sixteen- to nineteen-year-olds on reservations, 27 percent neither are enrolled in high school nor are high school graduates. As of 1986, only 0.7 percent of college students were Native Americans. The unemployment rate for Indians is twice the rate for the population as a whole; 25 percent of Native Americans live below the poverty line, compared with 10 percent of the general population; and median income for Native Americans is only two-thirds that for all Americans (*Statistical Abstract*, 1991, p. 39). On reservations, median income is less than half the national average, and over 41 percent of families live below the poverty line. More than half of those on reservations live in substandard housing, and 70 percent must haul their drinking water a mile or more (frequently from unsanitary sources).

Native Americans have a life expectancy ten years below the national average—the shortest of all American racial and ethnic groups (Yetman, 1992). They also have unusually high rates of accidents, homicide, suicide, alcoholism, influenza, pneumonia, and diabetes (see Figure 10.6). Indeed, the American Indian Policy Review Commission regards alcohol abuse as "the most severe and widespread health problem among Indians today" (Dorris, 1989). Nearly all crimes for which Native Americans are jailed or imprisoned are alcohol-related (Hodgkinson, Outtz, and Obarakpor, 1990; Yetman, 1992).

Asian-Americans

In the 1980s, Asian-Americans became not only the fastest-growing ethnic group in the United States but also one of the most diversified in terms of national origins, social class, income, education, and skills (see Figure 10.7). Unlike Hispanic-Americans, who are unified by the Spanish language and Roman Catholic religion, Asian-Americans speak many languages and practice a wide range of religions, including Buddhism, Christianity, Hinduism, and Islam. Whereas the increase in the Hispanic population reflected growth in groups that have a long history in this country, many of the new Asian immigrants have few cultural connections on this continent. They are also more economically stratified, with a highly visible and successful layer of professionals, a strong middle class, and a lower stratum of poor peasants, forced from their homelands by political upheavals. Depending on their background and circumstances, in this country they may work as physicians or engineers, grocers or nurses, or waiters or peddlers.

Today's Asian-Americans are widely regarded as a "model minority," but this was not always the case. The two Asian groups that have been in the United States longest—the Chinese and Japanese—have encountered more intense prejudice and discrimination than any group of European or Hispanic immigrants.

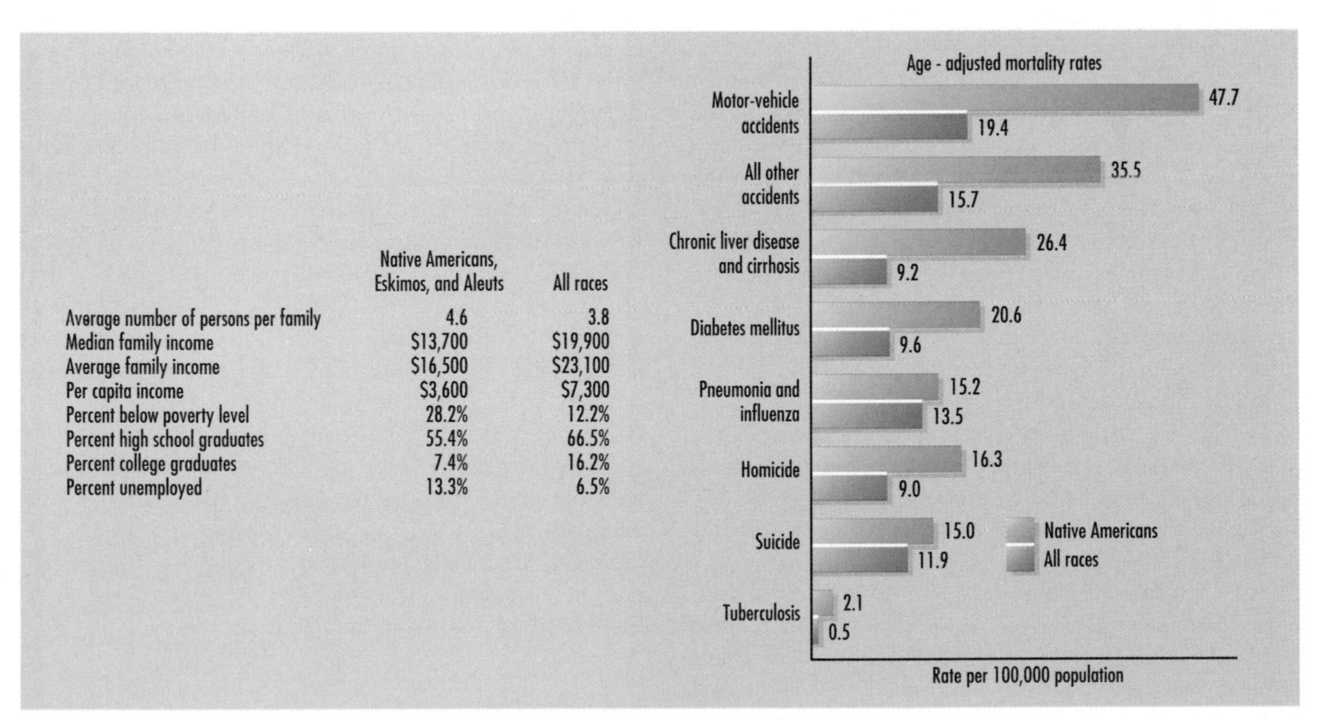

	Native Americans, Eskimos, and Aleuts	All races
Average number of persons per family	4.6	3.8
Median family income	$13,700	$19,900
Average family income	$16,500	$23,100
Per capita income	$3,600	$7,300
Percent below poverty level	28.2%	12.2%
Percent high school graduates	55.4%	66.5%
Percent college graduates	7.4%	16.2%
Percent unemployed	13.3%	6.5%

FIGURE 10.6 / Socioeconomic Characteristics of Native Americans

Sources: (Left) Data for American Indians in the thirty-three reservation states in 1980, from the U.S. Department of Health and Human Services, *Health Status of Minorities and Low-Income Groups*, 1991. (Right) U.S. Department of Health and Human Services, Indian Health Service, *Trends in Indian Health*, 1989, table 4.9, p. 39.

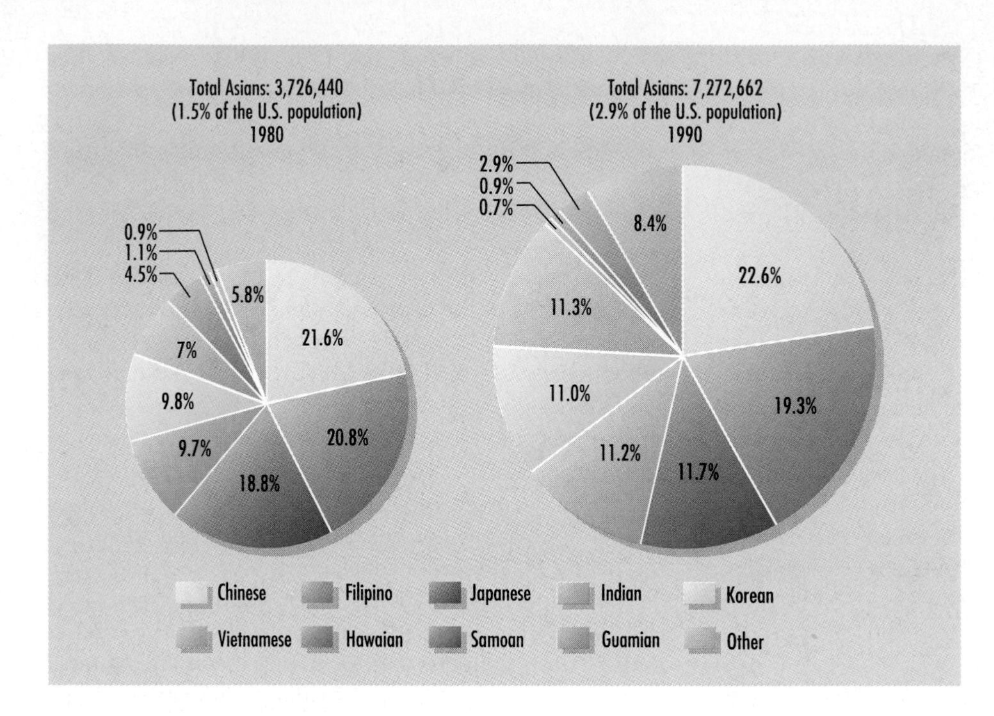

FIGURE 10.7 / The Increase in the Asian-American Population of the United States, by Country of Origin, 1980–1990

Source: *The New York Times*, June 21, 1991, p. D25.

A Brief Social History

Chinese people began immigrating to the West Coast in the middle of the eighteenth century. Their labor on the railroads, in laundries, and in restaurants earned them a reputation as hard workers. When the railroad was finished and unemployment began to rise, white working people turned on the Chinese. Lynchings, expulsions, and arson were not uncommon. The Chinese Exclusion Act of 1882 halted further immigration and denied Chinese the right to become naturalized citizens or to own land in the United States. In most places they were also denied schooling, jobs, and housing. They withdrew to ethnic enclaves (termed *Chinatowns*), keeping to themselves until anti-Chinese feelings subsided. Finally, in 1965, national-origins immigration quotas were abolished, and for the first time Chinese immigrants were treated on a par with other nationalities (Wong, 1982).

Since 1965, more Chinese have come here than arrived during the first eighty years of Chinese immigration. More than 60 percent of today's 1.6 million Chinese-Americans are recent immigrants, primarily from Taiwan and Hong Kong rather than mainland China (*New York Times*, June 12, 1991, A1, D25).

Japanese immigration to the United States began in the 1870s. These newcomers established groceries, flower shops, and other small businesses and took jobs as truck farmers and laborers in the lumber mills and fish canneries of the West Coast. Some became professionals. Anti-Oriental sentiments ran high, however, and in 1924 all immigration from East Asia was halted. After Japan attacked Pearl Harbor, the United States turned on its Japanese residents. On the West Coast more than 120,000 Japanese, including 70,000 who were American citizens, were rounded up and moved inland to guarded camps, or "relocation centers." While they were interned, whites seized their lands and took over their businesses. Not until 1988 did the U.S. Senate approve a bill to apologize officially for this violation of human and civil rights and pay a token $20,000 in reparations to every living Japanese-American who had been interned during the war.

In recent years Japanese immigration has slowed, largely because Japan's prosperous economy has offered people abundant opportunities at home. Most of today's 847,000 Japanese-Americans are second-, third-, and fourth-generation American citizens. They are among the most highly assimilated Asian immigrant groups.

Current Socioeconomic Status

Even Asians who immigrated more recently, under extremely difficult conditions and with few personal resources—such as refugees from Vietnam, Cambodia, and

These recently arrived Vietnamese immigrants face an extremely challenging and uncertain future in the United States. They must learn English and they must learn how to negotiate a totally different culture, from the food they find at McDonald's to the subtleties of everyday social interaction. Friendship groups, like the one shown here, are crucial to the long and painful process of assimilating to a new society.

Laos—have done remarkably well in the United States. By almost every measure, Asian-Americans have equaled and often surpassed other groups of Americans (Winnick, 1990). The median Asian-American income of $42,250 is higher than the white median of $36,920 (U.S. Bureau of the Census, 1991); Asian-American adults are overrepresented in the professions and other high-status occupations; and Asian-American students score higher on standardized tests (especially in math and science) than other American students and are twice as likely to obtain college degrees.

A Model Minority?

Asian success is real, but it has been exaggerated into a stereotype. Like other stereotypes, the image of Asians as a model minority is a half-truth at best (Crystal, 1989). First, the higher median income of Asian-Americans is due in part to the fact that most Asian households send more members into the work force than do other American households. Naturally, having more family members work boosts family income, even if each person's wages are not higher than average. And while averages show that many Asians are doing well, many others continue to struggle. In the 1980s, the poverty and welfare-dependency rates for Indochinese refugees were much higher than those for any other minority (ranging from 50 percent for Vietnamese to almost 90 percent for Hmong) (Rumbaut, 1991).

Second, despite high educational attainments, Asian-Americans tend to earn less than mainstream Americans with equivalent educations; discrimination is still a problem. Educational credentials and professional experience from Asian countries of origin often are devalued by universities and other employers. As a result, many Asian immigrants are underemployed; an engineer may have to take a job as a technician, a physician as a lab assistant, and so on. Even those with American college degrees earn less than whites with equivalent credentials (Jencks, 1992, p. 3).

Third, the apparent stability of Asian families and adjustment of Asians as individuals (evidenced by low levels of use of mental health and other social services) to some extent reflect the tradition among Asians of "saving face," or avoiding shame, by keeping their troubles to themselves.

Even positive stereotypes can be dangerous, for several reasons (Crystal, 1989). The belief that Asians can make it on their own has been used to justify their exclusion from minority programs, so that many are not getting help they need. Further, the idea of a model minority can be used against other groups, as "proof" that the United States is a racially tolerant society and that groups whose members are trapped in poverty have only themselves to blame. Finally, stereotypes about Asian success may fuel resentment among other American ethnic groups, as was evident in the hostility toward Koreans expressed by some blacks during the 1992 riot in Los Angeles (see Chapter 21).

Explaining the Asian Success Story

The most frequent explanation of the achievements of Asian immigrants involves a constellation of values embedded in ***culture***: a devotion to, and willingness to sacrifice for, education; strong family ties; a tendency toward thrift and self-denial and toward working long hours in order to accumulate capital; a strong inclination toward self-employment and small-business ownership; and a tradition of pooling funds and hiring family members and compatriots.

Asian cultures include a strong, ancient value on literacy, which distinguishes them from most other ethnic groups. (One notable exception is Jews.) Almost all Europeans, for example, were illiterate not just in the Middle Ages but into the modern era. For well over a thousand years, even aristocrats saw no reason to learn to read; the church taught that only priests needed to be literate so that they could interpret scripture for others. By comparison, literacy in the Chinese elite goes back thousands of years without a break; the literate traditions of Japan and Korea are almost as old. The value of studying hard is not a new idea for Asians.

Asian cultures teach that each person must strive not just for his or her own sake but for that of the family. This idea is closely related to the cultural value of strong respect for parents, which leads children to meet their parents' expectations—for example, that they will study hard. At the same time, parents are willing to sacrifice themselves for their children. Many work two jobs or extra hours to provide their children with social mobility for themselves as for the family through their children.

The ***functional integration*** of family and community has played an important role in the Asian success story. Although migration has often disrupted family life, Asians have been particularly successful in reuniting families and making them the backbone of social organization. They have also been able to knit together strong communities, providing links for mutual benefit. In New York City's Chinatown, for example, a strong network of social exchange and functional division of labor links Chinese lawyers, restaurant owners, doctors, shopkeepers, accountants, and teachers. Each group makes a point of doing business with the others.

Recent Asian immigrants also seized ***social-structural*** opportunities that other Americans overlooked or shunned (Winnick, 1990). For example, Korean immigrants took advantage of the low rents and lack of services in deteriorating urban neighborhoods to open greengroceries. This type of cash business did not require a large investment, could be run by family members and other Koreans, and filled a local need.

Finally, the Asian success story is a recent development, even though Asians have been part of American society for more than a century. The Chinese "coolies" who worked on the railroads did not climb to the top of the socioeconomic ladder. Indeed, most died destitute. But their descendants and more recent Asian immigrants have benefited from growing support for multiculturalism in the United States. Thus, their success story has been made possible not just by ancient values in Chinese and other Asian cultures, but by some changes in American culture as well.

Thinking Back on the Key Concepts

Perhaps one young Japanese-American woman can stand as a symbol of the mixture of good news and bad in America's multicultural experience. In 1992, Americans of all ethnic backgrounds cheered as figure skater Kristi Yamaguchi defeated Japan's Midori Ito to win an Olympic gold medal. No one doubted that Kristi, the daughter of a Sacramento, California, dentist, was "100 percent American." There was even a special, if ironic, satisfaction in watching an American of Japanese ancestry compete against a Japanese citizen. Yet fifty years earlier, Kristi's mother had been born behind barbed wire in the California camp where her grandparents were interned during World War II. Her grandparents had thought they were American, too, until the U.S. government seized their property and imprisoned them without trial.

To understand the complex pattern of intergroup relations in the United States today, we need to remember that inequalities among ethnic groups—from income differences to levels of segregation—remain entrenched in the ***social structure***. These inequities are in part the result of the patterns of institutional discrimination that have long been ***functionally integrated*** into American society, reproducing an unequal system generation after generation. It is easier for athletes to break out of this vicious circle because they perform in areas where winning or losing is clearly visible and it is difficult to deny individual success.

Nevertheless, the success of minorities in athletics and other fields depends on a long chain of ***social actions*** aimed at changing the racist heritage of the United States. Because of social action by civil rights advocates and government officials, Michael Jordan was able to attend and play basketball at the University of North Carolina en route to participating in the Olympic gold medal dream team and becoming a multimillionaire sports celebrity. When Jordan's parents were of college age, no African-Americans were being admitted to UNC under any circumstances.

Social action was needed not just because of structural or cultural factors, but because of the ***power*** many Americans used to maintain their positions of racial superiority—by jailing civil rights activists in the South, driving Native Americans onto reservations, trying to limit Puerto Ricans' access to the U.S. mainland even while requiring them to serve in the U.S. Army, and interning Kristi Yamaguchi's grandparents.

Those were the bad old days, you might say. Perhaps. Although overt prejudice has declined significantly in American ***culture*** over the last quarter century, there are signs that racial and ethnic tensions are heating up. No American, of any cultural background, can yet afford to be complacent about the state of race relations in the United States.

SUMMARY

1. The United States is one of the most culturally diverse nations on earth. In recent years immigration to the United States has risen as a result of changes in immigration laws and in the international situation.

2. Minority groups, whose members are denied equal treatment, are found in every society. Often these categories are defined in terms of physical appearance (race) or cultural characteristics (ethnicity).

3. Race and ethnicity are social constructs. A race is a population that perceives itself and is perceived by others to have distinctive, inherited characteristics. Ethnicity is a social identification based on perceived cultural differences of a group.

4. When different racial and ethnic groups meet, the result may be either conflict or accommodation. Patterns of conflict often grow out of a combination of ethnocentrism and competition for resources. Sometimes one group economically and politically subjugates another, as in colonialism. At other times, the more powerful group displaces, enslaves, or segregates the weaker group. Segregation physically and socially separates groups by race or ethnicity; integration unites them.

5. Prejudice is a positive or negative attitude toward a group of people based on their real or imagined social characteristics. Not merely a personal opinion, prejudice is grounded in cultural norms and values. Discrimination is social action based on presumed differences between groups.

6. Minorities may react to prejudice and discrimination with self-segregation, covert aggression, nonviolent resistance, or violent protest and outright rebellion.

7. Sometimes groups meet with a minimum of conflict, as when they blend, assimilate, or exist in a pluralistic mosaic. Assimilation has been the dominant pattern for white European immigrants to the United States. However, the melting pot may be more a figment of political ideology than a reflection of reality. Nor is the United States a pluralistic society: White Anglo-Saxon Protestant values and ideals predominate.

8. Efforts to achieve racial and ethnic equality in the United States have been only partly successful. African-Americans, the largest minority group in the country, have made many gains since the 1960s, but they still lag behind whites. Housing is highly segregated; educational opportunities and achievement are unequal; the growth of a black middle class has been paralleled by an increase in ghetto poverty; African-Americans have been elected to almost every political office, but not in proportion to their numbers; only in the military are racial equality and integration becoming realities.

9. Hispanic-Americans may surpass African-Americans as the country's largest minority group early in the twenty-first century. Coming from many different Latin American societies, at different times, and under different circumstances, Hispanics share a language, religion, and customs that make them a distinct ethnic group.

10. Native Americans are the poorest minority group in the United States and have suffered all the tragic effects of racism.

11. The fastest-growing category in the United States, Asian-Americans are often cited as a "model minority." Although many come from urban, educated, elite families in their land of origin and have prospered here, others are uprooted peasants who still struggle to find a foothold; others fall between these extremes.

REVIEW QUESTIONS

1. What are the factors that contribute to the tension between the ideals of cultural unity and tolerance and the realities of cultural diversity?

2. What are the factors that contribute to the maintenance of cultural and racial biases?

3. How are minority groups different from racial and ethnic groups? Give an example of each.

4. How do the patterns of conflict and domination differ from each other?

5. How have acceptance and integration occurred?

6. Develop brief profiles of the minority groups discussed in the chapter: African-Americans, Hispanic-Americans, Native Americans, and Asian-Americans.

CRITICAL THINKING QUESTIONS

1. Examine immigration using at least three of the five key concepts (social structure, social action, functional integration, power, and culture).

2. Develop some policy suggestions for reducing both prejudice and discrimination.

3. The "melting pot" metaphor may not accurately reflect the relations among ethnic and racial groups in the United States. Construct another metaphor that you think would be more accurate and explain your rationale for it.

4. Use at least three of the five key concepts to analyze the situation of one of the minority groups profiled in the chapter.

GLOSSARY

Affirmative action Special consideration and preferential treatment accorded to members of minority groups to remedy past discrimination.

Assimilation The incorporation of a minority group into the culture and social life of the dominant group so that the minority eventually disappears as a separate, identifiable unit.

Colonialism The economic takeover of one nation by another, more powerful nation, and the subsequent political and social domination of the native population.

De facto segregation Racial separation that results from unofficial social patterns.

De jure segregation Segregation imposed by law.

Discrimination Exclusion or exploitation on the basis of group membership. While sometimes intentional, discrimination may also be institutional—that is, caused as a by-product of the regular operation of social institutions which affect groups unequally.

Ethnic group A category of people who perceive themselves and are perceived by others as possessing shared cultural traits.

Integration The unimpeded interaction and contact between different racial and ethnic groups. This is sometimes termed "social" integration to distinguish it from functional integration.

Minority groups People who are singled out for unequal treatment in the society in which they live and who consider themselves to be victims of collective discrimination.

Multiculturalism An approach to life in a pluralistic society which calls for finding ways for people to understand and interact with one another that do not depend on their sameness but rather on respect for their differences. This view differs from other forms of pluralism in its emphasis on interaction and equality among groups.

Pluralism The coexistence of different racial or ethnic groups, each of which retains its own cultural identity and social networks, while participating in the same economic and political systems.

Prejudice A categorical predisposition to like or dislike people for their real or imagined social characteristics.

Race A group of people who believe themselves and whom others believe to be genetically distinct.

Racism The doctrine that some races are inherently inferior and some inherently superior to others.

Segregation The legal or customary restriction or prohibition of contact between groups according to such criteria as race, ethnicity, sex, and age.

CHAPTER 11

Sex and Gender

> Exposure to danger is not combat. Being shot at, even being killed, is not combat. Combat is finding . . . closing with . .,. and killing or capturing the enemy. It's KILLING. . . . And women CAN'T DO IT! Nor should they even be thought of as doing it. The requirements for strength and endurance render them UNABLE to do it. And I may be old-fashioned, but I think the very nature of women disqualifies them from doing it. Women give life. Sustain life. Nurture life. They don't TAKE it. (In *New York Times*, July 21, 1991, p. E3)

So declared General Robert H. Barrow, retired commandant of the Marine Corps, at the 1991 Senate Armed Services Committee hearings to determine whether women pilots should be allowed to fly combat missions. (The committee voted to study the issue further.) As more women have joined the U.S. military and have acquired advanced skills, they are calling for promotions and opportunities to serve that match their training and performance. They have met strong resistance from people, like General Barrow, who believe that war is "men's work."

Women have played a role in every U.S. military operation, beginning with the Revolutionary War. But never before the Persian Gulf war of 1990–1991 have American women participated in a military action in such large numbers and in such a variety of jobs. Today, more than one in ten American soldiers are women. An estimated 35,000 served in the Persian Gulf. Eleven were killed—five in action—and two were taken prisoner.

In some ways, the armed forces today are a model of equality between the sexes. A woman was chosen head cadet at West Point. Day-care centers are standard on military bases. Women commanders led troops through desert minefields during the gulf war. Yet women are still banned from the military's main activity: combat.

The official reason is that women are not as physically strong as men and are therefore less able to defend themselves. Women soldiers counter that they are already risking death or capture in communications, transport, intelligence, and medical units. Besides, today's advanced military technology requires brains as much as brawn. Hand-to-hand combat is increasingly rare, and women can "plot coordinates and push buttons as fast as men can" (*Newsweek*, August 5, 1991, p. 25). Some worry that women soldiers might become pregnant and leave their units shorthanded, but more soldiers were taken out of service in the Persian Gulf because of sports injuries than because of pregnancies (*Newsweek*, August 5, 1991). Still others argue that the presence of women interferes with strong "male bonding" among soldiers. Many women suspect that the real issue is **sexism**—the unequal treatment of men and women on grounds of sex or gender—and male antagonism against women who are entering military roles once reserved for men. Reports to a Senate panel about the sexual abuse of women soldiers by their fellow soldiers in the Persian Gulf have suggested that bias against women is at least as common in the military as it is in the larger society. In 1991, for example, a number of women—including navy officers—were assaulted at a convention of naval aviators in Las Vegas. Subsequent investigations revealed widespread sexual harassment and led to the resignation or reassignment of several admirals and the navy secretary who tolerated it. Women also suspect that the combat prohibition serves the self-interest of military men. "By pretending they were protecting women from harm," says Representative Pat Schroeder, "all they were really protecting them from was promotions" (in Quindlen, 1991, p. E19).

Combat restrictions clearly limit career opportunities for women in the military. In today's army one in six lieutenants is female, but only one in thirty colonels and only three of 407 generals are women (Moskos, 1990). Advancement to the top ranks usually depends on flying bombing raids and leading troops into battle. In sociological terms, the *manifest function* of banning women from combat may be to protect them, but a *latent function* is to restrict their military careers.

The debate over women in combat reflects fundamental, unresolved questions about the roles of males and females in our society and about their relationships to one another. We address these underlying questions in this chapter. In the first section we consider which differences between males and females are biological and which are imposed by ***culture***. Next, we analyze the different roles that our culture has prescribed for males and females, and describe how these cultural expectations are passed from generation to generation. In the third section we focus on the ***social structures*** of gender inequality on the job, in the family, and in politics. We consider how ***power*** shapes relations between men and women, and we use examples from other societies to examine how gender differences are ***functionally integrated*** into different kinds of social organizations. Throughout the chapter, we consider the extent to which ***social action*** enables people to alter patterns of gender difference and inequality.

THE SOCIAL CONSTRUCTION OF GENDER

From the moment a baby is born, that baby is classified as either a girl or a boy on the basis of physical appearance.

Biological differences are basic to the distinction between male and female. The harder question to answer is *how* people should be male or female, because biology leaves a great deal to social construction. The first time new parents dress their newborn boy in blue or their baby girl in pink, the sexual identity of the child is being socially constructed. That is, society establishes a set of cultural expectations for each gender; children are taught to conform to what their society expects of them as either a boy or a girl.

Sociologists use the term **gender** to refer to nonbiological, culturally and socially produced distinctions between men and women and between masculinity and femininity (Laslett and Brenner, 1989; Oakley, 1972; Scott, 1986). While the term *sex* is often used to refer to male and female characteristics in general, it is more properly restricted to the biological differences that are relevant to reproduction. Sex differences are the products of heredity and biology; gender differences result from socialization.

All societies, from the most primitive to the most advanced, use gender as an organizing principle, dividing the chores and rewards of social life into men's and women's roles. "[N]o aspect of social life—whether the gathering of crops, the ritual of religion, the formal dinner party, or the organization of government—is free from the dichotomous thinking that casts the world in categories of 'male' and 'female' " (Epstein, 1988, p. 232). From clothing styles to careers, men and women are expected to be different.

Historically, men and women have been viewed not simply as different, but also as unequal. In most times and places, the work, pastimes, personality traits, ideas, and even virtues ascribed to women have been viewed as less desirable and less worthy than those attributed to men. This is still true in modern Western cultures, despite social change: Being rational (a supposedly masculine trait) is viewed as superior to being emotional (a feminine trait); being competitive (a masculine trait) as more valuable than being caring (a feminine trait); making money (until recently a male role) as more important than rearing children (still primarily a feminine pursuit). Almost always, males have enjoyed far greater wealth, power, and prestige than have females.

Gender inequality is virtually universal. Many people hold that the ultimate reason gender differences are so widespread is biology.

Is Biology Destiny?

Clearly, biology has a great deal to do with differentiating men and women and shaping their behavior, especially when it comes to sex and reproduction. But sociologists believe that although biology shapes our behavior and potential, it does not rigidly determine what kind of people we will be. Human beings are extremely adaptive animals, capable of living in many ways in all kinds of environments. Compared with other species, humans have few instincts or innate behavior patterns and a much greater capacity to learn and to change. As the evolutionary biologist Stephen Jay Gould (1984) warns, simplistic biological theories that stress the "naturalness" of gender inequality too often emphasize genetic limitations (which are few) rather than the range of potentialities (which are vast).

Women have gained power by approximating male roles in the U.S. armed forces, but cultural values have limited how far women may rise in the military. Deeply held beliefs about gender that were supposedly intended to protect women have the effect of limiting their social mobility.

Arguers on both sides of the debate over whether gender differences are determined by biology tend to assume that there are clear differences between men and women and then set out to find the reasons for these. In fact, there is a great deal of *similarity* between men and women; we need to be careful not to assume differences that cannot be demonstrated scientifically. Reviewing more than 2,000 books and articles on sex differences, Maccoby and Jacklin (1974) concluded that, on average, males and females do not differ significantly in terms of sociability, suggestibility, self-esteem, achievement motivation, rote learning, analytical skills, and responses to auditory and visual stimulation. Psychological testing produced only a few areas in which males and females consistently differed, and these differences were small. Males seemed to be more aggressive than females and to perform better on visual–spatial tasks and in mathematics. In contast, females seemed to be better in verbal abilities. Since Maccoby and Jacklin's study, one research project has found that girls are somewhat more likely than boys to be timid and boys somewhat more likely to be aggressive, but otherwise they are remarkably similar (Jacklin, Maccoby, Doering, and King, 1984; see also Hyde, 1981; J. Sherman, 1978; Tavris and Wade, 1984).

Differences between boys and girls are especially small before puberty. At the onset of adolescence, sexual maturation and cultural norms combine to produce a new differentiation of behavior and experience. Adolescent girls often have crises of self-esteem and begin to lower their expectations for themselves (Gilligan, 1982). By high school, the division between male and female worlds is clear-cut (Richmond-Abbott, 1992). Biological factors may play some role in this process, but cultural influences are so pervasive that it is almost impossible to isolate the effects of biology.

There is another reason to be cautious in drawing conclusions from evidence of biological differences: the wide range of individual variation in the expression of any given trait. On average, thus, men may be able to lift heavier weights than women, but this does not mean that any particular man is stronger than any particular woman. For virtually every behavior, there is far greater variation within each sex than there is, on average, between the sexes (Bleier, 1984; Hyde, 1984).

Even for physiological differences, it is not clear that there are purely biological explanations. Male athletic champions can run faster and jump higher than their female counterparts. But this apparent evidence for innate biological differences between the sexes is not as conclusive as it appears. First, American culture (and most others) provides much more encouragement, even pressure, for boys to participate in sports. It should not be surprising that they excel. Second, over the last twenty-five years, girls and women have become much more active in sports—including the same sports that boys and men play. As a result, the gap between male and female champions has steadily narrowed (Doyle and Paludi, 1986; Jordan, 1983). In some sports, women are breaking records once held by men. At the 1992 Olympics, for example, gold medalist Jackie Joyner-Kersee long-jumped 7.10 meters; forty years earlier, Bob Mathias had won a gold medal by jumping 6.98 meters—and eighty years earlier, in 1912, the great Jim Thorpe had jumped 6.79 meters. The fact that women athletes now surpass the records of recent male champions shows the impact that both cultural change (greater acceptance of female athletes) and individual social action (improved training) can have on the "raw material" that biology gives us.

Cross-Cultural Comparisons

If gender characteristics were simply a matter of biology, then one would expect to find that gender roles do not vary much from one culture to another. But that is not the case. What people consider masculine or feminine behavior is actually quite variable. Americans, for instance, think of men as naturally stronger and tougher than women and better suited to perform the most strenuous physical labor. In many traditional societies, however, particularly in sub-Saharan Africa and South America, women do most of the heavy work—carrying goods to market, hauling firewood, and constucting houses. Men hunt—and spend a lot of time talking. Similarly, in the United States most doctors are men; in Russia most are women. Among some peoples men are the main storytellers; among others women are. Among some peoples agriculture is restricted to men, in some societies farming is regarded as women's work, and in still others men and women work in the fields side by side. Whatever innate biological differences exist between men and women, they allow for wide variation in actual social life.

The anthropologist Margaret Mead (1935/1963) was one of the first to study societies whose gender arrangements differ from our own. In three neighboring New Guinea tribes, she found evidence of aggression in women, passivity in men, and minimal differences in the roles of men and women. According to Mead, the mild-mannered Arapesh expected both sexes to be gentle, cooperative, and maternal. In contrast, the neighboring Mundugumor believed both sexes were fierce, combative, and selfish. Both men and women exhibited exaggerated **machismo**, or compulsive masculinity, involving posturing, boasting, and an exploitative attitude. In the third tribe, the Tchambuli, ideals of masculinity and femininity were the opposite of ours. Women were the primary food providers for their families, shaved their heads, wore no ornaments, and dominated their men. The men were preoccupied with beauty and romance, and spent their days primping and gossiping.

This Tchambuli woman of New Guinea is fulfilling her culture's notion of the woman's role—that of hunter and provider. Cross-cultural evidence of wide variation in gender roles undercuts the notion that biology is all-determining.

Mead took a relatively extreme position on the issue of social construction of gender. As she wrote, "Many, if not all, of the personality traits which we have called masculine or feminine are as lightly linked to sex as are the clothing, the manners, and the form of head-dress that a society at a given period assigns to either sex. . . . [T]he evidence is overwhelming in favor of the strength of social conditioning" (in Chafetz, 1970, p. 260). While no sociologist believes that biology completely determines gender roles, many believe that there is more cross-cultural consistency in male and female roles than Mead indicated. In hunting and gathering societies all over the world, for example, men are nearly always the hunters (Lenski, Lenski, and Nolan, 1991).

Furthermore, in nearly every culture gender roles are structured so that the skills and traits that are considered masculine are valued more highly than are those considered feminine (Chafetz, 1984). Mead (1928/1968) recognized this and summed it up nicely: There are societies where men farm and women fish, and societies where men fish and women farm; but whatever form the division of labor takes, the man's jobs are considered vitally important and the woman's tasks are viewed as routine and mundane. For example, before the Industrial Revolution in England, spinning was seen as women's work and weaving was men's work; weaving was better paid. When spinning machines were introduced, however, men claimed the right to operate them because they were the high technology of the day and their operators were paid better than hand spinners or weavers. As weaving was devalued, more women became weavers (Pinchbeck, 1930; Thompson, 1968).

Cross-cultural comparisons, thus, show that there is a wide range of variation in what different cultures consider to be "male" or "female," "masculine" or "feminine." At first men were able to dominate women because they were physically stronger—a biological difference. The longer this domination went on, however, the more resources men could accumulate and thus the greater the inequality between men and women became. Male dominance became part of the social structure, supported by cultural norms and values as well as physical force, or power.

The key concept of ***power*** helps to explain why there are cross-cultural differences in the extent of inequality between men and women, even though some inequality is always present. In the modern era, for example, technological changes reduced the importance of physical strength in production; capitalism stressed monetary wealth, which could be owned by either men or women, rather than military power, which was controlled by men; and democracy spread ideas of equality, which gradually changed the relations between the sexes.

The question of whether gender differences are based on biology or on ***culture***, ***social structure***, and ***power*** has been highly controversial. If biology were shown to be the basis of gender differences, then continued male dominance over women, and continued division of labor by sex, would be justified. However, if other sources of gender variation were identified, men and women should be able to organize their relations and division of labor in any way they wanted. Societies would still have to achieve ***functional integration*** by ensuring that such essential jobs as rearing children and protecting the community got done. But each person's place in that system would not be determined by his or her sex.

Many people have assumed that if men and women are to become equal, gender differences will have to be eradicated; but this is not necessarily true. The goal is to end men's oppression of women, not to eliminate the differences between them. In fact, many contemporary feminist scholars have stressed the value of the style of reasoning that women bring to moral and other decisions (Benhabib and Cornell, 1986; Gilligan, 1982). While men commonly try to narrow decisions down to a small number of clear and generalizable principles, women consider a wider range of contextual factors; men are more likely to accept the limits within which an issue is initially posed, while women are more likely to consider other possibilities.

One of the most important contributions of cross-cultural comparisons is their demonstration that there is no one "essence" of maleness or femaleness (Fuss, 1989).

There are different ways to be male and female, and cultures attach different values to the same sorts of activities. All societies do distinguish between men and women, although not all regard sex as an inflexible and dominant aspect of identity, the way modern Westerners typically do. In varying degrees, thus, gender is a source of differences among people around the world. These differences are socially and culturally constructed, however, not just given by biology.

Gender Roles and Stereotypes

The 1950s and early 1960s might be called "the era of the housewife" in the United States. It was during these prosperous years after World War II that a large proportion of the U.S. population belonged to families in which the man was the sole provider and the woman was a full-time homemaker. Dad went off to his steady, secure job and earned a "family wage"; Mom devoted herself to rearing their 2.4 children, keeping the house spick-and-span, and perhaps doing volunteer charity work or community service. Many of our notions of masculinity and femininity date from this historically unusual period.

Gender roles are the expected behaviors, attitudes, obligations, and privileges that a society assigns to each sex. Even though more women are working today and new job opportunities for women are opening in formerly all-male fields, the gender roles formed during the 1950s persist as an ideal, even though they are based on a set of gender stereotypes that have been challenged by both social science and the women's movement (Richmond-Abbott, 1992; Roger, 1984).

Gender stereotypes are oversimplified but strongly held ideas about the characteristics of males and females (Basow, 1986). They help maintain gender roles by shaping ideas about the tasks to which men and women are "naturally" suited. Thus, a 1990 Gallup Poll found that nearly six out of ten respondents believed that males and females have different personalities, interests, and abilities. When asked to identify personality traits characteristic of the two sexes, most people described men as aggressive, strong, proud, disorganized, courageous, and confident, while women were described as emotional, talkative, sensitive, affectionate, and patient (see Table 11.1 for additional responses). Opinion was divided on whether these differences were due to biological makeup (45 percent) or upbringing (40 percent).

Gender roles and stereotypes influence one another in both directions. While stereotypes help to set up our expectations about the tasks men and women should per-

Gender stereotypes help to perpetuate traditional gender roles. In the United States and many other countries, these stereotypes hold that males should be tough and self-sufficient and females should be gentle and cooperative, so the gender-role socialization that boys and girls receive encourages them to behave accordingly.

TABLE 11.1

How Different Do Men and Women Think the Sexes Are?

Question: Now I want to ask about some more specific characteristics of men and women. For each one I read, please tell me whether you think it is generally more true of men or more true of women.

Fifteen characteristics most often said to describe men

		OPINIONS OF	
	Total	Men	Women
1. Aggressive	64%	68%	61%
2. Strong	61	66	57
3. Proud	59	62	55
4. Disorganized	56	55	57
5. Courageous	54	55	53
6. Confident	54	58	49
7. Independent	50	58	43
8. Ambitious	48	51	44
9. Selfish	47	49	44
10. Logical	45	53	37
11. Easy-going	44	48	40
12. Demanding	43	39	46
13. Possessive	42	38	45
14. Funny	40	47	34
15. Level-headed	39	46	34

Fifteen characteristics most often said to describe women

		OPINIONS OF	
	Total	Men	Women
1. Emotional	81%	79%	83%
2. Talkative	73	73	74
3. Sensitive	72	74	71
4. Affectionate	66	69	64
5. Patient	64	60	68
6. Romantic	60	59	61
7. Moody	58	63	52
8. Cautious	57	55	59
9. Creative	54	48	60
10. Thrifty	52	51	53
11. Manipulative	51	54	48
12. Honest	42	44	41
13. Critical	42	43	41
14. Happy	39	38	39
15. Possessive	37	43	32

Source: Linda DeStefano and Dr. Diane Colasanto, "Unlike 1975, Today Most Americans Think Men Have It Better," The Gallup Poll Monthly, *February 1990, p. 29.*

form, seeing people in traditional roles every day reinforces our belief that gender stereotypes are valid. For instance, we think that men are strong and forceful and therefore suited to police work; when we observe that most police officers are indeed male, we conclude that our gender stereotypes must be right. The problem with such reasoning is that it is circular. Because we don't routinely see men and women outside traditional gender roles, we have few opportunities to test our assumptions. Hence we mentally write off the policewoman or male nurse as an exception who proves the rule. As more women assume previously male roles (and vice versa), these stereotypes tend to weaken. However, they still retain the power to create major *role conflicts*—clashes between the demands associated with different roles—for both men and women.

Role conflicts may pose special problems for women, many of whom find themselves torn between the demands of motherhood and career (not to mention husbands and housework, as we'll see later). A woman may feel she isn't doing either job very well. Even if she is able to manage both responsibilities, her employer and colleagues may see her as a bad bet for promotion. Fatherhood does not carry the same stigma in the workplace or create such strong role conflict. Indeed, the more successful men are, the more likely they are to marry and have a family. For women the pattern is reversed. Only about 40 percent of top female executives today have children, compared with 95 percent of their male counterparts (Ehrenreich and English, 1989). At the same time, women who decide not to become mothers tend to be stigmatized (Fisher, 1991). Clearly, the choice between career and family is more stressful and the cost more apparent for women than for men (Rubin, 1984).

Despite its advantages in power and prestige, however, the male role in American society can be a source of stress. Fear of inadequacy and failure is the dark side of the pres-

The role of the white male in American society may confer power and prestige, but it is also likely to impose a stressful degree of rigidity, isolation, and responsibility.

sure on men to achieve. Men are supposed to maintain an impression of strength and courage at all times. Forbidden by gender stereotyping to express warmth, tenderness, and sensitivity, men may find themselves hampered in their relationships with their wives and children. Moreover, the emphasis men place on toughness and superiority can lead them to test and prove these attributes repeatedly by engaging in acts of aggression and violence.

The male role takes its toll in ill health. Men's life expectancy is eight years shorter than women's, and men suffer more heart attacks, stress-related illnesses, and alcoholism.

While members of both sexes complain about the constraints imposed by traditional gender roles, these roles tend to persist. Most men still choose predominantly male occupations; most women are in charge of child care and housework even if they work full-time outside the home.

GENDER SOCIALIZATION

When we hear that a friend has had a baby, our first question is likely to be, "Boy or girl?" It is as though we need to identify the infant's sex before we can form a mental picture of him or her. Language reinforces this: We need to know whether to say "him" or "her" because "it" doesn't sound very nice. To be spoken of as a human being, the baby needs a gender.

As soon as the infant's gender is established, the sociocultural world into which he or she has been born starts to socialize him or her into male or female roles. Admiring grandparents will say "she" is pretty and "he" is handsome. When the baby becomes a toddler, "he" will get toy cars and "she" will get dolls. Even parents who want to raise their child with no gender stereotypes find this impossible, because friends, family, school, the media, and society as a whole pressure youngsters to conform. Mom and Dad may think that Barbie dolls promote an objectionable stereotype, but that won't stop their daughter from wanting one if her friends have one.

Although we learn cultural norms and values from all our social interactions, the most important sources of gender learning are parents, peers, teachers, and the mass media.

The Influence of Parents

A recent review of the literature on gender and socialization found that parents treat boys and girls equally in many ways (Lytton and Romney, 1991). Differences in verbal interaction, physical play, warmth and responsiveness, encouragement of achievement, and strictness and discipline were slight. But parents do perceive their children in gender-related ways and encourage "gender-appropriate" activities.

Gender-role socialization by parents begins at birth (Paludi and Gullo, 1986; J. Z. Rubin, Provenzano, and Luria, 1974). Parents see their daughters as "weak," "soft," "fine-featured," "awkward," and "delicate," while their sons are "strong," "firm," "large-featured," "well-coordinated," and "hard." Parents tend to be upset when a stranger perceives an infant or toddler as a member of the opposite sex (McGuire, 1988). Fathers are particularly gender-conscious in relation to boys, and tend to react more strongly to "inappropriate" behavior in a son than a daughter, even when the child is only one year old (M. E. Snow, Jacklin, and Maccoby, 1983).

Today's parents are more likely than past generations of parents to encourage girls to participate in sports and are somewhat less likely to tolerate aggression in sons. But other forms of gender stereotyping persist. The parent who gives a truck to a girl or a doll to a boy is rare indeed (Stern and Karraker, 1989). And most parents assign their children traditional domestic chores, asking girls to help with cooking and baby-sitting and boys to do yard work and small repairs (Baker, 1984). Higher-income parents tend to be less stereotyped in the activities they encourage, and girls who are only children are more likely to learn both "helper" and "handyman" skills (Burns and Homel, 1989).

Parents may also apply gender stereotyping to intellectual achievements. They tend to attribute a girl's success in math to effort and a boy's success to talent (Yee and Eccles, 1988). Since talent presumably is a stable quality, parents may subtly communicate confidence in their son's future math success and doubt about their daughter's. This tendency may explain why from junior high school on, girls often have negative attitudes toward math and lower estimates of their own abilities, regardless of their actual performance.

What parents teach their children may not be as important as what parents themselves do (whether the mother works outside the home, and if so, what kind of job she has), how they relate to each other at home (such as whether they share the housework), and what the general structure of the family and other institutions is. For example, Nancy Chodorow (1989) argues that many gender differences reflect the traditional division of family

The increase in two-career families may be helping to broaden the gender-role horizon for both boys and girls. When both parents work outside the home and share household chores, their children are less likely to subscribe to traditional gender stereotypes.

labor, with women as the primary caretakers of children. Girls identify with their mother and so take on many of her traits, including her "feminine" capacity for love, warmth, and nurturance. Girls tend to define themselves in terms of intimacy and to value empathy. Boys are supposed to identify with their father or other adult males. This leads boys to shun the feminine mothering role and turn instead to the impersonal world of work and life outside the home. Boys tend to define themselves in terms of separateness and to value individualism. According to Chodorow, this cycle of gender socialization will continue as long as women are mainly responsible for the emotional nurturance of infants and toddlers.

The Influence of Peers

Peers exert a powerful influence on the development of gender roles. From an early age, peers promote and reinforce ideas about what is acceptable dress and play, often drawing on the media and advertising for notions of what is right. (Ninja Turtles are toys for boys to play with, and My Little Ponies are for girls.) As children get older, peer groups shape attitudes about dating and other social interactions with the opposite sex. Peers also influence career aspirations and choices—laughing at a boy who wants to be a nurse and supporting one who wants to be a fireman, for example. Peer pressure may also keep girls from competing with boys in their academic work (Gilligan, 1982).

Differences among peer groups reflect in part differences in children's values and styles of social action as these were developed in the home. But it is hard for parents to exert control over their children's playmates once the children reach school age. Although different peer groups may have different interests and values (a group of rap music fans versus a church youth group, for example), all will tend to promote and reinforce gender distinctions—just somewhat different ones.

The Influence of School

Most studies find that schools reinforce what parents and peers have begun. Boys may be asked to wash blackboards or move tables, while girls are asked to pass cookies (Richmond-Abbott, 1992). Even in nursery school, girls most often get attention and praise for being obedient and helpful, while boys more often get attention and reprimands for misbehavior. In the elementary grades, girls are more likely to be praised for neatness and boys for the quality of their work. Teachers tend to think that boys contribute more ideas to a discussion or project, even when independent scorers find that both sexes participate equally (Ben Tsvi-Mayer, Hertz-Lazarowitz, and Safir, 1989; Dweck, Davidson, Nelson, and Enna, 1978; T. Evans, 1988).

Gender lessons are also built into the social structure of a typical school. For instance, while 85 percent of elementary school teachers are women, 79 percent of principals are male (Baker 1984). And while more mothers than fathers are active in the PTA and various school clubs, men tend to dominate school boards and councils (T. Evans, 1988). Repeatedly seeing men in positions of authority over women makes an impression on children. Louis Paradiso and Shauvan Wall (1986) found that first-graders attending schools with female principals had less stereotypical views about gender roles than did children in schools with male principals. School curricula may reinforce gender roles. Although home economics classes are now open to boys and shop classes to girls, these programs remain largely segregated by sex. The same is true of school sports programs. Since the 1970s many schools have tried to combat gender discrimination by organizing coeducational teams. But contact sports (football, ice hockey, wrestling) are still primarily the province of males.

Sex stereotyping continues into middle school, junior high, and high school. Indeed, young adolescents may be among the most sexist age groups in our society. In 1956, when the genders were sharply differentiated in our culture, Miriam Lewin questioned adolescents (Lewin, 1957). She found that both sexes felt it was important for boys to be leaders, to stick by their decisions, to drive a car, and to like sports, while girls should like music and art, be quiet and not call attention to themselves, and be cheerful and good-natured. In 1982, Lewin and a colleague asked adolescents the same questions (Lewin and Tragos, 1987). To their surprise, the answers were much the same; if anything, adolescents in the 1980s are more rigid than their counterparts a quarter century ago. The one difference was that the self-image of girls had improved.

The Influence of the Media

Of course, parents, peers, and schools are not children's only sources of information. The mass media—TV, radio, magazines, books—are filled with illustrations of tradi-

American commercial television is a powerful agent of socialization not only in the United States but in Samoa, where much of the programming is American.

tional gender roles. From their first years, children are bombarded with media messages about the "right" behavior for males and for females.

A classic study of prize-winning children's books found that nearly all presented highly stereotyped and unrealistic images of girls and boys, men and women (Weitzman and Eifler, 1972). The ratio of pictures of males to females was eleven to one; one-third of the books involved males only. When girls did appear, they were nearly always indoors, helping, watching, or loving the book's hero. When another team of researchers (J. A. Williams, Vernon, Williams, and Malecha, 1987) replicated this study, focusing on prize-winning books of the 1980s, they found the picture had changed—but not that much. Male and female characters were represented about equally; a third of the leading characters were female; and girls and women were more often pictured outdoors. But only one female character worked outside the home, and she was a waitress. Although females were more visible, males still had more adventures, more responsibilities, and more fun.

Television programs and commercials reinforce these sex-role stereotypes. Children's shows have more than twice as many male as female characters, and the males are portrayed more favorably. Typically, males are active, constructive, and rewarded for their actions, whereas females defer to males and often manipulate others to get their way (Basow, 1986).

Women take a backseat to men on adult TV programs as well. Nancy Signorielli (1989) analyzed prime-time network dramas broadcast between 1969 and 1985. She found that the number of women has increased significantly; further, every season has brought a few modern, nontraditional roles for women. But men still outnumber women by almost three to one on prime-time TV. Female characters are less likely than male characters to be seen working outside the home. If they do work, they are likely to be in low-pay, low-prestige occupations (waitress, secretary, nurse) and also likely to be single or divorced. Conversely, if they are married and have children, they usually do not have a job. Most women on prime-time TV are young and attractive. In contrast, male characters tend to be older, to work in high-status occupations (physician, attorney, police officer), and to be in charge. Signorielli concludes that, with a few exceptions, gender-role images on TV remained stable, traditional, and conservative over the fifteen years she analyzed.

As for the print media, a study of the images of women and men in newspapers (Luebke, 1989) found that women are "out of focus," both literally and figuratively. The photographs on page one are usually of men, portrayed in their roles as professionals, politicians, or athletes. When photographs of women do appear on page one, they are usually illustrating a "human interest" story (a woman eats lunch in the park on the first day of spring). Even when women are shown in their roles as professionals, the story is likely to appear in the "lifestyle" pages rather than the hard-news section. Although the 1980 census found that nearly 25 percent of professional athletes in the United States were female, less than 7 percent of the photos on the sports pages show women.

Magazine ads also exploit gender stereotypes (Masse and Rosenblum, 1988). Men are usually portrayed as alone and aloof, independent and strong. Women are more often pictured as submissive, as seeking contact (through their gestures and glances), or as sexual props for male-oriented products like cars and razor blades. As on prime-time TV, women are rarely seen as they see themselves, but rather as male advertisers and consumers imagine them. "For the male consumer, the implicit message is that, if you buy product x, you will also get the sweet young thing associated with it. For the female, the dynamics are those of incorporation: buy product x and *be* the sweet young thing" (p. 143). Stereotyped images of men as competent and women as cute also dominate TV commercials (Courtney and Whipple, 1983). In more than 90 percent of TV ads, the knowledgeable, authoritative voice-overs that describe a product's benefits are male (Bretl and Cantor, 1988).

What is the cumulative impact of this barrage of stereotypes? Studies have found that children who watch network TV a lot are more likely to describe males and females in stereotyped terms, and to choose gender-typed activities, than are children who rarely watch TV or watch mainly educational programs (Fruch and McGhee, 1975; Kimball, 1986; Repetti, 1984; Rothschild, 1984). With some exceptions, the mass media both reflect and perpetuate the ambivalence that prevails in our society about the changing roles of women and men.

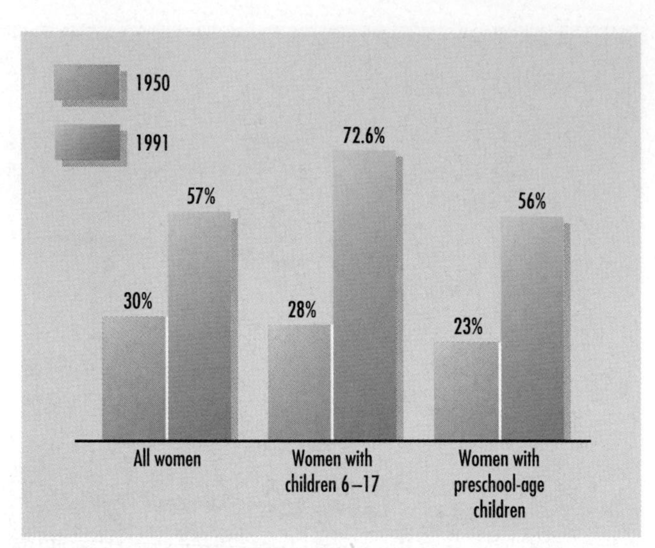

FIGURE 11.1 / Percentage of American Women in the Paid Labor Force, 1950 and 1991

Source: U.S. Bureau of the Census, *Statistical Abstract of the United States*, 1992.

PATTERNS OF GENDER INEQUALITY

There is no denying that gender roles are far more open in the United States and other societies today than they were even a generation ago, and that today's women enjoy a much greater degree of equality with men than their mothers or grandmothers did. Yet inequalities persist, affecting all of us, male and female. Both inequality and changes are particularly clear in two areas of public life where we expect antidiscrimination laws to have strong effects: jobs and politics.

Gender Stratification in the Workplace

Women's movement into the paid labor force has been called "the basic social revolution of our time" (Hochschild, 1989, p. 249). The number of American women who work outside the home has been growing since the turn of the century, but in recent years the increase has been staggering (see Figure 11.1). The greatest change has occurred among white middle-class women. Substantial numbers of black and other minority women, as well as

Cultural beliefs that many people take for granted define "women's work" as nurturing, family-oriented, and "people-centered." In truth, conceptions of gender and work are highly variable, even in a brief time period within the same society. Top left: *At the beginning of the industrial era women worked in factories doing the same physically demanding and dangerous jobs as did men. As industrial capitalism contracted and required a smaller labor force, American society redefined "women's work," confining it to the home.* Top right: *During World War II, when able-bodied men were in military service, women reentered the factories to build the ships, airplanes, and tanks required by the war effort. After the war, a massive propaganda campaign encouraged women to return to child rearing and homemaking.* Left: *In recent decades spiraling divorce rates and general economic hardship have led women to seek jobs that had previously been defined as "men's work."*

working-class women, have always worked outside the home (Woody, 1989).

In the past, white middle-class American women entered the wage market primarily during "emergencies"—for example, during the Great Depression, when many men were unemployed, and during World War II, when women "filled in" for men who had entered the military. After the war, women were pushed out of the labor force to make room for returning servicemen. Then, in the 1970s, women began going to work in increasing numbers—this time, to stay. A number of factors contributed to this trend (Maxwell, 1990). Some were economic. The number of service jobs traditionally filled by women—sales clerk, secretary, waitress, or nurse—was increasing rapidly. At the same time, the real value of men's wages was declining (see Chapter 16). To maintain their standard of living, many couples needed two salaries.

Another factor was the divorce rate, which doubled between 1960 and 1990 (Sorrentino, 1990; U.S. Department of Commerce, Bureau of the Census). Many divorced fathers pay little or no child support. Married women whose husbands earn enough to support a family may pursue careers as a form of insurance, so that they won't be stranded without work experience if they should get divorced in the future.

Finally, attitudes about working wives have changed. A majority of both men and women now approve of married women who work outside the home (see Table 11.2).

TABLE 11.2

Attitudes toward Wives Working

Question: Do you approve or disapprove of a married woman earning money in business or industry if she has a husband capable of supporting her?

	1938		1986	
	Women	Men	Women	Men
Approve	25%	19%	76%	78%
Disapprove	75	81	23	21
No opinion	0	0	1	1

Source: Rita J. Simon and Jean M. Landis, "The Polls—A Report. Women's and Men's Attitudes about a Woman's Place and Role," Public Opinion Quarterly 53 *(Summer 1989), p. 270 (1938 data from Gallup Poll; 1986, National Opinion Research Council—General Social Survey).*

"Women's Work" Today

Despite changes in attitude, the U.S. occupational and wage structure still reflects the old notion that the man is the breadwinner and women work only for spending money. By and large, women are segregated into female jobs—the "pink-collar ghettoes" (L. K. Howe, 1977) of nursing, secretarial work, and child care (see Table 11.3). In contrast, they account for less than 5 percent of the airline pilots, fire fighters, and mechanics (U.S. Bureau of Labor Statistics, 1989). Women hold just 2 percent of the seats on the boards of major corporations (*The Economist*, March 28, 1992).

Jobs that are considered "women's work" tend to offer lower pay, fewer opportunities for advancement, and less prestige than do jobs occupied primarily by men (Coser, 1983). There is a wide gap between secretaries and corporate executives, teachers and school superintendents, sales clerks and sales managers, nurses and physicians. In virtually every industry in which both men and women work, women tend to be concentrated at the bottom of the hierarchy while men monopolize the top. Promotion from lower-paying jobs into higher-paying ones is rare. An excellent secretary, for instance, might become a supervisor of other secretaries, or she might be offered a secretarial job for a more important executive. There is little chance that she will get her feet on the rungs of the managerial ladder (Blau and Jusenius, 1976). The movie *Working Girl*, in which a secretary becomes an investment banker, is an updated Cinderella story.

As we saw in Chapter 9, even when lower-status male jobs are compared with typical female ones, men earn more. Sewers and stitchers, for example, who are primarily women, earn a median income just over half that of carpet installers, who are primarily men. Even men working in traditionally female jobs are typically paid more than their female colleagues. Education does not eliminate this inequity. The average female college graduate earns less than a male worker with only a high school diploma (see Figure 11.2). Minority women are doubly disadvantaged: On average, black female college graduates with full-time jobs earn no more than white male high school dropouts (Rhode, 1990).

The average woman's annual pay is 65 percent of the average man's (National Committee on Pay Equity, 1987), an improvement of only 5 percent since 1950. Just 18 percent of workers earning $50,000–$75,000 (a managerial salary) are female (*The Economist*, March 28, 1992). These numbers do not capture the full extent of gender inequality: Only half of all employed women work full-time for the whole year, and many do not receive the same employee benefits (such as health insurance and pension plans) as do male workers (Kamerman and Kahn, 1987).

TABLE 11.3

Gender Segregation of the Work Force (Selected Occupations)

Occupation	Total Employed (Thousands)	Percent Female
Secretary	4,788	98.3%
Receptionist	815	97.2
Bookkeeper	1,926	91.7
Bank teller	503	91.0
Computer operator	870	64.2
Computer programmer	561	35.2
Sales supervisor and proprietor	3,828	34.8
Sales worker	6,186	67.8
Licensed practical nurse	414	96.1
Dental hygienist	80	99.2
Child-care worker	358	97.1
Cleaner or servant	464	94.9
Waiter or waitress	1,389	80.6
Sewing machine operator	757	90.5
Precision production occupation	3,988	23.2
Mechanic and repairer	4,550	3.4
Carpenter	1,369	1.2
Firefighter	208	3.9
Police and detective	803	12.6
Truck driver	2,616	3.9
Airplane pilot and navigator	109	3.8

Source: U.S. Bureau of Labor Statistics, Monthly Labor Review; *November 1989, table 652, pp. 396–397.*

The picture for minority women, especially African-Americans, is more complicated (Woody, 1989). Historically, black women have been the most segregated group in the labor force, largely confined to such low-status and low-paying occupations as domestic worker, factory worker, and field hand. In the 1970s, with the passage of antidiscrimination legislation, African-American women made significant gains: By 1985, black women earned almost 90 percent as much as white women. Their most significant gains were in government and public administration, transportation and communications, health, education, and social services. Not all benefited equally: In some cases black women just "moved over" into low-paying sales and office jobs, while white women "moved up." On the whole, however, the occupational status and incomes of black women improved. But these gains were offset by the sharp decline in employment opportunities and pay for black men, which left many African-American women as their family's sole earners. In 1991, 50 percent of households headed by black or Hispanic women had incomes below the poverty line (*Current Population Reports*, Series P-60, no. 181, 1991).

Occupational segregation and wage discrimination are global phenomena (United Nations, 1991). Virtually everywhere in the world, the workplace is segregated by sex. Yet increasing numbers of women are working for wages, and many are major or sole providers for their families (often including elderly parents). Women's work still tends to be defined as less important, and women earn much less than men—even when they move into occupations traditionally dominated by men. The average wage gap worldwide is 30 to 40 percent and shows little sign of closing.

All these inequities make it harder than ever to decide whether to combine career and family (see the Making Choices box on pages 284–285)—and have given rise to the debate over comparable worth.

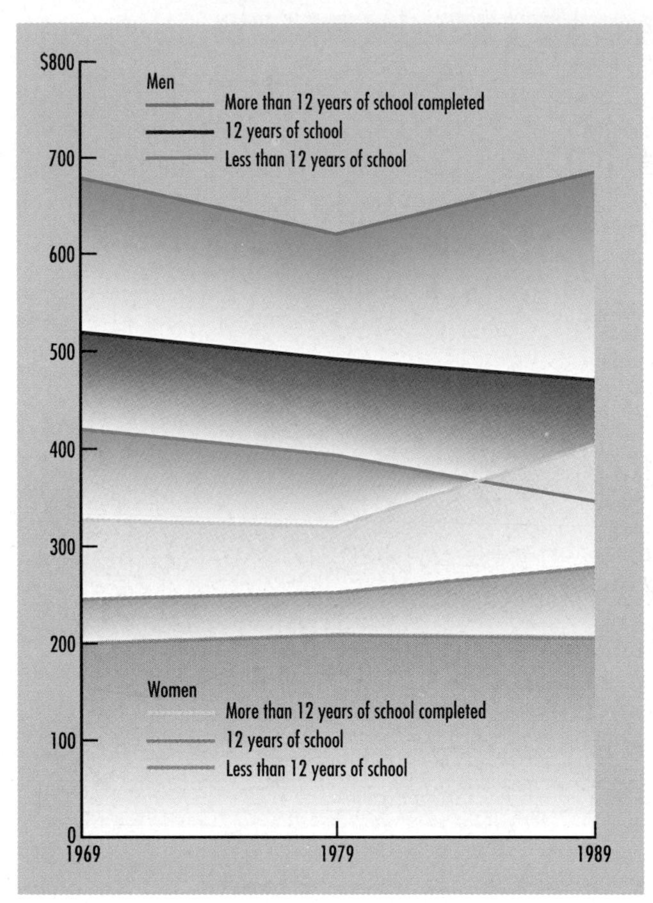

FIGURE 11.2 / Average Weekly Earnings for Working Adults (in 1989 Dollars)

Source: Professor Rebecca M. Blank, Northwestern University, in *The New York Times*, July 26, 1992.

The Comparable-Worth Debate

Title VI of the 1964 Civil Rights Act prohibits discrimination because of sex or race in the U.S. workplace. Employers are required to provide equal pay for equal work; this is usually interpreted as meaning *identical* work. Thus a telephone repairwoman must be paid as much as a telephone repairman with the same amount of work experience. As we have seen, however, the job market is strongly segregated by sex. Most women and men do not work in gender-integrated or gender-neutral jobs. As a result, enforcing equal pay statutes does little to close the gender gap in earnings. This raises the issue of **comparable worth**: basing wages for a job category on the amount of skill, effort, responsibility, and risk the job entails, plus the amount of income the job produces, rather than other criteria.

Advocates hold that comparable worth fulfills both the spirit and the letter of antidiscrimination statutes. When wages for a job category dominated by women or minority males are lower than wages for a job filled predominantly by white males, and the two jobs are of comparable value to the employer, then discrimination is a strong possibility. Statistics clearly show that jobs traditionally performed by women and/or minorities have been systematically devalued (Treiman and Hartmann, 1981; Wittig and Lowe, 1989). Figure 11.3 shows the typical salaries for pairs of jobs that have been judged to be of equal value by the state of Minnesota, which has led the way in exploring issues involved in the comparable-worth debate.

Comparable-worth programs are designed to correct these inequities. Advocates do not say that everyone should be paid the *same* salary; they do not suggest that a secretary should earn as much as a physician. Rather, they argue that wages should be based on the difficulty and importance of the job, not on the sex or race of the jobholder. Under comparable-worth programs, jobs are rated in terms of educational requirements, working hours and conditions, and other concrete measures; equal salaries are paid for jobs with equal ratings, with seniority, merit, and productivity taken into account.

Opponents argue that equal-pay provisions alone are sufficient to eliminate gender discrimination. By implication, if women want higher salaries, they should prepare for higher-paying jobs and careers. This argument overlooks the fact that many of the jobs traditionally filled by women, such as nursing and teaching, are vital to society. Because the pay is low, women are leaving these occupations, with serious social consequences (Lewin and Tragos, 1987). Advocates maintain that comparable worth is sound business practice that will enhance the recruitment, retention, performance, and satisfaction of skilled workers in such vital "feminine" occupations (S. Taylor, 1989).

A second argument against comparable pay is that it would be too costly, with estimates of cost ranging from $2 billion to $150 billion per year for the U.S. work force (Remick and Steinberg, 1984). But studies of employers who have implemented comparable-pay policies here and abroad indicate that the cost has been greatly exaggerated. When phased in gradually, such reforms account for only 5 to 10 percent of the average American employer's payroll (Hartmann, 1987). Equally important, opponents of comparable pay do not take into account the hidden costs of unequal pay to society as a whole and to taxpayers (who foot the bill for poverty, in terms of both antipoverty programs and crime). "At the bottom line, comparable worth puts money in the hands and pockets of women and minorities who are at the lowest end of the pay scale" (Evans

FIGURE 11.3 / Comparison of Monthly Salaries for Equally Valued Jobs Held Mostly by Men or by Women

Source: Minnesota Department of Employee Relations, in Sara M. Evans and Barbara J. Nelson, "Comparable Worth: The Paradox of Technocratic Reform," *Feminist Studies* 15, no. 1 (1989): 174.

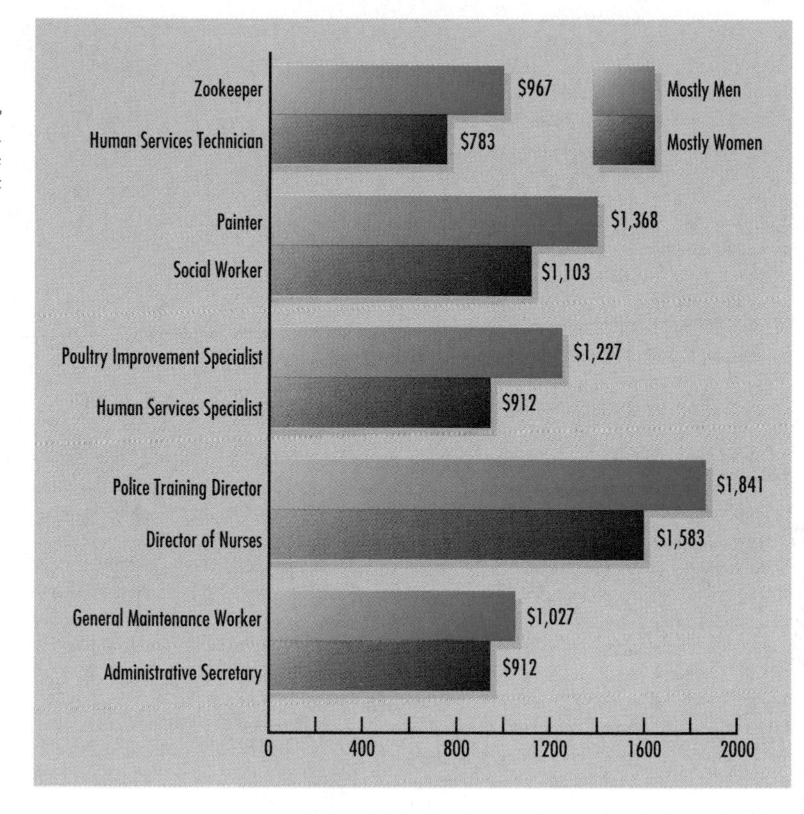

and Nelson, 1989, pp. 185–186).

To date, comparable-worth programs have been implemented for the entire economy of Australia, the Canadian government, seven state governments in the United States, and an unknown number of local municipalities and private-sector businesses. Because most of these programs are new, it is too soon to evaluate the long-term results. Sara Evans and Barbara Nelson (1989) studied the implementation of comparable worth in Minnesota at the state level, where things proceeded smoothly, and in local jurisdictions, where dissent and abuse were fairly common. They concluded that two important reasons for success at the state level were committed political leaders and the integration of women into existing power structures.

Gender Bias on the Job

Even if comparable worth is not widely accepted in the United States, equal opportunity and equal pay are the law. Why then do so many women work in low-paying occupations? A large part of the answer has to do with the key concept of ***culture***. As we discussed earlier, boys in our culture are socialized to develop qualities such as assertiveness, competitiveness, and emotional detachment, which lead to vocational achievement, while girls are encouraged to cultivate qualities such as deference, sensitivity, and self-sacrifice, which may be handicaps on the job. From an early age, children know which occupations are considered feminine and which masculine. As they approach the age when they have to make decisions about education and occupation, families and peers may pressure girls to make choices that are suitably "feminine" and will not interfere with raising a family.

Gender socialization continues on the job, where women in unconventional roles may be the butt of jokes or sexual harassment, are not offered valuable business contacts, and the like (Epstein, 1988). (The Key Concepts in Action box on page 286 discusses the issue of sexual harassment in more detail.) To be sure, cultural stereotypes are weakening and more women are entering nontraditional fields such as electrical engineering, architecture, agribusiness, military intelligence, banking, bartending, and mail delivery (Baber and Monaghan, 1988; Machung, 1989; Rix, 1990). Women also are swelling the ranks of doctors, attorneys, and business executives. But their num-

MAKING CHOICES

Combining Career and Family

Recently several sociologists have asked college students about their plans for the future (Machung, 1989; Maines and Hardesty, 1987; Spade and Reese, 1991). They have found that young men and women want to "have it all"—a good marriage and happy children combined with a fulfilling career.

Men's and Women's Expectations

In describing their future family life, however, both sexes tend to follow traditional gender roles (Machung, 1989). When asked whose job comes first, most say the husband's does. Both sexes are unanimous in declaring that primary care of children is the wife's job. Although young women hope their husband will share household chores equally, most young men express only willingness to "help"—a word that implies, not taking their share of the responsibility, but assisting with tasks that are really the wife's responsibility.

Although both sexes anticipate having careers, males and females hold different attitudes toward work (Maines and Hardesty, 1987). Male students see their future in terms of a steady line of work and achievement. Most have clear ideas about where they want to go and how to get there. They expect to work for the rest of their lives and to be the main providers for their families, even if their wife works. By comparison, women seem tentative and vague about their career goals. They want to work, but see their career plans as depending on the needs of their husband and children. They expect their careers to be interrupted or even halted at various times.

In short, neither sex anticipates a symmetrical marriage in which husband and wife assume equal responsibility for supporting the family and raising the children. If compromises need to be made, both sexes assume that the wife will sacrifice her career for the family (and the husband his family life for his career). Given the fact that women usually earn less than men and that the workplace is not structured to accommodate family commitments, these expectations may be realistic (Spade and Reese, 1991).

Indifference in the Workplace

The American workplace is not designed for people who want to make equal commitments to their family and their job (Rhode, 1990). The law does not guarantee American women maternity leave, and very few companies offer men paternity leave though one of the first bills that President Bill Clinton signed into law in 1993 required large companies to offer their workers unpaid leave for births, adoptions, and family emergencies. Although more than half the mothers of small children work, few employers provide any form of child-care assistance (such as on-site day care or allowances for baby-sitters). The federal government's support for day care has been minimal. Because caring for children is still seen as women's work, the burden of trying to balance work and parenthood falls on women. Our culture still expects men to be part-time parents, just filling in for Mom now and then.

There are alternatives. In Sweden, where nine out of ten women ages twenty-five to thirty-four work, the government provides public day care for all children. Parents of either sex who choose to stay home with a newborn or newly adopted baby are guaranteed eighteen months' leave, receive social security payments corresponding to their current salary, and must be given their old jobs back when their leave ends. The government also requires employers to allow parents time off to care for a sick child and the option of part-time work while children are preschoolers. Either parent may take advantage of these pro-

bers are still small, and, within organizations dominated by men, they still face a "glass ceiling"—unofficial and often invisible barriers to the upper levels of management (Blum and Smith, 1988; J. Hagan, 1990; Kanter, 1977, 1983).

Female attorneys are an example. Between the 1970s and the 1980s, the number of female lawyers in the United States increased tenfold (J. Hagan, 1990). One might expect that in this prestigious and highly paid profession, which deals directly with the issue of equal treatment under the law, women would have achieved equality with men. They have not. Ten years after graduation, women lawyers earn an average of $40,000 a year less than their male peers. They are more likely than male lawyers to work in small firms that represent individuals rather than in large firms that represent major organizations. Even when they work in large firms, they tend to work in less prestigious areas of the law and to receive fewer promotions. In the 1980s, female attorneys made up 25 percent of associates (lawyers working as nonpermanent employees) but only 6 percent of partners (permanent members) in U.S. law firms (American Bar Association, 1988).

Gender bias may take the form of deciding in advance that women are not temperamentally suited to certain positions or of devaluing certain jobs because they are traditionally performed by women. The evidence suggests grams, or mothers and fathers may take turns (Sorrentino, 1990). Of all the industrial nations, only the United States and South Africa do not provide new parents with some form of support (see Wiatrowski, 1990). But the structure of the workplace does not tell the full story; cultural forces also come into play. Even in Sweden, few men take advantage of paternity leave, and those who do often are ridiculed by their co-workers (Moen, 1989). As a result, most women today hold two full-time jobs, one at the workplace and one at home.

Women's Second Shift

The sociologist Arlie Hochschild (1989) characterizes the state of gender relations in America today as a "stalled revolution." The work force has changed, women have changed, but most workplaces and many men have not changed in response.

The most visible sign of the stalled revolution is the phenomenon that has come to be known as women's "second shift." Growing numbers of women work an eight-hour shift at their jobs and then put in another full shift at home, cooking, cleaning, and caring for children. From her own research and other time-use studies, Hochschild calculates that working women do fifteen more hours of work a week than their husbands do. This adds up to an extra month of twenty-four-hour days each year. Even when husbands are willing to put in as much time on child care and housework, women feel more responsible for the functioning of the family and the home. Women are the ones who keep track of doctor appointments, arrange for children's visits with friends, and call from work to check on the baby-sitter. Women do more of the daily jobs, like cooking and cleaning up, that lock them into fixed routines. Men take care of the car, the yard, and household repairs—nonroutine chores that are less frequent and often can be done whenever time permits. Most of the time men spend working at home is devoted to the children, not the laundry. Moreover, men are more likely to do "fun" things with the children (such as trips to the zoo), while women more often perform such routine child-care tasks as feeding and bathing. Just as there is a wage gap in the workplace, so there is a "leisure gap" at home. Husbands sleep longer and have more time to watch TV or pursue hobbies. Wives talk about sleep "the way a hungry person talks about food" (p. 9).

Hochschild suggests that women give in to their husbands on the "second-shift" issue because they are locked into marriage in a way that men are not. For one thing, women earn less than men and so have more of an economic need for marriage. For another, marriage is less stable than it used to be, and divorce is more economically damaging to women than to men. To make matters worse, many divorced mothers receive little emotional or other support from traditionally minded friends and relatives.

Hochschild sees the "stalled revolution" as the result of colliding social forces. On the one hand, new economic opportunities and needs have drawn women into the work force, which puts pressure on men to share the second shift. On the other hand, the wage gap between men and women and the high rate of divorce lead women to hold on to their marriages—and men to hold out on sharing housework. Hochschild suggests that many modern women feel doubly oppressed by men, not only on the first shift (where the boss is male, privileged, and better paid than they are) but also on the second shift (where husbands opt out).

that both types of discrimination occur more or less regularly. A number of laboratory studies have shown that the same résumé is given a lower rating and offered a lower starting salary when evaluators are told the applicant is a female rather than a male; that jobs labeled "feminine" are seen as requiring less effort and skill than identical jobs labeled "masculine"; and that successful performances by females are likely to be attributed to luck, while the same accomplishments by men are attributed to effort (Wittig and Lowe, 1989). In particular, both women and men tend to have negative attitudes toward female managers, as if they believed that women do not belong in positions of authority (E. J. Frank, 1988; B. Rosen and Jerdee, 1978; Statham, 1987). Female managers are caught in a double bind: If they conform to traditional definitions of femininity, they are seen as lacking necessary assertiveness; if they conform to masculine models, they are seen as "bitchy" and difficult to work for (Rhode, 1990).

Gender bias can be especially strong when women choose traditionally masculine occupations, such as the military, as we saw at the beginning of this chapter, and police work (Ott, 1989). Women police officers report that they are constantly being watched and tested by their male colleagues, expected to do such "female" chores as making coffee and tidying up, and subjected to coarse sexist remarks and rude jokes. Male officers do not want them as

KEY CONCEPTS IN ACTION

Sexual Harassment

Sexual harassment—the demand that someone respond to or tolerate unwanted sexual advances from a person who has power over the victim—made headlines in 1991 during the Senate hearings on President George Bush's appointment of Clarence Thomas to the Supreme Court. In the course of the hearings, Anita Hill, a law professor, accused Judge Thomas of having sexually harassed her when she worked on his staff. He had persistently asked her for dates, she said, and made offensive sexual comments when she refused. Thomas denied the accusations and was eventually confirmed as a Supreme Court justice. We will probably never know for sure who was telling the truth. But what scandalized many women was the fact that the Senate Judiciary Committee evaluating Judge Thomas's appointment initially ignored the charge of sexual harassment. The public learned of Professor Hill's accusation only because it was leaked to the press; the all-male Senate committee apparently saw the issue as insignificant.

Several themes illustrating the key sociological concepts came together in the Hill–Thomas episode. First of all, the ***social structure*** of the Senate was (and is) extremely unbalanced in gender terms: Of 100 senators in 1991, only two were women. Second, in part because of this social structure, women lacked the ***power*** to insist that issues important to them be taken seriously. This is part of a broader ***cultural*** pattern in which male harassment of women is not treated as a major problem. Indeed, women are reluctant to report instances of harassment; existing patterns of ***functional integration*** fail to offer procedures for responding to women's complaints. In addition, functional links between school and workplace, and between one workplace and another, discourage women from speaking out when to do so would mean losing a valuable work recommendation. When faced with reports of harassment, it is functional for men in positions of power to ignore comparatively powerless women. One result of the Thomas hearings was to make many women resolve to take political ***action*** to make sure that their voices were heard, that more women were elected to Congress, and that men would take seriously the hardships that sexual harassment causes women.

Sexual harassment is a particular problem in workplaces and in relationships of unequal power. It takes place because men (harassers are usually, though not always, men) abuse their power, and because our culture denies that this is serious—suggesting in effect that "boys will be boys." Sexual harassment can be limited to sexual jokes in a classroom or on the job that make women feel uncomfortable. It is more serious when a woman's professor or boss or co-worker makes a sexual advance, especially when the woman has clearly indicated that such attentions are unwelcome. It is extremely serious when a woman's refusal of a sexual advance results in punitive treatment or denial of a promotion. This is also illegal, although male-dominated judges and grievance committees have been slow to enforce the law.

Sexual harassment causes difficulties not just when women who reject sexual advances are penalized, but whenever women work in an atmosphere where they fear they must either tolerate harassment or lose their jobs. Harassment illustrates the fears—small and large—that women in our society are forced to live with because of the unequal power relationship between men and women. The Hill–Thomas case suggests that women's fear of speaking out is realistic, given the gender inequality built into the social structure.

Sexual harassment is not as extreme a crime as rape, but the underlying problems are similar. Both are products of a culture that encourages male sexual aggressiveness, and both have been dismissed by the "powers that be" because of the comparative powerlessness of women. It is still difficult, for example, to get **date rape** (forced sexual intercourse with a person the victim went out with voluntarily) taken seriously as a crime. Men, who have the power through the legal system to define what constitutes rape, typically consider this sort of assault trivial or even blame the victim for having provoked it. In one famous case of date rape, the boxer Mike Tyson was convicted of raping a contestant in the Miss Black America beauty pageant. In an echo of the Hill–Thomas case, thousands of African-American church women were startled to hear the head of their religious denomination say that Tyson should be given a light sentence or set free—and some other ministers backed him up. As the women noted, all the ministers were male. Even though women were a majority of the church members, the men dominated the leadership of the church.

partners on patrol, and supervisors see them as suited only to desk jobs. Men entering traditionally female occupations have the opposite experience. Male nurses win quick acceptance. Both physicians and patients tend to take them more seriously than female nurses, asking them for technical or medical assistance rather than routine care. Supervisors criticize them less often, give them more freedom in planning their own schedules, and are more likely to recommend that they upgrade their skills and move into higher-paying positions (Ott, 1989).

Sexual harassment on the job finally became a serious issue for Americans—one that needed to be brought into the open—as a result of Anita Hill's allegations during the confirmation hearings of Supreme Court nominee Clarence Thomas in 1991.

Discrimination against women is not inevitable, even in formerly all-male settings. A study of gender integration of the Coast Guard showed that biases can be overcome if those in power are clearly committed to equality. Preliminary surveys found that male cadets deeply resented the presence of females in their ranks and held hostile, sexist attitudes toward female cadets in particular and women in general. Most held traditional attitudes about a woman's place—which did not include issuing commands to men. But male cadets and future seamen were not given a choice: They were *ordered* to treat female cadets as equals and were reminded that their own futures depended on obeying orders. A follow-up study in 1986 found that sexist attitudes had declined markedly and that male cadets' estimates of female cadets' abilities had risen substantially (Stevens and Gardner, 1987). Thus, changes in behavior led to changes in attitudes. Required to treat females as equals, the cadets began to perceive them as equals. The implication is that as more men (and women) are exposed to women in positions of authority—in settings where antidiscrimination codes are strictly enforced—they become more likely to judge the women in terms of their roles and abilities, rather than in terms of prejudices and stereotypes.

The Politics of Gender

Politics has long been regarded as a man's world (Epstein, 1988). Prevailing stereotypes have held that women lack the driving ambition, the lust for power, that is required for politics; that they are too "nice" to dirty their hands in struggles for power. Women were not granted the right to vote in this country until 1920, after decades of struggle. (We consider the rise of feminism and the contemporary women's movement in Chapter 21.) Over the next half century, millions of women worked as volunteers for the major political parties and particular candidates. Hardly any were nominated for political office themselves; nor were women admitted to the "smoke-filled rooms" where the real business of bargaining and brokering took place before parties issued decisions, platforms, and statements for public consumption.

In the 1970s, as the modern women's movement gathered momentum, women's role in American politics began to change, and "the changes were swift and dramatic" (Epstein, 1988, p. 166). The proportion of women who voted, traditionally low, came to equal and sometimes surpass the number of male voters. Women played major roles in elections nationwide in 1992, which some commentators dubbed "the year of the woman." Much of the attention focused on Hillary Clinton, the first president's wife with an outside career (as a lawyer). As Table 11.4 shows, the

TABLE 11.4

Women in Elective Office, Selected Offices, 1975–1993

	PERCENT FEMALE			NUMBER OF WOMEN
Elected Officeholders	1975	1981	1993	1993
Members of U.S. Congress	4	3	9.9	53
Statewide elective officials	10	11	22.2	72
Members of state legislatures	8	12	20.2	1,503

Source: Center for the American Woman and Politics, Eagleton Institute of Politics, Rutgers University.

number of women elected to office increased in 1992, but the percentage of women elected to office remained disproportionately small.

Moreover, as the sociologist Cynthia Fuchs Epstein (1988) points out, the upper echelons of politics are still largely closed to women. When women do become heads of state, the reason is often that they are widows or daughters of prominent political leaders (the late Indira Gandhi in India or Corazon Aquino in the Philippines, for example). And despite gains, women are still underrepresented among elected and appointed officials. This is true not only in the United States, but around the world. Of the 159 member states in the United Nations, as of 1990 only six were headed by women (Iceland, Ireland, Nicaragua, Norway, Dominica, and the Philippines). The business of governing, like other businesses, is gender-stratified. Large numbers of women work at low-level jobs in public administration, political parties, trade unions, and other political organizations. But very few hold decision-making posts. The percentage of female ministers (the equivalent of U.S. cabinet secretaries) ranges from a third (in Iceland) to zero (in fifty countries on all continents) (see Figure 11.4). The United States, where 5.6 percent of cabinet secretaries are female, is not a world leader in this area (United Nations, 1991).

In other ways, however, American women may be better off than women in other industrialized nations (Davis and Robinson, 1991). They're much more likely to go to college, they are more likely to be employed, and young American women, in particular, report less discrimination than older generations faced. For them, gender equality seems within reach. But many are still single and childless. Whether they will be as optimistic when they begin struggling to balance careers with domestic responsibilities remains to be seen.

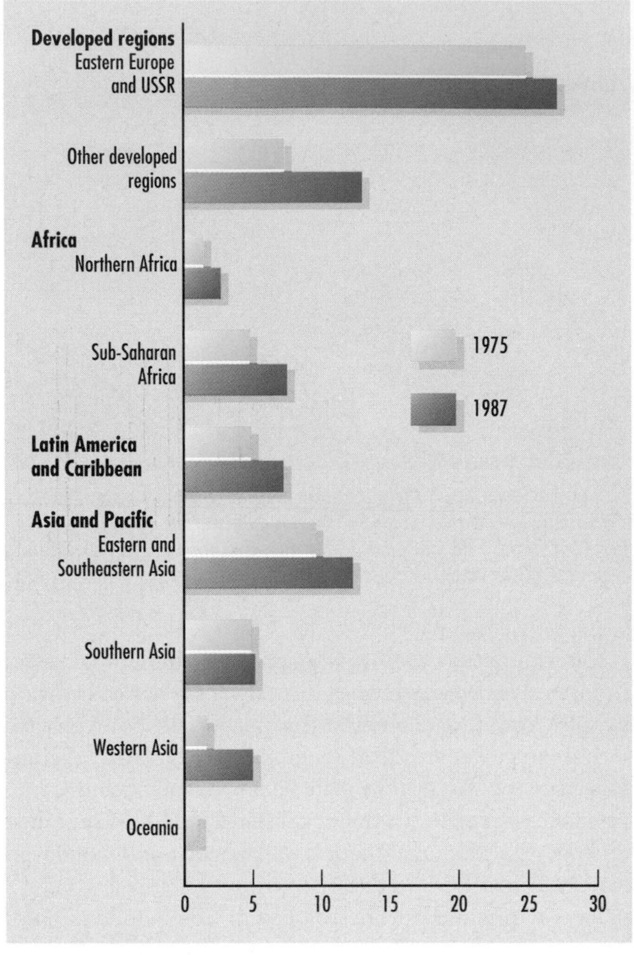

FIGURE 11.4 / Average Percentage of Women Members of National Parliamentary Assemblies, by Region, 1975 and 1987

Source: United Nations, *The World's Women, 1970–1990: Trends and Statistics*, 1991, p. 32.

Thinking Back on the Key Concepts

We began this chapter with a notable example of changing gender roles: women serving in the military during the Persian Gulf war. Women were performing military tasks—***social actions***—in that conflict that were far beyond women's role in the armed services only a few years before. Yet, as we saw, women's role in the military is still a matter of debate; women are not allowed to serve in combat. One reason cited for women's unsuitability as fighters is their biological difference from men—yet although biology shapes the possibilities open to men and women, it does not rigidly determine what they can do.

Distinctions between men and women are a part of ***culture*** and ***social structure*** everywhere in the world. We saw obvious structural inequality between men and women in the United States reflected in the worlds of work and politics. We saw that while all cultures distinguish between the genders and have stereotypes of men and women, the actual characteristics they assign to the genders are somewhat different. So are the specific roles that cultures assign to men and women (no combat for American women soldiers, for example). But one feature that runs through nearly every culture and social situation is men's greater ***power***. This power may have originated in biological differences, but it has been used by men to create whole systems of social life—social structures—that ensure their dominance. Thus, gender bias has come to be woven into systems of ***functional integration*** that shape everyday life and social institutions. In the military and the civilian workplace, men are still reluctant to accept women as equals. Their resistance is made possible not only by their structurally greater number but also by the power they hold and the entrenched gender bias of the social system and the larger culture.

SUMMARY

1. The debate over female soldiers highlights unresolved questions about the similarities and differences between men and women. Sociologists distinguish between sex (male or female biology) and gender (the set of conceptions that people have regarding masculine and feminine characteristics). Gender is a social construct; thus, we cannot assume that males and females are born with different abilities and temperaments.

2. Biology lays the foundation for all human behavior, creates physiological differences between the sexes, and determines what role a person may play in reproduction. But biology does not explain the belief that males and females are opposites; indeed, research shows the sexes are more alike than different. Cross-cultural studies show that men and women are both capable of a wide range of activities and responsibilities; nevertheless, virtually all societies distinguish between men's and women's work and place a higher value on the former.

3. Gender roles are sets of cultural expectations about how a man or woman is supposed to think, feel, and behave. Gender roles are based on stereotyped ideas about the differences between the sexes. Although social behavior is changing, gender stereotypes linger, creating role conflict for both women and men.

4. We learn gender roles through socialization. This process begins at home, is continued in peer groups and school, and is amplified by the mass media. Gender socialization illustrates how patterns of social behavior (such as parent–child interaction) and social structures (such as the division of labor in the home) combine, reinforcing one another.

5. The number of women in the U.S. work force (especially, white working- and middle-class women) has increased dramatically in recent decades because of such factors as increasing opportunities for (traditionally female) service jobs, decreasing wages for (traditionally male) manufacturing jobs, the rising divorce rate, and changes in attitudes. But a pattern of gender inequality on the job continues. Many women still tend to be channeled into traditionally "feminine" occupations and to earn less than men even when they perform identical jobs. Current efforts to close this gap focus on the notion of comparable worth.

6. The movement of women into the paid work force is felt most directly in the home. Changes in attitudes toward men's and women's responsibilities for housework and child care have not kept pace with changes in women's work and married lives. Regardless of the type of work they do, most wives work a second shift at home.

7. Women are playing a more active and visible role in American politics today than ever before. But they still are excluded from the highest levels and backstage areas of political decision making. The same pattern is seen through much of the world.

REVIEW QUESTIONS

1. Why do sociologists use the term *gender* in their analyses of females and males?

2. Assess the arguments for the existence of biological differences between males and females.

3. Document the cross-cultural differences between females and males.

4. How do gender roles and stereotypes influence each other?

5. What contributions do parents, peers, and the media make to gender socialization?

6. Review the state of gender stratification in the workplace.

CRITICAL THINKING QUESTIONS

1. Why are many people interested in explaining the differences between males and females? Do you think analysts are more interested in gender differences than in age differences?

2. Examine gender roles using at least three of the five key concepts (social structure, social action, functional integration, power, and culture).

3. Given what you have learned about sociology thus far, develop some specific policy suggestions for reducing gender stereotypes.

4. What is your view of the comparable-worth argument? Bring some basic sociological concepts and theories into your discussion.

5. What are some instances of gender stereotyping that you have experienced or performed?

6. Use the five key concepts to think about how—if at all—the armed forces would have to change for women and men to be treated equally.

GLOSSARY

Comparable worth The practice of basing wages for a job category on the amount of skill, effort, responsibility, and risk the job entails, to offset inequalities based on the sex or race of incumbents.

Date rape Forced sexual intercourse with a person the victim went out with voluntarily.

Gender All the socially constructed, nonbiological traits assigned to men and women.

Gender roles The distinct tasks and activities that society assigns to each sex and defines as masculine or feminine.

Gender stereotypes Oversimplified but strongly held ideas about the characteristics of males and females.

Gender stratification The assigning of men and women to unequal positions in the social hierarchy (including the work force, the political system, and the family).

Machismo Compulsive masculinity, evidenced in posturing, boasting, and an exploitative attitude toward women.

Sexism The unequal treatment of men and women on grounds of sex or gender; usually refers to prejudice and discrimination against women.

Sexual harassment The demand that someone respond to or tolerate unwanted sexual advances from a person who has power over the victim.

CHAPTER PROJECTS

1. **Individual Project** Find a copy of a children's book in your school or public library. Study the book to determine whether it shows sexual stereotypes. Write a brief report detailing the book you studied and any examples of stereotypes it includes.

2. **Cooperative Learning Project** Working in groups of four, study and discuss the table on page 273. Then interview 10 people, asking them the same question that the pollster in the table asked. Tally your results and combine them with the results of the other groups in your class. Do the polls conducted by your class approximate the professional poll results?

PART 4

Social Institutions

CHAPTER 12

The Family

Allen came home one day and found that his wife had run off with one of his friends. He was left with the house and two children. Allen had known things were shaky in the marriage, but he had not expected this. Suddenly he was left with a number of brewing crises. He had to decide what to tell the children. He had to go to work and arrange for child care. He had to figure out how to do the housework, handle the laundry, and prepare meals. Finally, he had to sort things out for himself. There were many things about his failed marriage he did not understand. Three months later, Allen's wife returned. Her new relationship had fallen apart, and she wanted the children and the house. Allen said no, and they went to court. The judge thought the children were better off staying where they were: Allen won. (Greif, 1985, p. 1)

In 1991, 1.36 million American fathers were raising children under the age of eighteen by themselves (*Current Population Reports*, 1990). Although many more mothers are single parents (almost 8.8 million in 1991), the proportion of single fathers is increasing. One reason is that sex roles have become less rigid, making child-rearing an acceptable activity for men. Men are becoming more involved in the role of father, in both intact and divorced families. A wife's income also gives a man more leisure time to spend with his children. Many men consciously strive to be different from their own fathers, many of whom were preoccupied with work and were distant from their children. Finally, changes in the divorce laws have made the courts more likely to view men and women as equal in family responsibilities; as a result, child custody is no longer automatically awarded to the mother.

Geoffrey Greif's survey of 1,136 single fathers (1985) found that the most difficult problem for them, as for single mothers, was in balancing the demands of work and child care. Most single fathers discovered that they had to choose between being successful at work and being successful as a parent. They could not play both roles equally well. The more children there were to raise, the younger the children, and the younger and less established the father was in his career, the greater were the problems. Most of the men in the study had to cut back on the time they spent at work; sixty-six changed jobs, and forty-three were fired. When they got married, these men had thought of themselves as workers first and fathers second; now those priorities were reversed. This affected the way they saw themselves as men.

The implications of Greif's study go beyond the observation that fathers can make good parents. If men can rear children successfully, then our notion of separate male and female "realms" may have to be reexamined. Trends in family patterns have also thrown into question the traditional definition of what constitutes a family. It may be more accurate today to think of a **family** as any group of people who are united by ties of marriage, ancestry, or adoption, having the responsibility for rearing children. Nevertheless, most Americans still see a two-parent family, grounded in a marriage that lasts a lifetime, as the ideal. Yet in 1991 only 70 percent of American households consisted of a husband, wife, and their dependent children (*Current Population Reports*, 1990). The small but growing number of single fathers, and the much larger number of single mothers, are only part of this story.

Sex, marriage, and childbearing are no longer considered part of a single, tightly wrapped package in American society (Cherlin, 1990). Compared with twenty-five years ago, fewer Americans are getting married and those who do are marrying later in life. Married couples are having fewer children (or no children); and more marriages are ending in divorce (Poponoe, 1990). Many more Americans are living alone, cohabiting with someone to whom they are not married, bearing children outside of marriage, or marrying more than once and creating stepfamilies. Thus, the average American today will live in several different types of family over the course of a lifetime (Cherlin, 1990).

There is much debate about whether these variations on the traditional two-parent family are good or bad for society and for individuals, especially children. On one side are those who believe that these changes signal the decline of the family as a central, indispensable social institution. On the other side are those who see them as evidence of the family's continuing importance and vitality—as a liberating increase in the range of options for social action available to individuals (see Blankenhorn, Bayme, and Elshtain, 1990; Dizard and Gadlin, 1990; Stacey, 1990).

In this chapter we will examine the debate about the role of the family in American society today from a sociological perspective. This debate involves a discussion of basic changes in ***social structure*** such as the trend toward smaller families, childlessness, and living alone. Many of these structural changes are the result of ***social actions*** including divorce, decisions to limit the number of children one has, and the decision for both parents to pursue careers while raising young children. Modern society has increased the range of choices people have for their family structures. Yet American ***culture*** still stresses the value of a more traditional family structure. Politicians often make family values a political issue to court those who hold strong traditional values and are opposed to alternative lifestyle and family choices. In fact, those who value one kind of family structure sometimes try to use ***power*** to impose this value on others. On an individual level, power within the family is often abused, both physically (as in the case of child abuse) and emotionally.

Much of the debate over the role of the family hinges on the fact that the ***functional integration*** of family life into American society is changing. Families no longer perform many of their traditional functions as providers of basic child care, education, jobs, health care, and so on. As social institutions outside the family have taken on these roles, families have come to be increasingly specialized in providing nurturing and emotional support. Yet families in the traditional sense have also come to seem more optional to many Americans.

We will begin by looking at the social functions that the family serves and the evolution of the family structure. We will then consider marriage and divorce in a variety of cultural settings. We will look at how social forces affect the choice of marriage partner, the age at which people marry, and the decision to divorce. After this, we will examine changes in the nuclear family and consider the array of alternatives to the traditional husband, wife, and children arrangement. Finally, we will look at two of the most important problems for American families today, teenage pregnancy and domestic violence.

FAMILY FUNCTIONS AND STRUCTURE

The family in some form is part of the social organization in all societies. Indeed, it is sometimes called the most basic of all social institutions. The family is considered so important to individuals and society because it responds to some of the most fundamental human needs, both individual and collective.

Functions of the Family

One function of the family is to meet the individual members' *need for love and emotional security*. The family involves a set of "loving obligations" to share both material and emotional resources among its members. Ideally, the family offers warmth, loyalty, concern, willingness to sacrifice for the good of others, and unconditional love (Dizard and Gadlin, 1990).

The family also fulfills the societal *need to regulate sexual behavior*. All societies place limits on the sexual behavior of their members, including limits regarding who can have sexual relations with whom. Forbidding sex between close family members (called the *incest taboo*) is a universal restriction.

Another societal need that the family fulfills is the *need to produce new generations*. At the same time, the family fulfills the *need to socialize children*. Children are society's "raw recruits." They must be taught the elements of culture needed for competent participation in social life. The family is the primary arena in which this cultural learning takes place.

The *need to protect the young and the disabled* is served by the family as well. During infancy and early childhood, humans are dependent on their parents for food, clothing, shelter, and basic care. Even as adults, many people experience episodes of illness or disability during which they can't take care of themselves. The family sees its members through these times when special help is needed.

Finally, the family fulfills the *need to "place" people in the social order*. The structure of a society is an intricate web of social roles and statuses. People must somehow be placed within these statuses and motivated to play the appropriate roles. Even in the United States and other societies that stress equal opportunity and social mobility, people's ascribed statuses, including their national, ethnic, racial, religious, class, and community identities, derive largely from family membership.

Cross-Cultural Variations in Family Structure

Like any other social institution, the American family is a set of patterned behaviors and role relationships that fulfill certain basic societal needs. This does not mean that the family is the only way to fulfill those needs. Americans tend to see their society's way of organizing the family as the way that is natural and right; yet to people in other societies, different ways of structuring family life seem equally correct.

■ To the Nayar of Kerala, India, it is natural for a woman's brother to share in the raising of her children, instead of the children's biological father. During adolescence, a Nayar girl is encouraged to have several lovers. If she becomes pregnant, one or more of these lovers acknowledges paternity and pays the costs of delivering the baby. Beyond this, however, none of the lovers has any obligations toward the girl or her child. The girl's kin are responsible for caring for her and her baby. Property and privileged status are transmitted not from father to son but from mother's brother to nephew (Gough, 1974).

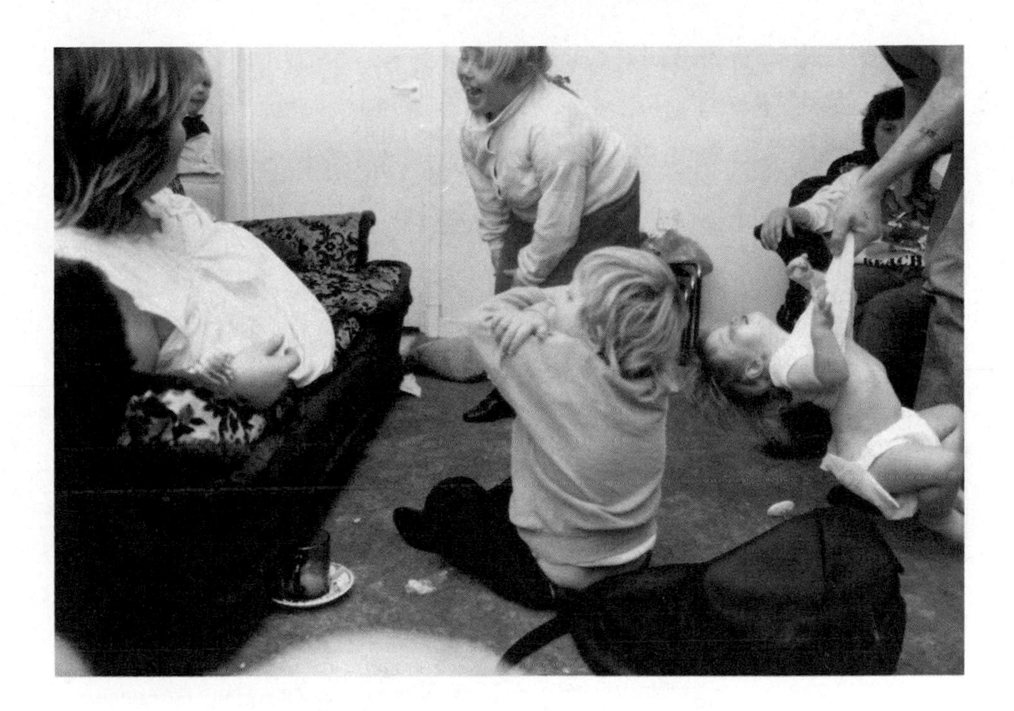

The middle and upper classes have resources to devote to lessons, vacations, private tutors, and extensive private spaces for the children in the house. In contrast, the children of the working classes are physically and socially integrated into the crowded but intimate life of their families. This photograph documents working-class family life in a British suburb.

■ Among the Betsileo of Madagascar, a man is allowed to have several wives. Each wife is housed in the village adjoining one of the rice fields that the man owns. Wealthier men have more rice fields and so can support more wives. The first and most senior wife, called the *big wife*, lives in the village next to the husband's best, most productive field. The husband lives mainly with this woman, but visits the others periodically as he oversees his other fields (Kottak, 1991).

■ In the foothills of the western Himalayas, brothers share a wife. The oldest brother arranges the marriage, and his brothers become co-husbands, with all of them living together in a single household. Any children the wife bears call all the brothers "father." The brothers are free as a group to marry additional women if they wish, in which case all the wives are shared by all the husbands.

Social scientists have categorized such variations in family structure using a number of criteria. One is the number of partners involved in a marriage. Both culturally and legally, U.S. society advocates **monogamy**, marriage between one man and one woman. Other societies permit **polygamy**, marriage involving more than two partners at the same time. In our examples above, the Betsileo practice a form of polygamy known as **polygyny**, in which a man has more than one wife at the same time. Much less common is **polyandry**, in which a woman has more than one husband at the same time.

Another structural criterion is the degree of importance given to marital ties, as opposed to blood ties. When marital ties are of paramount importance, a husband and wife and their immature children form a core unit, called the **nuclear family**. This arrangement is the preferred family structure in the United States and most other modern Western countries. It also exists in some traditional societies, such as that of the Betsileo, in which a man may establish several nuclear families in separate villages. Of course, multiple marriages aren't required for a person to belong to more than one nuclear family. In the United States, for example, most people are eventually members of two nuclear families. The first consists of oneself and one's parents and siblings, called the **family of orientation**. The second consists of oneself and one's spouse and children, called the **family of procreation**.

When family structure gives priority to blood ties, the arrangement is called an **extended family**. An extended family consists of blood relatives (groups of adult siblings, for example, or adult siblings and their parents) who live together in a single household. The blood relatives may bring with them their various spouses, but the spouses are considered peripheral to the core family unit. A common form is the three-generation extended family, in which some of a couple's married adult children (typically either

In an extended family, three or more generations live together or nearby, so that members can provide one another with financial, social, and emotional support. In contrast, the nuclear family, often isolated from relatives, relies on itself to fulfill these needs of its members.

the sons *or* the daughters) live with their parents, along with their own spouses and children. The extended family living together on a ranch in the television series "Dallas" illustrated this pattern, which is not very common in the United States. In other societies, in contrast, the three-generation extended family is the preferred form of family organization.

Three-generation extended families can usually be subclassified as either patrilocal or matrilocal in their pattern of residence. With **patrilocal residence**, a newly married couple live with or near the husband's family. That is, married sons stay at home with their parents while married daughters move away. With a **matrilocal residence**, in contrast, a son leaves his family and sets up housekeeping with or near his wife's family. In the United States and other societies that favor the nuclear family, **neolocal residence** is preferred, in which a newly married couple establish a new home of their own.

Family structure can also be categorized according to rules of descent. In American society, children are thought of as descended from both their mother's and their father's kin group, and they may inherit from both their maternal and paternal lines—a system called **bilateral descent**. In George Peter Murdock's (1949) survey of some 250 societies, 30 percent of them followed this pattern. More common in Murdock's sample (40 percent of the societies) was **patrilineal descent**, in which people are considered members of their father's kin group, not their mother's. About 20 percent of the societies in Murdock's survey practiced **matrilineal descent**, in which kinship is traced through the female line only. Not surprisingly, matrilineal descent is often found with matrilocal residence, while patrilineal descent is often found with patrilocal residence.

A final set of criteria for categorizing family structure are norms regarding who wields authority in the home. In theory three types of authority patterns are possible: Power may be vested in males (**patriarchy**), in females (**matriarchy**), or relatively equally between the two (**egalitarian**). Throughout history the predominant pattern has been patriarchy, the system found among the ancient Greeks, Romans, and Hebrews, as well as in most other societies. Despite legends of Amazon women, matriarchy has not been the norm in any society. The authority of women, however, varies from family to family, depending upon the personalities of the spouses and the nature of their relationship. As a general rule, egalitarian patterns are becoming more prevalent in modern societies.

MARRIAGE AND DIVORCE

Marriage may be defined as a socially recognized union between two or more people that involves sexual and economic rights and duties. In no society are the choice of marriage partner and the age at first marriage left completely to personal preference. The rate of divorce is also affected by social forces.

Deciding Whom to Marry

Even in the United States, where we feel we are "free" to marry whomever we wish, powerful social forces push us into marriage with an "appropriate" partner (Turner and Helms, 1988). Like members of all other societies, Americans have norms defining the range of acceptable mates from whom a person can choose. Some of these norms require that people marry *within* their own social group (their own tribe, nationality, religion, race, community, and so forth). These are called rules of **endogamy**. Others require that people marry *outside* a group to which they belong. These are called rules of **exogamy**. Often these rules operate as a circle within a circle. Rules of exogamy bar marriage within a small inner circle (such as one's own close relatives), while rules of endogamy establish an outer circle that defines how far afield people can go in search of a mate (not outside one's own race or social class, for instance).

Arranged Marriages

Societies vary in the strictness with which they enforce rules of endogamy and exogamy, and in the degree to which they allow young people to be involved in the choice of a spouse. In many societies, people believe that this decision is too important to leave to the young. As a result, adults arrange marriages for their children, often without consulting the young people. The couple may not even meet until their wedding day.

In the societies that prefer them, arranged marriages are considered desirable for a number of reasons. In societies where newlyweds become part of an extended family, the family has a heavy stake in the type of spouse chosen. It is important to choose a person who will share the family's ideas about what is good and proper, just as it is important to choose someone who will adjust to the family's codes of behavior and pull his or her weight in the household. Intense emotional attachment between the newlyweds could have a disruptive effect, imperiling customary family relationships and practices. Finally, in many of these societies a substantial amount of wealth is exchanged when a couple gets married (as a bride price or dowry), so both families have a strong financial interest in ensuring that

Sociologists recognize that the more elaborate a ritual, and the more the ritual overlaps other parts of people's lives (such as religion), the greater the ritual's power. In many settings wedding rituals unite whole families and extend their economic as well as social dependence. However, this Las Vegas wedding seems to have no social impact beyond the formalization of a bond between two individuals.

Recent studies report that children who are abused or severely neglected may experience a drop in intelligence and increased risk of depression and suicide (*New York Times*, February 18, 1991, p. 11). As young children, they tend to be hyperactive, easily distracted, and unpopular with their peers. As adolescents and adults, they are more likely to abuse drugs or alcohol and to become involved in juvenile delinquency and violent crime.

Abuse does not have to be severe to cause problems. Our culture has long supported parental use of physical punishment, in the belief that spanking will control aggression in children and make them obey. "Spare the rod and spoil the child," the old saying goes. In fact, however, an adult who strikes a child is supplying the child with a model for physical aggression. Studies have found that frequent use of physical punishment results in a marked *increase* in the child's own aggression (Patterson, 1982; Walters and Grusec, 1977). Moreover, regular spanking and other forms of physical discipline can lay the groundwork for child abuse.

The good news is that a recent national poll found that the proportion of parents who admitted hitting a child even once in the preceding year dropped sharply, from 60 percent in 1989 to 50 percent in 1990 (*Chicago Tribune*, April 8, 1990, sec. 1, p. 5). This does not necessarily mean that fewer parents hit their children. It may mean instead that more of those who did so felt guilty enough to deny it. Still, these changing attitudes may be the first step toward changing behavior.

Some sociologists maintain that child abuse can end only when the social conditions that bring it about are alleviated (Gelles, 1974, 1985; Gil, 1974). This would involve identifying families at risk for abuse and providing them with the various forms of support and assistance they need (child-rearing classes, rent supplements, drug treatment, day care, and so forth). In general, researchers find that people use violence as a last resort, when they feel the need to compensate for a lack of such other resources as money, knowledge, and respect (D. A. Wolfe, 1985). Moreover, abusive parents are often socially isolated, with no one to turn to in times of stress. Parents Anonymous organizes support groups for abusive parents. Another approach is to make the physical punishment of children illegal, as Sweden has done. Removing society's stamp of approval for "spanking" makes relatives, neighbors, and others feel entitled to intervene. In the short term, it is important to identify child abusers and try to get them into treatment. All fifty states now have laws requiring doctors and teachers to report child abuse and neglect to the police; and public and private social services have been enlisted to help treat and prevent these problems (Straus and Gelles, 1986).

Wife Abuse

Force or the threat of force between husband and wife is also common in America. In nearly all cases, the husband is the attacker and the wife the victim. When a wife attacks her husband, the reason usually is that he has beaten her.

According to a national survey, about 1.4 million wives, or thirty in 1,000 women, are assaulted by their husbands in any given year (Gelles and Straus, 1988). The typical wife beater is young (between the ages of eighteen and twenty-four), has been married for less than ten years, and is employed part-time or not at all. He feels a need to play the role of male provider and to dominate his wife and children, but he lacks the social and economic resources to do so without physical force.

A number of researchers have tied wife battering to *status inconsistency*—that is, a gap between the role the man thinks he ought to play in relation to others and the actual position in which he finds himself. Although economic strain is most common among the poor and less educated, status inconsistency can occur at any social level. A man who has a college degree but drives a taxicab for a living experiences status inconsistency; so does a man whose wife is more steadily employed or earns more than he does. *Status ambiguity* may also lead to wife beating: A recent study found that cohabiting men are more likely to beat their partners than are husbands, perhaps because their role in the household is less clearly defined (Ellis, 1989).

Ultimately, the roots of wife abuse lie in our culture (Okun, 1986). The tradition of male superiority prescribes that the husband should always be in charge. Indeed, Western culture has traditionally approved the use of violence by husbands to "keep their wives in line." For most of recorded history a man who killed an unfaithful wife had the law on his side. Moreover, males are socialized in ways that reward them for acting tough. And male folklore and pornography portray females as enjoying aggressive treatment by males. (According to their wives, abusive husbands read more pornography than do nonabusive husbands; Sommers and Check, 1987.)

Many battered wives stay with abusive husbands. Compared with women who seek help or move out, they are more likely to be young, to have few job skills, to be unemployed, and to be mothers of small children (Gelles and Straus, 1988). Thus, they lack the social and economic resources, and in some cases the will, to leave. Typically, beatings alternate with periods of kindness and contrition, allowing the woman to hope that the problem has gone away (Walker, 1979). Often, battered wives are ashamed to admit to anyone what is happening; many blame them-

This photograph of an actual incident of wife beating is a shocking reminder that—despite the function of the family to institutionalize the love between two people, and despite cultural values that disapprove of domestic violence—for many women, marriage becomes a kind of prison.

selves for provoking their husbands. But contrary to popular belief, few passively accept abuse. Most report that they fight back during an attack and seek help to stop the violence (Gelles and Straus, 1988; Gondolf and Fisher, 1991).

Most experts agree that the most effective way to reduce wife abuse is to combine criminal sanctions for abusers with counseling and shelter for victims (Lerman and Cahn, 1991). Many communities lack the resources to implement this advice. At present, there are only about 1,000 shelters for battered women and their children in the United States—or one shelter for every 1,400 abused wives (Gelles and Straus, 1988).

Elder Abuse

The abuse of elderly people by members of their families is on the rise in our society. A survey conducted by the House of Representatives Select Committee on Aging (1990) found that at least 1.5 million elderly Americans, or one in twenty of the elderly population, are abused each year. Since maltreatment of older people is even less likely to be reported than child abuse is, the actual number may be even higher. Elder abuse may take the form of physical assaults (including sexual abuse), neglect (withholding food, medical treatment, or personal care necessary for well-being), financial abuse (theft or misuse of the older person's assets), or psychological abuse (including threats to abandon the elderly person in a nursing home).

Karl Pillemer (1986) compared forty-two physically abused elderly people with forty-two nonabused controls. The aim of the study was to determine what makes some older people victims of abuse. One common belief is that those who are physically impaired and therefore dependent on family members for feeding, bathing, and other sorts of care are most at risk because their needs put stress on the family member who is the caregiver. Pillemer found this hypothesis to be false. If anything, the abused elderly in the study were in better health and more independent than the controls. The critical difference between the two sets of families was that the abusers were dependent on the elders for housing, help with household repairs, financial assistance, and transportation. The abusers responded with violence to their own ongoing need for their aging parent, not to the parent's neediness. Pillemer also found that two-thirds of the abusers had mental or emotional problems or were alcoholics. There was no evidence that the abusers had been victims of family violence themselves; nor were they under chronic financial stress. This study suggests that the degree to which elderly Americans are at risk for abuse depends primarily on the characteristics of their caregivers.

THE FUTURE OF AMERICAN FAMILIES

No one would presume to predict the future of American families in every detail. Nevertheless, certain trends stand out. Clearly, "the normative imperatives to marry, to remain married, to have children, to restrict intimate relations to marriage, and to maintain separate roles for males and females" have weakened (Thornton, 1989, p. 873). Americans are much more tolerant of such unconventional arrangements and lifestyles as cohabitation, divorce, and childlessness. When researchers probe deeper, however, they find that Americans still place a high value on marriage, parenthood, and family life. In other words, a majority of Americans think it is all right for *other* people to remain single or voluntarily childless, or to divorce and remarry more than once, but they do not want these lifestyles for themselves.

The rates of cohabitation, single parenthood, divorce, and childless marriages—all of which increased steadily during the 1960s and 1970s—appear to be stabilizing. A 1991 Gallup Poll found that 93 percent of baby boomers (then aged thirty-six to forty-seven) said that family life was "very important" to them, and 73 percent said they expected to have a "happier family life" than their parents had. In another poll, two-thirds of the respondents said they thought "family values had grown weaker" across the country, but an equal number said they were "very" or "extremely" happy with their own family life (*New York Times*, December 29, 1991, p. E2). Thus, Americans may not be returning to the nuclear families of the 1950s, but neither are they giving up on the family. The challenge for society is to accommodate new family structures, especially to take them into account in deciding how schools and workplaces are to be run.

Thinking Back on the Key Concepts

Throughout this chapter we have seen how the five key concepts in sociology can help us understand important issues concerning the family in contemporary society. The family is the basic unit of ***functional integration*** for most people. It provides nurturance and support. Children of divorced parents may be faced with a situation in which their parents' distress inhibits this family function and may try to compensate for its loss. For some impoverished people, having a child out of wedlock enables them to get maximum benefits out of the welfare system and thus take advantage of the only means of functional integration available to them.

Basic changes in ***social structure*** have had far-reaching consequences for the family. The widespread incidence of divorce and remarriage has led to a greater variety of family organizations; single-parent families, blended families, dual-career families, and greater involvement of grandparents in child-rearing are all on the rise. As a result, people today face a wider range of possible ***social actions*** related to family life. Each of us must face the decision to marry, divorce, or pursue an alternative to the nuclear family, such as remaining single. These social actions play an important part in shaping the family and in enabling the family to fulfill its basic functions.

We have seen that ***culture*** also plays a critical role in shaping our values about family life, such as attitudes about love and marriage, the traditional nuclear family, and divorce. Indeed, the very definition of family depends on culture. For example, in polygamous societies the typical family consists of a husband or wife and two or more partners.

The role of ***power*** in the family is an issue of growing concern. As in the case of arranged marriages, power may become institutionalized. Abuse of power in the family is manifested by increased reports of violence against children, spouses, and elders.

SUMMARY

1. The family is a key element of social organization, charged with providing love and emotional security and regulating sexual behavior, reproduction, socialization, protection, and social placement.

2. Patterns of family organization vary among cultures and over time. Two basic forms are the nuclear family, emphasizing marital bonds, and the extended family, emphasizing blood ties. Rules of descent, residence, number of partners, and authority also vary among cultures.

3. Decisions involving marriage and divorce are both cultural and economic. Some societies arrange marriages, others value marriage for love, and many promote elements of both. Some societies do not permit divorce, while in others, such as our own, divorce is common.

4. Some marriages are more vulnerable to divorce than others. Women and children tend to experience a decline in their standard of living after divorce. The long-term effects of divorce can create serious problems for many individuals.

5. Although the traditional nuclear family is still valued in our society, the reality of American life is that this form is no longer prevalent. People are marrying later, delaying childbearing, and having smaller families. Nontraditional nuclear families include dual-career families, families in which grandparents play an active part, and blended families. Diverse household patterns—alternatives to the nuclear family—have become more common, including singlehood, childless marriages, and single-parent families.

6. Teenage pregnancy has reached record high levels in recent years. This seems to correlate most strongly with poverty, although there are also large ethnic variations in the teenage pregnancy rate. The social consequences of teenage pregnancy are drastic, for both the parent and the child.

7. Domestic violence causes serious and lasting problems for victims. Typical victims are wives who lack economic resources and job skills, children of young, impoverished parents, and dependent elderly. Some of the roots of domestic violence are cultural. Current efforts in the legal system and recent research attention have focused on the importance of preventing domestic violence.

REVIEW QUESTIONS

1. What functions are served by the family? Which one do you think is the most important, and why?

2. Provide some examples of how the family varies cross-culturally.

3. Explain the usefulness of such concepts as patrilocal, matrilocal, and neolocal residence; bilateral, patrilineal, and matrilineal descent; and patriarchy, matriarchy, and egalitarian authority patterns.

4. What are some of the sociological reasons behind the decisions whom and when to marry?

5. What are some sociological reasons for the current high divorce rate?

6. Compare the modern-day family with the traditional ideal.

7. Provide some basic data on alternatives to the nuclear family: singlehood, childless marriages, and single-parent families.

8. Provide some basic data on teenage pregnancy and family violence.

CRITICAL THINKING QUESTIONS

1. Describe your own family of orientation, family of procreation (present or future), and extended family.

2. The chapter notes that matriarchy has not been the norm in any society. Explain why this is so, drawing on at least three of the five key concepts (social structure, social action, functional integration, power, and culture).

3. Do you think the high divorce rate is good or bad? Using some sociological concepts and theories, explain your position.

4. Describe people you know who fit the alternatives to the nuclear family: singlehood, childless marriages, and single-parent families. Compare them with the profiles provided in the chapter.

5. Extend the chapter's analysis of the future of the family by drawing on the five key concepts and other family-related issues raised in previous chapters.

GLOSSARY

Bilateral descent The reckoning of descent through both the father's and mother's families.

Blended families Families formed by the marriage of two people one or both of whom also have children. Also called stepfamilies.

Dual-career family A family in which both husband and wife hold jobs that offer opportunities for professional advancement.

Egalitarian authority A pattern in which power within the family is vested equally in males and females.

Endogamy A rule that requires a person to marry someone from within his or her own group—tribe, nationality, religion, race, community, or other social grouping.

Exogamy A rule that requires a person to marry someone from outside his or her own group.

Extended family A household consisting of married couples from different generations, their children, and other relatives; the core family consists of blood relatives, with spouses being functionally marginal and peripheral.

Family Any group of people who are united by ties of marriage, ancestry, or adoption, having the responsibility for rearing children.

Family of orientation A nuclear family consisting of oneself and one's father, mother, and siblings.

Family of procreation A nuclear family consisting of oneself and one's spouse and children.

Marriage A socially recognized union between two or more individuals that typically involves sexual and economic rights and duties.

Matriarchy A pattern in which power within the family is invested in females.

Matrilineal descent The reckoning of descent through the mother's family only.

Matrilocal residence An arrangement in which the married couple, upon marriage, sets up housekeeping with or near the wife's family.

Monogamy Marriage restricted to one husband and one wife.

Neolocal residence An arrangement in which the married couple, upon marriage, sets up a new residence.

Nuclear family A household consisting of husband, wife, and their immature children; blood relatives are functionally marginal and peripheral.

Patriarchy A pattern in which power within the family is vested in males.

Patrilineal descent The reckoning of descent through the father's family only.

Patrilocal residence An arrangement in which the married couple, upon marriage, sets up housekeeping with or near the husband's family.

Polyandry Marriage consisting of one wife and two or more husbands.

Polygamy A marriage arrangement consisting of a husband or wife and more than one spouse.

Polygyny Marriage consisting of one husband and two or more wives.

CHAPTER PROJECTS

1. **Individual Project** Construct a chart contrasting the social structures of the nuclear and the extended family. Your chart should include a brief description of each type of social structure as well as the advantages and disadvantages of each.

2. **Cooperative Learning Project** The class should organize into three groups. The first group should find information on the nuclear family in the United States today. The second group should do the same with singlehood; the third with single-parent families. Each group should prepare a class presentation that includes charts and graphs showing recent statistical trends.

CHAPTER 13

Education

Cyril Simmons (1990), a British teacher and educational researcher, once asked a class of high school students to list all the Japanese products that they or their parents owned. A long list of consumer goods from Japan soon filled the blackboard. Then Simmons informed his students that in Japan, teenagers can quit school at fifteen if they wish. He asked them to guess the proportion of Japanese students who complete the remaining three years of high school. What do *you* think the proportion might be? If, like Simmons's students, your guess is 75 or 80 percent, you have not guessed high enough. In Japan almost 100 percent of adolescents finish their secondary schooling. What's more, Japanese students work very hard at their education. They spend more hours a day and more days a year in the classroom and do more homework than their Western counterparts. Whereas American teenagers spend their after-school hours hanging out or working at part-time jobs, a large percentage of Japanese adolescents sign up for after-school enrichment classes in academic subjects, privately paid for by their parents.

What could motivate young Japanese to devote so much more time and effort to schooling than most American or British teenagers do? And could their diligence be part of the secret to Japan's success in selling its cars and other goods all over the world? That possibility dawned on Simmons's students. Maybe, they thought, there is a connection between the Japanese enthusiasm for education and the high-quality Japanese products used so widely throughout the world. Education, after all, is related not just to an individual's success but also to an entire nation's ability to compete successfully in international markets. Awareness of this connection has led many Americans to question their own educational system and propose ways to improve it.

In this chapter we explore some of those proposals, as well as many other aspects of education. To sociologists, **education** is a structured form of socialization in which a culture's knowledge, skills, and values are formally transmitted from one generation to the next. In addition to the school, education may take place in a workplace, in a club, in a governmental organization, or even in front of a home computer or a television set. Whatever the setting, education is a conscious, intentional process. Those involved are aware that learning is *expected* to occur.

Although education is closely tied to the key concept of ***culture***, other key concepts are involved in it as well. Thus, education is shaped by ***power*** relations, such as the power of school administrators to determine a curriculum, or the power of teachers to decide which students pass and which ones fail. Moreover, every school and classroom has its own ***social structure***, its own patterns of social relationships, social positions, and numbers of people. At the same time, access to education is influenced by the structure of society as a whole, especially by the structured inequality that exists there. Society's ***functional integration*** affects education, too. For instance, when a country's economic system is changing, with old industries dying and new ones springing up, the disruptions to functional integration that occur put demands on education to teach young people new skills. Finally, educational experiences are always shaped by individual ***social action***. For example, when an adolescent decides to follow his brother's lead and work hard to get into college, he is assessing his situation, making a choice, and engaging in actions that involve not just himself, but other people too (family members, teachers, college personnel, and so forth).

In this chapter we begin with a look at the functions that educational institutions serve in society—the ways in which schools are connected to and support other parts of the social order. We then turn to the question of who gets what kind of education—that is, which American children get the best of public education and which get the worst. We move on to the issue of whether schools can do more to foster equal educational opportunity. We look particularly at the school's role relative to that of the family, and also at the impact that school desegregation has had. We next take up the current crisis in our public schools, especially the problem of illiteracy and the measures proposed to combat it. Finally, we consider higher education in our society: its structure, its benefits, and the millions of Americans who are currently involved in it.

THE SOCIAL FUNCTIONS OF SCHOOLS

In preindustrial societies, children are educated by their elders and peers in the course of daily activities. Girls watch women garden, cook, clean house, and care for children. Boys watch men farm, fish, hunt, herd livestock, and make tools. Through these informal observations, children learn the skills they will need when they grow up. They also acquire the beliefs and values of their culture informally, often by listening to the stories and myths that the elders tell. In modern societies, by contrast, there is too much to learn for all of education to be this loosely structured and informal. Instead, most of education is carried out in formal, specialized institutions, namely, schools.

Sociologists have studied how the "hidden curriculum" of the schools—the training in obedience, discipline, and conformity—has prepared the great masses of American society for jobs in factories and bureaucracies in which conformity and the repetition of simple tasks are much more important than creativity and problem-solving ability.

Schools teach reading, writing, arithmetic, and other academic skills, but they also do much more. They play a vital role in fostering the ***functional integration*** of society and in maintaining its hierarchical ***social structure***. This they do not only by teaching specific skills but also by instilling in children certain attitudes, beliefs, and behaviors that most people don't even think of as part of formal education. Learning self-discipline and the value of hard work, acquiring pride in one's country and its economic and political institutions, and becoming aware of one's "place" in society and being shaped to fit it well are some of the many lessons that are taught in schools. These lessons help produce people for the next generation who have internalized the established culture and who "fit" the existing social structure. Schools also support structural hierarchy by serving as a sorting mechanism that selects students for higher or lower social positions based on their academic performance.

In this section we look at several ways in which American schools perform these and other social functions. We begin by considering the school's role in teaching children the self-discipline they need to live in a world of impersonal rules and hierarchical organizations. This process has been called the *hidden curriculum.*

To Instill Self-Discipline

The **hidden curriculum** is the set of unwritten rules of behavior taught in school to prepare children for life outside the small, informally structured world of the family—that is, to prepare them for the world of large, formally structured organizations (Jackson, 1968). Learning self-discipline is a crucial part of this process. To succeed academically as well as socially, children must learn to be quiet, to line up, to wait, to act interested even when they are not, and to please their teachers without alienating their peers. These and other aspects of the hidden curriculum are taught alongside the regular, academic curriculum.

Kindergarten is the child's initiation into the world of formal organizations. In kindergarten, children learn to do what the teacher wants, when the teacher wants it done. The kindergarten teacher is the child's first boss. Learning to obey orders from a boss, to cope with contradictory evaluations, to tolerate frustration, and to be one among many are the very qualities people need if they are to function effectively in an office or a factory. In effect, the hidden curriculum is designed to mold students into good workers.

Most Americans agree that the hidden curriculum is necessary and desirable. When asked what qualities are important in a child's development, nearly as many adults answer "the ability to get along with others" as "learning to think for oneself." When asked how to improve the overall quality of education, people say "enforce stricter discipline" as often as "devote more time to teaching basic skills" (Gallup, 1983). Indeed, most Americans consider a lack of discipline to be one of the biggest problems in our schools. When parents are asked what factors would be most important if they had a choice in selecting their children's school, 95 percent say student discipline (Elam, 1990).

To Transmit and Reproduce Culture

Schools also help to keep alive many ideas and values of the ***culture*** by transmitting them to each new generation of children. They are taught what it means to be American or English or Russian or Chinese. This training involves the whole range of elements of culture (see Chapter 3), including values, beliefs, and language, as well as knowledge.

The elements of culture are not just passed along unaltered, like a book handed down from grandparent to parent to child. Rather, the transmission of culture in schools is more like a story that is adapted to fit the needs of a new generation when it's retold to them. For instance, a century ago American schools placed a much greater emphasis on discipline and obedience than they do today, because they were helping to turn out the thousands of factory workers needed to staff the new assembly lines. Today, as the number of people employed in factory jobs declines, employers are placing more emphasis on literacy and the conceptual skills needed by workers in the service and information industries. Schools have responded by revising their curriculums to encourage these abilities, but in the process they have not lost sight of traditional cultural values and assumptions. Hard work and diligence are still stressed within the new framework, and the cultural belief persists that schools should serve the needs of employers. In this way there is continuity to the culture transmitted by schools, even if some of the details of the lessons change with changing times.

As we saw in Chapter 3, however, American culture is not just one homogeneous whole in which every person and group shares equally. There are many subcultures, and there are disputes over some important elements of culture, such as whether our constitutional separation of church and state should prohibit the teaching or practice of religion in public schools. For the most part, schools teach a fairly generalized, mainstream version of American culture (although recently more effort has been made to reflect

In the one-room schoolhouses of the rural United States, older students learned advanced skills and helped the teacher with the instruction of their younger schoolmates. While this system of education now seems old-fashioned, there is no doubt that an educational setting in which learning and teaching roles are integrated provides for a more "organic" education.

American society's multicultural diversity in textbooks and classes). What is generally taught is a version of American culture that fits most closely the experience of white middle-class children; in schools, they learn more or less the same values and cultural orientations that their parents and grandparents learned before them. Children from working-class families, minority groups, and immigrant populations have a different experience; schools serve to draw them into the cultural mainstream in a way that diverges from the experience of their families and what they learn informally at home.

In school, cultural transmission is both direct (as when lessons are given in American history and government) and indirect (as when teachers give approval to students who show the "right" norms and values). Direct attempts to use schools to draw people into the cultural mainstream have been made in the United States throughout much of its history. For example, in response to the influx of immigrants at the turn of the century, the American Legion called for the "Americanization of America" through required classes in civics for students in public schools. At the same time, various states required schools to offer courses in American history, government, citizenship, the Constitution, and patriotism. Some states required that all schools teach only in English. For example, until the late 1960s, Texas law forbade that state's public schools to teach in any other language. These efforts persist today. In 1986, California passed a law that made English the state's "official language," partly as a reaction against bilingual education in the public schools.

From the standpoint of ***functional integration***, drawing people into the cultural mainstream is extremely valuable. For one thing, it is assumed to reduce the friction that cultural heterogeneity can bring. When a culture is homogeneous—that is, when people have the same beliefs, share the same values, and think in the same ways—the likelihood of interpersonal conflict is reduced. Widespread acceptance of the mainstream culture also reduces the chances that those at the bottom of the social hierarchy will rebel against the system. This rationale has long been offered for preserving free public schooling in the United States. During the Great Depression, for example, school boards were urged to maintain their support for universal education because it was good insurance against social radicalism. Thus, while our system of public education aims to prepare Americans to participate in a democratic society, it also emphasizes the creation of "good" citizens—that is, citizens who accept the basic rightness of American institutions. Schools try to mold such citizens by emphasizing the merits of the American way of life: our political and economic processes, our form of family life, even our educational system itself. In doing so, our schools give people a sense of shared identity and belonging, which fosters commitment and loyalty to the nation.

When we think about social ***power***, however, we must ask whether schools are *forcing* young people into the cultural mainstream, even against their will and the will of their parents. Observations of schools in African-American communities, in Mexican-American communities, and on Native American reservations support this view. For example, approximately a third of all Native American children attend boarding schools run by the federal government's white-dominated Bureau of Indian Affairs (Cornell, 1984). These schools were instituted in the nineteenth century for the express purpose of separating the children from their "savage" parents so that they might learn to be "Americans." Visits to and from the parents are discouraged. The result is that as many as 16,000 Native American children do not go to school at all because their parents refuse to send them away. Moreover, every year hundreds of other Native American youngsters run away from school, an indication of their deep dissatisfaction with being "Americanized."

Educational efforts to draw people into the cultural mainstream also mean that minority children find their heritages ignored or slighted in school curricula. Most American textbooks, for example, still give only brief consideration to Native Americans, Mexican-Americans, and African-Americans. The assumption in the schools has always been that minorities must be assimilated—for their own good—and that they cannot become truly Americanized unless they abandon their different ways. This view defines minority cultures as inferior and not worth preserving.

In the past fifteen to twenty years, largely as a result of the civil rights and women's movements, courses geared to minorities, such as black history, black literature, and women's studies, have been added to school curricula. But this has happened mainly in higher education. Minority students who do not go on to college are seldom exposed in school to information about any culture except the dominant one.

To Perpetuate the Socioeconomic Power Structure

Some sociologists have argued that schools are agencies by which those who hold power in capitalist societies perpetuate existing ***social structures*** and social-class ***power*** relations. This they do partly by saturating students with the language, symbols, values, and concepts of capitalism and by excluding those of any other ideology (Apple, 1979, 1982). Capitalism is also bolstered by the fact that schools in many ways mirror the capitalist workplace, and so prepare people to fit into the economic system. Schools, it is argued, are authoritarian in structure, much like a bureaucratic corporation, and schools promote submissiveness and diligence, characteristics desired by capitalist enterprise (Bowles and Gintis, 1976).

Sociologists who focus on the school's role in perpetuating the capitalist power structure believe that schools don't socialize everyone for the same social roles. Schools, they maintain, socialize students from different social backgrounds differently, in ways that are consistent with their future places in society. Schools, in other words, teach different "status cultures" (a concept of Max Weber's); they teach the culture that is typical of a certain social status. Thus, teachers in middle- and upper-class schools stress proper English, whereas teachers in working-class or slum schools may permit ethnic slang and street grammar in the classroom. Topics brought up for class discussion are also likely to differ, reflecting social-class differences in leisure-time activities, entertainment, and so forth. The result of all these differences is that middle-class students will fit more easily into society's higher-status positions. They will know how to speak and act in these positions and will have that important (if intangible) asset, a middle-class "background." Less advantaged students, in contrast, marked by their speech, manners, and past experiences, will have been socialized to fit into the status culture of the blue-collar worker. A study by Paul Willis (1977), which we discussed in detail in Chapter 5, indicated that working-class students may even contribute to their own deprivation by rebelling against the school culture that is biased against them—and thus may fail to benefit from the advantages it does offer them.

Martin Carnoy and Henry Levin (1985) argue that schools not only perpetuate the existing socioeconomic order but challenge it. Schools mirror many aspects of the larger social order (particularly the workplace), but they are also generally characterized by greater equality than exists in the rest of society. In short, "public education both reproduces the unequal hierarchical relations of the nuclear family and capitalist workplace and also presents opportunities for social mobility and the extension of democratic rights" (Carnoy and Levin, 1985, p. 76). According to Carnoy and Levin, there is an inherent tension between the ideological goals on which the American educational system was partially based and the practical needs of capitalist employers. On the one hand, there are pressures to make schools serve the democratic purpose of training citizens for political participation. On the other hand, there are pressures to make education serve the needs of capitalism by supplying the kind of work force it requires. Throughout their history, American schools have responded to both types of pressures, sometimes being more oriented toward the demands of capitalism and sometimes being more democratically oriented.

These cross-pressures can be seen in the history of community colleges. Based on the model of earlier two-year colleges aimed largely at female students who were not thought to need four-year programs, community colleges were greatly expanded in the 1960s. The reasons came from the pressure for democracy. Community colleges were to provide access to higher education for students with limited financial resources, who did poorly in high school, who want to stay close to their families, or who choose careers whose credentials do not require longer courses of study (Richard J. Ernst, "The Community College: Separate But Equal," *Washington Post*, 21 May 1989). However, in many states and localities, the capitalist pressure soon made itself felt. Local businesses began to rely on community colleges to provide students with basic job skills. Often, indeed, employers explicitly lobbied community college administrators to get them to place greater emphasis on the specific skills they needed in their companies, so that they would not have to bear the training costs themselves (Brint and Karabel, 1989). The proportion of community college students studying liberal arts courses with the intention of transferring to a four-year school declined in those states where this business dominance of community colleges was strongest. In these cases, the democratic idea of increasing opportunities for upward social mobility was limited by the capitalist demand for trained workers.

To Select Talent

Ideally, from the standpoint of ***functional integration***, the educational system should ignore a student's social-class background and prepare him or her for whatever career that student has the ability to fill. Providing equal opportunity to all students so that anyone with talent can rise to the top is a fundamental rationale for American public education.

In fact, however, the selection of students for high achievement at school is determined by many factors other than just talent. Social ***power*** can play an important part. For one thing, wealthier parents are able to ensure that their children go to better schools. For another, teachers are often prejudiced in favor of students with middle- or upper-class manners, speech, and dress. This was suggested by findings that researcher Ray Rist made when he studied an all-black kindergarten with a black faculty (Rist, 1970). After only eight days of school, the students were permanently assigned to three separate worktables based on the teacher's perception of their academic abilities. Table 3, the lowest-ability table, was at the back of the classroom, farthest away from the teacher; table 2 was in the middle; and table 1, assigned to the highest-ability pupils, was at the front of the room. Rist discovered that the teacher's perceptions of ability were based on socioeconomic criteria: Middle-class students were assigned to table 1, and those from poorer families were assigned to tables 2 and 3.

These table assignments wouldn't be important if the teacher had given all her students equal encouragement and attention; but she didn't. She tended to ignore the children whom she presumed to be "slow," and in time they disengaged from classroom activities. When reading-readiness tests were given at the end of the year, the table 1 children scored highest. Moreover, as the children progressed through elementary school, the categories and labels stuck. In the first grade, table 1 students were dubbed the Tigers and were placed in the "high" group. The children from tables 2 and 3 became Cardinals and Clowns and were given less demanding readers. The IQ scores of the Cardinals and Clowns were not significantly lower than those of the Tigers, but the Cardinals and Clowns were never really given a chance to catch up.

This study suggests that teachers' perceptions of ability based on social class can become *self-fulfilling prophecies*—that is, they can evoke behavior that helps to make those perceptions come true. By the time a child is categorized as a Clown, teachers and fellow students have formed an idea of how he or she will behave in school. Clowns, as the name suggests, are not expected to do well; and given this expectation, they are unlikely to. So even if the initial negative assessments are based on completely irrelevant grounds, the Clowns are encouraged to behave as others expect, thus fulfilling the prophecy of poor academic performance. The underlying force behind the self-fulfilling prophecy is labeling (discussed in Chapter 7). When students are called Clowns and are viewed by others as being "the dumb group," they may eventually accept these negative labels and stop trying to do well.

The self-fulfilling prophecy helps to explain why throughout the twentieth century, despite our society's equal-opportunity ideal, the privileged classes have maintained their advantage over the poorer classes in being singled out for higher education and completing more years of schooling (Mare, 1981). Granted, between 1965 (when the Higher Education Act was passed as part of President Lyndon Johnson's War on Poverty) and the mid-

1970s, there were modest gains in college enrollments among low-income students. At least half these gains were lost during the 1980s, however, so that today a student whose family is in the bottom quarter of the income range is only about a tenth as likely as an affluent student (in the top income quarter) to complete four years of college by the age of twenty-four (Mortenson, 1991).

One of the ways in which opportunities remain open for talented students from less wealthy families is through the community college system. Community colleges and other two-year institutions have expanded rapidly since the 1960s, and now enroll nearly 40% of American undergraduates (*Digest of Educational Statistics*, 1990). Students attending community colleges are more likely than those at four-year institutions to come from families in which the parents have no more than a high school education (Astin, Korn, and Berz, 1989). They have also increased access to higher education for minority students and immigrants.

Community colleges are significant in regard to the talent selection function of higher education both for students seeking to transfer to four-year schools and for those seeking job skills and credentials in two years.

First, community colleges provide an opportunity for students who would not otherwise have a chance at college degrees to demonstrate their potential. Thus a student who could not afford to attend a four-year college or university may be able to go to a community college. So can a student whose high school grades would not enable him or her to get into a competitive college or university. If he or she does well in community college courses, transfer places and even scholarships are open at many of the country's best four-year schools.

Second, community colleges are crucial in helping employers select the most talented students for jobs that do not require college degrees. High school diplomas are now common enough that they do not distinguish adequately among the talents and preparation of potential applicants even for jobs that require no specific credentials. Grades and letters of recommendation from community college instructors enable prospective employers to choose the best applicants. In many fields, community colleges also provide job-specific training to assist students in developing talents that do not require four-year college degrees.

Despite the availability of community colleges, the selection of students for advancement in American higher education is not on the basis of talent alone. At all levels, students' social backgrounds make a difference too. Women are more likely to be advised to become nurses or bookkeepers, men to become doctors or accountants. Working class students are less likely to attend the most elite colleges and universities—and these are the ones that

For centuries, education in basic skills took place within the family. As specific trades developed, such as blacksmithing, a formal method of training emerged called apprenticeship. This system moved training out of the family but preserved the traditional pattern in which sons followed fathers' occupations.

bring the biggest payoff in expected lifetime earnings. In addition to bias on the part of admissions offices, key reasons include the fact that working class students often need to work full-time and attend school only part-time, that they cannot afford to live away from home, and that their communities do not offer as much information about which educational opportunities might bring them the biggest return on their investment of time and effort.

At the same time, higher education in the United States remains relatively open to selection on the basis of talent. While the U.S. does not have the highest college graduation rate in the world (Canada does), the U.S. has the highest rate of entry into full-time higher education (*Education at a Glance*. OECD *Indicators*. Paris: OECD Publications, 1993). This means that more people at least get a chance to prove themselves or discover their talents in college. And one of the biggest differences is the increasing openness to "non-traditional students," especially those who didn't complete college when they were 18–22 years old, but instead are getting their college educations after several years in other occupations. In many other countries (as to a large extent in the U.S. in earlier years), such students would have been frozen out of a chance at college education, no matter what their talents.

To Teach Skills

We turn last to the most obvious function of schools: to equip people with the capabilities they need for effective participation in modern societies. This task involves teaching young people basic skills (reading, writing, and arithmetic); developing their ability to reason and solve problems; and providing them with both general knowledge and specific information to be used in their jobs.

Most respondents in a 1990 Gallup Poll said that mathematics, English, history and American government, science, computers, careers, and business should be required courses for all high school students, whether they are college-bound or not. For those students who intend to go to college, most people felt that geography and foreign languages should be required too (Elam, 1990). Most people think American schools are not stressing these courses. In the same poll, a majority of respondents said that every one of these subjects should be emphasized more in high school than they currently are.

Considerable evidence suggests that public schools are failing in the all-important task of teaching basic skills. Even if the United States does well by those students who go on to college, this is a serious problem. As many as one young adult in three is functionally illiterate—that is, unable to read at an eighth-grade level (Fiske, 1986a). The rate of functional illiteracy among minority youth is even higher than the national average: about 40 percent. Few seventeen-year-olds can express their thoughts effectively in writing. Although their spelling and grammar are adequate, they use short, childlike sentences and cannot organize coherent paragraphs (National Commission on Excellence in Education, 1983). A similar pattern is evident in arithmetic skills. Most young adults can perform basic mathematical operations, but they have trouble using these operations to solve problems. Less than half can figure out the most economical size of a product, like laundry detergent; only 45 percent can read a federal income tax table; and just 1 percent can balance a checkbook (National Assessment of Educational Progress, 1979). Between 1975 and 1980, remedial math courses in public four-year colleges increased by 72 percent and now constitute a fourth of all math courses taught in these institutions (National Commission on Excellence in Education, 1983). In the area of vocational education, community colleges now increasingly are called on to provide students with the minimum credentials and skills needed for first jobs. This may involve partly the ineffectiveness of high-school based vocational education. It also reflects the enormous range of technical skills needed by workers in today's society. Northern Virginia Community College alone, for example, offers 87 highly specialized technical and occupational programs in such fields as aviation technology, dental hygiene, electronics, computer maintenance, nursing and veterinary technology. Many students seeking these technical skills do not come straight out of high school, but attend community college courses for new training after working for many years and even after earlier college education in other fields.

WHO GETS WHAT KIND OF EDUCATION?

A high level of attainment at high-quality schools is the gateway to economic and professional opportunity. A high level of educational attainment also means credentials (diplomas, degrees, certifications), a kind of educational seal of approval, which is increasingly important in American society. Yet in the United States high educational achievement is far more readily available to some kinds of people than to others.

Discrimination, Tracking, and Ability

We have already said that going to college depends in part on students' socioeconomic backgrounds (Lee, 1985).

While education is theoretically available to all, the reality of local funding for education produces schools that match their social and economic settings. Thus poor children, often isolated in inner cities, attend dangerous, overcrowded, and poorly equipped schools in which teachers are typically less well trained and more overworked than their suburban counterparts. At this New York City high school an armed guard screens all who enter.

cially for the lowest-income students), modern buildings, up-to-date texts and curricula, and higher expenditures per pupil did not. Rather, it was the child's social environment—especially the attitudes and behaviors of family members and peers—that seemed to set the stage for academic success or failure. Schools, in other words, were seldom able to compensate for a child's lack of opportunity to practice important cognitive skills (reading, writing, computation, listening and speaking, problem solving) outside the classroom (R. Clark, 1990).

The crucial finding of the Coleman Report was that the social environment of students was the main factor related to their school achievement; socially advantaged children were more likely to do well in school. The courts, interpreting the report, drew the conclusion that every child within a school district had an equal right to be in a school with a comparable distribution of "advantaged" and "disadvantaged" children. Since advantaged status was correlated with race, this interpretation provided a rationale for redistributing children throughout a school system—usually by busing (see the next section). Coleman himself thought that focusing directly on the "contextual" factors that affected learning (exposure to reading and writing, for example) made more sense than trying to solve problems of inequality by moving children around. (He has since elaborated this view and argued against the use the courts made of his findings; see Coleman and Hoffer, 1987.) The Coleman Report did provide a strong rationale for **compensatory education**, enrichment programs that help students from disadvantaged backgrounds to "catch up" with more privileged students. Coleman argued that to achieve true equality of opportunity, American society must provide each person with an equal chance of achieving a certain level of success. In education, equal opportunity will exist when no children are at a disadvantage in school simply because they lack the learning experiences outside the classroom that other children enjoy.

A few years after the Coleman Report was published, Christopher Jencks and his colleagues took Coleman's diagnosis one step further in a book called *Inequality* (1972). The Jencks group, too, found that social inequality outside the classroom is the major determinant of inequality within it. Jencks argued that schools could do nothing about this fact; they could not be miracle workers and "fix" social inequality in society as a whole. Reforming the schools would not alter the differences in power and privilege that have always been part of the American social structure. Instead, Jencks argued that inequality should be attacked directly, not through educational reform.

Other researchers have challenged both the methods and conclusions of Coleman's and Jencks's work. They argue that there are indeed qualitative differences in schools, and that these differences do affect scholastic achievement and students' opportunities in the larger society. For instance, an English group headed by Michael Rutter criticized Coleman's study for using crude measures and for never finding out what actually went on inside the schools (Rutter et al., 1979). (Jencks's study has been criticized on similar grounds.) Rutter and his colleagues also pointed out that a cross-sectional survey like Coleman's cannot measure changes over time, as a longitudinal study can.

In their study, Rutter and his colleagues carefully assessed ten-year-olds in inner-city London schools, measuring their verbal and reading abilities, their family backgrounds, their behavior problems, and so forth. They also assessed in detail the quality of the schools, using surveys, classroom observations, and interviews. They then repeated the process four years later to see whether anything had changed for these students. Unlike Coleman, these researchers found that some schools were superior to others in that their students performed and behaved better than students of similar background and ability did at other schools. What made good schools good was primarily how teachers taught. In good schools there was a strong emphasis on academic achievement. Students were given regular homework, and their work was carefully checked. They were expected to master their assignments, and they were rewarded for good performance. Although the teachers enforced clear standards of discipline, they made school a comfortable place for students by doing such things as decorating their classrooms and being available to talk about personal problems.

These findings have been supported by a study of effective schools in the United States conducted by researchers at the Harvard School of Education (Williams, Huck, Ma, and Monroe, 1981). Apparently, good teaching can make more of a difference to scholastic achievement among children from disadvantaged backgrounds than Coleman originally believed.

More recently, Jonathan Kozol (1992) has documented the "savage inequalities" that distinguish schools in relatively rich, often suburban, districts from those in inner-city and rural areas. While some schools have enough computers for every student to practice with, for example, others have none. Such inequalities affect children's learning opportunities. Studies like Rutter's and Kozol's provide support for the courts' attempts to promote greater equality of opportunity by providing a more equal distribution of races and resources in schools.

Desegregation and Busing

As we noted above, the Coleman Report was commissioned by the Civil Rights Act of 1964. The courts therefore approached it not as an academic exercise, but in the context of cases that alleged that segregated schools violated the constitutional rights of students like Linda Brown. It was not the task of the courts to attack broader community factors that affected learning, or to attack inequality directly (as Jencks would urge), but to decide whether it was in their power to right the wrongs caused by segregation. They chose to do this by ordering the busing of students to create roughly the same racial balance in each of a school district's schools. Busing proved to be very effective (Sheppard, 1981). In the late 1960s it prompted a massive reduction in public school segregation, especially in the South. Fewer blacks now attend highly segregated schools in the South than in the North (Fiske, 1987).

Despite its effectiveness in achieving desegregation (and despite support of integration by a majority of the American people), busing has never been popular (Formisano, 1991). Opponents of busing—particularly middle-class whites, but also many blacks—say that its costs outweigh its benefits. Parents feel unfamiliar with their children's new school and worry about its safety. They think that the time spent riding the bus to and from school could be better spent on homework or extracurricular activities, and they believe that community spirit declines without a neighborhood school (Armor, 1989). Perhaps most important, they raise the issue of **white flight**. Given mandatory busing, some white parents remove their children from public schools, either sending them to private schools or moving to a predominantly white suburb not affected by busing. As a result, the ratio of blacks to whites in inner-city schools has risen significantly, until some of these schools closely resemble the old segregated schools of the past. Of course, massive white flight hasn't occurred in every city with mandatory busing, but in some cities the exodus has been sizable enough to cause great concern (Armor, 1989; Taeuber, 1990). In Norfolk, Virginia, for instance, the federal courts actually ordered a halt to busing in the lower elementary grades in an effort to halt white flight (Armor, 1991). This effort has been controversial, however, because some believe that white flight from the cities is a trend that would continue even without

Although forced busing has equalized educational experiences to some extent, it has often reinforced the prevailing racism, which children learn from their elders.

mandatory busing (Carr and Zeigler, 1990; F. Wilson, 1985). In many Southern towns where busing was never used to achieve integration, private schools were still founded to provide less integrated education for white children.

The growing proportion of black and Hispanic students in many inner-city schools creates new challenges for public policy. Should we find new ways to bring more whites into these school districts (perhaps busing them from distant suburbs), or should we focus on improving the quality of inner-city schools without worrying so much about the racial mix of their students? The answer depends partly on one's reason for supporting school desegregation. If the main reason is to increase educational opportunity for minority students until their level of scholastic achievement is on a par with that of whites, there may be other, even more effective, ways of achieving this goal than racial integration (J. S. Coleman, 1990a). If the main reason for supporting desegregation is to lay the groundwork for a truly multiracial society, however, then the problem of white flight from the cities cannot be ignored. Probably, throughout the 1990s, both these issues will remain on the public agenda. Certainly the issue of improving the quality of public schools is important not just in inner-city districts, but throughout the country. It is the central focus of what has become a crisis in American education.

PUBLIC SCHOOLS IN CRISIS

In a 1990 Gallup Poll on attitudes toward public schools, only 22 percent of Americans felt that the schools in their communities had improved over the last five years. Drug abuse, lack of discipline, inadequate financial support, and poor curricula and academic standards were cited as the four biggest problems that American public schools face (Elam, 1990).

Criticisms of public education come from all segments of society (see the box "How Americans Grade the Public School System"). Parents, educators, politicians, and journalists charge that American public schools today are failing to meet many of the basic goals for education that we discussed at the beginning of this chapter. Schools are not imposing the discipline needed to prepare young people for their adult roles as workers. Schools are not sufficiently stressing the core American values required to integrate our heterogeneous population and reduce divisive conflicts. Schools have lowered academic standards so far that a person can now graduate from high school and barely be literate. Employers complain of job candidates who can't read and write well enough to fill out an application. Studies reveal that a disturbing number of high school graduates lack a basic knowledge of our country's geography and governmental system, let alone those of other nations (Ravitch and Finn, 1987). Schools also seem slow to respond to the needs of a changing society. Many students graduate from high school today with little knowledge of computers and no ability to speak a foreign language, despite the increasing globalization of the American economy.

What are the reasons for this growing crisis in American education? It is not that today's students are less capable than they once were, less talented than those in other countries with higher levels of academic achievement. This is suggested by the fact that some schools *are* able to extract a high level of performance, particularly private schools. James Coleman and his associates (1987) have found that private school students in general have higher levels of academic achievement than their public school peers from similar socioeconomic backgrounds. This is true not just of students in elite boarding schools, but also of those who attend Catholic and other religious schools, many of whom are from working-class homes. Private school students are also more likely to go to college than their public school peers. This difference exists even when factors such as academic track, ability, educational aspirations, and socioeconomic class are held constant.

The superior record of private schools is probably due in part to the higher levels of order and discipline that they demand from students. It may also result from the extra encouragement that a private school teacher can offer, from the fact that many private schools consider college an important goal for most of their students, and from the greater commitment that parents who choose private schools have to their children's education. Most Catholic schools, for instance, place in an academic track many students who in a public high school would receive a general or vocational curriculum. They also require more advanced work from

Despite all the problems of education in the United States, there are many well-run, successfully integrated public schools in which children of different ethnic groups and social classes work together happily.

students and give them more homework assignments, especially their students from disadvantaged backgrounds (J. S. Coleman, 1990a). The students, it seems, live up to these higher demands and expectations and perform better than they would in most public schools. So, if public schools are failing in this country, it is not because the students who attend them lack academic potential.

The Increase in Functional Illiteracy

One of the most disturbing aspects of the crisis in public education is the fact that 25 million Americans are functionally illiterate—that is, they emerge from school unable to read and write at the fourth-grade level or better. Although the United States, as a nation of immigrants, has always had a sizable number of citizens who have trouble

How Americans Grade the Public School System

In the midst of the current debate over how well American schools are serving the needs of American society and its students, *Business Week* magazine (Segal, 1992) decided to conduct a sociological survey to find out what Americans think about the subject. They hired the well-known opinion-polling firm of Louis Harris & Associates to do the research in August 1992. The polltakers followed the general procedures for survey research that we discussed in Chapter 2. They began by establishing a representative sample of the entire U.S. population. In this case, they located 1,250 adults who fit the national pattern of variation in such characteristics as sex, racial and ethnic background, and level of education and income. Each respondent was then called on the telephone and asked to choose from a list of possible answers to various questions. From the responses, the researchers were able to get the following picture (accurate to within 3 percentage points) of what Americans think about their public schools and how the schools might be improved.

Improvements Needed

■ In general, how would you rate the quality of American public schools—excellent, pretty good, only fair, or poor?

Response	%
Excellent	3%
Pretty good	36%
Only fair	36%
Poor	23%
Not sure	2%

A Direct Stake

■ Do you have a child or grandchild who is currently attending or has attended U.S. public schools in the past five years, or not?

Yes . . 52% No . . 47% Not sure . . 1%

Family Report

■ (If yes:) How would you rate the quality of those schools—excellent, pretty good, only fair, or poor?

Response	%
Excellent	16%
Pretty good	44%
Only fair	29%
Poor	10%
Not sure	1%

Neighbors' View

■ (If no:) How would you rate the quality of the public schools in your local community—excellent, pretty good, only fair, or poor?

Response	%
Excellent	12%
Pretty good	43%
Only fair	25%
Poor	17%
Not sure	3%

What's Going Wrong

■ Within the public school system, is each of the following a very serious problem, a somewhat serious problem, not a very serious problem, or not a problem at all?

	Very serious	Somewhat serious	Not very serious	Not a problem	Not sure
A lack of parental involvement with children's education	56%	26%	9%	6%	3%
A shortage of teachers	37%	23%	18%	18%	4%
An insufficiently challenging curriculum	33%	31%	16%	13%	7%
Too many administrative rules governing individual schools	25%	37%	22%	9%	7%
A lack of up-to-date computers and equipment	24%	30%	24%	16%	6%
A short school year	18%	24%	25%	28%	5%

School Bucks

■ Even if it might mean higher taxes, would you favor spending more money on your community's public schools, or would you favor spending less or about the same amount of money?

Response	%
More	47%
Less	8%
About the same	43%
Not sure	2%

reading and writing (Graubard, 1990), the problem seems to be growing. This is an unprecedented reversal. Through American history, until ten or fifteen years ago, our society made continual progress in the proportion of adults who could read and write. Now, however, we seem to be moving backward and experiencing an increase in the percentage of functionally illiterate Americans.

According to a study supported by the federal government, one young adult in three is barely literate (Kirsch and Jungeblut, 1986). About 20 percent can't understand what the label on a can of drain cleaner says to do if a child swallows some of the contents. About 30 percent can't compose a simple letter to report an error on a bill. The proportion who lack this fundamental writing skill rises to 60 percent among blacks, and between 60 and 80 percent among high school dropouts (depending on the

Leveling the Learning Field

■ Now I'd like to read you a series of statements about public school education in this country. Tell me whether you agree or disagree with each statement.

	Agree	Disagree	Not sure
School districts that decide to raise more money to pay for better schools should be allowed to do so	86%	13%	1%
Children should be able to attend any school they qualify for, including public, parochial, or private schools, with government money going to poor or middle-income children attending private or parochial schools	69%	29%	2%
Children should be able to attend the public school of their choice, including one out of their district, with government money going to the school they attend	63%	35%	2%
To ensure more equal spending among districts, financing of the public school system should be taken out of the hands of local government and moved toward federal or state governments	43%	52%	5%
Most of the money for schools should continue to come from local taxes, not state or federal taxes	41%	56%	3%

Back to Basics

■ Do you favor or oppose each of the following proposed changes to the curriculum in public schools?

	Favor	Oppose	Not sure
Putting more emphasis on teaching tougher, more challenging basics such as reading, writing, math, and science	96%	3%	1%
Teaching more practical skills that can be used in the work force	92%	7%	1%
Raising requirements for passing courses and graduating	80%	18%	2%
Teaching more about foreign countries and languages	71%	27%	2%
Teaching a broader, more enriched curriculum, including more arts and music	67%	32%	1%

Teachers' Paychecks

■ Bearing in mind that they are paid out of taxes, do you think public school teachers are paid enough, too little, or too much?

Enough	35%
Too little	55%
Too much	6%
Not sure	4%

number of years of school they've completed). At the lowest level of competence, about 6 percent of all American adults can't read and write at the fourth-grade level (educators' cutoff point for basic literacy). This means that they can't understand a typical newspaper headline, a road sign, or a fast-food restaurant menu (King and Weaver, 1986; Mikulecky, 1990). About 75 percent of those who are unemployed are functionally illiterate, which is not surprising since reading skills are required for most jobs in our society (Public Agenda Foundation, 1990).

Schools alone are not responsible for the problem of illiteracy. Many social forces besides formal education influence the learning of reading and writing skills. Still, schools are assumed to have failed in a fundamental way if they turn out a great many students who cannot read a road map, make sense of a train schedule, or comprehend simple written instructions. The reasons for this failure are a matter for debate. David Hawkins (1990) argues that schools have taught the rudiments of reading and writing, such as letter and word recognition, spelling, and grammar. But they have done little to develop the motivation to read by supplying children with a rich assortment of good, appropriate books. When students are exposed only to textbooks and worksheets, they don't acquire an interest in reading and writing that stays with them outside the classroom. The process is rather like using charts and verbal instruction to teach someone to swim, instead of letting him or her spend time in the pool. The person will know the principles of swimming, but is unlikely to be a good swimmer.

Reactions and Reforms

In 1983, a commission appointed to study the problems of American education published a report entitled *A Nation at Risk: The Imperative for Educational Reform.* The commission declared that the educational system was deficient in major ways. Schools weren't emphasizing the right subjects, teachers weren't demanding enough effort from students, and young people were graduating with an appalling lack of basic skills and knowledge. The commission wasn't alone in its criticisms, moreover. Many other studies at the time were concluding the same thing: American public education simply wasn't working, and it was time for fundamental change.

Many politicians and others took up the education crusade. George Bush declared that he wished to be the "education president." He asked the nation's governors to help put together a plan to achieve educational excellence by the year 2000. The late 1980s saw a wave of educational reforms in many states, including mandatory kindergartens, more hours in the classroom, stiffer graduation requirements, literacy tests for teachers, and administrative reorganizations. But today, although the bill for public education is over 30 percent higher than it was in the early 1980s, the improvement curve is virtually flat (Doyle, Cooper, and Trachtman, 1991). President Bush's lack of effective action on education was an issue that gave an edge to Democratic candidate Bill Clinton in their 1992 presidential race.

Achievement-test scores aren't rising. In international comparisons of performance in math and science, American students continue to score near the bottom (see Figure 13.4). American students also display a dismal lack of knowledge regarding basic facts about history, government, economics, and geography. Most can't say when Lincoln was president, what a budget deficit is, or where Greece is located on a map of Europe (Finn, 1989b).

Most observers now agree that far-reaching changes are needed to turn American education around. Many have urged improving the quality of teachers. Some steps toward this goal were taken in the 1980s when many states raised their standards for teacher certification and introduced some kind of performance-based pay (master teacher classifications, incentive programs, merit pay, and so forth). Measures to improve teacher training have also been proposed (Goodlad, 1990). The Holmes Group, consisting of deans of education and other academic officers from universities across the country, has suggested that teachers' undergraduate work should provide a solid liberal arts background and that they should take education courses only at the graduate level. Several other task forces and panels have echoed this proposal (Fiske, 1986b). The assumption is that "four years of college education is not enough time to master the subjects to be taught and acquire the skills to teach them" (Carnegie Task Force on Teaching as a Profession, 1986, p. 73).

Another proposal is to provide alternatives to schools of education as the route to teacher certification. The rationale is to open up a career in teaching to a broad range of bright, committed, well-educated college graduates who are now effectively screened out of the teaching profession because they have no formal training in education. In order to be eligible for a teaching certificate, such a person normally has to return to college for two or three more years and then do a semester of student teaching without pay. In an alternative certification program, a person would receive teacher training as an intern in a public school, while also taking graduate education courses in a nearby university. The interns, who get modest salaries, are under the supervision of a master teacher who serves

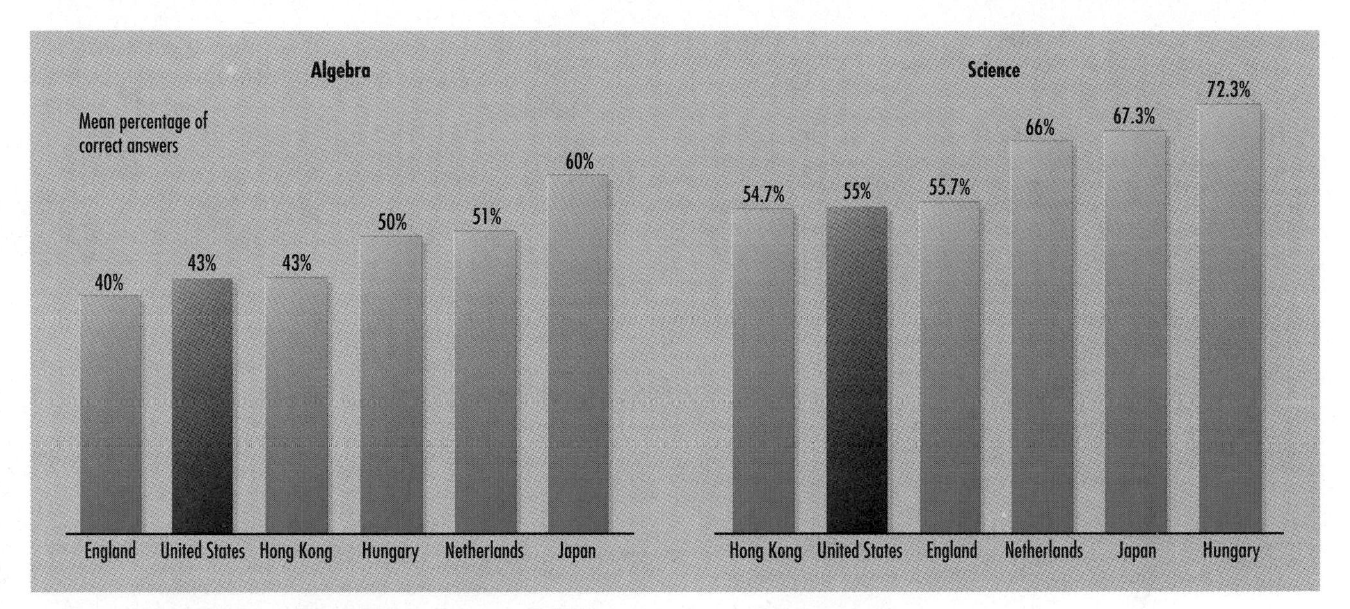

FIGURE 13.4 / Performance on Math and Science Achievement Tests by Junior High School Students in Six Countries

Source: International Association for the Evaluation of Education Achievement, in Public Agenda Foundation, *Regaining the Competitive Edge* (Kendall/Hunt, Dubuque, Iowa, 1990), p. 34.

as their mentor. In Texas, minority-group teachers certified through the new alternative route tend to score significantly higher on the traditional exit exam than those certified in the conventional way (Dill, 1990).

A third approach to educational reform is the empowerment of individual schools to make important decisions about budgets, staffing, and curricula, rather than having these decisions made by centralized state bureaucracies. The assumption is that when local school committees of administrators, teachers, parents, and community leaders are given the power to structure their schools as they wish, they will work harder and smarter to find ways of improving the quality of education (Glickman, 1990).

A fourth approach is educational choice, which refers to giving parents the freedom to choose which schools their children attend. Schools with poor records of achievement would be forced to improve the quality of their programs or lose students and the funding they bring (Chubb and Moe, 1990). Minnesota, for example, now has a statewide system of educational choice, with enrollment in all of its public schools open to any state resident. Since this system was started in the late 1980s, some Minnesota public high schools have upgraded their curricula in an effort to attract good students (Segal, 1992). (However, only 1 percent of the state's 500,000 students have actually changed schools.) A different kind of educational choice is being tried in the city of Milwaukee, where some students from low-income families are being given public funds, in the form of "vouchers," to leave the ailing public school system and enroll in private schools instead (Doyle, Cooper, and Trachtman, 1991). As yet, students who have chosen private school have not made substantial academic gains, and 25 percent of the participants left the program in 1992 (Segal, 1992).

Another proposal has been to create more schools that will break the mold of traditional education and develop more effective, innovative ways of teaching. This idea builds on the concept of magnet schools that has flourished since the 1980s. Many **magnet schools** are public schools with high academic standards and curricula that are specialized in a particular field, such as math, science, or the arts. There are now about 5,000 magnet schools in the United States. Most are located in urban areas, and many have excellent records of achievement (Toch, Linnon, and Cooper, 1991). The New American School idea is a way of extending the kinds of innovations that exist in the best magnet programs to a larger number of communities across the country.

The need to innovate in American education, to pass on knowledge in a more effective, compelling way, intensifies every year. The National Commission on Excellence in Education stressed this need in *A Nation at Risk*:

> The world is indeed one global village. We live among determined, well-educated, and strongly motivated competitors. We compete with them for international standing and markets, not only with products but also with the ideas of our laboratories and neighborhood workshops. . . . Knowledge, learning, information, and skilled intelligence are the new raw materials of international commerce and are today spreading throughout the world as vigorously as miracle drugs, synthetic fertilizers, and blue jeans did earlier. . . . Learning is the indispensable investment required for success in the "information age" we are entering. (1983, pp. 6–7)

TODAY'S COLLEGE STUDENTS

In 1991, over 20 percent of our adult population had completed four years of college or more, and that proportion was growing (U.S. Bureau of the Census, 1991b, p. 1). In this section we profile this ever-increasing pool of college-educated people.

The average age of the American college student has increased to almost twenty-two years. This is partly because a growing number of students take time off from college to decide what they want to do and then return to school when they are somewhat older. It is also because middle-aged adults have been going back to college to improve their job skills. In fact, probably the most dramatic change in higher education today is taking place in adult education, both degree and nondegree, as colleges, universities, corporations, and other organizations provide adults with literacy classes, enrichment courses, and career retraining (Eurich, 1985).

Just over half of all college students are now women, and the majority are white (Casale and Lerman, 1986). College freshmen in 1991 were 84 percent white, 9 percent black, 3 percent Asian, 2 percent Hispanic, and 2 percent from other minority groups (*Chronicle of Higher Education*, 1991). A sizable proportion came from families in which the parents were well-educated. About 41 percent had fathers with at least a bachelor's degree.

Freshmen in 1991 reported that several factors influenced their decision to go to college. These included the desire to prepare for graduate or professional school (53 percent), to get a general education and appreciation of ideas (63 percent), and to learn more about things that interested them (73 percent). Topping the list, however, was the desire to get a better job, mentioned by 78 percent of the students.

Politically, most college students consider themselves middle-of-the-roaders (55 percent of the 1991 freshmen). The self-labeled liberals are about equal in number to those who call themselves conservatives (among 1991 freshmen, 23 percent and 20 percent, respectively). Only very small proportions say they are far to the right or far to the left (less than 2 percent each). Yet there seems to be a growing activism among college students (Dodge, 1990a). Nearly 40 percent of freshmen in 1991 said they had participated

Technological or vocational schools offer valuable job training in an era of scarce employment, but community colleges have also become a means through which the working class is rechanneled into traditional working-class jobs such as auto repair.

MAKING CHOICES

The Value of a Bachelor's Degree

In 1987, about 63 percent of all American college students were enrolled in four-year public or private institutions, and many of those in two-year colleges hoped someday to transfer to a four-year school. Four years of higher education is a sizable investment in money, time, and effort. Is that investment worth it—does going to college "pay off"? Answers to this question can help you to make more informed choices about your own education.

In American society a college degree opens doors to high-paying, prestigious jobs. In 1991, the median annual income of men with a college degree was 55 percent higher than that of men with only a high school diploma. Among women who possessed a college degree, the median income was 36 percent more than that of women who had just a high school education (U.S. Bureau of the Census, 1991b, pp. 94–95). When the differences in median income are multiplied by a working life of forty years, a college degree (compared with a high school diploma) increases lifetime earnings by about $442,000 for men and $319,000 for women.

A degree from an elite school boosts earnings even more. In one study conducted in the 1970s, the 15 percent of students who attended the country's most elite private institutions could expect to earn 85 percent more on average than those who had not graduated from college (Coleman and Rainwater, 1978). More recent research shows that it is still a good investment to attend an elite private institution. Going to Harvard or Yale, for example, typically "pays for itself" in the long run. Attending a state university can give a good return on investment, too, especially if a person studies the right subjects and earns good grades. For example, degrees in business, management, economics, and engineering all tend to yield relatively high future incomes (Kominski, 1990). How well students do, and which fields they major in, matter as much as, or even more than, which school they go to (James, Alsalam, Conaty, and To, 1989).

Community college education has its greatest economic pay-off for students who transfer after two years and complete bachelor's degrees. Vocational degrees enhance job-market chances compared to high school diplomas, but not to four-year degrees in most fields (Monk-Turner, 1988).

The selection of certain majors can also tend to lower future earnings. For example, people with bachelor's degrees in education, home economics, or nursing tend to earn relatively less than college graduates with degrees in other fields (Kominski, 1990).

One reason for the lower monetary worth of some bachelor's degrees is educational "inflation," whereby more college degrees have been granted than there are jobs requiring a college education. As the following table shows, in 1969 college graduates made up only about one in eight U.S. workers, but by 1990, they made up nearly one in four workers (Samuelson, 1992):

	1969	1990
	(% of U.S. Workers)	
College (4 years +)	12.6%	23.2%
College (1–3 years)	12.6	21.3
High school graduate	38.4	39.4
High school dropout	36.4	16.2

As a result of educational inflation, some jobs that were once done by high school or technical school graduates are now being done by college graduates, with little relative increase in pay.

However, the value of a college education can't be measured solely in dollars and cents. Howard Bowen (1977) argues that the college experience significantly improves the quality of people's lives. He cites studies that show that college work increases cognitive abilities (particularly verbal and mathematical skills), fosters logical thinking, broadens a person's fund of knowledge, boosts intellectual curiosity, and enhances interest in and responsiveness to the arts. The research of sociologist Herbert H. Hyman and his colleagues (1975, 1979) has confirmed that higher education increases receptivity to further learning, stimulates a quest for knowledge, encourages respect for civil liberties, and enhances emotional and moral development.

in demonstrations in the past year. More than 50 percent supported greater consumer protection, more pollution control, preservation of abortion rights, busing to achieve racial balance in schools, gun control, and a national health-care program. In addition, an increasing number of today's college students are volunteering some of their time in community service (M. Duncan, 1990).

Outside of the classroom, many college students today also spend time working. In fact, nearly 30 percent of full-time students and 84 percent of part-time ones work

Religion

להבדיל בין קדש לחול
ובין אור לחשך ובין
ישראל לעמים ובין יום
השביעי לששת ימי
המעשה כשם שהבדלתנו
יי אלהנו מעמי הארצות
וממשפחות האדמה
משטן רע ומפגע רע
ומכל גזרות קשות
ורעות המתרגשות

In all the broad universe, there is no other hope for man than ourselves. This is a tremendous responsibility. I have borne it too long alone. You share it with me now. (L. Ron Hubbard, founder of Scientology)

[Scientology] contains the secrets of the universe. That may be hard for people to handle sometimes, hearing that. [Actor John Travolta (in *Time*, May 6, 1991)]

Scientology is quite likely the most ruthless, the most classically terroristic, the most litigious and the most lucrative cult the country has ever seen. [Vicki Aznaran, former leader of Scientology (in *Time*, May 6, 1991)]

[Scientology] made a business of selling religion [and] conspired for almost a decade to defraud the United States Government by impeding the IRS. [U.S. Tax Court, 1984 (in *Los Angeles Times*, June 24, 1990)]

In this chapter we examine religion in general and various types of religious institutions, both mainstream and marginal. To lead into our topic, let's consider the special and controversial case of Scientology.

The Church of Scientology was founded in the late 1950s by the former science fiction writer L. Ron Hubbard (B. R. Wilson, 1990). In his best-selling book *Dianetics: The Modern Science of Mental Health* (1950) and countless later publications, some available on paperback stands in supermarkets and airports and others held secret from nonbelievers, Hubbard described his unique vision. According to Hubbard, the human body is a temporary vehicle occupied by a "thetan," or soul, that passes through innumerable reincarnations over trillions of years. Although not part of the material world, thetans created the universe and everything in it, and have the capacity to control that universe. But thetans are also vulnerable to painful emotional and physical experiences, or "engrams," that interfere with rational intelligence. The goal of Scientology is to release individuals from the grip of engrams, to replace grief and apathy with enthusiasm and exhilaration. To achieve this goal, church members must enroll in a series of courses, each rationally planned and measured (hence the name "*Scien*tology"). The process may cost thousands of dollars and take years to complete. Only a small number of those who embark on this quest achieve the upper level: harmony with the universe and mastery over their fate.

In a mere four decades, Scientology has grown from a handful of self-help groups composed of devoted Hubbard fans to a multimillion-dollar organization that boasts 700 centers in sixty-five countries and some 6.5 million followers (*Los Angeles Times*, June 24, 1990; *Time*, May 6, 1991). It has also outlived its founder, who died in 1986. From the beginning, Scientology has been controversial. Respected psychiatrists denounced Hubbard's first book as bogus psychology. Sociologists have dismissed it as "modern magic" (Bainbridge and Stark, 1980). Investigative journalists have exposed gaps and apparent lies in Hubbard's official biography. Numerous lawsuits have been filed against Scientology for terrorizing its critics, brainwashing and exploiting its recruits, and defrauding its members of thousands of dollars through high-pressure sales techniques. Eleven of its top leaders—including Hubbard's second wife—were imprisoned for burglarizing the U.S. Justice Department and other federal agencies that were investigating the organization.

Scientology is not the first religion that has been condemned by government officials. To cite some well-known examples, the Romans attempted to stamp out Christianity, and the Spanish expelled the Moors (or Muslims) and forced Jews to convert to Christianity. Nor is Scientology the first religion whose beliefs may seem bizarre to outsiders. Many non-Christians find the ideas of Jesus's virgin birth and resurrection after death improbable.

Is Scientology really a religion? The answer is of more than academic interest. It matters to parents who want the courts' help in retrieving and "deprogramming" children who have joined the Church of Scientology. It matters to individuals who believe that Scientology has damaged their emotional health, depleted their savings, or broken their families. It matters to members of the Church of Scientology, who want public recognition and tax deductions for their contributions. And it matters to society as a whole. Because of the constitutional separation of church and state, the U.S. government normally does not become involved in decisions about whether a group does or does not qualify as a religion. But the Internal Revenue Service can deny tax-exempt status to any self-proclaimed religious organization if it commits crimes, engages in partisan politics, operates as a business, or enriches private individuals. Traditionally the IRS also requires that a religion have an established place of worship, regular services, a formal doctrine, ordained ministers, and sincerely held beliefs (Podus, 1992). The IRS has repeatedly denied the Church of Scientology tax-exempt status. The government of Spain has gone further, expelling Scientology from the country. But the High Court of Australia has formally recognized it as a church (B. R. Wilson, 1990).

As the example of Scientology shows, defining religion is exceedingly difficult. Must religion involve a belief in a supernatural being? If so, then Chinese Confucianism, which teaches proper ways to live in this world, would be disqualified because its founder is remembered as an exceptionally wise (but mortal) human being. Must there be an idea of one supreme being or God? If so, religions such as Hinduism, which recognize many gods, would be left out. Is the notion of "salvation" sufficient to identify a group as a religion? If so, then EST and other therapy groups from the human potential movement within psychology would have to be included. In fact, religion has never been defined in a way that satisfies everyone because the various definitions have tended to favor some claims to be a religion over others.

Sociological definitions of **religion** focus in varying degrees on three basic elements, all stressed by the most influential founder of the sociology of religion, Émile Durkheim (1912/1965). The first element is *beliefs*. As we saw in Chapter 3, beliefs are basic elements of culture. For many religious people belief in God or a supreme being is crucial. Second, religion is not just a matter of what people believe but also of what they do, so many sociological definitions of religion focus on the presence of distinctive *social practices* that represent organized, highly patterned forms of social action. The most significant of these are rituals, such as ceremonies of worship. Religion also shapes social action by instructing believers to perform certain actions or refrain from others. The Ten Commandments and the Golden Rule are two examples of such instructions. Third, in defining religion, sociologists ask whether a group has created a *moral community*. Religions, they suggest, must draw people together and organize social relations in terms of moral commitment and standards of right or good behavior.

In this chapter we will consider religions that are both conventional and unconventional, familiar and unfamiliar. We will begin by looking further at how sociology's key concepts are used in the study of religion, relating them to the three elements discussed above. Next, we will consider different types of religious organizations. We will then analyze the sources and directions of change in religion. Finally, we will survey religion in the United States today.

KEY CONCEPTS IN THE STUDY OF RELIGION

The five key concepts in sociology can help us understand the basic elements of religion. Religious beliefs and symbols reflect ***culture***, rituals and ceremonies are ***social action***, religious communities reflect a ***social structure***, and religions help to achieve ***functional integration*** at several levels. ***Power*** and conflict can affect the nature and significance of each of these basic elements of religion. Let us look further at each of these points.

Culture: Religious Beliefs and Symbols

In Chapter 3 we learned that beliefs and symbols are crucial elements of ***culture***. At the heart of religion lies a system of sacred beliefs and symbols. Beliefs are cultural certainties that do not require empirical proof to be accepted as true or real. The Mbuti Pygmies of Africa believe that the forest in which they live is a supernatural being. They personify it as Mother and Father, Life-Giver, and occasionally Death-Giver. The Pygmies' belief is an example of **animism**, or the idea that things in the world (a forest, a tree, an animal, a mountain, or a river, for instance) have active, animate spirits. In some religions people believe in the existence of ancestral spirits. An example is Shintoism, most of whose 3.2 million followers are Japanese.

More familiar to Westerners is the religious belief known as **theism**, the idea that powerful supernatural beings are involved with events and conditions on earth. *Monotheists*, such as the world's 1.8 billion Christians, 17 million Jews, and 950 million Muslims (*Encyclopaedia Britannica*, 1992), believe in a single supernatural being, called God, Yahweh, or Allah. *Polytheists*, in contrast, believe in several deities. Today's 720 million Hindus, most of whom live in India, have a pantheon of many minor gods and five major ones, who are in turn reflections of a higher, more sacred principle of Brahman, or "Oneness."

In other religions, beliefs center on a supernatural force rather than a supernatural being. Polynesians, for example, believe in a supernatural force called *mana*, which can inhabit objects and people. A canoe that is able to withstand intense storms or a farmer whose crops flourish is said to possess mana. This kind of religious belief is most common in preindustrial societies.

Émile Durkheim was one of the first sociologists to propose explanations for the religious beliefs that people develop. Durkheim (1912/1965) identified the distinction between the *sacred* and the *profane* as an essential part of a religion. By sacred he meant that which is set apart from everyday experience and inspires awe and reverence. In contrast, the profane is that which is mundane and ordinary. The concept of community is important in this distinction because it is the community that bestows sacredness on things. Religion, in turn, functions to promote social unity and to create moral and intellectual consensus. So, according to Durkheim, a central element in the def-

The word religion *comes from Latin* re-, *back, and* ligare, *to bind or fasten. Religion binds one to the past, to the natural world, and to other members of one's society. It also reinforces a sense of mystery about the world and one's place in it. The origin and purpose of these prehistoric monoliths at England's Stonehenge are not fully understood, yet they fill us with an awe that echoes, perhaps, the awe of the builders confronting their world.*

inition of religion is that it pertains to what the community has determined to be sacred.

Durkheim began by studying Australian aboriginal clans, which he believed were the simplest kind of human society and therefore should have elementary forms of religion. A central part of aboriginal religion is the **totem**: an object (usually an animal or plant) that symbolizes both the clan itself and that which the clan considers sacred. Durkheim was intrigued by this dual symbolism of the clan and the sacred. He argued that in worshiping a totem, the aborigines were essentially revering their own society or social group. This insight led Durkheim to the conclusion that religious beliefs stem from people's experiences with the social forces that shape their lives. For instance, a belief in divine creation arises from the fact that we are products of a culture that seems outside us and is not of our own making. "We speak a language that we did not make," wrote Durkheim; "we use instruments that we did not invent, we invoke rights that we did not found, a treasury of knowledge is transmitted to each generation that it did not gather itself" (Durkheim, 1912/1965, p. 212). By extension, we ourselves are fashioned by external forces beyond our control, forces that deserve our awe and devotion. The same idea is embodied in the belief in a god who created the world.

In addition to beliefs in deities, spirits, or supernatural forces, most religions also incorporate moral principles. These beliefs about what is right and wrong, good and bad, proper and improper, are not just abstract ideas, but prescriptions for behavior. Adherents of the religion are expected to use these principles as guides in their daily lives (Gellner, 1972). In some nontheistic religions (those without ideas of a deity) the moral principles are paramount. Buddhists, for instance, are less concerned with revering the Buddha than with achieving the ethical and spiritual ideas that the Buddha set forth in his message of the "four noble truths." Other religions that focus on a striving toward moral goals are Confucianism and Taoism, both of which originated in China.

Virtually all religions are expressed through *symbols*, or things that stand for something other than themselves. As we said in Chapter 3, nothing is symbolic in and of itself. People agree among themselves about what the symbolic meanings are and assign those meanings to various words, actions, and objects. The Christian communion ceremony, for example, includes both symbolic acts (drinking wine and eating bread as a symbolic reenactment of the Last Supper) and symbolic objects (the wine and bread themselves, which symbolize the blood and body of Christ). Durkheim argued that the use of such religious symbols often involves what he called *collective representation*: communication from larger social bodies to individuals. Thus, the various symbols employed in a Christian communion speak from all those who share the Christian faith

Emile Durkheim proposed that societies create religions that reflect their basic structures, and in so doing end up worshiping an image of their actual social relations. A totem like this painted rock in Australia is an object, usually from the natural world, that reflects the clan or other elementary social form and serves as a focus of worship.

(including all past generations) to all those who are currently participating in the ceremony.

Social Action: Religious Practices and Experiences

The rituals and ceremonies of religion are a form of ***social action***. Sociologists often refer to "ritual practices" or "religious practices" to indicate actions that are performed repeatedly in accord with rules or an understanding of a deeper, shared meaning. Rituals can satisfy personal religious needs, such as creating a link to God through prayer. But they also can establish a religious community, as when members of a Catholic congregation gather to celebrate the sacrament of the Eucharist (Holy Communion).

Religion is also a form of social action whereby believers express their faith, communicate it to others, seek supernatural guidance or intervention, honor their deities, affirm their sacred beliefs, or simply produce religious experiences. Religious practices take many forms. They may be shared or solitary, compulsory or optional, rigidly structured or open to creative innovations. Music, dance, prayer, meditation, feasting, and fasting are just a few of the many activities carried out in the name of religion.

Some religious practices can be classified as **rituals**, or standardized sets of actions used in particular ceremonies or on other specific occasions. Rituals rely on symbols to convey their meaning and to reinforce that meaning for participants. Some rituals are secular rather than religious. For instance, the customs of requiring people to stand when a judge enters a courtroom, witnesses to raise their right hand when swearing to tell the truth, and a jury foreman to rise when delivering the verdict are all rituals that lend symbolic respect and gravity to a court of law. Religious rituals are usually accorded even greater sanctity. The ritual cleansing with water in a Christian baptism or the ritual reading from the Torah in a Jewish bar mitzvah are solemn acts that convey deep spiritual meaning to participants and help to give them a sense of religious community (Douglas, 1970; Gluckman, 1962; Turner, 1970).

Religions also prescribe actions that are not rituals. These include moral instructions such as rules for living one's daily life and prohibitions. Jews are told to eat only kosher foods. Christians are told to "do unto others as you would have them do unto you." Muslims are told that it is immoral to charge interest on a loan to other Muslims. Some versions of Christianity have encouraged large families to bring new souls into the world and expand the numbers of Christians. Others have encouraged celibacy in the belief that refraining from sex keeps one's thoughts closer to heavenly purity. As each of these examples shows, religions help to organize the social actions people take (or refrain from taking) as well as their beliefs.

People who claim to be followers of a particular religion do not necessarily observe all of that religion's rituals and other practices. Not all professed Christians go to church, for example, and not all who go to church take communion. According to recent Gallup Polls, two out of three Americans belong to a church or synagogue, but only about 32 percent of Americans attend religious services once a week or more (see Figure 14.1; *The American Enterprise*, November–December 1990; *The Gallup Report*, September 1989). Regular attendance is greatest among Roman Catholics, followed by Protestants, and then Jews (*Emerging Trends*, November/December 1987). In part, these differences reflect the different meanings that the various religious groups attach to attendance at services.

Religious symbolism is a complex language of images and gestures. This fifteenth-century painting, Jan Van Eyck's Giovanni Arnolfini and His Bride, *appears to be a simple domestic portrait of husband and wife, but symbolic elements—the husband's raised hand, the single candle burning in the chandelier, the fruit on the windowsill, and in fact virtually every detail in the painting—transform it into a powerful commentary on the sacredness of marriage.*

Religion is also characterized by powerful and important experiences that reaffirm members' faith (Stark and Bainbridge, 1985). Sometimes religious experiences involve intensified awareness of a supernatural being or power. This may be accompanied by a sense of spiritual cleansing or purification. The so-called born-again experience associated with conversion to fundamentalist Christianity often takes this form (Tipton, 1982). Other religious experiences involve transcending the here and now in deep emotional experiences or ecstasies (Evans and Peacock, 1990). Certain Muslim groups, for instance, use violent whirling, dancing, and shouting to reach states of altered consciousness. In other religions drugs may be ritually used to achieve the same goal. Religious experiences also include the feeling of having attained personal contact with a deity. People may even report being given divine revelations. Closely related is a sense of oneness with other people (especially members of one's own religious group) or a strong identity with nature. Ritual provides occasions for religious experience to take place on a regular basis. Both rituals and the experiences they encourage are shaped by religious symbols and beliefs.

Social Structure: Religious Community

One of the most important features of religion is its creation of what Durkheim called **moral community**. This community is composed of people whose shared beliefs, symbols, practices, and experiences bind them together into a larger social whole. So important is community to the life of a religion that its absence is seen as a serious problem. One reason many contemporary clergy are concerned about the spread of TV evangelism is that it promotes religion without community. Religious broadcasts may create the illusion that viewers are in church, talking face-to-face with the minister; but in fact they are alone in their homes and strangers to one another. They can connect and disconnect their religious attachments simply by turning their sets on and off.

Religious communities are not just groups of people who happen to share beliefs and engage in rituals. They have an organized, and usually enduring, ***social structure***. In the United States today, many religious groups, such as the United Methodist church, have formal organizations that give them a national structure. The Roman Catholic church, with its system of priests, bishops, and cardinals under a pope, has a fully international structure. The social structure of religious groups encompasses a variety of organizations. These include central offices, seminaries for training new religious leaders, publishers of material such as prayer books, distributors of articles such as communion wafers and choir gowns, youth camps, and overseas missions and organizations. Religious groups also have a structure in terms of the relationships between members. People are more likely to marry within their religion. Prayer groups of Christian businesspeople establish a network of links that promotes business as well as religion.

The scope of a religious community varies with the type of society involved. In a small tribe, religion encompasses everyone and affects every aspect of life. People might seek the guidance of ancestral spirits regarding how to handle family concerns, how to decide political matters, when to plant and harvest or hunt and fish, or how to cure an illness. The religious community and the society are virtually one and the same (Calhoun, 1980; Evans-Pritchard, 1965; Fortes, 1969). In larger, more complex societies,

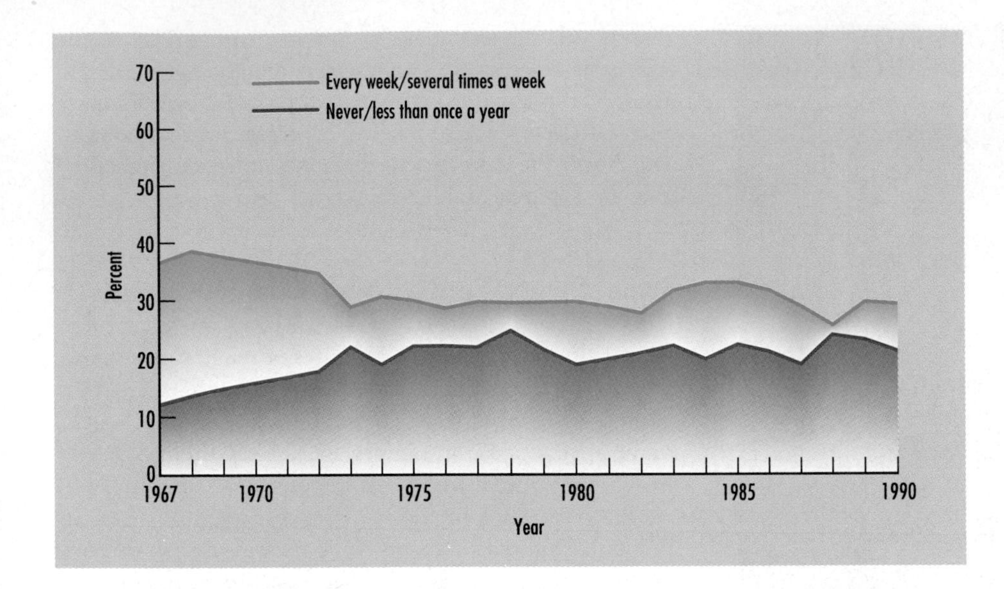

FIGURE 14.1 / Percentages of Americans Who Reported Attending Religious Services "Often" and "Seldom or Never," 1967–1990

Source: Surveys by the National Opinion Research Center, in "America: Land of the Faithful," *The American Enterprise*, November–December 1990, p. 97.

religion is more compartmentalized. People may seek guidance on family matters from their minister, but turn to a physician when a family member is ill or to a banker for advice on investments. Furthermore, larger societies often encompass a variety of religions, each with its own churches, schools, charities, and so forth.

Religion and Functional Integration

Even in large, complex societies, religions help achieve ***functional integration*** in both the religious community and society at large. Religious involvement helps knit society together in several ways. First, it encourages adherence to and sharing of moral standards. It helps to create meaningful social bonds among people in local religious communities. For example, in the United States, churches have often helped immigrants adapt to their new homeland (Greeley, 1972). Churches modeled after those in the immigrants' homelands provide a haven of traditional beliefs and customs that help ease the transition to a new way of life. Second, religions link local communities together through national and international organizations, as well as shared rituals. Finally, when respect for secular social institutions is made part of religious beliefs and practices, religions help to legitimate the established social order.

The extent to which religious institutions help to achieve functional integration varies from one society to another. In some societies, nearly everyone is a member of the same religion. For example, in both France and Ireland, Catholicism is predominant. In others, like the United States and India, there are many different religions. The extent of religious involvement also varies. The United States has one of the highest rates of attendance at religious services in the world. In some societies, such as Iran and Great Britain, the government officially supports one religion. In others, including the United States, church and state are officially kept separate.

Religion may legitimate the established social order by sanctioning the prevailing social arrangements. Guy Swanson (1974) showed this in a study of fifty non-Western societies. Just as Durkheim had suggested, each society tended to reflect itself in its religion. For instance, in societies where elders occupied important positions, ancestors were worshiped; and in societies with large inequalities in wealth, religion tended to support a wide gap between rich and poor. In our own society, when television preachers encourage people to fulfill their individual potential, they are endorsing the American cultural values of ambition and individual opportunity (see Chapter 3).

Religious legitimation of the established social order also can be seen in what the sociologist Robert Bellah (1970) calls national, or civil, religion. **Civil religion** is essentially a sanctifying of the nation by associating its history, values, and institutions with God's special favor. One study of civil religion among elementary school children found that 85 percent believed that America "has been placed on this earth for a special purpose," that it is God's chosen nation, and that its success is a reward for its goodness (Smidt, 1980). Most adults also feel that our country was created "under God," and that from God the government derives its ultimate legitimacy. The American Constitution expressly forbids any ties between the state and particular religions, however, so civil religion involves a very general seeking of blessings from God. God's aid on behalf of the nation is invoked at the opening of Congress, at political party conventions, at swearing-in ceremonies, and in political speeches, including every presidential inaugural address but one (Washington's second, which was only two paragraphs long). Civil religion, then, creates links between the sacred and the secular. In so doing, it encourages a willingness to care about and sacrifice for the public good (Bellah and Hammond, 1980; J. A. Coleman, 1983). Civil religion can come in both conservative and liberal forms, and can stress both our freedom to choose and our obligations to one another (Wuthnow, 1988).

Sometimes the idea of religious community is used in more radical ways. For example, during the Middle Ages the Franciscan order of Catholic monks renounced all personal property in favor of a communal sharing of possessions. This lifestyle, which was intended as a message to the world about proper Christlike behavior, created conflict with the church hierarchy. A similar process has occurred in modern times with the rise of liberation theology. Liberation theology was originally a movement among Catholic priests in Brazil and other Latin American countries. The priests pursued economic justice as well as spiritual salvation partly because of a belief that a Christian community is destroyed by too wide a gap between rich and poor. Ministering especially to the poor and landless, these priests founded "base communities," or settlements in which, like early Christians, they emphasized a common struggle against oppression (Gutierrez, 1973, 1983). Liberation theology has now spread to many American Christian churches, both Catholic and Protestant (Tabb, 1986).

Power in Religious Communities

As the contrasting examples of civil religion and liberation theology showed, religious faith may be the basis for involvement with ***power*** relations, either supporting them

In Poland during the 1980s, the Solidarity movement and social unrest were motivated by economic factors, but the Catholic faith provided a source of strength and a sense of community for workers in separate industries and cities. At left, a portrait of Polish-born Pope John Paul II hangs above workers as they block a factory gate. Above, a Vietnamese man prays to his ancestors at a Shinto shrine, which resembles the Catholic shrine and reminds us that nearly all religions revolve around rituals centered on symbols of the sacred.

A heresy is an opinion or doctrine that differs from accepted church doctrine. During the Spanish Inquisition, which began in the fifteenth century, the Catholic Church tortured thousands of suspected heretics to obtain confessions. Those who did confess lost all their property (half to the church) and were publicly flogged. Those who refused to confess were burned at the stake. The power of the church to require strict adherence to its beliefs was granted by a society that was convinced that those beliefs were the one path to salvation.

through civil religion or struggling to change them as in liberation theology.

Although many religious groups emphasize equality, or at least community, among believers, they give greater power to some members than others. Generally, we can distinguish two roles in a religious group: the leadership role accorded to priests and the follower role characteristic of other members. (Note that sociologists use *priest* or *clergy* to refer to all official religious leaders.)

Priests have played a crucial role in defining modern religions and giving them their distinctive culture. As the sociologist Pierre Bourdieu (1991) notes, religious leaders have the power to mobilize religious communities and to divide the sacred from the profane. The history of many religions can be viewed as a struggle among various groups for the power to designate correct beliefs and practices and thereby to dominate the organization. According to Bourdieu, every religious body represents the power of its current leaders as well as previous struggles over how to define that religion and organize religious life.

The establishment of an individual priest's power is often a critical factor in defining a religious community, because a local minister or rabbi can give a church or synagogue much of its distinctive identity. In many of the world's religions priests have had a near-monopoly on the interpretation of sacred texts because they were among the few members of the society who could read.

In addition, religious factions or different religions may compete for authority. Each church carves out its own religious community, and different churches tend to be at odds over the kind of community the larger society should build and the share in that community each church should have. This has been a recurring theme in American religious history. Periodically, new sects have broken off from established churches and searched for places (often on the Western frontiers) where they could fashion their own ideal communities. The Mormons who settled in Utah are one example. (We discuss the founding of Mormonism later in this chapter.) Other American sects have followed a similar pattern (Marty, 1984). As religions become more formally organized, developing national or international church bureaucracies, these organizations tend to become weapons in power struggles among believers over what the church should do. (For example, should Christian churches accept homosexual members, even letting them preach? In 1992, the Southern Baptist Convention decided it would not and expelled two North Carolina congregations that disobeyed.) And as societies become larger and include members of different religions (as well as people who are nonreligious), occasions for competition and conflict multiply. For example, Jews and other non-Christians in the United States protest when Christians use their power to spend public money on religious symbols (such as Christmas decorations) or to promote religious practices (such as specifically Christian prayers in schools).

TYPES OF RELIGIOUS INSTITUTIONS

Most religious communities organize themselves into some type of institution: some set of relatively stable roles, statuses, groups, and values. The forms that religious institutions take vary greatly, however, depending on such factors as their size, doctrines, membership, origins, and relations with the rest of society. On the basis of such factors, sociologists recognize *church*, *sect*, and *cult* as the three major forms of religious institutions.

Churches and Sects

The sociologist Ernst Troeltsch (1931) viewed religious institutions as typically falling in the categories of either churches or sects. Table 14.1 lists some of the characteristics of church and sect according to Troeltsch and his followers. Note that any given religious group need not conform 100 percent to one or the other list of features. These descriptions are merely *ideal types*, which serve as conceptual tools that can be used to measure reality and to make comparisons (see Chapter 1).

Troeltsch defined a **sect** as a small, exclusive, uncompromising fellowship of people seeking spiritual perfection. Members are voluntary converts, and their lives are largely controlled by the sect. Troeltsch found that a sect is usually characterized by asceticism; members adopt austere, dis-

TABLE 14.1

Church and Sect

Characteristic	Church	Sect
Size	Large	Small
Relationship with other religious groups	Tolerant	Rejects; feels it has sole truth
Wealth	Extensive	Limited
Religious services	Limited congregational participation; formal; intellectual emphasis	Extensive congregational participation; spontaneous; emotional emphasis
Clergy	Specialized; professional	Unspecialized; little training; part-time
Doctrines	Liberal interpretation of Scriptures; emphasis upon this world	Literal interpretation of Scriptures; emphasis upon other world
Membership	By birth or ritual participation; social institution embracing all socially compatible	By conversion; moral community excluding unworthy
Social class of members	Mainly middle class	Mainly lower class
Relationship with secular world	Endorses prevailing culture and social organization	Renounces or opposes prevailing cultural standards; requires strict adherence to biblical standards

Source: Adapted from Lifton Pope, Millhands and Preachers: A Study of Gastonia *(Yale University Press, New Haven, Conn., 1942).*

ciplined lifestyles. Most sects are concerned strictly with their own religious doctrines. They see themselves as select groups that have been granted special enlightenment. Often they discourage their members from extensive participation in worldly affairs because they consider the world outside the sect to be decadent, corrupt, and sinful.

As a sect grows, Troeltsch believed, it typically evolves into a **church**, a large, conservative, universalist religious institution. Its growth increasingly comes from those born into the group, not from conversion. A church is more tolerant of other religious groups than a sect is. Because it is large, a church tends to acquire a certain amount of social and political power, and often it retains that power by becoming associated with the government or the ruling class. A church thus accommodates itself to the claims of powerful groups and the dominant institutions, and it tends to support the society's status quo. The Church of England, the Catholic church in Spain, and the Muslim Shiites in Iran come close to this ideal type.

Although Troeltsch's descriptions offer many valuable insights about church and sect, some sociologists think that his models may lead to confusion over how to classify certain real-life religious institutions. Granted, there are both churches and sects with all the traits in Troeltsch's definitions—but there are also churches with some of the traits of sects, as well as sects with some of the traits of churches. That is why some sociologists prefer to classify religious institutions according to just one dimension: the institution's acceptance or rejection of its social environment (B. Johnson, 1963; Stark and Bainbridge, 1985). At one end of this continuum is the church that is at one with its social environment; at the other end is the sect that exists in a perpetual state of tension with the larger society. Most religious groups fall somewhere between these two extremes.

This model has the advantage of emphasizing the dynamics of an organization as it moves up or down the scale of tension with its environment. For example, as a sect gains stability and respectability, it begins to coexist more harmoniously with the surrounding society, thus moving closer to the "church" end of the continuum.

Cults

Stark and Bainbridge (1985) reserve the label *sect* for schismatic institutions that are formed when dissidents break away from an established church, claiming that they are the authentic, cleansed version of the faith from which they split. The Puritans who broke with the Church of England and formed their own religious community are one example of a sect. In contrast, other religious institutions in tension with their environment are imported from other cultures or are formed when people create entirely new religious beliefs and practices. These institutions have no prior ties to established religious bodies in the same society. Stark and Bainbridge refer to these more innovative institutions as **cults**. In its early years Christianity was considered a cult. In fact, all the major religions of the world started as cults.

Stark and Bainbridge categorized cults into three types on the basis of how tightly they are organized. *Audience cults* have practically no formal organization. The members are actually consumers of cult doctrines delivered over the airwaves or in books, magazines, and newspaper columns. In *client cults*, the religious leaders offer specific services to those who follow them. Although the leaders are well-organized, the clients are not members of congregations. Scientology is often cited as an example of a client cult because it uses an organized network of paid staff members to teach cult doctrine to groups of clients. Some client cults evolve into *cult movements* as they become larger and more tightly organized. This happened with the Reverend Sun Myung Moon's Unification church, and may be happening to the Church of Scientology. In the process of becoming larger and better organized, cult movements often generate opposition in their social environment. Cults that permit their members to pursue normal lives and occupations typically arouse less opposition than do cults whose members abandon their normal activities to become full-time followers. Why is the larger community more hostile to cults that consume all their members' energies? One reason is that these cults rupture the convert's ties to conventional institutions, including the family.

The question of whether a religious group is a church, sect, or cult can become part of the competition for power and authority. As we noted in our discussion of Scientology, one person's cult is another person's legitimate religion. Also, cults or sects that thrive tend to become more institutionalized and to take on the characteristics of churches. Ironically, this process can disillusion members because institutionalization tends to make religion seem more "everyday" and less "sacred," weakening the religious experience. Max Weber studied this transformation intensively. He held that one particular cycle of innovation and institutionalization, the Protestant Reformation, played a pivotal role in producing the modern era.

SOCIAL CHANGE AND RELIGION

We tend to think of religions as relatively conservative forces that lend their support to the status quo. This is not always the case, however. Religious communities can be powerful forces for social change. This can happen when the religions themselves undergo change, which is what happened to the Roman Catholic church in the sixteenth century when local religious leaders and their followers came into conflict with authorities in the church's hierarchy. The Protestant Reformation resulted in the foundation of the Baptist, Methodist, Lutheran, Presbyterian, and other religions, all of which nevertheless consider themselves Christians. Similar divisions exist among American Jews and Muslims. In this section we will explore how religion can promote massive social change.

The way religious groups react to innovations also influences social change. For example, the common availability of safe and effective methods of contraception challenged religious groups to determine whether they should encourage or discourage the practice of birth control. Religious groups have had to determine if this was in accord with their religious teachings on sexuality and reproduction. Sometimes such changes outside religious communities cause religious leaders to promote a revival of faith as a way to meet the challenges of a changing secular world. Sociologists and historians of religion (Marty, 1984) have identified a tendency for religious groups to alternate periods of revival with periods of increasing institutionalization during which religious communities become more stable and better integrated into the established social structure of the larger society.

The Religious Roots of Modernization

The Protestant Reformation was itself a period of radical religious revival and innovation. Max Weber argued that some of the Protestant reforms laid the groundwork for modern capitalism by promoting new attitudes toward work and investment. He began with the observations that capitalism emerged in Christian-dominated Europe, not in Asia or Africa, and that Germany, which was largely Protestant, was more industrialized than the parts of Europe that remained largely Catholic. Weber also noticed that Protestants were more likely than Catholics to become industrial millionaires. He wondered what could explain these patterns. To find an answer, he examined Protestant beliefs, particularly those of John Calvin (1509–1564) and his followers.

At the heart of Calvinist doctrine is the concept of predestination, the belief that a person's fate after death, whether it be salvation or damnation, is determined at birth. Eternal life, according to Calvinists, is bestowed by God's grace, not by individual merit. Thus, Calvinists could not turn to a priest for intercession with God or obtain a promise of absolution from a church hierarchy. No human efforts, even by members of the clergy, could alter God's plan. Nor could mere humans hope to learn God's particular intentions for them. These beliefs left Calvinists with a profound uncertainty about their future and a deep sense of isolation. Many responded by trying to prove they had a place among God's chosen few by achieving success in life. This meant hard work, frugality, self-denial, and astute investment for future gain—in short, a kind of worldly asceticism. The Calvinist outlook is captured in such traditional sayings as "The devil finds work for idle hands" and "A penny saved is a penny earned." Weber called this outlook the *Protestant ethic*.

The Protestant ethic, according to Weber, fostered the spirit of capitalism because it consisted of ideas and attitudes that encouraged the growth of privately owned businesses. This it did especially by encouraging the owners of the means of production to reinvest their profits rather than spending them all on luxuries (as many earlier aristocrats had done). Calvinists were highly motivated to make this personal sacrifice, for they saw self-denial of material pleasures as the road to business success; and success, in their minds, was proof of God's favor.

Weber's theory that Protestant values laid the groundwork for capitalism and economic modernization has been much debated since he first proposed it over eighty years ago. Critics have argued, for example, that the changes Weber described were not confined to Protestants, but affected some Catholics as well. Others argue that religious changes followed capitalist development rather than paving the way for it. All the same, Weber's theory is an excellent example of the interplay between religion and the secular world. As religious beliefs were changed in an effort to purify Christianity, those beliefs set in motion forces that had the potential to alter the economic system. Thus, Weber showed how religious reform and change in the secular spheres of society can go hand in hand.

Religious Responses to Secularization

Once capitalism and other aspects of modern society were established, **secularization** began to occur in the new social order: It became more concerned with worldly matters and less concerned with spiritual ones (D. Martin, 1978). Secularization occurred for several reasons.

- First, modernization has involved the creation and growth of science, which endorses reason and systematic

Within a single religion such as Christianity there can be a great deal of variety in the practice of worship. Both of these churches attempt to orient worshipers' attention to sacred matters, but one does it through extreme simplicity that focuses attention on heaven, the other by elaborate and beautiful images of saints and other sacred objects of veneration. Though we now regard such differences as simply matters of style or taste, they mattered enough to some people during the Protestant Reformation to lead them to kill one another over the issue.

observation as the supreme authorities in our knowledge of the world. As people have come to "believe in" science, to accept its rationalistic outlook, the capacity for faith in the supernatural may have gradually eroded.

- Second, modern societies are much more heterogeneous than traditional societies, not just in terms of racial and ethnic diversity, but also in terms of religious diversity. With such a large number of religious beliefs to choose from, it is hard to think of any one of them as embodying absolute truth, and so the traditional authority of religion may be eroded further.

- Finally, the nature of modern life, with its complex machines and rapid pace, is not always compatible with spirituality. If the angels spoke to us all the time, observes sociologist Peter Berger (1979), the business of modern living would probably grind to a halt. A substantial degree of concern with secular matters is essential if modern societies are to keep running.

From the eighteenth century to the present day, many scientific or rationalistic thinkers have predicted that relentless secularization would eventually spell the end of religion. Marx thought that when socialism made society more scientifically planned and egalitarian, religion would no longer have a function to perform because it existed largely to bind people to the old order and protect it from rebellion. Durkheim and Weber didn't go quite so far, but both thought that secular views and interests would become so predominant that there would be little room left for spiritual concerns. Despite such gloomy predictions, however, religious faith is not disappearing in the modern world. In fact, it remains pervasive and strong. Even in highly industrialized societies such as the United States, religion is still a powerful force. In recent polls 55 percent of Americans said that religion was "extremely important" or "very important" in their lives; 63 percent said that they thought religion could answer all or most of today's problems; and 53 percent said that they pray at least once a day (*The American Enterprise*, November/December 1990).

Religion can stay so vital in the face of secularization because secularization tends to encourage two opposing trends (Stark and Bainbridge, 1985). One trend is **religious innovation**: an effort to create new religions or to change existing ones to better meet people's current needs. The other is **religious revival**: an effort to restore more traditional, more deeply spiritual features to religions that are believed to be weakening under the influence of secular society. Although the word *revival* is sometimes used to refer to all visits from evangelical preachers, sociologists generally use it to describe only those periods when calls for revival actually succeed and social movements of considerable scope and duration are produced. These two trends together—innovation and revival—counteract the influence of secularization so that the importance of religion remains relatively constant.

Religious Innovation: The Founding of the Mormon Faith

The Church of Jesus Christ of Latter-Day Saints, better known as Mormonism, is an example of religious innovation. The denomination was founded in upstate New York in 1830 by Joseph Smith, who claimed to have been inspired by a series of sacred visions. The first took place while Smith was still a teenager. Confused by the many modern Christian sects that were all competing for followers, Smith decided to ask God which faith was right. So he went alone to the woods to seek divine guidance. As he described his experience:

> . . . immediately I was seized upon by some power which entirely overcame me, and had such astonishing influence over me as to bind my tongue so that I could not speak. Thick darkness gathered around me, and it seemed to me for a time as if I were doomed to sudden destruction. . . . Just at this moment of great alarm, I saw a pillar of light exactly over my head, above the brightness of the sun, which descended gradually until it fell upon me. (Quoted in Marty, 1985, p. 199)

Out of the light appeared two persons, suspended in the sky and dazzling Smith with their brightness. One identified the other as his "beloved Son" and instructed Smith to listen to what he had to say. Smith boldly asked which of all the sects was right. He was told that all were wrong, that all in fact were corrupt and abominations.

A Methodist preacher later advised Smith that this apparition was the work of the devil, who was trying to weaken Christian faith on earth. Other people told Smith that the vision was an hallucination, perhaps a sign of mental strain. But Smith interpreted the event as a visitation from God, whose purpose it was to express strong dissatisfaction with the existing churches. Later, Smith claimed to have had a second vision, in which a messenger of God revealed to him the whereabouts of a sacred text written on golden tablets. According to his account, Smith found the tablets, translated them, and published them as the Book of Mormon. Shortly thereafter, he confirmed his two brothers and three other young men as the first followers of the Mormon faith. Thus the seeds of a new religion were sown.

What is extraordinary about the Mormon faith is not the fact that it began as a reaction against the increasingly secularized religions of the nineteenth century; many new religions start this way. Rather, Mormonism is remarkable for its phenomenal growth. While most new religions eventually dwindle and die out, Mormonism has enjoyed the highest growth rate of any new faith in American history (Stark, 1984). By 1840, only ten years after Smith and his five followers declared themselves the first Mormons, membership in the church had reached about 30,000. Ten years later, in 1850, there were 60,000 Mormons. This doubling of membership took place despite persecution from non-Mormons, a change in leadership following the death of Joseph Smith, and a grueling migration across the Great Plains and Rocky Mountains to start a new community in Utah. By 1950, there were over 1 million Mormons, and by 1990, 7.5 million in 129 countries and territories. With approximately 300,000 conversions and/or baptisms each year, Mormons continue to expand both their membership and their geographic reach, adding missions in places as diverse as Romania, Bulgaria, Lesotho, Swaziland, El Salvador, and Nicaragua during 1990 (Marty, 1991).

Religious Revival and Fundamentalism

Fundamentalism is a kind of religious movement that seeks to establish or reestablish a pure way of life that is grounded in religious teachings and principles that followers believe to be under siege. Fundamentalism arises from confrontations with others who do not share the beliefs, either because they are members of competing religions or because they are not religious. Fundamentalist movements are most likely to develop in modern, pluralistic, secular societies where cultural certainties and traditional communities have been supplanted or challenged. As one scholar put it, they "seem to be a way of coping with the experience of chaos, the loss of identity, meaning and secure social structures created by the rapid introduction of modern social and political patterns, secularism, scientific culture and economic development" (Ruether, 1992). In the last several decades, fundamentalism has had an impact in most parts of the world. Here we will focus on two recent episodes of fundamentalist revival, Islamic fundamentalism in the Middle East and Hindu fundamentalism in India.

Islamic Fundamentalism

The 1979 revolution in Iran caught most Westerners off guard. The Shah of Iran had ruled for more than twenty years. With oil revenues and American military backing, he seemed in total control. Although not an "enlightened" ruler in terms of human rights, the Shah had brought Iran (formerly Persia) into the modern world. Under his rule the number of industrial factories went from 1,000 to 8,000, university enrollments increased tenfold, and per capita annual income grew from $160 to $1,600 year. But a general strike in 1978 led to a year of mass protests that forced the Shah to resign and brought to power a fundamentalist Shiite Islamic regime led by the Ayatollah Ruhollah Khomeini (Abrahamian, 1985). To understand this apparently abrupt change from a secular, modern state to a theocracy (or rule by religious leaders), one must look at the history of Islam.

Islam dates back to the seventh century A.D., when (followers believe) an angel of Allah, or God, revealed himself to an Arab trader named Mohammed. The religion that Mohammed founded shares many elements with Judaism, Christianity, and other earlier traditions. Followers of Islam, known as Muslims, see Mohammed as the last and greatest of a line of prophets extending back to Jesus and Abraham; the feast of Eid, one of the most important days on the Islamic calendar, celebrates the sparing of Abraham's son Isaac, a story told in the Judeo-Christian Bible. Mohammed recorded Allah's message in the Islamic holy book, the Koran (or Qur'an). Muslims revere the Koran as the literal dictations of the thoughts of Allah, which are not subject to interpretation or even translation. Many non-Arabic-speaking Muslims in places like Pakistan and Indonesia, as well as illiterate Arab herders and peasants, learn the Koran by heart. Verses from the Koran are posted in homes, offices, restaurants, and taxis—much as Catholics display the crucifix or pictures of saints.

Islam, like Christianity, spread throughout much of the world and developed many local variations. But all Muslims share certain important traditions, called "the pillars of Islam." These include affirming that "there is no God but Allah and Mohammed is his last prophet"; praying at regular intervals during the day; contributing a portion of one's income to charity; fasting from daybreak to nightfall during the month of Ramadan, when the Koran was revealed; and if possible, making a pilgrimage to the holy city of Mecca, in Saudi Arabia, at least once in a lifetime. This pilgrimage, called the *Haj*, is one of the most important goals of a Muslim's life.

From the beginning, Islam was a messianic religion, oriented to converting others and spreading its message universally (a characteristic it shares with Christianity but not some other religions, such as Judaism and Hinduism, that do not actively seek converts). The drive to expand and the duty to protect the religious community led to the tradition of the *jihad*, or holy war against those who threaten the community, and the belief that a soldier who dies fighting the infidel would be a martyr, revered on earth and reserved a special place in heaven. (This tradition of martyrdom is particularly strong among the Shiite Muslims; see Chapter 1.) Islam's early history was one of military conquest, religious conversion, and cultural achievements. Muslims ruled most of the Mediterranean world and the East almost as far as China, repelling European Crusaders, conquering most of north and central India under the Mogul Empire, and remaining in power (through the Ottoman Empire, ruled from Istanbul) up until World War I. Despite the Muslim dedication to winning converts, minorities (such as Jews and Christians) generally were allowed to live and pursue their own religion as they liked under Islamic rulers (B. Lewis, 1985).

Islam's glorious past has been overshadowed by recent humiliations as Arabs and other Muslims were conquered by European colonial powers, forced to accept the creation of the state of Israel, and several times defeated by Israeli armies backed by the United States and other Western powers. Islamic fundamentalism can be seen as an attempt to "salvage that history" (J. D. Hunter, 1990, p. 60). The first wave of Islamic revivals occurred in the early eighteenth and nineteenth centuries when, for example, Sudanese Muslims armed only with spears defeated a massive British force armed with guns and artillery. The second wave began in the mid-twentieth century, and continues to spread. The revolution in Iran was but one expression of this movement.

Why Iran and why the late 1970s? The modernization of Iran did not result from pressure for change by the Iranian people, but was imposed by the Shah with little regard for the people's traditions and sensibilities. A small number of Iranians profited handsomely from the country's new-found oil wealth and adapted readily to the influx of Western ideas and lifestyles. For most people, though, modernization meant dislocation in the cities, unemployment, and a repressive secret police force. The mosques of the Muslim sect known as Shiism, a sect that had a long history of blending politics and religion, provided ready-made sanctuaries for dissidents to meet and organize. In these mosques young Iranians heard idealized accounts of the pure Islam of old, represented by the exiled leader Khomeini. Here plans began to take shape for a revolution that would restore the traditions of early Islam. Shiism provided Iranians not only with a cultural identity and a purpose in the midst of cultural and social chaos but also with education, jobs, emergency food and medicine, and a degree of social security. Shiite clergy had long maintained close connections with Iran's traditional bazaar shopkeepers, who were willing and able to support the urban poor—and future revolutionaries.

The revolution in Iran reverberated throughout the region, indeed throughout the world. Most Arab leaders belong to the Sunni branch of Islam. They consider themselves—or at least present themselves—as devout Muslims (much as Western leaders who go out of their way to testify to their Judeo-Christian values, whether or not they are actively religious). But, again like most Western leaders, they are committed to the separation of church (or mosque) and state. The presence of a revolutionary Shiite state, intent on exporting Islamic fundamentalism, represents a constant threat (which is why many of these leaders supported Iraq in its war with Iran during the 1980s; see Chapter 1). Adding to their fears, many Middle Eastern states (Saudi Arabia, Lebanon, Syria) have substantial Shiite minorities within their borders. The Ayatollah Khomeini and his successors have been accused of instigating Shiite rebellion against Sunni Arab leaders, as well as Islamic revolution against the infidel West. Meanwhile, Islamic fundamentalism has become a political force elsewhere in the Muslim world, especially North Africa. The Sudan declared itself an Islamic state in 1990; on a visit to Iran, Sudan's leader General Bashir declared that the two countries had a common duty to promote Islamic rule. In Algeria in 1991, when Islamic fundamentalists won resounding victories in free elections, the military stepped in and declared the elections void. This created a quandary for Western leaders, who champion free elections but at the same time support more "moderate" Sunni Muslim regimes. A major foreign-policy question is whether religious and secular states, like democratic and communist states during previous decades, must always be opposed to each other. The clash between religious and secular values also reaches into local communities, as the Global Issues/Local Consequences box explains.

Hindu Fundamentalism

Religion has also played a key role in the history and politics of India. The great majority of Indians are Hindu, but the nation's population includes substantial numbers of Muslims, Sikhs, Christians, Jains, Parsees, and Buddhists. Although there have been long periods of relative tolerance in India's history, religious divisions have been a frequent cause for violence and bloodshed. Shortly before India became independent of the British Empire in 1948, Muslim dissidents broke away to form Pakistan (the eastern part of which later split off to become Bangladesh). Pacifist leader Mahatma Gandhi was assassinated by a

GLOBAL ISSUES/LOCAL CONSEQUENCES

Fundamentalism versus Freedom of Expression

The uproar over Salman Rushdie's 1989 novel *The Satanic Verses* (which we touched on at the end of Chapter 3) illustrated how international fundamentalism can reach into local communities, affecting what books people read, what thoughts and images they can express, and even how safe they are (Fischer and Abedi, 1990; Kramer, 1991).

One section of the novel describes a controversial dream of Mohammed's, in which the prophet seems to be tempted by the devil. This scene in the book was widely regarded as blasphemous. The book was banned in India, Pakistan, and other countries that either are predominantly Muslim or have large Muslim minorities. But the reaction was strongest among Muslim immigrants in England, where a widely publicized book burning in Yorkshire was followed by a massive march on Parliament. Soon after, Iran's Ayatollah Khomeini issued a *fatwa*, or edict, promising heaven to any Muslim who killed Rushdie or any of his publishers. This threat forced Rushdie into hiding. His Italian and Japanese translators both were stabbed, the latter fatally. A paperback edition of the book was long postponed because no one wanted to take the risk of publishing it.

The demonstrations in England, in particular, were a direct expression of the clash between the fundamentalist concepts of blasphemy and heresy and the secular value of freedom of expression. What Rushdie and most Westerners saw as a work of fiction, many Indian, Pakistani, Bengali, and other Muslim immigrants to Britain saw as a direct attack on their religion and an indirect attack on themselves. For the demonstrators, Islam is the one true faith, not a matter of choice or a subject for discussion and debate. Many were small shopkeepers and mill workers, who came from peasant backgrounds and had had strict religious upbringings in their homelands. Unlike Rushdie, they did not travel in celebrity circles. No matter how long they had lived in Britain, they were still viewed as backward foreigners. They resented Asian artists, like Rushdie, and scholars who claimed to explain the immigrant experience to the ruling majority. Until the Rushdie affair, however, they were a community without a leader or a focus. *The Satanic Verses* gave them a rallying point and an identity as members of the nation of Islam, which in their eyes transcended secular government or citizenship.

For a time at least, their voices were heard. Even the fact that the native British elite stood more or less solidly behind Rushdie and their own cultural principle of freedom of speech, dismissing the demonstrators as "crazies," lifted the veil of anonymity. The British had to face the fact that they didn't really know the Asians whose shops they patronized; nor did they have a plan or vision for an England that included large numbers of people who were not white, Anglo-Saxon, and Christian, and did not think or behave as they did (Kramer, 1991).

Hindu religious fanatic for allegedly being "pro-Muslim." In 1984 Prime Minister Indira Gandhi was assassinated by her Sikh bodyguards, provoking bloody interreligious riots throughout the country. Her son Rajiv also was killed by religious fanatics. Thousands of other Indians have been killed in this ongoing violence, which became even more intense in 1992, after Hindu militants stormed a mosque in Ayodhya.

Hinduism is an ancient religion that has given rise to innumerable independent and sometimes conflicting religious beliefs, practices, experiences, and organizations (Klostermaier, 1989). The main Hindu texts, especially the Vedas, offer sociopolitical, ethical, and spiritual guidance, couched in great narratives about the adventures of gods, kings, heroes, and lesser mortals. Unlike Muslims and Christians, Hindus do not worship a single God but recognize an enormous pantheon of deities, some (like Rama and Shiva) more important than others. At the heart of the Hindu religion is the concept of *dharma*, a code of conduct for people in various social categories (or castes), situations, and stages of life. Hindus believe that every person, every living creature, every act, has its place in the cosmic order. If that order is violated, chaos results. Hinduism has never recognized the borders that Westerners place around religion today; instead, it sees politics, social relations, health, sex, science—literally every aspect of life—as part of the divine order. Hinduism predates the other religions practiced in India, and has shaped all of them (Mahmood, 1989; Madan, 1989).

Hindu fundamentalism is not new, but rather is experiencing a revival. The idea of a past golden age of Hinduism, the belief that first Muslim and then British invaders had defiled this heritage, and the conviction that India could not regenerate itself until the rules of *dharma* were restored—all played key roles in the movement for Indian independence. But the great leaders of that movement—Gandhi, Nehru, and other members of the Congress party—all advocated the creation of a secular, democratic state in which members of different religions would live together in peace. In a much quoted statement, Gandhi declared, "I am a Hindu, a Sikh, a Muslim, and a Christian" (in Mahmood, 1989, p. 340).

In the Hindu religion the concept of dharma, *or duty, is related to belief in* karma *(loosely translated as "result"), which leads to a person's reincarnation at either a higher or a lower social status. The Ganges River is considered sacred by Hindus, and corpses are often burned on the shores and the ashes scattered over the water.*

Ironically, the very success of modernization, democracy, and the protection of minority rights has contributed to the divisions and violence in India today (Malik and Vajpeyi, 1989). Under the protection of Indian laws, minorities are seeking a larger share of India's prosperity, and Hindus are resisting their advances. Today's Hindu revival takes many forms, including increased attendance at temples; the revival of religious symbols and rituals; organizations dedicated to "liberating" Hindu temples that were converted to mosques by Mogul rulers; attempts to "reconvert" Muslims and Christians back to Hinduism; demonstrations against "affirmative action" programs for lower-caste Hindus; electoral victories for the Hindu nationalist party, Bharatiya Janata; and even the resurgence of the once discredited, paramilitary Rashtryia Swayamsevak Sangh (RSS), or National Pure Service Society which was widely held responsible for the assassination of Gandhi. Separatist movements have arisen in Muslim-dominated Kashmir and Sikh-dominated Punjab.

Current clashes must be seen in historical and international context. Under the Mogul Empire and British Raj, Hindus were a persecuted "minority" in their own land. Today, in Pakistan and Bangladesh, both of which are Muslim states, those Hindus who remain are denied full rights under the law, and in Sri Lanka Tamil-speaking Hindus are fighting for survival against the Sinhala-speaking Buddhist majority. In addition, many Hindus in India see the government as appeasing minorities, for example, by allowing Muslims to apply their own family laws (e.g., restricting women's rights in divorce cases). Even members of India's Westernized middle class appear to be responding to the call for Hindu nationalism (Malik and Vajpeyi, 1989), which is also supported by many Hindus living abroad.

Where these conflicts will lead is impossible to predict. But religion clearly has become a major source of political mobilization, and seems likely to play a key role in national and international relations for some time to come. There are Islamic revivals in Malaysia and Indonesia, Buddhist movements in Thailand, Confucian renewals in Japan, Korea, and Taiwan—not to mention the increased visibility of Christian and Jewish fundamentalists in the United States (Marty and Appleby, 1992).

RELIGION IN THE UNITED STATES TODAY

Unlike societies in which a single religion predominates, the United States is characterized by religious pluralism (see Figure 14.2). This means that Americans can choose among dozens of religious denominations, from Presbyterian to Rastafarian.

Many Americans choose no denomination in particular. They practice a private form of religion that the sociologist Thomas Luckmann (1967) has called **invisible religion**: They think of religion as a subjective, personal experience, not as a group doctrine. Studies suggest that this outlook is widespread. For instance, in a survey of Christians in

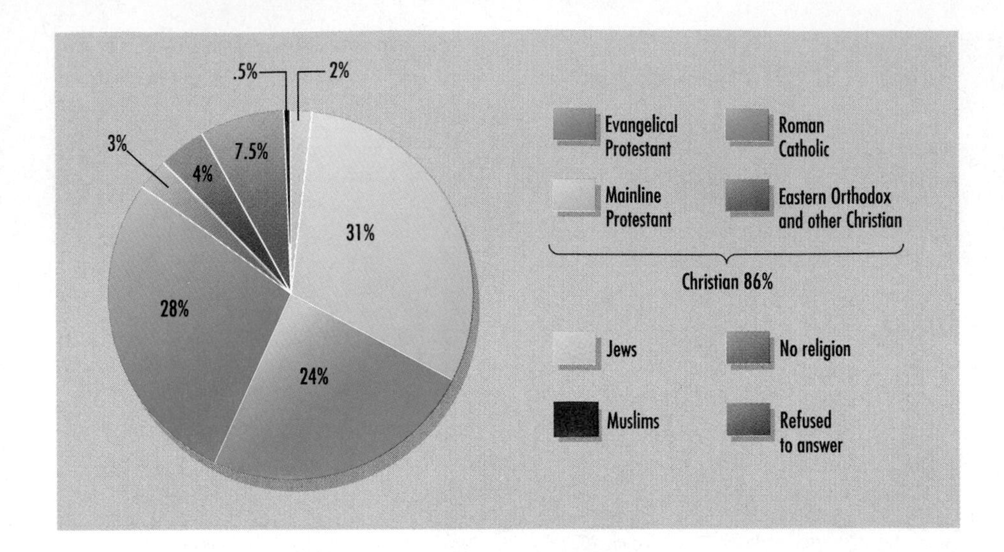

FIGURE 14.2 / Religious Affiliations of the American People

Sources: *New York Times*, April 10, 1991, pp. A1, A11; *Time*, May 22, 1989, pp. 94–96.

Minnesota two-thirds said that people could "reject some church teachings and continue to have deep Christian faith" (Chittister and Marty, 1983, p. 79). These "unaffiliates" usually are not members of traditional churches and congregations. They do not proselytize, nor do they even talk about their religious beliefs except to very close relatives and friends. They tend to keep their faith, worship, and spiritual life to themselves (Hart, 1987). This does not mean they lack religious beliefs. Almost half believe in life after death, and two-fifths believe in a literal interpretation of the Bible (Greeley, 1989). The existence of invisible religion helps explain why, although between 90 and 95 percent of Americans say they believe in God, only about 32 percent regularly attend religious services (Harris, 1987). In terms of the three dimensions of religion introduced at the beginning of this chapter, these people emphasize belief more than practices or religious community. Some theologians are concerned about the pervasiveness of invisible religion because they fear it can undermine the sense of community that churches offer.

There is a lot of talk about religious change in the United States. In the 1960s, many asked "Is God dead?" in the wake of the publication of a best-selling book on that theme by the theologian Harvey Cox. In the 1970s a new fundamentalist and evangelical movement became prominent. Audiences for TV ministers became enormous. Religion and politics mixed in new ways. In this section we will examine each of these changes—but it is important not to exaggerate the extent of religious change. Reviewing major studies of religion in the United States over the past quarter century, the sociologist Andrew M. Greeley (1989) found more stability than change. Today as in the past, Americans are more religious than their European counterparts (about a third of whom say they have no religion). Moreover, religious beliefs and practices have not changed very much since the eve of World War II (when data were first collected). A majority of Americans still hold traditional religious beliefs in God, the divinity of Jesus (if they are Christian), and the afterlife (see Table 14.2). Although fewer accept the literal truth of the Bible, more say that they read the Bible daily and exhibit accurate knowledge of its contents. About 40 percent of Americans today say they attended religious services in the last seven days—the same proportion as in 1939 (Gallup Organization survey, June 1990).

This does not mean that religion in the United States is completely static. While beliefs and rituals have been relatively stable, the organization of religious communities, their patterns of social action, and their relations with the broader society have changed significantly. Religious affiliation is a dynamic process. As one denomination loses followers, another gains in strength. As one sect disappears from the social landscape, a new one emerges and attracts adherents. One of today's major changes, suggests the sociologist Robert Wuthnow (1988), is an overall decline in denominationalism. There is much less competition among Protestant denominations like Baptists and Methodists; Protestant and Catholic leaders are more cooperative. The boundaries between denominations are more fluid, with people moving fairly readily from one denomination to another. As a result, there has been a good deal of reshuffling of religious membership and restructuring of religious organizations. Data on changes in church membership tell us little about any changes taking place in how

TABLE 14.2

Religious Beliefs

	Year	Percentage Answering Yes
A. Do you believe in the existence of God or a universal spirit?		
	1944	97%
	1954	96
	1967	97
	1981	95
B. Do you believe that Jesus Christ ever actually lived? Do you think He was God or just another leader like Mohammed or Buddha?		
	1952	77
	1965	75
	1983	76
C. Do you believe there is a life after death?		
	1944	76
	1952	77
	1965	75
	1975	76
	1985	74
D. Do you think there is a heaven where people who have led good lives are eternally rewarded?		
	1952	72
	1965	68
	1980	71
E. Do you believe there is a hell?		
	1952	58
	1965	54
	1980	53

Source: Andrew M. Greeley, Religious Change in America (*Harvard University Press, Cambridge, Mass., 1989), p. 14, table 2.1.*

the people in each religious group feel and think. For this we must look more closely at events occurring in each of the major religions in the United States today.

Trends in Mainline American Churches

Although some Americans have recently looked for new avenues of religious expression, for the most part Americans have sought to make the existing churches more responsive to their needs. In the 1980s this meant both a search for stronger spiritual moorings and an increased activism among church leaders in response to social issues (*Gallup Report*, 1985). Partly as a result, religion in America has become more polarized: growing numbers of people with no religious affiliation at one extreme and growing numbers of religious conservatives at the other (Himmelstein, 1990). Likewise, religion has become more polarized politically (Wuthnow, 1988). Recent developments among American Roman Catholics, Protestants, and Jews illustrate these trends.

Roman Catholics

The reforms instituted by the Second Vatican Council marked a turning point for traditional Roman Catholicism in the United States. Vatican II, held in Rome between 1962 and 1965, eliminated the Latin mass and meatless Fridays, allowed laity to receive communion wafers in their own hands and to take wine from the chalice, redefined non-Catholics as separated brothers and sisters (not "heretics"), and repudiated anti-Semitism. In addition, lay Catholics were permitted to take on administrative and liturgical duties once reserved for priests, including the reading aloud of Scripture and the distribution of communion. Vatican II can be seen as the result of a long power struggle within the Catholic church between those who wanted to maintain the church's hierarchical structure and the priestly power to decide what it means to be Christian, and those who saw the modern church as "people of God," in which lay Catholics are invited to examine their own consciences and think for themselves.

The impact of Vatican II was dramatic and far-reaching, especially in the United States. Catholicism became more personalized, with individuals deciding spiritual matters and moral issues for themselves. For instance, more than four-fifths of young-adult Catholics reject their church's teachings on birth control, premarital sex, divorce, and remarriage; many also reject the doctrine of papal infallibility. Yet they remain solidly Catholic in their fundamental convictions about life, death, and God, and they say they intend to remain in the church, though on their own terms. In large degree, "Catholic" has come to be an ethnic or cultural identity (Greeley, 1990).

These challenges to priestly authority have provoked counterreactions among church officials (Segers, 1990). (As a measure of the turmoil within American Catholicism in the wake of Vatican II, a fifth of all Catholic priests left the ministry, and an even higher proportion of nuns withdrew from religious orders.) Some priests and higher church officials have responded by attempting to meet their parishioners' call for a more liberal and activist church, for example, by endorsing such unconventional activities as support groups for divorced Catholics and for homosexuals. A new political advocacy first emerged in

The rituals of pilgrimage and penance have largely disappeared from religion in the United States but are still common in rural areas of Europe. Penitents come from all over the world to Fatima, Portugal, to ask holy favors and give thanks at a site where in 1917 three shepherd children reported being visited by the Virgin Mary. In 1930, at the same site, thousands of pilgrims witnessed the "sun miracle of Fatima," in which the sun appeared to move closer to the earth.

the spring of 1983, when the U.S. College of Roman Catholic Bishops issued a letter calling for nuclear disarmament. Another pastoral letter, in 1984, called for efforts to eliminate poverty and unemployment, as well as a policy of increased aid to Third World nations. Suddenly, the Catholic church seemed to be adopting the role of social conscience and liberal advocate for change that some of the mainline Protestant churches had played in the 1960s (Marty, 1985).

Other Catholic leaders (most notably in Rome) have attempted to slow the pace of change and insist on traditional values. Pope John Paul II has spoken out strongly against liberalizing and politicizing the church. The result has been mounting strain between Vatican officials and American church leaders who suggest different interpretations of God's laws. The role of women has become the source of much controversy. Nuns, who outnumber priests by two to one, have taken the lead in the movement to expand the role of women in the church. The issues of contraception and abortion remain strongly divisive. Moreover, the church still emphasizes the priorities of marriage and family over careers for women.

Protestants

For generations, the Methodist, Presbyterian, Episcopalian, and Congregationalist churches have been integral parts of nearly every American community. But these mainline, established, predominantly white denominations belonging to the National Council of Churches are in decline. Since 1965, membership in the Congregationalist denomination (or United Church of Christ) has shrunk by 20 percent, the Presbyterian church by 25 percent, the Episcopal church by 28 percent, the United Methodist by 18 percent, and the Christian church (Disciples of Christ) by 43 percent (after a schism). All told, these denominations lost 5.2 million members while the U.S. population grew by 47 million (*Time*, May 22, 1989). Of the more than 40 percent of Americans born into mainline churches during this period, one in five left (Greeley, 1989). At the same time, the evangelical movement within the Protestant churches was attracting new members in record numbers. Membership in the fundamentalist, conservative Southern Baptist Convention rose 20 percent; in the Seventh-Day Adventists, 36 percent; and in the Assemblies of God, 62 percent.

Evangelical movements share three distinguishing beliefs: The Bible is the highest authority on the word of God; eternal salvation comes only through acceptance of Jesus Christ, who atoned for humanity's sins; and "the kindest thing one person can do for another is to tell him or her of this gospel promise of salvation" (Marsden, 1990, p. 23).

Recall from our earlier discussion that fundamentalist movements are likely to develop in modern, pluralistic, secular societies where cultural certainties and traditional communities have been supplanted. Fundamentalists believe that biblical tenets and religious traditions alone should guide both individual and collective life. Evangelicals (mainly a Christian designation) stress telling the "good news" of God's saving grace. As we saw in looking at Islamic fundamentalism, fundamentalism inherently advocates cultural conservatism; evangelicalism may or may not. While some evangelicals are fundamentalists, many are not (and vice versa).

Most evangelicals describe themselves as born-again Christians: people who have had a significant conversion experience in which they came to accept Jesus as their Lord and Savior. Most also oppose such "barroom vices" as drinking, smoking, dancing, gambling, and sex outside of marriage (Marsden, 1990).

Greeley and others (for example, Kelly, 1977) suspect that evangelical groups are thriving because mainline denominations became too liberal and too activist for many Americans. In the 1960s and 1970s many were on the cutting edge of social change, promoting such causes as women's liberation and gay rights before the majority of Americans were ready to accept them. Social crusading began to replace spiritual matters in Sunday services, and many people were alienated. Evangelicalism appeals "to those who still want 'religion' with their religion" (Greeley, 1989, p. 36). In support of this explanation, Greeley notes that people who have moved toward evangelicalism attend church more often, pray more frequently, feel closer to God, are more active in church-related organizations, and are more likely to describe themselves as "strongly religious" than others.

Jews

Jews have been part of the American religious scene since the nation's beginning. In general, Jews have had an easier time gaining acceptance in the United States than in European countries, where national identity is based on membership in a common ethnic group and a state church. Although Jews make up less than 2 percent of the population, they have long been accepted as one of the three major religious groups in America, along with Protestants and Catholics. Anti-Semitism has sometimes limited opportunities for Jews (for example, when many universities restricted the number of Jewish students), but Jews have prospered in the United States, finding most social, economic, and political doors open to them at least since the 1960s (Eisenstadt, 1978), although incidents of anti-Semitism—such as vandalism of synagogues—have increased in the past few years. Tensions are especially high between Jews and some African-American groups like Louis Farrakhan's Nation of Islam.

Like Christianity, American Judaism is divided into a number of denominations. Orthodox Judaism is the most traditional in its beliefs, ethnic loyalties, and religious practices (such as wearing skullcaps or *yarmulkes*, keeping the strict dietary laws of *Kasreuth*, and strictly observing the sabbath); most members of Orthodox synagogues trace their ancestry to the urban ghettoes and villages of Eastern Europe; and many still speak Yiddish—the traditional language of Eastern European Jews. Reform Judaism is the most liberal and assimilated branch of the Jewish faith; members of Reform congregations tend to be middle or upper class and to trace their ancestry several generations to German Jews who migrated before the rise of Hitler in the 1930s. Conservative Judaism falls between these two, providing a religious home for those Eastern European Jews who are more assimilated to American culture and are more likely to be highly educated professionals than are the Orthodox Jews, but tend to be more traditionally religious than the Reform Jews (Lipset, 1990). Despite these broad patterns of development, the boundaries between the groups are not rigid. Jews sometimes choose a synagogue because they like the rabbi or the "feeling" of the congregation—just the way many Christians choose which parish to join. Sometimes local rivalries or immigration patterns shape the predominance of one or another denomination in a community (Morowska, 1991).

Despite these religious and socioeconomic differences, many Jews share certain concerns (Glazer, 1990). One is the memory of the Holocaust, in which more than 6 million European Jews were slaughtered in Nazi death camps. Few Jews take for granted their survival as a people, and periodic flare-ups of anti-Semitism, here and abroad, keep this experience a living memory.

Closely related to the fear that the Holocaust could happen again is fear for Israel's survival. Even if they are not religious, most Jews feel a kinship with Israel, identify with Israeli victories and defeats, and support Israel through financial contributions and votes for pro-Israeli politicians in America. But the election of a conservative and seemingly intransigent government in Israel, and the debates over settlement of the West Bank in Jordan and treatment of Palestinians, have created a quandary for many American Jews, who tend to be liberal. Should they support Israel no matter what, or assist peace groups within Israel? The 1992 election of a more moderate Israeli government brought rising hopes for peace and new optimism among American Jews.

A third concern is for the survival of Jews and Judaism in America. In this context, *survival* refers not to physical safety but to cultural identity. Nine out of ten Jewish youths attend universities, where they are likely to adopt universalist values that discourage ethnic loyalty. Jewish intermarriage rates are approaching 50 percent, and birth rates are low. Because American Jews are a small minority in a predominantly Christian country, and because Judaism does not encourage conversion (even of spouses), there is concern that their distinct heritage may disappear. However, in recent years there has been a revival of interest among American Jews in the rituals, symbols, and activities of Jewish social groups.

Christian Fundamentalism

As in other parts of the world, fundamentalism, especially Christian fundamentalism, has become a significant voice in American religion (Marsden, 1990). Like their counterparts in other cultures, Christian fundamentalists are opposed to moderate liberal theologies, especially "secular humanism," which emphasizes cultural and religious relativity. Upset by many trends in modern secular culture, they are willing to fight for their beliefs. Fundamentalists believe that the Bible is the ultimate authority on spiritual matters and that its historical and scientific assertions are literally true. This is known as the *doctrine of biblical inerrancy*. Most fundamentalists, for example, reject the theory of evolution in favor of the biblical story of divine creation. They believe that in winning converts they are not only saving souls, but ultimately fighting to save America—sounding a nationalist theme found in many forms of fundamentalism. They believe that the world is divided between the forces of good and evil, that they know who the enemy is, and that they can accept no compromise. Fundamentalists are linked together outside the church's traditional structure by a range of organizations and by concern about threats to their social values.

Recent Developments in American Fundamentalism

American fundamentalism has undergone changes in the past two decades. Once identified mainly with rural and small-town people, it has come to flourish in major metropolitan areas. Though Southerners are prominent, the stereotype of fundamentalism as a Southern phenomenon is false. Fundamentalism has seen some of its most rapid growth in California. While earlier fundamentalists were often workers and farmers without much formal education, many contemporary fundamentalists are well-educated. They are especially common among those whose families are new to the middle class and among the lower and middle levels of the middle class. Their educational background tends to be in technical fields rather than the liberal arts. Fundamentalists are united by strong beliefs about divine inspiration and the accuracy of the Bible as well as by a sense that trends in secular society are threatening them. Concern about protecting children from perceived evil influences is an important part of fundamentalism. Fundamentalists have also begun to take a more active role in political life, partly because they see trends such as acceptance of homosexuality, rising divorce rates, single-parent families, and teenage drug use as threats to the social values they hold dear. This is what links them to the conservatives who are not part of any fundamentalist Christian movement. This also distinguishes them from many people in the upper middle class whose social values became more liberal in the 1960s and 1970s. Fundamentalists are linked together outside the traditional structures of church denominations by a range of new organizations, including nondenominational seminaries for training ministers. Christian music, special bookstores, and Christian schools also provide a sense of community and a way of disseminating religious culture. Members of the fundamentalist movement have been concerned with building alternative cultural institutions and communities, not simply with advocating certain beliefs. Members of fundamentalist congregations spend much time and energy on providing support for those who seek to depend less on secular or non-Christian social institutions.

Christian fundamentalism grew more prominent in the 1970s. But comparing survey data over time, Greeley (1989) has shown that this is not because more Americans hold fundamentalist beliefs. On three fundamentalist questions, there was little evidence of change between 1976 and 1984. The proportion of respondents who had had a born-again experience had increased slightly, while the percentages who believed in a literal interpretation of the Bible and who believed they should encourage others to accept Jesus remained about the same. About one-fifth of Americans are fundamentalists, a figure that has remained more or less stable for decades. The crucial changes are the rising number of middle-class fundamentalists and the increasing political activity of fundamentalist groups. The political involvement of fundamentalists has been called *the new Christian right*.

The new Christian right emerged in the context of a broader conservative movement. Many forces contributed to the politicization of fundamentalists (Himmelstein, 1990; Wuthnow, 1988). One was the presidency of born-again Christian Jimmy Carter, which increased the public's recognition of evangelicals and gave them more legitimacy. A second reason was the emergence of a new set of social issues, including abortion rights, the Equal Rights Amendment and feminism generally, sexual liberation, gay and lesbian rights, drug abuse, prohibitions on school prayer, and pornography. Suddenly, important political issues seemed intertwined with moral questions. In the 1950s and 1960s, fundamentalists had seen the United States as being engaged in a life-or-death struggle with the Soviet Union and world communism; in the 1970s and 1980s, they began to believe that moral permissiveness in the government and the public at large had set the country on a course toward self-destruction. The third reason for the new political visibility of fundamentalists was that they had developed an extensive infrastructure—including superchurches, broad communication networks, up-to-date methods of computerized fund-raising, targeted lobbying, and an electronic ministry—that enabled them to mobilize political conservatives and religious traditionalists who usually shied away from politics.

During the 1980s, evangelical Christianity rose to renewed prominence in the United States, thanks partly to preachers like Robert Schuller (shown here) who used television. Taken from the word for several key books of the New Testament, "evangelism" refers to spreading the "good news" of Christ's promised salvation and seeking converts or renewals of faith.

Televangelism

In 1960, the Federal Communications Commission (FCC) ruled that broadcasters could satisfy their public-service requirement by selling air time to religious organizations. This decision, along with the advent of cable and satellite TV technology, opened the door for a new brand of television minister, who combined evangelical themes (personal salvation, biblical inerrancy, and the evils of secular humanism) with on-the-air fund-raising for Christian projects and causes (Himmelstein, 1990). Known as *televangelism*, this phenomenon played a major role in the increased visibility of the fundamentalist message.

A 1985 Nielsen poll found that 60 million Americans tuned in to at least one of the evangelical programs weekly (*The Economist*, May 16, 1987). By 1987, the electronic church had become a $2 billion enterprise ("Religion in America," 1987). Surveys found that the audience for religious TV was socially and religiously diverse (Wuthnow, 1990). Although most electronic ministries were headquartered in the South, only one out of three viewers lived in that region. Most were white evangelical Protestants, but one in five was black, about the same proportion was Roman Catholic, and a third belonged to mainline Protestant groups. Most were heavy consumers of conventional as well as religious TV. Like other regular TV viewers, they tended to be older and less educated than the average American, and to feel that they had been left behind. A majority said they were distressed by "the way moral standards have been changing in America" (p. 97). In the late 1970s they also began hearing a conservative Republican message. President Ronald Reagan became the fundamentalists' champion. Although not a regular churchgoer himself, Reagan actively courted the new Christian right and sided with it on most issues.

The influence of televangelists and the new Christian right peaked in the 1980s. Many fundamentalists were disappointed in the results of their participation in mainstream politics, feeling they received little more than lip service from Presidents Reagan and Bush. Some turned increasingly to opposing abortion and homosexuality; others retreated from organized politics. The viewing audience fell off sharply after a series of scandals involving televangelists rocked the new Christian right. Despite these setbacks, fundamentalists remain a powerful, well-organized segment of American society and are likely to continue to exert an influence.

Thinking Back on the Key Concepts

Religion is one of the most important aspects of ***culture***. As we saw in this chapter, religion includes beliefs (one God or many) and cultural distinctions (between the sacred and the profane). We also saw that religion responds to cultural changes, for example, when secularization brings revival or innovation. Religion is also a matter of ***social action***, first of all in the way every religion prescribes specific kinds of action for its members. These actions include both rituals and rules for everyday life. Religions are also founded through social action, as we saw in the case of Mormonism, and are changed or renewed through social action, as we saw in the case of Islamic fundamentalism.

Religious action and religious belief are usually organized into religious institutions with specific ***social structures***. Thus, for example, we saw that in the United States today practicing religious people are divided into a number of churches and sects, and particularly into the various Catholic and Protestant Christian denominations and different branches of Judaism. Each of these includes formal and informal organizational structures that provide training for clergy, reports to the press, and printing of sacred texts. All such activities have to be functionally integrated within each religious group, and it is usually important for members of a religion to develop a religious community that links them to one another in terms of both structure and ***functional integration***. Religion also plays an important role in reproducing the functional integration of society as a whole. One way this happens—especially in the United States—is through civil religion, which provides for religious reaffirmation of secular institutions.

Although religion is largely concerned with issues of community, sacred values, and worship, we also saw that it involves ***power***. Religious leaders have the power to define what is sacred or profane, sinful or good. The founder of Scientology, L. Ron Hubbard, used his power to start what he considered a new religion. And religious leaders like the Ayatollah Khomeini have used their power to intervene in the politics of their countries.

SUMMARY

1. In defining religion, sociologists focus on three basic elements: beliefs, social practices, and moral community. Durkheim defined religion as a set of beliefs and practices pertaining to sacred things that unite people into a moral community. Other definitions focus on the role of power, the concept of supernatural forces, and experiences that transcend everyday life.

2. Regardless of the specific characteristics of different religions, all have certain elements in common. These include religious beliefs and symbols, which are elements of ***culture***; rituals and ceremonies, which are forms of ***social action***; and religious community, a form of ***social structure***. Religion may support or contest the existing social order, or contribute to ***functional integration*** or to schisms based on ***power*** conflicts.

3. Sociologists distinguish among three types of religious institutions: church, sect, and cult. A church is a large, conservative religious institution that tends to coexist harmoniously with the larger society. A sect, in contrast, is a small, uncompromising fellowship of people who seek spiritual perfection and tend to reject the larger society. Sects form when people break away from established churches and claim to have adopted a more authentic, purer version of their faith. A cult is like a sect in most respects except its origins. Cults are imported from other cultures or are formed when people create entirely new religious beliefs and practices.

4. Max Weber believed that the rise of modern capitalism had important roots in certain religious ideas of the Protestant Reformation. In particular, the Calvinist concept of predestination encouraged hard work, frugality, and astute investment in order to be successful in life and thus provide proof of God's favor. Weber's theory is a good example of how religious change can promote change in other aspects of society.

5. Modernization has generally been accompanied by secularization, which entails a greater concern with worldly matters than with spiritual ones. But secularization has not spelled the end of religion. Religion remains a powerful force because of two countervailing trends: religious innovation (an effort to create new religions or to change existing ones to better meet people's needs) and religious revival (an effort to restore more traditional, spiritual features to established religions). The Mormon faith, founded in the United States in 1830, is an example of religious innovation; Islamic and Hindu fundamentalism in the East are examples of contemporary religious revivals.

6. Contrary to popular impressions, religious beliefs and practices in the United States have remained remarkably stable over the years. But religious organizations have undergone significant restructuring. Since Vatican II, the Catholic laity have become more active in their church and also more independent in deciding moral and social issues. Mainline Protestant churches have lost members, while evangelical denominations have grown. For third- and fourth-generation American Jews, religion plays an important role in maintaining ethnic identity. Fundamentalist churches became more visible and more active during the 1980s. At the same time many more people described religion as a personal or private matter.

REVIEW QUESTIONS

1. What are the three basic elements of religion?

2. What is the difference between churches, sects, and cults? Give an example of each.

3. How has religion helped to bring about social change?

4. What is meant by religious pluralism, and what are the implications?

5. Summarize the current trends in mainline American churches.

CRITICAL THINKING QUESTIONS

1. Using the five key concepts—social structure, social action, functional integration, power, and culture—examine your own religion or some religion with which you are familiar.

2. The chapter describes how religion can bring about social change. Using what you have learned in this and other chapters, predict some social changes that religion may help to bring about.

3. The chapter notes that Americans are more religious than Europeans. Using what you know about the culture and social structure of American and European societies, develop some possible explanations for the difference.

4. Using what you have learned in this and other chapters, project trends in mainline American churches.

5. How has reading this chapter affected your approach to or understanding of both your own religion and religiosity in general?

GLOSSARY

Animism The idea that things in the world are imbued with active, animate spirits.

Church According to Troeltsch, a large, conservative, universalist religious institution that makes few demands on its members and accommodates itself to the larger society.

Civil religion Bellah's term for a sanctifying of the nation by associating its history, values, and institutions with God's special favor.

Cult According to Stark and Bainbridge, a religious group that tends to exist in a state of tension with the surrounding culture and that has no prior ties to any established religious body in the larger society.

Evangelicals Christians who feel a calling to emphasize the teachings of the Scriptures and to bear witness to God's influence on earth.

Fundamentalism The view that religious teachings and principles have eroded in modern societies, and a pure way of life must be reestablished by returning to religious basics (or "fundamentals").

Invisible religion The view that religion is a subjective, personal experience, not a matter of group doctrine.

Moral community A group of people who share religious beliefs, symbols, and practices that bind them together into a social whole.

Religion According to Durkheim, a set of beliefs and practices pertaining to sacred things that unite people into a moral community. According to Stark and Bainbridge, organizations primarily engaged in providing people with the hope of future rewards to compensate for things they greatly desire but have not obtained in life; this hope is based on a set of beliefs in supernatural forces, beings, or places.

Religious innovation An effort to create new religions or to change existing ones to better meet people's needs.

Religious revival An effort to restore more traditional, spiritual features to established religions.

Ritual A standardized set of actions used in a particular ceremony or on some other specific occasion.

Sect As defined by Troeltsch, a small, exclusive, uncompromising fellowship that makes heavy demands on its members and sets them apart from the larger society. As defined by Stark and Bainbridge, a religious group formed by breaking away from an established religious body.

Secularization The process by which people and their social institutions become more concerned with worldly matters and less concerned with spiritual ones. Secularization is often associated with modernization.

Theism The idea that powerful supernatural beings are involved with events and conditions on earth.

Totem An object, plant, or animal that is worshiped as the mystical ancestor of a society or other special group.

CHAPTER 15

Health and Health Care

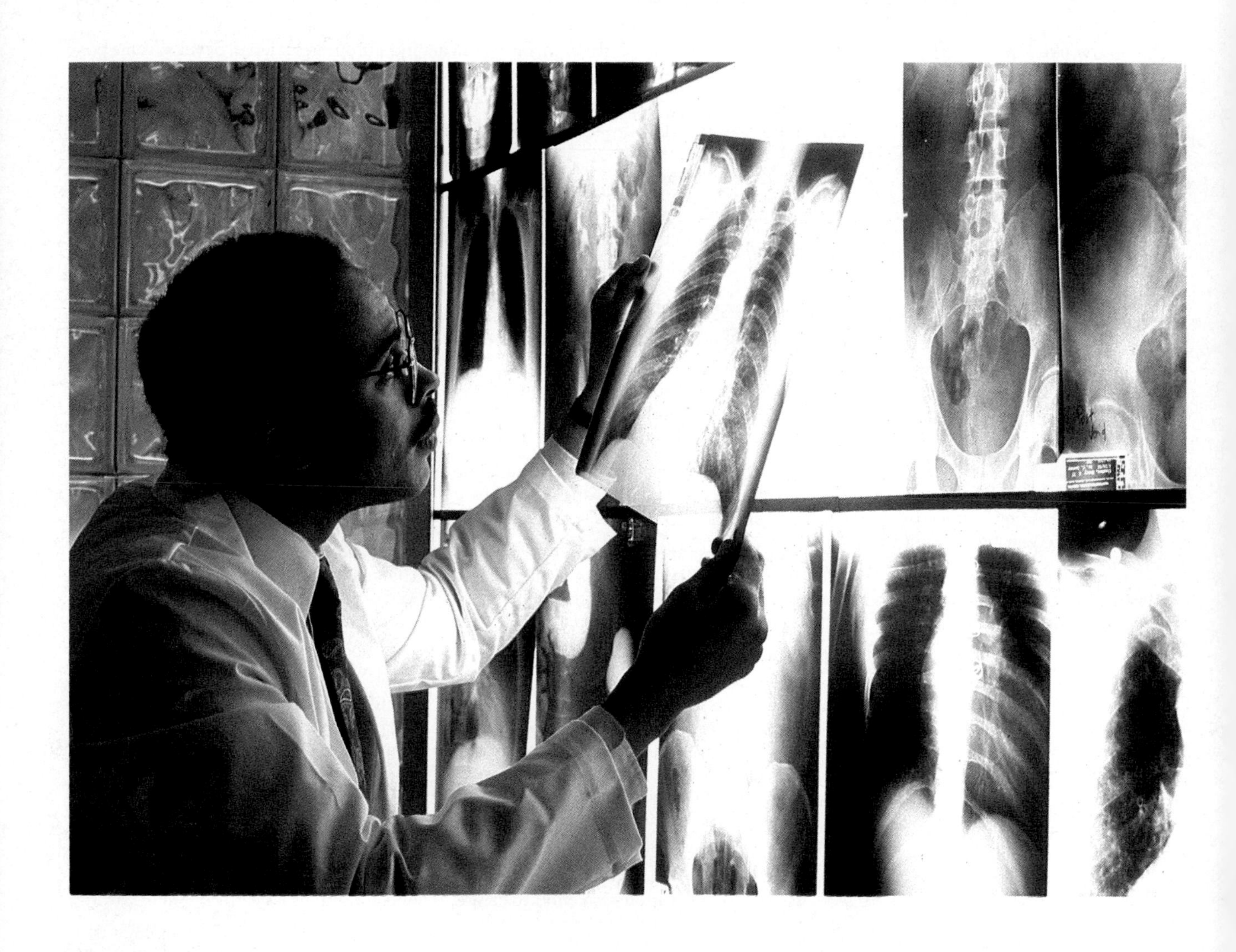

One February morning in an East Coast city a young Hispanic woman brought her twenty-month-old daughter to a public health-care clinic. The mother reported that the child had falling spells, sometimes vomited, complained of pains in her head, and had "sandy" diarrhea. The fourth-year medical student on duty, alert to the possible meaning of the last symptom, asked the mother, "Does your daughter ever eat paint chips or plaster?" "Oh, yes," the mother replied. "She eats the walls all the time. I can't stop her; she eats them right down to the wood." Tests confirmed what the medical student suspected: The child had severe lead poisoning from eating lead-based paint. Although the mother had considered her daughter's habit annoying, she didn't know it was dangerous. After all, other children in her neighborhood of deteriorating buildings had done the same and seemed all right. And because paint chips and plaster are sweet-tasting, she would have had to watch her daughter every waking minute of the day to prevent her from eating them (Light, Phipps, and Sorbello, 1982).

Understanding issues related to health and health care requires more than medical knowledge. As the story above suggests, to get a full picture, we must also apply sociological analysis. The problem of lead poisoning, for example, is related to ***social structure***. The poorest American children are most likely to suffer from lead poisoning because they are most likely to live in run-down housing built before 1940 when lead paint was still commonly used. (The use of lead paint is now restricted.) Whether or not parents know about the dangers of eating paint chips and the speed with which a child is taken to a doctor are partly a matter of ***culture*** because different social groups have different levels of knowledge about health issues. Developing a public health-care system that includes clinics, such as the one in the example above, is an instance of ***social action***. Public clinics can be supported by both government funding and private charities. Many medical professionals choose to work long hours at reduced salaries to help people who could not otherwise afford health care. Health care in the United States remains expensive and inaccessible to many in part because of the ***power*** of the American Medical Association and other groups that work to protect the existing system. The health-care system is ***functionally integrated*** with American society because it must respond to the health problems that society creates. In addition to the high rate of illness among the poor, the system must contend with occupational injuries, health problems created by exposure to hazardous wastes, and a wide variety of infectious diseases. Its costs, in turn, are borne by society as a whole, and can be a strain on the economy.

In studying the social dimensions of health care and medicine, sociologists distinguish among three concepts: disease, illness, and sickness. **Disease** is a medically diagnosed pathology (such as lead poisoning, bacterial or viral infection, or cancer). **Illness**, in contrast, is a person's own subjective sense of not feeling well. **Sickness** is social acceptance of a person as ill, as is the case when a company allows its employees "sick days" home from work. These three concepts are often closely related. Someone with the disease of lead poisoning, for example, often feels ill and is frequently treated as a sick person in a hospital. All three of these concepts, moreover, are affected by social factors such as age, sex, ethnicity, social class, and subculture.

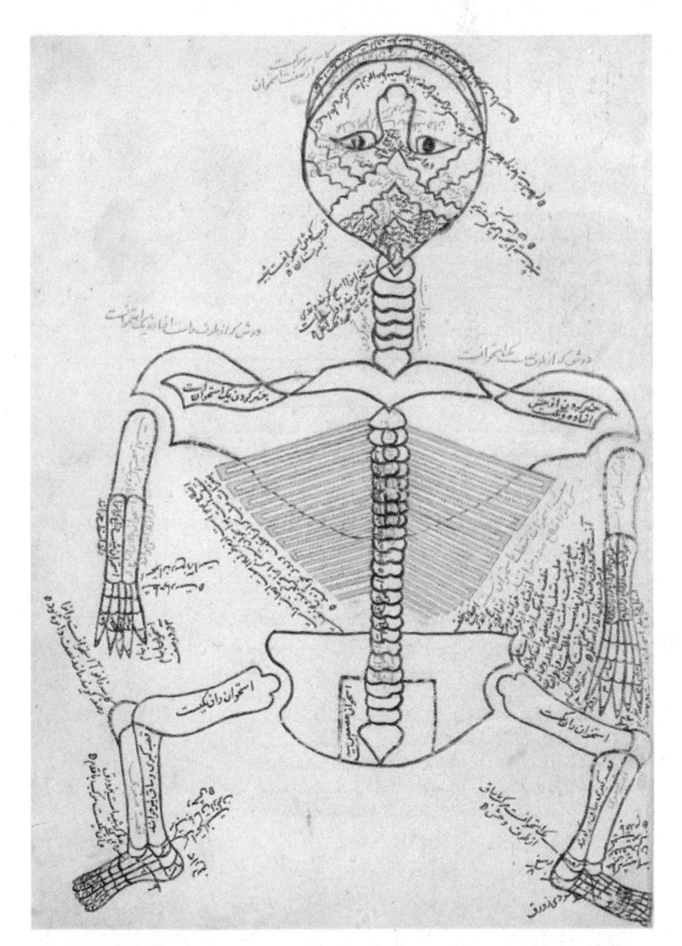

The fact that healers must invade the body to cure was not widely accepted until relatively recently. Thus, the nature of the body beneath the skin had to be guessed at by the probing minds of early medical practitioners. This fifteenth-century Islamic drawing pictures the human skeletal system.

Very elderly people, for instance, are more vulnerable to certain diseases (such as cancers), tend to experience more symptoms of illness, and are more readily accepted by others into the sick role.

In the first section of this chapter we look at social patterns of disease. We explore how modern society has helped to spawn its own set of physical ailments, and how the people who become afflicted with these disorders vary by social background. Next we turn to the sociological dimensions of three major health problems: hunger, smoking, and AIDS. Here we see how the experiences of health and illness can differ markedly among social groups. After that, we take up the topic of how the U.S. health-care industry has grown into a huge, multibillion-dollar enterprise. We then address the major dilemmas in our society's current system of health-care delivery: unequal access, spiraling costs, and the crisis in medical insurance. Finally, we examine solutions to the high cost of health care.

SOCIAL PATTERNS OF DISEASE

The Chronic Diseases of Modern Life

In 1900 the leading causes of death in the United States were pneumonia, influenza, and tuberculosis. Today these acute infectious diseases rarely kill; instead, most people die of chronic diseases such as heart disorders or cancer (see Figure 15.1). The primary reason for the change is that we now have antibiotics and other drugs that can cure infectious diseases. In addition, standards of living and public health have greatly improved. More people today eat a healthier diet, drink comparatively clean water and uncontaminated milk, and live in environments relatively free of insects, rats, and other carriers of disease. These factors tend to protect people from *acute* infections so that they may live long enough to develop the *chronic* diseases of "civilization" (those associated with modern life in highly developed countries). For example, lack of exercise and a diet high in fats and salt have been linked to the development of heart and vascular disorders. Similarly, modern dietary patterns and long exposure to low-level carcinogens (cancer-causing substances) have been associated with certain malignancies. Prosperity can thus have negative physical consequences.

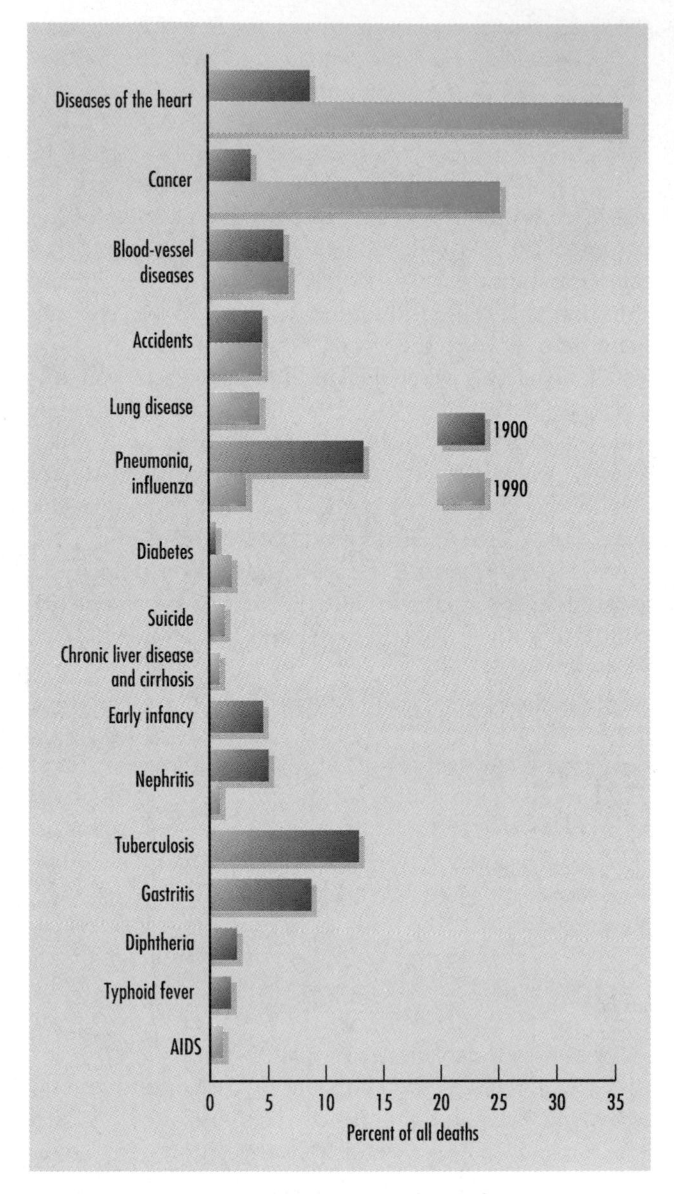

FIGURE 15.1 / Leading Causes of Death in the United States, 1900 and 1990

Sources: (1900) *Vital Statistics of the United States*, Vol. 1 (U.S. Government Printing Office, Washington, D.C., 1954), p. 170, and U.S. Bureau of the Census, *Mortality Statistics, 1900–1904* (U.S. Government Printing Office, Washington, D.C., 1906), pp. xx–xxi; (1990) National Center for Health Statistics, *Vital Statistics of the United States, Monthly Vital Statistics Report*, June 12, 1991.

What would happen if these risks of modern life were greatly reduced or even eliminated? What if most people in the industrialized world quit smoking, ate a healthier diet, got regular exercise, and avoided carcinogens? Of course, everyone would still die eventually. But according to James F. Fries (1983) of the Stanford University School of Medicine, people would live longer, more active lives and would remain comparatively free of disease until their last few years. He calls this process a **compression of morbidity** (morbidity is another word for disease). With a compression of morbidity, suffering from disease would be confined to the very end of life for most people.

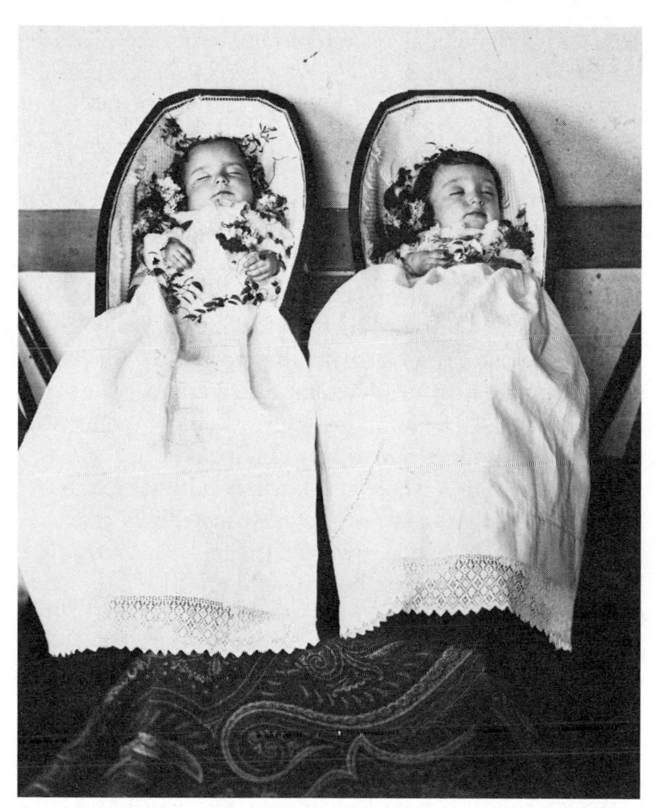

Left: *During the nineteenth century in the United States, epidemics of infectious diseases such as diphtheria led to the deaths of great numbers of children—many of whom were photographed only after death, for their grieving parents' remembrance. The prevailing pattern of childhood morbidity was reflected in cultural values (attitudes toward children, religion, and family life), socially structured strain (depletion of resources), and changes in behavior associated with begetting and raising children.* Right: *These Greek peasants integrate death into their culture. People are buried in a ceremony in which the whole village takes part and in which deep grief is expressed. After the body has been buried for some years, it is dug up for another elaborate ritual in which the villagers examine the condition of the remains to see if their loved one has entered heaven.*

How likely is it that a widespread compression of morbidity will occur in this country in your lifetime? The answer depends mainly on how much we are able to reduce the factors that give rise to chronic diseases. Some reductions people can undertake by themselves, such as giving up smoking, drinking less alcohol, eating a diet low in fats and salt, and getting more exercise. Reduction of environmental pollution, in contrast, is more a matter of collective effort. Emissions from smokestacks, cars, toxic waste dumps, and nuclear reactors have been implicated in many cancers and other diseases. The workplace, too, contains many health hazards, and certain occupations pose particular risk by exposing people to carcinogens. Controlling the environmental pollutants and toxins that cause work-related cancers requires that society adopt a "get-tough" policy with businesses that don't meet minimum safety standards. The compression of morbidity, in other words, depends very much on social policies.

Social Status and Disease

Morbidity will probably be compressed for some groups much faster than others because of the social inequalities that exist in society. The incidence of many diseases differs significantly among Americans by sex, race and ethnic background, and socioeconomic status.

Differences by Sex and by Race and Ethnic Background

Although some evidence exists that women experience more minor illness than men (Gove and Hughes, 1979), women outlive men by an average of more than seven years. No one knows why this is so, but sociologists and others have proposed explanations that take into account differences in lifestyle, diet, activity level, and social circumstances between men and women. Some point to the fact that more men smoke cigarettes and engage in other risky behaviors (drinking too much, participating in dangerous sports, driving too fast), and until recently men experienced more stresses and strains of the workplace and of the breadwinner role. Others maintain that certain genetic factors make women physiologically hardier than men. Female hormones, for example, seem to play a role in protecting premenopausal women from heart disease, and women seem less prone to high blood pressure than men are.

There are also health differences based on race and ethnicity. For instance, African-Americans and Hispanic-Americans have higher **mortality rates**, or death rates, than white Americans do. The cancer rate among black men is nearly one and a half times what it is among white men, and more than double what it is among white women. And black men have twice as many strokes as white men. Blacks and Hispanics are also far more likely to report themselves in "fair" or "poor" health, as opposed to "excellent" or "good" (U.S. Department of Health and Human Services, 1991). These racial and ethnic differences point to the role of social factors, such as poverty, in illness and disease. Blacks and Hispanics are on average poorer than whites, and lack of material resources is linked to ill health throughout the world.

The Impact of Poverty

Poverty means inadequate nourishment; unsanitary, poorly heated housing; and more exposure to stress and violence that can cause injury and disease. It also means lack of access to preventive health-care measures such as prenatal care and well-child checkups in addition to fewer trips to the doctor for treating minor illnesses before they become major. The frustration of poverty may also foster self-destructive behavior such as alcoholism, smoking, drug abuse, and other forms of risk-taking that weaken the body's immune system and leave a person more vulnerable to disease and infection.

Although Americans spend more on health care than do the people in any other country, statistically the United States is not the world's healthiest nation. One of the main reasons is the high poverty rate; another is the lack of a national system of affordable health care. Statistics on the death rate among infants show the problem. The overall infant mortality rate has been falling, but it is edging upward again in some areas, particularly in states with high levels of poverty that have suffered cutbacks in government aid for prenatal, maternal, and preventive health services. In cities such as Washington, D.C., with a substantial population of poor families, the infant mortality rate is higher than in such countries as Jamaica, Cuba, and Costa Rica. Overall, the U.S. mortality rate is 11.2 per 1,000 among infants less than one year old, compared with Finland's 6.4, Japan's 6.6, and Sweden's 6.8 (Creighton-Zollar, 1990).

Not surprisingly, life expectancy tends to be highest in industrialized countries—such as Iceland, Norway, Sweden, Switzerland, the Netherlands, and Japan—countries that have the most nearly equal distributions of income (Wilkinson, 1990). Not surprisingly, when the majority of people get adequate nutrition and adequate health care, the population as a whole is healthier and lives longer.

For the poor, in contrast, poverty and illness often go hand in hand. The poorer you are, the less healthy you are likely to be; and the less healthy you are, the more your income declines. Moreover, the poor not only get the diseases of poverty, such as infections and illnesses related to diet deficiencies; they are also more likely to suffer from the so-called diseases of affluence—cancer and heart disease. The explanation of this paradox is that poor people's diet is fattier, they are exposed to more pollutants, and, above all, their lives are frequently more stressful.

The connection between poverty and poor health is worldwide. There is a strong correlation between per capita gross national product and such indices of health as infant mortality and life expectancy. In the more developed nations the infant mortality rate averages 15 per 1,000 infants; in the least developed countries it averages 122 per 1,000. Similarly, life expectancy at birth averages seventy-four years in the more developed countries, but only forty-nine in the least developed ones (*UN World Population Chart*, 1990).

The patterns of disease in underdeveloped countries differ appreciably from those in developed countries. Infectious, parasitic, and respiratory diseases cause more than 40 percent of the deaths in underdeveloped countries, but only about 10 percent of deaths in industrialized countries. The most widespread diseases in poorer regions are diarrheal transmitted by human fecal contamination of food, water, and soil; only about a third of the people in underdeveloped countries have access to safe water. Parasitic diseases such as malaria and schistosomiasis also tend to be widespread in poorer countries, infecting a quarter of the world's population overall. Malaria, which is transmitted by mosquitoes, is the most prevalent disease worldwide—around 100 million new cases every year—despite the fact that it can be prevented by routine administration of inexpensive drugs (*World Malaria Situation*, 1987).

Schistosomiasis—caused by a snail-borne parasite—chronically infects some 200 million people. Both malaria and schistosomiasis are debilitating diseases that sap energy and strength.

Many underdeveloped countries spend much of their health budgets establishing medical schools and building hospital complexes. But this approach addresses the health care of only 10 to 15 percent of the population, usually the elite. The resources are used mainly to cure chronic disease using increasingly expensive technology (intensive care units, bypass surgery, life-support systems, whole-body scanners). The health needs of the population at large would be better served by campaigns to eliminate parasitic and infectious agents, hunger, and contaminated drinking water. Since most of these conditions can be dramatically reduced at relatively modest cost, the suffering they cause is largely preventable.

Currently, four-fifths of the world's population does not have access to *any* permanent form of health care. The public health services of the sixty-seven poorest countries, excluding China, spend less on health care than the richer countries spend on tranquilizers alone. Moreover, richer countries (chiefly, Australia, Canada, Germany, the United Kingdom, and the United States) are attracting physicians from the poorer ones. Although it costs eight times more to train a physician than to train a medical auxiliary, many poorer countries continue to emphasize training physicians. If the goal of good health is to be achieved for the great masses of the world's population, existing health-care strategies will have to be dramatically transformed (Mahler, 1980, 1981).

The Impact of Unemployment

Given the relationship between poverty and disease, it is hardly surprising that unemployment exerts a detrimental effect on health. For many of the approximately 500 million people worldwide who have lost (or never had) a job, unemployment means having to do without many of life's necessities. In poor countries, medical care may not be easily accessible even for working people. For those with no income, it is simply unavailable. Moreover, many countries have no "safety net," such as welfare programs or disability benefits, for people who lose their jobs. When these countries suffer economic recession and unemployment rates rise sharply (as happened in the Latin American nations in the wake of their debt crisis in the mid-1980s), the impact on national health can be devastating (Musgrove, 1987).

The effects of unemployment on health extend beyond loss of income. Even in the United States, where workers' compensation and other programs offer some assistance and where many families have two wage earners, the experience of unemployment itself can still undermine health. One study (Brenner, 1987) stirred controversy by showing that the death rate from heart disease increases when unemployment rises. Unemployment has also been linked to anxiety, depression, and abuse of alcohol and tranquilizers (Kessler, House, and Turner, 1987). This is true even when preexisting conditions and behaviors that may have contributed to job loss are taken into account. Apparently, unemployment statistics can serve as barometers of health, and reductions in unemployment can yield health improvements.

SOCIOLOGICAL DIMENSIONS OF THREE MAJOR HEALTH PROBLEMS

Every illness or disease has its sociological dimensions, its recurring patterns caused by social forces and its variations among different social groups. We can illustrate this point by analyzing three major health problems: hunger, smoking, and AIDS. Each takes an enormous toll in terms of human suffering and social costs.

Hunger

To most Americans, hunger means a slight feeling of discomfort brought on by dieting or skipping a meal. But to as many as 20 million people in this country (Brown, 1987), hunger means chronic misery and impaired health. A great many of the hungry in the United States are children. One recent survey found that 5.5 million American children go hungry much of the time (Pear, 1991). This figure probably understates the true total, for homeless people were not included in the survey sample, and the interviews were conducted before the recession that began in 1991 took its toll on family income.

In the 1960s, when hunger in the United States first came to public attention, several government programs were enacted to make sure that food was available to the poor. Among these were food stamps, school lunch and breakfast programs, and a program to provide free food to pregnant women, babies, and young children. By the mid-1970s, these programs had made considerable headway in ensuring that most Americans had enough to eat (Brown, 1987). In 1981, however, the federal government started to withdraw funds for social programs, forcing several public agencies to close their doors and putting a strain on private efforts to feed the poor. Within five years, churches and social-service agencies were once again being overwhelmed by needy people, who flocked to soup kitchens and food pantries that had been set up in urban centers and in areas of high unemployment. Many of these food-distribution centers reported that they were feeding entire families, not just the "down-and-out" individual adults who had lined up for free food in the past.

The increase in hunger can also be traced to a surge in unemployment in 1982–1984 and to a tightening of eligibility requirements for virtually every federal assistance program. Many of those who lost their jobs were deemed ineligible for unemployment benefits, food stamps, or Medicaid, and their children were unable to qualify for free or subsidized meals at school. During the same period, inflation (especially in the cost of housing) meant that a family hit by unemployment had to stretch its reduced income even further. The result was a sharp rise in the numbers of people seeking food from charitable organizations, as well as an increase in the infant mortality rate in eleven states and several urban areas (Brown, 1987). Inadequate diets are partly to blame for the rise in infant mortality, for poorly nourished mothers give birth to smaller, frailer babies.

As we noted earlier, hunger remains a widespread problem. Paradoxically, hunger failed to decline even during the prosperous years of the late 1980s (Brown and Gershoff, 1989). Despite a rising median income, millions of Americans were hungry, including many who participated in government-sponsored food-assistance programs (Pear, 1991). The situation worsened during the economic recession of the early 1990s. As we saw in Chapter 9, the numbers of poor people grew even while the stock market boomed. At the same time, the government cut some programs designed to help poor people get enough to eat. This is one reason for the persistence of hunger in the world's richest nation.

Hunger and malnutrition are even more widespread in poorer countries. Famine is a frequent disaster in much of Africa and parts of Latin America as well as South and Southeast Asia. Even when climate conditions are good for farming, many countries are unable to grow enough food to feed their population. Countries like China that have made a policy of encouraging local farming rather than developing large crops for export have been more successful in combating hunger. (Chapter 19 discusses the problem of Third World hunger in detail.)

Smoking

The surgeon general of the United States declared in 1982 that cigarette smoking is "the chief, single, avoidable cause of death in our society and the most important public health issue of our time" (Davis, 1987). Despite this dramatic statement, and many other warnings that "smoking is hazardous to your health," millions of Americans continue to smoke. Even worse, every year substantial numbers of young people take up the habit. The health consequences are devastating. Smoking-related diseases, such as lung cancer, emphysema, and heart disease, kill an estimated 350,000 Americans a year and account for about one-sixth of this country's death toll (Davis, 1987).

One reason many people smoke is that cigarettes are the most heavily advertised consumer product. Every year, tobacco companies spend nearly $4 billion on cigarette advertising and promotion in the United States alone (*The Economist*, May 16, 1992). Much of this persuasion is aimed at those groups that smoke most or have shown less inclination to quit smoking: women, blue-collar workers, blacks and Hispanics, and members of the military. Although the tobacco companies deny slanting their advertising toward children and teenagers, they do advertise frequently in magazines that have millions of young readers (*TV Guide*, *Sports Illustrated*, *Glamour*, *Cosmopolitan*), and ads often feature attractive young models in poses that suggest that smokers are independent, fun-loving, and sexy.

Perhaps more significant, tobacco companies' massive advertising budgets give them what comes close to veto power over the editorial content of magazines that accept cigarette ads. Any magazine that runs articles on the health risks of smoking or on antismoking campaigns is likely to find itself losing millions of dollars of advertising. The result is that "the media's dependence on revenue from cigarette advertising has repeatedly led to suppression of discussion of smoking and health matters" (K. E. Warner, 1985, p. 385).

The modern antismoking movement began in the late 1950s, when scientific evidence on the health risks of smoking began to accumulate. Opponents of smoking try to undermine the tobacco companies' message that smoking is a harmless personal pleasure, something people choose of their own free will because of the enjoyment it gives. They argue that smokers take up cigarettes in their youth in response to advertising and peer pressure, continue to smoke because they become addicted to the nicotine in tobacco, and are at high risk for developing a number of life-threatening diseases. These competing definitions of smoking—as a pleasant pastime and as a

It seems shocking, with today's awareness of the medical effects of smoking, to think that doctors would endorse a particular brand of cigarettes. This 1947 ad appeared in a national news magazine, and was typical for its day. Even though we now know that smoking is the single leading threat to public health, tobacco continues to be grown and aggressively marketed—a reminder that social and economic power are intricately intertwined with each other and with public health.

health-destroying addiction—are at the heart of the battle over tobacco.

Some evidence suggests that the antismoking campaign is changing people's ideas about smoking. By 1990, twenty-six years after the surgeon general first reported that cigarette smoking is hazardous to health, 38 million American adults had given up smoking, almost 50 percent of all those who ever smoked (Surgeon General, 1990). Moreover, growing evidence that "passive smoking"—breathing the smoke of others—is harmful to nonsmokers has led to the passage of many antismoking ordinances. For example, the Federal Aviation Administration no longer permits smoking on domestic airplane flights, and in a number of cities smoking has been banned in public buildings.

As tobacco companies saw their U.S. markets shrink, they began to market their products aggressively in Europe, Asia, and many Third World countries (Barry, 1991). They have fought back at home, too, spending more for advertising and attempting to overcome tobacco's unhealthy image by promoting low-tar and "light" brands. They have also promoted the idea of "smokers' rights" and challenged the government's authority to ban smoking.

These efforts at influencing public opinion have paid off in some ways, especially among certain segments of the population. For instance, the prevalence of smoking has declined much more sharply among men than women. This is not so much because fewer women than men are quitting smoking as because more teenage girls and young adult women are taking up the cigarette habit (Fiore, Novotny, Pierce, Hatziandreu, Patel, and Davis, 1989). The reasons for this are still being investigated. Some of the factors involved may be that young women are less likely than men to participate in sports and exercise (activities that tend to discourage smoking), that they are more often trying to lose weight (smoking is associated in the public mind with eating less and staying thin), and that they may be more inclined to use smoking to cope with stress (Waldron, Lye, and Brandon, 1991).

Many have charged that women smoke more because cigarette advertising and promotion aimed at women encourages them to do so. Tobacco companies have tried to associate smoking with "womanly" qualities, such as femininity, sophistication, sexiness, and fashionableness (Amos, 1990). They have introduced brands designed to appeal to women, such as Virginia Slims, Eve, Satin, and Ritz. Female models in cigarette ads are beautiful, dressed in the height of fashion, and often pictured in affectionate or provocative poses with men. Another theme in cigarette advertising is thinness, conveyed even in the cigarettes' names: slims, thins, lights.

What explanations do women themselves give for cigarette smoking? One study found that smoking among women is closely tied to the idea of relaxation, often as part of a coffee break or a few moments of peace and quiet snatched in a day devoted to the care of other members of the family. As one smoker noted, "I think it gives me a break. Having a cigarette is an excuse to stop for five minutes" (Graham, 1987, p. 52). The women in the study looked to smoking as their one item of self-indulgence in budgets that didn't allow for new clothes, makeup, restaurant meals, or other treats.

Unfortunately, smoking is not a benign means of relaxation and self-indulgence. It has highly negative effects on health. Smoking kills more than half a million women yearly in the industrialized world, and many more in developing countries (Barry, 1991). Approximately 20 to 25 percent of women who smoke will die of smoking-related diseases, a third of them before the age of sixty-five.

In addition, smoking has detrimental effects on children. Women who smoke while pregnant are more likely to give birth to premature, low-birth-weight babies (Graham, 1987). Passive smoking has been linked to a number of respiratory conditions in children, such as asthma, bronchitis, and pneumonia, as well as problems such as stomachaches, ear infections, and behavioral disorders. Children of smokers are more likely to become smokers themselves (Graham, 1987).

AIDS

> [The patient] was suffering from oral candidiasis, a yeast infection of the mouth. One of the woman's children had already died of a respiratory ailment stemming from strange problems with her immune system, problems that started with a case of this candidiasis. Within a few weeks of her arrival in Brussels, the mother was also suffering from a severe infection of cytomegalovirus. The doctors could do nothing as waves of infection washed over the mother's body. By January 1978, as she withered away from severe diarrhea caused by an untreatable salmonella infection in her intestines, she flew back to Kinshasa, where she died a month later. (Shilts, 1987)

In 1977, when this Congolese woman brought her daughter to Brussels for treatment, the mysterious disorder of the immune system from which they both suffered did not yet have a name. Today we know it as **AIDS**, acquired immune deficiency syndrome, a devastating disease that has profoundly affected individuals and communities worldwide.

The Nature of AIDS

AIDS is caused by the human immunodeficiency virus (HIV), which destroys the body's ability to fight off infections and cancers. AIDS kills by allowing other diseases and infections to run rampant through a body unprotected by a healthy immune system. The virus is spread through contact with the blood, semen, vaginal secretions, or breast milk of an infected person. Thus, a person may become infected by having unprotected sexual intercourse with an infected partner, sharing a hypodermic needle with an infected person, getting a contaminated blood transfusion, or (in the case of babies) being in the womb of an infected mother.

Once in a new host's body, the virus may remain inactive for years. During this period, unless the infected person is tested for HIV, he or she may unknowingly transmit it to other people. No one knows how HIV is eventually activated, but once this happens the immune system is progressively weakened so that the person is vulnerable to the so-called *opportunistic infections* that ravage the body and eventually lead to death. The most common opportunistic infections include virulent and disfiguring forms of herpes, cryptococcus, salmonella, and yeast infections. Pneumonia, meningitis, a rare form of cancer known as Kaposi's sarcoma, and tuberculosis also occur frequently in people who have AIDS. In fact, tuberculosis, which had been almost eradicated in the United States, is once again on the rise, largely because AIDS has given it an opportunity to develop and spread in densely populated urban areas. TB is also spreading because vaccination has been lax and follow-up treatment—especially for poor, minority populations—is often difficult to obtain.

In the United States, as of 1992, an estimated 1 million to 1.5 million people had tested positive for the HIV virus. Of this number, about 50 percent will develop AIDS within ten years, and at the ten-year mark another 35 percent will show early signs of weakened immune systems (Scott and Zonana, 1990). Because AIDS is a new disease, it is not yet known whether the remaining 15 percent of infected people who show no impairment after ten years of living with HIV will eventually succumb to it. Although new drugs and treatments for AIDS are being developed and doctors are now more successful in treating opportunistic infections, the long-term outlook remains bleak. So far, of those who have developed full-blown cases of AIDS, not a single person has recovered.

Social Structure and the Spread of AIDS

The HIV virus can spread with alarming speed through a population. Among intravenous drug users in Thailand, for instance, infection with HIV grew from a mere 1 percent in 1987 to 40 percent just three years later (Mann, 1990). Similarly, among a sample of homosexual men in San Francisco, who had a history of other sexually transmitted diseases, the rate of infection rose from under 4 percent to over 75 percent in less than eight years. What causes the AIDS virus to spread so quickly? The answer, according to the sociologist Peter Bearman (1992), lies in ***social structure***. A high degree of interconnectedness among members of population segments that engage in risky behavior allows the virus to spread quickly in those segments. For example, in the United States, the close networks among and risky behavior associated with two populations—gay men and intravenous drug users—have resulted in very high rates of HIV infection in those groups.

If population segments infected with AIDS had no risky contact with outsiders, AIDS would spread into other segments very slowly. The fact is, though, that the groups initially most affected by AIDS are not *bounded*, or isolated from other groups. For example, a bisexual man who contracts AIDS through unprotected homosexual intercourse may pass AIDS on to a female partner through unprotected sex. She may in turn pass it on to another sexual partner, or, if pregnant or nursing, she may pass it on to her baby. In the 1980s, a bridge between infected and uninfected populations was the medical blood supply. Before the mode of AIDS transmission was understood, HIV-infected blood donors unwittingly passed the virus on to hemophiliacs and others who received contaminated transfusions.

Cases of AIDS in the general population may remain widely dispersed, except where the infection enters a tightly linked social network. High levels of interconnectedness within a population and the extent to which populations are bounded are important social-structural variables in the spread of an infectious disease like AIDS.

The impact of social-structural variables is apparent in the different social patterns that underlie the transmission of AIDS in other countries. For instance, the AIDS virus has spread rapidly in eastern and central Africa, the area where it first appeared. In Malawi, a third of the population is HIV-positive, and in some cities of Tanzania, 40 percent of adults are infected. Worst off is Uganda, where, among the urban population, 24 percent of members of low-risk populations and 86 percent of members of high-risk populations test positive for HIV. In contrast to the United States, the AIDS virus in Africa is transmitted overwhelmingly by heterosexual intercourse. One study found that in eastern and central Africa in general, 80 percent of the HIV-positive adults had acquired the virus through heterosexual contact and another 10 percent through contaminated blood transfusions. That left only 10 percent for unprotected homosexual contact and sharing of contaminated needles, the most prevalent means of transmission in the United States (N'galy and Ryder, 1988).

Some observers believe that the patterns seen in Africa foreshadow what will eventually happen in the United States. They argue that the AIDS epidemic is older and therefore more mature in eastern and central Africa, so that what is happening there will soon happen in other parts of the world. Thus, whereas in 1985 only 3 percent of all AIDS cases in the United States were contracted by heterosexual intercourse, by 1991 this proportion had doubled to 6 percent, and by 1992 it had climbed to 7 percent (Nullis, 1992).

Social Action and the Spread of AIDS

The specific mode of transmission of an infectious disease like AIDS determines what sorts of actions are defined as risky for the disease. Sociologists study the transmission of disease in order to see how social factors contribute to it. Such research can be particularly helpful in determining how ***social action*** might be modified to reduce the risk and incidence of the disease. As we will see, social action is also involved in the extent and quality of the treatment and support that people with AIDS receive.

Peter Bearman (1992) argues that to predict the spread of AIDS in the years ahead, we must focus on the fact that AIDS can spread from person to person, and from group to group, only through an exchange of contaminated body fluids. Bearman emphasizes that it is people's actions, not attributes like their gender, race, age, or sexual orientation, that determine who is most at risk of contracting AIDS:

> . . . if IV drug users didn't share dirty needles, they would not be at risk to AIDS. It is not the drug abuse that defines risk to HIV. In the same manner, men who do not exchange fluids during sex are not at risk to HIV. It is not homosexuality, but the exchange of fluids during sex which defines risk behaviors. (Bearman, 1992)

Since intravenous drug users do not share needles with people who do not use drugs, and since the medical supply of blood is now free of the AIDS virus, AIDS is now spread from one group to another primarily through unprotected sexual intercourse. While gay men are a strongly bounded population, bisexual men who have sexual relations with both men and women can serve as bridges for the AIDS virus to move from the gay community into other populations. The more such bridges there are, the greater the rate of sexual mixing between groups and the faster the spread of the virus.

Among intravenous drug users there are even more bridges to other segments of the population. Although they tend to have stable sexual relationships with men who also use drugs, female drug users frequently resort to prostitution to help support their drug habit. Heterosexual non-drug-using men who buy these sexual services are putting themselves at risk for infection with HIV. Similarly, heterosexual male intravenous drug users tend to have many non-drug-using partners, and these men rarely practice safer sex. Not surprisingly, 62 percent of the cases of heterosexually transmitted AIDS among women come from unprotected sexual contact with a male drug user (National Research Council, 1990).

Accordingly, the non-drug-using heterosexual population may be on the verge of a sudden, rapid increase in the incidence of AIDS. This is the pattern that most epidemics of infectious diseases have taken: a period during which tightly bounded groups of people are ravaged by the disease and a deceptive sense of calm prevails among people who are unaffected, followed by increasingly numerous infections as the disease spreads throughout the population.

The problem in predicting the extent to which AIDS will follow this pattern among the heterosexual population of the United States lies in the specific ways in which AIDS is transmitted: an exchange of body fluid, usually during sex. Many factors influence who will have sex with whom and in what fashion, as well as who will take action to protect themselves during sexual intercourse and to what extent. Thus, it is very hard to foresee the course of this country's AIDS epidemic.

Cultural Values and the Spread of AIDS

The AIDS epidemic has changed the American social landscape. For one thing, it has caused changes in sexual behavior, putting a damper on the "sexual revolution" of the 1960s and 1970s. These changes are most apparent among gay men, many of whom are now having sex with fewer partners and are avoiding other sexual behaviors that put them at risk of contracting the AIDS virus (Friedman, Des Jarlais, Sotheran, Garber, Cohen, and Smith, 1987). For instance, the average number of sexual partners that gay men have per month dropped from nearly seven in 1981 to roughly two in 1989. There has also been a decrease in the gay community in the use of recreational drugs, which can impair judgment in assessing the risk of sexual behavior (Siegel, Mesagno, Chen, and Christ, 1989).

While the most effective ***social action*** against AIDS is clearly activity aimed at decreasing the incidence of risky behaviors, many measures are opposed by people whose ***cultural*** values lead them to oppose programs and strategies for various moral reasons. For instance, programs that allow intravenous drug users to exchange used needles for sterile ones, or that give out bleaching kits to addicts with instructions on sterilizing needles, have come under fire from groups who claim that these efforts condone illegal drug use and make it easier. Efforts to teach safer-sex guidelines to students in public schools face opposition from those who consider sexual abstinence to be the only appropriate form of safer sex for unmarried teens. These groups worry that any form of sex education will encourage sexual behavior among young people. (They are correct in their assertion that sexual abstinence *is* the only 100 percent effective protection against AIDS.)

In spite of all the controversy, the need to educate the public about how AIDS is spread has made sex a topic for national discussion. In 1988, the surgeon general of the United States sent a brochure to every household in the country explicitly describing safe and unsafe sexual behaviors.

The AIDS epidemic has also produced responses different from the sympathy usually shown toward seriously ill people. Anyone who becomes infected with HIV may become a social outcast. One couple's house was burned to the ground after townspeople learned that their three hemophiliac sons were infected with HIV. Some people have an exaggerated fear of catching AIDS through casual contact; others believe that AIDS is a punishment for wicked behavior. Because of such attitudes, the AIDS epidemic has undermined some of the progress toward full civil rights that homosexuals have made over the last decades. In many places, it has occasioned a backlash of violence and discrimination. The epidemic has also fostered greater prejudice toward inner-city blacks and Hispanics, who are disproportionately represented among AIDS patients because of their relatively high rate of intravenous drug use (Mays and Cochran, 1987).

Another important consequence of AIDS is the challenge it poses to civil liberties. As fear of AIDS has grown, suggestions have been made that some or even all Americans should be tested for HIV and that those who test positive should be quarantined. William F. Buckley, Jr., a conservative writer, has advocated mandatory universal HIV testing, with all those who test positive to be tattooed on their forearms and buttocks (Brandt, 1986). In 1986, one-third of California voters supported a proposition that would have required a quarantine of people with AIDS, even though such forcible restrictions are probably unconstitutional.

Many other questions regarding civil liberties have been raised by the AIDS epidemic. Should employers be allowed to fire people who are HIV-positive? Should insurance companies be allowed to deny them coverage? Should public schools be able to bar them from classrooms? Although antidiscrimination ordinances that protect people with AIDS are in effect in some large cities in the United States, American society in general has not yet decided what rights those with AIDS or HIV should have.

The Black Death, or bubonic plague, ravaged Europe in waves from the fourteenth through the seventeenth century. These epidemics reduced Europe's population by more than 50 percent and created social chaos and economic stagnation. The Black Death is a classic case study of social and cultural responses to a medical catastrophe. Some observers refer to AIDS as the Black Death of modern times.

The Battle against AIDS

In his preface to *And the Band Played On* (1987), a history of the initial stages of the worldwide AIDS epidemic, especially its first five years in the United States, the journalist Randy Shilts comments:

> AIDS did not just happen to America—it was allowed to happen by an array of institutions, all of which failed to perform their appropriate tasks to safeguard the public health. This failure of the system leaves a legacy of unnecessary suffering that will haunt the Western world for decades to come.

Since the beginning of the epidemic, people with AIDS and their advocates have claimed that the federal government's commitment of funds for research and prevention has never been proportionate to the impact and threat of the disease—and that this inadequate response is a reflection of widespread prejudice against homosexuals and intravenous drug users. Not until AIDS became perceived as a threat to the non-drug-using, heterosexual population, activists argue, did there seem to be much national concern about developing strategies for prevention and treatment.

The government's and the health-care community's slow start in responding to the AIDS crisis in the United States is one reason more than a million Americans are now HIV-positive. The alarming fact that this number is still growing has created uncertainty about whether the already overburdened health-care system can cope with the avalanche of new AIDS cases that is expected by the year 2000. People with AIDS require a considerable amount of care and treatment, much of which they are unable to pay for themselves. In 1990 alone, $8.5 billion was spent on Americans with AIDS, and as the epidemic progresses these costs will spiral higher (Makadon, Seage, Thorpe, and Fineberg, 1990).

From the beginning of the U.S. AIDS crisis, homosexual communities throughout the country have mobilized to take up some of the slack in AIDS treatment and prevention. In San Francisco, for example, a number of volunteer organizations have provided information, medical referrals, help with housing, financial assistance, counseling, home-attendant services, and hospice care (Arno, 1986). These efforts not only have been of immense help to people with AIDS but also have helped to minimize the burden on public institutions. (Patients who can live at home with help, for example, do not have to be hospitalized.) Drug users and drug-treatment agencies have made some efforts to provide similar services for people with AIDS, but their efforts have not been as effective as those of gay advocacy groups (Friedman et al., 1987).

Advocacy groups that began in the gay community have also made significant progress in raising public awareness about AIDS. As AIDS has continued to affect larger and more varied groups of people, these organizations have expanded in order to benefit all people affected by AIDS. A group in New York, the People with AIDS Coalition (PWAC), was founded by and for people with AIDS. Originally a primarily white, gay, male organization, PWAC now publishes a Spanish as well as an English version of its monthly magazine, *PWA Coalition Newsline*. It has a variety of support groups geared to specific populations including Spanish-speaking, African-American, bisexual, and heterosexual people with AIDS and their loved ones.

The work of groups like PWAC tends to focus on three points. First, they seek to change risky behavior through education. This effort has been particularly effective in the gay community, where the incidence of new infections has gone down (although gay men remain at high risk for infection). Second, groups strive to build general public awareness through media exposure (talk shows, radio spots, bus and subway posters, and speaker bureaus, for example). Third, groups may involve themselves in lobbying and activist work in order to pressure health-care organizations to provide better services and to secure greater government and public support for medical care, educational activities, and research.

The Outlook for AIDS Treatment and Prevention

Despite the slow response of government officials and the lack of funding for research, the life expectancy of people with AIDS has improved over the last few years. New drugs are currently in development, and others, such as AZT, have proved effective in slowing the pace of the disease's development in HIV-positive people. Unfortunately, many of these drugs are highly toxic; most people with AIDS can tolerate them only for short periods of time, if at all.

Equally important are drugs that have proved effective against specific opportunistic infections. For example, aerosolized pentamidine is now regularly used to prevent *Pneumocystis carinii* pneumonia. Such treatment breakthroughs, though, remain out of reach for many people who are HIV-positive or who have AIDS, because they are extremely expensive. AIDS patients who have medical insurance either lose it once they become too ill to work or exhaust their benefits.

Researchers are working on a vaccine that would keep HIV from developing into full-blown AIDS. Some experts believe that a vaccine will be developed within fifteen years—a short time from the scientific standpoint, but an externity for people who are already sick.

THE DEVELOPMENT OF THE HEALTH-CARE INDUSTRY

The health-care industry in the United States is huge and rapidly growing. This vast enterprise now employs more than 5 million people: doctors, nurses, technicians, therapists, pharmacists, and others who work in a variety of settings. In 1992 health-care expenses accounted for 13 percent of the country's gross national product, some $738 billion. It has been estimated that by the year 2030, when the baby-boom generation will be well into old age, 26 percent of GNP will be allotted to medical services, supplies, and equipment (Morganthau and Hager, 1992). This is why health care reform became one of the top priorities of the new Clinton administration in 1993 (also see the Making Choices box). In exploring how the health-care industry developed its present size and form, we begin with a look at how so many personal and social problems came to be seen as requiring medical attention.

Medicalization: Redefining Illness

An important by-product of the growth of the health-care industry and the prestige of physicians, discussed in the next two sections, is an increase in the number of conditions that are thought to be of medical concern. In the not-too-distant past, birth and death usually occurred at home, with family members and friends at hand. Now most people are born and die in a hospital, surrounded by bright lights and expensive machines. People who were addicted to alcohol or drugs were once considered sinners or weaklings. Now such addictions are considered illnesses. Conditions that used to be accepted as part of life—baldness, wrinkles, obesity, acne, small breasts, lack of interest in sex, anxiety, sleeplessness, infertility, hyperactivity in children—are today deemed appropriate for medical intervention. Some criminologists have even defined antisocial behavior as a medical problem. Lawbreakers of all kinds, from shoplifters to mass murderers, may be labeled "sick." This trend toward including personal problems in the realm of medicine has been called **medicalization**.

Medicalization has given doctors wide leeway to intervene in people's private lives. Doctors may now scrutinize patients' entire lifestyles—what they eat, whether they smoke, how much they drink and exercise, how many hours they spend at work, and what the various stresses in their lives are. A modern doctor's "prescription" might be to stop smoking, eat fewer fatty foods, or begin an exercise program. Going further, physicians may attempt to influence the habits of an entire society—promoting restrictions on smoking, for example.

Another sign of medicalization is the use of medical arguments to help advance causes not immediately or directly connected with the treatment of illness (Zola, 1972). For example, loud rock music is cited as being damaging to hearing and bad for children's mental health. Environmental pollution is condemned not only for being destructive to plants and animals but also for causing some forms of human cancer. One great exploiter of medical rhetoric has been the advertising industry, which touts the health benefits of everything from high-fiber cereals to low-calorie sweeteners and "lite" beer.

Medicalization also involves a redefinition of social issues and a reassignment of blame. For example, to characterize homeless people as mentally ill is to obscure the fact that much homelessness is related to unemployment among unskilled workers and a lack of affordable housing (Snow, Baker, Anderson, and Martin, 1986). Although considering some deviant behavior (such as alcoholism and drug abuse) as illness would seem to be compassionate, doing so raises questions of social control. For instance, can a company's random drug testing violate the employees' rights if the stated goal is to protect their health? As medicalization reaches into more areas of people's lives, such questions are of growing concern.

Through ***social action***, opponents of medicalization have attempted to recapture some aspects of human behavior from organized medicine (Fox, 1977). For instance, women's health groups have pressed for the demedicalization of the birth process, setting up birthing centers and clinics in which babies can be born in a homelike setting and mothers can be spared as much medical intervention as possible (often they are attended only by nurse-midwives). Similarly, patients' advocates have maintained that terminally ill people should be allowed to die without heroic medical intervention if they wish. Other attempts at demedicalization can be seen in self-help groups. People who have a problem in common—obesity, gambling, spouse abuse—have formed such groups to help one another cope with their problem without turning to medical authorities. However, these efforts have made only minor inroads in reversing the medicalization trend. In general, American society now thinks of a great many human activities as appropriate for medical intervention.

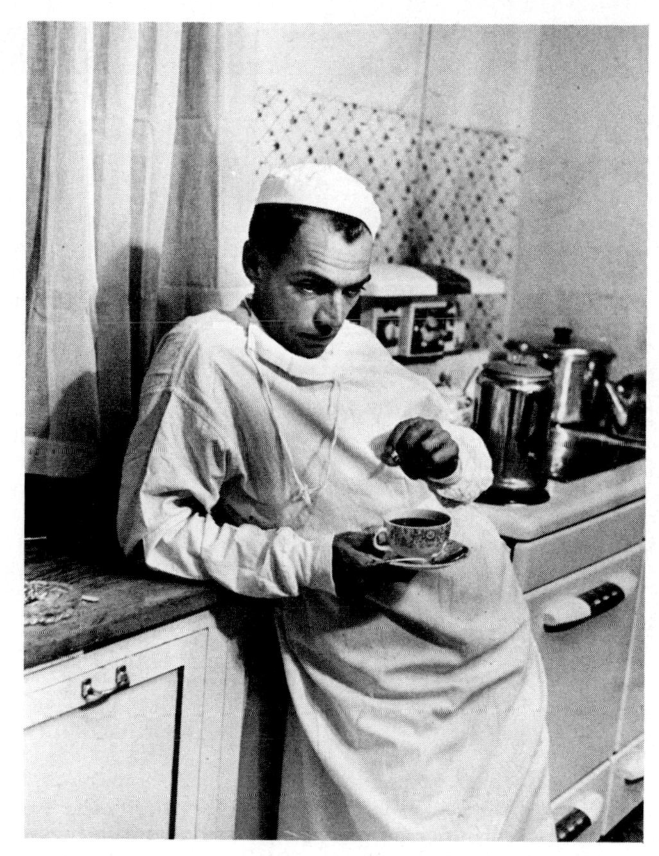

Until well into this century, a single doctor could master much of the medical knowledge that was available. The modern system has moved away from the treatment of the whole person by a single doctor and toward greater specialization. While the modern system may do well in treating specific, complicated medical problems, many people in and out of the medical field lament the loss of the family doctor who knew his or her patients all their lives and stressed prevention as well as cure.

The Status Elevation of Doctors

Doctors occupy a position of such esteem in the United States that it is hard to believe that they have not always done so. Yet through much of American history a doctor's social position and income were little better than that of a manual worker. In colonial America, for instance, anyone could become a doctor merely by calling himself or herself one. There were no medical schools or medical societies to license or regulate what was a free-for-all trade.

MAKING CHOICES

Toward a National Health-Care System

Near downtown Montreal, a pregnant woman arrives at a centre local de services communautaires. *Here at the CLSC, as the center is called, she receives regular checkups and counseling on the right foods to eat during her pregnancy.*

When it's time for her to deliver, she will go to a local hospital. One of the two doctors who has been caring for her will deliver the baby. After the baby is born, she can bring it back to the CLSC for immunizations and follow-up care. . . .

The woman will pay nothing for these services. She simply presents her orange-and-yellow health card, issued by the government of Quebec. That card entitles her to free medical care at any of the 158 CLSCs in the province or from any doctor or hospital she chooses. (Consumer Reports, *1990a, p. 614)*

In Tennessee, twenty-four-year-old construction worker Terry Takewell suffers from diabetes, has been unable to buy health insurance, and has run up a large bill at the local hospital. One afternoon, a neighbor finds him very ill and calls an ambulance. He is found to be suffering from a diabetic condition known as acute ketoacidosis and is admitted to the hospital.

Terry had been in the hospital less than an hour when word reached the acting administrator that he had been admitted. Alarmed at the prospect of the young man incurring another bill that he would be unable to pay, he went to Terry's hospital room, lifted him under the arms, and dragged him out of the building, leaving him propped under a tree in the hospital parking lot. . . . The neighbor took Terry back home . . . and tried to make him as comfortable as she could. That's where he was found, dead, the following morning. (Bonnyman, 1992, p. 12)

Such stories of how the American system of health care fails show "the inevitable consequence of treating health care, like CD players or designer jeans, as simply another commodity for sale. Those who can afford it, get it (sometimes even when it is not necessary). Those who can't, don't" (Bonnyman, 1992, pp. 13–14).

Many Americans concerned about the health-care system look with great interest across the border to the north. In the United States, medical costs keep spiraling upward at the rate of about 10 percent a year (well above the 5 percent rate of inflation). In 1991, U.S. per capita health-care expenditures reached a record $2,900. Twenty years earlier, in 1971, when Canada first implemented its health-care system, both the United States and Canada spent 7.4 percent of their respective GNPs on health care. By 1992, the U.S. expenditure had risen to 13 percent of GNP—4.1 percentage points higher than Canada. That difference represented $125 billion (*Consumer Reports*, 1992). As the accompanying graph shows, the United States spends more on health care than any other developed country.

Moreover, access to the U.S. health-care system is declining. About 32.1 million people have no health insurance of any kind (U.S. Bureau of the Census, 1992). Medicaid now covers only half as many poor Americans as it did in the 1960s. Many working Americans now are employed by companies that can afford only health-insurance policies that offer less than complete coverage.

In Canada, in contrast, everyone receives health care paid for out of tax revenues; yet the Canadian per capita expenditures for it are about 30 percent less than in the United States. The health of Canadians, moreover, isn't suffering because of this system. Their infant mortality rate is actually lower than that in the United States, and their life expectancy is higher.

Proposals for a national health-insurance system similar to Canada's have been introduced into the U.S. Congress. Although they differ in their details, all these plans assume that every person in this country, regardless of income, job status, or health, is entitled to medical services paid for through a universal health-insurance plan supported by taxes and run by federal and state governments. Proponents of such a system consider health care a right, not a privilege, and say it shouldn't be denied to anyone. What is needed, they say, is a system of real risk sharing that covers those who are poor and sick as well as those who are well-off and healthy.

Such a plan has several advantages. For one thing, *everyone* would be covered for health care; no one would be unable to get treatment because that person couldn't afford it. For another, universal national health insurance would almost certainly help contain medical costs. It would eliminate the bureaucratic expenses involved in having some 1,500 private insurance companies reimbursing patients for their medical expenses or paying doctors and hospitals directly. (Administrative costs now account for some 15 to 20 percent of American health-care expenses, for a total of more than $100 billion a year; Public Agenda Foundation, 1992.) It would also help to put a ceiling on what could be charged for certain medical procedures by establishing medical budgets and medical pay scales. And by covering people for *all* their medical expenses, it would encourage more Americans to get preventive health care, thus reducing the number of serious illnesses that occur.

A national health-insurance system also has some drawbacks. The Canadian system involves substantial waiting periods for elective (optional and non-emergency) surgery and for high-tech special procedures when the patient's life is not in jeopardy. (This is a way of helping to reduce the number of costly, nonessential treatments.) To pay for the national health insurance, taxes must increase. Moreover, it is not clear that a government bureaucracy would be more efficient than private insurance companies.

A major alternative to a national health-insurance system is mandatory insurance coverage purchased by private employers. If all companies were required to buy medical insurance for their workers, only the unemployed, the self-employed with very low incomes, the "uninsurable" with preexisting medical conditions, and those who took early retirement would be left outside the insurance net. (The elderly and disabled would be covered by Medicare.) For those not covered, an expanded system of public insurance could fill in the gap.

Critics question what right government has to tell firms they must either buy health insurance for their workers or pay penalties in the form of higher payroll taxes. Is this fair, they ask, especially to the many small businesses that are struggling to survive? It is, after all, just a historical accident that we have as much employer-paid health insurance as we do. During World War II, when the War Labor Board put a ceiling on wage increases to ward off inflation, companies desperate for workers began to offer health insurance to help attract employees. After the war, this policy simply continued, and it worked fairly well until medical costs began to rise sharply (Public Agenda Foundation, 1992). Now it may be outmoded because it has become such a burden to employers and because an employer-paid system does little to help contain health-care costs.

One proposal for helping to reduce the cost of medical insurance for most Americans is to offer government-paid coverage for people with preexisting

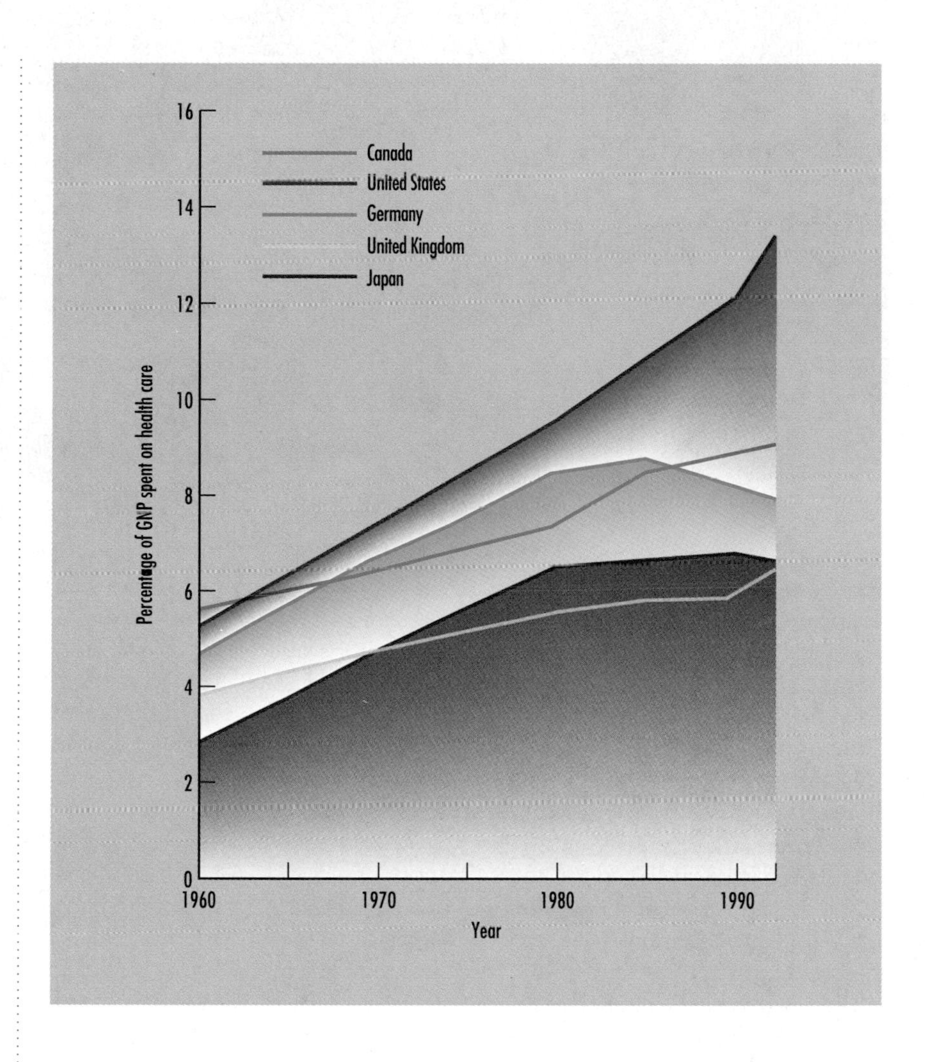

medical conditions that put them at high risk. This would allow insurance companies to essentially insure only healthy people, thus reducing the premiums they must charge for comprehensive policies. The problem with this idea is that it doesn't really reduce costs; it just shifts them from private business to government. The health care of people with serious illness remains as high as ever whether it is paid for by company profits or by tax dollars. Would state governments, many of which are already in financial crisis, be able to meet this huge additional expenditure?

Because of the relative poverty of the rural American South, black midwives delivered babies in thousands of isolated and impoverished hamlets. The midwife, a specialist with relatively little training, had very high rates of success in both delivering babies and teaching mothers and families the rudiments of pre- and postnatal care. The rural midwife reminds us that fine health care may depend more on the dedication of medical personnel than on elaborate technology and formal training.

Sometimes clergymen tried to provide medical care to their parishioners. Documents of the time record a doctor who sold "tea, sugar, olives, grapes, anchovies, raisins, and prunes" along with medicines, and also tell of a woman who "Acts here in the Double Capacity of a Doctoress and Coffee Woman" (quoted in Starr, 1982, p. 39).

Medicine became a full-time vocation in the United States (though still not an established profession) in the early years of the nineteenth century, when medical schools began to open around the country (Conrad and Schneider, 1980). This change did not mean that all doctors were educated in medical schools. Many still learned their trade through apprenticeship. Moreover, in addition to those who called themselves doctors, there were a variety of medical "specialists": abortionists, midwives, bonesetters, and cancer curers, for instance (Starr, 1982). One reason so many of these people found clients at this time was the primitive nature of medical science. Effective anesthesia was unknown, as was the crucial fact that microscopic agents—germs—cause many diseases. Even doctors who received medical school training used crude techniques and had little understanding of disease. In such circumstances, the efforts of trained physicians to distinguish themselves from ordinary people who concocted herbal remedies, or traveling peddlers who sold elixirs, had only modest success.

During the 1920s scientific advances, coupled with the rise of the American Medical Association (the AMA, the physicians' major professional organization), enabled doctors to acquire enough political and social ***power*** to prevail over other people who claimed to be healers (Burrow, 1971; Larson, 1977; Starr, 1982). The widespread acceptance of scientific medicine as superior to traditional attempts at curing put trained physicians in a position to assert that medical education was a prerequisite to becoming a legitimate doctor. In essence, medicine began to define itself as a true profession—one that, because of its expertise, deserved to dominate the care of sick people. New laws set licensing requirements for doctors and made medicine a legally defined monopoly (Conrad and Schneider, 1980; Freidson, 1970). The AMA also pressed for legislation that limited the kinds of drugs that could be sold to the public directly. Previously, preparations containing opium, cocaine, and other powerful drugs could be bought by anyone; now a doctor's prescription was needed to obtain these substances (Starr, 1982). At the same time, physicians secured the right to set their own fees; before the mid-nineteenth century, some states set limits on the amounts that doctors could charge. Such autonomy in setting fees and making other decisions about one's services is an important part of professional status. Soon after World War I, the medical profession as we know it had begun to appear, and subsequent decades have seen its prestige continue to rise.

One measure of physicians' dominance of the modern health-care system is that only they have the authority to diagnose illness, prescribe and evaluate treatments, and convey information to patients. Seriously ill people may not be fully informed about what is wrong with them, often because their doctors assume that they lack the expertise to understand medical information or are so upset by their condition that they will misinterpret any information given. As a result, many patients develop a childlike dependence on their doctors. In recent years, some patients have rejected this position, asserting that they have a right to know about their health status and to participate in their own medical care. However, the voice of the doctor is still supreme in most cases.

The preeminent position of doctors also implies a hierarchical relationship to other health-care workers. The physician's dominance is sustained by a number of subservient professionals and semiprofessionals (nurses, physical therapists, pharmacists, and so forth). According to the sociologist Eliot Freidson (1970), people in these "lesser" fields are often reduced simply to following doctors' orders, and so may become alienated from their work, like factory workers and others who have little autonomy. For example, problems of morale are probably as important as low pay in the current shortage of nurses in the United States.

Doctors assume their position at the top of the health-care system after a long period of socialization into the practice of medicine. As medical students, interns, and residents, those who train to be doctors internalize the ideals of the profession. Some of these ideals involve dedication to caring for the sick. But others involve maintaining the prestige of the profession (learning never to criticize another doctor in front of lay people, for instance) and accepting the idea that the practice of medicine involves a high degree of autonomy. Since the work entailed is thought to be very complicated, it is often assumed that those who do it must be extraordinarily gifted. Accordingly, many young doctors go beyond professional pride to a sense of superiority or arrogance (Freidson, 1970).

High social status, combined with the power to control access to health care, have enabled physicians to demand some of the highest pay levels of any group in the United States. American doctors also earn far more than their colleagues in other countries. This has a good deal to do with how health care in the United States is organized as a business.

Corporatization: Health Care as a Business

It is hardly surprising that in a country as devoted to free enterprise as the United States an enormous industry like health care would be an arena for entrepreneurship and profit making. Increasingly, the provision of medical services is being taken over by for-profit corporations, and these corporations are being consolidated into even larger corporations—what some have called the "medical-industrial complex" (D. W. Light, 1986; Relman, 1980).

This corporatization has important consequences for health care. As one researcher has written:

> As health care becomes a profitable market for corporate investment, health services are treated as commodities—products that are bought and sold in the marketplace like automobiles, hats, iron, or oil. The deciding factor as to whether to provide a service or produce a particular piece of equipment is made according to whether that "product" will sell. The bottom line is marketability and whether the company providing the service will make a profit on its sale. (Levitt, 1986, p. 483)

Corporatization is a fairly recent phenomenon in health care. It might be dated from 1968, the year a Nashville doctor and a former executive of Kentucky Fried Chicken formed the Hospital Corporation of America, an investor-owned for-profit hospital chain (D. W. Light, 1986). There is evidence that for-profit hospitals have positioned themselves in a health-care niche in which sizable profits can be made. In many cases, they have done this by refusing to offer services that tend to lose money, such as obstetrics, and by locating where few poor or uninsured people live. When poor patients arrive in the emergency room of a for-profit hospital, they may be turned away (D. W. Light, 1986).

Hospitals are not the only profit-making enterprises in the health-care field (Stoesz and Karger, 1991). In recent years, medical laboratories, kidney dialysis centers, CT

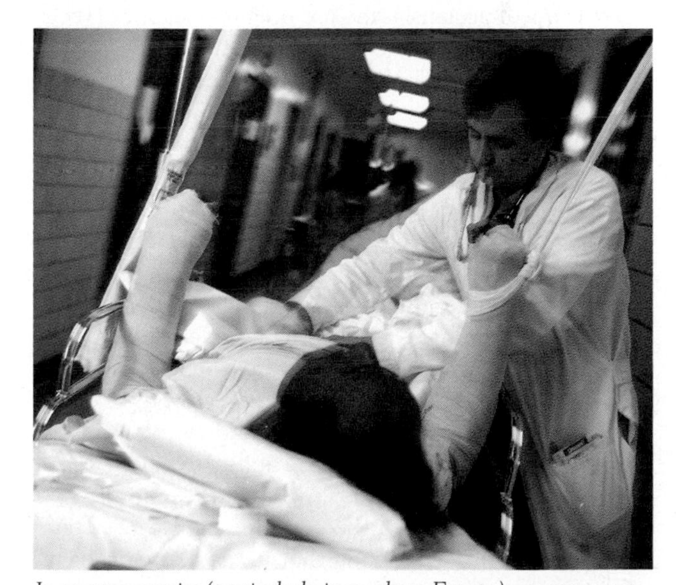

In many countries (particularly in northern Europe), governments have tried to minimize the correlation between social class and the availability of health care. But in the United States, the inequities of social class are ever more sharply reflected in the unequal availability of health care and in the very experience of illness. Here a doctor takes the medical history of a patient "parked" in the hallway of a hospital emergency room.

scan units, ambulatory-care clinics, nursing homes, and many other enterprises have been organized as corporate ventures. Doctors, too, are becoming more entrepreneurial, incorporating themselves in group practices and investing in expensive medical equipment so that they can perform costly tests and procedures in their offices. And like hospitals, groups of doctors are establishing women's health centers, psychiatric centers, and other clinics. In such an atmosphere of corporatization, the independent physician may find it increasingly hard to compete.

MAJOR PROBLEMS OF THE U.S. HEALTH-CARE SYSTEM

The structure of the U.S. health-care system has created many problems that must be addressed. These include unequal access, spiraling costs, and a health insurance crisis.

Unequal Access

American health care is essentially a system of intervention rather than prevention: The system is oriented toward treating and curing disease rather than preventing it. As a result, Americans do not usually come into contact with the health-care system unless they feel ill. When this happens, the health-care providers they encounter are often highly trained specialists who use the most advanced technology to provide treatment—if the patient can afford it. Moreover, the United States is the only industrialized nation besides South Africa that does not provide comprehensive health care for all its citizens, regardless of their ability to pay.

The American system of health care has three tiers: one for the well-off and well-insured (the upper classes, the elderly through Medicare, and the middle class with "good" jobs at large companies), one for the poor who are eligible for government-funded Medicaid, and one for the 32.1 million citizens with no insurance and too little income to afford a serious illness (U.S. Bureau of the Census, 1992). In short, access to the health-care system is highly unequal because it is based on the ability to pay.

An abundance of evidence shows that the uninsured are at a great disadvantage in the current health-care system. For instance, one study found that insured Americans receive 90 percent more hospital care than the uninsured do, and the reason is not that they experience 90 percent more serious illness (Davis and Rowland, 1983). When the uninsured get seriously ill for a long period of time, they are often forced to go begging for treatment, hoping that doctors and public hospitals will not turn them away. Many of the uninsured also forgo preventive health care (routine checkups and screenings). As a result, they tend not to detect health problems until they are well-advanced and more expensive treatment is needed, or even until it is too late to treat them at all.

Spiraling Costs

The spiraling costs of health care make the problem of unequal access even worse. In a sense, the health-care system is a victim of its own success. Its guiding philosophy—vigorous and even heroic efforts to cure disease—has led to an array of extremely expensive high-tech treatments, such as organ transplants and coronary bypass surgery. Once these procedures are available, the demand for them spreads quickly, for everyone understandably wants the best and the latest that medical science has to offer. As a result, lives are saved but medical costs rise spectacularly, to the point that private insurance companies and Medicare/Medicaid have begun to balk at paying the bills.

New medical technologies also add to the cost of health care by requiring highly trained workers to operate the new equipment and perform the new procedures. Ironically, the growing number of doctors in the United States boosts health-care costs as well. Young doctors, eager to attract patients, are quick to offer the new high-tech treatments. Older doctors must then do the same to stay competitive, so the nation's health-care bill rises ever higher.

The skyrocketing cost of malpractice insurance adds to the dilemma, as more people are suing physicians for treatment that has gone wrong. In 1990, American doctors paid $4.5 billion in malpractice insurance premiums. This extra cost is paid by all insured doctors—good, bad, or mediocre—and it is inevitably passed on to patients. In response to the threat of being sued for malpractice, doctors are increasingly practicing what is called "defensive medicine." They give patients every conceivable diagnostic test and routinely call in consultants to protect themselves from patients' charges that they were not careful enough. The American Medical Association estimates that defensive medicine costs between $12 billion and $14 billion a year (P. G. Marshall, 1990).

Another factor is the aging of the American population: Older people, in general, use more medical services than younger ones. Between 1940 and 1990, the proportion of the population that is elderly nearly doubled, from about 7 to about 12 percent. This trend will continue as the baby-boom generation ages. By 2030 an estimated 25 percent of Americans will be elderly, a fact that has ominous implications for the total cost of health care.

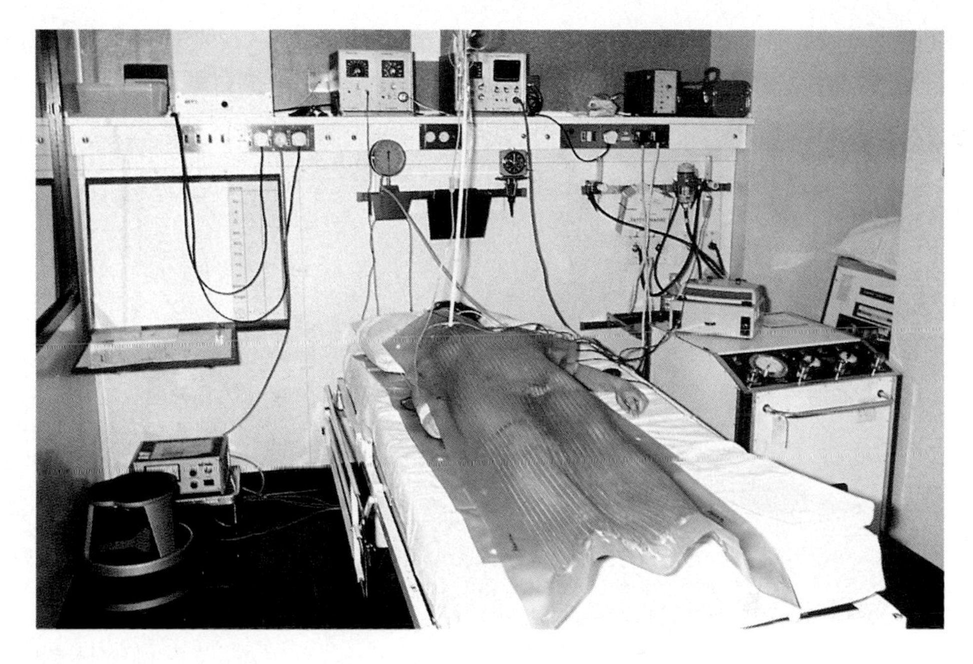

Medical technology has advanced so far that it has given rise to such issues as whether a brain-dead person is still truly alive and whether scarce resources should be spent for drastic life-support procedures when vast numbers of people have difficulty obtaining basic medical services.

Finally, many of the millions of Americans who lack health insurance not only may not get the care they need but also place a financial burden on taxpayers, hospitals, and other patients. In 1988, unpaid hospital bills alone amounted to over $8 billion (*Consumer Reports*, 1990b). Hospitals and doctors who care for the uninsured typically raise the fees they charge insured patients in an effort to compensate for their losses. In New Jersey, for example, hospitals add onto each patient's bill a 13 percent surcharge to cover the cost of treating people who are unable to pay. As a result of such measures, medical charges rise, insurance premiums spiral, and adequate health care moves beyond the reach of more people.

The Health Insurance Crisis

This cycle has led to a crisis of health insurance in the United States. The higher the cost of medical insurance rises (recently at rates between 10 percent and 25 percent a year), the greater the number of Americans who either do without insurance or buy reduced coverage. Particularly hard hit are the unemployed, the self-employed, and part-time workers, all of whom must pay the entire health insurance premium themselves. Also affected are people who work for small businesses, which often have enough trouble surviving without having to foot the bill for employee medical insurance. Even large firms are feeling the health insurance pinch. Whereas in 1984, 37 percent of large American companies paid the entire health insurance premium for their employees, just four years later only 24 percent did (*Consumer Reports*, 1990b). Today, the majority of American firms ask their workers to pay some of their health-care costs through out-of-pocket deductibles and premium copayments. Of course, those who are earning relatively low wages may not be able to afford the copayments, so they too give up their health insurance, expanding the pool of people who have no safeguard.

Many people believe that they have good health insurance but fail to realize how vulnerable to disaster they are should serious illness strike. This vulnerability arises from the way in which insurance companies do business. In response to the skyrocketing costs of health care, insurance companies are refusing to issue policies to people with medical conditions that might prove expensive. If one of their policyholders falls seriously ill, they may raise the premiums charged to that person by as much as 200 percent (*Consumer Reports*, 1990b). These tactics allow the insurance firm to offer more competitively priced premiums to their healthy clients, but the person who is seriously ill is left in a dilemma. He or she can neither do without insurance nor switch to another insurance company, because no other carrier wants to insure a person who is already sick. So that unlucky person is stuck with staggeringly high premiums, no matter how much money has already been paid for premiums. Even worse, the insurance firm may refuse to renew the policy, leaving the high-risk individual or his or her employer unable to purchase insurance at any cost.

Although in the past this problem has affected mainly individual or small-group buyers of insurance, that pattern is changing. Large-group purchasers of insurance are no

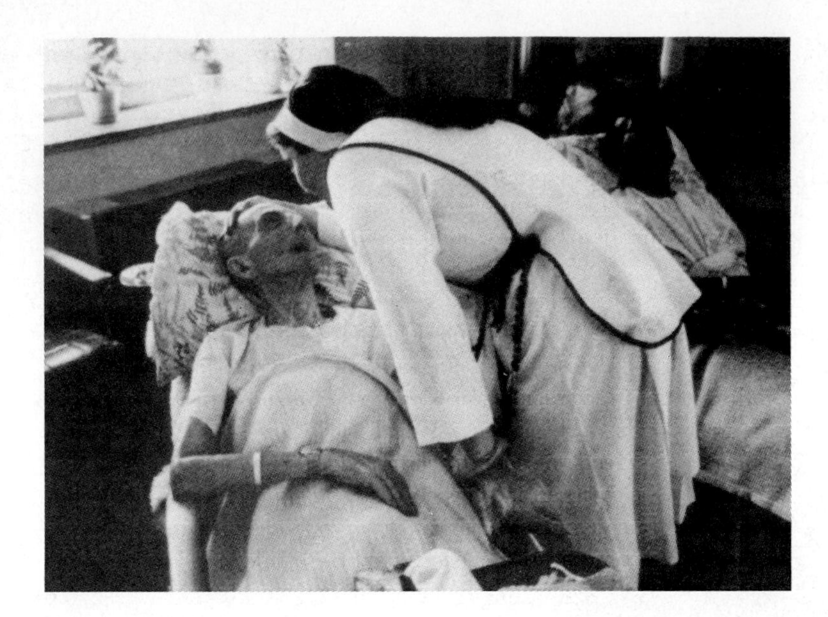

A growing hospice movement has made it possible for terminally ill people to die in a homelike setting where the emphasis is on comfort and caring rather than on prolonging life.

longer always bastions of security. One woman in California who purchased insurance through a group of thousands of college alumni saw her premium rise to $16,000 a year after it was discovered that her eight-year-old daughter had been born with only one kidney, which didn't function completely. According to one expert on health insurance, "No one in this country with private health insurance coverage who is in any kind of group plan is free from the kind of uncertainty that competition is producing" (Daniels, quoted in Kolata, 1992, p. A1).

SEARCHING FOR SOLUTIONS TO THE HIGH COST OF HEALTH CARE

Americans have started to search for solutions to the serious problems created by the spiraling costs of medical treatment and health insurance. The pressure for a national health-care system grows stronger every year. Meanwhile, doctors and hospitals are being urged to control costs, and doctors' professional judgments have come under scrutiny. Questions such as, "Is this expensive test or procedure really needed?" and "Can this patient be discharged from the hospital a few days earlier than the doctor recommends?" herald the beginning of an era in which doctors are held accountable for their decisions and medical costs are shaved wherever possible.

One of the most significant by-products of this new era is an altered balance of ***power***, with those who pay the bills—the government (through Medicare and Medicaid), employers, and insurance companies—chipping away at physicians' traditionally absolute power to make decisions about patient care. As one commentator has put it, "[P]ower so carefully accumulated and nurtured for the better part of five decades has begun to shift from those who provide care to those who pay for it. . . . Increasingly, those who pay for care are demanding economic accountability from those who provide it and are altering many of the historic ground rules" (Goldsmith, 1984, p. 453).

Signs of this fundamental change are everywhere (Burke and Jain, 1991). Insurance companies, for example, have started managed-care programs in which the company reviews a policyholder's hospital stay and treatment before it is undertaken and while it is under way. If the insurance company decides that a procedure is not essential, it may refuse to pay for it. Employers who pay for medical insurance are also entering into people's health-care choices. For instance, some are gathering data on the fees charged by different hospitals and doctors, identifying particularly expensive ones and discouraging employees from using them. Others are requiring their employers to get a second opinion when a doctor tells them they need surgery. Still others are putting "service contracts" out for competitive bid—that is, they are offering a health-care provider the chance to "service" all their employees *if* it can do so at an attractive price (Leyerle, 1984; D. W. Light, 1988).

The federal government, too, is cutting back on its two major health-insurance programs: Medicare for the elderly and Medicaid for the poor. Eligibility requirements for Medicaid have been tightened substantially. Once offered to more than 70 percent of the country's poor, by 1983 this program was available to only 47 percent, and by 1990 to only 38 percent (*Consumer Reports*, 1990a; Davis and Rowland, 1983). Two-parent families, for example, are usually ineligible for Medicaid, and single adults are rarely covered unless they are elderly or disabled (Davis and Rowland, 1983). Besides reducing the numbers of people eligible for Medicaid, recent cutbacks have limited benefits and the fees paid to physicians and hospitals (Kern and Windham, 1986). This means that many low-income people who are covered by Medicaid can't always get the medical care they need. As a result, public hospitals that provide free care to the poor have been flooded with patients who can't pay.

Another belt-tightening measure is the prospective payment system (PPS), a new way of compensating hospitals for treating Medicare patients. Previously, a hospital submitted a bill for services rendered and Medicare paid it. Under the PPS, the hospital receives a fixed amount from Medicare for a given procedure (gall bladder removal, cataract surgery, appendectomy). Analyses suggest that PPS does indeed reduce Medicare expenditures (Russell and Manning, 1989). However, it also provides an incentive to discharge patients early, because hospitals are paid the same amount for a particular service whether they keep the patient for three days or ten. Under the old system of reimbursement, hospitals earned more money by providing more care. Under PPS, they earn more by providing *less* (Guterman and Dobson, 1986).

In response to PPS and the managed-care programs of private health-insurance providers, hospitals have changed some of their procedures. First, they have found various ways to reduce the number of days a patient stays in the hospital. They now do all the preliminary tests and paperwork before admission. Patients scheduled for some kinds of surgery are often admitted to the hospital early in the morning of the same day their surgery is scheduled. In addition, some hospitals are designating certain rooms as reduced-rate areas to accommodate patients who need further recuperation but require fewer services than other patients.

Cost concerns have also led to new forms of health-care delivery. One is the **health maintenance organization**, or **HMO**, a health-care organization that provides medical services to its subscribers for a fixed price each year. Since HMOs lose money if patients require many expensive treatments, they usually stress preventive care to keep people healthy. Another new and growing form of health-care delivery is the **preferred provider organization**, or **PPO**. A PPO is a group of doctors that offers specific services to specific groups of patients (such as all the employees of a company) at discount prices. The organization's clients get a price break, and doctors get a steady stream of patients. A PPO also allows considerable freedom: A patient can choose to go to a doctor outside the PPO (but must pay the difference in the fees). Similarly, doctors who see PPO patients are free to see non-PPO patients. PPOs come in many forms and sizes. They may be organized by doctors, by employers, by insurance companies, or by hospitals that want to expand their range of services.

The problems of the American health-care system aren't likely to be solved overnight, even though most Americans believe that it needs many improvements, even fundamental overhaul (Steinbrook, 1990). The great majority of Americans say they want the government to step in and control medical costs, improve medical insurance coverage, and increase access to health care; yet policymakers are still undecided about what actions to take. One reason for their indecision is the pressure from powerful elites and interest groups who feel they stand to lose from particular health-care reform proposals. Another reason is the complexity of the health-care issue. There are a great many alternatives to be weighed, and a great many competing values are involved. All these social forces have kept the subject of health care on the public agenda.

Thinking Back on the Key Concepts

This chapter has shown us each of the five key sociological concepts at work in understanding health and the health-care system. ***Social structure*** provides an explanation of how diseases spread among different groups at different rates. The division between rich and poor, for example, helps to explain differences in how often Americans see doctors and the quality of medical care they receive. Networks of interpersonal relationships help to explain the patterns by which sexually transmitted diseases like AIDS are spread.

Culture plays an important part in the way people respond to health issues. It shapes, for example, the ways people react to efforts to prevent the spread of AIDS, as when the cultural orientation of some Americans leads them to discourage TV ads urging the use of condoms or free needle-exchange programs for intravenous drug users.

Culture also shapes the way different groups of people react toward individuals who have diseases such as AIDS.

The key concept of ***functional integration*** shows us how spiraling health-care costs are the result of changes in American society, including not only higher pay for physicians but also larger numbers of elderly Americans. It also shows us how the costs of health care in turn affect our entire economy.

Power is a crucial factor in the development and maintenance of the American health-care system. Governmental power has mandated that health care will be extended to older Americans and to some who cannot afford to pay for it themselves. The power of some doctors and for-profit hospital corporations and others who benefit from the current health-care arrangements has slowed efforts to control costs. However, through ***social action*** many Americans have begun to campaign for a better system of health care, one that would be both more effective in serving *all* Americans and more economical. Social action by AIDS advocacy groups has also been and continues to be crucial to making the health-care system responsive to the needs of those who suffer from AIDS and to raising public awareness of the need to combat the epidemic.

SUMMARY

1. The major causes of death in this country have changed in the past century from acute, infectious diseases (such as pneumonia and influenza) to chronic disorders (such as heart disease and cancer). This change is due mainly to the development of antibiotics and vaccines that reduce or prevent many formerly deadly infections, allowing people to live long enough to contract chronic conditions. These chronic conditions are said to be "diseases of civilization" because they arise from factors associated with modern life (a sedentary lifestyle, a diet high in salt and fats, exposure to low-level carcinogens, and so forth). If these negative influences on health could be reduced, Americans would enjoy a compression of morbidity, meaning that disease would be confined to the last few years of life in most cases.

2. The incidences of many diseases differ significantly among Americans by sex, race and ethnic background, and socioeconomic status. For instance, women outlive men by an average of more than seven years, and blacks, Hispanics, and the poor have higher mortality rates than middle-class whites. Factors contributing to health problems among the poor are inadequate food and housing, less medical care, and more stress. Unemployment, too, is related to ill health. It deprives people of medical insurance and of income to pay for health care, and the stress connected with not working in itself contributes to health problems.

3. Every illness or disease has its sociological dimensions, its recurring patterns caused by social forces and its variations among different social groups. This is illustrated by analyzing some major health problems, such as hunger, smoking, and AIDS. Hunger in the United States has emerged again as a major social problem. Budget cuts and unemployment during the 1980s, along with the recession of the early 1990s, combined with a rising cost of living to make many people unable to afford enough to eat. Smoking, too, is increasingly recognized as a critical public health problem. Although many people have quit smoking, heavy promotion of cigarettes constantly attracts new smokers. AIDS has brought a number of social consequences in its wake. These include changes in sexual behavior and attitudes, more openness in discussion of sexual matters, increased discrimination against homosexuals and other high-risk groups, and challenges to civil liberties.

4. The health-care industry in the United States is enormous and still growing. Part of its expansion has involved the status elevation of doctors. Doctors enjoy an unusual degree of autonomy in their profession. Until recently they have been protected from intervention, competition, and evaluation. A by-product of the medical profession's prestige has been the medicalization of American society. Many problems that were once the province of clergy, the family, or the courts are now taken to doctors. At the same time, medical care has undergone a process of corporatization: It has become a profitable market for corporate investment. For-profit hospitals have expanded, doctors have become entrepreneurs, and all kinds of health-related industries have sprung up as profit-driven enterprises.

5. The American system of health care has three tiers: one for the well-off and well-insured, one for the poor who are eligible for Medicaid, and one for the roughly 35 million to 40 million people who have no insurance and not enough income to pay for a serious illness. Thus, the American health-care system offers first-class care to those who can pay and ignores the needs of those who cannot.

6. Exacerbating the problem of unequal access to health care in America are its spiraling costs. These rising costs are due to a number of factors: many high-tech treatments and highly trained medical workers to operate new equipment and carry out new procedures, the skyrocketing costs of both malpractice insurance and the defensive medicine doctors practice in response to malpractice suits, the fact that the American population is growing older and elderly people have more medical problems, and the millions of uninsured families who cannot pay their hospital bills and so boost the prices charged to those who have insurance coverage.

7. Another major problem with the health-care system in the United States today is the crisis in health insurance. Because premiums are rising at a very rapid rate, insurance companies are reluctant to increase those premiums further by including people with serious illnesses among their policyholders. As a result, people who are seriously ill sometimes find their policies canceled or are singled out to pay extremely high rates.

8. Rising medical costs led to a variety of cost-containment measures during the 1970s and 1980s. For instance, insurance companies have started managed-care programs in which the company reviews a policyholder's hospital stay and treatment before treatment is undertaken and while it is under way. If the insurance company feels that any procedure is unessential, it may refuse to pay for it. The government, too, has tried to reduce what it pays for Medicaid and Medicare. Eligibility requirements for Medicaid have been tightened substantially, and fixed payments are now given for Medicare-covered treatments. Cost concerns have also led to new forms of health-care delivery, such as health maintenance organizations and preferred provider organizations. Both seek to offer health care to groups of people in a less expensive way than conventional care entails.

REVIEW QUESTIONS

1. What is the difference between disease, illness, and sickness? Give an example of each.

2. What is the relationship between poverty on the one hand and health and health care on the other?

3. Why has the incidence of hunger increased?

4. How did AIDS become an epidemic in the United States?

5. How has the social status of doctors increased over time?

6. What are some of the consequences, both positive and negative, of the high social status of doctors?

7. How does medicalization involve a redefinition of social issues?

8. What are some ways of reducing the high cost of health care?

CRITICAL THINKING QUESTIONS

1. Develop some suggestions for social policies designed to reduce the effects of poverty on health and health care.

2. Choose one of the major health problems discussed in the chapter—hunger, smoking, or AIDS—and analyze it from the perspective of at least three of the five key concepts (social structure, social action, functional integration, power, and culture).

3. Develop some suggestions for social policies designed to reduce the incidence of hunger, smoking, or AIDS cases.

4. Have you or someone you know had an experience with medicalization or demedicalization? Describe it in the terms used in the chapter.

5. What is your opinion about a national health-care system for the United States?

6. From a sociological perspective, which strategy for reducing health-care costs would work best? Why?

GLOSSARY

AIDS Acquired immune deficiency syndrome, a fatal disease caused by the HIV virus and transmitted through contact with infected body fluids.

Compression of morbidity A hypothetical situation in which people live longer, more active lives and would remain comparatively free of disease until their last few years.

Disease A medically diagnosed pathology.

Health maintenance organization (HMO) A health-care organization that provides medical services to its subscribers for a fixed yearly price.

Illness An individual's subjective sense of not being well.

Medicalization The trend toward including personal problems in the realm of medicine.

Mortality rate The relative frequency of deaths among members of a population segment.

Preferred provider organization (PPO) A group of doctors offering specific services to groups of patients, such as the employees of a particular company, at discount rates.

Sickness The social acceptance of a person as ill.

CHAPTER 16

Economics and Work

Rockefeller Center: a cluster of Art Deco buildings in midtown Manhattan, built in the 1930s when almost no one had much money, except people like the multimillionaire descendants of John D. Rockefeller. Dominating its plaza is a statue of Prometheus, Titan of Greek mythology and symbol of benevolent power and strength. The tourists who flock there in December—to gaze at the enormous Christmas tree, take in the show at Radio City Music Hall, and watch the skaters gliding around the ice rink—seldom stop to think that someone *owns* this complex. To them, it is just there, like the noisy traffic, the bustling crowds, and the hazy smog overhead.

That is why many Americans had an unsettling surprise when they learned in 1989 that Mitsubishi Estate, probably the largest real estate development company in Japan, had purchased a controlling interest in Rockefeller Center. Suddenly, they were reminded that Rockefeller Center is not just an American monument, like the Statue of Liberty. It is part of an **economic system.** In functional terms, an economic system is the social institution that fulfills our basic societal need for goods and services. A building complex like Rockefeller Center is an investment. The Rockefeller heirs created it to house businesses that need places to carry out their work. Consumers, in turn, buy the products of these businesses, contributing to their profits and to the rents collected by the owners of the buildings they use. Without the wheels of an economic system endlessly turning behind the scenes, there would be no Rockefeller Center—in fact, no New York City and no United States.

The American economic system is more than just the web that connects producers and consumers in our own society. Increasingly, it operates on a worldwide scale, entwined in a global economy that stretches from New York to Paris, from Cairo to New Delhi, from Sydney to Tokyo and Hong Kong. The American economic system is the largest component of this global economy, but it is no longer the unquestioned world leader. The United States' share in the worldwide sale of many products has declined steadily, while those of various Asian and Western European countries have grown. Older "rust-belt" American industries, like steel and cars, are not the only ones that have lost out to international competition. Sales of American-made high-technology products—from computers to medical equipment, from electronic instruments to telecommunication devices—have also suffered. The U.S. military now relies on Japanese suppliers for semiconductors and other high-tech equipment needed for its "smart" weapons. While the U.S. gross domestic product (GDP—the total value of the goods and services produced each year) is still the largest in the world, for years it has been growing more slowly than those of many competing countries. Japanese economists estimate that their country's GDP could outstrip that of the United States by the end of this decade, even though Japan has only half as many people (Reich, 1991).

In addition to the sagging competitiveness of many American industries and a flood of foreign imports into the U.S. market, another economic trend has foreign companies buying American businesses and manufacturing on American soil. The Japanese alone have been making several hundred acquisitions each year in the United States. The purchase of Rockefeller Center is just one recent example. Others are Panasonic's purchase of MCA (owner of Universal Studios) and Sony's purchase of Columbia Pictures. A group of Japanese investors bought Pebble Beach Golf Club in California for an estimated $1 billion. In the booming consumer electronics industry, fully half of all American-based firms were foreign-owned in 1990 (Reich, 1991). Many Americans have the vague sense that their country is becoming an economic colony.

Sociologists apply our key concepts as they seek to understand the workings of all economic systems, from small and relatively self-contained ones to those that span the entire globe. Sociologists point out that ***social action*** and ***social structure*** combine to produce a ***functionally integrated*** economy. The economic role of social action is not new to most people. Economies, especially capitalist ones, are often thought of as being shaped by rational choices made by millions of people as they decide what to buy and sell and at what prices (J. Coleman, 1992). From this perspective, economies are created by people, and the actions of people are what bring about economic stability or change. Social structure, too, has an influence on the workings of economic systems. The social structure of an economy refers to the patterns of social relationships, social positions, and numbers of people that are involved in determining what is produced, how it is produced, and how it is distributed. From the perspective of social structure, a modern economy involves the actions of individuals and corporations, the operation of markets, and government intervention (DiMaggio and Powell, 1992). Economic systems are also shaped by elements of ***culture***—that is, by the beliefs and values that people hold about work, property, and the production of services and goods. ***Power*** is involved in economic systems, too, since ownership and control of the means of production are crucial bases of influence in any economy.

Economies are often thought of as huge, impersonal, and impossibly complex systems of cash transfer. Yet much of the economy takes place in small-scale situations like this one, with an Amish work team reroofing a house while a father-and-son construction crew repairs a chimney. The informality of the arrangements obscures the fact that a quiet division of labor guides this work to completion.

In this chapter we first examine the two major forms of economic organization in the world today: capitalism and socialism. Each is partly a product of different cultural values. Under capitalism, a high value is placed on private ownership, while socialism puts a high value on shared responsibility for social welfare. We then turn to the organizations that conduct America's business—from giant corporations down to small family-owned grocery stores. The vast global power of large corporations sharply sets them apart from individuals. Finally, we look at work in the United States, one of the social activities that underlie our economic system.

CAPITALIST ECONOMIES

There are different ways of structuring an economic system, different ways of patterning social relationships and positions to produce and distribute goods and services. In this section we look at one kind of economic system, capitalism, which is now the predominant form of economic structure in the world.

The Nature of Capitalism

Thousands of employees of NBC (the National Broadcasting Corporation) work in its Rockefeller Center headquarters. As they skim financial reports, produce TV shows, and enter computer data, they are engaging in some of the millions of different activities that make up American capitalism. **Capitalism** is a way of organizing economic activity that has four essential characteristics: (1) *private ownership* of the means of production; (2) *self-interest and the profit motive* as the major economic incentives; (3) *free competition* in the markets for labor, raw materials, and products; and (4) repeated investment for the purpose of *capital accumulation*. These four attributes constitute a pure model, or ideal type, of capitalism.

The first of these characteristics is probably the easiest to understand. In a pure capitalist system all the material means of production—from farmlands to oil refineries to factories producing ballpoint pens—are owned by private individuals or corporations rather than by the state. These means of production are forms of **capital**, or wealth that is invested in generating more wealth by producing goods and services. Capitalist ideology holds that private ownership of capital is an inalienable right. At the same time, capitalism gives power mainly to owners of capital—capitalists—not to the workers who contribute labor rather than capital to the production process.

In a capitalist system, people base their economic decisions on self-interest. Consumers buy the goods and services they want (limited only by their ability to pay). Workers choose the jobs they wish to hold (constrained only by their individual backgrounds, training, and experience). Producers select the goods and services they wish to sell (restricted only by the availability of investment dollars, the interests of consumers, and the ability to earn a profit). Although these may seem self-centered ways of making economic choices, their cumulative results can be quite beneficial for society as a whole. According to Adam Smith, whose books, especially *The Wealth of Nations* (1776/1976), helped to develop modern capitalist ideology (see Chapter 1), economic choices motivated purely by self-interest ultimately lead to the production of the goods consumers want and a corresponding rise in society's wealth. In this view, the rational choices of individuals combine to produce the functional integration of the economy as a whole.

Acting in accordance with self-interest motivates producers to maximize their profits. They do this to increase their own wealth and prestige, but at the same time they are also contributing to the greater good of the economy. In trying to maximize profits, producers are constantly searching both for new products that meet consumers' wants and needs and for new cost-reducing methods of manufacturing those products (lower costs mean both a larger volume of sales and a greater return on each item sold). As a result, from society's standpoint, resources are being used efficiently. Everyone benefits, not just the entrepreneur.

What is to prevent an enterprising capitalist from charging exorbitant prices to maximize profits? The answer is the free competition that exists in a capitalist economy. If one firm's products are overpriced, consumers will simply reject them in favor of similar products produced by other firms. The same competitive forces operate in the market for labor and other resources. If one firm tries to boost its profits by paying workers less than the going wage, its best employees will find work elsewhere, resulting in poorer-quality products and loss of sales. In the end, such a firm will probably be forced to increase its wages or be driven out of business. The result, again, is that society benefits. Products are priced fairly, workers are paid fairly, resources are used efficiently, and capitalists earn a "normal" profit. At least this is how the pure model of capitalism works. In real life, giant corporations may compete unfairly with smaller businesses or try to hold down the wages of workers who cannot easily find other jobs. At this point, however, we are concerned only with the workings of pure capitalism.

Another result of free competition in a pure capitalist system is that producers are motivated to invest part of what they earn in improving their businesses. As Max Weber put it, capitalism means "production for the pursuit of profit and *ever-renewed* profit" (1904/1958). Capitalists can't sit back and let their existing companies give them a high income and a comfortable way of life. If they do, they are likely to fall behind their competitors and be driven out of business. So capitalists use some of their profits to make their products or manufacturing methods even better, thus keeping or even increasing their competitive edge.

Goods from all over the Mediterranean world filled the shops of this busy commercial street in a fifteenth-century Italian city-state. Centers of international trade, ruled by wealthy merchant oligarchies, these dynamic city-states provided the context for the social and cultural movement toward secularism and humanism that became known as the Italian Renaissance.

The Rise of Modern Capitalism

Although capitalism seems natural to us in modern Western nations, it has not always existed. Its features came together and began to dominate the economic landscape only in the late eighteenth and early nineteenth centuries. This is when Britain began its Industrial Revolution; Germany, France, and the United States followed soon after. Before this, agriculture had been the main source of wealth and the dominant occupation in every society.

The key to the Industrial Revolution was dramatically improved methods of production. First, agricultural production increased dramatically. With fewer people needed to produce food, more could live in cities and work in manufacturing jobs. Industrial productivity then improved as manufacturers began to use *specialization and division of labor.* No longer did a single craftsman make a product from beginning to end. Instead, the manufacturing process was broken down into small steps, and each step was performed by a worker who specialized in doing that task as efficiently as possible. As labor was divided, tasks also became simpler. This meant both that less skilled workers could be hired and that machines could be developed to perform some of the work. Every investment in laborsaving machinery further increased productivity—that is, allowed the same number of workers to produce even more goods. As a result, some workers lost their jobs, but society's total wealth increased.

The ability of industrial capitalism to expand the wealth of nations served as a moral justification for it. Before the rise of capitalism, the profit motive had been equated with personal greed. Now it was seen as benefiting society as a whole. The social theorist Bernard de Mandeville summed up this new outlook by declaring that certain "private vices" can become "public goods." He meant that from the viewpoint of individual morality, it might in fact be selfish and greedy to seek wealth aggressively; but if in doing so you created more wealth, not just for yourself but for others, you were also serving the public good, even if unintentionally (Dumont, 1977; A. O. Hirschman, 1977).

Modern capitalism not only transformed the production of goods; it also expanded their distribution enormously. Previously, most trade had been local because long-distance shipping was difficult and risky. Capitalism led to the integration of national markets as roads and railroads were built, and to a great expansion and regularization of international trade. A market now extended as far as ships could travel. Raw materials were imported from faraway

In the 1970s, when American automobile manufacturers failed to respond to changing social and economic conditions, the Japanese dramatically expanded sales of their smaller, more fuel-efficient, and better-engineered cars in the United States. The vast influx of Japanese products has prompted Americans to question everything from the adequacies of their educational system to the appropriateness of their social goals in general.

rural places to the increasingly industrialized nations of the West, and manufactured goods found buyers worldwide. As Karl Marx and Friedrich Engels wrote: "The need of a constantly expanding market for its products chases the bourgeoisie over the whole surface of the globe. It must nestle everywhere, settle everywhere, establish connexions everywhere" (Marx and Engels, 1848/1976, p. 451). The global reach of capitalism has continued to expand ever since the initial Industrial Revolution. It was, for example, one of the major factors behind the efforts of Europeans to colonize much of the rest of the world, especially in the nineteenth and twentieth centuries. In addition to importing raw materials, capitalists needed ever-bigger markets for their products. Thus after the British conquered India, they set out to eliminate the local textile industry there so that Indians would have to buy British cloth.

From the late 1940s through the 1960s, the United States was the unquestioned leader of the capitalist world, with more goods sold abroad and more international investments. Since the 1970s, however, the global market has changed. We opened this chapter with one dramatic example: the purchase of Rockefeller Center by a Japanese corporation. Such takeovers are signs of a new global economy in which the United States is no longer the clear leader and in which competition is intense. Not only Japan but several other Asian countries like Korea and Taiwan have become serious competitors in many areas of the global economy (see Figure 16.1). At the same time, European countries, especially Germany, have rebuilt after the ravages of World War II and become formidable economic powers. Thus, the global economy has changed from one with a single leader to one with several major players. The United States is still trying to adjust to this change (see the Global Issues/Local Consequences box).

At the same time, the relentless globalization of economic markets has led to new conceptions of "domestic" economies. It is increasingly difficult to speak of the U.S., British, French, or Japanese economy as though it were

FIGURE 16.1 / The Changing Balance of International Trade

Source: World Bank, *World Development Report, 1991,* table 18, pp. 238–239.

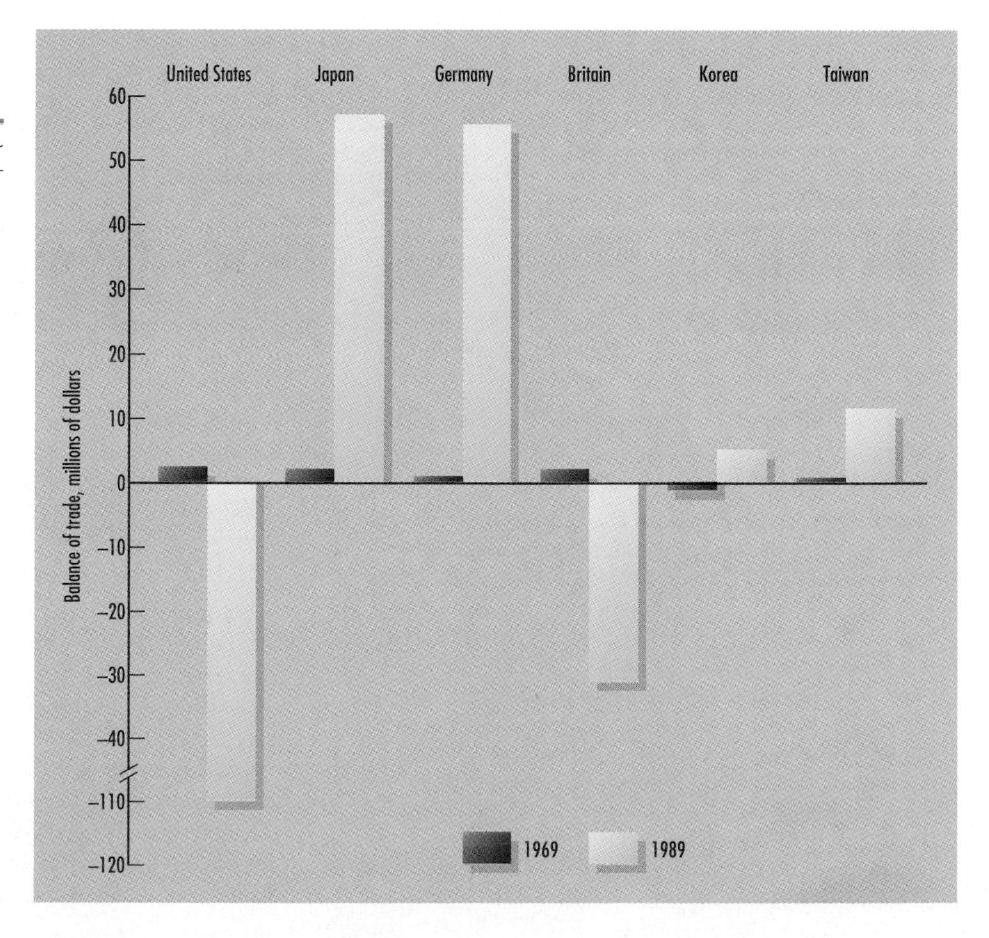

GLOBAL ISSUES/LOCAL CONSEQUENCES

Competing in the New Global Economy

Statistics show that foreign competitors are relentlessly eroding America's economic supremacy. For example, between 1980 and 1988, America's worldwide share of machine-tool exports dropped by 17 percent, of microelectronic exports by 26 percent, of computer exports by 36 percent, and of automobile exports by 46 percent (Judis, 1990). Similarly, a study of fifteen major industries showed that although the United States had the largest market share in all of them in 1970, by 1986 it had lost ground in every one but two (aerospace and paper products), and foreign competitors had actually outstripped the United States in five of the fifteen (banking, chemicals, electrical equipment and electronics, iron and steel, and nonferrous metals) (Franko, 1989).

Even in our own country we are losing ground to foreign competition. During the 1980s we not only failed to increase our share of sales abroad; we also failed to stop the growing American preference for foreign products of many different kinds. By 1987, for example, we were importing more than 26 percent of our cars, 31 percent of our engineering and scientific instruments, and 60 percent of our radios and TVs (U.S. Bureau of the Census, 1990c). In 1990, the value of what we imported was over $100 billion more than the value of what we exported, a huge trade deficit.

Some Americans believe that it may not matter that we are losing ground in manufacturing to production overseas. They say that if Americans can't make certain goods at competitive prices (presumably because our workers earn such high wages), we should let these industries decline and specialize instead in ones in which we have a clear-cut competitive advantage. But many social scientists argue that there are serious flaws in this logic. For example, Linda Stearns (1992) persuasively argues that when our country's manufacturing sector declines, the vast majority of Americans suffer, directly or indirectly. Loss of manufacturing jobs is accompanied by a decline in factory wages. Between 1980 and 1989, for example, as more than a million manufacturing jobs were eliminated from our economy, the average real hourly wage of American factory workers dropped by 8.5 percent. Today, factory workers in Japan, France, Italy, Germany, and Great Britain all earn more on average than their counterparts in the United States (*Economic Report of the President*, 1991).

Workers who lose jobs in manufacturing often seek new ones in the service sector. But without a healthy manufacturing base on which to build, higher-paid service jobs (in communications, research and development, transportation, insurance, law, advertising, accounting, finance, and so forth) are not as abundant as they otherwise would be. What are available are a great many low-paying service jobs—retail salespeople and cashiers, waiters and waitresses, food counter and food preparation workers, janitors and cleaners, nurse's aides and hospital orderlies (Stearns, 1992).

Given this general decline in higher-paying jobs, it is no wonder that Americans have suffered a drop in their standard of living. This decline has occurred both in absolute terms and in comparison with citizens of other countries. In terms of per capita wealth, the United States currently ranks ninth, behind the

a separate unit with clear boundaries. As Robert Reich puts it:

> When an American buys a Pontiac Le Mans from General Motors, he or she is engaging unwittingly in an international transaction. Of the $10,000 paid to GM, about $3,000 goes to South Korea for routine labor and assembly operations, $1,750 to Japan for advanced components (engines, transaxles, and electronics), $750 to West Germany for styling and design engineering, $400 to Taiwan, Singapore, and Japan for small components, $250 to Britain for advertising and marketing services, and about $50 to Ireland and Barbados for data processing. The rest—less than $4,000—goes to strategists in Detroit, lawyers and bankers in New York, lobbyists in Washington, insurance and health-care workers all over the country, and General Motors shareholders—most of whom live in the United States, but an increasing number of whom are foreign nationals. The proud owner of the Pontiac is not aware of having bought so much from overseas, of course. General Motors did all the trading, within its global web. (Reich, 1991, p. 113)

According to Reich, we can no longer count on American corporations to be the "national champions" they once were. In the 1950s, the health of the large American corporations meant the health of the U.S. domestic economy. These companies primarily employed American workers, paid dividends to American stockholders, and made products for American consumers. Consequently, relatively little of their wealth "leaked out" abroad, and they linked their fortunes with those of the country as a whole. "As steel goes, so goes the nation," was the motto four Scandinavian countries, as well as Germany, Iceland, Switzerland, and Japan (Organization for Economic Cooperation and Development, 1990). Clearly, the personal consequences of America's loss of a competitive edge in the global economy are highly significant.

A high level of investment in domestic production is the main reason some of our competitors are now outperforming us. The Japanese, for instance, didn't invent products that U.S. manufacturers couldn't produce. What the Japanese did, above all, was to develop better ways of making the same sorts of products. They invested in new technology, with the result that by the 1980s their factories were much more automated than those in America. They also invested in more and better training for their workers and in research and development for new production processes. Thus, during the 1960s and 1970s, while American companies were devoting only 2 or 3 percent of their profits toward improving the efficiency of production, the Japanese were investing 10 to 12 percent (Reich, 1991).

However, American firms must be willing to invest in domestic production, not only by buying new machines and equipment of their own but also by supporting public investment in education, job training, transportation, and other government spending programs that are needed for a healthy domestic economy. In recent years, many have instead favored increases in military spending to maintain the stable international environment in which global trade and investment can flourish (Ferguson and Rogers, 1986). As a result, the domestic U.S. economic base has weakened.

Some sociologists suggest that to boost investment at home, the United States needs a national industrial policy, like those of its major competitors (Stearns, 1992). In countries like Germany and Japan, government and business see themselves as partners in promoting national economic interests. The government deliberately aids the growth of certain industries that it deems essential to the economy's well-being. In the 1950s, for example, the Japanese government set out to build a competitive computer industry by establishing protective tariffs and quotas, sponsoring research and development projects, and giving financial assistance to firms. By 1970, [illegible] puter [illegible] (Stearns, 1992).

Linda Stearns (1992) proposes that an American national industrial policy would entail three things. First, it would foster the development of new industries with high growth potential (robotics or biogenetics, for example). This it would do by providing a well-educated work force, research and development assistance, and long-term loans at low interest. Second, a national industrial policy would encourage the modernization of older industries (like steel) that still have the potential to become internationally competitive. Here it would limit foreign imports to give firms a period of protection during which they could invest in new technologies. Third, a national industrial policy would help to ease the demise of uncompetitive industries with no potential for growth. It could, for example, offer job training to displaced workers and discourage declining firms from wasting money on additional capital investments. Only in these ways, Stearns believes, can the United States revitalize its economic strength in the new global economy.

of U.S. Steel, and it contained a great deal of truth. Today, however, with the increased globalization of production, we can no longer expect that thriving "American" companies necessarily mean a thriving domestic economy. Much of the money American firms now spend goes to citizens of other nations. For example, in 1990, 40 percent of IBM employees were foreign nationals, and this percentage was growing. Employees of Whirlpool, another large "American" business, are now mostly from other countries, as are employees of Seagate Technology, a California-based world leader in making hard-disk drives for computers. As Charles Exley, head of National Cash Register, recently told the *New York Times*: "National Cash Register is not a U.S. corporation. It is a *world* corporation that happens to be headquartered in the United States" (quoted in G. Epstein, 1990–1991).

Government Intervention in Capitalist Systems

Adam Smith was a brilliant thinker, but he never imagined that capitalism would someday operate on the vast global scale it does today. He also didn't anticipate that national governments would intervene in economic activities to the extent that they do today. Smith had a basically functional view. He thought that all the economic actions of individuals would combine to produce the best overall integration of the economic system. Government, he believed, should adopt a *laissez-faire* policy, leaving businesspeople, workers, and consumers alone to make economic choices as they pleased. In Smith's view, competition would provide the rewards and punishments needed to make the whole system work. Governments would only be

Could a national energy policy stabilize the cycles of economic expansion and contraction, and create an investment plan that would create sustained economic growth? While sociologists who study the economy often rely on the same statistics used by economists, we must also remember how social experience is influenced by economic cycles. During the Great Depression of the 1930s, about 25 percent of the American labor force was unemployed, families disintegrated, and social institutions were in crisis. Thousands of people, like this man, migrated from the Midwestern "Dust Bowl" to the West Coast in search of work.

called on to act as "enablers," providing the public the goods and services (such as money, roads, and civil courts) necessary for people and businesses to carry out their economic transactions.

From the beginning, however, others thought that governments needed to do more because an ideal functional integration of the economy would not come about "naturally." For the most part, this latter view has prevailed. "Enabler" is only the first of three principal roles governments play in all modern capitalist systems. The second is that of "assister," offering help to various social groups. One form of assistance is protection for capitalists and workers, as when the U.S. government imposes tariffs on imported clothing so that American garment workers have a better chance of keeping their jobs, and their employers of keeping their profits. Governments also assist those who face serious economic problems beyond their control, thus compensating for some of the negative effects of capitalism. Examples include government assistance programs for the poor, the unemployed, and the disabled. More controversially, governments can assist one group in its struggle against another, as in helping businesses to break up labor unions. Third, governments are "regulators": They protect businesses from unfair forms of competition, consumers from potentially harmful products, minorities from unfair discrimination, and so forth. Throughout the modern capitalist world these three roles of government have become increasingly prominent in the twentieth century.

In the United States, government intervention in economic life started to increase rapidly during the Great Depression, when our capitalist system seemed on the verge of collapse. The New Deal programs of President Franklin D. Roosevelt were attempts to use government resources to boost the devastated economy and relieve personal hardship. During the same era, an English economist, John Maynard Keynes, argued persuasively for an expanded role of government in regulating the capitalist economy's cyclical ups and downs. Keynes believed that government should increase its spending (through borrowing, if necessary) whenever business activity declined. The additional spending would both stimulate economic recovery and cushion the effects of unemployment. Until the late 1970s, government policymakers throughout the world followed Keynes's prescription. The result was dramatic growth in government social programs, peacetime military spending, and the number of government employees.

A prominent American Keynesian economist, John Kenneth Galbraith (1978), has argued that big government has become essential in the modern capitalist world. Big corporations, according to Galbraith, need a stable environment within which to plan new products and make large investments, an environment that only government can maintain. Moreover, government contracts provide long-term guaranteed business for corporations and make it possible for them to conduct extensive research and development. This research and development, in turn, results in new inventions that benefit society. Development of the modern computer industry, for example, including the vast array of personal computers and software, was supported largely by contracts from the military and other government agencies, such as the IRS (Burnham, 1983). In short, the "welfare state" provides many public benefits besides financial assistance to the poor. Assistance to the poor, in fact, accounts for a relatively small proportion (5 to 12 percent) of total government spending.

In the late 1970s, however, Keynesian economics came under attack. Many economists argued that the cost of government programs outweighed their benefits. Some sociologists and economists suggested that government assistance programs were not only too expensive but too difficult to administer effectively and thus prone to abuses. Still others argued that the government's best economic tool was regulation of the money supply (mainly through the lending practices of the Federal Reserve Board), rather than direct government spending. In an effort to cut back government spending, the Reagan administration curtailed many of the social programs previously supported on both economic and humanitarian grounds. Yet, overall, government spending continued to rise. The federal budget grew from $590.9 billion in 1980 (the year before Reagan took office) to $1,118.3 billion in 1988 (the last year of his administration). This is nearly a twofold increase in a period of eight years. The largest increases were in military and defense spending. Although Reagan denounced government borrowing to spend more than the revenues it receives, he actually raised the national debt more than any previous president. Government economic intervention, in short, does not come only from Keynesians, and it continues in both Democratic and Republican administrations, though with different emphases.

SOCIALIST ECONOMIES

From its beginnings, capitalism has had critics. Some have been conservatives who have denounced the tendency of capitalist economies to push for continual innovation and so disrupt established social practices. Others, ultimately more influential, have been socialists. **Socialism** has come in many varieties since the early nineteenth century. The unifying feature, and the source of the name, is an emphasis on putting social cooperation ahead of individual competition and placing the needs of society as a whole ahead of the benefits of a wealthy class. The most common means for achieving socialism has been ownership or control of the means of production by society as a whole or by communities of workers. Before we see how experiments in socialism have fared, we need to look at the socialist critique of capitalism.

The Socialist Critique of Capitalism

Capitalism at the time of the Industrial Revolution was shocking to many people. Early coal-powered factories caused terrible air pollution. New technologies put thousands of craftsmen out of work. All the profits seemed to go to owners, not workers. Owners tried to deny workers the right of free assembly because they feared it would lead (as it often did) to the formation of unions. Greed seemed to be winning out over morality and the collective good, and many workers and others clamored for a "moral economy" (E. P. Thompson, 1968). They wanted an economy that would not just avoid capitalism's abuses (child labor, dangerous working conditions, long hours for very low wages) but would also save traditional community life, which capitalism seemed to be destroying. It was in this context that socialism arose.

A number of socialist critics challenged the ideology of capitalism, especially the importance it gave to individual self-interest, its notion that profit making supersedes moral responsibility to others, and its belief that capitalists are more deserving of rewards than workers who actually produce goods and services. Many of the early socialists were Christians whose religious beliefs condemned the seemingly unbridled greed of capitalism. Others were workers in skilled crafts who found themselves jobless due to the rise of factories. Still others were utopian thinkers trying to conceive of the best possible society. Among these early critics of capitalism, Karl Marx has been by far the most influential. Marx was not primarily a moral critic of capitalism, an advocate of traditional crafts, or a utopian thinker. He was a social scientist trying to develop an empirically based theory that related economics to social organization.

As we saw in Chapters 1 and 9, Marx focused on the exploitation of the working class by the capitalist class. He argued that this abuse was an unavoidable structural consequence of capitalism, not just a moral failing of capitalists. Capitalist profits came mainly from paying workers less than the full value of the goods they produced. Raising workers' pay would reduce or eliminate profits. Yet workers who weren't paid much couldn't afford to buy the goods that capitalist industry produced in ever-greater quantities. Thus, there was a tension between individual rational action and an irrational system. Capitalists made a rational decision to maintain their profits by paying only subsistence wages and investing in new technology to increase productivity. For the class of capitalists as a whole, however, this decision created twin problems of overproduction (too many goods) and underconsumption (not enough people with enough money to buy them). When the demand for goods fell, each capitalist would naturally lay off workers, but this action would only make matters worse by reducing demand still further, since unemployed workers do not buy much. If capitalism didn't collapse in the midst of one of these crises, workers, in Marx's view, would eventually recognize their common interests and join together to overthrow capitalism.

Marx was right in some of his predictions, wrong in others. He correctly predicted the series of worsening crises that culminated in the Great Depression of the 1930s. He even predicted that capitalists would sometimes resort to war as a solution to the crises of overproduction and underconsumption that produced depressions. What Marx did not predict was that capitalists would accept the government economic intervention that since the 1930s has prevented the recurrence of another Great Depression (although the milder economic downturns called recessions continue to plague capitalist economies around the world; Wallerstein, 1984). Marx was also wrong in thinking that workers in advanced capitalist societies would inevitably slide into such abject poverty that they would join together and revolt. In modern, industrialized capitalist states over the last 200 years, workers generally have become better off, even though they haven't closed the gap between themselves and capitalists. Does this mean that Marx was totally wrong in believing that exploitation was inherent in capitalism? Perhaps not, if we consider the global capitalist order. It may be that the rising incomes of workers in wealthy capitalist states are made possible in part by the exploitation and poverty of those in underdeveloped parts of the capitalist world. Indeed, the socialist revolutions that have occurred have not been in advanced capitalist countries, but in poorer countries making the transition to capitalist development.

In addition to the exploitation of workers and the tendency toward cycles of boom and bust, capitalism has produced a number of other problems, according to its critics. One is its emphasis on competition at the expense of economic cooperation. Capitalism not only sets people against one another within societies; it also produces tensions, even wars, between countries (the world's most devastating wars have been fought in the capitalist era). At the same time, economic competition makes it hard to alleviate poverty and hunger, not only in Appalachia and inner cities but also in the Third World (see Chapter 18).

Another problem that capitalism produces, in the view of its critics, is intense exploitation and destruction of the environment. Under capitalism, businesses are encouraged to use natural resources, especially nonrenewable fossil fuels like coal, oil, and gas. Conservation is encouraged only when it immediately saves a firm money. The capitalist urge to produce ever-more goods also contributes to pollution, the production of dangerous wastes, and other health hazards.

Last but not least, critics fault unbridled capitalism for a severely unequal distribution of wealth. While a little economic inequality can serve to motivate people, there is no need for a company to pay its managers as much as thirty times the wages it pays its workers, as is typical in the United States today.

Experiments in Socialism

Socialists have not only criticized capitalism; they have tried to produce better economic systems. In the United States, their efforts have focused on reforms designed to bring more social responsibility to capitalism. American socialists have thus helped to achieve such reforms as the enactment of a minimum wage, unemployment insurance, and welfare benefits for the poor. In Western Europe, socialists have brought about greater reforms of capitalism, especially stronger protections for workers, more help for the poor, and free or low-cost health care. As a result, many European countries are often called *social democracies*. Elsewhere, for example in Russia and China, socialists waged revolutions to try to replace capitalism altogether.

While the socialist reforms of Western Europe have been widely successful—so much so that many are now accepted by procapitalist conservative parties—the record of revolutionary socialism has not been so favorable. In the following sections we look first at socialist reform in Western Europe, then at socialist revolution in the Soviet Union, and finally at Third World socialism.

Socialist Reform: Western Europe

In most of the democratic states of Western Europe, socialists of various kinds, both Marxist and non-Marxist, joined forces with trade unions and other groups to compete for power through elections. The most successful democratic socialist parties have been those of Scandinavia, but socialists have also been in control for extended periods in Austria, Germany, France, and Great Britain, and they have shared power in Italy.

Western European socialism differs from the socialist economic system that Marx envisioned. For one thing, it does not involve public ownership of all the means of production. In Sweden, socialist governments regulated industry but did not take it over. In France, socialists called for public ownership of only certain essential industries. At the same time, most Western European socialist systems do not involve extensive central planning of what to produce, how to produce it, and how to distribute it. Instead, there is a great deal of free competition for goods and services, raw materials, and labor. Thus, the democratic socialist states of Western Europe have not overthrown capitalism. But they *have* used government to limit capitalism's excesses and to protect the welfare of workers.

Some aspects of Western European socialism have worked better than others. Public takeover of essential industries (called *nationalization*) has had mixed success. While some nationalized businesses have flourished, others have not. Problems are particularly common when the government has taken over a nearly bankrupt firm to prevent its employees from losing their jobs. Democratic socialist efforts to provide for the welfare of private-sector workers have met with more consistent success. They have resulted in extensive unemployment benefits (thus cushioning the impact of recessions), national health-care systems, old-age pensions, and programs to help the poor. They have also brought about better working conditions, such as higher minimum wages and more stringent safety standards in the workplace. All these welfare provisions have not cost Western European countries their prosperity. For instance, Sweden (which has had a socialist government for most of the time since 1945) has long had a higher average standard of living than the United States; and recently, under socialist presidents, both Italy and France have enjoyed higher rates of growth than the United States has.

Socialist Revolution: The Soviet Union

The most important distinguishing feature of Western European socialist systems is that they are democratic. Indeed, many say they are pursuing economic democracy to go along with political democracy. This has not been the case where Communist parties have come to rule. Though officially committed to democracy, most of the world's Communist parties have in fact been undemocratic, committed to a "proletarian dictatorship" in which the party itself retains most social power. This is not inconsistent with what Marx envisioned. In Marx's view, capitalism would ultimately be replaced by a totally classless society, in which all people contributed according to their abilities and all received according to their needs. During this stage, called **communism**, the state would wither away because it was no longer needed. First, however, there would be a stage of socialism, in which collective control of the means of production would eliminate the evils of capitalism.

CENTRAL ECONOMIC PLANNING The first successful communist revolution occurred in October 1917 when the Bolsheviks (Lenin's faction in Russian politics) seized power. Especially under Lenin's successor, Joseph Stalin, the Bolsheviks created a dictatorial central government dominated by members of the Communist party. All important means of production became publicly owned. Economic decisions, instead of being left to the workings of the market, were placed in the hands of a central planning board. Creating a series of annual and five-year plans, the central planners in Moscow determined which goods to produce and in what quantities, where and how to produce them, and how to distribute the output. They passed their directives down to regional planners, which in turn transmitted more specific goals to local ministries in charge of particular industries or resources. These ministries then set output quotas for Soviet factories and other enterprises, all of which were staffed by state-paid workers. In this way, the planners hoped to establish a production and distribution system that was less wasteful and more just than a capitalist one, and also less prone to capitalism's vicious cycles of overproduction and underconsumption.

From the beginning there were problems. One of the first moves was to force small farmers to work together as members of collective farms rather than on their own plots of land. Many of these peasants resisted, and the collective farms were never very productive or efficient. For most of its history, the Soviet Union was unable consistently to feed its people despite having a sizable quantity of farmland.

In industrial development, the Soviet central planners were more successful at first. They boosted production rapidly and transformed the primitive economy of the old Russian Empire into an industrial power. Steel and heavy equipment were essential to a modern army, and the creation of such an army was a high priority for the Soviet government. The priority given to military production meant that the needs of the Soviet people took second place. Consumer goods from toilet paper to cars and TV sets were chronically in short supply and of poor quality. In addition, the centrally planned economy became bogged down in bureaucracy and corruption, encouraged by the dictatorial control of a small governing class of Communist party members.

To varying degrees, the other communist states of Eastern Europe and Asia (especially China and North Korea, where communism still survives) experienced the same problems. After initial postrevolutionary gains (often focused on rebuilding a war-ravaged society), the communist system failed to provide for sustained economic growth.

THE COLLAPSE OF THE SOVIET ECONOMY Although many political and cultural issues were involved, it was above all economic failure that brought about the breakup of the Soviet Union. A major problem was a lack of incentive to produce desirable, high-quality products in cost-conscious ways. Soviet state-owned enterprises were not subject to the laws of supply and demand, as they would have been under capitalism. If their costs outstripped their revenues, the state subsidized them. All a Soviet manager had to do was meet production goals. The state was responsible for supplying raw materials, and the state purchased all the finished products, for delivery to state-run stores. The careers of managers depended more on pleasing higher-ups in the bureaucracy than on satisfying the people who bought their products. Thus, there was little motivation to improve the quality of products or to design new ones not called for by the central planners. There was also little motivation to operate efficiently, which is why the Soviet system used two and a half to three times more resources than the American capitalist system to produce a given amount of output (Aganbegyan, 1988). Those who received defective or overpriced products—whether consumers or other businesses—had no effective way to demand change, so the dysfunctions just built up in the system.

Another vexing problem of the Soviet economy was the difficulty of setting output quotas in ways that didn't backfire on the central planners. For instance, if the planners specified quotas by weight (so many tons of nails or sheet metal, for example), producers were encouraged to make their goods heavier so as to meet the quota more easily. One result was chandeliers so heavy they pulled ceilings down (Roberts and LaFollette, 1990). If the planners then switched to quotas specified by numbers (so many paper clips or toasters per month, for instance), they inadvertently encouraged overproduction of small-sized goods, or products that were carelessly made. Almost any way Soviet planners tried to express quotas, backfire effects occurred. For example, the quotas for oil-exploration teams were set by the number of meters drilled, which led to an excess of shallow wells that did not yield major oil finds. Deep drilling through bedrock was avoided, even though it was the best way to strike oil, because it took longer and led to fewer total meters drilled. Some Soviet geological expeditions hadn't found a major deposit in years (Goldman, 1983).

A third problem inherent in the Soviet centrally planned economy was the overwhelming job of coordinating producers and suppliers. Imagine being in charge of supplying all the businesses in the United States with each and every material they need in the right amounts at the right times. The task is mind-boggling in scope. No wonder shortages and late deliveries of raw materials were the norm in the Soviet Union. These problems, in turn, led to a practice called "storming." During the first couple of weeks of a new month, when deliveries of materials were late, Soviet workers in many factories were idle. Then production picked up late in the month when supplies finally came, reaching a feverish pitch in the last few days so that the factories would make their monthly quotas. The haste in which the products were made was another source of poor quality. Chronic shortages of supplies also led to the use of inferior substitute materials—whatever it took to get the products out. Ironically, then, although central planning was meant to create greater economic integration than capitalism could, the result was just the reverse: a dysfunctional production and distribution system in which the different parts of the economy were poorly integrated.

From the Soviet people's point of view the economic system became intolerable. Defective consumer goods were everywhere (Aslund, 1989). Hair dryers short-circuited, vacuum cleaners had no suction, washing machines did little more than get laundry wet, and televisions had a disconcerting habit of bursting into flames (in Moscow alone more than 2,000 such fires were reported every year) (*Ogonek*, November 29, 1987, p. 5). Consumer products were also chronically scarce. Because production of heavy industrial equipment, steel, and military goods took priority over consumer needs, people had to spend hours every day tracking down necessities like soap and toothpaste, sugar, bread, and meat. They formed long lines at the mere rumor that some desirable item was about to be delivered to a certain store—a big part of the reason worker absenteeism was so high in the Soviet Union (Shmelev and Popov, 1989).

By the mid-1980s, the problems of the system had reached crisis proportions, which only far-reaching

measures could remedy. Soviet Premier Mikhail Gorbachev launched a campaign for *perestroika*, a restructuring of the Soviet economy. *Perestroika* was intended to gradually introduce a number of economic reforms traditionally associated with a market system. These included running businesses on a profit basis (the revenues a firm received from the sale of its goods had to meet or exceed the costs of production); pay scales that were related to worker productivity; investments that were financed out of a company's earnings; freedom on the part of business managers to purchase their own supplies, determine their own output, and establish their own production processes; and negotiation of prices between buyers and sellers (Zaslavskaya, 1990). In short, *perestroika* entailed a marriage of socialist ownership and ideals with some of the personal incentives found in capitalism. But the reforms of *perestroika* came too little and too late. Although the Soviet economy improved a little in Gorbachev's first years in power, by 1988 it was in shambles and growing worse by the day. In 1991, an attempted coup by Communist party hard-liners provided a rallying point for popular discontent, and the communist regime was overthrown.

The various republics that were part of the old Soviet Union have formed a Commonwealth of Independent States. Although they all renounce communism, and most call for capitalism, it is not clear how quickly these new nations will be able to change. The difficulties in fashion-

Shoppers in Moscow express their dismay over food shortages (top), *while in an open market* (bottom) *a man buys with the hard currency of U.S. dollars. These photographs suggest how economic paralysis in the former Soviet Union continues to shape the lives of the common people.*

Agriculture was once a craft system based primarily on production for local consumption. The modern reality is that locally situated agricultural businesses, like this plant nursery, must compete with an international agricultural system in which the productive centers are located thousands of miles away and which often profit from a poorly paid labor force.

involved, or due to local changes in the business environment (as when a neighborhood declines and customers move out).

Despite these problems, hundreds of thousands of new small businesses are started each year. Owning one's own store, restaurant, or office seems to reflect the value Americans place on independence. Small-business people like being their own bosses. Since Americans also value hard work, they are often unconcerned about the many hours involved in running a small business. Small-business owners typically work far more than forty hours a week, and often entire families help out.

The many ethnic minority members who own small businesses are often recent immigrants. For example, in New York City, a sample of restaurants in 1980 revealed that 60 percent were immigrant-owned (Aldrich and Auster, 1986). One motivation for owning a small business is the desire to avoid the discrimination that minorities often experience in the larger economy, especially against those whose language and culture are markedly different from those of the American mainstream. For some ethnic entrepreneurs, self-employment, with all its risks, is more attractive than a low-paying job working for someone else. Many ethnic entrepreneurs are also attracted by the business opportunities in their neighborhoods, where the demand for ethnic services and products is often high. When an ethnic minority is characterized by extended families, the incentive to start a small business is often combined with the ability to do so. Family members can serve as a pool of much needed and low-wage labor.

Small businesses of all kinds are born in hope every year, but the mortality rate among them is very high. Over 50 percent fail within two years; 75 percent within five years; and 90 percent within ten years (Aldrich and Auster, 1986). Smallness and newness are definitely liabilities in the business world.

Small businesses, however, are extremely important to the American economy. They generate many more new jobs than do large companies (although large companies account for a greater percentage of existing jobs) (Birch, 1988). Table 16.2 compares the percentage of jobs created by small businesses with those spawned by middle-sized and larger firms. Jobs are central. After all, it is mainly through our work—and the income it generates—that most of us are integrated into the economic system.

WORK IN THE UNITED STATES

> All I do now is get up in the morning, go there, and I don't be thinking about that. Like a machine, that's about the only way I can feel. (Will Robinson, bus driver, in Terkel, 1972, p. 201)

> I run into people who say how much they admire what I do. It's embarrassing. I don't make any judgments about my work, whether it's great or worthless. It's just what I do best. It's the only job I want to do. I work hard because I have to. I get tired. At four I feel as though I'm ready to die. (Laughs.) I don't feel bad about it. This is my life. I just am. (Pat Zimmerman, alternative school teacher, in Terkel, 1972, p. 493)

Work. It is how we spend most of the waking hours of our adult lives. It is what provides us not only with an income to live on but also with an important part of our sense of identity and purpose. Few things are more rewarding than meaningful, enjoyable work, and few things are more discouraging than work that is boring or stressful.

TABLE 16.2

Percentage of Jobs Created, by Size of Firm and Region

Number of Employees in Firm	PERCENT OF JOBS CREATED				
	Northeast	North Central	South	West	U.S. Average
0–20	177.1%	67.2%	53.5%	59.5%	66.9%
21–50	6.5	12.0	11.2	11.6	11.2
51–100	−17.4	5.2	5.5	6.3	4.3
101–500	−33.3	3.1	9.4	9.3	5.2
501+	−32.9	12.4	20.4	13.3	13.3
Total	100.0%	100.0%	100.0%	100.0%	100.0%

Source: Birch, 1988; M.I.T. Program on Neighborhood and Regional Changes.

Work is clearly a form of ***social action***, since it is oriented toward and coordinated with the actions of other people. As such, work is distinctly human, as Karl Marx (1867/1976) pointed out. Animals may build and produce things—birds make their nests, bees their honey—but they don't work. They don't devise a plan and self-consciously execute it, keeping the needs and actions of others in mind.

The Meaning of Work

The importance with which Americans view work can be appreciated if we think of the first question we often ask when we meet someone new: "What do you do?" By this we mean not what are your hobbies or how do you spend your leisure time, but what is your occupation, what *work* do you do? Work is one way of defining other people and ourselves. If the man sitting next to you on a plane says he is a prizefighter, you get a very different impression than if he says he is a psychiatrist. For most occupations—factory worker, nurse, physical education teacher, stockbroker, dairy farmer, scientist, hairdresser, auto mechanic, priest—we have certain expectations about the kind of people who fill them. At the same time, when we ourselves enter an occupation, we tend to mold our behavior to conform to what we think is appropriate for that particular social role.

Most Americans have favorable opinions about their work, particularly those in white-collar, professional and technical occupations for which substantial training is required. Mathematicians, biologists, lawyers, and journalists are among the most satisfied. Between 80 and 90 percent of them report they would choose the same kind of work again. By comparison, only 24 percent of blue-collar workers say that they would choose the same kind of work (Tausky, 1984).

You might assume that job satisfaction is higher among professionals because their jobs bring relatively high pay and prestige. These rewards are important aspects of job satisfaction, but they are not the only reasons people express pleasure with their work. Others include the inherent interest of the work itself, the sense that one is doing something worthwhile and contributing to society, the sense that one is supporting oneself and one's family and doing what is expected of an adult, the pleasure of developing competence at something and exercising a skill, and the enjoyment of being with co-workers. Unfortunately, not all jobs offer these satisfactions. Many blue-collar factory jobs, for instance, are inherently boring, unchallenging, and socially isolating, as well as poorly paid and without prestige. (It is not that manual work is inherently unsatisfying; craftspeople with high levels of skill, autonomy, and opportunity for creativity report high levels of satisfaction.) Workers who do the same manual tasks all day, who are pressed to do these tasks as quickly as possible, and who never have the sense of seeing a process from beginning to end are especially likely to find their jobs dissatisfying. They are likely to feel alienated from their work environment, even from society as a whole. To them a job is just a means of earning a paycheck. This view of work is one reason that trade unions have focused so intently on increasing wages for blue-collar workers. When people are convinced that life's pleasures are all outside the workplace, having enough money to pursue outside interests becomes of paramount importance (Calhoun, 1981).

Karl Marx believed that worker dissatisfaction was inherent in a capitalist system, where the organization and management of production are separate from the manual labor involved. Blue-collar workers have no control over the production process, their work is not organized in any socially unifying way, and they labor for the enrichment of capitalist employers whose goal of maximizing profits tends to encourage worker exploitation. To Marx, it was inevitable that workers under capitalism would feel alienated, dehumanized, and unfulfilled. They are treated merely like cogs in the overall production process, not like skilled employees who are performing a meaningful and valued role.

Power in the Workplace

Control is the most important issue in contemporary sociological studies of the organization of work (Simpson, 1985). Because the production of goods now involves hundreds of people interacting with one another like parts in a giant machine, considerable planning and coordination are needed. In most modern work settings, coordination is bound up with control, with managers seeking to maximize their ***power*** in relation to workers. From the perspective of workers, relations with bosses are a major source of dissatisfaction.

Control in the workplace is related to the size of an organization (Edwards, 1979). In small firms, control is direct and face to face, usually exercised by the owner of the company and a few top managers. This kind of control—called *simple control*—can be both arbitrary and harsh. Workers question or disobey the manager's wishes at their own risk. As organizations grow and become more complex, simple control is impossible. For one thing, there is a limit to the number of workers any one manager can supervise directly. For another, workers may become unionized and thus have some protection against arbitrary dismissal or discipline from management.

To deal with the demands of a large organization, managers have devised two new styles of control that are built right into the way work is structured. One is *technical control*, or control that arises from work's technical organization. A prime example is the assembly line, which compels workers to perform their tasks in a certain way at a certain pace. On a car assembly line, for instance, workers who install the axles must do so quickly and correctly before the car is passed along for wheel installation. Although technical control is usually associated with blue-collar jobs, office automation has introduced it into the white-collar workplace as well. The output of employees who work at computers, for example, can be precisely moni-

The rise of industrial capitalism created a new class of workers, who were brought together in factories and cities where conditions were often squalid. They were pressed to learn new kinds of work and were subjected to stricter discipline and greater pressure to produce than earlier craft workers had been. At the same time, factory owners lacked the established legitimacy of older, aristocratic elites. All these factors combined to produce a widespread struggle between owners and workers over economic power. Strikes were among the most important weapons that workers could employ. Early capitalists often used violence or state power to repress strikes. Here, the Massachusetts militia guards a plant entrance from striking workers in Lawrence in 1912.

tored by management, and these employees can be pressured to work faster, just as factory workers can be pressured to tighten more bolts or solder more connections per hour. A more prevalent form of control in the office workplace is *bureaucratic control.* Here control is exerted by a hierarchical system that assigns rewards according to a job's level. Employees work harder to obtain special privileges like their own letterhead stationery, a reserved parking spot, access to the executive dining room, and so on. We will look again at the issue of control when we focus on technology in the workplace.

Changing Patterns of Work

The American paid labor force has traditionally been dominated by men. For the past 100 years, the proportion of men aged sixteen and older holding a paid job has remained quite steady at about 80 percent. By contrast, the proportion of women in the paid labor force during the same time period has increased from 15 percent to 63 percent (U.S. Bureau of Labor Statistics, 1990). This striking change in ***social structure*** has significant implications for marriage, family, the birth rate, and other aspects of social life (see Chapters 11 and 12).

The proportion of women in the paid work force has fluctuated since the Industrial Revolution first drew women from farms to factories and sweatshops. When they could afford it, or their husbands demanded it, women tended to give up paid jobs to care for their families. During World War II, when millions of American men were enlisted in the military, women were needed to work in munitions factories and other wartime industries. After the war, most women were pushed out of or persuaded to leave their jobs. But in the 1960s and 1970s the pattern seems to have changed permanently. A number of social changes encouraged more women to find paid employment: an increase in the divorce rate, the development of reliable contraception, the revival of the feminist movement, and the need for a second family income to counter the effects of inflation. The increase in women workers went hand in hand with another major shift in labor patterns: a dramatic rise in the number of service-oriented jobs. Such occupations have traditionally been held by women; so as more of these jobs were created, they provided increased employment opportunities for women (Shank and Getz, 1986). Most of these service jobs, although white-collar, have been relatively low-paying.

Accompanying the increase in service occupations has been a sharp drop in agricultural work and, as well, a decline in manufacturing jobs (see Figure 16.3). The decline

Until recently, most occupations dominated by women, such as nursing and grade-school teaching, were able to claim only semiprofessional status. The increase in the number of women entering the professions of law, medicine, and college teaching has profoundly affected the gender-based division of labor, as well as the nature of the professions themselves. President Bill Clinton is shown with Janet Reno, the first female attorney general of the United States.

in farm work has been due primarily to mechanization in agriculture, which has increased the amount of land each farmer can cultivate. Manufacturing jobs have also declined because of technological innovations, such as computers and industrial robots (B. Jones, 1982). Other causes have to do with changes in the global economy, such as a shift in manufacturing production to other countries where labor costs are cheaper. As a result of these changes, a great many American factory workers have found themselves laid off. Many have had to accept jobs at a fraction of their former pay, and others have not been able to find work at all in their ailing local economies (Schwartz and Neikirk, 1983). These major declines in agricultural and manufacturing jobs are likely to continue in the United States.

The decline in the number of farm and industrial jobs is one reason that Americans now need higher minimum credentials to enter the work force. So many jobs now require technical skills, like operating or programming a computer, that people with little formal education simply are not qualified for them. What's more, even when no specific technical skills are needed in a certain job, it has become common for employers to require high school diplomas (see Chapter 13).

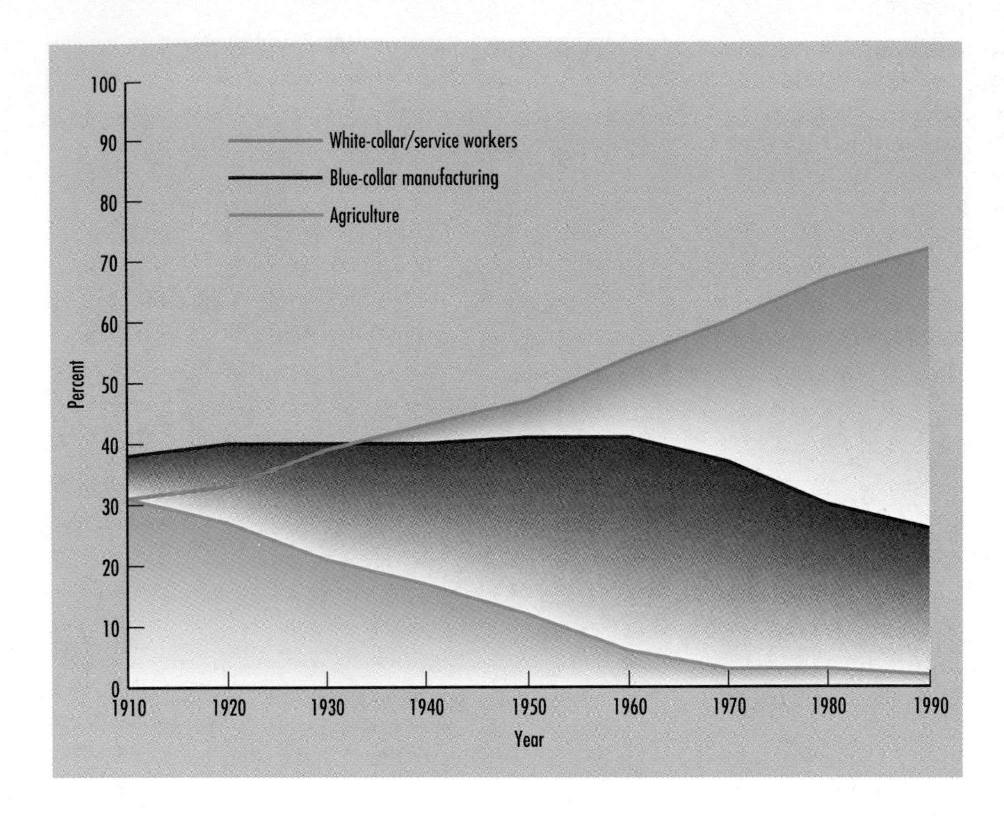

FIGURE 16.3 / Percentage of the Labor Force in Various Sectors of the U.S. Economy, 1910–1990

Source: Data from U.S. Bureau of the Census and U.S. Bureau of Labor Statistics.

Labor Markets

The job that a person is able to find depends on a number of personal attributes. Education, experience, and various skills (like leadership ability in a manager and manual dexterity in an assembly-line worker) are considered legitimate advantages that one person can have over another in trying to land a job. Race, gender, and social-class background are not considered legitimate grounds for employment, but they are usually involved in the hiring decision anyway. However, personal attributes do not determine jobs by themselves; it is crucial to know the structure of opportunities, the availability of vacancies. This is the basis of labor markets, and is determined by many factors including the numbers of people competing for similar jobs and the state of the economy as a whole. But workers with different starting personal attributes and structural starting points tend to face different labor markets.

Sociologists distinguish two broad labor markets in modern capitalist economies: the primary and the secondary (Sabel, 1982). The **primary labor market** is that in which workers are employed by stable, successful, usually relatively large firms. These workers have job security, health-care and retirement benefits, and relatively good incomes. Most workers who are advantaged in terms of education, experience, and socioeconomic background find employment in the primary labor market.

The **secondary labor market** is smaller and much less stable than the primary labor market. Workers in the secondary market are employed in domestic service, in fast-food restaurants, and in small businesses like florists, caterers, and liquor stores, many of which don't survive very long. Jobs in the secondary labor market are often part-time or seasonal. Wages are low and layoffs are frequent, especially during recessions. Health insurance and other benefits are rarely provided. Most jobs in the secondary labor market offer no chance for career advancement and seldom teach skills that could lead to better positions. Many workers in this market struggle to make ends meet even when they are employed full-time.

Changes in technology and in the organization of production affect demand in labor markets. At any given time, certain skills are in high demand while others are not. As computers came into widespread use, the position of computer programmers was boosted while that of bookkeepers was undercut. If people whose current skills are devalued in the primary labor market fail to develop new, more marketable skills, they may find that they have to accept jobs in the secondary labor market. As an example, a laid-off steelworker might have to take a job delivering pizzas or working for a small carpet-cleaning business. The alternative may be long-term, sometimes permanent, unemployment.

The Problem of Unemployment

Unemployment is a "normal" characteristic of capitalist economies. Sociologists are interested mainly in the unemployment rate (as a percentage of the total number of people in the labor market), and in the question of which people suffer unemployment.

There is always some unemployment as a result of changing patterns of jobs available and changing patterns of workers with various skills living in various locations. This is called *structural unemployment* because it is tied to the structure of an economic system as it undergoes market changes. For instance, technological innovations always cause some industries to decline, as new ones develop and expand. When the automobile was invented, there was a steady drop in the demand for goods and services related to horse-drawn vehicles, and eventually these products virtually disappeared from the market. In the process, many workers (from blacksmiths, to wagonmakers, to producers of buggy whips) were forced out of work. Unless these people acquired new skills or were willing to work for lower wages in unskilled occupations, they could remain without a job for a substantial period of time. Structural unemployment also occurs when firms lose out in competition with other firms because they are either inefficiently run or produce inferior products. If these firms go out of business, their employees lose their jobs and may have trouble finding new work if other firms in their area don't need their skills. Then, too, corporate mergers and other kinds of business reorganization can make some employees redundant and cause them to be laid off.

The periodic downturns in capitalist economies also create unemployment, called *cyclical unemployment.* When supply outstrips demand, businesses cut back on employees, and the resulting drop in income and spending can trigger more job layoffs, until a recession sets in. The threat of unemployment from one or more of these causes, and the presence of many people looking for work, serves to keep workers disciplined in a capitalist system and to discourage them from demanding substantially higher wages.

Temporary joblessness is very common in our own capitalist economy. In fact, an estimated two out of three Americans will lose a job at some time in their lives. One out of five Americans was unemployed at some point during the recession year of 1991 (*U.S. News & World Report,* January 13, 1992). Many of these people found new jobs quickly. But some suffered long periods of anxiety, economic deprivation, personal humiliation, and a devastated sense of self-worth.

Government statistics seldom reveal the true magnitude of unemployment at any given time, because the official unemployment rate is determined by counting only those who are actively seeking a full-time job. It does not include those who are looking for part-time employment, nor those who have grown so discouraged that they have virtually given up trying to find a job. For instance, during 1991, at least 1 million unemployed Americans had stopped looking for work. Still more had been pushed into early retirement. There were also many young people who delayed entering the labor force because they knew that opportunities were limited. Only when these people are added to the 8.6 million who were actively seeking work do we get a true picture of the extent of unemployment in that year. In fact, we might also count the 5.9 million American workers who currently hold part-time jobs but would prefer full-time ones. In short, the official unemployment rate doesn't tell us all we need to know about the state of unemployment. Figure 16.4 shows the various components which, when added to the official unemployment rate of 7.8 percent, give the real unemployment rate.

Unemployment happens disproportionately to the poor, who are least able to weather financial crises. For instance, the rate of unemployment for young, lower-class high school dropouts is an alarming 25 percent or even higher during periods of recession (Kasarda and Appold, 1990).

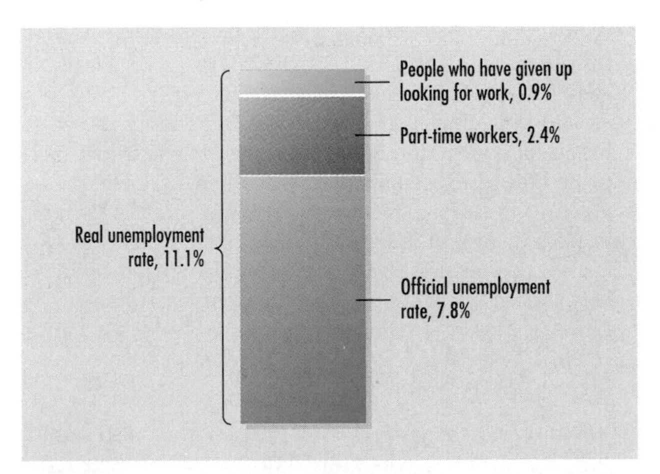

FIGURE 16.4 / The Real Unemployment Rate (When Part-Time Workers and People Who Have Given Up Looking for Work Are Included), 1991

Source: *U.S. News & World Report,* January 13, 1992.

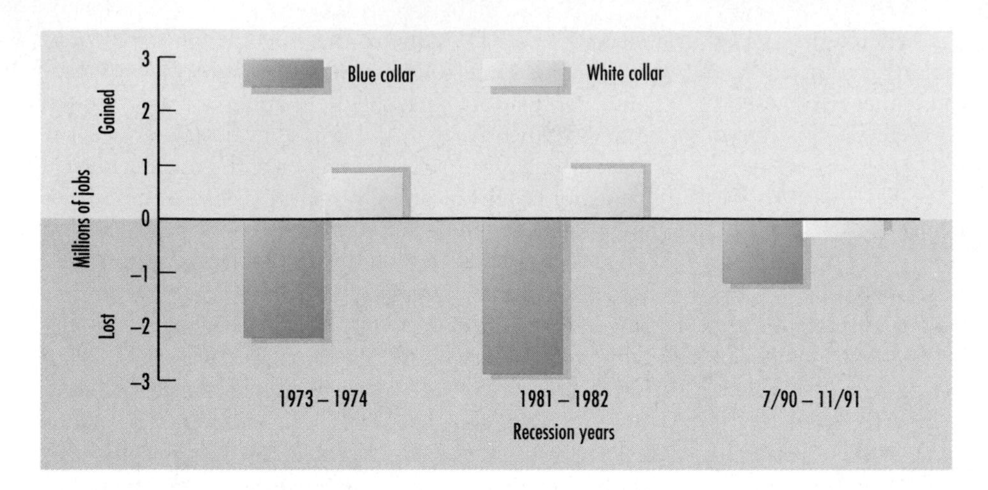

FIGURE 16.5 / Net Change in Blue-Collar and White-Collar Employment during the Three Most Recent Recessions

Source: *U.S. News & World Report*, January 13, 1992.

But unemployment also strikes the middle class and even the wealthy. For instance, in the wave of corporate mergers during the 1980s, many senior executives lost their jobs. Similarly, when the computer industry took a downturn in the late 1980s and early 1990s, highly paid engineers and other computer specialists suddenly found themselves out of work and unlikely to find new jobs very soon. The recession of the early 1990s cut middle- and even top-level jobs, which had been largely immune in previous recessions (see Figure 16.5).

Although the upper-middle-class unemployed usually have savings to help them through, they also have a high standard of living to support. Seeing their lifestyle disintegrate around them can be a very stressful experience. As one put it:

> At the beginning I had quite a few leads, interviews. And then there came a period of nothing. It was a time of utter mental turmoil for me. . . . I was at home all day typing up letters, sending out résumés. I felt like I was a rubber band that was wound up and stretched to the breaking point. Little things, things that would normally not bother me, really got to me. Nothing was coming through. I was bucking up against a stone wall. No matter which way I turned, nothing. I was very quickly falling into a bottomless pit. [Somehow I felt] I was on the outside looking in. I had a feeling of complete uselessness, and I felt I was too young to be useless. The days were filled with uncertainty. (in Newman, 1988, p. 64)

Unemployed executives and professionals also feel a strong sense of social isolation. The privacy of their large homes cuts them off from neighbors. They can no longer afford to socialize at their clubs and favorite restaurants. They feel embarrassed about calling old friends at work because they think those people will be expecting to be asked for a job. The upper-middle-class unemployed are also likely to blame themselves, rather than economic conditions, for their joblessness. After a while, they start to question their own ability to hold down a high-paying job. In job interviews they often feel that potential employers can see through their falsely confident exterior to their many shortcomings (Newman, 1988).

The problems of unemployment are not just matters of self-image; they include very real material deprivations. The unemployment during the recession of the early 1990s was a major factor in causing the total assets or net worth of American households to drop by more than $1 billion between 1989 and 1990 (see Figure 16.6)—the biggest annual drop since 1947. By the end of 1992, median family income in America had dipped below 1980 levels. During times of high unemployment many people also lose employer-paid health insurance. If they or their children get sick, they may not be able to afford to see a doctor or they may be devastated by medical bills.

How well people cope with unemployment depends largely on the social and institutional support available to them. This includes the support of family and friends, who can help the unemployed person maintain a sense of competence and self-worth. It also includes financial support, such as severance pay and unemployment benefits, as well as agencies that offer counseling and job-hunting assistance. When many such supports exist, prolonged unemployment is more bearable.

Professionalization

Professionalization has been an important trend in the primary labor market. **Professions** are categories of jobs in

FIGURE 16.6 / Real Household Net Worth, 1985–1990

Source: *U.S. News & World Report*, January 13, 1992.

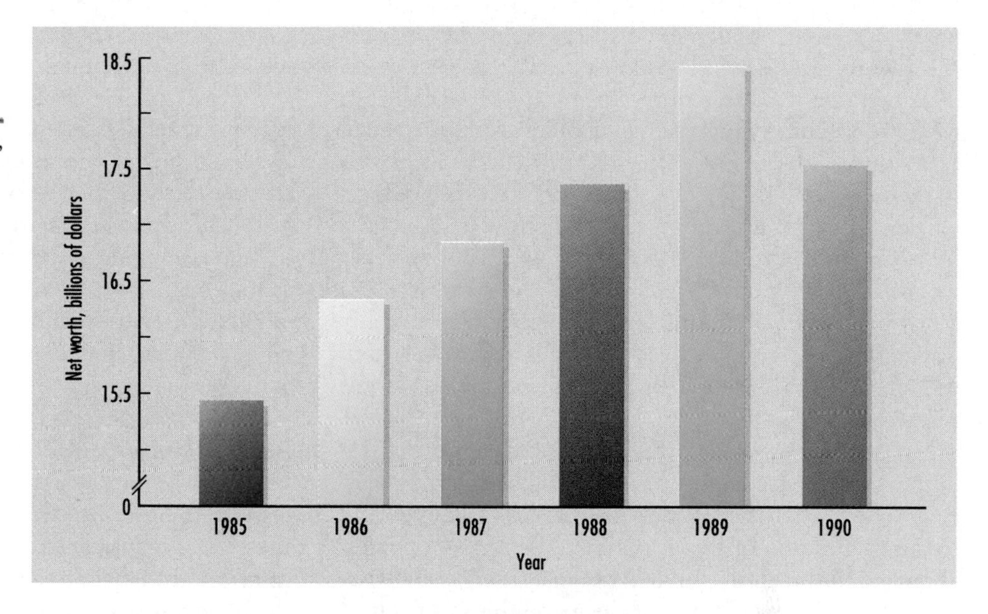

which entrance is restricted to those who possess specialized knowledge and skills that they have acquired from a relatively long period of formal education. Evaluation of the members of a profession is performed by other members (not by "outsiders"), and the members are largely self-organized in their work. The oldest and most respected professions are law and medicine. Religious ministry, in some other countries and historical periods the most elite profession, is less prestigious in the United States today, partly because we have no state church and no government certification of clergy.

Because their numbers are restricted by the educational credentials they must obtain, professionals often command good incomes. Many are self-employed, with their own offices or partnerships. Instead of being supervised by a boss, they are governed by professional codes of ethics and the desire for a good reputation. The majority of professionals, however, work for large organizations. While privileged when compared with most other workers, corporate professionals are subject to some degree of bureaucratic control (Friedson, 1985; Powell, 1985). In general, though, professionals resist interference by others in the regulation of their work. Doctors, for instance, hold that only another doctor can judge the quality of a physician's services. This attempted exercise of power is sometimes contested, as when a patient sues a doctor for malpractice, in effect asking the courts to evaluate that doctor's work (Abbott, 1988).

In recent years, people in a number of traditionally nonprofessional occupations have sought to organize themselves as professionals. Some have succeeded fairly well (dentists, accountants), while others have been less successful (nurses, social workers). Because professionals typically enjoy high prestige, pay, and autonomy, there is an incentive for occupational groups to try to achieve professional status. As this occurs, more credentials are needed to enter these fields. An oversupply of members, which occurs when credential requirements are not very stringent, tends to weaken a claim to professional status (Friedson, 1985).

Productivity and Automation

Productivity refers to the amount of labor, land, machinery, or other factor of production that is required to produce a given amount of output. For example, an acre of land might yield five tons of soybeans or ten tons depending on a farmer's skill, the amount of fertilizer used, the quality of the land, and so on. For sociologists, the main concern is the productivity of labor: how much human work is needed to produce a given amount of goods. Better tools and technology, better work organization (an efficient division of labor, for example), and greater effort are all ways of increasing the productivity of labor.

One of the most important social and economic trends since the Industrial Revolution has been rapid and continuing increases in labor productivity. Rising productivity has been the basis for the generally high standard of living in the United States. During the 1950s and 1960s the productivity of American labor grew at an annual rate of nearly 3 percent, enough to double in only thirty years. If this rate of increase were sustained, each new generation of Americans would produce twice as much as the last, with an accompanying rise in earnings (Public Agenda Foundation, 1990). The problem is that this rapid growth in productivity has *not* been sustained. After the Arab oil embargo of 1973, the annual rate of increase in American labor's productivity took a dive from which it has never recovered. It now hovers at 1 percent a year or even less. Many believe that boosting labor productivity is the only way to cure our country's economic ills and restore it to the preeminent position it enjoyed for much of this century.

Yet the ways in which higher labor productivity has traditionally been accomplished are not without negative effects. The introduction of new laborsaving machinery and the reorganization of the workplace around it—a process known as **automation**—sometimes makes work less satisfying. The sociologist David Halle found this in a study of New Jersey's highly automated chemical industry. As one worker told Halle, the work left behind after automation can be dismal:

> It's hard, brutal work in poor air and bad fumes. There is tremendous heat from the kettles. No brains or talent are required. You blindly follow orders from insecure, unfeeling, insensitive clods. You smash up material with sledgehammers in bad heat like a convict, constantly worried about being caught sneaking a smoke or standing still. It's great to develop muscles and petrify brains. (1984, p. 105)

Even more glamorous technologies can be mixed blessings. Workers may initially welcome the challenge of mastering and putting to efficient use a new technological tool, such as computerized equipment, but then find themselves excluded from programming it and even from controlling the on/off switch. The result can be damaged self-esteem and a gnawing sense of alienation (R. Howard, 1985).

The feeling of alienation and lack of control is not restricted to shop-floor workers. Even highly educated and well-paid specialists are subjected to new forms of control in high-technology companies. Many of these are based on subtle combinations of special incentives and management of emotions. For example, Robert Howard (1985) has examined the development of corporate campuses in Silicon Valley, where in times of prosperity highly skilled computer workers have been treated to free company gyms, health-food bars, and counseling services. Although such benefits are very attractive on the surface, they sometimes come with hidden costs. They are an exercise of ***power*** on the part of management designed to promote loyalty and motivation among workers by enmeshing them in a system that dominates much of their lives. Howard writes, for example, of workers who were expected not just to do their jobs well, but to smile constantly to show how much they liked working at their particular computer firm. This kind of emotional control may be an increasing part of the modern workplace (Hochschild, 1983). Howard calls this vision the "brave new workplace," after the title of Aldous Huxley's *Brave New World.* That novel describes a nightmarish twenty-fifth-century society in which governmental control over people is so complete that possibilities for individuality and creativity are lost, but various automated pleasures are provided to keep everyone superficially happy. Long before the twenty-fifth century, we face the challenge of figuring out how to increase efficiency and productivity without surrendering individuality and the satisfactions of creativity.

Thinking Back on the Key Concepts

Economic reports on the evening news ("The Dow Jones average fell ten points today." "The U.S. economy grew in May for the twenty-second consecutive month") may make us think of the economy as a natural force, almost like the weather. This view tends to blind us to the fact that economies are created, sustained, and changed by the ***social actions*** of people. People analyze economic options from their own perspectives, deciding what to buy, where to work, and how to make what they produce. Economic events don't just happen on their own. They are the result of people making economic choices in response to, and in coordination with, the economic choices of others.

Adam Smith believed that, in a capitalist free-market economy, all these individual choices together would bring about a ***functionally integrated*** economic system. Consumers would "vote" with their dollars for the goods and services they wanted, and businesses would try to provide these products in the most efficient ways possible so as to maximize profits. Economic resources (land, labor, machinery) would therefore be put to desirable uses from society's point of view, and the prices these resources commanded in the market would be bid up to reasonable levels as firms competed for the workers and materials they needed. In reality, of course, no economic system has ever achieved perfect functional integration. There are always some goods being produced that consumers don't wish to buy, and others being offered at excessive prices or produced in inefficient ways. Under capitalism, however, these market dysfunctions are assumed to correct themselves eventually if free competition is allowed to prevail.

However, the modern reality of capitalism is that competition is never completely free. Some actors in any economic system have more ***power*** than others. In our own capitalist economy, for instance, oligopolistic industries are dominated by a few giant firms that are able to stifle competition, create demand for their products through extensive advertising, and charge the maximum that consumers are willing and able to pay. Similarly, in international markets, a few huge multinational corporations are so powerful they can actually affect the prosperity of the countries in which they do business.

Corporations are an important part of our economy's ***structure***, its way of organizing economic relationships and positions to produce goods and services. Studying the various components of economic structure and their effects is an important contribution of sociology to economic analysis. For instance, sociologists point out that unemployment has many structural causes, as when technological change alters the patterns of jobs being offered, eliminating many that are outmoded and creating relatively fewer new ones. Here patterns of available jobs relative to the number of people wanting work—two elements of social structure—are critical to determining the unemployment rate.

Another contribution of sociology to economic analysis is the study of how ***culture*** affects economic life. Cultural values underlie the two major forms of economic organization in the world today: capitalism and socialism. The first rests on the values of private ownership, competition, freedom of choice, and personal achievement; the second on the values of shared responsibility, cooperation, concern for others, and collective welfare. Culture also influences personal economic choices, from the products people buy to the kinds of work they seek. It is no accident, for instance, that with the strong value our culture places on independence, a great many Americans want to own and run their own businesses.

SUMMARY

1. The economy is a social institution that accomplishes the production and distribution of goods and services. Capitalism is the most widespread and important form of economic organization today. In a pure capitalist system the means of production are all privately owned, workers and consumers make economic choices in accordance with their own self-interest, producers are governed by the profit motive, free competition exists in virtually all markets, and the owners of businesses repeatedly invest for the purpose of capital accumulation.

2. Modern capitalism operates on a global scale unimagined by its founders. Capitalist corporations today do not simply buy and sell abroad; they also produce there. High-volume standardized production is now largely being done in countries where wages are low, while more costly skills are being purchased in whatever parts of the world these talents can be found.

3. Government intervenes to a great extent in modern capitalist systems. In the United States this trend has been dramatic since the Great Depression. The influential economist John Maynard Keynes suggested that government spending programs are needed to control economic swings from unemployment to inflation. The welfare state that resulted has been challenged in recent years.

4. Another economic arrangement is socialism, which arose in response to some of the abuses of nineteenth-century capitalism. Socialism involves public ownership and control of at least some of the means of production. In the former Soviet Union, extensive public ownership was combined with extensive centralized planning regarding economic decisions. Such centralized planning is enormously complex and gives rise to many problems.

5. Many of America's large corporations are multinational, with operations in many different countries. Multinational corporations influence both the economic and political life of countries in which they operate. The stockholders of such large corporations are too diffuse to exert much control over policy, so decisions affecting both the corporations and the host countries are largely in the hands of corporate managers.

6. Although large corporations dominate business in the United States, small businesses also play an important role because they employ a sizable number of people and create many new jobs. For a variety of reasons, recent immigrants to the United States are especially attracted to owning a small business. In part because they are often underfinanced and run by inexperienced people, small businesses have a high mortality rate.

7. Work is rewarded not only by pay but by the sense of identity it gives to people. Today, white-collar workers are more prevalent than blue-collar workers and seem to be more satisfied as well, particularly those in professional and technical occupations for which substantial training is required. All people employed by someone else are subject to control, or the coordination of their work effort. Blue-collar workers are controlled by the technical requirements of the production line, while white-collar workers are controlled by the promise of nonmonetary rewards built into a bureaucratic system.

8. Two current work trends in America are an increasing proportion of women in the paid labor force and a decline in farm and factory work coupled with an increase in service occupations, including many low-paying ones. Many women (and minorities) work in the secondary labor market, where jobs are part-time or seasonal and offer few career opportunities. The better-paying and more secure primary labor market is reserved for those with academic degrees and other job credentials. Because these credentials have risen in recent years, unskilled workers who cannot find jobs in the shrinking farm and factory sectors are often forced into the secondary labor market. At the high end of the primary labor market are the professions, such as law and medicine, which offer the best pay, most prestige, and most autonomy. Unemployment is most common in the secondary labor market, but in the 1990s it has begun to affect increasing numbers of highly skilled workers in the primary labor market.

9. The productivity of labor (or output per labor-hour) has been increased by automation, which involves the introduction of machinery and reorganization of the workplace around it. But automation often has reduced job satisfaction by making jobs less interesting.

REVIEW QUESTIONS

1. What are the four basic features of capitalism?

2. Explain the origins of capitalism and socialism, with particular attention to social developments during the eras in which they arose.

3. List some of the positive and negative aspects of corporate life in the United States.

4. Why must any comprehensive approach to understanding corporations take a global perspective?

5. Identify several factors that affect satisfaction with work.

6. How has work in the United States changed over the last century?

CRITICAL THINKING QUESTIONS

1. Some economists argue that capitalism may not survive in the Western world. Others argue that capitalism's dominance demonstrates its survivability regardless of social changes. Present your own views and your reasons for holding them.

2. Do you think Marx would have had more or less impact had he written today rather than 150 years ago? How do you think he would have responded to the social and economic changes of the past few years in the former Soviet Union and in Eastern Europe?

3. Some argue that socialism could work if it were given a realistic chance. Do you agree or disagree, and why?

4. Develop a speech to a group of senior business students about improving corporate life in the United States. Include specific strategies and provide a rationale for each.

5. Develop the essentials of a program to improve work in the United States. Be specific about what you mean by "improve" and about your strategies.

GLOSSARY

Automation The use of machinery to replace human workers and the reorganization of the workplace around it.

Capital Wealth that is invested in the production of more wealth, such as factories which are investments in the manufacture of goods.

Capitalism An economic system based on private ownership of the means of production, self-interest, and the profit motive as the major economic incentives; free competition in the markets for labor, raw materials, and products; and repeated investment for the purpose of capital accumulation.

Communism In Marx's theory, the stage of a truly classless society in which totalitarian control by the state would no longer be needed.

Corporation An organization created by law that has an ongoing existence, powers, and liabilities independent from those of its owners, managers, and employees.

Economic system The social institution that accomplishes the goal of producing and distributing goods and services within a society.

Interlocking directorships Networks of people who serve on the boards of directors of two or more corporations.

Multinational corporation A very large and usually diversified corporation that has operations and subsidiaries in many countries.

Oligopoly An industry dominated by only a few very large firms.

Primary labor market The labor market in which workers are employed by stable, successful, usually large firms that offer job security, health-care and retirement benefits, and relatively good pay.

Productivity The amount of output that a given input of labor or other resource can create.

Professions Categories of jobs in which entrance is restricted to those who possess specialized knowledge and skills that they have acquired from a relatively long period of formal education.

Secondary labor market A small, relatively unstable sector of the labor market, one in which jobs are generally insecure, low-paying, and dead-end.

Socialism An attempt to replace the individualistic competition of capitalism by some form of social cooperation, placing the needs of society as a whole ahead of the benefits of a wealthy class. The most common means suggested for achieving socialism was ownership or control of the means of production by society as a whole or by communities of workers.

CHAPTER PROJECTS

1. Individual Project Create a chart of socialist economic systems based on the information given in this chapter. Include entries for socialism in Western Europe, communism in the Soviet Union, and socialism in the Third World. On your chart, detail the advantages and disadvantages of the economic system as it operated in each region.

2. Cooperative Learning Project Working in pairs, choose one of the corporations listed in the table on page 412. (Make certain that each pair chooses a different corporation.) Do research on your corporation to update the chart with this year's information. Then, working as a class, create a new chart giving the corporations their current rankings.

CHAPTER 17

Politics, the State, and War

In the mid-1980s, newspapers the world over carried grim stories of terrorism: A truck bomb blew up the U.S. marine barracks in Beirut, Lebanon, killing hundreds of soldiers; the cruise ship *Achille Lauro* was hijacked in the Mediterranean and an elderly man on board was murdered; a TWA plane was hijacked in Athens and a young soldier was killed. These terrorist acts of the 1980s were nothing new. The 1970s saw more than 5,000 acts of terrorism, 40 percent of them in Western Europe, 25 percent in Latin America, and 10 percent in the United States (Rubenstein, 1987). Terrorism—and fear of terrorism—continues in the 1990s. During the Persian Gulf war, the United States automatically braced itself for a wave of Iraqi terrorism. Though that never came, terrorism did strike in the United States in a major way with the 1993 bombing of the World Trade Center in New York. Terrorism has become part of the modern world.

Many Americans think of terrorism as the work of deranged, violent individuals who are out of touch with social norms. Sociological research shows otherwise. Terrorism is a form of ***social action***. It is relatively extreme, but like other social action, it does involve patterns of organization. It is generally a response to ***social-structural*** conditions, such as those that exist when people who consider themselves a national group lack a state to represent them.

An essential factor in both terrorism and the social-structural conditions to which it responds is the distribution of ***power***. Terrorists usually lack the power to achieve their aims by more conventional political or military means; they calculate that spreading terror will undermine the power of those who hold governmental authority. The spread of terror does this by disrupting the everyday ***functional integration*** of a society—by making people afraid to fly on airplanes, shop in public places, or take jobs in countries like Lebanon. These disruptions in the functional integration of economic activity, communication, or other areas of life impose a cost on both governments and ordinary people that may lead them to give in to terrorists' demands.

Terrorism is also shaped by ***culture*** in two major ways. First, many of the disputes that provoke terrorist actions are matters of cultural identity and autonomy—whether the rights of Catholics in Northern Ireland or of Palestinians in the Middle East. Second, terrorism works not by actually killing so many people that functional integration is disrupted—as in war—but by promoting a widespread sense of insecurity, by making fear part of everday culture.

Nationalism is often a motive for terrorism, as can be seen in the Middle East. For generations, Palestine and the lands around it have been a battleground between two contending groups: Jews and Arabs. In the late nineteenth century, a movement began among European Jews to settle in Palestine (then a predominantly Arab protectorate of Britain), the home of the Jewish nation in ancient times, in the hopes of establishing a country of their own there. This idea, known as *Zionism*, was a reaction to feelings of statelessness. Dispersed throughout many countries of the world, Jews had no home of their own where they could escape persecution. At the beginning of World War II, some of the Jews who settled in Palestine became terrorists in response to new British restrictions on Jewish immigration. They attacked the British regime there, blowing up buildings and committing other violent acts. After World War II, when Nazi efforts to exterminate Europe's Jews became public knowledge, hundreds of thousands of Jews joined the Zionist movement. When Israel was finally created in 1948, the 700,000 Arabs living in Palestine suddenly found themselves "foreigners" in the land of their ancestors. Some turned to terrorism in the effort to carve out an independent Palestinian state. Thus, one stateless group—Jews—had gained a homeland at the expense of another—Palestinian Arabs.

In this chapter we focus much of our attention on the state, the political unit that plays an important part in giving people a sense of collective identity. Next, we discuss the rise of modern states and examine the emergence of nations and nationalism and the development of the welfare state. We consider the contest for political power—fundamental to all politics—and how power is distributed in societies. We also look at democracy, a widespread form of political organization in the world today. We consider democracy's foundations, the way democracy functions in the United States, and the struggle to establish it in Eastern Europe and the former Soviet republics. Finally, we take up the question of war, a political act that occurs when states can't settle their differences peacefully.

THE CONTEST FOR POWER

Politics is the process by which people gain, use, and lose power. Accordingly, there is an element of politics in almost all social relationships. Parents seek to maintain power over their children; husbands and wives exercise power over each other; teachers wield power over their students, and business executives over their employees. This breadth is part of what makes ***power*** a key sociological concept. In this chapter, however, our focus is on politics in a narrower sense—on specialized institutions of power, especially those related to government.

When we speak of politics as the pursuit of power, we are usually referring to **power** in the sense of the ability to exert control over other people's behavior or experience, even when they resist (Weber, 1922/1978). Bear in mind, though, that politics can also be the pursuit of increased power for everyone—the increased collective capacity to get things done (to manufacture products, for example, or to build skyscrapers) through social organization (Parsons, 1960; Rueschemeyer, 1986). The government, thus, exercises power not just when it uses police or soldiers to force people to perform some action but also when it prints money to make it easier for people to conduct business.

Legitimacy and Authority

Legitimacy is an important issue in the study of power. It refers to the extent to which power is recognized as valid and justified, not just by those who wield it but also by those who are subject to it. For instance, the power of Congress to pass legislation is widely considered legitimate, but not the power of an armed robber to take money from a bank. Sociologists often refer to legitimate power as **authority**. Authority is a matter of right, and ideally should not need to be backed up by coercive power, or force. Power is illegitimate when it is solely a matter of coercion.

Most political systems rest on the exercise of both authority and coercion. In the United States, for instance, some force is used in support of authority, as when police give out tickets for speeding and judges sentence criminals to prison. Even governments that use much more force than our own usually also have at least *some* legitimacy, or consent from the governed. Power based exclusively on coercion tends to be unstable both because it is inefficient and because people submit to it out of fear rather than allegiance. Eventually such a regime is likely to encounter rebellion and be overthrown. Such was the case in Iran under the Shah, in the Philippines under Ferdinand Marcos, and in the former Soviet Union under communism. A continued reliance on force undermined the authority of these rulers, and their bases of power crumbled.

Sociologists use various criteria to determine when a government is legitimate. Some look for the absence of widespread, overt public opposition (Lipset, 1981). According to this view, as long as people are not openly rebelling, they must consider their regime at least moderately legitimate. This is a fairly loose yardstick for measuring legitimacy. People may be losing faith in their political system and not actively revolt against it. Sometimes they are too apathetic to do so, or too fearful of the consequences. Thus, the government of the Soviet Union seems to have lost legitimacy before any real rebellion broke out. That is why other sociologists use stricter criteria for measuring legitimacy (Habermas, 1989; C. Taylor, 1985). Some say that a political system is legitimate only if the people in it have the power to make changes they desire. Others go further, arguing that legitimacy requires power to be exercised in the people's best interest. When it is not, the system is illegitimate (Connolly, 1984).

Americans often assume that democracy is the only kind of political system that people willingly consider legitimate and voluntarily support. This, however, is not so. Dictatorships may also have a great deal of legitimacy in the eyes of those who live under them. In this case, relatively little force is needed to gain the people's compliance.

Max Weber identified three forms of legitimate power, or authority: traditional, charismatic and legal/rational. **Traditional authority** has historically been the most common form of authority. It stems from beliefs and practices passed down from generation to generation, and usually consists of inherited positions based on kinship and descent, like those of king, chief, or even father. People accept traditional authority because they have always done so. In some societies, traditional authority is considered sacred, and political leaders are part of the sacred order. Such views of a sacred order can provide certain limits to the free exercise of traditional authority.

Charismatic authority derives from the belief that leaders have exceptional personal qualities that deserve respect and devotion. There is no objective way to determine whether leaders actually have such gifts; by definition, charisma is in the eye of the beholder. Charismatic authority is unstable because it is closely tied to the individual personality of the leader; so successors are not easily found. Examples of charismatic leaders in recent history are Mahatma Gandhi, who led the nonviolent struggle for independence in India; Martin Luther King, Jr., and Malcolm X, black leaders in the United States; and Cesar Chavez, a spokesman for Mexican-American farm workers.

Legal/rational authority derives from a system of explicit laws that define legitimate uses of power. Power is vested in offices or positions, not in their temporary occupants. It is also limited to "official business"; it cannot be extended beyond the law without people's express consent. For example, the president of the United States can't order American couples to limit themselves to two children, because the president's legal/rational authority under the Constitution doesn't extend into this sphere. Legal/rational authority permits officeholders to exercise power

Three types of authority: traditional, charismatic, and legal/rational. Top left: *Swaziland's king, Mswati III, "The Lion," is a traditional leader from a family that has ruled this small kingdom for generations.* Bottom left: *Martin Luther King, Jr., held no public office, but his courage and vision made him a charismatic source of power and direction for the civil rights movement.* Above: *Margaret Thatcher, Britain's former prime minister, had legal/rational authority that was vested in her office by explicit rules and within specified limits.*

only within specified limits. They act within the context of a "rational" system defined by rules and regulations.

In any given instance of legitimate power, authority usually takes just one of these three foundations identified by Weber. Sometimes, however, several foundations are combined. John F. Kennedy, for example, had legal/rational authority because he was elected to the presidency; he had the traditional authority that surrounds this high political office; and to many Americans he had charismatic authority as well.

The Social Structure of Power

Power is not distributed equally or randomly among people; it has a hierarchical ***social structure***. By the very nature of power, some people have more than others, although some systems distribute power more equitably than others do. There are three basic sociological views on the structure of power in industrial capitalist societies like the modern United States. Marxists argue that the most important forms of power are controlled by the capitalist class. Power-elite theorists agree that a relatively small group wields far more than its share of power, but think there are routes to membership in this elite besides ownership of economic capital. Pluralists suggest that there are multiple bases for power which enable different groups to contend with and balance one another. Let's examine these three views in more detail.

The Marxist View

Karl Marx was one of the first to draw attention to the economic roots of power. He argued that those who own the means of production tend to control the rest of society through their domination of the economy. In an agricultural society, land is the most important means of production; so those who control land have the most power. In the Middle Ages in Europe, this meant that feudal lords were the ruling class. In order to exercise their power, however, they needed the help of other groups. They were supported by a military apparatus, which was centered on knights in armor. These knights gained a good deal of power themselves through their roles as protectors of the feudal lords. Equally important was the Catholic church, whose support gave feudal lords legitimacy and authority. In addition, priests and monks provided many services—including doing much of the writing for kings and lords, who were often illiterate. Indeed, the church came to control a good deal of property of its own, and thus was in a position to challenge the feudal lords on occasion.

With the rise of modern capitalist industry, Marxists argue, power passed gradually from feudal lords to the owners of businesses. Of course, this did not mean that every president or prime minister of a capitalist country was a businessman. On the contrary, most were trained in law, diplomacy, or other fields; many came from the old aristocracy. But, according to the Marxist analysis, they were able to exercise their official power only when they served the interests of capitalist elites. When American workers started to form unions, it was no accident that the government took the side of big business against the workers. The government served the interests of the dominant class. Because the bourgeoisie controls the means of production in a capitalist society, it directs not only economic activity but also the institutions that shape the moral and intellectual life of the country, including law, government, art, literature, science, and philosophy.

In analyzing American society's power structure, Marxists note the extent to which giant corporations dominate government and other power relations (E. O. Wright, 1986). When President George Bush traveled to Japan in 1992, for example, he took top auto executives with him, but no labor leaders. The secretary of labor is usually a businessman, while major labor leaders are excluded from government office. President Ronald Reagan's tax cuts benefited corporations and the rich more than the poor and the middle class.

Since power comes from control over the means of production, the Marxist view implies that nationalizing these means of production would greatly reduce the inequality of political power. If the government were to take over industry and run it in the interests of all workers, class power would be eliminated.

The Power-Elite View

Marx's overwhelming focus on economics as the source of power and his predictions about the coming of a classless society have been challenged by a number of sociologists. Two Italians, Vilfredo Pareto (1848–1923) and Gaetano Mosca (1858–1941), argued early on that inequalities of power are inherent in any social order. They considered a classless society to be an impossibility. In any society some lawyers are inevitably more clever than others, some royal mistresses more influential, some thieves more successful, and so forth. According to Pareto and Mosca, the main reason for inequality of power is that talent is unequally distributed. Other sociologists have emphasized structural reasons, which apply regardless of inequalities of talent.

Writing in the first decades of the twentieth century, the German economist and sociologist Robert Michels echoed this view. He claimed that in all organizations power tends to end up in the hands of a small group of leaders. As organizations grow larger and more complex, this tendency toward **oligarchy** (rule by a few) becomes stronger (Mayhew and Levinger, 1976; Michels, 1915/1949). Leaders chosen for their special talents in administration and public relations gradually take command. In time, these leaders develop a vested interest in maintaining their positions. The ruling clique becomes more conservative, seeks compromise with its enemies, avoids risk-taking, and erects barriers to challenges by opponents—all measures designed to protect its position and advance its fortunes. Michel's proposition that large-scale organization always leads to rule by a small minority has become known as the **iron law of oligarchy**.

The ideal of the early elite theorists was for a "circulation of elites"—an open possibility for all people of talent to rise to the top. The American sociologist C. Wright Mills (1959/1970), however, showed how elites became entrenched and closed. The **power elite** that he identified in the United States consists of a coalition of military leaders, government officials, and business executives that effectively runs American government and business. According to Mills, this small group makes most major policy decisions, especially those related to war and peace. While the power elite generally supports and is supported by the capitalist class, it is a smaller, more elite group than the whole capitalist class. Sometimes, to retain power, it works out compromises that are not immediately in the interests of capitalists—as when the U.S. government legalized labor unions and introduced much of the welfare system in the 1930s.

Several social scientists have collected evidence on the American power elite (Domhoff, 1978, 1983, 1993; Useem, 1984). They have found that about one-half of 1 percent of the U.S. population controls up to 25 percent of the country's wealth and holds a disproportionate number of high-level positions in government and business. Members of "the governing class" attend the same schools, belong to the same clubs and civic associations, and intermarry, producing a fairly tightly knit inner circle. This system is less structurally fixed than the Marxist view of a ruling class based solely on capitalist economic relations, but it is not open and democratic, either.

Mills argued that the different branches of the power elite are interlocking. Congress approves billions of dollars in military appropriations every year, dollars that end up in corporate pockets. Why does Congress make these appropriations? In part for national defense, in part because military contracts create jobs, and in part because business leaders are important campaign contributors. Thus, politicians tend to support big business, and business leaders often support politicians. All three sectors—economic, political, and military—have a vested interest in what Mills called "military capitalism."

The Pluralist View

While acknowledging that elites are more powerful than the unorganized masses, sociologists who take a pluralist view don't believe that a single ruling clique dominates America. Rather, **pluralists** argue that ***social power*** is dispersed among a variety of competing interest groups—the oil industry and the coal industry, car manufacturers and environmentalists, union and business associations, hunters' lobbies and wildlife foundations, the navy and the air force, General Motors and Ford. All these groups control resources and influence policy decisions with varying degrees of success, but no one group is in command. In most cases each can do little more than stop programs that threaten its interests (Dahl, 1961; Keller, 1963; Kornhauser, 1961; Riesman, 1951). Thus, society's problem may not be too little pluralism, but too much of it. With competing groups constantly erecting barriers to programs they do not like, major social and economic problems become impossible to solve (Thurow, 1985). Either decision making becomes deadlocked or legislation is filled with so many compromises that it is ineffectual.

Some observers think we don't need to choose between the pluralist and power-elite views, because *both* have validity. For instance, the sociologist Arnold Rose (1967) concludes that foreign affairs seem to be dominated by a small group of people who resemble Mills's power elite, but the growth of the federal government and the emergence of certain interest groups (such as civil rights organizations) have undercut the power of big business. In Rose's view, there are many power structures in America, not just one, and nationwide decisions are made through a process of bargaining (the pluralist view). However, the power structures themselves (political parties, government agencies, legislatures, businesses, and so on) tend to be dominated by oligarchies (the power-elite perspective). The power structure of American society, in short, consists of a complex plurality of elites.

Others who have studied how policy decisions are made in America tend to agree with Rose. For instance, when the sociologist J. Allen Whitt (1982) investigated the making of important decisions regarding mass transit in California, he found that power was exercised in a number of ways. Different interest groups (the highway lobby and central-city leaders, for example) were able to influence some legislators and government administrators (the pluralist view). But business leaders, who often cooperated closely with one another, were heavily involved in all the decisions (the power-elite view). Finally, the very need for mass transit was in part related to the capitalist quest for ever-increasing profits (the Marxist perspective). In short, an integration of all three approaches may broaden our understanding of how power is distributed in the United States.

THE STATE

A distinctive feature of modern societies is the existence of complex institutions and organizations that are specialized for exercising authority. These include courts, police departments, legislatures, regulatory agencies, executive offices (the presidency, governors), and the military. Taken together, these specialized political institutions and organizations form the **state**. The state has a monopoly

Great kings like France's Louis XIV, "the Sun King," were fawned over by their courtiers, venerated by their subjects, and given great power; but they did not have the capacity to affect the lives of ordinary people that modern states, with their more impersonal bureaucracies, have developed.

over the legitimate use of force within a given territory. People who try to use force outside the authority of the state are considered criminals, terrorists, or revolutionaries.

Note that the concept of the state is not the same as the concept of government. While the state is all the specialized organizations and institutions in which power over a given geographic region is concentrated, a government is a body of elected and nonelected officials who direct the state at any given time. Thus, people can be loyal to their state even while detesting a particular government.

The Rise of Modern States

Throughout most of human history, states as we know them did not exist. Tribes or other small groups formed the basic social units, and kinship was the foundation of the social order. Power was concentrated in people, usually elders or heads of families, not in a collection of organizations. Personal power and official power were one.

The state came into being largely through ever-greater distinctions between officials as private persons and officials in their public capacities. This gradual process began with the emergence of tribal chieftains, then kings. Eventually, the office of king came to be understood as something separate from the person who held it (Gluckman, 1965; Kantorowicz, 1957).

As the state grew and empowered more officials, it became increasingly accepted that authority should not be given on the basis of heredity, but on the basis of qualifications (Weber, 1922/1978). The result was a growing separation between public and private spheres. Today we consider it highly improper for officials to let personal relationships influence their actions. For instance, governors cannot appoint their relatives to state jobs or treat public funds as their own without risking criminal prosecution.

Between the sixteenth and nineteenth centuries the states of Europe grew in size and strength. Two major forces were behind this growth: the expansion and consolidation of political territories and the expansion of international trade. These in turn were linked to other historical trends: the uniting of principalities through inheritance and royal marriage; improvements in transportation; wars of conquest; and the colonization of the Americas, Africa, and Asia. Rulers now found it necessary to maintain control over large, often far-flung regions. To do so, they had to impose taxes, build roads, and assemble large armies. At the same time, merchants were demanding that their goods be protected from marauders and that the safety of their shipping be guaranteed. Rulers had to see that treaties were negotiated, roads and seas policed, and domestic peace ensured (P. Anderson, 1974; J. A. Hall, 1985; M. Mann, 1986).

In order to accomplish all these tasks, the rulers of European states developed new governmental institutions, which operated on two basic principles: (1) the strict separation of public duties from private lives and personal connections and (2) formal rules to govern official behavior. Officeholders were not to profit, for example, from privileged information obtained in their public roles. A new class of "public servants" came to staff what we now call *bureaucracies*. As you learned in Chapter 8, a bureaucracy is an organizational structure characterized by specialization and division of labor, a hierarchy of offices, explicit rules and regulations, impersonality in decision making, and rewards and promotions based on merit. Bureaucracies continue to be central to the operation of every modern state (Badie and Birnbaum, 1983).

In some countries—particularly communist ones—the state bureaucracy seems ever-present. This is because it controls industry and economic life, in addition to its political functions. In capitalist countries, state bureaucracies also play an economic role, but private bureaucracies, in the form of large corporations, dominate the economy (de Jassay, 1985; Lindblom, 1977). Bureaucracy has also spread throughout the less developed countries of the Third World (Thomas and Meyer, 1984). Although personal relationships continue to play a large role in distributing power in many Third World countries, the ideology of a state free from personal rule—one of the principles of a bureaucracy—is widespread. Even in countries in which changes of regime are common, each successive coup is likely to be justified in terms of the corruption of the previous rulers. What corruption means in this context is largely a failure to conform to the notion of a state in which the public and private realms are kept separate.

Nations and Nationalism

Related to the rise of the modern state and state bureaucracies is the emergence of nations and nationalism (Anderson, 1991; Gellner, 1983). **Nation** refers to the cultural bonds that give a sense of shared identity to a group of people who occupy or aspire to occupy the same geographic territory. When states started to develop, a number of languages and dialects were spoken in a single country, and customs often varied greatly from one region of the country to another. Gradually, as political boundaries were solidified, transportation improved, and government became more centralized, local differences began to decline. By the nineteenth century, all the citizens of a single state were expected to share a single ***culture***. Thus, Frenchmen now contrasted themselves with Englishmen or with Germans, rather than just with other Frenchmen in the next valley. Institutions like nationally organized schools promoted this unified view.

Not all Frenchmen (or all Englishmen, or all Germans) necessarily had a great deal in common. The ideal of nationhood is based on an imagined community among people who don't know one another directly (Anderson, 1991; Calhoun, 1991). It tends to obscure internal differences, especially in areas of the world where state boundaries were imposed from the outside rather than developed through a long historical process of unification. In Africa, for example, and in the Middle East (as we saw in Chapter 1), European invaders carved up colonial territories without regard for tribal boundaries (Wolf, 1982). This has been the source of much later conflict. In the same way, the collapse of communism in the Soviet Union and Eastern Europe revealed that communist states governed many very different peoples. Russians, Ukrainians, Georgians, and others claimed to be separate nations in the breakup of the USSR. In the former Yugoslavia, Slovenes, Croats, and Serbs all asserted claims to national identity—in some cases fighting bloody battles over the territory they claimed. Bosnia-Herzegovina, once a province in Yugoslavia, tried to become a multinational, multireligious republic; but it was attacked by Serbian nationalists.

Along with the modern concept of nationhood grew a parallel belief: that all people with a distinct culture should have their own autonomous state (Gellner, 1983). This belief became known as **nationalism** (Greenfeld, 1992; Williams, 1976). Nationalism has encouraged pressure for statehood among many dispossessed peoples, such as the Basques in Spain; the Kurds in Iraq, Iran, and Turkey; the Jews before Israel was created; and the Palestinians today. Nationalism has become a rationale for many acts of terrorism (Rubenstein, 1987), including the use of rape and murder as part of the "ethnic cleansing" by which some Serbs in the former Yugoslavia sought to drive Muslims out of their home towns to make way for Serbian occupation. Nationalism has also motivated wars as neighboring nations struggled over territory claimed by both. The rise of nationalism also marked a shift in citizens' relationship to their state. Their loyalty was no longer directed toward an emperor or king, but toward the nation-state (Breuilly, 1985; Morgenthau and Thompson, 1985). According to the ideology of nationalism, people are joined together by common descent or common culture, not merely a common ruler. This belief can be a support for democracy, but it has also been a basis for fascism like that of Nazi Germany. Nationalism (as we saw in our discussion of the Persian Gulf war in Chapter 1) is one of the most powerful—and unstable—political forces in the world today (Calhoun, 1991).

The Modern Welfare State

In the United States and in other relatively rich, industrialized, democratic countries—Canada, New Zealand, Australia, most of the countries of Western Europe—the role of the state has expanded dramatically since the early nineteenth century. At first the state limited itself to such tasks as expanding transportation and communication systems; but then it became involved with education, health care, housing, social security, and working conditions. A state that takes responsibility for the welfare of its people in such areas is called a **welfare state**. Particularly in the last fifty years, the trend toward the welfare state has involved not only social-democratic countries such as Austria and Sweden (countries that combine elements of socialism and capitalism under political democracy) but also more completely capitalist countries such as the United States. The trend, in fact, is a major sociological and political phenomenon of our times (Flora and Heidenheimer, 1981; Przeworski, 1985; Skocpol, 1985). Even when, as in Sweden in 1991, a taxpayers' revolt has brought advocates of smaller government to office, they have generally not reversed the basic principle of the welfare state, just tried to cut its costs.

In the United States, the development of a welfare state began with President Franklin Roosevelt's New Deal. This set of wide-ranging government programs was launched in the 1930s to deal with the economic problems and personal hardships of the Great Depression. Other countries began expanding the roles of their state governments at about the same time. The most influential theorist supporting an expanded role for government was the English economist John Maynard Keynes (Schott, 1983). As we discussed in Chapter 16, Keynesian theory encouraged enormous growth in government social programs for the poor and unemployed, in the peacetime military (including defense research), and in the government work force, all of which meant a tremendous increase in the size of the state bureaucracy.

The modern welfare state provides many **collective goods and services**, things that individuals can't readily buy because they're too expensive and can't be easily divided into "shares." Examples are national defense, clean air and water, public transportation, and the services provided by regulatory government agencies such as the Food and Drug Administration and the Civil Rights Commission. In addition, the modern welfare state is deeply involved in managing the economy. Through its monetary and fiscal policies it attempts to dampen the cyclical swings in unemployment and inflation that occur under capitalism. Some sociologists argue that these roles of government evolved to counteract problems inherent in capitalism (O'Connor, 1973; Offe, 1984, 1985). For instance, a capitalist system necessarily creates hardships for those who lose out in economic competition. These hardships may prompt disadvantaged people to question the system's legitimacy. To reassure them and to maintain the existing power structure, the government spends money on welfare programs. If these programs become too costly, however, middle-class taxpayers may resist them. Thus, a delicate balance is required in the effort to keep the welfare state functioning.

In recent years criticisms of big government have become widespread. Ronald Reagan was elected president twice on a platform that included a promise to reduce the size of the federal government's regulatory and social programs. One response by Congress was the Family Support Act of 1988, which was intended to reduce the scope of the welfare state by encouraging welfare recipients to acquire job skills and become self-supporting. It now appears that this reduction will not amount to much. The Congressional Budget Office has estimated that over its first five years the law reduced welfare caseloads by only a little over 1 percent.

The welfare system remains the focus of debate over the size and scope of the welfare state. As we discussed in Chapter 9, some observers suggest eliminating many welfare payments entirely because they encourage dependency and take away financial need as an incentive for people to try to help themselves (Gilder, 1981). Others contend that this view unfairly blames poverty on its victims. They say that American society must continue to help people who are placed at an economic disadvantage by the workings of our free-market system. But we must do so, they argue, with economic assistance programs that are short-term, cost-effective, and geared toward giving the poor a real chance to succeed in our economy.

DEMOCRACY

The idea of democracy, or government by the people, is very old, dating back to ancient Greece. The word itself comes from the Greek: *demos*, meaning "the people," and *kratos*, meaning "authority." In a **democratic state**, authority is rooted in the consent of the people. This doesn't mean that the people are always directly involved in political choices. Most democratic countries are **representative democracies**, in which the people elect public officials to represent their wishes and interests. Representative democracies impose clear, legally established limits to what elected officials can do. All participants in the system must obey the rules regarding such principles as open elections, one person/one vote, and acceptance of majority decisions while respecting a minority's right to dissent. A democracy does not claim exclusive, unquestioning loyalty from its people. In fact, if those in power overstep their authority, the people have a right—even a duty—to vote them out of office.

The opposite of democracy is **totalitarianism**, in which the government attempts to control every aspect of the lives and even the thoughts of its citizens. No opposing view is tolerated in a totalitarian system. Cultural institutions from schools to art are used to reinforce the official ideology. Power is concentrated in the hands of one ruling party that is permanently identified with the state. The power of political leaders is so great that it may be exercised in capricious and arbitrary ways, creating insecurity, even fear, among the people.

Although we're accustomed to thinking of states as either democratic or totalitarian, in reality there are no perfect democracies and no successful complete totalitarianisms. For instance, for much of American history, blacks and women were denied the right to vote, meaning that our political system was not purely democratic. Even today, some citizens (the very rich, the heads of huge corporations and other influential organizations) have a much stronger voice in the political system than others. By the same token, most totalitarian regimes do not completely disregard the rights and wishes of the people. For instance, the Chinese totalitarian state holds elections, and citizens are given many chances to participate in local affairs—as long as they stick to the party line. Most totalitarian rulers realize that "there are certain bounds to their power beyond which they cannot expect compliance" (Moore, 1978, p. 18). Leaders who consistently overstep those bounds—who seek to increase their personal wealth and power at the expense of society—are usually challenged and eventually overthrown.

The Foundations of Democracy

Through most of human history, elites considered mass democracy to be little more than "mob rule"—and for good reason. Society lacked the foundations needed for democratic rule to be stable and orderly. One of the most important of these is universal education. Literacy is needed to help people become informed about public issues. In modern, complex societies, citizens are asked to decide on a wide range of issues involving technology, economics, health care, and other specialized fields of knowledge. If they are not to be ruled by self-proclaimed experts, they need education to understand those social issues.

Democracy also requires that citizens be able to exchange ideas with one another, not just one-to-one but in a public discourse (Habermas, 1989); so they must have freedom from censorship and from reprisals for expressing unpopular views. Citizens also need places for open discussion, whether at town meetings in a rural school's basketball gymnasium or in the formal auditoriums of state capitals, or just over coffee at a café. When the Solidarity movement was trying to bring democracy to communist Poland in the 1980s, Catholic churches were often the only places where public meetings were safe from disruption by government forces. In addition, the free exchange of ideas requires a communication system through which people throughout a country can both learn about current issues and make their own opinions and experiences known. Because the Soviet Union's communist government wanted to stifle free public discourse, it banned citizens from owning copy machines and even limited the availability of telephones. It encouraged only those communications technologies (like TV and newspapers) that the government could control and use to speak to the people without enabling them to communicate with one another.

Still another important foundation for democracy is a society that treats most, if not all, citizens as approximately equal. If the gulf between a wealthy elite and a mass of poor people is too wide, they may have too few interests in common for democracy to succeed. The existence of a large middle class is a ***structural*** support for democracy. In contrast to those who are very poor and discontented, middle-class people are more likely to have a vested interest in their political system. They are also likely to feel free to express their views, even when they oppose elites. The fact that high productivity in the wealthier capitalist countries tends to create a strong middle class is one reason capitalism is often linked with democracy (Berger, 1987; Schumpeter, 1942). In poorer capitalist countries, with smaller middle classes, democracy is less likely.

Cultural factors can also promote democracy. Capitalism, for example, may provide a foundation for democracy through its emphasis on individual economic choice, which can serve as a model of individual freedom in the political realm. Beyond this, democracy requires a shared sense of basic values. In the United States, some of the most important of these are enshrined in the Bill of Rights, the first ten amendments to the U.S. Constitution (Dworkin, 1977, 1986). They include the freedom to associate with whomever one chooses, freedom of speech and the press, and freedom from unreasonable search and seizure. If people don't value such personal freedom and if government doesn't respect them, then the culture is not conducive to democracy.

Finally, democracy depends on the people's willingness to get involved in their political system—to inform themselves about political issues, to work for candidates of their choice, to volunteer their help in solving social problems, and to cast their votes in elections. Alexis de Tocqueville, a Frenchman who closely observed American society a century and a half ago, praised Americans for these very qualities. However, Americans' willingness to participate in the political process may be on the wane. As we discuss in more detail below, relatively few Americans even vote regularly. They may be eager to express their views on phone-in radio shows, but most seem apathetic when it comes to organized politics. Thus, if the United States has a government "by the people," it is only by *some* of the people, a fact that tends to undermine the cohesiveness of the American political system (Teixeira, 1988).

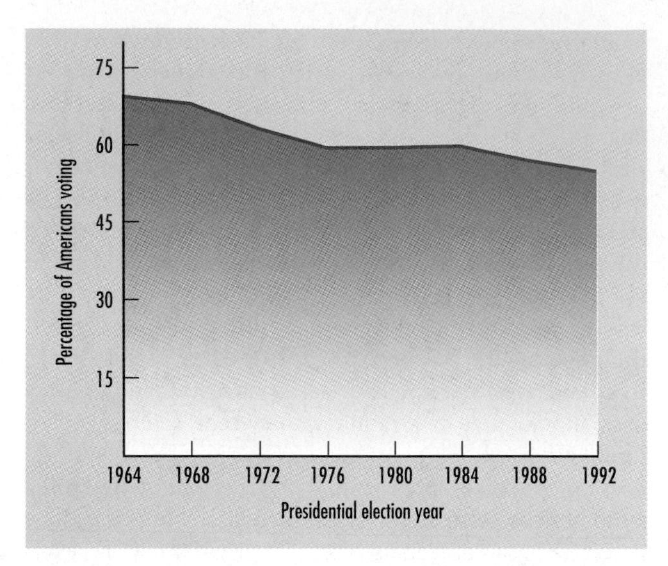

FIGURE 17.1 / Percentage of Americans Voting in Presidential Elections, 1964–1992

Source: U.S. Bureau of the Census, *Current Population Reports.*

Participation in American Democracy

In addition to voting, two other traditional means of political involvement in the United States are participation in political parties and participation in interest groups. In this section we look at trends in these three areas.

Voter Turnout

American representative democracy is based on mass participation through periodic elections. Ideally, the principle of one person/one vote offsets inequalities of social class, sex, and race in the United States. But because many Americans fail to vote, the validity of this assumption is questionable. Whereas in Western Europe 80 to 90 percent of voters regularly turn out for national elections, only 55 percent of Americans eligible to vote did so in the 1992 presidential election (see Figure 17.1). Even fewer Americans bother to cast their ballots in congressional elections—less than half in every year since 1974.

Perhaps the central explanation of this low voter turnout is that many Americans feel their votes don't matter; they believe that things will go on in much the same way whether or not they vote (see Figure 17.2). Surveys indicate that many Americans ignore political issues because they find them confusing or incomprehensible (Neuman, 1986). In addition, elections themselves can make people apathetic toward politics. With the media, special-interest groups, and politicians setting the political agenda, people tend to think that politics is something that "other people take care of" (Hirschman, 1982; Kettering Foundation, 1991). There are also institutional barriers to full participation in U.S. elections (Piven and Cloward, 1979). For example, restrictions on voter registration (such as a registration deadline months before election day) can help to keep people away from the polls. Finally, people seem to vote their resentments and fears; when there is little to ignite these emotions, they are less likely to vote (Adelman, 1980).

The factors that encourage low voter turnout tend to affect some Americans more than others. Figure 17.3 shows that those least likely to exercise their right to vote are the young, the less educated, the unemployed, and the poor. People in these groups may fail to vote because they lack education about citizenship, because they are less well integrated into American society generally, because politicians do not represent their interests, or because they are the least likely to belong to organizations (such as unions or chambers of commerce) that take a political stand or help their members clarify their values or the issues. Hispanic-Americans are significantly less likely to vote than are blacks or whites, possibly because language is a barrier. Many nonvoters are more mobile than voters, moving in search of opportunities for education or employment. To the extent that these groups have different political preferences than voting Americans do, their

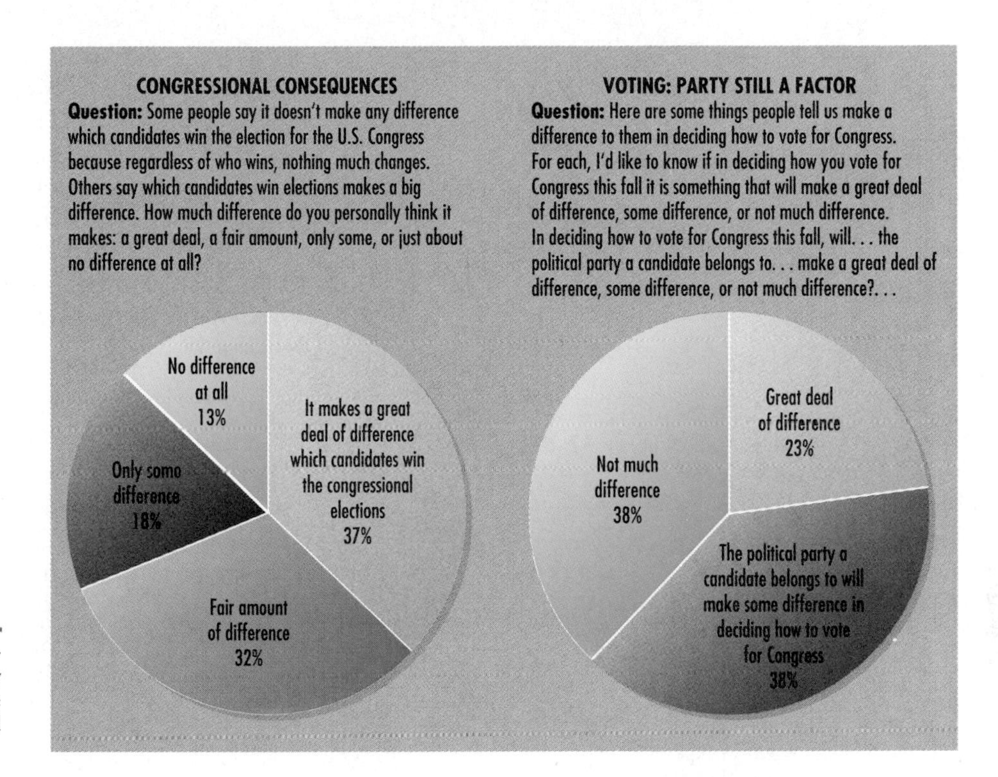

FIGURE 17.2 / Americans' Beliefs about the Significance of Congressional Elections

Source: Sample of 1,602 voters in *Public Opinion* 5, no. 6 (December–January 1983): 21. Copyright © 1982 by the New York Times Company. Reprinted by permission.

views are not being adequately represented at the ballot box. The Making Choices box on pages 442–443 raises sociological questions about the decision to get involved in politics—including that most basic involvement, voting.

Political Parties

The kinds of choices an electoral system offers are closely related to the nature of its political parties. A **political party** is an organization designed for gaining and holding legitimate political power.

Parties perform several crucial functions in large, complex political systems. They link citizens with their government, transmitting public opinion to policymakers and mobilizing grass-roots support for policy decisions. They also serve as a link between different branches and levels of government (executive and legislative, federal and state) and between governmental and nongovernmental power structures. In addition, parties play a dominant role in recruiting candidates for elective office (Dowse and Hughes, 1972).

Ideally, parties fulfill two other functions as well. First, parties lead people to work out the connections between different issues, to make compromises with each other, and to develop an overall program or platform on which to base policy. This function of parties is undermined by the growing number of single-issue voters who ignore overall party platforms and concentrate on one area, like gun control or abortion. The use of direct-mail campaigns and computer targeting of voters is a means to promote single-issue voting, usually at the expense of parties (Calhoun, 1988). Second, in principle, parties represent the range of public opinions, interests, and values. This function is challenged both by the dominant roles of established politicians in the Democratic and Republican parties and by the fact that to succeed, they must appeal to an extremely broad cross section of the American people, rather than representing the strong views of different groups.

Americans are accustomed to thinking in terms of two major political parties, while some countries have five or more and others have only one. The reason for these national differences lies largely in the structure of a country's electoral system. In the United States, officials are elected by a *simple-plurality system*: The candidate who gets the most votes wins, and everyone else loses. This system discourages smaller third parties, because their candidates have no chance of winning. A vote for a third party seems like a wasted vote. In *proportional-vote systems*, such as Italy's, a party receives the same proportion of representatives as the proportion of votes it gets in the election. If a

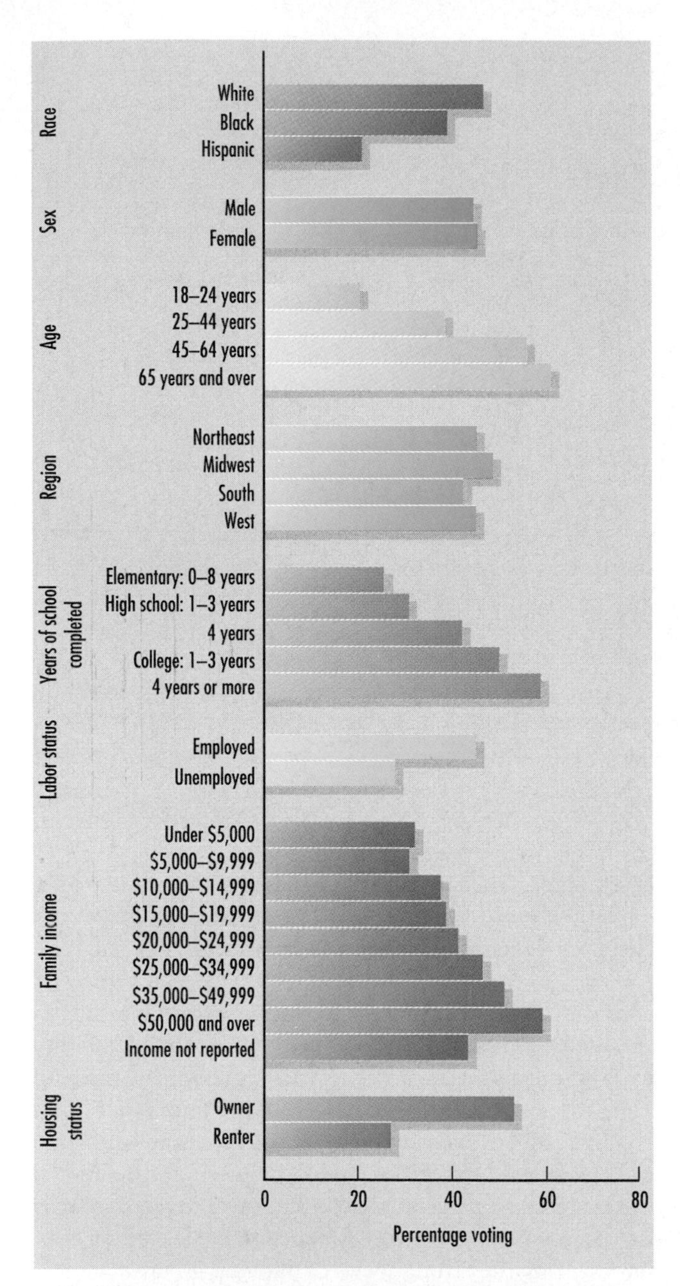

FIGURE 17.3 / Percentage of Americans Voting, by Structure of Population, Election of 1990

Source: U.S. Bureau of the Census, *Voting and Registration in the Election of 1990*. Doc. P-20, no. 453, October 1991.

minority party receives only 10 percent of the votes, it still gets 10 percent of the seats in the legislature. In this kind of electoral system, a vote for a minority party is *not* wasted, and a multiparty system is encouraged.

The simple-plurality system thus has the dysfunctional effect of discouraging clear representation of divergent views and interests. This affects not only the number of parties in the United States but also their character. Because they must appeal to the lowest common denominator to win state and national elections, American parties must either appeal to some basic emotion, such as fear, or take bland positions that will offend no one. This system discourages debate among holders of different positions on a range of issues.

SOCIAL BACKGROUND AND PARTY PREFERENCE The two major American political parties appeal to different kinds of voters. Studies show that there are indeed correlations between voting patterns and ***social-structural*** factors such as class, race, age, and education.

Among people with a yearly income under $15,000, only 30 percent are Republicans, compared to 57 percent of people with an annual income over $50,000 (*New York Times*, January 21, 1990, p. A-15). Similarly, in terms of occupation, professionals and managers exhibit stronger support for the Republican party than do lower-status workers (*Public Opinion*, October/November 1985). Yet at every income level and in virtually every occupation, there are both Republicans *and* Democrats, as well as many who consider themselves independents (roughly a third of all voters). This is a far cry from strict class-based voting.

Race is a social characteristic that tends to be closely linked to party preference. Blacks remain overwhelmingly Democratic, even as they move up the economic ladder (*Statistical Abstract*, 1992, p. 270). Religion is only slightly correlated with party preference today, although in the past it was strongly influential, with Catholics and Jews much more likely than Protestants to vote Democratic. The relationship between age and party choice has changed over time. During the 1960s and 1970s, younger voters tended to be Democratic. In the 1980s, young people became more conservative and more likely to vote Republican. At the same time, the aging baby-boom generation did not shed all its leftist, liberal views; its members are still more likely to vote Democratic than Republican, but they are also particularly likely to describe themselves as independents—not committed to either major party. (With the election of Democrats Bill Clinton and Al Gore in 1992, the baby-boom generation took over the national administration for the first time.)

One of the most-discussed differences between supporters of Democrats and Republicans is the "gender gap"—a reference to the fact that women are much more likely than men to be Democrats. This gap is a recent phenomenon that emerged in the 1980s when many men moved to the right and began to vote Republican. Men are more likely to respond favorably to "tough" foreign-policy and military positions; women are more likely to favor less militaristic candidates who are concerned with domestic welfare issues. So far, however, this difference has not translated into great success for female candidates in either party. Women remain dramatically underrepresented in Congress and other levels of government.

The effect of education level on party preference is less straightforward. Voters with less education—including manual workers, for example—are more likely to vote Democratic. People with college educations are more likely to vote Republican. But people with elite college educations are more likely to vote Democratic. To some extent this really reflects class: The Democrats have traditionally been the party of working Americans, while the Republicans have been more business-oriented. At the same time, liberalism, which is associated with the Democratic party, has been more common among more educated people. However, this correlation often depends on the kind of school attended. In a study of voting in the 1984 presidential election, Republican incumbent Ronald Reagan won by a landslide at religious colleges and military schools, and also did quite well at many less elite, large state universities. Yet at elite private colleges, like Amherst and Oberlin, at the most elite and traditionally liberal state universities (for example, Michigan, Wisconsin), and at predominantly black schools, Democratic candidate Walter Mondale was the overwhelming favorite (*Congressional Quarterly*, 1985).

THE INFLUENCE OF PARTIES Since the 1960s, parties seem to have become weaker and less important in American politics (Gibson, 1985). This can be seen in the fact that fewer American voters are identifying with either of the two major political parties (Salmore and Salmore, 1985). Growing numbers now label themselves independents. This trend has encouraged elections to be less party-oriented and more candidate-centered (Price, 1986; Salmore and Salmore, 1985). At the same time, there has been much less party cohesiveness in Congress. On a variety of political issues, numerous members of Congress have increasingly departed from the official position of their party. In addition, the president's control over legislators who belong to his own party can no longer be taken for granted. As a result, the role of the party in shaping public policy has eroded.

Technological advances in communications have contributed to this decline of American political parties. With more voters calling themselves independents, candidates are increasingly inclined to run more personalized campaigns, aided by computerized direct-mail advertising. The mass media, particularly television, have taken over some of the campaign functions traditionally performed by parties. One of these is informing voters about candidates

Televised political debates—like this one among 1992 presidential candidates Bill Clinton, George Bush, and Ross Perot—allow politicians to present themselves to voters and to explain their views on issues. The use of television and other mass media for political advertising, however, raises the costs of campaigns and sometimes leads candidates to rely more on misleading, brief commercials than on the presentation of well-developed rational arguments.

torious troops). Neither did the battles generally destroy the productive capacity of the countries in which they were fought, as modern bombing does.

The three Punic wars between Rome and Carthage (264–146 B.C.) came perhaps the closest of all ancient wars to total war between modern superpowers. At the height of the conflict, nearly a third of Rome's male citizens were serving in the army, a figure seldom matched in modern wars, and 10 percent of Rome's adult men were killed (Hopkins, 1978). When Rome finally defeated Carthage, the city was completely demolished; salt was ground into the earth so that the very soil could not support life. Carthaginian captives were sold into slavery, and no one lived on the site of the city for 100 years. Thus, even though the technology of this era was primitive, it was possible to achieve a devastation not much different (except perhaps for the numbers of civilian casualties) from that which a nuclear bomb would have caused (Dyer, 1985). What kept such total destruction from being common was not so much level of technology as social organization: If the goal of warfare was to extend an empire or demand payment of tribute, it made no sense to destroy the enemy's country.

Over 21 centuries ago, Rome left defeated Carthage in ruins, thus ending the large-scale, 100-year-long Punic wars. The utter destruction of Carthage was on a scale that today can be compared to the effect of a bomb dropped on the city.

Hand-to-hand confrontations between large groups of mainly mercenary soldiers continued to be the basic pattern of warfare until the late Middle Ages. After that, warfare began to change. The crucial reason was the rise of modern states, with their centralized power structures, tighter control over their territories, and growing national integration (discussed earlier in this chapter). Wars increasingly involved civilians, and a larger percentage of citizens participated as people came to understand wars as being waged between peoples or nations, not just rulers. Defeat could mean destruction not only of their state but also of their distinctive way of life.

These broad political changes paved the way for a new kind of social organization in armed forces. Armies were gradually transformed from mere collections of hired men into bodies of citizen soldiers. The first great example of this was the mass mobilization of the French in 1793, which turned some 770,000 Frenchmen into soldiers in a matter of months (Dyer, 1985). Because citizen soldiers were motivated not just by money but also by a desire to defend their state, they did not need to be as tightly controlled as mercenaries did. As a result, they could be deployed in new ways. For instance, small groups of citizen soldiers could carry out raids on larger armies that occupied their lands, using their superior knowledge of the terrain, as well as the support of friendly civilians. This pattern of fighting, known as *guerrilla warfare*, is characteristic of many wars today (*guerrilla* in Spanish means "little war"). Guerrilla warfare works best against a foreign invader, when repeated raids make it increasingly costly for the foreign army to remain. (This was essentially the problem U.S. forces faced in Vietnam.)

Modern warfare, thus, has always had two faces. On one side were the ongoing struggles of guerrilla movements, often aiming at national liberation. On the other side were "conventional wars," the large-scale conflicts between massive citizen armies, culminating in the slaughter and destruction of World Wars I and II. Because the division of the world into nation-states was accompanied by political-cultural alliances and an increasingly global integration of economies, wars spread much more widely.

The Industrial Revolution further transformed warfare. One aspect was the development of new weapon technologies. Starting with improvements to the rifle at the end of the eighteenth century, and continuing with the development of machine guns, missiles, and bombs, military technology has become more lethal and the distance between killer and killed much greater. In addition, with the development of improved methods of transportation, deployment of troops and supplies has become easier. Armies no longer have to live off the land they fight in. They can now bring their own provisions with them, even to remote regions in inhospitable weather.

Although technology has made war "easier" and more "efficient," it has also made it more expensive. Modern armies depend on costly weapons and great quantities of materials, which are rapidly used up in battle. The high cost of modern warfare makes any major war partly a matter of domestic production. It is no coincidence that both world wars were won by the side with superior industrial capacity (McNeill, 1982). The victors outproduced the losers and ultimately outlasted the losers' resources. When two sides are badly mismatched in their productive capacities, the superior side may simply overwhelm the enemy, as the United States did in the Persian Gulf war against Iraq.

War has the unanticipated consequence of advancing technology, sometimes with benign implications. The computer technology that was developed for nuclear capability may be used to organize vast social development. This is an underground air force command post in Colorado.

Some Problems of Waging Modern War

To prepare for modern warfare and the huge quantities of weapons it requires, societies must have enormous stockpiles of armaments. In capitalist countries, these stockpiles are produced by private business. Dwight Eisenhower, who commanded the Allied forces in Europe during World War II (and later became president), was well aware of the role that private industry plays in winning wars. But Eisenhower worried that suppliers of military goods would earn unfair profits at taxpayers' expense. He was also concerned that corporations would join forces with Defense Department officials to push for ever-more expensive weapons, regardless of whether they were needed or even whether they worked. Eisenhower's fears about what he called the military-industrial complex were not groundless. In recent years, taxpayers have begun to object to the staggeringly high prices paid to military contractors for everything from $500 hammers to the $300 million B-1 bomber.

The modern military also faces serious work-force problems, both at the top and at the bottom. At the top, each of the branches of the U.S. military has developed a huge bureaucracy, advancement in which depends on the individual's organizational and political skills. As a result, officers with the greatest potential for leadership in combat may not rise to the top. At the bottom of the military hierarchy, at the level of the average recruit, many soldiers lack the intellectual skills needed to cope with today's complex weaponry. As one military consultant has asked:

> What happens when you have an antitank missile which, if it strikes an enemy tank, has a 100 percent probability of disabling or destroying that tank, but in which the system for aiming and firing the missile is really only capable of being used by someone with an IQ of over 100—whereas most of the people in forward combat units in your army have an IQ of about 85 or 90, and the smart ones have a lot of other jobs to do? (Quoted in Dyer, 1985, p. 193)

Some people consider such problems minor, noting that in the war with Iraq the U.S. military performed well (though since the war, there have been more indications of technical problems). Others contend that the Iraqi war did not put U.S. forces to an adequate test, because Iraq was a much less formidable opponent than originally thought. Much of its equipment was outmoded, its tactics were often inept, and its troops lacked strong motivation

War is hell, but it is also an escape from the routine of life. Popular culture has always reinforced the idea that war is glorious because it offers men the opportunity to show their capacity for heroism and valor. The Hollywood popularization of the air ace of World War I did not stress the reality that most of these early combat pilots died horrible, if dramatic, deaths.

to continue fighting. In other circumstances, the American military might not fare as well.

Views about the capabilities of American military forces are closely tied to views about the soundness of American society (McNeill, 1982). A modern army needs literate (even computer-literate) soldiers and dependable, state-of-the-art equipment. The military relies on the larger society to fulfill these important needs. Military effectiveness is therefore very much a matter of ***functional integration***. Not only must the military be well-integrated internally; it must be well-supported by a society's industrial capacity, public opinion, transport systems, and other resources. If the civilian parts of a society cannot deliver the needed resources, the armed forces are less likely to do their job well.

The Threat of Nuclear War

Ever since atomic bombs were dropped on the Japanese cities of Hiroshima and Nagasaki to end World War II, the nature of war has changed. Indeed, the word *war*, which brings to mind armies, generals, columns of tanks, and so forth, seems inappropriate to describe what would happen in a nuclear catastrophe. Although some military theorists claim that the destruction caused by nuclear weapons could be limited to "surgical strikes" on specific targets, others believe that a limited nuclear war is an impossibility (S. Zuckerman, 1983). In a war between two nuclear powers, a nuclear strike would inevitably provoke nuclear retaliation, which could cause the conflict to escalate and end in mutual annihilation (Schell, 1982). In the process, much of the rest of the world would also be destroyed.

The massive stockpiles of nuclear weapons in the hands of the United States and the former USSR are products of the cold war policy known as *deterrence*. The theory was that each side would restrain the other from a nuclear attack by its power to inflict "unacceptable losses" in retaliation. Proponents of deterrence argued that if the two sides had equal nuclear strength, neither would dare to start a war. The problem was that each side inevitably tried to gain an advantage by producing even more nuclear weapons with even greater destructive capacities. This upset the balance of power and prompted the other side to respond by expanding its nuclear arsenal. The result was a nuclear arms race that grew to irrational proportions:

> By 1962 the buildup of the American nuclear forces and, correspondingly, those of the Soviet Union, had already gone well beyond the rational requirements of any mutual deterrent threat. Not only did the buildup never stop, it . . . surpassed any reasonable level. . . . (S. Zuckerman, 1983, pp. 47–48)

In the 1970s and 1980s, while the arms race continued, the United States and the Soviet Union tried to negotiate arms control treaties. The two superpowers signed a number of agreements, but verification—allowing the other country's observers to monitor compliance with the treaties—was always a sticking point. Nevertheless, in 1988 each country destroyed some missiles by agreement, a ma-

The hopeful flags of United Nations members contrast with the wreckage of Berlin toward the end of World War II. Those who speak of world peace, of a time when nation-states will be superseded by world government and a global sense of community, are often accused of naiveté and innocence. Innocence *comes from the Latin* in, *not, and* nocere, *to harm. Perhaps such innocence is called for in a world where everyone lives in the awareness that humans both possess and have used the capacity to kill each other as faceless and near numberless masses in the name of war.*

jor milestone. Today, with the downfall of communism in Eastern Europe and the political reorganization of the former Soviet republics, the concept of mutual deterrence is rapidly becoming a thing of the past. Much larger reductions in nuclear stockpiles could begin. However, the damage is not yet past, because many of the old Soviet Union's nuclear weapons are now in the hands of insecure nationalist groups with little experience of international relations and a tendency to armed combat.

The threat of war today is not between communism and capitalism—the possibility that the U.S. military has prepared for ever since World War II. Rather, conflicts are most likely between rival nationalist groups in the former communist countries or among Third World countries. Some of these might result in a threat of nuclear terrorism against the United States and other rich countries. This is made possible by the spread of nuclear weapons. One of the issues in the Persian Gulf war, as we saw in Chapter 1, was the U.S. fear that Iraq was on the verge of achieving nuclear weapons. Thus, a major goal of American foreign policy in the 1990s is to halt nuclear proliferation among smaller potential adversaries around the world.

Thinking Back on the Key Concepts

This chapter has been mainly about ***power*** and the conflicts that result from power struggles. Power struggles are matters of ***social action***, from voting, to running for office, to engaging in terrorism and warfare. The working of a democratic political system depends on certain ***cultural*** conditions, such as education and communication among citizens and a willingness to accept defeat peacefully.

Power, as we saw, has a ***social structure*** of its own. As Marxists, power-elite theorists, and pluralists have observed in different ways, power may be distributed more equally or more unequally, depending on whether the society uses inheritance, elections, wealth, or some other factor as the basis for distribution. The most basic social structure of power in modern societies is the state.

Finally, a society's political arrangements need to remain ***functionally integrated*** with other social institutions. The ways in which communist political power undermined the economy of the former Soviet Union, for example, were among the reasons for its collapse.

SUMMARY

1. Politics is the process by which people gain, use, and lose power. One type of power is the ability to exert control over others even when they resist. Another is the increased collective capacity to get things done through social organization.

2. Legitimacy is the extent to which power is recognized as valid and justified, not just by those who wield it but also by those who are subject to it. Legitimate power is known as authority. Weber distinguished three types of authority: traditional authority deriving from beliefs and practices passed down from generation to generation, charismatic authority deriving from exceptional personal qualities, and legal/rational authority deriving from law. In contrast to authority, illegitimate power is exercised without social approval and tends to involve force. Most political systems rest on the exercise of both authority and force.

3. There are different views of how power is distributed in societies. Marxists believe that in capitalist societies power is lodged in the hands of the owners of the means of production, who dominate and manipulate the workers in pursuit of their own class interests. Marxists also contend that this power distribution is inherently unstable because it generates class conflict that can lead to revolution. Power-elite theorists agree that power is monopolized by a relative few, but they maintain that this pattern is inevitable and unlikely to change. In contrast, pluralists see power as more broadly dispersed. They believe that the distribution of power is constantly shifting, as groups compete with one another for influence and as alliances are formed and broken.

4. The state is the sum of the institutions that specialize in wielding power and authority. These include the courts, police, legislatures, executive offices, the military, regulatory agencies, and other official bodies. Throughout most of history, states did not exist. States arose as rulers sought to expand their territories and commercial interests. The modern state is based upon a distinct separation of private and public lives. It also involves bureaucracy, a formal, rule-governed hierarchical organization of public servants.

5. The idea of nationhood and nationality arose as states and bureaucracies took shape. The advent of easy transportation and the centralization of government led to increased communication among previously isolated localities and a sense of common identity and culture. The parallel rise of nationalism toward the end of the 1700s meant that citizens had begun to identify with their state. In our day, stateless peoples who want to establish their own states are sometimes motivated by nationalism to commit terrorist acts.

6. A welfare state is a state that has considerably expanded its social and governmental programs to take more responsibility for the welfare of its citizens. It provides goods and services that are not easily purchased by individuals, such as assistance to the poor, collective goods like national defense, and regulatory activities. The modern welfare state also manages the economy.

7. In a democratic state, authority derives from the consent of the people. This doesn't mean that the people are always *directly* involved in political choices. More likely they elect public officials to represent their wishes and interests (called representative democracy). The opposite of democracy is totalitarianism, in which government attempts to totally control the lives and thoughts of its citizens. No opposing view is tolerated in a totalitarian system.

8. Mass participation in the political process is an important right to citizens in a democratic state. But only around 55 percent of the American electorate votes (less in nonpresidential election years). Political parties—collective groups designed for gaining and holding legitimate government power—may be declining in importance in the United States, as politics becomes less party-oriented and more candidate-centered.

9. U.S. public officials are elected through a simple-plurality system in which the candidate with the most votes wins. This system reinforces the American two-party structure. In some other Western nations, a proportional-vote system prevails: A party receives the same proportion of representatives as votes. Such a system tends to encourage many parties, since a vote for a minority party isn't a wasted vote. In any political system, various social factors—such as race, gender, income, and education—influence the preference of voters for a particular party and candidate.

10. Interest groups and political action committees seem to be gaining influence, especially as campaigns grow more expensive, and technology allows candidates to reach voters and supporters directly, without a party's help.

11. Modern warfare began with the development of settled agricultural societies and fortified states. Early wars were fought by large armies of foot soldiers, often mercenaries, and rarely involved civilians. With the rise of national states, citizen armies developed. These armies identified with their state and were willing to fight for their national way of life. Modern warfare depends increasingly on technology and productive capacity. As a result, the military-industrial complex has grown quite large and powerful. The military today finds itself challenged to find literate, educated recruits who are well-equipped to handle the demands of modern weapons.

REVIEW QUESTIONS

1. Define *politics*, *legitimacy*, and *authority*, and give an example of each.

2. What are the three sociological views on the structure of power in industrial capitalist societies?

3. What is the difference between a nation and a state?

4. Summarize the research on voter turnout and party preference presented in the chapter.

5. How is waging war today different from waging war fifty or 150 years ago?

CRITICAL THINKING QUESTIONS

1. When people feel that the government is not functioning very well, they often put the blame on "politics." How is this use of the term different from the sociological use?

2. How much traditional authority, charismatic authority, and legal/rational authority does the current president of the United States have?

3. "Democracy is clearly the best way to run a government." Do you agree or disagree with this statement? Explain your answer.

4. Develop a program of policies to help increase the voter turnout in elections.

5. Present an argument for increasing the number of political parties in the United States.

6. "World War III is inevitable." Is this a statement of fact or of opinion? Explain your answer.

GLOSSARY

Authority Power viewed as legitimate and exercised with the social approval of most individuals in a group or society.

Bureaucracy Formal, rule-governed hierarchical organization of public servants.

Charismatic authority A type of authority identified by Weber that derives from public recognition of exceptional personal qualities.

Collective goods Goods including services not easily bought and sold by individuals and so provided to citizens by the modern welfare state.

Democratic state A state based on rule by the people or their elected representatives.

Interest groups Organizations created to influence political decisions that directly concern their members.

Iron law of oligarchy According to Robert Michels, the chain of events that leads to the concentration of power in the hands of a few.

Legal/rational authority A type of authority identified by Weber that derives from explicit laws defining the legitimate uses of power. It is vested in positions, not in individuals.

Legitimacy The extent to which power is recognized as valid and justified by people in a social relationship and by society at large.

Nation A group united by shared cultural bonds who usually share a state.

Nationalism The belief that a people with a distinct culture (that is, a nation) should have their own state. Pride in one's nation is linked with this belief.

Oligarchy Rule by a few.

Pluralism The view that a political power structure is composed of a variety of competing elites and interest groups.

Political action committees (PACs) Organizations designed to further an interest group's political goals partly through financial support of candidates for political office.

Political party An organization designed for gaining and holding legitimate political power.

Politics The social process by which people gain, use, and lose power.

Power Either (a) the ability to control people's behavior or experience even when they resist or (b) the capacity to accomplish some end.

Power elite A coalition of military leaders, government officials, and business executives united by common interests and social background. In C. Wright Mills's view, such a coalition rules America.

Propaganda A communication technique that presents an issue in such a way as to build support for one side and against the other side.

Representative democracy A democratic system in which the people aren't *directly* involved in making political choices, but rather elect public officials to represent their wishes and interests.

State An abstract entity composed of the political institutions and other organizations that are specialized for exercising authority within a given territory (may include welfare administration, public schools, and the like).

Totalitarianism A political system in which no opposing opinion or party is tolerated and in which the government controls many aspects of citizens' lives.

Traditional authority A type of authority identified by Weber that stems from traditional beliefs and practices passed down from generation to generation.

War The use of military means to resolve a dispute between societies or between factions within a society.

Welfare state A state that takes responsibility for the welfare of its people in such areas as education, health care, housing, social security, and working conditions.

CHAPTER PROJECTS

1. Individual Project Choose a nation and research its history. Write a two-page report detailing the steps that the nation went through to consolidate its power as a state.

2. Cooperative Learning Project Work in groups of four to locate advertisements in magazines and newspapers. Classify each advertisement as an example of glittering generalities, testimonials, plain-folks technique, name-calling, scapegoating, or transfer. Note that an advertisement may include more than one propaganda technique. Also, examine the advertisements carefully to determine what parts of them are factual and what parts are mere opinions.

PART 5

Global Challenges

CHAPTER 18

The Third World

"The rich get richer and the poor get poorer." Ordinarily we apply this bit of folk wisdom to individuals and families (the usual focus of research in social stratification; see Chapter 9). However, the concepts of rich and poor also apply to different communities within a country and to entire countries. Thus in New York City, midtown Manhattan is richer than the South Bronx; the state of California is richer than Arkansas; and the United States is far richer than, say, Mali or Sudan. This does not mean that there are no poor people in Manhattan, California, or the United States as a whole, or that there are no prosperous or even wealthy individuals in Mali and Sudan. But the average wealth of individuals is less in poor places, and less wealth is available for such public purposes as building schools, hospitals, and roads. Moreover, the wealth and power of European, North American, and other industrialized nations (especially Japan) have grown enormously in recent times ("the rich get richer"), while the poor, non-Western countries of the Third World have developed slowly if at all. Many have suffered one economic, environmental, or political crisis after another, undercutting any progress they manage to make ("the poor get poorer").

Mali and Manhattan illustrate how uneven levels of development are in the world today. The glass and steel canyons of midtown Manhattan are monuments to the rapid growth of corporate America, especially since World War II. The shops lining Fifth Avenue offer the best of everything, from toys at F. A. O. Schwarz to diamonds at Tiffany's. Apartments in midtown Manhattan sell for $1 million or more; hotel rooms rent for $300 a night and up; lunch for two at one of the better restaurants might run $150. Tourists flock to Manhattan to visit its museums and theaters and to gaze at its shop windows. Despite its problems—crime, homelessness, overcrowding—Manhattan is one of the world's centers of wealth: the Big Apple.

The nation of Mali, in West Africa, is a study in contrast. With a gross national product of only $270 per person, it is one of the poorest countries in the world (World Bank, 1991). The average secretary in midtown Manhattan earns more in a year than the average Malian earns in a lifetime. Life expectancy in Mali is forty-eight years; one in two children dies before the age of five years. There is only one physician for every 25,000 people (compared with one per 470 in the United States). Since 1970, Mali has been hit by two major droughts and widespread famine. The average daily calorie intake is 2,181 (compared with 3,666 in the United States). More than 80 percent of adults are illiterate, and less than 20 percent of children are enrolled in school. The few young people who complete secondary school are unlikely to find jobs at home and are forced to migrate to the Ivory Coast or France, either seasonally or permanently, where they usually work in menial jobs.

Mali's current poverty contrasts with its rich history as the cradle of West African civilization (Imperato, 1989). In 1200 B.C., Mali was the cultural and technological equal of Rome. Three great empires—Ghana, Mali, and Songhay—with ministers, bureaucrats, scribes, and court musicians, thrived within its traditional borders. Strategically located on the trade routes from North Africa across the Sahara to the Guinea Coast, all three were trade or "market empires" (Crowder, in P. Harrison, 1984). Their wealth derived primarily from the exchange of gold, ivory, and slaves from the south for horses, salt, beads, and cloth from the north. The kings of Ghana lived in a separate royal city, where they entertained traders from all over North Africa; the Keita dynasty of Mali ruled for more than four centuries. In the fifteenth century their fabled city of Timbuktoo was a center of Islamic scholarship as well as trans-African commerce. Being wealthy and powerful at one stage of world history, however, is no guarantee of future wealth and power. With the rest of West Africa, Mali suffered its first loss of wealth and power when Europeans invaded and greatly expanded the slave trade that Arabs and indigenous peoples had started. It became poorer and weaker when colonial powers split the region into smaller states. Cut off from the sea and many valuable resources along the coast, Mali was left a large but landlocked and resource-poor country. There is little in Mali today to attract foreign investors. Its colonial history all but guaranteed its current poverty.

Why should Americans care about Mali in particular, and the Third World in general? The central problem facing Mali today—**underdevelopment**, or the lack of modern economic growth—is a global problem. The Third World, in which three-quarters of humanity lives, consists of most countries outside of Europe and North America. The effects of its underdevelopment are felt everywhere, even in the richest countries. Especially since the breakup of the Soviet bloc and the end of the cold war, the Third World's struggle for survival and social justice is perhaps the greatest story of our time. Narrowing the gap between the rich and poor countries is a moral and economic issue not just for hungry citizens and impoverished nations but for well-fed citizens of affluent nations as well, because our world has become increasingly interdependent. Americans depend on workers in South Korea to make cars, computers, stereos, and other products that we use every day. We buy copper from Zambia, oil from the Arabian peninsula, and coffee from Central America. We depend on Third World countries not just for material goods but also for cooperation in the quest for a clean environment and for world peace. In short, Americans should be concerned about Mali because the problems of the Third World are our problems.

We begin this chapter by looking at the distinguishing characteristics of the nations of the Third World, especially the lingering heritage of colonialism, the rural foundations of these countries, and the recent explosion in their urban populations. Next we consider three leading sociological explanations of the gap between developed and underdeveloped nations: modernization theory, which stresses ***culture*** and ***functional integration***; dependency theory, which emphasizes ***power*** relations; and world systems theory, which stresses global ***social structure***. Then we look ahead, focusing on the Republic of Korea as one of the success stories in the Third World, an indication that ***social action*** can bring development.

CHARACTERISTICS OF THE THIRD WORLD

The concept of the Third World originated in Europe (Merriam, 1988; Worsley, 1984). The term is rooted in the old French notion of society being divided into three classes: the nobility, the clergy, and the common people, known as the first, second, and third estates. The notion was revived in the 1950s to describe the emergence of militant anticolonial movements, which would become new countries and would combine as a new force in global politics. Bound neither to Western capitalism nor to Soviet communism, these new nations sought a "third way."

As used today, the term ***Third World*** implies that the nations of the world are divided into three groups. The ***First World*** consists of the rich, industrialized nations of North America, Europe, and Japan, whose economies are based on private property, wage labor, and competition. The ***Second World*** refers to those countries that pulled out of the capitalist world system (at least for a time) and whose economies were based on collective or state ownership of the means of production and on centrally planned production and distribution of goods—especially the Soviet Union and the countries of Eastern Europe (rather than China or North Korea, which, though communist, are more commonly counted as part of the Third World). Once a solid bloc, the Second World began to unravel in the late 1980s. How these countries' economies will fare, and how they will fit into the world system a decade from now, is difficult to predict. Despite changes in East–West relations, the Third World is still very much with us.

The **Third World** is made up of the relatively poor, nonindustrial nations of Latin America, Africa, and Asia (including China), most of which were either colonies or clients of First World countries until they gained political independence, in many cases shortly after World War II. Although courted by both the United States and the USSR during the cold war years, most were not permanently aligned with either side. Other ways of looking at global inequalities have been proposed, such as North versus South (most rich countries lie in the Northern Hemisphere and most poor countries in the Southern Hemisphere). But the concept of the Third World is widely accepted by political leaders and scholars alike.*

The nations that see themselves and are seen by others as belonging to the Third World are not a homogeneous group in terms of politics, economics, history, culture, or other common criterion. Many are one-party states or dictatorships, but some are democracies, and some are constitutional monarchies. Thailand's royal family, the Chakri, is as old as the Windsors of Great Britain. Most Third World nations are poor, but some have amassed great wealth—notably the oil-producing Arab nations. Some, such as Taiwan and Korea, have industrialized rapidly in recent decades and produce high-tech goods that rival those manufactured in the First World. Nevertheless, they have certain characteristics in common: a colonial heritage, an economy rooted in agriculture, and rapidly growing cities.

The Legacy of Colonialism

One common theme in the Third World is consciousness of a history of domination by Western powers and the legacy of that domination, underdevelopment (Worsley, 1984). History is full of examples of large powers invading, conquering, and annexing smaller ones. Western imperialism, which began in the late fifteenth century and continued into this century, was unique in at least three respects (P. Harrison, 1984; Magdoff, 1982).

First, whereas earlier empires, in both the West and the East, were the result of political ambitions and the desire

*A few would add a "Fourth World" to this scheme to describe indigenous peoples, such as the Lapps of Scandinavia and the Yanomamo of the Amazon rain forest, who are victims of a kind of internal colonization by the ethnic majorities in their respective countries.

King Njoya, ruler of the Kingdom of Bamum in the western part of Cameroon, ascended to the throne around 1895 as the sixteenth ruler of the kingdom, shortly after the future of Cameroon was decided at the Berlin conference as colonial Europe and America carved Africa into colonial parcels. The ideology that justified colonialism defined Europeans as inherently superior to the countries they came to control. The reality of colonialism is that many of the countries that fell into the colonial system were complex and sophisticated states which had existed for several centuries.

for power, Western imperialism usually was driven by the profit motive and the individual pursuit of wealth. For example, the *conquistadores* were not members of royal armies, sent out to acquire the Americas for Spain and Portugal. Rather, they were entrepreneurs who signed contracts with their kings and queens, used their own or their friends' wealth to buy and equip ships, hired mercenaries, and expected a share of the booty as a return on their investment. The first British and Dutch outposts in Asia and Africa were trading posts, not forts, and were the result of private enterprise, not government initiative. Only when merchants were threatened by "uncooperative" local leaders, by pirates, or by rival trading companies did the state reluctantly step in. For the most part, "the flag followed trade, rather than vice versa" (Harrison, 1984, p. 43). In some places (notably China and Japan) outright conquest never occurred; rather, Europeans used threats of invasion or brief demonstrations of military prowess to make favorable trade agreements. The exception to this pattern was Africa, which was not subjugated until the 1800s. By then so many European nations had entered the race for territory that political considerations took priority.

Second, earlier empires built on existing social and economic structures. The conquerors may have carried off slaves and treasure, but they usually left local modes of production intact, content to skim a tribute off the top. At first, European conquerors followed the traditional route of plunder, for example, carting off the gold and silver artifacts of the decimated Inca and Aztec empires. But the rise of capitalism and spread of industrialization in Europe created new demands: Factories needed raw materials, and growing urban populations needed food. To meet these demands, Europeans began to restructure the traditional economies of their colonies. Large tracts of land were bought or simply seized for plantations, and egalitarian systems of communal landholding were replaced with private property. New, commercial crops (sugar, coffee, cotton, rubber) were introduced. Slaves were abducted from Africa and "coolie" laborers imported from Asia. In addition, colonial settler societies were established in North America, Australia, and New Zealand. As the volume of their machine-made goods increased, Europeans needed new and bigger markets. Again they turned to the colonies. In some places they intentionally destroyed local industry to create demand for their own manufactured goods, as in India, where the existing textile industry was virtually destroyed to open markets for British cloth. In settler colonies such as the United States, local peoples were either moved onto reservations or killed off to make room for an expanding population of European farmers. Traditional rulers and systems of authority were also destroyed, replaced by Western governors and administrators, who sometimes worked with local collaborators and puppets, established Western laws and courts, and used the

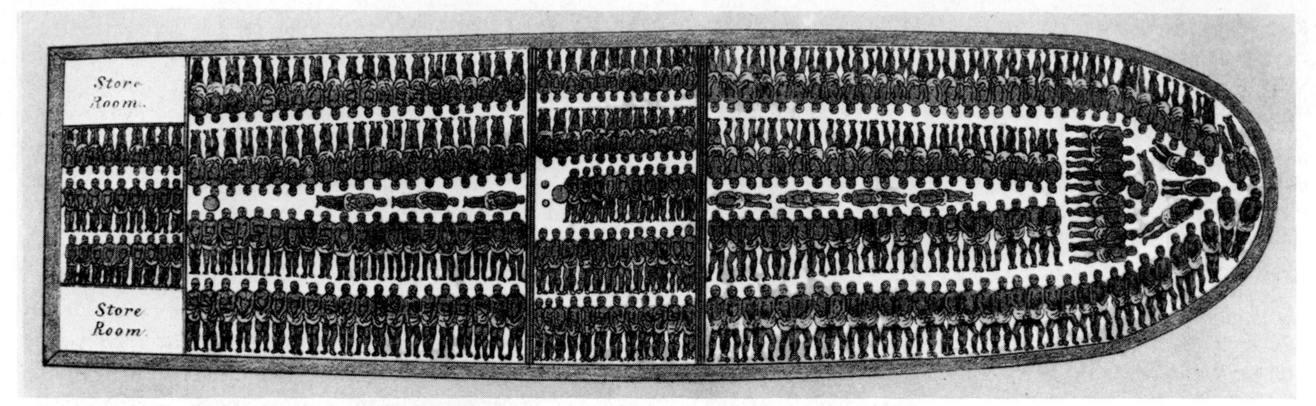

Slaves from Africa were first imported into Central and South America as a labor force after the native populations were killed, fled, or died from the diseases introduced by European conquerors. This diagram of an efficient way to load a slave ship shows the "rationality" of a system in which humans are, in fact, dehumanized.

police and armies to enforce them. By 1914, European colonial powers directly or indirectly controlled almost 85 percent of the earth (Magdoff, 1982).

A third unique aspect of Western colonialism was cultural imperialism (Harrison, 1984). Earlier conquerors usually settled into their new territories, intermarried with local peoples, and adopted many of their customs. European colonials were different. Some were more racist than others, but virtually all were culturally arrogant. They viewed their religion, their language, their manners and morals, as innately superior to those of non-Europeans, and made little or no effort to assimilate. Through missionary and later government schools, small native elites were indoctrinated with the ways of Western culture. Others were indoctrinated by exclusion—that is, by countless daily experiences designed to make them ashamed of their own race and culture. The only route to upward social mobility in European colonies was through acceptance and imitation of white ways. To be Western in appearance and attitude meant to be modern, a goal toward which much of the world aspired (including the elites of countries that had not been colonized, such as Japan).

After World War I, European powers began to loosen their grip. Ownership of colonies was reshuffled and boundaries redrawn to suit the needs of the victors. The Communist Revolution in Russia illustrated an alternative to the capitalist/colonial system, inspiring nationalist leaders in the colonies as well as labor leaders and intellectuals in Europe and the United States. Further, the United States and Japan began to rival Great Britain and Europe as naval, industrial, and quasi-colonial powers. Japan invaded Manchuria and in 1937 began a campaign to conquer all of China. Although the United States never officially owned colonies, it established dominance over the "protectorates" of Guam, Puerto Rico, the Panama Canal Zone, and Alaska and Hawaii. It also began to use military intervention and economic infiltration to establish dominance in Latin America and to a lesser degree the oil producing Arab world. After World War II, the United States emerged as the undisputed economic leader of the First World. The Soviet Union consolidated its hegemony over Eastern Europe, establishing a political bloc and a largely self-contained trade network—a Second World. After its own Communist Revolution in 1949, China chose an independent route, closing its borders, rejecting economic aid even from the Soviet Union (after the middle 1950s), and relying on its own resources. One former European colony after another fought for and won independence, beginning with India in 1947. And so the Third World came into being.

Political independence did not automatically mean economic independence, however. U.S. policy toward nationalist movements and newly independent countries depended in large part on whether they sought to remain in the world capitalist system. (Likewise, Soviet policy depended on whether the emerging nations wanted to join that country's sphere of influence.) Aid to developing nations was usually geared toward making the world safe—and profitable—for multinational corporations. Advertising and marketing, reinforced by Western-style entertainment, paved the way for Western goods, from jeans and Coca-Cola to tractors and tanks.

In short, Western colonialism created a global economy that was almost impossible for new nations to avoid. The

Karl Marx wrote that after the establishment of the English colonial system, "the plains of India were littered with the bleached bones of native cotton manufacturers." Marx understood that cotton could be mass produced and shipped more cheaply in England than in India. Eighty years later, Mahatma Gandhi led a movement of national liberation based on the economic revitalization of India through the combined efforts of millions of individuals at spinning wheels.

once self-sufficient societies of what we now call the Third World were transformed into appendages of European imperial powers, into suppliers of raw materials and agricultural products and consumers of manufactured goods. A global division of labor was established that, with some modifications, persists today. Not only have the rich countries gotten richer, but many of the poor countries have gotten poorer (see Table 18.1 on page 462).

If independence failed to bring wealth to Third World countries, neither did it bring political stability. Few of them are nations as we defined that term in Chapter 17: one people with a common history and culture. This is particularly evident in Africa. The boundaries of today's African nations were drawn by colonial powers with little regard for the distribution of people and resources. Some countries are torn by civil war because traditional enemies were thrown together into a single nation. In colonizing Sudan, for example, the British not only joined two geographically and culturally dissimilar peoples but also widened the gap between them by encouraging Christian missionaries in the south to oppose the spread of Islam from the north. Other African countries are perpetually at odds with their neighbors either because they must compete for scarce resources or because artificial borders divided a single tribe or cultural group into two. Some countries are landlocked, like Mali, because colonial authorities wanted to separate the interior from the coast. With many different factions vying for power, plus shortages of the expertise and capital needed to run modern economies, African governments tend to be weak. The allure of urban, semi-Western lifestyles further undermines the vestiges of traditional social organization and authority.

As a result of their colonial experience, Third World nations—and peoples—have more in common with one another than with the nations of either the First or Second World. "More than merely a socioeconomic designation, [the term *Third World*] connotes a psychological condition, a state of mind encompassing the hopes and aspirations of three-fourths of humanity" (Merriam, 1988, p. 20). Third World status is thus a matter of ***culture*** as well as of the ***power*** of rich countries, the ***social structure*** of unequal wealth distribution, and the ***functional integration*** of the global economy. The problems of underdevelopment have proved hard to tackle by short-term ***social action***; they call

TABLE 18.1

Levels of Development and Structural Characteristics: Basic Indicators (Selected Countries)

	Population (Millions) Mid-1990	Area (Thousands of Square Kilometers)	GNP PER CAPITA: Dollars 1990	GNP PER CAPITA: Average Annual Growth Rate (Percent) 1965–1990	Life Expectancy at Birth (Years) 1990	ADULT ILLITERACY (PERCENT): Female 1990	ADULT ILLITERACY (PERCENT): Total 1990
Low-income countries	**3,058.3**	**37,780**	**350**	**2.9**	**62**	**52**	**40**
Mali	8.5	1,240	270	1.7	48	76	68
Kenya	24.2	580	370	1.9	59	42	31
Sri Lanka	17.0	66	470	2.9	71	17	12
Middle-income countries	**1,087.5**	**41,139**	**2,220**	**2.2**	**66**	**27**	**22**
Bolivia	7.2	1,099	630	−0.7	60	29	23
Peru	21.7	1,285	1,160	−0.2	63	21	15
Iran	55.8	1,648	2,490	0.1	63	57	46
Mexico	86.2	1,958	2,490	2.8	70	15	13
South Korea	42.8	99	5,400	7.1	71	*	*
High-income countries	**816.4**	**31,790**	**19,590**	**2.4**	**77**	**5**	**4**
Singapore	3.0	1	11,160	6.5	74	N.A.	N.A.
United States	250.0	9,373	21,790	1.7	76	*	*
Norway	4.2	324	23,120	3.4	77	*	*

According to UNESCO, illiteracy is less than 5 percent.

Source: World Bank, World Development Report 1992 (Oxford University Press, Oxford, 1992), pp. 218–219.

for enduring efforts at social action continued over decades.

Agriculture: The Base

A second distinguishing feature of the Third World is its overwhelming dependence on agriculture (see Figure 18.1). Even though Americans are sentimental about their country's agricultural past, fewer than 2 percent of Americans today are farmers. By contrast, in most of the Third World farming is by far the most common occupation. Even so, agricultural development in the Third World tends to be stagnant, accounting for only a small proportion of economic growth—if any (Morgan, 1988). Poverty is concentrated in rural areas (Bandyopadhyaya, 1988). Often people in the countryside lack not only adequate food, clothing, and shelter but also such basic necessities as a pure water supply, sanitation, health care, education, and public transport (see Table 18.2 on page 464).

The farmers of the Third World fall into two main groups, peasants and landless laborers. A knowledge of the situation of these two groups is critical for understanding why poverty and underdevelopment are so widespread in these countries.

Peasants

Peasants are small farmers who, working with family labor and simple technology, grow crops and raise livestock primarily for their own consumption (Shanin, 1990). Economically, socially, and culturally, peasants are tied to the land. They may or may not own the ground they till. In some cases the land is held by the tribe or community and parceled out to families according to need; in others it belongs to a landlord, who is owed a certain percentage of the produce as rent; in still others it belongs to the state. The family household is the center of peasant life, providing for most of its members' needs. The peasant family is

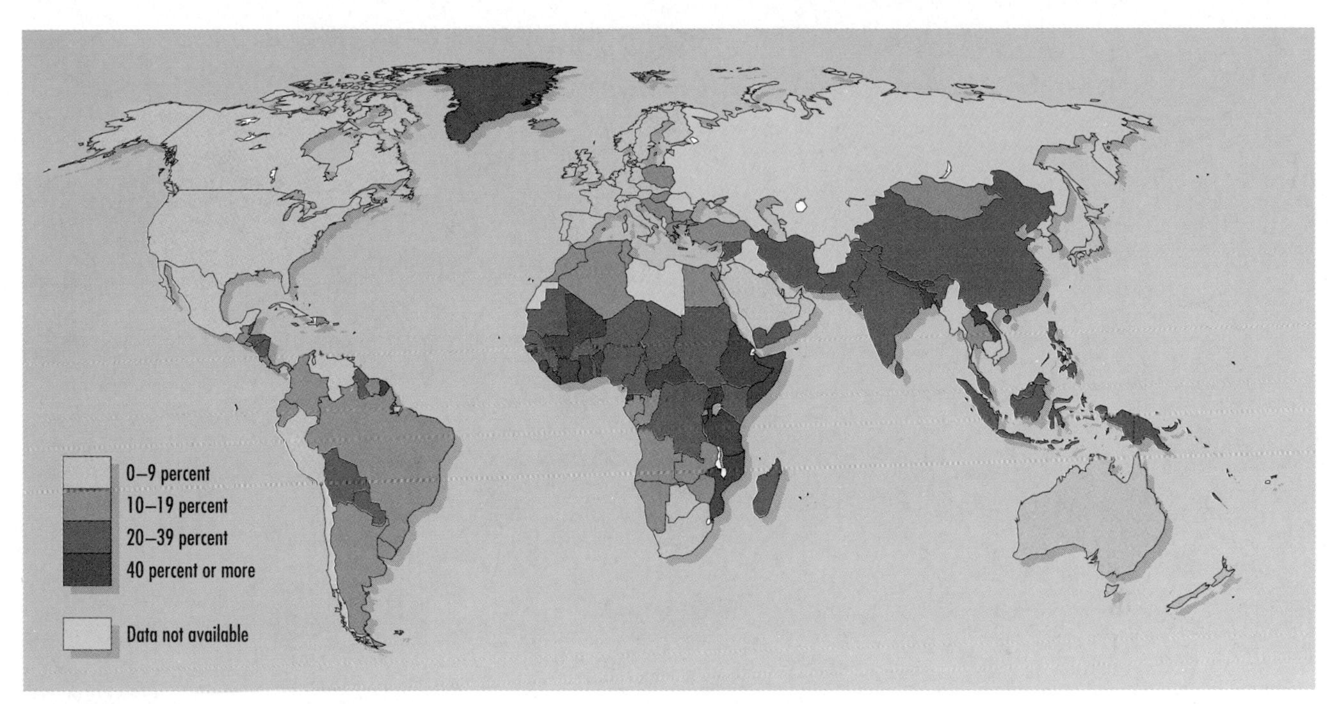

FIGURE 18.1 / Agriculture's Contribution to Individual Countries' Gross Domestic Product

Source: World Bank, *World Development Report 1992*, pp. 222–223.

also embedded in a community that tends to be highly traditional and conformist. The individual's status in the community depends on his or her family's position.

In many ways, today's Third World peasants resemble the traditional family farmers of the United States. Two main differences are that peasants usually reside in a village rather than isolated houses and that they own or control tiny plots of land rather than larger spreads. Indeed, many American farm families are descended from European peasants—German, Swedish, Irish—who immigrated to America in search of more land. Peasants become modern farmers when they begin to commercialize, producing crops and livestock for the marketplace first and home consumption second, and when they specialize, for example, by raising dairy cattle or growing oranges to sell and buying whatever else they need with their earnings.

Peasants are not necessarily poor. Given enough land and labor, plus good weather, they may produce a substantial surplus to sell or trade. But most Third World peasants live close to the edge. As an English visitor to prerevolutionary China put it, "There are districts in which the position of the rural population is that of a man standing permanently up to the neck in water, so that even a ripple is sufficient to drown him" (Tawney, in Scott, 1976, p. 1). This description still applies in much of the Third World and helps to explain some important aspects of peasant culture. Most peasants remember times when food was so scarce that the young and the weak died, while others were reduced to eating their last livestock, seeds for next year's crop, or food they ordinarily fed to animals. Many are living under such conditions today. Constant uncertainty encourages what James Scott (1976) called a "subsistence ethic." On the one hand, peasants feel that everyone in the community is entitled to a minimal living, so rich peasants are expected to give to poor ones, communal land and communal work act to redistribute risks and rewards, and favors must be reciprocated. On the other hand, peasants tend to be suspicious of outsiders and of innovations, clinging to methods and practices that have worked in the past. This can be the source of resistance to the changes that might bring economic development—like new farm techniques or population control.

Author Paul Harrison (1984) describes the household of sixty-year-old Moumouni Ouedraogo, in a northern corner of the African nation of Burkina Faso (formerly Upper Volta), illustrating some of the problems of Third World peasants. First, they often have too little land, water, fertilizer, and other resources to produce even a minimal liv-

TABLE 18.2

Rural and Urban Poverty in the Third World (Selected Countries)

Region and Country	Rural Population as Percentage of Total	Rural Poor as Percentage of Total	Infant Mortality (per Thousand Live Births)		Access to Safe Water (Percentage of Population)	
			Rural	Urban	Rural	Urban
Sub-Saharan Africa						
Côte d'Ivoire	57	86	121	70	10	30
Ghana	65	80	87	67	39	93
Kenya	80	96	59	57	21	61
Asia						
India	77	79	105	57	50	76
Indonesia	73	91	74	57	36	43
Malaysia	62	80	—	—	76	96
Philippines	60	67	55	42	54	49
Thailand	70	80	43	28	66	56
Latin America						
Guatemala	59	66	85	65	26	89
Mexico	31	37	79	29	51	79
Panama	50	59	28	22	63	100
Peru	44	52	101	54	17	73
Venezuela	15	20	—	—	80	80

Source: World Bank, *World Development Report 1990: Poverty,* p. 31, table 2.2.

ing. When Moumouni was a child, his father's compound included twelve people; today it has thirty-four members, not counting five young men working in the Ivory Coast. Other families in the village have also expanded. The village chief allots land to each family according to its needs. But while the village population has grown, its traditional lands—hemmed in by other villages on every side—have not. So bigger families must get by with less land.

Second, peasants often farm by relatively primitive techniques. Moumouni's people traditionally practiced slash-and-burn agriculture, a method well suited to thin tropical soils. The farmer clears a patch of brush, allows it to dry, then sets it on fire. The ash fertilizes the soil; the tree stumps, which are left in place, help to prevent soil erosion; and crops are planted around them, using hoes and digging sticks. After two or three years, the soil is exhausted and the farmer clears another plot. The old garden is allowed to return to forest, a process that takes about fifteen years, after which it can be farmed again. This system works well for a sparse population with abundant land, but not for a growing population with limited land, as in Burkina Faso and much of Africa. Why don't Moumouni and his neighbors use plows, fertilizers, and other more modern techniques? Even in fat years, Moumouni does not sell extra grain, but rather stores it for the inevitable lean years. So he does not have cash for extra supplies. Moreover, there is some doubt that European-style plows and mixed agriculture (using cattle for plowing, manure, and meat and using grain to feed cattle) would work in the thinner soils and the hotter, drier climate.

A third problem is ecological damage. Moumouni lives in the Sahel, the dry region that stretches across a dozen countries just south of the Sahara. Throughout this region overcultivation and overdrilling for water have taken their toll. Around Moumouni's village there is no ground cover—not even weeds—to soften the impact of the rain, which washes away precious topsoil, leaving hard, infertile red clay to bake in the sun. The possibility of revitalizing this moonscape seems remote. Burkina Faso is one of the places where the Sahara is slowly moving southward, forcing people and animals to migrate south and start the cycle of environmental degradation and desertification over

Peasants are small farmers whose livelihood depends on what they can grow by themselves. Consequently, they put in long days of backbreaking labor. Yet peasant farms are usually tiny and often face competition from large landholders, so the chances of getting ahead are generally slight.

again (see Chapter 19). Yet Moumouni is better off than some, particularly many landless laborers.

Landless Laborers

Paul Harrison (1984) visited a tea plantation in Sri Lanka in 1975. From the air the plantation looked lush and green; on the ground, however, conditions were grim. Hundreds of Tamil tea workers lived in rows of single-room barracks built by the British in the nineteenth century. Thirty-seven-year-old Puryana Supaya's home was a windowless ten-foot-square cell in a row of twenty identical dwellings. This dank room served as kitchen, bedroom, and living room for Supaya, his wife, and their three children. Their only possessions two cooking pots, the Supayas slept on sacks spread on the cement floor. Puryana earned about sixty cents a day hoeing, weeding, and pruning (when there was work); his wife made about forty-five cents a day picking tea leaves. The government provided free education and health care and subsidized food prices. Even so, they could afford little but food.

The Supayas are part of an army of **landless laborers**—peasants who have lost the rights to land, children of landless peasants, or, in much of Latin America, Indians who formerly lived by hunting and gathering. For the most part they work as hired hands on plantations and other large farms. Because they do not own or have rights to land of their own, they always lack autonomy. This is the ***social-structural*** constant in their situation around the world. But their living conditions are variable. In some cases the landowner provides decent housing, living wages, health care, schools for children, and the like, but in others laborers are subjected to near-slave conditions. In some cases they are steadily employed, but in others they are only seasonally employed or work as day laborers. Many come to the United States from Latin America and the Caribbean as migrant workers. Contrary to stereotypes, most are legal "guest workers," under contract to middlemen who supply large farms with cheap labor as needed. (Guest workers in the United States are not legally entitled to the minimum wage paid Americans.) Likewise, France employs landless laborers from Morocco and Algeria; Germany employs Turks; oil-producing Arab states hire Egyptians, Palestinians, and others; and Great Britain depends on workers from all over the Commonwealth (especially India, the West Indies, Pakistan, and Bangladesh). Often living conditions are deplorable, pay is low, and the availability of work is uncertain. But there are always workers. Estimates in 1980 put the number of migrants worldwide at 20 million (Harrison, 1984). If anything, the numbers have increased since then. The steady flow of landless laborers from the Third to the First World and to the cities and privileged sectors of Third World economies is testimony to the degree and scope of rural poverty.

Leaving the land is rarely voluntary. "It means going into exile, leaving your home village, leaving the supportive network of the extended family, leaving the complex culture of status and ceremony in which you hoped to one day play your part. It is a last resort, when all else has failed" (Harrison, 1984, p. 140). People may be forced off the land for a number of reasons, including population growth; inheritance systems, which may favor older sons or divide the land into plots too small to provide a living; wars, which create refugees who are forced to accept whatever work they can get; and pestilences and droughts, which may bankrupt peasants and allow rich landowners to move in and buy (or take) their land, and then possibly hire them.

Landlessness is often an outgrowth of colonialism and the ***power*** of Westerners who conquered indigenous people in what is now the Third World. In Latin America, *conquistadores* and their descendants took the best land, forcing Indians onto land too meager to farm, and thus eventually compelling them to labor on the new landlord's estate. When Indians fled or died from starvation rations and diseases from Europe for which they had no immunity, colonists imported slaves from Africa. In the nineteenth century, when slavery and indentured servitude were outlawed, the landlords introduced peonage—granting workers loans to buy food, clothes, and other necessities at inflated prices, while ensuring that they never earned enough to pay off the accumulating debt. Further, under a system that victims call "the yoke," laborers were (and in some places still are) required to provide landlords with several weeks of free labor each year. Most large landowners in Latin America today are descended from Spanish and Portuguese colonists, while those who work the land tend to be descended from local Indians and African slaves.

European colonists were not the only villains in this sad history. To escape racism in the United States, freed slaves founded a new country in Africa, Liberia. In doing so, they appropriated land from the indigenous populations (sometimes with U.S. military backing) and joined with multinational corporations to exploit the newly landless laborers. Liberia's Firestone rubber plantations were among the largest in the world until the price of rubber collapsed with the introduction of synthetics and left thousands of workers unemployed but still landless. In 1980 indigenous Liberians staged a revolution against the "Americo-Liberians" descended from the ex-slaves. Civil war continues to plague Liberia.

The ongoing consolidation of landownership and displacement of peasants has numerous side-effects. Modern agriculture requires sizable parcels of land, large-scale irrigation, fertilizers and insecticides, mechanization, and some degree of specialization. The yield from a large, mechanized and irrigated farm usually is much higher than that from hundreds of small plots, worked by hand and watered by rain. But the people who used to work the land often cannot afford to buy food produced by modern methods. Moreover, much of the food is not intended for local consumption but for sale on the international market. And often plantations are used to produce cash crops like rubber and coffee. People grow rubber not for their own consumption but to sell, and in Third World countries like Liberia they sell mainly to multinational corporations.

In a nutshell, commercialization—the shift from village-based food production to the production of cash crops on private property—undermines self-sufficiency, at both the individual and the national levels. It also increases vulnerability. Many Third World countries depend on the export of primary commodities (fuel, minerals, metals, and agricultural goods). The prices that commodities command on the global market fluctuate widely, making it difficult for developing countries to budget and plan (see Figure 18.2, page 468). While large, mechanized or better-irrigated farms may produce higher yields than hundreds of small plots do, the large farms' products are commonly intended for sale on international markets because that's where the money is. They fail to provide for local dietary needs, as small farms do. Many Third World countries use more acres to produce fruits, vegetables, and cotton for sale to the First World than to grow food for their own people. While the rich countries import luxuries (coffee, sugar, bananas), the poor agricultural countries are forced to import staples (wheat, corn, rice). In many Third World countries, dependency on food imports and aid has increased in recent years (see Table 18.3, page 469).

Private property and commercialization tend to lead to economic polarization, opening a wide gap between the rich and the poor. Thus in Latin America there are the *latifundia* (huge estates) and the *minifundio* (tiny holdings, often on steep hillsides and other marginal land), wealthy landowners and landless laborers or marginal peasants, and very little in between. The gap between the wealthy and everyone else is probably more extreme in Latin America than anywhere else, but it exists in Asia and Africa as well. Land reform—redistribution of large holdings to small peasants and landless laborers—is often a top priority for revolutionaries. In El Salvador, where a tiny elite controls most of the countryside, land reform was the major issue in a twenty-year civil war. The Sandinistas, who threw Anastasio Somoza out of power in Nicaragua in 1979, were backed by landless laborers who sought land redistribution

Three phases in the process of commercialization are illustrated here. Top left: *Commercialization drives people off the land, creating landless migrant workers like these men advertising their skills in Mexico City.* Top right: *This plantation in Brazil produces coffee mainly for export and is probably owned by an international corporation.* Right: *This Brazilian factory packages cashews for export. These images suggest the dependency and loss of meaningful social existence that accompany the social-structural changes brought about by commercialization.*

and reorganization of the ownership of that country's coffee plantations. In these two countries and elsewhere, colonists created a highly inegalitarian pattern of land distribution; this pattern usually persisted after colonialism ended.

When peasants control food production, they have an incentive both to care for the land and to increase the yield; surpluses can be sold for hard cash. But when there are so many landless laborers that landowners can keep wages low regardless of how high a commodity's price rises on the world market, this incentive disappears. Low productivity and ecological damage result (Lipton and Longhurst, 1989). State-controlled farming can have a similar effect, as China discovered in the 1980s, when it decollectivized agriculture and allowed peasants to raise crops on their own land again. Production jumped, making peasants richer and providing the country as a whole with more food (see Chapter 16).

Land reform—giving peasants and landless laborers access to land of their own—is often considered the solution to social and agricultural problems in the Third World. However, with the overpopulation present in many of these countries, bringing more land under cultivation may cause ecological catastrophe—and even, eventually, fa-

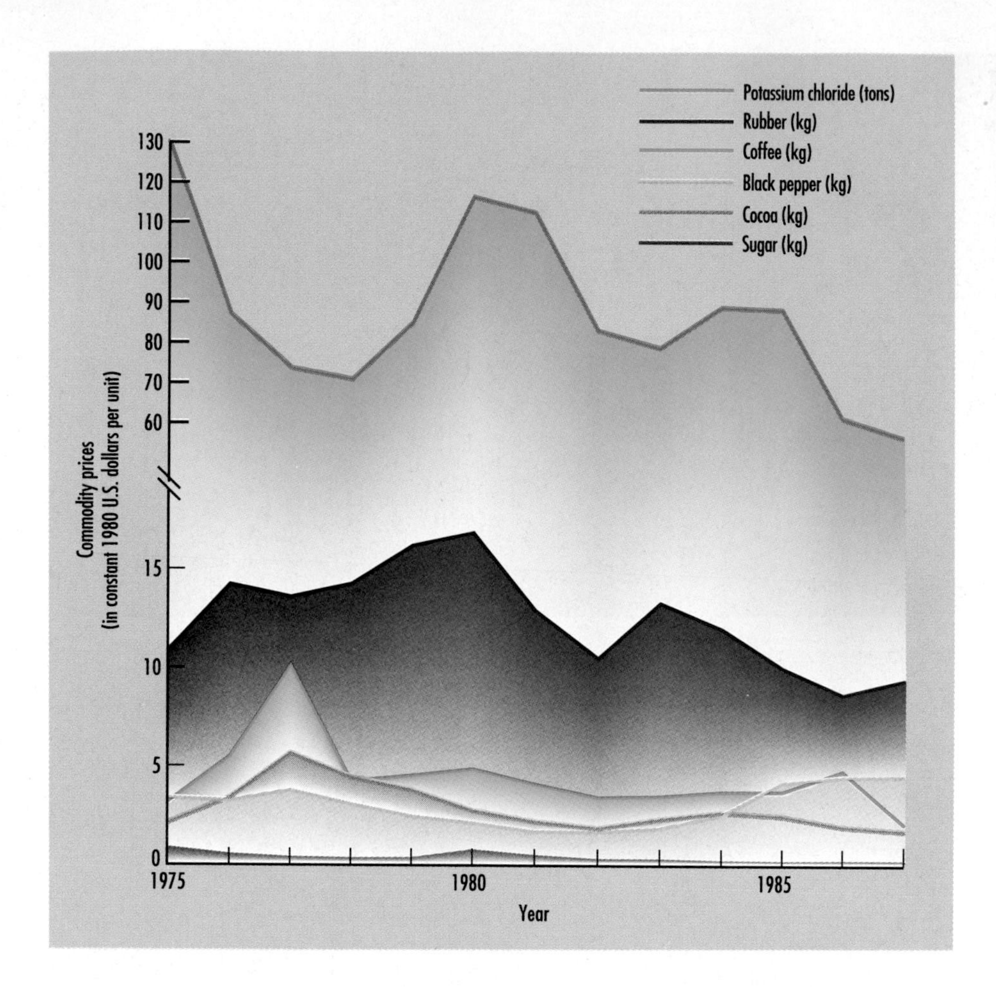

FIGURE 18.2 / World Price Fluctuations for Six Commodities, 1975–1988

Source: World Bank, in World Resources Institute, *World Resources 1990–1991* (Oxford University Press, New York, 1990).

mine (see Chapter 19). In Brazil, the Amazon rain forest is being cut down to enable landless laborers to become peasants—causing ecological problems that may affect the entire world. In much of Africa, deforestation and soil erosion caused by farming on land not able to support it are turning vast areas into deserts (as described above, in Burkina Faso). Repeated famines in Africa have killed millions of people, as a single year of drought forces farmers to eat the seed grain they would have planted the next year, or the rain that follows the drought washes away the fertile soil. Since Third World governments are usually too poor to stockpile agricultural reserves, natural disasters cause severe suffering among peasants and landless laborers. Nine out of ten disaster deaths occur in the Third World (Sen, 1990). The Making Choices box on pages 470–471 describes what people in richer countries can do to help.

Swelling Cities

Faced with population pressures and shortages of land and opportunity in the countryside, Third World citizens have moved to the cities in record numbers. The result has been an explosion in the size of Third World cities, some of which are larger than the major cities of the industrial world (see Table 18.4). The rate of growth is also unprecedented. Estimates are that the total urban population of poor countries will grow by 2 billion, or 160,000 people per day, during the 1990s (Kasarda and Crenshaw, 1991). This is more than twice the growth rate of First World cities at a comparable stage in their development. Even the most sophisticated traveler may be overwhelmed by the size and density of the population of Third World cit-

TABLE 18.3

Agriculture and Food Production, Aid, and Imports

	Value Added in Agriculture* (Millions of Dollars) 1990	Cereal Imports (Thousands of Metric Tons) 1990	Food Aid in Cereals (Thousands of Metric Tons) 1989–1990	Average Index of Food Production per Capita** (1979–1981 = 100) 1988–1990
Low-income countries	**287,958**	**35,748**	**6,599**	**119**
Mali	1,125	61	38	97
Burkina Faso	970	145	44	114
Kenya	2,131	188	62	106
Sri Lanka	1,910	996	231	87
Middle-income countries	**290,333**	**77,607**	**4,483**	**102**
Bolivia	1,069	147	93	98
Peru	2,420	1,562	194	100
Iran	24,484	6,250	22	104
Mexico	21,074	7,648	341	102
South Korea	21,364	9,087	0	106
High-income countries	**N.A.**	**73,797**	**0**	**100**
Singapore	97	737	0	69
United States	N.A.	2,217	0	92
Norway	2,551	379	0	100

"Value added" refers to the amount of new wealth created in a production process.

***In indexes like this, numbers are percentages of a starting point. Thus "100" means that 1988–1990 production equaled that of 1979–1981; it was 100 percent of the earlier, "index" number.*

Source: World Bank, *World Development Report 1992* (Oxford University Press, Oxford, 1992), pp. 224–225.

TABLE 18.4

The World's Ten Largest Cities, by Population and Density, 1990

	1990 Population	Projected 2000 Population	Density (Number of People per Square Mile)
Tokyo–Yokohama, Japan	26,952,000	29,972,000	24,463
Mexico City, Mexico	20,207,000	27,872,000	37,314
São Paulo, Brazil	18,052,000	25,354,000	38,528
Seoul, South Korea	16,268,000	21,976,000	45,953
New York, United States	14,622,000	14,648,000	11,473
Osaka–Kobe–Kyoto, Japan	13,826,000	14,287,000	27,833
Bombay, India	11,777,000	15,357,000	120,299
Calcutta, India	11,663,000	14,088,000	54,607
Buenos Aires, Argentina	11,518,000	12,911,000	21,233
Rio de Janeiro, Brazil	11,426,000	14,169,000	42,894

Source: U.S. *Bureau of the Census*, Current Population Reports.

MAKING CHOICES

How Can You Help the Third World?

On some days in 1992, more than 1,000 people died in Somalia's famine. Bitter civil war and drought had helped to create the conditions for widespread famine. At year's end, more than 1.5 million people, mostly children, were in imminent danger of death from starvation or disease. Halfway around the globe, in Guatemala, there was no sudden crisis, no civil war, and no drought. Yet thousands of children arrived at school too hungry to pay attention; thousands more were at risk of death or permanent physical damage from malnutrition.

What can be done about problems like these? Sometimes when we look at all the pictures of starving children on television, it seems as though there is nothing anyone can do to make the situation any better. However, this is not the case. Both private charities and governments around the world work to prevent or reduce famine and to aid development. They face an uphill battle, but they do have some successes.

People from the world's rich countries offer those in the Third World two main kinds of assistance. First, they offer immediate food aid and other supplies to help cope with emergencies. This emergency relief goes not only to victims of drought but also to those displaced from their homes after earthquakes and floods and to those whose homes or crops have been destroyed by fighting, like the victims of civil war in Bosnia-Hercegovina and other parts of what was once Yugoslavia. Some of the most important emergency relief work is done by religious organizations like Lutheran World Relief and Church World Services. The International Medical Corps and *Medecins sans frontiers* (Doctors without Borders) send volunteer medical teams to provide emergency care, vaccinations, and therapeutic feeding. The Food and Agriculture Organization of the United Nations coordinates emergency food relief.

Second, citizens and governments from the world's richer countries assist in long-term programs designed to foster economic and social development in Third World countries. They build roads and dig wells, provide seeds, run schools, offer assistance in population planning, and train factory managers. In these ways they lay foundations for growth that they hope will permanently lift countries out of poverty. Some of the agencies mentioned above provide development assistance as well as emergency relief, although much important work in this area is done by government agencies of richer countries. The United States operates the Agency for International Development, for example, a wing of the State Department that runs development programs around the world. In addition to such country-to-country programs, organizations like the United Nations Development Program and the World Bank (officially, the International Bank for Reconstruction and Development) unite countries in support of development programs.

Although the United States is one of the world's richest countries, it is not one of the most generous—at least not where government aid is concerned. Most of its aid is in the form of military support for its allies, not development programs or emergency relief. The United States, like the other wealthy members of the Organization for Economic Cooperation and Development (OECD), has set itself the goal of giving 0.7 percent of its gross national product for development assistance to the Third World. The accompanying graph shows that in 1990 only four member countries met that goal: Norway, the Netherlands, Denmark, and Sweden. The United States ranked seventeenth, lower than all the other OECD members except Ireland.

When it comes to private charities, however, Americans are more generous. U.S. charities received over $122 billion in donations in 1990—only 4 percent of which went toward international development assistance or emergency relief (*Christian Science Monitor*, June 17, 1991, p. 17; *Statistical Abstract of the United States*, 1992, p. 379). Americans gave three times as much in private donations to arts and culture organizations in this country as they gave to all international assistance programs.

What these figures indicate is that you can make a personal choice to help the

ies. Paul Harrison describes arriving in Calcutta during a hot, damp, evening rush hour:

> It is the nearest human thing to an ant heap, a dense sea of people washing over roads hopelessly jammed as taxis swerve round handpulled rickshaws, buses run into handcarts, pony stagecoaches and private cars and even flocks of goats fight it out for the limited space. (1984, pp. 165–166)

One result of mass migration from the country to the city is **hyper-urbanization**: a rate of urban growth that outstrips industrial and other forms of economic growth, leading to widespread unemployment and overburdened public services. No economy, no matter how rich, could absorb the huge, steady stream of job seekers that is flowing into Third World cities. No city could build houses, hospitals, and schools, pave roads and provide buses, dig sewers and lay water pipes and electric cables fast enough to keep up with this human tide. And most Third World cities and nations are not rich. Except where immigration is controlled (as in some oil-producing Arab states), urban

Third World. One thing you can do is ask the U.S. government to do more to help poorer countries. For example, between 1980 and 1992 the United States did not pay its full share of dues to the United Nations, leaving many U.N. programs without enough money to operate. If you believe the United States should pay its U.N. dues in full or should increase the budget of the U.S. Agency for International Development, you can write your congressional representatives and say so.

You can also give privately to charities that work in the Third World. To choose a charity, you can send for printed materials that describe the work different groups do. Remember that charities are social organizations, and like all others can be more or less effective at what they do, and more or less focused on their main goal. You can ask for information on what percentage of contributions goes directly to programs to help Third World people. In most reputable groups, this figure is 85 percent or higher. CARE, for example, is involved in relief efforts around the globe. Of its donations, 93.5 percent goes directly into programs; only 2.5 percent is spent on central management and 3.6 percent on fund-raising efforts (Roha, 1992, p. 130). Some other international relief organizations that are particularly effective and responsible are OXFAM, International Red Cross, AmeriCares, and Save the Children Foundation.

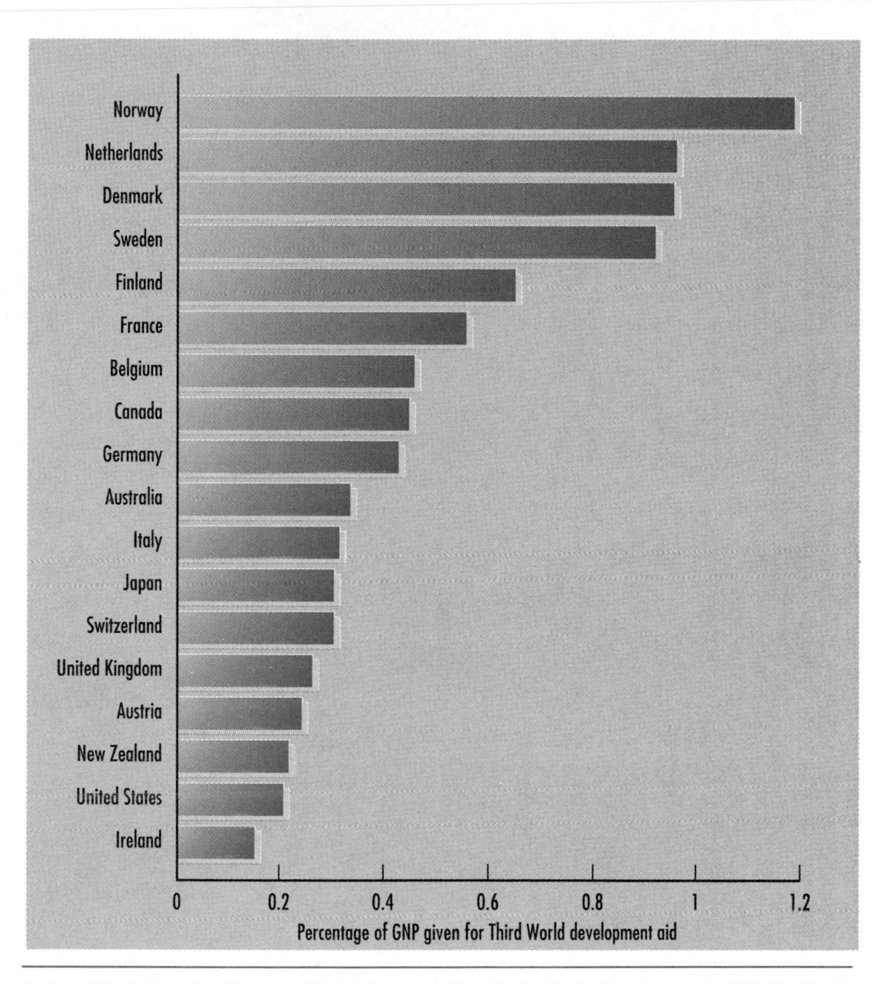

Source: "The Industrialized Countries Slightly Increased Their Public Aid for Development in 1990," *Le Monde*, October 2, 1991, sec. B, p. 21.

planning and budgets are overwhelmed. In all Third World cities, housing is scarce and expensive.

Poverty and Affluence

In Third World cities, poverty and affluence exist side by side. Skyscrapers tower over slums, and shantytowns spring up next door to luxurious apartment blocks and villas, continental restaurants, and nightclubs. In most Third World cities, a small middle and upper class lives in an affluent style familiar to their American and European counterparts. They own color televisions and VCRs, send their children to private schools, wear Italian suits and French fashions, and drive Japanese or German cars. Indeed, they have privileges beyond the reach of most middle-class Americans, such as full-time, live-in household help (which they can afford because of the large numbers of unemployed).

At the opposite extreme are the great majority of urban residents, who live in conditions most Americans cannot

Agricultural crises, high birth rates, and social dislocation due to famine and conflict have led to vast increases in the populations of Third World cities, which have suffered over-stressed infrastructure and public services. This photograph shows downtown traffic, air pollution, and the visual clutter of billboards in Jakarta, Indonesia.

imagine—not only without electricity, but without solid buildings, streets, sewers, toilets, or even running water. Every Third World city has its shantytowns (Worsley, 1984). These squatter settlements currently house over a billion people and are growing at an average rate of more than 15 percent a year.

In Calcutta, about a third of the city's 10 million residents are packed into slums, or *bustees* (Harrison, 1984; Worsley, 1984). The typical *bustee* dwelling is a ramshackle structure built of mud, brick, corrugated iron, thatch, or whatever other material is available. Entire families crowd into single rooms, perhaps twelve feet square, arranged around a central courtyard with a privy that may serve fifty people or more. Strictly speaking, *bustees* are not squatter settlements. The land is privately owned and the "apartments" rented out by a resident manager. Many of Calcutta's poor cannot afford even to rent space in these slums and live in makeshift camps and hovels on the outskirts of the city or in any vacant space. Then there are the people who live and die in the streets. In Calcutta they number between 200,000 and 400,000, making this city a world capital of misery and despair.

Periodically, city officials may tear down squatter settlements, but they tend to pop back up in the same or other sites. Some last long enough for the inhabitants to develop a sense of community, complete with networks of social support and neighborhood organizations that provide a degree of self-government (Castells, 1983). These settlements also serve as a buffer between rural and urban life. People from the same villages and regions tend to settle near one another, and so do not suffer either a complete break with their past or total anonymity.

The juxtaposition of poverty and affluence explains other features of Third World cities. Almost all have relatively high crime rates; petty theft, such as pickpocketing, is especially common. The reason is much the same as in New York City or any other place where the rich and poor are thrown together: The pickings are good and there are people in need who have little to lose. Prostitution is rampant in Third World cities from Bangkok, Thailand, to Rio de Janeiro, Brazil, and Nairobi, Kenya. The reason is much the same: the simultaneous presence of men with money to spend and women with few alternatives.

Cities in the First World have homeless people, too, but the numbers of destitute people are much higher in the Third World. Few developing countries have any social welfare system, unemployment benefits, or other forms of public assistance, so people depend on charity. Many first-time visitors to Mexico City are shocked by the number of beggars. For miles, the main road into the city from the airport is lined with women and their children, begging or selling a few meager handicrafts. In every public park, on almost every street corner, women sit silently, watching their children tug on the elbows of tourists and hoping for a handout.

The dual city, with its islands of affluence in a sea of poverty and unemployment, is in part a legacy of colonial times (Harrison, 1984). To house themselves and their administrations, European colonists built models of the cities they knew back home. But they needed porters, tea boys, junior clerks, and the like, so they allowed local people to camp on the outskirts of their new cities. The dual city survived and expanded after independence, as new nations poured resources into Western-style government buildings, boulevards, industries, and homes for government workers and neglected the well-being of the country's traditional, rural way of life. Rural citizens joined the ranks of urban squatters and urban unemployed in ever-increasing numbers.

The post-colonial era has seen the rise of a new social class in Brazil and other Third World countries: a small bourgeoisie with comparatively great wealth and social power, largely responsible for development, yet often tied to political or economic groups that make autonomous development impossible.

The Informal Sector

A quarter to two-thirds of Third World residents do not hold regular, salaried jobs (Sethuraman, 1987). They survive through the **informal sector** of the economy. This term (coined by the anthropologist Keith Hart) refers to the economic activity that takes place outside of regular employer/employee relations and government scrutiny and taxation. The cornerstones of the informal economy are bartering and cash deals. If you paint your brother's house and he gives you his old car in return, you are bartering and have entered the informal sector. Similarly, if you pay a mechanic cash to repair your car so that he doesn't have to report it on his income tax return and he gives you a lower rate, you are operating in the informal sector.

An informal sector exists in the United States and other industrial nations, but it is a relatively small part of the economy, located on the fringes. In Third World countries, however, the informal sector is central. As Hart (1973) argued on the basis of his fieldwork in Ghana, the informal sector provides migrants from the rural north to the capital city of Accra with goods, services, and income they could not obtain otherwise. The formal sector is out of bounds for most of the poor. They cannot afford to buy its products or use its accommodations; nor are they qualified for its jobs. The main advantage of the informal sector is that it does not require significant amounts of capital or formal schooling (see Figure 18.3 for other differences). Virtually anyone can set up shop.

One aspect of the informal sector is the *black market*, the illegal trade in stolen, untaxed, or other illegally distributed goods, drugs and other contraband, and foreign currency. The informal sector also includes restaurants and bars, barber and beauty shops, tailors, scribes (to help the illiterate), photographers, impromptu "factories," and all manner of repair shops, often set up in temporary quarters to serve the residents of shantytowns and slums. These activities are part of the informal sector not because they are illegal, but because they are not licensed, inspected, and taxed. Shoeshiners, who need no permanent address

Informal
- Ease of entry
- Reliance on local resources
- Family ownership of enterprises
- Small-scale
- Labor-intensive and innovative, ad hoc technology
- Skills acquired outside the formal school system
- Unregulated and competitive markets

Formal
- Difficult to enter
- Dependence on imports
- Corporate ownership
- Large-scale
- Capital-intensive, imported technology
- Skills often acquired abroad
- Markets protected by tariffs, import, and exchange licenses

FIGURE 18.3 / Characteristics of the Formal and Informal Sectors of the Economy

Source: Peter Worsley, *The Three Worlds* (University of Chicago Press, Chicago, 1984), p. 210.

as are Western Europe and Japan to a lesser degree. What lies beyond the consumption stage, writes Rostow, is impossible to predict.

Perhaps the most important contribution of modernization theory is its emphasis on ***culture***, on the ideas and attitudes that promote savings, investment, and economic innovation (see Eisenstadt, 1973; Inkeles, 1983).

Another strength of modernization theory is its emphasis on ***functional integration***. Adherents maintain that many different elements of a society must be working together for development to occur. For example, Rostow points out that some countries have made the mistake of neglecting agricultural development in their rush to industrialize, with disastrous consequences. Likewise, some countries have devoted too few resources to the physical infrastructure (roads, railroads, telephones, and the repair services that go with them). Other analysts have focused on cultural dysfunctions, such as the absence of a work ethic, with its emphasis on punctuality and productivity.

In the 1950s and 1960s, the First World's policy toward Third World nations was based on modernization theory. The relatively rich Western countries offered aid to poor countries to help them overcome the deficiencies described above. Schools were built, scholarships to Western universities provided, roads and factories constructed, and government ministries reorganized. The goal was to make the poorer countries of the world richer, and the assumption was that the way to do this was through Western-style economic and social development.

Modernization theorists can point to a number of successes. Clearly, the "Little Tigers" of Asia—South Korea, Taiwan, Hong Kong, and Singapore—have taken off. So, in Rostow's view, has India, and Thailand and Malaysia are not far behind. Several countries in Latin America (especially Brazil and Mexico) could take off if their burden of international debt were lifted. China could also move forward if the government does not "frustrate its extraordinary intellectual and entrepreneurial potential as it did in the Great Leap Forward, in the Cultural Revolution, and in June 1989 [when the prodemocracy movement was crushed]" (Rostow, 1990, p. xvii). In all, Rostow identifies four "graduating classes" in the school of modernization (see Figure 18.4).

Unfortunately, the expected modernization failed to occur as planned in most (if not quite all) of the world's poor countries, a number of which suffered damaging civil wars, military takeovers, and other forms of repression. As a result, some scholars and politicians, in both rich and poor countries, are disillusioned with modernization theory. They see its major weaknesses as, first, the assumption that following in the footsteps of Great Britain and the United States is the only path to development; second, the failure to acknowledge the role that actions of the colonial powers played in making the Third World poor; and, third, the neglect of the unequal international structure, which gives greater economic and political power to the already developed countries and stacks the cards against newcomers in the global market. In short, while modernization theory focused on culture and functional integration, it neglected action, power, and structure. This, plus a tendency to focus on the success stories and gloss over the failures, made it overly optimistic.

Dependency Theory: The Role of Power

The first critics of the modernization view to emphasize the importance of ***power*** were dependency theorists, notably André Gunder Frank (1967, 1980), an American who worked much of his career in Latin America. According to **dependency theory**, the main reason Third World countries have failed to "take off," in Rostow's terms, is that they are dependent on the already developed nations of the First World. By supporting Third World governing elites—buying raw materials from them, building factories in their cities, hiring their citizens, and even providing them aid—rich nations do more harm than good. Dependency theory is particularly oriented to explaining the stunted growth of Latin America rather than the nonexistent growth of Africa or the successful development of parts of Asia. Chile, Brazil, and Argentina, for example, all have substantial natural resources—exceptional resources in the case of Brazil. All three of these countries were relatively well off at the beginning of the twentieth century; indeed, Argentina was one of the ten richest countries in the world (Waisman, 1987). Moreover, all have received substantial investments from the United States and other developed countries. But all have lost economic ground relative to the First World. None has developed a strong, modern industrial sector with a secure, capitalist middle class. And all have been politically unstable and ruled by authoritarian military governments.

One problem was that the political leaders of these (and other) Third World countries were not fully autonomous, but were dominated by one or more First World allies. The leaders of the United States and other industrial nations were selective in their assistance, giving the most aid to countries they considered friendly. Likewise, First World business leaders invested only in countries they perceived as hospitable. This meant, first, that Third World govern-

FIGURE 18.4 / Four Classes of Countries "Graduating" into Rostow's Take-Off Stages of Economic Growth

Source: W. W. Rostow, *The Stages of Economic Growth: A Noncommunist Manifesto*, 3d ed. (Cambridge University Press, New York, 1990), chap. 1, p. xviii.

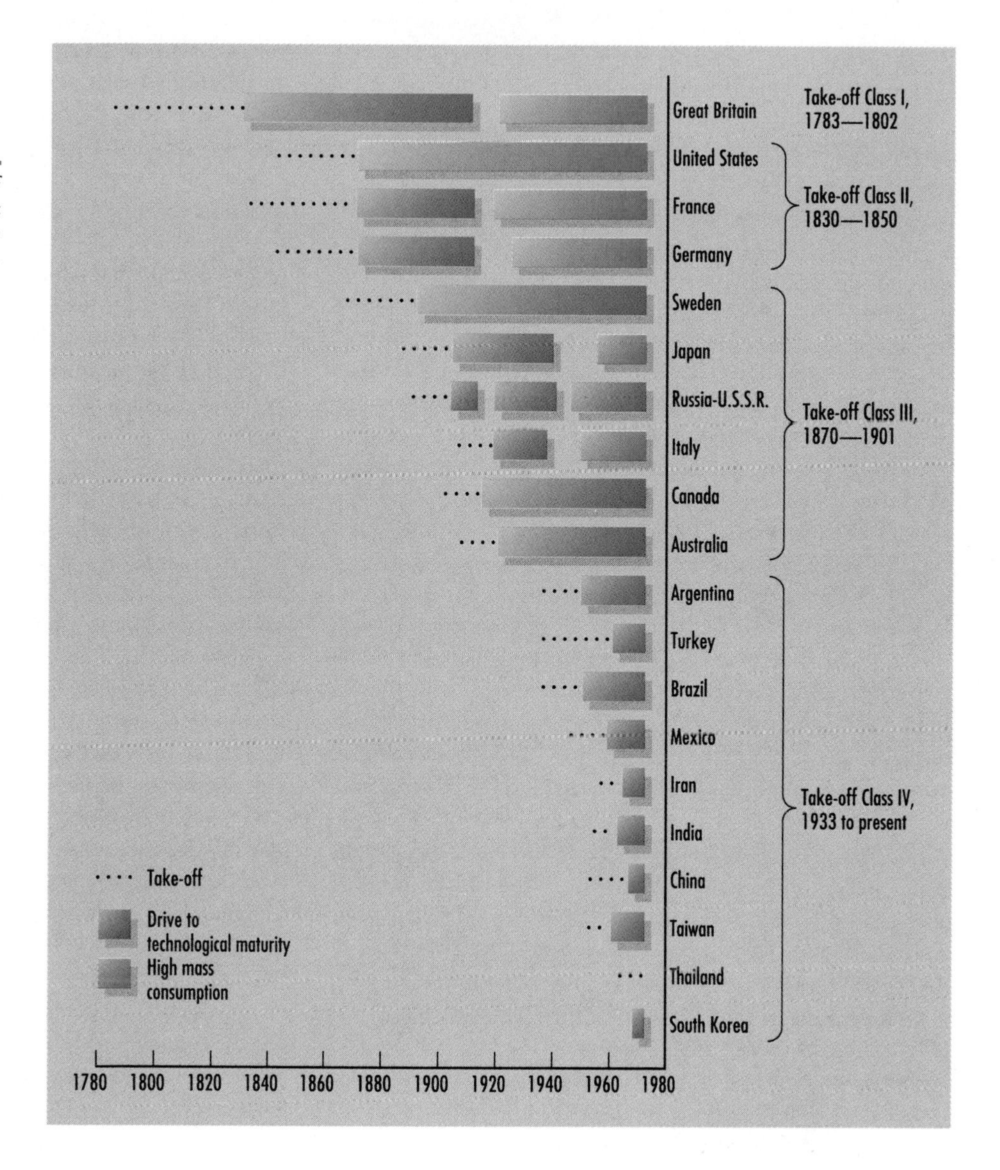

ments had to be at least as attentive to the foreigners who gave them aid or did business in their country as they were to the needs and wishes of their own people. To a greater or lesser degree, they became agents of the world economy whose main role was to keep their country's work force in line. As a result, democracy often was put on hold. Second, this meant that the United States supported a number of repressive dictatorships, such as those of Anastasio Somoza in Nicaragua and Ferdinand Marcos in the Philippines.

For similar reasons, dependent development tended to slow or prevent the emergence of a strong, autonomous middle class, another essential condition for development and for democracy (see Chapter 17). Members of local business elites commonly became dependent on their governments, which were often corrupt. For example, the government might grant a businessman a license to be the sole importer of automobiles (in exchange for a bribe or share of his profits). The importer could then reap high profits without having to take the risk of being an industrial capitalist and without investing much in his own country. Often, the only way local entrepreneurs could operate was by working with the political-military elite. Others became middlemen or agents for foreign-owned corporations. Instead of starting their own businesses to compete with foreign companies, they worked for those companies, selling their products or managing their plants. This dependent middle class did not create new local jobs or a dynamic economy full of domestic enterprises. The middle class also hindered development by imitating the lifestyles of foreign elites, buying imported goods and thus depriving their countries of potential investment money. Moreover, the best-educated and most ambitious citizens often moved to New York, London, or other Western cities.

Even foreign aid, which obviously helps in some ways, can slow development in the long run. Foreign technology can throw the local economy off balance by making it dependent on foreign supplies and expertise. A new shoe factory built with American aid, for example, would provide a few jobs but at the same time would put local shoemakers out of work. If the equipment in the factory broke down, the owners would have to pay for new American parts with scarce American dollars. Often no one in the receiving country would fully understand the machinery, so that foreign technicians would have to be brought in. All this would be bad enough if aid were only a matter of gifts, but foreign assistance often came in the form of loans. When development did not occur as planned, the receiving countries had trouble making their loan payments. The richer First World governments often encouraged banks to lend the receiving countries still more money; the result was the current international loan crisis. The problems arose not so much with humanitarian aid (such as money for health care) as with inappropriate development aid, which was often based on modernization theory's assumption that Third World countries should imitate First World countries.

Dependency theory shows the economic problems of underdevelopment to be closely linked to political difficulties. Dictatorship is the most prevalent form of government in the Third World. Authoritarian (often military) rule, undemocratic institutions that cater to a small elite, corruption, inefficiency, instability, and revolutions are all widespread. Why should this be? Peter Evans's classic study of Brazil (1979) showed how Brazil's authoritarian government was linked to its dependent position in relation to the United States and other foreign countries.

In the early 1970s Brazil was widely hailed as an economic miracle, a country that had developed from little more than a huge coffee plantation in the world system to an industrial state. This process of industrialization was very beneficial to certain urban elites; rural landlords also prospered by selling produce like coffee and bananas to the United States. Most other classes did not share in the benefits. Brazil's rapid but imbalanced rise was largely the result of partnerships the government formed with multinational corporations—private companies with operations and subsidiaries in many countries (see Chapter 16). In order to attract and keep foreign investment, a country has to be hospitable and dependable. Authoritarian governments are in a position to provide what multinational corporations are looking for—and thereby to satisfy the domestic elites that benefit from the presence of the multinationals.

What multinationals are looking for, first and foremost, is political stability. A government has to demonstrate that it is in control and will not be seriously threatened by radical political movements, militant nationalists who oppose foreign business, or powerful labor movements. The military government that came to power in Brazil in the early 1960s was able to deliver this assurance. Second, multinationals need an inexpensive and docile supply of labor, which the Brazilian government ensured by systematically preventing the formation of unions. Third, multinationals need a developed infrastructure (transportation, communications, energy, access to raw materials). The Brazilian government met this requirement by gradually taking control of these sectors of the economy. Finally, multinationals need favorable terms that enable them to profit from their investment. The Brazilian government offered tax credits, low export fees, and minimal regulation. As a result, Brazil's economy grew steadily. But as one former president commented, "Brazil is doing well, but the people are not."

One of the costs of doing business with multinationals, and of dependent development generally, is that profits flow out of the country, rather than being invested in local businesses. Wages are kept artificially low, so that most workers do not benefit from development. Moreover, both the state and business elites (local people who work for management) are likely to socialize with their counterparts in the multinationals, develop international tastes and lifestyles, and so become further removed from their fellow citizens. All these factors—perhaps especially the gap between the rich and poor within the country—generate social unrest. Typically, the government's response is to crack down on dissenters.

And so dependent development creates a vicious cycle. Lack of economic growth leads to civil uprisings and authoritarian (often military) rule. Seeking development to strengthen their position, the government and the elites that support it enter into partnerships with multinational corporations. The country develops, though only within limits; elites are enriched, but the majority of the population reaps little benefit. This inequality leads to rebellion, which provokes more repressive government, and so it continues. The only true winners in this situation are the multinational corporations, at least temporarily.

The main strength of dependency theory is that it shows how reliance on the First World limited and distorted Third World development, particularly in Latin America and a few other places where abundant natural resources made possible an initial, but stunted, growth. It shows how the power of the First World combined with that of local Third World elites to provide benefits for them at the expense of balanced development that would have benefited the population as a whole.

Dependency theory is less helpful in specifying what policies work best to promote development. At one time many dependency theorists thought that socialist governments were the answer. While these governments often have done better than capitalist governments in some areas—such as health care and education—they have done worse in overall economic development. As Rostow (1980) has emphasized, agriculture and the physical infrastructure still matter, whether a country is dependent or not. So does its position in the overall social structure of the world system.

World Systems Theory: Global Social Structure

Sociology's third important contribution to understanding uneven development is **world systems theory**. Whereas dependency theory emphasizes power relations and the actions of multinational corporations and Third World elites, world systems theory emphasizes the ***social structure*** of global inequality. As defined by the American sociologist Immanuel Wallerstein (1974, 1984, 1988), the modern, capitalist world system is the web of production and consumption relations that has linked the First and Third worlds since the rise of capitalism. It is a global social system with a structure and logic of its own. Its main feature is that it is capitalist, and thus driven by competitive pressures, which give international trade its structure. Those countries with high levels of accumulated capital investment always have an advantage over those with less productive industries. Rich countries have advanced technology, skilled labor forces, and other advantages. Poorer countries that want to develop can't compete with them at all in high-technology fields, and in other areas their only tactic is to keep wages as low as possible. There are always lots of poor countries with cheap labor, though, so this doesn't give them much of an advantage.

Throughout the modern era, a system of unequal trade has moved resources from the Third World to the First. Colonialism was one factor in this process, but even ordinary trade is structured so that more rewards go to producers of industrial or high-technology goods than to those who mine or farm. Multinational corporations build their headquarters in the First World and keep most of their profits there. When Third World countries try to advance themselves, they are always forced to try to catch up with richer, more productive First World countries. As a result, poor countries today can't take the path England or the United States followed 150 to 200 years ago, because England and the United States already block that path. The First World countries continue to reap advantages from having industrialized first.

The world system develops a global division of labor that has three levels or parts: the core, the periphery, and the semiperiphery. The **core nations** consist of the world's powerful industrial economies, which now include the United States, most Western European nations, and Japan. The core nations provide the management and much of the essential machinery for the production of the world's goods. They control the main multinational corporations. They also reap most of the profits.

The Third World countries that we have been discussing, which contain the vast majority of the world's population, usually are **peripheral nations**. These countries are on the edges of the world system—not because they are traditional or because they are in a transitional stage, but because they are the sellers of low-priced raw materials. Most are predominantly agricultural, depend to some degree on foreign aid, and participate in the world system only on terms set by the core countries. Many are not able to enter large-scale international trade at all, having nothing valuable to sell to the world markets. Countries like Chad, Botswana, Peru, and Guatemala are in this category. Most have experienced very little economic growth in recent years, and some have slipped backward.

Between the core and the periphery are the **semiperipheral nations**, those which are moving up or down in the system. They are actively involved in the world system but are limited in their ability to influence it. The newly industrialized countries of Asia developed out of this group. Turkey, Mexico, and Malaysia, all of which have improved their global position in recent years, are part of the semiperiphery. A formerly powerful core country can slide down into the semiperiphery if it fails to keep investing enough in technology and other sources of industrial productivity to stay competitive in the world market. Some would argue that this is happening in Great Britain today—although it may yet recover, especially as part of a more integrated Europe. Some critics (for example, Rostow, 1990) object that the semiperiphery is a catchall category, designed to cover nations that do not fit neatly into either of the other two groups. Wallerstein (1974, 1979) counters that semiperipheral countries play a vital role in the world system, acting as a buffer between the poor countries of the periphery, which might rise up in revolt, and the rich nations of the core, which prefer the status quo. In effect, the semiperiphery is the middle class in the world system.

A country's opportunities for development, according to Wallerstein, depend largely on where it fits into the world system of capitalist trade. By and large, the core nations are able to set the terms of this trade. They control the world's currency system, shipping, communications, and markets. Further, they are in a position to trade high-priced machines and technology for raw materials, agricultural products, and low-priced goods that require little technology or skill to manufacture. The latter sell for lower prices, provide jobs for fewer people in the countries where they are produced, and are highly vulnerable to oversupply and market crashes (as happened in many sectors in the 1970s and 1980s). One problem is that too many peripheral and semiperipheral countries are trying to produce the same sorts of goods, like sugar and rubber. Another is that the core countries entered the competition well before these other countries, a fact that in itself confers a major advantage.

The main strategy for self-improvement by a semiperipheral country is to keep its wages very low and its rate of investment—especially domestic investment—very high. The structure of the capitalist world system encourages countries like Mexico and Korea to adopt strategies that enrich their elites and keep their masses relatively poor. The payoff for the workers in such countries is deferred to the distant future. They are told they can't have higher wages until development really takes off (even though those who own the factories they work in get high rewards for their investments). This strategy works well only in countries like Mexico that are endowed with high-priced natural resources (oil, in the case of Mexico) or in countries like Korea that have histories of previous high development that leave better-skilled work forces, sound roads, and other advantages. It also works best where countries are not torn by deep ethnic tensions produced by colonial boundary drawing, as in Africa.

World systems theory has been criticized for its narrow focus on market structure. The theory is best seen as correcting and supplementing, rather than completely replacing, modernization and dependency approaches. Whereas modernization theory sees different countries as more or less developed but all moving on essentially the same path, world systems theory stresses the basic structure of the worldwide economy, revealing the forces that put different countries on different paths. It also shows that analyses that address the culture of developing countries without also taking account of their structural positions in the world's economic system cannot offer effective explanations.

World systems theory offers advances on dependency theory, too. It shows how structural factors set limits to what Third World countries can do, even if they change counterproductive patterns of action (like government corruption) and limit the power of the military or of multinational corporations. Though it focuses on structure, world systems theory does point to the one strategy of action that seems to offer a successful—though difficult—path to development. In doing so, world systems theory also helps explain why dependency theory fits Latin America best, and why Asia and Africa have diverged from that model. First, countries like Argentina, Chile, and Brazil were never part of the core, even when they were relatively wealthy by world standards. They did not call the shots in the world economy; their currencies were not used in international trade; and they could not dictate terms of trade to the United States or other rich countries. When there was a coup in one of these countries, world stock markets did not crash as they probably would have if a political revolution had occurred in the United States or Japan. Yet because these Latin American countries offered minerals and agriculture for export, they came to be fairly well integrated into the world system: They produce goods that are in demand on the world market (although not always at high prices); they are involved with multinational corporations, albeit in minor roles; and they are important markets for goods produced in the First World.

By contrast, most African nations are on the periphery and are barely part of the world system. Multinational corporations see little reason to do business in Africa; when they do, it is usually limited to selling a few popular consumer goods (such as Coke and Pepsi), or purchasing minerals or small amounts of agricultural products (such as coffee). Many African countries are especially vulnerable to outside influences because they have only one major export. Thus, when the world price of copper plunged in the 1970s, Zambia, dependent on copper exports, was left destitute.

Asian countries provide the main examples of the progression from peripheral to semiperipheral to core countries. Japan showed the way. Japan had a strong government and a high level of cultural homogeneity (unlike Latin America and Africa) because it was not created or carved up by European colonial powers. It used both governmental and corporate ***power*** and aspects of traditional ***culture*** to discipline its citizens. They became good industrial workers, accepted low wages, did not attempt to overthrow the government, and saved a high percentage of their salaries, making additional domestic investment possible. In addition, its relatively wealthy past gave Japan some initial capital to work with. As we'll see in the next section, Korea is another Asian country that is following Japan's example.

NEWLY INDUSTRIALIZED COUNTRIES: ACTION FOR CHANGE IN SOUTH KOREA

In the years following independence in the Third World, a single goal dominated the thinking and behavior of developing nations, development agencies, and already developed countries alike. "Development, all but a few radical spirits agreed, involved following the yellow brick road painted by Western societies toward an Oz of industrialization and consumerism" (Harrison, 1983, p. 23). Yet one, two, three, and even (in Latin America) fifteen decades later, the gap between rich and poor nations is as wide as ever. Neither massive inputs of aid nor forced modernization has led to the gains expected a generation ago. The situation is not all bleak, however. Some nations have made rapid economic progress and are on the brink of graduating into the ranks of rich industrialized nations. This has not come as easily as moderization theory predicted. It has happened more—especially in Asia—than dependency theorists expected. But as world systems theory showed, the path to development called for a highly disciplined, often authoritarian model of social action, with high costs.

The case of South Korea illustrates one path to economic development. Occupied by the Japanese even before World War II, torn by the Korean war (1950–1953), which divided the country in half and cut off the industrial centers in the North, the Republic of Korea faced a future that looked dim. In the 1950s South Korea depended heavily on U.S. aid and imports but, after a military coup in 1961, embarked on an ambitious program of economic expansion (Griffin, 1989; Haggard, 1990). Korea focused on industrial development rather than agriculture or mining, because manufacturing offered the best possibility of long-term advancement in the world system. The first factories used pirated designs to produce parts for the international market. But Koreans soon began to produce finished goods for export, targeting industries where they could underprice core countries, such as consumer electronics, steelmaking, and shipbuilding. They deliberately diversified to avoid becoming dependent on a single export. And instead of importing technology, machinery, and products from core countries, Koreans learned how to manufacture for their own consumption. Foreign investment was tightly controlled. In most cases, only joint ventures in which Koreans were part owners were permitted, and plans included the systematic replacement of foreign technicians and managers with Koreans.

From the beginning, expansion was guided and directed by the government. One of the military government's first acts was to repossess privately owned shares in commercial banks and to open two state-run financial institutions. An Economic Planning Board oversaw planning and budgeting and used loans, tax policy, and price controls to reward companies that complied with government plans and to penalize those that did not. The emphasis was on goods for the world market, and an Export Development Committee was involved in every stage of the process, from technical and design assistance to quality control, marketing, arranging visits by foreign buyers, and even packaging.

Korea's business community, like Taiwan's and to some extent Japan's, is dominated by a small number of family-owned businesses and closely held firms. This entrepreneurial elite is something like a European aristocracy, growing in part by mergers and by marrying their sons and daughters to one another. Both social ties and formal business associations serve to limit unnecessary domestic competition and in some cases to pool resources for international competition. These families are extremely wealthy by any standard, but the distribution of income among Korea's factory workers and farmers is more equitable than in many other Third World countries. A series of land reforms created a peasant agricultural system, based on owner-operated farms; Korea does not have the masses of landless agricultural laborers found elsewhere. And although factory wages are low, so is unemployment. Korea's factories are labor-intensive, employing people rather than machines where possible. In addition, the government has invested heavily in "human capital," especially through public health care and education, including a competitive university system that emphasizes science and technology.

In short, Korea's success has not been a matter of luck, but one of planning. Korea is a decidedly capitalistic country, with a high level of private ownership. But its rise as an industrial power was planned and coordinated by the government, in collaboration with a more or less unified, entrepreneurial elite. In purely economic terms, the results have been spectacular. Between 1961 and 1972, Korea's total exports increased by forty times, and manufactured exports, 170 times.

The social cost of this "violent rush to modernization," however, has been an extremely repressive political regime (Wariavwalla, 1988, p. 258). In the early stages of development, authoritarian government was largely tolerated as the population sought to recover from the war and rebuild

Increased wealth in newly modernizing states often leads to more education and higher economic aspirations for common people—and to harsh political repression. This clash between students and police took place in 1988 at South Korea's University of Yon Sei. Despite violent suppression, the social movements of students, opposition political leaders, and even peasant associations in South Korea continue.

its economic foundation. However, as Korea's wealth increased while that of the average Korean did not, demonstrations against the government became more common. In response, the Korean government moved from a policy of "restricted democracy" to a state of martial law: Opposition political leaders were exiled, jailed, and sent to work camps; peasant associations and labor unions were outlawed; and student uprisings were violently suppressed. But the demonstrations continue, as workers seek higher wages and better working conditions and students seek the freedoms and the voice in government that they see in other relatively rich countries. The very success of Korea's "dictatorship of development," which transformed a traditional society into an industrial one, may prove its undoing.

With the cold war over, issues of trade, money, and energy are likely to overtake security on the world's political agenda. Korea and other newly industrialized countries (especially Taiwan, Singapore, and Hong Kong) will become increasingly important, perhaps in some cases even core countries. Whether the Third World can develop, and whether its forms of development will contribute to environmental destruction, are basic questions for the future of the whole world. In the time it takes to read this paragraph, 100 children will be born—six in industrial countries and ninety-four in developing countries. As the World Bank (1991) puts it, "No matter what the outlook in the industrial economies, the world's long-term prosperity and security—by sheer force of numbers—depend on development" (p. 157).

Thinking Back on the Key Concepts

The division between the poor nations of the Third World and richer countries like the United States involves all five of our key sociological concepts. It is rooted, first of all, in colonization, a ***social action*** by European countries that conquered and dominated the parts of the globe that now make up the Third World. Other social actions followed in response, including eventually the revolutionary struggles by which many Third World countries achieved their independence, and the successful struggles of some, like South Korea, to achieve economic development.

Most Third World countries have not been so fortunate as South Korea, however, largely because colonialism joined with capitalism to produce a ***social structure*** that keeps rich and poor divided. As world systems theory shows, this social structure operates on a global scale to limit the opportunities that poor countries have for development and to make trade work primarily for the benefit of richer countries. At the same time, the social structure within most Third World countries sharply divides rich from poor, with most of the population consisting of peasants or landless laborers.

Closely related to this sharply unequal social structure is the continued exercise of ***power***, both on a global scale and within individual countries. The richer or stronger countries used their power to make poorer and weaker ones into colonies, and they have continued to use it by stopping revolutions and attempts to distribute land in favor of poor peasants and landless laborers but at the expense of multinational corporations. Within much of the Third World, power relations perpetuate the poverty of masses of people by denying them not only land but access to education and other sources of opportunity. Third World elites sometimes join with First World governments and multinational corporations against the interests of poor people in their own countries.

Colonialism brought not only armies and navies but also missionaries and teachers. The Third World has been shaped by the spread of ***culture*** from the First World. Television, radio, and tourism perpetuate this process of "cultural imperialism"—a process in which the ideas and values of the richer countries are spread much more widely than those of the poorer countries. According to modernization theory, however, cultural differences are a source of inequality between countries. "Entrepreneurial spirit," "work ethic," and "good business sense" are more prominent in First World countries, theorists suggest, and Third World countries need these cultural characteristics. Success stories like that of South Korea depend on them, but also reveal that they are not unique to the West or the First World. Still another important cultural aspect of Third World underdevelopment is the shortage of teachers and educated people who are needed for economic advancement.

Finally, it is important to recognize that the poverty of the Third World and the wealth of the First World are joined to each other in a system of ***functional integration***. Americans are able to buy clothes, coffee, and other consumer goods at relatively low prices because the Third World workers who produce them are paid much less than workers in the United States and receive much less health care, education, food, and other benefits. At the same time, the many forms of inequality between the First and Third worlds, and the First World's domination of the Third World, make it hard for Third World countries to achieve functional integration. The interference of multinational companies, for example, may reduce opportunities for locally owned business. American support for "friendly" dictators may contribute not only to poverty but also to revolution and political instability. These disruptions prevent the functional integration needed for economic development. Ironically, being integrated into a very unequal worldwide economic system may have a *disintegrating* impact on the internal affairs of Third World countries.

SUMMARY

1. The First World consists of the wealthy, industrialized nations of the Northern Hemisphere; the Second World is made up of the formerly communist nations that were part of the Soviet bloc from World War II to 1990, when that bloc fell apart; and the Third World comprises the world's relatively poor and underdeveloped nations, most of which are located in the Southern Hemisphere.

2. One common thread among Third World nations is the legacy of colonialism. European imperialism was guided by the profit motive and the need for raw materials and open markets. To this end, European colonials usually replaced local leaders, reorganized local modes of production, imposed European cultural standards on local peoples, and redrew boundaries to suit their own interests. The result was a global division of labor and system of social stratification that persisted long after former colonies achieved political independence.

3. In a world of high technology, Third World countries are still predominantly agricultural. Most of their populations are either peasants, who use simple technology to eke a subsistence living from small plots of land, or landless laborers, who have been forced off their traditional lands and now work for meager wages, often under deplorable conditions. The commercialization of agriculture and overpopulation have undermined food self-sufficiency and caused serious environmental deterioration in much of the Third World.

4. The populations of Third World cities are exploding, as people are forced or enticed off the land. While the urban elite lead lives of luxury, the masses typically live in squatter settlements, without electricity, clean water, or plumbing, and many live on the street. Most depend on the informal sector of the economy for a marginal living, and many are forced to beg. Even so, people continue to migrate from rural areas to the city, because Third World governments tend to neglect the countryside and subsidize cities and because cities provide the only opportunities (however slight and risky) to get ahead.

5. Sociologists have proposed three explanations of the continuing poverty in the Third World: modernization theory, dependency theory, and world systems theory.

6. Modernization theory holds that development depends on certain prerequisites, especially positive cultural attitudes toward progress and willingness to invest in infrastructure.

7. Dependency theory traces the poverty of Third World nations to reliance on foreign governments and corporations, which may benefit a small elite, but at the cost of long-term development of the nation itself and the majority of the population. Dependency tends to delay the emergence of democratic political institutions and social welfare programs.

8. World systems theory holds that the rise of capitalism produced a global division of labor, in which core nations are the owners and managers of the most important technology and industries; semiperipheral nations provide the middlemen and smaller factories; and peripheral countries have been left behind, except as providers of raw materials (including cheap labor). Much of the Third World falls into the peripheral category.

9. The most hopeful signs for the future come from newly industrialized countries. South Korea, for example, has achieved rapid progress by investing heavily in industrialization geared toward the global market, limiting foreign involvement in local industry, reforming land ownership to maintain agricultural self-sufficiency, providing citizens health care and education (especially in science and technology), and maintaining strict control over business and finance—but at the cost of a highly repressive government.

REVIEW QUESTIONS

1. Why should Americans care about the Third World?

2. What are the First World, the Second World, and the Third World?

3. What differentiates Western imperialism from the imperialism of earlier empires?

4. What are the major problems faced by Third World peasants?

5. What are the advantages and disadvantages of the informal sector of the economy?

6. Compare the three theories of development discussed in the chapter.

CRITICAL THINKING QUESTIONS

1. Some people argue that First World countries should assist Third World countries, while others believe that such help is an intrusion and will simply contribute to even more rapid population growth that Third World countries cannot sustain. Which view do you agree with, and why?

2. Develop some policies that would help address the major problems faced by Third World peasants.

3. Review Chapter 16 and any two of the concepts or theories discussed there to explain one of the problems described in this chapter.

4. Select two or three of the concepts or theories discussed in Chapter 17, and use them to explain one of the problems described in this chapter.

5. Of the three theories of development discussed in this chapter, which one has the most potential for developing practical solutions to Third World problems? Suggest several social policies implicit in the theory.

GLOSSARY

Core nations In world systems theory, the rich industrial countries that provide most of the management, financing, and machinery for global production.

Dependency theory The view that the underdevelopment of Third World nations is due in large part to reliance on First World governments and corporations, which have a vested interest in maintaining a stable climate for investment, regardless of the local social and political costs.

First World The advanced, industrial, capitalistic nations of the Northern Hemisphere (including Japan).

Hyper-urbanization A rate of urban growth that outstrips industrial and other forms of economic growth, leading to widespread unemployment and overburdened public services.

Informal sector Economic activity that takes place outside of regular employer/employee relations and outside of regular government scrutiny and taxation.

Landless laborers Peasants who have lost the rights to land, children of landless peasants, or peoples who formerly lived by hunting and gathering but now must work as hired hands.

Modernization theory The view that economic development depends on cultural attitudes (and perhaps foreign aid) that promote investment in industrial enterprise and related support systems.

Peasants Small farmers who, with family labor and simple technology, grow crops and raise livestock primarily for their own use.

Peripheral nations In world systems theory, countries on the fringes of the global capitalist economy, whose role is largely limited to providing raw materials and purchasing minor consumer goods.

Second World The formerly communist nations of the old Soviet bloc, whose economies until recently were based on state ownership of the means of production and the centrally planned production and distribution of goods.

Semiperipheral nations In world systems theory, countries that actively participate in the global capitalist economy but have only limited influence on the terms and conditions of trade.

Third World The relatively poor, nonindustrial nations of Latin America, Africa, and Asia (including China), most of which were either colonies or clients of Western imperial powers in the past. (See First World and Second World.)

Underdevelopment The absence of modern economic growth that characterizes Third World countries by comparison with the developed nations of the West.

World systems theory Wallerstein's theory that a nation's development is determined by its place in a world system that is defined by capitalist trade and divides the world into three categories: core, peripheral, and semiperipheral nations.

CHAPTER 19

Population and Environment

A total of 1,133,682,501 (1.13 billion) people. That's the finding of the Fourth National Census of the People's Republic of China, conducted in 1990. More than a fifth of all the world's people live in China. With a territory only slightly larger than that of the United States (and with much less farmland), China must support a population four times as large.

China's huge population is largely the result of government-directed modernization, which brought more food, better medical care, and improved sanitation to a land where mass epidemics and famines had been common events. In the years following the Communist Revolution of 1949, birth rates stayed high and death rates fell. The most dramatic change was in child mortality: Between 1950 and 1975, the death rate for children under the age of five dropped from 266 per 1,000 live births to 83 (*World Resources, 1990–91*). China's health-care system stands as a model for developing countries. Rather than investing scarce resources in expensive technology, the government concentrated on preventive care, especially large-scale projects to improve sanitation and inoculate children. Today a baby born in Shanghai has a better chance of surviving infancy than a child born in New York City, and life expectancy there is 75.5 years, compared with seventy-three years for whites and seventy years for nonwhites in New York City (Kristoff, 1991). That's the good news.

The bad news is that China's population is growing at a rate that threatens to destroy the country's chances of improving or even maintaining its current standard of living. Even though China's economy is booming, just providing food and other necessities for everyone consumes most of its economic gains. Despite a record harvest in 1990, there was less to eat per person than five years earlier because there were more people (Oka, 1991). At current growth rates, China's population will increase by 140 million to 150 million in the 1990s, and all these new people will need housing and employment in the first quarter of the twenty-first century.

Even if China had the resources to create millions upon millions of new houses and jobs, the impact on the environment would be staggering. Already what novelist Pearl Buck called "the good earth" of China is turning bad (Smil, 1984, 1989). The area around Beijing used to be heavily wooded. Today the trees are gone, cut down for firewood by the growing population. At night a fine layer of dust, blown in from the naked hills, settles on the streets, only to be whisked into the air by the next day's traffic and mixed with the fumes from the soft coal now used for heating and cooking as well as industry. Beijing residents suffer constant respiratory problems. Deforestation is a problem throughout China, causing shortages of fuel, lumber, and paper and contributing to soil erosion and air pollution. China's Yellow River (the Huang He) gets its name from mud that runs off adjacent farmland, leaving cracks in the earth as deep as a man is tall. Because of erosion, overplanting, and housing construction, China loses more than a million acres of farmland a year (Smil, 1989). Long stretches of the Yangtse River are not only muddy but dead: Human and industrial pollution from cities along its course have killed all the fish. And industrialization is spreading from cities to small towns and suburbs, providing new jobs and products but also fouling country air and local waterways.

The news could be worse. During the years that revolutionary leader Mao Zedong was in power, the pressure of China's population on its resources was largely ignored. Mao subscribed to Marx's view that so-called population problems were merely symptoms of poor economic development or the unfair distribution of goods. The real problem, he thought, was not too many mouths, but too little food; not too many workers, but too few jobs. After Mao died in 1976, China's new leaders began to pay close attention to social research showing that population growth was the root of other problems (Smil, 1990). In 1979, after an unsuccessful campaign to encourage smaller families through education, the Chinese government launched a new policy of allowing only two children per couple, in the hopes of stabilizing the population at 1.2 billion by 2001 (Kane, 1987). By the early 1980s, the government realized that this was not a drastic enough action, and lowered the limit to one child per family. Had the government *not* imposed strict controls, the country's population today would be 240 million more than it is—an increase equal to the entire population of the United States (WuDunn, 1991a).

Under the one-child policy, a couple who plan to conceive a baby must obtain official permission in the form of a small red certificate. Otherwise, they are expected to use contraceptives or undergo sterilization, available from the state at no cost. To enforce this policy, the government has instituted a variety of incentives and penalties (Smil, 1990). Couples who have only one child receive a monthly stipend until the child is fourteen, special consideration for scarce housing, easier access to good schools, free medical care, and extra pension benefits. The pressure to conform is powerful. After one child, a woman may be required to undergo regular examinations to ensure that she has not conceived again. If she has, party officials, neighbors, and respected elders will visit her home to persuade her to have an abortion. Couples who resist this pressure and have additional children may be taxed, fined, denied land, or evicted from their homes.

Some nations, such as China, have adopted vigorous birth-control policies aimed at reducing birth rates. The billboard behind the Chinese couple at left reminds people of the social desirability of one-child families. In France and several other northern European countries, in contrast, fertility is at or below the replacement level. The governments of these nations encourage people to have children through billboards like the one above, which says: "There is more to life than sex. . . . France needs children."

Nonetheless, couples resist. Perhaps the most important reason is the desire to have at least one son to carry on the family line. (Daughters become part of their husbands' families, and so do not count as heirs.) The tradition of *duo zi duo fu* (more sons, more happiness) is particularly strong in the countryside. To combat violations, in 1983 the government decreed mandatory intrauterine birth-control devices (IUDs) for women with one child and sterilization or abortion for all couples with two or more children. Soon reports of forced abortions late in pregnancy, involuntary sterilization, and even female infanticide began to surface in the world press. How many of these actually occurred is not known, but about 10 million abortions are performed each year (Oka, 1991). Female babies are the most vulnerable. Chinese law now prohibits doctors from telling prospective parents the sex of the fetus after prenatal tests, but many will do so for a price. Females may be aborted, drowned at birth, given up for adoption, provided less food than male babies, or not taken to a doctor during a medical crisis. If the baby girl dies, the couple are legally free to try for a boy. Using data from China's 1990 census on the male-to-female ratio, demographers calculate that some 30 million females are "missing" in China (and millions more elsewhere in Asia and the Middle East). The Chinese government claims that the low proportion of females is the result of couples not registering girls at birth so that they can obtain permission to try for a son (Kristoff, 1991). Under international pressure the government relaxed the rules in the late 1980s, but since 1992 the use of force in birth-control programs has apparently increased (Kristoff, 1993).

Ironically, agrarian reforms instituted at about the same time as the one-child policy further undercut population-control goals (Greenhalgh, 1990). To increase food production, the government gave peasants the opportunity to sell much of what they grew on the open market. Newly prosperous farmers were willing and able to pay stiff fines (or bribes) for additional children who could work on the family farm, and local officials were willing to look the other way. The plan was successful in increasing food production, but millions of "illegal" babies were born.

Even with these problems, China's family-planning campaign has been remarkably effective: The average number of live births per woman dropped from five or six in the 1970s to two or three in the 1980s and to less than two in the 1990s. China alone accounts for most of the world's fertility reduction during the 1980s. But the larger goal—a stabilized population—is far from sight. Because so many children were born between 1965 and 1975 (and survived), nearly a quarter of China's population is now in or approaching childbearing age. Even if couples limit themselves to one child, the population will continue to grow at the rate of about 15 million people a year well into the twenty-first century. This is the equivalent of adding a population the size of the Netherlands every year or an Argentina every two years (Smil, 1989), and it may exceed the limit of what either the economy or the environment can bear.

This glimpse at China and its population dilemma dramatically illustrates an important way of telling a society's story: through the numbers, characteristics, and distribution of its people. Population data—information from periodic national censuses and from records of births, marriages, and deaths—are indispensable to an understanding of social life.

Sheer numbers are only part of this story. A society's **population structure**—the age, sex, education, income, occupation, marital status, race, and religion of its members—has important implications for the nature of relationships among its people. Traditionally, the Chinese have venerated old age in part because it was so rarely achieved. But the population is aging rapidly. The proportion of Chinese over the age of sixty-four is projected to grow from 5 percent in 1982 to 25 percent in 2050 (Chen, 1984). This changing age ratio could lead to radical change in Chinese social, economic, political, and cultural systems. At the family level, each child without siblings will have to care for two aging parents. At the national level, smaller generations of workers will have to produce for increasing numbers of retirees (a problem China shares with the United States and other developed nations). Culturally, old age may be transformed from a privilege into a problem, and children may suffer the "only-child syndrome" of being pampered on the one hand and pressured to excel on the other (WuDunn, 1991b).

Likewise, **population distribution**—people's location in world regions, countries, provinces, states, cities, neighborhoods, and blocks—has far-reaching consequences. The combination of population growth and agrarian reform in the 1980s freed tens of millions of rural Chinese from farm work (Smil, 1989). Some found jobs in small local factories, but at least 90 million flocked to China's already overcrowded cities (Tien, 1991). Their impact was overwhelming. Beijing's 10 million permanent residents were joined by a floating population of a million or more shoppers, peddlers, and job seekers. The city of Guangzhou had to ask for state help to cope with a deluge of 2.5 million migrants seeking jobs and shelter. Each day Shanghai's Nanjing Road is flooded with 1.5 million shoppers. Basic urban services are overloaded. In most Chinese cities the water supply is sporadic at best; air quality is poor even compared with that of Tokyo or Los Angeles; and despite a strong tradition of recycling, garbage removal has become an almost impossible task. Population size and concentration take on added significance for a nation's resources and environment. With a mere one-fifteenth of the world's farmland, China must feed almost a fourth of the world's people. So far it has succeeded, but only by using intensive agricultural techniques, including high levels of chemical fertilizers and pesticides. Intensive agriculture may lead to short-term gains but long-term losses, as fields are exhausted, toxic chemicals accumulate in the soil and water, and more people are forced off the land into cities.

The example of China illustrates how important population issues are to social life. **Demography** is the scientific study of how births, deaths, and migration affect the composition, size, and distribution of populations. Sociologists use demographic data in several ways pertaining to the five key sociological concepts. One is to describe ***social structure***, particularly age structure. Statistics on China show that most of the population is entering its working and childbearing years, old people are becoming more numerous, and fewer children are being born. Another use for demographic data is to illuminate the cumulative impact of individual ***social actions*** on society. Population size depends on the creation of children, an intensely personal issue. In most cases, whether to have children, when, and how many are matters of individual choice. Such choices are made within a social context, however, and sociologists study the social forces (not always as obvious as China's one-child rule) that lead people to have smaller or larger families, and the social consequences of their decisions. Demographic data may also reveal changes in ***functional integration***; for example, rapid population growth may

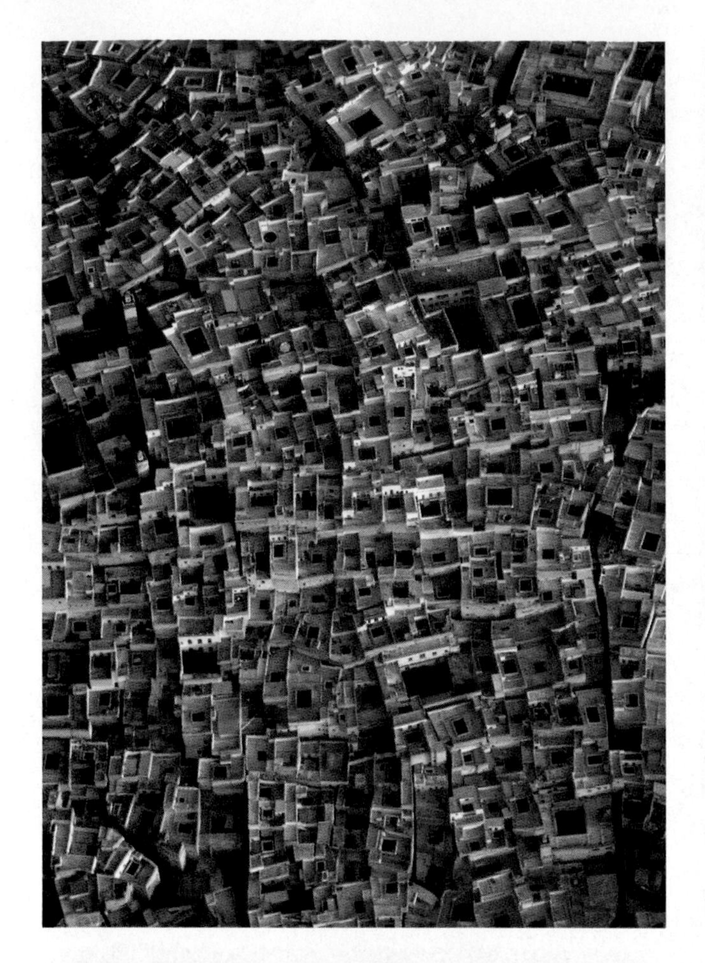

These aerial photographs from Georg Gerster's fascinating book Below from Above *show some extremes in habitation patterns. Each pattern has its own implications for population distribution, environmental impact, and social activity. The ancient city of Fez,* Morocco (top left), *with its jumble of closely packed living and working quarters, seems like an impenetrable maze to a Westerner. To the Islamic observer who is used to the bustle of Fez, the symmetrical and repetitive pattern of summer houses in* Denmark (top right) *may seem oppressively organized and wasteful of space. The village of Labbezanga* (left), *on an island in the Niger River in Mali, might seem too remote for the residents of Fez and too random for the Danes.*

leave a society without enough schools, houses, or health-care facilities to serve all its members. Sociologists who study population may find links between ***culture*** and ***power*** and demographic patterns—for instance, why some groups tend to have more children than others, and how agents of power (such as China's government) may affect these patterns.

The study of population and environment, and the interaction between the two, has moved to the forefront of the social sciences. Public-policy makers, business leaders, and ordinary citizens cannot afford to ignore the impact of human population on the global environment. We begin this chapter by looking at how sociologists identify and assess changes in the size and shape of populations. Next we consider current and future trends in the world's population. In the third section we use the issue of food supplies to illustrate the connection between population and environment. In the last section we look at why the planet is endangered and what can be done to halt or reverse the damage.

POPULATION DYNAMICS

China is unique. Nowhere else in the world have government policies brought about such dramatic changes in so short a time (*World Resources, 1990–91*). More often, shifts in the structure and dimensions of a population occur gradually and are barely perceptible. They are not events but trends, and can be appreciated only in hindsight or through careful statistical analysis. This is the work of demography, which helps sociologists not only to understand the past but also to predict trends and describe the problems that may lie ahead.

The most important source of demographic data is a **census**, a periodic count of an entire population, rather than a sample survey (see Chapter 2). Commonly, a census also describes the regional composition and distribution of people according to their origins, skills, incomes, and activities. The 1990 census of China was the largest ever taken. Even tallying the relatively small U.S. population is a major operation.

The U.S. Census

Article I of the U.S. Constitution requires that the population of the United States be counted every ten years. The 1990 census was a $2.5 billion-dollar undertaking, temporarily employing some 200,000 "enumerators," or census takers. Much rides on the results (Robey, 1989). Seats in the House of Representatives are based on census figures, which means that states (and political parties) may gain or lose power depending on the results. Every year some $40 billion in federal funds is distributed among states, counties, and cities on the basis of census figures. A minor miscount (one or two missing blocks or large apartment buildings) could cost a local program thousands of dollars. Governors and mayors, school boards and community services, political pollsters and news organizations, corporations and advertisers—all employ census data for planning, marketing, and forecasting consumer or client demand.

Here is how the U.S. census works (Edmondson, 1988). In May the Census Bureau mails forms to every address on its master list. This list is based on the bureau's own records, supplemented by commercial mailing lists and triple-checked by postal workers, bureau employees, and local officials. In 1990, the list included some 106 million residences. Not everyone on this list responds, however; in 1990, the return rate was a disappointing 64 percent. In April, census workers set out to visit each of the 37 million housing units that did not reply (*Science*, May 10, 1990). In most cases they interview residents directly; in others they are forced to rely on secondhand data from neighbors, postal workers, or building superintendents. For the 1990 census, data on more than 7 million households were based on such hearsay (*New York Times*, February 23, 1991, p. A10). The 1990 census added "S night" (*S* stands for *street* and *shelter*), on which census workers attempted to interview and count the homeless, and "T night" (*T* for *transients*), on which they tacked census questionnaires on the doors of 70,000 hotel and motel rooms. Information from all these questionnaires is fed into computers programmed to cross-check for such errors as double filing and to spot implausible data, such as individuals over the age of one hundred thirty (Gleik, 1990).

Inevitably, the census is controversial. Actually counting every man, woman, and child in the population is impossible, and both people and computers make mistakes. Most observers agree that the census undercounts the poor, the young, minorities, immigrants, and males, all of whom tend to be mobile and wary of government officials asking questions. This in turn hurts the cities and states where these groups are concentrated, and Democrats, for whom they tend to vote. When New York and fourteen other cities sued for a recount after the 1990 census, the Commerce Department (which oversees the census) agreed to check its results by a postcensus sampling. This survey suggested that the census may have missed 4 million to 6 million people, but other studies indicated the opposite

(*New York Times*, October 17, 1990; April 19, 1991). In standard statistical terms, then, the current U.S. population is 250 million, plus or minus 4 million. Nonetheless, census data offer the most detailed and accurate picture available of the country's people. Even if the census is flawed, it reveals patterns and trends that might otherwise be overlooked (see Figure 19.1). Because it can change the way we see ourselves as a nation, the census is itself a historic event.

Assessing Population Change

In order to assess change in the overall numbers of a population, demographers focus on three variables: fertility (births), mortality (deaths), and migration (movement into or out of an area).

Fertility

The crude birth rate is the number of births per 1,000 people during a given year. In 1947, at the beginning of the baby boom, the crude birth rate in the United States was about twenty-seven per 1,000. In 1975, by contrast, it was down to 14.6 per 1,000. Though useful for some purposes, the crude birth rate is not a reliable basis for long-term analysis. For this we need the total **fertility rate** (often referred to simply as **fertility**). This is the average number of births a woman will have in her lifetime. The fertility rate in the United States hit a peak of 3.77 in 1957 and then dropped to 1.77 in the bicentennial year of 1976. This "baby bust" was largely the result of delayed childbearing: Many baby boomers postponed starting families from their twenties to their thirties. When they began having babies in the mid-1980s, the fertility rate climbed to 2.1 in 1990, then declined somewhat (Haub, 1991; *New York Times*, November 3, 1991). Demographers refer to a fertility level of 2.1 as the **replacement rate**, or the rate at which a population will remain stable (in the absence of immigration); that is, each parent "replaces" himself or herself but does not add to the population. Whether U.S. fertility rates have leveled off or will decline as baby boomers move out of their childbearing years depends on what size families the next generation's potential parents decide to have.

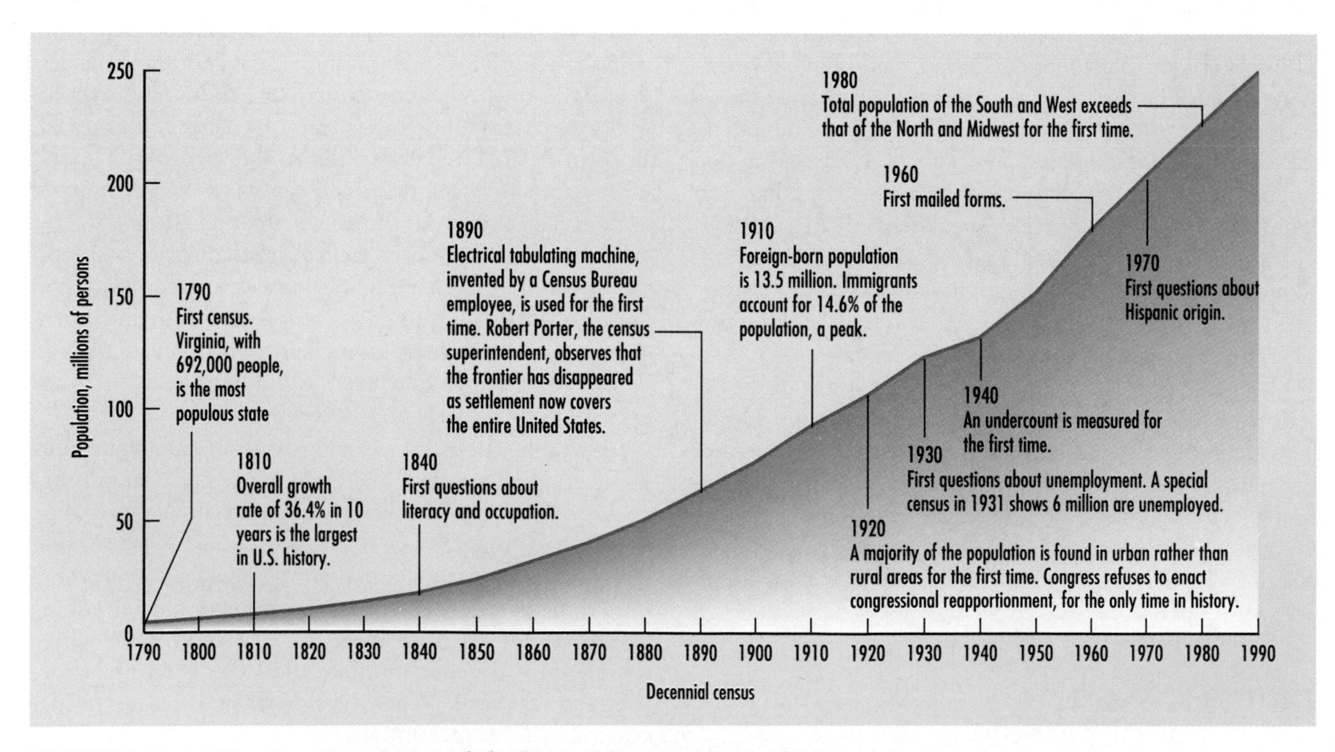

FIGURE 19.1 / Resident Population of the United States at Each Census, 1790–1990

Sources: *New York Times*, April 1, 1990, p. 27; U.S. Bureau of the Census, *Statistical Abstract of the United States, 1982–1983*, Washington, D.C., table 1.

Overall, the trend in the United States has been toward smaller families. At the turn of the century, most Americans preferred a family of three or more children. Nowadays a two-child family is the ideal (Gallup, 1986)—a cultural change with a predictable effect on fertility patterns. Except for the baby boom and recent "baby boomlet," birth and fertility rates in the United States have been declining more or less steadily, as we described in Chapter 6 (Rindfuss, Morgan, and Swicegood, 1988). The pattern of the decline has varied according to socioeconomic status. Birth rates dropped first in upper- and middle-class families and later in poorer families. Also, the white birth rate began declining earlier than did that of African-Americans. The overall black birth rate is now declining, but socioeconomic stratification is at work here too: Middle-class black families have fewer children than middle-class whites, but poor blacks have more children than poor whites. Moreover, Hispanic and Asian birth rates still are much higher than white or black rates. Even so, the total U.S. fertility rate today is just below the replacement level. This is one reason the U.S. population is aging.

Figure 19.2 shows fertility rates around the world. Fertility in developed, or industrialized, countries such as the United States is relatively low compared with that of the rest of the world (especially the least developed countries)—a point to which we will return.

Mortality

The crude death rate is the number of deaths per 1,000 people during a given year. In 1991, there were just over 2.1 million deaths in the United States, for a rate of 8.6 deaths per 1,000 population (U.S. Department of Health and Human Services, 1992, p. 1). The *number* of people who die is not particularly revealing, however, because everyone dies sooner or later. More important are age-adjusted mortality rates.

The **infant mortality rate** is the number of deaths among infants under one year of age per 1,000 live births in a given year. In 1991, there were 8.8 infant deaths per 1,000 live births in the United States, the lowest rate ever recorded in this country. Even so, this rate is higher than in most other developed nations. Japan has the lowest infant mortality rate in the world (4.4 per 1,000 live births), followed by Sweden (5.7), Finland (5.8), Taiwan (6.0), and Switzerland (7.3). Infant death rates in this country are much higher among blacks (17.9) than among whites

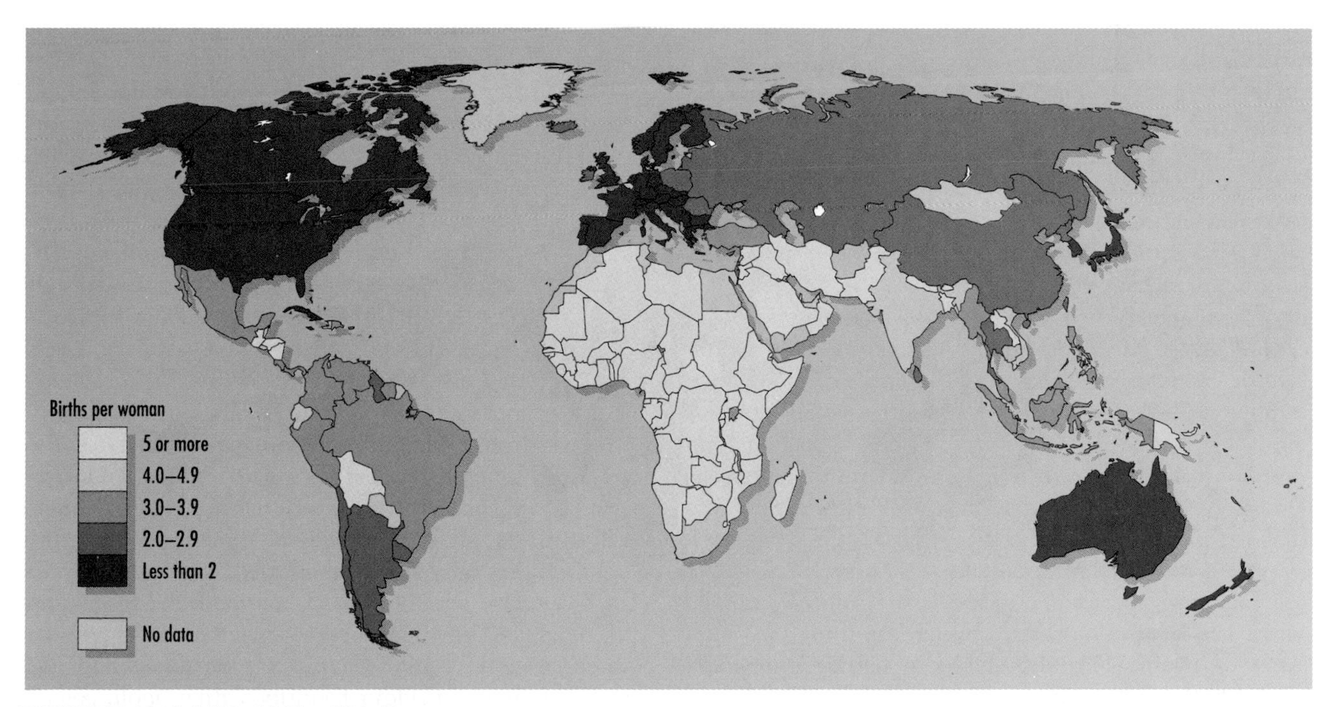

FIGURE 19.2 / World Fertility Rates

Source: *The World Bank Atlas 1990* (World Bank, Washington, D.C., 1990), pp. 22–23.

Hispanic populations are growing rapidly; indeed, sometime in the early twenty-first century, the Hispanic population will probably overtake the African-American population as the largest minority group in the United States. Recently, immigration has brought similar changes to Europe, to the dismay of many traditionalists (Brubaker, 1992). While the United States is a society of relatively recent settlers and continuous immigration, European countries have understood themselves more as senders than receivers of immigrants. This situation has changed in recent years, with disturbing results. For many Europeans, it has come as a shock to see television news of Germans storming the buildings where Southeast Asian refugees are housed, or French youth attacking mosques built by Arab immigrants, or British "skinheads" beating up Pakistani immigrants.

Age Structure

The impact of the birth, death, and migration rates is best seen in the **age structure**, the pattern that emerges when people in a society are grouped by age (see Chapter 6). The population pyramid, as shown in Figure 19.5, is a graphic representation of age structure. In societies where birth rates are high but death rates are also high, age structure takes the form of a triangle. The pattern in which many children are born, but few reach old age, is typical of developing countries. In contrast, with lower birth rates and fewer people dying young, the age structure of developed countries is more rectangular, narrowing only near the top of the pyramid. Birth and death rates have both declined, with the result that the numbers of people in each age group are roughly equal.

A large increase in births, deaths, or migration will also change the shape of the pyramid. The baby boom of 1946–1957 created a uniquely large **birth cohort**—which (as we saw in Chapter 6) is a category of people who were born in the same year or in a small number of consecutive years. This huge bulge in the U.S. population is composed mainly of people now in their late thirties and forties (see Figure 19.6), and thus is swelling the proportion of middle-aged Americans. After the year 2000, this large cohort will begin turning sixty and retiring. At the peak of the baby-

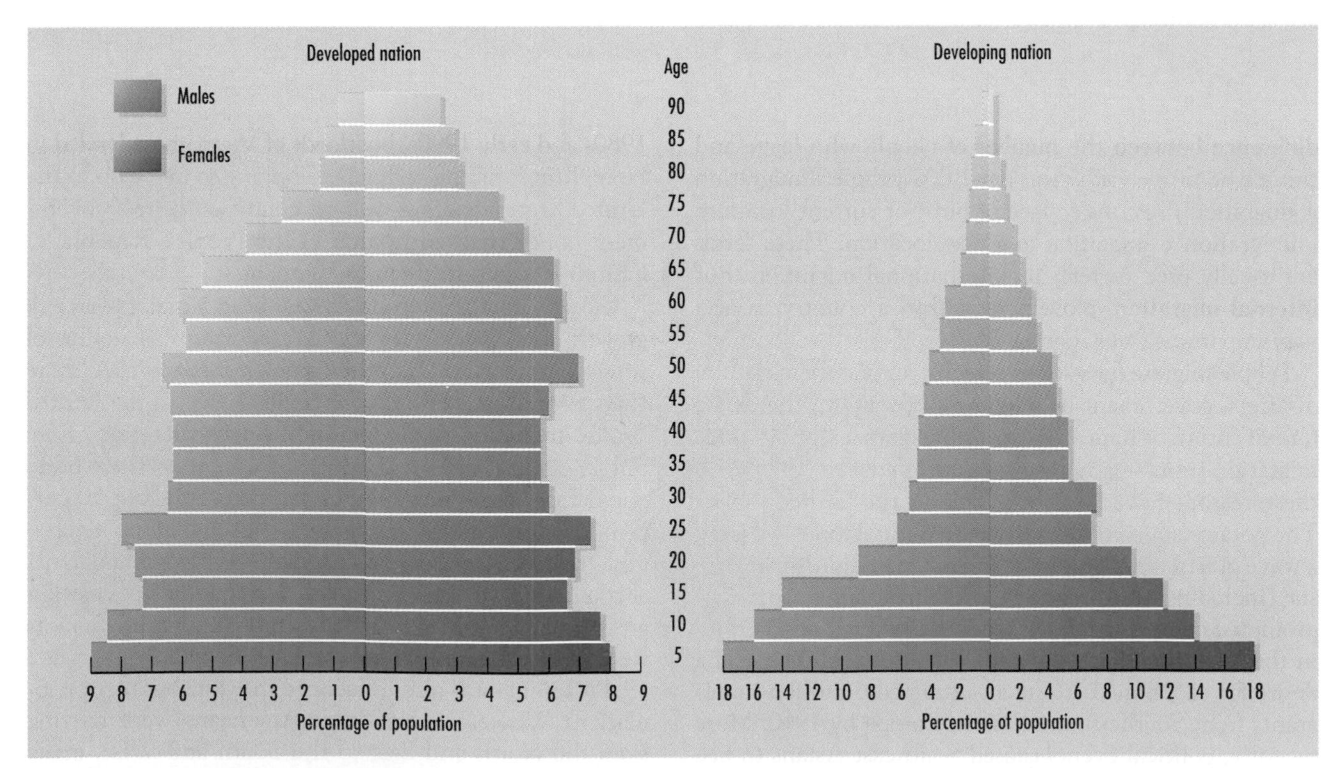

FIGURE 19.5 / Typical Population Structures of Developed and Developing Nations

Source: *Scientific American* 243 (September 1980): 196.

FIGURE 19.6 / The Age Structure of the United States, 1989

Source: Carl Haub, "World and United States Population Prospects," *Population and Environment: A Journal of Interdisciplinary Studies* 12, no. 3 (1991), p. 304.

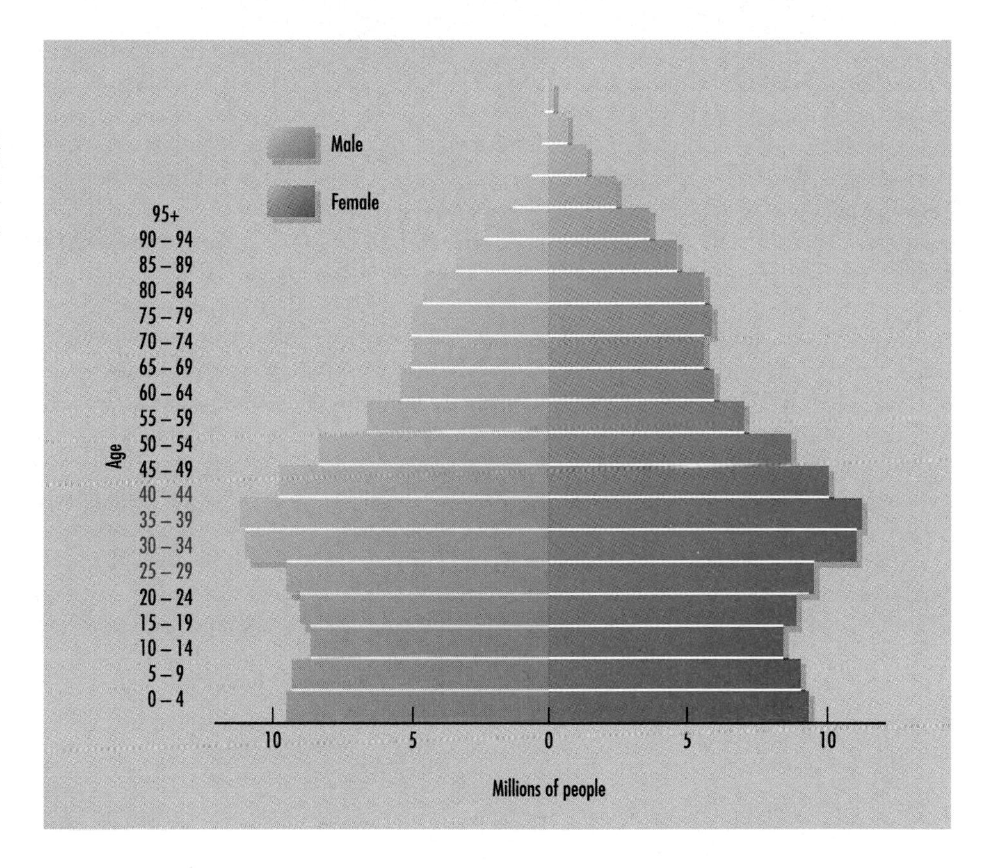

boom generation's retirement years (about 2020), there may be as many as 58 million elderly Americans. A similar bulge has been created in Israel's population structure by the mass immigration of Jews from the former Soviet Union in recent years. In contrast, mass emigration or war may create a shortage of adults in their productive years. For example, the Soviet Union lost 20 million people in World War II and another 15 million to Stalin's purges; all those deaths left a huge gap in the country's population pyramid. The recent wars between Iraq and Iran, and Iraq and the United States, have nearly wiped out a generation of young men in both Middle Eastern countries. This loss will affect everything from the national economies and political strategies to marriage chances for young women.

Knowing the age structure of a society helps policymakers and social planners predict what sorts of goods and services may be needed in the future. A large proportion of children means a growing demand for schools; a large number of people entering their childbearing years signals probable population growth; increasing numbers of elderly people may strain pension plans and health services.

Age structure also affects growth rates. As Paul Ehrlich and Anne Ehrlich (1990) point out, populations that have been growing rapidly keep growing even when birth rates slow down to replacement levels. In 1989, about 40 percent of the population of less developed nations were in their youth. More than a billion young people in these countries have yet to enter their prime reproductive years (ages fifteen to thirty). Even if they were to sharply reduce the number of children each woman has, more women will be having children in the years ahead. So the population will continue to expand. The impact of demographic forces does not stop at a nation's boundaries; it has global implications as well.

WORLD POPULATION PRESSURES

Earth's human population got off to a slow start (Ehrlich and Ehrlich, 1990). The earliest humans probably appeared some 4 million years ago; our own species, *Homo sapiens*, evolved about 300,000 years ago. The size of these prehistoric populations was small (a few hundred thousand) compared with that of other species. When agriculture was invented, about 10,000 years ago, probably no more than 5 million people were on the entire earth—about as many as currently live in the San Francisco Bay Area. In the time of Christ, a mere 2,000 years ago, the entire human population was no larger than that of the United States today. By the mid-1800s, the world population had reached 1 billion (Wilford, 1981). Until then the pattern was one of dramatic ups and downs, as populations swelled in good times, only to be cut back by famines, wars, and disease. In the fourteenth century, for example, the European population was decimated by the plague. A long period of continuous population growth began in the late seventeenth century. The global population reached 2 billion by 1930. The third billion was added by 1960, and the fourth by 1975. The 5-billion mark was passed in 1987 (see Figure 19.7). Even though the world's population is growing more slowly today than it was in the 1960s and 1970s, 275 new humans are born each minute, 16,482 an hour, 395,579 a day, 144 million a year. Unless massive famine, epidemics, or nuclear holocaust intervenes, the world's population is predicted to reach 6.4 billion by the year 2000 and 8.5 billion by 2025 (*World Resources*, 1990–91, p. 50).

Another significant pattern involves changes in population distribution. The developed nations' share of world population has been dropping steadily since 1950, when it was about one-third. Of the 3.2 billion people projected to join the human race over the next thirty-five years, 3 billion—95 percent—will be born in the less developed countries of the Southern Hemisphere, compared to fewer than 200 million in the developed countries of the Northern Hemisphere (Keyfitz, 1989). The population of Sweden will take about 350 years to double if current growth rates are maintained. At the other extreme, India's population is expected to double within twenty years, at which point India will be even more populous than China. Thus, the world population is becoming more polarized, with fewer people (relatively speaking) in the rich areas of the world and more people concentrated in those regions that are the least able to provide for them. In 2025, four out of five people on earth will be living in the less developed countries, or Third World.

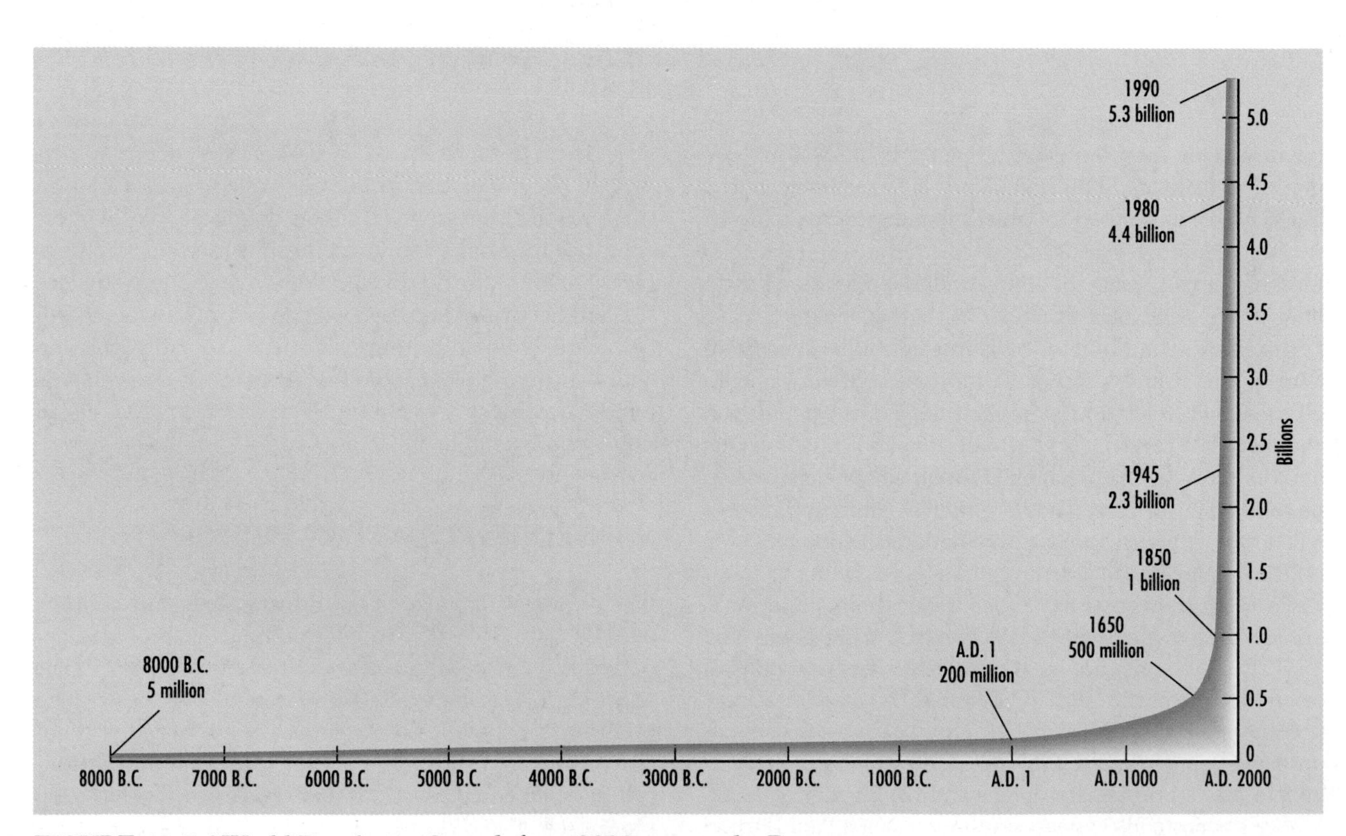

FIGURE 19.7 / World Population Growth from 8000 B.C. to the Present

Source: *World Population Data Sheet*, Population Reference Bureau, Inc., Washington, D.C.

Malthus versus Marx

How large can world population ultimately become, and, more particularly, how many human beings can the planet feed and the environment sustain? These questions are not new. They haunted the influential English scholar Thomas Malthus (1766–1834), whose theories appeared in 1798 in "An Essay on the Principles of Population." Malthus took an exceedingly pessimistic view, arguing that human populations are inescapably caught in a conflict between their "need for food" and the "passion between the sexes." Population, he maintained, increases geometrically (2, 4, 8, 16, . . . , thus doubling and redoubling), while food supplies increase only arithmetically (2, 3, 4, 5, . . .). No population can continue to grow indefinitely, because people will increase their numbers to the limit of subsistence. Since populations increase to the ultimate point of subsistence, low standards of living must prevail. Whenever advances in food production improve people's standard of living, thought Malthus, the population inevitably catches up and literally eats away the higher standard of living. The only way to stave off doom was to teach people to restrain their natural sexual urges—to marry later and have fewer children (Malthus did not approve of birth control or abortion). If this was not done, population growth would continue until checked by drastic means: starvation, pestilence, or war.

One of the foremost critics of Malthus was Karl Marx (1867/1976). Malthus had placed the blame for overpopulation and poverty on the individual members of society who succumbed to their sexual urges. For Marx, however, the issue was not overpopulation but underproduction. Marx thought that Malthus had failed to anticipate the full possibilities of the Industrial Revolution, especially technological advances in agriculture. In the United States, for example, modern farm machinery, fertilizers, pesticides, irrigation, hybrid plants, and genetically selected animals have contributed to a more rapid growth in the nation's produce than in its population (though U.S. agricultural surpluses have not ended hunger and starvation in other parts of the world). In fact, for the past fifty years the U.S. government has sponsored programs designed to cut back agricultural production: Farmers receive subsidies to let fields lie fallow. Marx believed that the system of capitalism had the capacity to produce food and other necessities for an indefinitely expanding population. It was only capitalism's unequal distribution of social wealth that made it seem that there had to be a natural limit on population. Moreover, in Marx's view, the system of property relations in capitalism skewed production away from meeting the needs of poor people and toward increasing the accumulation of capital. Capitalists further benefited from the fact that a surplus population created competition for jobs, thus driving down wages and maximizing profits. Marx's solution to the problem of overpopulation was socialism. Thus, whereas Malthus focused on individual actions and sought the answer to population problems in moral restraint, Marx focused on the economic structure of society and sought the solution in a new social order.

Mao Zedong was following Marx's lead when he decreed that China did not need population control, only economic expansion. However, as we saw earlier in this chapter, Mao's successors in the Chinese government disagreed. They believed that if population growth was not slowed drastically, all the benefits of economic improvement would go toward providing basic subsistence for the larger population instead of raising the standard of living. Hence they imposed the limit of one child per family.

Marx may have been too optimistic, but Malthus was too pessimistic. Despite many crises, the world's population (and that of most individual countries) has continued to grow. Marx was right in believing that technological and social factors—not just natural limits—determine how many people the earth can support. Neither Marx nor Malthus, however, anticipated the most basic contribution that modern demography has made to this ongoing debate: the observation that economic development not only increases the food supply and lowers death rates (thus allowing for a larger population), but over the long term generally leads to choices of smaller families and thus to reductions in the rate of population growth. This process is known as the *demographic transition.*

The Demographic Transition

The idea of a **demographic transition** is a generalization from the historical experience of Western Europe (Teitelbaum, 1975). As Europe industrialized during the nineteenth century, fertility rates fell. Demographers theorized that such declining fertility rates could always be expected as a consequence of industrialization. This left two questions open, however. First, what specific characteristics of industrialization caused the decline in fertility rates? Second, must other countries follow the same path? As we will see in the next section, more recent research has improved on the basic idea of demographic transition in response to both these questions. The basic model is still important, however, for even if it doesn't specify the underlying causes of fertility changes, it does indicate the pattern of stages in which population first increases and then levels off in response to decreasing mortality and fertility rates.

The model of the demographic transition consists of four stages that characterize the population dynamics of societies undergoing industrialization (see Figure 19.8). In the first, or preindustrial, stage, both the birth rate and the death rate are high, so the population is relatively stable. In stage 2, the birth rate stays high while the death rate declines as nutrition, health, and sanitation improve. In particular, the infant mortality rate drops, and more babies survive and in due course become parents themselves. Hence, this stage has the potential for explosive population growth. In stage 3, the birth rate also drops as families realize they don't need so many children to provide for their old age and as new economic opportunities develop, especially for women. In stage 4, both the birth rate and the death rate are low and in balance again.

Few countries today are still in stage 1, with high birth and death rates, although this pattern is characteristic of some tribal peoples in Africa. It was also true of China in the years before the Communist Revolution. India, Nigeria, Brazil, and most other developing countries are in stage 2, with transitional high population growth. China, where birth control is becoming widespread, is an example of stage 3. Europe, North America, and Japan are in the fourth and (apparently) final phase, with a low but fluctuating birth rate and a low, steady death rate. Indeed, the number of births has fallen below the number of deaths in some industrialized countries, such as Germany.

The demographic transition should not be seen as a fixed sequence that all industrializing countries inevitably experience. Under some conditions, cultural, political, and other factors have altered fertility and mortality patterns more profoundly than economic development. Right now, for example, in the former communist countries of Eastern Europe, fertility rates are falling much faster than death rates—which may actually be rising. In the midst of great economic uncertainty, people are deciding not to have children. Between 1989 and 1991, Russia's birth rate went down by 15 to 20 percent, and Romania's by 30 percent (*New York Times*, December 31, 1991). At the same time, the quality of health care and nutrition has suffered in communism's collapse.

Stage 2 of the demographic transition brings acute problems in many developing nations. The death rate has dropped precipitously in India, for example, primarily because of the introduction of vaccines and other imported technology (improvements in nutrition and sanitation, crucial to lowering the death rate elsewhere, have been relatively slow). The words of an elderly man in Calcutta capture the suddenness of this change:

> When I was a boy, they took away forty or fifty bodies after a cholera epidemic. It happened every five or ten years. Now they come and vaccinate our children. I have lived here almost seventy years. The biggest change in my time

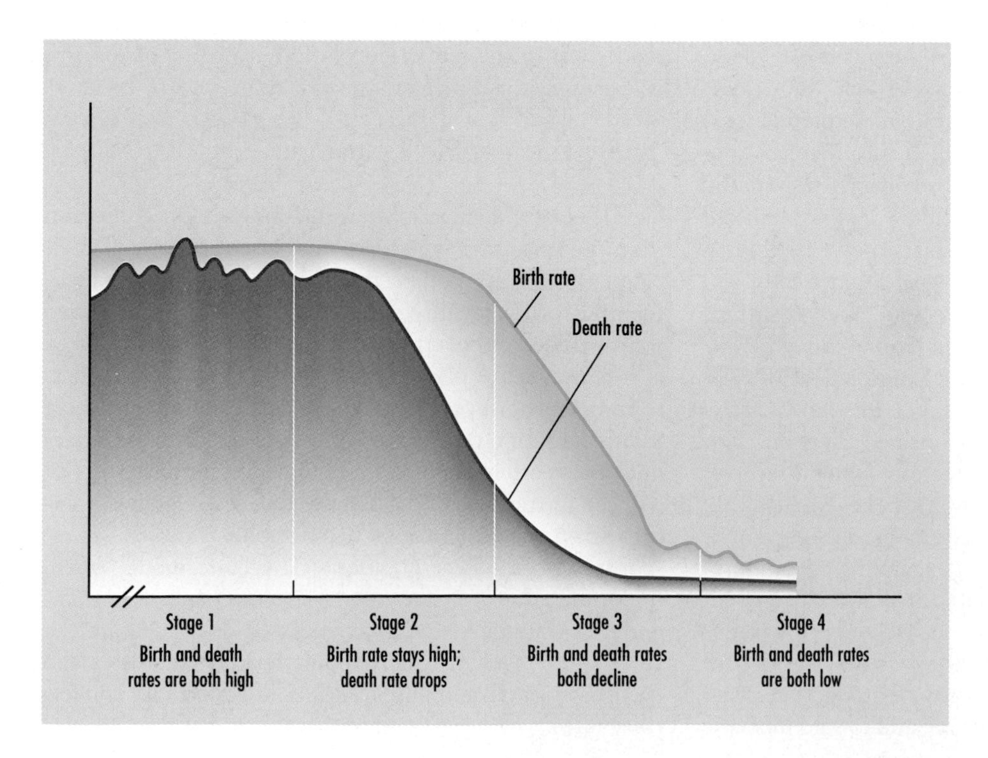

FIGURE 19.8 / The Four Stages of the Demographic Transition in Industrializing Nations

has been health. We've learned to keep from dying. (Quoted in Thomlinson, 1976, p. 29)

Changes that took place over a century or two in the Western world have been compressed into just a few decades in the Third World. The high value that many people place on large families has not changed as rapidly as the technologies that have lowered death rates.

Lowering Fertility Rates

Many groups and organizations today are working to hurry the demographic transition along, encouraging population planning worldwide. Within most developing countries, governments set population policies and charge ministries of health or other agencies with carrying them out. Most of these policies are based on the awareness that high population levels and continued rapid population growth cause social, economic, and environmental problems. Policymakers also want to offer individual parents the opportunity to plan their families better. For example, children are likely to be healthier if they are spaced two years or more apart and if their mothers are neither very young nor very old. These measures also contribute to the control of population growth. When lower rates of population growth become national policy, however, private and public values are likely to clash.

From the perspective of the individual parent, having a large family is likely to make sense. In agricultural societies, for example, children typically produce more than they cost. From the perspective of society as a whole and over the long term, however, population growth is "the master lock on the national poverty trap" (Harrison, 1984, p. 250), not to mention a threat to the global environment and world peace. Paul Harrison draws an analogy between the Third World's desire for many children and the First World's love affair with cars:

> Every household wants [at least one] car to increase its freedom and mobility, but when too many people have one they get stuck in traffic jams, motorways are pushed through their neighborhoods, public transport . . . declines so that eventually people take far longer to get to work than their grandfathers did on the trams. Because everyone strives for individual freedom and mobility, eventually their freedom and mobility are restricted more than ever before. So it is with children. People have large families in a bid to escape poverty, yet their poverty is increased because everyone else is following the same strategy. (1984, pp. 226–227)

People's desire to have children is profoundly influenced by cultural beliefs and economic realities. In much of the Third World, the family functions as a basic economic unit whose success depends on the contributions of children as well as adults.

Cultural Influences on Fertility Rates

The most important influence on a nation's fertility rate is whether people want to have children, and this decision is shaped by ***cultural*** attitudes as well as economic opportunities (Harrison, 1984). Love of children is a universal reason for having them, but culturally specific reasons also play a part. For example, the tradition of *machismo* encourages men in Latin countries to prove their virility by fathering as many children as they can. Even more basically, cultural values and traditional economic incentives combine to make large families attractive. In much of the Third World, the family functions something like a private corporation (Harrison, 1984). The head of the family, usually a man, is responsible for the fortunes of all its members (or stockholders). His success depends not on the accumulation of capital in the modern sense, but on the accumulation of people. Family members, including children, are either the mainstay or the whole of his work force. Children begin performing chores as soon as they are able, and by about age thirteen are full-fledged workers. In the countryside, they work in fields or tend animals; in the city, they may be sent out to peddle small goods or to beg. The head of a large family is likely to wield considerable power and influence in his community. He commands an "army" of kin and through marriages forms alliances with other families, all of whom can be called on in time of need or during feuds over land, water rights, or debts. Equally important, a large family provides extra insurance against old age in countries that do not provide old-age assistance programs. The more children a couple have, the better off they will be in old age.

In particular, families want sons. The reason is not simply that sons often carry on the family name (as we noted in considering China). In general, men earn more than women do, so sons add more to the family coffers before they marry and are better able to support their parents in old age. Furthermore, in Asia sons traditionally receive dowries (money or goods from the bride's family) when they marry. The more sons a couple have, the more they stand to gain (conversely, the more daughters, the more they lose). In countries where death in infancy or childhood is still common, one son is not enough, because he might not survive. According to a Chinese proverb, "One son is no son, two sons are an undependable son, and only three sons can be counted as a real son"; Iranians say, "The first two sons are for the crows" (Harrison, 1984, p. 220). So men envy fathers with several strong sons and women envy the mothers who bore them, because these families often enjoy extra wealth, power, and status.

Changing this cultural outlook is not easy, even when medical advances and better nutrition enable more children to live into adulthood. For many decades, prevailing wisdom held that the key to population control was economic development. According to this view, a country must reach a certain level of modernization (in such areas as industrialization, urbanization, and education) before people will realize the economic advantage of small families. Supporters of this argument (which is central to the supposedly "natural" workings of the demographic transition) point to the rapid fall in birth rates experienced by such newly industrialized countries as Singapore and Korea. However, the pattern is not uniform. Fertility has also declined in countries that have not experienced such major economic gains (Sri Lanka and Costa Rica, for example), but it has remained high in countries that have made substantial economic progress (Brazil and Mexico) (Ehrlich and Ehrlich, 1990).

Contraception and the Status of Women

Rapid population growth can be an enemy of development, so policymakers seek more immediate ways to lower fertility rates. One clearly effective strategy is to make contraception readily available. While it is possible to limit births without modern birth-control devices, it is difficult. Even where such devices are available, they are not always used. Family-planning programs have had to be creative and persistent. Thailand, for example, has used a combination of community involvement and economic incentives to break down taboos against birth control. Carnivals, village fairs, and even weddings feature such birth-control games as condom "balloon-blowing" contests. Vasectomy marathons are held on Labor Day and the king's birthday, with teams of doctors and nurses competing to perform the highest number. Registered family planners, who promote birth control in their home communities, may be rewarded with discounts on the rental of buffaloes to plow their fields, on purchases of fertilizer and seed, and on transport of their goods to market. More than 16,000 villages have their own family-planning centers. About 60 percent of Thai couples practice birth control, and total fertility dropped from 6.1 in 1965–1970 to 2.8 in 1985 (World Bank, 1990). Not all programs are so successful. For example, Kenya initiated family-planning programs in 1967, but with less effective organization and less government support. Kenya still has one of the highest fertility rates and fastest-growing populations in the world (*Euromonitor*, 1992, pp. 179–181).

There are some signs that the overall situation is improving. In 1965, Third World women averaged more than six children each; by 1991, this fertility rate had fallen to 3.9 children. China accounts for much of the improvement, but not all. Demographers estimate that more than 50 percent of Third World women are using some form of contraception (Sinding and Segal, 1991). It is well worth examining the factors that lead women to decide whether or not to take the ***social action*** of limiting family size.

Paul Harrison (1984, p. 231) suggests that deep-seated opposition to birth control is a reflection of sexual politics, specifically men's fear that if women control their own fertility, fathers will lose control over their daughters and husbands over their wives. Women in such settings who want no more babies may be afraid to do so because they fear their husbands will beat them if they find out. Or they may believe that using birth-control devices is sinful because it is against the teachings of the Catholic church. These fears suggest that family planning will be accepted only when and where the status of women improves.

In most Third World countries, women (and children) are "the poorest of the poor" (Harrison, 1984). In many places women cannot inherit land or other property from their fathers or husbands, nor are they permitted to acquire property on their own. Although they supply most of the agricultural labor, they have no rights to the land or to any profits. Agricultural development programs may be run by and restricted to men, on the grounds that admitting women would violate cultural norms. Industrialization often reduces the market for the handicrafts women traditionally produce, and factory jobs may be unattainable because women lack the educational credentials to compete with men. Although Latin American and Caribbean girls are catching up to boys, African and Asian girls are far less likely to attend school than their brothers are. Three-quarters of the women aged twenty-five and older in these regions are illiterate (*The World's Women*, 1991). The net result of all these handicaps is that for many Third World women, marrying and bearing children (preferably sons) is the only way they can achieve security and status. Typically, women marry young and have numerous pregnancies, often losing several children in infancy.

A growing body of research shows that the more education women receive, the fewer children they are likely to bear. One study analyzed the impact on a woman's total fertility of her age at first marriage, level of education, place of residence (rural versus urban), marital status, religion, contraceptive use, and work status in Kenya (Agyei and Mbamanyo, 1989). The researchers found that of all these factors, education had the most impact. Women with secondary or higher education had an average of 3.12 fewer children than did women with no formal education. The second most important factor in reducing fertility was age at first marriage. The two often go together: Women who have equal access to education are likely to postpone marriage longer than those who do not.

A United Nations report (*State of the World Population Report*, 1989) cites education and equal rights for women as two of the prerequisites for lowering fertility. Education provides women with both the know-how and the motivation to limit the size of their families. Educated women are more likely to obtain salaried jobs and so to delay marriage and childbearing. Paid employment not only makes women less dependent on their fathers and husbands but also provides an alternative status to motherhood. Educated women are more likely to know about birth-control services and to be able to use contraceptives properly. Furthermore, schooling presents both sexes with ideas of alternative futures and helps to reduce suspicion of social change, making contraception a less frightening idea.

SUSTAINING THE WORLD'S POPULATION: THE EXAMPLE OF FOOD SUPPLY

The future of humanity and the future of the environment are tightly intertwined. Human beings have colonized some two-thirds of the world's land, and most of the rest is either inaccessible or unproductive mountaintops, ice caps, tundra, or desert (A. Ehrlich, 1991). Technological advances are sometimes described as "freeing" humanity from dependency on nature. But this global takeover has made humankind dependent on the physical environment in new ways—and in the process has threatened that very environment. Already we are straining the earth's capacities to the limit.

It is important to bear in mind that high levels of population are not the only way in which we put stress on the earth's **ecology**—the pattern of relationships between organisms (including humans) and between organisms and their environments. Consumers in the world's rich countries put far more than their share of strain on the earth by demanding abundant energy and foods (like beef), whose production uses up enormous natural resources, and by producing enormous amounts of waste (much of it hazardous). The earth is challenged not just by the numbers of people, in other words, but by how they live. A small number of car-driving, beef-eating, waste-producing Americans pumping water long distances and using air-conditioning so they can live comfortably in the desert may do more ecological damage than ten times as many poor people in the Third World.

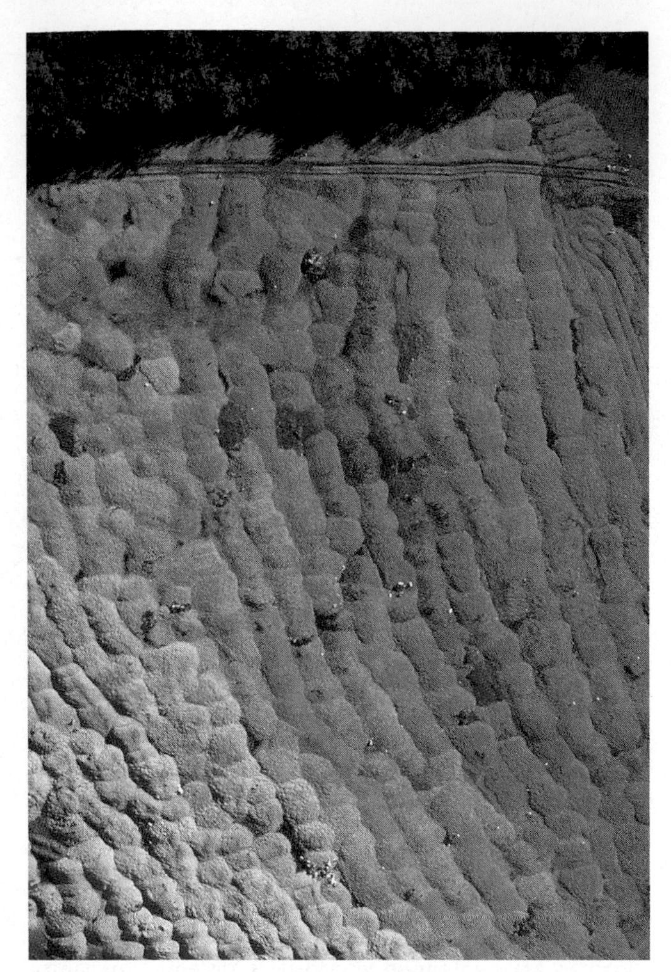

In the developed world, pesticides and herbicides are used to produce food that looks flawless. Many of these chemicals are harmful to human health and to the environment in general—and, ironically, food ends up being thrown out by the ton anyway because it is less than perfect. Each small hill in this aerial photograph (from George Gerster's Below from Above*) is a truckload of discarded, rotting tomatoes or pumpkins.*

Nonetheless, large populations are a source of environmental problems and a strain on resources. Even at a low level of technology, a swelling population is likely to strip land of its forests, largely for fuel. It is likely to overtax water supplies and to foul them with its waste. Perhaps the best example of the tension between population growth and resource allocation has to do with the food supply.

About 1 billion of the earth's 5 billion people have more than enough to eat (Ehrlich and Ehrlich, 1990). Approximately a third of the world's grain is fed to livestock so that the well-to-do, most of whom live in the rich countries of the First World, are supplied with meat, eggs, and dairy products. Perhaps 3 billion more people get enough to eat, though their diets are primarily vegetarian. That leaves nearly a billion people who are chronically hungry, and as many as 400 million who are so undernourished that their health is threatened or their growth is stunted. Severe hunger is concentrated in the Third World, especially Latin America and Africa. The almost continuous famine in the Sahel, the area just south of the Sahara, is virtually the Malthusian nightmare come true. Overpopulation led to excess grazing, cultivation, and water pumping; combined with civil war, it resulted ultimately in mass starvation. In the 1980s, one out of every five children born in this region—5 million infants—died each year from hunger-related causes (Independent Commission on International Humanitarian Issues, 1985).

If all the food produced in the world were distributed equally (and if Westerners ate less meat and milk products), there might be enough to feed everyone on earth today. But there would not be enough left over to accommodate the 95 million additional people who join the population each year. Lester Brown, an agricultural economist and president of the Worldwatch Institute, estimates that 28 million more tons of grain must be harvested each year just to keep pace with population growth in the 1990s (Brown et al., 1990). In Brown's estimation, such expanded food production is unlikely.

From 1950 to about 1984, worldwide grain production increased steadily (though distribution was uneven). The main reason was the so-called **Green Revolution**—the invention of new strains of cereal crops such as corn, wheat, and rice that doubled or tripled the yield per acre. When they were introduced in the 1950s, in countries such as India and Pakistan, these high-yielding grains were hailed as the solution to world hunger. The Green Revolution did produce spectacular short-term gains, but at the price of long-term damage to the environment.

Green Revolution crops depend on intensive agriculture, using high levels of irrigation, fertilizers, and pesticides. This combination takes a toll on the environment. One problem is soil erosion. Every year farmers lose about 24 billions tons of topsoil worldwide (Brown et al., 1990). In addition, much land is exhausted by intensive farming. As a result, more acres must be taken out of cultivation each year. Not enough new fields can be added to replace them, because the amount of land suitable for farming is dwindling. Chemical fertilizers do not replace the soil that is washed away, nor do they substitute for the natural fertility of soil (Ehrlich and Ehrlich, 1990). Rather, they temporarily mask the loss of certain nutrients to crops and erosion. When these fertilizers are washed into rivers and streams, they contribute to pollution by promoting the growth of algae, which consume oxygen and lead to the death of fish. To irrigate high-yield crops, farmers must

In many Third World countries, arable land (suitable for farming) is in very short supply, so every bit must be used. On this hillside in Peru, walls have been built to form terraced plots that can be cultivated. Population growth often makes it necessary to divide land into smaller and smaller plots over the years, making it increasingly hard to use modern farming technology and to support a family.

drill wells ever deeper into the water table, withdrawing more water than nature can replenish. Any successful irrigation is temporary, because it often causes salt buildup or waterlogging, again rendering the land unusable. In short, the Green Revolution is reaching the point of diminishing returns.

Brown holds that farmers will have a difficult time producing grain increases of more than 0.9 percent a year in the 1990s—which is only half the expected population growth rate of 1.8 percent. Even without considering such influences on agricultural output as pollution and global warming, feeding the world in the 1990s and beyond will be a problem. World grain production may continue to increase, but the amount of food per person will decline (see Table 19.1). Brown and others do not see a technological solution on the horizon. Most current research in biotechnology (especially genetic engineering) is aimed at reducing the input or cost of agricultural production, not increasing the output. In the final analysis, the solution is a social one. Writes the French agronomist René Dumont, "The future of the world hinges above all on whether or not we can curb, and then stop, the world's terrifying population explosion" (1990, p. 37).

Besides straining the world's food-producing capacities, rapid population growth means increased pressure to exploit limited, often irreplaceable, natural resources and in-

TABLE 19.1

World Grain Production, Total and Per Capita, 1950–2000

	WORLD GRAIN PRODUCTION			PER CAPITA		
Year	Total (Million Tons)	Change per Decade (Million Tons)	Change per Decade (Percent)	Total (Kilograms)	Change per Decade (Kilograms)	Change per Decade (Percent)
1950	631			246		
1960	847	+216	+34	278	+32	+13
1970	1,103	+256	+30	296	+18	+ 6
1980	1,441	+338	+31	322	+26	+ 9
1990	1,684	+243	+17	316	− 6	− 2
2000 (est.)	1,842	+158	+ 9	295	−21	− 7

Source: Lester R. Brown et al., State of the World 1990. *Worldwatch Institute (Norton, New York, 1990)*, p. 76.

creased pollution of the air and water that sustain all life. Without careful management and international cooperation, the planet itself is endangered.

THE ENDANGERED PLANET

The First Earth Day, in April 1970, was a national event organized by groups of activists whom many Americans regarded as alarmists and kooks. Today, Earth Day is celebrated each year by people of all ages and walks of life in 140 countries. Three out of four Americans describe themselves as "environmentalists," and even many corporate executives have stopped arguing that saving the environment will kill jobs and have begun competing to show how "green" they are (Wald, 1990). The bald eagle, once threatened by DDT, is about to be moved off the endangered species list; the Cuyahoga River no longer bursts into flames as it winds through Cleveland; the tailpipes of new cars emit 75 to 95 percent fewer toxic gases than old models did.

Unfortunately, the good news about the environment is offset by bad. The increasing number of cars means that despite tighter regulations on auto emissions, almost half of Americans live in communities that violate federal clean air standards. The fish that have returned to the Cuyahoga River have so many poisons in their flesh that they are inedible. Worldwide, some 500 million acres of forest (an area equal to that of the United States east of the Mississippi River) were cut down between 1970 and 1990; deserts are spreading on every continent; aquifers (underground water reservoirs formed during the last Ice Age) are being drained; and the air quality in dozens of cities often is so poor that it is dangerous for children to play outdoors. Moreover, new problems, which no one had heard of on the first Earth Day, have surfaced, including the greenhouse effect, holes in the ozone layer, and acid rain.

In this section we will look at the social causes and consequences of *resource depletion* and *pollution*. While it is useful for the sake of discussion to separate these two types of assault on the environment, in reality they are intertwined. Both are results of capitalist economic development. As the sociologist James O'Connor points out, "The natural wealth of the world is depleted and turned into garbage, often dangerous garbage, through global capital accumulation. And the unwanted by-products—pollution—have the effect of depleting [or] exhausting resources." For example, oil is extracted from the earth (depleting resources) and transported to industrial centers, where it is used as fuel (causing pollution) or turned into virtually indestructible products such as plastics (causing further pollution).

This system has also accelerated the division between rich and poor, First World and Third World nations. The Third World provides most of the raw materials for capitalist growth and so suffers greater resource depletion, while industrial nations generate more than their share of pollution. The First World also "exports" pollution to the Third World, not only in the form of dangerous airborne and waterborne chemicals but also as cars, factories, soda cans, and in some cases products and production methods that have been deemed unsafe and banned in the home countries.

Resource Depletion

Human beings have always exploited nature, in the sense of breathing the air, eating plants and animals (probably more of the former than the latter), drinking fresh water, and using skins and tree branches for clothing and shelter. But all these natural resources are renewable, and for most of human existence the population was small and widely scattered. "[H]uman groups therefore consumed [natural resources] no faster than natural processes produced them" (Ehrlich and Ehrlich, 1990, p. 49). Only in recent times did this balance begin to tip. One reason was that humans began to use *nonrenewable resources*—first metals and then fossil fuels (oil, coal, natural gas, and peat)—which took millions of years to form and cannot be replaced. The second reason was population growth, which, combined with increasing demand for goods, has led to the consumption of renewable resources (such as trees and water) faster than they can be replenished, often along with damage to the earth.

Consumption of Fossil Fuels

The fossil fuel we burn today took roughly a million years to develop (Gibbons, Blair, and Gwin, 1989). Oil provides about 40 percent of the world's energy, coal about 30 percent, and natural gas about 20 percent. (Nuclear and hydroelectric plants and, in the Third World, wood and organic wastes such as animal dung provide most of the rest.) Consumption of these resources is not distributed evenly. With less than a quarter of the world's population, industrialized nations consume more than half of the world's available energy (*World Resources, 1990–91*). The United States accounts for the largest share by far: One American

The lifestyle that the typical middle-class American family takes for granted requires wealth, caloric input, and consumption of natural resources at levels that are unthinkable in much of the Third World. The water being used to wash this car is cleaner than the drinking water available in many poor countries. Not many Third World families can afford a car in the first place, or the gasoline required to run it.

uses as much energy as two Japanese or Germans, five Mexicans, thirty-five Indians or Indonesians, and fifty-six Nigerians (Durning, 1990). The root of Americans' dependence on oil is the automobile (Flavin, 1991). Two out of three barrels of oil used in the United States go into the tanks of cars and other light vehicles. Worldwide, the number of vehicles on the road (almost half a billion in 1989) is growing even faster than population (*Euromonitor*, 1992, p. 642). Most cars and drivers are in industrialized nations, but the Third World (especially Asia and South America) is catching up. Although Third World nations use far less oil than First World countries do, their citizens spend a larger proportion of their incomes on fuel, and are the hardest hit when the flow of oil and gas is interrupted.

Dependence on fossil fuels is problematic for several reasons (Flavin and Lenssen, 1991). One is location. About two-thirds of the world's proven oil reserves are in the Persian Gulf area. The same is true for natural gas. As Iraq's invasion of Kuwait in 1990 demonstrated, the Middle East is politically unstable, which makes the global supply of oil unpredictable. A second problem with the current energy system is pollution. Fossil fuels are the major source of both local smog and such world problems as acid rain and global warming (discussed below). Unfortunately, coal, the one fossil fuel available in large quantities on every continent, is also the dirtiest (Gibbons, Blair, and Gwin, 1989). Mining it scars the land, and burning it produces two or three times as much air pollution as the combustion of other fuels.

The third problem is both social and political. People around the world have rebelled against their governments' proposed solutions to energy problems. Some of the first demonstrations against the central government in the Soviet Union were sparked by environmental issues, even before the accident at the nuclear reactor in Chernobyl in April 1986. Because people fear nuclear accidents, radioactive wastes, regular exposure to low levels of radiation (as can occur when people work in nuclear power plants or live near them), and the use of energy technology for secret production of nuclear bombs (as in Iraq), worldwide construction of nuclear plants has almost stopped. Citizens of Germany have voted down nuclear expansion in their country. Plans to build hydroelectric plants in India have been met with massive public protests. Coal-powered, as well as nuclear, energy plants have been blocked by voters in the United States. Citizens may not know exactly what kind of energy they want, but are passionate about what they do *not* want. As a result, U.S. energy policies and practices have shifted from one extreme to another.

For decades, Americans took the availability of cheap energy—and the desirability of huge, gas-guzzling cars—for granted. Then, in the early 1970s, the Organization of Petroleum Exporting Countries (OPEC) imposed an embargo on the sale of oil to the United States. The price of gas skyrocketed, and the federal and many state governments set up a number of programs to encourage conservation: Energy prices were deregulated, minimum efficiency standards set for cars and appliances, tax credits offered for better home insulation, and funds made available for research and development of renewable sources of energy. Between 1973 and 1986, energy efficiency in the United States increased by about 30 percent, oil imports fell from 9 billion barrels a day to 5 billion, and the nation's annual fuel bill decreased by $150 billion (Flavin, 1991). New technologies were developed, such as the photovoltaic cell, which converts sunlight directly into electricity (and which probably powers your pocket calculator). Research funding increased for solar, geothermal, and other non-fuel-consuming energy technologies. Old technologies, such as windmills and wind turbines, were revived. Then, in 1985–1986, when world petroleum prices fell, oil imports and consumption began to creep upward again, and today are back near their peak (Flavin, 1991). Under the Reagan and Bush administrations, regulations were relaxed and conservation programs allowed to lapse, on the grounds that they hurt the economy. Symbolically, the solar-energy panels that used to save on water-heating bills were removed from the White House roof.

This brief history of energy use in the United States shows, first, that people can be motivated to change their energy habits. Further, the technology for more efficient sources of energy already exists. During the war in the Persian Gulf, for example, solar panels in Jordan, Israel, and Cyprus continued to operate, undisturbed by the threat of disrupted oil supplies. Some 6,000 villages in India rely on photovoltaic cells for electricity (Flavin and Lenssen, 1991). "Superinsulated," airtight homes in Sweden use 90 percent less energy than the average American home (*World Resources, 1990–91*). Some homes in California get 40 percent of their electricity from wind turbines (Flavin, 1991). Electronic communications could greatly reduce the energy spent on business travel (Ehrlich and Ehrlich, 1990). None of these technologies alone will replace fossil fuels, but in combination they could help to reduce dependence on more dangerous and less dependable energy sources.

Deforestation

Forests are the lungs of the earth: They absorb carbon dioxide from the atmosphere and exhale oxygen. They also store energy from the sun, bind topsoil to the land, and aid in climate control by capturing and releasing water. They also provide a habitat for innumerable species of plants and animals, serving as a global storehouse of genetic diversity. Ancient forests are not a renewable resource in the sense that they can be replaced simply by replanting and waiting; they represent special ecosystems that developed over hundreds of years and may never be regenerated. But in the 1980s, ancient forests were being cut down at the rate of about 70,000 acres a year (*New York Times*, November 3, 1991, p. E3).

Deforestation is not a new phenomenon; it dates back to the beginnings of agriculture. The ancient Greek philosophers warned of the dangers of overcultivation and overgrazing, especially by goats. They were right: Today Greece is almost a desert, its forests gone and its soil poor and thin (Ehrlich and Ehrlich, 1990). Only about 5 percent of the virgin forests that European settlers found in what is now the United States remain; most were cut down to make way for cattle and crops. Concern is growing that the tropical rain forests of the Southern Hemisphere will suffer the same fate, with severe consequences both for local inhabitants and for the world as a whole.

Some 140 square miles of rain forest are cut down every day (Jagger, 1991). There are two main reasons for this deforestation. One is population pressure: Many people in Third World nations use wood for cooking, heating, and lighting, as well as for houses and furniture. The more people, the more trees they cut down. New trees do not spring up to replace the old ones, especially in the tropics; rather, the deforested land reverts to grass or scrubland, or in some cases desert. So people have to travel farther every day to find wood, and the process of environmental degradation spreads.

The second main reason for rain-forest depletion is commercial development for the global market. Foreign investors or local entrepreneurs strip large areas of rain forest to obtain export lumber and minerals or to make way for ranches and plantations. Examining data on thirty-six countries, the environmental scholar Thomas Rudel (1989) concluded that the main reason for high rates of deforestation in the Third World is population growth. However, in countries with large rain forests, political and economic factors also play a role. Thus the cattle farms in the Amazon produce cheap meat for sale in fast-food chains in the United States, while wood from the forests of Papua New Guinea, Thailand, Malaysia, Colombia, and Cameroon is ground up to make cardboard for packaging electronic equipment in Japan (Ehrlich and Ehrlich, 1990).

Brazil illustrates both patterns of population pressure and commercial development. In the Amazon, Brazil has both the largest remaining tropical forest and the highest rate of deforestation in the world (Goldemberg, 1989; *World Resources, 1990–91*). Under a program begun in the

The tropical rain forest is being destroyed because of population pressure, commercial development for the global timber market, and the need for additional arable land.

1960s, the Brazilian government opened this area for development by building the Trans-Amazonia Highway and other roads, and by offering plots of land at giveaway prices, tax credits, and even a year's wages to people who would settle there (Harrison, 1984). The program was designed both to tap the resources of the Amazon and to solve the problem of overpopulation in northeastern and southern Brazil, where commercial agriculture had left many peasants landless. However, it was carried out with little attention to the ecology of the Amazon basin or its traditional inhabitants. The one requirement was that settlers "improve" or clear their land, usually by cutting and burning off trees. Settlers came in droves, but as often as not the land would not support conventional farming for more than a few years. Most of the energy in rain forests is stored in the trees, not the soil; once they are cut down, the soil's nutrient value deteriorates rapidly. This is why traditional inhabitants practice slash-and-burn agriculture, in which small fields are rotated frequently, allowing the forest to grow back in the unplanted areas. Some settlers made a living by clearing land, selling it to large-scale commercial ranchers, and moving on.

In the late 1980s the invasion and destruction of the Amazon rain forest began to capture world attention. Under international pressure, the Brazilian government suspended tax credits for developers and joined other nations in an Amazon Pact, dedicated to conservation, sustainable use of the area's natural resources, and protection of indigenous peoples. At the same time, however, it began to negotiate with Japan for funds to build a highway connecting the forest with the Pacific seaport of Lima, Peru, to facilitate export of hardwoods. And large landowners still receive tax credits for clearing land to graze cattle (World Bank, 1990).

With some justification, the Brazilian government argues that the United States and other industrialized nations, whose citizens use fifteen times more energy than Brazilians, have no right to demand that Brazil become a leader in conservation. Since deforestation helped to "buy" the development of today's rich countries, perhaps we must pay if we want the citizens of poorer countries to restrict their development to save forests. The future of the Amazon and other tropical forests will require international effort, perhaps in the form of an international protection fund or arrangements with Third World nations to forgive part of their foreign debt in exchange for preservation of natural areas (see the Global Issues/Local Consequences box).

Pollution

Snow in Mexico City? That is what residents of the northern suburb of Ecatepec call the fine white dust that blan-

GLOBAL ISSUES/LOCAL CONSEQUENCES

At Home in the Rain Forest

When environmentalists talk about the impact of destruction of the rain forest, they usually focus on the possible effect on the global climate or the loss of biological and genetic diversity. To many thousands of people, however, losing the forest means losing their home.

Tu'O, from the Malaysian island of Borneo, is a hunter-gatherer turned environmental activist. "To us the forest is everything," he says. "It is like our supermarket and also our bank" (quoted in Ryan, 1991, p. 8). Tu'O's people, the Penan, have lived in the Sarawak forest for as long as they can remember, collecting, hunting, fishing, and growing crops in small clearings. In the last decade, commercial loggers have invaded the region, displacing local people, polluting rivers, eroding hillsides, and leaving ruined forest in their wake. With some companies operating twenty-four hours a day, nearly 2,200 acres of forest are lost daily (Carothers, 1990; Ryan, 1991). The wood is sold internationally for lumber. The Penan and their neighbors, the Kelabit, are fighting back. Thousands have participated in roadblocks, and hundreds have been arrested. The Malaysian courts rejected the first arrests, but a new law makes interfering with logging a state crime.

Resisters to development of the Amazon region in Brazil have fared better in some ways, but worse in others. After much controversy and many deaths, a reserve the size of Missouri was set aside for the Amazon's Yanomamo Indians in 1991. Brazilian labor leader Chico Mendes helped to organize another group, Amazonian rubber tappers, into a national political force. The rubber tappers, who make a living by bleeding natural latex from trees and gathering Brazil nuts (neither of which depletes the resource base), were being squeezed out by ranchers. Under Mendes's leadership the union won four protected areas from the Brazilian government and convinced the Inter-American Development Bank to place environmental restrictions on future loans to Brazil. Mendes paid for his achievements with his life: He was assassinated in December 1988. Amnesty International (1989) estimates that as many as 1,000 union leaders, rubber tappers, peasants, and Indians were killed in the fight over the Amazon during the 1980s.

The activities of the Penan in Sarawak and the Yanomamo and rubber tappers of the Amazon illustrate that deforestation is not simply an enviromental issue, but involves questions of social justice (*World Resources, 1990–91*). The global ecological crisis—a product in part of our affluent lifestyles and our energy- and resource-intensive form of social organization—threatens the local habitats and ecologically benign lifestyles of hundreds of thousands of indigenous people.

kets their houses and streets every morning. The cloud of chemical dust produced by a nearby caustic-soda plant kills trees and shrubs, burns residents' eyes and throats, and is probably responsible for their frequent skin rashes and respiratory diseases. This toxic snow is only one symptom of the growing environmental crisis in Mexico City. In the past forty years the population has grown from 5 million to 16 million, making it the largest metropolitan area on earth and one of the most polluted. Nearly 3 million vehicles and tens of thousands of poorly regulated factories, some of which burn tires or sawdust soaked in fuel oil, pour an estimated 4.35 million tons of pollutants into the atmosphere each year. In the city's vast squatter settlements, latrines and sewers are rare; the dust carries dried fecal matter and such infectious microorganisms as salmonella and streptococcus. The banks of the Rio de los Remedios are lined with trash, and the river itself is a stream of black sludge. Oil from industrial discharge shimmers on the surface, while untreated sewage decaying below the surface sends up bubbles of gas. The U.S. government pays its diplomatic staff a 10 percent hardship bonus for having to breathe Mexico City's air, rents them houses outside the city, and advises women not to have babies while on duty there (*New York Times*, May 12, 1991, pp. A1, 7).

Mexico City may be a worst-case pollution scenario, but it captures the impact of uncontrolled population growth, urbanization, and industrialization on the environment—and serves as a warning. The production of waste is a natural part of life. Waste becomes **pollution** when so much is produced that it overloads natural recycling processes, or when human beings produce materials (such as plastics and radioactive dust) that cannot be broken down by natural processes. Pollution is made into a crisis by two social factors: (1) new technologies with new waste products and (2) levels of population density (the number of people per square mile) unprecedented in world history.

Population growth must be viewed in the context of the environmental, social, and other problems of Third World cities. This photograph of Mexico City shows air pollution so severe that it is health-threatening—a dramatic example of urban growth that has outstripped the social infrastructure's ability to prevent or control it.

Air Pollution

Air pollution first became a problem during the Industrial Revolution. By the beginning of the twentieth century, many cities in Europe and North America were blanketed with smoke, soot, and ash—the by-products of industrialization (*World Resources, 1990–91*). In 1952, a "black fog" covered London, killing 4,000 people and making tens of thousands sick (French, 1990). At mid-century, air pollution was mainly a local problem, but since then its impact has become global—for example, with the destruction of the earth's ozone layer.

Efforts to control air pollution have brought progress in some places (*World Resources, 1990–91*). The concentrations of such common pollutants as sulfur dioxide, which contributes to respiratory diseases and acid rain, have declined in twenty of the thirty-three cities that participate in the United Nations' Global Environmental Monitoring System (GEMS). By restricting automobile emissions and requiring power plants to install cleaning devices, Sweden, Austria, Switzerland, and western Germany have cut pollution rates by almost two-thirds.

For every success story, however, there are failures and setbacks. The former communist countries were among the world's worst polluters, driven by the imperative to produce industrial goods at all costs (see Chapter 16). In Eastern Europe, the former Soviet Union, and much of the developing world, there are still no emission controls on industry or vehicles. In the beautiful ancient city of Krakow, Poland, damage to historical buildings is so severe that people speak of the stone as "melting." In fourteen of the cities GEMS monitors in China, sulfur dioxide levels are rising and now stand three to five times as high as in North America.

In addition to these local pollution problems, many modern practices and technologies are contributing to a more general destruction of the earth's atmosphere. The atmosphere functions like a blanket to trap warmth from the sun and keep rivers and oceans from freezing, and to shield the earth from harmful ultraviolet rays. In recent years, pollution from human activities has begun to threaten both functions. The **greenhouse effect** refers to the way atmospheric gases, like the roof of a greenhouse, trap heat. The most common "greenhouse gases" are water vapor, carbon dioxide, methane, nitrous oxide, and ozone. Life on earth depends on the maintenance of a certain level of concentration of greenhouse gases in the atmosphere. With too few, the earth would be as frozen as Mars, and with too many, as hot as Venus. The concentration of these gases, which has been growing since the beginning of the Industrial Revolution, has accelerated rapidly in recent decades. The main reasons are the burning of fossil fuels and the cutting and burning of forests (live trees collect and store carbon, but burning trees releases it).

The current scientific consensus is that if this trend continues, it will probably cause global warming (*World Resources, 1990–91*). This increase in average temperatures, in turn, might cause the polar ice caps to melt and the oceans to rise, flooding many cities; droughts in the major breadbaskets of the world, such as the American Midwest; mass migrations and extinctions of plant and animal species; and changes in the distribution of disease-bearing organisms. No one knows exactly how severe global warming might be, but there is clear cause for concern. Although developed nations are prime contributors to the greenhouse effect, developing nations also make a contribution, which increases as their populations grow (see Figure 19.9).

Of special concern are the chlorofluorocarbons (CFCs), synthetic chemicals used in refrigeration, air conditioners, plastics, and aerosol sprays. When they reach the lower levels of the atmosphere, CFCs act as greenhouse gases, trapping heat; in the upper atmosphere, CFCs damage the layer of ozone that protects people, animals, and plants from the sun's ultraviolet rays. Ultraviolet rays not only increase the risk of skin cancer and cataracts in humans but also weaken the human immune system, interfere with photosynthesis (especially in algae and broadleaf plants like soybeans), and damage DNA (the genetic material on which all life depends) (Ehrlich and Ehrlich, 1990). How much damage has already been done to the ozone layer and what effect this will have on earth are uncertain.

It is certain that acid rain, the result of air pollutants trapped in water vapors, falls on every continent, changing the chemistry of lakes and rivers so that fish can no longer survive and damaging crops and trees. In Northern Europe alone, 125 million acres of forest have been affected. Acid rain illustrates that pollution does not respect political boundaries: Often the sources of pollution are far from the effects.

Water Pollution

Water pollution from human activity dates back to antiquity, but the scope and severity of the problem are increasing. There are three basic sources of pollution of the earth's fresh water (*World Resources, 1990–91*). One is domestic waste, which has become a critical problem in Third World cities like Mexico's capital. Untreated sewage dumped into waterways not only carries health-threatening bacteria but also depletes the water of oxygen that is essential to aquatic life. A second source is industrial waste, a problem in all cities and, increasingly, industrialized suburbs. A third source is land use. As we noted earlier, when land is cleared for agriculture, erosion becomes more common and pesticides and fertilizers leach into both

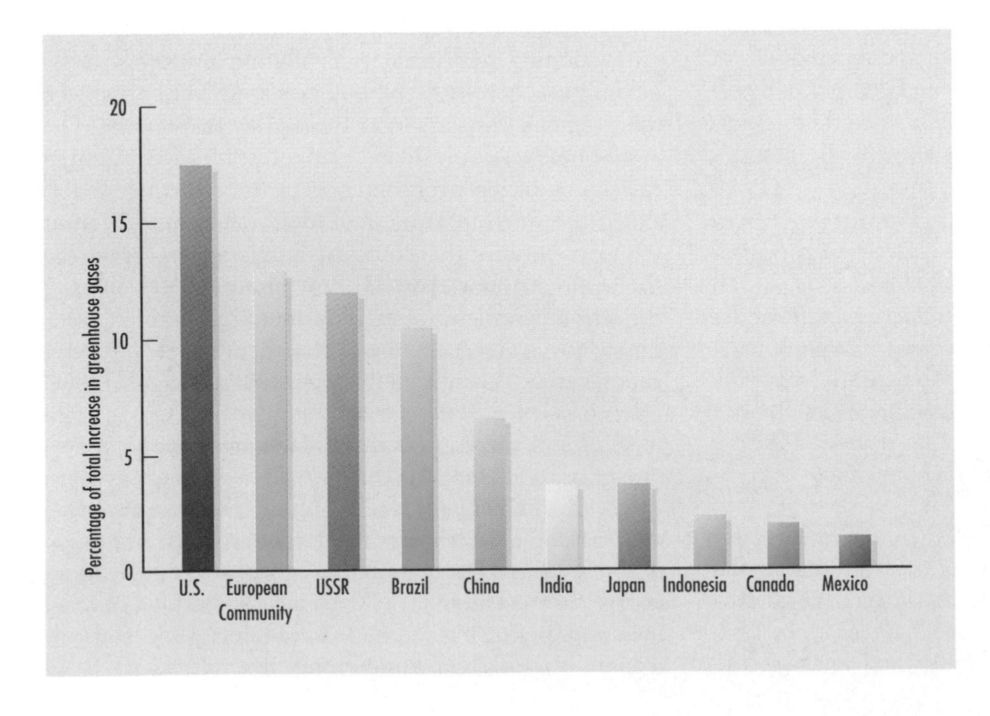

FIGURE 19.9 / The Ten Countries with the Most Greenhouse-Gas Emissions, 1987

Source: *World Resources, 1990–91* (World Bank, Washington, D.C., 1991), p. 3.

groundwater and waterways. Dense human habitation—cities—is even more destructive than agriculture.

Water pollution combines with depletion of water reserves to threaten a critical shortage of clean drinking water. Already, many people in the world lack access to safe drinking water, and most of the lakes and rivers in the world (including most of the United States) are polluted to some degree. We tend to behave as if water is so plentiful that it's almost free, but in many developing countries people now pay a significant percentage of their disposable incomes for drinking water. Others must walk as much as two hours a day to haul it. This is a clear example of a more general sociological phenomenon: As supplies of natural resources dwindle and pollution spreads, access to the resources that once seemed equally given to all humankind comes to depend more on ability to pay. Those who can afford it move from central cities to suburbs for clean air. Cities like Los Angeles buy water from hundreds of miles away, often pricing it out of the reach of farmers nearer the source. Oil and gas are already out of the reach of most Third World consumers.

There is little doubt that human activity, particularly during the last century, has endangered the planet. The question is whether human activity can save it.

Toward a Sustainable World

A sustainable world is one in which economic growth and development are limited to levels that maintain the earth's ecology (Ruckelshaus, 1989). In the words of Lester Brown,

> An environmentally sustainable global economy is one where trees cut and those planted are in balance, where soil erosion does not exceed new soil formation, where carbon emissions do not exceed carbon fixation, where human births and deaths are in balance, where the ozone layer is stable, and where the extinction of plant and animal species does not exceed the rate at which new species evolve. (1990, p. 2)

Brown recommends a number of conservation measures, all of which have been implemented by some countries, but not everywhere or in a consistent manner. These include:

Stabilizing population size. China cut its population growth in half in just six years by imposing its one-child policy; Japan and Thailand did the same in about eight years with less severe methods.

Raising energy efficiency. In the United States, more energy leaks out of poorly insulated buildings than flows through the Alaska pipeline. Much of the Third World's energy literally goes up in smoke. The technology to end both sources of waste already exists.

Harnessing the sun's energy. Thousands of villages in India and elsewhere are already collecting energy from free-standing photovoltaic installations; a solar plant in the Mojave Desert is producing electricity at a lower cost than that of nuclear power.

Reusing and recycling materials. The one-way flow of raw materials to consumption-oriented societies can be reduced significantly by minimizing packaging, reusing glass and hard plastic containers, recycling paper and tin cans, and using waste for fuel. Japan and the Netherlands have already taken giant steps in this direction. Many U.S. cities and communities are also moving in this direction.

Reforesting. Planting trees may be the easiest way to combat global warming. Australia and the United States have plans to create millions of acres of new forest.

Stabilizing the soil. Deteriorating cropland should be retired where possible. Elsewhere, efforts should be made to plant living fences of trees or hedges to stop wind erosion, to do terracing and soil contouring, and to implement other soil-conservation techniques.

This is not to suggest that recycling newspapers, bottles, and cans will save the earth; the problems run very deep. As Brown suggests, these are just first steps in a needed "wholesale restructuring of priorities." Eliminating acid rain will require international cooperation; reversing deforestation will cost jobs in rich as well as poor countries; slowing population growth entails major changes in cultural values; so would a shift from reliance on private cars to public transportation. But here, too, precedents exist. When threatened with war, societies have accomplished seemingly impossible feats of mobilization. Now, as in wartime, the survival of the world is at stake. As the leading consumers of resources and polluters of the air and water, developed nations must lead the way. But poorer nations must also be armed for the battle.

Thinking Back on the Key Concepts

Population structure is among the most important and most basic aspects of ***social structure***. Population structure includes not only the numbers of various groups within a population but also their distribution in space and in relation to social categories such as age. Population structure, as we have seen in this chapter, changes in response to ***social action*** and to changing patterns of ***culture***. Individual people make decisions about bearing children, but the action in question is always social—it always takes two people, even if they are not married. Decisions to marry later (or not at all), to use contraception, and to send daughters to school are all factors that contribute to lower fertility rates, which in turn shape population structure. Changes in cultural values can have the same effect: Americans now hold an ideal of a two-child family; citizens of China are encouraged to have just one child, and the government is trying to change cultural ideas like the strong preference for sons over daughters.

Population changes are ***functionally integrated*** with many other aspects of social life and with the natural environments of which human beings are a part. Decisions to have smaller families, for example, fit functionally with the transition from agricultural societies (where children can contribute to farm labor) to industrial and even postindustrial ones (where children are costly and offer less economically and where it may be more common for both parents to work outside the home).

Finally, we noted that many of the factors that stand in the way of solutions to worldwide ecological problems have to do with social ***power***. For example, independent countries are unwilling to give up power over their own economic, demographic, and other decisions in order to make possible international action on environmental issues like saving rain forests. Multinational corporations sometimes use their power to get Third World governments to allow them to conduct business in ecologically unsound ways, such as by polluting the air or water.

SUMMARY

1. Demography is the study of how births, deaths, and migration affect the composition, size, and distribution of populations. Sociologists use demographic information to describe social structure, to evaluate the cumulative impact of individual decisions, and to predict future trends.

2. China is the world's most populous country, with nearly a fifth of the world's people. Through the use of rigidly enforced family planning policies, it has also become one of the most successful Third World examples of population control, accounting for most of the world's reduction in fertility during the 1980s.

3. The main source of population data is the census, a periodic counting of the population and a collection of information about it. A full census of the U.S. population is conducted every ten years. The census attempts to reach every person in the country, but may underestimate the numbers of poor, males, minorities, and immigrants especially.

4. Population growth depends on the relationship among three demographic variables: fertility (the number of births an average woman will have in her lifetime), mortality (usually expressed as the number of deaths in a given age group), and migration. In the twentieth century, fertility rates in the United States have dropped steadily (except for the post–World War II baby boom); mortality rates have also dropped; and life expectancy has increased. But the main source of population growth has been immigration. The age structure of a population depends on the proportion of people in different age groups.

5. Until fairly recently the world's human population grew slowly, in fits and starts. Beginning in about 1850, our population began to spiral upward. Barring mass epidemics, famine, or nuclear holocaust, it will reach 8.5 billion in 2025, and four out of five people will live in the Third World.

6. Thomas Malthus was the first scholar to analyze population growth and to worry about its consequences for humankind. He felt that increases in the food supply could never keep pace with population growth. The only way to halt population growth, in his opinion, was voluntary abstinence from sexual relations; otherwise population growth would be checked drastically by war, pestilence, or starvation.

7. Karl Marx took exception to Malthusian doctrine, believing that the problem was not one of overpopulation but of underproduction and the inequitable distribution of the world's wealth. Whereas Malthus saw the solution to the world's problems in moral restraint, Marx sought the solution in socialism.

8. The basic model of population change in the West over the past two centuries is known as the *demographic transition.* In stage 1, high birth and death rates keep population size stable. In stage 2, the death rate begins to decline as public hygiene and sanitation improves and better food supplies become available. Population grows rapidly. In stage 3, the birth rate drops, too. Finally, in stage 4, as in the industrialized nations today, the birth and death rates are low and in balance again.

9. Demographers are cautious about applying the model of the demographic transition to the developing world, however. In much of the Third World, death rates have dropped precipitously in a very short time because of imported technology. But birth rates are high and are likely to remain so as long as large families provide individual advantages. A number of studies show that the surest way to reduce fertility is to raise the status of women.

10. Already the Malthusian nightmare is a reality for millions of people. As population growth puts a strain on available resources, hunger, starvation, environmental deterioration, underemployment, and civil unrest become increasingly common.

11. Awareness of human threats to the environment has grown, but not enough to halt or significantly slow the depletion of natural resources and pollution. Resource depletion is most obvious in the use of nonrenewable fossil fuels (especially by American drivers), which entails political as well as environmental risks, and in destruction of forests (often tropical forests in the Southern Hemisphere).

12. Pollution is most obvious in Third World cities. Scientists now realize that pollution is not merely a local problem but has global consequences, especially the greenhouse effect and global warming, destruction of the ozone layer, and acid rain. Likewise, reversing such trends will require a reordering of priorities on a global scale.

REVIEW QUESTIONS

1. How is population structure different from population distribution? (Illustrate your definitions with examples.)

2. How does the U.S. census work?

3. Discuss the role of the three central variables in demographic analysis: fertility, mortality, and migration.

4. What is the demographic transition?

5. How do resource depletion and pollution endanger the planet?

6. What is meant by a sustainable world?

CRITICAL THINKING QUESTIONS

1. Think of a city or town that you know well. How would you describe its population structure?

2. Malthus and Marx disagreed over the question of whether the world's population could grow indefinitely or would necessarily be blocked by natural limits. What factors did both of them overlook? If they had stressed the key sociological concept of culture, how would their thinking have been helped?

3. What factors could prevent the demographic transition from proceeding through all its potential stages to the point where lowered fertility rates match lowered death rates?

4. The chapter focuses on resource depletion and pollution as two major factors endangering the earth. Identify at least two other factors and explain why they might be important as well.

5. The chapter describes a number of conservation measures that might contribute to a sustainable world. Do you think these measures alone will accomplish the goal? Are there others that would help? What are some strategies that might make more people comply with conservation measures?

GLOSSARY

Age structure The pattern that results from the distribution of members of a population into different age categories.

Birth cohort A category of people who were born in the same year or in a small number of consecutive years.

Census A periodic counting of a population, in which certain facts on age, sex, occupation, and the like, are also recorded.

Demographic transition A three-stage process in which a population shifts from a high birth rate and a high death rate, to a high birth rate but a low death rate and hence rapid population growth, to a low birth rate, a low death rate, and a more or less stable population.

Demography The scientific study of how births, deaths, and migration affect the composition, size, and distribution of populations.

Ecology The pattern of relationships between organisms (including humans) and between organisms and their environments.

Emigration The movement of people *out* of an area.

Fertility rate (fertility) The average number of births a woman will have in her lifetime.

Green Revolution The creation of new strains of wheat, rice, and other grains that doubled and tripled the yield per acre, in the late 1950s.

Greenhouse effect The collection of gases in the earth's atmosphere that trap heat and may lead to global warming.

Immigration The movement of people *into* an area.

Infant mortality rate The number of deaths among infants under one year of age per 1,000 live births in a given year.

Internal migration Movement from one location to another *within* a society.

Life expectancy The average number of years of life remaining for an individual of a given age.

Life span The maximum number of years of human life.

Migration rate The difference between the number of people who leave and those who arrive each year, per 1,000 people.

Pollution Damage to the environment caused by waste levels that overload natural recycling systems or by synthetic materials that cannot be broken down by natural processes.

Population distribution The proportions of people in world regions, countries, provinces, states, cities, neighborhoods, and blocks.

Population structure The pattern that results from the age, sex, education, income, occupation, marital status, race, and religion of members of a population.

Replacement rate The fertility rate at which a population will remain stable (in the absence of immigration).

CHAPTER 20

Communities and Urbanization

Diagonal, Iowa, is the kind of place most Americans picture when they think about small towns (Hundley, 1989). Main Street climbs three blocks, past a collection of storefronts, to the top of a gentle hill. From there one can see the surrounding countryside spread out toward the horizon like a patchwork quilt in amber, green, and brown. The heart of Diagonal is the high school gymnasium, which holds about 1,000 spectators. On winter nights, when the basketball team is playing, the gym is packed to the rafters, even though the entire population of Diagonal is only 362. In 1938, the tiny school won the state championship, overpowering big-city schools in a season that seemed like a Hollywood movie script. That championship season has become part of local legend, passed from generation to generation.

The legend lives on: Fifty years later the high school is still producing winning basketball teams, despite an enrollment of just forty-two students. Almost every boy in the school turns out for the team, and hopes for this season—as usual—are running high. A five-foot, eleven-inch senior is reputed to be one of the slickest guards in the state, and sure to earn a small-college scholarship. The old-timers in bib overalls who gather for coffee in the Lion's Club on Main Street are speculating on how far the Maroons will go this year. So are pairs of small boys who dig into chocolate fudge sundaes at the counter of the local café, under the watchful eyes of older women in print dresses who exchange recipes and gardening tips over shortcake.

Except for basketball nights, teenagers find Diagonal deadly dull; but the adults, many born and raised in the town, can't imagine a better life. Says one who returned after a spell in Philadelphia:

> People don't get lost. It's a sense of things being small enough that you can have an impact. A school play or a band recital is a major community activity in a small town. People are involved. They aren't home flipping the remote control in front of the TV set. When you walk down the street or go into a grocery store, people are glad to see you. It's totally different from when I used to go into a supermarket in Philadelphia. (Quoted in Hundley, 1989, p. 21)

New York City is 1,000 miles away from Diagonal, but considering its lifestyle, the distance seems more like 200,000. On Manhattan's Upper West Side, Columbus Avenue is a center of conspicuous consumption. Young urban professionals stroll through its stores on weekends, buying $400 sports jackets and $200 slacks, perfect for sitting in a fashionable café sipping Perrier at $5 a glass. On a typical Sunday thousands of people are part of this Yuppie scene. Some come from the suburbs and some from other sections of New York City, but a great many are Upper West Siders. They all live in the same small area (five blocks wide by about twenty-seven blocks long). Yet while browsing through a new shop, dining in a restaurant, or drinking at a bar, they usually do not know *any* of the people around them. The Upper West Side is decidedly a "community" of strangers. Each resident is acquainted with only a tiny fraction of its population of 100,000 (McKeon, 1985; Morrisroe, 1985).

In almost every way, Diagonal and the Upper West Side of Manhattan appear to be opposites. In Diagonal everyone knows everyone else personally; people are involved in a continual round of community-centered activities (the few who do not participate are thought aloof and antisocial); and everyone's activities are subject to close scrutiny. Gossip keeps most Diagonal residents from stepping very far out of line. Of course, sexual transgressions, public drunkenness, and teenage vandalism occasionally take place, but serious crime is rare. On the Upper West Side most people know only a few of the people who live in their apartment building; everyone has his or her own circle of friends; and community-based activities are rare (such as the occasional block party). Neighborliness is often considered nosiness. Anonymity is the norm, and widely different lifestyles are tolerated or simply ignored. At the same time, crime is common: Most Upper West Side residents either have been the victim of a mugging or robbery or know someone who has been.

Can we therefore conclude that the Upper West Side is nothing at all like Diagonal? Not quite. As you will see later in this chapter, traditional communities—and sometimes entirely new kinds of communities—thrive in even the most urbanized settings.

This chapter takes a sociological look at life in towns, suburbs, and cities, focusing on Europe and the United States (see Chapter 18 for a look at community life in the Third World). The organization of these communities is ***functionally integrated*** with that of the larger societies of which they are parts; they are joined economically, for example, to places that sell them goods and buy what they produce and politically to a government that regulates life throughout the country. Indeed, functional integration on a global scale now links American communities to others throughout the world. Communities are also units of ***social structure***. They are among the building blocks that make up the organization of whole countries, and at the same

A small town like Diagonal, Iowa (above), *and a big city like New York* (right) *develop very different kinds of community life and social organization. Diagonal has only 362 residents, while New York City has 7 million. If the state closes Diagonal's school for lack of students, the town will lose a social institution that holds the community together and gives it identity. In New York, it is impossible for everybody to know everybody else, as people do in Diagonal; crowding, crime, and ethnic conflict undercut the sense of community; but some social institutions—like the city's professional sports teams—still give New Yorkers a strong sense of shared identity.*

time they are internally structured by differences in wealth and ethnicity.

Urbanization, the process by which small towns grow into cities, is a transformation of social structure. Urbanization also affects ***culture***. Communities have their own local cultural traditions. Community is also valued as a way of life, and Americans want to know whether growth and other changes threaten to undermine the close connections associated with the culture of small towns. Urbanization is not entirely a "natural" process; it is a result of ***social action*** and ***power***. Individual people decide whether to move to big cities or stay put in small towns; but their decisions are shaped by the power of those in charge of corporations to close factories and offices in or near older cities in order to build new facilities in rural areas or small towns where costs are lower. Different sorts of communities are also the contexts for different kinds of social action—from charity to crime—and for the use of power to promote one and try to control the other. The role of both police and churches thus is shaped by whether they exist in large, relatively impersonal urban areas or in small towns where most people know one another.

We begin this chapter by examining whether urbanization—the growth of big cities—has destroyed community or has simply given new form to the kinds of close, enduring relationships found in small towns like Diagonal. Second, we consider the historical process of urbanization: where and when cities first appeared and why and how they developed. Third, we look more closely at the contemporary urban environment and evaluate several theories that attempt to explain its spatial organization. We conclude the chapter by examining current trends in rural, urban, and suburban communities.

THE EFFECTS OF URBANIZATION ON COMMUNITY

Urbanization is the process whereby large numbers of people leave the countryside and small towns to settle in cities and surrounding metropolitan areas. Thus, urbanization involves migration from sparsely populated regions to densely populated ones. The scope of this migration has been enormous in the twentieth century. In 1900, 86.4

percent of the world's population lived in rural areas, and only 13.6 percent lived in cities. Today, 45 percent of the world's population are city dwellers (Palen, 1987). Densely populated urban regions have become a dominant feature of the modern landscape.

Sociologists have disagreed sharply on the consequences of urbanization. Some emphasize the positive. They view cities as the high point of human civilization: as places where people of different backgrounds can mingle and exchange ideas and outlooks, places that encourage innovations in business, science, technology, and the arts. Other sociologists contend that the problems of city life outweigh the benefits. Cities, they say, are polluted, crime-ridden, hectic environments that promote stress and mental illness. This debate centers on whether urbanization has meant a loss of community. By *community*, sociologists mean more than a particular place inhabited by people; the term also describes a certain quality of relationships. People who form a **community** have common values and interests, engage in frequent face-to-face interactions, feel close to one another, and tend to think of themselves as part of a group (they have a sense of "we-ness"). In effect, a community is a large primary group (see Chapter 8).

What effect has urbanization had on community? Sociologists suggest three different answers (A. Hunter, 1978). One is that large, densely populated urban areas like the Upper West Side have destroyed all possibility of community. A second view holds that a sense of community similar to that of Diagonal persists within the neighborhoods of even the biggest, most populated cities: New York, Chicago, and Boston have enclaves where relationships are in some ways like those in small towns. A third view argues that urbanization has given rise to a new kind of community, one that does not depend on people living near one another. In the following sections we will explore the evidence for each of these perspectives.

The Disintegration of Community

The idea that urbanization destroys community has deep roots in sociology. As early as 1887 the German sociologist Ferdinand Tönnies contrasted social relations in a community (which he called a *Gemeinschaft*) to those in a society or "association" (which he called a *Gesellschaft*). Tönnies viewed small towns as the model for *Gemeinschaft*. In a ***Gemeinschaft***, each person is embedded in a close-knit network of relatives and friends. Members of the community have a common ancestry and common values, aspirations, and traditions, as well as many common roles. Shared histories, common activities, and frequent face-to-face relations help to create strong social and emotional bonds. In a *Gemeinschaft*, status tends to be ascribed at birth: The squire's son does not become a tenant farmer, and the tenant farmer's son does not marry a daughter of the gentry. People tend to remain what they were born to be. Geographic mobility is also limited: Most individuals live and die in the same small area. As a result, people think of their identity in terms of their place within the community.

Urban, industrial society, according to Tönnies, is dramatically different. It is a ***Gesellschaft*** because people are linked together through formal organizations and markets, rather than informal relations and a sense of belonging. Big cities epitomize *Gesellschaft*. Their dense populations guarantee that many of the people who encounter each other in the course of a typical day will be strangers, and their interactions will be impersonal. Relationships tend to be very superficial, even with neighbors. Often neighbors come from very different backgrounds, so they may not share ancestry, values, norms, or attitudes. Nor are they likely to have the same work roles, since work in urban society is highly specialized. All these differences create social distance. Those ties which urban dwellers do have tend to be fragmented. Friends may live across town, co-workers miles away, and relatives on the other side of the country. Finally, urbanites are extremely mobile. In the United States, one out of every ten people moves each year. Urbanites also move socially, leaving old friends behind as they make new ones.

Tönnies saw urbanization, the shift from *Gemeinschaft* to *Gesellschaft*, as one of the defining trends of the modern era. He regretted this development, for he thought it meant a loss of community. He was not the only European sociologist to believe that urbanization exacts a toll. In a classic essay, "The Metropolis and Mental Life" (1902–1903/1950), the German sociologist Georg Simmel also looked at interaction patterns in urban areas. He focused partly on the effects of the noisy, crowded, hectic backdrop to urbanites' everyday dealings with one another. According to Simmel, such constant stimulation encourages people to develop a blasé attitude toward what is going on around them. This attitude enables them to screen out much of what they see and hear, thus shielding them from emotional exhaustion or what we today call *psychic overload* (Milgram, 1970). The result is that city dwellers seem to be cold and heartless, indifferent to the feelings and actions of others. This protective shell contrasts sharply with the mutual concern and caring typical of people in very small towns. On the other hand, Simmel thought that urban life was much more conducive to the development of individuality, partly because its ***social structure*** allows

The word "community" describes the kind of social bond that exists among people as well as the physical layout of their settlement. Many Native American tribes were nomadic hunters and gatherers. After their defeat by the U.S. military in the nineteenth century, they were forced to live permanently on isolated reservations that often lacked a subsistence base. As a result of this destruction of their culture, for many decades the community of Native Americans was in steep decline.

anonymity and a wide variety of personal relationships.

In the United States, Louis Wirth (1938) echoed the ideas of Tönnies and Simmel. Wirth was a member of the University of Chicago's department of sociology, which did a great deal to develop the field of urban sociology. On the basis of his studies of Chicago during the 1920s and 1930s, Wirth argued that city populations have three main structural characteristics: large size, high density (crowding), and great heterogeneity (many differences among people). Each of these characteristics, according to Wirth, tends to discourage close personal relationships. For instance, a large population makes it impossible for everyone to know everyone else. Because the Upper West Side of Manhattan has 100,000 residents and is part of a city of 7 million and a metropolitan region of 19 million, most social encounters are necessarily superficial. Similarly, dense populations can give rise to friction and irritation, as people find it hard to obtain space and privacy. Wirth agreed with Simmel that the closer the physical contact that people must have with strangers, the more distant their social relations will be. Finally, a heterogeneous population can undermine close personal ties. When neighbors do not share values, norms, and attitudes, they tend to lose the sense of "we-ness" characteristic of community.

Wirth linked the impersonal nature of city life to the spread of serious social problems. When people feel isolated and cut off from emotional support, they are more vulnerable to mental breakdowns, depression, and suicide. Similarly, an indifferent attitude toward others can permit increased rates of crime, delinquency, and corruption. Urban residents are more likely to prey upon each other because they think of their neighbors as anonymous faces, not as individuals. Moreover, deviance in cities is difficult to control because people do not keep an eye on one another and condemn wrongdoers, as small-town residents do. Instead, city dwellers try to maintain social order through formal mechanisms of control: the law, the police, the courts. These are seldom as effective as the informal social pressures that operate in villages and towns.

Empirical evidence suggests that Wirth may have overstated his case in claiming that urban life breeds serious social problems. After reviewing a number of studies, Harvey Choldin (1978) concluded that population density is not the primary cause of crime and juvenile delinquency. Rather, these social problems are based on a variety of ***social-structural*** factors, such as the racial mix of a population or the distribution of wealth and jobs, which vary considerably from one city to another.

The Persistence of Community

Other sociologists have questioned the notion that traditional community ties cannot survive in large, modern cities. In their view, many urban neighborhoods are similar to small towns in both social structure and interaction patterns. Herbert Gans was one of the first sociologists to collect evidence for this view. In 1957, he rented an apartment in Boston's West End so that he could observe life there firsthand. At the time, the West End of Boston was a low-income, working-class district of about 7,000 people living in three- and five-story tenement buildings. Most of the residents were second- and third-generation Italian-Americans, although enclaves of Poles, Jews, Greeks, Ukrainians, and other nationalities could be found there, too. Government officials considered the West End a decaying slum and planned to demolish it; but Gans found that the area's ***social structure*** made it far from the depersonalized, alienating kind of place that Wirth had described. In fact, he discovered that the West End was a community with the same close, enduring ties and networks of mutual support thought to exist only in very small towns. When Gans wrote a book about West End residents, he aptly titled it *The Urban Villagers* (1962).

Gans believed that what made the West End an urban village was interpersonal relationships. Obviously, all 7,000 West End residents were not intimately acquainted; but they did know and routinely talked with the neighbors on their own blocks. A very active social life took place in the hallways of apartment buildings, in shops, on stoops, and on the streets. Neighbors would greet one another, stop to chat, and catch up on gossip. In this way West Enders learned about other members of their own ethnic groups, even about people they had never met. They might hear that a friend's second cousin three blocks away had just given birth to twins, or that the father-in-law of another friend's niece had lost his job. Through such intimate personal information, West Enders felt connected to hundreds of others around them. They knew one another's joys and sorrows, strengths and weaknesses, triumphs and failures. By no means a collection of strangers, they enjoyed the close social ties characteristic of a true community, even though they lived in the midst of a modern city.

The most intensive social interactions among West Enders took place among their small peer groups made up of relatives and close friends who got together several times a week in someone's home. The men would congregate in the living room, the women around the kitchen table. For hours on end they would talk, joke, laugh, swap stories, report the latest gossip, and simply enjoy being part of the group. For the Italian West Enders on whom Gans focused, group life was all-important. Peer groups started to form in early childhood and continued into adolescence and adulthood. They provided companionship, emotional support, and even outlets for expressing individuality; West Enders felt lost without them.

The West End of Boston is not unique. The sociologist Gerald Suttles (1968) found similar patterns in Chicago. The Near West Side of Chicago was clearly divided into ethnic neighborhoods—Italian, Mexican, black, Puerto Rican—each a village unto itself. Like Boston's West Enders, Near West Siders were well acquainted with neighbors from their own ethnic groups. To walk along their block was not to pass through a sea of strangers, but to greet people they had known all their lives—people who shared their ***culture.***

Local stores, catering to the dominant ethnic group in the neighborhood, helped to create a small-town atmosphere. An Italian-owned grocery store, a black-owned barber shop, a Mexican-owned café—all were places where people of these ethnic backgrounds could find the products and services they preferred. At the same time, these establishments became centers of neighborhood social life. People would stop by to banter and gossip, discuss their problems, and air their views. Very often customers left without purchasing anything. Economic transactions were considered secondary to the real business of social give-and-take. If someone was a little short of cash, credit would be extended with no embarrassment or fuss. These social patterns are very similar to those in small towns like Diagonal, where residents often visit the shops of Main Street just to see and chat with their friends. They bear little relationship to the stereotyped view of cold and highly depersonalized life in a large city.

Gans, Suttles, and like-minded researchers argue that community may persist *despite* urbanization. They point out that even in the largest cities, the residents of a neighborhood may develop a shared sense of belonging, intimacy, and caring. Often these urban villagers are immigrants from small rural towns in Europe or South America, or the children or grandchildren of such immigrants. They are maintaining the kind of community ties that their families have always thought of as natural and right.

The Transformation of Community

Close-knit ethnic neighborhoods are not the only places where community survives in big cities. Other sociologists have proposed that the high concentration of people in urban settings gives rise to a distinctive ***social structure,*** which in turn fosters new forms of community attachment, not necessarily based on common origins or residential proximity. According to this view, city dwellers often form social networks (see Chapter 4) that transcend neighborhood boundaries and even city lines (Webber, 1966). These networks are based on shared interests, occupations, and activities. Thus, feminists from different parts of a city might meet regularly to share their views and undertake joint projects. Or people who love classical music might form an amateur chamber orchestra and play together once a week. Rural villagers are not conducive to these kinds of interest-based networks, for their populations are not large and diverse enough to support them. Only the city, with its huge concentration of people, allows such urban subcultures to form. Ironically, then, population size and density (the very traits that Wirth thought alienated people from one another) cause new kinds of social ties to develop and help perpetuate community.

The sociologist Claude Fischer (1982) tested this theory by interviewing more than 1,000 men and women who lived in places that varied greatly in their degree of urbanism. He found that urbanism did encourage people to find friends in a wider geographic area, and the physical distance between friends didn't weaken the personal bonds they formed. Friends who lived in widely separated sections of a city were just as likely to feel close to one another as friends who lived next door. Urbanism, in other words, did not destroy community. It transformed it by broadening the geographic boundaries within which community was built up. Fischer also found that living in an urban area changed the composition of people's social networks. Relationships tended to be based less on kinship and membership in the same church, and more on shared work roles and shared involvement in secular associations (clubs, interest groups, and civic organizations).

If community survives in cities, why do we get the sense that urbanites are remote and uncaring? The answer, according to Fischer, is that city dwellers differ from rural residents in their general distrust of strangers. One reason for this distrust is a greater fear of crime and other forms of victimization. In public, urbanites don a protective shell of aloofness, as Simmel described. In their private lives, however, they have close and caring relationships just as people in villages and small towns do.

All the same, there is a ***structural*** difference between cities and smaller communities. The various relationships of city dwellers are less likely to overlap so as to form a single, tightly knit community. In small towns, by contrast, neighbors are more likely to be co-workers, to attend the same church, and to participate in the same leisure activities (Calhoun, 1980).

All these views of urban life are correct to some extent. The sense of community in cities may be disintegrating, persisting, and changing, all at the same time. Depending on which particular urban districts we look at, we can find empirical support for each of the three theories we have outlined in this section. The task for sociologists is to identify the specific conditions under which urbanization destroys, sustains, or creates community ties. We will return to this task later in this chapter.

CHANGING PATTERNS OF URBAN LIFE: A TALE OF THREE CITIES

A **city** is a relatively large, densely populated, and permanent settlement of people who are socially diverse and who do not directly produce their own food. In general, cities dominate the surrounding countryside and smaller towns. This characterization applies to cities through the ages, from ancient Thebes in Egypt and Athens in Greece to modern-day New York, Tokyo, and Paris.

At the dawn of human culture, people lived in small bands, hunting, fishing, and foraging for their food. In most places, wild foods were not plentiful enough to support more than a small number of people, so humans were forced to be nomadic: They would settle in a place for only a short time, moving on when the food supply ran short.

Why did people begin to live in villages, towns, and cities? What led to these new forms of social organization? To answer these questions, we must look back 10,000 years, to the era when people first began to domesticate plants and animals. Probably in areas where natural supplies were scarce, people began weeding and watering stands of edible plants, adding organic matter to fertilize the soil, and saving the seeds from the strongest, most desirable plants to sow the next spring. At the same time, they began protecting herds of small wild animals such as goats and sheep from predators, moving them to more plentiful pastures during the dry months of summer and supplementing their diets during the harshest periods of winter. These innovations, coupled with a few simple techniques for storing grain and meat, enabled people to settle in small, semipermanent villages. These villages, which consisted of only 200 to 400 people, were the basic form of human social organization for the next several thousand years (Childe, 1952).

Then, sometime between 6000 and 5000 B.C., in the basins of the Nile, Tigris-Euphrates, and Indus river valleys, settlements emerged more than ten times the size of any earlier ones. Housing between 7,000 and 20,000 people, these first true cities developed largely because innovations in agriculture and transportation enabled people to take advantage of the valleys' exceptionally fertile soils. The domestication of new, higher-yield grains and the development of the ox-drawn plow, metalworking, and irrigation made possible large surpluses of food. These sur-

The earliest urban centers grew out of advances in agriculture and in the means of transporting surplus food from farm to town. Here an Egyptian pharaoh oversees the harvest on his estates and makes decisions on how much food will reach the people, and by what means.

pluses permitted some of the population to become full-time artisans, merchants, teachers, soldiers, and priests, rather than farmers. Specialization of labor, in turn, required that people live close to others on whose skills they depended. Densely populated areas became necessities, and cities began to increase in size and number (K. Davis, 1955).

Yet the emergence of cities cannot be explained solely in terms of a more complex division of labor. For cities to grow and flourish, a centralized system of ***power*** was needed, both to coordinate the new diversity of social and economic activities and to settle conflicts between groups with competing interests (Sjoberg, 1960). Not accidentally, then, the development of the first true cities coincided with the emergence of powerful governments, administrators, lawmakers, and judges. This was the basis of Rome, Beijing, Istanbul, and Cairo—all of which were capitals of great empires.

During the Middle Ages (from the fall of Rome in the fifth century A.D. until about 1350), urban development in Europe came to a standstill (though cities did grow and flourish in India, China, and elsewhere). With the coming of the Renaissance, European cities began to grow again, not only in size but also in political, technological, and artistic achievements. Fairly typical of cities during this period was Venice, in northeast Italy on the Adriatic Sea.

The Preindustrial City: Venice in Its Golden Age

Venice was built on a cluster of small islands nestled close together in a large lagoon and linked by an intricate network of 177 canals, which still serve as roads to move people and goods throughout the city. By 1492 (ten centuries after its founding) Venice boasted an estimated 190,000 inhabitants, all crowded into a very small space (K. Davis, 1955).

Even if Venice had not been built on islands, it would still have remained geographically small by today's standards. The reason is that transportation was limited to horse- and ox-drawn wagons, small boats, or foot. In order for residents to get fairly quickly from one point to another, a preindustrial city could be no more than a few miles across. Before the nineteenth century, the cities of the world were mostly small, concentrated settlements dotting a vast and otherwise rural landscape. Urban sprawl, in other words, is a modern-day phenomenon.

Preindustrial cities were also limited in population. Only so many people could be packed within their borders, because of the problems of supply. For example, food for Venice first had to be carried by wagon to the water's edge, then conveyed by barge to the islands and by gondola through the city. Because this system was so slow, food had to originate in the countryside very near to Venice, and farmers there produced only a limited amount.

Without modern technology, a city with such a dense population tended to be a breeding ground for disease. Rotting garbage and raw sewage were dumped into the canals, causing foul odors to permeate the city. In 1438, a Spanish visitor to Venice described how residents tried to camouflage the stench by burning sweet-smelling spices in the streets (Chambers, 1970). Spices could do nothing to halt the spread of bacterial and viral infections, however. Epidemics were common.

The absence of modern lighting also made Venice dark and dangerous at night. The city's narrow alleys and shadowy canals were the scenes of many murders and other acts of violence—some the result of personal conflicts, others politically motivated. A special police force, the *signori di notte* ("lords of the night"), patrolled the city after dark. Anyone found carrying a sharp knife was automatically fined and imprisoned for two weeks. Even so, Venice's crime rate remained quite high (Chambers, 1970).

Life in preindustrial Venice nevertheless had its attractions. Venice was a beautiful city, an architectural masterpiece. Magnificent churches, piazzas, and houses, many built during the fifteenth and sixteenth centuries, graced (and still grace) the major canals. Wealthy Venetians were the patrons of many great painters, and the city's glassware and textiles were coveted throughout Europe (J. H. Davis, 1973). Like other preindustrial cities, Venice was a center for the arts, handicrafts, the sciences, and learning.

Although life in preindustrial Venice was generally harmonious, the population was sharply divided by social class. A huge gap in wealth existed between the *tabarro* (ordinary citizens) and the *toga* (aristocrats). Aristocratic families lived in great palaces that had large, richly furnished rooms with glass windows; ate lavish meals with silver utensils; and slept on beds with real mattresses (Davis, 1973). A common laborer would have had to work for a year to earn the price of a single aristocrat's cloak. Still, the commoners of Venice were better off than the commoners in most other European cities. The employment rate in preindustrial Venice usually remained high. Although the city had its beggars, they were not as numerous nor as destitute as their counterparts in Rome, Paris, or London. The relative well-being of the common working people is one reason that intense class conflict never erupted in Venice. Another reason was the absolute power of the ruling class. Secret "inquisitors of state" identified those disloyal to the existing regime, keeping most Venetians in line (Rowdon, 1970).

Industrialization and Urbanization: Nineteenth-Century Boston

The next explosion in urban growth was linked to industrialization. We tend to think of the Industrial Revolution only in terms of transforming the production of things like iron and steel, textiles and clothing. But the Industrial Revolution also affected farming. The introduction of new agricultural equipment (tractors, cultivators, harvesters, milking machines) reduced the need for farm labor while greatly increasing yields. Mass-produced and mass-applied pesticides, herbicides, fertilizers, and feeds had the same effects, as did new, mechanized methods of irrigation. The result was a tremendous leap in the number of people a single farmer could supply. Whereas in 1820 one American farmer fed only four people (including himself), by 1900 one American farmer fed seven people. Over the next eighty years even more impressive gains were made. Such massive food production has made it possible to support huge urban settlements.

Just as industrialization made urban growth possible, so urban growth made industrialization possible. The two processes were interdependent. Workers no longer needed on farms flocked to cities, where they supplied the labor force needed to run the growing number of factories. In the Boston area, early industrialists built factories in small towns to tap surplus farm labor (mainly women and children). By the 1840s, however, the new steamships were delivering waves of immigrants (many of whom were displaced farmers, desperate for work) to Boston's harbor. To employ this cheap labor pool, industrialists began locating factories in Boston itself. Thus, immigrants played a central role in the industrialization and urbanization of the United States (S. B. Warner, 1962).

Boston and other growing cities could support a huge industrial labor force for several reasons. One reason, already mentioned, was the great increase in agricultural productivity. Another was the development of railroad systems, which tremendously improved the speed and efficiency of transportation. Trains could deliver large amounts of food to downtown Boston, much more than could be hauled in with horses, carts, and wagons. The invention of refrigerated freight cars and warehouses further improved this system, making it possible to feed huge concentrations of city dwellers. At the same time, new building materials, such as steel and reinforced concrete, plus the invention of the elevator, enabled architects to design much taller buildings in their efforts to accommodate the increasingly dense population. Finally, improvements in public hygiene (indoor plumbing, municipal sewer systems, citywide garbage collection) cut the mortality rate caused by contagious diseases.

Nineteenth-century Boston differed from preindustrial cities in other ways as well. One way was physical layout. While fifteenth-century Venice was a city of narrow, crooked alleys and canals, nineteenth-century Boston was increasingly developed in a gridlike pattern, with rows of parallel streets intersecting other rows at right angles. The square blocks of land thus formed were divided into uniform lots, each with a relatively narrow frontage on the street. This grid arrangement became the norm for neighborhoods of all kinds, from the tightly spaced three- and five-story tenements of the West End to the spacious one-family houses of the outlying suburbs.

In the nineteenth century, the railroad and the steam engine were central symbols for human society's invasion of the natural world. In Claude Monet's painting "Train in the Country" (left), *nature still holds the foreground, but the black, boxlike railroad cars suggest that society's dream of life in an unspoiled garden was about to end. The photograph at right shows the reality of early twentieth-century industrialization, in which the railroad was both the means to the industrial end and a product of the industrial system.*

Suburbs themselves were another new feature of industrial urbanization. In nineteenth-century Boston and other cities of that era, suburbs tended to spring up along expanding trolley lines (first horse-drawn trolleys and then electrically powered ones). From an aerial view, Boston began to look like a giant bicycle wheel: The crowded industrial district lay at the center, and suburbs extended out along the fixed-rail spokes. Later, manufacturing plants also started to migrate from the city's central hub to suburbs, where land was less expensive (S. B. Warner, 1962). The factories remained close to train depots, however, for they depended on the railroads to deliver raw materials and ship finished products.

The development of nineteenth-century suburbs intensified residential segregation of social class. Because of the small size of preindustrial cities, the rich and the poor never lived very far apart. On the canals of preindustrial Venice, for example, the crowded houses of working-class people sat side by side with the palaces of aristocratic families. Nineteenth-century Boston, in contrast, was developing into a divided city. By 1900, mainly lower-income families lived in the central core, within walking distance of the large factories in which they worked. Most middle- and upper-income families had moved to the suburbs, where the surroundings were less noisy, hectic, and dirty. Still, the distance between rich and poor was not very great. In the 1880s and 1890s, the distance from Boston City Hall to the farthest outlying suburb was only about six miles. Beyond the outermost ring of commuter housing lay great stretches of farms and undeveloped woodland.

The Modern Metropolis: Los Angeles Today

This picture of nineteenth-century Boston bears little resemblance to the huge, contemporary **metropolis**, a major city with surrounding municipalities caught up in its economic and social orbit (Herbers, 1983). Greater Los Angeles, for instance, covers some 4,100 square miles, an area about *forty times* larger than greater Boston at the turn of the century. Rather than being dominated by a single downtown district, Los Angeles consists of some eighteen diverse urban centers, all fluidly linked by an enormous system of freeways. Urban experts describe Los Angeles as a metropolitan "galaxy" with numerous "constellations" (Lockwood and Leinberger, 1988). In sharp contrast to the pattern of older industrial cities in the East, Los Angeles's settlement pattern is relatively low in density (S. B. Warner, 1972). The single-family unit is the most common form of housing; high-rise apartment buildings are relatively rare. Housing subdivisions, retail shopping districts, entertainment centers, and industrial parks stretch for miles.

The Bureau of the Census calls a metropolis like this one a **Consolidated Metropolitan Statistical Area (CMSA),** or an interlinked cluster of one or more cities and their surrounding suburbs that together have a population of over 1 million people. There are nineteen CMSAs in the United States. Greater Los Angeles, with its 14 million inhabitants, is the second largest in population size. (The greater New York CMSA is first, with a total population of more than 19 million.)

Many think that the single most important reason Los Angeles is so spread out is the automobile. At the turn of the century, what we now call Los Angeles was a collection of several dozen towns, linked by the Red Trolley network. Californians were among the first to embrace Henry Ford's Model T. With the coming of the private automobile, people were much less restricted by where they could live and still be able to commute to work. No longer did they have to build houses near trolley or train lines. They could settle in any area *between* these fixed transportation routes, or even in districts beyond them. The same freedom applied to businesses deciding where to locate plants. With trucks delivering raw materials and transporting finished products, a factory could now be far removed from railroad facilities. Relatively inexpensive roads were all that were needed to link one place with any other. In the 1920s, Los Angeles residents voted down a proposal for a system of subways and elevated trains in favor of expanding the street system and building the first "parkway." General Motors, Standard Oil, and Firestone Tire & Rubber pushed hard for the new automobile system, which brought them profits because Los Angeles residents came to depend heavily on autos, gas, and tires (Clifford, 1989a; M. P. Smith, 1988). The average Los Angeleno today drives 117 miles a week (Clifford, 1989b); see Figure 20.1.

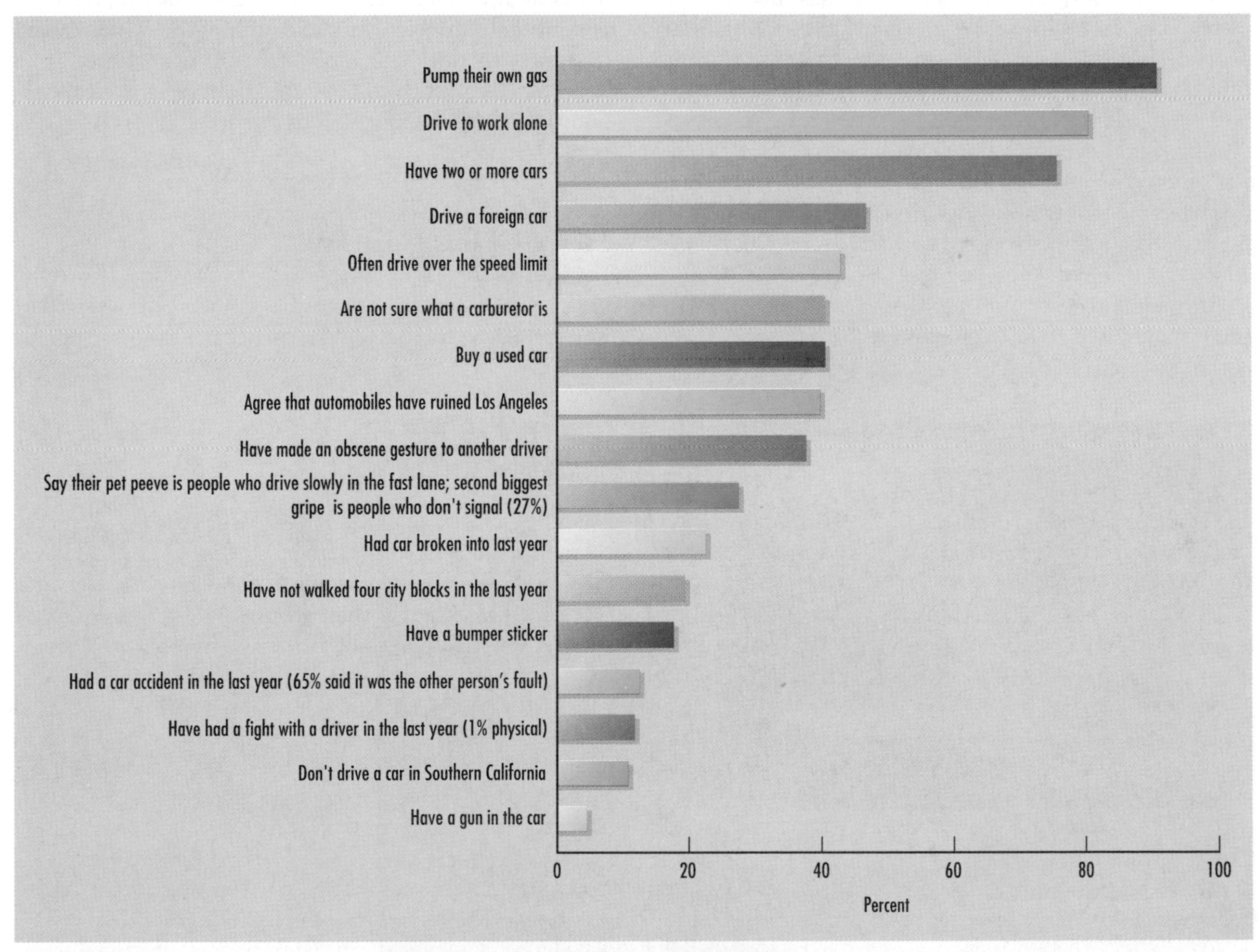

FIGURE 20.1 / *Southern California Residents as Drivers: A Profile*

Extensive car travel and sprawling development make life in a modern metropolis like Los Angeles very different from that in an early industrial city like Boston. While nineteenth-century Bostonians considered ten miles a substantial round-trip commute, many modern-day residents of Los Angeles travel 100 miles to and from work. Moreover, unlike their nineteenth-century counterparts, relatively few Angelenos commute to the central city. The majority have jobs in outlying areas, making daily commuting an immense crisscrossing of the entire metropolitan area. Most retail shops and entertainment centers are located in the suburbs. Vast indoor shopping malls, usually situated at the intersections of freeways, offer all the attractions of a central city—restaurants, theaters, department stores, boutiques, and gourmet food shops—without the parking problems. The stores of downtown Los Angeles account for only 3 percent of all retail sales in the metropolitan region (Brodsly, 1981).

A complex system of freeways was constructed to accommodate all this travel. With each additional highway, people, businesses, and jobs were dispersed even farther, thus creating a need for more freeways. Even so, the system is overloaded. Rush hours often last 3 hours, mornings and evenings, and even on "good" days freeways are clogged with motorists creeping along at fifteen miles per hour. Estimates are that Los Angeles drivers waste some 100,000 hours a day in traffic jams (Lockwood and Leinberger, 1988).

Although no other U.S. city is as spread out as Los Angeles, some CMSAs have grown to the point where their outermost edges are starting to merge with those of neighboring metropolises. Such a vast urban stretch, hundreds of miles long, is called a **megalopolis** (literally, "great city"). The urban sprawl between Los Angeles and San Diego to the south forms a megalopolis. At its northern end this huge urban region may soon start to merge with the southernmost tip of the San Francisco metropolis. On the East Coast, a megalopolis extends from Kittery, Maine—through Boston, New York City, Philadelphia, Baltimore, and Washington—to Quantico, Virginia. More than 40 million people, a fifth of the nation's population, live in this sprawling 500-mile belt. Other growing megalopolises are Palm Beach–Miami, Dallas–Fort Worth, Pittsburgh–Youngstown–Canton–Akron–Cleveland, and Milwaukee–Chicago–Detroit.

As extraordinary as Los Angeles and other American megalopolises are, they are not the fastest-growing or the largest cities in the world. As we saw in Chapter 18, several Third World cities, such as Cairo and Calcutta, have experienced stunning growth, and most of the world's largest cities are in developing countries. We analyzed Third World urban growth in Chapter 18; here we concentrate on patterns and explanations of urban growth in the United States.

HOW CITIES GROW

No city ever develops at random. Affluent housing does not spring up in the middle of decaying slums, nor do

Urban experts describe greater Los Angeles as a "galaxy" with constellations of neighborhoods and suburbs—which makes the automobile the spacecraft in which people must ride to get from one "planet" to another. The urban environment of Los Angeles is about as hospitable to the pedestrian as outer space would be to an unprotected space traveler.

smoke-belching factories suddenly get built next to elegant office towers. The shape of a city, in other words, is not haphazard. It is the product of social, economic, political, and geographic forces. In this section we consider two influential sociological perspectives on how cities grow: the urban-ecology approach and the political-economy view.

Urban Ecology

Ecology is a subfield of biology that studies how living organisms interact with their physical environments and with one another to affect the development of their communities. In the early and mid-twentieth century, a number of sociologists began to borrow ecological concepts and apply them to the study of cities. Based at the University of Chicago, Louis Wirth, Robert Park, and Ernest Burgess developed the **urban-ecology** approach. They examined how the social uses of urban land result from an interaction between diverse groups of people and their physical and geographic environment. The urban-ecology perspective has produced three major models of urban area development.

Three Models of Urban Land Use

The earliest model of urban land use was that proposed by Ernest Burgess. Burgess argued that as the size of an urban population increases, people begin to compete for space (Park, Burgess, and McKenzie, 1925). This competition tends to produce six **concentric zones** of development, each serving a different function (see Figure 20.2a). The first zone, at the center of the city, is the business district, made up of stores and offices. The second zone, which surrounds the first, is in a state of transition and is characterized by residential instability, low rents, high crime rates, and various forms of vice. Businesses and light manufacturing are beginning to move in. Beyond the zone in transition lie four residential zones. The first is inhabited by the working class; the second and third are occupied by the middle and upper classes; the fourth is a zone of wealthy commuter suburbs outside the city limits. Burgess's concentric-zone model best describes a city like Chicago, which developed very rapidly after the Industrial Revolution, before the introduction of the automobile.

In the 1930s, the sociologist Homer Hoyt (1943) proposed a second model of urban development. Hoyt em-

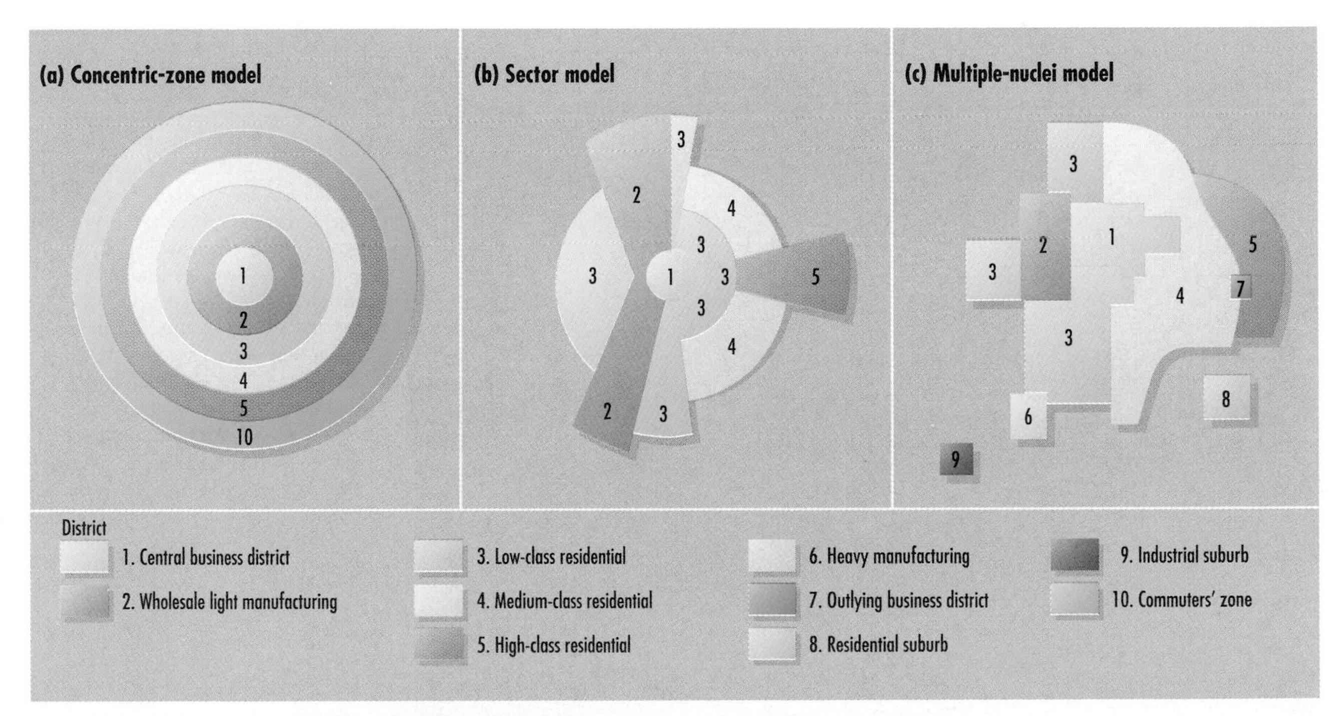

FIGURE 20.2 / Three Models of Urban Land Use

Source: Chauncy D. Harris and Edward Ullman, "The Nature of Cities," in Paul K. Hatt and A. J. Reiss, Jr. (eds.), *Cities and Society* (Free Press, Peoria, Ill., 1957).

phasized the importance of transportation routes—such as railroad lines, highways, rivers, and canals—as a structural basis for the growth of cities. His **sector model** also featured an outward movement of population, but in the form of pie-shaped sectors surrounding a central business district (see Figure 20.2b). According to Hoyt, the various zones of urban land use tend to be distributed along major transportation routes radiating out from the downtown area. As land use of a certain type expands, it tends to do so within its particular sector, extending outward toward the edge of the metropolis. One example is the development of the Boston suburbs along trolley lines. Another is the recent development of California's Silicon Valley, where computer firms have settled along freeways running south out of Oakland and San Francisco.

Both the concentric-zone and the sector models assume that cities expand outward from a single business district in the city center. This pattern does not hold for all urban areas, however. To describe those that have followed a different pattern, Chauncy Harris and Edward Ullman (1945) proposed the **multiple-nuclei model.** In this model, cities develop a series of separate centers, called *nuclei*, each with its own specialized functions (see Figure 20.2c). Four basic factors encourage this pattern of functional specialization:

- First, certain activities require specialized facilities. Heavy manufacturing, for example, requires nearness to highways or railroad lines, just as international importing requires nearness to a port.
- Second, certain activities (such as retail trade) benefit when those involved in it are clustered close together (clusters of retail stores increase the pool of shoppers in an area).
- Third, certain dissimilar activities can harm each other when located close together. Warehousing, for example, with its high demand for truck traffic, discourages pedestrian shopping, and vice versa.
- Fourth, certain activities (such as wholesaling, which requires a great deal of space) cannot afford to be located in high-rent districts.

These four factors together give rise to various specialized districts within a city. The city grows as the specialized districts expand and increase in number.

Ecological Processes and Neighborhood Change

To understand why patterns of urban land use change as a city's population grows, consider the dramatic change in

A moshav *is an Israeli cooperative village of land-owning small farmers. This is Nahalal, the oldest moshav, founded in the 1920s. The farmers live on the outer circle; on the other side of the circular street live the community members who provide services for the farmers. Jointly owned buildings and administrative offices are in the center of the settlement. This layout accentuates the equality of the community's members and creates a boundary that ensures that the village will not grow beyond a certain size.*

the use of an urban neighborhood that occurred many years ago in the Harlem section of New York City. Today Harlem is one of America's best-known urban slums, but it was not always so. In the late nineteenth century, it was among the most fashionable residential districts of the city. Harlem's transformation began around the turn of the twentieth century, when it was at its peak of affluence (Osofsky, 1982).

In the late 1890s the city government announced that construction would soon begin on a new subway line extending from midtown Manhattan into Harlem. The news set off a wave of speculation in Harlem real estate. People were convinced that property values, which were already high, would double and triple when the subway link to the central city was completed. Developers began to build apartments on every piece of vacant land. Because of Harlem's reputation as the home of the genteel and wealthy, most of the new buildings offered elegant accommodations, designed to reap high rents for developers. The apartments were large and richly detailed, with spacious living and dining rooms, maids' quarters, butler's pantries, dumbwaiters, and elevators. The building boom soon led to a glut of new housing at highly inflated prices; many units were completed years before the new subway began to operate; and the massive influx of wealthy new residents that everyone expected never materialized. Buildings stood partly or even entirely vacant, and rents began to drop precipitously. Developers stood to lose their investments.

One group in the city was in desperate need of more and better housing: the large black population. Taking advantage of the plummeting rents in Harlem, black realtors began trying to place their clients there. At first only a few black families settled in Harlem, all of them in the newly developed west section. Many white apartment owners tried to prevent more from coming by signing agreements among themselves that they would not rent to blacks. These efforts proved ineffective, however, because the whites could not create a unified front. Some were willing to cut their losses by opening their buildings to blacks. Others engaged in panic selling (disposing of their property to whoever would buy it at whatever price they could get). The result was a steady movement of blacks into west Harlem and from there into other parts of the district. By World War I, Harlem was predominantly black.

For a time, Harlem was the most luxurious black community in American history. Occupying elegant apartments intended for the rich, middle-class black families finally had a decent neighborhood to live in. The problem was that the steady stream of blacks wanting to move to Harlem pushed rents higher than most of them could afford. Some families were forced to take in boarders, and many smaller buildings were converted to rooming houses. Conditions became increasingly overcrowded:

> People were packed together to the point of "indecency." Some landlords, after opening houses to Negro tenants, lost interest in caring for their property and permitted it to run down—halls were left dark and dirty, broken pipes were permitted to rot, steam heat was cut off as heating apparatus wore out, dumbwaiters broke down and were boarded up, homes became vermin-infested. (Osofsky, 1982, p. 192)

By the 1920s, Harlem had become one of the worst slums in the country.

Park, Burgess, and McKenzie (1925) introduced the **invasion/succession model** to explain neighborhood change like that which occurred in Harlem. The concepts of invasion and succession are borrowed from plant and animal ecology. *Invasion* refers to the appearance in an environment of a new species, and *succession* refers to a change in the mix of different species present until a new, stable community is formed. In urban ecology, the invasion/succession process begins when social forces bring change, as when rising or falling land values attract a new kind of resident to an urban district, a resident who is socially or racially different from those who are already there. In turn-of-the-century Harlem, the new residents were black families. The perceived invasion is met with resistance by established residents, who are forced to compete with the newcomers for available land. Competition may give way to ***conflict*** as the groups vie for space. Sometimes an accommodation is reached and the two manage to live together. Other times, no compromise is achieved and one or the other group abandons the area. When the established residents leave, as occurred in Harlem, a kind of succession has taken place. Of course, succession is not always a gradual, seemingly natural occurrence; often it is advanced or resisted by power struggles—as when white suburbanites try to keep blacks out of their neighborhoods despite civil rights laws.

Complementing the invasion/succession model of neighborhood change is the **neighborhood life-cycle model** (Hoover and Vernon, 1959). This approach sees change in urban districts as part of a larger series of invasion/succession episodes. A neighborhood may begin its life cycle undergoing extensive *development*, just as Harlem did in the late nineteenth century. Then a period of *transition* may occur in which major social forces change (the overbuilding in Harlem, for example, followed by plummeting land values and the movement of black people into the district). A *downgrading* of the area may follow, as occurred in Harlem when landlords let their property run down. Eventually stores and houses may be so decayed that a *thinning out* of population occurs. The final stage may be urban *renewal* and a new wave of development. City neighborhoods do not necessarily pass through all these stages. Sometimes a neighborhood will become stable at a certain point. Thus, Harlem today remains "downgraded," despite some pockets of attempted renewal (public housing projects, some restoration of old housing, and the construction of New York State office buildings). Research suggests that movement through the stages depends on a number of factors, including the extent to which population and new housing are expanding, area residents have access to jobs, resources are mobilized to resist change, and public officials pursue redevelopment (Schwirian, 1983).

The ecological perspective remains influential in urban sociology today, but ecologists have expanded their research beyond central cities to look at the organization of whole regions and their relation to national and international economic change. The idea of interdependence has become increasingly prominent. It draws on the key sociological concept of ***functional integration*** to counterbalance the traditional ecological emphasis on competition for resources (Berry and Kasarda, 1977; Frisbie and Kasarda, 1988). Contemporary urban ecologists see metropolitan areas as integrated wholes, each part serving functions that complement and support those being served by other parts. Thus, as one part adapts to a changing environment, adjustments are needed in other parts so that the whole remains vital. For instance, if a certain district of the city is invaded by manufacturing, nearby areas will develop working-class housing for the workers that the new factories need. Note that these manufacturing and residential districts are mutually beneficial and interdependent. The factories need the workers and provide jobs for them, just as the workers need the factories and supply them with labor. In this functional view, regions and cities constantly adapt so as to improve their chances of survival in a certain environment (Hawley, 1971). Major economic changes can disrupt these adaptive processes, however. For example, it took years for some industrial Midwestern cities to find new economic bases to replace closed factories. Some have never recovered and are still floundering. In others, office buildings replaced factories, posing new adaptive challenges for the cities and their environs.

The Political Economy of Urban Space

Urban ecologists see the development of cities as a more or less natural process of adaptation to the changing social and technological environment. Other sociologists, taking a **political-economy view,** emphasize ***power*** and ***social action*** rather than functional adaptation (Gottdiener and Feagin, 1988; M. P. Smith, 1988). They see the changing shapes of cities as reflecting deliberate decisions that have been made by powerful groups and coalitions in order to direct urban growth to their own advantage. These powerful groups control the major economic and political institutions of the city: its corporations, banks, financial markets, real estate and construction industries, local government, and government programs. Their decisions, in turn, are based on the logic of the capitalist economy: maximizing profits and minimizing costs. Thus, according to the political-economy view, "Changing urban development patterns are best understood as the long-term outcomes of actions taken by economic and political *actors* operating within a complex and changing matrix of global and national economic and political *forces*" (Smith and Feagin, 1987, p. 17).

The Rise of the Corporate City

Across the country, old, industrial cities have largely been replaced by modern corporate cities, in which the center city is dominated by corporate headquarters and the firms that serve them (banks, law firms, advertising agencies, and the like). Factories and warehouses are now located in the suburbs. According to urban ecologists, the emergence of corporate cities was largely the result of structural factors such as innovations in transportation and communications, especially the advent of cars, trucks, and highways. Looking at this development from the political-economy view, David Gordon (1984) argues that while these changes in technology *enabled* the corporate city to emerge, they were not its fundamental cause. Rather, the corporate city was the product of capitalist profit making carried out by huge, wealthy corporations with immense control over worldwide markets.

One change that these corporations deliberately brought about was the relocation of production plants from the downtown district to the periphery of the city, or even beyond city limits. The major motivation for this shift was a need to control labor unions and reduce worker–management conflict. In the early twentieth century, capitalists were increasingly faced with picketing, strikes, and even sabotage of their operations. The clustering of factories in central cities made the problem worse, for workers in different plants could compare conditions and demand changes from exploitative employers. One solution was to move to the suburbs, where employees would be more isolated from incidents of labor unrest. So corporations moved out in ever-increasing numbers. This exodus of production from the central cities was made possible by the wave of corporate mergers and rapid corporate growth that occurred between 1898 and 1903. Many corporations became large enough and sufficiently well-financed to afford the investment in new facilities. The move to the suburbs fit the growing size and wealth of American business.

The proliferation of downtown corporate headquarters lodged in towering skyscrapers also fit the character of twentieth-century capitalism. By the 1920s, many American corporations had acquired control over vast markets. "They were now large enough to separate administrative functions from the production process, leaving plant managers to oversee the factories while corporate managers supervised the far-flung empire" (Gordon, 1984, p. 43). As anyone knows who has ever stood at the foot of a huge corporate tower, this feature of the modern city is the very symbol of enormous, highly centralized economic power. However, changing forms of capitalism also bring changing symbols. For every giant central-city corporate office tower built today, there are several corporate "campuses" dispersed through megalopolises and even outside them. Global capitalism, aided by new technologies, makes centralization less of a benefit (Harvey, 1989).

The City as Growth Machine

While Gordon and Harvey have tried to explain the spatial organization of capitalist cities, other sociologists with a political-economy perspective have looked at the forces that fuel the general process of urban expansion (Logan and Molotch, 1987). According to the sociologist Harvey Molotch (1987), "The city is, for those who count, a growth machine" (p. 310). By this he means that the city is a giant human-produced device that helps make it possible for business and commerce to expand, for the labor force to increase, and for more intensive and widespread use of land resources to be made. Growth, in short, is the essence of cities in capitalistic nations like the United States. The reason is simple. Growth is a source of greater wealth and power for those who own the city's land resources. Through growth, an acre that once sold for a few hundred dollars becomes worth millions. Through growth, urban landowning elites multiply their profits many times over.

Molotch sees the American city as an aggregate of land-based interests: a coalition of individuals, groups, and organizations that stand to gain or lose financially from the way the city's land resources are developed. The objective is more intensive use of land, which means greater profits.

Industrialization has nearly always brought waves of migrants to cities. As industrial cities grew in nineteenth- and early twentieth-century Europe and the United States, millions of people were crowded into squalid housing, often without basic public services like running water and garbage collection. The same pattern is being repeated today in many Third World cities. These crowded and poorly maintained urban districts are home to deep and interlocked social problems that are hard to solve without changing the basic organization of urban life.

Many of the property owners in New York's Harlem, for instance, broke up large apartments into one-room flats in order to maximize their profits. By the 1920s, space in Harlem that would normally have earned only $40 a month was earning $100 or $125 because of intensified use. Some landlords even rented out space in basements and coalbins to get the most they could from their landholdings (Osofsky, 1982). This example shows how powerful coalitions of interests can promote growth regardless of other considerations (such as the availability of services and the impact on the urban environment).

Local government is eager to assist urban growth, because elected officials are often deeply involved with the city's land interests. Many are large landowners themselves, or they are bankers, realtors, and investment brokers whose success and income depend on a growing community. These officeholders try to maintain a favorable "growth climate," which means sizable tax breaks for developers and investors, harmonious labor relations to attract new industry, and a police force that gives high priority to protecting private property.

Molotch stresses that growth is not good for the whole community, as those in power contend. Urban growth can bring many distressing problems such as air and water pollution, traffic congestion, and residential overcrowding. It can also increase what people must pay for public utilities, police and fire protection, and other city services. And growth does not necessarily make jobs for residents, as proponents usually claim. Most of the jobs created in the corporate city are either in the high-wage information sector (which attract highly educated workers from around the country and so do not necessarily increase employment for residents) or in the low-wage service sector (restaurants, laundries, residential construction, and the like, which offer little job security and few benefits) (Smith and Feagin, 1987). Urban growth, in other words, bestows the greatest benefits on those who own the resources used in the process—namely, the community's economic elite.

The notion that the city is a "growth machine" has implications for the international economy, as the Global Issues/Local Consequences box explains.

CURRENT TRENDS IN AMERICAN COMMUNITIES

Cities are a defining feature of the modern era. For most of this century, the trend in the United States has been toward increasing urbanization. Yet every day we read about the exodus from cities, cities cutting back on services, cities going bankrupt. Is the era of cities drawing to a close? In this section we will look at current trends and future prospects for all three types of American settlements: small towns, big cities, and suburbs.

The Crisis of Rural America

"$1,000 Reward!" shouts a poster seen all over Jefferson, Iowa, a rural county seat eighty miles north of Des Moines. The text under the headline promises this bounty to anyone who helps to attract an employer who will provide at least fifteen jobs (*New York Times*, September 11, 1990, p. A20). Like Jefferson, other small towns across the United States are threatened with extinction. No one knows how many small towns have been wiped off the map in recent decades. The Census Bureau calculates that 200 vanish each decade, but many experts believe the actual number is much higher (*New York Times*, January 3, 1990, p. A16). As small towns disappear, a way of life is dying with them.

In 1950, about 36 percent of Americans lived in small towns and rural areas; by 1990, only 25 percent did (see Figure 20.3). The depopulation of rural America is due in large part to advances in technology, starting with the tractor. In the 1950s and 1960s, the size of farms increased while the number of farmers decreased. A brief agricultural boom in the 1970s led many farmers to mortgage their land to purchase new and expensive equipment. When the demand for U.S. farm products on the world market and commodity prices within the United States fell in the

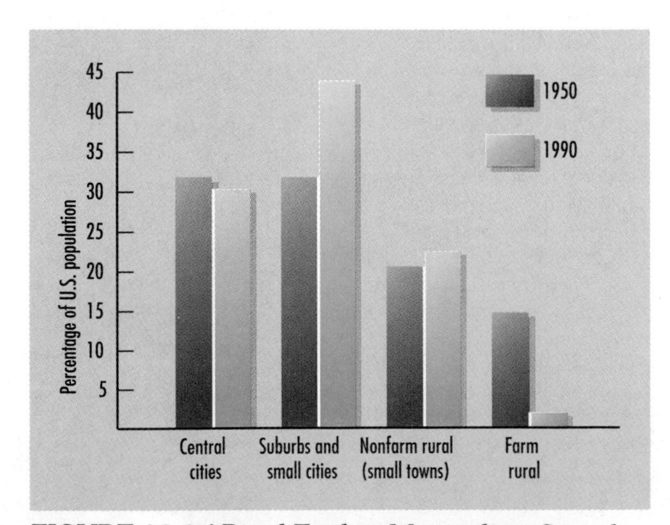

FIGURE 20.3 / Rural Exodus, Metropolitan Sprawl: Changes in U.S. Residential Patterns, 1950–1990

Sources: U.S. Bureau of the Census, Washington, D.C., and Department of Agriculture, Washington, D.C.

GLOBAL ISSUES/LOCAL CONSEQUENCES

Urban Growth and the World Economy

The sociologist Joe Feagin (1985, 1988) looks at the concept of the city as a growth machine within the context of a worldwide capitalist economy. He argues that the expansion of many modern metropolises can be understood only with this broader global picture as background. The impressive growth of Houston, Texas, the center of a worldwide oil and petrochemical production system, illustrates Feagin's view.

By every measure, Houston has grown phenomenally. Population there increased at least 29 percent in every decade from 1850 to 1980, and in one decade (the 1920s) it more than doubled. Whereas in 1890 Houston ranked only 112th in population among all U.S. cities, today it ranks fourth (after New York, Los Angeles, and Chicago). This dramatic growth has been accomplished partly by a huge migration of people to Houston and partly by the city's annexation of surrounding land. Houston covered only nine square miles in 1900 (the year before oil was first discovered ninety miles to the east). By 1980, it had annexed 550 additional square miles (Feagin, 1985).

Feagin attributes this impressive rate of growth not just to the push of local land-based interests but also to the pull of the worldwide demand for oil and oil products. Over the years, Houston has become a global center for the export of oil technology and equipment, as well as for oil refining and the manufacture of oil-based chemicals. Thirty-four of America's top thirty-five oil companies have major research, production, or administrative facilities in Houston, and 400 other major oil and gas companies have operations there. In all, about 25 percent of America's oil-refining output and 50 percent of its petrochemical production take place in Houston (Hill and Feagin, 1987). Houston thus occupies a vital niche in the global capitalist system.

Because of this niche, Houston's fate is tied more to global economic trends (especially the price of crude oil) than it is to national ones. When the price of crude oil rises (as it did in the 1970s), Houston is a boomtown. In 1973–1974, for example, when oil prices soared, there was a surge in oil exploration and drilling that stimulated Houston's economy even though the rest of the United States was in an economic recession. While cities like Dallas at the time suffered a 6 percent employment drop in manufacturing industries, Houston enjoyed an 18 percent *increase* because it manufactures mainly for the world oil market (Hill and Feagin, 1987). In contrast, when the price of oil falls (as it did in the 1980s), Houston sinks into serious recession even if other parts of the country are prospering.

This boom-or-bust cycle in Houston during the last two decades illustrates how sensitive the city's development is to changes in the global economy. Because Houston is a major component of a worldwide capitalist market system, its fortunes ebb and flow with decisions made in the boardrooms of multinational corporations. These changing fortunes, in turn, affect the daily lives of Houston's citizens. Whether it is easy or hard to find a job there, what kinds of jobs are scarce or plentiful, how much money is being channeled into urban development, and whether local taxes must be raised to compensate for falling corporate profits are all matters that are intimately connected to Houston's niche in the world capitalist system.

The growth or decline of other cities throughout the modern world is likewise tied to trends in the global capitalist economy and to the niches occupied by these cities within that worldwide economic order. For instance, many Third World cities have now become centers for the modern capitalist assembly line. As a result of this trend, employment in these cities has increased significantly, giving jobs to thousands of people. At the same time, however, this global trend has contributed to the decline of local industries and trade, neglect of rural areas, overcrowding in the major centers of production and export, and stagnation in Third World cities not selected for large-scale capitalist investment. Thus, local events in one city are often intricately linked to local events in other cities within one vast economic system (Feagin and Smith, 1987).

1980s, many of these mortgages were foreclosed and former farmers were forced to look elsewhere for work. Iowa—the heart of the Midwestern farm belt—lost more than 5 percent of its population in the 1980s alone. Young people (especially those with higher education) are most likely to move away, often leaving their parents behind. As a result, rural America is aging: The average age in Greene County, Iowa, is over fifty (*New York Times*, September 11, 1990, p. A20).

The quality of life in rural America is also declining (Hundley, 1989). Contrary to stereotypes, only a small proportion of rural Americans (less than 2 percent) make their living from farming; even in farm families, at least one spouse usually works off the farm. Because many small towns depend on a single employer, their economies are fragile. Moreover, with more people than jobs, employers are able to pay just the minimum wage. The poverty rate for young people in rural areas more than doubled in the

1980s (to more than 35 percent), and the unemployment rate is twice the national average (C. Duncan, 1991).

Town after town has seen its Main Street close down. In the 1980s, small towns in Iowa lost 41 percent of their gas stations, 27 percent of their grocery stores, and 37 percent of their variety stores. Part of the reason is simply that there are fewer customers, and part that local stores face stiff competition from national chains like Walmart and K Mart, which offer a big-city array of goods at bargain prices.

Health care in rural America is deteriorating. Of the 300 hospitals that closed in the 1980s, more than half were in small towns. The country doctor is also disappearing. Many small towns have only a part-time physician who serves several communities, and some have no doctor at all. Twelve of eighteen counties in southern Illinois do not have a single obstetrician. The reason is not only that small towns have too few patients to support a doctor but also that Medicare reimburses rural doctors 20 to 50 percent less than city doctors for the same procedure, on the grounds that their overhead is less. With $50,000 to $100,000 in medical school debts, even those new doctors who would like to establish small-town practices cannot afford to do so.

Small-town schools are also in trouble. With dwindling numbers of students, the cost of educating a single student often becomes prohibitive, and many small districts have been forced to merge. In 1945, Missouri had 8,607 school districts; today the state has only 545. In the 1980s alone, enrollment in Missouri schools dropped by 20 percent. In consolidated districts, students may be forced to travel fifty miles back and forth to school each day. Athletic and other school events used to be the high points of small-town life. "When you lose your school," says the principal of tiny Diagonal High, "you lose your town" (quoted in Hundley, 1989, p. 13).

The crisis in rural America is taking its toll on residents. A recent study of Iowa farmers found that one in three suffered symptoms of depression (Belyea and Labao, 1990). A University of Minnesota study of rural adolescents found that they are far more prone to depression and suicidal thoughts than are their urban counterparts (in Hundley, 1989).

Not all small, rural towns are in decline, however. A few have succeeded in attracting big industry, such as the multibillion-dollar plant General Motors built in Spring Hill, Tennessee (former population 1,100); some have attracted large numbers of retirees; and a few have become weekend spots for restless urbanites, or even suburbs of suburbs. Rural development can be a mixed blessing, though: Some residents may prosper, but traditional community ties may be torn in the process (Brown, Greersten, and Krannich, 1989; Summers and Branch, 1984). Moreover, these success stories are the exception to the rule. At the moment, the prognosis for America's small towns is not good.

The Restructuring of America's Cities

In the early 1980s, U.S. cities seemed on the verge of a revival. **Gentrification**—the conversion of working-class, often run-down areas of a city into middle- and upper-middle-class neighborhoods—was hailed as the wave of the future. City after city launched massive urban renewal projects. Blocks of abandoned and dilapidated buildings were razed, and office complexes, recreation centers (with hotels, restaurants, theaters, and attractions like aquariums), and luxury condominiums constructed in their place. This optimism turned out to be premature (Kasinitz, 1988).

Today's cities are a study in contrasts: between affluence and poverty, chaos and creativity, optimism and fear. For example, one section of downtown Los Angeles boasts sixty major corporate headquarters, a dozen banks with assets of more than $1 billion, five of the eight biggest international accounting firms, a battalion of corporate law firms, condominiums selling for $11 million—and the highest concentration of homeless people in the nation (Soja, 1989).

From Industry to Information

The most profound change in American cities is a ***functional*** one: their transformation from centers for the production and distribution of goods to centers of administration, finance, and information processing (Castells, 1989; Kasarda, 1989). Gone are the "smokestack," or heavy manufacturing, industries built up in the nineteenth and early twentieth centuries. Los Angeles once had the second largest automobile assembly complex in the country; today, only one factory remains (Soja, 1989). Gone, too, are the skilled, unionized, better-paying blue-collar jobs that used to be the backbone of urban economies. Center cities have also lost large numbers of sales and clerical jobs to suburbs and smaller cities.

To some extent, manufacturing jobs have been replaced by white-collar, managerial, and professional jobs in such knowledge-intensive fields as finance, law, accounting, and advertising (see Chapter 16). These jobs generally require at least a college degree, which many urban residents lack;

This is a residential section of Reston, Virginia, the first effort in the United States to create a fully planned community near a major urban center (Washington, D.C.). Reston's master plan allocates 45 percent of the usable space to public purposes, including schools, parks, roads, walkways, churches, golf courses, swimming pools, tennis courts, and malls. While planned communities have long been discussed in the United States, little large-scale urban planning has actually been carried out—in sharp contrast to most other industrialized countries.

so they are filled by suburban commuters. Minorities have been hardest hit by the changes in urban jobs and educational requirements. In particular, blacks with high school educations or less may be trapped in urban ghettoes, unable to find work in the city and unable to move or commute to jobs in the suburbs (see Chapter 10). Lack of opportunity, in turn, contributes to high rates of school dropouts, crime, drugs, and the swell of social problems plaguing cities today.

The number of low-skill and low-wage service and light-manufacturing jobs in cities has also increased. For example, in the 1970s the garment industry in Los Angeles grew by almost 60 percent, creating an estimated 125,000 new jobs (Soja, 1989). In many ways, though, the new garment factories resemble the sweatshops of the nineteenth century: Violations of minimum-wage laws, mandatory overtime, unsafe working conditions, and child labor are widespread. Perhaps 80 percent of garment workers are undocumented aliens (and thus unable to protest exploitation), and 90 percent are women.

Temporary and part-time jobs have also increased. Los Angeles has a growing number of self-employed people who work as free-lance consultants out of their homes, "telecommuting" to their jobs via computer modems and fax machines and moving in and out of the labor force (Lockwood and Leinberger, 1988). While such work may pay well, it is not steady; nor do self-employed people enjoy such benefits as health insurance, sick leave, pension plans, and paid vacations.

In short, the occupational structure of cities has changed. Employment has increased at the top and the bottom of the occupational hierarchy, but the middle is shrinking. A few displaced blue-collar laborers work their way up into white-collar jobs, but many more slide downward into marginal jobs—a process that has been called the "K Marting" of the labor force. (When the president of the United Electrical Workers Local was asked what her 1,000 members—mostly skilled women earning $10 to $12 an hour—would do when General Electric closed its plant in Ontario, California, she replied, "become clerks at K Mart" [Soja, 1989, p. 207].) Some working- and lower-middle-class residents have fled the city, and others have fallen out of the working class. As a result, cities have become more polarized, with a small number of highly affluent residents, a large number of residents who are scraping by, and fewer middle-class residents in between.

The Global City

In addition, the ethnic composition of some U.S. cities has changed. In the past two decades, for example, almost 2 million people from Third World countries (mostly in Asia and Latin America) have immigrated to Los Angeles (Lockwood and Leinberger, 1988; Rieff, 1991; Soja, 1989). In one of the largest in-migrations on record, almost

CHAPTER 21

Social Movements and Collective Action

On April 29, 1992, a jury in Ventura County, California, acquitted four Los Angeles police officers on charges of using excessive force in the arrest of black motorist Rodney C. King.* The trial featured a videotape, made by a witness in an apartment across the street, of the officers kicking and clubbing King as he rolled on the ground. Black leaders had long charged the Los Angeles Police Department with systematic brutality toward African-Americans. The 81-second videotape, shown over and over on national TV, seemed to offer proof of these charges. King was hit not once or twice, but fifty-six times. Yet the jurors, none of whom were black, found three of the officers innocent and could not reach a decision on the fourth. (Charges had been dismissed against seventeen other police officers who had observed but not participated in the beating.) On the steps outside the courtroom, Councilwoman Patricia Moore called the verdict "a modern-day lynching." Another observer predicted, "This is a time bomb. It's going to blow up" (*Newsweek*, May 11, 1992, p. 33). He was right.

The first hint of unrest came over the police radio band between 4:30 and 5:00 p.m. A group of "gangbangers" had gone into Tom's Liquor Store, on the corner of Florence and Normandie Streets in the South-Central district of Los Angeles, helped themselves to bottles of liquor, and started out the door without paying. When the son of the store's Korean owner tried to block them, he was hit over the head with a beer bottle. Police arriving at the scene found a crowd of black youths hurling cans and bottles at passing motorists. When officers attempted an arrest, the crowd turned on them. At 5:45 the field commander ordered the outnumbered police to withdraw. They retreated to their cars and reassembled at a bus depot, where they waited for further instructions for several hours.

More than a thousand South-Central residents had gathered at the First African Methodist Episcopalian church to sing gospel music and listen to black leaders denounce the injustice but plead for calm. Outside, groups of youths were blocking traffic, attacking drivers, and torching their cars when they fled. At about 6:45, white truck driver Reginald Denny stopped at a red light. Several men surrounded the truck, dragged Denny from the cab, beat and kicked him, robbed him, and left him lying in a pool of blood. News helicopters whirled overhead, feeding live coverage to horrified television audiences. There was no sign of police, but four black residents later braved rocks and bottles to drive Denny to a hospital.

*Except where noted, descriptions of the King trial and the violence that followed are drawn from coverage in the *Los Angeles Times*, April 30–May 11, 1992.

Across town another crowd had gathered outside police headquarters, demanding the resignation of Police Chief Daryl Gates. In effect, the police there were under siege, unable to move in or out. For a time this multiethnic crowd was vocal but nonviolent; later they fanned out, smashing doors and windows and lighting fires as they went. By 10:00 p.m., four emergency calls a minute were pouring in to the fire department, but snipers and bands of angry youths, coupled with a lack of police escorts, prevented fire fighters from handling more than a few. In one case fire fighters had to barricade themselves inside the home of a nearby Latino family, awaiting police rescue. The smoke from out-of-control fires was so thick that Los Angeles International Airport was able to keep only one runway open.

For reasons that were never made clear, city officials were slow to react to the growing violence. Full police mobilization was not ordered until 7:30 p.m.; by then many officers had trouble getting to their posts. At 8:55 p.m. Mayor Tom Bradley declared a state of emergency, imposed a curfew, and asked California Governor Pete Wilson to send in the National Guard. But guardsmen were not deployed to the streets until mid-afternoon Thursday. On Friday President George Bush ordered 4,500 military troops and 1,000 federal law enforcement officers into Los Angeles.

On Thursday, carloads of youths armed with baseball bats, crowbars, and guns roamed the city. Normal activities ground to a halt: Buses and trains stopped running; schools closed; banks, businesses, and even some post offices shut their doors. Looters emerged from stores with their arms full of stolen merchandise, clowning for TV cameras and calling out, "Everything is free." Some arrived by car, filled their trunks, went home, and came back for another load. Anything that could be moved—from cigarettes to personal computers, couches, and even a cash machine—was carted away. Typically, after a store was emptied, it was set afire. Hopelessly outnumbered, the police could only watch. In self-defense African-American store owners taped "black-owned" signs on their doors, while Korean shopkeepers cleared their shelves or stood guard, guns drawn.

The violence and looting spread through Hollywood toward Beverly Hills and wealthy, mostly white West Los Angeles. Violence erupted in other cities as well, from San Francisco and Las Vegas to Atlanta, Tampa, and even Toronto, Canada. Not until Friday evening did the Los Angeles police, backed by guardsmen and federal troops, begin to restore order. By then, sixty people were dead, some 2,400 were injured, and more than 15,000 had been arrested. Nearly 5,200 buildings had been destroyed or

Left: *National Guardsmen patrol a deserted street in Detroit during the riot of 1967. Far from being the work of mindless mobs or a hard core of agitators, the ghetto riots of the 1960s were a spontaneous but purposeful response to unacceptable social and economic conditions.* Above: *In 1992, Los Angeles and other American cities erupted in mostly unplanned, uncontrolled, and violent mass actions in response to the verdict in the Rodney King beating case. That trial was the precipitating event, but the underlying reasons for these riots, too, were long-term social problems.*

severely damaged by arson and vandalism, many of them businesses, at an estimated cost of $1 billion and 40,000 jobs.

The media verdict was clear: This was the worst urban riot in recent U.S. history. There can be no doubting the violence or the cost. It is important, though, to remember that "riot" is only one possible label for the upheaval. For many African-American observers and participants, it was a "rebellion" against long-standing abuse.

The events in Los Angeles illustrate what sociologists call **collective action**, socially shared but relatively nonroutine responses to events, things, or ideas. Collective action usually involves large numbers of people who may not even know one another and differs, often strikingly, from the habitual patterns of everyday life (G. B. Rose, 1982). A clothing fashion that sweeps the country, a bizarre rumor that spreads from city to city, a sudden mass hysteria or panic, a riot or other unusual form of mob action are all incidents of collective action. In some cases collective action is a more or less isolated event, which subsides as suddenly as it erupted. In other cases it is part of a **social movement**, which is "a conscious, collective, organized attempt to bring about or resist large-scale change in the social order by noninstitutionalized means" (J. Wilson, 1973, p. 8).

It is easy to recognize collective action as a variety of ***social action***. Other key sociological concepts are also important in understanding collective action and social movements. We will see, for example, that participation in social movements is shaped by ***social structure***, both through the networks of personal relationships that help people mobilize and through the way in which such large-scale structures as class shape people's decisions to participate. ***Culture*** shapes collective actions by determining both their form (violent or nonviolent, for example) and their goals (such as racial equality, women's rights, world peace, or an end to abortion). According to some sociological theories, collective action is best understood as a response to failures of ***functional integration***, for example, when social systems fail to meet the needs of one segment of the population, like inner-city African-Americans in the United States today. Other theories place more emphasis on ***power***, and we will see how social movements and the official response to them reflect the distribution of social power. Indeed, perhaps the most important reason people join together for collective action is to wield power that they would lack if they acted separately.

CROWDS AND COLLECTIVE ACTION

A **crowd** is a temporary collection of people who gather around some person or event and who are conscious of and influenced by one another. Crowds differ from other social groups primarily in that they are short-lived, are only loosely structured, and use conventional spaces or buildings for unconventional purposes (Snow, Zurcher, and Peters, 1981).

Types of Crowds

In his classic essay "Collective Behavior" (1939/1951), the sociologist Herbert Blumer described four kinds of crowds: *casual, conventional, expressive,* and *acting.* A **casual crowd** forms spontaneously when something attracts the attention of passersby. For instance, when a number of people walking along a city street stop to view a window washer high overhead, they form a casual crowd. The members of such a crowd, writes Blumer, "come and go, giving but temporary attention to the object which has awakened [their] interest . . . and entering into only feeble association with one another" (p. 178).

Passengers on a plane, shoppers in a store, or the audience at a concert illustrate what Blumer called a **conventional crowd.** Members of a conventional crowd gather for a specific purpose and behave according to established norms. For example, although booing is expected of the crowd at a football game, it is considered inappropriate for the crowd at a classical music concert. Relatively little interaction occurs in a conventional crowd. People are pursuing a common goal, but they tend to do so as individuals. Exchanges among such people are usually highly routinized and impersonal.

People at rock festivals, revival meetings, and Mardi Gras celebrations present examples of **expressive crowds.** The emotionally charged members of an expressive crowd get carried away by their enthusiasm and intense feelings, behaving in ways they would consider unacceptable in other settings. Expressing their feelings becomes their primary aim. The legendary Woodstock Music and Art Fair, held in New York's Catskill Mountains in August 1969, provides an example of such a crowd. An impressive array of rock stars drew more than 300,000 young people to the farm where the festival was held. The mood of the crowd became increasingly joyous, and today the event is remembered perhaps more for this experience and expression of good feeling than for the concert itself.

The emotional tone of an acting crowd is different from that of an expressive crowd. An **acting crowd** is an excited, volatile collection of people who focus on a controversial event that provokes their indignation, anger, and desire to act. Examples of acting crowds might be gang members who beat up a youth from another neighborhood who strays onto their turf and fans at a soccer match who go on a rampage when a referee makes a questionable call. Unlike members of an expressive crowd, who see release of their feelings as an end in itself, members of an acting crowd seek redress of a perceived wrong. When a large acting crowd engages in violence or threatens to do so, it is often referred to as a **mob** (Hoult, 1969). Because the social effects of crowd action can be far-reaching, we will examine it in some detail.

Crowd Action

For centuries, mass uprisings and destructive riots have been the nightmare of people in power. Crowd action was common in eighteenth- and nineteenth-century Europe (Rudé, 1964). In town and country, throngs of armed men and women took over markets and warehouses, demanding the rollback of prices and sometimes seizing goods. In England, angry bands of craftspeople burned factories and destroyed the machines that threatened their livelihood. On July 14, 1789, Parisians stormed the ancient Bastille prison in the most famous confrontation of the French Revolution.

Violent crowds have also figured importantly in American history. The nineteenth century was marked by farmers' revolts, miners' rebellions, bloody battles between unions and police, lynchings, and urban riots. The 1863 Civil War draft riot in New York City, which raged for four days and left 1,000 dead, was probably the worst riot in this country's history. Crowd action has also turned violent in the twentieth century. In the 1960s especially, one black ghetto after another exploded; the nation as a whole seemed threatened. The recent violence in Los Angeles frightened the whole country and led people to demand answers to questions like these: Why do riots break out? Why do crowds engage in actions that most people ordinarily condemn? Were rioters just emotionally upset, or were they consciously choosing their actions, perhaps as a kind of rebellion?

The Social Psychology of Crowds

Until recently, mobs were seen as little more than unchained beasts, spurred by powerful, violent urges and with no sense of reason. What people did in crowds was seen not as the collective *action* of rational humans, but as collective *behavior* that was the result of regression to primitive levels of psychology. A chief proponent of this psychological perspective was the Frenchman Gustave Le Bon. Le Bon (1841–1931) was an aristocrat in an era when the masses of common people were challenging the hereditary ruling class. As far as Le Bon was concerned, the old social system, with its privileges and security for elites like himself, was being threatened by emotionally volatile mobs. Le Bon regarded mobs as purely irrational and destructive, capable of tearing apart the social order. He developed a deep distrust of all political dissent, whether it was in support of parliamentary democracy or socialism. "The age we are about to enter," wrote Le Bon, "will be in truth the era of crowds." He meant this as a dire warning.

In his book *The Crowd* (1895/1960), Le Bon argued that involvement in a crowd puts individuals "in possession of a collective mind" that makes them think, feel, and act quite differently than they would if each person were alone. Contemporary psychologists refer to this as *deindividuation*: Members of mobs become anonymous to themselves and others, and inhibitions are lost in the thrill of being part of something larger than oneself (Wallace and Zamichow, 1992, p. A25). Crowds, Le Bon maintained, gain control over people much as hypnotists do. Individuals in crowds become highly suggestible; they "will undertake . . . acts with irresistible impetuosity." Waves of emotion sweep through crowds, "infecting" one person after another. This phenomenon is known as **social contagion**: the rapid spread of a mood or behavior from one individual to another. As Le Bon saw it, the thin veneer of civilization falls away, allowing primitive motivations and antisocial impulses to rise to the surface.

In the 1950s, the sociologist Herbert Blumer (1939/1951) refined Le Bon's ideas. He traced the social contagion to an "exciting event" (such as the verdict in the King case) that creates unrest in a group of people. The people begin milling about, "as if seeking to find or avoid something, but without knowing what it is they are trying to find or avoid" (p. 173). As they search for clues, excited behavior or rhetoric catches their attention. Instead of judging these actions, as they ordinarily would, they respond impulsively and model their own behavior after them. This reaction reinforces the original actors, making them still more excited (what Blumer called the *circular reaction*). As excitement builds, people become more inclined to act on their mounting feelings of agitation. Often the result is *mass hysteria.*

Mass hysteria can be seen not only in mobs and crowds but also in fads and crazes. In one famous case, Seattle newspapers in the spring of 1954 carried the first of several stories about damage to automobile windshields in a town eighty miles to the north of the city. The windshields had small pit marks and bubbles in them, and tiny, metallic-looking particles were sometimes found embedded in the glass. The cause of this curious damage was unknown, but police suspected vandals. On the evening of April 14, the mysterious destructive agent appeared to hit Seattle itself. During the next two days, nearly 250 people called the Seattle police, reporting windshield damage to more than 3,000 cars. By far the most frequently rumored explanation for the epidemic was radioactive fallout from H-bomb tests in the north Pacific. As this rumor swept Seattle, frightened residents desperately tried to devise ways of protecting their windshields. On the evening of April 15, the mayor of Seattle appealed to the governor and to the president for emergency help. Then, as quickly as it had arisen, the mass hysteria died down. Later, a team of experts determined that the windshields had always been pitted. People simply had not noticed them before because drivers customarily look *through* their windshields, not *at* them. Their own fear had made them imagine a threat that did not exist (Medalia and Larson, 1958).

Communication: Rumors and the Mass Media

For any type of collective action to take place, people must have some means of communicating their fears or frenzy to one another. Rumors play a prominent role in mob action. A **rumor** is an unverified story that circulates from person to person and is accepted as fact, although its original source may be vague or unknown. Rumors proliferate in tense and ambiguous situations, when people are unable to learn the facts or when, for one reason or another, they distrust the information they receive (Rosnow and Fine, 1976). Rumors reflect people's desire to find meaning in events, and thus represent a form of group problem solving. In Seattle, residents thought the pits in their windshields were caused by radioactive fallout from H-bomb tests. Although this interpretation turned out to be wrong, it did temporarily solve their problem of finding some explanation of the mysterious damage they believed they saw.

Most rumors are born, live, and die within a relatively short period. After studying the transmission of rumors in the laboratory and in the field, the psychologists Gordon W. Allport and Leo Postman (1947) discovered a basic pattern. A person hears a story that seems interesting and repeats it—or what is remembered of it—to a friend. Gradually, the original story is reduced to a few essential details that are easy to tell. Allport and Postman call this process *leveling*: "As a rumor travels, it tends to grow shorter, more concise, more easily grasped and told. In successive versions, fewer words are used and fewer details are mentioned" (p. 75). People also tend to alter details to make the story more coherent and more in keeping with their preconceptions. In the early stages of the 1992 disturbance in Los Angeles, rumors that police had donned riot gear apparently inflamed the crowd, encouraging them to arm themselves with stones, bottles, clubs, or whatever was handy. In fact, only one police officer had put on a helmet. But the rumor of police preparations for attack conformed to widespread beliefs about police brutality, confirming the crowd's expectations. The next day, rumors that carloads of African-American youth were "invading" affluent white suburbs caused panic and sent residents to supermarkets to stock up for the expected siege.

The mass media also play an important role in crowd action today. In the Los Angeles incident, television was both a catalyst and a target. Throughout the trial of the police officers, TV networks had replayed the video of the King beating. The fact that it was a "home movie," rather than a glossy professional report, added to people's sense of its truthfulness. When people see an event on television, they tend to believe that they saw it firsthand, for themselves—and to disbelieve people who interpret the images differently.

The verdict in the King case was broadcast live, followed by shouts of disbelief among customers at an African-American barber shop on one station and outraged statements by public officials (including Mayor Bradley) on others. When the mood on the street turned ugly, news stations competed for the most sensational footage. In watching the news on TV, people tend to forget that reporting is selective, with editors deciding which events are newsworthy and which are not (Gans, 1979; Gitlin, 1985). As is often the case, shots of violence were selected over shots of calm. One TV station superimposed images of street violence over choir music from the church gathering. Another actually reported the news *before* it happened: the reporter commented that he hadn't seen "any fires *yet*" (*Newsweek*, May 11, 1992, p. 43). Simply by being there, reporters created news—namely, assaults on themselves and their equipment. Television reporters also broadcast the message that the police were not responding to the violence and looting. In effect, the cameras showed potential participants where the action was. In the words of one commentator, "Helicopter one-upmanship on Wednesday night led to a two-hour invitation, delivered by an airborne minicam, to riot" (Hewitt, 1992, p. M1). At the very least, television reinforced the feeling that law and order had broken down. Moreover, without media coverage it seems unlikely that the violence would have spread to other cities.

Emergent Norms and Social Relationships

Few contemporary sociologists dispute the observation that emotions and behavior sometimes spread through crowds, whether via rumors or the mass media, as if they were contagious. However, most contemporary sociologists believe that Le Bon and Blumer underestimated the organization of crowds and their capacity for rational behavior. It is simplistic, they argue, to view people in crowds as impulsive, unpredictable creatures who can no longer control their own behavior. Ralph Turner and Lewis Killian (1972), for example, question the implicit assumption that social conformity no longer operates in a crowd. According to their **emergent-norm theory**, people develop new social norms as they interact in situations that lack firm guidelines for coping. These norms then exert a powerful influence on their behavior.

The new norms evolve through a gradual process of social exploration and testing. One or more people may suggest a course of action (shouting obscenities or hurling bottles, for example). Other suggestions follow. The crowd begins to define the situation, to develop a justification for acts that would in other circumstances seem questionable. In this way new norms may emerge that condone violence and destruction, but still impose some limits on crowd behavior. For example, all the motorists assaulted during the Los Angeles violence were Caucasian, Hispanic, or Asian; none were black, though many more African-Americans were accidentally injured or killed by gunfire. Similarly, Asian (mostly Korean) businesses seem to have been singled out for looting because of special resentment against their owners as outsiders and successful immigrants who were apparently taking opportunities away from African-Americans.

The emergence of new norms, Turner and Killian argue, does not mean that members of a crowd come to think and feel as one. Although it may appear to outsiders that a crowd is a unanimous whole, some participants may just be going along to avoid disapproval and ridicule. Thus, unlike Le Bon and Blumer, Turner and Killian believe that crowd unanimity is little more than an illusion. The illusion is created by the fact that crowd members tend to demand at least surface conformity to the new norms that have evolved.

Extending Turner and Killian's ideas, other sociologists have argued that new social relationships also emerge in crowds (Weller and Quarantelli, 1973). Consider lynching, a fairly common form of crowd violence in the early American West and, until recent decades, in the South as well. A lynch mob dispenses with conventional norms of trial by jury, rule of law, and execution only by the state, replacing them with the norms of a vigilante trial and punishment by mob consensus. But new social relationships develop, too. Participants, improvising a division of labor, informally designate such roles as prosecutor, witnesses, jury members, and executioners. Crowds, in short, are neither normless nor totally lacking in social organization. Both norms and social relationships always emerge in them, making them much more structured than they seem at first glance.

Crowd Action as Rational Decision Making

Contrary to the common view of "crowd madness" and "irrational rioting," rational-choice theories (see Chapter 1) have shown that people do not always "lose their heads" (their rationality) simply because they are part of a crowd (Berk, 1974). They continue to weigh the costs and benefits of possible courses of action. The costs associated with rioting are the risk of personal injury and the likelihood of being arrested. In a crowd that greatly outnumbers police, these risks are relatively small. Moreover, the benefits of mob action may outweigh the risks for people who are disadvantaged and have many pent-up frustrations. These benefits may be either tangible, such as looted merchandise, or intangible, such as social recognition and emotional release. In any case, Berk argues, people in mobs calculate that violence will pay off in their particular situation.

Not all sociologists agree that crowd action is this calculated. But riots clearly do gain attention. In the aftermath of the riot in the Watts section of Los Angeles in 1965, Martin Luther King, Jr., toured the ruins. He was approached by a group of young men claiming victory. "How can you say you won when 34 Negroes are dead, your community is destroyed and whites are using the riots as an excuse for inaction?" King asked. The youths replied, "We won because we made them pay attention to us" (quoted in *Los Angeles Times*, May 2, 1992, p. A2). And so it was in 1992. President Bush ordered the Justice Department to press federal civil rights charges against the officers who beat Rodney King only *after* the riot. Before the riot, neither the president nor Congress had paid serious attention to the problems of inner cities. Program after program had been cut back or canceled. After the riot, politicians scrambled to be associated with urban initiatives. Within a week of the violence, President Bush had pledged $600 million for restoration, Congress had introduced emergency legislation for $300 million in small-business loans, and California Governor Pete Wilson had proposed $20 million in state funds for job training. Many community leaders—and sociologists—hold that these measures do not address the underlying causes of the riot. Nonetheless, whether the violence is called a riot or a rebellion, it did call public attention to the desperate situation of South-Central Los Angeles.

USING THE KEY CONCEPTS TO ANALYZE THE LOS ANGELES "RIOT"

Everyday explanations of the Los Angeles violence focus on the verdict in the Rodney King case. Certainly the trial touched off the riot or rebellion. It was what the sociologist Neil Smelser (1963) called a **precipitating event**, an incident that confirms people's suspicions and fears—in this case, about how the criminal justice system is biased against African-Americans. But injustices occur every day; riots and rebellions do not. Our five key concepts can help explain the underlying causes and significance of the events in Los Angeles.

Crowd Action as Social Action

The behavior of a crowd is ***social action*** by definition, because crowd members' actions are in response to, or coordinated with, or oriented toward, one another. As we noted earlier, people sometimes try to explain crowd action by the characteristics of the individuals who participate. This was certainly true of the Los Angeles events. One popular explanation was a kind of "riffraff theory." It held that only criminal types participate in riots, and that a hard core of agitators incites violence despite the strong disapproval of area residents. Thus, many outsiders blamed the violence on criminals and opportunists, especially gang members (Merina and Mitchell, 1992). However, eyewitnesses reported that a broad spectrum of citizens—young and old, African-American and Hispanic, Asian and Caucasian—joined the action. "You had 7- and 8-year-olds all the way up to 60-year-olds," said one South-Central resident. "You had everyday citizens. . . . I thought about participating myself" (p. A12). While some people in the crowds saw themselves as making a political statement or avenging past insults, others seized the opportunity to acquire goods they could not afford, and still others felt compelled to steal before the stores were stripped bare and they would not be able to feed and care for their families. (Along with televisions, sneakers, and guns, disposable diapers were among the most popular items seized by looters.)

This mixture of motives is common to many crowd actions. It was also the case in the ghetto riots of 1967, as the National Advisory Commission on Civil Disorders (1968), appointed by President Lyndon Johnson, pointed out. In Detroit, for instance, the commission found that nearly 40 percent of ghetto residents either participated in the crowd action or were bystanders to it. This hardly represents a deviant minority. The Detroit "rioters," moreover, were on average better-educated, better-informed, and more involved in the community than were the nonrioters. And most of the rioters were employed, although many thought their jobs were beneath them.

Even a riot has a kind of social organization. In Los Angeles, groups of young men—not simply thousands of isolated individuals—were drawn into collective action. For some, this meant deciding to burn down a store. For others, it meant organizing to try to protect their homes. In South-Central Los Angeles, crowds gathered at specific places, not randomly throughout the area. In particular, they gathered wherever the police were congregated—partly to taunt them—and wherever the media were present. In these crowds, some young men performed while larger groups served as their audience: The young men shouted insults at police, ran out in front of the crowd to throw a rock or bottle, and threatened any white passersby. These actions can be understood only in terms of the relationship between the individuals who performed them and the audiences who watched and sometimes shouted their approval. However, all these kinds of crowd action depended not just on the other people around but on the patterns of social organization by which people were both motivated to join the crowd and organized within it. For example, people in the crowds were often with small groups of friends; this helped to reduce their fear. Bigger, more structural factors were also involved.

Structural Conduciveness

Smelser (1963) coined the term **structural conduciveness** to describe aspects of ***social structure*** that facilitate collective action. Perhaps the most important structural issue behind the Los Angeles upheaval—and smaller crowd actions that took place around the country—was the deterioration of inner cities in recent decades (see Chapter 20). Ghetto residents were left in a state of economic isolation. At least one member of most inner-city families, especially young men, was unemployed. With more than half a million people, South-Central Los Angeles had only thirty-five supermarkets and fewer than twenty bank branches (*Los Angeles Times*, May 1, 1992). Many residents had to either take two bus rides to shop for food or patronize higher-priced neighborhood grocery stores. For those who had jobs, cashing a paycheck meant waiting in long lines or paying high fees at check-cashing stores. About one in four South-Central residents was poor, almost twice the rate for urban whites. Yet the poor watched the same TV shows, with their tantalizing portrayals of goods and lifestyles they could not afford, that the middle class did. Such economic frustration is one of the structural preconditions for crowd action.

Significantly, the main targets of the 1992 crowds were not the police, as in earlier riots, but retail stores, factories, and other enterprises. Much of the rioters' wrath was aimed specifically at shops owned by Korean-Americans. Immigrants, with only small amounts of capital to invest, often fill the need for goods and services in inner-city neighborhoods. They succeed in part by working long hours themselves and hiring family members; but as a result, they are less likely to hire local residents and more likely to be cut off socially from the neighborhoods they serve. Their success, however modest, also invites the envy of local residents. "They just charge high prices and take our money," said one looter of Korean businesses. "Now we are taking some back" (quoted in *Los Angeles Times*, May 1, 1992, p. A24). Relations between African-American residents and Asian store owners in South-Central were particularly tense because a Korean storekeeper had recently been given probation for shooting to death a fifteen-year-old girl she suspected of shoplifting.

The fact that poor African-Americans are crowded together in inner cities also facilitates crowd action. Residents live in close proximity to one another, and substandard housing encourages many to spend a great deal of time outdoors. In addition, many are unemployed or employed at irregular hours. As a result, the streets are normally filled with people. If an incident enraged, say, Irish-Americans, who are dispersed all over the Los

Angeles suburbs, mobilization for immediate crowd action would be difficult. But when something happens in South-Central, crowds gather rapidly. News of the verdict in the King case, broadcast live on radio and TV, spread like wildfire. So did news that a riot was under way.

Functional *Dis*-Integration

Under optimal conditions, the different elements of a social system work together, each contributing to the smooth functioning of the whole. When this ***functional integration*** breaks down, collective action is more likely.

To a large degree, American society has passed inner cities by. Businesses have moved their factories to the countryside or even to Third World nations and their retail outlets and offices to the suburbs. The middle class, both black and white, has largely abandoned the city as well. As a result, big-city mayors and political machines no longer play a pivotal role in politics. Beltways enable commuters to avoid even driving through urban neighborhoods. In a way, today's inner cities are like yesterday's rural backwaters: They are literally *dis*-integrated, cut off from the mainstream of economic, political, and social life.

The Los Angeles riot provided an example of disintegration at the local political level. Los Angeles is the only major city in the United States in which the mayor cannot hire and fire the chief of police. Rather, the chief reports to a Police Commission. To remove a chief, the Police Commission must file formal charges with the Civil Service Commission, a procedure that can take months. Moreover, the City Council can override the Police Commission. In short, there is no clear chain of command. Mayor Bradley had tried to force Chief Gates to resign after the Rodney King beating, but without success. At the time of the riot, the two men apparently had not spoken to each other for almost a year. Mayor Bradley did not have the authority to order police into neighborhoods where the riot was gathering force, and Chief Gates decided to avoid confrontation. When the mayor asked Governor Wilson to send in the National Guard, on the first night of rioting, it was the governor who had to arrange a conference call to convince Chief Gates and his deputy to agree. The second day of the riot, guardsmen sat in armories awaiting orders; again, the governor had to step in to demand action. Thus, divisions within local government prevented a quick police response, which might have prevented a full-scale riot or at least cut it short.

Cultural Clashes

Most Americans, including President Bush, were surprised by the not-guilty verdicts in the Rodney King case. Polls found that a majority of white as well as black Americans thought that the verdicts were wrong and that the federal government should bring charges (*Newsweek*, May 11, 1992). This surface agreement obscured the legacy of racism in American ***culture***, and the long-term, continuing separation between black and white Americans. A white person watching the videotape of King's beating might feel sickened: "How can they do that to that poor guy?" An African-American would probably feel threatened as well: "That poor guy could be me!" To a degree that most white Americans cannot imagine, most African-Americans (especially males) live in fear of police brutality, not to mention insults from white cab drivers, store clerks, headwaiters, and others. The verdict in the King case seemed to confirm that however innocent they might be and however badly they have been treated by authorities, African-Americans are presumed to be guilty by white authorities. At the same time, many white Americans live in fear of black crime and violence. "For blacks the acquittal, and for whites the aftermath, tended to confirm each race's worst fears and suspicions about the other" (*Time*, May 11, 1992, p. 20).

Blacks and whites also tended to differ in their explanations of the events in Los Angeles (Lauter and Fluwood, 1992). Many African-Americans saw the basic problem as racial oppression, the product of a system that routinely neglects and often brutalizes blacks. Many white Americans saw the primary problem as social pathology, due in part to individual irresponsibility and irreverence for basic family and community values. These differences helped produce the contrasting labels among blacks ("rebellion") and whites ("riot").

The division between black and white Americans was not the only cultural gap that surfaced in Los Angeles, however. As we have noted, much of the violence was directed against Korean-Americans. Ghetto residents saw Asian shopkeepers not only as exploitative, but also as arrogant and exclusive (Koppel, 1992). In a meeting held to bring the two groups together, African-Americans complained that Koreans typically put change on the counter rather than in the customer's hand, which they perceived as an act of disdain. Koreans explained that in their culture it is insulting to physically touch a nonrelative, particularly a woman. Koreans expect customers to ask for what they want; African-Americans like to browse. Under conditions of economic conflict and inequality, violations of such minor cultural norms can lead to major hostility.

Other cultural groups were drawn into the conflict. Japanese- and Chinese-Americans admitted worrying that they would be mistaken for Korean-Americans and also feeling guilty about wanting to dissociate themselves from other Asians (Woo, 1992). Hispanics occupied an ambiguous role in the upheaval, sometimes becoming the victims of mob violence and other times joining the mob. White Anglo-Americans joined the crowd outside police headquarters the night the riot erupted, and sometimes participated in the looting on subsequent days. Los Angeles had often been cited as a "world city," a model of the changing ethnic mix in the United States. The events of 1992 showed just how volatile that mixture could be.

Power and Powerlessness

Riots are an assertion of ***power*** by the powerless—the last resort of people who cannot make themselves heard through conventional political and economic channels. They nearly always pit the poor against the rich. To the upper classes, riots may look like senseless, self-destructive, emotional outbursts. To participants, however, such collective action may be a form of collective bargaining (Piven and Cloward, 1979; Thompson, 1971). By creating or threatening to create civil disorder, rioters prod government into action. That action may be repressive, but very poor people may feel they have little to lose. The dangers they face may seem well worth the feeling of being in control for once, however briefly. Shortly after midnight on the first night of the Los Angeles disturbance, Police Chief Gates announced that the city was calming down. But a rioter told reporters, "It ain't over till *we* say it's over"—and he, not Gates, proved to be right (Koppel, 1992).

In the urban riots that swept the United States in the 1960s, violence was confined almost entirely to the African-American ghetto. White-owned stores may have been destroyed, but white neighborhoods were not threatened. In Los Angeles in 1992, violence did spill over ghetto borders and involve other ethnic groups. The number of rioters who left downtown for the beaches, the hills, and the malls was small, and the damage relatively slight; but the danger seemed real to well-to-do whites who were used to feeling protected by the power their wealth bestowed and who were not accustomed to seeing poor blacks try to exert power directly. "There was a siege mentality out here—a sense of the have-nots coming after the haves," said the owner of a suburban bookstore (quoted in *Los Angeles Times*, May 7, 1992, p. J1). Suddenly, affluent Angelenos who had been watching the riots from a safe distance, on TV, smelled smoke. Although few stores outside South-Central were looted and few homes burned, the psychological barrier—the feeling of suburban invulnerability—was breached.

SOCIAL MOVEMENTS

Social movements are special cases of collective action. Riots, panics, fads, and other types of collective action are generally short-lived and, though sometimes calculated, typically heedless and emotional. In contrast, social movements are sustained and deliberate efforts to bring about or resist social change. Although they may attract crowds, most social movements include formal organizations with hierarchical structures and formal ties to one another. They differ from more institutionalized efforts to influence social patterns in their willingness to use unconventional tactics. Social movements frequently employ mass marches and rallies, sit-ins, boycotts, and sometimes even violence, sabotage, and other illegal acts (especially when agents of social control try to suppress them) to make their grievances known.

Because they challenge existing patterns of ***functional integration***, social movements nearly always face a variety of obstacles. Some people may actively oppose them, while others remain indifferent. Social movements succeed only when they are able to wield significant ***power***. Revolutions do this by attempting to seize control of the government or state and use its power to bring about social change. Other social movements, such as the women's movement, focus on altering the ***culture***—on changing people's attitudes, beliefs, and values, and thereby their behavior.

Explaining Social Movements

Let's turn now to the reasons that a social movement arises—to what makes people engage in unconventional, often risky, collective action in order to bring about or resist change.

Social and Economic Deprivation

Social movements may arise from social and economic deprivation. When discontent with existing social arrangements becomes deep and broad enough, people join together and fight back. Karl Marx held that the basic causes of revolutions and other social movements were structural. The owners of the means of production in a society are driven to increase their privileges by exploiting

The social movements of the 1960s were based on the hopes and frustrations of certain groups, such as African-Americans; but they also brought very different groups together. Top left: *Bob Dylan jams with Student Nonviolent Coordinating Committee (SNCC) workers.* Top right: *Vietnam war veterans lead an antiwar demonstration.* Bottom: *National Guardsmen rough up a photographer at a black civil-rights demonstration.*

the laboring masses. Over time this exploitative economic structure leads to widespread poverty and deprivation, which in turn sparks revolution. The French Revolution, for instance, was preceded by a sharp increase in the price of bread (the highest price in seventy years) as a result of poor harvests in 1787 and 1788. Workers in the cities and even rural residents faced severe hunger. In 1789 they rebelled.

As we discussed in Chapter 16, Marx contended that in capitalist societies, the ever-increasing use of machinery and factory production would condemn workers to more and more menial tasks, thus continually depressing their wages and feeding their sense of alienation. The economic cycle of boom and bust that characterizes capitalist societies would aggravate the misery of the working class. Eventually, workers would find their exploitation intolerable and would organize to overthrow their oppressors.

Not all sociologists agree with the view that progressive impoverishment puts people in a revolutionary frame of mind. The French observer Alexis de Tocqueville (1856) emphasized the role of ***culture*** in revolutions and social movements. People's actual conditions may not get very much worse (indeed, they may improve); but new cultural beliefs and ideas may cause them to view their situation as intolerable. Thus the notion of continual progress, faith that democracy could solve all sorts of social problems, and belief in the value of individualism—all new to the eighteenth century—were destabilizing. When the downtrodden begin to believe that a better life is possible, they react by reaching for it. "Evils which are patiently endured when they seem inevitable," wrote Tocqueville, "become intolerable once the idea of escape from them is suggested" (p. 214). Sociologists call this gap between people's expectations and their actual conditions **relative deprivation** (Gurr, 1970).

Relative deprivation occurs under a variety of circumstances. Tocqueville identified one condition, that of *rising expectations*. It was a sense of rising expectations, some sociologists say, that bred the black protest movement and the ghetto outbreaks of the 1960s (Abeles, 1976; Geschwender, 1964). The economic prosperity of the 1950s and the early gains of the civil rights movement led African-Americans to believe that their circumstances would soon improve substantially. The new civil rights legislation and President Lyndon Johnson's War on Poverty program, however, delivered little. The Johnson administration's promise of a Great Society faded as the United States became increasingly preoccupied with the war in Vietnam. To raise people's expectations of a feast and then deliver crumbs is to create a socially explosive situation. In this case, the explosion included the ghetto riots and the Black Power movement of the late 1960s.

The sociologist James Davies (1962, 1974) has described this pattern as a "J-curve" because a graph of a sudden, sharp reversal in a pattern of long-term improvement can look like an upside-down "J" (see Figure 21.1). Davies bases his analysis on the observation of such events as Dorr's Rebellion in Rhode Island in 1842, the Pullman strike of 1894, the Russian Revolution of 1917, and the Egyptian Revolution of 1953. Davies concludes that revolutionary movements are most likely to spring up when a prolonged period of economic and social improvement is followed by a drastic reversal in people's fortunes. The first period presumably creates an expectation that things will steadily get better; the second period stimulates a terrible fear that all past progress will suddenly be irretrievably lost. Davies believes that the actual conditions prevailing in the period of reversal are less important than the psychological state they foster. Revolutions flare up when the gap between what people expect and what they actually receive suddenly widens.

Resource Mobilization

Most contemporary sociologists see deprivation alone as an insufficient explanation for the rise of a social movement (McAdam, McCarthy, and Zald, 1988; Tilly, 1978). They contend that discontent is always widespread; yet full-fledged social movements are relatively infrequent. The reason, they argue, is that discontent must be coupled with the ability to mobilize resources on behalf of a group's collective interests. Without sufficient resources and the organization to use those resources effectively, even the most aggrieved people cannot launch a social movement.

The resources that can be mobilized in support of a social movement consist of tangible assets and human skills (Freeman, 1979; McCarthy and Zald, 1977). Among the primary tangible assets are money (which can purchase many other assets), channels of mass communication (leaflets, newspapers, radio, and television) to publicize the movement's goals, and space to house its headquarters. Human skills include leadership, organizational talent, personal prestige (which is helpful in attracting followers and in gaining social acceptance), and intimate knowledge of the people or institutions the movement hopes to change. Also crucial are the time to devote to movement activities and a commitment to the cause (that is, a willingness to endure risk and inconvenience so that the movement's goals can be achieved). Support may come from people who are not directly involved but are sympathetic with the cause as well as from inside.

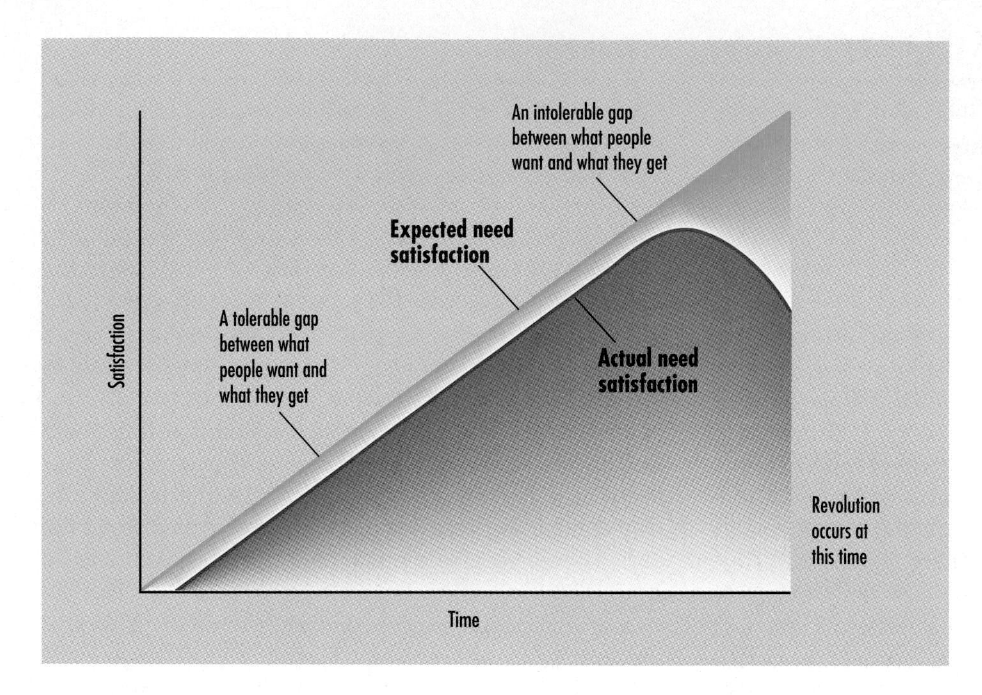

FIGURE 21.1 / Davies's J-Curve Theory of Revolution

Source: Adapted from James C. Davies, "Toward a Theory of Revolution," *American Sociological Review* 27 (February 1962), fig. 1, p. 6.

The ability to mobilize resources also depends on favorable opportunities in the social environment (Tilly, 1978; Zald and McCarthy, 1987). It was not an accident that the prosperous 1950s and 1960s gave birth to a number of social movements, including the civil rights, women's, and environmental movements, which we will analyze below. During times of prosperity people generally are more receptive to calls to improve the conditions of underprivileged groups and more willing to give time, money, and other resources to causes than they are when they are struggling to keep their own heads above water.

Still another factor conducive to resource mobilization is what Doug McAdam (1982) calls *cognitive liberation.* Cognitive (or mental) liberation occurs when members of an aggrieved group come to view their situation both as unjust and as potentially changeable through collective action. People must come to see their troubles as the result of social injustice, not personal failure; identify with others in the same situation; and put combined interests ahead of personal gain. Cognitive liberation depends on both a favorable opportunity structure (which holds out hope that change is possible) and organization (which allows insurgents to share their views). The result of all these factors is collective action.

Whether or not collective action is successful is another matter. Usually, a social movement owes much of its success to effective leadership. Sociologists have identified several types of leaders, ranging from the "agitator" or "prophet," whose skills at articulating some demand compel public attention, to the "administrator," who puts together the nuts and bolts of an organized campaign (Wilson, 1973). Sometimes a single leader exerts several kinds of leadership simultaneously. Martin Luther King, Jr., and Betty Friedan were both influential prophets who voiced the concerns of blacks and women, respectively. In addition, both functioned as administrators. King was spokesperson for the Southern Christian Leadership Conference and Friedan for the National Organization for Women. Such versatile leaders tend to be the exception. More often, a movement develops a division of labor among several leaders who have different kinds of skills.

The sociologists John McCarthy and Mayer Zald (1973, 1977; Zald and McCarthy, 1987) have proposed that many modern-day social movements are largely the creation of outside leadership. They say that a groundswell of discontent among aggrieved individuals is of secondary importance in generating a social movement. Skilled leaders can take weak and ill-defined discontent and broaden its base. For this reason, grass-roots support for some social movements actually comes *after* the movement is under way. For example, the movement to provide federally funded health care for the elderly in the United States did not derive initially from an outcry among senior citizens. Instead, the movement's principal organization, the National Council for Senior Citizens for Health Care through Social Security (NCSC), was staffed primarily by young and middle-aged professionals and funded by the AFL-CIO. Organizers staged rallies across the country and encouraged mass petitioning. Later, when the movement encountered opposition from the American Medical Association, the NCSC began to use its resources to mobilize a large membership base among the elderly. Thus, active support from the aggrieved group was sought only after the movement was in full swing. Far from involving a popular outcry of discontent, this social movement was professionally planned and directed by outsiders (A. Rose, 1967).

Social Revolution as Structural Change

Many of the movements studied by sociologists seek only moderate reforms—like the improvement of access to public transportation and buildings sought by the movement for the rights of handicapped people. Other movements seek more basic change, and these can result in revolutions. The sociologist Theda Skocpol defines **social revolutions** as "rapid, basic transformations of a society's state and class structures . . . accompanied and in part carried through by class-based revolts from below" (1979, p. 4). The simultaneous occurrence of class upheaval and sociopolitical transformation distinguishes a social revolution from a rebellion (which does not result in any structural change), from political revolution (which involves no change in social structure), and from such revolutionary processes as industrialization (which involve no change in political structure).

Skocpol explains social revolution by combining aspects of Marxist and resource-mobilization theories. She finds that although underlying class conflict is fundamental to revolution, it is also necessary to consider how the class members are organized and what their resources are. Rather than attempting to create a general theory for all revolutions, she has tried to construct an explanation for social revolutions in three agrarian states: France at the time of the overthrow of Louis XVI (1789), Russia at the time Czar Nicholas II was deposed (1917), and China when the Qing dynasty was ousted (1911) and again when the communist government was established (1949).

On the basis of her careful study of these revolutions, Skocpol highlights three factors that tend to be ignored in other theories of revolution. First, revolutions are rarely started intentionally; they generally emerge from structural crises, such as government budgetary deficits or wars. Both the cost and the unpopularity of World War I contributed to the Russian Revolution of 1917, for example. Second, revolutions are not purely products of internal forces. International relations and developments (particularly long-drawn-out wars and military defeats) contribute to the emergence of crises and revolutions by undermining old political regimes. Third, states have an existence of their own and are not necessarily dependent on the interests and structure of the dominant class. Revolutions are against states, not directly against ruling classes.

Skocpol's account of revolution places major emphasis on ***social structure***, on the basic conditions that make states vulnerable. Jack Goldstone (1991) has extended this line of argument, showing how rapid population growth helps to produce government crises by creating more job seekers, inflation in food prices, and other demands on government treasuries. All weaken the support structures for the state.

Three Social Movements That Changed American Society

The late twentieth century will surely be remembered as an era of protest, not just in the United States but around the globe. The overthrow of communist governments in Eastern Europe and the breakup of the Soviet Union may stand out as the most dramatic episodes of this period. In some ways the social movements that swept the United States were just as revolutionary as the events in Europe. These social movements had a profound impact on American ***culture***, on the ***social structure*** of the United States, and on the distribution of ***power*** in American society. Collective action ranged from the antiwar and the gay rights movements at one end of the political spectrum to the right-to-life and fundamentalist Christian movements (for the latter, see Chapter 14) at the other. Here we will focus on three movements that have had basic, long-term effects on American society: the civil rights movement, the women's movement, and the environmental movement. All have roots deep in the past, and all have scored significant victories. None has run its course, but continues to shape the political, cultural, and social agendas of American society.

The Civil Rights Movement

The 1992 riot in Los Angeles might be seen as an echo or aftershock of the civil rights movement of the 1950s and 1960s. One of the most sweeping and effective crusades in modern U.S. history, the civil rights movement has nevertheless left many issues unresolved, among them the plight of the inner-city poor.

The civil rights movement began in the South in the 1950s, as a grass-roots protest against the so-called Jim

The storming of the Bastille (an old prison and arsenal in Paris) was a key moment in the French Revolution, but it was only one action in a long, socially organized process. As in all revolutions, different groups played a part, each using its special resources to compete for power and influence. Underlying structural conditions, such as inequality between social classes and the government's financial crisis, helped to make the French Revolution happen.

Crow laws that enforced racial segregation and excused racial terrorism. African-Americans had never accepted white domination, even under slavery, but they had seldom confronted the existing power structure directly. Why did a movement take shape in the 1950s? One reason had to do with relative deprivation. In World War II, black and white soldiers fought together against a common enemy, the Nazi regime of Adolf Hitler, whose racist policies were universally condemned. In the army and in Europe, they had been treated as full citizens. Yet many black veterans returned to Southern communities where they were forbidden to vote, or even to drink water from a public fountain. Laws and customs that had once seemed inevitable became intolerable (A. D. Morris, 1984).

A second reason was rising expectations. In its 1954 decision in *Brown* v. *Board of Education*, the U.S. Supreme Court had rejected the separate-but-equal doctrine, declaring segregated schools "inherently unequal." By implication, any form of segregation was unconstitutional. But black hopes for integration soon crashed against organized, sometimes violent, white opposition. Southern governors declared that they would ignore the Court's order; white citizen's councils were formed to keep blacks "in their place" by any means necessary; and neither Republican

President Eisenhower nor the Democratic Congress was offering wholehearted support (A. D. Morris, 1984).

A third factor was structural opportunity (Evans and Boyte, 1992; Tilly, 1978). The mechanization of agriculture in the 1950s had pushed sharecroppers off farms into Southern cities (as well as to the North). No longer so dispersed, black communities had achieved the "critical mass" necessary for effective collective action.

The precipitating event in the civil rights movement was the 1956 arrest of Rosa Parks, a black seamstress and former secretary of the Alabama chapter of the National Association for the Advancement of Colored People (NAACP), for refusing to give up her seat on a public bus to a white passenger. Within a week, the local black community founded the Montgomery Improvement Association, elected as president the young minister Martin Luther King, Jr., and organized a boycott of city buses. Planned to last one day, the boycott continued for a year and became the model for the civil rights movement as a whole.

As head of the Southern Christian Leadership Conference (SCLC), King led the movement from Montgomery on to Selma and then Birmingham, Alabama. King was an advocate of nonviolent confrontation. Lacking conventional political power, he argued, black people could use civil disobedience, economic boycotts, and public shame to pressure white legislatures to grant them their rights. In the spring of 1960 the movement was joined by students from predominantly black colleges across the South, who began holding sit-ins at restaurants and other public accommodations under the auspices of the Student Nonviolent Coordinating Committee (SNCC). Soon "black America was on the march" (Newman, Amidei, Cater, Day, Kruvant, and Russell, 1978, p. 19). In 1960 alone, some 50,000 people (most African-American) participated in demonstrations in a hundred cities. The demonstrators were threatened; attacked with police dogs, fire hoses, and electric cattle prods; jailed; fired from their jobs; evicted from their homes; and driven from their churches by firebombs. But the demonstrations continued. White sympathy for the protesters grew—as much from revulsion at the brutal attacks and mass jailings as from agreement with the movement's goals. In 1963, an estimated 250,000 demonstrators, including many whites, marched on Washington, D.C., to hear King deliver his famous "I have a dream" speech. Finally, in 1964 President Johnson convinced Congress that the finest monument to the assassinated John F. Kennedy would be passage of a Civil Rights Act. The movement was by no means over, but a milestone in American history had been passed.

Although King was its acknowledged leader, and organizations like SCLC, SNCC, CORE (Congress of Racial Equality, founded in 1942), and the NAACP (founded in 1909) were important, the drive for civil rights was a true grass-roots movement, composed of dozens of local protest groups with their own organizations, leaders, and strategies. The most important way local people were mobilized was through black churches (A. D. Morris, 1984). Religion was the one institution in which white Southerners permitted blacks any organizational freedom during the Jim Crow years. The black churches were what sociologists call *free spaces*, where people can think, talk, and socialize among themselves and can discover their true identities and aspirations, away from the scrutiny and control of those who hold power over other aspects of their lives (Evans and Boyte, 1992). Churches provided Southern blacks with experience in owning and directing an organization of their own; with leaders—ministers—who were largely independent of white society; with communications networks; and with the cultural traditions of gospel music and oratory for expressing shared hopes and fears.

The civil rights movement also had outside support. The mass media helped to mobilize white sympathy in the North. Images of police turning fire hoses and attack dogs on unresisting black men, women, and children—whether seen on television or the pages of *Life* magazine—awakened the nation's conscience. In the early days of the movement, a number of the students who risked their lives to demonstrate in the South were Northern whites; their characteristics are discussed in the Making Choices box. The Supreme Court stood squarely behind black civil rights during this period. So did some members of the government. Thus John Kennedy, while still a presidential candidate, helped to win Martin Luther King's release from jail, and, as we have noted, Lyndon Johnson used his power to push civil rights legislation through Congress. The mainstays of the movement, however, were poor, rural, often elderly and poorly educated Southern blacks who gave shelter and support to young activists (Newman et al., 1978).

By the late 1960s, the civil rights movement seemed to be losing momentum. Even before King was assassinated in 1968, there were disputes over leadership and the direction the movement should be taking. Often the arguments followed generational lines. Younger blacks tended to be more militant than their elders, to focus on the problems of the urban poor in Northern cities, to question the effectiveness of nonviolent action, to call for separatism (rather than integration), to identify with Africa and the Third World, and to talk of revolution (Newman et al., 1978). After the 1963 march on Washington, the news media, too, began to lose interest in peaceful protest and to search for more dramatic stories. When Stokely Car-

MAKING CHOICES

Characteristics of Active Participants in a Social Movement

Suppose this were the early 1960s, the height of the civil rights movement. Would you become an active participant in the movement, or would you remain on the sidelines as a sympathetic bystander? Sociologists cannot answer this hypothetical question about you, personally, but they have identified some of the characteristics that distinguished activists from spectators during the 1960s.

Doug McAdam (1986, 1989) studied participants in the Freedom Summer of 1964. This project drew hundreds of Northern college students, most of whom were white, to Mississippi to help staff freedom schools, register black voters, and dramatize the continuing violation of African-Americans' civil rights in the South. It is difficult to imagine a more dangerous or demanding example of social activism. The students literally put their lives on the line: Just days after the project began, three volunteers—Michael Schwerner, James Chaney, and Andrew Goodman—were kidnapped and murdered by a group of hard-core segregationists. All the remaining volunteers suffered beatings, bombings, and arrests. And all shared the grinding poverty and constant stress of the black families who housed them.

To participate in Freedom Summer, volunteers were required to fill out a lengthy application. Using these forms, now stored in archives, McAdam compared the 720 participants with the 239 students who had been accepted but later withdrew. He found very little difference in attitudes between the two groups: All were strongly committed to the goals of the civil rights movement. Nor did he find significant differences in their educational, employment, or marital status, all of which might have influenced their availability for active participation.

The main differences were, first, that participants were more likely than withdrawers to belong to several political organizations. They were joiners, not simply observers. Second, participants were more likely to list other volunteers and activists as people they would want to be kept informed of their summer activities. Thus, they were already linked to activist networks, and perhaps more subject to social pressure to honor their applications (and less pressure to put their personal safety first). Finally, participants had more prior experience in high-risk/high-cost activities (such as freedom rides and sit-ins) as compared with low-risk/low-cost activities (such as listening to speakers or giving money). McAdam concludes that although beliefs and attitudes were important, the deciding factors were ***structural***—namely, the participants' preexisting organizational and interpersonal ties to the civil rights movement.

McAdam also studied the consequences of activism, interviewing more than 200 participants and 100 withdrawers twenty years later (McAdam, 1989). He found that for many participants, Freedom Summer marked the beginning of an "activist career." When white involvement in the civil rights movement became problematic, many redirected their energies into the student, antiwar, and women's movements. More than a third had worked as paid activists at some point. And nearly half reported that they were still active in some social movement. Compared with withdrawers, participants had lower incomes and were less likely to be currently married—suggesting to McAdam that they tended to value political over personal goals. Activists emerged from Freedom Summer even more committed than before, and with even stronger ties to activist networks. "For many," McAdam (1989) writes, "New Left politics became the organizing principle of their lives, personal as well as political" (p. 758).

michael, a young member of SNCC, called for "Black Power," the media seized the phrase as signifying a change of heart in the movement. Although African-Americans interpreted the slogan in different ways (ranging from an assertion of black pride, to a call for greater participation in electoral politics, to endorsement of militancy), many whites were convinced that Black Power could mean only one thing: violence against them.

As if to confirm the change, a riot erupted in the largely black Watts section of Los Angeles in the summer of 1965, leaving thirty-four dead. Riots broke out across the country in the summers of 1966 and 1967, when sixty-seven cities were affected, and again in 1968, following the assassination of Dr. King (U.S. National Advisory Commission on Civil Disorders, 1968). The riots inflamed white fears, but they also worried many black leaders, who saw them as destroying black communities. This is a common problem with social movements. To attract public attention and demonstrate the importance of the cause, a movement needs to grow; but it may outgrow the organizational capacities of the original leaders and take directions they never intended. New recruits often lack the discipline and dedication of original members.

Partly in response to the riots and partly as the result of the long years of peaceful agitation by the civil rights movement, the government of the United States began to increase its efforts to overcome racial inequality. In addition to enforcing laws against segregation and discrimination, the government began to make—and to require other organizations to make—positive efforts to ensure integration and equal opportunity. One reason the growth of the civil rights movement slowed after the late 1960s was that the government appeared to be taking on many of the movement's goals.

The civil rights movement did not end unequal treatment of African-Americans, but it was a special chapter in U.S. history. Its impact reached beyond black communities, influencing society as a whole. In many ways, the civil rights movement changed the shape of politics in the United States. The concept of nonviolent confrontation in the form of marches, sit-ins, and other demonstrations to achieve goals not attainable through conventional channels has become part of the political culture. In more concrete terms, the civil rights movement was the model and often the training ground for leaders of other social movements, including the student and antiwar movements of the 1960s, the modern women's movement, the migrant farm workers' movement, the pan-Indian movement, the gay rights movement, and most recently the environmental movement.

The Women's Movement

Organized political protest by women has a long history in the United States. In the early twentieth century a strong women's movement arose to demand the right to vote. Following this victory, feminist protest waned as women entered a period that has been called the *barren years* (E. Klein, 1984). Even then, some activism remained, keeping women's issues alive until social forces set the stage for renewed grass-roots support (Rupp and Taylor, 1987).

One of those social forces was the publication in 1963 of Betty Friedan's book *The Feminine Mystique*. This book was so influential that many scholars equate its publication with the birth of the modern women's, or feminist, movement. In it, Friedan spoke to millions of American women about "the problem that has no name." Trained from childhood to relinquish self-reliance, careers, and personal autonomy and to dedicate their lives to the full-time care of home and children, many women felt dependent, isolated, and unfulfilled. Friedan helped them to identify the causes of these feelings. She also brought to public attention the private grievances of women who worked outside the home and were trapped in dead-end, low-paying, unchallenging jobs. Thus, women across the country became aware of a shared discontent and the possibility that together they might improve their lives. It was the start of their "cognitive liberation" (McAdam, 1989).

A number of factors besides Friedan's book triggered the drive for equal rights for women. One was the black civil rights movement, which stimulated increased awareness of injustice and oppression in a number of groups. Interestingly, women's experiences in the civil rights, student, and antiwar movements served as important catalysts. In these movements, women were often relegated to routine jobs such as typing, answering phones, and making coffee. They were forced to confront the contradiction of working for equal rights for others without enjoying equal rights themselves.

A social movement requires not just a sense of shared injustice but also the mobilization of resources. This mobilization is, in turn, facilitated by organization. Especially important were the commissions to investigate the status of women that were established in each of the fifty states in 1963. The sociologist Jo Freeman (1973) argues that the women's movement of the 1960s would not have materialized without the communications network that these commissions provided. They brought together large numbers of knowledgeable and politically active women and gave them channels for discussing common problems and planning collective solutions. Thus, although the position of women in the 1960s was the same as it had been for decades, something critical had changed. "What changed," writes Freeman (1973), "was the organizational situation. It was not until a communications network developed between like-minded people beyond local boundaries that the movement could emerge and develop past the point of occasional, spontaneous uprising" (p. 804).

The resurgent women's movement worked at two levels (Boles, 1991; Stoper, 1991). The first was an effort to secure equality of official rights between men and women. Most activists who focused on women's rights emphasized moderate reforms, especially the opportunity for women to enter the work force on an equal footing with men. At the same time, a number of other activists sought deeper changes in the way women fit into society. These radical feminists emphasized the need for more profound changes in American cultural institutions, especially the family. These changes, activists suggested, would have to go beyond the recognition of equal public rights for men and women. As a popular slogan put it, "The personal is political." In other words, ***power*** differences that shaped people's personal relations needed to be made the object of public attention and political activism.

The women's movement mobilized for action through both large formal organizations and small, more informal groups. By far the most important organization was the National Organization for Women (NOW). NOW was founded in June 1966 when a small group of women attending the Third National Conference of Commissions on the Status of Women met in Betty Friedan's hotel room. They were concerned that the work of the commissions was not going far enough or fast enough. With Friedan as president, NOW began to attract women in the professions, labor, government, and the communications industry. NOW received a major boost in 1969 when the national media began to carry news stories on women's liberation.

Through its national board and 800 or more local chapters, NOW has used lawsuits, lobbying, demonstrations, boycotts, and other methods to press for such goals as educational reform; nonstereotyped portrayal of women in the media; repeal of laws outlawing abortion; lesbian rights; enhanced roles for women in religion, politics, and sports; and passage of the Equal Rights Amendment (ERA). A number of other organizations of professional women have been formed, such as WEAL (Women's Equity Action League), which focuses on legal questions, and the NWPC (National Women's Political Caucus), which works to get women elected to public office.

While usually supporting the work of organizations like NOW, many feminists also sought to develop a grass-roots movement with many independent local groups. Some of these activists were concerned about keeping NOW from working only on "safe" issues like equal access to higher education and making sure that it would represent the needs of lesbians, battered wives, and others who were usually ignored by the media and the political mainstream. Many radical feminists also rejected hierarchical, highly structured organizations, believing that they inevitably stifled those at the bottom. Instead, they created egalitarian groups, which sought not only to increase opportunities for women but also to change the structure of human relationships and roles. Many of the groups emphasized consciousness-raising: Through sharing their ideas and experiences, members attempted to identify their previously unconscious attitudes and behaviors in dealing with both males and females. This new awareness, they hoped, would help to change their attitudes and behaviors, fostering a more egalitarian society. Many local activists branched out into educational and service projects, establishing women's centers, abortion-counseling clinics, shelters for rape victims and battered wives, feminist bookstores and publications, and day-care facilities.

By the 1970s the women's movement had made substantial progress in expanding female career opportunities. Barriers and inequalities still remained, but women were entering fields once considered the domain of men and their salaries were rising. The entry of many women into full-time professional jobs, however, raised a new issue: namely, how to manage both career commitments and family roles. Women activists have responded to this problem by pressing for affordable day care, paid maternity and parental leaves, more flexible work hours, and job sharing between husband and wife (E. Klein, 1984).

A countermovement to passage of the ERA posed a major obstacle to the progress of the women's movement in the 1970s. A **countermovement** is a social movement that forms to resist a movement already under way. As we discussed in Chapter 12, the leaders of the antifeminist countermovement blamed the women's movement for a variety of social changes (from no-fault divorce laws to legal abortion) that they saw as threats to family stability. To them, the ERA represented the final assault on the traditional roles of wife and mother. To block its ratification, they formed countermovement groups, such as Humanitarians Opposed to Degrading Our Girls (HOTDOG) in Utah, Protect Our Women (POW) in Wisconsin, and Women Who Want to Be Women (WWWW) in Texas (S. E. Marshall, 1985). Leading the countermovement at the national level was Phyllis Schlafly, who organized several thousand women in a campaign called Stop-ERA.

Although most of these countermovement groups remained much smaller than NOW and other leading feminist organizations, they were very damaging to the women's movement. In particular, they gave legitimacy to antifeminist men by allowing them to point out that many women were antifeminist too. The antifeminist countermovement was heavily supported by money from conservative political groups, which tried to portray all feminists as extremely radical and "antifamily." Although this charge was not true, it led many women's rights activists to shy away from the label *feminist.* All these efforts proved at least partially successful. The strong initial momentum in favor of the ERA slowed dramatically after 1973 and came to a halt by 1977. Between 1977 and the deadline for ratification, in 1982, not a single additional state voted to ratify the amendment.

The battle lines between the women's movement and the antifeminist countermovement have become closely drawn. On one side are mostly younger, better-educated, professionally employed women who want to extend the gains of the 1960s and 1970s. On the other side are primarily older, less educated women, who are often full-time homemakers with strong religious beliefs (Burris, 1983; Deutchman and Prince-Embury, 1981; Luker, 1984; Mueller and Dimieri, 1982). With the ERA defeated, these antifeminists have set new goals, such as making abortion

The social movements on each side of the debate over women's right to choose abortion have radicalized groups that had not previously been involved in anything remotely resembling a mass movement. They were galvanized into participation by the fact that the debate engages a basic issue—the question of when life begins—and does so in what is, for many abortion-rights opponents, a clear-cut religious context. In 1993, one man opposed abortion so strongly that he shot and killed a doctor who performed abortions.

illegal again and banning affirmative-action programs for women. Members of NOW and other women's movement organizations are forced to devote much of their time, energy, and money defending against these attacks (Chavez, 1987). The ongoing debate has helped to put new issues on the national political agenda, including women's health care, day care, domestic violence, sexual assault, reproductive rights, and the plight of displaced homemakers.

At the national level, the women's movement has become institutionalized (Boles, 1991). Women's rights organizations such as NOW rely in large part on paid leaders and professional staffs (Staggenborg, 1988). Many of their members are "conscience constituents," who contribute money and may occasionally participate in protests, such as marches, but are not true activists (Zald and McCarthy, 1987). Moreover, the tactics these groups use are often the same as those used by mainstream pressure groups—lobbying and forming electoral alliances. Women's groups are facing the same problems faced by other "mature" movements, namely, complacency, an aging core of activists, and low visibility.

Examining whether the women's movement is fading into the past, Virginia Sapiro (1991) has focused on ***culture***, on changes in attitudes and beliefs over the life of the contemporary women's movement. She finds that the daughters of the generation that launched the movement—young women now entering their twenties and starting families—are "liberated" in some ways but not others. The great majority (more than nine in ten) support equality in the workplace, but a substantial minority (about one in four) believe families suffer when women work. A majority of young women feel that men do not take women seriously in the workplace, despite many gains. Among those who are married, most say they take more responsibility for housework and child care than their husbands do, but most also say their husband is doing his fair share. Many accept the cultural myth that women who are raped (especially by an acquaintance) or beaten by their husband somehow "asked for" the violent abuse.

Thus, in some ways, less has changed than one might expect. Sapiro does not conclude, however, that the women's movement's days are numbered. Most people surveyed say that while the movement has achieved some goals, much remains to be done and "the United States continues to need a strong women's movement to push for changes that benefit women" (Dionne, in Sapiro, 1991, p. 21).

The Environmental Movement

Much as Friedan's *The Feminine Mystique* was the spark that ignited the contemporary women's movement, so Rachel Carson's book *Silent Spring* (1962) played a central role in the formation of the environmental movement. The book described a future in which the indiscriminate use of pesticides would "still the songs of birds and the leaping fish in the streams." Carson's warning led President John F. Kennedy to direct federal agencies to look at the issue. The book also prompted a flurry of local and state regulations on pesticide use; it began a groundswell of support that led to the creation of the Environmental Protection Agency (EPA); and it generally helped to make environmental protection a popular cause (McDowell, 1982).

Carson's book was needed because many threats to the environment are invisible and most people simply did not realize the extent of the ecological damage. Carson pulled together a large number of facts pointing to the gradual destruction of the environment and the threat to human survival. She made clear that even invisible pollutants can have devastating effects on human health and welfare, and she exposed some of the vested interests in the business and scientific communities that were knowingly engaged in environmental degradation. The exposé aroused public anger and indignation. Concerned experts, media commentators, and other authors took up the cause, and the shared discontent was born that is required for the formation of a social movement.

The environmental movement differs from the others we have discussed in several ways. First, it presents itself as universal, rather than as working on behalf of just one segment of the population. Everyone wants to save the planet, and everyone wants a safe environment. For the movement's supporters, the environment is the one social issue that overrides all others, from unrest in Eastern Europe, to shelter for the homeless, to equal pay for women. Victory on these other fronts will not mean much if the environment collapses (*Newsweek*, June 1, 1992). Where individuals, groups, and nations differ is in the perception of how immediate and severe the threats to the environment are and of what ought to be done and by whom.

Second, the environmental movement is global. Every nation has its own environmental problems—from acid rain in Canada to severely polluted water in Czechoslovakia, high birth rates in Kenya, soil erosion in China, and deforestation in Thailand and Malaysia. Beyond these local problems, pollution does not respect national borders. Thus, much of the acid rain in Canada is caused by industrial pollutants produced in the United States, and the severe floods in Pakistan and Bangladesh in recent years can be traced to deforestation of the Himalayas in Nepal.

The United Nations Conference on Environment and Development, known as the Earth Summit, held in Rio de Janeiro in June 1992 and attended by more than 100 heads of state, reflected the growing awareness that environmental problems require global solutions. Three main treaties were proposed at that conference:

- A treaty to reduce global warming (a result of the greenhouse effect—see Chapter 19). While some scientists believe that human activity is altering the global climate in ways that could prove disastrous in the next century, others are not convinced. The United States agreed to sign this treaty only if there were no fixed targets or timetables.

- A treaty to preserve biodiversity by conserving all animal and plant species, many of which have not been discovered and many of which are located in tropical rain forests. Many scientists believe that without concerted effort, as many as one-fourth of existing species could disappear in the next fifty years; some of these species might provide new medicines and food sources (Brown et al., 1990). Every year pharmaceutical companies test thousands of tropical plants for potential curative properties. The treaty suggested that drug companies pay royalties to the countries in which useful species are discovered, many of which lie in the Southern Hemisphere. The United States was the only major power that refused to sign this treaty, although it did propose a plan for preserving the world's dwindling rain forests.

- Agenda 21, a nonbinding blueprint for a global cleanup. This treaty called on industrialized nations to assist developing nations in protecting and preserving their environments.

The Earth Summit underscored the political dimensions of the environmental movement, which pits growth against conservation, the industrialized nations of the North against the developing nations of the South.

A final difference between the environmental movement and the civil rights and women's movements is that concern for the environment is not a single, unified drive, but is embodied in many movements, each with its own focus and strategies (W. T. Anderson, 1989). One group, the *politicos*, consists of established organizations like the Sierra Club, the Audubon Society, and the World Wildlife Fund. These groups maintain lobbies in Washington (and other national capitals) and concentrate on getting proenvironment laws passed and influencing government agencies. They are staffed by paid professionals and funded primarily by large numbers of conscience constituents. Many have corporate sponsors as well. One new group of environmental politicos is the Business Council for Sustainable Development, made up of forty-eight chief executives from major companies such as Du Pont, Chevron, Nissan, and Mitsubishi (*Newsweek*, June 1, 1992).

Environmentalism became a mass movement because of highly visible disasters such as the Amoco Cadiz *shipwreck and oil spill just off the coast of France in 1978. The challenge for the environmental movement has been to transfer the awareness stimulated by these dramatic episodes to the more complex—but even more significant—environmental issues that lack such vivid symbols.*

The second branch of the environmental movement may be called the *greens*—environmental activists who tend to be highly suspicious of government and big business and of groups (like the environmental politicos) that seek change through these channels. Greens tend to believe that the environment can be saved only through drastic changes in people's attitudes, values, and lifestyles. Greens generally pursue their goals through various forms of protest. Whereas politicos are based in capital cities, greens are typically found on college and university campuses.

A third environmental group consists of *grass-roots activists*—people who fight to keep their local communities from being polluted or destroyed by developers. Although most members of such local groups are middle-class home owners, they often have proved willing to use radical strategies to achieve their goals. Even though they are primarily concerned with local issues, these groups maintain communication networks with one another. They are sometimes mocked for having a NIMBY ("Not in my backyard") attitude, but one grass-roots network recently adopted the slogan "Not in *anybody's* backyard."

A final category is the *globals*—individuals and groups that focus on the big picture and worry about the future of the planet as a whole. In Washington, D.C., the globals are represented by groups like the Worldwatch Institute and the World Resources Institute. Many members of global groups are scientists, and many of their concerns—such as global warming, biodiversity, and the ozone layer—are based on scientific data. The globals are largely responsible for calling attention to the link between environmental issues and development in the Third World; it was they who formulated the concept of "sustainable development"—economic growth that does not deplete resources.

Even though it is divided into so many categories, the environmental movement has succeeded in raising the world's consciousness on ecological issues. However, true worldwide commitment to environmental conservation and protection remains a distant goal. Recycling cans, bottles, and newspapers and demonstrating to save the rain forests are worthy activities, but they are not enough to save the planet. The environmental movement still faces its greatest challenge: inspiring global cooperation and lasting social change.

Thinking Back on the Key Concepts

When the environmental movement sought to change the way people thought about renewable energy sources or the problems of disposing of waste, it was seeking to change ***culture***. The women's and civil rights movements also sought to change culture because they wanted to change people's ideas, beliefs, knowledge, and values. One reason these movements tried to bring about cultural change was that they wanted to change ***social action***, which depends on culture (for example, beliefs about the environment influence willingness to recycle). Activists also sought laws and other ways of reinforcing certain patterns of action by engaging in a special form of social action themselves—collective action, especially the long-term organization of collective action in social movements.

In this chapter, we have seen that ***social structure*** determines who joins social movements and how successful they are. For example, the Making Choices box showed how previously established networks of relationships with other activists encouraged people to participate in the Freedom Summer of 1964. The close proximity of African-Americans in South-Central Los Angeles made it easier for them to join in collective action in 1992.

When people engage in collective action and social movements, they are usually seeking to exercise a degree of ***power*** that they would not have if they acted alone. Such power comes partly through numbers and partly through organization. The civil rights movement was a major exercise of power, which changed American history in basic ways; but it took millions of people working together, often in highly disciplined ways, for many years. One explanation of the need for this sort of collective action is based on the idea that ***functional integration*** is faltering—is not meeting the needs of all members of a society. In the United States, for example, social institutions have never functioned to provide black people with opportunities equal to those of whites; in many cases they have functioned instead to segregate large numbers of African-Americans in impoverished, inner-city neighborhoods. In this view, the problems of black Americans are not simply accidental dysfunctions; they are the result of the way American institutions normally work and are thus a reason to change the whole pattern of functional integration. This is what many social movements seek to do.

SUMMARY

1. Collective action is a special form of ***social action***, in which people depart from everyday routines, responding to events, things, or ideas in unconventional ways. A social movement is a sustained, coordinated effort by relatively large numbers of people to change or resist change in the social order.

2. Collective action often begins with a crowd, or a temporary collection of people drawn together by some common experience. Crowds may be casual, conventional, expressive, or acting. A mob is an acting crowd that has become violent.

3. Theories of crowd action have focused on group psychology (especially social contagion); the spread of rumors and, in modern times, the impact of the media; the emergence of new norms and relationships under ambiguous circumstances; and rational calculation.

4. Conventional wisdom usually traces an event like the Los Angeles riot of 1992 to a specific incident or series of incidents (the precipitating event). Sociology shows that a number of conditions also must be met for crowd action to take place.

5. The first condition is "structural conduciveness," meaning that elements of the ***social structure*** promote or at least allow crowd action. An example would be large numbers of people in close contact with one another and with time on their hands.

6. Second, crowd action often reflects ***functional dis-integration***. The crowd may be composed of people who are not well integrated into the mainstream of society, and/or the crowd may take violent actions because social controls are not functioning adequately.

7. Third, crowd action may reflect the buildup of ***cultural*** misunderstandings, especially under conditions where groups are in economic competition.

8. Fourth, crowd action often is a "last-ditch effort" by people who feel they lack ***power*** and see no other way of making their grievances known.

9. Social movements are sustained efforts by large numbers of people to bring about or resist social change through noninstitutionalized means. Most social movements press for cultural change. In revolutions, the movement attempts to seize control of the government.

10. Some social theorists have traced the formation of social movements to social and economic deprivation, such as alienation from the means of production (Marx); new cultural ideas that lead to feelings of relative deprivation (Tocqueville); and sudden economic reversals (Davies).

11. Deprivation alone does not explain social movements. They also require the mobilization of resources, including human capital (in the form of leadership, organizational skill, and the like) and tangible assets (including funds, means of communication, and space).

12. Opportunity is also important in the formation of social movements, especially social revolutions, which are rapid and basic transformations of government and class structure. Some theorists hold that revolutions are often influenced by structural forces, such as the international situation or population pressures, more than by ideology.

13. Three social movements that have had enormous impact on American society are the civil rights, women's, and environmental movements. Each illustrates the importance of organization, opportunity, communication, and "conscience constituents" to social movements.

REVIEW QUESTIONS

1. What is the difference between collective action and a social movement? Give an example of each.

2. Define the four types of crowds—casual, conventional, expressive, and acting—and give examples of each.

3. Why do social movements arise?

4. How does Skocpol's explanation of social revolutions differ from Marxist and resource-mobilization theories?

5. Summarize the explanations for the rise of the civil rights movement, emphasizing the role of concepts and theories discussed in the chapter.

6. Summarize the explanations for the rise of the modern women's movement, emphasizing the role of concepts and theories discussed in the chapter.

7. Summarize the explanations for the rise of the environmental movement, emphasizing the role of concepts and theories discussed in the chapter.

CRITICAL THINKING QUESTIONS

1. The section on crowd action in the chapter analyzes the social psychology of crowds, the role of communication, norms and relationships, and crowd action. Summarize this discussion in light of at least three of the five key concepts—social structure, social action, functional integration, power, and culture.

2. Examine the three explanations given for the rise of social movements from the perspective of at least three of the five key concepts—social structure, social action, functional integration, power, and culture.

3. Use the concepts raised in the chapter to analyze a social movement or social revolution that you have studied in a history, political science, or some other course.

4. The chapter discusses the civil rights movement, the women's movement, and the environmental movement. Select one of these three social movements and make projections about what will happen to it in the next ten to twenty years, basing your analysis on what you have learned in this and other chapters.

5. Think of a social movement that you or someone you know has been involved in, and describe the experience in the context of the points, concepts, and theories discussed in the chapter.

GLOSSARY

Acting crowd Herbert Blumer's term for an excited, volatile collection of people who are focused on a controversial event that provokes their indignation, anger, and desire to act.

Casual crowd Herbert Blumer's term for a spontaneous gathering whose members give temporary attention to an object or event and then go their separate ways.

Collective action Socially shared but relatively nonroutine responses to events, things, or ideas. (Also called *collective behavior.*)

Conventional crowd Herbert Blumer's term for people who gather for a specific purpose and behave according to established norms.

Countermovement A social movement that forms to resist a movement already under way.

Crowd A temporary collection of people who are gathered around some person or event and are conscious of and influenced by one another.

Emergent-norm theory The principle that crowds develop new norms in order to define an ambiguous situation.

Expressive crowd Herbert Blumer's term for a crowd whose members express feelings and behave in ways they would not consider acceptable in other settings.

Mob A large crowd whose members are emotionally aroused and are engaged in, or threaten to engage in, violent action.

Precipitating event An incident that sparks collective action by confirming people's suspicions and fears.

Relative deprivation The gap between people's expectations and their actual conditions.

Rumor An unverified story that circulates from person to person and is accepted as fact, although its original source may be vague or unknown.

Social contagion The relatively rapid and unintentional spread of a mood or behavior from one individual to another.

Social movement A deliberate, organized effort to change or resist large-scale change through noninstitutionalized means.

Social revolution According to Theda Skocpol's definition, a rapid and basic transformation of a society's state and class structures.

Structural conduciveness Neal Smelser's term to describe aspects of social structure that facilitate collective action.

CHAPTER 22

Social Change

In 1992, the world took note of the 500th anniversary of Christopher Columbus's voyage from Europe to America. The Spanish city of Seville spent more than $7 billion on a World's Fair to commemorate the event. The Dominican Republic, where Columbus first landed, invested $10 million in a lighthouse-museum that would be the world's largest Columbus monument, while the United States spent about $80 million to ensure, in the words of President George Bush, "that this commemoration will have the significant global impact that such a milestone deserves" (Sale, 1990b, p. 444). Such extravaganzas are not unprecedented: In 1892, at the 400th anniversary of Columbus's voyage, the World's Columbian Exposition in Chicago did more than celebrate the European discovery of America (Sanoff, 1990). That fair announced to all that the United States—having survived a bloody civil war, now building factories and manufacturing goods at dizzying rates, tempering this raw industrialization with progressive social reforms—had surpassed the Old World that Columbus had left behind.

While almost everyone agrees that Columbus's explorations changed the course of human history, scholars five centuries later continue to disagree on just what happened in 1492, and they heatedly dispute the meaning and significance of Columbus's accomplishment. Some of the controversy centers on the historical details of the event. Was Columbus in fact the first European to set foot in North America, or had the Vikings successfully crossed the North Atlantic centuries before? Where exactly is Columbus's landfall, and what were those "natives" he met there really like? Did the Arawaks naively welcome the *Niña*, the *Pinta*, and the *Santa Maria*, or, learning from their earlier encounters with the warlike Caribs, were they prepared for battle? What about Columbus the man—was he a dashing Italian, a skillful sailor, a risk-taking entrepreneur, or a shifty scoundrel who was a merely average seaman, a selfish megalomaniac out for his own glory and not for the glory of Spain or Christianity? Did he really leave Spain in search of spices and to "test" a theory that the earth is round, or did Columbus know full well that he was not—in his pursuit of gold—at any risk of falling off the edge (Crosby, 1976, 1989; Fagan, 1990; Larner, 1988; Sale, 1990a)?

While these questions may fascinate historians, sociologists are more interested in the longer-range consequences of Columbus's achievement—whatever the details may be. If the arrival of Columbus in the West Indies was indeed a turning point in human history, it is sociologically important to ask: What did human society turn *from*, and what did it turn *to*? One interpretation is captured in the simple and seemingly incontestable claim that "Columbus discovered America." Setting aside the question of whether it was Erik the Red who beat Columbus to these shores, saying that Columbus *discovered* America means ignoring the native people who had lived on the continent for several thousand years before any Europeans arrived. We shall never know the identity of those hardy people who first discovered America by crossing the ice from eastern Asia into what is now Alaska. To celebrate Columbus's feat as the *discovery* of America is an obviously ethnocentric point of view (see Chapter 3), a story told to celebrate the winners, the survivors. It is a familiar story to most Americans: The hero Columbus brought civilization to the naked savages he met on the beach; he brought Christianity to pagans (Morison, 1974); he brought technological superiority (people who knew nothing of metal were no match for swords); and he opened up the possibility of a *New* World. From this ethnocentric, Eurocentric perspective, the New World would have virtually nothing to do with the culture Columbus found when he landed in Hispaniola. Rather, it was a New World in the form of a blank slate—an unknown, empty frontier—where transplanted Europeans could build a brand-new social order free from the constraints imposed by settled civilization of the Old World.

Even if one takes a balanced view of Columbus's voyage, the initial encounter between Europeans and native "Americans" (the Arawak) remains perhaps the single most important event shaping human history. At that moment, two independent lines of human culture—which had developed separately over the millennia into distinctive sets of beliefs, values, practices, and social institutions—met for the first time. Whether that moment is described as a discovery, an encounter, an exchange, a clash, or simply a contact depends on one's political and theoretical assumptions. This initial cultural contact had consequences that have profoundly shaped the five centuries since. Columbus set in motion the rise of Europe to worldwide dominance, the accumulation of unsurpassed wealth and unchallenged power in the hands of a few new nation-states. The encounter in 1492 set the stage for the eventual triumph of capitalism, inaugurating a pattern of colonialism and imperialism in which the natural resources and human labor of what would become the Third World would feed the desires of the First World in Western Europe (Koning, 1976). It also marked the triumph of the scientific world view and its technological by-products, not only the Europeans' superior weapons but their possession of navigational and astronomical knowledge that enabled Columbus to get across the Atlantic. With all this coming in its wake, the first contact between Europeans and the natives of America has been called the "most influential

For almost 500 years the so-called discovery of America by Christopher Columbus was simply thought of as the imposition of a superior culture onto primitive people. Only in recent years have the descendants of the Europeans who followed Columbus—that is, the majority of today's North Americans—begun to question what the "discovery" meant to those who were already here, and to those who were brought here as slaves after the native populations had been killed, starved, or driven from their lands.

event on this planet since the retreat of the continental glaciers" (Crosby, 1989, p. 668).

The "encounter" becomes a "catastrophe" when viewed from the perspective of those who were here to greet Columbus and his crew. It is estimated that there were about 8 million inhabitants of Hispaniola when Columbus arrived in 1492; just twenty-two years after that, their number had dwindled to 28,000; and by 1550 the Arawak on the island were essentially extinct. The people died of deadly diseases introduced by the Europeans or of forced labor and other forms of abuse, and their culture died with them. The triumph of Western science brought an end to the natives' own understanding and appreciation of nature. In contrast to modern "utilitarian" attitudes toward nature—conquer it, control it, use it—the Arawak evidently revered the environment around them (Sale, 1990a). They had learned how to raise crops in a way that did not deplete or erode the delicate island ecosystem, and managed to feed themselves with only about two to three hours of work per week. Columbus's arrival set in motion the heavy-handed transformation of a primal environment that the Arawak had only lightly touched.

In this chapter we consider large changes in human societies, ones that bring about fundamental and enduring transformations—like the changes brought on by the arrival of Columbus in North America. The task of understanding such huge changes is difficult because such massive societal transformations are often invisible to those who live through them—the individual life is too short, and each person's perspective too narrow, to be able to grasp the "big picture." We begin with classical sociological theories of large-scale social change, not just as an exercise in intellectual history but as a source of ideas about where our global society today may be headed. Then we consider various causes of social change, giving special attention to two especially potent sources of "the new":

science and technology. We end the chapter—and this text—with a question perhaps impossible to answer but vital to ask: Has the world become *smaller* in the 500 years since "in fourteen hundred and ninety-two, Columbus sailed the ocean blue"? Or is there something bigger than an ocean that keeps people apart?

Social change refers to alterations, over time, in the behavior patterns, culture, and structure of a society. Not all changes that are of interest to sociologists fall into the category of "social change" as defined here. For instance, the socialization that we experience as children profoundly changes our personal lives, but it does not alter the basic organization of the family or the larger society and, therefore, is not social change. The maturation of an individual through the life course is not the kind of social change we consider here. In contrast, the creation of communal child-care centers in Israel's kibbutzim (collective farms), where the young are housed, fed, and taught, does constitute a major social change (Talmon, 1972). The *structure* and *process* of socialization in kibbutzim are fundamentally different from the conventional modern pattern in which children experience such primary socialization within the nuclear family.

Each of the five key concepts will enter our discussion of social change—both as cause and as consequence. Patterns of ***social structure***, such as the size of the human population, cause changes in social life, such as increased density in urban centers; and at the same time they are consequences of earlier developments, such as the discovery of cures for diseases that used to keep the population in check. Most social changes can ultimately be traced to ***social action***. For example, the invention of the birth-control pill resulted from research, or social action, by Dr. Carl Djerassi and his co-workers; a couple's decision to have a child or to use the pill or some other contraceptive is a social action, too. ***Culture*** is a potent source of social change: Beliefs and values surrounding the decision to have one, two, or many children will bring about changes in the size of the population; but those beliefs and values are themselves shaped by technological and social-structural developments such as the recent increase in the labor-force participation of women during their childbearing years. Not everyone contributes equally to the direction of social change: As in all other aspects of social life, those individuals and groups with greater ***power*** do more to shape the future than do those without power. Much significant social change results from struggles *for* power, such as revolutionary uprisings by peasants in developing countries seeking greater control over land and working conditions. None of these large-scale social changes occur in a vacuum: Each development is a consequence of those changes that came before it and a cause of changes that come after it. The key concept of ***functional integration*** serves as a reminder of this interdependence of society's parts.

CLASSICAL THEORIES OF SOCIAL CHANGE

Social change occurs in all aspects of social life. It affects both the everyday patterns of social interaction, as can be seen in the kibbutz experience, and the larger structures of social institutions. Consider, for example, how technological and institutional developments have transformed work and the occupational structure. Some observers believe that we are now entering a new era in human history, restructuring society from an industrial to an information base. Just as the steam engine brought an end to the predominance of agricultural work and moved huge numbers of workers from farms to factories, so the computer (and related information technologies) is moving huge numbers of workers out of factories and into offices. Automation and robotics have eliminated jobs in manufacturing, but the need to create, evaluate, and distribute information has created new jobs in the service sector. Many names have been proposed to describe this ongoing transformation (see Figure 22.1).

Sociologists are interested in four basic questions about social change:

1. What is the fundamental "engine" of social change? That is, what causes the macro-level transformation from, say, autocratic to democratic political arrangements?

2. Is there a direction to social change? Do human societies consistently move from one set of conditions toward something else, or does history tend to repeat itself? In short, is social change linear, cyclical, or just random?

3. Are the causes and direction of social change identical in human societies everywhere and at all times? Or does social change itself assume various forms in different cultural and historical settings?

4. What are the consequences of social change? How is social change in one sphere of life related to changes in other spheres?

The founding theorists of sociology had much to say about each of these four questions.

1959	**Postcapitalist society**
1960	**Postmaturity economy**
1964	**Global village**
	Postcivilized era
	Technological society
1967	**New industrial state**
1968	**Postmodern society**
1969	**Age of discontinuity**
1970	**Computerized society**
1971	**Information age**
	Postindustrial society
1972	**Posttraditional society**
1973	**New service society**
1975	**Communications age**
1978	**Network nation**
	Wired society
1979	**Credential society**
1980	**Micro revolution**
	Third wave
1983	**Gene age**

FIGURE 22.1 / Name That Era

Most sociologists agree that we are in the midst of a major transformation of social life, but they cannot agree on what we should call this new era. Here are several names and the year each label was proposed. It appears to be relatively simple for us to look *back* into human history and label one era "agrarian" and another "industrial." But even the most astute social observers at the time, as today, would probably have disagreed with such tags and would have proposed alternatives. Each term listed here captures *part* of what seems to be happening these days. The latest addition to the list is "postmodern age." Maybe the most appropriate label will become clear only when humans have moved on to the next epoch of history.

Source: James R. Beniger, *The Control Revolution: Technological and Economic Origins of the Information Society* (Harvard University Press, Cambridge, Mass. 1986), pp. 4–5.

Marx's Theory of Social Change through Power and Conflict

In Chapters 1 and 17, we saw that Karl Marx's perspective on society emphasized relations of power and conflict. Those in a position of ***power***—those who own the means of production in a capitalistic society—are locked in conflict with those they dominate, the workers who sell their labor in the marketplace. The interest of the owners lies in maintaining their authority and control over economic decisions, whereas the interest of the workers lies in overthrowing that class in order to be able to reap the profits of their own labor. Marx's views of social change focus on the process of struggle, which is of two kinds.

The Struggle with Nature

The first kind of struggle is common to all people: using existing technology to overcome the limits imposed by nature. For example, in a hunting-and-gathering society, the availability of animals and fruits in the surrounding area sets a natural limit on that society's population and standard of living. If the members of that society "invent" agriculture, however, their numbers can increase and they can live better. Marx believed that at every stage in the Industrial Revolution, advances in productive capacity radically altered what were believed to be natural limits and established the basis for subsequent social changes.

According to Marx, advances in production almost always change social organization. For example, a factory is a *social* organization of relationships among people, just as it is a *technical* organization of relationships among machines (Marx, 1867/1976). As industry and productive technology have become more complex, so has the social organization necessary to support it—elaborate division of labor, sprawling factory and office complexes, multinational financial institutions.

The Struggle between Classes

Marx saw an inevitable problem with this scheme of things. Even though workers and owners were linked together in increasingly complicated organizational relationships, the ownership and control of the means of production were being concentrated in the hands of a relatively small elite class. This development set the scene for the second kind of struggle Marx described: the struggle between classes for control of the production process and, by extension, for control of social life (Marx and Engels, 1848/1976). For Marx, class struggle was not just an economic battle but a political struggle to shape the whole of social organization. To Marxists, there are strong links between economic struggles and political struggles of all kinds involving age, gender, or race (Poulantzas, 1974; Vogel, 1983).

Whereas the first, economic, struggle provides the opportunity for social change, the second, political, struggle shapes the specific course that social change will take. Advances in production make new forms of social organization possible, but relations of power determine how such advances will be used and whether social organization will be fundamentally changed. Old elites whose power is based on old ways of production may be overthrown by new elites who have control over new means of production. The class struggle determines which elites will dominate and how much freedom they will have. Thus, kings and feudal lords had to be overthrown by early revolutions to make the growth of modern capitalism possible. Marx believed that the working classes in capitalist society would, in turn, revolt against the capitalist owners in order, first, to create a socialist society in which the workers would dominate and, second, to give way to a new kind of society without classes or state—that is, a communist state. As many nations these days abandon Marxism as an official state ideology and try to convert from a socialist to a market economy, it begins to appear that Marx's theory may be more successful as an explanation for the social changes that led us to the Industrial Revolution, and less successful as a prediction of what has come after.

Marxist socialism was a powerful force in the United States at the turn of the century. Americans understood that the Marxian analysis of class struggle explained a great deal about their socioeconomic circumstances, including the cyclical crises of capitalism and the great battles between workers and capitalists in the early years of the labor movement.

Weber's Theory: The Influence of Culture

Max Weber argued that no single factor could explain all the major social changes of history. The many different ideas and beliefs of a ***culture***—not just its material means of production—play an important role in bringing about social change. Although Weber recognized the huge impact of advances in productive capacity, he considered it impossible to say whether those advances constituted "progress." As we shall see in a later section, progress itself is as much a value judgment as an objective fact, and changing ideas of progress have themselves brought about important social changes. The point, for Weber, is that the realm of culture (which includes ideas like "progress") is at least as significant for social change as the realm of material production.

Although Weber disputed the idea of a single "engine" driving social change, he did identify a consistent and cumulative pattern in the recent past. He labeled this pattern **rationalization**, the tendency to base action on a logical assessment of anticipated effects. For example, a young woman who chooses a college for its ability to prepare her for a desired profession is making a rational choice; in contrast, if she were to choose a college simply because her parents and grandparents went there, she would be following a tradition. Weber believed that most societies throughout history were governed by tradition. Occasionally (as we saw in Chapter 8) a charismatic leader might rise to challenge the established authorities; but once that leader died, traditional structures and practices would typically be reinstated. A fundamental and irreversible overthrow of traditional authority came from currents of rationalization in Western Europe starting in the Renaissance.

The Protestant Reformation in the West, argued Weber, set in motion enduring and sweeping processes of rationalization that continue today. As we saw in Chapter 18, traditional patterns of religious authority—reaching their peak of power during the medieval period—gradually gave way to a rational, disenchanted world view that spread from religion to other social institutions. For example, Protestant religious groups that sought refuge in the New World helped set in motion the events that led to the creation of the United States, the world's first large-scale democracy and the first to separate church and state. This "first new nation" (Lipset, 1963a) was an explicit effort to break from traditional forms of political authority (the monarchy) and create a different social order grounded in rational principles of equality and liberty.

Most significantly, the upheavals initiated by the Protestant Reformation did not lead back toward a new traditionalism. Tradition itself was replaced in Western Europe (and its colonies) by a more rational outlook on life, government, and the economy. This new pattern of ra-

Max Weber understood that modern life would be increasingly directed by the rational assessment of knowable outcomes. Because such a perspective and means of operation are efficient, Weber believed them to be inevitable; nevertheless, he regarded them as an "iron cage," drained of all emotion. George Orwell's 1949 novel 1984 *(and the film based on it) portrayed such a world of totalitarian rationality.*

tionalization set the course for many social changes: increasingly bureaucratic states, increasingly specialized work tasks, and more rules and regulations to bring order to an increasingly complex society. Capitalist economies have become more rationalized, with large corporations, "scientific" management techniques, computer systems, and the like. Few companies today, for example, would rely on a hunch—or on "history"—to decide whether to introduce a new product. Instead, companies conduct market research with sophisticated scientific tools. Similarly, politics has become increasingly rationalized, creating governments dominated by bureaucratic officeholders and formal rules. Even private life has become more rationalized; we now structure our activities by the clock rather than by the more natural rhythms of night and day or the seasons (Young, 1988). Life choices are no longer largely predetermined by nature or by tradition, but are made after a careful calculation of costs and benefits. For Weber, since the Reformation, social change has meant increasing rationalization, a process that is now extending into non-Western cultures as well.

Weber was profoundly ambivalent about this rationalization of human societies, which involved—in the words of the social theorist Robert Nisbet (1966, p. 293)—"the conversion of social values and relationships from the primary, communal and traditional shapes they once held to the larger, impersonal and bureaucratized shapes of modern society." On the one hand, Weber appreciated the greater efficiency produced by the bureaucratic organization of work, and noted that rationalization had freed humanity from reliance on superstition and from the frequently exploitative tyranny of traditional authority. On the other hand, Weber feared that rationalization would become an end in itself, and the disenchantment, mechanization, and regimentation of all social life would lead to a world in which the incessant pursuit of more efficient *means* would make it difficult to evaluate (or even remember) the *ends*. Clearly, Weber worried that rationalization had the power to diminish humanity even as it increased efficiency: In his classic essay, "Politics as a Vocation," Weber wrote, "Not a summer's bloom lies ahead of us, but rather a polar night of icy darkness and hardness" (Weber, 1918/1947, p. 128).

Durkheim's Functional View of Social Change

Émile Durkheim's views on social change center on the different types of social solidarity, the ways in which people are ***functionally integrated*** in a society. As we saw in Chapter 1, mechanical solidarity binds together people who are essentially alike, those who live in simple societies and share similar beliefs and practices. Such societies are integrated by the essential sameness of each member: Everyone thinks and behaves the same way. Organic solidarity binds together people who are different from one another but who need to find a way to live together in complex modern societies. Because of the variety of social roles available to people in modern societies, we are drawn together by our mutual dependence on others who can provide the things we cannot provide for ourselves. People in simple societies grow their own food, make their own clothes, build their own houses; people in modern societies rely on others to do these things. Modern societies create integration through the interdependence of people who maintain diversity in their beliefs and practices. Not surprisingly, Durkheim identified the growing and increasingly specialized division of labor as a crucial element of social change.

At least in the West, the prevailing direction of social change led from mechanical to organic solidarity. Durkheim also identified the mechanism that produced this change. The onset of modernity—marked by a shift to organic solidarity as the basis of societal integration—is brought about by increases in the dynamic density of social interaction. **Dynamic density** refers to the frequency of interactions among members of the population. Three social-structural factors combine to increase dynamic density: growing population size, the proliferation of different kinds of jobs, and new technologies of communication and transportation. Increases in dynamic density—coupled with increasingly dysfunctional competition among similar people all trying to play the same social roles—brought on the transition from mechanical to organic solidarity.

In the same way that Weber worried about the consequences of rationalization, Durkheim feared that rampant individualism and rapid social change might blind people to their functional interdependence. When society changes rapidly—for better or worse—people tend to lose their bearings, to become unsure about which social rules apply, and to lose connections to supportive groups and relationships. Durkheim characterized such conditions as *anomie*, which (as we saw in Chapter 1) is a state of disruption in the rules and understandings that guide and integrate social life. Despite the higher risk of anomie in modern societies, Durkheim generally had an optimistic view of society's journey from mechanical to organic solidarity. The capacity for material production was enhanced. Cultural life was improved by the substitution of science for mythology. Individuals had a wider choice of actions than in primitive societies, as well as greater opportunities for creativity and individual development.

Evolutionary and Cyclical Theories of Social Change

In the mid-nineteenth century, Charles Darwin offered his biological theory of evolution as an explanation for the diversity of species in the worlds of plants and animals. Since that time (and perhaps before), sociologists have wondered whether a theory of *social* evolution could explain the diversity of human societies—that is, explain processes and patterns of change that bring about diversity in ***social structure***. The key to Darwin's evolutionary theory was his identification of natural selection as the general mechanism that drives the diversification of life-forms. Evolution results from random genetic variations among species, which produce distinctive characteristics or traits that prove to be advantageous or disadvantageous in a particular environment. Species whose characteristics are well-matched to their environments are "selected" for successful reproduction, and their traits are passed on to successive generations; species whose traits are poorly matched with their environments eventually fail to reproduce and die out. Although Darwin identified natural selection as the mechanism of "natural change" (that is, of the diversification of species), his theory said nothing about the ultimate direction or goal of evolution. Genetic variations and mutations are random or nondirectional; they do not come about in anticipation of making a species more fit for its environment. Once traits appear, however, the environment selects some of them for reproduction. If the environment happens to change, traits that were once advantages could become disadvantages (Mayr, 1988).

Evolutionary Models

Sociologists who have thought about the possibility of applying **evolutionary models** to social change face the same two questions as Darwin: Is there a general mechanism of social change, and is there a direction to social change? Different theorists have offered different answers to those questions. Herbert Spencer (1820–1903), a contemporary of Darwin, offered a complete theory of social evolution that identified both the direction and the general mechanism of social change. Spencer drew elaborate parallels between the development and evolution of biological species and the development and evolution of human societies. Like Darwin, Spencer saw adaptation to the environment as the general mechanism of social change. In the struggle for existence in an environment of scarcity, only the "fittest" *social* forms survive.

Spencer differed from Darwin in two important ways. First, while Darwin saw genetic variation as a random, nondirectional process, Spencer argued that human societies intentionally adjust to changing environments in ways that increase their chances of survival. Spencer suggested that human societies have the capacity to learn about themselves and their place in the environment, and with this information they can choose new adaptive strategies for survival—a good example of ***social action***. Those strategies that "work" are retained and institutionalized in subsequent generations (Haines, 1988). Second, Spencer did not hesitate to identify the long-range direction of social change: All societies undergo change from simple, homogeneous forms (namely, tribes) to complex, differentiated forms (that is, nation-states). This universal pattern of change is much like Durkheim's idea of the shift from mechanical to organic solidarity.

Some contemporary sociologists continue to pursue Spencer's goal of an evolutionary theory of social change. Gerhard Lenski sees direct parallels between biological and social evolution, but he recognizes a cultural heritage as well as a genetic heritage in every human society. Human societies, in interacting with their natural and social world, develop characteristics that enable them to cope and to grow. These characteristics get encoded in the society's information systems, just as a plant or animal species' record of experience in an environment gets encoded in its genes (Lenski, Lenski, and Nolan, 1991).

Lenski believes that to grow in size, complexity, wealth, or power, a society must create and use new information that can, in turn, lead to new sources of energy needed to sustain their enlarged activities. The more information used, the more energy there is; the more energy, the more a society can grow. Advances in technology stimulate further advances, leading to further growth. The process of societal development, once set in motion, tends to be self-sustaining. The society that does not make advances in technology will not grow and in the long run will not survive. Lenski does call attention to factors that can limit a society's growth, such as its physical environment, beliefs, and values. These can produce obstacles or resistance to innovation and social change. The fluoridation controversy, discussed later in this chapter, is an example of sustained resistance to a new scientific idea.

Other sociologists—both classical and modern—are less inclined to believe that societies "evolve" in anything like a Darwinian manner. Some believe that it will never be possible to arrive at a single, general mechanism that causes social change. That is, they argue that there is simply no social equivalent of the environment in Darwin's natural-selection theory (Ragin and Zaret, 1983). Following Weber's methodological prescriptions, these sociologists argue that the discipline will never do more than provide limited generalizations about the mechanisms of change. Thus, while Weber argued that increasing rationalization characterizes modern social change throughout the West, he held that the *causes* of this pattern are multiple, specific to a particular setting, and changeable over time. In other words, there is no single underlying mechanism ultimately driving all social change. Sociologists who accept this view are suspicious both of Durkheim's idea that dynamic density drives the shift from mechanical to organic solidarity and of Marx's idea that contradictions between productive technology and its social surroundings lead to revolutionary transformations.

The Cyclical Perspective

Still other sociologists question Spencer's position that society moves in a certain direction through history, from simpler to more complex organization. Other theorists argue that social change goes in cycles—that history repeats itself. Those who take this **cyclical perspective** believe that social change is neither cumulative nor progressive. Every society has a natural life cycle: birth, adolescence, maturation, decay, and eventual death, followed by the birth of some new social order.

Oswald Spengler may be the most famous proponent of the idea that just as Western society could rise, so it could fall. In his widely read book *The Decline of the West* (1926–1928), Spengler argued that all societies are destined to follow a course of growth followed by decay. In its youth a society is most creative and most idealistic. As it matures, a society becomes less flexible, more materialistic, and more prone to decay—war and social disintegration (in the form of crime and other types of deviance) become more common. Spengler was convinced that Western society had already reached its golden years and was on the decline. Few contemporary sociologists share Spengler's pessimism, in part because his theories tend to be more philosophical than scientific.

Arnold Toynbee (1946), a British historian, has offered a more optimistic cyclical theory of social change. Central to his theory are the concepts of "challenge and response": The measure of a civilization's success is found in its responses to specific challenges posed by its physical and social environment. All civilizations, in his view, rise and fall according to their ability to meet these challenges, although later civilizations have the benefit of learning from the mistakes of civilizations before them.

Cyclical theories of social change persist today, but few of them share the sweeping generalities of Spengler and Toynbee. In his recent book *The Rise and Fall of the Great Powers* (1987), historian Paul Kennedy argues that since 1500 the great powers—Spain, the Netherlands, France, the British Empire, and the United States—have risen and fallen relative to one another. One nation tends to rise to political and economic power as the others fall. Kennedy identifies three related factors that drive this cyclical rise and fall: productive economic resources, revenue-raising capacity (that is, the ability of a central government to build wealth through taxes), and military strength. Great powers on the rise often take special advantage of a technological innovation (sailing ships, steam engines, computer chips) to boost their economic production, which can be taxed to increase the national treasury; they then turn that revenue into the development and production of military weapons. The "conquest" of falling nations by rising new powers is both an economic and a military accomplishment. Although Kennedy's thesis has received considerable criticism, the post–World War II "Asian miracle"—the economic and political rise of Japan to its present status as a great power—at least raises the question: Does the Japanese rise signal an American fall?

CAUSES OF SOCIAL CHANGE

The abstract theories that we have been describing provide only a general idea of the sources of social change, and they explain only sketchily how particular changes come about. For example, what specific causes and processes explain Japan's recent rise to global prominence? A complete answer would start with a description of the environmental and demographic contexts of the recent economic explosion. It is important to know, for instance, that Japan is an island nation with relatively few of the natural resources needed to fuel a modern industrial society. Also, with little territory available for expansion, the population density is extremely high. The Japanese have been adept at exploiting recent scientific and technological innovations—the computer chip, as one obvious example—routinely turning discoveries and inventions into profitable goods. The Japanese have certainly *borrowed* from other cultures (the assembly-line system of mass production has American and European origins), but they have also *shared* their own creations. For example, as we saw in Chapter 8, some Japanese management techniques are being borrowed by American and European corporations. Let's take a closer look at each of the four causes of social change just indicated: the natural environment, population, innovation, and diffusion.

The Natural Environment

The physical environment provides the opportunity for social change, but it also constrains or limits the kinds of changes humans might choose to make. Availability of natural resources—clean water, easily retrievable fuels, fertile soil, abundant food supplies—has done much to shape human history. Those societies in which resources are abundant have developed in substantially different ways from those living in environments where they are scarce. Remarkably diverse technological innovations have been developed to enable human societies to survive in diverse ecosystems. Think of the variety of traditional agricultural practices in different regions of the world: Cultivation of rice paddies makes sense only where periodic flooding takes place—as it does in Southeast Asia; the herding of sheep in the Scottish highlands is an effective response to the thin, rocky soil found there. However, technology cannot always conquer environmental limitations: How long can Southern California's growing population survive in what is essentially a desert, drawing water from increasingly depleted reservoirs and rivers?

The natural environment shapes social change in at least two other ways. First, natural disasters or catastrophes have brought some civilizations to an end: The volcanic eruption of Vesuvius destroyed the thriving Roman town of Pompeii in A.D. 79, just as floods from the Indus River have periodically destroyed ancient Indian civilizations. Interestingly, however, human societies have typically bounced back from such natural disasters—by moving to a more benign site or simply by rebuilding where they were. Earthquakes in and around San Francisco—the "big one" of 1906 and the "pretty big one" of 1989—have not driven people away from the Bay Area. Instead, they have led to a set of social changes: building codes that require skyscrapers and bridges to be able to withstand the next major quake. Second, the geographic location of a human society also shapes its development. Civilizations that develop at the crossroads of transportation or communication lines are likely to learn about and to exploit innovations and ideas from diverse cultures; civilizations at the margins or periphery generally develop in a more insular way, and perhaps at a slower pace. Location at the crossroads creates problems as well: Nation-states located between powerful neighbors sometimes find it difficult to defend their political autonomy and cultural distinctiveness (as has been the case for Poland in recent decades, situated between Germany and the Soviet Union).

For much of human history, the natural environment imposed itself on social change—it was an external force that operated more or less independently from the people who had to deal with it. That is scarcely the case today: We find ourselves in a complex interaction with the physical environment. Many of the social changes we choose to make are so massive that they bring about environmental changes that, in turn, force new patterns of human response. The growing threat of global warming, described in Chapter 19, is a good example (Adler, 1991; Lacayo, 1991). Global warming is due to human activity—chiefly, the burning of coal and oil—which has increased the amount of carbon dioxide in the atmosphere, trapping more of the sun's heat. Since the warming is a global trend, the resulting problems will require perhaps unprecedented

Because our advanced technology seems to shield us from natural disasters, our memory of disasters in our own country is short and our empathy with the victims of natural disasters in other parts of the world is curiously limited. Will it take a replay of the devastating San Francisco earthquake of 1906 to make today's Americans place themselves in an appropriately humble relationship with the natural world?

cooperation among all nations—especially those in the industrialized world, which contribute more to environmental pollution than simpler societies do. Sustained global warming could change our environment to such a degree that it would force social changes of considerable magnitude. The dire predictions of rising temperatures and drought in some areas, flooding in other areas, and massive changes in ecosystems that could cause disruptions in agriculture have led to an international effort to halt this warming trend. This effort will itself require dramatic social changes. Massive reductions in auto emissions would certainly help, but will people in the industrialized world give up the convenience and relatively low cost of "the family car"?

Population

The importance of population trends as a cause of social change cannot be overestimated. Increases or decreases in the size of a population, or in the relative numbers of young and old, male and female, urban and rural inhabitants, will have profound effects on social behavior and social organization. As we saw in Chapters 6 and 19, sharp increases in the birth rate after World War II created the baby-boom generation that—as it heads into middle age, looking toward retirement—will eventually bring about a "graying" of the American population. The changes accompanying this demographic shift will be far-reaching: everything from more retirement communities to more hospices.

Continued growth in the total size of the human population will also lead to social changes. There is considerable disagreement about how many people the earth can comfortably hold, and many suggest that the real issue is not overall population size in the future but the distribution of necessary resources (food, water, shelter, health care, education, jobs) among those already here (Simon, 1990). However, no one disputes that the global population continues to surge upward. There are now about 5.4 billion people on earth, and United Nations projections call for a leveling off probably at 11 billion—but perhaps as high as 14 billion—during the twenty-first century (Fornos, 1991; Haub, 1989).

These extraordinary increases are not evenly distributed over the globe. Ninety percent of population growth occurs in the developing countries, which can least afford it. The case of Ethiopia is especially tragic. Despite recurrent famine, deforestation, drought, desertification, and civil war, Ethiopia's population may double in the next twenty-three years (from about 50 million to 100 million people). The average Ethiopian woman has seven children. Continued growth of the world's population will exacerbate social and environmental problems already obvious throughout the Third World: rapidly increasing urbanization (which creates high unemployment, substandard housing, sewage and waste disposal problems, and rising crime); food shortages (the world now consumes more food in a year than it produces, a recent trend that obviously cannot continue for long); environmental degradation (the elimination of global forests and scrub trees for fuel, for profit, and for the expansion of urban areas is one obvious example). The social changes needed to avert these disasters are just as massive (Donaldson, 1990): What would need to happen to reduce the birth rate in ten African countries where 90 percent of the women had never even heard of birth control (Fornos, 1991, p. 49)?

Innovation

The old adage "There is nothing new under the sun" is, fortunately for all of us, a gross exaggeration. Indeed, "under the sun" these days one is likely to find huge fields of solar collectors and batteries gathering up and storing the sun's energy as a supplement to other—mainly dirtier or riskier—sources of power. The development of solar energy systems is an **innovation**: the social creation and institutionalization of new ideas, products, processes, or structures. Let's consider three types of innovation that bring about social change: discoveries, new ideas, and inventions.

Discoveries

A **discovery** might be defined as new knowledge about the external world. From the standpoint of Europeans in 1492, Columbus's voyage was indeed one of "discovery": They learned for the first time about an autonomous culture living on the other side of the Atlantic. The first systematic measurements of carbon dioxide in the atmosphere and the first reliable counts of the world's population are also discoveries—the first about the natural world and the second about the social world. By themselves, discoveries probably do not directly contribute much to social change; but when people begin to make choices on the basis of the new knowledge that discoveries provide—different choices, or even choices that had never before been imagined—the social changes involved are immense.

These days, most people associate the process of discovery with science, and sociologists who have examined scientists' practices have learned a great deal about how new knowledge comes into existence. Take one of the most significant scientific discoveries of this century: James Watson and Francis Crick's discovery of the structure of DNA, the "hereditary molecule" containing genetic information that determines every physical characteristic of every living thing. The young American Watson and the more senior Briton Crick announced to the world in 1953 that DNA took the shape of a double helix, two twisted strands of chemicals connected by a patterned sequence of bridges that carry the genetic code (Judson, 1979). Their discovery initiated the science of molecular biology, which has, in turn, given rise to biotechnology: attempts to engineer new life forms (or alter existing ones) by manipulating the genetic material in DNA.

Were Watson and Crick reclusive but creative geniuses, working away as hermits in their laboratory, unknown to others, suddenly shouting "Eureka!" (literally: "I have found it!") when they first saw the double helix? Hardly. Scientific discovery is an intensely *social* activity. Watson and Crick could not have made their discovery alone, for several reasons. First, their discovery built on knowledge accumulated by countless scientists before them. For example, chemists had already ascertained that DNA consisted of phosphates, sugar, and several nitrogen-containing bases—but it was left for Watson and Crick to figure out how these various pieces were assembled. Second, Watson and Crick worked with a large team of fellow investigators, at renowned institutions of scientific inquiry (Cavendish Labs at Cambridge and Kings College in London): Maurice Wilkins's and Rosalind Franklin's x-ray diffraction photographs provided crucial support for the idea of a double helix. Like other forms of work, modern science is characterized by a highly specialized division of labor (Watson, for instance, needed a crash course in crystallography, a body of skills and procedures that others had worked hard to develop). Third, Watson and Crick were pushed to their discovery in an intense and frantic competition to be the first to announce the structure of DNA. Wilkins and Franklin were out to unlock the same mystery, and Linus Pauling at Cal Tech was thought to be close to the double helix as well (Watson, 1968). The social institution of science—which offers copious rewards and recognition (Nobel Prizes, for example) for priority in making a discovery—stimulates a competitive atmosphere which, in part, accounts for the rapid rate at which modern scientists add to the storehouse of reliable knowledge.

New Ideas

Unlike the discovery of the double helix, innovative ideas do not always take the form of explicit descriptions of the external world. Some new ideas—like the idea of "progress"—are moral evaluations about the state of the world, and these are more easily translated into individual attitudes and choices. Such new ideas can be potent sources of social change. The idea of progress—that is, the notion that life is always improving, that the present is better than the past, and that the future will be even better than the present—is not a cultural universal. At different times and in different cultures, people have questioned whether human history is advancing in a linear and cumulative way: For some, degeneration seems a better description for where we have come from and where we are going. Critics of progress, often labeled romantics, have found "golden ages" of the past against which the present looks notably inferior.

FAITH IN PROGRESS However, in most Western cultural traditions, the idea of progress—an optimistic reading of human history and its future—has long roots. It may have originated in religious thought during the medieval period (Alexander and Sztompka, 1990; Nisbet, 1980). If mortals were indeed winning the war of good against evil, were they not moving closer to achieving heaven on earth? Such faith in progress was an important part of the ideology that inspired European Christians to join the Crusades to destroy infidels in the Holy Land. The Enlightenment of the eighteenth century put this commitment to progress into secular form by replacing "faith" with "reason." The Parisians in 1789 who sought the head of King Louis XVI were driven in part by the *idea* that popular representative government was an improvement over the divine right of kings. By the nineteenth century, progress assumed a materialist tone: The manufacture and consumption of more goods, new goods, improved goods, became the measure of progress. However, it was also at this time that some began to question the inevitability of progress as they looked around at sooty factories, children in sweatshops, and what the social critic Thorstein Veblen (1899) called the "conspicuous consumption" of luxuries.

Not even two world wars were enough to kill the idea of progress, though the enhanced possibility of human annihilation via nuclear war seemed an odd definition of progress. Materialist visions of progress kept people buoyant during the 1950s, as families in new homes and cars with V-8 engines saw their lives as a definite improvement over their parents' experience with the Great Depression in the 1930s. The counterculture of the 1960s was a mix of romantic celebrations of the past—recovering "tribal" roots at Woodstock, for example—coupled with progressive ideas about better living through chemistry (in the form of drug-induced altered states). The go-go 1980s put progress in a nakedly monetary form: Getting richer faster was an improvement in itself (and homeless people had brought their problems on themselves). Only lately, with increased concerns about the ability of a very polluted planet to sustain human life, have we begun to lose faith in the idea that progress always means improvement.

RECONSIDERING PROGRESS Christopher Lasch, in his book *The True and Only Heaven* (1991), argues that continued faith in progress—as it has come to be defined in American culture—not only is refuted by the historical changes of our past but is suicidal when pushed into the future. Lasch traces one strand of the American idea of progress back to the eighteenth-century economist and moralist Adam Smith, who put forth the idea that the advancement of human civilization comes from increases in the consumption of goods and services. From Smith through the "greedy" 1980s, progress has come to be seen as the increased ability to satisfy private, material wants. From this point of view, human wants are infinite: There is always something more, something better, something different to be desired. The insatiability of human wants is not seen as a character flaw but rather as an economic virtue: It is the stimulus to increased production and perpetual economic expansion. Since human wants are limitless, the productive machinery—technical, social—that provides the sought-after goods and services must also be limitless. The *idea* of progress has, in part, driven and legitimated over 200 years of growth in the productive capacities of the American economy.

And therein lies the problem for Lasch. The belief in progress has created a "culture of consumption" that cannot endure in the face of now-obvious signals of resource exhaustion and environmental degradation. Lasch hopes for a cultural change that will have far-reaching consequences: Can we replace the idea of progress with the idea of limits? Where can we find a language for talking about our future, with ideas that recognize the dangers of resource depletion and environmental pollution and are not grounded on the assumption that "bigger is better"? Lasch finds such a language in a nineteenth-century view of the world held by artisans, shopkeepers, tradesmen, and farmers. He calls this view "populist" or "republican," and in its apparent conservatism it contrasts sharply with both radical and liberal traditions of thought. In the values of these lower-middle-class Americans of a century ago, Lasch discovers a formula that he thinks should replace the long-standing idea of progress as a guide to our future. These values emphasize an awareness that everything has its price, a sense of civic responsibility, a respect for limits, a skepticism of change for its own sake, and a belief that human existence is a struggle, with trade-offs and compromises, rather than an inevitable improvement. Interestingly, nineteenth-century small landowners and merchants had no sense of the environmental crisis that would first be recognized in the 1950s and fully appreciated in the decades that followed. Yet, Lasch suggests, their traditional values are precisely the ones on which we should base the new social order that is being compelled by ecological limitations and constraints.

This new age of limits would be dominated by small-town values of family, community, and tradition. This complex of commitments would put the brakes on our insatiable material wants and would lead to a society more in tune with undeniable environmental limitations, and to a people more content with their lives. Lasch would like to see American society move in the direction of a cultural conservatism and economic egalitarianism, encouraging the decentralization of political power and decision making coupled with the breakup of massive corporations into smaller-scale production units. These traditional values run counter to liberal positions on social issues: Working-class commitments to community and family have fueled, for example, the antibusing and antiabortion movements. Moreover, Lasch is aware that working-class values can be pushed to negative extremes—racism, for example, or other forms of intolerance—that are unacceptable not just for liberals but for most other people regardless of their political convictions. In no sense does Lasch want to turn back the clock to a time when racial prejudice was tolerated and widespread, but neither does he believe that liberalism—with its faith in progress, its commitment to limitless expansion of production and consumption of goods—holds much hope for the future. He seeks to recover from traditional working-class populism those values that could be effective in a world of declining economic growth and diminished material expectations. A concern for the common good would replace an unrestrained pursuit of self-interest, and the health of the community would become as important as the health of the individual.

Lasch concludes his argument by making a distinction between optimism and hope. Both words convey a feeling about the future, and the differences between them are not obvious. Optimism is closely linked to the idea of progress, for it is grounded in the presumption that the future will be better. Optimism about the future draws on a belief in the perfectibility of human societies, that there will always be improvement in how we live with one another. Too often, says Lasch, that improvement is assessed only by looking at the kinds of changes that are most easily measured; few would deny that, at least for Western society, there is a continuing "democratization of consumption" as more goods become available to more people. However, such beliefs can easily lead to the blind faith that things will inevitably work out for the best.

The idea of hope, by contrast, seems better suited to a future that does not always work out as desired. Hope, unlike optimism, does not presume confidence in a future that is bigger and better. Its confidence comes not from tomorrow but from yesterday: Time-honored values that got us through difficulties of the past are good candidates for getting us through inevitable difficulties of the future. Hope is linked not to a belief in progress, but to a belief in justice—to the idea that past and present wrongs will be righted. Environmental degradation will be reversed, social injustices will be remedied. Hope, unlike optimism, sees the future not as an endless improvement but as the occasion to fix things that went wrong in the past. Clearly, Lasch prefers hope to optimism as the desired image of our future.

In sum, just as a belief in progress has in the past been a potent motivator of human action and a source of social change, Lasch hopes that an abandonment of the idea of progress will yield social and behavioral changes that will enhance the odds of human survival.

Inventions

The third category of innovation is **invention**: the making of a new product or process. We tend to think that material inventions have only recently begun to shape social changes; actually, they have been around since the dawn of human life. Consider only one example from the Middle Ages, often incorrectly remembered as "the Dark Ages," a time of stagnation. The relatively simple invention of the stirrup, which allowed the rider of a horse to stay firmly seated in the saddle, produced far-reaching social changes. This medieval innovation led to a completely new battle tactic in which a warrior on a horse could slash and jab at his opponent without fear of tumbling unchivalrously to the ground. This new mode of fighting, in turn, made novel demands on soldiering. No longer could a freeman simply take up arms and declare himself fit for battle. Mounted combat required many years of training, not to mention the great expense of horses, attendants, and equipment. Thus, a whole new social aristocracy was born—the knightly class—and with it a new set of social patterns that were attuned to the needs of a mounted warrior's way of life. Indeed, the emergence of feudalism is associated with these other changes brought about by the invention of the stirrup. So that they could afford the increasingly expensive equipment needed for mounted shock

Clockwise from top left: *A Roman cart, an eighteenth-century mill wheel, and a trimming wheel at a modern paper-manufacturing plant. Though the wheel first appeared thousands of years ago in Mesopotamia, succeeding ages and societies—including our own—have continued the process of innovation by which this invention has become an ever more useful tool.*

combat, knights were given land and the right to tax the peasants or serfs who lived and worked on it. "Few inventions have been so simple as the stirrup," wrote Lynn White, Jr. (1962, p. 38), "but few have had so catalytic an influence on history."

In our own day, several technological changes have had equally profound effects. Consider the automobile. On a personal level, it has had an enormous impact on everyday patterns of social life. It has enabled greater mobility for visiting, vacationing, participating in community activities, engaging in sports and other recreation, and even dating and courtship. The vast influence of the automobile on society as a whole is also apparent. The car has encouraged the development of many major industries, in addition to car manufacturing, shipping, and marketing: supplying materials to automakers, servicing and repairing cars, producing the fuels to run them, and providing the roads they drive on. In this way, the automobile directly or indirectly employs many millions of American workers. The car has greatly affected settlement patterns as well. Without the car, it is unlikely that today's sprawling suburbs would have evolved as they have. Accompanying these changes in residence patterns are other transformations. For instance, the car has promoted great change in retail distribution: The small, main-street merchants are being replaced by huge shopping malls located on the outskirts of town. The car, in short, has virtually revolutionized the American way of life.

Not all inventions are of a material kind. Some of the most consequential inventions are not new durable goods, but rather new social processes or techniques. Consider the invention of the public opinion poll. The systematic process of asking a representative sample of people about their preferences, and then extrapolating from their answers to the entire population, began only in the 1930s. Before that time, politicians interested in knowing their chances for election, and manufacturers of consumer goods interested in knowing potential demand for a new product, could only make educated guesses based on experience and common sense. Today, no candidate can survive the early months of an election campaign unless the polls show some minimal public enthusiasm, and few companies would consider manufacturing a new product without doing market research beforehand. Interestingly, when Abraham Lincoln said that "Public opinion is everything. . . . With it nothing can fail. Without it nothing can succeed," there was no reliable process for knowing public preferences. Now—thanks to the invention of public opinion polls and other techniques of survey research—results published everywhere on every subject by Gallup, Roper, Harris, Yankelovich, and the National Opinion Research Center sometimes make it seem that no secrets are left (Bogart, 1972; Crespi, 1989; P. M. Hauser, 1975).

Diffusion

When did you first see a bar code? These symbols have become so omnipresent in contemporary life that it is probably impossible for you to remember the first time you looked quizzically at the meaningless string of vertical stripes (of varying thickness) above a random sequence of numbers. The bars and numbers stuck or printed on everything are hardly meaningless and random to the computers that read them. Bar codes are now essential for keeping track of sales (and other) transactions, for taking stock of the inventory of goods, and for organizing production sequences (L. Davis, 1989; Nulty, 1982).

You probably first saw a bar code at the supermarket, on a can of cat food or a box of cereal. Now you can't avoid them. Bar codes will greet you when you go to the library: Each book has a unique bar-code number on a sticker, and so does your library ID card. Whisk the wand over both of them—matching book title to borrower—and the library's computer instantly knows everything it needs to know about the circulation of its collection. People are getting bar-coded, too: The New York City Marathon puts bar codes on each of its runners, so that race officials can wave the wand over them as they cross the finish line and get an instant and accurate list of their finishing times. And take a look at the back cover of this book.

The bar-coding of America illustrates **diffusion**: the spread of innovations from one social setting to another. In this case the innovation of bar codes spread throughout a single culture, from grocery stores, to libraries, to marathon runners. Just as consequential for social change are innovations that move from one *cultural* setting to another—in effect, the transplantation of ideas or products into the social life of a different group of people. Soldiers, colonial administrators, missionaries, migrants, traders, visiting scholars and artists, exchange students, tourists—all are potential agents of diffusion between societies. We can see the cross-cultural results of diffusion even in something as all-American as the United States Constitution. It was written in English, a language borrowed from the British Isles, using an alphabet that came from ancient Phoenicia by way of the Greeks and Romans. The various sections of the document are denoted by Roman and Arabic numerals. It was printed by means of a process invented in Germany; the paper it was printed on was derived from an invention of the ancient Egyptians. Finally, many of the political ideas incorporated in the Constitution were cultural legacies of French and English philosophers.

Rates and patterns of diffusion vary considerably. At one extreme, contact between societies may result in a cultural "takeover." For example, the Dutch colonials transformed Indonesians from subsistence farmers who lived in small, egalitarian villages into a competitive, stratified society that was oriented toward the world market (Plog, Jolly, and Bates, 1976). At the other extreme, contact may prompt people to withdraw and cling to their traditions. Although the Sumu Indians of Nicaragua have been trading with neighboring groups for centuries, until recently they shut their doors when strangers entered their villages, kept their ways secret, and married only among themselves.

Between these two extremes are numerous examples of societies selectively borrowing elements of other cultures. For instance, Marco Polo introduced his Italian countrymen to the long, thin, round noodles eaten by the Chinese. The noodles soon became popular in Italy, where they were called *spaghetti*. Italian immigrants later brought spaghetti to America. Similarly, the Incas of Peru discovered quinine and passed it along to their Spanish conquerors, who then shared it with other Europeans, who in turn used it in Africa to offset malaria attacks. (Thus, were it not for the Incas, Europeans might never have colonized Africa.)

questionable and possibly dangerous intrusion into people's lives.

Perhaps the most significant feature of the fluoridation controversy is the fact that it has gone on for forty-five years, with no sign of being resolved soon. The endless debate shows the limits of science in deciding public-policy decisions where evidence and logic, politics and ethics, get jumbled together. Pro-fluoridation scientists, dentists, and government officials depicted the earliest opponents of fluoridation as right-wing libertarian extremists, as ignorant people who also believed that the earth was flat. Now that scientific evidence hints at a risk of cancer from fluoride, however, opposition to fluoridation has taken on a new legitimacy. On the one hand, this turnabout suggests that any belief becomes more credible if science can be brought to its defense. On the other hand, the fluoridation controversy suggests that science alone is not enough to decide policy decisions that are questions of values as much as of fact.

The Impact of Technology

Technology is the application of knowledge to the solution of practical problems. The impact of technology on social life is not limited to new machines that enable people to do miraculous new things—like fly, or send images through space, or compute. Just as the rise of science is both an increase in new knowledge and the transformation of cultural authority, technology is simultaneously new machines or tools *and* new social and cultural arrangements. These transformed institutional structures are, on one level, *consequences* of new technical inventions; but just as important—and more often overlooked—is the fact that these revamped social and cultural circumstances become *causes* of the creation, manufacture, and diffusion of the next generation of new tools, machines, and processes. The relationship between technology and society is interactive: Causal forces push in both directions, as the story of Caliente and the coming of the diesel engine, below, illustrates.

Death by Dieselization: Analyzing Technological Choices

Caliente was in every way a model American small town. Its homes, stores, streets, and parks were attractive and well-maintained. Its schools were good; its local government was honest; its citizens were public-spirited and hard-working. But Caliente was a railroad town, and it died during the 1940s. According to W. F. Cottrell, a sociologist who published a classic 1951 paper on the fate of Caliente, it was a case of "death by dieselization." The new technology of diesel power "killed" the town.

Caliente was built in the desert of the American Southwest for the sole purpose of maintaining the steam-powered locomotives that passed through it daily. The steel boilers of these locomotives were under tremendous stress from the high temperature and pressure needed to keep up a head of steam. So every hundred miles the boilers were disconnected from the train, checked for damage, and repaired or replaced. Caliente was one of the "division points" where this work took place. Most of the men who lived in Caliente were employed by the railroad. Others provided the goods and services that the railroad workers needed.

The introduction of diesel trains spelled disaster for Caliente. Diesel locomotives do not require frequent servicing, so some of the former division points, including Caliente, became obsolete. Except for a handful of men offered jobs elsewhere in the railroad system, most of the men of Caliente found themselves out of work. Because of the widespread unemployment, the town's whole economy suffered. Sales in the business district plummeted, and many stores closed. Property values collapsed, causing many families to lose most of their life savings.

To make matters worse, the situation seemed permanent. Try as they might, the residents of Caliente could not attract another large employer to their isolated part of the country. The case of Caliente is, in retrospect, hardly unique. Other towns and even cities have been thoroughly transformed by the closing of a factory that once employed most of the residents. In some of these cases, factory closings were precipitated by the same kind of technological changes that brought an end to Caliente.

Cottrell's case study of the impact of dieselization illustrates the *interactive* relationship between technology and society. The negative consequences of dieselization are obvious: The citizens of Caliente, who had tied their fortunes to the future of steam locomotion, lost not only their livelihood but their town as well. However, while the railroad company initially lost money from declining property values in Caliente after the trains no longer stopped there (the railroad owned much of the town), it saved money in the long run because diesel engines were cheaper to run, and abandonment of division points such as Caliente meant fewer workers to pay. Oil companies also stood to gain from increased sales of diesel fuel.

Technological changes, then, are likely to be evaluated differently by people who are affected by them in different ways. Dieselization was money-saving modernization for

Some observers see great freedom in the "postmodern" condition; others see only fragmentation and alienation. Much of our society's art reflects this profound ambivalence, which typifies the contemporary social situation.

the railroad and oil companies, and rail passengers certainly enjoyed the cleaner and faster ride that diesel enabled. But for Caliente, dieselization was doom. It is impossible, in this episode, to say that dieselization was progress. One must ask, progress *for whom?*

The Caliente case illustrates a second point about the interaction of technology and society: The rate and direction of change in technology is not determined by the technology itself. That is, the choice to replace steam power with diesel power is not inherent in the technology of dieselization. Sociologists must look for social and cultural factors that shape the eventual decision to "go diesel." The promise of greater efficiency for the railroad company and greater profits for some oil companies is certainly part of the economic context shaping the rise of diesel trains' engines; but there were other, less obvious, factors. For example, why didn't organized labor unions resist dieselization on grounds that it would eliminate the jobs of their members? The historical timing of the shift to diesel becomes an all-important cultural context. During the labor shortages caused by American involvement in World War II, it would have been almost unpatriotic to protest a technological change that eliminated the need for workers who were badly needed elsewhere. Perhaps this is why the U.S. Interstate Commerce Commission ruled against the request from Caliente citizens to have all trains stop there even if the diesel engines no longer required it.

This is just a beginning to the long list of social and cultural factors shaping the technological choices that culminated in the death of Caliente. Where did this new engine come from, and why is it referred to as a "diesel"? A look at the life and accomplishments of Rudolf Diesel (1858–1913) suggests that new technologies do not come into being in a straightforward, inevitable way—as if the eventually greater efficiency and profitability of diesel were obvious from the very start. It was not so; the early years of diesel power were marked by more failures than successes, bitter controversies over patent rights, many false starts and blind alleys, cooperation between two of Germany's largest companies, financial losses, disappointed consumers, and ultimately the suicide of the man who gave his name to today's diesel engine. For sociologists, bringing a new technology into being involves all these social and cultural elements—personalities, patent laws, corporate cooperation, trial and error—along with the valves, cylinders, air chambers, blowers, and crankshafts that make up the machine itself (Bryant, 1969, 1976; Latour, 1987; D. E. Thomas, 1987).

If Rudolf Diesel is today recognized as the father of the diesel engine, it is a paternity that he shares with many other individuals and organizations. To make his engine a reality, Diesel needed much more than an idea and a few spare parts. Indeed, even the idea for a "rational engine" was not Diesel's alone. It was inspired by thermodynamic principles set down decades before by Diesel's hero, the French physicist Sadi Carnot. Diesel developed the central idea behind his new engine in 1890–1891: He believed that ignition could occur without a rise in temperature (a process known as *isothermal combustion*), and that such an engine would be far more efficient to run than a steam engine. In order to move his invention closer to reality, Diesel wrote down "the idea in his head," submitted it to the patent office, and was granted a patent in 1893. The engine still existed only on paper; now Diesel had to turn his plans and drawings into steel.

For this step, Diesel needed to be more than an engineer—he needed to become an entrepreneur. He had to sell the idea of his new engine to those with the capital and equipment to build a prototype, or working model. So Diesel wrote a book about his invention, one that included as much promotional material as technical specifications. For example, Diesel suggested that his new engine would be economical and efficient even in small sizes, in contrast to steam engines, which were efficient only when they were built on a large scale. His small engine would make possible the decentralization of manufacturing and could, Diesel argued optimistically, restore the small craftsman to his former position of importance. Diesel's book convinced Maschinenfabrik-Augsburg and Krupp, two makers of steam engines, to invest in the development of the new engine. From 1893 to 1897, Diesel worked mainly with other engineers at Augsburg, trying to put together a machine that worked.

The first model never ran successfully under its own power, and the Augsburg team tinkered for almost a decade as they tried to solve the fundamental technical problem of how to get a good mixture of air and fuel into the cylinder in the short time available. Diesel himself faced an additional problem: In order to benefit financially from a successful engine, and in order to be able to call it his, Diesel needed to make certain that the various prototypes and models did not differ dramatically from the drawings and descriptions he had provided in his patent application. That is, Diesel sought a machine that not only worked, but that was still protected by the patent he had been granted in 1893. Unfortunately, both goals could not be achieved, and it soon became clear at Augsburg that—for example—in an effective "diesel" engine, the temperature would have to rise to 1,000°C after ignition. By 1897, Maschinenfabrik-Augsburg negotiated licensing and manufacturing agreements with several firms, but none of the engines built away from Augsburg worked properly. There were significant financial losses around this period (both corporate and personal), and even general despair about whether a successful "rational engine" would ever be built. Diesel himself suffered a nervous breakdown, and his family's financial situation was perilous.

From this point on, Diesel contributed virtually nothing to the design of "his" engine; that was left entirely to the engineers at Augsburg. They eventually succeeded, and by 1908, there were about 1,000 working diesel engines at twelve companies in six countries. In 1912, historians convened at a conference to discuss the invention and development of the diesel engine. Diesel wrote his own account, arguing that the eventually successful machine was his idea, his design. Other historians disagreed, saying the working machine bore little resemblance to Diesel's plans, and that credit for the invention should go to the Augsburg engineers. One year later, Diesel—near financial ruin, and in despair about losing control of the engine named for him—drowned himself.

It is a long way from Augsburg in the 1890s to Caliente in the 1940s. But the choice by the railroad to abandon steam in favor of diesel power could not have been made without the events in Germany a half century before. As we have seen, the invention and development of a working diesel engine required not just technical solutions to technical problems, but social solutions to social problems. These two related episodes show that technological innovations shape social change, and that social and cultural contexts shape the development of new technologies.

WORLDS APART: THE NEED FOR GLOBAL CHANGE

The first contact some 500 years ago between Europeans and natives of the Americas brought the people of the world closer together. Changes in science and technology have made the world seem an ever-smaller place. Electronic bar codes and diesel engines can now be found everywhere on the globe. However, in spite of revolutionary developments in communication and transportation, for example, people in other ways remain "worlds apart."

> Year by year the world becomes more sharply divided into two. On the one hand there are the advanced, industrial, developed, mature economies. And then there are the rest—developing, less developed, underdeveloped, undeveloped, pre-industrial or backward. The precise shade of

When humans journey to the airless and lifeless spaces of our solar system, we are reminded that Earth is a fragile jewel in an indescribably hostile environment.

> euphemistic description is unimportant; for the basic division is, of course, one between Rich and Poor. (Donaldson, 1986, p. 11)

This gap did not always exist. Less than 150 years ago the preindustrial economies held 74 percent of the world's population and 72 percent of the world's income. But by 1960 their population share was 65 percent and their income share a mere 22 percent. If the poorer countries continue to grow in output per year at their present rate, they will take 191 years to reach the present American level. By then, of course, the American economy will have grown at an even faster rate (Donaldson, 1986).

What created this great gap? For one thing, as we noted in Chapter 18, the modernized rich nations had the luxury of developing over centuries, without the interference of more advanced countries setting the rules for modernization. By contrast, most developing nations were colonies and as such were the prey of colonial powers, who manipulated the conditions of trade to serve their own purposes. In some cases the colonial powers actually destroyed local production to create a market for their own manufactured goods; Britain, for example, destroyed the textile industry in India in the last century. Colonial America was also subjected to trade restraints that favored the mother country, but the independent-minded American settlers were able to overthrow their colonial ruler while time was still left to get into the capitalistic race.

At the same time that the developing nations have been futilely trying to compete in a game that seems to be rigged against them, they have been bombarded with images of Western-style affluence (Harrison, 1984). As Peter Donaldson notes, "No longer do the poor remain in blissful (or even miserable) ignorance of what is going on elsewhere.

The cinema, radio and other mass media have opened the eyes of the poor two-thirds of the world to the levels of affluence achieved elsewhere. Increasingly, they will demand their share of it. This is the so-called 'revolution of rising expectations' " (1986, p. 16). Another problem in the developing nations is a consequence of population pressures; as we saw in Chapter 19, many poor nations have grown beyond the capacity of the land to support them with food, firewood, and clean water. Finally, not only are the poor people of the world largely discontented and needy, but they are also often neglected or exploited by their own corrupt government leaders and administrators.

Marx would not be surprised that contemporary Third World countries are breeding grounds of revolution and civil war. The ideologies may vary widely, from fundamentalist Islam to nationalism to communism, but the conflict is basically the same—between those who have and those who have not. Nicaragua, Argentina, Chile, Brazil, Panama, Guatemala, Cuba, San Salvador, Iran, Lebanon, Libya, Uganda, Kenya, Ethiopia, Sudan, Zambia, Mozambique, Vietnam, Cambodia, Laos, India, Sri Lanka—all have experienced (or are still undergoing) violent upheavals in their social and political organizations. The common thread is the desperation of people who have little reason to believe that the existing system will ever help them. This frustration has spread beyond national boundaries in alarming ways in the form of international terrorism.

It is a sad irony that in a world growing ever smaller and more unified through technological advances in communications and transportation, nations are being pulled away from one another economically, politically, and socially. Absorbed in our own *lifeworld*—our everyday experience and network of relationships—we find it difficult to take in, much less analyze, the dimensions of the social ills manifested in the large-scale *system*, the term used by the German sociologist Jürgen Habermas (1984, 1988) to describe the global system of indirect relationships of markets, technology, governments, and mass media. In time, perhaps, the world's citizens will turn their collective attention to the needs of this huge, diverse system world and find a way to harmonize their interests and to channel social change in beneficial ways. Columbus's arrival in the Americas provided the beginning of a fine opportunity for such cooperation. Perhaps the next 500 years will see greater progress toward the harmony amidst diversity of one world.

Thinking Back on the Key Concepts

The five key sociological concepts are useful for understanding both the causes and consequences of social change. The town of Caliente's "death by dieselization" is a good illustration of the large-scale changes in ***social structure*** that have been the subject of this chapter. The decision by the railroad company to switch from steam-powered to diesel locomotives was shaped by the structural context of a capitalist economy, in which owners of the means of production encourage technological developments that increase their profits. That decision had massive significance for the social structure of Caliente: Without a need for engines to take on water, the town lost its reason for existence and eventually lost most of its residents as well. Marx's theory of social change draws attention to the fundamental role played by the social structure of capitalism, in particular, the necessarily opposed interests of two social classes—workers and owners. Durkheim's theory also suggests that social structure drives social change in certain directions but not others. However, Durkheim was less interested in the effects of capitalist organization than in changes in population size, density, and occupational specialization—all vital aspects of social structure.

Too much attention to the social-structural sources of change could lead one to forget that most such changes are the result of meaningful ***social action*** by identifiable individuals or groups. Thus, Caliente was doomed by the invention and development of the diesel engine by Rudolf Diesel. This example is important because it brings seemingly impersonal forces of social change—capitalism, technology—back down to the level of individuals, like Diesel and other engineers, whose choices and accomplishments were essential for the transformation of society.

Social action is also visible in the fluoridation controversy—and so is the concept of ***power***. Who has the power to decide whether fluoride should be used; scientific experts, elected representatives, or local citizens? The controversy would never have emerged if some concerned citizens had not engaged in social action to protest its use. The unresolved conflict pits two potent sources of power against each other: science and politics. Much social change results from struggles for power between experts and ordinary citizens, owners and workers, rich and poor.

Such struggles for power go on against the backdrop of ***culture.*** Max Weber called attention to cultural beliefs and values as sources of social change, and in particular described the centuries of "rationalization" that have transformed Western societies. The increasing bureaucratization of social life is a major consequence of rationalization, but so is the growth of science as a cultural authority. Consider how the rationalizing force of science has changed the way humans think about plants and animals. Where once humans had to "make do" with the natural characteristics of a particular species, now—with discoveries of the logic of DNA and of the manipulation of genetic material—scientists hope to engineer new kinds of plants and animals that "nature" never dreamed of.

The expression "What goes around, comes around" certainly describes these processes of large-scale social change, though modern societies of the West may be reminded of its truth in particularly painful ways. Capitalism and rationalization have driven the search for ever-more powerful and efficient ways to produce the goods and services Westerners demand—from farms to factories, from books to computers, from horse-drawn carriages to automobiles. Now scientists warn that unwanted by-products of all this progress are causing environmental degradation—loss of the earth's protective ozone layer, greenhouse effects, and acid rain. The concept of ***functional integration*** reminds us that all these social changes are interrelated—that developments in one area force changes in another. Perhaps the continued pollution of the atmosphere will require that we adjust our cultural definition of progress away from "bigger and better" to "smaller and cleaner." It could also lead to intensified social action by environmental activists and "green" parties challenging anew the power of capitalists to set agendas for future technological change.

SUMMARY

1. Social changes are the alterations, over time, in the behavior patterns, culture, and structure of a society. Changes over the life course of an individual are not included under this definition. Rather, social change includes the enduring and fundamental transformations of human societies—like the many structural, institutional, and environmental changes initiated by Columbus's arrival in the Americas in 1492.

2. Classical theorists offer different interpretations of the causes and forms of social change. For Karl Marx, social change is rooted in the struggle between social classes over control of the means of production and the social relations of production. For Max Weber, social change in Western societies is characterized by increasing rationalization: the growing tendency to base decisions on logical evaluation of anticipated effects. For Émile Durkheim, social change was driven by an increasingly specialized division of labor, which shifted the basis for social integration from mechanic to organic solidarity.

3. Evolutionary theorists (such as Herbert Spencer) argue that all societies move from the simple to the complex (in terms of social organization). Those social patterns that survive and thrive are ones best suited to environmental opportunities and constraints. Cyclical theories imply that history repeats itself in a cyclical fashion and that all human societies move through a rise-and-fall life cycle.

4. The natural environment creates opportunities for social change, but limits the directions human action might take. Increasingly, societal choices (for example, the decision to burn oil and gas in huge quantities) have altered the natural environment (for example, global warming) in ways that require further social changes to ensure survival.

5. Demographic shifts—such as increases or decreases in the size of a population, or changes in its age structure (like the graying of America)—are potent sources of social change.

6. Innovations take three forms. Discoveries consist of new knowledge about nature (such as Watson and Crick's realization that DNA has a structure like a double helix). Not all new ideas take the form of descriptions of nature; others are philosophical or ethical evaluation of present or future states of affairs (like the idea of progress). Finally, invention is the making of a new product or process. Some inventions are material ones (like the stirrup), while others are social (like public opinion polls).

7. Another source of social change is diffusion: the spread of innovations from one social setting to another. Material innovations such as bar codes seem to diffuse more easily and quickly than cultural innovations (like the idea of progress).

8. In the modern world, science and technology are two of the most significant sources of social change. Science has not only enlarged the stock of reliable knowledge about the external world. As the case of the fluoridation controversy suggests, science has also become a voice of authority in political debate—but not so authoritative that scientific facts necessarily overrule ethical judgments or economic interests.

9. The relationship between technology and society is interactive. New technology has profound impact on social life: Dieselization of one railroad line brought a certain death to a small Western town. But new technologies emerge and develop in social and cultural contexts as well. The invention of the diesel engine involved not just pistons and valves but also profits, personalities, and patents.

REVIEW QUESTIONS

1. Define social change and provide some examples relevant to you.
2. Contrast the classical theories of social change.
3. What are the basic causes of social change? Provide one or more examples.
4. What is the difference between new ideas and inventions? Give an example of each.
5. Contrast the basic theories for explaining global change.

CRITICAL THINKING QUESTIONS

1. Assess social change in the United States over the past fifty years in terms of each of the four classical theories of social change.
2. What do you consider the three most important discoveries ever made, and why?
3. What do you consider the three most important new ideas, and why?
4. What do you consider the three most important inventions, and why?
5. Why do you think the authors discuss science and technology in the same section of this chapter?
6. What three major directions do you think global change will take in the next twenty-five years, and why?

GLOSSARY

Cyclical perspective The belief that history repeats itself in cycles that are neither cumulative nor progressive.

Diffusion The spread of innovations from one social setting to another.

Discovery New knowledge about the external world.

Dynamic density The frequency of interactions among members of the population; a concept identified by Emile Durkheim to explain social change.

Evolutionary models Theories that explain processes and patterns of changes that lead to diversity, based on Charles Darwin's concept of natural selection—the idea that survival is dependent on adaptation to changing environments.

Innovation The social creation and institutionalization of new ideas, products, processes, or structures.

Invention The making of a new product or process.

Rationalization The tendency to base action on a logical assessment of anticipated effects.

Science A method for establishing reliable and useful knowledge about natural and social phenomena.

Social change Basic alterations, over time, in the behavior patterns, culture, and structure of a society.

Technology The application of knowledge to the solution of practical problems.

CHAPTER PROJECTS

1. **Individual Project** This chapter highlights the theories of social change formulated by Karl Marx, Max Weber, Émile Durkheim, and Herbert Spencer. Choose one of these theorists and write a two-page report describing the major points of his theory.

2. **Cooperative Learning Project** We live in an era of unprecedented technological change. Working in pairs, interview at least three adults over 40 years old to get their perspective on how technology has affected them. Present your findings to the class.

REFERENCES

The number in brackets at the end of each entry is the number of the chapter in which the work is cited.

Abadinsky, Howard. 1981. *Organized Crime*. Boston: Allyn and Bacon. [7]

Abbott, Andrew. 1988. *The System of Professions: An Essay on the Division of Expert Labor*. Chicago: University of Chicago Press. [16]

Abeles, Ronald P. 1976. Relative deprivation, rising expectations, and black militancy. *Journal of Social Issues*, 32:119–137. [21]

Abrahamian, V. 1985. Structural causes of the Iranian revolution. In J. Goldstone, Ed., *Revolutions* (pp. 119–127). San Diego: Harcourt Brace Jovanovich. [14]

Adelman, Kenneth L. 1980. Non-voting: A sign of decay or health? *Wall Street Journal* (October 15):20. [17]

Adler, Freda, Gerhard O. W. Mueller, and William S. Laufer. 1991. *Criminology*. New York: McGraw-Hill. [7]

Adler, Jerry. 1990. Survival. *Newsweek* (December 31): 300–303. [22]

Adler, Peter, and Patricia A. Adler. 1985. From idealism to pragmatic detachment: The academic performance of college athletes. *Sociology of Education*, 58:241–250. [5]

Aganbegyan, Abel. 1988. *The Economic Challenge of Perestroika*. Bloomington: Indiana University Press. [16]

Agnew, Robert. 1990. The origins of delinquent events: An examination of offender accounts. *Journal of Research in Crime and Delinquency* 27 (3, August): 267–294. [7]

Agyei, William K.A., and Joseph Mbamanyo. 1989. Determinants of cumulative fertility in Kenya. *Journal of Biosocial Science*, 21 (3, April): 135–144. [19]

Akers, Ronald L. 1985. *Deviant Behavior: A Social Learning Approach*, 3d ed. Belmont, CA: Wadsworth. [7]

Aldrich, Howard, and Ellen R. Auster. 1986. Even dwarfs started small: Liabilities of age and size and their strategic implications. *Research in Organizational Behavior*, 8:165–198. [16]

Aldrich, Howard E., and Jeffrey Pfeffer. 1976. Environments of organization. *Annual Review of Sociology*, 2:79–105. [8]

Alexander, Herbert E., and Brian Haggerty. 1981. *The Federal Election Campaign Act*. Citizens Research Foundation. Los Angeles: University of Southern California. [17]

Alexander, Jeffrey, Ed. 1988. *Durkheimian Sociology*. New York: Columbia University Press. [1]

Alexander, Jeffrey, and Piotr Sztompka, Eds. 1990. *Rethinking Progress*. Boston: Unwin Hyman. [22]

al-Khalil, Samir. 1990. *Republic of Fear: The Inside Story of Saddam's Iraq*. New York: Pantheon. [1]

Allen, Walter R., and Reynolds Farley. 1986. The shifting social and economic tides of black America, 1950–1980. *American Review of Sociology*, 12:277–306. [10]

Allport, Gordon W., and Leo Postman. 1947. *The Psychology of Rumor*. New York: Holt. [21]

American Bar Association (ABA), Commission of Women in the Professions. 1988. *Report to the House of Delegates*. Chicago: ABA. [11]

Ammerman, Robert T., Martin J. Lubetsky, and Karen F. Drudy. 1991. Maltreatment of handicapped children. In Robert T. Ammerman and Michael Gersen, Eds., *Case Studies in Family Violence* (pp. 209–230). New York: Plenum Press. [12]

Amnesty International. 1989. Amnesty International Brazil briefing. Background paper released in September. Washington, D.C. [19]

Amos, Amanda. 1990. How women are targeted by the tobacco industry. *World Health Forum*, 11(4):416–422. [15]

Anderson, Benedict. 1991. *Imagined Communities: Reflections on the Origin and Spread of Nationalism* (rev. ed.). London and New York: Verso. [17]

Anderson, P. 1974. *Lineages of the Absolutist State*. Chicago: University of Chicago Press. [17]

Anderson, Walter Truett. 1989. Green politics now comes in four distinct shades. *Pacific News Service* (December 15). [21]

Andrews, Lori B. 1984. Exhibit A: Language. *Psychology Today* (February):28–33. [3]

Apple, Michael W. 1979. *Ideology and Curriculum*. London: Routledge & Kegan Paul. [13]

Apple, Michael W. 1982. *Education and Power: Reproduction and Contradiction in Education*. London: Routledge & Kegan Paul. [13]

Applebombe, Peter. 1987. 1,000 new inmates a week jam too few cells. *New York Times* (March 7). [7]

Arensberg, Conrad M., and Arthur H. Niehoff. 1964. *Introducing Social Change*. Chicago: Aldine. [3]

Ariès, Philippe. 1962. *Centuries of Childhood*. R. Baldick (Trans.). New York: Random House. [6]

Armor, David J. 1989. After busing: Education and choice. *The Public Interest*, 95 (Spring):24–37. [13]

Armor, David J. 1991. Response to Carr and Zeigler's 'White Flight and White Return to Norfolk.' *Sociology of Education*, 64 (April):134–139. [13]

Arno, Peter S. 1986. The non-profit sector's response to the AIDS epidemic: Community-based services in San Francisco. *American Journal of Public Health*, 76 (11):1325–1330. [15]

Aronowitz, Stanley. 1992. *The Politics of Identity*. Minneapolis: University of Minnesota Press. [10]

Aronson, Elliot, and J. Merrill Carlsmith. 1968. Experimentation in social psychology. In G. Lindzey and E. Aronson, Eds., *The Handbook of Social Psychology*, Vol. 2, 2d ed., Reading, MA: Addison-Wesley. [2]

Aronson, Elliot, and J. Mills, 1959. The effect of severity on liking for a group. *Journal of Abnormal and Social Psychology*, 59:177–181. [2]

Aslund, Anders. 1989. *Gorbachev's Struggle for Economic Reform*. Ithaca, NY: Cornell University Press. [16]

Astin, Alexander W., William S. Korn, and Ellyne R. Berz. 1989. *The American Freshman: National Norms for Fall 1989*. Los Angeles: Higher Education Research Institute, University of California. [3, 13]

Atkinson, J.M., and P. Drew. 1979. *Order in the Court*. London: Macmillan. [4]

Atkinson, Paul. 1988. Ethnomethodology: A critical review. *American Sociological Review*. 14:441–465. [4]

Baber, Kristine M., and Patricia Monaghan. 1988. College women's career options and motherhood expectations: New options, old dilemmas. *Sex Roles*. 19(3/4):189–203. [11]

Bachrach, Christine, and W. Mosher. 1984. Use of contraception in the United States, 1982. *Advance Data from Vital and Health Statistics*, 102. [12]

Badie, Bertrand, and Pierre Birnbaum. 1983. *The Sociology of the State*. Chicago: University of Chicago Press. [17]

Bailey, Thomas. 1989. Black employment oppportunities. In C. Brecher and R.D. Horton, Eds., *Setting Municipal Priorities, 1990* (pp. 80–111). New York: New York University Press. [9]

Bainbridge, William Sims, and Rodney Stark. 1980. Scientology: To be perfectly clear. *Sociological Analysis*. 41 (Summer, 2):128–136. [14]

Baker, P. 1984. Age differences and age changes in the division of labor by sex: Reanalysis of White and Brinherhoff. *Social Forces*, 62:808–814. [11]

Bales, Robert F., and Fred L. Strodtbeck. 1951. Phases in group problem solving. *Journal of Abnormal and Social Psychology*, 46:485–495. [8]

Bandura, Albert. 1977. *Social Learning Theory*. Englewood Cliffs, N.J.: Prentice-Hall. [7]

Bandura, Albert. 1986. *Social Foundations of Thought and Action: A Social Cognitive Theory*. Englewood Cliffs, NJ: Prentice-Hall. [7]

Bandura, Albert, and Richard H. Walters. 1959. *Adolescent Aggression*. New York: Ronald Press. [7]

Bandyopadhyaya, Jayantanuja. 1988. *The Poverty of Nations: A Global Perspective of Mass Poverty in the Third World*. Ahmedabad, India: Allied Publishers. [18]

Bane, Mary Jo, and David T. Ellwood. 1989. One fifth of the nation's children: Why are they poor? *Science, 245* (September 8):1047–1053. [9]

Barry, Michele. 1991. The influence of the U.S. tobacco industry on the health economy, and environment of developing countries. *The New England Journal of Medicine*, 324 (March 28):917–920. [15]

Bartal, David. 1989. Volvo's back-to-the-future factory. *U.S. News and World Report*, 107 (August 21):42. [8]

Basow, Susan A. 1986. *Gender Stereotypes*. Pacific Grove, CA: Brooks/Cole. [11]

Bates, J.E. 1987. Temperament in infancy. In J.D. Osofsky, Ed., *Handbook of Infant Development*, 2d ed. (pp. 1101–1149). New York: Wiley. [5]

Baumeister, A. 1987. The new morbidity. Poverty and handicapping conditions in America. Paper presented at the Institute for Developmental Disabilities, University of Minnesota, November. [9]

Bearman, Peter. 1992. AIDS and sociology. In Craig Calhoun and George Ritzer, Eds., *Social Problems*. New York: McGraw-Hill. [15]

Becker, Howard S. 1963. *Outsiders: Studies in the Sociology of Deviance*. New York: Free Press. [7]

Becker, Howard, 1984. *Art Worlds*. Berkeley: University of California Press. [3]

Becker, Howard. 1986. *Doing Things Together*. Evanston, IL: Northwestern University Press. [3].

Begley, Sharon. 1990. Don't Drink the Water? [Fluoride] *Newsweek*, 115 (February 5):60–61. [22]

Bell, Daniel. 1980. *The Winding Passage: Essays and Sociological Journeys*, 1960–1980. Cambridge, MA: Abt Books. [3]

Bellah, Robert N. 1970. *Beyond Belief*. New York: Harper & Row. [14]

Bellah, Robert N., and Phillip E. Hammond. 1980. *Varieties of Civil Religion*. New York: Harper & Row. [14]

Bellah, Robert N., Richard Madsen, William M. Sullivan, Ann Swidler, and Steven M. Tipton, 1985. *Habits of the Heart: Individualism and Commitment in American Life*. New York: Harper & Row. [3]

Belsky, J., M. Fish, and R. Isabella. 1991. Continuity and discontinuity in infant negative and positive emotionality: Family antecedents and attachment consequences. *Developmental Psychology*, 27:421–431. [5]

Belyea, Michael J., and Linda M. Labao. 1990. Psychosocial consequences of agricultural transformation: The farm crisis and depression. *Rural Sociology*, 55(1):58–75. [20]

Benet, Sula. 1976. *How to Live to Be a Hundred*. New York: Dial. [6]

Benhabib, Seyla, and Drucilla Cornell, Eds. 1986. *Feminism as Cultural Critique*. Minneapolis: University of Minnesota Press. [11]

Bensman, David, and Roberta Lynch. 1987. *Rusted Dreams*. New York: McGraw-Hill. [16]

Bentham, Jeremy. 1789/1970. *An Introduction to the Principals of Morals and Legislation*. London: Methuen. [1]

Ben Tsvi-Mayer, Shushanna, Rachel Hertz-Lazarowitz, and Marilyn P. Safir. 1989. Teachers' selection of boys and girls as prominent pupils. *Sex Roles*, 21 (3/4):231–239. [11]

Ben-Yehuda, Nachman. 1985. *Deviance and Moral Boundaries: Witchcraft, the Occult, Science Fiction, Deviant Sciences and Scientists*. University of Chicago Press. [7]

Ben-Yehuda, Nachman. 1990. *The Politics and Morality of Deviance*. Albany: State University of New York Press. [7]

Berger, Peter L. 1963. *Invitation to Sociology*. New York: Doubleday. [4]

Berger, Peter L. 1979. *The Heretical Imperative: Contemporary Possibilities of Religious Affirmation*. Garden City, NY: Doubleday/Anchor. [14]

Berger, Peter L. 1987. *50 Propositions about Capitalism*. New York: Basic Books. [17]

Berger, Peter L., and Brigitte Berger. 1979. Becoming a member of society. In P. Rose, Ed., *Socialization and the Life Cycle*. New York: St. Martin's Press. [5]

Berk, A.R. 1974. *Collective Behavior*. New York: Brown. [21]

Berk, Richard A., William P. Bridges, and Anthony Shih. 1981. Does IQ really matter? A study of the use of IQ scores for the tracking of the mentally retarded. *American Sociological Review*, 46:58–71. [13]

Bernardi, B. 1955. The age-system of the Masai. *Annali Lateranensi*, 18:257–318. [6]

Berry, Brian J.L., and John D. Kasarda. 1977. *Contemporary Urban Ecology*. New York: Macmillan. [20]

Beteille, Andre. 1985. Stratification. In Adam Kuper and Jessica Kuper, Eds., *The Social Science Encyclopedia* (pp. 831–833). London: Routledge. [9]

Biggart, Nicole Woolsey. 1989. *Charismatic Capitalism: Direct Selling Organizations in America*. Chicago: University of Chicago Press. [8]

Billy, John, and J. R. Udry, 1985. The influence of male and female best friends on adolescent sexual behavior. *Adolescence*, 20:21–32. [6]

Birch, David L. 1988. *Job Creation in America: How Our Smallest Companies Put the Most People to Work*. New York: Free Press. [16]

Blake, Judith. 1986. *Family Size and Achievement*. Berkeley: University of California Press. [5]

Blankenhorn, David, Steven Bayme, and Jean Bethke Elshtain, Eds. 1990. *Rebuilding the Nest. A New Commitment to the American Family*. Milwaukee: Family Service America. [12]

Blau, Francine, and Carol Jusenius. 1976. Economists' approaches to sex segregation in the labor market: An appraisal. In M. Blaxall and B. Reagan, Eds., *Women in the Workplace: The Implications of Occupational Segregation* (pp. 181–199). Chicago: University of Chicago Press. [11]

Blau, Peter M. 1964. *Exchange and Power in Social Life*. New York: Wiley. [4]

Blau, Peter M. 1977. *Inequality and Heterogeneity: A Primitive Theory of Social Structure*. New York: Free Press. [4]

Blau, Peter M., and Otis Dudley Duncan. 1967. *The American Occupational Structure*. New York: Wiley. [9]

Blau, Peter M., and Marshall W. Meyer. 1987. *Bureaucracy in Modern Society*, 3rd ed. New York: Random House. [8]

Blau, Peter M., and Joseph E. Schwartz. 1983. *Cross-Cutting Social*

Circles: Testing a Macrostructural Theory of Inter-group Relations. New York: Academic Press. [4, 10]

Bleier, Ruth. 1984. *Science and Gender*. New York: Pergamon Press. [11]

Bluestone, Barry, and Bennet Harrison. 1982. *The Deindustrialization of America*. New York: Basic Books. [16]

Blum, Linda, and Vicki Smith. 1988. Women's mobility in the corporation: A critique of the politics of optimism. *Signs*, 13(3)528–545. [11]

Blumer, Herbert. 1939/1951. Collective behavior. In A.M. Lee, Ed., *New Outline of the Principles of Sociology*. New York: Barnes & Noble. [21]

Blumer, Herbert. 1969/1986. *Symbolic Interactionism: Perspective and Method*. Berkeley: University of California Press. [1, 3, 4]

Bogart, Leo. 1972. *Silent Politics: Polls and the Awareness of Public Opinion*. New York: Wiley. [22]

Bohannan, Paul, and Rosemary Erickson. 1978. Stepping in. *Psychology Today*, 11(January):11. [12]

Boles, Janet K. 1991. Form follows function: The evolution of feminist strategies. *Annals of the American Academy of Political and Social Science*, 515(May):38–49. [21]

Bonnyman, Gordon. 1992. Moral malpractice. *Sojourners* (April: 12–17. [15]

Booth, A., and D. Johnson. 1988. Premarital cohabitation and marital success. *Journal of Family Issues*, 9:255–272. [12]

Booth, Alan, and Lynn White. 1980. Thinking about divorce. *Journal of Marriage and the Family*, 42(3):605–616. [12]

Bornschier, Volker, and Thanh-Huyen Ballmer-Cao. 1979. Income inequality: A cross-national study of the relationships between MNC-penetration, dimensions of the power structure and income distribution. *American Sociological Review*, 44(June): 487–506. [16]

Bornschier, Volker, and Jean-Pierre Hoby. 1981. Economic policy and multinational corporations in development: The measurable impacts in cross-national perspective. *Social Problems*, 28:363–377. [16]

Bourdieu, Pierre. 1965. *Travail et Travailleurs en Algeria*. Paris: Editions Mouton. [9]

Bourdieu, Pierre. 1984. *Distinction: A Social Critique of the Judgment of Taste*. R. Nice (Trans.). Cambridge, MA: Harvard University Press. [3, 9]

Bourdieu, Pierre. 1987. *Choses Dites*. Paris: Edition de Minuit. [9]

Bourdieu, Pierre. 1990a. *Photography: A Middle-Brow Art*. Stanford, CA: Stanford University Press. [3]

Bourdieu, Pierre. 1990b. *The Logic of Practice*. Stanford, CA: Stanford University Press. [3]

Bourdieu, Pierre. 1991. Genesis and structure of the religious field. *Comparative Social Research*, 13: 1–43. [14]

Bourdieu, Pierre. In press. *The Economy of Linguistic Exchanges*. Stanford, CA: Stanford University Press. [3]

Bourdieu, Pierre, Jean-Claude Chamboredon, and Jean-Claude Passeron. 1991. *The Craft of Sociology: Epistemological Preliminaries*. New York: de Gruyter. [1]

Bourdieu, Pierre, and A. Darbel. 1990. *The Love of Art*. Stanford, CA: Stanford University Press. [3]

Bourdieu, Pierre, and Jean-Claude Passeron. 1991. *Reproduction in Education, Culture, and Society* (rev. ed.). Newbury Park, CA: Sage. [13]

Bowen, Howard R. 1977. *Investment in Learning: The Individual and Social Values of Higher Education*. San Francisco: Jossey-Bass. [13]

Bowlby, John. 1973. *Separation: Anxiety and Anger*. New York: Basic Books. [5]

Bowles, Samuel, and Herbert Gintis. 1976. *Schooling and Capitalist America*. New York: Basic Books. [13]

Brain, R. 1976. *Friends and Lovers*. New York: Basic Books. [3]

Brandt, Allan M. 1986. AIDS: From social history to social policy. *Law, Medicine and Health Care*, 14(5–6):231–242. [15]

Brenner, Harvey M. 1987. Economic instability, unemployment rates, behavioral risks, and mortality rates in Scotland, 1952–1983. *International Journal of Health Services*, 17(3):475–487. [15]

Bretl, G., and M. Cantor. 1988. Portrayal of men and women in U.S. television advertisements: Recent content analysis and fifteen-year trends. *Sex Roles*, 18(4/5):545–609. [11]

Breuilly, John. 1985. *Nationalism and the State*. Chicago: University of Chicago Press. [17]

Brint, Steven, and Jerome Karabel. 1989. *The Diverted Dream: Community Colleges and the Promise of Educational Opportunity in America, 1900–1985*. New York: Oxford University Press. [13]

Brint, Steven, and Jerome Karabel. 1991. *The Dream Deferred*. New Haven, CT: Yale University Press.

Brodsly, David. 1981. *LA Freeway*. Berkeley: University of California Press. [20]

Brown, Buck. 1989. FTC Puts a damper on Tupperware party. *Wall Street Journal* (November 14):B1. [8]

Brown, Dee. 1971/1984. *Bury My Heart at Wounded Knee*. New York: Doubleday. [10]

Brown, J. Larry. 1987. Hunger in the U.S. *Scientific American*, 256(2):37. [15]

Brown, J. Larry, and Stanley N. Gershoff. 1989. The paradox of hunger and economic prosperity in America. *Journal of Public Health and Policy*, 10(4):425–443. [15]

Brown, Jane D., and Kenneth Campbell. 1986. Race and gender in music videos: The same beat but a different drummer. *Journal of Communication*, 36 (Winter):94–106. [2]

Brown, Lester R. 1990. Assessing the planet's condition. *EPA Journal* (July/August): 2–6. [19]

Brown, Lester R., et al. 1990. *State of the World, 1990*. New York: Norton. [19, 21]

Brown, Ralph B., H. Reed Greersten, and Richard S. Krannich. 1989. Community satisfaction and social integration in a boomtown: A longitudinal analysis. *Rural Sociology* 54(4):568–586. [20]

Brubaker, Rogers. 1984. *The Limits of Rationality*. London: George, Allen and Unwin. [1]

Brubaker, Rogers. 1992. *The Politics of Citizenship*. Cambridge, MA: Harvard University Press. [19]

Bryant, Lynwood. 1969. Rudolf Diesel and his rational engine. *Scientific American*, 221:108–117. [22]

Bryant, Lynwood. 1976. The development of the diesel engine. *Technology and Culture*, 17:432–446. [22]

Buchmann, Marlis. 1989. *The script of life in modern society*. Chicago: University of Chicago Press. [6]

Bumpass, Larry L. 1990. What's happening to the family? Interactions between demographic and institutional change. Population Association of America, 1990 Presidential Address. *Demography*, 27 (4, November):483–498. [12]

Bumpass, Larry L., Teresa Castro Martin and James A. Sweet. In press. Background and early marital factors in marital disruption. *Journal of Family Issues*. [12]

Bumpass, Larry L., and James A. Sweet. 1989a. National estimates of cohabitation: Cohort levels and union stability. *Demography*, 26:615–625. [12]

Bumpass, Larry L., and James A. Sweet. 1989b. Children's experience in single-parent families: Implications of cohabitation and marital transitions. *Family Planning Perspectives*, 21 (6, November/December):256–260. [12]

Bumpass, Larry L., James A. Sweet, and Andrew Cherlin. 1989. *The Role of Cohabitation in Declining Rates of Marriage*. NSFH Working Paper 5. Madison: University of Wisconsin, Center for Demography and Ecology. [12]

Bumpass, Larry L., James A. Sweet, and Teresa Castro Martin. 1990. Changing patterns of remarriage. *Journal of Marriage and the Family*, 52 (August):747–756. [12]

Burke, Thomas P., and Rita S. Jain. 1991. Trends in employer-provided health care benefits. *Monthly Labor Review*, 114(2):24–30. [15]

Burnham, David. 1983. *The Rise of the Computer State*. New York: Random House. [16]

Burns, Alisa, and Ross Homel. 1989. Gender division of tasks by parents and their children. *Psychology of Women Quarterly*, 13:113–125. [11]

Burridge, Kenelm O.L. 1957. A Tangu Game. *Man*, 57:88–89. [3]

Burris, Beverly H. 1991. Employed mothers: The impact of class and marital status on the prioritizing of family and work. *Social Science Quarterly*, 72 (1, March):50–66. [12]

Burris, Val. 1983. Who opposed the ERA? An analysis of the social bases of antifeminism. *Social Science Quarterly*, 64:305–317. [21]

Burrow, James G. 1971. *Organized Medicine in the Progressive Era: The Move Toward Monopoly*. Baltimore: Johns Hopkins University Press. [15]

Burt, Ronald S. 1990. Kinds of relations in American discussion networks. In C. Calhoun, M.W. Meyer, and W.R. Scott, Eds., *Structures of Power and Constraint: Papers in Honor of Peter M. Blau* (pp. 411–451). New York: Cambridge University Press. [4]

Butler, Robert N. 1975. *Why Survive: Being Old in America*. New York: Harper & Row. [6]

Butler, Robert N. 1989. Dispelling ageism. *Annals*, 503 (May): 138–147. [6]

Button, James, and Walter Rosenbaum. 1990. Gray power, gray peril or gray myth? *Social Science Quarterly*, 71 (March):25–38. [6]

Cairns, Robert B., Beverley D. Cairns, and Holly J. Neckerman. 1989. Early school dropout: Configurations and determinants. *Child Development*, 60:1437–1452. [13]

Calhoun, Craig. 1980. The authority of ancestors. *Man*, 5(2):304–319. [14, 20]

Calhoun, Craig. 1981. The political economy of work. In S.G. McNall, Ed., *Political Economy: Critique of American Society*. Glenview, IL: Scott, Foresman. [16]

Calhoun, Craig. 1988. Populist politics, communications media, and large scale social integration. *Sociological Theory*, 6(2):219–241. [17]

Calhoun, Craig. 1989. Tiananmen, television and the public sphere: Internationalization of culture and the beijing spring of 1989. *Public Culture*, 12(1):54–72. [3]

Calhoun, Craig. 1991. Imagined communities and indirect relationships: Large-scale social integration and the transformation of everyday Life. In P. Bourdieu and J.S. Coleman, Eds., *Social Theory for a Changing Society* (pp. 95–120). Boulder, CO: Westview Press. [17]

Calhoun, Craig, and Henryk Hiller. 1988. Coping with insidious injuries: The case of Johns-Mansville Corporation and asbestos exposure. *Social Problems*, 35(2):162–181. [7, 16]

Callahan, Daniel. 1987. *Setting Limits*. New York: Simon and Schuster. [6]

Callahan, Parnell. 1979. *How to Serve on a Jury*, 2d ed. Dobbs Ferry, NY: Oceana. [7]

Carnegie Task Force on Teaching as a Profession. 1986. *A Nation Prepared: Teachers for the 21st Century*. New York: Carnegie Forum in Education and the Economy. [13]

Carnoy, Martin, and Henry M. Levin. 1985. *Schooling and Work in the Democratic State*. Stanford, CA: Stanford University Press. [13]

Carothers, Andre. 1990. Defenders of the forest. *Greenpeace*, 15(4, July–August):8–12. [19]

Carr, Leslie G., and Donald J. Zeigler. 1990. White flight and white return to Norfolk: A test of predictions. *Sociology of Education*, 63:272–282. [13]

Carson, Rachel. 1962. *Silent Spring*. Boston: Houghton Mifflin. [21]

Casale, Anthony M., and Philip Lerman. 1986. *USA Today: Tracking Tomorrow's Trends*. Kansas City, MO: Andrews, McMeel & Parker. [13]

Castells, Manuel. 1983. *The City and the Grassroots*. Berkeley: University of California Press. [18]

Castells, Manuel. 1989. *The Informational City: Information Technology, Economic Restructuring, and the Urban-Regional Process*. New York: Basil Blackwell. [20]

Cater, Douglass, and Stephen Strickland. 1975. *TV Violence and the Child: The Evolution and Fate of the Surgeon General's Report*. New York: Russell Sage Foundation. [5]

Cattan, Peter. 1988. The growing presence of Hispanics in the U.S. work force. *Monthly Labor Review* (August):9–14. [10]

Chafetz, Janet. 1970. *Masculine, Feminine, or Human?* 2d ed. Itasca, IL: Peacock. [11]

Chafetz, Janet. 1984. *Sex and Advantage*. Totowa, NJ: Rowman & Allenheld. [11]

Chambers, D.S. 1970. *The Imperial Age of Venice*. New York: Harcourt Brace Jovanovich. [20]

Chambliss, William J. 1973. The Saints and Roughnecks. *Society*, 11 (December):24–31. [7]

Chambliss, William J., and Robert B. Seidman. 1972. *Law, Order, and Power*. Reading, MA: Addison-Wesley.

Chandler, Alfred D., Jr. 1962. *Strategy and Structure: Chapters in the History of the Industrial Enterprise*. Cambridge, MA: MIT Press. [8]

Chandler, Alfred. 1976. *The Visible Hand*. Cambridge, MA: Harvard University Press. [16]

Chase-Dunn, Christopher. 1975. The effects of international economic dependence on development and inequality: A cross-national study. *American Sociological Review*, 40 (December):720–738. [16]

Chavez, Lydia. 1987. Women's movement, its ideals accepted, faces subtler issues. *New York Times* (July 17). [21]

Chen, Pi-Chao. 1984. Birth planning and fertility transition. *Annuals of the American Academy of Political and Social Science*, 476 (November):128. [19]

Cherlin, Andrew. 1990. Recent Changes in American Fertility, Marriage, and Divorce. *Annals of the American Academy of Political and Social Science*, 510 (July):145–154. [12]

Cherlin, Andrew, and Frank Furstenberg. 1986. *The new grandparent: A place in the family, a life apart*. New York: Basic Books. [12]

Childe, V. Gordon. 1952. *Man Makes Himself*. New York: New American Library. [20]

Children's Defense Fund. 1987. *The State of the World's Children*. New York: Oxford University Press. [19]

Children's Defense Fund. 1989. *S.O.S. America! A Children's Defense Fund Budget*. Washington, D.C.: Children's Defense Fund. [12]

Children's Defense Fund. 1991. *The Adolescent and Young Adult Fact Book*. Washington, D.C.: Children's Defense Fund. [12]

Chittister, Joan D., and Martin E. Marty. 1983. *Faith & Ferment*. Minneapolis: Augsburg. [14]

Chodorow, Nancy. 1989. *Feminism and Psychoanalytic Theory*. New Haven, CT: Yale University Press.

Choldin, Harvey M. 1978. Urban density and pathology. *Annual Review of Sociology*, 4:91–113. [20]

Chronicle of Higher Education. 1991. This year's college freshmen: Attitudes and characteristics. *Chronicle of Higher Education*, 37(20): A30–A31. [13]

Chubb, John E., and Terry M. Moe. 1990. *Politics, Markets, and America's Schools*. Washington, DC: Brookings Institute. [13]

Chudacoff, Howard P. 1989. *How Old Are You?* Princeton, NJ: Princeton University Press. [6]

Clark, Reginald M. 1983. *Family Life and School Achievement: Why*

Poor Black Children Succeed or Fail. Chicago: University of Chicago Press. [13]

Clark, Reginald M. 1990. Why disadvantaged students succeed. *Public Welfare*, 48(2):17–23. [13]

Clausen, John A. 1986. *The Life Course: A Sociological Perspective*. Englewood Cliffs, NJ: Prentice-Hall. [6]

Clifford, Frank. 1989a. Driving passion for cars fuels California style. *Los Angeles Times* (October 1). [20]

Clifford, Frank. 1989b. We curse the traffic, but won't give up our cars. *Los Angeles Times* (October 4). [20]

Clinard, Marshall B., and Peter C. Yeager. 1980. *Corporate Crime*. New York: Free Press. [7]

Cohen, Albert K. 1966. *Deviance and Control*. Englewood Cliffs, NJ: Prentice Hall. [7]

Cohen, Albert K. 1965. The sociology of the deviant act: Anomie theory and beyond. *American Sociological Review*, 30 (February):5–14. [7]

Cole, Robert E. 1989. *Strategies for Learning: Small-Group Activities in American, Japanese and Swedish Industry*. Berkeley: University of California Press. [8]

Cole, Stephen. 1986. Sex discrimination and admission to medical school, 1929–1984. *American Journal of Sociology*, 92 (November):549–567. [4]

Coleman, James S. 1961. *The Adolescent Society*. New York: Free Press. [6]

Coleman, James S. 1966. *Equality of Educational Opportunity*. Washington, DC: U.S. Government Printing Office. [13]

Coleman, James S. 1982. *The Asymmetric Society*. New York: Syracuse University Press. [16]

Coleman, James S. 1987a. Families and schools. *Educational Researcher*, 16(6):32–38. [13]

Coleman, James S. 1987b. *Public and Private High School: The Impact of Communities*. New York: Basic Books. [13]

Coleman, James S. 1990a. *Equality and Achievement in Education*. Boulder, CO: Westview Press. [13]

Coleman, James S. 1990b. *Foundations of Social Theory*. Cambridge, MA: Harvard University Press. [1, 16]

Coleman, James S., Ed. 1992. *Rational Choice Theory: Advocacy and Critique*. Newbury Park, CA: Sage. [1, 11, 16]

Coleman, James S. and T. Hoffer, 1987. *Public and Private High Schools: The Impact of Communities*. New York: Basic Books. [13]

Coleman, John A. 1983. The Christian as citizen. *Commonweal*, 110:457–462. [14]

Coleman, Marilyn, and Lawrence H. Ganong. 1990. Remarriage and stepfamily research in the 1980s: Increased interest in an old family form. *Journal of Marriage and the Family*, 52 (November):925–940. [12]

Coleman, R.P., and L. Rainwater. 1978. *Social Standing in America: New Dimensions of Class*. New York: Basic Books. [13]

Coll, C.T. Garcia. 1990. Developmental outcome of minority infants: A process-oriented look into our beginnings. *Child Development*, 61:270–289. [9]

Collins, Glenn. 1987. As the nation grays, a mighty advocate flexes its muscles. *New York Times* (April 2):B1, C7. [6]

Collins, Randall. 1971. Functional and conflict theories of educational stratification. *American Sociological Review*, 36 (December):1002–1018. [13]

Collins, Randall. 1975. *Conflict Sociology*. New York: Academic Press. [9]

Collins, Randall. 1979. *The Credential Society*. New York: Academic Press. [13]

Connolly, William. 1984. The dilemma of legitimacy. In W. Connolly and S. Lukes, Eds., *Legitimacy and the State* (pp. 122–149). New York: New York University Press. [17]

Conrad, Peter, and Joseph Schneider. 1980. *Deviance and Medicalization: From Badness to Sickness*. St. Louis: Mosby. [15]

Consumer Reports. 1990a. The crisis in health insurance: Health insurance for all? *Consumer Reports*, 55(9):608–617. [15]

Consumer Reports. 1990b. The crisis in health insurance: Who loses it? What happens? *Consumer Reports*, 55(8):533–549. [15]

Cook, K. 1990. Linking actors and structures: An exchange network analysis. In C. Calhoun, M. Meyer, and W. R. Scott, Eds., *Structures of Power and Constraint: Essays in Honor of Peter M. Blau*. New York: Cambridge University Press. [1]

Cook, Karen S., Richard M. Emerson, Mary R. Gillmore, and Toshio Yamagishi. 1983. *American Journal of Sociology*, 83(2):275–305. [4]

Cooley, Charles H. 1909/1929. *Social Organization*. New York: Scribners. [8]

Cooley, Charles H. 1956. *Social Organization: A Study of the Larger Mind*. Peoria, IL: Free Press. [5]

Cooley, Charles H. 1964. *Human Nature and the Social Order*. New York: Schocken. [5]

Cornell, Stephen. 1984. Crisis and response in Indian-white relations: 1960–1984. *Social Problems*, 32 (1):44–59. [10, 13]

Corsaro, William A. 1985. *Friendship and Peer Culture in the Early Years*. Norwood, NJ: Ablex. [2, 6]

Corsaro, William, and Donna Eder. 1990. Children's peer culture. *Annual Review of Sociology*, 16:197–220. [5, 6]

Coser, Lewis A. 1974. *Greedy Institutions: Patterns of Undivided Commitment*. New York: Free Press. [8]

Coser, Rose Laub. 1983. Where have all the women gone? In L. Richardson and V. Taylor, Eds., *Feminist Frontiers*. Reading, MA: Addison-Wesley. [11]

Cottrell, W.F. 1951. Death by dieselization: A case study in the reaction to technological change. *American Sociological Review*, 16:358–365. [22]

Courtney, Alice E., and Thomas W. Whipple. 1983. *Sex Stereotyping in Advertising*. Lexington, MA: Lexington Books. [11]

Cowen, R. 1990. Panel finds fluoride–cancer link equivocal. *Science News*, 137 (April 28):278. [22]

Creighton-Zollar, Ann. 1990. Infant mortality by socioeconomic status and race in Richmond, Virginia, 1979–1981. *Sociological Spectrum*, 10:133–142. [15]

Crespi, Irving. 1989. *Public Opinion, Polls and Democracy*. Boulder, CO: Westview. [22]

Crosby, Alfred W. 1976. *The Columbian Exchange: Biological and Cultural Consequences of 1492*. Westport, CT: Greenwood Press. [22]

Crosby, Alfred W. 1989. Reassessing 1492. *American Quarterly*, 41 (December):661–669. [22]

Crystal, David. 1989. Asian Americans and the myth of the model minority. *Journal of Contemporary Social Work*, 70 (7): 405–413. [10]

Crystal, Stephen, and Dennis Shea. 1990. Cumulative advantage, cumulative disadvantage, and inequality among elderly people. *Gerontologist*, 30:437–443. [6]

Current Population Reports. 1986. Washington, DC: U.S. Government Printing Office. [10]

Current Population Reports. 1990 (March). Washington, DC: U.S. Government Printing Office. [12]

Current Population Reports. 1990 (July). Series P-60, No. 166. Washington, DC: U.S. Government Printing Office. [12]

Current Population Reports. 1990 (December). Washington, DC: U.S. Government Printing Office. [12]

Currie, Elliott. 1985. *Confronting Crime: An American Challenge*. New York: Pantheon. [7]

Curtiss, Susan. 1977. *Genie: A Psycholinguistic Study of a Modern-Day "Wild-Child."* New York: Academic Press. [5]

Dahl, Robert. 1961. *Who Governs?* New Haven, CT: Yale University Press. [17]

Damon, W. 1977. *The Social World of the Child*. San Francisco: Jossey-Bass. [5]

Dan-Cohen, M. 1986. *Rights, Persons and Organizations*. Berkeley: University of California Press. [16]

Davidson, Osha Gray. 1990. *Broken Heartland: The Rise of America's Rural Ghetto*. New York: Free Press. [9]

Davies, James C. 1962. Toward a theory of revolution. *American Sociological Review*, 27:5–19. [21]

Davies, James. 1974. The J-curve and power struggle theories of collective violence. *American Sociological Review*, 39:607–619. [21]

Davies, Mark, and Denise B. Kandel. 1981. Parental and peer influence on adolescents' educational plans: Some further evidence. *American Journal of Sociology*, 87:363–387. [5]

Davis, John Hagy. 1973. Venice. *Newsweek*. [20]

Davis, Karen, and Diane Rowland. 1983. Uninsured and underserved: Inequities in health care in the United States. *Milbank Memorial Fund Quarterly/Health and Society*, 61 (2):149–176. [15]

Davis, Kingsley. 1949. *Human Society*. New York: Macmillan. [5]

Davis, Kingsley. 1955. The origin and growth of urbanization in the world. *American Journal of Sociology* 60:429–437. [20]

Davis, Kingsley, and Wilbert E. Moore. 1945. Some principles of stratification. *American Sociological Review*, 10(April):242–249. [9]

Davis, Leila. 1989. Wider uses for bar codes. *Nation's Business*, 77(March):34–36. [22]

Davis, Nancy J., and Robert J. Robinson. 1991. Men's and Women's Consciousness of Gender Inequality: Austria, West Germany, Great Britain, and the United States. *American Sociological Review*, 56 (February):72–84. [11]

Davis, Ronald M. 1987. Current trends in cigarette advertising and marketing. *New England Journal of Medicine*, 316(12):725–747. [15]

Day, Christine L. 1990. *What Older Americans Think*. Princeton, NJ: Princeton University Press. [6]

de Jassay, Anthony. 1985. *The State*. Oxford, England: Basil Blackwell. [17]

de Rougemont, Denis. 1940/1983. *Love in the Western World*. Princeton, NJ: Princeton University Press. [12]

de Tocqueville, Alexis. 1856. *The Old Regime and the French Revolution*. J. Bonner (Trans.). New York: Harper & Row. [21]

Denton, Nancy A., and Douglas S. Massey. 1988. Residential segregation of blacks, Hispanics, and Asians by socioeconomic status and generation. *Social Science Quarterly*, 69 (4, December):797–817. [10]

DeParle, Jason. 1991. Covering the war. *New York Times* (May 5):A1, A20; (May 6):A9. [13]

Department of Health and Human Services (HHS). 1990. *Child Abuse and Neglect: Critical First Steps in Response to a National Emergency* (August). U.S. Advisory Board on Child Abuse and Neglect, Washington, DC. [12]

Deutchman, Iva E., and Sandra Prince-Embury. 1981. Political ideology of pro- and anti-ERA women. *Women and Politics*, 1:39–55. [21]

Digest of Education Statistics. 1990. National Center for Education Statistics, U.S. Department of Education. [13]

Dill, Vicky S. 1990. Support for the 'Unsupportable.' *Phi Delta Kappan*, 72(3):198–199. [13]

DiMaggio, Paul, and Walter Powell. 1992. *The New Institutionalism*. Chicago: University of Chicago Press. [16]

Dizard, Jan E., and Howard Gadlin. 1990. *The Minimal Family*. Amherst: University of Massachusetts Press. [12]

Dodge, Susan. 1990a. More college students choose academic majors that meet social and environmental concerns. *Chronicle of Higher Education* (April 25):B2. [13]

Dodge, Susan. 1990b. The typical student owns a car, watches TV 6 hours a week, and reads few books. *Chronicle of Higher Education*, 36(5):A37. [13]

Domhoff, G. William. 1978. *The Powers That Be*. New York: Random House. [17]

Domhoff, G. William. 1983. *Who Rules America Now?* Englewood Cliffs, NJ: Prentice Hall. [17]

Domhoff, G. William. 1993. *Who Rules America?* In C. Calhoun and G. Ritzer, Eds., *Introduction to Social Problems*. New York: McGraw-Hill/Primis. [9, 17]

Donaldson, Peter. 1986. *Worlds Apart: The Economic Gulf Between Nations*. London: Penguin. [18, 22]

Donaldson, Peter J. 1990. *Nature Against Us: The United States and the World Population Crisis, 1965–80*. Chapel Hill: University of North Carolina Press. [22]

Dornbusch, Sanford M. 1989. The sociology of adolescence. *Annual Review of Sociology*, 15:233–259. [5]

Dornbusch, Sanford M. 1990. The sociology of adolescence. *Annual Review of Sociology*, 15:233–259. [6]

Dorris, Michael A. 1981. The grass still grows, the rivers still flow: Contemporary Native Americans. *Daedalus*, 110. [10]

Dorris, Michael A. 1989. *The Broken Cord*. New York: Harper & Row. [10]

Douglas, Jack D. 1967. *The Social Meaning of Suicide*. Princeton, NJ: Princeton University Press. [2]

Douglas, M. 1970. *Purity and Danger*. New York: Penguin. [14]

Dowd, Maureen. 1991. Bush's holy war: The crusader's cloak can grow heavy on the shoulders. *New York Times* (February 3):E1, E4. [1]

Dowse, Robert E., and John A. Hughes. 1972. *Political Science*. New York: Wiley. [17]

Dowty, Allen. 1987. *Closed Borders: The Contemporary Assault on Freedom of Movement*. New Haven, CT: Yale University Press. [10]

Doyle, Denis P., Bruce S. Cooper, and Roberta Trachtman. 1991. Education: Ideas and strategies for the 1990s. *The American Enterprise*, 2(2):25–33. [13]

Doyle, James A., and Michele A. Paludi. 1986. *Sex and Gender: The Human Experience*. 2d ed. Dubuque, IA: Brown and Benchmark. [11]

Drucker, Peter F. 1983. Squeezing the firm's midriff bulge. *Wall Street Journal* (March 25):14. [8]

Dumont, Louis. 1977. *From Mandeville to Marx: The Genesis and Triumph of Economic Ideology*. Chicago: University of Chicago Press. [16]

Dumont, René. 1990. The coming food crisis. *World Press Review, Le Monde* (January):35–37. [19]

Duncan, A. 1987. The Values, Aspirations, and Opportunities of the Urban Underclass. B.A. honors thesis, Harvard University, Cambridge, MA. [9]

Duncan, Cynthia. 1991. Stagnation in the countryside. *Dissent* (Spring):279–281. [20]

Duncan, Greg J. 1982. "Who gets ahead? And who gets left behind?" *American Demographics*, 4 (July–August):38–41. [11]

Duncan, Greg J. 1984. *Years of Poverty, Years of Plenty*. Ann Arbor: Institute for Social Research, University of Michigan. [9]

Duncan, Greg, and Ken Moore. 1989. The Rising Affluence of the Elderly. *Annual Review of Sociology*, 15:261–289. [6]

Duncan, Marsha. 1990. Contrary to public perceptions, the students of the 90's are committed social activists. *Chronicle of Higher Education* (April 25):B2. [13]

Dupuy, R. Ernest, and Trevor N. Dupuy. 1986. *The Encyclopedia of Military History from 3500 B.C. to the Present*, 2d rev. ed. New York: Harper & Row. [8]

Durkheim, Émile. 1893/1985. *The Division of Labor in Society*. New York: Free Press. [1, 9]

Durkheim, Émile. 1895/1982. *Rules of Sociological Method*. New York: Free Press. [1, 7]

Durkheim, Émile. 1897/1951. *Suicide: A Study of Sociology*. J.A. Spaulding and G. Simpson (Trans.). New York: Free Press. [2]

Durkheim, Émile. 1912/1965. *The Elementary Forms of Religious Life*. J.W. Swain (Trans.). New York: Free Press. [1, 14]
Durning, Alan. 1990. How much is "enough"? *WorldWatch*, 3 (6, November/December):12–19. [19]
Dweck, C. S., W. Davidson, S. Nelson, and B. Enna. 1978. Sex Differences in Learned Helplessness. *Developmental Psychology*, 14:268–276. [11]
Dworkin, Ronald. 1977. *Taking Rights Seriously*. Cambridge, MA: Harvard University Press. [17]
Dworkin, Ronald. 1986. *Law's Empire*. Cambridge, MA: Harvard University Press. [17]
Dyer, Gwynn. 1985. *War*. New York: Crown Books. [17]

Easterbrooks, M. Ann, and Wendy A. Goldberg. 1984. Toddler development in the family: Impact of father involvement and parenting characteristics. *Child Development*, 55:740–752. [5]
Ebaugh, Helen Rose Fuchs. 1987. *Becoming an Ex: The Process of Role Exit*. Chicago: University of Chicago Press. [4]
Economic Report of the President. 1991. Washington, DC: U.S. Government Printing Office. [16]
Edelman, Marian Wright. 1987. *Families in Peril*. Cambridge, MA: Harvard University Press. [12]
Edmondson, Brad. 1988. Hide and seek. *Atlantic*, 262 (6):18–26. [19]
Education at a Glance. 1993. Paris: OECD Publications. [13]
Educational Testing Service. 1990. *1990 Profile of SAT and Achievement Test Takers*. New York: College Entrance Examination Board. [13]
Edwards, Richard. 1979. *Contested Terrain: The Transformation of the Workplace in the Twentieth Century*. New York: Basic Books. [16]
Ehrenreich, Barbara, and Diedre English. 1989. Blowing the whistle on the "mommy track." *Ms.* (July/August):56, 58. [11]
Ehrlich, Anne H. 1991. People and food. *Population and Environment: A Journal of Interdisciplinary Studies*, 12 (3, Spring):221–229. [19]
Ehrlich, Paul R., and Ehrlich, Anne H. 1990. *The Population Explosion*. New York: Simon and Schuster. [19]
Eisenstadt, S.N. 1973. *Tradition, Change, and Modernity*. New York: Wiley. [18]
Eisenstadt, S.N. 1978. *Revolution and the Transformation of Societies*. New York: Free Press. [14]
Eisenstein, Elizabeth. 1979. *The Printing Press as an Agent of Change* (2 vols.). New York: Cambridge University Press. [3]
Eisslin, M. 1982. *The Age of Television*. New York: Freeman Press. [3]
Ekstrom, Ruth B., Margaret E. Goertz, Judith M. Pollack, and Donald A. Rock. 1986. Who drops out of high school and why? Findings from a national study. *Teachers College Record*, 87 (3):356–373. [13]
Elam, Stanley M. 1990. The 22nd annual Gallup poll of the public's attitudes toward the public schools. *Phi Delta Kappan*, 72(1):41–55. [13]
Elder, Glen H., Jr. 1974. *Children of the Great Depression*. Chicago: University of Chicago Press. [6]
Elder, Glen H., Jr. 1978. Approaches to social change and the family. *American Journal of Sociology*, 84 (suppl.):170–199. [6]
Elder, Glen H., Jr. 1987. Families and lives: Some developments in life-course studies. *Journal of Family History*, 12 (1–2):170–199. [6]
Elkin, Frederick, and Gerald Handel. 1984. *The Child and Society: The Process of Socialization*, 4th ed. New York: Random House. [5]
Ellis, Desmond. 1989. Male abuse of a married or cohabiting female partner: The application of sociological theory to research findings. *Violence and Victims*, 4 (4):235–255. [12]
Ellwood, David T. 1988. *Poor Support: Poverty in the American Family*. New York: Basic Books. [17]
Ember, Carol R., and Melvin Ember. 1988. *Anthropology* (5th ed.). Englewood Cliffs, NJ: Prentice-Hall. [3]
Emerson, Richard M. 1962. Power-dependence relations. *American Sociological Review*, 27:31–40. [4]
Emerson, Richard M. 1976. Social exchange theory. *Annual Reviews*, pp. 335–362. [4]
Epstein, Cynthia Fuchs. 1988. *Deceptive Distinctions: Sex, Gender, and the Social Order*. New Haven, CT: Yale University Press, and New York: Russell Sage Foundation. [11]
Epstein, Gerald. (1990–1991). Mortgaging America. *World Policy Journal*, VIII (1):27–59. [16]
Epstein, J.L. 1986. Parents' Reactions to Teacher Practices of Parent Involvement. *Elementary School Journal*, 86 (3):277–294. [13]
Epstein, J.L. 1987. Parent involvement: What researchers say to administrators. *Education and Urban Society*, 19 (2):119–136. [13]
Erikson, Erik. 1950. *Childhood and Society*. New York: Norton. [6]
Erikson, Erik. 1982. *The Life Cycle Completed: A Review*. New York: Norton. [6]
Ermann, M. David, and Richard J. Lundman. 1982. *Corporate Deviance*. New York: Holt, Rinehart and Winston. [7]
Etzioni, Amitai. 1982. Making interest groups work for the public. *Public Opinion*, 5 (August–September):52–55. [17]
Eurich, N. 1985. *The Corporate Classroom*. New York: Carnegie Foundation for the Advancement of Teaching. [13]
Euromonitor. 1992. *International Marketing Data and Statistics, 1992*. London: Euromonitor. [19]
Evans, Peter. 1979. *Dependent Development: The Alliance of Multinational, State, and Local Capital in Brazil*. Princeton, NJ: Princeton University Press. [18]
Evans, Sara M., and Harry C. Boyte. 1992. *Free Spaces: The Sources of Democratic Change in America*. Chicago: University of Chicago Press. [21]
Evans, Sara M., and Barbara J. Nelson. 1989. Comparable worth: The paradox of technocratic reform. *Feminist Studies*, 15 (1):171–190. [11]
Evans, Terence, and James Peacock, Eds. 1990. *Case Studies in Transcendence: Comparative Social Research*, Supplement No. 1. Greenwich, CT: JAI Press. [14]
Evans, Terry. 1988. *A Gender Agenda: A Sociological Study of Teachers, Parents and Pupils in Their Primary Schools*. Sydney, Australia: Allen & Unwin. [11]
Evans-Pritchard, E.E. 1965. *Theories of Primitive Religion*. London: Oxford University Press. [14]

Fagan, Brian. 1990. A clash of cultures. *Archaeology*, 43 (January–February):32–37. [22]
Fallows, James. 1989. What's wrong with testing? *Washington Monthly* (May):12–24. [13]
Farley, Reynolds. 1984. *Blacks and Whites: Narrowing the Gap?* Cambridge, MA: Harvard University Press. [10]
Farley, Reynolds, and Walter R. Allen. 1987. *The Color Line and the Quality of Life in America*. New York: Russell Sage. [10]
Feagin, Joe R. 1985. The global context of metropolitan growth: Houston and the oil industry. *American Journal of Sociology*, 90 (6):1204–1227. [20]
Feagin, Joe R. 1988. *The Free Enterprise City: Houston in Political-Economic Perspective*. New Brunswick, NJ: Rutgers University Press. [20]
Feagin, Joe R., and Michael Peter Smith. 1987. Cities and the new

international division of labor: An overview. In Michael Peter Smith and Joe R. Feagin, Eds., *The Capitalist City: Global Restructuring and Community Politics*. London: Basil Blackwell. [20]

Featherman, David L., and Robert Hauser. 1978. *Opportunity and Change*. New York: Academic Press. [9]

Federal Bureau of Investigation. 1991. *Uniform Crime Reports for the United States*. Washington, DC: FBI. [7]

Federal Election Commission. 1992. Spending jumped to $504 million by '92 congressional candidates. Press release (December 30). [17]

Ferguson, Thomas, and Joel Rogers. 1986. *Right Turn: The Decline of the Democrats and the Future of American Politics*. New York: Hill and Wang. [16]

Fine, Gary Alan. 1987. *With the Boys: Little League Baseball and Preadolescent Culture*. Chicago: University of Chicago Press. [3,5]

Fine, Gary Alan, and Sherryl Kleinman. 1979. Rethinking subculture: An interactionist analysis. *American Journal of Sociology*, 85(1):1–20. [3]

Finn, Chester E., Jr. 1989a. Dropouts and grownups. *Public Interest*, 131–136. [13]

Finn, Chester E., Jr. May 1989b. A nation still at risk. *Commentary*, 87(5):17–23. [13]

Fiore, Michael C., Thomas E. Novotny, John P. Pierce, Evridiki J. Hatziandreu, Kantelal M. Patel, and Ronald M. Davis. 1989. Trends in cigarette smoking in the United States: The changing influence of gender and race. *Journal of the American Medical Association*, 261(1):49–55. [15]

Fischer, Claude S. 1982. *To Dwell Among Friends: Personal Networks in Town and City*. Chicago: University of Chicago Press. [4,20]

Fischer, Michael M.J., and Mehdi Abedi. 1990. *Debating Muslims: Cultural Dialogues in Postmodernity and Tradition*. Madison: University of Wisconsin Press. [14]

Fisher, Bernice. 1991. Affirming Social Value: Women Without Children. In David R. Maines, Ed., *Social Organization and Social Process: Essays in Honor of Anselm Strauss* (pp. 87–104). New York: De Gruyter. [11]

Fishman, Paula. 1978. Interaction: The Work Women Do. *Social Problems*, 28:387–406 [4]

Fiske, Edward B. 1986a. Literacy in America: Beyond the basics. *New York Times* (September 26):A15. [13]

Fiske, Edward B. 1986b. Teacher quality becomes top school issue. *New York Times* (October 17):B1, B2. [13]

Fiske, Edward B. 1987. Integration lags at public schools. *New York Times* (July 26):1. [13]

Fitzpatrick, Joseph P. 1971. *Puerto Rican Americans: The Meaning of Migration to the Mainland*. Englewood Cliffs, NJ: Prentice Hall. [3]

Flavin, Christopher. 1991. Conquering U.S. oil dependence. *World Watch*, 4 (1, January–February):28–36. [19]

Flavin, Christopher, and Nicholas Lenssen. 1991. Designing a sustainable energy system. In *State of the World, 1991* (pp. 21–38). New York: Norton. [19]

Fligstein, Neil. 1990. *The Transformation of Corporate Control*. Cambridge, MA: Harvard University Press. [16]

Flora, Peter, and Arnold J. Heidenheimer, Eds. 1981. *The Development of Welfare States in Europe and America*. New Brunswick, NJ: Transaction Books. [17]

Foner, Anne. 1986. *Aging and Old Age: New Perspectives*. Englewood Cliffs, NJ: Prentice Hall. [6]

Forer, Lucille K. 1976. *The Birth Order Factor—How Your Personality Is Influenced by Your Place in the Family*. New York: David McKay. [5]

Formisano, Ronald P. 1991. *Boston Against Busing: Race, Class, and Ethnicity in the 1960s and 1970s*. Chapel Hill: University of North Carolina Press. [13]

Fornos, Werner. 1991. Population politics. *Technology Review*, 94(February–March):42–52. [22]

Forste, Renata, and T.B. Heaton. 1988. Initiation of sexual activity among female adolescents. *Youth and Society*, 19:250–268. [6]

Fortes, Meyer. 1969. *Kinship and the Social Order*. Chicago: Aldine. [14]

Fox, Renée C. 1977. The medicalization and demedicalization of American society. *Daedalus* (Winter). [15]

Fox, Robin. 1970. The cultural animal. *Encounters*, 35 (July):31–42. [4]

Frank, André Gunder. 1967. *Capitalism and Underdevelopment in Latin America*. New York: Monthly Review Press. [18]

Frank, André Gunder. 1980. *Crisis in the Third World*. New York: Holmes and Meier. [18]

Frank, Ellen J. 1988. Business students' perceptions of women in management. *Sex Roles*, 19 (1/2):107–118. [11]

Franko, L.G. 1989. Global corporate competition: Who's winning, who's losing, and the R&D factor as one reason why. *Strategic Management Journal*:449–474. [16]

Freeman, Jo. 1973. The origins of the women's liberation movement. *American Journal of Sociology*, 78:792–811. [21]

Freeman, Jo. 1979. Resource mobilization and strategy. In M.N. Zald and J.D. McCarthy, Eds., *The Dynamics of Social Movements*. Cambridge, MA: Winthrop. [21]

Freeman, John H., and Michael T. Hannan. 1983. Niche width and the dynamics of organizational populations. *American Journal of Sociology*, 88 (6). [8]

Freeman, John H., Glenn R. Carroll, and Michael T. Hannan. 1983. The liability of newness: Age dependence in organizational death rates. *American Sociological Review*, 48:692–710. [8]

Freidson, Eliot. 1970. *Professional Dominance: The Social Structure of Medical Care*. New York: Atherton Press. [15]

Freidson, Eliot. 1985. *The Power of Profession*. Chicago: University of Chicago Press. [16]

French, Hilary F. 1990. Clearing the air in WorldWatch Institute, *State of the World, 1990* (pp. 98–118). New York: Norton. [19]

Freud, Sigmund. 1920/1953. Beyond the pleasure principle. In J. Strachey (Ed. and Trans.), *The Standard Edition of the Complete Psychological Works of Sigmund Freud* (Vol. 18). London: Hogarth Press. [5]

Freud, Sigmund. 1923/1947. *The Ego and the Id*. London: Hogarth Press. [5]

Frey, William H. 1990. Metropolitan America: Beyond the transition. *Population Bulletin*, 45(2):3–49. [20]

Friedman, Samuel R., Don C. Des Jarlais, Jo L. Sotheran, Jonathan Garber, Henry Cohen, and Donald Smith. 1987. AIDS and self-organization among intravenous drug users. *The International Journal of the Addictions*, 22 (3):201–219. [15]

Fries, James F. 1983. The compression of morbidity. *Midbank Memorial Fund Quarterly/Health and Society*, 61 (3):397–419. [15]

Frisbie, W. Parker, and John D. Kasarda. 1988. In Neil J. Smelser, Ed., *Handbook of Sociology*. Newbury Park, CA: Sage. [20]

Fruch, Terry, and Paul E. McGhee. 1975. Traditional sex role development and amount of time spent watching television. *Developmental Psychology*, 11 (1):109. [11]

Fucini, Joseph J., and Suzy Fucini. 1990. *Working for the Japanese. Inside Mazda's American Auto Plant*. New York: Free Press. [5]

Furstenberg, Frank F., Jr., Judith A. Levine, and Jeanne Brooks-Gunn. 1990. The children of teenage mothers: Patterns of early childbearing in two generations. *Family Planning Perspectives*, 22 (2, March/April):54–61. [12]

Fuss, Diana. 1989. *Essentially Speaking: Feminism, Nature and Difference*. New York: Routledge. [11]

Fyfe, Alec. 1989. *Child Labour*. Cambridge, England: Polity. [6]

Galbraith, John Kenneth. 1978. *The New Industrial State*, 3d ed., Boston: Houghton Mifflin. [16]
Gallup, George. 1986. *The Gallup Poll: Public Opinion 1985*. Wilmington, DE: Scholarly Resources. [19]
Gallup, George. 1983. *The Gallup Poll: Public Opinion 1982*. Wilmington, DE: Scholarly Resources. [6,13]
Gallup Report. 1985. *Fifty Years of Gallup Surveys on Religion*. (Report No. 236, May). [14]
Gamoran, Adam, and Martin Nystrand. 1990. Tracking, instruction, and achievement. Paper prepared for the World Congress of Sociology, Madrid, Spain. [13]
Gans, Herbert J. 1962. *The Urban Villagers*. New York: Free Press. [20]
Gans, Herbert J. 1979. *Deciding What's News*. New York: Pantheon. [21]
Gans, Herbert J. 1988. *Middle American Individualism: The Future of Liberal Democracy*. New York: Free Press. [3]
Gans, Herbert J. 1990. Deconstructing the underclass: The term's danger as a planning concept. *Journal of the American Planning Association*. 56 (Summer):271–277. [9]
Garb, Paula. 1984. *From Childhood to Centenarian*. Moscow: Progress. [6]
Garfinkel, Harold. 1967. *Studies in Ethnomethodology*. Englewood Cliffs, NJ: Prentice Hall. [4]
Garfinkel, Irwin, and Sara S. McLanahan. 1986. *Single Mothers and Their Children: A New American Dilemma*. Washington, DC: Urban Institute Press. [12]
Gaylord, Mark S., and John F. Galliher. 1988. *The Criminology of Edwin Sutherland*. New Brunswick, NJ: Transacton. [7]
Gecas, Viktor, and Monica Seff. 1990. Families and adolescents. *Journal of Marriage and the Family*, 52:941–958. [6]
Geertz, Clifford. 1973. *The Interpretation of Culture*. New York: Basic Books. [3]
Gellerman, Saul W. 1986. Why good managers make bad ethical choices. *Harvard Business Review* (July–August):85–90. [7]
Gelles, Richard J. 1974. Child abuse as psychopathology: A sociological critique and reformulation. In S.K. Steinmetz and M.A. Straus, Eds., *Violence in the Family*. New York: Harper & Row. [12]
Gelles, Richard J. 1983. Violence in the family. In D.H. Olson and B.C. Miller, Eds., *Family Studies Review Yearbook* (Vol. 1). Beverly Hills, CA: Sage. [12]
Gelles, Richard. 1985. Family violence. *Annual Review of Sociology*, 11:347–367. [12]
Gelles, Richard J., and Murray A. Straus. 1988. *Intimate Violence*. New York: Simon and Schuster. [12]
Gellner, Ernest. 1972. *Legitimation of Belief*. London: Weidenfeld and Nicholson. [14]
Gellner, Ernest. 1983. *Nations and Nationalism*. Oxford, England: Basil Blackwell. [17]
Gelman, David. 1990. A much riskier passage. *Newsweek* (Special Issue: The New Teens): 10–16. [6]
George, Katherine. 1968. The civilized West looks at primitive Africa: 1400–1800. In A. Dundes, Ed., *Every Man His Way: Readings in Cultural Anthropology*. Englewood Cliffs, NJ: Prentice Hall. [3]
Gerber, Jerry, et al. 1989. *Lifetrends*. New York: Stonesong/Macmillan. [6]
Geschwender, James A. 1964. Social structure and the Negro revolt: An examination of some hypotheses. *Social Forces*, 43:248–256. [21]
Gibbons, John H., Peter D. Blair, and Holly I. Gwin. 1989. Strategies for energy use. *Scientific American* (September):136–143. [19]
Gibson, J.L. 1985. Whither the local parties? A cross-sectional and longitudinal analysis of the strength of party organization. *American Journal of Political Science*. [17]
Giddens, Anthony. 1985. *The National State and Violence*. Berkeley: University of California Press. [17]
Giddens, Anthony. 1990. *The Consequences of Modernity*. Stanford, CA: Stanford University Press. [3, 12]
Gil, David G. 1974. Helping parents and protecting children. In S.K. Steinmetz and M.A. Straus, Eds., *Violence in the Family*. New York: Harper & Row. [12]
Gilder, George. 1981. *Wealth and Poverty*. [17]
Gilligan, Carol. 1982. *In a Different Voice: Psychological Theory and Women's Development*. Cambridge, MA: Harvard University Press. [11]
Gitlin, Todd. 1985. *Inside Prime Time*. New York: Pantheon. [21]
Glazer, Sarah. 1990. Why schools still have tracking. *Congressional Quarterly's Editorial Research Reports*, 1(48):746–758. [13,14]
Gleik, James. 1990. The census: Why we can't count. *New York Times Magazine* (July 15):22. [19]
Glick, Paul C. 1989. Remarried families, stepfamilies, and stepchildren: A brief demographic profile. *Family Relations*, 38:24–27. [12]
Glickman, Carl D. 1990. Pushing school reform to a new edge: The seven ironies of school empowerment. *Phi Delta Kappan*, 72(1):68–75. [13]
Gluckman, Max. (ed.). 1962. *Essays on the Ritual of Social Relations*. Manchester, England: Manchester University Press. [14]
Gluckman, Max. 1965. *Politics, Law and Ritual in Tribal Society*. New York: New American Library. [1]
Goffman, Erving. 1959. *The Presentation of Self in Everyday Life*. Garden City, NY: Doubleday. [4]
Goffman, Erving. 1961. *Asylums*. Chicago: Aldine. [5]
Goffman, Erving. 1963. *Stigma: Notes on the Management of Spoiled Identity*. Englewood Cliffs, NJ: Prentice-Hall. [7]
Goffman, Erving. 1967. *Interaction Ritual*. New York: Doubleday. [4]
Goffman, Erving. 1974. *Frame Analysis: An Essay on the Organization of Experience*. Cambridge, MA: Harvard University Press. [4]
Goldemberg, José. 1989. *Amazonia: Facts, Problems and Solutions*. Sao Paulo, Brazil: University of Sao Paulo and Institute for Space Research (INPE). [19]
Golding, William. 1954. *Lord of the Flies*. New York: Coward-McCann. [8]
Goldman, Marshall I. 1983. *USSR in Crisis*. New York: Norton. [16]
Goldsmith, Jeff. 1984. Death of a paradigm. *Health Affairs*, 3 (3):5–19. [15]
Goldstone, Jack. 1991. *Revolutions in the Early Modern World*. Berkeley: University of California Press. [21]
Gondolf, Edward W., and Ellen R. Fisher. 1991. Wife battering. In Robert T. Ammerman and Michael Gersen, Eds., *Case Studies in Family Violence* (pp. 273–292). New York: Plenum Press. [12]
Goode, William J. 1960. A theory of role strain. *American Sociological Review*, 25:483–496. [4]
Goode, William J. 1963. The role of the family in industrialization. In *Social Problems of Development* (Vol. 7). The U.S. Papers Prepared for the UN Conference on the Application of Science and Technology for the Benefit of the Less Developed Areas. Washington, DC: U.S. Government Printing Office. [12]
Goode, William J. 1967. The protection of the inept. *American Sociological Review*, 32 (February):5–19. [8]
Goode, William J. 1972. The place of force in American society. *American Sociological Review*, 73:507–519. [8]
Goode, William J. 1978. *The Celebration of Heroes: Prestige as a Control System*. Berkeley: University of California Press. [9]
Goodlad, John I. 1990. Better teachers for our nation's schools. *Phi Delta Kappan*, 72 (3):185–194. [13]
Gopian, J. D. 1984. What makes PACs tick? *American Journal of Political Science*, 28 (2):259–281. [17]
Gordon, David M. 1984. Capitalist development and the history of American cities. In W.K. Tabb and L. Sawers, Eds., *Marxism and the Metropolis*, 2d ed., New York: Oxford University Press. [20]
Gordon, Milton M. 1978. *Human Nature, Class and Ethnicity*. New York: Oxford University Press. [10]

Goring, Charles. 1913. *The English Convict.* London: His Majesty's Stationery Office. [7]
Gottdiener, M., and Joe R. Feagin. 1988. The paradigm shift in urban sociology. *Urban Affairs Quarterly,* 24(2):163–187. [20]
Gottfredson, Michael, and Travis Hirschi. 1990. *A General Theory of Crime.* Stanford, CA: Stanford University Press. [7]
Gough, E. Kathleen. 1974. Nayar: Central Kerala. In D. Schneider and E.K. Gough, Eds., *Matrilineal Kinship.* Berkeley: University of California Press. [12]
Gould, Harold. 1971. Caste and class: A comparative view. *Module.* 11:1–24. [9]
Gould, Stephen J. 1984. Similarities between the sexes. Review of *A Critique of Biology and Its Theories on Women,* by Ruth Bleier. *New York Times Book Review* (August 12):7. [11]
Gouldner, Alvin W. 1973. The norm of reciprocity. In *For Sociology* (Chap. 8). New York: Basic Books. [4]
Gove, Walter R. 1975. *The Labeling of Deviance: Evaluating a Perspective.* New York: Sage. [7]
Gove, Walter R. 1979. The labeling versus the psychiatric explanation of mental illness: A debate that has become substantially irrelevant. *Journal of Health and Social Behavior,* 20(September):301–303. [7]
Gove, Walter R., and Michael Hughes. 1979. Possible causes of the apparent sex differences in physical health: An empirical investigation. *American Sociological Review,* 44(February): 126–146. [15]
Gove, Walter, Suzanne Ortega, and Carolyn Briggs Style. 1989. The maturational and role perspectives on aging and self through the adult years. *American Journal of Sociology,* 94:1117–1145. [6]
Graham, Hilary. 1987. Women's smoking and family health. *Social Science and Medicine,* 25(1):47–56. [15]
Granovetter, Mark S. 1974. *Getting a Job: A Study of Contacts and Careers.* Cambridge, MA: Harvard University Press. [4]
Granovetter, Mark S. 1984. The strength of weak ties: A network theory revisited. In R. Collins, Ed., *Sociological Theory 1983* (Chap. 7). San Francisco: Jossey-Bass. [4]
Graubard, Stephen R. 1990. Doing badly and feeling confused. *Daedalus,* 19(2):257–279. [13]
Greeley, Andrew M. 1972. *The Denominational Society.* Glenview, IL: Scott, Foresman. [14]
Greeley, Andrew M. 1989. *Religious Change in America.* Cambridge, MA: Harvard University Press. [14]
Greeley, Andrew M. 1990. *The Catholic Myth.* New York: Scribners. [14].
Green, Arthur H. 1991. Child neglect. In Robert T. Ammerman and Michael Gersen, Eds., *Case Studies in Family Violence* (pp. 135–152). New York: Plenum Press. [12]
Greenfeld, Liah. 1992. *Nationalism: Five Roads to Modernity.* Cambridge, MA: Harvard University Press. [17]
Greenhalgh, Susan. 1990. Socialism and fertility in China. *Annals of the American Academy of Political and Social Science,* 510(July):73–86. [19]
Greenstein, Robert, and Scott Barancik. 1990. *Drifting Apart: New Findings on Growing Income Disparities Betweeen the Rich, the Poor, and the Middle Class.* Washington, DC: Center on Budget and Policy Priorities. [9]
Greif, Geoffrey L. 1985. *Single Fathers.* Lexington, MA: Heath. [12]
Griffin, Keith. 1989. *Alternative Strategies for Economic Development.* New York: Macmillan and OECD Development Centre. [18]
Griswold, Wendy. 1989. Formulaic fiction: The author as agent of elective affinity. *Comparative Social Research,* 11:75–130. [3]
Grusec, Joan E., and Hugh Lytton. 1988. *Social Development: History, Theory, and Research.* New York: Springer-Verlag. [5]
Gumperz, John J., Ed. 1982. *Language and Social Identity.* New York: Cambridge University Press. [3]
Gurr, Ted Robert. 1970. *Why Men Rebel.* Princeton, NJ: Princeton University Press. [21]
Guterman, Stuart, and Allen Dobson. 1986. Impact of medicare prospective payment for hospitals. *Health Care Financing Review,* 7(3):97–114. [15]
Gutierrez, G. 1973. *A Theory of Liberation.* Maryknoll, NY: Orbis. [14]
Gutierrez, G. 1983. *The Power of the Poor in History.* Maryknoll, NY: Orbis. [14]

Habermas, Jürgen. 1984. *The Theory of Communicative Action,* Vol. 1. Boston: Beacon Press. [22]
Habermas, Jürgen. 1987. *The Philosophical Discourse of Modernity: Twelve Lectures.* Cambridge, MA: MIT Press. [17]
Habermas, Jürgen. 1988. *The Theory of Communicative Action,* Vol. 2. Boston: Beacon Press. [1, 22]
Habermas, Jürgen. 1989. *The Structural Transformation of the Public Sphere.* Cambridge, MA: MIT Press. [17]
Habib, Jack. 1990. Population aging and the economy. In R. Binstock and L. George, Eds., *Aging and the Social Sciences,* 3d ed. San Diego: Academic Press. [6]
Hagan, John. 1990. The gender stratification of income inequality among lawyers. *Social Forces,* 68(3, March):835–855. [11]
Hagan, John, and Alberto Palloni. 1990. The social reproduction of a criminal class in working-class London, circa 1950–1980. *American Journal of Sociology,* 96(2)(September):265–299. [7]
Haggard, Stephan. 1990. *Pathways from the Periphery: The Politics of Growth in the Newly Industrializing Countries.* Ithaca, NY: Cornell University Press. [18]
Haines, Valerie. 1988. Is Spencer's theory an evolutionary theory? *American Journal of Sociology,* 93(5):1200–1223. [22]
Halbenstein, Robert U., Charles H. Mindel, and Roosevelt Wright, Jr. 1988. *Ethnic Families in America: Patterns and Variations,* 3d ed. New York: Elsevier. [11]
Hale, Christiane B. 1990. Infant mortality: An American tragedy. *The Black Scholar* (Jan.–Feb.–March):17–26. [9]
Hall, G. Stanley. 1905/1981. *Adolescence: Its Psychology and Its Relations to Physiology, Anthropology, Sociology, Sex, Crime, Religion, and Education* (2 vols.). Norwood, PA: Telegraph Books. [6]
Hall, John A. 1985. *Powers and Liberties.* Berkeley: University of California Press. [17]
Hall, Richard H. 1963–1964. The concept of bureaucracy: An empirical assessment. *American Journal of Sociology,* 69:32–40. [8]
Hall, Richard H. 1982. *Organizations: Structure and Process,* 3d ed. Englewood Cliffs, NJ: Prentice Hall. [8]
Halle, David. 1984. *America's Working Man: Work, Home and Politics Among Blue-Collar Property Owners.* Chicago: University of Chicago Press. [16]
Halperin, David M. 1989. *One Hundred Years of Homosexuality.* New York: Routledge. [11]
Hannan, Michael T., and John Freeman. 1977. The population ecology of organizations. *American Journal of Sociology,* 82(5): 929–964. [8]
Hanson, Kerry. 1987. Party animal (Tupperware). *Forbes* (November 16):262. [8]
Hanson, Sandra L. 1983. A family life-cycle approach to the socioeconomic attainment of working women. *Journal of Marriage and the Family,* 45(2):323–338. [6]
Harrington, Michael. 1959/1963. *The Other America: Poverty in the United States.* Baltimore: Penguin. [9]
Harrington, Michael. 1988. *Who Are the Poor?* New York: Institute for Democratic Socialism. [9]
Harris, Chauncy D., and Edward L. Ullman. 1945. The nature of

cities. *Annals of the American Academy of Political and Social Science*, 242(November):7–17. [20]
Harris, Louis. 1987. *Inside America*. New York: Vintage. [14]
Harris, Marvin. 1975. *Cows, Pigs, Wars, and Witches: The Riddles of Culture*. New York: Random House. [3]
Harrison, Paul. 1983. *The Third World Tomorrow: A Report from the Battlefront in the War Against Poverty*, 2d ed. New York: Pilgrim Press. [18]
Harrison, Paul. 1984. *Inside the Third World*, 2d rev. ed. Harmondsworth, England: Penguin. [18, 19, 22]
Hart, Keith. 1973. Informal Income Opportunities and Urban Employment in Ghana. *Journal of Modern African Studies*, 11(1):61–89. [18]
Hart, Stephen. 1987. Privatization in American religion and society. *Sociological Analysis*, 47(4):319–334. [14]
Hartmann, Heidi I. 1987. *Pay Equity: Empirical Inquiries*. Washington, DC: Academy Press. [11]
Harvey, David. 1989. *The Condition of Postmodernity: An Enquiry into the Origins of Cultural Change*. New York: Basil Blackwell. [20]
Haub, Carl. 1989. Trial by numbers. *Sierra* (November–December):40–42. [22]
Haub, Carl. 1991. World and United States population prospects. *Population and Environment: A Journal of Interdisciplinary Studies*, 12(3, Spring):297–310. [19]
Hauser, Philip M. 1975. *Social Statistics in Use*. New York: Russell Sage Foundation. [22]
Hauser, Robert M., Archibald O. Haller, David Mechanic, and Taissa S. Hauser, Eds. 1982. *Social Structure and Behavior*. New York: Academic Press. [9]
Hauser, Robert M., Shu-Ling Tsai, and William H. Sewell. 1983. A model of stratification with response error in social and psychological variables. *Sociology of Education*, 56:20–46. [9]
Hawkins, David. (1990). The Roots of Literacy. *Daedalus*, 19(2):1–14. [13]
Hawley, Amos H. 1971. *Urban Society: An Ecological Approach*. New York: Ronald Press. [20]
Hayes, C.D. 1987. *Risking the Future: Adolescent Sexuality, Pregnancy, and Childbearing*, Vol. 1. Washington, DC: National Academic Press. [12]
Hearn, James C. 1984. The relative roles of academic, ascribed, and socioeconomic characteristics in college destinations. *Sociology of Education*, 57(January):22–30. [13]
Heath, Stephen. 1982. *The Sexual Fix*. New York: Schocken. [6]
Heilbroner, Robert L. 1976. *Business Civilization in Decline*. New York: Norton. [16]
Helson, Ravenna, and Geraldine Moore. 1987. Personality change in women from college to midlife. *Journal of Personality and Social Psychology*, 53:126–186. [6]
Herbers, John. 1983. Large cities and suburbs giving way to the sprawl of small urban areas. *New York Times* (July 8):1. [20]
Herdt, Gilbert H. 1984. A comment on cultural attributes and fluidity of bisexuality. *Journal of Homosexuality*, 10(3/4):53–61. [11]
Herman, Edward. 1981. *Corporate Control, Corporate Power*. New York: Cambridge University Press. [16]
Hess, Beth, and Elizabeth Markson. 1991. *Growing Old in America*, 4th ed. New Brunswick, NJ: Transaction. [6]
Hess, John L. 1990. Confessions of a greedy geezer. *Nation*, 250(April 2):1, 42. [6]
Hewitt, Hugh. 1992. When television throws a riot. *Los Angeles Times* (May 3):M1,M3. [21]
Hill, Richard Child, and Joe R. Feagin. 1987. Detroit and Houston: Two cities in global perspective. In Michael Peter Smith and Joe R. Feagin, Eds., *The Capitalist City: Global Restructuring and Community Politics*. London: Basil Blackwell. [20]
Himmelstein, Jerome L. 1990. *To the Right: The Transformation of American Conservatism*. Berkeley: University of California Press. [14]
Hirsch, Paul M. 1971. Processing fads and fashions: An organization-set analysis of cultural industry systems. *American Journal of Sociology*, 77(4):639–659. [3]
Hirschi, Travis. 1969. *Causes of Delinquency*. Berkeley: University of California Press.
Hirschi, Travis, and Michael Gottfredson. 1988. Towards a general theory of crime. In W. Buikhuisen and S.A. Mednick, Eds., *Explaining Criminal Behaviors* (pp. 8–26). Leiden: Brill. [7]
Hirschman, Albert O. 1977. *The Passions and the Interests: Political Arguments for Capitalism Before Its Triumph*. Princeton, NJ: Princeton University Press. [16]
Hirschman, Albert. 1982. *Shifting Involvements*. Princeton, NJ: Princeton University Press. [17]
Hochschild, Arlie Russell. 1983. *The Managed Heart: Commercialization of Human Feeling*. Berkeley: University of California Press. [3,16]
Hochschild, Arlie Russell, with Anne Machung. 1989. *The Second Shift: Working Parents and the Revolution at Home*. New York: Viking. [11, 12]
Hodge, Robert, and David Tripp. 1986. *Children and Television: A Semiotic Approach*. Cambridge, England: Polity Press. [5]
Hodgkinson, Harold L., Janice Hamilton Outtz, and Anita M. Obarakpor. 1990. *The Demographics of American Indians*. Washington, DC.: Institute for Educational Leadership. [10]
Hogan, Dennis, and E. Kitagawa. 1985. The impact of social status, family structure and neighborhood on the fertility of black adolescents. *American Journal of Sociology*, 90:825–836. [6]
Holstein, William J. 1990. Hands across America: The rise of Mitsubishi. *Business Week* (September 24):102–107. [8]
Homans, George C. 1974. *Social Behavior: Its Elementary Forms*, rev. ed. New York: Harcourt Brace Jovanovich. [4]
Hoover, E.M., and R. Vernon. 1959. *Anatomy of a Metropolis*. Cambridge, MA: Harvard University Press. [20]
Hopkins, K. 1978. *Conquerors and Slaves: Sociological Studies in Roman History*. New York: Cambridge University Press. [17]
Horn, Jack C., and Jeff Meer. 1987. The vintage years. *Psychology Today*, 21(5):76–90. [6]
Hostetler, John A. 1980. *Amish Society*, 3d ed. Baltimore: Johns Hopkins University Press. [8]
Hoult, Thomas Ford. 1969. *A Dictionary of Modern Sociology*. Totowa, NJ: Littlefield, Adams. [21]
House, J., and G. Kasper. 1981. Politeness markers in English and German. In F. Coulmas, Ed., *Conversational Routine: Explorations in Standardized Communication Situations and Prepatterned Speech* (pp. 157–185). The Hague: Mouton. [3]
House of Representatives Select Committee on Aging, Subcommittee on Health and Long-Term Care. 1990. *Elder Abuse: A Decade of Shame and Inaction*. Washington, DC: U.S. Government Printing Office. [12]
Howard, Robert. 1985. *Brave New Workplace*. New York: Viking. [16]
Howe, Louise Knapp. 1977. *Pink Collar Workers*. New York: Putnam. [10, 11]
Hoyt, Homer. 1943. The structure of American cities in the post-war era. *American Journal of Sociology*, 48(January):475–492. [20]
Huber, Joan, and Glenna Spitze. 1980. Considering divorce: An expansion of Becker's theory of marital instability. *American Journal of Sociology*, 86(1):75–89. [12]
Hughes, Robert. 1987. *The Fatal Shore*. New York: Knopf. [7]
Hughes, Thomas P. 1987. The evolution of large technological systems. In W. Bijker, T.P. Hughes, and T. Pinch, Eds., *The Social Construction of Technological Systems* (pp. 51–81). Cambridge, MA: MIT Press. [20]
Hundley, T. 1989. Small-town blues. *Chicago Tribune Magazine* (January 29):9–21. [20]

Hunt, Morton. 1985. *Profiles of Social Research.* New York: Russell Sage Foundation. [2]
Hunter, Albert. 1978. Persistence of local sentiments in mass society. In D. Street et al., Eds., *Handbook of Contemporary Urban Life* (pp. 134–156). San Francisco: Jossey-Bass. [20]
Hunter, James Davison. 1990. Fundamentalism in its global contours. In Normal J. Cohen, Ed., *The Fundamentalist Phenomenon: A View From Within; A Response from Without* (pp. 56–71). Grand Rapids, MI: Eerdmans. [14]
Hyde, Janet S. 1981. How large are cognitive gender differences? *American Psychologist,* 36:892–901. [11]
Hyde, Janet S. 1984. How large are gender differences in aggression? A developmental meta-analysis. *Developmental Psychology,* 20:722–736. [11]
Hyman, Herbert H., and Charles R. Wright. 1979. *Education's Lasting Influence on Values.* Chicago: University of Chicago Press. [13]
Hyman, Herbert H., Charles R. Wright, and John Shelton Reed. 1975. *The Enduring Effects of Education.* Chicago: University of Chicago Press. [13]

Ianni, Francis A.J. 1989. *The Search for Structure: A Report on American Youth Today.* New York: Free Press. [6]
Imperato, Pascal James. 1989. *Mali: A Search for Direction.* Boulder: Westview Press. [18]
Independent Commission on International Humanitarian Issues. 1985. *Famine: A Manmade Disaster?* New York: Vintage. [19]
Inkeles, Alex. 1983. *Exploring Individual Modernity.* New York: Columbia University Press. [18]
Isaac, Rael J., and Virginia C. Armat. 1990. *Madness in the Streets: How Psychiatry and the Law Abandoned the Mentally Ill.* New York: Free Press. [9]
Ivins, Molly. 1990. Good ol debs. *Ms.,* 18(August):22. [6]

Jackall, Robert. 1988. *Moral Mazes: The World of Corporate Managers.* New York: Oxford University Press. [16]
Jacklin, Carol N., Eleanor E. Maccoby, Charles H. Doering, and David R. King. 1984. Neonatal sex-steroid hormones and muscular strength of boys and girls in the first three years. *Developmental Psychobiology,* 20(3), May):459–472. [11]
Jackson, Philip, W. 1968. *Life in Classrooms.* New York: Holt, Rinehart and Winston. [13]
Jacoby, Tamar. 1991. Thinking about the homeless. *Dissent* (Spring):249–253. [9]
Jagger, Bianca. 1991. Save the rain forest in Nicaragua. *New York Times* (November 12):A25. [19]
James, Estelle, Nabeel Alsalam, Joseph C. Conaty, and Duc-Le To. 1989. College quality and future earnings: Where should you send your child to college? *American Economic Review,* 79(2):247–252. [13]
Jankowski, Martin Sánchez. 1991. *Islands in the Street.* Berkeley: University of California Press. [7]
Janis, Irving L. 1972. *Victims of Groupthink: A Psychological Study of Foreign-Policy Decisions and Fiascos.* Boston: Houghton Mifflin. [8]
Janis, Irving L. 1982. *Groupthink: Psychological Studies of Policy Decisions and Fiascoes.* Boston: Houghton Mifflin. [8]
Janis, Irving L. 1989. *Crucial Decisions.* New York: Free Press. [8]
Jencks, Christopher. 1972. *Inequality: A Reassessment of the Effect of Family and Schooling in America.* New York: Basic Books. [13]
Jencks, Christopher. 1992. *Rethinking Social Policy: Race, Poverty, and the Underclass.* Cambridge, MA: Harvard University Press. [10]
Jiao, Shulan, Guiping Ji, and Qicheng Jing (C.C. Ching). 1986. Comparative study of behavioral qualities of only children and sibling children. *Child Development,* 57:357–361. [5]
Johnson, Ann Braden. 1990. *Out of Bedlam: The Truth About Deinstitutionalization.* New York: Basic Books. [9]
Johnson, Barbara A., and Jonathan H. Turner. 1984. A formalization and reformalization of anomie theory. *South African Journal of Sociology,* 15(4):151–158. [7]
Johnson, Benton. 1963. On church and sect. *American Sociological Review,* 28:539–549. [14]
Jones, Barry. 1982. *Sleepers, Wake!: Technology and the Future of Work.* Melbourne, Australia: Oxford University Press. [16]
Jones, Landon Y. 1980. *Great Expectations: America and the Baby Boom Generation.* New York: Coward, McCann & Geoghegan. [6]
Jönsson, Berth. 1991. Production philosophy at Volvo. In Michael Maccoby, Ed., *Sweden at the Edge.* Philadelphia: University of Pennsylvania Press. [8]
Jordan, Nick. 1983. You've run a long way, baby. *Psychology Today* (June):79. [11]
Judis, John. 1990. Goodbye to all that. *In These Times* (November):7–13. [16]
Judson, Horace Freeland. 1979. *The Eighth Day of Creation.* New York: Simon and Schuster. [22]

Kadushin, Charles. 1983. Mental health and the interpersonal environment: A reexamination of some effects of social structure on mental health. *American Sociological Review.* 46:393–405. [4]
Kalifon, S. Zev. 1989. Homelessness and mental illness: Who resorts to state hospitals? *Human Organization,* 48(3, Fall):268–273. [9]
Kalmuss, Debra, and Judith A. Seltzer. 1989. A framework for studying family socialization over the life cycle. *Journal of Family Issues,* 10(3, September):339–358. [5]
Kamerman, Jack B. 1988. *Death in the Midst of Life.* Englewood Cliffs, NJ: Prentice Hall. [6]
Kamerman, Sheila B., and Alfred J. Kahn. 1987. *The Responsive Workplace.* New York: Columbia University Press. [11]
Kamin, Leon J. 1986. Is crime in the genes? The answer may depend on who chooses what evidence. *Scientific American* (February):22–27. [7]
Kane, Penny. 1987. *The Second Billion: Population and Family Planning in China.* New York: Penguin. [19]
Kanter, Rosabeth Moss. 1972. *Commitment and Community: Communes and Utopias in Sociological Perspective.* Cambridge, MA: Harvard University Press. [8]
Kanter, Rosabeth Moss. 1977. *Men and Women of the Corporation.* New York: Basic Books. [8, 11]
Kanter, Rosabeth Moss. 1983. *The Changemasters: Innovation and Entrepreneurship in the American Corporation.* New York: Simon and Schuster. [11]
Kantorowicz, Ernest. 1957. *The King's Two Bodies.* Princeton, NJ: Princeton University Press. [17]
Kapstein, Jonathan. 1989. Volvo's radical new plant. *Business Week* (August 28):92–93. [8]
Kasarda, John D. 1989. Urban industrial transition and the underclass. *Annals of the American Academy of Political and Social Science* 501(January):26–47. [20]
Kasarda, John D., and Stephen J. Appold. 1990. Urban industrial transition and workforce skill mismatches: The U.S., U.K. and R.G. Chapel Hill, NC: Frank Hawkins Kenan Institute of Private Enterprise, Working Paper Series. [9, 16]
Kasarda, John D., and Edward M. Crenshaw. 1991. Third world urbanization: Dimensions, theories and determinants. *Annual Review of Sociology,* 17:467–501. [18]

Kasinitz, P. 1986. Gentrification and homelessness: The single room occupant and the inner city revival. In J. Erickson and C. Wilhelm, Eds., *Housing the Homeless*. New Brunswick, NJ: Center for Urban Policy Research. [9]

Kasinitz, Philip. 1988. The gentrification of "Boerum Hill": Neighborhood change and conflicts over definitions. *Qualitative Sociology* 11(3)(Fall):163–182. [20]

Keith, Jennie. 1990. Age in social and cultural context. In R. Binstock and L. George, Eds., *Aging and the Social Sciences*, 3d ed. San Diego: Academic Press. [6]

Keller, Suzanne. 1963. *Beyond the Ruling Class: Strategic Elites in Modern Society*. New York: Random House. [17]

Kelly, Dean M. 1977. *Why Conservative Churches Are Growing*. New York: Harper & Row [14]

Kennedy, Paul. 1987. *The Rise and Fall of the Great Powers*. New York: Random House. [22]

Kerbo, Harold R. 1991. *Social Stratification and Inequality*. New York: McGraw-Hill. [9]

Kerckhoff, Alan C., and Robert A. Jackson. 1982. Types of education and the occupational attainments of young men. *Social Forces*, 61:24–45. [13]

Kern, Rosemary Gibson, and Susan R. Windham, with Paula Griswold. 1986. *Medicaid and Other Experiments in State Health Policy*. Washington, DC: American Enterprise Institute for Public Policy Research. [15]

Kerr, Peter. 1987. Drug smugglers: New breed of ethnic gangs. *New York Times* (March 21):A1, 31. [7]

Kessen, William, Ed. 1975. *Children in China*. New Haven, CT: Yale University Press. [5]

Kessler, Ronald C., James S. House, and J. Blake Turner. 1987. Unemployment and health in a community sample. *Journal of Health and Social Behavior*, 28(March):51–59. [15]

Kett, Joseph F. 1977. *Rites of Passage: Adolescence in America, 1790 to the Present*. New York: Basic Books. [6]

Keyfitz, Nathan. 1989. The growing human population. *Scientific American*, 261(3, September):119–126. [9, 19]

Kilgore, Sally B. 1991. The organizational context of tracking in schools. *American Sociological Review*, 56, (April):189–203. [13]

Kimball, M.M. 1986. Television and sex-role attitudes. In T.M. Williams, Ed., *The Impact of Television: A Natural Experiment in Three Communities*. Orlando, FL: Academic Press. [11]

King, Wayne, and Warren Weaver, Jr. 1986. Briefing: Alarming words. *New York Times* (October 8):B10. [13]

Kirsch, Irwin S., and Ann Jungeblut. 1986. *Literacy: Profiles of America's Young Adults*. Princeton, NJ: Educational Testing Service. [13]

Klein, Bruce W., and Philip L. Rones. 1989. A profile of the working poor. *Monthly Labor Review* (October):3–13. [9]

Klein, Ethel. 1984. *Gender Politics: From Consciousness to Mass Politics*. Cambridge, MA: Harvard University Press. [21]

Klostermaier, Klaus K. 1989. *A Survey of Hinduism*. Albany: State University of New York Press. [14]

Kohn, Melvin L. 1959. Social class and parental values. *American Journal of Sociology*, 64(January)337–351. [5]

Kohn, Melvin L. 1976. Occupational structure and alienation. *American Journal of Sociology*, 82(July):111–130. [5]

Kohn, Melvin L. 1981. Personality, occupation, and social stratification: A frame of reference. In D.J. Treiman and R.V. Robinson, Eds., *Research in Social Stratification and Mobility: A Research Annual*, Vol. 1(pp. 276–297). Greenwich, CT: JAI Press. [5]

Kohn, Melvin L., and Carmi Schooler. 1978. The reciprocal effects of the substantive complexities of work and intellectual flexibility: A longitudinal assessment. *American Journal of Sociology*, 84(July):24–52. [5]

Kohn, Melvin L., and Carmi Schooler. 1983. *Work and Personality: An Inquiry into the Impact of Social Stratification*. Norwood, NJ: Ablex. [5]

Kohn, Melvin I., Atushi Naoi, Carrie Schoenbach, Carmi Schooler, and Kazimierz M. Slomczynski. 1990. Position in the class structure and psychological functioning in the United States, Japan, and Poland. *American Journal of Sociology*, 95(4, January): 964–1008. [5]

Kohn, Melvin I., Kazimierz M. Slomczynski, and Carrie Schoenbach. 1986. Social stratification and the transmission of values in the family: A Cross-National Assessment. *Social Forces*, 1(1):73–102. [5]

Kolata, Gina. 1992. New insurance practice. Dividing sick from well. *New York Times* (March 4):A1, A15. [15]

Kominski, Robert. 1990. *What's it worth? Educational background and economic status: Spring 1987*. Current Population Reports: Household Economic Studies, Series P-70, No. 21. Washington, DC: U.S. Government Printing Office. [13]

Koning, Hans. 1976. *Columbus: His Enterprise*. New York: Monthly Review Press. [22]

Koppel, Ted. 1992. Moment of crisis: Anatomy of a riot. *ABC Nightline Special Investigation* (May). [21]

Koretz, Gene. 1989. The rise in births is only an echo of the baby boom. *Business Week* (July 10):18. [6]

Kornhauser, William. 1961. "Power Elite" or "Veto Groups"? In S.M. Lipset and L. Lowenthal, Eds., *Cultural and Social Character*. Peoria, IL: Free Press. [17]

Kosofsky-Sedgwick, Eve. 1990. *Epistemology of the Closet*. Berkeley: University of California Press. [11]

Kottak, Conrad Phillip. 1991. *Anthropology: The Exploration of Human Diversity*. New York: McGraw-Hill. [12]

Kozol, Jonathan. 1988. *Rachel and Her Children: Homeless Families in America*. New York: Crown. [9]

Kozol, Jonathan. 1992. *Savage Inequities: Children in America's Schools*. New York: HarperCollins. [13]

Kramer, Jane. 1991. Letter from Europe. *New Yorker* (January 14):60–75. [3, 14]

Kristoff, Nicholas D. 1991. Chinese grow healthier from cradle to grave. *New York Times* (April 14):A1,6. [19]

Kristoff, Nicholas D. 1993. In China's crackdown on population growth, force is a big weapon. *International Herald Tribune* (April 28):4. [19]

Krosnick, Jon A., and Charles M. Judd. 1982. Transition in social influence at adolescence: Who induces cigarette smoking? *Developmental Psychology*, 18:359–368. [5]

Kübler-Ross, Elisabeth. 1969. *On Death and Dying*. New York: Macmillan. [6]

Kuper, Leo, and M.G. Smith. 1969. *Plural Societies*. Chicago: Aldine. [10]

Lacayo, Richard. 1987. Considering the alternatives. *Time* (February 2):60–61. [7]

Lacayo, Richard. 1991. Global warming: A new warning. *Time*, 137(April 22):32. [22]

Ladd, Everett Carl, Jr., and Charles D. Hadley. 1975. *Transformation of the American Party System*. New York: Norton. [17]

Landry, Bart. 1991. The enduring dilemma of race in America. In Alan Wolfe, Ed., *America at Century's End* (pp. 185–207). Berkeley: University of California Press. [10]

Lang, Michael H. 1989. *Homelessness Amid Affluence: Structure and Paradox in the American Political Economy*. New York: Praeger. [9]

Lareau, Annette. 1989. *Home Advantage: Social Class and Parental Intervention in Elementary Education*. Philadelphia: Falmer Press. [13]

Larner, John. 1988. The certainty of Columbus: Some recent studies. *History*, 73(February):3–23. [22]

Larson, Magali Sarfalti. 1977. *The Rise of Professionalism: A Sociological Analysis*. Berkeley: University of California Press. [15]

Lasch, Christopher. 1991. *The True and Only Heaven: Progress and Its Critics*. New York: Norton. [22]

Laslett, Barbara, and Johanna Brenner. 1989. Gender and social production: Historical perspectives. *American Sociological Review*, 15:381–404. [11]

Laslett, Peter. 1973. *The World We Have Lost*, 2d ed. New York: Scribners. [1]

Latané, B., K. Williams, and S. Harkins. 1979. Many hands make light the work: The causes and consequences of social loafing. *Journal of Social Psychology*, 37:822–832. [2]

Latour, Bruno. 1987. *Science in Action*. Cambridge, MA: Harvard University Press. [22]

Lauter, David, and Sam Fluwood, III. 1992. U.S. racial slumber ends in jolt. *Los Angeles Times* (May 3):A1, A8. [21]

Lawrence, Peter A., and Tony Spybey. 1986. *Management and Society in Sweden*. London: Routledge and Kegan Paul. [8]

Lazare, Daniel. 1991. Collapse of a city: Growth and decay of Camden, New Jersey. *Dissent* (Spring):267–275. [20]

Le Bon, Gustave. 1895/1960. *The Crowd: A Study of the Popular Mind*. New York: Viking. [21]

Lee, Benjamin. 1991. Critical internationalism. Working paper of the Center for Psychosocial Studies, Chicago. [10]

Lee, Renselaer W., III. 1989. *The White Labyrinth: Cocaine and Political Power*. New Brunswick, NJ: Transaction. [7]

Lee, Valerie. 1985. *Access to Higher Education: The Experience of Blacks, Hispanics, and Low Socio-Economic Status Whites*. Washington, DC: American Council on Education, Division of Policy Analysis and Research. [13]

Leek, Margaret Guminski, and Pearson, T. Allan. 1991. Demographic subgroup contributions to divorce cause constellations. *Journal of Divorce and Remarriage*, 15(1/2):33–49. [12]

Leiss, W., S. Kline, and S. Shelly. 1986. *Social Communication in Advertising: Persons, Products, and Images of Well-Being*. Toronto: Methuen. [3]

Lemert, Edwin M. 1951. *Human Deviance, Social Problems, and Social Control*. New York: McGraw-Hill. [7]

Lenski, Gerhard E. 1966. *Power and Privilege: A Theory of Social Stratification*. New York: McGraw-Hill. [9]

Lenski, Gerhard E., Jean Lenski, and Patrick Nolan. 1991. *Human Societies: An Introduction to Macrosociology*. New York: McGraw-Hill. [9, 11, 22]

Lerman, Lisa G., and Naomi R. Cahn. 1991. Legal issues in violence towards adults. In *Case Studies in Family Violence*, Robert T. Ammerman and Michael Gersen, Eds. (pp. 73–85). New York: Plenum Press. [12]

Levin, Jack, and William C. Levin. 1980. *Ageism*. Belmont, MA: Wadsworth. [6]

Levinson, Daniel J., et al. 1978. *The Seasons of a Man's Life*. New York: Knopf. [6]

Levinson, S.C. 1983. *Pragmatics*. New York: Cambridge University Press. [3]

Levitas, Mitchel. 1990. Homelessness in America. *New York Times Magazine* (June 10):45. [9]

Levitt, Jane. 1986. The Corporation of health care. In S. Jonas, Ed., *Health Care Delivery in the United States*. New York: Springer. [15]

Levy, Frank. 1987. *Dollars and Dreams: The Changing American Income Distribution*. New York: Norton. [9]

Lewin, Miriam Papanek. 1957. *Authority and Interpersonal Relations in the Family*. Doctoral Dissertation. Radcliffe College, Harvard University, Cambridge, MA. [11]

Lewin, Miriam P., and Lilli M. Tragos. 1987. Has the feminist movement influenced adolescent sex role attitudes? A reassessment after a quarter century. *Sex Roles*. 16(3/4):125–135. [11]

Lewis, Bernard. 1985. *The Jews of Islam*. Princeton, NJ: Princeton University Press. [14]

Lewis, Catherine C. 1989. Cooperation and control in Japanese nursery schools. In James J. Shields, Jr., Ed., *Japanese Schooling* (pp. 28–44). University Park: State University Press. [5]

Leyerle, Betty. 1984. *Moving and Shaking American Medicine: The Structure of a Socioeconomic Transformation*. Westport, CT: Greenwood Press. [15]

Lieberson, Stanley. 1961. A societal theory of race relations. *American Sociological Review*, 26:902–910. [10]

Lieberson, Stanley. 1980. *A Piece of the Pie: Black and White Immigrants Since 1880*. Berkeley: University of California Press. [9]

Lieberson, Stanley. 1982. Stereotypes: their consequences for race and ethnic interaction. In Robert M. Hauser et al., Eds., *Social Structure and Behavior: Essays in Honor of William Hamilton Sewell*. New York: Academic Press. [10]

Liebow, Elliot. 1967. *Tally's Corner: A Study of Negro Streetcorner Men*. Boston: Little, Brown. [4]

Light, Donald W. 1986. Corporate medicine for profit. *Scientific American*, 255(6):38–45. [15]

Light, Donald W. 1988. Social control and the American health care system. In H.E. Freeman and S. Levine, Eds., *Handbook of Medical Sociology*, 4th ed. Englewood Cliffs, NJ: Prentice Hall. [15]

Light, Donald W., Etienne Phipps, and Alfred Sorbello. 1982. Dilemma of comprehensive care. *The New Physician*, 31(5):39–40. [15]

Light, Paul. 1988. *Baby Boomers*. New York: Norton. [6]

Lin, Nan, Walter M. Ensel, and John C. Vaughn. 1981. Social resources and strength of ties: Structural factors in occupational status attainment. *American Sociological Review*, 46:393–405. [4]

Lincoln, Alan Jay, and Murray A. Straus. 1985. *Crime and the Family*. Springfield, IL: Charles C. Thomas. [12]

Lincoln, James, and Arne Kalleberg. 1990. *Culture, Control, and Commitment: A Study of Work Organizations and Work Attitudes in the U.S. and Japan*. New York: Cambridge University Press. [2, 8]

Lindblom, C. 1977. *Politics and Markets*. New York: Basic Books. [17]

Linton, Ralph. 1947. *The Study of Man*. New York: Appleton-Century-Crofts. [3, 4]

Lipset, Seymour Martin. 1963a. *The First New Nation*. New York: Basic Books. [22]

Lipset, Seymour Martin. 1963b. *Political Man*. New York: Doubleday/Anchor. [17]

Lipset, Seymour Martin. 1981. *Political Man*, 2d ed. Chicago: University of Chicago Press. [17]

Lipset, Seymour Martin, and William Schneider. 1983. *The Confidence Gap*. New York: Free Press. [17]

Lipton, Michael, and Richard Longhurst. 1989. *New Seeds and Poor People*. Baltimore: Johns Hopkins University Press. [18]

Littman, Mark S. 1989. Poverty in the 1980's: Are the poor getting poorer? *Monthly Labor Review* (June):13–18. [9]

Livingston, E. 1987. *Making Sense of Ethnomethodology*. London: Routledge & Kegan Paul. [4]

Lockwood, Charles, and Christopher B. Leinberger. 1988. Los Angeles Comes of Age. *Atlantic Monthly* 261(1)(January):31–56. [20]

Logan, Charles H. 1985. Incarceration, Inc.: The Privatization of Prisons. Paper presented at the Society for Study of Social Problems annual meeting, Washington, DC, August 23–26. [7]

Logan, J.R., and H.L. Molotch. 1987. *Urban Fortunes: The Political Economy of Place*. Berkeley: University of California Press. [20]

Louis, Arthur M. 1973. The new rich of the seventies. *Fortune*, 88(September):170–175. [9]

Lowenthal, Marjorie F., Majda Thurnher, and David Chiriboga. 1975. *Four Stages of Life*. San Francisco: Jossey-Bass. [6]

Luckmann, Thomas. 1967. *The Invisible Religion*. New York: Macmillan. [14]

Luebke, Barbara F. 1989. Out of focus: Images of women and men in newspaper photographs. *Sex Roles*. 20(3/4):121–133. [11]

Luhmann, Niklas. 1986. *Love as Passion*. Cambridge, MA: Harvard University Press. [3, 12]

Luker, Kristin. 1984. *Abortion and the Politics of Motherhood*. Berkeley: University of California Press. [21]

Lytton, Hugh, and David M. Romney. 1991. Parents differential socialization of boys and girls: A meta-analysis. *Psychological Bulletin*, 109(2):267–296. [11]

Maccoby, Eleanor E., and Carol N. Jacklin. 1974. *The Psychology of Sex Differences*. Stanford, CA: Stanford University Press. [11]

Machung, Anne. 1989. Talking career, thinking job: Gender differences in career and family expectations of Berkeley seniors. *Feminist Studies*, 15(1, Spring):35–58. [11]

Madan, T.N. 1989. Religion in India. *Daedalus*, 118(4, Fall):115–146. [14]

Magdoff, Harry. 1982. Imperialism: A historical survey. In Hamza Alavi and Teodor Shanin, eds., *Introduction to the Sociology of "Developing Societies"* (pp. 11–28). New York: Monthly Review Press. [18]

Mahler, Halfdan. 1980. People. *Scientific American*, 243(September):67–77. [15]

Mahler, Halfdan. 1981. The Meaning of Health for All by the Year 2000. *World Health Forum*, 2:5–22. [15]

Mahmood, Cynthia Keppley. 1989. Sikh rebellion and the Hindu concept of order. *Asian Survey*, 29(3, March):327–340. [14]

Maines, David R., and Monica J. Hardesty. 1987. Temporality and gender: Young adults' career choices and family plans. *Social Forces*. 66:102–120. [11]

Makadon, Harvey, George Seage, Kenneth Thorpe, and Harvey Fineberg. 1990. Paying the medical cost of the HIV epidemic: A review of policy options. *Journal of Acquired Immune Deficiency Syndromes*, 3:123–133. [15]

Malik, Yogendra K., and Dhirendra K. Vajpeyi. 1989. The rise of Hindu militancy: India's secular democracy at risk. *Asian Survey*, 29(3, March):308–325. [14]

Mann, Dale. 1986. Can we help dropouts: Thinking about the undoable. *Teachers College Record*, 87(3):307–323. [13]

Mann, Jonathan M. 1990. Global AIDS into the 1990s. *Journal of Acquired Immune Deficiency Syndromes*, 3:438–442. [15]

Mann, Michael. 1986. *The Sources of Social Power Vol. 1: Power from the Beginning to 1760 A.D.* New York: Cambridge University Press. [17]

Mare, Robert D. 1981. Change and stability in educational stratification. *American Sociological Review*, 46:72–87. [13]

Marger, Martin N. 1991. *Race and Ethnic Relations: American and Global Perspectives*. Belmont, CA: Wadsworth. [3]

Margolis, Richard J. 1990. *Risking Old Age in America*. Boulder, CO: Westview. [6]

Markovsky, Barry, David Willer, and Travis Patton. 1988. Power relations in exchange networks. *American Sociological Review*, 53(April):220–236. [4]

Marr, Phoebe. 1991. Iraq's uncertain future. *Current History* 90(552):1–42. [1]

Marris, Peter. 1990. "Witnesses, engineers or storytellers? Roles of sociologists in social policy. In H. Gans, Ed., *Sociology in America* (pp. 75–87) Newbury Park, CA: Sage. [1]

Marsden, George M. 1990. Defining American fundamentalism. In Norman J. Cohen, Ed., *The Fundamentalist Phenomenon: A View from Within, a Response from Without* (pp. 22–37). Grand Rapids, MI: Eerdmans. [14]

Marsden, Peter V. 1983. Restricted access in networks and models of power. *American Journal of Sociology*. 88(4, January): 686–715. [4]

Marsden, Peter V. 1987. Core discussion networks of Americans. *American Sociological Review*, 52(February):122–131. [4]

Marsden, Peter V. 1990a. Network diversity, substructures, and opportunities for contact. In C. Calhoun, M.W. Meyer, and W.R. Scott, Eds., *Structures of Power and Constraint: Papers in Honor of Peter M. Blau* (pp. 397–410). New York: Cambridge University Press. [4]

Marsden, Peter V. 1990b. Network data and measurement. *Annual Review of Sociology*, 16:435–463. [4]

Marshall, Eliot. 1990. The fluoride debate: One more time. *Science*, 247 (January 19):276–277. [22]

Marshall, Patrick G. 1990. Setting limits on medical care. *Congressional Quarterly's Editorial Research Reports*, 1(4):666–678. [15]

Marshall, Susan E. 1985. Ladies against women: Mobilization dilemmas of anti-feminist movements. *Social Problems*, 32(4): 348–362. [21]

Martin, Brian. 1991. *Scientific Knowledge in Controversy: The Social Dynamics of the Fluoridation Debate*. Albany: State University of New York Press. [22]

Martin, David. 1978. *A General Theory of Secularization*. New York: Harper & Row. [14]

Martin, Teresa Castro, and Larry L. Bumpass. 1989. Recent trends in marital disruption. *Demography*, 26(February):37–51. [12]

Martin, William, and Ivan Szelenyi. 1991. *The New Class Theory*. Boulder, CO: Westview. [13]

Marty, Martin E. 1984. *Pilgrims in Their Own Land: 500 Years of Religion in America*. New York: Penguin. [14]

Marty, Martin E. 1985. Transpositions: American religion in the 1980s. *Annals of the American Academy of Politics and Social Science* 480(July):11–23. [14]

Marty, Martin E. 1991. Two years that shook the world of religion. *Encyclopedia Britannica, 1991 Book of the Year*. Chicago. [14]

Marty, Martin E., and R. Scott Appleby, Eds. 1992. *Fundamentalism Observed*. Chicago: University of Chicago Press. [14]

Marx, Karl. 1852/1979. The eighteenth brumaire of Louis Bonaparte. In *Collected Works*, Vol. 11 (pp. 99–197). London: Lawrence and Wishart. [1]

Marx, Karl. 1867/1976. *Capital*, Vol. 1. B. Fowkes (Trans.). Harmondsworth, England: Penguin. [1, 9, 16, 19, 22]

Marx, Karl, and Friedrich Engels. 1848/1976. Manifesto of the Communist Party. In *Collected Works*, Vol. 6. London: Lawrence and Wishart. [16, 22]

Marx, Karl, and Friedrich Engels. 1848/1967. *Communist Manifesto*. New York: Pantheon. [9]

Masse, Michelle A., and Karen Rosenblum. 1988. Male and Female created they them: The depiction of gender in the advertising of traditional women's and men's magazines. *Women's Studies International Forum*, 11(2):127–144. [11]

Massey, Douglas S., and Nancy A. Denton, 1987. Trends in residential segregation of Blacks, Hispanics, and Asians: 1970–1980. *American Sociological Review*, 52(December):802–825. [10]

Massey, Douglas S., and Nancy A. Denton. 1992. *American Apartheid: Segregation and the Making of the American Underclass*. Cambridge, MA: Harvard University Press.

Massey, Douglas S., and Mitchell L. Eggers. 1990. The ecology of inequality: Minorities and concentration of poverty, 1970–1980. *American Journal of Sociology*, 96(5, March): 1153–1188. [10]

Maxwell, Nan L. 1990. Changing female labor force participation: Influences on income inequality and distribution. *Social Forces*, 68(4):1251–1266. [11]

Mayhew, Bruce, and T. Levinger. 1976. On the emergence of oligarchy in human interaction. *American Journal of Sociology*, 81:1017–1049. [17]

Mayr, Ernest. 1988. *Toward a New Philosophy of Biology: Observations of an Evolutionist.* Cambridge, MA: Belknap Press of Harvard University Press. [22]

Mays, Vickie M., and Susan D. Cochran. 1987. Acquired immunodeficiency syndrome and black Americans: Special psychosocial issues. *Public Health Reports*, 102(2):224–231. [15]

McAdam, Doug. 1982. *Political Process and the Development of Black Insurgency.* Chicago: University of Chicago Press. [21]

McAdam, Doug. 1986. Recruitment to high-risk activism: The case of freedom summer. *American Journal of Sociology*, 92, 1(July):64–90. [21]

McAdam, Doug. 1989. The biographical consequences of activism. *American Sociological Review*, 54(October):744–760. [21]

McAdam, Doug, John D. McCarthy, and Mayer N. Zald. 1988. Social Movements. In N.J. Smelser, Ed., *Handbook of Sociology* (pp. 695–738). Beverly Hills, CA: Sage. [21]

McCartan, Anne-Marie. 1988. Students Who Work. *Change*, 20(5):11–20. [13]

McCarthy, John D. 1977. Resource mobilization and social movements: A partial theory. *American Journal of Sociology*, 82:1212–1241. [21]

McCarthy, John D., and Mayer N. Zald. 1977. Resource mobilization and social movements: A partial theory. *American Journal of Sociology*, 82:1212–1214. [21]

McCarthy, John D., and Mayer N. Zald. 1973. *The Trend of Social Movements in America.* Morristown, NJ: General Learning Press. [21]

McCarthy, Paul. 1989. Ageless sex. *Psychology Today*, 23(March):62. [6]

McDowell, Edwin. 1982. "Silent Spring," 20 Years a Milestone. *New York Times* (September 27):C16. [21]

McGuire, Jacqueline. 1988. Gender stereotypes of parents with two-year-olds and beliefs about gender differences in behavior. *Sex Roles*, 19(3/4):233–240. [11]

McHoul, A.W. 1978. The organization of turns at formal talk in the classroom. *Language Sociology*, 7:183–213. [4]

McKeon, Nancy. 1985. Consuming passions. *New York*, (May 13):62–68. [20]

McLanahan, Sara, and Karen Booth. 1989. Mother-only families: Problems, prospect, and politics. *Journal of Marriage and the Family*, 51(August):557–580. [12]

McNeill, William H. 1982. *The Pursuit of Power.* Chicago: University of Chicago Press. [17]

Mead, George Herbert. 1934. *Mind, Self and Society.* Chicago: University of Chicago Press. [1, 4, 5]

Mead, Margaret. 1928/1968. *Coming of Age in Samoa.* New York: Morrow. [11]

Mead, Margaret. 1935/1963. *Sex and Temperament in Three Primitive Societies.* New York: William Morrow. [11]

Medalia, Nehum Z., and Otto N. Larson. 1958. Diffusion and belief in a collective delusion: The Seattle windshield pitting epidemic. *American Sociological Review*, 23:221–232. [21]

Mehan, H. 1979. *Learning Lessons.* Cambridge, MA: Harvard University Press. [4]

Menken, Jane. 1985. Age and fertility—How late can you wait? *Demography*, 22(4):469–483. [12]

Mensh, Elaine, and Harry Mensh. 1991. *The IQ Mythology: Class, Race, Gender, and Inequality.* Carbondale: Southern Illinois University Press. [13]

Merina, Victoria, and John Mitchell. 1992. Opportunists, criminals get blame and riots. *Los Angeles Times* (May 1):A1, 12. [21]

Merriam, Allen H. 1988. What does 'Third World' mean? In Jim Norwine and Alfonso Gonzalez, Eds., *The Third World: States of Mind and Being* (pp. 14–22). Boston: Unwin Hyman. [18]

Merton, Robert K. 1957. *Social Theory and Social Structures.* New York: Free Press. [10]

Merton, Robert K. 1968a. *Social Theory and Social Structure.* New York: Free Press. [1, 7, 8]

Merton, Robert K. 1968b. Social problems and social theory. In R. Merton and R. Nisbet, Eds., *Contemporary Social Problems* (p. 447). New York: Harcourt, Brace and World. [1]

Merton, Robert K. 1982. The unintended consequences of purposive social action. In *Sociological Ambivalence.* New York: Free Press. [1]

Meyrowitz, J. 1985. *No Sense of Place: The Impact of Electronic Media on Social Behavior.* New York: Oxford University Press. [3]

Michels, Robert. 1915/1949. *First Lectures in Political Science.* A. de Grazia (Trans.). Minneapolis: University of Minnesota Press. [17]

Mikulecky, Larry. 1990. National adult literacy and lifelong learning goals. *Phi Delta Kappan*, 72(4):304–309. [13]

Milgram, Stanley. 1970. The experience of living in cities. *Science*, 167(March 13):1461–1468. [20]

Miller, Brent C., and C.R. Bingham. 1989. Family configuration in relation to the sexual behavior of female adolescents. *Journal of Marriage and the Family*, 51:499–506. [6]

Miller, Brent C., and Kristin A. Moore. 1990. Adolescent sexual behavior, pregnancy and parenting. *Journal of Marriage and the Family*, 52:1025–1044. [6, 12]

Miller, Judith, and Laurie Mylroie. 1990. *Saddam Hussein and the Crisis in the Gulf.* New York: Times Books/Random House. [1]

Miller, Louisa F., and Jeanne E. Moorman. 1989. *Married-Couple Families with Children. Current Population Reports*: Special Studies, Series P-23, No. 162. Washington, DC: U.S. Government Printing Office. [12]

Mills, C. Wright. 1951. *White Collar.* New York: Oxford University Press. [16]

Mills, C. Wright. 1959/1970. *The Sociological Imagination.* New York: Pelican. [1]

Mills, C. Wright. 1959. *The Power Elite.* New York: Oxford University Press. [17]

Mills, D. Quinn. 1987. *Not Like Our Parents.* New York: Morrow. [6]

Mintz, Beth, and Michael Schwartz. 1981. Interlocking directorates and interest group formation. *American Sociological Review*, 46:851–869. [16]

Mintz, Beth, and Michael Schwartz. 1985. *The Power Structure of American Business.* Chicago: University of Chicago Press. [16]

Mishel, Lawrence, and Jacqueline Simon. 1988. *The State of Working America.* Washington, DC: Economic Policy Institute. [9]

Mishima, Yasuo. 1989. *The Mitsubishi: Its Challenge and Strategy.* Greenwich, CT: JAI Press. [8]

Moen, P. 1989. *Working Parents: Transformations in Gender Roles and Public Policies in Sweden.* Madison: University of Wisconsin Press. [11]

Moffat, Michael. 1989. *Coming of Age in New Jersey.* New Brunswick, NJ: Rutgers University Press. [6]

Moffitt, Terrie E. 1987. *Causes of Crime.* New York: Cambridge University Press. [7]

Moffitt, Terrie E., and Sarnoff A. Mednick, Eds. 1988. *Biological Contributions to Crime Causation.* Boston: Martinus Nijoff. [7]

Molm, Linda D. 1990. Structure, action, and outcomes: The dynamics of power in social exchange. *American Sociological Review*, 55(June):427–447. [4]

Monk-Turner, Elizabeth. 1988. Educational differentiation and status attainment: The community college controversy. *Sociological Focus*, 21(2):141–151. [13]

Moore, Barrington, Jr. 1978. *Injustice: The Social Bases of Obedience and Revolt.* White Plains, NY: Sharpe. [17]

Moreland, J.P., and Norman L. Geisler. 1990. *The Life and Death Debate.* New York: Greenwood. [6]

Morgan, Leslie A. 1991. Economic security of older women. In B. Hess and E. Markson, Eds., *Growing Old in America*, 4th ed. New Brunswick, NJ: Transaction. [6]

Morgan, W.B. 1988. Agrarian structure. In Michael Pacione, Ed., *The Geography of the Third World: Progress and Prospect* (pp. 77–113). London: Routledge. [18]

Morganthau, Tom, and Mary Hager. 1992. Cutting through the gobbledygook. *Newsweek* (February 3):24–25. [15]

Morgenthau, Hans J., and Kenneth W. Thompson. 1985. *Politics Among Nations*, 6th rev. ed. New York: Knopf. [17]

Morison, Samuel Eliot. 1974. *The European Discovery of America: The Southern Voyages, 1492–1616*. New York: Oxford University Press. [22]

Morowska, Eva. 1991. Small town, small place: Transformation of the religious life in the Jewish community of Johnstown, Pennsylvania (1920–1940). *Comparative Social Research*, 13:127–178. [14]

Morris, Aldon D. 1984. *The Origins of the Civil Rights Movement: Black Communities Organizing for Change*. New York: Free Press. [21]

Morris, Robert, and Scott Bass. 1988. A new class in America. *Social Policy* (Spring):38–43. [6]

Morrisroe, Patricia. 1985. The new class. *New York* (May 13):34–39. [20]

Mortenson, Thomas G. 1991. Equity of Higher Educational Opportunity for Women, Black, Hispanic, and Low Income Students. ACT Student Financial Aid Research Report Series (January). [13]

Mortimer, Jeylan T., and Roberta G. Simmons. 1978. Adult socialization. *Annual Review of Sociology*, 4:421–454. [5]

Moskos, Charles. 1990. Army women. *The Atlantic Monthly* (August):71–78. [11]

Moynihan, Daniel P. 1986. *Family and Nation*. San Diego: Harcourt Brace Jovanovich. [1]

Mueller, Carol, and Thomas Dimieri. 1982. The structure of belief systems among contending ERA activists. *Social Forces*, 60:657–675. [21]

Murdock, George Peter. 1949. *Social Structure*. New York: Macmillan. [12]

Murray, Charles, 1984. *Losing Ground: American Social Policy*, 1950–80. New York: Basic Books. [1]

Musgrove, Philip. 1987. The economic crisis and its impact on health and health care in Latin America and the Caribbean. *International Journal of Health Services*, 17(3):411–441. [15]

Mydans, Seth. 1991. For These Americans, Mexico Not Left Behind. *New York Times* (June 30):A12. [3]

Myers, George C. 1990. Demography of aging. In R. Binstock and L. George, Eds., *Aging and the Social Sciences*, 3d ed. San Diego: Academic Press. [6]

Myrdal, Gunnar. 1944. *An American Dilemma*. New York: Harper & Row. [10]

National Advisory Commission on Civil Disorders. 1968. *Report of the National Advisory Commission on Civil Disorders (Kerner Commission)*. New York: Bantam. [21]

National Assessment of Educational Progress (NAEP). 1979. *Changes in Mathematical Achievement*, 1973–1978. Denver: Educational Commission of the States. [13]

National Center for Health Statistics. 1988. *Monthly Vital Statistics Report: Births, Marriages, Divorces and Deaths for 1987*, 36 (March). [12]

National Commission on Excellence in Education. 1983. *A Nation at Risk*. Washington, DC: U.S. Government Printing Office. [13]

National Committee on Pay Equity. 1987. *Briefing on the Wage Gap*. Washington, DC: National Committee on Pay Equity. [11]

National Educational Association (NEA). 1990. Academic Tracking. Report of the NEA's Executive Subcommittee on Tracking, (June). [13]

National Housing Task Force. 1988. *A Decent Place to Live*. Washington, DC: National Housing Task Force. [9]

National Research Council. 1989. *A Common Destiny: Blacks and American Society*. Gerald Davis Jaynes and Robin M. Williams, Jr., Eds., Washington, DC: National Academy Press. [10]

National Research Council. 1990. *AIDS: The Second Decade*. Washington, DC: National Academy Press. [15]

Natriello, Gary, Aaron M. Pallas, and Edward L. McDill. 1986. Taking stock: Renewing our research agenda on the causes and consequences of dropping out. *Teachers College Review*, 87(3):430–440. [13]

Neckerman, Kathryn M., and Joleen Kirschenman. 1990. Statistical discrimination and inner-city workers: An investigation of employers' hiring decisions. Paper presented at the Annual Meeting of the American Sociological Association, Washington, DC, August 11–15. [9]

Nee, Victor, and David Stark, Eds. 1989. *Remaking the Economic Institutions of Socialism: China and Eastern Europe*. Stanford, CA: Stanford University Press. [2]

Neff, Robert. 1990. Mighty Mitsubishi is on the move. *Business Week* (September 24):98–101. [8]

Neill, D. Monty, and Noe J. Medina. 1989. Standardized testing: Harmful to educational health. *Phi Delta Kappan*, 70:688–697. [13]

Nelkin, Dorothy, Ed. 1984. *Controversy: Politics of Technical Decision*, 2d ed. Beverly Hills, CA. Sage. [22]

Neugarten, Bernice L., and Dail A. Neugarten, 1987. The changing meanings of age. *Psychology Today*, 21(5):29–33. [6]

Neuman, W. Russell. 1986. *The Paradox of Mass Politics: Knowledge and Opinion in the American Electorate*. Cambridge, MA: Harvard University Press. [17]

Newcomer, Susan F., and J.R. Udry. 1984. Parental marital status effects on adolescent sexual behavior. *Journal of Marriage and the Family*, 49:235–240. [6]

Newhouse, John. 1991. The Diplomatic round: Misreadings. *New Yorker* (February 18):72–78. [1]

Newman, Catherine. 1988. *Falling from Grace. The Experience of Downward Mobility in the American Middle Class*. New York: Free Press. [9, 16]

Newman, Catherine. 1991. In A. Wolfe, Ed., *America at Century's End*. Berkeley: University of California Press. [9]

Newman, Dorothy K., Nancy J. Amidei, Betty L. Cater, Dawn Day, William J. Kruvant, and Jack S. Russell. 1978. *Protest, Politics, and Prosperity: Black Americans and White Institutions, 1940–1975*. New York: Pantheon Books. [21]

N'galy, Bosenge, and Robert Ryder. 1988. Epidemiology of HIV infection in Africa. *Journal of Acquired Immune Deficiency Syndromes*, 1:551–558. [15]

Nisbert, Robert A. 1966. *Social Change in History*. London: Heinemann. [22]

Nisbet, Robert A. 1980. *History of the Idea of Progress*. New York: Basic Books. [22]

Nisbet, Robert, and Robert G. Perrin. 1977. *The Social Bond*, 2d ed. New York: Knopf. [1]

Nullis, Claire. 1992. One million more AIDS victims: Report blames heterosexuals. *Providence Journal* (February 13):A-1, A-13. [15]

Nulty, Peter. 1982. The bar-coding of America. *Fortune*, 106(December 27):98–101. [22]

Oakes, Jeannie. 1990. *Multiplying Inequalities: The Effects of Race, Social Class, and Tracking on Opportunities to Learn Mathematics and Science*. Santa Monica, CA: RAND Corp. [13]

Oakley, Ann. 1972. *Sex, Gender and Society*. London: Temple Smith. [11]

Oates, R. Kim. 1991. Child Physical Abuse. In Robert T. Ammerman and Michael Gersen, Eds., *Case Studies in Family Violence* (pp. 113–134). New York: Plenum Press. [12]

Oberdorfer, Don. 1991. Mixed signals in the Middle East. *Washington Post Magazine* (March 17):19–41. [1]

O'Connor, James. 1973. *The Fiscal Crisis of the State*. New York: St. Martin's Press. [17]

Offe, Claus. 1984. *Contradictions of the Welfare State*. J. Keane, Ed. Cambridge, MA: MIT Press. [17]

Offe, Claus. 1985. *Disorganized Capitalism: Contemporary Transformations of Work and Politics*. J. Keane (Trans.). Cambridge, MA: MIT Press. [17]

O'Hare, William P., Kenneth M. Pollard, Taynia L. Mann, Mary M. Kent. 1991. African Americans in the 1990s. *Population Bulletin*, 46(1, July). [10]

Oka, Takashi. 1991. The anomalies of China's one-child policy. *Christian Science Monitor* (January 11):18. [19]

Okun, Lewis. 1986. *Woman Abuse*. Albany: State University of New York Press. [12]

Ole Saitoti, Tepilit, and Carol Beckwith. 1980. *Masai*. New York: Abrams. [6]

Oliver, Melvin L., and Thomas M. Shapiro. 1990. Wealth of a nation: a reassessment of asset inequality in America shows at least one third of households are asset-poor. *American Journal of Economics and Sociology*, 49(2, April):129–151. [9]

Oliver, Pamela. 1984. "If you don't do it, nobody will": Active and token contributors to local collective action. *American Sociological Review*, 49:601–610. [4]

O'Rand, Angela, and Margaret Krecker. 1990. Concepts of the life cycle. *Annual Review of Sociology*, 16:241–262. [6]

Orfield, Gary, 1983. *Public School Desegregation in the United States, 1968–1980*. Washington, DC: Joint Center for Political Studies. [13]

Organization for Economic Cooperation and Development (OECD). 1990. *OECD Economic Surveys, USA, 1989/1990*. Paris: OECD. [16]

Orwell, George. 1933/1972. *Down and Out in Paris and London*. San Diego: Harcourt Brace Jovanovich. [4]

O'Shaughnessy, Nicholas J. 1990. *The Phenomenon of Political Marketing*. New York: St. Martin's Press. [17]

Osofsky, Gilbert. 1982. *The Making of a Ghetto*. New York: Harper & Row. [20]

Ott, E. Marlies. 1989. Effects of the male–female ratio at work: Policewomen and male nurses. *Psychology of Women Quarterly*, 13:41–57. [11]

Ouchi, William G. 1981. *Theory Z*. Reading, MA: Addison-Wesley. [8]

Oxford Analytica. 1986. *America in Perspective: Major Trends in the United States Through the 1990s*. Boston: Houghton Mifflin. [3, 19]

Palen, J. John. 1987. *The Urban World*. New York: McGraw-Hill. [20]

Paludi, Michele A., and Dominic F. Gullo. 1986. The effect of sex labels on adults' knowledge of infant development. *Sex Roles*, 16(1/2):19–30. [11]

Paradiso, Louis V., and Shauvan M. Wall. 1986. Children's perceptions of male and female principals and teachers. *Sex Roles*, 14(1/2):1–7. [11]

Park, Robert E., Ernest W. Burgess, and Roderick D. McKenzie, Eds. 1925. *The City*. Chicago: University of Chicago Press. [10, 20]

Parkin, Frank. 1976. *Marxism and Class Theory: A Bourgeois Critique*. New York: Columbia University Press. [9]

Parkinson, C. Northcote. 1957. *Parkinson's Law*. Boston: Houghton Mifflin. [8]

Parsons, Talcott. 1951. *The Social System*. Glencoe, IL: Free Press. [1]

Parsons, Talcott. 1959. The social class as a social system: Some of its functions in American society. *Harvard Educational Review*, 29(Fall):297–318. [5]

Parsons, Talcott. 1960. *Structure and Process in Modern Societies*. New York: Free Press. [1, 17]

Patterson, Gerald R. 1982. *Coercive Family Process*. Eugene, OR: Castalia Press. [12]

Pear, Robert. 1991. Hungry children put at 5.5 million. *New York Times* (March 27):A18. [15]

Pebley, Anne R., and David E. Bloom. 1982. Childless Americans. *American Demographics*, 4 (January):18–21. [12]

Peretz, Don. 1990. *The Middle East Today*, 4th ed. New York: Praeger. [1]

Pescosolido, Bernice A., and Robert Mendelsohn. 1986. Social causation or social construction of suicide? An investigation into the social organization of official rates. *American Sociological Review*, 51:80–101. [2]

Peter, Laurence F., and Raymond Hull. 1969. *The Peter Principle*. New York: William Morrow. [8]

Peterson, Richard A. 1979. Revitalizing the culture concept. *Annual Review of Sociology*, 5:137–166. [3]

Petersen, William. 1975. *Population*, 3d ed. New York: Macmillan. [19]

Petras, Kathryn, and Ross Petras. 1989. *The Only Job Hunting Guide You'll Ever Need*. New York: Poseidon Press. [4]

Pfaff, William. 1991. Islam and the West. *New Yorker* (January 28):83–88. [1]

Phillips, David P. 1974. The influence of suggestion on suicide: Substantive and theoretical implications of the Werther effect. *American Sociological Review*, 39:340–354. [2]

Phillips, David P. 1986. The found experiment: A new technique for assessing the impact of mass media violence on real-world aggressive behavior. In G. Comstock, Ed., *Public Communication and Behavior*, Vol. 1. San Diego: Academic Press. [2]

Phillips, David P., and Lundie L. Carstensen. 1986. Clustering of teenage suicides after television and news stories about suicide. *New England Journal of Medicine*, 315(September 11):685–689. [2]

Phillips, David, and Lundie Carstensen. 1988. The effect of suicide stories on various demographic groups, 1968–1985. *Suicide and Life-Threatening Behavior*, 18(1):100–114. [2]

Phillips, Kevin. 1991. *The Politics of Rich and Poor*. New York: Simon and Schuster. [9]

Pill, Cynthia J. 1990. Stepfamilies: Redefining the family. *Family Relations*, 36:186–193. [12]

Pillemer, Karl A. 1986. Risk factors in elder abuse: Results from a case-control study. In K.A. Pillemer and R.S. Wolf, Eds., *Elder Abuse: Conflict in the Family* (pp. 239–263). Dover, MA: Auburn House. [12]

Pinchbeck, Ivy. 1930. *Women and the Industrial Revolution, 1750–1850*. London: Cass. [11]

Pittman, Karen. 1993. Teenage pregnancy. In Craig Calhoun and G. Ritzer, *Social Problems*. New York: McGraw-Hill.

Piven, F.F., and R. Cloward. 1979. *Poor People's Movements*. New York: Vintage. [17, 21]

Plog, Fred, Clifford J. Jolly, and Daniel G. Bates. 1976. *Anthropology: Decisions, Adaptation, and Evolution*. New York: Knopf. [22]

Podus, Deborah. 1992. Churches, tax exemption, and the social organization of religion. *Comparative Social Research*, 13:179–202. [14]

Pomper, Gerald. 1980. *Party Renewal in America*. New York: Praeger. [17]

Poponoe, David. 1990. Family decline in America. In D. Blankenhorn, S. Bayme, J.B. Elshtain, Eds., *Rebuilding the Nest: A New Commitment to the American Family*, (Chapter 3, pp. 39–51). Milwaukee: Family Service America. [12]

Portes, Alejandro, and Rubén G. Rumbaut. 1990. *Immigrant America: A Portrait*. Berkeley: University of California Press. [5]

Postman, Neil. 1982. *The Disappearance of Childhood*. New York: Delacorte. [6]

Postman, Neil. 1986. *Amusing Ourselves to Death*. New York: Penguin. [3]

Poulantzas, Nicos. 1974. *Political Power and Social Classes*. London: New Left Books. [22]

Powell, Michael J. 1985. Developments in the regulations of lawyers: Competing segments, and market, client, and government controls. *Social Forces*, 64 (2):281–305. [16]

Preston, Samuel. 1984. Children and the elderly: Divergent paths for America's dependents. *Demography*, 21 (4):435–457. [9]

Preston, Samuel, and John McDonald. 1979. The incidence of divorce within cohorts of American marriages contracted since the Civil War. *Demography*, 16 (February):1–26. [12]

Price, David. 1986. *Bringing Back the Parties*. Washington, DC: Congressional Quarterly. [17]

Prokesch, Steven. 1991. Edges fray on Volvo's brave new humanistic world. *New York Times* (July 7):5. [8]

Przeworski, Adam. 1985. *Capitalism and Social Democracy*. New York: Cambridge University Press. [17]

Public Agenda Foundation. 1990. *Regaining the Competitive Edge: Are We Up to the Job?* Booklet prepared for National Issues Forums Institute. Dubuque, IO: Kendall/Hunt Publishing. [13, 16]

Public Agenda Foundation. 1992. *The Health Care Crisis: Containing Costs, Expanding Coverage*. New York: McGraw-Hill. [15]

Public Opinion. 1985. October–November. [17]

Public Opinion. 1988. September–October. [17]

Quadagno, Jill. 1980. *Aging, the Individual, and Society*. New York: St. Martin's Press. [12]

Quadagno, Jill. 1986. Aging. In G. Ritzer, Ed., *Social Problems*, 2d ed. New York: Random House. [6]

Quindlen, Anna. 1991. Women Warriors. *New York Times* (February 3):E19. [11]

Ragin, Charles. 1987. *Beyond Qualitative and Quantitative Approaches: Methods of Comparative Sociology*. Berkeley: University of California Press. [2]

Ragin, Charles, and David Zaret. 1983. "Theory and Methods in Comparative Research: Two Strategies." *Social Forces* 61:731–754. [22]

Ravitch, Diane, and Chester E. Finn, Jr. 1987. *What Do Our 17-Year-Olds Know? A Report on the First National Assessment of History and Literature*. New York: Harper & Row. [13]

Reich, Robert B. 1991. *The Work of Nations: Preparing Ourselves for 21st Century Capitalism*. New York: Knopf. [16]

Reinhold, Robert. 1991. Class struggle. *New York Times Magazine* (September 29):26–29, 46–52. [3]

Reiter, Laura. 1989. Sexual orientation, sexual identity, and the question of choice. *Clinical Social Work Journal*, 17(2). [11]

Relman, Arnold S. 1980. The new medical-industrial complex. *New England Journal of Medicine*, 303:963–970. [15]

Remick, Helen, and Ronnie Steinberg. 1984. Technical possibilities and political realities: Concluding remarks. In Helen Remick, Ed., *Comparable Worth and Wage Discrimination*. Philadelphia: Temple University Press. [11]

Remnick, David. 1991. *Providence Journal* (August 5):1.

Rendon, Laura L., and Terri B. Mathews. 1989. Success of community college students: Current issues. *Educational and Urban Society*, 21(3):312–327. [13]

Repetti, Rena L. 1984. Determinants of children's sex stereotyping: Parental sex-role traits and television viewing. *Personality and Social Psychology Bulletin*, 10:456–468. [11]

Report on Minorities in Higher Education. 1988. Hearing before the Committee on Education and Labor, House of Representatives, September 13. Serial No. 100-92. Washington, DC: U.S. Government Printing Office. [10]

Rhode, Deborah L. 1990. Gender equality and employment policy. In Sara E. Rix, Ed., *The American Woman, 1990–1991: A Status Report* (pp. 170–200), Women's Research & Education Institute. New York: Norton. [11]

Rich, Adrienne. 1980. Compulsory heterosexuality and lesbian existence. In C.R. Stimson and E.S. Person, Eds., *Women, Sex and Sexuality* (pp. 62–91). Chicago: University of Chicago Press. [11]

Rich, Sharon Lee, and Ariel Phillips, Eds. 1985. *Women's Experience, and Education*. Cambridge, MA: Harvard Education Review. [13]

Riche, Martha Farnsworth. 1990. The boomerang age. *American Demographics*, 12:24–27. [6]

Richmond-Abbott, Marie. 1992. *Masculine and Feminine: Gender Roles Over the Life Cycle*. New York: McGraw-Hill. [11]

Ridgeway, Celia L., Joseph Berger, and LeRoy Smith. 1985. Nonverbal cues and status: An expectation status approach. *American Journal of Sociology*, 90(5):955–978. [4]

Rieff, David. 1991. *Los Angeles: Capital of the Third World*. New York: Simon & Schuster. [20]

Riesman, David, with Nathan Glazer and Reuel Denney. 1951. *The Lonely Crowd*. New Haven: Yale University Press. [3, 17]

Riley, John W., Jr. 1983. Dying and the meaning of death: Sociological inquiries. *Annual Review of Sociology*, 9:191–216. [6]

Riley, Matilda W. 1987. On the significance of age in sociology. *American Sociological Review*, 52(February):1–14. [6]

Rindfuss, Ronald R., S. Phillip Morgan, and G. Swicegood. 1988. *First Births in America: Changes in the Timing of Parenthood*. Berkeley: University of California Press. [19]

Rist, Ray C. 1970. Student social class and teacher expectations: The self-fulfilling prophecy in ghetto education. *Harvard Educational Review*, 40. [13]

Rix, Sara E., Ed. 1990. *The American Woman, 1990–1991: A Status Report* (Women's Research & Education Institute). New York: Norton. [11]

Roberts, Paul Craig, and Karen LaFollette. 1990. *Meltdown: Inside the Soviet Economy*. Washington, DC: Cato Institute. [16]

Robey, Bryant. 1989. Two hundred years and counting: The 1990 census. *Population Bulletin*, 44 (1, April):3–39. [19]

Robinson, Ann. 1990. Cooperation or exploitation? The argument against cooperative learning for talented students. *Journal for the Education of the Gifted* (Fall). [13]

Roeder, Edward, Ed. 1986. *PACs Americana: The Directory of Political Action Committees and Their Interests*, 2d ed. Washington, DC: Sunshine Services. [17]

Roethlisberger, F.J., and William J. Dickson (with H.A. Wright). 1939/1961. *Management and the Worker*. Cambridge, MA: Harvard University Press. [2, 8]

Rogers, Everett. 1979. Network analysis of the diffusion of innovations. In P.W. Holland and S. Leinhardt, Eds., *Perspectives on Social Network Research* (pp. 137–164). New York: Academic Press. [4]

Rogers, E.M. 1986. *Communications Technology: The New Media in Society*. New York: Free Press [3]

Roha, Ronaleen R. 1992. Giving back: Helping victims of this year's many disasters. *Kiplinger Personal Finance Magazine* (December):130. [18]

Ropp, Theodore. 1959. *War in the Modern World*. Durham, NC: Duke University Press. [8]

Rose, Arnold M. 1967. *The Power Structure*. New York: Oxford University Press. [17, 21]

Rose, Gerry B. 1982. *Outbreaks*. New York: Free Press. [21]

Rosen, B., and T. Jerdee. 1978. Perceived sex differences in managerially relevant characteristics. *Sex Roles*, 4:837–843. [11]

Rosen, Jay. 1991. The Trashing of Our Public Time. *The Raleigh (NC) News and Observer* (April 4):17A. [3]

Rosenbaum, James E., and Takehiko Kariya. 1989. From high school to work: Market and institutional mechanisms in Japan. *American Journal of Sociology*, 94(6):1334–1365. [4]

Rosenbaum, James E., Takehiko Kariya, Rick Settersten, and Tony Maier. 1991. Market and network theories of the transition from high school to work: Their application to industrialized societies. *Annual Review of Sociology*, 16:263–299. [4]

Rosenfeld, Anne, and Elizabeth Stark. 1987. The prime of our lives. *Psychology Today* (May):62–72. [6]

Rosnow, Ralph L., and Gary Alan Fine. 1976. *Rumor and Gossip: The Social Psychology of Hearsay*. New York: Elsevier. [21]

Rossi, Peter H. 1989. *Down and Out in America: The Origins of Homelessness*. Chicago: University of Chicago Press. [9]

Rostow, Walt Whitman. 1952. *The Process of Economic Growth*. New York: Norton. [18]

Rostow, Walt Whitman. 1980. *The World Economy: History and Prospect*. Austin: University of Texas Press. [18]

Rostow, Walt Whitman. 1990. *The Stages of Economic Growth: A Noncommunist Manifesto*, 3d ed. New York: Cambridge University Press. [18]

Roth, Guenther, and Wolfgang Schluchter. 1979. *Max Weber's Theory of History*. Berkeley: University of California Press. [1]

Rothbart, M.K. (1986). Longitudinal observation of infant temperament. *Developmental Psychology*, 22(3):356–365. [5]

Rothschild, N. 1984. Small group affiliation as a mediating factor in the cultivation process. In G. Melischek, K.E. Rosengren, and J. Stappers, Eds., *Cultural Indicators: An International Symposium*. Vienna: Osterreichischen Akademie der Wissenschaften. [11]

Rowdon, Maurice. 1970. *The Silver Age of Venice*. New York: Praeger. [20]

Roy, Donald F. 1960. "Banana time": Job satisfaction and informal interaction. *Human Organization*, 18:156–168. [4]

Rubenstein, Richard E. 1987. *Alchemist of Revolution: Terrorism in the Modern World*. New York: Basic Books. [17]

Rubin, Deborah Kaplan. 1984. Fifth annual salary survey. *Working Woman* (January):59–63. [11]

Rubin, J.Z., F.J. Provenzano, and Z. Luria. 1974. The eye of the beholder: Parents' views on sex and newborns. *American Journal of Orthopsychiatry*, 44:512–519. [11]

Rubin, Lillian Breslow. 1976. *Worlds of Pain: Life in the Working-Class Family*. New York: Basic Books. [5]

Ruckelshaus, William D. 1989. Toward a sustainable world. *Scientific American* (September):166–174. [19]

Rudé, George. 1964. *The Crowd in History: A Study of Popular Disturbances in France and England, 1730–1848*. New York: Wiley. [21]

Rudel, Thomas K. 1989. Population, development, and tropical deforestation: A Cross-national Study. *Rural Sociology*, 54(3):327–338. [19]

Rueschemeyer, Dietrich. 1986. *Power and the Division of Labor*. Stanford, CA: Stanford University Press. [17]

Ruether, Rosemary Radford. 1992. A world on fire with faith. *New York Times Book Review* (January 26):10–11. [14]

Ruggles, Patricia. 1990. The poverty line—Too low for the 1990s. *New York Times* (April 26):A31. [9]

Rumbaut, Rubén G. 1991. Passages to America: Perspectives on the new immigration. In Alan Wolfe, Ed., *America at Century's End* (pp. 208–244). Berkeley: University of California Press. [10]

Rupp, Leila J., and Verta Taylor. 1987. *Survival in the Doldrums: The American Women's Rights Movement, 1945 to the 1960s*. New York: Oxford University Press. [21]

Russell, Charles H. 1989. *Good News About Aging*. New York: Wiley. [6]

Russell, Cheryl. 1987. *100 Predictions for the Baby Boom*. New York: Plenum Press. [6]

Russell, George. 1986a. The fall of a Wall Street superstar. *Time* (November 24):71–72. [7]

Russell, George. 1986b. Going after the crooks. *Time* (December 1):48–56. [7]

Russell, Louise B., and Carrie Lynn Manning. 1989. The effect of prospective payment on Medicare expenditures. *New England Journal of Medicine*, 320(7):439–444. [15]

Rutter, Michael, et al. 1979. *Fifteen Thousand Hours*. Cambridge, MA: Harvard University Press. [13]

Ryan, John C. 1991. Plywood vs. People in Sarawak. *World Watch*, 4 (1, January-February):8–9. [19]

Ryan, William. 1976. *Blaming the Victim*, rev. ed. New York: Vintage Books. [9]

Sabel, Charles. 1982. *Work and Politics: The Division of Labor in Industry*. Cambridge, England: Cambridge University Press. [16]

Sahlins, Marshall D. 1958. *Social Stratification in Polynesia*. Seattle: University of Washington Press. [9]

Sale, Kirkpatrick. 1990a. *The Conquest of Paradise: Christopher Columbus and the Columbian Legacy*. New York: Knopf. [22]

Sale, Kirkpatrick. 1990b. What Columbus Discovered. *Nation*, 251(October 22):444–446. [22]

Salmore, Stephen A., and Barbara G. Salmore. 1985. *Candidates, Parties, and Campaigns: Electoral Policies in America*. Washington, DC: Congressional Quarterly Press. [17]

Samuelson, Robert J. 1992. The value of college. *Newsweek* (August 31):75. [13]

Sanoff, Alvin P. 1990. The myths of Columbus. *U.S. News and World Report*, 109 (October 8):74. [22]

Sapiro, Virginia. 1991. Feminism: A generation later. *Annals of the American Academy of Political and Social Science*, 515 (May):10–22. [21]

Schein, Edgar H. 1978. *Career Dynamics: Matching Individual and Organizational Needs*. Reading, MA: Addison-Wesley. [5]

Schell, Jonathan. 1982. *The Fate of the Earth*. New York: Knopf. [17]

Schell, O. 1989. *Discos and Democracy: China in the Throes of Reform*. New York: Anchor. [3]

Scherer, Klaus R., and Howard Giles, Eds. 1979. *Social Markers in Speech*. New York: Cambridge University Press. [3]

Schlesinger, Arthur, Jr. 1979. Crisis of the party system. *Wall Street Journal* (May 10):22. [17]

Schott, K. 1983. The rise of Keynesian economics. In D. Held, J. Anderson, B. Gieben, S. Hall, L. Harris, P. Lewis, N. Parker, and B. Turok, Eds., *States and Society* (pp. 338–362). New York: New York University Press. [17]

Schruger, Scott. 1990. Who are the homeless? *Washington Monthly* (March):38–49. [9]

Schudson, Michael. 1984. *Advertising: The Uneasy Persuasion*. New York: Basic Books. [3]

Schuman, Howard, and Stanley Presser. 1981. *Questions and Answers in Attitude Surveys*. New York: Academic Press. [2]

Schumpeter, Joseph A. 1942. *Capitalism, Socialism, and Democracy*. New York: Harper & Row. [17]

Schutz, Alfred, and Thomas Luckmann. 1973. *Structures of the Life World.* London: Heinemann Educational Books. [1, 4]

Schwartz, Gail Garfield, and William Neikirk. 1983. *The Work Revolution.* New York: Rawson Associates. [16]

Schwartz, Joe. 1991. The baby boom talks to the dead. *American Demographics* (April):14. [6]

Schwebel, Andrew I., Mark A. Fine, Maureen A. Renner. 1991. A study of perceptions of the stepparent role. *Journal of Family Issues,* 12(1, March):43–57. [12]

Schwirian, Kent P. 1983. Models of neighborhood change. *Annual Review of Sociology,* 9:83–102. [20]

Scott, James C. 1976. *The Moral Economy of the Peasant.* New Haven, CT: Yale University Press. [18]

Scott, James C. 1985. *Weapons of the Weak.* New Haven, CT: Yale University Press. [10]

Scott, James C. 1987. Resistance without protest and without organization. *Comparative Studies in Society and History,* 29. [10]

Scott, Janny, and Victor Zonana. 1990. AIDS conference ends on note of confidence. *Los Angeles Times* (June 25):A1. [15]

Scott, Joan W. 1986. Gender: A useful category of historical analysis. *American Historical Review,* 91(5):1053–1075. [11]

Scott, Peter Dale, and Marshall, Jonathan. 1991. *Cocaine Politics: Drugs, Armies, and the CIA in Central America.* Berkeley: University of California Press. [7]

Scott, W. Richard. 1981. *Organizations: Rational, Natural, and Open Systems.* Englewood Cliffs, NJ: Prentice Hall. [8]

Secord, Paul F., and Carl W. Backman. 1974. *Social Psychology,* 2d ed. New York: McGraw-Hill. [8]

Segal, Troy. 1992. Saving our schools. *Business Week* (September 14):70–78. [13]

Segers, Mary C., Ed. 1990. *Church Polity and American Politics: Issues in Contemporary American Catholicism.* New York: Garland. [14]

Seligman, Martin E.P. 1988. Boomer blues. *Psychology Today,* 22(October):55. [6]

Selznick, Philip. 1949. *TVA and the Grass Roots: A Study of Politics and Organizations.* Berkeley: University of California Press. [8]

Sen, Amartya. 1990. *Disasters.* Cambridge, England: Cambridge University Press. [18]

Sethuraman, S.V. 1987. The Informal Sector and the Urban Poor in the Third World. Paper presented to the conference "Universitat und Dritte Welt," University of Giessen, Giessen, Germany. [18]

Sewell, William H., and Robert M. Hauser. 1976. Causes and consequences of higher education: Models of the status attainment process. In W.H. Sewell and R.M. Hauser, Eds., *Schooling and Achievement in American Society.* New York: Academic Press. [9]

Shanin, Teodor. 1990. *Defining Peasants.* Oxford, England: Basil Blackwell. [18]

Shank, Susan E., and Patricia M. Getz. 1986. Employment and unemployment: Developments in 1985. *Monthly Labor Review,* 109 (2):3–12. [16]

Shapiro, Walter. 1991. The birth and—maybe—death of yuppiedom. *Time* (April 8):65. [6]

Shaw, Clifford R. 1930. *The Jack-Roller.* Chicago: University of Chicago Press. [7]

Shaw, Clifford R., and Henry D. McKay. 1969. *Juvenile Delinquency and Urban Areas.* Chicago: University of Chicago Press. [7]

Shenon, Philip. 1983. What's new with dual-career couples. *New York Times* (March 6):F29. [12]

Sheppard, Nathaniel, Jr. 1981. Schools ending chapter in U.S. desegregation saga. *New York Times* (June 10):A28. [13]

Sherman, Barry L., and Joseph R. Dominick. 1986. Violence and sex in music videos: TV and rock and roll. *Journal of Communication,* 36 (Winter):79–93. [2]

Sherman, Julia. 1978. *Sex-Related Cognitive Differences.* Springfield, IL: Charles C. Thomas. [11]

Shields, James J., Jr., Ed. 1989. *Japanese Schooling: Patterns of Socialization, Equality, and Political Control.* University Park: Pennsylvania State University Press. [5]

Shilts, Randy. 1987. *And the Band Played On: Politics, People, and the AIDS Epidemic.* New York: Penguin. [15]

Shmelev, N., and V. Popov. 1989. *The Turning Point: Revitalizing the Soviet Economy.* M.A. Brady (Trans.). New York: Doubleday. [16]

Shorter, Edward. 1975. *The Making of the Modern Family.* New York: Basic Books. [6]

Siegel, Larry J., Ed. 1990. *American Justice: Research of the National Institute of Justice.* St. Paul, MN: West Publishing. [7]

Siegel, Karolynn, Frances Mesagno, Jin-Yi Chen, and Grace Christ. 1989. Factors distinguishing homosexual males practicing risky and safer sex. *Social Science and Medicine,* 28(6):561–569. [15]

Signorielli, Nancy. 1989. Television and conceptions about sex roles: Maintaining conventionality and the status quo. *Sex Roles,* 21 (5/6):341–360. [11]

Silberman, Charles E. 1980. *Criminal Violence, Criminal Justice.* New York: Vintage. [7]

Simmel, Georg. 1902–1903/1950. The metropolis and mental life. In Kurt Wolff, Ed. and Trans., *The Sociology of George Simmel* (pp. 409–424). New York: Free Press. [20]

Simmons, Cyril. 1990. *Growing Up and Going to School in Japan: Traditions and Trends.* Bristol, PA: Open University Press. [13]

Simon, Julian L. 1990. *Population Matters.* New Brunswick: Transaction. [22]

Simpson, Richard L. 1985. Social control of occupations and Work. *Annual Review of Sociology,* 11:415–436. [16]

Sinding, Steven W., and Sheldon J. Segal. 1991. Birth rate news. *New York Times* (December 19):A19. [19]

Singer, Dorothy G. 1983. A time to reexamine the role of television in our lives. *American Psychologist,* 38:815–816. [5]

Singer, Jerome L., and Dorothy G. Singer. 1981. *Television, Imagination, and Aggression: A Study of Preschoolers.* Hillsdale, NJ: Erlbaum. [5]

Singh, Jitendra V., and Charles J. Lumsden. 1990. Theory and Research in Organizational Ecology. *Annual Review of Sociology,* 16:161–196. [8]

Sjoberg, Gideon. 1960. *The Preindustrial City: Past and Present.* Peoria, IL: Free Press. [20]

Skocpol, Theda. 1979. *States and Social Revolutions: A Comparative Analysis of France, Russia, and China.* New York: Cambridge University Press. [2, 21]

Skocpol, Theda. 1985. Bringing the state back in: Strategies of analysis in current research. In P.B. Evans, D. Rueschemeyer, and T. Skocpol, Eds., *Bringing the State Back In* (pp. 3–43). New York: Cambridge University Press. [17]

Skolnick, Jerome H., and David H. Bayley. 1986. *The New Blue Line: Police Innovation in Six American Cities.* New York: Free Press. [7]

Slater, Philip E. 1976. *The Pursuit of Loneliness: American Culture at the Breaking Point,* rev. ed. Boston: Beacon Press. [3]

Slavin, Robert E. 1990. Achievement effects of ability grouping in secondary schools: A best-evidence synthesis. *Review of Educational Research,* 60 (3):471–499. [13]

Smelser, Neil J. 1963. *Theory of Collective Behavior.* New York: Free Press. [21]

Smidt, Corwin. 1980. Civil religious orientations among elementary school children. *Sociological Analysis,* 41:24–40. [14]

Smil, Vacal. 1984. *The Bad Earth: Environmental Degradation in China.* Armonk, NY: Sharpe. [19]

Smil, Vacal. 1989. China's environmental morass. *Current History* (September):257–277. [19]

Smil, Vacal. 1990. Feeding China's people. *Current History* (September):257–277. [19]

Smith, Adam. 1776/1976. *The Wealth of Nations.* Chicago: University of Chicago Press. [1, 16]

Smith, M.G. 1974. Pre-industrial stratification systems. In *Corporations and Society*. London: Duckworth. [9]

Smith, M.G. 1991. Pluralism and social stratification. In Selwyn Ryan, Ed., *Social and Occupational Stratification in Contemporary Trinidad and Tobago* (pp. 3–35). St. Augustine, Trinidad: Institute of Social and Economic Research, University of the West Indies. [9]

Smith, Michael Peter. 1988. *City, State and Market: The Political Economy of Urban Society*. New York: Basil Blackwell. [20]

Smith, Michael Peter, and Joe R. Feagin, Eds. 1987. *The Capitalist City: Global Restructuring and Community Politics*. New York: Basil Blackwell. [20]

Smolak, L. 1986. *Infancy*. Englewood Cliffs, NJ: Prentice Hall. [5]

Snow, David A., Susan G. Baker, Leon Anderson, and Michael Martin. 1986. The myth of pervasive mental illness among the homeless. *Social Problems*, 33 (5):45. [15]

Snow, David A., Louis A. Zurcher, Jr., and Robert Peters. 1981. Victory celebrations as theater: A dramaturgical approach to crowd behavior. *Symbolic Interaction*, 4(1). [21]

Snow, Margaret E., Carol Nagy Jacklin, and Eleanor E. Maccoby. 1981. Birth-order differences in peer sociability at thirty-three months. *Child Development*, 52:589–595. [5]

Snow, Margaret Ellis, Carol Nagy Jacklin, and Eleanor E. Maccoby. 1983. Sex-of-child differences in father–child interactions at one year of age. *Child Development*, 54:227–232. [11]

Soja, Edward W. 1989. *Postmodern Geographics: The Reassertion of Space in Critical Social Theory*. London: Verso. [20]

Sommers, E.K., and J.V.P. Check. 1987. An empirical investigation of the role of pornography in the verbal and physical abuse of women. *Violence amd Victims*, 2:189–209. [12]

Sorrentino, Constance. 1990. The changing family in international perspective. *Monthly Labor Review* (March):41–58. [11]

Sourcebook of Criminal Justice Statistics, 1989. 1990. Washington, DC: U.S. Department of Justice. [7]

Spade, Joan Z., and Carole A. Reese. 1991. We've come a long way, maybe: College students' plans for work and family. *Sex Roles*, 24(5/6):309–321. [11]

Spencer, Herbert. 1974. *The Evolution of Society: Selections from Herbert Spencer's "Principles of Sociology."* Robert L. Carniero, Ed. Chicago: University of Chicago Press. [9]

Spencer, Paul. 1988. *The Maasai of Matapato*. Bloomington: Indiana University Press. [6]

Spengler, Oswald. 1926–1928. *The Decline of the West*. New York: Knopf. [22]

Spicer, Edward H. 1980. American Indians. In S. Thernstrom, Ed., *Harvard Encyclopedia of American Ethnic Groups*. Cambridge: MA: Harvard University Press. [10]

Spitz, R.D. 1951. The psychogenic diseases of infancy: An attempt at their etiological classification. *Psychoanalytic Study of the Child*, 6:255–275. [5]

Stacey, Judith. 1990. *Brave New Families: Stories of Domestic Upheaval in Late Twentieth Century America*. New York: Basic Books. [12]

Staggenborg, Suzanne. 1988. The consequences of professionalization and formalization in the pro-choice movement. *American Sociological Review*, 53 (August):35–50. [21]

Stark, Rodney. 1984. The rise of a new world faith. *Review of Religious Research*, 26 (1). [14]

Stark, Rodney, and William Sims Bainbridge. 1985. *The Future of Religion: Secularization, Revival and Cult Formation*. Berkeley: University of California Press. [14]

Starr, Paul. 1982. *The Social Transformation of American Medicine*. New York: Basic Books. [15]

State of the World Population Report. 1989. Status of women key to future. *Development Forum*. May–June. [19]

Statham, Anne. 1987. The gender model revisited: Differences in the management styles of men and women. *Sex Roles*, 16 (7/8):409–429. [11]

Statistical Abstract of the United States. 1990. U.S. Bureau of the Census. Washington, DC: U.S. Government Printing Office. [9, 17]

Statistical Abstract of the United States. 1991. U.S. Bureau of the Census. Washington, DC: U.S. Government Printing Office. [10, 11]

Stearns, Linda Brewster. 1992. How America can best compete in a global economy. In C. Calhoun and G. Ritzer, Eds., *Social Problems*. New York: McGraw-Hill/PRIMIS. [16]

Steinbrook, Robert. 1990. The Times Poll: Most Americans favor reforms in nation's health care system. *Los Angeles Times* (February 4):A1, A26. [15]

Steinmetz, Suzanne K., and Murray A. Straus, Eds. 1974. *Violence in the Family*. New York: Harper & Row. [12]

Stern, Marilyn, and Katherine Hildebrandt Karraker. 1989. Sex stereotyping of infants: A review of gender labeling studies. *Sex Roles*, 20 (9/10):501–522. [11]

Sterngold, James. 1987. With key executives' arrest, Wall Street faces challenge. *New York Times* (February):A1, A38. [7]

Stevens, Gwendolyn, and Sheldon Gardner. 1987. But can she command a ship? Acceptance of women by peers at the Coast Guard Academy. *Sex Roles*, 16 (3/4):181–188. [11]

Stoesz, David, and Howard Karger. 1991. The corporatisation of the United States welfare state. *Journal of Social Policy*, 20(1):157–171. [15, 17]

Stoper, Emily. 1991. Women's work, women's movement: Taking stock. *Annals of the American Academy of Political and Social Science*, 515(May):151–162. [21]

Straus, Murray A., and Richard J. Gelles. 1986. Societal change and change in family violence from 1975 to 1985 as revealed by two national surveys. *Journal of Marriage and the Family*, 48 (August):465–479. [12]

Sullivan, Harry Stack. 1953. *The Interpersonal Theory of Psychiatry*. New York: Norton. [5]

Sullivan, Scott. 1986. Europe's population bomb. *Newsweek* (December 15):52. [10]

Summers, Gene F., and Kristi Branch. 1984. Economic development and community social change. *Annual Review of Sociology*, 10:141–166. [20]

Suransky, Valerie Polakow. 1982. *The Erosion of Childhood*. Chicago: University of Chicago Press. [6]

Surgeon General's 1990 Report on the Health Benefits of Smoking Cessation: Executive Summary. *Morbidity and Mortality Weekly Report*, 39(RR-12):1–10.

Suro, Roberto. 1990. Behind the census numbers, swirling nodes of movement. *New York Times* (September 16):E4. [19]

Sutherland, Edwin. 1949. *White Collar Crime*. New York: Dryden Press. [7]

Suttles, Gerald D. 1968. *The Social Order of the Slum*. Chicago: University of Chicago Press. [20]

Swanson, Guy E. 1974. *The Birth of the Gods*. Ann Arbor: University of Michigan Press. [14]

Swidler, A. 1986. Culture in action: Symbols and strategies. *American Sociological Review* 51:273–286. [3]

Tabb, William. 1986. *Churches in Struggle: Liberation Theology and Social Change in North America*. New York: Monthly Review Press. [14]

Taeuber, Karl. 1990. Desegregation of public school districts. *Phi Delta Kappan*, 72(1):18–40. [13]

Talmon, Yonina. 1972. *Family and Community in the Kibbutz*. Cambridge, MA: Harvard University Press. [22]

Tausky, Curt. 1984. *Work and Society: An Introduction to Industrial Sociology*. Itasca, IL: Peacock. [16]

Tavris, Carol, and Carole Wade. 1984. *The Longest War: Sex Difference in Perspective*, 2d ed. San Diego: Harcourt Brace Jovanovich. [11]

Taylor, Charles. 1985. Legitimation crisis? In *Philosophy and the Sciences of Man*. New York: Cambridge University Press. [17]

Taylor, Charles. 1992. *The Politics of Recognition*. Princeton, NJ: Princeton University Press. [3, 10]

Taylor, M. Susan, and Janet A. Sniezek. 1984. The college recruitment interview: Topical content and applicant reactions. *Journal of Occupational Psychology*, 57:157–168. [4]

Taylor, Robert Joseph, Linda M. Chatters, M. Belinda Tucker, and Edith Lewis. 1990. Developments in research on black families: A decade review. *Journal of Marriage and the Family*, 52 (November):993–1014. [12]

Taylor, Susan H. 1989. The case for comparable worth. *Journal of Social Issues*, 45 (4):23–37. [11]

Teitelbaum, Michael S. 1975. Relevance of demographic transition theory for developing countries. *Science*, 188:420–425. [19]

Teixeira, R. 1988. Will the real non-voters please stand up? *Public Opinion* (July–August):41–59. [17]

Telles, Edward E., and Edward Murguia. 1990. Phenotypic discrimination and income differences among Mexican Americans. *Social Science Quarterly*, 71(4, December):682–696. [10]

Terkel, Studs. 1972. *Working: People Talk About What They Do All Day and How They Feel About It*. New York: Pantheon. [16]

Testa, Mark, and Marilyn Krogh. 1989. The Effect of Employment on Marriage Among Black Males in Inner-City Chicago. Unpublished manuscript, University of Chicago. [9]

Thomas, Donald E. 1987. *Diesel*. Tuscaloosa: University of Alabama Press. [22]

Thomas, Elizabeth Marshall. 1959. *The Harmless People*. New York: Vintage. [9]

Thomas, G.M., and J. Meyer. 1984. The expansion of the state. *Annual Review of Sociology*, 10:461–482. [17]

Thomas, William I., and Dorothy Swaine Thomas. 1928. *The Child in America*. New York: Knopf. [1, 4]

Thomlinson, Ralph. 1976. *Population Dynamics*, 2d ed. New York: Random House. [19]

Thompson, E.P. 1968. *The Making of the English Working Class*. Harmondsworth, England: Penguin. [11, 16]

Thompson, E.P. 1971. The moral economy of the English crowd in the eighteenth century. *Past and Present*, 50:76–136. [21]

Thornton, Arland. 1989. Cohabitation and marriage in the 1980s. 1988. *Demography*, 25:497–508. [12]

Thurow, Lester C. 1985. *The Management Challenge: Japanese Views*. Cambridge, MA: MIT Press. [17]

Tien, H. Yuan. 1991. The new census of China. *Population Today* (January):6–8. [19]

Tilly, Charles. 1978. *From Mobilization to Revolution*. Reading, MA: Addison-Wesley. [21]

Tipton, Steven M. 1982. *Getting Saved from the Sixties: Moral Meaning in Conversion and Cultural Change*. Berkeley: University of California Press. [14]

Tischler, Henry L., and Brewton Berry, Eds. 1978. *Race and Ethnic Relations*, 4th ed. Boston: Houghton Mifflin. [10]

Tobin, Joseph J., David Y.H. Wu, and Dana H. Davidson. 1989. *Preschool in Three Cultures: Japan, China, and the United States*. New Haven, CT: Yale University Press. [12]

Toby, Jackson. 1989. Of dropouts and stay-ins: The Gershwin approach. *Public Interest* (95):3–13. [13]

Toch, Thomas, Nancy Linnon, and Matthew Cooper. 1991. Schools that Work. *U.S. News & World Report* (May 27):58–66. [13]

Tönnies, Ferdinand. 1887/1963. *Gemeinschaft and Gesellschaft*. C.P. Loomis (Trans.). New York: American Book. [20]

Toynbee, Arnold. 1946. *A Study of History*. New York: Oxford University Press. [22]

Treiman, D.J., and H.I. Hartmann, Eds. 1981. *Women, Work, and Wages: Equal Pay for Jobs of Equal Value* (Committee on Occupational Classification and Analysis, National Research Council). Washington, DC: National Academy of Sciences. [11]

Troeltsch, Ernst. 1931. *The Social Teaching of the Christian Churches*. New York: Macmillan. [14]

Troiden, Richard. 1984. Self, self-concept, identity and homosexual identity. *Journal of Homosexuality*, 10(3/4):97–109. [11]

Tumin, Melvin M. 1953. Some principles of stratification: A critical analysis. *American Sociological Review*, 18(August):387–393. [9, 11]

Turnbull, Sharon K., and James M. Turnbull. 1983. To dream the impossible dream: An agenda for discussion with stepparents. *Family Relations*, 32:227–230. [12]

Turner, Jeffrey S., and Donald B. Helms. 1988. *Marriage and Family*. New York: Harcourt Brace Jovanovich. [12]

Turner, Ralph H., and Lewis M. Killian. 1972. *Collective Behavior*, 2d ed. Englewood Cliffs, NJ: Prentice Hall. [21]

Turner, Victor W. 1970. *The Ritual Process*. Chicago: Aldine. [14]

Udry, J.R., and John Billy. 1987. Initiation of coitus in early adolescence. *American Sociological Review*, 52:841–855. [6]

Udy, Stanley H., Jr. 1959. "Bureaucracy" and "rationality" in Weber's organizational theory: An empirical study. *American Sociological Review*, 24 (December):791–795. [8]

Uniform Crime Reports for the United States. 1991. Washington, DC: Federal Bureau of Investigation, U.S. Department of Justice. [7]

United Nations. 1991. *The World's Women, 1970–1990: Trends and Statistics*. New York: United Nations. [11]

U.N. Commission on Transnational Corporations. 1978. Transnational corporations in world development: A re-examination. Fourth session. New York (May 15–26). [16]

U.S. Bureau of the Census. 1990a. Current Population Reports: Series P-20. Washington, DC: U.S. Government Printing Office. [16]

U.S. Bureau of the Census. 1990b. *Money Income of Households, Families, and Persons in the United States: 1990*. Current Population Reports: Series P-60, No. 174. Washington, DC: U.S. Government Printing Office. [10]

U.S. Bureau of the Census. 1987, 1990c, 1991. *Statistical Abstract of the United States*. Washington, DC: U.S. Government Printing Office. [6, 9, 10, 11, 16, 17]

U.S. Bureau of the Census. 1991a. *The Asian and Pacific Islander Population of the United States: March 1991 and 1990*. Current Population Reports: Series P-20, No. 459. Washington, DC: U.S. Government Printing Office. [10]

U.S. Bureau of the Census. 1991b. *Educational Attainment in the United States: March 1991 and 1990*. Current Population Reports: Series P-20, No. 462. Washington, DC: U.S. Government Printing Office. [13]

U.S. Bureau of the Census. 1991c. *Money Income of Households, Families, and Persons in the United States: 1991*. Current Population Reports: Series P-60, No. 180. Washington, DC: U.S. Government Printing Office. [13]

U.S. Bureau of the Census. 1992. *Health Insurance Coverage, 1987–1990*. Current Population Reports: Household Economic Studies, Series P-70, No. 29. Washington, DC: U.S. Government Printing Office. [15]

U.S. Congress, House of Representatives. 1990. *Emptying the Elderly's Pocketbook: Growing Impact of Rising Health Care Costs*. Select Committee on Aging, Washington, DC. [6, 12]

U.S. Department of Education. 1990. *Digest of Education Statistics*. National Center for Educational Statistics, Publication 91-660, table 159. [6]

U.S. Department of Health and Human Services. 1991. Health status and utilization (pp. 32–33). In *Health United States: 1990.* Hyattsville, MD: U.S. Department of Health and Human Services. [15]

U.S. Department of Health and Human Services. 1992. *Monthly Vital Statistics Report*, 41(2, June 26). [19]

U.S. Department of Justice. 1989. *Correctional Population in the United States.* Washington, DC: U.S. Department of Justice. [7]

U.S. Department of Justice. 1990. *Tracking Offenders, 1987.* Bulletin NCJ-125315. Washington, DC: U.S. Department of Justice. [7]

U.S. Department of Labor. 1988. Employment and Earnings (January):183–188. Washington, DC: U.S. Government Printing Office. [4]

U.S. Department of Labor. 1992. *Employment and Earnings* (August). Washington, DC: U.S. Government Printing Office. [10]

Useem, Michael. 1980. Corporations and the corporate elite. *Annual Review of Sociology*, 6:41–77. [16]

Useem, Michael. 1984. *The Inner Circle: Large Corporations and the Rise of Business Political Activity in the U.S. and U.K.* New York: Oxford University Press. [16, 17]

Vaillant, George. 1977. *Adaptation to Life.* Boston: Little, Brown. [6]

Van Creveld, Martin., 1985. *Command in War.* Cambridge, MA: Harvard University Press. [8]

Van den Berghe, Pierre. 1978. *Race and Racism: A Comparative Perspective*, 2d ed. New York: Wiley. [10]

Van Evra, Judith. 1990. *Television and Child Development.* Hillsdale, NJ: Erlbaum. [5]

Van Gennep, Arnold. 1908/1961. *Rites of Passage.* M.B. Vizedon and G.L. Caffee (Trans.). Chicago: University of Chicago Press [6]

Van Maanen, John. 1976. Breaking-in: Socialization to work. In R. Dubin, Ed., *Handbook of Work, Organization and Society.* Indianapolis, IN: Bobbs-Merrill. [5]

Veblen, Thorstein. 1899. *Theory of the Leisure Class.* New York: Macmillan. [9, 22]

Velez, William. 1985. Finishing college: The effects of college type. *Sociology of Education*, 58 (July):191–200. [13]

Velez, William. 1989. High school attrition among Hispanic and non-Hispanic white youth. *Sociology of Education*, 62:119–133. [13]

Vera Institute of Justice. 1977. *Felony Arrests: Their Prosecution and Disposition in New York City's Courts.* New York: Vera Institute of Justice. [7]

Viorst, Milton. 1991. The house of Hashem. *New Yorker* (January 7):32–52. [1]

Vogel, Ezra F. 1979. *Japan as Number One: Lessons for America.* Cambridge, MA: Harvard University Press. [22]

Vogel, Lise. 1983. *Marxism and the Oppression of Women.* New Brunswick, NJ: Rutgers University Press. [22]

Wacquant, L.J.D. 1989. The ghetto, the state, and the new capitalist economy. *Discent* (Fall):508–520. [9]

Wacquant, L.J.D. and William J. Wilson. 1989. The cost of racial and class exclusion in the inner city. *Annals of the American Academy of Political and Social Science*, 501 (January):8–25. [9]

Waisman, Carlos. 1987. *Reversal of Development in Argentina.* Princeton, NJ: Princeton University Press. [18]

Waite, Linda J., and Lee A. Lillard. 1991. Children and marital disruption. *American Journal of Sociology*, 96 (4, January):930–953. [12]

Wald, Matthew I. 1990. Guarding the environment: A world of challenges. *New York Times* (April 22):A1, A24–25. [19]

Waldron, Ingrid, Dianne Lye, and Anastasia Brandon. 1991. Gender differences in teenage smoking. *Women and Health*, 17(2):65–90. [15]

Walker, Lenore. 1979. *The Battered Woman.* New York: Harper & Row. [12]

Wallace, Amy, and Nora Zamichow. 1992. When right and wrong blur. *Los Angeles Times* (May 2):A2, A25. [21]

Wallerstein, Immanuel. 1974. *The Modern World System*, Vol. I. New York: Academic Press. [18]

Wallerstein, Immanuel. 1979. *The Capitalist World Economy*, New York: Academic Press. [18]

Wallerstein, Immanuel. 1984. *The Modern World System*, Vol. II. New York: Cambridge University Press. [16, 18]

Wallerstein, Immanuel. 1988. *The Modern World System*, Vol. III. New York: Cambridge University Press. [18]

Wallerstein, Immanuel. 1991. The construction of peoplehood: Racism, nationalism, ethnicity. In Etienne Balibar and Immanuel Wallerstein, Eds., *Race, Nation, Class: Ambiguous Identities* (pp. 71–85). London: Verso. [10]

Wallerstein, Judith S., and Sandra Blakeslee. 1989. *Second Chances: Men, Women, and Children a Decade After Divorce.* New York: Ticknor & Fields. [12]

Wallerstein, Judith S., and Joan Berlin Kelly. 1980. *Surviving the Breakup: How Children and Parents Cope with Divorce.* New York: Basic Books. [12]

Walters, Gary C., and Joan E. Grusec. 1977. *Punishment.* San Francisco: Freeman. [12]

Walters, Glenn D. 1992. *Foundations of Criminal Science*, Vol. 1. New York: Praeger. [7]

Wariavwalla, Bharat. 1988. Interdependence and domestic political regimes: The case of the newly industrializing countries. *Alternatives* 13:253–270. [18]

Warner, Kenneth E. 1985. Cigarette advertising and media coverage of smoking and health. *New England Journal of Medicine*, 312 (6):384–388. [15]

Warner, Michael. 1992. Critical Multiculturalism. *Critical Inquiry.* [10]

Warner, Sam Bass, Jr. 1962. *Streetcar Suburbs: The Process of Growth in Boston, 1870–1900.* Cambridge, MA: Harvard and MIT Press. [20]

Warner, Sam Bass, Jr. 1972. *The Urban Wilderness.* New York: Harper & Row. [20]

Waters, Mary C. 1990. *Ethnic Options: Choosing Identities in America.* Berkeley: University of California Press. [10]

Watson, James D. 1968. *The Double Helix.* New York: Signet.

Watson, John B. 1925/1970. *Behaviorism.* New York: Norton. [5]

Webber, Melvin. 1966. Order in diversity: Community without propinquitz. In L. Wingo, Ed., *Cities and Space: The Future Use of Urban Land* (pp. 23–54). Baltimore: Johns Hopkins Press. [20]

Weber, Eugen. 1976. *Peasants into Frenchmen: The Modernization of Rural France, 1870–1914.* Stanford, CA: Stanford University Press. [10]

Weber, Max. 1904/1958. *The Protestant Ethic and the Spirit of Capitalism.* Talcott Parsons (Trans.). New York: Scribner's. [1, 16]

Weber, Max. 1918/1947. *From Max Weber: Essays in Sociology*, 2d ed. H.H. Gerth and C.W. Mills (Trans.). New York: Oxford University Press. [22]

Weber, Max. 1922/1978. *Economy and Society.* E. Fischoff et al. (Trans.). New York: Bedminster Press. [1, 17]

Weed, James A. 1982. Divorce: Americans' style. *American Demographics*, 4 (March):13–17. [12]

Weinberg, Martin S., and Colin J. Williams. 1975. Gay baths and the social organization of impersonal sex. *Social Problems*, 23 (2):124–136. [2]

Weitzman, Lenore. 1985. *The Divorce Revolution: The Unexpected Consequences for Women and Children in America.* New York: Free Press. [12]

Weitzman, Lenore J., and Deborah Eifler. 1972. Sex role socialization in picture books for preschool children. *American Journal of Sociology*, 77 (May):1125–1144. [11]

Weller, Jack M., and E.L. Quarantelli. 1973. Neglected characteristics of collective behavior. *American Journal of Sociology*, 79 (November): 665–685. [21]

Wender, Paul H., and Donald F. Klein. 1981. The Promise of Biological Psychiatry. *Psychology Today*, 15 (February):25–41. [7]

West, C. 1984. *Routine complications: Troubles with talk between doctors and patients*. Bloomington: Indiana University Press. [4]

West, C., and D.H. Zimmerman. 1977. Women's place in everyday talk: Reflections on parent–child interactions. *Social Problems*, 24:521–528. [4]

Wheeler, Stanton, 1966. The structure of formally organized socialization settings. In O.G. Brim and S. Wheeler, eds., *Socialization After Childhood*. New York: Wiley. [5]

White, Burton L., Barbara T. Kaban, and Jane S. Attanucci. 1979. *The Origins of Human Competence*. Lexington, MA: Heath. [5]

White, Lynn, Jr., 1962. *Medieval Technology and Social Change*. New York: Oxford University Press. [22]

White, Lynn K. 1990. Determinants of divorce: A review of research in the eighties. *Journal of Marriage and the family*, 52 (November):904–912. [12]

White, Lynn, and John N. Edwards. 1990. Emptying the nest and parental well-being. *American Sociological Review*, 55:235–242. [6]

Whitt, J. Allen. 1982. *Urban Elites and Mass Transportation: The Dialectics of Power*. Princeton, NJ: Princeton University Press. [17]

Wiatrowski, William J. 1990. Family-related benefits in the workplace. *Monthly Labor Review* (March):28–33. [11]

Wilford, John Noble. 1981. 9 Percent of everyone who ever lived is alive now. *New York Times* (October 6):13, 14. [19]

Wilkinson, Richard G. 1990. Income distribution and mortality: A natural experiment. *Sociology of Health and Illness*, 12 (4):391–412. [15]

Williams, D.A., J. Huck, C. Ma, and S. Monroe. 1981. Why public schools fail. *Newsweek* (April 20):62–73. [13]

Williams, J. Allen, Jr., Joetta A. Vernon, Martha C. Williams, and Karen Malecha. 1987. Sex role socialization in picture books: An update. *Social Science Quarterly*, 68 (March):148–156. [5, 11]

Williams, Raymond. 1976. *Keywords: A Vocabulary of Culture and Society*. London: Fontana. [17]

Williams, Raymond. 1982. *The Sociology of Culture*. New York: Schocken. [3]

Williams, Robin. 1970. *American Society*, 3d ed. New York: Knopf. [3]

Willie, Charles V. 1983. *Race, Ethnicity and Socioeconomic Status*. New York: General Hall. [1]

Willis, Paul. 1977. *Learning to Labor: How Working Class Kids Get Working Class Jobs*. New York: Columbia University Press, 1977. [5]

Willis, Paul. 1990. *Common Culture: Symbolic Work at Play in the Everyday Cultures of the Young*. Boulder, CO: Westview Press. [5]

Wilson, Bryan R. 1990. *The Social Dimensions of Sectarianism: Sect and New Religious Movements in Contemporary Society*. Oxford, England: Clarendon Press. [14]

Wilson, Edward O. 1978. *On Human Nature*. Cambridge, MA: Harvard University Press. [5]

Wilson, Franklin. 1985. The impact of school desegregation programs on white public-school enrollment, 1968–1976. *Sociology of Education*, 58 (July):137–153. [13]

Wilson, James Q. 1983. *Crime and Public Policy*. New York: ICS Press. [7]

Wilson, John. 1973. *Introduction to Social Movements*. New York: Basic Books. [21]

Wilson, Lillie. 1988. The aging of aquarius. *American Demographics*, 10(September):34–37. [6]

Wilson, William J. 1980. *The Declining Significance of Race: Blacks and Changing American Institutions*. New York: Basic Books. [9]

Wilson, William J. 1987. *The Truly Disadvantaged: The Inner City, the Underclass, and Public Policy*. Chicago: University of Chicago Press. [1, 9]

Wilson, William J. 1991. Studying inner-city social dislocations: The challenge of public agenda research (1990 Presidential Address). *American Sociological Review*. 56 (February):1–14. [9]

Winn, Marie. 1984. *Children Without Childhood*. New York: Penguin. [6]

Winn, Marie. 1985. *The Plug-in Drug: Television, Children and the Family*. New York: Penguin. [5]

Winnick, Louis. 1990. America's "Model minority." *Commentary*. 90 (2, August):22–29. [10]

Wirth, Louis, 1938. Urbanism as a way of life. *American Journal of Sociology*, 44:1–24. [20]

Wittig, Michele Andrisin, and Rosemary Hays Lowe. 1989. Comparable worth theory and policy. *Journal of Social Issues*. 45 (4):1–21. [11]

Wolf, Eric. 1982. *Europe and the People Without History*. Berkeley: University of California Press. [17]

Wolfe, David A. 1985. Child abusive parents: An empirical review and analysis. *Psychological Bulletin*, 97:462–482. [12]

Womack, James P. et al. 1990. *The Machine that Changed the World*. New York: Macmillan/Rawson Associates. [8]

Wong, Bernard P. 1982. *Chinatown: Economic Adaptation and Ethnic Identity of the Chinese*. New York: Holt, Rinehart and Winston. [10]

Woo, Elaine. 1992. Fissures of race tear L.A. fabric. *Los Angeles Times* (May 5):A1, 12.[21]

Wood, Floris W., Ed. 1990. *An American Profile—Opinions and Behavior, 1972–1989*. Detroit: Gale Research. [12]

Woody, Bette. 1989. Black women in the emerging services economy. *Sex Roles*, 21 (1/2):45–67. [11]

World Bank. 1990. *World Development Report 1990: Poverty*. New York: Oxford University Press. [18, 19]

World Bank. 1991. *World Development Report 1991: The Challenge of Development*. New York: Oxford University Press. [18]

World Resources, 1990–91. 1990. Report by the World Resources Institute in collaboration with the United Nations Environment Programme and The United Nations Development Programme. New York: Oxford University Press. [19]

The World's Women, 1970–1990: Trends and Statistics. 1991. Social Statistics and Indicators, Series K, No. 8. New York: United Nations. [19]

Worsley, Peter. 1984. *The Three Worlds*. Chicago: University of Chicago Press. [18]

Wray, William D. 1984. *Mitsubishi and the N.Y.K. 1870–1914*. Cambridge, MA: Harvard University Press. [8]

Wright, Erik Olin. 1986. *Classes*. London: New Left Books. [17]

Wright, James D. 1989. Address unknown: Homelessness in contemporary America. *Society*. 26 (6, Sept./Oct.):45–53.[9]

Wright, J.R. 1985. PACs, contributions and roll calls: An organizational perspective *American Political Science Review*, 79 (2):400–414. [17]

Wrong, Dennis H. 1961. The oversocialized conception of man in modern sociology. *American Sociological Review*, 26:183–193. [5]

WuDunn, Sheryl. 1991a. China, with ever more to feed, pushes anew for small families. *New York Times* (June 16):A1, A4. [19]

WuDunn, Sheryl. 1991b. For China, it's the year of the spoiled child. *New York Times* (February 17):A10. [19]

Wuthnow, Robert. 1988. *The Restructuring of American Religion*. Princeton, NJ: Princeton University Press. [14]

Wuthnow, Robert. 1990. The social significance of religious television. In Robert Abelman and Stuart M. Hoover, Eds., *Religious Television: Controversies and Conclusions* (pp. 87–98). Norwood, NJ: Ablex. [14]

Yamagishi, Toshio, Mary R. Gillmore, and Karen S. Cook. 1988. Network connections and the distribution of power in exchange networks. *American Journal of Sociology*, 93 (4, January):833–851. [4]

Yee, Doris K., and Jacquelynne S. Eccles. 1988. Parent perceptions and attributions for children's math achievement. *Sex Roles*, 19 (5/6):317–333. [11]

Yetman, Norman R. 1992. Race and ethnic inequality. In C. Calhoun and G. Ritzer, Eds., *Social Problems*. New York: McGraw-Hill/PRIMIS. [10]

Yoder, Jan D., and Robert C. Nichols. 1980. A life perspective comparison of married and divorced persons. *Journal of Marriage and the Family*, 42 (2):413–419. [12]

Young, Michael D. 1988. *The Metronomic Society: Natural Rhythms and Human Timetables*. Cambridge, MA: Harvard University Press. [22]

Zald, Mayer N.M., and John D. McCarthy. 1987. Introduction. In Zald and McCarthy, eds., *Social Movements in an Organizational Society*. New Brunswick, NJ: Transaction. [21]

Zangwill, Israel. 1909. *The Melting Pot*. New York: Jewish Publishing Society of America. [10]

Zaslavskaya, Tatyana. 1990. *The Second Socialist Revolution: An Alternative Soviet Strategy*. Bloomington: Indiana University Press. [16]

Zelizer, Viviana. 1985. *Pricing the Priceless Child*. New York: Basic Books. [6]

Zelnik, Melvin, Michael A. Koenig, and Yong J. Kim. 1984. Source of prescription contraceptives and subsequent pregnancy among women. *Family Planning Perspectives*, 16:6–13. [12]

Zeman, Ned. 1990. The new rules of courtship. *Newsweek* (Special Issue: The New Teens):25–27. [6]

Zey-Ferrell, Mary. 1981. Criticisms of the dominant perspective on organizations. *Sociological Quarterly*, 22:181–205. [8]

Zinn, Maxine B., and D. Stanley Eitzen, Eds. 1989. *The Reshaping of America: Social Consequences of a Changing Economy*. Englewood Cliffs, NJ: Prentice Hall. [9]

Zola, Irving Kenneth. 1972. Medicine as an institution of social control. *Sociological Review*, 20 (November):487–504. [15]

Zolberg, Aristede. 1991. The next waves: Migration theory for a changing world. In Norman R. Yetman, Ed., *Majority and Minority: The Dynamics of Race and Ethnicity in American Life*, 5th ed. (pp. 523–537). Boston: Allyn and Bacon. [10]

Zuckerman, Harriet. 1972. Interviewing an ultra-elite. *Public Opinion Quarterly*, 36:159–175. [2]

Zuckerman, Solly. 1983. *Nuclear Illusion and Reality*. New York: Vintage. [17]

TEXT CREDITS

Table 2.1 and Table 2.2 From David P. Phillips, "The Influence of Suggestion on Suicide: Substantive and Theoretical Implications of the Werther Effect," *American Sociological Review*, 39, 1974, pp. 340–354. Reprinted by permission of the American Sociological Association.

Figure 3.3 From *Rotten Reviews: A Literary Companion*, edited by Bill Henderson. © 1987 Pushcart Press. Reprinted by permission.

Figure 5.2 and Figure 5.3 From *Work and Personality: An Inquiry into the Impact of Social Stratification* by Melvin L. Kohn and Carmi Schooler, 1983. Reprinted with permission from Ablex Publishing Corporation.

Figure 6.2 Reproduced from *The Life Cycle Completed: A Review*, by Erik H. Erikson, by permission of W. W. Norton & Company, Inc. Copyright © 1982 by Rikan Enterprises, Ltd.

Figure 6.3 From *The Seasons of a Man's Life* by Daniel J. Levinson et al. Copyright © 1978 by Daniel J. Levinson. Reprinted by permission of Alfred A. Knopf, Inc., and Sterling Lord Agency.

Chapter 7 Excerpts from *Islands in the Street* by Martin Sanchez Jankowski, 1991, pp. 42, 43, 45, 103, 143, 182, 185. Reprinted by permission of University of California Press.

Figure 7.1 Adapted with the permission of The Free Press, A Division of Macmillan, Inc., from *Social Theory and Social Structure*, Revised and Enlarged Edition by Robert K. Merton. Copyright © 1968, 1967 by Robert K. Merton.

Table 7.1 Adapted from Graeme Newman, "Comparative Deviance: Perception and Law in Six Cultures," Elsevier Science Publishing, 1976, p. 116. Reprinted by permission of the author.

Chapter 8 Excerpts reprinted by permission of The Putnam Publishing Group from *Lord of the Flies* by William Golding. Copyright © 1954, 1982 by William Golding. Also by permission of Faber and Faber Ltd.

Figure 8.1 From *General Social Surveys 1972–1990: Cumulative Guidebook*, National Opinion Research Center, 1990, p. 369. Reprinted by permission.

Table 8.1 Reprinted with the permission of The Free Press, a Division of Macmillan, Inc., from *Handbook of Small Group Research*, Second Edition, by A. Paul Hare. Copyright © 1976 by The Free Press.

Chapter 9 Excerpt from *Down and Out in America* by Peter Rossi, pp. 1–8. Copyright © 1989. Reprinted by permission of The University of Chicago Press.

Table 9.1 Adapted from *General Social Surveys, 1972–1983: Cumulative Codebook*, National Opinion Research Center, 1983, pp. 338–349. Reprinted by permission.

Figure 9.4 From "Solutions on Welfare: They All Cost Money," *The New York Times*, July 26, 1992. Copyright © 1992 by The New York Times Company. Reprinted by permission.

Figure 9.5 From *The State of Working America* by Lawrence Mishel and Jared Bernstein, 93, 1992, p. 194. Copyright © 1993 by M. E. Sharpe, Inc.

Figure 10.1 From *Racial and Ethnic Groups*, 2nd Edition, by Richard T. Schaefer. Copyright © 1984 by Richard T. Schaefer. Reprinted by permission of HarperCollins Publishers.

Figure 10.7 From "Total Asians—1980," and "Total Asians—1990," *The New York Times*, June 21, 1991. Copyright © 1991 by The New York Times Company. Reprinted by permission.

Table 10.1 From Charles C. Moskos and John S. Butler, "Blacks in the Military Since World War II." Reprinted with permission from *A Common Destiny: Blacks and American Society*. Copyright 1989 by the National Academy of Sciences. Courtesy of the National Academy Press, Washington, D.C.

Figure 11.2 From "Solutions on Welfare: They All Cost Money," *The New York Times*, July 26, 1992. Copyright © 1992 by The New York Times Company. Reprinted by permission.

Figure 11.3 From Sara M. Evans and Barbara J. Nelson, "Comparable Worth: The Paradox of Technocratic Reform," *Feminist Studies*, 15, no. 1, 1989, p. 174. Reprinted by permission.

Table 11.2 From Rita J. Simon and Jean M. Landis, "The Polls—a Report: Women's and Men's Attitudes about a Woman's Place and Role," *Public Opinion Quarterly*, 53, Summer 1989, p. 270. Reprinted by permission of The University of Chicago Press, the Gallup Organization, and the National Opinion Research Center.

Figure 13.1 and Figure 13.2 From *1990 Profile of SAT and Achievement Test Takers*. Reprinted by permission of Educational Testing Services, the copyright owner.

Figure 14.1 From "America: Land of the Faithful," *The American Enterprise*, November/December 1990, p. 97. Reprinted by permission of National Opinion Research Center.

Figure 14.2 From "Religious Affiliations of the American People," *The New York Times*, April 10, 1991. Copyright © 1991 by The New York Times Company. Reprinted by permission.

Table 14.1 Adapted from *Millhands and Preachers: A Study of Gastonia* by Lifton Pope. Copyright © 1983. Reprinted by permission of Yale University Press.

Chapter 15 Article from David Remnick © 1991 the Washington Post. Reprinted with permission.

Figure 15.A Chart, "Health Care: Cutting Through the Gobbledygook," *Newsweek*, February 3, 1992, p. 24. © 1992, Newsweek, Inc. All rights reserved. Reprinted by permission.

Figure 16.2 From Beth Mintz and Michael Schwartz, "Interlocking Directorates and Interest Group Formation," *American Sociological Review*, 46, December 1981, p. 857. Reprinted by permission of the American Sociological Association.

Figure 16.4, Figure 16.5, and Figure 16.6 From *U.S. News & World Report*. Copyright, January 13, 1992, U.S. News & World Report.

Table 16.1 From *Fortune* Magazine, April 20, 1992, p. 226. © 1992 Time Inc. All rights reserved.

Figure 17.2 Graph "Americans' Beliefs about the Significance of Congressional Elections," copyright © 1982 by The New York Times Company. Reprinted by permission. And from "Sample of 1,602 Voters," *Public Opinion*, 5, no. 6, December/January 1983, p. 21. Reprinted by permission of American Enterprise Institute.

Figure 18.3 From *The Three Worlds* by Peter Worsley, p. 210. Copyright © 1984. Reprinted by permission of The University of Chicago Press.

Figure 18.4 From *The Stages of Economic Growth: A Noncommunist Manifesto*, 3rd Edition, by W. W. Rostow, p. xviii. Copyright © 1990. Reprinted by permission of Cambridge University Press.

Figure 19.1 "Resident Population of the U.S. at Each Census, 1970–1990," from *The New York Times*, April 1, 1990. Copyright © 1990 by The New York Times Company. Reprinted by permission.

Figure 19.2 From *The World Bank Atlas 1990*, pp. 22–23. Reprinted by permission of International Bank for Reconstruction and Development/The World Bank.

Figure 19.4 From *The World Bank Atlas 1990*, pp. 20–21. Reprinted by permission of International Bank for Reconstruction and Development/The World Bank.

Figure 19.5 Illustration by Gabor Kiss, adapted from "Economic Development" by K. K. S. Dadzie, *Scientific American*, September 1980. Copyright © 1980 by Scientific American, Inc. All rights reserved.

Figure 19.6 From Carl Haub, "World and United States Population Prospects," *Population and Environment: A Journal of Interdisciplinary Studies*, 12, no. 3, 1991, p. 304. Reprinted by permission of Human Sciences Press, Inc.

Figure 19.7 From *World Population Data Sheet*, Population Reference Bureau, Inc., Washington, D.C.

Figure 20.1 From Frank Clifford, "We Curse the Traffic, but Won't Give Up Our Cars," *Los Angeles Times*, October 4, 1989. Copyright 1989 Los Angeles Times. Reprinted by permission.

Figure 22.1 Reprinted by permission of the publishers from *The Control Revolution* by James R. Beniger, Cambridge, Mass.: Harvard University Press, Copyright © 1986 by the President and Fellows of Harvard College.

PHOTO CREDITS

Chapter 1
2 Debra P. Hershkowitz. 4 Association des Amis de Jacques Henri Lartigue, Paris. 6 Charles Gupton/Stock, Boston. 11 Bob Daemmrich/Stock, Boston. 12 Courtesy of Lorna Price and the Estate of Ernest Born. From "The Plan of St. Gall," by Walter Norn and Ernest Born, University of California Press. 13 Adjan van Sleeuwen, Amsterdam, The Netherlands. 14 Susan Melselas/Magnum. 15 Mildred Constantine & Alan Fern, "Revolutionary Soviet Film Posters," The Johns Hopkins University Press, Baltimore and London, 1974, p. 88. 19 Barnardo Film Library, England. 20 *top and bottom*, Bettmann. 21 Courtesy of the German Information Center. 22 Courtesy of the University of Chicago, Joseph Regenstein Library.

Chapter 2
28 Debra P. Hershkowitz. 30 *top left*, AP/Wide World Photos; *top right*, U.S. Navy; *bottom left*, David Powers/Stock, Boston; *bottom right*, UPI/Bettmann Newsphotos. 36 Bill Foley/Black Star. 37 Washington Post/Frank Johnston/Woodfin Camp & Associates. 39 Bill Bachman/Stock, Boston. 41 *left and right*, Professor Philip G. Zimbardo/Stanford University. 43 Professor Douglas Harper, University of South Florida, Tampa. 45 *left*, Craig Calhoun; *right*, Luis Villota/The Stock Market.

Chapter 3
51 George Olson/Woodfin Camp & Associates. 53 Lynton Gardiner, Department of Library Services American Museum of Natural History. 54 Fortune Magazine, August 1933. 58 Rene Burri/Magnum. 59 *left*, Art Stein/Photo Researchers; *middle*, Ellis Herwig/Stock, Boston; *right*, John Chiasson/Gamma Liaison. 61 Professor Douglas Harper, University of South Florida, Tampa. 65 *left*, Bob Daemmrich/Stock, Boston; *right*, Eli Reed/Magnum. 70 S. Franklin/Magnum.

Chapter 4
75 Comstock. 78 Paul Ekman. 80 *top left*, Rick Friedman/The Picture Cube; *top right*, Bettmann; *bottom*, David S. Strickler/The Picture Cube. 82 John Eastcott/VVA Momatiuk/The Image Works. 84 *left*, UPI/Bettmann Newsphotos; *right*, David Hurn/Magnum. 86 American Museum of Natural History. 87 *left*, Jamie Tnaka/Bruce Coleman; *right*, Bohdan Hrynewych/Southern Light. 95 de Wildenberg/Sygma. 97 Professor Douglas Harper, University of South Florida, Tampa.

Chapter 5
104 Eastcott/Momatiuk/Woodfin Camp & Associates. 109 Ivan Polunin/Bruce Coleman. 110 Peeter Vilms/Jeroboam. 113 *top*, Bruce Davidson/Magnum; *bottom*, Bill Owens, Hayward, CA. 115 UPI/Bettmann Newsphotos. 116 International Museum of Photography at George Eastman House. 118 Mike Greenlar/The Image Works. 120 J. Chiasson/Gamma Liaison. 121 Steve Uzzell/Woodfin Camp & Associates. 122 Charles Gupton/The Stock Market.

Chapter 6
127 J. Eastcott/Y. Momatiuk/Woodfin Camp & Associates. 129 Bruce Davidson/Magnum. 130 National Archives. 133 Bettmann. 134 Sepp Seitz/Woodfin Camp & Associates. 138 Larry Mulvehill/Edinburgh Castle, Edinburgh, Scotland. 139 Lewis Hine/Bettmann. 141 Photo Researchers. 142 Dick Spahr/Liaison International. 143 Kenneth Chen/Sygma. 145 *left*, Culver Pictures; *right*, Steven McCurry, Magnum. 147 Tim Simpson, University of South Florida, Tampa.

Chapter 7
154 Blaine Harrington III/The Stock Market. 156 *top left*, Francois Gohier/Photo Researchers; *top right*, "Going Home," Bethlehem's Kayford Branch Mine, Cabin Creek, W. V., by Builder Levy, © 1978 from his exhibition of photographs and book, "Images of Appalachian Coalfields," Temple University Press; *bottom left*, Tomas Muscionico/Contact Press. 157 *left*, Dennis Stock/Magnum; *right*, David Austen. 163 Dale Wittner/West Stock. 165 Michael S. Yamashita/Woodfin Camp & Associates. 168 Comstock. 172 N. Tully/Sygma. 175 Gilles Peress/Magnum. 177 Anders Petersen/MIRA, Stockholm, Sweden.

Chapter 8
180 Richard Pasley/Stock, Boston. 183 Jeff Lowenthal/Woodfin Camp & Associates. 185 *left*, Cyril Toker/Photo Researchers; *right*, John Launois/Black Star. 187 Bettmann. 189 Michael L. Abramson/Woodfin Camp & Associates. 191 Blair Seitz/Photo Researchers. 194 Stacy Pick/Stock, Boston. 196 General Electric Hall of History Foundation, Schenectady, NY. 199 Comstock. 201 Hiroji Kubota/Magnum.

Chapter 9
207 Stephanie Maze/Woodfin Camp & Associates. 210 Photo by Nicole Mitchell, age 11. From "Shooting Back: A Photographic View of Life by Homeless Children," by Jim Hubbard,

San Francisco: Chronicle Books, 1991. **217** *left*, Will McIntyre/Photo Researchers; *right*, George D. Lepp/Comstock. **219** *left*, Giraudon/Art Resource; *right*, Roy Morsch/The Stock Market. **224** Hodge/Gamma Liaison. **230** Photo by Chris Heflin, age 9. From "Shooting Back: A Photographic View of Life by Homeless Children," by Jim Hubbard, San Francisco: Chronicle Books, 1991.

Chapter 10
236 Joe Sohm/The Image Works. **238** Professor Steven Gold, Whittier College, California. **240** Jacques Langevin/Sygma. **244** Collection Musee de l'Homme. **245** *top*, AP/Wide World Photos; *bottom*, Stanly Forman/Boston Herald. **250** Professor Douglas Harper, University of South Florida, Tampa. **256** Garth Lumley/Gamma Liaison. **257** Alex Harris, "White Blue and God Bless You: A Portrait of Northern New Mexico," New Mexico University Press, 1992, p. 87. **260** © Skeet McAuley, 1989. Reproduced with permission from "Sign Language: Contemporary Southwest Native America," Apeture, New York, 1989. **263** Professor Steven Gold, Whittier College, California.

Chapter 11
267 Cameron Davidson/Comstock. **269** Eric Bouvet/Gamma Liaison. **271** Agnes Estioko-Griffin and P. Bion Griffin. **272** *top*, Rob Nelson/Picture Group; *bottom*, Ulrike Welsch. **274** Charles Harbutt. **275** Carol Palmer/The Picture Cube. **277** Thomas Nebbia/Woodfin Camp & Associates. **279** *top left*, Bettmann; *top right*, National Archives; *bottom left*, "Brenda Ward," by Builder Levy, © 1982 from his exhibition of photographs and book, "Images of Appalachian Coalfields," Temple University Press. **287** Brad Markel/Gamma Liaison.

Chapter 12
292 Ronnie Kaufman/The Stock Market. **295** Nick Waplington from Living Room by Nick Waplington, © 1991 Aperture N.Y. **296** *left*, Craig Aurness/West Light; *right*, Susan McCartney/Photo Researchers. **297** Alan Weiner/Gamma Liaison. **298** *left*, Bettmann; *right*, Everett Collection. **302** Nina Leen/Life Magazine © Time Warner. **304** Peter Menzel/Stock, Boston. **307** J. L. Atlan/Sygma. **308** *left and right*, Ricabeth Steiger, Basel, Switzerland. **311** Rick Friedman/Black Star. **313** Donna Ferrato/Black Star.

Chapter 13
317 Bill Weems/Woodfin Camp & Associates. **319** *top*, National Archives/FPG International; *middle*, FPG International; *bottom*, Jon Feingersh/Stock, Boston. **321** M. E. Warren Collection/Photo Researchers. **324** Culver Pictures. **332** Yvonne Hemsey/Gamma Liaison. **333** *left*, George Skadding/Time Life Picture Agency; *right*, McGraw-Hill College Division Photo Library. **335** E. Hartmann/Magnum. **342** R. Bossu/Sygma.

Chapter 14
346 Stephanie Maze/Woodfin Camp & Associates. **349** Adam Woolfitt/Woodfin Camp & Associates. **350** Bill Bachman/Photo Researchers. **351** London National Gallery. **353** *left*, Alain Dejean/Sygma; *right*, G. Clifford/Woodfin Camp & Associates. **354** Topham Photo Library/The Image Works. **358** *top*, Adam Woolfitt/Woodfin Camp & Associates; *bottom*, C. T. Seymour/The Picture Cube. **363** Arvind Garg/Photo Researchers. **366** Marrie Bot, Rotterdam, Netherlands. **369** Tom Zimberoff/Gamma Liaison.

Chapter 15
372 Steve Dunwell/The Image Bank. **373** National Library of Medicine/Science Photo Library/Photo Researchers. **375** *left*, State Historical Society of Wisconsin; *right*, Alexander Tsiaras, "The Death Rituals of Rural Greece," by Loring M. Danforth, Princeton University Press, 1982. **379** The Photo Works. **383** Mary Evans Picture Library/Photo Researchers. **385** W. Eugene Smith/Life Magazine © Time Warner. **388** W. Eugene Smith/Life Magazine © Time Warner. **389** Will & Deni McIntyre/Photo Researchers. **391** Biophoto Associates/Photo Researchers. **392** Abraham Menashe/Photo Researchers.

Chapter 16
396 Paul Chesley/TSW. **398** Professor Douglas Harper, University of South Florida, Tampa. **399** Art Resource. **400** J. P. Laffont/Sygma. **406** Library of Congress. **409** *top*, Jeremy Nicholl/Woodfin Camp & Associates; *below*, Jeck Reznicki/The Stock Market. **411** Michael L. Abramson/Woodfin Camp & Associates. **416** Professor Douglas Harper, University of South Florida, Tampa. **418** Photo Researchers. **419** Markel/Liaison/Gamma Liaison.

Chapter 17
428 Alon Reininger/Woodfin Camp & Associates. **431** *top left*, Francois Von Sury/Sygma; *top right*, Peter Turnley/Black Star; *left*, Dan Budnik/Woodfin Camp & Associates. **434** *bottom*, Bettmann; *right*, Perry Alan Werner/The Image Works. **441** Cynthia Johnson/Gamma Liaison. **445** Burt Glinn/Magnum. **448** Editorial Photocolor Archives/Art Resource. **449** C. Mulvehill/The Image Works. **450** National Air and Space Museum, Smithsonian Institution. **451** *top*, G. Vandystadt/Photo Researchers; *bottom*, Bettmann.

Chapter 18
456 Armen Kojoyian. **459** Fotoarchiv des Rautenstrauch-Joest Museums für Völkerkunde, Köln. Images from Bamum, Christaud M. Geary, Smithsonian Press, 1988, p. 51. **460** Bettmann. **461** Margaret Bourke-White/Life Magazine © Time Warner. **465** David Austen/Woodfin Camp & Associates. **467** *top left*, Stephanie Maze/Woodfin Camp & Associates; *top right*, Dmitri Kessel/The Stock Market; *bottom*, Paula Lerner/Woodfin Camp & Associates. **472** Chuck O'Rear/Woodfin Camp & Associates. **473** Paolo Fridman/Sygma. **482** A. Tannenbaum/Sygma.

Chapter 19
486 Martin Rogers/Stock, Boston. **488** *left*, Owen Franken; *right*, Ilhami/SIPA. **490** *top left, bottom left, and bottom right*, Georg Gerster/Comstock. **501** Michele Burgess/The Stock Market. **504** Georg Gerster/Comstock. **505** Mireille Vautier/Woodfin Camp & Associates. **507** Paul Barton/The Stock Market. **509** David R. Austen/Stock, Boston. **511** Wesley Bocxe/Photo Researchers.

Chapter 20
517 Craig Aurness/Woodfin Camp & Associates. **519** *left*, Dave & Liz Wiley, Diagonal, Iowa; *right*, Michael Radigan/The Stock Market. **521** Weiner/Gamma Liaison. **524** Egyptian Expedition of the Metropolitan Museum of Art, Rogers Fund, 1930. **526** *left*, Art Resource; *right*, Caufield & Shook Collection, Photographic Archives, University of Louisville, Kentucky. From "Real Life: Louisville in the Twenties," Michael Lesy, Pantheon, p. 71. **528** Tony Freeman/PhotoEdit. **530** Georg Gerster/Comstock. **533** Bettmann. **537** Robert Llewellyn, from "Virginia: An Aerial Portrait," by Robert Llewellyn, Thomasson, Grant and Howell, 1985, p. 108. **539** Professor Douglas Harper, University of South Florida, Tampa.

Chapter 21
544 J. R. Holland/Stock, Boston. **546** *left*, Dennis Brack/Black Star; *right*, Allan Tannenbaum/Sygma. **554** *top left and bottom*, Danny Lyon/Magnum; *top right*, Professor Douglas Harper, University of South Florida, Tampa. **558** ARCHIV/Photo Researchers. **563** John Chiasson/Gamma Liaison. **565** Martin Rogers/Stock, Boston.

Chapter 22
568 Ricardo Beliel/Gamma Liaison. **570** The Image Works. **573** Courtesy Temple University Press, from "Art for the Masses," by Rebecca Zurier, Temple University Press, Philadelphia, 1988. **574** Columbia Pictures, from Jerry Ohlingers Movie Material, New York. **578** Bettmann. **582** *top left*, Art Resource; *bottom left*, Gabe Palmer/The Stock Market; *right*, Lohn Blaustein/Woodfin Camp & Associates. **587** Molly Harper, Lutz, Florida. **589** Vance Brand, NASA.

GLOSSARY INDEX

NAME INDEX

SUBJECT INDEX

THE SOCIOLOGIST'S CODE OF ETHICS

In conducting research, sociologists must follow a strict code of ethics. Below is an excerpt from this code of ethics as stipulated by the American Sociological Association (ASA).

A. *Objectivity and Integrity*
Sociologists should strive to maintain objectivity and integrity in the conduct of sociological research and practice.

1. Sociologists should adhere to the highest possible technical standards in their research, teaching and practice.
2. Since individual sociologists vary in their research modes, skills, and experience, sociologists should always set forth *ex ante* the limits of their knowledge and the disciplinary and personal limitations that condition the validity of findings which affect whether or not a research project can be successfully completed.
3. In practice or other situations in which sociologists are requested to render a professional judgment, they should accurately and fairly represent their areas and degrees of expertise.
4. In presenting their work, sociologists are obligated to report their findings fully and should not misrepresent the findings of their research. When work is presented, they are obligated to report their findings fully and without omission of significant data. To the best of their ability, sociologists should also disclose details of their theories, methods and research designs that might bear upon interpretations of research findings.
5. Sociologists must report fully all sources of financial support in their publications and must note any special relations to the sponsor.
6. Sociologists should not make any guarantees to respondents, individuals, groups or organizations—unless there is full intention and ability to honor such commitments. All such guarantees, once made, must be honored.
7. Consistent with the spirit of full disclosure of method and analysis, sociologists, after they have completed their own analyses, should cooperate in efforts to make raw data and pertinent documentation collected and prepared at public expense available to other social scientists, at reasonable costs, except in cases where confidentiality, the client's rights to proprietary information and privacy, or the claims of a fieldworker to the privacy of personal notes necessarily would be violated. The timeliness of this cooperation is especially critical.
8. Sociologists should provide adequate information and citations concerning scales and other measures used in their research.
9. Sociologists must not accept grants, contracts or research assignments that appear likely to require violation of the principles enunciated in this Code, and should dissociate themselves from research when they discover a violation and are unable to achieve its correction.
10. When financial support for a project has been accepted, sociologists must make every reasonable effort to complete the proposed work on schedule, including reports to the funding source.
11. When several sociologists, including students, are involved in joint projects, there should be mutually accepted explicit agreements at the outset with respect to division of work, compensation, access to data, rights of authorship, and other rights and responsibilities. Such agreements may need to be modified as the project evolves and such modifications must be agreed upon jointly.
12. Sociologists should take particular care to state all significant qualifications on the findings and interpretations of their research.
13. Sociologists have the obligation to disseminate research findings, except those likely to cause harm to clients, collaborators and participants, or those which are proprietary under a formal or informal agreement.
14. In their roles as practitioners, researchers, teachers, and administrators, sociologists have an important social responsibility because their recommendations, decisions, and actions may alter the lives of others. They should be aware of the situations and pressures that might lead to the misuse of their influence and authority. In these various roles, sociologists should also recognize that professional problems and conflicts may interfere with professional effectiveness. Sociologists should take steps to insure that these conflicts do not produce deleterious results for clients, research participants, colleagues, students and employees.

B. *Disclosure and Respect for the Rights of Research Populations*. Disparities in wealth, power, and social status between the sociologist and respondents and clients may reflect and create problems of equity in research collaboration. Conflict of interest for the sociologist may occur in research and practice. Also to follow the precepts of the scientific method—such as those requiring full disclosure—may entail adverse consequences or personal risks for individuals and groups. Finally, irresponsible actions by a single researcher or research team can eliminate or reduce future access to a category of respondents by the entire profession and its allied fields.

1. Sociologists should not misuse their positions as professional social scientists for fraudulent purposes or as a pretext for gathering intelligence for any organization or government. Sociologists should not mislead respondents involved in a research project as to the purpose for which the research is being conducted.
2. Subjects of research are entitled to rights of biographical anonymity.
3. Information about subjects obtained from records that are opened to public scrutiny cannot be protected by guarantees of privacy or confidentiality.
4. The process of conducting sociological research must not expose respondents to substantial risk of personal harm. Informed consent must be obtained when the risks of research are greater than the risks of everyday life. Where modest risk or harm is anticipated, informed consent must be obtained.
5. Sociologists should take culturally appropriate steps to secure informed consent and to avoid invasions of privacy. Special actions may be necessary where the individuals studied are illiterate, have very low social status, or are unfamiliar with social research.
6. To the extent possible in a given study sociologists should anticipate potential threats to confidentiality. Such means as the removal of identifiers, the use of randomized responses and other statistical solutions to problems of privacy should be used where appropriate.
7. Confidential information provided by research participants must be treated as such by sociologists, even when this information enjoys no legal protection or privilege and legal force is applied. The obligation to respect confidentiality also applies to members of research organizations (interviewers, coders, clerical staff, etc.) who have access to the information. It is the responsibility of administrators and chief investigators to instruct staff members on this point and to make every effort to insure that access to confidential information is restricted.
8. While generally adhering to the norm of acknowledging the contributions of all collaborators, sociologists should be sensitive to harm that may arise from disclosure and respect a collaborator's wish or need for anonymity. Full disclosure may be made later if circumstances permit.
9. Study design and information gathering techniques should conform to regulations protecting the rights of human subjects, irrespective of source of funding, as outlined by the American Association of University Professors (AAUP) in "Regulations Governing Research On Human Subjects: Academic Freedom and the Institutional Review Board," *Academe*, December 1981: 358–370.
10. Sociologists should comply with appropriate federal and institutional requirements pertaining to the conduct of research. These requirements might include but are not necessarily limited to failure to obtain proper review and approval for research that involves human subjects and failure to follow recommendations made by responsible committees concerning research subjects, materials, and procedures.